PRINCIPLES OF ACCOUNTING

FIFTH EDITION

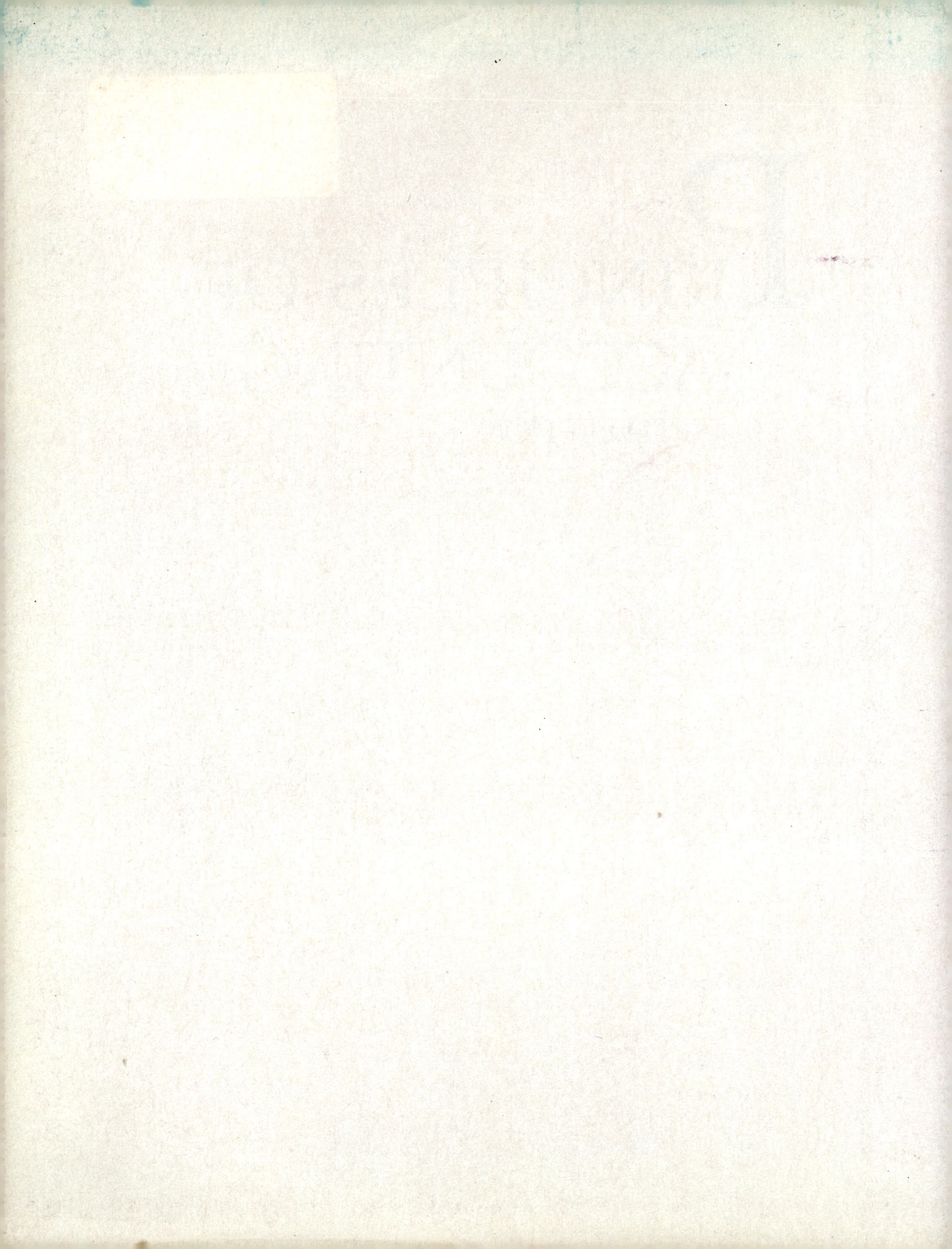

PRINCIPLES OF ACCOUNTING

FIFTH EDITION

PAUL H. WALGENBACH
University of Wisconsin

ERNEST I. HANSON
University of Wisconsin

JAMES C. HAMRE
University of Wisconsin

Harcourt Brace Jovanovich, Publishers
San Diego New York Chicago Austin Washington, D.C.
London Sydney Tokyo Toronto

ISBN: 0-15-571393-0

Library of Congress Catalog Card Number: 89–85892

Printed in the United States of America

PREFACE

The Fifth Edition of *Principles of Accounting* provides a comprehensive first course in accounting and is designed both for students planning a career in the field and for students desiring a general understanding of the subject. The textbook presents a balance of conceptual and procedural material for both financial and managerial accounting, using carefully designed examples and illustrations, a large variety of problems, and a complete program of integrated study aids. Learning objectives are integrated throughout the textbook; and the instructor's materials and the student study aids ensure that the entire package is pedagogically consistent and thorough.

Prominent features of this edition include the following:

- *Chapter Objectives* at the beginning of each chapter, now with page references, indicate what students should understand when they complete the chapter. All teaching and study aids are tied to these objectives.
- A *boxed insert* in each chapter reprints a business article or focuses on a related point to show the real-life complexities of accounting. Classic boxed inserts have been retained, but many are new.
- *Key Points for Chapter Objectives,* with Chapter Objectives repeated, clearly summarize each chapter.
- *Key Terms Used in This Chapter* list, with page references, the boldfaced major terms introduced in each chapter. A comprehensive glossary of all major terms, referenced by chapter, appears at the back of the book.
- *Self-Test Questions for Review.* Five multiple-choice questions, with answers at the end of each chapter, give students immediate feedback on their grasp of each chapter.
- A *Demonstration Problem for Review,* with complete solution, now follows each chapter in the textbook.
- *Questions, Exercises, Problems,* and *Alternate Problems* provide students with a wide variety of single- and multiple-topic work assignments at varying levels of difficulty. All exercises and problem material are new or revised and are clearly labeled for topic coverage. Problems that can be worked using the *Computer Resource Guide,* Third Edition, are marked with a computer logo. The number of alternate problems has been increased so that each problem has an alternate.
- A *Business Decision Problem* at the end of every chapter provides a case situation for applying many of the key ideas.
- *Annual Report Problems* are provided at the close of five of the six parts in the text (an *Accounting Practice Problem* concludes Part 5). These problems ask students to interpret excerpts from the published annual reports of actual corporations and organizations (or, for Part 5, the practices of a CPA firm). Data are presented for A. Shulman, Inc.; Bush Industries; Emery Air Freight Corporation; Fay's Drug Company, Inc.; House of Fabrics, Inc.; J. P. Industries,

Inc.; Kelly Services, Inc.; Nature's Sunshine Products, Inc.; Perry Drug Stores, Inc.; Pfizer, Inc.; and Tubby's, Inc. The complete financial portion of the 1988 annual report of Whirlpool Corporation is presented at the end of the text, providing full financial data and disclosures for the Annual Report Problem for Part 6. Data from the annual reports of other firms are also used to illustrate financial disclosures at various points throughout the text.

- An expanded *Glossary* at the end of the text permits students to look up key terms at any point in their study.
- *Checklist of Key Figures,* on the front and back endpapers, aids students in working homework assignments.

CHANGES AND ADDITIONS TO THE FIFTH EDITION

The changes in the Fifth Edition were designed to clarify and simplify difficult topic areas and to provide instructors with greater flexibility in course organization and pedagogy.

Chapter 1 A new exhibit shows the articulation among the income statement, the statement of owner's equity, and the balance sheet.

Chapters 3 and 4 The accounting cycle discussion has been expanded from six to nine steps.

Chapter 5 More examples and entries for Freight Prepaid and Collect are included. A new appendix, with worksheet and problems, focuses on the alternate (adjusting entry) method for recording inventories.

Chapter 6 New material on electronic data processing, with new diagrams, succinctly contrasts manual and computerized accounting.

Chapter 7 The concept of internal control structure from *Statement on Auditing Standards No. 55* is discussed.

Chapter 9 The discussion of lower of cost or market inventory costing has been simplified.

Chapter 12 A new diagram and an expanded explanation clarifying accounting for property taxes are presented.

Chapter 13 A new exhibit integrates the various components of the conceptual framework of financial reporting. Newly selected footnotes from the financial statements of actual companies illustrate disclosures.

Chapter 15 The discussion of stock splits has been moved to this chapter from Chapter 16. The section on redemption of preferred stock is eliminated. A new stockholders' equity exhibit illustrates the presentation of various types of paid-in capital.

Chapter 16 The sequence of material has been changed to present retained earnings first, dividends second, and earnings disclosures last. A new exhibit illustrates a statement of stockholders' equity.

Chapter 17 The discussion of deferred income taxes has been completely revised to reflect the most recent FASB standard on this topic. A discussion of future value, together with problems and future value tables, has been added to the appendix on effective interest amortization.

Chapter 19 The discussion of cash flow statements has been thoroughly revised and updated, with a revised worksheet for the direct method and simplified examples, to reflect the most recent FASB changes. A new appendix details an alternate method of preparation (the T-account approach).

Chapter 21 A new appendix, with worksheet and problems, presents the alternate (adjusting entry) method of recording materials, work in process, and finished goods inventory.

Chapter 23 A new appendix, with problems, illustrates the use of the weighted average method in a process costing system.

Chapter 24 The discussion of break-even analysis and net income planning has been simplified and expanded.

Chapter 26 Coverage of standard costs has been expanded and separate variances for variable and fixed overhead have been incorporated. Discussion of two-variance and three-variance methods of total overhead analysis has been expanded and coordinated.

Chapter 27 Unequal cash flows in the cash payback and average rate of return methods are now discussed.

Chapter 28 The computations for phasing out the low-bracket tax rate and personal exemptions have been simplified.

SUPPLEMENTARY AIDS

For the Instructor

INSTRUCTOR'S EDITION For this version of the textbook, 64 pages have been added at the very end consisting of complete answers to all the end-of-chapter questions in the textbook, alternate syllabuses for two-semester and three-quarter courses, and an index of teaching transparencies.

INSTRUCTOR'S MANUAL WITH SOLUTIONS TO PRACTICE SETS This manual, prepared by Richard Metcalf and Orville Keister (both of the University of Akron) and Thomas E. Balke (University of Nebraska—Lincoln) has been expanded. For each text chapter it now includes key points for chapter objectives, lecture notes, an overview of all exercises and problems, an additional self study problem, and two 10-minute quizzes with worked solutions.

SOLUTIONS MANUAL Answers for all exercises and problem material in the textbook are included.

TEST RESOURCE MANUAL This class-tested booklet is integral to the instructional package. And for this edition we have revised and expanded the manual to provide 70 objective questions and 10 short problems, organized by chapter objectives, for each chapter. Questions and problems are also included for each appendix in the text. The manual also includes Achievement Tests A and B, two sets of selected questions, and problems for testing purposes. Each version contains 14 two-chapter tests suitable for 50-minute class periods, and two comprehensive tests, each covering 14 chapters of the textbook. Annotated answers, with computations when appropriate, are given for all questions and problems in the manual.

COMPUTERIZED TEST RESOURCE SYSTEM For the IBM-PC and compatibles, for Apple II, and for Macintosh, this system allows instructors to edit, add, and generate multiple versions of examinations with answer keys.

SOLUTIONS TRANSPARENCIES 1 AND 2 Transparencies for solutions to all exercises and problem material are available. They are contained in two packages, one for Chapters 1–14 and one for Chapters 15–28 of the textbook.

TEACHING TRANSPARENCIES Designed by Sharyll A. B. Plato (Central State University), 100 color teaching transparencies are available to adopters. Many have been created for this package; the rest are reprinted or adapted from the textbook.

ELECTRONIC TRANSPARENCIES Demonstration problems or exhibits from every chapter have been placed on a disk in the form of spreadsheet templates. Schools using Lotus 1-2-3 and appropriate microcomputer display equipment can do spreadsheet demonstrations and "what if" analysis in the classroom or computer lab.

VIDEO LECTURES A series of video lectures consists of two fifty-minute videotapes for each chapter of the textbook. The first tape is a lecture covering chapter material; the second tape reviews selected problems.

MILLER GAAP GUIDE: COLLEGE EDITION 1990, AND GAAP GUIDE UPDATE SERVICE All current FASB and AICPA pronouncements are restated and analyzed, cross-referenced, organized by topic, and indexed. The Update Service provides technical analyses of GAAP within weeks of release of official pronouncements.

For the Student

STUDY GUIDE Prepared by Imogene A. Posey (University of Tennessee), the Study Guide reprints the Chapter Objectives for each text chapter and includes a brief Chapter Summary and a detailed Chapter Review outline. A Check Your Knowledge section consists of true/false and completion questions and exercises, organized by chapter objectives and followed by worked solutions.

WORKING PAPERS Working papers (in two volumes) are available for all problems, alternate problems, business decision problems, and annual report problems. The working papers are identified by problem number and name and contain headings, columns, cross-references to related pages, and other necessary aids to assist students in organizing answers and solutions. When appropriate, given problem data have been entered to save the students time. Volume 1 consists of chapters 1–16; Volume 2 contains papers for chapters 14–28. Thus working papers related to two corporate chapters (15 and 16) are included in each set, so that this material may be covered in either the first or second semester.

COMPUTER RESOURCE GUIDE: PRINCIPLES OF ACCOUNTING, THIRD EDITION In a major revision of this combined general ledger, practice set, and spreadsheet package, the *Computer Resource Guide* by John Wanlass (De Anza College) allows students to work selected problems from Chapters 2–27 of the text using powerful software requiring no prior computer training. It is available for use with IBM PC and PS/2.

MICROSTUDY: COMPUTERIZED STUDY GUIDE This copyable $5\frac{1}{4}$-inch disk is provided free to adopters. It can be used with an IBM PC or PC-compatible with a minimum of 192K memory, and it may be transferred to a $3\frac{1}{2}$-inch disk. The Guide is also available in a Macintosh version. For each textbook chapter, the guide contains chapter objectives, true/false questions, matching exercises, and multiple-choice questions. Page number references to the textbook are now provided, as well as complete answers to true/false questions. All questions are scored and scrambled.

PRACTICE SET A, "LET THERE BE LIGHT" Prepared by Ron Burnette (Macomb Community College), it covers the basic steps in the accounting cycle (Chapters 1–6), using a sole proprietorship business that sells light fixtures. Students are asked to record a month's transactions, post, perform ending procedures, and prepare financial statements. The estimated time for completion is 15–18 hours.

COMPUTERIZED PRACTICE SET A, "LET THERE BE LIGHT" Prepared by Carol Asplund (College of Lake County) and Ron Burnette (Macomb Community College), it includes special instructions for the computerized version, and a disk. The $5\frac{1}{4}$-inch disk is for use with an IBM PC or PC-compatible with at least one $5\frac{1}{4}$-inch floppy disk drive and an IBM compatible printer. It may be installed on a hard disk for use with the IBM. It requires 256K RAM, PC-DOS, or MS-DOS version 2.1 or higher.

PRACTICE SET A WITH BUSINESS PAPERS, "TRAVIS APPAREL SHOP" It also covers the basic steps in the accounting cycle (Chapters 1–6) using a sole proprietorship, but it provides business documents (invoices, checks, receipts, etc.) for students to work with. This practice set has been revised to improve its clarity for this edition. The estimated time for completion is 18–20 hours.

PRACTICE SET B, "'IN' FREQUENCIES, INC." Prepared by Ron Burnette (Macomb Community College), it covers the accounting cycle and certain other topics for a corporation. Students can work this revised practice set after they have completed Chapter 16. The estimated time for completion is 15–18 hours.

PRACTICE SET C, "EXCELL MANUFACTURING, INC." This manual practice set illustrates the operation of a job order costing system. Students can work this practice set after they have completed chapter 22. The estimated time for completion is 18–20 hours.

ACKNOWLEDGMENTS

We are especially grateful to the following for their contributions to the textbook and supplements for the Fifth Edition: Thomas Balke, Ron Burnette, Orville Keister, Richard Metcalf, Sharyll Plato, Imogene Posey, David Ravetch, and John Wanlass.

We are deeply indebted to the many perceptive reviewers, questionnaire respondents, and focus group participants who helped in the development of the Fifth Edition:

John C. Arnsparger (Red Rocks Community College)
George F. Aulbach, Jr. (West Texas State University)
William H. Barnett II (Walters State College)
David Bayley (Santa Monica College)
Don Baynham (Eastfield College)
John R. Biglin (Muhlenberg College)
Sheila Bradford (Tulsa Junior College)
Virginia Brunell (Diablo Valley College)
Sandra D. Byrd (Southwest Missouri State University)
Jane Calvert (Central State University)
Janet Cassagio (Nassau Community College)
Judith M. Cook (Grossmont College)
Anthony Cottell (Bergen Community College)
Rosalind Cranor (Virginia Polytechnic Institute and State University
Billie M. Cunningham (Collin County Community College)
Nona Demetre (Santa Monica College)
Robert J. DePasquale (St. Vincent College)
JoAnn Devries (Central State University)
G. DiLorenzo (Gloucester County College)
Walter Doehring (Genesee Community College)
Patricia L. Duckworth (Metropolitan State College)
Bob Englard (College of Staten Island)
Richard Fleischman (John Carroll University)
Mike Foland (Belleville Area College)
Clyde J. Galbraith (West Chester University)
Daniel J. Galvin (Diablo Valley College)
Helen Gerrard (Miami University)
Martin Ginsberg (Rockland Community College)
Shirley Glass (Macomb Community College)
Max P. Godwin (Southwest Texas State University)
Ellsworth C. Granger, Jr. (Mankato State University)
Kenneth Gustafson (Bergen Community College)
Clo Hampton (West Valley College)

Bill Hansen (Indian Hills Community College)
Quenton E. Hanson (University of Minnesota—Duluth)
Mark A. Hoffman (McDonnell Douglas Technologies Incorporated)
Thomas Holowaty (St. Vincent College)
Jean Marie Hudson (Lamar University)
Harry Hughes (University of Tennessee)
Kirstin Johnston (Eastern Montana College)
Alvin Koslofsky (San Jose City College)
Hana Kovanic (Bergen Community College)
Joseph A. Kreutle (Miami-Dade Community College)
Kyle Laws (Pueblo Community College)
Linda Lessing (State University of New York at Farmingdale)
Bruce A. Lindsey (Genesee Community College)
Nelson H. Long (Kutztown University)
Jay Mackie (Drexel University)
Audrey Mansfield (Brookdale Community College)
Geoff Mather (Liberty University)
Keith McBee (University of Wisconsin—Marathon Center)
Florence McGovern (Bergen Community College)
Charles V. Neal (Alfred State College)
Lynn M. Paluska (Nassau Community College)
Robert Picard (Mankato State University)
Sharyll A. B. Plato (Central State University)
David Ravetch (University of California—Los Angeles
E. Thomas Robinson (University of Alaska—Fairbanks
Audrey Roche (Santa Monica College)
Leo A. Ruggle (Mankato State University)
Charles Savana (Burlington County College)
Edward W. Scott, Jr. (Olympic College)
Suzanne Sevalstad (University of Nevada)
Eugene H. Shepard (Georgia College)
Eleanor Simon (Santa Monica College)
Brent T. Sjaardema (Muhlenburg College)
Kursheed Smer (Arkansas College)
Bruce W. Smith (Mankato State University)
William A. Stahlen (Drexel University)
John Stancil (Cumberland College)
Beverly B. Terry (Central Piedmont Community College)
Rosemary Thomas (Olympic College)
Jack Topiol (Community College of Philadelphia)
Gerald A. Unruh (Arapahoe Community College)
David D. Wagaman (Kutztown University)
Ronald T. Walters (Community College of Aurora)
S. Churchill Ward (Austin Community College)
P. R. Wheaton (University of Michigan—Dearborn)
James S. Worthington (Auburn University)
Marilyn J. Young (Tulsa Junior College)
Richard Zaleski (Camden County College)
E. Robert Zoeller (Brookdale Community College)

We wish to thank the members of the book team at Harcourt Brace Jovanovich for their tireless efforts on behalf of the project: Ken Rethmeier, executive editor; Bill Teague, software editor; Craig Avery, manuscript editor and project coordinator; Sheila Spahn, production editor; Diane Southworth, Chris Cohn, and Ken Fine, production managers; Diane Pella and Kay Faust, designers; and Paulette Russo, art editor.

Paul H. Walgenbach
Ernest I. Hanson
James C. Hamre

CONTENTS

PART 6 PLANNING, CONTROL, AND DECISION MAKING 925

PRINCIPLES OF ACCOUNTING

FIFTH EDITION

PART 1

THE BASIC FRAMEWORK OF ACCOUNTING

1

ACCOUNTING: AN INFORMATION SYSTEM

CHAPTER OBJECTIVES

1. Provide a basis for understanding the goals of the accounting process and flows of accounting information (pp. 3–7).
2. Describe the various fields of accounting activity (pp. 7–9).
3. Provide an overview of the basic financial reports and their underlying concepts (pp. 10–13).
4. Explain and illustrate the effect of transactions on the balance sheet (pp. 13–20).
5. Describe and illustrate the relationship of the income statement to the statement of owners' equity and the balance sheet (pp. 20–22).
6. Explain the forms of business organization (pp. 22–24).

Ours is the Age of the Machine.
Also, it is the Age of the Accountant.
A little literacy in accounting has become a
prime necessity.

PAUL A. SAMUELSON

Modern accounting is widely recognized as a basic component of business management. Accounting is the means by which managers are informed of the financial status and progress of their companies, thus contributing to the continuing processes of planning, control of operations, and decision making. Accounting provides a method of systematically recording and evaluating business activities. This is, perhaps, the fundamental reason for business managers and business students to familiarize themselves with the accounting discipline.

A large portion of the information that a business manager requires is derived from accounting data. The ability to analyze and use these data helps managers accomplish their objectives. Through your study of accounting, you will discover the types of business activities that can be accounted for usefully, the methods used to collect accounting data, and the implications of the resulting information. Furthermore—and often just as important—you will become aware of the limitations of accounting reports.

ACCOUNTING AS AN INFORMATION SYSTEM

Virtually all profit-seeking organizations and most nonprofit organizations maintain extensive accounting records. One reason is that these records are often required by law. A more basic reason is that, even in a very small organization, a manager is confronted with a multitude of complex variables. Not even the most brilliant manager can be sufficiently informed just by observing daily operations. Instead, he or she must depend on the accounting process to convert business transactions into useful statistical data that can be abstracted and summarized in accounting reports. In every sense, this process is essential to the coordinated and rational management of most organizations—regardless of their size. Thus, accounting is an *information system* necessitated by the great complexity of modern business.

In today's society, many persons and agencies outside of management are involved in the economic life of an organization. These persons frequently require financial data. For example, stockholders must have financial information in order to measure management's performance and to evaluate their own holdings. Potential investors need financial data in order to compare prospective investments. Creditors must consider the financial strength of an organization before permitting it to borrow funds. Also, labor unions, financial analysts, and economists often expect a considerable amount of reliable financial data. Finally, many laws require that extensive financial information be reported to the various levels of government. As an information system, the accounting process serves persons both inside and outside an organization.

THE ACCOUNTING PROCESS

Accounting can be defined as the process of (1) *recording*, (2) *classifying*, (3) *reporting*, and (4) *interpreting* the financial data of an organization. Once an accounting system has been designed and installed, recording and classifying data may become somewhat routine and repetitive. While it is important for accountants to have a sound knowledge of this phase of the accounting process, it is often a relatively minor part of their total responsibility. Accountants direct most of their attention to the reporting and interpretation of the meaningful implications of the data.

Except in small businesses, much routine accounting work has become highly mechanized and automatic. Thus, many persons not acquainted with current accounting trends think that the profession is becoming progressively narrower. Quite the contrary is true. The emergence of electronic data processing has freed accountants from the routine aspects of recording and classifying data, enabling them to concentrate more on the analytical and interpretive aspects of the accounting function. These are the areas most affected by the new demands for accounting information. Indeed, the number of licensed accountants in the United States has grown from about 60,000 in the early 1960s to an estimated 300,000 today. The demand for better educated and more experienced accountants will undoubtedly continue to rise in the future.

Whether the accounting records for a given organization should be maintained manually or electronically will depend on several things, such as the size of the organization, the amount of data to be processed, the amount of information required, and the need for prompt access to stored data. The recent introduction of inexpensive microcomputers and related software programs (see Chapter 6) has enabled even small firms to process accounting data electronically.

Regardless of the method used, the underlying accounting concepts are essentially the same. Because a manually maintained system is most easily handled in the classroom and in problem situations, we use this type of system throughout this book. Where appropriate, however, we include comments relating to electronic systems. Also, certain of the exercises and problems in the text, identified by a computer logo, may be worked using the Computer Resource Guide, a supplement to this text (see the Preface).

THE REPORTING PROCESS

The reporting process, comprising four main channels of information flow, is graphically represented in Exhibit 1–1.

Channel A: Managerial Data and Reports

A major function of accounting is to provide management with the data needed for decision making and for efficient operation of the firm. Although management people routinely receive the financial reports, tax returns, and special reports prepared for outsiders, they also require various other information, such as the unit cost of a product, estimates of the profit earned from a specific sales campaign, cost comparisons of alternative courses of action, and long-range budgets. Because of the strategic nature of some of this information, it may be available only to the firm's high-level management. The process of generating and analyzing such data is often referred to as **managerial accounting.** Emphasis on this area of accounting has increased in recent years as a result of the implementation of computers and sophisticated quantitative tools.

EXHIBIT 1–1

TYPICAL FLOWS OF ACCOUNTING INFORMATION

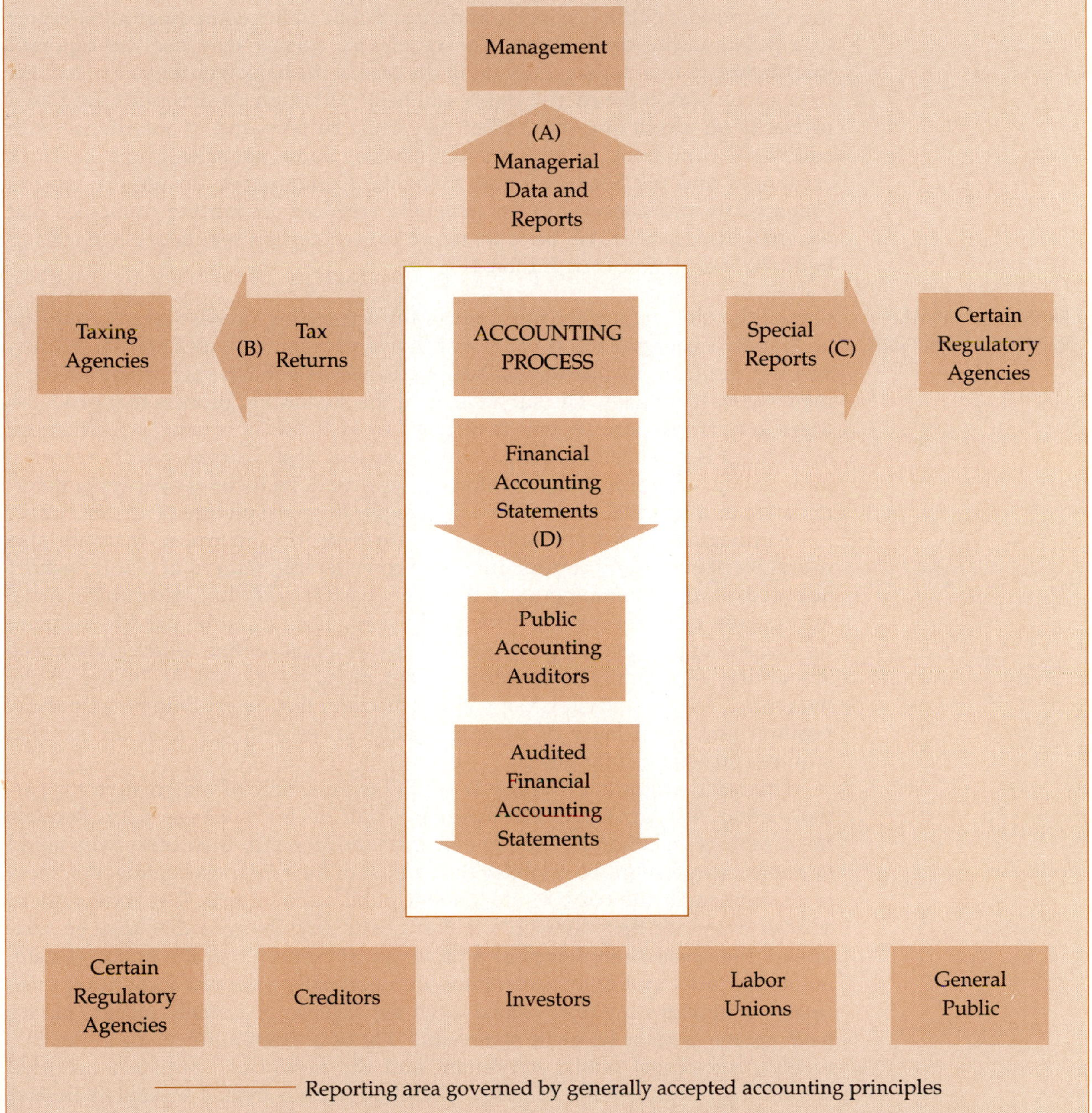

Channel B: Tax Returns Most businesses are required to file many kinds of tax returns—for example, federal, state, and municipal income taxes, excise taxes, and payroll taxes. The preparation of these returns is governed by the rulings and special reporting requirements of the taxing agencies involved. Proper compliance is generally a matter of law and can be quite complicated. Consequently, many firms, especially when preparing income tax returns, retain certified public accountants or attorneys specializing in taxation.

Channel C: Special Reports

Some companies, by the nature of their activities, are required to report periodically to certain regulatory agencies. For example, certain banks must report to the Comptroller of the Currency, and most public utility companies must report to a public utility commission. The regulatory agency may use the reported information to monitor solvency (as in the case of the banks) or the rate of income to be earned (as in the case of public utilities). Although these reports are based primarily on accounting data, often they must be prepared in accordance with additional conditions, rules, and definitions. Some agencies, such as stock exchanges and the Securities and Exchange Commission, do require reports prepared in accordance with the generally accepted accounting principles that we shall discuss later. We have therefore shown certain regulatory agencies in both channels C and D of Exhibit 1–1.

Channel D: Financial Accounting Statements

One of the most important functions of the accounting process is to accumulate and report accounting information that shows an organization's financial position and the results of its operations. Many businesses publish such financial statements at least annually. The subdivision of the accounting process that produces these general-purpose reports is referred to as **financial accounting.** Financial accounting is essentially retrospective, because it deals primarily with historical information, or events that have already happened. Its focus is on income determination and financial position as an aggregate financial picture of an enterprise.

Although financial accounting data are primarily historical, they are also useful for planning and control. Indeed, a considerable amount of planning must be based on what has happened in the recent past. In addition, historical financial information is inherently a control mechanism, since it can be used to measure the success of past planning. We should also emphasize that, although financial accounting is primarily historical, it is not merely a process of "filling in the numbers." As you study further, you will discover that determining the financial position and profitability of an enterprise is an exceedingly complex job that requires professional judgment.

Financial accounting statements are the main source of information for parties—other than governmental agencies—outside the business firm. Because these reports will often be used to evaluate management, their objectivity could be subject to question. To establish the validity of their financial statements, most firms have them audited by independent public accountants. The independent auditor examines the statements and suggests any changes that may be warranted. He or she then expresses a professional opinion that the financial statements are fairly stated "in accordance with generally accepted accounting principles" or indicates any reservations about the statements. Usually, outside parties have greater faith in financial statements that have been audited. Both the role of the professional public accountant and the nature of "generally accepted accounting principles" are complex. Therefore, each is treated separately in later sections of this chapter.

ACCOUNTING PRINCIPLES

To be useful, financial accounting information must be assembled and reported objectively. Those who must rely on such information have a right to be assured that the data are free from bias and inconsistency, whether deliberate or not. For this reason, financial accounting relies on certain standards or guides that have proved useful over the years in imparting economic data. These standards are called **generally accepted accounting principles (GAAP).** Because accounting is more an art than a science, these principles are not immutable laws like those in the physical sciences. Instead, they are *guides to action* and may change over time. Sometimes specific principles must be altered or new principles must be formulated to fit changed economic circumstances or changes in business practices.

Because accounting principles are based on a combination of theory and practice, there has always been, and probably always will be, some controversy about their propriety. A number of organizations are concerned with the formulation of accounting principles. The most prominent among these is the Financial Accounting Standards Board (FASB). The FASB, organized in 1973, is a nongovernmental body whose pronouncements have the force of setting authoritative rules for the general practice of financial accounting. Before the creation of the FASB, the Accounting Principles Board (APB) of the American Institute of Certified Public Accountants (AICPA) fulfilled the function of formulating accounting principles. If the *attest* function (auditing and independent reporting) of the independent certified public accountant is to be meaningful, the business enterprises of this country must generally observe substantially comparable accounting principles.

Various regulatory bodies—such as the Securities and Exchange Commission and the Internal Revenue Service—also prescribe rules to be used in financial reporting. Because these rules often touch upon accounting principles and may conflict with the rules and practices specified by other agencies, compromises sometimes have to be made in financial reporting. This has been especially true when the rules of a regulatory body have conflicted with those considered "generally accepted" by accounting practitioners.

Often, income determined by tax regulations differs from that determined by generally accepted accounting principles. When rules or methods prescribed by the Internal Revenue Service for the determination of taxable income conflict with those acceptable for business reporting, an enterprise may keep more than one set of records to satisfy both reporting requirements. Uninformed people may think that this practice is illegal or unethical; actually, there is nothing sinister or illegal about keeping separate records to fulfill separate needs, as long as all the records are subject to examination by the appropriate parties.

As Exhibit 1–1 indicates, generally accepted accounting principles are primarily relevant to financial accounting. In managerial accounting, the main objective is to assist management in making decisions and in operating effectively, and in such cases it is frequently useful to depart from concepts utilized in financial accounting. On many occasions, financial accounting data must be reassembled or altered to be most useful in solving internal business problems.

FIELDS OF ACCOUNTING ACTIVITY

Accountants perform many diverse services and are engaged in various types of employment. The three major fields of accounting activity are *private accounting, public accounting,* and *governmental accounting*. Because each of these may comprise many aspects of accounting activity, it is possible to give only a broad description for each type of accounting employment.

Private Accounting

More accountants are employed in private accounting than in any other field. Private employers of accountants include manufacturers, wholesalers, retailers, and service firms. Depending on the size and complexity of the business, the private accountant's duties may vary from routine reporting to the design and implementation of electronic accounting systems. The major objective of the private accountant, however, is to assist management in planning and controlling the firm's operations. In many large business firms, the head of the accounting department is called the **controller** and is a key executive who works closely with other management personnel.

Frequently, a large company will have an **internal auditing** staff that reports to a high-ranking management officer or to an audit committee of the board of directors. Internal auditing is an appraisal activity conducted within the business firm to determine if management's financial and operating controls are effective and are being properly utilized. An internal auditor investigates policies and procedures designed to safeguard assets, promote operational efficiency, and provide reliable information.

Public Accounting

The field of public accounting is composed of firms that render independent, expert reports on financial statements of business enterprises. Public accounting firms also perform a wide variety of accounting and managerial services, acting as consultants to their clients. Most accountants in public accounting firms are *certified public accountants* (CPAs), holding certificates from the particular states in which they work.[1] These certificates declare that the CPA has passed a rigorous examination and has met the requirements for education and experience set by the state to ensure high standards of performance. The CPA profession, like the older professions of law and medicine, has a comprehensive code of ethics—a set of rules of professional conduct—that governs the behavior of its practitioners in the performance of their work.

The professional responsibility of the certified public accountant is unique. While the attorney and the physician are responsible only to their clients and patients, the certified public accountant may be professionally responsible to third parties who rely on the financial statements the CPA has audited. This is true even though the third party in no way contributes to the fee paid for the audit and has no contractual relationship whatsoever with the accountant.

Governmental Accounting

A large number of accountants are employed by federal, state, and local governmental agencies. The services performed by these accountants parallel those of private and public accountants and may cover the entire spectrum of financial and managerial accounting. For example, the General Accounting Office of the federal government and the Department of Audit in the various state governments engage in auditing activities similar to those of public accountants. Audits may be conducted not only of governmental agencies but also of private firms doing business with a governmental unit. Accounting personnel of the Internal Revenue Service and the corresponding state agencies conduct accounting investigations of firms and individuals in connection with their tax liabilities. Among the many other governmental agencies and regulatory bodies that employ accountants are the Securities and Exchange Commission, the Department of Defense, the Federal Power Commission, the Interstate Commerce Commission, and state utility commissions and agencies.

[1]Most states still allow certain accountants who are not certified to practice public accounting.

THE MODERN ACCOUNTANT: IMAGE AND PROSPECTS

A little over 25 years ago, two social scientists who conducted a government survey of attitudes among 1,000 students at five unnamed but "highly selective" universities found that in the students' eyes, "the accountant is the anti-hero of the occupational world. . . . The accountant is a conformist, with a minimum of social skills. . . . He is rated as passive, weak, soft, shallow, and cold."*

This stereotyped image has been dramatically erased in the past two decades and replaced by that of a dynamic, sophisticated, professional person. Recently, a prominent business magazine quoted the chairman of the accounting department of a major university as saying, "Suddenly students see accounting as glamorous, sexy. Many of our best students who would have gone to law school a couple of years ago are now going into public accounting." Today's young men and women know that the field can be a lot more challenging and rewarding than merely balancing debits and credits. In a recent newspaper article, James R. MacNeill of the American Institute of Certified Public Accountants was quoted as saying, "Thanks to the computer, a lot of the pencil-pushing has been done away with. The emphasis is on people who are sophisticated in business, finance, and communications."

An estimated 60,000 college graduates with bachelor's degrees and 8,500 with advanced degrees entered the accounting field in 1985—more than three times the number entering the field fifteen years before. Not only are there plenty of job openings with increasingly attractive salaries, but the positions available also have more dimension and challenge than ever before. In fact, the immediate and long-term prospects for accounting graduates are better than for most other professions, such as law. The U.S. Bureau of Labor Statistics indicates that employment of accountants and auditors is expected to grow faster than average through the 1990s.

Slightly more than one-fourth of current accounting graduates enter public accounting (described in this chapter); the remainder may become management accountants or internal auditors, working in industry, in government, for financial institutions, or for not-for-profit organizations. Many graduates who enter the public accounting field may "opt out" after several years of experience in this field to take high-level positions with clients. For example, many chief financial officers, treasurers, and controllers have prior CPA firm experience.

Both industry and government offer a broad spectrum of opportunities for accounting graduates. A graduate with good grades and course work in another specialty, such as hospital administration or information systems, will fare well in private accounting.† Students interested in auditing for the private sector will find that the field of internal auditing has expanded dramatically just during the last decade. For most companies, the present-day focus of internal auditing is operational auditing—auditing for efficiency, economy, and profits. Internal auditors are therefore in a good position to learn about all facets of a firm's operations, and subsequently can often work their way into top management positions within their firms.

Government positions also offer a wide variety of opportunities with outstanding fringe benefits. For example, the Federal Bureau of Investigation, in recent years, has been hiring more accountants than lawyers, and the Internal Revenue Service recruits accountants at most colleges and universities with an accounting program. Overall, government and industry offer better job security than CPA firms, and job security rates high among job criteria by many accounting graduates.

Women and minority accounting graduates are in particular demand by all accounting fields. In 1985, roughly 40% of the accounting graduates hired by public accounting firms were women—up from 24% ten years before. The major difficulty in recruiting minority graduates is that not many go into accounting as undergraduates, so there is a limited pool from which to draw. The minority student who enters a good accounting program and achieves high grades is in an enviable competitive position.

*Steve Lohr, "Good-bye to the Ink-stained Wretch," *Atlantic Monthly,* August, 1980, p. 68.
†Robert E. Jensen and John D. Rice, "The Times Are Changing," *New Accountant*, September, 1985, p. 8.

BASIC FINANCIAL REPORTS

As we mentioned earlier, one of the major functions of accounting is to provide periodic reports to management, owners, and outsiders. The two principal reports resulting from the process of financial accounting are the balance sheet and the income statement. Although the form of these financial statements may vary among different business firms or other economic units, their basic purpose is the same. The **balance sheet** portrays the financial position of the organization at a particular point in time. The **income statement** portrays the operating results for a period of time. These financial statements are prepared at least yearly, but quarterly or monthly reports are also customary.

Another basic statement, called the **statement of cash flows,** is generally required in reporting to outsiders. This statement will be discussed in Chapter 19.

Although the balance sheet and income statement are the end result of the process of financial accounting, we will introduce them in simplified form here, early in our study. Having some knowledge of the ultimate objective of financial accounting will help you understand the various steps in the accounting process.

THE BALANCE SHEET

The balance sheet, sometimes called the **statement of financial position,** is a listing of a firm's assets, liabilities, and owners' equity on a given date (these terms are explained below). Exhibit 1–2 is a balance sheet prepared for Art Graphics, a single-owner business, showing its financial position at December 31, 19XX.

The proper heading of a balance sheet consists of (1) the name of the organization, (2) the title of the statement, and (3) the date for which the statement was prepared.

The body of the statement in Exhibit 1–2 contains three major sections: assets, liabilities, and owner's equity. With this presentation, the reader can tell at a

EXHIBIT 1–2

Art Graphics
Balance Sheet
December 31, 19XX

Assets		**Liabilities**		
Cash	$ 6,000	Accounts Payable	$ 5,000	
Accounts Receivable	8,000	Mortgage Payable	35,000	
Supplies on Hand	4,000			
Land	10,000	Total Liabilities		$ 40,000
Building (Less Accumulated Depreciation)	32,000	**Owner's Equity**		
		George Taylor, Capital		80,000
Equipment (Less Accumulated Depreciation)	60,000			
Total Assets	$120,000	Total Liabilities and Owner's Equity		$120,000

glance that the resources of this firm total $120,000 and that these assets are being financed by two sources—$40,000 by the creditors (liabilities) and $80,000 by the owner (owner's equity). Occasionally, the right-hand portion of this statement is called *Equities,* with subdivisions called *Creditors' Equity* and *Owners' Equity.* The total assets always equal the sum of the creditors' and owners' equities. This balancing is sometimes described as the **accounting equation,** which dictates that all of the listed resources are attributed to claims of creditors and owners. Conversely, the claims of both creditors and owners must be balanced by total listed resources. These relationships can be diagrammed as follows:

Technical terms:	**Assets**	=	**Liabilities**	+	**Owners' Equity**
Basic meanings:	Business resources	=	Outsiders' claims	+	Owners' claims
Amounts (Exhibit 1–2):	$120,000	=	$40,000	+	$80,000

We now briefly explain each of the three elements in the accounting equation.

Assets

Assets are the economic resources of the business that can usefully be expressed in monetary terms. Assets may take many forms. Some assets—such as land, buildings, and equipment—may have readily identifiable physical characteristics. Others may simply represent claims for payment or services, such as amounts due from customers (accounts receivable), or prepayments for future services (for example, prepaid insurance). As a convenience to the reader of the balance sheet, the assets are usually listed in an established order, with the most liquid assets (cash, receivables, supplies, and so on) preceding the more permanent assets (land, buildings, and equipment).

Assets are usually recorded at their acquisition price, or cost. The recorded costs of assets may be reduced for a variety of reasons. Supplies are used up, and assets such as buildings and equipment depreciate. For example, in Exhibit 1–2, Art Graphics' buildings and equipment have both been reduced by accumulated depreciation over the years. We will develop the concept of depreciation in Chapter 3 and discuss it fully in Chapter 10.

Accounting principles do not permit upward valuation of assets, simply because it is often difficult or impossible to determine the *actual value* of an asset at regular intervals in a completely *objective* way. Assume, for example, that 10 years ago a firm purchased some real estate for $20,000. Today the property may well be worth considerably more. Assigning a current market value to the real estate may be helpful, but it would be difficult to accomplish unless the property were offered for sale. However, most business firms plan to use their long-term operating assets, not to sell them. Therefore, the accounting convention of reflecting assets in financial statements at acquisition cost has persisted, although criticism is frequently leveled at this practice.

Liabilities

Liabilities, or creditors' equity, are the obligations, or debts, that the firm must pay in money or services at some time in the future. They therefore represent creditors' claims on the firm's assets. Liabilities are listed on the balance sheet in the order that they will come due. Short-term liabilities—such as notes payable given for money borrowed for relatively short periods, accounts payable to creditors, and salaries owed employees—are shown first. Below the short-term liabilities, the long-term debt is presented. Normally, long-term debt—for example, mortgages and bonds payable—will not be repaid in full for several years.

Although most liabilities are payable in cash, some may involve the performance of services. A magazine publisher, for example, may receive advance payments for three- or five-year subscriptions. These payments constitute a liability that the publishing company will reduce periodically by supplying the publication during the subscription period. Should the publisher be unable to fulfill this commitment, the unexpired portion of the subscription amount must be refunded.

Owners' Equity

The **owners' equity** in the resources, or assets, of the firm is shown below the liabilities. The owners' interest is equal to the *net assets* of the business, which is defined as the difference between the assets and the liabilities. Thus, owners' equity is a *residual claim*—a claim to the assets remaining after the debts to creditors have been discharged. Formerly, the term *net worth* was frequently used to describe owners' equity. This expression is no longer considered good terminology, because it conveys an impression of value, and as we have seen, the value, or current worth, of assets may not be portrayed in the balance sheet. We also often use the term *capital* to describe owners' interest in a firm. (This practice is derived from legal usage of the term.) Sometimes in economic literature the assets of a business are referred to as the firm's "capital." This use of the term is avoided in accounting literature.

The owner's equity in Art Graphics amounts to $80,000. It consists of the amounts invested in the organization and the net earnings of the organization that have not been withdrawn by the owner.

UNDERLYING ACCOUNTING CONCEPTS

Certain fundamental concepts provide a framework for recording and reporting business transactions. These concepts have been developed over time to provide general guides to making financial reports as objective and as useful as possible. Although various terms—such as *principles, standards, assumptions,* and *conventions*—are often used to describe such guides, a distinction among these terms is not essential to an understanding of the guides. At this point, a brief discussion of certain of these guides may be helpful in understanding the structure of the accounting process. A more thorough discussion is given in Chapter 13.

The Accounting Entity

Any business enterprise—whether a sole proprietorship, a partnership, or a corporation—is an individual accounting unit separate and distinct from the other economic activities and the personal affairs of the owners. Thus, if sole proprietor George Taylor owned other businesses or participated in other economic ventures, these activities would be accounted for separately and would not affect the accounting for the sole proprietorship art graphics business. A separate set of accounting records would be maintained, and a separate set of financial statements would be prepared for each enterprise.

Historical Cost

We have mentioned that assets are recorded and subsequently reported at their acquisition price, or **historical cost.** Although other measurements, such as appraised values or market prices, might be used for reporting in subsequent periods, accountants have long recognized that historical cost is probably the most objective and verifiable basis for reporting assets. As you will learn, reported asset costs are often *reduced* over time to reflect expiration, and in some cases, they may be reduced to market values; upward revaluations, however, are not permitted in conventional financial statements. We explain later how certain reported *supplemental* information departs from the cost principle.

Objectivity

Because accounting data are most useful when they are objective and verifiable, the recording of transactions should be based on actual invoices, physical counts, and other relatively bias-free evidence whenever possible. Undocumented opinions of management or others do not provide a good basis for accounting determinations. Even when a certain amount of subjectivity cannot be avoided—as in estimating the useful lives of plant assets, collectibility of accounts receivable, or possible liability for product warranties—it is important that such estimates be supported by some sort of objective analysis.

Going Concern

The **going concern** concept is based on the presumption that a business will continue indefinitely and will not be sold or liquidated. This assumption permits the accountant to carry certain incurred costs such as plant assets and supplies into future periods and to reflect them as costs of operation when the items are used in operations. The concept also supports the cost principle, because it assumes that such assets will be *used* in operating the business rather than sold; hence, it is considered rational to use cost, rather than market price or liquidation value, as the basis for measurement.

The Measuring Unit

Accounting transactions and their results appearing in financial statements are expressed in terms of a monetary unit (the dollar in the United States). Unfortunately, the U.S. dollar (as well as the currencies of other countries) is not a stable unit of measure. Inflation causes a currency's purchasing power to decline through time. As a result, use of the cost principle may distort the financial statements of business firms, because the amounts appearing in the statements are expressed in dollars of different vintages. Over the years, there have been many proposals to adjust the amounts in financial statements by the use of price indexes or to substitute some current value such as replacement cost or appraisal value. Currently, conventional financial statements prepared in this country are still unadjusted, cost-based statements. However, the Financial Accounting Standards Board does encourage firms to make supplementary disclosures concerning the effects of inflation on their operations. A more detailed discussion of the problem will be given in Chapter 13.

EFFECT OF TRANSACTIONS ON THE BALANCE SHEET

An *accounting transaction* is a business activity or event that requires accounting recognition. Therefore, an event that affects any of the elements in the accounting equation (assets, liabilities, or owners' equity) must be recorded. Some activities—for example, ordering supplies, bidding for an engagement or contract, and negotiating for the acquisition of assets—may represent business activities, but an accounting transaction does not occur until such activities result in a change in the firm's assets, liabilities, or owners' equity.

Earlier, we observed that the balance sheet of a business indicates the firm's financial position at a particular point in time. We emphasized that the total assets should always equal the sum of the creditors' and owners' equities. If a balance sheet were prepared after each accounting transaction was completed, this equality of assets and equities would always hold true. Obviously, no one would care to do this, since the statements are required only periodically. However, keep in mind that although each transaction changes the complexion of the balance sheet, equality of assets and equities is always maintained.

Transactions Not Affecting Owners' Equity

Certain transactions may change the character and amounts of assets or liabilities, or both, but have no effect on owners' equity. For example, if George Taylor of Art Graphics (see Exhibit 1–2) purchases additional equipment for $1,000 cash, the asset Equipment will increase by $1,000, but the asset Cash will decrease by $1,000. Obviously, this transaction causes only a shift in assets on the balance sheet. In the same way, collection of accounts receivable causes a shift of assets. Collection of $500 of Accounts Receivable would result in a decrease in this asset and an increase in Cash of $500.

If the $1,000 worth of equipment had been purchased on credit rather than for cash, the result would have been a $1,000 increase in Equipment and an equal increase in the liability Accounts Payable. On the other hand, payment of liabilities reduces both assets and liabilities. If Taylor paid $500 to his creditors, both Cash and Accounts Payable would decrease by $500.

Transactions Affecting Owners' Equity

The following four types of transactions change the amount of owners' equity:

	Effect on Owners' Equity
1. Owner contributions	Increase
2. Owner withdrawals	Decrease
3. Revenue	Increase
4. Expenses	Decrease

When an owner contributes cash or other assets to a business firm, the firm's balance sheet shows an increase in assets and an increase in owners' equity. Conversely, when an owner withdraws assets from the firm, both assets and owners' equity decrease. The primary goal of any business, however, is to increase the owners' equity by earning profits, or **net income.** The net income of a firm is determined by subtracting *expenses incurred* from *revenue earned*. Owners' equity is increased by revenue and decreased by expenses. Let us examine the nature of revenue and expenses.

Revenue

Revenue is the increase in owners' equity a firm earns by providing goods or services for its customers. The revenue earned is measured by the *assets received* in exchange, usually in the form of cash or an account receivable. It is important to recognize that *revenue is earned and reflected in the accounting process at the time that goods or services are provided.* Receipt of cash by a business does not necessarily indicate that revenue has been earned. In a cash sale, revenue is earned at the time that the cash is received. Revenue is also reflected when services are rendered on *credit;* assets are increased when Accounts Receivable is increased. Subsequent collection of an account does not increase revenue—it merely results in a shift in assets from Accounts Receivable to Cash. Neither is revenue earned when a business borrows money or when the owners contribute assets. Such increases in assets are not earned, because the business firm has provided no goods or services.

Expenses

Expenses are costs incurred by the firm in the process of earning revenue. Generally, expenses are measured by the costs of *assets consumed* or *services used* during an accounting period. Depreciation on equipment, rent, employees' salaries, and costs of heat, light, and other utilities are examples of expenses incurred in producing revenue.

Because expenses are deducted from revenue to determine net income, the accounting process must relate expenses in a period to the revenue of that same period. For example, January rent—no matter when it is paid—should be related to January revenue in determining that month's net income. If an annual rent of $6,000 is prepaid on January 1, only 1/12 of the $6,000, or $500, is considered expense for January. At the end of January, the remaining prepayment of $5,500 constitutes an asset (called Prepaid Rent) to be apportioned over the remaining 11 months. Other examples of assets that are used up over a period of time are Prepaid Insurance and Prepaid Advertising.

Cash expenditures made to acquire assets do not represent expenses and do not affect owners' equity. Cash expenditures made to pay liabilities, such as the payment of an account payable, also do not represent expenses and do not affect owners' equity. Similarly, owners' withdrawals, although they reduce owners' equity, do not represent expenses. Expenses are directly related to the earning of revenue. They are determined by measuring the amount of assets or services consumed (or expired) during an accounting period.

Accrual Basis

The foregoing concepts of revenue and expenses apply to firms that employ an **accrual basis** accounting system. In accrual accounting, expenses incurred are matched with related revenue earned to determine a meaningful net income figure for a particular period. As we mentioned earlier, the revenue and expenses for determining net income do not depend on when cash is actually received or expended.

Certain businesses, principally service enterprises (such as law, architecture, or hairdressing) often use a **cash basis** mode of accounting. In contrast to accrual basis accounting, the cash basis system recognizes revenue when money is received and expenses when money is paid. Cash basis accounting is used primarily because it can provide certain income tax benefits and because it is simple. Cash basis financial statements, however, may distort the portrayal of financial position and operating results of a business. Consequently, most business firms use accrual basis accounting.

TRANSACTIONS AND THE BALANCE SHEET: AN ILLUSTRATION

Now that we have described the basic concepts underlying the preparation of financial statements, let us illustrate their application with an example.

Experienced driver education instructor John King established a private driving school called Westgate Driving School. King intends to buy a lot for vehicle storage and driver instruction, but to lease training vehicles. The transactions for June, the first month of operations, are analyzed below. A balance sheet is presented after each transaction so that the effect on the balance sheet may be examined.[2]

[2]Note that the totals in the various financial statements shown in this chapter have been double ruled. Accountants do this principally to signify that all necessary calculations have been performed and to emphasize final amounts for the benefit of readers. We will also employ double rulings in various other accounting records and forms illustrated in this text for these reasons and also to separate certain recorded data by time periods.

Initial Investment in Firm

TRANSACTION 1 On June 1, King invested $60,000 of his personal funds in the school. This first business transaction increased the asset Cash and increased King's equity (Capital) on the school's balance sheet.

Westgate Driving School
Balance Sheet

Assets		Liabilities	
Cash	$60,000	(none)	
		Owner's Equity	
		J. King, Capital	$60,000
		Total Liabilities and	
Total Assets	$60,000	Owner's Equity	$60,000

Purchase of Land

TRANSACTION 2 On June 2, King paid $24,000 cash for a lot to be used for storing vehicles and for some driving instruction. This transaction reduced the asset Cash and created another asset, Land, for an equivalent amount. This transaction was merely the conversion of one asset to another.

Westgate Driving School
Balance Sheet

Assets		Liabilities	
Cash	$36,000	(none)	
Land	24,000		
		Owner's Equity	
		J. King, Capital	$60,000
		Total Liabilities and	
Total Assets	$60,000	Owner's Equity	$60,000

Payment of Rent

TRANSACTION 3 On June 3, King paid $800 to rent a furnished office near the parking lot for June, and $5,000 to lease training vehicles. These items are June expenses, the cost of services received (use of office and vehicles) for the month. The transaction reduced assets (Cash) and owner's equity (J. King, Capital) by $5,800.

Westgate Driving School
Balance Sheet

Assets		Liabilities	
Cash	$30,200	(none)	
Land	24,000		
		Owner's Equity	
		J. King, Capital	$54,200
		Total Liabilities and	
Total Assets	$54,200	Owner's Equity	$54,200

Prepayment of Insurance

TRANSACTION 4 On June 4, King paid vehicle insurance premiums of $7,200 for three years. This payment for future coverage created a new asset, Prepaid Insurance, and reduced Cash. As each month passes, $\frac{1}{36}$ of the amount, or $200, will appear on the income statement as Insurance Expense, the cost of that month's insurance coverage.

Westgate Driving School
Balance Sheet

Assets		**Liabilities**	
Cash	$23,000	(none)	
Prepaid Insurance	7,200		
Land	24,000		
		Owner's Equity	
		J. King, Capital	$54,200
Total Assets	$54,200	Total Liabilities and Owner's Equity	$54,200

Purchase of Supplies on Account

TRANSACTION 5 On June 5, King purchased fuel and other supplies on account for $3,600. This transaction increased assets (Supplies on Hand) by $3,600 and resulted in a liability (Accounts Payable) of $3,600. The increase in assets did not change owner's equity; it merely created a liability on the balance sheet. Because King could not anticipate the amount of supplies that would be *used* (become expense) in June, he classified the entire $3,600 as an asset. Later, when the amount of supplies used is determined, an expense will be reflected.

Westgate Driving School
Balance Sheet

Assets		**Liabilities**	
Cash	$23,000	Accounts Payable	$ 3,600
Prepaid Insurance	7,200		
Supplies on Hand	3,600	**Owner's Equity**	
Land	24,000	J. King, Capital	54,200
Total Assets	$57,800	Total Liabilities and Owner's Equity	$57,800

Billing for Fee Revenue

TRANSACTION 6 On June 26, students were billed $21,500 for June instructional fees. Providing instruction during the month generated an asset, Accounts Receivable, and revenue, which increased owner's equity (J. King, Capital), even though payment may not be received until a later period.

Westgate Driving School
Balance Sheet

Assets		**Liabilities**	
Cash	$23,000	Accounts Payable	$ 3,600
Accounts Receivable	21,500		
Prepaid Insurance	7,200		
Supplies on Hand	3,600	**Owner's Equity**	
Land	24,000	J. King, Capital	75,700
Total Assets	$79,300	Total Liabilities and Owner's Equity	$79,300

Payment of Salaries

TRANSACTION 7 On June 30, King paid instructors' salaries of $9,000 for June. This amount was June expense, because it represented the cost of employees' services used during June. Therefore, the Cash account and J. King, Capital were both reduced by $9,000.

Westgate Driving School
Balance Sheet

Assets		Liabilities	
Cash	$14,000	Accounts Payable	$ 3,600
Accounts Receivable	21,500		
Prepaid Insurance	7,200		
Supplies on Hand	3,600	**Owner's Equity**	
Land	24,000	J. King, Capital	66,700
		Total Liabilities and	
Total Assets	$70,300	Owner's Equity	$70,300

Collection of Accounts Receivable

TRANSACTION 8 On June 30, the school collected $18,000 on account from students billed in transaction 6. This transaction increased Cash and decreased Accounts Receivable—merely a shift in assets. Note that the revenue, which increased owner's equity, had already been reflected when the month's billings were made on June 26.

Westgate Driving School
Balance Sheet

Assets		Liabilities	
Cash	$32,000	Accounts Payable	$ 3,600
Accounts Receivable	3,500		
Prepaid Insurance	7,200		
Supplies on Hand	3,600	**Owner's Equity**	
Land	24,000	J. King, Capital	66,700
		Total Liabilities and	
Total Assets	$70,300	Owner's Equity	$70,300

Payment on Accounts Payable

TRANSACTION 9 On June 30, the school paid $1,600 on account for the fuel and supplies purchased in transaction 5. Paying $1,600 of the $3,600 owed reduced both Cash and Accounts Payable, therefore reducing both assets and liabilities. This payment was the partial settlement of a previously recorded obligation—*not* an expense.

Westgate Driving School
Balance Sheet

Assets		Liabilities	
Cash	$30,400	Accounts Payable	$ 2,000
Accounts Receivable	3,500		
Prepaid Insurance	7,200		
Supplies on Hand	3,600	**Owner's Equity**	
Land	24,000	J. King, Capital	66,700
		Total Liabilities and	
Total Assets	$68,700	Owner's Equity	$68,700

Payment of Utilities

TRANSACTION 10 On June 30, King paid $250 for office utilities (electricity and telephone). This amount was a June expense decreasing both assets and owner's equity because the amount represented the cost of utility services used during the month. Cash and J. King, Capital were reduced by $250.

Westgate Driving School
Balance Sheet

Assets		Liabilities	
Cash	$30,150	Accounts Payable	$ 2,000
Accounts Receivable	3,500		
Prepaid Insurance	7,200		
Supplies on Hand	3,600	**Owner's Equity**	
Land	24,000	J. King, Capital	66,450
		Total Liabilities and	
Total Assets	$68,450	Owner's Equity	$68,450

Withdrawal by Owner

TRANSACTION 11 On June 30, King withdrew $2,000 from the firm for personal use. This withdrawal reduced Cash and J. King, Capital by $2,000. Note that the effect of this transaction was the reverse of transaction 1, in which King invested personal funds in the school.

Westgate Driving School
Balance Sheet

Assets		Liabilities	
Cash	$28,150	Accounts Payable	$ 2,000
Accounts Receivable	3,500		
Prepaid Insurance	7,200		
Supplies on Hand	3,600	**Owner's Equity**	
Land	24,000	J. King, Capital	64,450
		Total Liabilities and	
Total Assets	$66,450	Owner's Equity	$66,450

Recording Insurance Expense

TRANSACTION 12 On June 30, $\frac{1}{36}$ (one month) of the three years' prepaid insurance, or $200, had expired and no longer represented an asset; it became insurance expense for June. (Recall that in transaction 4 on June 4, the firm paid $7,200 for a 36-month policy.) Therefore, both the asset, Prepaid Insurance, and J. King, Capital were reduced by $200.

Westgate Driving School
Balance Sheet

Assets		Liabilities	
Cash	$28,150	Accounts Payable	$ 2,000
Accounts Receivable	3,500		
Prepaid Insurance	7,000		
Supplies on Hand	3,600	**Owner's Equity**	
Land	24,000	J. King, Capital	64,250
		Total Liabilities and	
Total Assets	$66,250	Owner's Equity	$66,250

Recording Supplies Expense

TRANSACTION 13 On June 30, supplies were counted, and only $1,350 worth of supplies remained on hand. Because supplies purchased for $3,600 in transaction 5 on June 5 were reflected as an asset, that portion of the purchase no longer on hand, $2,250, represented supplies used, or the supplies expense for the month. The result was a $2,250 decrease in both Supplies on Hand and J. King, Capital.

Westgate Driving School
Balance Sheet

Assets		Liabilities	
Cash	$28,150	Accounts Payable	$ 2,000
Accounts Receivable	3,500		
Prepaid Insurance	7,000		
Supplies on Hand	1,350	**Owner's Equity**	
Land	24,000	J. King, Capital	62,000
		Total Liabilities and	
Total Assets	$64,000	Owner's Equity	$64,000

Transactions 12 and 13 are reflected on the balance sheet to ensure that the items on that statement reflect the current end-of-period amounts. Because $200 of prepaid insurance has expired and $2,250 of supplies on hand are used during June, the related assets are reduced, and the amounts, representing June expenses, must be subtracted from the owner's capital account. These transactions are referred to as *adjustments.* A thorough discussion of adjustments is given in Chapter 3.

Summary of June Activities

Exhibit 1–3 summarizes the June activities of the Westgate Driving School and shows their effect on the balance sheet equation. The final results are, of course, identical with those given on the balance sheet prepared after transaction 13. The June 30 balance sheet is the only one that the Westgate Driving School would actually prepare, because June 30 is the end of the accounting period.

As a result of the driving school's June activities, John King's capital increased from his original investment of $60,000 to $62,000, an increase of $2,000. Had King not withdrawn $2,000 for personal use, the increase would have been $4,000, which represents the net income, or net earnings, for June.

THE INCOME STATEMENT

Although it is important to know the amount of net income, it is equally important to know how it was earned. To show the results of operations for a period, we prepare an income statement, which lists the revenue and expenses. When total revenue exceeds total expenses, the resulting amount is net income; when expenses exceed revenue, the resulting amount is a net loss. To prepare a June income statement for the Westgate Driving School, we must identify the revenue and expenses by analyzing the changes in owner's equity for the period. The changes in John King's capital, taken from Exhibit 1–3, are shown below, with an explanation of each change:

(1) Capital contribution	+	$60,000
(3) Rent expense	−	5,800
(6) Billings to students	+	21,500
(7) Salaries expense	−	9,000
(10) Utilities expense	−	250
(11) Withdrawal by King	−	2,000
(12) Insurance expense	−	200
(13) Supplies expense	−	2,250
Ending Capital Balance		$62,000

EXHIBIT 1–3

SUMMARY OF JUNE ACTIVITIES
AND THEIR EFFECT ON THE BALANCE SHEET EQUATION

	Assets									=	Liabilities	+	Owner's Equity
Transaction	Cash	+	Accounts Receivable	+	Prepaid Insurance	+	Supplies on Hand	+	Land	=	Accounts Payable	+	J. King, Capital
(1)	+ $60,000												+ $60,000
(2)	− 24,000								+ $24,000				
(3)	− 5,800												− 5,800
(4)	− 7,200				+ $7,200								
(5)							+ $3,600				+ $3,600		
(6)			+ $21,500										+ 21,500
(7)	− 9,000												− 9,000
(8)	+ 18,000		− 18,000										
(9)	− 1,600										− 1,600		
(10)	− 250												− 250
(11)	− 2,000												− 2,000
(12)					− 200								− 200
(13)							− 2,250						− 2,250
	$28,150	+	$ 3,500	+	$7,000	+	$1,350	+	$24,000	=	$2,000	+	$62,000
	$64,000										$64,000		

From this list of transactions and adjustments, we see that revenue, or instructional fees earned, equals $21,500, the June billings to students in transaction 6. The expenses are derived from transactions 3, 7, 10, 12, and 13 for rent, salaries, utilities, insurance, and supplies. Items 1 and 11, representing contributions and withdrawals by King, are ignored in preparing the income statement.

Westgate Driving School's formal income statement for the month of June, which would be prepared to accompany the June 30 balance sheet, appears in Exhibit 1–4.

STATEMENT OF OWNER'S EQUITY

Frequently at the end of an accounting period, a **statement of owners' equity** is prepared to accompany the balance sheet and income statement. This is simply a summary of the changes in the owners' capital balance during the period. Exhibit 1–5 shows this type of statement for the Westgate Driving School. Note that the ending balance on this statement agrees with the owner's capital balance on the balance sheet at June 30, 19XX. (See Exhibit 1–3.)

RELATIONSHIP OF INCOME STATEMENT, STATEMENT OF OWNERS' EQUITY, AND BALANCE SHEET

The income statement, the statement of owners' equity, and the balance sheet complement each other. As you can see in Exhibit 1–6, the net income (or net

EXHIBIT 1–4

Westgate Driving School
Income Statement
For the Month of June, 19XX

Revenue		
Instructional Fees Earned		$21,500
Expenses		
Rent Expense	$5,800	
Salaries Expense	9,000	
Utilities Expense	250	
Insurance Expense	200	
Supplies Expense	2,250	
Total Expenses		17,500
Net Income		$ 4,000

loss) for a period is an input into the statement of owners' equity, while the ending owners' equity balance on the statement is an input into the balance sheet at the end of the period. When financial statements are prepared, the sequence suggested by this relationship is customarily followed; that is, the income statement is prepared first, then the statement of owners' equity, and then the balance sheet. The statements of Westgate Driving School in Exhibit 1–6 are shown in condensed form.

FORMS OF BUSINESS ORGANIZATION

The principal forms of business organization are the **sole proprietorship,** the **partnership,** and the **corporation.** Although sole proprietorships, or single-owner businesses, are probably the most numerous, the corporate form of business is the most important in our economy. The partnership form is often used when two or more sole proprietorships merge into one business. For many years, professional people such as physicians, attorneys, and public accountants oper-

EXHIBIT 1–5

Westgate Driving School
Statement of Owner's Equity
For the Month of June, 19XX

J. King, Capital, June 1, 19XX	$ –0–
Add: Capital Contributed in June	60,000
Net Income for June	4,000
	$64,000
Less: Capital Withdrawn in June	2,000
J. King, Capital, June 30, 19XX	$62,000

EXHIBIT 1–6

Condensed Statements of Westgate Driving School

Income Statement	
Revenue	$21,500
Expenses: (itemized)	17,500
Net Income	$ 4,000

Statement of Owner's Equity	
King, Capital, June 1	$ –0–
Capital Contributed in June	60,000
Net Income	4,000
	$64,000
Capital Withdrawn in June	2,000
King, Capital, June 30	$62,000

Balance Sheet			
Assets (itemized)	$64,000	Liabilities (itemized)	$ 2,000
		Owner's Equity King, Capital	62,000
Total Assets	$64,000	Total Liabilities and Owner's Equity	$64,000

ated as partnerships because their codes of ethics or state laws prohibited incorporation. Most states now permit a special type of incorporation or association, and professional organizations have changed their codes of ethics to accommodate this change. Most professional firms, however, still operate as partnerships. For large-scale operations, the corporate form of organization has many advantages. These will be discussed in Chapter 15.

The principal differences in the balance sheets for the three types of business organizations just described appear in the owners' equity section. State corporation laws require that corporations segregate, in their balance sheets, the owners' investment (the amount paid for their stock) and any accumulated earnings. Because there are no comparable legal restrictions on sole proprietorships and partnerships, these types of businesses do not have to distinguish between amounts invested by owners and undistributed earnings.

The following illustrations demonstrate the variations in the balance sheet presentation of owners' equity for the three forms of business organization. In Chapters 14–18, we will consider in more detail the distinctive features of corporation and partnership accounting.

Case I: Sole Proprietorship

George Taylor originally invested $50,000 in a graphics business. Subsequent earnings left in the business amounted to $30,000. The owner's equity section of the firm's balance sheet would appear as follows:

Owner's Equity	
G. Taylor, Capital	$80,000

Case II: Partnership

George Taylor, Eva Williams, and John Young invested $25,000, $15,000, and $10,000, respectively, in a graphics business. Each partner's share of the subsequent earnings of $30,000 not withdrawn from the business was $10,000. The owners' equity section of this firm's balance sheet would appear as follows:

Owners' Equity	
G. Taylor, Capital	$35,000
E. Williams, Capital	25,000
J. Young, Capital	20,000
Total Owners' Equity	$80,000

Case III: Corporation

George Taylor, Eva Williams, and John Young began a corporation investing $25,000, $15,000, and $10,000, respectively, and receiving shares of stock for those amounts, totaling $50,000. This amount, called Capital Stock, is not available for distribution to the owners (stockholders). Unlike sole proprietorships and partnerships, in which owners are personally liable for the firm's debts, corporate stockholders' liability is usually limited to their investment. Therefore, the capital stock amount is kept intact to protect the firm's creditors. Because there may be many shareholders and because the shares of stock are freely transferable, the identity of the stockholders cannot be shown. Corporate earnings, amounting to $30,000, that have not been distributed are identified as *retained earnings* in the corporate balance sheet. Ordinarily, this is the maximum amount that can still be distributed to the shareholders. The stockholders' equity section of the firm's balance sheet would appear as follows:

Stockholders' Equity	
Capital Stock	$50,000
Retained Earnings	30,000
	$80,000

In sole proprietorships and partnerships the owners may make withdrawals quite informally, at their own discretion. A withdrawal results in a decrease to cash and a decrease in the owner's capital account. In a corporation, a formal procedure is needed. The board of directors, elected by the stockholders, must meet and "declare a dividend" before the distribution can be made to the stockholders. If the firm in our illustration declared and paid a dividend of $5,000, both cash and retained earnings would be reduced by that amount, and the retained earnings balance would be $25,000.

KEY POINTS FOR CHAPTER OBJECTIVES

1 Provide a basis for understanding the goals of the accounting process and flows of accounting information (pp. 3–7):

- Accounting is the process of (1) recording, (2) classifying, (3) reporting, and (4) interpreting financial data.
- Much of the recording and classifying of data is fairly routine and is often done by computer.
- Reporting to management, taxing agencies, and some regulatory agencies is in accordance with their directives or regulations; reporting to most other users is in accordance with generally accepted accounting principles.

2 Describe the various fields of accounting activity (pp. 7–9):

- Private accountants assist their employers (manufacturing, wholesale, retail, and service firms) in planning, controlling, and reporting operations.
- Public accountants render independent audit reports and provide other services for client firms.
- Government accountants are employed by federal, state, and local government agencies.

3 Provide an overview of the basic financial reports and their underlying concepts (pp. 10–13):

- Although a balance sheet and an income statement are usually prepared at the same time, a balance sheet presents financial position *at a point in time*, whereas the income statement presents operating results *for a period of time*.
- The accounting equation, Assets = Liabilities + Owners' Equity, represents the basic structure of the balance sheet and holds true after each accounting transaction.
- Some of the major underlying accounting concepts are:
  accounting entity: Each business venture is a separate unit, accounted for separately.
  historical cost: Assets are reported at acquisition price and are not adjusted upward.
  objectivity: Where possible, recording of transactions should be supported by verifiable evidence.
  going concern: The assumption is made in accounting that a business will continue indefinitely.
  measuring unit: Conventional accounting statements are expressed in money amounts, unadjusted for changes in the value of the dollar.

4 Explain and illustrate the effect of transactions on the balance sheet (pp. 13–20):

- Certain transactions may change the character and amounts of assets or liabilities, or both, but have no effect on owners' equity.
- Owners' equity is increased by contributions from owners and by revenue. It is decreased by withdrawals and expenses. Only revenue and expenses are used in determining net income. In determining revenue and expense on an *accrual basis*, revenue is recognized *when earned* rather than when cash is received, and expenses are recognized *when goods and services are used* rather than when they are paid for.

5 Describe and illustrate the relationship of the income statement to the statement of owners' equity and the balance sheet (pp. 20–22):

- First, net income is determined by subtracting the total expenses from revenue on the income statement.

- Next, net income is added to the owners' beginning capital and current contributions; withdrawals are subtracted to determine owners' ending capital.
- Finally, the balance sheet is prepared showing the owners' ending capital.

6 Explain the forms of business organization (pp. 22–24):

- The major differences in accounting for sole proprietorships, partnerships, and corporations appear in the presentation of owners' equity. In sole proprietorships and partnerships, the amount of equity shown for each owner is simply the sum of the amounts invested plus undistributed net income. A single amount is shown for each owner. For a corporation, state laws require the owners' investment to be shown separately, as capital stock, and the undistributed net income shown separately as retained earnings. Generally, only the retained earnings of corporations is available for distribution to the owners (stockholders).

KEY TERMS USED IN THIS CHAPTER

accrual basis 15*
accounting equation 11
assets 11
balance sheet 10
cash basis 15
controller 8
corporation 22
expense 14
financial accounting 6
generally accepted accounting principles 7
going concern 13
historical cost 12
income statement 10
internal auditing 8
liabilities 11
managerial accounting 4
measuring unit 13
net income 14
objectivity 13
owners' equity 12
partnership 22
revenue 14
sole proprietorship 22
statement of cash flows 10
statement of financial position 10
statement of owners' equity 21

SELF-TEST QUESTIONS FOR REVIEW

(Answers are at the end of this chapter.)

1. Which of the following types of accountants should be completely independent of the firm or organization whose financial data is being examined?
   (a) Controller
   (b) Certified public accountant
   (c) Internal auditor
   (d) Firm's budget director

2. A sole proprietor decided to use the same bank account for his personal affairs as for his business. Which of the following accounting concepts is violated?
   (a) Going concern
   (b) Accounting entity
   (c) Measuring unit
   (d) Objectivity

*The number in color following each term corresponds to the page number on which the term is first discussed.

3. Which of the following transactions does not affect the balance sheet totals?
   (a) Purchasing $500 supplies on account.
   (b) Paying a $3,000 note payable.
   (c) Collecting $4,000 from customers on account.
   (d) Withdrawal of $800 by the firm's owner.

4. The ending balance of owner's equity is $67,000. During the year, the owner contributed $5,000 and withdrew $4,000. If the firm had $10,000 net income for the year, what was the beginning owner's equity?
   (a) $56,000
   (b) $58,000
   (c) $78,000
   (d) $76,000

5. The beginning and ending balances of owner's equity for the year were $30,000 and $35,000, respectively. If owner's withdrawals exceeded contributions during the year by $3,000, what was the net income or net loss for the year?
   (a) $8,000 net loss
   (b) $14,000 net income
   (c) $2,000 net income
   (d) $8,000 net income

DEMONSTRATION PROBLEM FOR REVIEW

L. D. Ford operates the Ford Courier Service, a single proprietorship. The firm utilizes leased vehicles, and specializes in delivery services to banks, computer centers, film dealers, pharmacies, and various small businesses. On January 1 of the current year, the assets and liabilities of the business were as follows: Cash, $8,000; Accounts Receivable, $4,200; Supplies on Hand, $1,200; Prepaid Insurance, $1,800; and Accounts Payable, $1,400. The January business activities were as follows:

(1) Paid $600 on Accounts Payable.
(2) Paid January rent, $3,600.
(3) Received $2,000 on account from customers.
(4) Purchased supplies on account, $500.
(5) Billed customers for delivery services performed on account, $11,500.
(6) Paid employees' wages, $2,400.
(7) Received $2,000 for delivery services performed for cash customers.
(8) Paid utilities expense, $180.
(9) Withdrew $900 cash for Ford's personal use.
(10) Counted supplies on hand at the end of January, $980.
(11) Determined that $150 insurance premiums had expired during January.

REQUIRED

(a) From the data in the first paragraph, prepare a balance sheet equation for Ford Courier Service as of January 1 of the current year. Use the horizontal form illustrated in Exhibit 1–3 and place the amounts on the first line of the form.

(b) Following the form of Exhibit 1–3, show how transactions 1–11 affect the beginning balance sheet amounts, and total the columns to prove that total assets equal liabilities plus owner's equity at January 31.

(c) Prepare an income statement for January.

SOLUTION TO DEMONSTRATION PROBLEM

		Cash	+ Accounts Receivable	+ Supplies on Hand	+ Prepaid Insurance	=	Accounts Payable	+ L. D. Ford, Capital
(a)		$8,000	+ $ 4,200	+ $1,200	+ $1,800	=	$1,400	+ $13,800
(b)	(1)	− 600					− 600	
	(2)	− 3,600						− 3,600
	(3)	+ 2,000	− 2,000					
	(4)			+ 500			+ 500	
	(5)		+ 11,500					+ 11,500
	(6)	− 2,400						− 2,400
	(7)	+ 2,000						+ 2,000
	(8)	− 180						− 180
	(9)	− 900						− 900
	(10)			− 720				− 720
	(11)				− 150			− 150
		$4,320	+ $13,700	+ $ 980	+ $1,650	=	$1,300	+ $19,350
		$20,650					$20,650	

(c)

Ford Courier Service
Income Statement
For the Month of January, 19XX

Revenue		
Delivery Fees Earned		$13,500
Expenses		
Rent Expense	$3,600	
Wages Expense	2,400	
Utilities Expense	180	
Supplies Expense	720	
Insurance Expense	150	
Total Expenses		7,050
Net Income		$ 6,450

QUESTIONS

1–1 Distinguish between *financial* and *managerial* accounting.

1–2 Name some outside groups that may be interested in a company's financial data and state their particular interests.

1–3 What factors are important in determining a firm's need for electronic data processing?

1–4 Since financial accounting data are primarily historical, how are they useful for control purposes?

1–5 What are *generally accepted accounting principles*, and by whom are they established?

1–6 Why do business firms frequently keep more than one set of records on certain aspects of their financial activities?

1–7 How do the functions of private accountants and public accountants differ?

1–8 What is the purpose of a balance sheet? An income statement?

1–9 Define *assets, liabilities,* and *owners' equity.*

1–10 Explain how the presentation of owners' equity in the balance sheet of a corporation differs from that of a single proprietorship.

1–11 What is meant by the *accounting entity?*

1–12 Explain the concepts of *historical cost, objectivity,* and *going concern*. How are they related?

1–13 When the owners of a business withdraw cash, do the withdrawals appear as expenses on the income statement? Explain.

1–14 The owner's capital on a particular balance sheet is $70,000. Without seeing the rest of this financial statement, can you say that the owner should be able to withdraw $70,000 cash from the business? Justify your answer.

1–15 How do the accrual basis and the cash basis of accounting differ?

1–16 Describe a transaction that would
(a) Increase one asset but not change the amount of total assets.
(b) Decrease an asset and a liability.
(c) Decrease an asset and owners' equity.
(d) Increase an asset and a liability.

1–17 Indicate whether each of the following would increase, decrease, or have no effect on owners' equity:
(a) Purchased supplies for cash.
(b) Withdrew supplies for personal use.
(c) Paid salaries.
(d) Purchased equipment for cash.
(e) Invested cash in business.
(f) Rendered service to customers, on account.
(g) Rendered service to customers, for cash.

1–18 On December 31 of the current year, the Moran Company had $400,000 in total assets and owed $140,000 to creditors. If this corporation's capital stock amounted to $200,000, what amount of retained earnings should appear on a December 31 balance sheet?

1–19 During 19XX, the owners' equity of the Bailey Sport Shop increased from $80,000 to $94,000 even though the owners withdrew $10,000 for personal use. What was the net income (or loss) during 19XX if capital contributions were $9,000?

1–20 A business had total liabilities of $60,000 at the beginning of the year and $50,000 at year-end. At year-end, owner's equity was $80,000 and total assets were $20,000 greater than at the beginning of the year. If capital contributed exceeded capital withdrawn by $18,000, what was the net income for the year?

EXERCISES

Transaction analysis

1–21 Following the example shown in (a) below, indicate the effects of the listed transactions on the assets, liabilities, and owner's equity of the balance sheet of Linda Miller, certified public accountant, a sole proprietorship.
(a) Purchased, for cash, a typewriter for use in office.
ANSWER: Increase assets (Office Equipment)
Decrease assets (Cash)
(b) Rendered accounting services and billed customer.
(c) Paid rent for month.
(d) Rendered tax services to customer for cash.
(e) Received amount due from customer in (b).
(f) Purchased, on account, supplies estimated to last two years.
(g) Paid employees' salaries for month.
(h) Paid for supplies purchased in (f).
(i) Withdrew cash for personal use.

Balance sheet and net income determination

1–22 At the beginning of the current year, Dunn's Masonry had the following balance sheet:

Assets		Liabilities	
Cash	$ 8,400	Accounts Payable	$12,000
Accounts Receivable	9,600		
Equipment (Less Accumulated Depreciation)	30,000	**Owner's Equity**	
		Dunn, Capital	36,000
Total Assets	$48,000	Total Liabilities and Owner's Equity	$48,000

(a) At the end of the current year, Dunn had the following assets and liabilities: Cash, $16,200; Accounts Receivable, $19,800; Equipment (less Accumulated Depreciation), $28,000; and Accounts Payable, $10,000. Prepare a year-end balance sheet for Dunn's Masonry.

(b) Assuming that Dunn did not invest any money in the business during the year, but withdrew $6,000 for personal use, what was the net income or net loss for the current year?

(c) Assuming that Dunn invested an additional $8,000 early in the year, but withdrew $12,000 before the end of the year, what was the net income or net loss for the current year?

Transaction analysis and net income determination

1–23 The balance sheet of B. Lyons, attorney, at the beginning of an accounting period is given in equation form below, followed by seven transactions whose effects on the equation are shown.

(a) For each numbered item, describe the transaction that occurred. Of all the transactions affecting B. Lyons, Capital, only transaction 5 had no effect on net income for the period.

(b) What is the amount of net income for the period?

	Cash	+	Accounts Receivable	+	Supplies on Hand	+	Prepaid Rent	=	Accounts Payable	+	B. Lyons, Capital
Balance	$7,600	+	$9,000	+	$800	+	$3,600	=	$600	+	$20,400
(1)	+ 4,200		− 4,200								
(2)					+ 200				+ 200		
(3)			+ 5,000								+ 5,000
(4)	− 500								− 500		
(5)	− 1,600										− 1,600
(6)					− 480						− 480
(7)							− 600				− 600
	$9,700	+	$9,800	+	$520	+	$3,000	=	$300	+	$22,720

Determination of net income and ending capital

1–24 The following income statement and balance sheet information is available for Benson Appraisers at the end of the current month:

Supplies on Hand	$ 2,500	Accounts Payable	$ 7,000
Accounts Receivable	17,000	Salaries Expense	20,000
Utilities Expense	400	Appraisal Service Fees Earned	32,000
Supplies Expense	600		
Rent Expense	2,000	R. Benson, Capital (at beginning of month)	24,000
Cash	18,500		

(a) Without preparing a formal income statement, calculate the net income or net loss for the month.

(b) If R. Benson made no additional investment during the month, but withdrew $2,000, what is the amount of her capital at the end of the month?

Determination of omitted financial statement data

1–25 For the four unrelated situations below, compute the unknown amounts indicated by the letters appearing in each column.

	A	B	C	D
Beginning:				
Assets	$ 8,000	$12,000	$28,000	$ (d)
Liabilities	3,600	4,000	6,000	9,000
Ending:				
Assets	10,000	18,000	38,000	40,000
Liabilities	2,600	(b)	8,000	12,000
During year:				
Capital Contributed	4,000	1,500	(c)	2,500
Revenue	(a)	15,000	18,000	20,000
Capital Withdrawn	3,000	500	1,000	3,500
Expenses	7,500	12,000	14,000	15,000

Determination of retained earnings and net income

1–26 The following information appears in the records of Allison Corporation at the end of the current year:

Accounts Receivable	$36,000	Retained Earnings	$?
Accounts Payable	16,000	Supplies on Hand	4,000
Cash	18,000	Equipment	
Capital Stock	150,000	(Less Accumulated Depreciation)	138,000

(a) Without preparing a formal balance sheet, calculate the amount of retained earnings at the end of the current year.

(b) If the amount of the retained earnings at the beginning of the current year was $24,000, and $8,000 in dividends were declared and paid this year, what was the net income for the year?

PROBLEMS

Transaction analysis, income statement, and owner's equity statement

1–27 R. L. Harding Appraisal Service is a sole proprietorship providing commercial and industrial appraisals and feasibility studies. On January 1 of the current year, the assets and liabilities of the business were the following: Cash, $12,500; Accounts Receivable, $15,500; Supplies on Hand, $500; and Accounts Payable, $2,500. The following business transactions occurred during January:

(1) Paid rent for three months, $1,500.
(2) Received $7,200 on customers' accounts.
(3) Paid $1,200 on accounts payable.
(4) Received $2,400 for services performed for cash customers.
(5) Purchased $600 worth of supplies on account.
(6) Billed the city for a feasibility study performed, $7,200, and various other credit customers, $5,400.
(7) Paid salary of assistant, $2,800.
(8) Paid utilities expense, $450.
(9) Withdrew $2,000 cash for personal use of R. L. Harding.
(10) Supplies on hand at the end of January amounted to $680.
(11) Determined that rent expense for the month was $500 (see transaction 1).

REQUIRED

(a) From the data in the first paragraph, prepare a balance sheet equation for R. L. Harding Appraisal Service as of January 1 of the current year. Use the horizontal form illustrated in Exhibit 1–3 and place the amounts on the first line of the form. The headings should be as follows: Cash, Accounts Receivable, Supplies on Hand, Prepaid Rent, Accounts Payable, and R. L. Harding, Capital.

(b) Following the form of Exhibit 1–3, show the effects of transactions 1–11 on the beginning balance sheet amounts, and total the columns to prove that assets equal liabilities plus owner's equity at January 31.

(c) Prepare an income statement for January.

(d) Prepare a statement of owner's equity for January.

Transaction analysis

1–28 An analysis (similar to Exhibit 1–3) of the transactions of Jackson Detective Agency for the month of May appears below. Line 1 summarizes Jackson's balance sheet data on May 1; lines 2–10 represent the business transactions for May.

	Cash	+ Accounts Receivable	+ Supplies on Hand	+ Prepaid Insurance	=	Notes Payable	+ Accounts Payable	+ Jackson, Capital
(1)	$8,400	+ $9,600	+ $540	+ $720	=	$3,000	+ $560	+ $15,700
(2)	+ 2,000					+ 2,000		
(3)	+ 5,400	− 5,400						
(4)			+ 480				+ 480	
(5)		+ 9,500						+ 9,500
(6)	− 600							− 600
(7)	+ 2,000							+ 2,000
(8)			− 400					− 400
(9)				− 60				− 60
(10)	− 1,500					− 1,500		

REQUIRED

(a) Prove that assets equal liabilities plus owner's equity at May 1.

(b) Describe the apparent transaction indicated by each line. (For example, line 2: Borrowed $2,000, giving a note payable.) If any line could reasonably represent more than one type of transaction, describe each type of transaction.

(c) Prove that assets equal liabilities plus owner's equity at May 31.

Income statement, owner's equity statement, and balance sheet

1–29 On March 1, Rita Holt began the Arrow Delivery Service, which provides delivery of bulk mailings to the post office, neighborhood delivery of weekly papers, data delivery to computer service centers, and various other delivery services via leased vans. On February 28, Holt invested $30,000 of her own funds in the firm and borrowed $10,000 from her father on a six-month, non-interest-bearing note payable. The following information is available at March 31:

Accounts Receivable	$28,400	Delivery Fees Earned	$32,500
Rent Expense	2,400	Cash	21,200
Advertising Expense	900	Supplies on Hand, March 31	6,500
Supplies Expense	3,100	Notes Payable	10,000
Accounts Payable	5,600	Prepaid Insurance, March 31	3,300
Salaries Expense	12,500	Insurance Expense	300
Miscellaneous Expense	500	R. Holt, Capital, March 1	30,000

Holt made a $4,000 additional investment during March, but withdrew $3,000 during the month.

REQUIRED

(a) Prepare an income statement for the month of March.

(b) Prepare a statement of owner's equity for the month of March.

(c) Prepare a balance sheet at March 31.

Balance sheets for a corporation

1–30 The following balance sheet data is given for the Brittany Catering Service, a corporation, at May 31 of the current year:

Accounts Receivable	$12,300	Accounts Payable	$ 5,300
Notes Payable	10,000	Cash	18,200
Equipment (Less Accumulated Depreciation)	52,500	Capital Stock	50,000
Supplies on Hand	8,700	Retained Earnings	?

Assume that, during the next two days, only the following transactions occurred:

June 1 Purchased additional equipment costing $8,000, giving $3,000 cash and a $5,000 note payable.

2 Declared and paid a dividend, $4,000.

REQUIRED

(a) Prepare a balance sheet at May 31 of the current year.

(b) Prepare a balance sheet at June 2 of the current year.

Transaction analysis and income statement for a corporation

1–31 On June 1 of the current year, a group of bush pilots in Thunder Bay, Ontario, formed the Wilderness Fly-In Service, Inc., by selling $80,000 capital stock for cash. The group then leased several amphibious aircraft and docking facilities, equipping them to transport fishermen and hunters to outpost camps owned by various resorts. The following transactions occurred during June of the current year:

(1) Sold capital stock for cash, $80,000.
(2) Paid June rent for aircraft, dockage, and dockside office, $4,800.
(3) Purchased fuel and other supplies on account, $3,600.
(4) Paid bill for June advertising in various sport magazines, $750.
(5) Paid insurance premiums for six months in advance, $7,200.
(6) Rendered fly-in services for various groups for cash, $21,000.
(7) Billed the Ministry of Natural Resources for transporting mapping personnel, $5,200, and also billed various firms for fly-in services, $10,000.
(8) Paid $2,400 on accounts payable.
(9) Received $8,500 on account from clients.
(10) Paid June wages, $10,500.
(11) Declared and paid a dividend, $2,500.
(12) Determined that supplies and fuel on hand at June 30 amounted to $750.
(13) Determined that $1,200 insurance premiums expired during June.

REQUIRED

(a) Using the horizontal form of the balance sheet equation illustrated in Exhibit 1–3, designate the following column headings: Cash, Accounts Receivable, Supplies on Hand, Prepaid Insurance, Accounts Payable, Capital Stock, and Retained Earnings.

(b) Following the form of Exhibit 1–3, show how the June transactions affect the balance sheet amounts, and total all columns to prove that assets equal liabilities plus stockholders' equity.

(c) Prepare an income statement for June.

Balance sheets and income determination

1–32 Balance sheet information for the Whitney Packaging Service at the end of the last two years is given below.

	December 31, This Year	December 31, Last Year
Accounts Receivable	$41,000	$32,000
Accounts Payable	2,400	1,800
Cash	24,000	18,000
Equipment (Less Accumulated Depreciation)	27,000	30,000
Prepaid Insurance	1,200	800
Supplies on Hand	2,800	2,400
Land	15,000	15,000
Building (Less Accumulated Depreciation)	48,000	50,000
Mortgage Payable	38,000	42,000
Whitney, Capital	?	?

REQUIRED
(a) Prepare balance sheets for December 31 of each year.
(b) Whitney contributed $5,000 to the business early this year but withdrew $12,000 in December of this year. Calculate the net income for this year.

ALTERNATE PROBLEMS

Transaction analysis, income statement, and owner's equity statement

1–27A Erica Stewart began the Stewart Answering Service, a sole proprietorship, during December of last year. The firm provides services for professional people and is currently operating with leased equipment. On January 1 of this year, the assets and liabilities of the business were: Cash, $5,400; Accounts Receivable, $6,700; Supplies on Hand, $480; and Accounts Payable, $350. The following transactions occurred during January.

(1) Paid rent on office and equipment for January through March, $1,800.
(2) Collected $4,500 on account from clients.
(3) Purchased supplies on account, $250.
(4) Billed clients for work performed on account, $9,400.
(5) Paid $320 on accounts payable.
(6) Paid advertising expense, $280.
(7) Paid salaries expense, $3,200.
(8) Paid utilities expense, $180.
(9) Withdrew $1,200 for Erica Stewart's personal use.
(10) Supplies on hand at the end of January amounted to $360.
(11) Determined that $600 of prepaid rent had expired (see transaction 1).

REQUIRED
(a) From the information in the first paragraph, prepare a balance sheet equation for Stewart Answering Service. Use the horizontal form illustrated in Exhibit 1–3 and place the balance sheet amounts at January 1 on the first line of the form. Column headings should include: Cash, Accounts Receivable, Supplies on Hand, Prepaid Rent, Accounts Payable, and E. Stewart, Capital.
(b) Following the form of Exhibit 1–3, show the effects of the January transactions on the balance sheet amounts, and total all columns to prove that assets equal liabilities plus owner's equity.
(c) Prepare an income statement for January.
(d) Prepare a statement of owner's equity for January.

Transaction analysis

1–28A Appearing below is an analysis (similar to Exhibit 1–3) of the June transactions for David Johnson, consulting engineer. Line 1 summarizes Johnson's balance sheet data on June 1; lines 2–10 are the business transactions for June.

	Cash	+	Accounts Receivable	+	Supplies on Hand	+	Prepaid Rent	=	Accounts Payable	+	Notes Payable	+	D. Johnson, Capital
(1)	$3,500	+	$5,800	+	$620	+	$850	=	$490	+	0	+	$10,280
(2)				+	270			+	270				
(3)	+ 4,000									+	4,000		
(4)	+ 3,700	−	3,700										
(5)		+	4,200									+	4,200
(6)	− 220											−	220
(7)	− 540							−	540				
(8)	− 4,000									−	4,000		
(9)				−	520							−	520
(10)						−	425					−	425

REQUIRED
(a) Prove that assets equal liabilities plus owner's equity at June 1.
(b) Describe the apparent transaction indicated by each line. For example, line 2: Purchased supplies on account, $270. If any line could reasonably represent more than one type of transaction, describe each type of transaction.
(c) Prove that assets equal liabilities plus owner's equity on June 30.

Income statement, owner's equity statement, and balance sheet

1–29A After all transactions and adjustments have been reflected for the current year, the records of R. Jennings, interior decorator, show the following information:

Notes Payable	$ 2,400	Supplies on Hand, December 31	$ 8,200
Prepaid Insurance, December 31	700	Cash	4,300
Decorating Fees Earned	54,620	Accounts Receivable	35,400
Supplies Expense	4,400	Advertising Expense	520
Insurance Expense	350	Salaries Expense	19,200
Miscellaneous Expense	250	Rent Expense	5,400
R. Jennings, Capital January 1	25,750	Accounts Payable	1,450

Jennings made an additional investment of $3,000 in the business during the year and withdrew $8,500 near the end of the year.

REQUIRED
(a) Prepare an income statement for the current year.
(b) Prepare a statement of owner's equity for the current year.
(c) Prepare a balance sheet at December 31 of the current year.

Balance sheets for a corporation

1–30A The following balance sheet data is given for Carr Plumbing Contractors, Inc., at June 30 of the current year:

Accounts Payable	$ 4,700	Capital Stock	$100,000
Cash	25,600	Retained Earnings	?
Supplies on Hand	6,200	Notes Payable	7,500
Equipment (Less Accumulated Depreciation)	92,000	Accounts Receivable	19,000
		Prepaid Insurance	900

Assume that, during the next two days, only the following transactions occurred:
June 1 Paid non-interest-bearing note due today, $7,500.
2 Purchased equipment for $6,000, paying $1,000 cash and giving a note payable for the balance.
2 Declared and paid a dividend, $2,000.

REQUIRED
(a) Prepare a balance sheet at June 30 of the current year.
(b) Prepare a balance sheet at July 2 of the current year.

Transaction analysis and income statement

1–31A On December 1 of the current year, James Atwood started Psychological Resources, a sole proprietorship furnishing career and vocational counseling services. The following transactions took place during December:
(1) Atwood invested $8,000 in the business.
(2) Paid rent for December on leased office equipment, $80.
(3) Paid rent for office space for three months, $1,500.
(4) Purchased office supplies on account, $650.
(5) Received $750 for counseling services rendered for cash.
(6) Billed certain governmental agencies and other clients for counseling services, $4,650.
(7) Paid secretary's salary, $1,800.

(8) Paid utilities expense, $140.
(9) Withdrew $500 for personal use of James Atwood.
(10) Determined that supplies on hand at the end of December amounted to $420.
(11) Determined that office rent expense for the month was $500 (see transaction 3).

REQUIRED
(a) Using the horizontal form of the balance sheet equation illustrated in Exhibit 1–3, designate the following column headings: Cash, Accounts Receivable, Supplies on Hand, Prepaid Rent, Accounts Payable, and J. Atwood, Capital.
(b) Following the form of Exhibit 1–3, show how the December transactions affect the balance sheet amounts, and total all columns to prove that assets equal liabilities plus owner's equity.
(c) Prepare an income statement for December.

Balance sheets and income determination for a corporation

1–32A Balance sheet information for Curtis Janitorial Service, Inc., at the end of the last two years is given below.

	December 31, This Year	December 31, Last Year
Accounts Payable	$ 10,000	$ 8,000
Cash	18,000	12,000
Accounts Receivable	28,000	19,000
Land	20,000	20,000
Building (Less Accumulated Depreciation)	50,000	52,000
Equipment (Less Accumulated Depreciation)	65,000	68,000
Mortgage Payable	40,000	42,000
Supplies on Hand	12,500	10,000
Prepaid Insurance	1,500	1,000
Capital Stock	100,000	100,000
Retained Earnings	?	?

REQUIRED
(a) Prepare balance sheets for December 31 of each year.
(b) The firm declared and paid a dividend of $5,000 in December of this year. Calculate the net income for this year. (*Hint:* The net increase in retained earnings is equal to the net income less the dividend.)

BUSINESS DECISION PROBLEM

James Scott, a friend of yours, is negotiating the purchase of a sanitation firm called Ideal Pest Control. Scott has been employed by a national pest control service and knows the technical side of the business. However, he knows little about accounting, so he asks for your assistance. The sole owner of the firm, G. Clark, has provided Scott with income statements for the past three years, which show an average net income of $40,000 per year. The latest balance sheet shows total assets of $140,000 and liabilities of $15,000. Included among the assets are buildings listed at $36,000 after accumulated depreciation and equipment listed at $70,000 after accumulated depreciation. Scott brings the following matters to your attention:

1. Clark is asking $160,000 for the firm. He has told Scott that, because the firm has been earning 32% on the owner's investment, the price should be higher than the net assets on the balance sheet.
2. Scott has noticed no salary for Clark on the income statements, even though he worked half-time in the business. Clark explained that because he had other income, he withdrew only $10,000 each year from the firm for personal use. If he purchases the firm, Scott will hire a full-time manager for the firm at an annual salary of $20,000.

3. Scott wonders whether the buildings and equipment are really worth $106,000, the net amount shown on the balance sheet.
4. Clark's tax returns for the past three years report a lower net income for the firm than the amounts shown in the financial statements. Scott is skeptical about the accounting principles used in preparing the financial statements.

REQUIRED

(a) How did Clark arrive at the 32% return figure given in point 1? If Scott accepts Clark's average annual income figure of $40,000, what would Scott's percentage return be, assuming that the net income remained at the same level and that the firm was purchased for $160,000?

(b) Should Clark's withdrawals affect the net income reported in the financial statements? What will Scott's percentage return be if he takes into consideration the $20,000 salary he plans to pay a full-time manager?

(c) What explanation would you give Scott with respect to the value of the buildings and equipment?

(d) Could there be legitimate reasons for the difference between net income shown in the financial statements and net income reported on the tax returns, as mentioned in point 4? How might Scott obtain additional assurance about the propriety of the financial statements?

ANSWERS TO SELF-TEST QUESTIONS

1. (b) **2.** (b) **3.** (c) **4.** (a) **5.** (d)

2

THE DOUBLE-ENTRY ACCOUNTING SYSTEM

CHAPTER OBJECTIVES

1 Illustrate the expanded form of the accounting equation (pp. 39–40).
2 Explain the nature and format of an account (pp. 41–43).
3 Describe the system of debits and credits (pp. 43–45).
4 Illustrate debit and credit analysis of transactions (pp. 46–53).
5 Explain the nature and format of a trial balance (p. 54).
6 Discuss common types of errors in transaction analysis (pp. 54–55).

What advantages does the Merchant derive b
by double-entry? It is amongst the f
of th

JOHANN WOLFGANG VON G

The format for analyzing and recording transactions illustrated in Chapter 1 was useful in conveying a basic understanding of how transactions affect financial statements. This approach is not effective, however, in meeting management's needs for timely financial information. The transactions of most business firms are numerous and complex, affecting many different items appearing on the financial statements. Therefore, a formal system of classification and recording is required so that data may be gathered for day-to-day management requirements and timely accounting reports. In this chapter, we will examine the classification and recording system commonly called *double-entry* accounting. At the same time, we will expand several of the basic ideas introduced in Chapter 1.

CATEGORIES OF DATA NEEDED

Exhibit 2–1 shows the balance sheet and the income statement forms explained in Chapter 1. To prepare both the balance sheet and the income statement, we need five categories of information from the accounting system: *assets, liabilities, owners' equity, revenue*, and *expenses*. The first three relate to the balance sheet and the last two relate to the income statement.

In Chapter 1 we analyzed the effects of transactions on the balance sheet equation by starting with the three major categories: assets, liabilities, and owners' equity. When we used the basic accounting equation (Assets = Liabilities + Owners' Equity), we noted that owners' equity included increases from revenue and decreases from expenses. Specifically, owners' equity at the balance sheet

EXHIBIT 2–1

THE BASIC FINANCIAL STATEMENTS

ABC Company
Balance Sheet
December 31, 19XX

(List of assets)	$ XX	(List of liabilities)	$ XX
	XX		XX
	XX		
	XX	Total Liabilities	$ XX
		Owners' Equity	XX
Total Assets	$XXX	Total Liabilities and Owners' Equity	$XXX

ABC Company
Income Statement
For the Month of December, 19XX

Revenue		$XXX
Expenses:	$XX	
	XX	
	XX	
	XX	
Total Expenses		XX
Net Income		$ XX

date consisted of (1) the beginning balance, (2) net capital contributions (additional contributions less withdrawals), and (3) net income for the period (revenue less expenses). In preparing an income statement, we analyzed changes in owners' equity to obtain the necessary revenue and expense data.

Since in a typical business most transactions relate to revenue and expense, it is more efficient to keep track of revenue and expense as a separate part of owners' equity. The following expanded form of the accounting equation is useful:[1]

ASSETS = LIABILITIES + ——— OWNERS' EQUITY ———

[Beginning Capital + Contributions − Withdrawals] + [Revenue − Expenses]

If we had used this expanded equation in summarizing the June transactions of the Westgate Driving School (see Exhibit 1–3, page 21), the changes in owner's equity would have been shown in three columns, as follows:

	J. King, Capital + Contributions − Withdrawals		**Revenue**		**Expenses**
(1) Capital contribution	+ $60,000				
(3) Rent expense					$ 5,800
(6) Billings to students			+ $21,500		
(7) Salaries expense				−	9,000
(10) Utilities expense				−	250
(11) Withdrawal by King	− 2,000				
(12) Insurance expense				−	200
(13) Supplies expense				−	2,250
	$58,000	+	$21,500	−	$17,500
			$62,000		

Observe that the column totals in the above illustration, when added together, amount to $62,000, exactly the amount of the ending owner's equity shown in Exhibit 1–3. Segregating revenue and expense amounts, however, permits us to prepare an income statement without first having to analyze all changes in the owner's capital for the period. The desirability of doing this is apparent even in a situation as simple as our Westgate Driving School example. In more complex business situations—with many sources of revenue and possibly hundreds of different types of expenses—separate recording of revenue and expenses is imperative.

So far, our discussion of transaction analysis has been conceptual; we have tried to convey an understanding of how transactions affect the financial statements. Obviously, the system of transaction recording we have illustrated would be entirely inadequate for even relatively simple businesses, since even they will usually have a substantial number of transactions involving a variety of data to be reported in financial statements. In practice, the necessary data are accumulated in a set of records called *accounts*.

[1]In a corporation, beginning capital consists of both capital stock and retained earnings. Contributions would equal additional capital stock sold, whereas withdrawals would be the amount of dividends declared during the period.

THE ACCOUNT

The basic component of the formal accounting system is the **account,** which is an individual record of increases and decreases in specific assets, liabilities, owner capital, revenue, and expenses. The Cash account for the Westgate Driving School might appear as shown in Exhibit 2–2.

The amounts in the Westgate Driving School Cash account consist of the additions and deductions in the cash column of Exhibit 1–3. Increases in the Cash account have been placed on the left side and the decreases on the right side. A formal system of placement for increases and decreases in various accounts is explained later in this chapter. In our example, there was no beginning amount (balance), because June was the first month of business. A beginning amount would have appeared with the increases, above the entry for $60,000.

The form illustrated in Exhibit 2–2, called a *two-column* account, is often used in a manually maintained record-keeping system. Another popular form, called a *running balance,* or *three-column* account, is illustrated later in this chapter. Most account forms facilitate recording the following information:

1. The account title and number.
2. Amounts reflecting increases and decreases.
3. Cross-references to other accounting records.
4. Dates and descriptive notations.

Each account has a short account title that describes the data being recorded in that account. Some common account titles are Cash, Accounts Receivable, Notes Payable, Professional Fees Earned, and Rent Expense. In manually maintained records, increases and decreases are recorded in ruled columns under headings that indicate the meaning of the amounts appearing there. These amounts are referred to as **entries.** In other words, making an entry in an account consists of recording an amount in a particular place to represent either an increase or a

EXHIBIT 2–2

CASH ACCOUNT FOR THE WESTGATE DRIVING SCHOOL

Cash Account No. ______

Date	Description	Post. Ref.	Amount	Date	Description	Post. Ref.	Amount
19XX				19XX			
June 1			60,000	June 2			24,000
30			18,000	3			5,800
				4			7,200
				30			9,000
				30			1,600
				30			250
				30			2,000

decrease in the account. The normal balance of any account is simply the excess of increases over decreases that have been recorded to date. In Exhibit 2–2, we have indicated this balance, $28,150, on the left side of the account beside the last entry for an increase. This is the difference between the sum of the increases, $78,000, and the sum of the decreases, $49,850, both of which are written in pencil to provide temporary totals. Finally, most accounts contain space for presentation of other types of information—for example, the date of any entry, possibly some memoranda explaining a particular entry, and a posting reference column (indicated by "Post. Ref."). The posting reference column is used for noting the records from which entries into this account may have been taken. This practice will be explained more fully in the next chapter.

The account is an extremely simple record that can be summarized in terms of four money elements:

1. Beginning balance.
2. Additions.
3. Deductions.
4. Ending balance.

Obviously, if any three elements are known, the fourth can easily be computed. Normally, after transactions have been recorded, only the ending balance needs to be computed. Accountants, however, are sometimes confronted with situations in which available data are incomplete and reconstruction of accounts is necessary. Let us demonstrate such an analysis with the following example:

	A	B	C	D
Beginning balance	$10	$70	$ 40	$?
Additions	40	30	?	100
Deductions	20	?	160	120
Ending balance	?	10	0	40

In column A, the ending balance must be $20 greater than the beginning balance, because the additions exceed the deductions by $20. The ending balance is therefore $30. In B, the account balance decreased by $60, so the deductions must exceed the additions by $60. Therefore, total deductions are $90. Show that the unknown variable in column C is $120 and in column D is $60.

A simplified form often used to represent the account in accounting textbooks and in the classroom is referred to as the **T account** (because it resembles the letter *T*). This is merely a skeleton version of the account illustrated for actual record keeping. A T-account form with the June changes in Cash entered for the Westgate Driving School follows:

Cash

(1)	60,000	(2)	24,000
(8)	18,000	(3)	5,800
	78,000	(4)	7,200
		(7)	9,000
		(9)	1,600
		(10)	250
		(11)	2,000
			49,850

Because dates and other related data are usually omitted in T accounts, it is customary to "key" the entries with a number or a letter to identify the transactions or entry. This permits a systematic review of the entries in the event that an error has been made. It also enables anyone to review a set of such accounts and match related entries. The numbers in this T account are the ones used to identify the June transactions for the Westgate Driving School in our Chapter 1 example.

The printed account form in Exhibit 2–2 is appropriate for classifying accounting data in manual record-keeping systems. In accounting systems using computers, the account form may not be obvious because the actual data might be stored on media such as magnetic tapes or discs. Every accounting system, however, whether manual or automated, must provide for the retrieval and printing out of the types of information shown in the manual form.

THE SYSTEM OF DEBITS AND CREDITS

One basic characteristic of all account forms is that entries recording increases and decreases are separated. In some accounts, such as the Cash account illustrated in Exhibit 2–2, increases are recorded on the left-hand side of the account and decreases on the right-hand side; in other accounts the reverse is true. The method used in different types of accounts is a matter of convention; that is, a simple set of rules is followed. The remainder of this chapter is devoted to the discussion and illustration of such rules.

The terms **debit** and **credit** are used to describe the left-hand and the right-hand sides of an account, as shown below.

(Any type of account)

Debit	**Credit**
Always the left side	Always the right side

Regardless of what is recorded in an account, an entry made on the left-hand side is a debit to the account, while an entry recorded on the right-hand side is a credit to the account. Sometimes the abbreviations "dr." and "cr." are used.

The terms *debit* and *credit* are not synonymous with the words *increase* and *decrease.* The system of debits and credits related to increases and decreases in each of the five categories of accounts—assets, liabilities, owners' equity, revenue, and expenses—is shown in Exhibit 2–3 (page 45).

The system of debits and credits illustrated here is the standard **double-entry** system, so-called because at least two entries, a debit and a credit, are made for each transaction. The system of rules is analogous to the set of traffic rules whereby everyone in this country agrees to drive on the right-hand side of the road. Obviously, the system would work if we reversed everything; the important point is that we all follow the same rules.

Observe the following relationships in Exhibit 2–3:

1. *Debit* always refers to the left side of any account; *credit* refers to the right side.
2. Increases in asset and expense accounts are debit entries, while increases in liability, owners' equity, and revenue accounts are credit entries.
3. Decreases are logically recorded on the side opposite increases.

THE ORIGINS OF RECORD KEEPING

Double-entry bookkeeping is simply a specialized form of keeping accounts. It is neither a discovery of science nor the inspiration of a happy moment, but the outcome of continued efforts to meet the changing necessities of trade.*

The origin of keeping accounts has been traced as far back as 8500 B.C., the date archaeologists have established for certain clay tokens—cones, disks, spheres, and pellets—found in Mesopotamia (modern Iraq). These tokens represented such commodities as sheep, jugs of oil, bread, or clothing and were used in the Middle East to keep records. The tokens were often sealed in clay balls, called *bullae,* which were broken on delivery so the shipment could be checked against the invoice; *bullae,* in effect, were the first bills of lading. Later, symbols impressed on wet clay tablets replaced the tokens. Some experts consider this stage of record keeping the beginning of the art of writing, which spread rapidly along the trade routes and took hold throughout the known civilized world.†

Development of more formal account keeping methods is attributed to the merchants and bankers of Florence, Venice, and Genoa during the thirteenth to fifteenth centuries. The earliest of these methods consisted of accounts kept by a Florentine banker in 1211 A.D. The system was fairly primitive; accounts were not related in any special way (in terms of equality for entries), and balancing of the accounts was lacking. Systematic bookkeeping evolved from these methods, however, and double-entry records first appeared in Genoa in 1340 A.D.‡

The first treatise on the art of systematic bookkeeping appeared in 1494, in Venice. "Everything About Arithmetic, Geometry, and Proportion" (*Summa de Arithmetica, Geometria, Proportioni et Proportionalita*) was written by the Franciscan monk, Fra Luca Paciolo, one of the most celebrated mathematicians of his day. The work was not, in fact, intended to give instruction in bookkeeping, but to summarize the existing knowledge of mathematics. The treatise on bookkeeping appeared in the arithmetical part of the work. Although Paciolo made no claim to developing the art of bookkeeping, he has been regarded as the father of double-entry accounting. In "An Historical Defense of Bookkeeping," eminent accountant Henry Rand Hatfield referred to the system as one "sired four hundred years ago by a monk, and today damned by thousands of university students."§

*Richard Brown, ed., *A History of Accounting and Accountants* (New York: Augustus M. Kelly Publishers, 1968), p. 93.
†"The Roots of Writing," *Time,* August 1, 1977, p. 76.
‡Richard Brown, p. 99.
§A paper read before the American Association of University Instructors in Accounting (now the American Accounting Association), December 29, 1923, and reprinted in *The Journal of Accountancy,* April 1924, p. 247.

4. The normal balance of any account is on the side on which increases a recorded—asset and expense accounts normally have debit balances, while the other three groups normally have credit balances. This result occurs because increases in an account are customarily greater than or equal to decreases.

Note that the pattern for assets is opposite that for liabilities and owners' equity. Also observe that the pattern for revenue is the same as for owners' equity. This is to be expected, because revenue increases owners' equity. Following the same logic, the pattern for expenses is opposite that of owners' equity, because expenses reduce owners' equity.

THE RUNNING BALANCE ACCOUNT

In manually maintained accounting records, the **running balance,** or three-column, ledger account is often used rather than the symmetrical two-column form illustrated in Exhibit 2–2. The Cash account for the Westgate Driving School

EXHIBIT 2–3

PATTERN OF INCREASES AND DECREASES, DEBITS AND CREDITS, AND NORMAL BALANCES

The Five Major Categories of Accounts

	Assets		**Liabilities**		**Owners' Equity**		**Revenue**		**Expenses**	
1. Always true	Debit	Credit	Debit	Credit	Debit	Credit	Debit	Credit	Debit	Credit
2. Increases	+			+		+		+	+	
3. Decreases		–	–		–		–			–
4. Normal balance	★			★		★		★	★	

in running balance form is shown in Exhibit 2–4. Notice that the account contains all the information shown in the two-column account but also provides a balance after each transaction.

The major advantage of this type of account over the two-column account is that the account balance is apparent for any date during the period. Use of the running balance account also avoids the monthly ruling of accounts, which is customarily done when the two-column account is used. A slight disadvantage is that one must be careful to note whether the account has a normal balance or not. An abnormal account balance should be placed in parentheses. For example, if we overdrew our bank balance, the Cash account balance would be abnormal (a credit balance).

EXHIBIT 2–4

CASH ACCOUNT FOR THE WESTGATE DRIVING SCHOOL

Cash Account No. ______

Date		**Description**	**Post. Ref.**	**Debit**★	**Credit**	**Balance**
19XX						
June	1			60,000		60,000
	2				24,000	36,000
	3				5,800	30,200
	4				7,200	23,000
	30				9,000	14,000
	30			18,000		32,000
	30				1,600	30,400
	30				250	30,150
	30				2,000	28,150

We will use the running balance account in our formal illustrations throughout the succeeding chapters. To assist you in the earlier chapters, we have placed an asterisk (*) in the column of the account that designates its normal balance. In illustrations in which detail is not needed and concepts are emphasized, we will use T accounts.

ILLUSTRATION OF DEBIT AND CREDIT ANALYSIS

The following illustration of debit and credit analysis uses the transactions given in Chapter 1 for the first month's operations of the Westgate Driving School. Each transaction is stated, analyzed, and followed by an illustration of the appropriate debit and credit entries in the various accounts, using T accounts for simplicity. We have numbered each transaction for reference as in Chapter 1. In the transaction analysis and the resulting debits and credits, each entry resulting from a particular transaction is parenthetically keyed to the transaction number.

TRANSACTION 1 On June 1, John King deposited $60,000 of his personal funds in a special checking account for the Westgate Driving School.

Analysis In the first transaction of Westgate Driving School, King's contribution of capital increases both the assets and the equities of the firm. Specifically, Cash increases by $60,000, and the owner's equity account, J. King, Capital, increases by the same amount. The entries are

Debit Cash $60,000 **Credit** J. King, Capital $60,000

The related accounts would appear as follows:

Cash			
(1)	60,000		

J. King Capital			
		(1)	60,000

TRANSACTION 2 On June 2, King paid $24,000 for a lot to be used for storing vehicles and for some driving instruction.

Analysis This transaction represents the conversion of one asset to another, resulting in an increase in the asset Land and a decrease in the asset Cash. The entries are

Debit Land $24,000 **Credit** Cash $24,000

The related accounts would appear as follows:

Land			
(2)	24,000		

Cash			
(1)	60,000	(2)	24,000

TRANSACTION 3 On June 3, King paid $800 to rent a furnished office and $5,000 for leasing training vehicles for June.

Analysis The cost of using the office and the training vehicles is a June operating expense. When financial statements are prepared at the end of June, the month's rent will appear on the income statement as an expense. The transaction reduces Cash and increases Rent Expense. The entries are

Debit Rent Expense $5,800 **Credit** Cash $5,800

The related accounts would appear as follows:

Rent Expense

(3)	5,800		

Cash

(1)	60,000	(2)	24,000
		(3)	5,800

TRANSACTION 4 On June 4, King paid vehicle insurance premiums of $7,200 for three years.

Analysis This payment for future coverage creates an asset, Prepaid Insurance, and reduces the asset Cash. As each month passes, $\frac{1}{36}$ of the amount, or $200, will appear on the income statement as Insurance Expense, the cost of that month's coverage (see transaction 12). The entries are

Debit Prepaid Insurance $7,200 **Credit** Cash $7,200

The related accounts would appear as follows:

Prepaid Insurance

(4)	7,200		

Cash

(1)	60,000	(2)	24,000
		(3)	5,800
		(4)	7,200

TRANSACTION 5 On June 5, King purchased fuel and other supplies on account for $3,600.

Analysis King has purchased the fuel and other supplies on credit terms rather than with cash. This transaction increases both an asset, Supplies on Hand, and a liability, Accounts Payable. At the end of the month, supplies will be counted to determine the amount used during the month. The asset will then be reduced and the related expense increased (see transaction 13). The entries are

Debit Supplies on Hand $3,600 **Credit** Accounts Payable $3,600

The related accounts would appear as follows:

Supplies on Hand

(5)	3,600		

Accounts Payable

		(5)	3,600

TRANSACTION 6 On June 26, the school's students were billed $21,500 for June instructional fees.

Analysis Providing instruction during the month generates an asset, Accounts Receivable, and revenue, Instructional Fees Earned. Note that the revenue is reflected in the month that instruction is given, even though the students may not pay the fees until a later period. The entries are

Debit Accounts Receivable $21,500 **Credit** Instructional Fees Earned $21,500

The related accounts would appear as follows:

Accounts Receivable			
(6)	21,500		

Instructional Fees Earned			
		(6)	21,500

TRANSACTION 7 On June 30, King paid instructors' salaries for June of $9,000.

Analysis The services received from driving instructors during the month represent an expense that will be shown on the June income statement. Therefore, this transaction increases an expense, Salaries Expense, and decreases an asset, Cash. The entries are

Debit Salaries Expense $9,000 **Credit** Cash $9,000

The related accounts would appear as follows:

Salaries Expense			
(7)	9,000		

Cash			
(1)	60,000	(2)	24,000
		(3)	5,800
		(4)	7,200
		(7)	9,000

TRANSACTION 8 On June 30, the school collected $18,000 on account from students billed in transaction 6.

Analysis Receipt of this amount represents the collection of students' accounts, not new revenue. Recall that the related revenue was recorded in transaction 6, when the claims against students were recognized as the asset Accounts Receivable. This transaction changes one asset form (accounts receivable) into another asset form (cash). Cash increases by $18,000 and Accounts Receivable decreases by the same amount. The entries are

Debit Cash $18,000 **Credit** Accounts Receivable $18,000

The related accounts would appear as follows:

Cash			
(1)	60,000	(2)	24,000
(8)	18,000	(3)	5,800
		(4)	7,200
		(7)	9,000

Accounts Receivable			
(6)	21,500	(8)	18,000

TRANSACTION 9 On June 30, the school paid $1,600 on account for the supplies purchased in transaction 5.

Analysis Paying $1,600 of the $3,600 owed reduces both Cash and Accounts Payable by $1,600, therefore reducing both assets and liabilities. This payment is the partial settlement of a previously recorded obligation, not an expense. The entries are

Debit Accounts Payable $1,600 **Credit** Cash $1,600

The related accounts would appear as follows:

Accounts Payable

(9)	1,600	(5)	3,600

Cash

(1)	60,000	(2)	24,000
(8)	18,000	(3)	5,800
		(4)	7,200
		(7)	9,000
		(9)	1,600

TRANSACTION 10 On June 30, King paid $250 for office utilities (electricity and telephone).

Analysis Since the utility services have been used in June, this amount is a June expense and will be reflected in the income statement prepared at June 30. Utilities Expense increases and Cash decreases by $250. The entries are

Debit Utilities Expense $250 **Credit** Cash $250

The related accounts would appear as follows:

Utilities Expense

(10)	250		

Cash

(1)	60,000	(2)	24,000
(8)	18,000	(3)	5,800
		(4)	7,200
		(7)	9,000
		(9)	1,600
		(10)	250

TRANSACTION 11 On June 30, King withdrew $2,000 from the firm for personal use.

Analysis King has withdrawn this amount for his personal living expenses. The transaction reduces Cash and decreases King's equity in the Westgate Driving School by $2,000.

Although the reduction in owner's equity may be entered as a debit to the J. King, Capital account, King prefers to show all his withdrawals in a separate account. A proprietor uses a separate account, called the **drawing** account, to determine quickly the total amount withdrawn during a period without having to analyze the capital account. Drawing accounts (sometimes called *personal* accounts) are commonly used in sole proprietorships and partnerships. The account, J. King, Drawing, is a **contra** account because its balance represents a reduction of its related account, J. King, Capital. Debiting the drawing account to reflect the reduction in owner's equity has the same effect as debiting the owner's capital account directly. At the end of the period, after the net income has been added to the owner's capital account, the debit balance in the drawing account is deducted to arrive at the ending amount of owner's capital. Thus, the entries for King's withdrawal are

Debit J. King, Drawing $2,000 **Credit** Cash $2,000

The related accounts would appear as follows:

J. King, Drawing

(11)	2,000		

Cash

(1)	60,000	(2)	24,000
(8)	18,000	(3)	5,800
		(4)	7,200
		(7)	9,000
		(9)	1,600
		(10)	250
		(11)	2,000

TRANSACTION 12 On June 30, $\frac{1}{36}$ (one month) of the three years' prepaid insurance, or $200, had expired.

Analysis In transaction 4, the firm paid $7,200 in insurance premiums for a 36-month policy. Because this amount represented payment for future coverage, the asset Prepaid Insurance was debited. At the end of June, $\frac{1}{36}$ of the premiums has expired and no longer represents an asset. It will appear as Insurance Expense on the income statement prepared on June 30. The entries are

Debit Insurance Expense $200 **Credit** Prepaid Insurance $200

The related accounts would appear as follows:

Insurance Expense

(12)	200		

Prepaid Insurance

(4)	7,200	(12)	200

TRANSACTION 13 On June 30, supplies were counted, and only $1,350 worth of supplies remained on hand.

Analysis In transaction 5, supplies costing $3,600 were purchased and recorded as an asset. Supplies on hand now amount to only $1,350, and the $2,250 difference represents the supplies used during June. As we explained in the analysis of transaction 5, supplies used are a June expense. Therefore, an entry should be made to reduce Supplies on Hand by $2,250 and increase Supplies Expense by $2,250. The entries are

Debit Supplies Expense $2,250 **Credit** Supplies on Hand $2,250

The related accounts would appear as follows:

Supplies Expense			
(13)	2,250		

Supplies on Hand			
(5)	3,600	(13)	2,250

After the foregoing transactions have been entered properly, the account balances can be determined. The accounts of the Westgate Driving School are shown in Exhibit 2–5 (see pages 52–53), together with the financial statements that would eventually be prepared from the balances of these accounts. Observe the following:

1. Accounts accumulate data, especially revenue and expense accounts, which provide data for the income statement.
2. Keying transactions permits tracing any entry to both its originating transaction and its related change in some other account.
3. John King's equity of $62,000 at the end of June results from:

(a) His original capital contribution	$60,000
(b) Plus his earnings for June	4,000
	$64,000
(c) Minus his withdrawals	2,000
Ending balance in balance sheet	$62,000

4. Using the contra account, J. King, Drawing, does not change the net amount of owner's equity shown on the financial statements.

The June activities of the Westgate Driving School that we have just analyzed included both transactions with individuals, for which documents such as bills or checks are usually available, and activities that are sometimes described as internal transactions. For example, transactions 12 and 13—reflecting insurance expense and supplies expense—are called internal because they represent account adjustments not initiated by documents. In Chapter 3 you will learn that entries for adjustments are usually made at a particular time and are a significant part of the accounting process.

The financial statements of the Westgate Driving School in Exhibit 2–5 are illustrated together with the accounts to show their relationship to the accounts. However, these statements would not be prepared until after a *trial balance* is taken, as explained in the next section.

THE GENERAL LEDGER AND THE TRIAL BALANCE

The **general ledger** is the grouping of the accounts that are used to prepare financial statements for a business. The 14 accounts that we used in our example for the Westgate Driving School would each constitute a page in the general ledger, which is usually maintained in a binder so that, when necessary, accounts may be added or removed. Usually, the accounts are grouped by category in the following order: (1) assets, (2) liabilities, (3) owners' equity, (4) revenue, and (5) expenses.

EXHIBIT 2–5

THE ACCOUNTS AND FINANCIAL STATEMENTS OF THE WESTGATE DRIVING SCHOOL

Assets = **Liabilities** + **Owner's Equity**

Assets

Cash

Debit	Credit
(1) 60,000	(2) 24,000
(8) 18,000	(3) 5,800
	(4) 7,200
	(7) 9,000
	(9) 1,600
	(10) 250
	(11) 2,000
Bal. 28,150	

Accounts Receivable

Debit	Credit
(6) 21,500	(8) 18,000
Bal. 3,500	

Prepaid Insurance

Debit	Credit
(4) 7,200	(12) 200
Bal. 7,000	

Supplies on Hand

Debit	Credit
(5) 3,600	(13) 2,250
Bal. 1,350	

Land

Debit	Credit
(2) 24,000	

Liabilities

Accounts Payable

Debit	Credit
(9) 1,600	(5) 3,600
	Bal. 2,000

Owner's Equity

J. King, Capital

Debit	Credit
	(1) 60,000

J. King, Drawing

Debit	Credit
(11) 2,000	

Instructional Fees Earned

Debit	Credit
	(6) 21,500

Rent Expense

Debit	Credit
(3) 5,800	

Salaries Expense

Debit	Credit
(7) 9,000	

Utilities Expense

Debit	Credit
(10) 250	

Insurance Expense

Debit	Credit
(12) 200	

Supplies Expense

Debit	Credit
(13) 2,250	

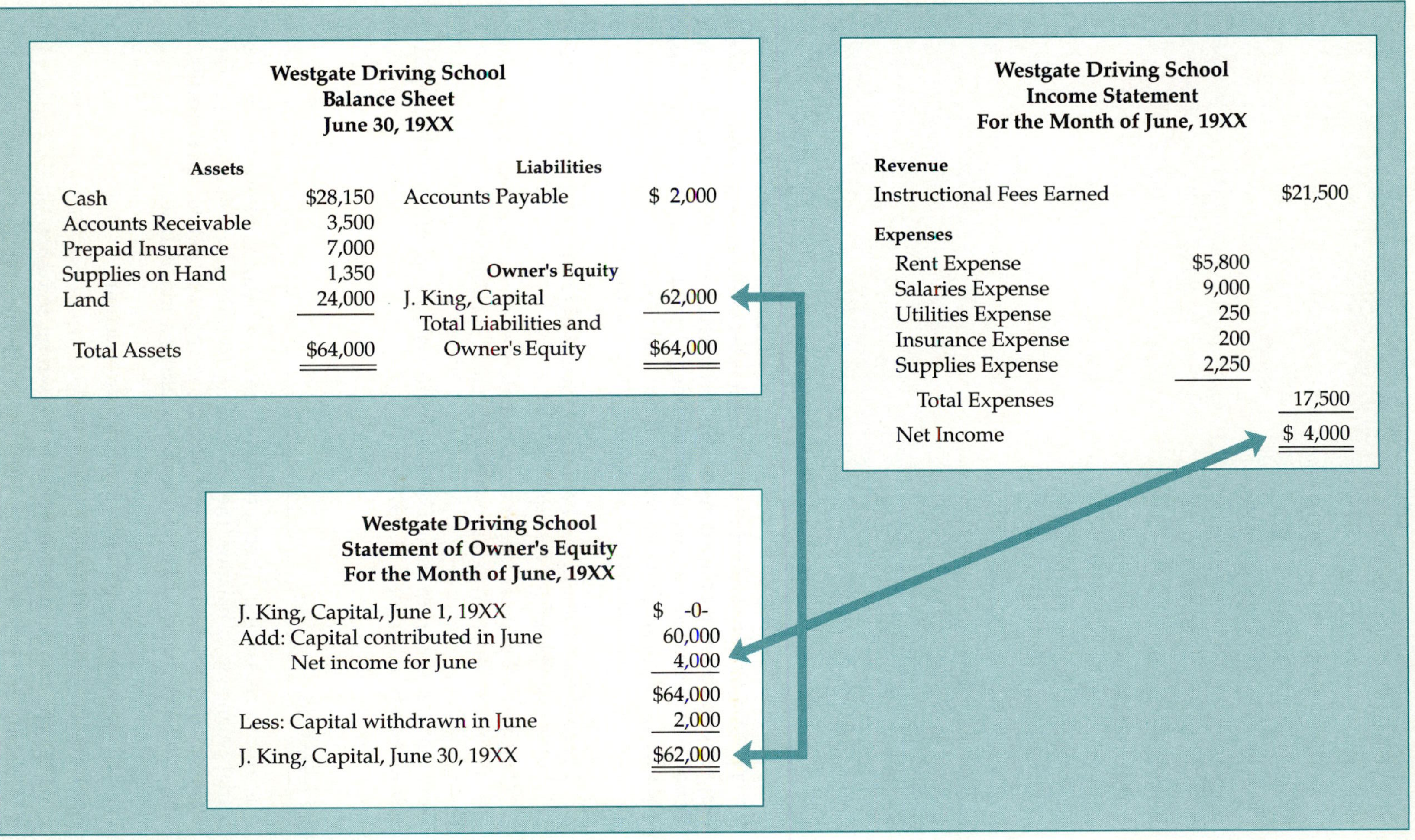

Westgate Driving School
Income Statement
For the Month of June, 19XX

Revenue		
Instructional Fees Earned		$21,500
Expenses		
Rent Expense	$5,800	
Salaries Expense	9,000	
Utilities Expense	250	
Insurance Expense	200	
Supplies Expense	2,250	
Total Expenses		17,500
Net Income		$ 4,000

Westgate Driving School
Statement of Owner's Equity
For the Month of June, 19XX

J. King, Capital, June 1, 19XX	$ -0-
Add: Capital contributed in June	60,000
Net income for June	4,000
	$64,000
Less: Capital withdrawn in June	2,000
J. King, Capital, June 30, 19XX	$62,000

Westgate Driving School
Balance Sheet
June 30, 19XX

Assets		**Liabilities**	
Cash	$28,150	Accounts Payable	$ 2,000
Accounts Receivable	3,500		
Prepaid Insurance	7,000		
Supplies on Hand	1,350	**Owner's Equity**	
Land	24,000	J. King, Capital	62,000
Total Assets	$64,000	Total Liabilities and Owner's Equity	$64,000

EXHIBIT 2–6

Westgate Driving School
Trial Balance
June 30, 19XX

	Debit	Credit
Cash	$28,150	
Accounts Receivable	3,500	
Prepaid Insurance	7,000	
Supplies on Hand	1,350	
Land	24,000	
Accounts Payable		$ 2,000
J. King, Capital		60,000
J. King, Drawing	2,000	
Instructional Fees Earned		21,500
Rent Expense	5,800	
Salaries Expense	9,000	
Utilities Expense	250	
Insurance Expense	200	
Supplies Expense	2,250	
	$83,500	$83,500

The **trial balance** is a list of the account titles in the general ledger with their respective debit or credit balances. It is prepared at the close of an accounting period after transactions have been recorded. Exhibit 2–6 illustrates a trial balance for the Westgate Driving School at the end of June.

The two main reasons for preparing a trial balance are:

1. To serve as an interim mechanical check to determine if the debits and credits in the general ledger are equal.
2. To show all general ledger account balances on one concise record. This is often convenient when preparing financial statements.

Note that a trial balance should be dated; the trial balance of the Westgate Driving School was taken at June 30, 19XX.

ERRORS IN TRANSACTION ANALYSIS

It is always reassuring when a trial balance does balance. However, even when a trial balance is in balance, the accounting records may still contain errors. A balanced trial balance simply proves that, *as recorded*, debits equal credits. The following errors may not be detected by taking a trial balance:

1. Failing to record or enter a particular transaction.
2. Entering a transaction more than once.
3. Entering one or more amounts in the wrong accounts.
4. Making an error that exactly offsets the effect of another error.

Several types of errors will cause a trial balance to be out of balance. If only one of these is present, it may be identified and located by one of the approaches suggested below. If several errors exist, however, often the only way to find them is to retrace each entry, check the arithmetic performed in balancing the accounts, and make certain that no error has occurred in transcribing amounts or in adding the trial balance. To search for errors, one should systematically follow certain procedures so that all steps are retraced only once and no steps are overlooked.

When there is a mistake in a trial balance, the first step is to determine the amount by which the total debits and credits disagree. Certain characteristics of this amount may provide a clue to identifying the type of error and finding where it was made.

DEBITS AND CREDITS INTERCHANGED When a debit is entered as a credit (or vice versa), the trial balance totals will differ by twice the amount involved. For example, if the credits exceed the debits by $246, one should first look for a $123 debit that has been treated as a credit. With this type of error, the amount of the discrepancy in the trial balance totals is divisible by two. If this is not the case, either another type of error or a number of errors are involved.

ARITHMETIC ERRORS Single arithmetic errors frequently cause trial balance totals to differ by amounts such as $1,000, $100, $1, and so on. Multiple arithmetic errors may either combine or offset and result in discrepancies such as $990 (errors of $1,000 and $10 offsetting) and $101 (errors of $100 and $1 combining).

TRANSPOSITION OF NUMBERS Transposing numbers means simply reversing their order. For example, transposing the first two digits in $360 would result in $630. This type of error usually occurs when amounts are transcribed from one record to another. The resulting discrepancy is easily identified because it is always divisible by nine ($630 − $360 = $270, and $270/9 = $30). Therefore, if total debits exceeded total credits by $270, one would suspect a transposition error.

AMOUNTS OMITTED An amount can be omitted if one enters only part of an entry, fails to include an entry when balancing an account, or leaves out an account balance in a trial balance. The resulting discrepancy is equal in amount to the omitted item. Of course, the omission of a debit amount will cause an excess of credits by that amount, and vice versa.

KEY POINTS FOR CHAPTER OBJECTIVES

1 Illustrate the expanded form of the accounting equation (pp. 39–40).

- This equation is illustrated as follows:

$$\text{Assets} = \text{Liabilities} + \overbrace{\left[\begin{matrix}\text{Beginning}\\ \text{Capital}\end{matrix} + \begin{matrix}\text{Contri-}\\ \text{butions}\end{matrix} - \begin{matrix}\text{With-}\\ \text{drawals}\end{matrix}\right] + \left[\text{Revenue} - \text{Expenses}\right]}^{\text{Owners' Equity}}$$

- In recording changes in owners' equity, the primary reason for segregating revenue and expense items is to facilitate preparation of the income statement.

2 Explain the nature and format of an account (pp. 41–43).

- An account is an individual record of increases and decreases in specific assets, liabilities, owner capital, revenue, and expenses.
- Information provided by the account includes title, amounts reflecting increases and decreases, cross-references to other accounting records, and dates and descriptive notations.

3 Describe the system of debits and credits (pp. 43–45).

- The left side of an account is always the debit side; the right side is always the credit side.
- Increases in assets and expenses are debit entries; increases in liabilities, owners' equity, and revenue are credit entries. Decreases are the opposite.
- The normal balance of any account appears on the side for recording increases.

4 Illustrate debit and credit analysis of transactions (pp. 46–53).

- Each accounting transaction should be analyzed into equal debits and credits.
- All accounting transactions are analyzed using one or more of the five basic account categories: (1) assets, (2) liabilities, (3) owners' equity, (4) revenue, and (5) expenses. Contra accounts, which offset related accounts in a basic category, may also be used.

5 Explain the nature and format of a trial balance (p. 54).

- The trial balance is a list of the accounts in the general ledger with their respective debit or credit balances; it is prepared after transactions have been recorded for an accounting period.
- The trial balance serves as a check to determine the equality of debits and credits.
- Showing all the account balances on one concise record facilitates preparation of the financial statements.

6 Discuss common types of errors in transaction analysis (pp. 54–55).

- Common errors that cause the trial balance not to balance include entering a debit as a credit (or vice versa), arithmetic errors, transposition errors, and omitted amounts.
- Errors that are not detected by a trial balance include failing to record a transaction, recording a transaction more than once, entering amounts in the wrong accounts but on the correct side, and offsetting errors.

KEY TERMS USED IN THIS CHAPTER

account 41
contra account 50
credit 43
debit 43
double-entry system 43
drawing account 49
entries 41
general ledger 51
running balance account 44
T account 42
trial balance 54

SELF-TEST QUESTIONS FOR REVIEW

(Answers are at the end of this chapter.)

1. In recording transactions
   (a) The word *debit* means to increase and the word *credit* means to decrease.
   (b) Assets, expenses, and owners' drawing accounts are debited for increases.
   (c) Liabilities, revenue, and owners' drawing accounts are debited for increases.
   (d) Assets, expenses, and owners' capital accounts are debited for increases.

2. Which of the following combinations of trial balance totals does not indicate a transposition?
   (a) $65,470 debit and $64,570 credit
   (b) $32,540 debit and $35,420 credit
   (c) $25,670 debit and $26,670 credit
   (d) $14,517 debit and $15,471 credit

3. Todd had a beginning credit balance of $27,000 in his capital account. At the close of the period, Todd's drawing account had a debit balance of $3,000. On the end-of-period balance sheet, Todd's capital balance is $38,000. If Todd contributed an additional $2,000 to the firm during the period, the period's net income is
   (a) $12,000 (b) $10,000 (c) $6,000 (d) $8,000

4. The ending balance of the Accounts Receivable account was $12,000. Services billed to customers for the period were $21,500, and collections on account from customers were $23,600. The beginning balance of Accounts Receivable was
   (a) $33,500 (b) $14,100 (c) $9,900 (d) $33,100

5. Which of the following is not true of a general ledger trial balance?
   (a) It proves that the total debits equal total credits, if it balances.
   (b) It facilitates preparation of financial statements.
   (c) It proves that no errors have been made in recording transactions, if it balances.
   (d) It will not detect an error where the accounts debited and credited are reversed in recording a particular transaction.

DEMONSTRATION PROBLEM FOR REVIEW

The following account balances, in alphabetical order, are from the ledger of Morton Graphics Service at January 31, 19XX. The firm's accounting year began on January 1. All accounts had normal balances.

Accounts Payable	$ 1,140	Prepaid Insurance	$ 440
Accounts Receivable	14,400	Rent Expense	560
Advertising Expense	150	Salaries Expense	3,000
Cash	9,200	Service Fees Earned	14,100
Insurance Expense	40	Supplies Expense	600
Morton, Capital, January 1	16,500	Supplies on Hand	1,600
Morton, Drawing	1,500	Utilities Expense	250

REQUIRED
(a) Prepare a trial balance in good form from the given data.
(b) Prepare an income statement for the month of January.
(c) Prepare a statement of owner's equity for the month of January.
(d) Prepare a balance sheet at January 31.

SOLUTION TO DEMONSTRATION PROBLEM

(a)

Morton Graphics Service
Trial Balance
January 31, 19XX

	Debit	Credit
Cash	$ 9,200	
Accounts Receivable	14,400	
Supplies on Hand	1,600	
Prepaid Insurance	440	
Accounts Payable		$ 1,140
Morton, Capital		16,500
Morton, Drawing	1,500	
Service Fees Earned		14,100
Advertising Expense	150	
Insurance Expense	40	
Rent Expense	560	
Salaries Expense	3,000	
Supplies Expense	600	
Utilities Expense	250	
	$31,740	$31,740

(b)

Morton Graphics Service
Income Statement
For the Month of January, 19XX

Revenue		
Service Fees Earned		$14,100
Expenses		
Advertising Expense	$ 150	
Insurance Expense	40	
Rent Expense	560	
Salaries Expense	3,000	
Supplies Expense	600	
Utilities Expense	250	
Total Expenses		4,600
Net Income		$ 9,500

(c)

Morton Graphics Service
Statement of Owner's Equity
For the Month of January, 19XX

Morton, Capital, January 1, 19XX	$16,500
Add: Net Income for January	9,500
	$26,000
Less: Capital Withdrawn in January	1,500
Morton, Capital, January 31, 19XX	$24,500

(d)

Morton Graphics Service
Balance Sheet
January 31, 19XX

Assets		**Liabilities**	
Cash	$ 9,200	Accounts Payable	$ 1,140
Accounts Receivable	14,400		
Supplies on Hand	1,600	**Owner's Equity**	
Prepaid Insurance	440	Morton, Capital	24,500
Total Assets	$25,640	Total Liabilities and Owner's Equity	$25,640

QUESTIONS

2–1 Why is it useful to record revenue and expenses separately from the owner's capital account?

2–2 Name the five categories of information needed to prepare the balance sheet and the income statement. Which categories are identified with the balance sheet? Which are identified with the income statement?

2–3 What information is recorded in an account?

2–4 Explain the terms *general ledger* and *trial balance*. What are the reasons for preparing a trial balance?

2–5 What general statement can be made about the *normal* side of an account?

2–6 Present three common business transactions that would not affect the amount of owners' equity.

2–7 Identify the following as asset, liability, owner's equity, revenue, or expense accounts and indicate whether a debit entry or a credit entry increases the balance of the account.

Professional Fees Earned	Adams, Capital
Accounts Receivable	Advertising Expense
Accounts Payable	Supplies on Hand
Cash	Adams, Drawing

2–8 Indicate the normal balance (debit or credit) of each account in Question 2–7.

2–9 What are the advantages and disadvantages of the running balance, or three-column, account form compared with the two-column form?

2–10 What is the justification for using a separate owner's drawing account?

2–11 "During the year, the total owner's equity of Jensen Gift Shop increased from $56,000 to $72,000. Therefore, the annual earnings must have been $16,000." Is this statement necessarily true? Explain.

2–12 Explain why purchases of supplies are usually charged to an asset account rather than to an expense account.

2–13 Describe three distinct types of errors that may be present even when a trial balance is in balance.

2–14 "A trial balance is a list showing all account titles in the general ledger and the total of debits and credits in each account." Do you agree with this statement? Why or why not?

2–15 Discuss the types of errors that may be present in each of the following five independent sets of trial balance totals:

Trial Balance	Trial Balance Totals Debit	Credit
A	$73,200	$74,200
B	41,540	41,180
C	35,746	35,695
D	63,471	64,907
E	54,840	54,620

2–16 The assistant bookkeeper of Wynn Sports prepared a trial balance that had total debits of $84,250 and total credits of $85,550. Compute the correct trial balance totals by assuming that only the following errors were involved:
(1) Accounts Payable of $4,250 was listed as a debit.
(2) During the current period, a $750 check for Utilities Expense was debited to Office Expense.
(3) Supplies on Hand of $2,800 had been omitted.
(4) Wynn, Drawing of $3,500 was included as a credit.

EXERCISES

Transaction analysis and trial balance

2–17 Make T accounts for the following accounts that appear in the general ledger of R. D. Blaine, a veterinarian: Cash; Accounts Receivable; Supplies on Hand; Office Equipment; Accounts Payable; R. D. Blaine, Capital; R. D. Blaine, Drawing; Professional Fees Earned; Salaries Expense; and Rent Expense. Record the following transactions in the T accounts and key all entries with the number identifying the transaction. Finally, prove equality of debits and credits by preparing a trial balance.
(1) Blaine opened a checking account on December 1 at the United Bank in the name of Animal Hospital and deposited $30,000.
(2) Paid rent for December, $750.
(3) Purchased office equipment on account, as follows: Desks, $850; typewriters, $1,250; filing cabinets, $600; and chairs, $500.
(4) Purchased supplies for cash, $900.
(5) Billed clients for services rendered, $6,400.
(6) Paid secretary's salary, $1,150.
(7) Paid $1,400 on account for the equipment purchased in transaction 3.
(8) Collected $4,200 from clients previously billed for services.
(9) Withdrew $1,500 for personal use.

Determination of omitted financial statement data

2–18 In the five independent situations below, replace the question marks with the amounts that should appear.

	A	B	C	D	E
Owner's Equity:					
Beginning Balance	$48,000	$72,000	$64,000	$?	$42,000
Capital Contributions	5,000	9,000	?	7,000	5,000
Net Income (Loss)	?	14,000	8,000	(6,000)	?
Capital Withdrawals	3,000	?	4,000	2,000	1,000
Ending Balance	$61,000	$90,000	$74,000	$54,000	$43,000

Transaction analysis

2–19 Match each of the following transactions of L. Cortez, Printer, with the appropriate letters, indicating the debits and credits to be made. The correct answer for transaction 1 is given.

	Answer
(1) The owner contributed cash to the business.	a, f
(2) Purchased equipment on account.	______
(3) Received and immediately paid advertising bill.	______
(4) Purchased supplies for cash.	______

(5) Borrowed money from bank, giving a note payable. ________
(6) Billed customers. ________
(7) Made partial payment on account for equipment. ________
(8) Paid employee's salary. ________
(9) Collected amounts due from customers billed in transaction 6. ________

Effect of Transaction

(a) Debit an asset	(f) Credit owner's capital
(b) Credit an asset	(g) Debit revenue
(c) Debit a liability	(h) Credit revenue
(d) Credit a liability	(i) Debit an expense
(e) Debit owner's capital	(j) Credit an expense

Transaction analysis

2–20 The accounts below are from the general ledger of a local accountant. For each letter given in the T accounts, describe the type of business transaction(s) or event(s) that would most probably be reflected by entries on that side of the account. For example, the answer to (a) is: The amounts of services performed for clients on account.

Accounts Receivable	
(a)	(b)

Supplies on Hand	
	(c)

Office Equipment	
(d)	

Prepaid Insurance	
(e)	

Professional Fees Earned	
	(f)

Owner's Drawing	
(g)	

Owner's Capital	
	(h)

Salaries Expense	
(i)	

Accounts Payable	
(j)	(k)

Analysis of accounts

2–21 Compute the unknown amount required in each of the following five independent situations. The answer to situation (a) is given as an example.

Account	Beginning Balance	Ending Balance	Other Information
(a) Cash	$ 6,100	$ 5,250	Total cash disbursed, $5,400.
(b) Accounts Receivable	8,500	6,700	Services on account, $16,400.
(c) Supplies on Hand	820	650	Supplies used, $450.
(d) Prepaid Insurance	180	720	Premiums paid in advance, $1,080.
(e) Ward, Capital	32,000	43,000	Capital contributions, $4,000.

Unknown Amounts Required

(a) Total cash received $4,550
(b) Total amount received from credit customers ________
(c) Supplies purchased during the period ________
(d) Amount of insurance expense for the period ________
(e) Net income, if no withdrawals were made ________

Effect of errors on trial balance

2–22 Indicate how each of the following errors would affect the trial balance totals. For each error, specify whether the debit or credit totals would be overstated, understated, or whether both totals would be unaffected.

(a) The Accounts Receivable balance of $54,600 was listed in the trial balance as $56,400.
(b) A $360 payment for Utilities Expense was debited to Miscellaneous Expense during the accounting period.
(c) The Accounts Payable balance of $28,300 was omitted from the trial balance.
(d) Salaries Expense of $4,500 was listed in the trial balance as a credit.
(e) The Owner's Drawing account, with a debit balance of $6,800, was listed as a credit in the trial balance.

PROBLEMS

Transaction analysis and trial balance

2–23 James Cruz, electrical contractor, began business on May 1 of the current year. The following transactions occurred during May:

(1) Cruz invested $30,000 of his personal funds in the business.
(2) Purchased equipment on account, $3,800.
(3) Paid the premium for a one-year liability insurance policy, $960.
(4) Purchased supplies on account, $840.
(5) Purchased a truck for $12,500. Cruz paid $5,000 cash and gave a note payable for the balance.
(6) Paid rent for May, $720.
(7) Paid fuel bill for truck, $60.
(8) Billed customers for services rendered, $11,500.
(9) Paid $2,000 on account for equipment purchased in transaction 2.
(10) Paid utilities expense for May, $140.
(11) Received invoice for May advertising expense, to be paid in June, $180.
(12) Paid employees' wages, $2,850.
(13) Collected $4,200 on accounts receivable.
(14) Withdrew $700 for personal expenses.
(15) Counted supplies on hand at May 31, $450 worth remained.
(16) Recorded the insurance expired at May 31, $80.

REQUIRED

(a) Record the above transactions in T accounts, and key entries with the numbers of the transactions. The following accounts will be needed to record the transactions for May: Cash; Accounts Receivable; Supplies on Hand; Prepaid Insurance; Equipment; Truck; Notes Payable; Accounts Payable; J. Cruz, Capital; J. Cruz, Drawing; Service Revenue; Rent Expense; Wages Expense; Utilities Expense; Truck Expense; Advertising Expense; Supplies Expense; and Insurance Expense.
(b) Prepare a trial balance of the general ledger as of May 31.

Trial balance, income statement, and balance sheet

2–24 The following account balances, in alphabetical order, are from the general ledger of Nolan's Waterproofing Service at January 31, 19XX. The firm's accounting year began on January 1. All accounts had normal balances.

Accounts Payable	$ 1,250	Nolan, Drawing	$1,200
Accounts Receivable	16,500	Prepaid Insurance	720
Advertising Expense	180	Rent Expense	650
Cash	9,200	Salaries Expense	3,600
Service Fees Earned	14,580	Supplies Expense	2,450
Insurance Expense	60	Supplies on Hand	7,850
Nolan, Capital, January 1	26,840	Utilities Expense	260

REQUIRED

(a) Prepare a trial balance in good form from the given data.
(b) Prepare an income statement for the month of January.
(c) Prepare a balance sheet at January 31.

Transaction analysis and the effect of errors on trial balance

2–25 The following T accounts contain numbered entries for the May transactions of Cynthia Martin, a market analyst, who opened her offices on May 1 of the current year:

Cash

(1)	20,000	(2)	5,400
(9)	3,400	(4)	800
		(6)	850
		(8)	900

C. Martin, Capital

		(1)	20,000

Accounts Receivable

(5)	6,200	(9)	3,400

C. Martin, Drawing

(8)	900		

Supplies on Hand

(3)	1,500	(7)	580

Professional Fees Earned

		(5)	6,200

Office Equipment

(2)	5,400		

Rent Expense

(4)	800		

Accounts Payable

(6)	850	(3)	1,500

Supplies Expense

(7)	580		

REQUIRED

(a) Give a reasonable description of each of the nine numbered transactions entered in the above accounts. Example: (1) Cynthia Martin invested $20,000 of her personal funds in her business.
(b) The following trial balance, taken for Martin's firm on May 31, contains several errors. Itemize the errors and indicate the correct totals for the trial balance.

Cynthia Martin, Market Analyst
Trial Balance
May 31, 19XX

	Debit	Credit
Cash	$15,540	
Accounts Receivable	6,200	
Supplies on Hand	920	
Office Equipment	5,400	
Accounts Payable		$ 650
C. Martin, Capital		20,000
C. Martin, Drawing		900
Professional Fees Earned		6,200
Rent Expense	800	
	$28,860	$27,750

Transaction analysis, trial balance, and financial statements

2–26 Susan Chen owns Artforms, a firm providing designs for advertisers, market analysts, and others. On July 1 of the current year, her general ledger showed the following account balances:

Cash	$11,500	Notes Payable	$ 5,000
Accounts Receivable	16,200	Accounts Payable	1,600
Prepaid Rent	1,200	S. Chen, Capital	29,700
Supplies on Hand	7,400		
	$36,300		$36,300

The following transactions occurred in July:

July 2 Collected $9,500 on account from customers.
5 Paid $2,000 installment due on the $5,000 non-interest-bearing note payable to a relative.
9 Billed customers for design services rendered on account, $17,850.
12 Rendered design services for cash customers, $750.
14 Purchased various art supplies on account, $1,860.
15 Paid $1,400 to creditors on account.
18 Collected $9,800 on account from customers.
21 Paid a delivery service for delivery of graphics to commercial firms, $230.
30 Paid July salaries, $2,750.
30 Received invoice for July advertising expense, to be paid in August, $520.
31 Paid utilities expense for July, $240.
31 Withdrew $800 for personal use.
31 Recorded rent expense for July, $600. (Note that on July 1, two months' rent, $1,200, was prepaid.)
31 Counted supplies on hand at July 31, $5,700 worth remained.

REQUIRED

(a) Set up the appropriate running balance accounts for the July 1 balance sheet and enter the beginning balances. Also provide the following running balance accounts: S. Chen, Drawing; Service Fees Earned; Rent Expense; Salaries Expense; Delivery Expense; Advertising Expense; Utilities Expense; and Supplies Expense. Record the listed transactions in the accounts.
(b) Prepare a trial balance at July 31.
(c) Prepare an income statement for July.
(d) Prepare a statement of owner's equity for July.
(e) Prepare a balance sheet at July 31.

Transaction analysis, trial balance, and financial statements

2–27 Wilderness Fly-In Service, Inc. (introduced in Problem 1–31) operates leased amphibious aircraft and docking facilities, equipping the firm to transport fishermen and hunters from Thunder Bay, Ontario, to outpost camps owned by various resorts in Ontario. On August 1 of the current year, the firm's trial balance was as follows:

Wilderness Fly-In Service, Inc.
Trial Balance
August 1, 19XX

	Debit	Credit
Cash	$ 54,650	
Accounts Receivable	31,500	
Supplies on Hand	19,200	
Prepaid Insurance	4,800	
Notes Payable		$ 2,500
Accounts Payable		4,200
Capital Stock		80,000
Retained Earnings		23,450
	$110,150	$110,150

During August the following transactions occurred:

Aug. 1 Paid August rental cost for aircraft, dockage, and dockside office, $4,800.
3 Purchased fuel and other supplies on account, $3,700.
5 Paid bill for August advertising in various sports magazines, $1,250.
6 Rendered fly-in services for various groups for cash, $18,250.
8 Billed the Ministry of Natural Resources for services in transporting mapping personnel, $4,700.
13 Received $19,500 on account from clients.
16 Paid $3,600 on accounts payable.
18 Paid miscellaneous expenses, $420.
24 Billed various clients for services, $16,800.
31 Paid August wages, $10,500.
31 Declared and paid a dividend, $4,000 (debit Retained Earnings).
31 Determined that $1,200 insurance premiums expired during August.
31 Determined that fuel and other supplies on hand at August 31 amounted to $16,800.

REQUIRED

(a) Set up running balance accounts for each item in the August 1 trial balance and enter the beginning balances. Also provide similar accounts for the following items: Service Fees Earned, Wages Expense, Advertising Expense, Rent Expense, Supplies Expense, Insurance Expense, and Miscellaneous Expense. Record the transactions for August in the accounts, using the dates given.
(b) Prepare a trial balance at August 31, 19XX.
(c) Prepare an income statement for August.
(d) Prepare a balance sheet at August 31.

Effect of errors on trial balance

2–28 The following trial balance for Ross Janitorial Service, prepared after its first month of operations on January 31 of the current year, does not balance because of a number of errors.

Ross Janitorial Service
Trial Balance
January 31, 19XX

	Debit	Credit
Cash	$ 6,360	
Accounts Receivable	9,720	
Supplies on Hand	3,670	
Prepaid Insurance	540	
Equipment	18,000	
Accounts Payable		$ 5,540
Ross, Capital		23,750
Ross, Drawing		1,200
Service Fees Earned		18,500
Wages Expense	4,500	
Insurance Expense	90	
Advertising Expense	270	
Supplies Expense	2,750	
	$45,900	$48,990

1. Utilities Expense, with a $160 balance, was omitted from the trial balance.
2. Supplies on Hand, listed in the trial balance as $3,670, should be $3,760.
3. During the period, a cash payment of $460 on accounts payable was recorded as a $640 credit to Cash.
4. A debit of $140 to Accounts Payable was erroneously recorded as a credit.
5. In determining the Accounts Receivable balance, a credit of $120 was overlooked.

6. The $1,200 balance of the Ross, Drawing account is listed as a credit in the trial balance.
7. The balance of the Service Fees Earned account was overfooted (overadded) by $100.

REQUIRED
Prepare a corrected trial balance as of January 31 of the current year.

ALTERNATE PROBLEMS

Transaction analysis and trial balance

2–23A Amy Tyson opened a tax practice on June 1 of the current year. The following accounts will be needed to record her transactions for June: Cash; Accounts Receivable; Office Supplies on Hand; Prepaid Insurance; Office Furniture and Fixtures; Notes Payable; Accounts Payable; A. Tyson, Capital; A. Tyson, Drawing; Professional Fees Earned; Rent Expense; Salaries Expense; Supplies Expense; Utilities Expense; and Insurance Expense. The following transactions occurred in June:

(1) Tyson opened a special checking account at the bank for the business, investing $15,000 in her practice.
(2) Purchased office furniture and fixtures for $2,800, paid $1,800 cash and gave a non-interest-bearing note payable for the balance.
(3) Paid the premium for a one-year liability insurance policy, $720.
(4) Purchased office supplies on account, $420.
(5) Paid rent for June, $750.
(6) Billed clients for professional services rendered, $6,500.
(7) Paid $300 on account to stationers for the office supplies purchased in transaction 4.
(8) Collected $4,300 on account from clients billed in transaction 6.
(9) Paid June salaries, $2,100.
(10) Withdrew $900 for personal use.
(11) Paid utilities for June, $190.
(12) Counted supplies on hand at June 30, $280 worth remained.
(13) One month's insurance premium expired during June (See transaction 3).

REQUIRED
(a) Record the above transactions in T accounts, and key entries with the numbers of the transactions.
(b) Prepare a trial balance of the general ledger as of June 30.

Trial balance, income statement, and balance sheet

2–24A The following account balances were taken (out of order) from the general ledger of R. Dodd, investment counselor, at January 31, 19XX. The firm's accounting year began on January 1. All accounts had normal balances.

Prepaid Insurance	$ 480	Rent Expense	$ 700
Insurance Expense	120	Supplies Expense	330
Supplies on Hand	810	Utilities Expense	180
Advertising Expense	350	Service Revenue	12,840
R. Dodd, Capital, January 1	23,220	Accounts Receivable	10,400
Cash	19,650	Salaries Expense	2,400
Accounts Payable	560	R. Dodd, Drawing	1,200

REQUIRED
(a) Prepare a trial balance in good form from the given data.
(b) Prepare an income statement for the month of January.
(c) Prepare a balance sheet at January 31.

Transaction analysis and the effect of errors on trial balance

2–25A The following T accounts contain numbered entries for the May transactions of Daniel Kelly, attorney, who opened his offices on May 1 of the current year:

Cash

(1)	17,000	(2)	4,800
(10)	4,200	(4)	850
		(6)	840
		(8)	750
		(9)	325

D. Kelly, Capital

		(1)	17,000

Accounts Receivable

(5)	5,750	(10)	4,200

D. Kelly, Drawing

(8)	750		

Prepaid Insurance

(6)	840	(11)	140

Professional Fees Earned

		(5)	5,750

Supplies on Hand

(3)	725	(7)	410

Rent Expense

(4)	850		

Office Equipment

(2)	4,800		

Insurance Expense

(11)	140		

Accounts Payable

(9)	325	(3)	725

Supplies Expense

(7)	410		

REQUIRED

(a) Give a reasonable description of each of the 11 numbered transactions entered in the above accounts. Example: (1) Daniel Kelly invested $17,000 of his personal funds in his law firm.

(b) The following trial balance, taken for Kelly's firm on May 31, contains several errors. Itemize the errors, and indicate the correct totals for the trial balance.

Daniel Kelly, Attorney
Trial Balance
May 31, 19XX

	Debit	Credit
Cash	$13,365	
Accounts Receivable	1,350	
Supplies on Hand	725	
Office Equipment	4,800	
Accounts Payable		$ 400
D. Kelly, Capital		17,000
D. Kelly, Drawing		750
Professional Fees Earned		5,750
Rent Expense	850	
Insurance Expense	140	
Supplies Expense	410	
	$21,640	$23,900

Transaction analysis, trial balance, and financial statements

2–26A June Thorp operates the Thorp Dance Studio. On June 1 of the current year, her general ledger contained the following information:

Cash	$12,600	Notes Payable	$ 3,000
Accounts Receivable	4,350	Accounts Payable	450
Prepaid Insurance	720	J. Thorp, Capital	14,870
Supplies on Hand	650		
	$18,320		$18,320

The following transactions occurred in June:

June 2 Paid June rent for practice and performance studio, $825.
3 Paid June piano rental, $75 (Rent Expense).
6 Collected $2,450 from students on account.
10 Paid $1,000 installment on non-interest-bearing note owed to a relative.
15 Billed students for June instructional fees, $4,820.
18 Purchased supplies (tickets, brochures, sheet music, and so on) on account, $350.
20 Paid $180 for advertising ballet performance.
21 Paid costume rental, $325 (Rent Expense).
25 Collected $3,260 from performances.
27 Paid Kleen Towel Company for June services, $70 (Miscellaneous Expense).
31 Paid utilities expense for June, $160.
31 Withdrew $700 for personal expenses.
31 Counted supplies on hand at June 30, $520 worth remained.
31 Determined that $120 insurance premiums had expired in June.

REQUIRED

(a) Set up the appropriate running balance accounts, and enter the beginning balances shown in the June 1 balance sheet. Also provide the following accounts: J. Thorp, Drawing; Instructional Fees Earned; Performance Revenue; Rent Expense; Supplies Expense; Insurance Expense; Utilities Expense; Advertising Expense; and Miscellaneous Expense. Record the listed transactions in the accounts.
(b) Prepare a trial balance at June 30.
(c) Prepare an income statement for June.
(d) Prepare a statement of owner's equity for June.
(e) Prepare a balance sheet as of June 30.

Transaction analysis, trial balance, and financial statements

2–27A On December 1 of the current year, a group of individuals formed a corporation to establish the *Cardinal*, a neighborhood weekly newspaper featuring want ads of individuals and advertising of local firms. The paper will be mailed free to about 5,000 local residents; revenue will be generated from advertising and want ads. The December transactions are summarized below:

Dec. 1 Sold capital stock of Cardinal, Inc., for cash, $40,000.
2 Paid December rent on office, $600.
4 Purchased office furniture and equipment for $9,000, paying $4,000 cash and giving a $5,000 note payable for the balance.
5 Purchased stationery and other office supplies on account, $840.
8 Collected want ad revenue in cash, $2,100.
12 Paid post office for bulk mailing expense, $520.
14 Billed for advertising in first two issues of the newspaper, $5,500.
15 Paid delivery expense to Acme Courier Service for transporting newspapers to post office, $65.

Dec. 16 Paid printing expense, $2,420.
18 Collected $2,200 want ad revenue in cash from various individuals.
28 Paid utilities expenses, $140.
31 Paid printing expense, $2,420.
31 Paid salaries expense, $3,600.
31 Billed for advertising in last two issues of the newspaper, $5,640.
31 Paid post office for bulk mailing expense, $560.
31 Paid delivery expense to Acme Courier Service for transporting newspapers to post office, $65.
31 Collected $7,200 on accounts receivable.

REQUIRED

(a) Set up three-column running balance accounts for the following: Cash, Accounts Receivable, Supplies on Hand, Office Furniture and Equipment, Notes Payable, Accounts Payable, Capital Stock, Advertising Revenue, Want Ad Revenue, Printing Expense, Mailing Expense, Utilities Expense, Salaries Expense, Rent Expense, and Delivery Expense. Record the foregoing transactions in the accounts.
(b) Take a trial balance at December 31.
(c) Assuming that unrecorded expenses—such as supplies expense, and so on—amount to $800, calculate the net income for December.
(d) If the firm decides to declare and pay a dividend of $1,500 on January 1 of the following year, what would be the amount of stockholders' equity immediately after paying the dividend?

Effect of errors on trial balance

2–28A The following trial balance for Bell Tree Service, prepared after its first month of operations on May 31 of the current year, does not balance because of a number of errors.

Bell Tree Service
Trial Balance
May 31, 19XX

	Debit	Credit
Cash	$ 6,570	
Accounts Receivable	8,450	
Supplies on Hand	4,850	
Prepaid Insurance	480	
Equipment	15,000	
Accounts Payable		$ 3,350
Bell, Capital		23,850
Bell, Drawing		1,200
Service Fees Earned		16,570
Wages Expense	4,500	
Rent Expense	480	
Supplies Expense	2,420	
Utilities Expense	200	
	$42,950	$44,970

1. Insurance Expense, with a $120 balance, was omitted from the trial balance.
2. Cash, listed in the trial balance as $6,570, should be $6,750.
3. In determining the Accounts Receivable balance, a $200 credit was overlooked.
4. The $1,200 balance of the Bell, Drawing account is listed as a credit in the trial balance.

5. A credit of $150 to Accounts Payable was erroneously recorded as a debit.
6. The balance in the Service Fees Earned account was underfooted (under-added) by $200.

REQUIRED
Prepare a corrected trial balance as of May 31 of the current year.

BUSINESS DECISION PROBLEM

Eileen Harris operates the Sunset Picture Gallery, selling original art and signed prints received on consignment (rather than purchased) from recognized wildlife artists throughout the country. The firm receives a 30% commission on all art sold and remits 70% of the sales price to the artists. Eileen began business in January of this year, but has not yet arranged for a formal set of records. She has prepared cash receipts and disbursements statements for each of the first three months of the year, but she is uneasy about relying on them to determine how well she is doing. She asks you to prepare a proper set of financial statements for the month of March.

By reviewing bank statements, check stubs, invoice files, and other data, you derive a set of balance sheets at March 1 and March 31. These are shown below, followed by a statement of cash receipts and disbursements for March.

Sunset Picture Gallery
Balance Sheets

Assets	**March 31, 19XX**	**March 1, 19XX**
Cash	$40,800	$22,400
Accounts Receivable	12,000	11,200
Supplies on Hand	2,600	2,400
Prepaid Insurance	1,600	2,000
	$57,000	$38,000
Liabilities and Owner's Equity		
Accounts Payable to Artists	$ 9,600	$ 8,800
E. Harris, Capital	47,400	29,200
	$57,000	$38,000

Sunset Picture Gallery
Statement of Cash Receipts and Disbursements
For the Month of March, 19XX

Cash Receipts		
Received on account from customers	$67,200	
Cash sales	12,000	
Total cash receipts		$79,200
Cash Disbursements		
Supplies purchased for cash	$ 1,800	
Payments to artists on account	55,200	
Payment of salaries	2,000	
Payment for March rent	1,500	
Payment for utilities expense	300	
Total cash disbursements		60,800
Net increase in cash balance		$18,400

REQUIRED

(a) From the above information, prepare an accrual basis income statement for the month of March. To obtain the data needed, you may wish to use T accounts to reconstruct the accounts.

(b) Illustrate the apparent correctness of your net income amount by preparing a statement of owner's equity for March.

ANSWERS TO SELF-TEST QUESTIONS

1. (b) **2.** (c) **3.** (a) **4.** (b) **5.** (c)

3

THE ACCOUNTING CYCLE

CHAPTER OBJECTIVES

1. Identify the first five steps in the accounting cycle (pp. 73–74).
2. Explain the role of source documents in transaction analysis (pp. 74–77).
3. Describe the general journal and the process of journalizing transactions (pp. 77–79).
4. Explain the process of posting information from the general journal to the general ledger accounts (pp. 79–88).
5. Review the nature and format of a trial balance (pp. 81, 88–89).
6. Describe the adjusting process and illustrate typical adjusting entries (pp. 88–99).

There is a right time for everything.

ECCLESIASTES 3:1

The double-entry accounting system provides a basic framework for the analysis of business activities. Now we wish to go into greater detail about the accounting procedures used to account for the operations of a business during a specific period. The accounting procedures of most businesses involve certain basic steps that are accomplished in a given order. This sequence of operations is known as the **accounting cycle.** We will divide the accounting cycle into nine steps. In this chapter we will explain the first five steps and in Chapter 4 we will discuss the remaining four steps.

THE FIRST FIVE STEPS IN THE ACCOUNTING CYCLE

The first five steps in the accounting cycle are listed below.

1. Analyze transactions from source documents.
2. Record transactions in journals.
3. Post journal entries to general ledger accounts.
4. Prepare a trial balance.
5. Adjust the general ledger accounts.

These initial steps in the accounting cycle do not occur with equal frequency. Usually, analyzing, journalizing, and posting (steps 1–3) take place regularly throughout each operating period. At a minimum, a trial balance is prepared (step 4) whenever the accounts are to be adjusted (step 5). The adjustments occur only when management requires financial statements, usually at monthly or quarterly intervals, but at least annually.

The annual accounting period adopted by a business firm is known as its **fiscal year.** Business firms whose fiscal year ends in December are said to be on a **calendar-year** basis. Many firms prefer to have their accounting year coincide with their "natural" business year; that is, the fiscal year ends when business is slow and inventory quantities are small and easy to count. Year-end accounting procedures are most efficiently accomplished at this time. For example, most department stores choose a fiscal year ending on the last day of January or February, when their inventories are depleted from the normally heavy holiday sales and from post-holiday clearance sales.

Exhibit 3–1 shows the percentage of companies (out of 600 industrial and merchandising firms recently surveyed) having fiscal years ending during the various months of the year. Note that the calendar year is clearly the most popular fiscal year, but 36% of the companies have fiscal years ending in some month other than December.

In the remainder of this chapter and in Chapter 4, we will use an example to help explain the various steps in the accounting cycle. Our example throughout will be the first month's transactions of Landen TV Service, a repair business begun by Mark Landen on December 1 of the current year. Landen TV Service's fiscal year-end will be December 31.

EXHIBIT 3–1

FREQUENCY OF FISCAL YEAR-END
FOR 600 COMPANIES

Month of Fiscal Year-End	Percentage of Companies
January	4%
February	2
March	2
April	1
May	3
June	7
July	2
August	3
September	6
October	4
November	2
December	64
Total	100%

Source: Based on data in American Institute of Certified Public Accountants, *Accounting Trends and Techniques—1987.*

ANALYZING TRANSACTIONS FROM SOURCE DOCUMENTS

Step 1: Analyze Transactions from Source Documents

Source documents are printed or written forms that are generated when the firm engages in business transactions. Even a brief source document usually specifies the dollar amounts involved, the date of the transaction, and possibly the party dealing with the firm. Some examples of source documents are (1) a sales invoice showing evidence of a purchase of supplies on account, (2) a bank check indicating payment of an obligation, (3) a deposit slip showing the amount of funds turned over to the bank, (4) a cash receipt indicating funds received from a customer, and (5) a cash register tape listing a day's over-the-counter sales to customers.

Exhibit 3–2 lists the December transactions of Landen TV Service, together with their related source documents. Ordinarily, source documents or business papers such as those listed in Exhibit 3–2 will alert the bookkeeper to the need for an entry in the records. Usually the bookkeeper is able to analyze the transaction by examining the documents to determine the appropriate accounts to be debited and credited. For example, in transaction 2, a scrutiny of the check stub from the rent payment would reveal the need for debiting Rent Expense and crediting Cash. In transaction 4, the seller's invoice or bill of sale would probably indicate both the cost of the equipment and the down payment. The check stub would further corroborate the amount paid, and the bookkeeper would debit Test Equipment for $3,600, credit Cash for $2,000, and credit Accounts Payable for $1,600, the amount still owing.

Some transactions can be analyzed only by making further inquiry or by referring to previously received documents and the accounting records

EXHIBIT 3–2

DECEMBER TRANSACTIONS
LANDEN TV SERVICE

Transaction	Date	Brief Description	Related Source Documents
(1)	Dec. 1	Mark Landen deposited $25,000 in the firm's bank account.	Bank deposit slip
(2)	1	Paid December rent, $600.	Bank check, lease contract
(3)	2	Purchased truck for $10,800 cash.	Seller's invoice, bank check
(4)	2	Purchased test equipment for $3,600; paid $2,000 down; remainder to be paid in 60 days.	Seller's invoice, bank check
(5)	2	Signed two service contracts to perform	
		(a) Service work for a local TV dealer for four months, December–March, at $250 per month. Received $1,000 in advance.	Contract, dealer's check
		(b) Service work for a local hotel at a rate of $16 per hour. Settlement to be made whenever 40 hours of service have been rendered.	Contract, periodic bills to hotel
(6)	3	Purchased supplies and parts on account, $950.	Seller's invoice
(7)	7	Performed TV service for various customers during first week of December and received $650 cash.	Duplicates of cash receipt forms
(8)	14	Billed various agencies and customers for TV service rendered on account, $900.	Bills to customers
(9)	14	Paid employee's wages for first two weeks of December, $540.	Bank check
(10)	14	Performed TV service for various customers during second week of December and received $680 cash.	Duplicates of cash receipt forms
(11)	17	Paid advertising bill, $80.	Seller's invoice, bank check
(12)	19	Received $500 on account from customers.	Customers' checks
(13)	21	Performed TV service for various customers during third week of December and received $520 cash.	Duplicates of cash receipt forms
(14)	28	Paid truck expenses (gas and oil), $160.	Seller's invoice, bank check
(15)	28	Billed various agencies and customers for TV service rendered on account, $2,400.	Bills to customers
(16)	28	Paid employee's wages for second two weeks of December, $540.	Bank check
(17)	28	Withdrew $800 for personal use.	Bank check
(18)	28	Performed TV service during fourth week in December and received $300 cash.	Duplicates of cash receipt forms

themselves. For example, consider the two contracts signed by Mark Landen on December 2 (transaction 5). The mere signing of the contracts would not require bookkeeping entries, since the contracts are just agreements to provide services. In transaction 5a, however, Landen TV Service received $1,000 in advance, which requires a debit to Cash and a credit to Unearned Service Fees. In this case, the Unearned Service Fees of $1,000 represent an obligation (liability) to provide services for four months. At the end of each of these months, an entry must be

ABOUT THOSE SOURCE DOCUMENTS . . . ?

Source documents underlie the recording of accounting transactions and, thus, are an integral part of the accounting process. The significance of source documents has not been overlooked by various embezzlers and swindlers who try to cover up their schemes with false accounting entries. Fictitious source documents are created to support the fake entries. A prominent example is the fraud perpetrated upon McKesson & Robbins, a pharmaceutical company, by Philip Musica and his three brothers during the period 1927–1938.

Philip Musica, alias William Johnson alias Frank D. Costa alias Dr. F. Donald Coster, bought control of McKesson & Robbins in 1926 and immediately assumed the presidency. Although convicted twice in earlier years (on charges of bribery and embezzlement), Musica had successfully managed to hide his unsavory past by 1926. In 1927, Musica organized McKesson & Robbins, Ltd., a Canadian subsidiary that ostensibly would buy and sell crude drugs outside the United States—*ostensibly*, because the entire operation was fictitious.

Musica put himself in charge of the Canadian subsidiary's activities. Within McKesson & Robbins, he was aided by his brothers George (assistant treasurer) and Robert (shipping department head). Both brothers used aliases. Another brother, Arthur (alias George Vernard), headed up two fictitious outside firms—W. W. Smith & Co., a trading agent for the Canadian subsidiary, and Manning & Co., a private banking firm. With this arrangement, Musica was ready to siphon funds from the parent McKesson & Robbins company to pay for the "purchase" of crude drugs by the Canadian subsidiary and to pay fees to W. W. Smith & Co.

According to the accounting records and source documents, the Canadian subsidiary traded millions of dollars' worth of crude drugs throughout the world. Yet no crude drugs were actually traded. About all that really existed in the subsidiary's Montreal location were a rented office, five rented (and empty) warehouses, and a vacant lot.

An elaborate facade of false documents concealed the fraud. Musica hired a printer to print letterheads, invoices, and receipts bearing the names of corporations all over the world. A secretary working with seven different typewriters typed all correspondence, trading orders, and inventory statements (she believed she was doing important work for an international business network). The Montreal locations were essentially mail drops—secretaries there received large envelopes sent by Arthur and remailed the smaller envelopes they contained to W. W. Smith & Co. The smaller envelopes, of course, contained forged documents. W. W. Smith & Co. provided McKesson & Robbins with documentation showing sales made, deliveries completed, payments received from customers, and deposits made in the Manning bank. Each month Manning & Co. sent the accounting department a detailed statement showing bills paid, deposits received from sales, and itemized inventories of the crude drugs in the warehouses.

By the end of 1937, the Canadian subsidiary showed accounts receivable and inventories of crude drugs totaling $18,000,000—all fictitious. Through the years, McKesson & Robbins' auditors did not detect the fraud. They never visited the Canadian warehouses, relying instead on statements of drugs on hand provided by the warehouses and carefully checking these statements against the source documents in McKesson & Robbins' headquarters. These forged documents, however, did contain some strange data that went unnoticed by the auditors. Some drug quantities on hand, for example, would supply the entire United States for years, and some shipping orders moved drugs from South America to Australia by truck.

The fraud was finally uncovered in 1938 by a company officer who became suspicious when he noted that the Canadian crude drug inventories were not insured. This fraud had a significant impact on auditing procedures. Shortly after the fraud was detected, the physical observation of inventory counts and the direct confirmation of receivables with customers became standard audit techniques—techniques that continue to this day.*

*For a complete story of Philip Musica and the McKesson & Robbins fraud, see Charles Keats, *Magnificent Masquerade: The Strange Case of Dr. Coster and Mr. Musica* (New York: Funk & Wagnalls Company, Inc., 1964).

made to reduce the obligation and to reflect an appropriate amount in the revenue account Service Fees Earned. To ensure the proper entry, the bookkeeper can refer to the contract terms or review the entry made when the advance was received.

As a result of transaction 5b, the bookkeeper would record an account receivable from the hotel and credit the revenue account Service Fees Earned at the end of each accounting period. To do this, the bookkeeper might check the contract terms to calculate the amounts of such entries. The periodic entries required to reflect properly the services rendered under these two contracts fall into the category of *adjusting entries*; we describe these in step 5 of the accounting cycle and show that such entries frequently require reference to previous accounting records.

JOURNALS

Step 2: Record Transactions in Journals

For simplicity, the entries used in Chapter 2 were made directly in the general ledger accounts. This method would not prove feasible, however, for even a modest-sized business. For instance, suppose an owner wished to investigate a $1,000 credit in the Cash account. If entries were actually recorded directly in the general ledger, the purpose of the $1,000 expenditure could be difficult to determine. The owner might be forced to search through the entire general ledger to discover the offsetting debit of $1,000. Consequently, accounting records include a set of journals, which show the total effect of a business transaction or adjustment in one location.

Journals, or **records of original entry,** are tabular records in which business activities are analyzed in terms of debits and credits and recorded in chronological order before they are entered in the general ledger. An accounting journal may be one of a group of special journals, or it may be a general journal. A *special journal* is designed to record a specific type of frequently occurring business transaction. For example, a business with 100 employees who are paid every two weeks would probably use a special journal for payrolls. Because two paydays would normally occur in a month, at least 200 payroll transactions would be recorded. Other types of transactions that are often kept in special journals are cash receipts, cash disbursements, merchandise sales, and merchandise purchases.

In contrast to the special journals, the *general journal* is a relatively simple record in which any type of business transaction or adjustment may be recorded. All adjustments are recorded in the general journal as are transactions that do not occur often enough to warrant entry in a special journal. All businesses, even those using many special journals, have a general journal. In this chapter, we shall illustrate only the use of a general journal; in Chapter 6, we will introduce the use of special journals.

Exhibit 3–3 shows the first four transactions from Exhibit 3–2 as they would be recorded in Landen's general journal. Most journal entries are based on information appearing on a source document resulting from a transaction between the business and an outside party. The procedure for recording entries in the general journal is as follows:

1. Indicate the year, month, and date of the entry. Usually the year and month are rewritten only at the top of each page of the journal or at the point where they change.

EXHIBIT 3–3

General Journal

Page 1

Date		Description	Post. Ref.	Debit	Credit
19XX					
Dec.	1	Cash		25,000	
		M. Landen, Capital			25,000
		Opened the TV Service's bank account using personal funds.			
	1	Rent Expense		600	
		Cash			600
		Paid rent for December.			
	2	Truck		10,800	
		Cash			10,800
		Purchased truck for cash.			
	2	Test Equipment		3,600	
		Cash			2,000
		Accounts Payable			1,600
		Purchased electronic test equipment for $3,600. Terms: $2,000 down, remainder due in 60 days.			

2. Enter titles of the accounts affected in the description column. Accounts to receive debits are entered close to the left-hand margin and are traditionally recorded first. Accounts to receive credits are then recorded, indented slightly.
3. Place the appropriate money amounts in the left-hand (debit) and right-hand (credit) money columns.
4. Write an explanation of the transaction or adjustment below the account titles. The explanation should be as brief as possible, disclosing all the information necessary to understand the event being recorded.

Each transaction and adjustment entered in the journal should be stated in terms of equal debits and credits. The account titles cited in the description column should correspond to those used for the related general ledger accounts. To separate clearly the various entries, we leave a line blank between entries. We explain the use of the column headed "Post.Ref." (posting reference) later in step 3 of the accounting cycle.

COMPOUND JOURNAL ENTRIES A journal entry that involves more than just two accounts is called a **compound journal entry.** The last journal entry in Exhibit 3–3 is an example of a compound journal entry involving three accounts. The debit of $3,600 to Test Equipment is offset by credits of $2,000 to Cash and $1,600 to Accounts Payable. Any number of accounts may appear in a compound entry;

but, regardless of how many accounts are used, the total of the debit amounts must always equal the total of the credit amounts.

CORRECTION OF JOURNAL ERRORS Certain procedures should be followed when errors are found in journal entries. Errors should not be erased, because erasures completely remove the original recording. As you might imagine, the acceptance of erasures might allow someone to falsify accounting records; consequently, other procedures are used.

If an erroneous journal entry has not been transferred to the general ledger, a single line is drawn through the erroneous amount or account title, and the correction is entered on the same line just above the error. Often the person correcting the entry must place his or her initials near the correction. This facilitates any subsequent inquiry about the nature of or reason for the correction. Once an erroneous journal entry has been transferred to the ledger accounts, both records contain the error. The recommended procedures for correcting this situation are discussed in step 3.

POSTING

Step 3: Post Journal Entries to General Ledger Accounts

After transactions have been journalized, the next step in the accounting cycle is to transcribe the debits and credits in each journal entry to the appropriate general ledger accounts. This transcribing process is called **posting** to the general ledger. Thus, data from a journal that stresses the total effect of particular transactions (such as the collection of accounts receivable) are transcribed to a ledger that stresses the total effect of many business transactions on a particular business variable (such as cash, accounts receivable, and so on). This latter type of data is specifically needed for the preparation of financial statements.

When records are kept by hand, posting from the general journal may be done daily, every few days, or at the end of each month. Journalizing and posting often occur simultaneously when the record-keeping process is automated. The posting of special journals is discussed in Chapter 6.

POSTING REFERENCES It is important to be able to trace any entry appearing in a ledger account to the journal from which it was posted. Consequently, accounting records use a system of references. Both journals and accounts have **posting reference** columns. Entries in the posting reference columns of journals indicate the account to which the related debit or credit has been posted. Posting references appearing in ledger accounts identify the journal from which the related entry was posted. The posting references in the journals and ledger accounts are entered when the journal entries are posted to the ledger accounts.

To keep accounting records uncluttered, we make posting references simple. For example, the posting reference of the general journal might be GJ or simply J. Similarly, special journals such as Cash Receipts and Payroll might be indicated by posting references of CR and PR, respectively. Because both general and special journals usually involve many pages of entries, journal pages are numbered in sequence. Thus, a posting reference of J9 appearing on the line with a $1,000 debit entry in the Cash account means that the ninth page of the general journal contains the entire entry in which the $1,000 debit to Cash appears.

Because all entries should be posted from some journal, every entry appearing in a ledger account should have a related posting reference. Posting references appearing in journals are usually the numbers that have been assigned to the general ledger accounts.

CHART OF ACCOUNTS In all but the simplest accounting systems, a number is assigned to each general ledger account. Such a numbering system permits easy reference to accounts even if the account title contains several words. For example, the account Depreciation Expense—Test Equipment might be referred to simply as account No. 57.

A **chart of accounts** is usually prepared in order to facilitate the analysis of activities and the formulation of journal entries. The chart of accounts is a list of the titles and numbers of all accounts found in the general ledger. The account titles should be grouped by, and in order of, the five major sections of the general ledger (assets, liabilities, owners' equity, revenue, and expenses). Exhibit 3–4 shows a chart of accounts for the Landen TV Service, indicating the account numbers that will now be used.

The method of assigning account numbers usually ensures that the numbers of all the accounts in a major section of the general ledger start with the same digit. In Exhibit 3–4, all asset accounts begin with 1, liabilities with 2, and so on. Complicated accounting systems may use three- or four-digit account numbers and may even employ suffixes to designate various branches, departments, or divisions.

EXHIBIT 3–4

LANDEN TV SERVICE
CHART OF ACCOUNTS

Assets

11. Cash
12. Accounts Receivable
14. Supplies and Parts on Hand
16. Test Equipment
17. Accumulated Depreciation—Test Equipment
18. Truck
19. Accumulated Depreciation—Truck

Liabilities

21. Accounts Payable
22. Utilities Payable
23. Wages Payable
24. Unearned Service Fees

Owner's Equity

31. M. Landen, Capital
32. M. Landen, Drawing
33. Income Summary

Revenue

41. Service Fees Earned

Expenses

51. Rent Expense
52. Wages Expense
53. Advertising Expense
54. Supplies and Parts Expense
55. Utilities Expense
56. Truck Expense
57. Depreciation Expense—Test Equipment
58. Depreciation Expense—Truck

ILLUSTRATION OF POSTING Exhibit 3–5 diagrams the posting of Landen TV Service's first transaction from the general journal to the ledger accounts. Each debit entry and each credit entry is posted as follows:

1. The date (year, month, and day) is entered in the appropriate account. Note that this is the date of the journal entry, not necessarily the date of the actual posting. As with journals, the year and month are restated only at the top of a new account page or at the point where they change.
2. The amount is entered in the account as a debit or a credit, as indicated in the journal's money columns, and the new balance is calculated.
3. The posting reference from the journal (both symbol and page number) is placed in the posting reference column of the ledger account.
4. The account number is placed in the posting reference column of the journal.

Regardless of the types of journals or the number of entries involved, the total debits posted should equal the total credits posted. Exhibit 3–6 (see pages 83–88) is a comprehensive illustration of the journalizing and posting of the December transactions of Landen TV Service. You should review each transaction in the illustration for (1) the nature of the transaction, (2) the related journal entry, and (3) the subsequent postings. Bear in mind that the account numbers in the posting reference column of the journal are not entered when the journal entry is recorded; they are inserted when the entry is posted.

CORRECTING ERRONEOUS POSTINGS Even the most carefully kept accounts will occasionally contain posting errors. An error involving only the wrong amount being posted may be corrected by drawing a line through the incorrect amount, entering the correct amount above, and initialing the correction. When an amount has been posted to the wrong account, however, the correction should be made with a journal entry. Let us assume that Landen TV Service purchased test equipment for $100 cash and that the bookkeeper erroneously debited the amount to Supplies and Parts on Hand instead of to Test Equipment. The following entry in the journal corrects the error by transferring the debit to the correct account:

Test Equipment	100	
Supplies and Parts on Hand		100
To correct entry for purchase of test equipment.		

TRIAL BALANCE

Step 4: Prepare a Trial Balance

After the journal entries have been posted to the general ledger accounts, a trial balance is prepared of all the general ledger accounts that show a balance. As noted in Chapter 2, the trial balance lists the general ledger accounts with their respective debit or credit balances. The debit balances and credit balances are each totaled to confirm their equality (that is, to confirm that the general ledger is "in balance"). We want to be sure the general ledger is in balance before we start to adjust the accounts. Because this trial balance shows the account balances before any adjustments have been made, it is sometimes called an **unadjusted trial balance.**

EXHIBIT 3–5

DIAGRAMS OF POSTING TO LEDGER ACCOUNTS

General Journal Page 1

Date		Description	Post. Ref.	Debit	Credit
19XX Dec.	1	Cash	11	25,000	
		M. Landen, Capital	31		25,000
		Opened the TV Service's bank account using personal funds.			

❶ ❷ ❸ ❹

General Ledger
Cash Account No. 11

Date		Description	Post. Ref.	Debit*	Credit	Balance
19XX Dec.	1		J1	25,000		25,000

General Journal Page 1

Date		Description	Post. Ref.	Debit	Credit
19XX Dec.	1	Cash	11	25,000	
		M. Landen, Capital	31		25,000
		Opened the TV Service's bank account using personal funds.			

❶ ❷ ❸ ❹

General Ledger
M. Landen, Capital Account No. 31

Date		Description	Post. Ref.	Debit	Credit*	Balance
19XX Dec.	1		J1		25,000	25,000

*Throughout this chapter, the asterisk indicates the column that designates the normal balance.

EXHIBIT 3–6

JOURNALIZING AND POSTING FOR LANDEN TV SERVICE

General Journal Page 1

Date		Description	Post. Ref.	Debit	Credit
19XX					
Dec.	1	Cash	11	25,000	
		M. Landen, Capital	31		25,000
		Opened the TV Service's bank account using personal funds.			
	1	Rent Expense	51	600	
		Cash	11		600
		Paid rent for December.			
	2	Truck	18	10,800	
		Cash	11		10,800
		Purchased truck for cash.			
	2	Test Equipment	16	3,600	
		Cash	11		2,000
		Accounts Payable	21		1,600
		Purchased electronic test equipment for $3,600. Terms: $2,000 down, remainder due in 60 days.			
	2	Cash	11	1,000	
		Unearned Service Fees	24		1,000
		Received advance on four-month contract at $250 per month.			
	3	Supplies and Parts on Hand	14	950	
		Accounts Payable	21		950
		Purchased supplies and parts on account; 60-day terms.			
	7	Cash	11	650	
		Service Fees Earned	41		650
		Services for cash, December 1–7.			
	14	Accounts Receivable	12	900	
		Service Fees Earned	41		900
		Services rendered on account.			
	14	Wages Expense	52	540	
		Cash	11		540
		Paid wages for first two weeks of December.			

EXH 3–6 (Continued)

General Journal — Page 2

Date		Description	Post. Ref.	Debit	Credit
19XX					
Dec.	14	Cash	11	680	
		Service Fees Earned	41		680
		Services for cash, December 8–14.			
	17	Advertising Expense	53	80	
		Cash	11		80
		Paid *Daily News* for December advertising.			
	19	Cash	11	500	
		Accounts Receivable	12		500
		Received $500 on account from credit customers.			
	21	Cash	11	520	
		Service Fees Earned	41		520
		Services for cash, December 15–21.			
	28	Truck Expense	56	160	
		Cash	11		160
		Gas and oil for December.			
	28	Accounts Receivable	12	2,400	
		Service Fees Earned	41		2,400
		Services rendered on account.			
	28	Wages Expense	52	540	
		Cash	11		540
		Paid wages for second two weeks of December.			
	28	M. Landen, Drawing	32	800	
		Cash	11		800
		Withdrew $800 for personal use.			
	28	Cash	11	300	
		Service Fees Earned	41		300
		Services for cash, December 22–28.			

EXH 3–6 (Continued)

General Ledger

Cash

Account No. 11

Date		Description	Post. Ref.	Debit*	Credit	Balance
19XX						
Dec.	1		J1	25,000		25,000
	1		J1		600	24,400
	2		J1		10,800	13,600
	2		J1		2,000	11,600
	2		J1	1,000		12,600
	7		J1	650		13,250
	14		J1		540	12,710
	14		J2	680		13,390
	17		J2		80	13,310
	19		J2	500		13,810
	21		J2	520		14,330
	28		J2		160	14,170
	28		J2		540	13,630
	28		J2		800	12,830
	28		J2	300		13,130

Accounts Receivable

Account No. 12

Date		Description	Post. Ref.	Debit*	Credit	Balance
19XX						
Dec.	14		J1	900		900
	19		J2		500	400
	28		J2	2,400		2,800

Supplies and Parts on Hand

Account No. 14

Date		Description	Post. Ref.	Debit*	Credit	Balance
19XX						
Dec.	3		J1	950		950

EXH 3–6 (Continued)

Test Equipment Account No. 16

Date		Description	Post. Ref.	Debit*	Credit	Balance
19XX Dec.	2		J1	3,600		3,600

Truck Account No. 18

Date		Description	Post. Ref.	Debit*	Credit	Balance
19XX Dec.	2		J1	10,800		10,800

Accounts Payable Account No. 21

Date		Description	Post. Ref.	Debit	Credit*	Balance
19XX Dec.	2		J1		1,600	1,600
	3		J1		950	2,550

Unearned Service Fees Account No. 24

Date		Description	Post. Ref.	Debit	Credit*	Balance
19XX Dec.	2		J1		1,000	1,000

M. Landen, Capital Account No. 31

Date		Description	Post. Ref.	Debit	Credit*	Balance
19XX Dec.	1		J1		25,000	25,000

EXH 3–6 (Continued)

M. Landen, Drawing Account No. 32

Date		Description	Post. Ref.	Debit*	Credit	Balance
19XX Dec.	28		J2	800		800

Service Fees Earned Account No. 41

Date		Description	Post. Ref.	Debit	Credit*	Balance
19XX Dec.	7		J1		650	650
	14		J1		900	1,550
	14		J2		680	2,230
	21		J2		520	2,750
	28		J2		2,400	5,150
	28		J2		300	5,450

Rent Expense Account No. 51

Date		Description	Post. Ref.	Debit*	Credit	Balance
19XX Dec.	1		J1	600		600

Wages Expense Account No. 52

Date		Description	Post. Ref.	Debit*	Credit	Balance
19XX Dec.	14		J1	540		540
	28		J2	540		1,080

Advertising Expense Account No. 53

Date		Description	Post. Ref.	Debit*	Credit	Balance
19XX Dec.	17		J2	80		80

EXH 3–6 (Continued)

Truck Expense Account No. 56

Date		Description	Post. Ref.	Debit*	Credit	Balance
19XX Dec.	28		J2	160		160

Because the trial balance is prepared as of a particular date, the heading for the trial balance should show that date. The trial balance of the Landen TV Service at December 31 is shown in Exhibit 3–7. Showing all the general ledger account balances in one place, as is done in this trial balance, makes it easier to review the accounts and determine which account balances need to be adjusted.

ADJUSTMENTS

Step 5: Adjust the General Ledger Accounts

It is important that accounts appearing in financial statements at the end of an accounting period be properly stated. Clearly, if the income statement is to portray a realistic net income figure based on accrual accounting, all revenues *earned* during the period and all expenses *incurred* must be shown. Therefore, revenues and costs must be properly aligned for the reporting period in question. This process of aligning costs and expenses with related revenue is the **matching** concept frequently mentioned in accounting literature.

Many of the transactions reflected in the accounting records through the first four steps in the accounting cycle affect the net income of more than one period. Therefore, to achieve a proper matching of costs and expenses with revenue, we must adjust the account balances at the end of each accounting period.

Four general types of adjustments are made at the end of an accounting period:

1. Aligning *recorded costs* with the appropriate accounting periods.
2. Aligning *recorded revenue* with the appropriate accounting periods.
3. Reflecting *unrecorded expenses* incurred during the accounting period.
4. Reflecting *unrecorded revenue* earned during the accounting period.

Adjustments in the first two categories—aligning recorded costs and revenue with the appropriate periods—are often referred to as **deferrals.** Adjustments in the last two categories—reflecting unrecorded expenses and revenue—are often referred to as **accruals.** The journal entries made to give effect to these various adjustments are known as **adjusting entries.**

ALIGNING RECORDED COSTS Many business outlays may benefit a number of accounting periods. Some common examples are purchases of buildings, equip-

EXHIBIT 3–7

Landen TV Service
Trial Balance
December, 19XX

	Debit	Credit
Cash	$13,130	
Accounts Receivable	2,800	
Supplies and Parts on Hand	950	
Test Equipment	3,600	
Truck	10,800	
Accounts Payable		$ 2,550
Unearned Service Fees		1,000
M. Landen, Capital		25,000
M. Landen, Drawing	800	
Service Fees Earned		5,450
Rent Expense	600	
Wages Expense	1,080	
Advertising Expense	80	
Truck Expense	160	
	$34,000	$34,000

ment, and supplies, and payments of insurance premiums covering a period of years. Ordinarily, these outlays are debited to an asset account at the time of expenditure. Then, at the end of each accounting period, the estimated portion of the outlay that has expired during the period or that has benefited the period is transferred to an expense account.

The preceding chapters included two examples of adjustments aligning recorded costs with the appropriate accounting period. One example allocated part of the cost of three years' insurance coverage to insurance expense for the current month. The total cost of the insurance premium had been debited initially to the asset account Prepaid Insurance. The adjustment then allocated the cost of one month's coverage ($\frac{1}{36}$ of the premium) to insurance expense. The other example dealt with the cost of supplies. The adjustment transferred the cost of supplies used during the current month from the asset account Supplies on Hand to the expense account Supplies Expense. We will consider another example involving supplies and parts in this chapter.

Under most circumstances, we can discover when adjustments of this type are needed by inspecting the monthly trial balance for costs that benefit several periods. By looking at the December 31 trial balance of Landen TV Service (Exhibit 3–7), for example, we would find that adjustments are required to apportion the costs of the supplies and parts, the test equipment, and the truck between December and subsequent periods.

Supplies and parts During December, Landen TV Service purchased supplies and parts and recorded the outlay in an asset account, Supplies and Parts on Hand, as follows:

Dec. 3	Supplies and Parts on Hand	950	
	Accounts Payable		950
	Purchased supplies and parts on account; 60-day terms.		

The firm could not conveniently keep a daily count of parts and supplies used in service work. Instead, at the end of December, it would count the items still on hand. Suppose the count shows $510 worth of supplies and parts on hand at the end of the month, indicating that $440 worth of supplies and parts have been used in service work during the month. Therefore, at the end of the period, an adjusting entry will transfer this amount to an expense account, Supplies and Parts Expense, as follows:

Dec. 31	Supplies and Parts Expense	440	
	Supplies and Parts on Hand		440
	To record expense of supplies and parts used in December.		

When this adjusting entry is posted, it will properly reflect the December expense for supplies and parts and will reduce the asset account Supplies and Parts on Hand to $510, the actual amount of the asset remaining at December 31. After the entry is posted, the related ledger accounts appear as follows:

Supplies and Parts on Hand Account No. 14

Date		Description	Post. Ref.	Debit*	Credit	Balance
19XX						
Dec.	3		J1	950		950
	31		J3		440	510

Supplies and Parts Expense Account No. 54

Date		Description	Post. Ref.	Debit*	Credit	Balance
19XX						
Dec.	31		J3	440		440

If financial statements were prepared without this adjustment, the December income statement would omit an important expense and would overstate net income by $440. Similarly, the balance sheet would overstate assets by $440, because the Supplies and Parts on Hand balance would remain at $950. As a result of overstating net income, owner's equity in the balance sheet would also be overstated by $440.

Depreciation The process of allocating the costs of a firm's equipment, vehicles, and buildings to the periods benefiting from their use is called **depreciation**

accounting. Because these long-lived assets help generate revenue in a company's operations, each accounting period in which the assets are used should reflect a portion of their cost as expense. This periodic expense is known as depreciation expense.

Periodic depreciation expense must be estimated by accountants. The procedure we use here estimates the annual amount of depreciation expense by dividing the cost of the asset by its estimated useful life in years. This method is called **straight-line depreciation.** (We will explore other methods in Chapter 10.)

When recording depreciation expense, the asset amount is not reduced directly. Instead, the reduction is recorded in a contra account called **Accumulated Depreciation.** Contra accounts are so named because they are used to record reductions in or offsets against a related account. The Accumulated Depreciation account will normally have a credit balance and will appear in the balance sheet as a deduction from the related asset amount. Use of the contra account Accumulated Depreciation allows the original cost of the related asset to be shown in the balance sheet, followed by the accumulated amount of depreciation.

Let us assume that the test equipment purchased by Landen TV Service for \$3,600 has an estimated life of five years and that the truck costing \$10,800 is expected to last six years. Straight-line depreciation recorded on the test equipment is therefore \$720 per year, or \$60 per month. Similarly, the depreciation on the truck is \$1,800 per year, or \$150 per month. At the end of December, we would make the following adjusting entries:

Dec. 31	Depreciation Expense—Test Equipment	60	
	Accumulated Depreciation—Test Equipment		60
	To record December depreciation on test equipment.		
Dec. 31	Depreciation Expense—Truck	150	
	Accumulated Depreciation—Truck		150
	To record December depreciation on truck.		

When the preceding entries are posted, they will properly reflect the cost of using these assets during December, and the correct expense will appear in the December income statement. After the adjusting entries have been posted, the asset accounts, accumulated depreciation accounts, and depreciation expense accounts appear as follows:

Test Equipment Account No. 16

Date		Description	Post. Ref.	Debit*	Credit	Balance
19XX Dec.	2		J1	3,600		3,600

Accumulated Depreciation—Test Equipment Account No. 17

Date		Description	Post. Ref.	Debit	Credit*	Balance
19XX Dec.	31		J3		60	60

Depreciation Expense—Test Equipment Account No. 57

Date		Description	Post. Ref.	Debit*	Credit	Balance
19XX Dec.	31		J3	60		60

Truck Account No. 18

Date		Description	Post. Ref.	Debit*	Credit	Balance
19XX Dec.	2		J1	10,800		10,800

Accumulated Depreciation—Truck Account No. 19

Date		Description	Post. Ref.	Debit	Credit*	Balance
19XX Dec.	31		J3		150	150

Depreciation Expense—Truck Account No. 58

Date		Description	Post. Ref.	Debit*	Credit	Balance
19XX Dec.	31		J3	150		150

If the firm failed to record the adjusting entries for depreciation, expenses would be omitted from the income statement. In the above situation, such an omission would result in an overstatement of net income by $210. Furthermore, assets and owner's equity would be overstated by the same amount on the balance sheet.

On the balance sheet, the accumulated depreciation amounts are subtracted from the related asset amounts. The resulting balances (cost less accumulated depreciation), which are the assets' **book values,** represent the unexpired asset costs to be applied as expenses against future operating periods. For example, the December 31, 19XX, balance sheet would show test equipment with a book value of $3,540, presented as follows:

Test Equipment	$3,600	
Less: Accumulated Depreciation	60	$3,540

ALIGNING RECORDED REVENUE Sometimes a business receives fees for services before service is rendered. Such transactions are ordinarily recorded by debiting Cash and crediting a liability account for the **unearned revenue.** The liability account in this situation may also be referred to as **deferred revenue** and shows the obligation for performing future service. For example, a monthly magazine publisher receiving $72 for a three-year subscription would debit Cash and credit Unearned Subscription Revenue for $72. Each month that magazines are supplied to the subscriber, $\frac{1}{36}$ of the publisher's obligation is fulfilled. At the end of each month, the bookkeeper would transfer $2 from the liability account Unearned Subscription Revenue to a revenue account, Subscription Revenue. This procedure reflects revenue when service is performed rather than when it is paid for.

During December, Landen TV Service entered one transaction that requires an end-of-month adjustment to recorded revenue. On December 2, the firm signed a four-month contract to perform service for a local TV dealer at $250 per month, with the entire contract price of $1,000 received in advance. The entry made on December 2 was as follows:

Dec. 2	Cash	1,000	
	Unearned Service Fees		1,000
	Received advance on four-month contract at $250 per month.		

On December 31, the following adjusting entry would be made to transfer $250, the revenue earned in December, to Service Fees Earned and reduce the liability Unearned Service Fees by the same amount:

Dec. 31	Unearned Service Fees	250	
	Service Fees Earned		250
	To record portion of advance earned in December.		

After this entry is posted, the liability account will show a balance of $750, the amount of future services still owing, and the Service Fees Earned account will reflect the $250 earned in December.

Unearned Service Fees Account No. 24

Date		Description	Post. Ref.	Debit	Credit*	Balance
19XX						
Dec.	2		J1		1,000	1,000
	31		J3	250		750

Service Fees Earned Account No. 41

Date		Description	Post. Ref.	Debit	Credit*	Balance
19XX						
Dec.	7		J1		650	650
	14		J1		900	1,550
	14		J2		680	2,230
	21		J2		520	2,750
	28		J2		2,400	5,150
	28		J2		300	5,450
	31		J3		250	5,700

A similar entry would be repeated at the end of each month of the contract period; $250 in revenue would be included in Service Fees Earned in the income statement, and the liability account in the balance sheet would be reduced by $250.

We emphasize here that if the adjusting entries are ignored, the revenue is never reflected in any income statement and the liability remains on the balance sheet after the obligation has been discharged. Therefore, it is important to make these adjustments carefully.

REFLECTING UNRECORDED EXPENSES Often a business will use certain services before paying for them. Obligations to pay for services such as salaries, utilities, and taxes may build up, or accrue, over a period of time. Most businesses make adjusting entries for such **accrued expenses** in order to reflect the proper cost in the period when the benefit was received. The bookkeeper must realize that services received have not yet been reflected in the accounts and make appropriate adjustments. If source documents are not available, amounts may be estimated.

Accrued utilities During December, Landen TV Service used telephone service and utility service for heat and light. Bills from the telephone and power companies will not arrive until January. Let us assume, however, that based on inquiries to the landlord and knowledge of local rates, the firm estimates that it received $120 worth of services during the month. On December 31, the bookkeeper makes the following adjusting entry:

Dec. 31	Utilities Expense	120	
	Utilities Payable		120
	To record estimated amount of December utilities expense.		

This adjustment reflects both the cost of services received during the period and the estimated amount owed for such services to be included on the balance sheet. If this adjustment were not made, net income would be overstated by $120 in the December income statement; on the December 31 balance sheet, liabilities would be understated and owner's equity overstated by $120.

Note that the credit in the adjusting entry above could have been made to Accounts Payable. Because the amount is an estimate, however, many businesses prefer to credit a separate account such as Utilities Payable.

After the bookkeeper posts the adjusting entry for estimated utilities expense, the expense and liability accounts would appear as follows:

Utilities Expense Account No. 55

Date		Description	Post. Ref.	Debit*	Credit	Balance
19XX Dec.	31		J3	120		120

Utilities Payable Account No. 22

Date		Description	Post. Ref.	Debit	Credit*	Balance
19XX Dec.	31		J3		120	120

Suppose the utility bill that arrives in early January is for $124, indicating that the firm has underestimated the December expense by $4. Obviously, $124 will be credited to Cash since the full amount of the bill must be paid. But what would be debited to balance the $124 credit? The firm might remove the liability by debiting $120 to Utilities Payable and debiting the remaining $4 to Utilities Expense for January. This tactic places some of December's utilities expense in January. Such a small discrepancy as $4 is not material, however, and most persons would not be disturbed about the minor inaccuracy. Another method of handling the accrual in the subsequent period, involving reversing entries, will be explained in Chapter 4.

Accrued wages A Landen TV Service employee is paid every two weeks at the rate of $270 for each six-day work week. The employee was paid $540 on December 14 and December 28. Let us assume that both these dates fell on Saturday and that Sunday is the employee's day off. If financial statements are prepared at the close of business on Tuesday, December 31, the employee will have worked two days (Monday and Tuesday) during December for which he will not be paid until January. Because the employee's wages are $45 per day ($270 ÷ 6 days), additional wages expense of $90 should be reflected in the income statement for December. The adjusting entry at the end of December would be as follows:

Dec. 31	Wages Expense	90	
	Wages Payable		90
	To record accrued wages for December 30 and 31.		

After posting, the Wages Expense and Wages Payable accounts would appear as follows:

Wages Expense Account No. 52

Date		Description	Post. Ref.	Debit*	Credit	Balance
19XX						
Dec.	14		J1	540		540
	28		J2	540		1,080
	31		J3	90		1,170

Wages Payable Account No. 23

Date		Description	Post. Ref.	Debit	Credit*	Balance
19XX						
Dec.	31		J3		90	90

This adjustment enables the firm to reflect as December expense all wages *earned* by the employee during the period rather than just the wages *paid*. In addition, the balance sheet will show the liability for unpaid wages at the end of the period. Omitting this adjustment would cause a $90 overstatement of net income in the December income statement, with a concurrent $90 overstatement of owner's equity and a $90 understatement of liabilities in the December 31 balance sheet.

When the employee is paid on the next regular payday in January, the bookkeeper must make sure that the two days' pay accrued at the end of December is not again charged to expense. If we assume that the employee is paid $540 on Saturday, January 11, the following entry can be made:

Jan. 11	Wages Payable	90	
	Wages Expense	450	
	Cash		540
	To record wages paid.		

This entry eliminates the liability recorded in Wages Payable at the end of December and debits January Wages Expense for only those wages earned by the employee in January. Another method of avoiding dual charges, that of reversing entries, will be explained in Chapter 4.

REFLECTING UNRECORDED REVENUE A company may provide services during a period that are neither billed nor paid for by the end of the period. Yet the value of these services represents revenue earned by the firm and should be reflected in the firm's income statement. Such accumulated revenue is often called **accrued revenue.** For example, a firm may have loaned money on which interest has been earned that is not collected by the end of the period. The amount of the interest should be reflected in the net income of the period in which it is earned. In this situation, an adjusting entry would be made debiting Interest Receivable and crediting Interest Income for the amount of interest earned.

In the case of Landen TV Service, the service contract with the local hotel negotiated on December 2 could result in accrued revenue. Under the terms of the contract, Landen TV Service will bill the hotel for work at $16 per hour whenever 40 hours of work have been completed. Suppose that by December 31, Landen has performed 15 hours of work for the hotel. Unbilled revenue of $240 (15 hours × $16) has accrued during the month and should be reflected in the accounts by the following adjusting entry:

Dec. 31	Accounts Receivable	240	
	Service Fees Earned		240
	To record unbilled revenue earned during December.		

This entry includes in the December accounts the revenue earned by performing services that are not yet billed to the hotel. It also enters the amount due from the hotel for these services as a receivable on the balance sheet. After the entry is posted, the related accounts would appear as follows:

Accounts Receivable Account No. 12

Date		Description	Post. Ref.	Debit*	Credit	Balance
19XX						
Dec.	14		J1	900		900
	19		J2		500	400
	28		J2	2,400		2,800
	31		J3	240		3,040

Service Fees Earned Account No. 41

Date		Description	Post. Ref.	Debit	Credit*	Balance
19XX						
Dec.	7		J1		650	650
	14		J1		900	1,550
	14		J2		680	2,230
	21		J2		520	2,750
	28		J2		2,400	5,150
	28		J2		300	5,450
	31		J3		250	5,700
	31		J3		240	5,940

The bookkeeper must be careful when the regular 40-hour billing is sent to the hotel in January. Let us assume that 40 hours of work has accumulated by January 21. Because the revenue from 15 hours of work ($240) was recorded in the December 31 adjusting entry, the billing made on January 21 contains only $400 (25 hours × $16) of revenue earned during January. The following entry could be made when the hotel is billed for $640 (40 hours × $16):

Jan. 21	Accounts Receivable	400	
	Service Fees Earned		400
	To record revenue earned during January; customer billed $640 for work performed in December and January.		

An alternative way of handling this situation, using reversing entries, is discussed in Chapter 4.

If we did not make the adjustment for accrued revenue, the December net income for Landen TV Service would be understated by $240, and the January net income would be overstated by the same amount. On the December 31 balance sheet, assets and owner's equity would also be understated.

PREPAYMENTS RECORDED IN EXPENSE AND REVENUE ACCOUNTS Expenditures made to benefit future periods and amounts received for services yet to be performed should be recorded initially in balance sheet accounts. Then the adjusting procedure consists of transferring the expired portion of prepaid expenses to expense accounts and transferring the earned portion of unearned revenue to revenue accounts. We have essentially just described these procedures.

Occasionally, an outlay benefiting future periods may be debited to an expense account rather than to prepaid expense, or an amount received for future services may be credited to a revenue account rather than to unearned revenue. In such situations, the adjusting procedure consists of transferring the unexpired or unearned portion of the recorded amount to the appropriate balance sheet account. For example, suppose that a one-year insurance premium of $1,200 was initially debited to Insurance Expense. At the end of the first month after the outlay, the following adjusting entry is appropriate:

Prepaid Insurance	1,100	
Insurance Expense		1,100
To transfer unexpired insurance cost to asset account.		

This entry sets up an asset of $1,100 and leaves $100 in the expense account.

Suppose also that the firm received a six-month prepayment of rent totaling $1,800 from a tenant and credited the entire amount to Rental Income (a revenue account). After the first month has elapsed, the appropriate adjusting entry is:

Rental Income	1,500	
Unearned Rental Income		1,500
To transfer unearned rental income to liability account.		

This adjustment records $1,500 as a liability and leaves a $300 balance in the revenue account.

It is important to note that the nature of the adjusting entry depends on how the transaction was recorded initially (a prepayment debited to either an asset or expense account and an advance receipt credited to either a liability or revenue

EXHIBIT 3–8

SUMMARY OF ADJUSTMENTS

Adjustment Category	Nature of Adjusting Entry	Examples: Text Page	Examples: Entry		
1. Aligning Recorded Costs					
a. Initially recorded as an asset	Increase expense	90	Supplies and Parts Expense	440	
	Decrease asset		Supplies and Parts on Hand		440
For depreciation	Increase expense	91	Depreciation Expense—Test Equipment	60	
	Increase contra asset (which decreases		Accumulated Depreciation—Test Equipment		60
	asset's book value)	91	Depreciation Expense—Truck	150	
			Accumulated Depreciation—Truck		150
b. Initially recorded as an expense	Increase asset	98	Prepaid Insurance	1,100	
	Decrease expense		Insurance Expense		1,100
2. Aligning Recorded Revenue					
a. Initially recorded as a liability	Decrease liability	93	Unearned Service Fees	250	
	Increase revenue		Service Fees Earned		250
b. Initially recorded as revenue	Decrease revenue	98	Rental Income	1,500	
	Increase liability		Unearned Rental Income		1,500
3. Reflecting Unrecorded Expenses	Increase expense	94	Utilities Expense	120	
	Increase liability		Utilities Payable		120
		95	Wages Expense	90	
			Wages Payable		90
4. Reflecting Unrecorded Revenue	Increase asset	97	Accounts Receivable	240	
	Increase revenue		Service Fees Earned		240

account). *After* the adjusting entry has been made and posted, however, the balances in the affected accounts will be the same regardless of how the transaction was initially recorded.

Exhibit 3–8 summarizes our discussion about the various types of adjustments.

KEY POINTS FOR CHAPTER OBJECTIVES

1 Identify the first five steps in the accounting cycle (pp. 73–74).

- The first five steps in the accounting cycle are:
  a. Analyze transactions from source documents.
  b. Record transactions in journals.
  c. Post journal entries to general ledger accounts.
  d. Prepare a trial balance.
  e. Adjust the general ledger accounts.

2 Explain the role of source documents in transaction analysis (pp. 74–77).

- Source documents usually provide the basis for analyzing business transactions.
- Source documents are printed or written forms that are generated when a transaction occurs.

3 Describe the general journal and the process of journalizing transactions (pp. 77–79).

- Accounting entries are initially recorded in a journal; the entries are in chronological order, and the journal shows the total effect of each transaction or adjustment.

4 Explain the process of posting information from the general journal to the general ledger accounts (pp. 79–88).

- Posting is the transfer of information from a journal to the general ledger accounts.
- Posting references are used to cross-reference the information in journals and the general ledger accounts.

5 Review the nature and format of a trial balance (pp. 81, 88–89).

- A trial balance lists the general ledger accounts with their respective debit or credit balances.

6 Describe the adjusting process and illustrate typical adjusting entries (pp. 88–99).

- Adjusting entries made to achieve the appropriate matching of expenses and revenue consist of the following four types:
  a. Aligning recorded costs with periods benefited.
  b. Aligning recorded revenue with periods in which it is earned.
  c. Reflecting unrecorded expenses incurred during the period.
  d. Reflecting unrecorded revenue earned during the period.

KEY TERMS USED IN THIS CHAPTER

accounting cycle 73
accruals 88
accrued expense 94
accrued revenue 96
accumulated depreciation 91
adjusting entries 88
book value (of depreciable asset) 92
calendar year 73
chart of accounts 80
compound journal entry 78
deferrals 88
deferred revenue 93
depreciation accounting 90
fiscal year 73
journals 77
matching concept 88
posting 79
posting reference 79
record of original entry 77
source document 74
straight-line depreciation 91
unadjusted trial balance 81
unearned revenue 93

SELF-TEST QUESTIONS FOR REVIEW

(Answers are at the end of this chapter.)

1. The first step in the accounting cycle is to
   (a) Record transactions in journals.
   (b) Analyze transactions from source documents.
   (c) Post journal entries to general ledger accounts.
   (d) Adjust the general ledger accounts.
2. A journal entry that contains more than just two accounts is called
   (a) A posted journal entry.
   (b) An adjusting journal entry.
   (c) An erroneous journal entry.
   (d) A compound journal entry.
3. Posting refers to the process of transferring information from
   (a) Journals to general ledger accounts.
   (b) General ledger accounts to journals.
   (c) Source documents to journals.
   (d) Journals to source documents.
4. Which of the following is an example of an adjusting entry?
   (a) Recording the purchase of supplies on account.
   (b) Recording depreciation expense on a truck.
   (c) Recording the billing of customers for services rendered.
   (d) Recording the payment of wages to employees.
5. An adjusting entry to accrue wages earned but not yet paid is an example of
   (a) Aligning recorded costs with the appropriate accounting periods.
   (b) Aligning recorded revenue with the appropriate accounting periods.
   (c) Reflecting unrecorded expenses incurred during the accounting period.
   (d) Reflecting unrecorded revenue earned during the accounting period.

DEMONSTRATION PROBLEM FOR REVIEW

Balke Laboratory began operations on July 1, 19X1, and provides various diagnostic services for physicians and clinics. Its fiscal year ends on June 30 and the accounts are adjusted annually on this date. Its unadjusted trial balance at June 30, 19X4, is as follows:

Balke Laboratory
Trial Balance
June 30, 19X4

	Debit	Credit
Cash	$ 1,000	
Accounts Receivable	9,200	
Prepaid Insurance	6,000	
Supplies on Hand	31,300	
Laboratory Equipment	270,000	
Accumulated Depreciation—Laboratory Equipment		$ 60,000
Accounts Payable		3,100
Diagnostic Fees Received in Advance		4,000
Balke, Capital		110,000
Diagnostic Fees Revenue		220,400
Wages Expense	58,000	
Rent Expense	22,000	
	$397,500	$397,500

The following information is also available:

1. The Prepaid Insurance account balance represents a premium paid on January 1, 19X4, for two years of fire and casualty insurance coverage. Before 19X4, Balke Laboratory had no insurance protection.
2. The supplies on hand were counted at June 30, 19X4. The total count was $6,300.
3. All laboratory equipment was purchased on July 1, 19X1. It is expected to last nine years.
4. Balke Laboratory received a $4,000 cash payment on April 1, 19X4, from Boll Clinic for diagnostic services to be provided uniformly over the four months beginning April 1, 19X4. Balke credited the payment to Diagnostic Fees Received in Advance. The services for April, May, and June have been provided to Boll Clinic.
5. Unpaid wages at June 30 were $600.
6. Balke Laboratory rents facilities for $2,000 per month. Because of cash flow problems, Balke was unable to pay the rent for June 19X4. The landlord gave Balke permission to delay the payment until July.

REQUIRED

Make the adjusting entries, in general journal form, needed at June 30.

SOLUTION TO DEMONSTRATION PROBLEM

Date	Account	Debit	Credit
June 30	Insurance Expense	1,500	
	Prepaid Insurance		1,500
	To record 6 months' insurance expense ($6,000 / 4 = $1,500).		
30	Supplies Expense	25,000	
	Supplies on Hand		25,000
	To record supplies expense for the year ($31,300 − $6,300 = $25,000).		
30	Depreciation Expense—Laboratory Equipment	30,000	
	Accumulated Depreciation—Laboratory Equipment		30,000
	To record depreciation for the year ($270,000 / 9 years = $30,000).		
30	Diagnostic Fees Received in Advance	3,000	
	Diagnostic Fees Revenue		3,000
	To record portion of advance payment that has been earned ($4,000 × $\frac{3}{4}$ = $3,000).		
30	Wages Expense	600	
	Wages Payable		600
	To record unpaid wages at June 30.		
30	Rent Expense	2,000	
	Rent Payable		2,000
	To record rent expense for June.		

QUESTIONS

3–1 List in their proper order the first five steps in the accounting cycle.

3–2 Define the term *fiscal year*.

3–3 Give three examples of source documents that underlie business transactions.

3–4 Explain the nature and purpose of a general journal.

3–5 What is a compound journal entry?

3–6 What is the appropriate procedure for correcting an erroneous general journal entry (a) before it has been posted and (b) after it has been posted?

3–7 Explain the technique of posting references. What is the justification for their use?

3–8 Describe a chart of accounts, and give an example of a coding system for identifying different types of accounts.

3–9 Why is the adjusting step of the accounting cycle necessary?

3–10 What four different types of adjustments are frequently necessary at the close of an accounting period? Give examples of each type.

3–11 On January 1, Prepaid Insurance was debited with the cost of a one-year premium, $912. What adjusting entry should be made on January 31 before financial statements are prepared for the month?

3–12 Referring to Question 3–11, suppose the bookkeeper had charged the entire $912 premium to Insurance Expense when it was paid on January 1. What adjusting entry should be made on January 31 before financial statements are prepared for the month?

3–13 At the beginning of January, the first month of the accounting year, the Supplies on Hand account had a debit balance of $700. During January, purchases of $800 worth of supplies were debited to the account. Although only $400 worth of supplies were on hand at the end of January, the necessary adjusting entry was omitted. How will the omission affect (a) the income statement for January and (b) the balance sheet prepared at January 31?

3–14 The publisher of *International Focus*, a monthly magazine, received two-year subscriptions totaling $7,800 on January 1. (a) What entry should be made to record the receipt of the $7,800? (b) What entry should be made at the end of January before financial statements are prepared for the month?

3–15 Davis Travel Agency pays an employee $400 in wages each Friday for the five-day work week ending on that day. The last Friday of January falls on January 27. What adjusting entry should be made on January 31, the fiscal year-end?

3–16 The Lopez Company earns interest amounting to $225 per month on its investments. The company receives the interest every six months, on December 31 and June 30. Monthly financial statements are prepared. What adjusting entry should be made on January 31?

EXERCISES

Transaction analysis

3–17 Creative Masters, a firm providing art services for advertisers, has the following accounts in its general ledger: Cash; Accounts Receivable; Supplies on Hand; Office Equipment; Accounts Payable; L. Wile, Capital; L. Wile, Drawing; Service Fees Earned; Rent Expense; Utilities Expense; and Salaries Expense. Record the following transactions for June in a two-column general journal:

June 1 Laura Wile invested $17,000 cash to begin the business.
2 Paid rent for June, $950.
3 Purchased office equipment on account, $6,300.
6 Purchased art materials and other supplies costing $2,500; paid $1,200 down with the remainder due within 30 days.
11 Billed clients for services, $4,200.
17 Collected $2,950 from clients.

June 19 Paid $3,000 on account to office equipment firm (see June 3).
25 Laura Wile withdrew $800 cash for personal use.
30 Paid utilities bill for June, $260.
30 Paid salaries for June, $2,200.

Source documents

3–18 For each transaction in Exercise 3–17, indicate the related source document or documents that evidence the transaction.

Error corrections

3–19 The following erroneous journal entries have been posted to the general ledger. Prepare the journal entries to correct the errors.

(a) A $250 cash collection of an account receivable was recorded as a debit to Cash and as a credit to Service Fees Earned.
(b) A $900 purchase of supplies on account was recorded as a debit to Supplies on Hand and as a credit to Cash.
(c) A $400 billing of customers for services rendered was recorded as a debit to Accounts Payable and as a credit to Service Fees Earned.
(d) A $375 cash payment for the current month's newspaper advertising was recorded as a debit to Rent Expense and as a credit to Cash.
(e) A $1,000 cash payment for office equipment was recorded as a debit to Cash and as a credit to Office Equipment.

Adjusting entries

3–20 Selected accounts of Ideal Properties, Inc., a real estate management firm, are shown below as of January 31 of the current year, before any adjusting entries have been made.

	Debit	Credit
Prepaid Insurance	$5,220	
Supplies on Hand	1,880	
Office Equipment	4,608	
Unearned Rental Fees		$ 4,500
Salaries Expense	2,800	
Rental Fees Earned		12,000

Monthly financial statements are prepared. Using the following information, record in a general journal the adjusting entries necessary on January 31:

(a) Prepaid Insurance represents a three-year premium paid on January 1.
(b) Supplies of $470 were on hand January 31.
(c) Office equipment is expected to last eight years.
(d) On January 1, the firm collected six months' rent in advance from a tenant renting space for $750 per month.
(e) Accrued salaries not recorded as of January 31 are $540.

Adjusting entries

3–21 Jody Bross began the Bross Refinishing Service on July 1 of the current year. Selected accounts are shown below as of July 31, before any adjusting entries have been made.

	Debit	Credit
Prepaid Rent	$3,480	
Prepaid Advertising	465	
Supplies on Hand	1,000	
Unearned Refinishing Fees		$ 360
Refinishing Fees Revenue		1,500

Using the following information, record in a general journal the adjusting entries necessary on July 31:

(a) On July 1, Bross paid one year's rent of $3,480.
(b) On July 1, $465 was paid to the local newspaper for an advertisement to run daily for the months of July, August, and September.

(c) Supplies on hand at July 31 total $400.
(d) At July 31, refinishing services of $500 have been performed but not yet billed to customers.
(e) One customer paid $360 in advance for a refinishing project. At July 31, the project is one-half complete.

Adjusting entries

3–22 For each of the following unrelated situations, prepare the necessary adjusting entry in general journal form.

(a) Unrecorded depreciation expense on equipment is $620.
(b) The Supplies on Hand account has a balance of $1,630. Supplies on hand at the end of the period total $910.
(c) On the date for preparing financial statements, an estimated utilities expense of $215 has been incurred, but no utility bill has yet been received.
(d) On the first day of the current month, rent for four months was paid and recorded as a $2,600 debit to Rent Expense and a $2,600 credit to Cash. Monthly statements are now being prepared.
(e) Nine months ago, Rocke Insurance Company sold a one-year policy to a customer and recorded the receipt of the premium by debiting Cash for $900 and crediting Premium Revenue for $900. No adjusting entries have been prepared during the nine-month period. Annual statements are now being prepared.
(f) At the end of the accounting period, wages expense of $780 has been incurred but not paid.
(g) At the end of the accounting period, $375 of repair services have been rendered to customers who have not yet been billed.

Transaction analysis and adjusting entries

3–23 Acme Building Maintenance Service offers janitorial services on both a contract basis and an hourly basis. On January 1 of the current year, Acme collected $14,400 in advance on six-month contracts for work to be performed evenly during the next six months.

(a) Give the general journal entry to record the receipt of $14,400 for contract work.
(b) Give the adjusting entry to be made on January 31 for the contract work done during January.
(c) At January 31, a total of 32 hours of hourly rate janitor work was unbilled. The billing rate is $15 per hour. Give the adjusting entry needed on January 31.

Analysis of adjusted data

3–24 Selected T-account balances for the Holt Company are shown below as of January 31 of the current year; adjusting entries have already been posted. The firm operates on a calendar year.

Supplies on Hand	
Jan. 31 Bal. 400	

Supplies Expense	
Jan. 31 Bal. 550	

Prepaid Insurance	
Jan. 31 Bal. 765	

Insurance Expense	
Jan. 31 Bal. 85	

Wages Payable	
	Jan 31 Bal. 400

Wages Expense	
Jan. 31 Bal. 3,500	

Truck	
Jan. 31 Bal. 8,100	

Accumulated Depreciation—Truck	
	Jan. 31 Bal. 2,565

(a) If the amount in Supplies Expense represents the January 31 adjustment for the supplies used in January, and $350 worth of supplies were purchased during January, what was the January 1 balance of Supplies on Hand?

(b) The amount in the Insurance Expense account represents the adjustment made at January 31 for January insurance expense. If the original premium was for one year, what was the amount of the premium and on what date did the insurance policy start?

(c) If we assume no balance existed in Wages Payable or Wages Expense on January 1, how much cash was paid as wages during January?

(d) If the truck has a useful life of five years, what is the monthly amount of depreciation expense and how many months has Holt owned the truck?

Analysis of the impact of adjustments on financial statements

3–25 At the end of the first month of operations, Bailey Company's bookkeeper prepared financial statements which showed the following amounts:

Assets	$40,000
Liabilities	15,000
Owners' Equity	25,000
Net Income	5,000

In preparing the statements, the bookkeeper overlooked the following items:
(a) Depreciation for the month of $700.
(b) Unbilled service revenue at month-end of $500.
(c) Accrued wages payable at month-end of $350.
Determine the correct amounts of assets, liabilities, and owners' equity at month-end and net income for the month.

PROBLEMS

Transaction analysis, posting, trial balance, and adjusting entries

3–26 Mark Ruff opened the Ruff Roofing Service on April 1 of the current year. Transactions for April are as follows:

Apr.	1	Ruff contributed $11,000 of his personal funds to begin the business.
	2	Purchased a used truck for $4,500 cash.
	2	Purchased ladders and other equipment for a total of $2,400, paid $1,000 cash, with the balance due in 30 days. (Classify this outlay as Equipment.)
	3	Paid three-year premium on liability insurance, $1,800.
	5	Purchased supplies on account, $1,500.
	5	Received an advance payment of $900 from a customer for roof repair work to be done during April and May.
	12	Billed customers for roofing services, $2,300.
	18	Collected $1,900 on account from customers.
	29	Paid bill for truck fuel used in April, $45.
	30	Paid April newspaper advertising, $90.
	30	Paid assistants' wages, $1,500.
	30	Billed customers for roofing services, $2,000.

REQUIRED
(a) Record these transactions in general journal form.
(b) Devise a chart of accounts for the firm and set up the general ledger. Allow for accounts that may be needed when adjusting entries are made at the close of the accounting period (see requirement [e]).
(c) Post journal entries to the ledger accounts.

(d) Take a trial balance.

(e) Make the journal entries to adjust the books for insurance expense, supplies expense, depreciation expense on the truck, depreciation expense on the equipment, and roofing fees earned. Supplies on hand on April 30 amounted to $700. Depreciation for April was $100 on the truck and $25 on the equipment. One-third of the roofing fee received in advance was earned by April 30. Post the adjusting entries.

Adjusting entries

3–27 Benson Carpet Cleaners ended its first month of operations on June 30 of the current year. Monthly financial statements will be prepared. The unadjusted account balances are as follows:

Benson Carpet Cleaners
Trial Balance
June 30, 19XX

	Debit	Credit
Cash	$ 820	
Accounts Receivable	300	
Prepaid Rent	1,200	
Supplies on Hand	1,000	
Equipment	4,680	
Accounts Payable		$ 600
Benson, Capital		5,500
Benson, Drawing	200	
Service Fees Earned		3,000
Wages Expense	900	
	$9,100	$9,100

The following information is also available:

1. The balance in Prepaid Rent was the amount paid on June 1 for the first four months' rent.
2. Supplies on hand at June 30 were $620.
3. The equipment, purchased June 1, has an estimated life of six years.
4. Unpaid wages at June 30 were $150.
5. Utility services used during June were estimated at $190. A bill is expected early in July.
6. Fees earned for services performed but not yet billed on June 30 were $400.

REQUIRED

In general journal form, make the adjusting entries needed at June 30.

Trial balance and adjusting entries

3–28 Phototake, Inc., a commercial photography studio, has just completed its first full year of operations on December 31 of the current year. The general ledger account balances before year-end adjustments follow. No adjusting entries have been made to the accounts at any time during the year. Assume that all balances are normal.

Cash	$ 950	Accounts Payable	$ 1,550
Accounts Receivable	2,500	Unearned Photography Fees	1,250
Prepaid Rent	7,560	Capital Stock	10,000
Prepaid Insurance	2,970	Photography Fees Earned	23,900
Supplies on Hand	3,240	Wages Expense	8,000
Equipment	9,100	Utilities Expense	2,380

An analysis of the firm's records discloses the following items:

1. Photography services of $700 have been rendered, but customers have not yet been billed.
2. The equipment, purchased January 1, has an estimated life of ten years.
3. Utilities expense for December is estimated to be $275, but the bill will not arrive until January of next year.
4. The balance in Prepaid Rent represents the amount paid on January 1 for a two-year lease on the studio.
5. In November, customers paid $1,250 in advance for pictures to be taken for the holiday season. When received, these fees were credited to Unearned Photography Fees. By December 31, all these fees are earned.
6. A three-year insurance premium paid on January 1 was debited to Prepaid Insurance.
7. Supplies on hand at December 31 are $1,120.
8. At December 31, wages expense of $180 has been incurred but not paid.

REQUIRED

(a) Prove that debits equal credits for the unadjusted account balances shown above by preparing a trial balance.
(b) Record adjusting entries in general journal form.

Transaction analysis, posting, trial balance, and adjusting entries

3–29 The Complete Catering Service had the following transactions in July, its first month of operations:

July 1 Heather Field contributed $13,000 of personal funds to the business.
1 Purchased the following items for cash from a catering firm that was going out of business (make a compound entry): delivery van, $3,420; equipment, $2,880; and supplies, $2,400.
2 Paid premium on a one-year liability insurance policy, $840.
2 Entered into a contract with a local service club to cater weekly luncheon meetings for one year at a fee of $500 per month. Received six months' fees in advance.
3 Paid rent for July, August, and September, $1,800.
12 Paid employee's two weeks' wages (five-day week), $1,200.
15 Billed customers for services rendered, $3,200.
18 Purchased supplies on account, $1,300.
26 Paid employee's two weeks' wages, $1,200.
30 Paid July bill for gas, oil, and repairs on delivery van, $450.
30 Collected $2,400 from customers on account.
31 Billed customers for services rendered, $3,600.
31 Field withdrew $1,000 for personal use.

REQUIRED

(a) Set up a general ledger that includes the following accounts, using the account numbers shown: Cash (11); Accounts Receivable (12); Supplies on Hand (13); Prepaid Rent (14); Prepaid Insurance (15); Delivery Van (16); Accumulated Depreciation—Delivery Van (17); Equipment (18); Accumulated Depreciation—Equipment (19); Accounts Payable (21); Wages Payable (22); Unearned Catering Fees (23); H. Field, Capital (31); H. Field, Drawing (32); Catering Fees Revenue (41); Wages Expense (51); Rent Expense (52); Supplies Expense (53); Insurance Expense (54); Delivery Van Expense (55); Depreciation Expense—Delivery Van (56); and Depreciation Expense—Equipment (57).
(b) Record July transactions in general journal form and post to the ledger accounts.
(c) Take a trial balance at July 31.

(d) Record adjusting journal entries in the general journal and post to the ledger accounts. The following information is available on July 31:

Supplies on hand, $1,100
Accrued wages, $360
Estimated life of delivery van, three years
Estimated life of equipment, six years

Also, make any necessary adjusting entries for insurance, rent, and catering fees indicated by the July transactions.

Adjusting entries

3–30 The following information relates to December 31 adjustments for Quality Print, a printing company:

1. Weekly salaries for a five-day week total $960, payable on Fridays. December 31 of the current year is a Monday.
2. Quality Print received $850 during December for printing services to be performed during the following year. When received, this amount was credited to Printing Revenue.
3. During December, Quality Print provided $500 of printing services to clients who will be billed on January 2.
4. All maintenance work on Quality Print's equipment is handled by Prompt Repair Company under an agreement whereby Quality Print pays a fixed monthly charge of $75. Quality Print paid six months' service charge in advance on December 1, debiting Prepaid Maintenance for $450.
5. The firm paid $510 on December 15 for a series of radio commercials to run during December and January. One-third of the commercials have aired by December 31. The $510 payment was debited to Advertising Expense.
6. Starting December 16, Quality Print rented 400 square feet of storage space from a neighboring business. The monthly rent of $0.50 per square foot is due in advance on the first of each month. Nothing was paid in December, however, because the neighbor agreed to add the rent for one-half of December to the January 1 payment.
7. Quality Print invested $5,000 in securities on December 1 and earned interest of $40 on these securities by December 31. No interest will be received until January.
8. The monthly depreciation on the firm's equipment is $175.

REQUIRED
Prepare the required December 31 adjusting entries in general journal form.

Alternative adjusting entries

3–31 Every summer the Harmonic Music Society sponsors a series of six classical music concerts. For 19X3, two concerts monthly are scheduled for June, July, and August.

Season tickets are on sale June 1–16, 19X3 (the first concert is June 16), and cost $45 for the six concerts. Tickets for individual concerts cost $9 each and go on sale June 15, 19X3. The society sold 500 season tickets during June 1–16 and credited the $22,500 proceeds to the Unearned Ticket Revenue account.

The concerts are given in a pavilion located in a city park. The society rents the facility from the city for $400 per concert. The city requires advance payment for all concerts by June 5. On June 3, 19X3, the society mailed a $2,400 check to the city and debited the amount to the Prepaid Rent account. The society incurs no other rent costs.

The two concerts for June were presented as scheduled. Individual tickets sold for the June concerts totaled $5,400 and were credited to the Ticket Revenue account.

Other than the season tickets sold during June 1–16, no advance tickets have been sold by June 30 for the July and August concerts.

REQUIRED

(a) Prepare the necessary adjusting entries at June 30, 19X3, for rent expense and ticket revenue.
(b) After the adjustments made in (a) have been posted, what are the June 30, 19X3, balances in the following accounts: Prepaid Rent, Unearned Ticket Revenue, Ticket Revenue, and Rent Expense?
(c) Assume the society credited the $22,500 season ticket sales amount to the Ticket Revenue account rather than to the Unearned Ticket Revenue account. Also assume the society debited Rent Expense rather than Prepaid Rent for the $2,400 payment on June 3, 19X3. Given these assumptions, prepare the necessary adjusting entries at June 30, 19X3, for rent expense and ticket revenue.
(d) After the adjustments made in (c) have been posted, what are the June 30, 19X3, balances in the following accounts: Prepaid Rent, Unearned Ticket Revenue, Ticket Revenue, and Rent Expense?

ALTERNATE PROBLEMS

Transaction analysis, posting, trial balance, and adjusting entries

3–26A The Lin Karate School began business on June 1 of the current year. Transactions for June were as follows:

June	1	Jay Lin contributed $5,000 of his personal funds to begin business.
	2	Purchased equipment for $1,950, paying $650 cash, with the balance due in 30 days.
	2	Paid six months' rent, $2,400.
	3	Paid one-year premium on liability insurance, $912.
	8	Paid June newspaper advertising, $130.
	15	Billed participants for karate lessons to date, $1,700.
	20	Received $480 from a local company to conduct a special three-session class on self-defense for its employees. The three sessions will be held on June 29, July 6, and July 13, at $160 per session.
	21	Collected $1,500 on account from participants.
	25	Paid $275 to repair damage to wall caused by an errant kick.
	30	Billed participants for karate lessons to date, $1,800.
	30	Paid assistant's wages, $540.

REQUIRED

(a) Record the given transactions in a general journal.
(b) Devise a chart of accounts for the firm and set up the general ledger. Allow for accounts that may be needed when adjusting entries are made at the close of the accounting period (see requirement [e]).
(c) Post journal entries to the ledger accounts.
(d) Take a trial balance.
(e) Make the adjusting entries for rent expense, insurance expense, depreciation expense, utilities expense, and karate fees earned. Depreciation expense for June is $25, estimated utilities expense for June is $90. Post the adjusting entries.

Adjusting entries

3–27A The Wheel House, Inc., began operations on March 1 of the current year to provide automotive wheel alignment and balancing services. On March 31, the unadjusted balances of the firm's accounts are as follows:

The Wheel House, Inc.
Trial Balance
March 31, 19XX

	Debit	Credit
Cash	$ 2,400	
Accounts Receivable	3,510	
Prepaid Rent	4,050	
Supplies on Hand	2,200	
Equipment	30,240	
Accounts Payable		$ 1,000
Unearned Service Revenue		800
Capital Stock		35,000
Service Revenue		9,200
Wages Expense	3,600	
	$46,000	$46,000

The following information is also available:

1. The balance in Prepaid Rent was the amount paid on March 1 to cover the first six months' rent.
2. Supplies on hand on March 31 amounted to $1,350.
3. The equipment has an estimated life of nine years.
4. Unpaid wages at March 31 were $380.
5. Utility services used during March were estimated at $410. A bill is expected early in April.
6. The balance in Unearned Service Revenue was the amount received on March 1 from a new car dealer to cover alignment and balancing services on all new cars sold by the dealer in March and April. Wheel House agreed to provide the services at a fixed fee of $400 each month.

REQUIRED

In general journal form, make the adjusting entries needed at March 31.

Trial balance and adjusting entries

3–28A Deliverit, a mailing service, has just completed its first full year of operations on December 31 of the current year. The firm's general ledger account balances before year-end adjustments are given below. No adjusting entries have been made to the accounts at any time during the year. Assume that all balances are normal.

Cash	$ 3,800	Lewis, Capital	$25,000
Accounts Receivable	4,360	Lewis, Drawing	6,600
Prepaid Advertising	1,320	Mailing Fees Earned	74,000
Supplies on Hand	4,790	Wages Expense	34,800
Equipment	36,000	Rent Expense	5,760
Accounts Payable	1,400	Utilities Expense	2,970

An analysis of the firm's records reveals the following:

1. The balance in Prepaid Advertising represents the amount paid for newspaper advertising for one year. The agreement, which calls for the same amount of space each month, covers the period from February 1 of the current year to January 31 next year. Deliverit did not advertise during its first month of operations.

2. The equipment, purchased January 1, has an estimated life of eight years.
3. Utilities expense does not include expense for December, estimated at $360. The bill will not arrive until January of next year.
4. At year-end, employees have earned $900 in wages that will not be paid until January.
5. Supplies on hand at year-end amounted to $1,100.
6. Mailing services amounting to $4,000 were rendered to customers who have not yet been billed for the services.
7. The firm's lease calls for rent of $480 per month payable on the first of each month, plus an amount equal to $\frac{1}{2}$% of annual mailing fees earned. The rental percentage is payable within 15 days after the end of the year.

REQUIRED

(a) Prove that debits equal credits for the unadjusted account balances shown above by preparing a trial balance.

(b) Record adjusting entries in general journal form.

Transaction analysis, posting, trial balance, and adjusting entries

3–29A Market-Touch, a market research firm, had the following transactions in June, its first month of operations.

June 1 J. Austin invested $22,000 of personal funds in the firm.

1 The firm purchased the following from an office supply company: office equipment, $10,080; office supplies, $1,620. Terms called for a cash payment of $4,000, with the remainder due in 60 days. (Make a compound entry.)

2 Paid June rent, $625.

2 Contracted for three months' advertising in a local newspaper at $300 per month and paid for the advertising in advance.

2 Signed a six-month contract with an electronics firm to provide research consulting services at a rate of $2,500 per month. Received two months' fees in advance. Work on the contract started immediately.

10 Billed various customers for services rendered, $3,600.

12 Paid two weeks' salaries (five-day week) to employees, $3,000.

15 Paid J. Austin's travel expenses to business conference, $920.

18 Paid post office for bulk mailing of survey research questionnaire, $460 (postage expense).

22 Billed various customers for services rendered, $4,900.

26 Paid two weeks' salaries to employees, $3,000.

30 Collected $6,100 from customers on account.

30 J. Austin withdrew $1,000 for personal use.

REQUIRED

(a) Set up a general ledger that includes the following accounts, using the account numbers shown: Cash (11); Accounts Receivable (12); Office Supplies on Hand (14); Prepaid Advertising (15); Office Equipment (16); Accumulated Depreciation—Office Equipment (17); Accounts Payable (21); Salaries Payable (22); Unearned Service Fees (23); J. Austin, Capital (31); J. Austin, Drawing (32); Service Fees Earned (41); Salaries Expense (51); Advertising Expense (52); Supplies Expense (53); Rent Expense (54); Travel Expense (55); Depreciation Expense—Office Equipment (56); and Postage Expense (57).

(b) Record June transactions in general journal form and post to the ledger accounts.

(c) Take a trial balance at June 30.

(d) Record adjusting journal entries in general journal form, and post to the ledger accounts. The following information is available on June 30:

Office supplies on hand, $910
Accrued salaries, $600
Estimated life of office equipment, eight years
Unbilled services rendered, $1,800

Also, make any necessary adjusting entries for advertising and for service fees indicated by the June transactions.

Adjusting entries

3–30A The following information relates to the December 31 adjustments for Water Guard, a firm providing waterproofing services for commercial and residential customers.

1. The firm paid a $2,340 premium for a three-year insurance policy, coverage to begin October 1 of the current year. The entire amount of the premium was debited to Insurance Expense; no other entry concerning this premium has been recorded.
2. Weekly wages for a five-day work week total $1,000, payable on Fridays. December 31 of the current year is a Tuesday.
3. Water Guard received $1,400 during December for services to be performed during the following year. When received, this amount was credited to Service Fees Earned.
4. During December, Water Guard provided $500 worth of services to clients who will not be billed until early January.
5. During December, fuel oil costs of $415 were incurred to heat the firm's buildings. Because the monthly bill from the oil company has not yet arrived, no entry has been made for this amount (fuel oil costs are charged to Utilities Expense).
6. The Supplies on Hand account has a balance of $12,900 on December 31. A count of supplies on December 31 indicates that $1,800 worth of supplies are still on hand.
7. On December 1, Water Guard borrowed $8,000 from the bank, giving an interest-bearing note payable. Interest is not payable until the note is due near the end of January. However, the interest expense for December is $60. No entries have been made for the interest expense or interest payable.
8. Water Guard rents parking spaces in its lot to firms in the office building next door. On December 1, Water Guard received $6,000 as advance payments to cover parking privileges in the lot for December through February. When received, the $6,000 was credited to Unearned Parking Fees.

REQUIRED
Prepare the necessary December 31 adjusting entries in general journal form.

Determination of adjustments from account balances

3–31A For the *unrelated* accounts given below, the current balances and the balances they should have after adjusting entries have been posted are indicated.

Account Title	Current Balance	Adjusted Balance
1. Supplies on Hand	$870	$450
2. Depreciation Expense—Building	600	750
3. Utilities Payable	—	375
4. Insurance Expense	490	560

5. Wages Payable	—	800
6. Unearned Service Fees	750	400
7. Accumulated Depreciation—Equipment	840	880
8. Prepaid Rent	900	675
9. Unearned Commissions Revenue	500	200
10. Prepaid Advertising	—	350
11. Interest Receivable	—	200

REQUIRED

For each item listed, prepare the *most probable* general journal entry (including an explanation) for each adjustment.

BUSINESS DECISION PROBLEM

Welker Consulting Services, a firm started several years ago by Brian Welker, offers consulting services for material handling and plant layout. The balance sheet prepared by the firm's bookkeeper at the close of the current year is shown below:

Welker Consulting Services
Balance Sheet
December 31, 19XX

Assets			**Liabilities**		
Cash		$ 3,100	Accounts Payable	$ 2,800	
Accounts Receivable		13,000	Notes Payable—Bank	17,000	
Supplies on Hand		8,900	Unearned Consulting Fees	8,200	
Equipment	$40,000		Total Liabilities		$28,000
Less: Accumulated			**Owner's Equity**		
Depreciation	12,000	28,000	B. Welker, Capital		25,000
			Total Liabilities and		
Total Assets		$53,000	Owner's Equity		$53,000

Earlier in the year, Welker obtained a bank loan of $17,000 for the firm. One of the provisions of the loan is that the year-end ratio of total liabilities to total owner's equity shall not exceed 1:1. Based on the above balance sheet, the ratio at the end of the current year is 1.12:1.

Welker is concerned about being in violation of the loan agreement and asks your assistance in reviewing the situation. Welker believes that his rather inexperienced bookkeeper may have overlooked some items at year-end.

In discussions with Welker and the bookkeeper, you learn the following:

1. On January 1, 19XX, the firm paid a $4,000 insurance premium for two years of coverage. The full amount was debited to Insurance Expense.
2. Depreciation on the equipment should be 12% of cost per year. The bookkeeper has recorded only one-half this amount for the current year.
3. Interest on the bank loan has been paid through the end of the current year.
4. The firm concluded a major consulting engagement in December, doing a plant layout analysis for a new factory. The $3,500 fee has not been billed or recorded in the accounts.
5. On December 1, 19XX, the firm received an $8,200 advance payment from Croy Corporation for consulting services to be rendered over a two-month period. This payment was credited to the Unearned Consulting Fees account. One-half of this fee was earned by December 31, 19XX.

6. Supplies costing $2,700 were on hand on December 31. The bookkeeper filed the record of the count but made no entry in the accounts.

REQUIRED

What is the correct ratio of total liabilities to total owner's equity at December 31, 19XX? Is the firm in violation of the loan agreement? Prepare a schedule to support your computation of the correct total liabilities and total owner's equity at December 31, 19XX.

ANSWERS TO SELF-TEST QUESTIONS

1. (b) **2.** (d) **3.** (a) **4.** (b) **5.** (c)

4

THE ACCOUNTING CYCLE CONCLUDED

CHAPTER OBJECTIVES

1. Explain the procedures for preparing a worksheet (pp. 117–22).
2. Identify the final four steps in the accounting cycle (p. 122).
3. Illustrate the financial statements prepared from a worksheet (pp. 122–23).
4. Illustrate the process of journalizing and posting adjusting entries (pp. 123–26).
5. Describe the process of closing the temporary accounts of a sole proprietorship and a corporation (pp. 126–29).
6. Explain the nature of a post-closing trial balance (pp. 129, 135).
7. Summarize the complete accounting cycle (pp. 135–36).
8. Discuss the purpose of reversing entries (pp. 135–40).

Everything ends that has a beginning.

QUINTILIAN

The first five steps in the accounting cycle—analyzing and recording transactions, posting to accounts, preparing a trial balance, and adjusting the accounts—are essential to the process of classifying financial data and, where necessary, aligning the data with appropriate periods. The goal of these procedures is to prepare the data so that they can be summarized in a set of meaningful financial statements.

Accountants typically use a *worksheet* to compile the information needed for financial statements. In this chapter, we will explain the preparation of a worksheet. Then we will discuss the remaining four steps in the accounting cycle. Our discussion continues to use the December financial data given in Chapter 3 for Landen TV Service.

PREPARING A WORKSHEET

The **worksheet** is a tool of the accountant, not part of a company's formal accounting records. The accountant prepares a worksheet at that stage of the accounting cycle when it is time to adjust the accounts and prepare financial statements.

The basic structure of the worksheet is presented in Exhibit 4–1, which includes an explanation of the format being used. The worksheet is prepared in the order indicated by the circled numbers in the exhibit. A completed worksheet for Landen TV Service appears in Exhibit 4–2. Refer to both of these exhibits when reading through the following procedures for preparing a worksheet.

❶ HEADING The worksheet *heading* should include (a) the name of the accounting entity involved, (b) the term "Worksheet" to indicate the type of analysis performed, and (c) a date describing the period covered. The worksheet includes both income statement data (for the period described) and balance sheet data (for the end of the period described).

The worksheet form we have illustrated has a description column and 10 amount (money) columns. A set of debit and credit columns is provided for each of the five headings, "Trial Balance," "Adjustments," "Adjusted Trial Balance," "Income Statement," and "Balance Sheet."

❷ TRIAL BALANCE Recall that a *trial balance* is taken as step 4 of the accounting cycle. This unadjusted trial balance becomes the starting point for the worksheet. The trial balance is entered in the worksheet's description column and the first pair of money columns. Once the trial balance is placed on the worksheet and double ruled, it reflects the state of the general ledger at the time the worksheet is prepared.

❸ ADJUSTMENTS *When a worksheet is used, all adjustments are first entered on the worksheet.* This procedure permits the adjustment to be reviewed for completeness and accuracy. To adjust accounts already appearing in the unadjusted trial balance, we simply enter the amounts in the appropriate side (debit or credit) of the adjustments columns on the lines containing the accounts. When accounts

EXHIBIT 4–1

BASIC STRUCTURE OF A WORKSHEET

1

(Heading for worksheet)

Description	Trial Balance		Adjustments		Adjusted Trial Balance		Income Statement		Balance Sheet	
	Debit	Credit	Debit	Credit	Debit	Credit	Debit	Credit	Debit	Credit
2 (The unadjusted trial balance)			3 (Amounts of adjustments)		4 (Amounts of adjusted account balances)		5 (Extension of adjusted account balances)			
							(Income statement accounts)		(Balance sheet accounts)	
(Titles of accounts not in unadjusted trial balance, added as needed)							6 (Balancing of columns for each statement)			

not appearing in the unadjusted trial balance require adjustment, their titles are listed as needed in the description column below the accounts already listed.

The adjustments recorded on the worksheet in Exhibit 4–2 are identical with those recorded in general journal form in step 5 of the accounting cycle (see Chapter 3). It is common practice to "key" the amounts of each adjusting entry with the same letter or number. Note that the numbers "(1)" through "(7)" are used in Exhibit 4–2. This procedure makes it easy to check the equality of debits and credits in each entry and to identify all the amounts related to a particular adjustment.

We repeat the adjusting entries made at the end of December for Landen TV Service and explain their placement on the worksheet (Exhibit 4–2). Remember, because we are preparing a worksheet, these adjustments are entered on the worksheet first; they are not yet recorded in the general journal.

(1)	Supplies and Parts Expense	440	
	Supplies and Parts on Hand		440

Because $510 worth of supplies were on hand at December 31, we needed to reduce the asset Supplies and Parts on Hand from $950 to $510 and to record the $440 difference as expense. Note that the expense account, Supplies and Parts Expense, does not appear in the unadjusted trial balance and must be added below the accounts already listed.

(2)	Depreciation Expense—Test Equipment	60	
	Accumulated Depreciation—Test Equipment		60

EXHIBIT 4–2

Landen TV Service
Worksheet
For the Month Ended December 31, 19XX

Description	Trial Balance Debit	Trial Balance Credit	Adjustments Debit	Adjustments Credit	Adjusted Trial Balance Debit	Adjusted Trial Balance Credit	Income Statement Debit	Income Statement Credit	Balance Sheet Debit	Balance Sheet Credit
Cash	13,130				13,130				13,130	
Accounts Receivable	2,800		(7) 240		3,040				3,040	
Supplies and Parts on Hand	950			(1) 440	510				510	
Test Equipment	3,600				3,600				3,600	
Truck	10,800				10,800				10,800	
Accounts Payable		2,550				2,550				2,550
Unearned Service Fees		1,000	(4) 250			750				750
M. Landen, Capital		25,000				25,000				25,000
M. Landen, Drawing	800				800				800	
Service Fees Earned		5,450		(4) 250 (7) 240		5,940		5,940		
Rent Expense	600				600		600			
Wages Expense	1,080		(6) 90		1,170		1,170			
Advertising Expense	80				80		80			
Truck Expense	160				160		160			
	34,000	34,000								
Supplies and Parts Expense			(1) 440		440		440			
Depreciation Expense—Test Equipment			(2) 60		60		60			
Accumulated Depreciation—Test Equipment				(2) 60		60				60
Depreciation Expense—Truck			(3) 150		150		150			
Accumulated Depreciation—Truck				(3) 150		150				150
Utilities Expense			(5) 120		120		120			
Utilities Payable				(5) 120		120				120
Wages Payable				(6) 90		90				90
			1,350	1,350	34,660	34,660	2,780	5,940	31,880	28,720
Net Income							3,160			3,160
							5,940	5,940	31,880	31,880

(3)	Depreciation Expense—Truck	150	
	Accumulated Depreciation—Truck		150

These entries recorded the expiration of the test equipment and truck costs for December. The entries to record depreciation expense and reduce the asset accounts (via accumulated depreciation contra accounts) require accounts that do not appear in the unadjusted trial balance. Therefore, the four accounts in entries 2 and 3 must be listed in the description column below the accounts in the trial balance.

(4)	Unearned Service Fees	250	
	Service Fees Earned		250

This adjustment was made to reflect the portion of a $1,000 advance earned in December. The liability account Unearned Service Fees, originally credited for the $1,000 advance, was reduced by a $250 debit, and a corresponding credit was made to the revenue account Service Fees Earned. Since both accounts appear in the unadjusted trial balance, we record this adjustment on the lines already provided for these accounts.

(5)	Utilities Expense	120	
	Utilities Payable		120
(6)	Wages Expense	90	
	Wages Payable		90

These adjusting entries reflected expenses incurred in December but not paid until January. The utilities expense was the estimated cost of services consumed in December. Wages were accrued for the last two days in December. Because no utilities expense was paid in December, the expense account does not appear in the unadjusted trial balance. Both the expense account and the liability Utilities Payable must be added below the accounts already listed. Since wages were paid during December, Wages Expense appears in the trial balance, but Wages Payable must be added.

(7)	Accounts Receivable	240	
	Service Fees Earned		240

This entry was made to reflect unbilled service fees earned in December. Since both accounts appear in the unadjusted trial balance, we record this adjustment on the lines already provided for these accounts.

After recording all the adjusting entries on the worksheet, we total the adjustments columns to prove that debits equal credits.

❹ ADJUSTED TRIAL BALANCE A trial balance of account balances after adjustments is called an **adjusted trial balance.** Once the adjustments have been entered on the worksheet, there is sufficient information available to compile an adjusted trial balance. The adjusted figures are determined by combining horizontally, line by line, the amounts in the first four money columns—that is, the unadjusted trial balance and the adjustments.

We review the calculations for the first three lines of Exhibit 4–2 to illustrate this process. The first line shows Cash with a debit of $13,130 in the trial balance. Because Cash is not affected by any adjustments, the $13,130 appears in the debit column of the adjusted trial balance. The second line shows a debit of $2,800 for Accounts Receivable in the trial balance and a debit of $240 in the adjustments columns. These two debit amounts are added, and the sum of $3,040 is shown in the debit column of the adjusted trial balance. On the third line, Supplies and Parts on Hand begins with a debit of $950 in the trial balance and then shows a credit of $440 in the adjustments columns. The $440 credit is subtracted from the $950 debit, and the remaining $510 is shown as a debit in the adjusted trial balance.

After computing the adjusted trial balance amounts for all the accounts on the worksheet, we total the two columns of the adjusted trial balance to confirm that they are equal and that, therefore, our worksheet still balances.

❺ EXTENSION OF ADJUSTED BALANCES The amounts in the adjusted trial balance columns are extended into the two remaining pairs of columns as follows:

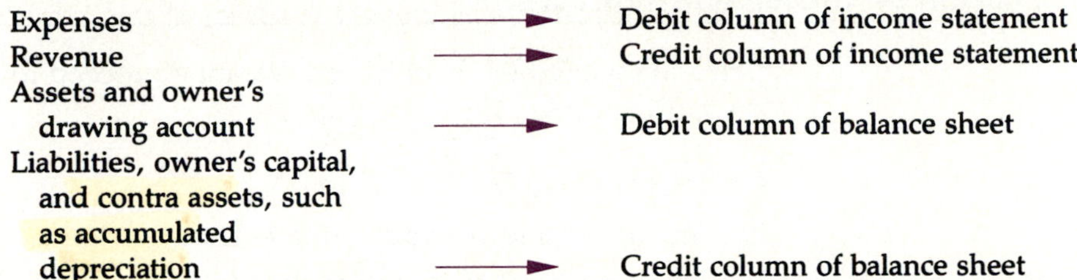

Expenses → Debit column of income statement
Revenue → Credit column of income statement
Assets and owner's drawing account → Debit column of balance sheet
Liabilities, owner's capital, and contra assets, such as accumulated depreciation → Credit column of balance sheet

Note that the positions of the adjusted balances in the worksheet correspond to the normal balances of the accounts. That is, expenses and assets are debits on the income statement and balance sheet, respectively; revenue is a credit on the income statement, and liabilities and owner's capital are credits on the balance sheet. The owner's drawing account is a debit in the balance sheet columns because it is a contra owner's equity account. The accumulated depreciation accounts are credits on the balance sheet because they are contra asset accounts. Once the proper extensions are made, the worksheet is complete except for the balancing of the two pairs of statement columns containing the adjusted balances.

❻ BALANCING THE WORKSHEET The first step in balancing is to add each of the income statement and balance sheet columns and record their respective totals on the same line as the totals of the adjusted trial balance columns. The difference between the total debits and total credits in the income statement columns will be the difference between total revenue and total expenses—that is, the net income for the period. The net income should also be the amount by which the debit and credit columns for the balance sheet differ. This is true because the capital account balance, as extended, does not yet reflect the net income for the current period.

When revenue exceeds expenses, we balance the two pairs of statement columns by adding the net income figure to both the debit column of the income statement and the credit column of the balance sheet. If expenses exceed revenue, we add the amount of net loss to the credit column of the income statement and to the debit column of the balance sheet. After we have added the net income (or loss) to the proper columns, we total and double rule the four columns. The worksheet is now complete and contains the account data necessary to prepare an income statement and a balance sheet.

A careful study of a worksheet's preparation shows the following advantages of the worksheet:

1. The balances of all general ledger accounts appear in one location and may be easily reviewed to determine whether any of them need adjusting.
2. The total effect of any adjustment—whether contemplated or actually made on the worksheet—can be readily determined. Because these adjustments are reviewed before adjusting entries are journalized and posted, the

likelihood of incorrect adjustments appearing in the formal accounting records is reduced.

3. Once all the adjustments have been made, the adjusted account balances can be determined and separated into a group for the income statement and a group for the balance sheet, simplifying the preparation of these statements.

COMPLETION OF THE ACCOUNTING CYCLE

Once the worksheet is prepared, we may proceed to the remaining steps in the accounting cycle. These steps are:

6. Prepare financial statements.
7. Journalize and post adjusting entries.
8. Journalize and post closing entries.
9. Prepare a post-closing trial balance.

Step 6: Prepare Financial Statements

Exhibits 4–3 and 4–4 illustrate an income statement and a balance sheet, respectively, for the Landen TV Service, prepared from the worksheet in Exhibit 4–2. The income statement is prepared from the income statement columns and the balance sheet is prepared from the balance sheet columns. To obtain the balance sheet amount for Mark Landen, Capital (his equity at December 31), we must combine three amounts appearing in the worksheet balance sheet columns, as follows:

Credit balance of capital account	$25,000
Debit balance of drawing account	(800)
Credit amount of net income to balance the balance sheet columns	3,160
Mark Landen's equity at end of period	$27,360

EXHIBIT 4–3

Landen TV Service
Income Statement
For the Month of December, 19XX

Revenue		
Service Fees Earned		$5,940
Expenses		
Rent Expense	$ 600	
Wages Expense	1,170	
Advertising Expense	80	
Truck Expense	160	
Supplies and Parts Expense	440	
Depreciation Expense—Test Equipment	60	
Depreciation Expense—Truck	150	
Utilities Expense	120	
Total Expenses		2,780
Net Income		$3,160

EXHIBIT 4–4

Landen TV Service
Balance Sheet
December 31, 19XX

Assets			**Liabilities**		
Cash		$13,130	Accounts Payable	$2,550	
Accounts Receivable		3,040	Utilities Payable	120	
Supplies and Parts on Hand		510	Wages Payable	90	
Test Equipment	$ 3,600		Unearned Service Fees	750	
Less: Accumulated Depreciation	60	3,540	Total Liabilities		$ 3,510
Truck	$10,800				
Less: Accumulated Depreciation	150	10,650	**Owner's Equity**		
			M. Landen, Capital		27,360
Total Assets		$30,870	Total Liabilities and Owner's Equity		$30,870

A formal set of financial statements frequently includes a statement of owner's equity. This statement simply lists the beginning balance, additions, deductions, and ending balance of owner's equity for the accounting period. Exhibit 4–5 illustrates such a statement for Landen TV Service for the month of December.

When capital contributions have been made during the accounting period, we cannot determine from the worksheet alone the beginning balance of owner's capital and amounts of capital contributions during a period. Consequently, in preparing a statement of owner's equity, we must examine the owner's capital account in the general ledger.

Step 7: Journalize and Post Adjusting Entries

At the close of the calendar or fiscal year, the adjusting entries on the worksheet must be recorded in the general journal and posted to the general ledger accounts in order to accomplish the proper closing procedures described in the next section. Although Landen TV Service has been in business only for December, its accounting year ends on December 31. Therefore, the adjusting entries are entered

EXHIBIT 4–5

Landen TV Service
Statement of Owner's Equity
For the Month of December, 19XX

Mark Landen, Capital, December 1, 19XX		$ -0-
Add: Capital Contributed in December	$25,000	
Net Income for December	3,160	28,160
		$28,160
Less: Capital Withdrawn in December		800
Mark Landen, Capital, December 31, 19XX		$27,360

EXHIBIT 4–6

ADJUSTING ENTRIES

General Journal

Page 3

Date		Description	Post. Ref.	Debit	Credit
19XX					
Dec.	31	Supplies and Parts Expense	54	440	
		Supplies and Parts on Hand	14		440
		To record expense of supplies and parts used in December.			
	31	Depreciation Expense—Test Equipment	57	60	
		Accumulated Depreciation—Test Equipment	17		60
		To record December depreciation on test equipment.			
	31	Depreciation Expense—Truck	58	150	
		Accumulated Depreciation—Truck	19		150
		To record December depreciation on truck.			
	31	Unearned Service Fees	24	250	
		Service Fees Earned	41		250
		To record portion of advance earned in December.			
	31	Utilities Expense	55	120	
		Utilities Payable	22		120
		To record estimated amount of December utilities expense.			
	31	Wages Expense	52	90	
		Wages Payable	23		90
		To record accrued wages for December 30 and 31.			
	31	Accounts Receivable	12	240	
		Service Fees Earned	41		240
		To record unbilled revenue earned during December.			

in the records and closing procedures are followed. The adjusting entries appear in the general journal as shown in Exhibit 4–6.

These journal entries are posted to the general ledger accounts of Landen TV Service shown in Exhibit 4–9 (pages 129–34). The entries are identified by the parenthetical notation "(adjusting)."

INTERIM FINANCIAL STATEMENTS Financial statements covering periods within a company's fiscal year—such as monthly or quarterly statements—are called **interim financial statements.** Most companies prepare interim financial statements from

REPORTS TO STOCKHOLDERS

Corporations include their financial statements in periodic reports to stockholders. The annual report to stockholders for large corporations may be quite extensive, often running 20–50 pages or more. In addition to financial statements, the annual report may include a message from the chairman of the board of directors and the chief executive officer, a review of the year's operations, a financial review, the accountants' report, and selected financial statistics for several years. Supplementing these items may be a variety of charts, graphs, and photographs of the company's products and facilities.

Reports to stockholders covering less than one year (interim reports) are much less extensive. They are intended to provide owners and potential investors with timely information on the corporation's progress and may include summarized financial information rather than a complete set of financial statements.

Comprehensive annual reports to stockholders are a relatively recent development in the United States. Before the 1900s, corporate management generally disclosed little, if any, financial information to stockholders. The first corporations were usually small and obtained much of their funding through short-term bank loans rather than from the public sale of stocks. Bankers who needed to assess the borrower's ability to repay short-term loans considered the balance sheet the primary financial statement because it revealed the total short-term obligations and the assets that would likely be converted to cash in the near future. By the late 1920s, however, corporate expansion led to increased financing through stock issuances and long-term debt. Owners and creditors used the income statement to judge earning power. Corporate reporting, then, evolved from providing balance sheets for bankers to providing income statements and balance sheets for stockholders and creditors.*

The first modern annual report was issued in 1902 by U.S. Steel Corporation. The report was lengthy and detailed, revealing so much about the corporation's operations that the directors were practically scandalized.† The extensive disclosures broke with tradition, and most corporations did not follow U.S. Steel's lead for many years.

Considerable variety exists in the length and detail of reports to stockholders. Remarks by the president of Diamond Match Company used 100 pages of the company's 1942 annual report.‡ In contrast, a 1972 semiannual report from North American Publishing of Philadelphia was more to the point. The report was poster size (three feet long) and featured letters eight inches high and six inches wide that stated: "We Had a BIG IMPROVEMENT for the First Six Months."§

Many corporations view the annual report, in part, as a public relations document. Imagine the chagrin, then, at Citizens Valley Bank in Albany, Oregon, a number of years ago. Half of the copies of the bank's 1973 annual report had been mailed before a particular omission was noted—the bank's name had been dropped from the report's cover and did not appear anywhere in the report.‖

*A. C. Littleton and V. K. Zimmerman, *Accounting Theory: Continuity and Change* (Englewood Cliffs, NJ: Prentice-Hall, Inc., 1962), pp. 92–97.

†"Annual Reports—No Longer Dry," *Fortune*, February 1944, p. 62.

‡*Ibid.*

§"The Numbers Game: A Few (Fairly) Kind Words," *Forbes*, May 1, 1973, p. 36.

‖"Business Bulletin," *The Wall Street Journal*, February 14, 1974, p. 1.

worksheet data, but they do not journalize and post the interim adjustments (they prefer to journalize and post adjusting entries only at year-end). Interim adjustments, then, are reflected only on the worksheet. When making interim adjusting entries on the worksheet, the bookkeeper must consider the period for which the adjustments are made. Some adjustment amounts will accumulate, while others will not. For example, in writing off a $1,200 one-year prepaid insurance premium paid on January 1 and debited to the asset account, the bookkeeper would debit Insurance Expense and credit Prepaid Insurance for $100 on the worksheet at January 31. The amount of the adjustment would be $200 at the end of February, $300 at the end of March, and so on. Similarly, the amount of the worksheet adjusting entry for depreciation will increase each month. On the other hand, an adjusting entry to accrue salaries at the end of any month will consist only of unpaid salaries at the date of adjustment, because salaries accrued at the end of each month are ordinarily paid during the ensuing month.

When the year-end worksheet is prepared, the adjusting data will pertain to the entire year. Therefore, the adjusting entries to be journalized and posted to the ledger accounts can be taken directly from this worksheet.

Step 8: Journalize and Post Closing Entries

Revenue, expense, and drawing accounts are temporary accounts that accumulate data related to a specific accounting year. These temporary accounts facilitate preparation of the income statement and provide additional information. At the end of each accounting year, the balances of these temporary accounts are transferred to the capital account (the Retained Earnings account for corporations). Therefore, the balance of the owner's capital account includes on a cumulative basis the net result of all revenue, expense, and drawing transactions. This phase in the accounting cycle is referred to as the **closing procedures.**

A temporary account is said to be *closed* when an entry is made that changes its balance to zero—that is, an entry that is equal in amount to the account's balance but is opposite to the balance as a debit or credit. An account that is closed is said to be closed *to* the account that receives the offsetting debit or credit. Thus, a closing entry simply transfers the balance of one account to another account. In this manner, closing procedures transfer the balances of temporary accounts to the capital account.

A summary account is traditionally used to close the temporary revenue and expense accounts. For our illustration, we will use an account titled "Income Summary," although a variety of titles are found in practice (Revenue and Expense Summary, Income and Expense Summary, or Profit and Loss Summary, for example). The entries for opening and closing Income Summary are quite simple and occur only during the closing procedures. The entries that close the temporary accounts are as follows:

1. Debit each revenue account in an amount equal to its balance, and credit Income Summary for the total revenue involved.
2. Credit each expense account in an amount equal to its balance, and debit Income Summary for the total expense involved.

After these temporary accounts have been closed, the balance of the Income Summary account is equal to the net income for the period—hence the title "Income Summary." The remaining closing steps are as follows:

3. Debit Income Summary for its balance, and credit the capital account (Retained Earnings for a corporation) for the same amount. In the case of a net loss, debit the capital account and credit Income Summary.
4. For noncorporate businesses, credit the drawing account in an amount equal to its balance and debit the capital account for the same amount.

In Exhibit 4–7, we illustrate the entries for closing the revenue and expense accounts to the Income Summary account of Landen TV Service as they would be recorded in the general journal. The effect of these two entries is shown using T accounts.

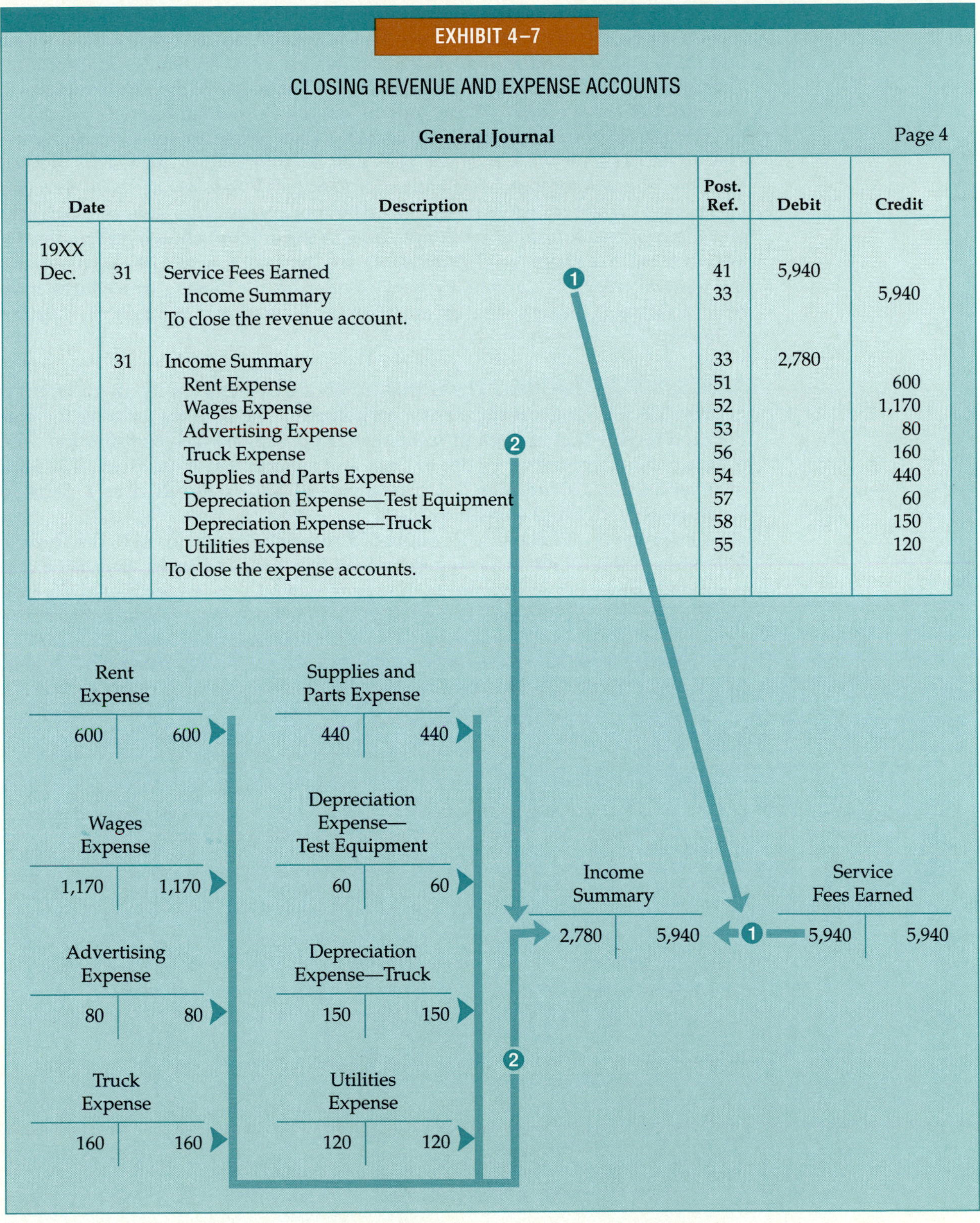

EXHIBIT 4–7

CLOSING REVENUE AND EXPENSE ACCOUNTS

General Journal Page 4

Date		Description	Post. Ref.	Debit	Credit
19XX					
Dec.	31	Service Fees Earned	41	5,940	
		Income Summary	33		5,940
		To close the revenue account.			
	31	Income Summary	33	2,780	
		Rent Expense	51		600
		Wages Expense	52		1,170
		Advertising Expense	53		80
		Truck Expense	56		160
		Supplies and Parts Expense	54		440
		Depreciation Expense—Test Equipment	57		60
		Depreciation Expense—Truck	58		150
		Utilities Expense	55		120
		To close the expense accounts.			

At this point, the balance of the Income Summary is a credit equal to the net income of $3,160. The closing procedure is completed by closing the Income Summary and M. Landen, Drawing accounts to the M. Landen, Capital account. These two entries are recorded in the general journal as shown in Exhibit 4–8. The effect of these entries on the general ledger is also diagrammed.

It is probably most convenient to take the data necessary for formulating the closing entries from the worksheet, although the information can also be derived from the ledger. After the closing entries for Landen TV Service have been recorded and posted to the firm's general ledger, all temporary accounts have zero balances and the capital account has a balance equal to the amount shown on Landen TV Service's balance sheet (see Exhibit 4–4). Exhibit 4–9 (pages 129–34) illustrates the general ledger of Landen TV Service after all the closing procedures have been followed. Closing entries are identified by the parenthetical notation "(closing)."

CORPORATION ACCOUNTING The entries involving owners' equity are different if Landen TV Service is organized as a corporation. The persons forming the corporation receive capital stock in exchange for the $25,000 cash contribution. The transaction is recorded as a debit to Cash and a credit to Capital Stock. The $800 cash withdrawal is considered a cash dividend and is recorded as a debit to Retained Earnings and a credit to Cash.

The revenue and expense accounts of a corporation are closed to the Income Summary account exactly as they are closed in a proprietorship. Because a corporation is subject to an income tax, however, it must close an additional expense account, Income Tax Expense. Disregarding income taxes, the revenue and expense

EXHIBIT 4–8

CLOSING THE INCOME SUMMARY AND DRAWING ACCOUNTS

General Journal Page 4

Date		Description	Post. Ref.	Debit	Credit
19XX					
Dec.	31	Income Summary	33	3,160	
		M. Landen, Capital ③	31		3,160
		To close the Income Summary account.			
	31	M. Landen, Capital	31	800	
		M. Landen, Drawing ④	32		800
		To close the drawing account.			

M. Landen, Drawing

Debit	Credit
800	800 ④

M. Landen, Capital

Debit	Credit
800	25,000
	3,160

Income Summary

Debit	Credit
2,780	5,940
③ 3,160	

accounts are closed as shown in Exhibit 4–7. Once the revenue and expense accounts are closed to Income Summary, the closing procedures for a corporation are completed by closing the Income Summary account to Retained Earnings. We show this in the T accounts below.

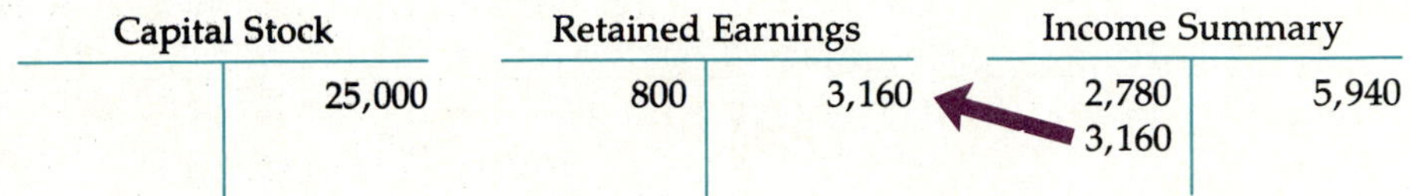

Capital Stock
25,000
Retained Earnings
800
3,160
Income Summary
2,780
3,160
5,940

After closing entries are posted, the Retained Earnings account reflects the $2,360 earned and retained in the business. Combined with the Capital Stock of $25,000, total stockholders' equity is $27,360.

Step 9: Prepare a Post-closing Trial Balance

A **post-closing trial balance** is taken after the completion of the closing process. The balancing of this trial balance is evidence that an equality of debits and credits has been maintained in the general ledger throughout the adjusting and closing process and that the general ledger is in balance to start the next accounting period. Because the temporary accounts have been closed, only balance sheet accounts appear in a post-closing trial balance. Exhibit 4–10 (p. 135) presents the post-closing trial balance for Landen TV Service.

EXHIBIT 4–9

LANDEN TV SERVICE GENERAL LEDGER

Cash Account No. 11

Date		Description	Post. Ref.	Debit*	Credit	Balance
19XX						
Dec.	1		J1	25,000		25,000
	1		J1		600	24,400
	2		J1		10,800	13,600
	2		J1		2,000	11,600
	2		J1	1,000		12,600
	7		J1	650		13,250
	14		J1		540	12,710
	14		J2	680		13,390
	17		J2		80	13,310
	19		J2	500		13,810
	21		J2	520		14,330
	28		J2		160	14,170
	28		J2		540	13,630
	28		J2		800	12,830
	28		J2	300		13,130

EXH 4–9 (Continued)

Accounts Receivable Account No. 12

Date		Description	Post. Ref.	Debit*	Credit	Balance
19XX						
Dec.	14		J1	900		900
	19		J2		500	400
	28		J2	2,400		2,800
	31	(adjusting)	J3	240		3,040

Supplies and Parts on Hand Account No. 14

Date		Description	Post. Ref.	Debit*	Credit	Balance
19XX						
Dec.	3		J1	950		950
	31	(adjusting)	J3		440	510

Test Equipment Account No. 16

Date		Description	Post. Ref.	Debit*	Credit	Balance
19XX						
Dec.	2		J1	3,600		3,600

Accumulated Depreciation—Test Equipment Account No. 17

Date		Description	Post. Ref.	Debit	Credit*	Balance
19XX						
Dec.	31	(adjusting)	J3		60	60

Truck Account No. 18

Date		Description	Post. Ref.	Debit*	Credit	Balance
19XX						
Dec.	2		J1	10,800		10,800

EXH 4–9 (Continued)

Accumulated Depreciation—Truck Account No. 19

Date		Description	Post. Ref.	Debit	Credit*	Balance
19XX Dec.	31	(adjusting)	J3		150	150

Accounts Payable Account No. 21

Date		Description	Post. Ref.	Debit	Credit*	Balance
19XX Dec.	2		J1		1,600	1,600
	3		J1		950	2,550

Utilities Payable Account No. 22

Date		Description	Post. Ref.	Debit	Credit*	Balance
19XX Dec.	31	(adjusting)	J3		120	120

Wages Payable Account No. 23

Date		Description	Post. Ref.	Debit	Credit*	Balance
19XX Dec.	31	(adjusting)	J3		90	90

Unearned Service Fees Account No. 24

Date		Description	Post. Ref.	Debit	Credit*	Balance
19XX Dec.	2		J1		1,000	1,000
	31	(adjusting)	J3	250		750

EXH 4–9 (Continued)

M. Landen, Capital Account No. 31

Date		Description	Post. Ref.	Debit	Credit*	Balance
19XX						
Dec.	1		J1		25,000	25,000
	31	(closing)	J4		3,160	28,160
	31	(closing)	J4	800		27,360

M. Landen, Drawing Account No. 32

Date		Description	Post. Ref.	Debit*	Credit	Balance
19XX						
Dec.	28		J2	800		800
	31	(closing)	J4		800	–0–

Income Summary Account No. 33

Date		Description	Post. Ref.	Debit	Credit*	Balance
19XX						
Dec.	31	(closing)	J4		5,940	5,940
	31	(closing)	J4	2,780		3,160
	31	(closing)	J4	3,160		–0–

Service Fees Earned Account No. 41

Date		Description	Post. Ref.	Debit	Credit*	Balance
19XX						
Dec.	7		J1		650	650
	14		J1		900	1,550
	14		J2		680	2,230
	21		J2		520	2,750
	28		J2		2,400	5,150
	28		J2		300	5,450
	31	(adjusting)	J3		250	5,700
	31	(adjusting)	J3		240	5,940
	31	(closing)	J4	5,940		–0–

EXH 4–9 (Continued)

Rent Expense Account No. 51

Date		Description	Post. Ref.	Debit*	Credit	Balance
19XX						
Dec.	1		J1	600		600
	31	(closing)	J4		600	–0–

Wages Expense Account No. 52

Date		Description	Post. Ref.	Debit*	Credit	Balance
19XX						
Dec.	14		J1	540		540
	28		J2	540		1,080
	31	(adjusting)	J3	90		1,170
	31	(closing)	J4		1,170	–0–

Advertising Expense Account No. 53

Date		Description	Post. Ref.	Debit*	Credit	Balance
19XX						
Dec.	17		J2	80		80
	31	(closing)	J4		80	–0–

Supplies and Parts Expense Account No. 54

Date		Description	Post. Ref.	Debit*	Credit	Balance
19XX						
Dec.	31	(adjusting)	J3	440		440
	31	(closing)	J4		440	–0–

EXH 4–9 (Continued)

Utilities Expense Account No. 55

Date		Description	Post. Ref.	Debit*	Credit	Balance
19XX						
Dec.	31	(adjusting)	J3	120		120
	31	(closing)	J4		120	–0–

Truck Expense Account No. 56

Date		Description	Post. Ref.	Debit*	Credit	Balance
19XX						
Dec.	28		J2	160		160
	31	(closing)	J4		160	–0–

Depreciation Expense—Test Equipment Account No. 57

Date		Description	Post. Ref.	Debit*	Credit	Balance
19XX						
Dec.	31	(adjusting)	J3	60		60
	31	(closing)	J4		60	–0–

Depreciation Expense—Truck Account No. 58

Date		Description	Post. Ref.	Debit*	Credit	Balance
19XX						
Dec.	31	(adjusting)	J3	150		150
	31	(closing)	J4		150	–0–

EXHIBIT 4–10

Landen TV Service
Post-closing Trial Balance
December 31, 19XX

	Debit	Credit
Cash	$13,130	
Accounts Receivable	3,040	
Supplies and Parts on Hand	510	
Test Equipment	3,600	
Accumulated Depreciation—Test Equipment		$ 60
Truck	10,800	
Accumulated Depreciation—Truck		150
Accounts Payable		2,550
Utilities Payable		120
Wages Payable		90
Unearned Service Fees		750
M. Landen, Capital		27,360
	$31,080	$31,080

SUMMARY OF THE ACCOUNTING CYCLE

We may now put together all the steps in the accounting cycle, integrating the use of a worksheet. The following sequence of accounting procedures occurs each fiscal year and represents a systematic process for analyzing, accumulating, classifying, and reporting the financial data of a business entity:

1. Analyze transactions from source documents.
2. Record transactions in journals.
3. Post journal entries to general ledger accounts.
4. Prepare a trial balance to start a worksheet.
5. Adjust the general ledger accounts on the worksheet and complete the worksheet.
6. Prepare financial statements.
7. Journalize and post adjusting entries.
8. Journalize and post closing entries.
9. Prepare a post-closing trial balance.

Exhibit 4–11 summarizes the actions taken in the accounting cycle and notes their frequency of occurrence and the related document or accounting record.

REVERSING ENTRIES: OPTIONAL FIRST STEP IN NEXT ACCOUNTING PERIOD

In our discussion of adjusting entries for accrued items in Chapter 3, we pointed out that certain precautions are necessary to avoid reflecting the same expense or revenue in two successive periods. We now review two alternative procedures

EXHIBIT 4–11

THE ACCOUNTING CYCLE

Frequency	Action Taken	Related Document or Record
Daily	1. Analyze transactions	Source documents
	2. Record transactions	Journal
	3. Post journal entries	General ledger
Whenever financial statements are desired	4. Prepare trial balance 5. Adjust general ledger accounts	Worksheet
	6. Prepare financial statements	Income statement Statement of owner's equity Balance sheet
End of period	7. Journalize and post adjusting entries 8. Journalize and post closing entries	Journal and General ledger
	9. Prepare post-closing trial balance	Post-closing trial balance

for recording the settlement of accrued items in the period after their accrual. We illustrate these procedures using wages expense for Landen TV Service.

Wages Expense in December

Recall from Chapter 3 that the Landen TV Service employee received wages of \$270 for each six-day work week (\$45 per day) and that the employee was paid every other Saturday. We assumed that the two paydays in December fell on

December 14 and 28. Wages expense of $90 was accrued for December 30 and 31. We made the following adjusting entry to reflect the proper expense for December:

Dec. 31	Wages Expense	90	
	Wages Payable		90
	To record accrued wages for December 30 and 31.		

After this adjusting entry was posted, the Wages Expense account had a debit balance of $1,170. This consisted of two debits of $540 made on December 14 and 28 and the $90 accrual on December 31. Along with other expenses, the Wages Expense account was closed to Income Summary on December 31. After the closing procedures, the Wages Expense and Wages Payable accounts appeared in the ledger as follows:

Wages Expense Account No. 52

Date		Description	Post. Ref.	Debit*	Credit	Balance
19XX						
Dec.	14		J1	540		540
	28		J2	540		1,080
	31	(adjusting)	J3	90		1,170
	31	(closing)	J4		1,170	–0–

Wages Payable Account No. 23

Date		Description	Post. Ref.	Debit	Credit*	Balance
19XX						
Dec.	31	(adjusting)	J3		90	90

January Accounting Without Using Reversals

On January 11, the employee will receive another $540 wage payment. Of this amount, only $450 should be reflected as January expense since only 10 days were worked in January (the other two days were worked in December and accrued as December wages expense). We may record the wage payment and the correct January wages expense by making the entry we presented in Chapter 3, as follows:

Jan. 11	Wages Payable	90	
	Wages Expense	450	
	Cash		540
	To record wages paid.		

This procedure, however, requires extreme vigilance in recording routine transactions on the part of the bookkeeper, who must keep in mind previously made accruals in order to record subsequent payments correctly. Many bookkeepers find this a nuisance and avoid the problem by reversing adjustments made for accruals.

January Accounting Using Reversals

As an alternative to the preceding procedure, then, a bookkeeper may use **reversing entries.** Reversing entries are made after all closing procedures have been completed and the post-closing trial balance has been prepared. Reversing entries are dated the first day of the following period and, therefore, are the first journal entries in that period. A reversing entry is so named because the entry exactly reverses the debits and credits of an adjusting entry. For example, the reversing entry for the accrual of wages would be

Jan. 1	Wages Payable	90	
	Wages Expense		90
	To reverse accrual made December 31.		

This entry reduces the liability Wages Payable to zero and results in a $90 abnormal credit balance in the Wages Expense account at the start of the new accounting period. On the next payday, however, the wage payment of $540 is recorded as all wage payments are recorded, as follows:

Jan. 11	Wages Expense	540	
	Cash		540
	Paid wages for two weeks ended January 11.		

When this entry is posted to the Wages Expense account, the $540 debit is combined with the $90 credit balance created by the reversing entry. As a result, the account balance is the proper wages expense for January 1–11 ($450). Afer the January 1 reversing entry and the January 11 payment have been posted, the Wages Expense and Wages Payable accounts appear as shown below. Note that the $90 abnormal balance is placed in parentheses.

Wages Expense Account No. 52

Date		Description	Post. Ref.	Debit*	Credit	Balance
19XX						
Dec.	14		J1	540		540
	28		J2	540		1,080
	31	(adjusting)	J3	90		1,170
	31	(closing)	J4		1,170	–0–
19X1						
Jan.	1	(reversing)	J5		90	(90)
	11		J6	540		450

Wages Payable Account No. 23

Date		Description	Post. Ref.	Debit	Credit*	Balance
19XX						
Dec.	31	(adjusting)	J3		90	90
19X1						
Jan.	1	(reversing)	J5	90		–0–

Both of the alternative procedures for handling the December accrued wages in January give the same result—the elimination of the $90 wages payable and the portrayal of $450 of wages expense for the first 11 days in January. By using reversals, however, the bookkeeper can record the first January payroll without having to consider the amount of wages accrued at December 31.

Other Reversals

A reversing entry may simplify the recording of a transaction that relates to an earlier adjusting entry. No hard-and-fast rule determines which adjusting entries should be reversed. Generally, though, *accruals* of revenue and expenses that relate to routine, repetitive transactions are the most appropriate adjustments to reverse. Of the adjustments made by Landen TV Service (in addition to the accrual of wages), reversing entries would be employed for the two other accruals—the $120 estimated utilities expense and the $240 unbilled service fees earned. The bookkeeper would therefore make two additional reversing entries after the books are closed:

Jan. 1	Utilities Payable	120	
	Utilities Expense		120
	To reverse accrual made December 31.		
Jan. 1	Service Fees Earned	240	
	Accounts Receivable		240
	To reverse accrual made December 31.		

These entries eliminate the accrued amounts from the liability and asset accounts and create an abnormal credit balance of $120 in Utilities Expense and an abnormal debit balance of $240 in Service Fees Earned.

The credit balance in Utilities Expense will be eliminated when the utility bills are received and paid in January. If we assume that bills amounting to $124 arrived and were paid on January 6, the entry would be:

Jan. 6	Utilities Expense	124	
	Cash		124
	To record payment of December utilities.		

After the entry for payment is posted, Utilities Expense will have a $4 debit balance to be absorbed in January. As we mentioned in Chapter 3, charging a small amount of one period's expense in another period must be tolerated when estimates are used.

The debit balance in Service Fees Earned is eliminated when Landen TV Service bills the local hotel after the completion of 40 hours of work (per its contract with the hotel). This billing, made on January 21, is recorded as follows:

Jan. 21	Accounts Receivable	640	
	Service Fees Earned		640
	To record billing for 40 hours of work at $16 per hour.		

This entry leaves a credit balance of $400 in the Service Fees Earned revenue account, reflecting the proper amount of revenue for work performed in January (25 hours × $16). The $640 debit to Accounts Receivable represents the amount of cash to be collected from the hotel.

Although the use of reversing entries is optional, it does permit us to analyze routine, repetitive transactions the same way all the time. For example, if reversals are used, a bookkeeper may be instructed (or a computer programmed) to debit Wages Expense and credit Cash every time wages are paid. Similarly, every utility payment may be analyzed as a debit to Utilities Expense and a credit to Cash, and every billing of service fees may be recorded as a debit to Accounts Receivable and a credit to Service Fees Earned. Reversals eliminate the need to remember the effects of previous accruals and, therefore, contribute to the more efficient processing of data.

Reversals normally are not appropriate for adjustments involving prepayments of expense or advance receipts of revenues. Only if a company's policy is to record expense prepayments in expense accounts and advance revenue receipts in revenue accounts might adjustments involving these items be reversed. In these cases, the reversals reestablish the remaining expense prepayments and advance revenue receipts in the appropriate expense and revenue accounts. These types of situations, however, are not common and will not be illustrated here.

KEY POINTS FOR CHAPTER OBJECTIVES

1 Explain the procedures for preparing a worksheet (pp. 117–22).

- The worksheet facilitates the preparation of financial statements.
- The worksheet begins with the unadjusted trial balance.
- Adjusted account balances, which are extended into the income statement and balance sheet columns of the worksheet, provide the data for the formal financial statements.

2 Identify the final four steps in the accounting cycle (p. 122).

- The final four steps in the accounting cycle are:
  a. Prepare financial statements.
  b. Journalize and post adjusting entries.
  c. Journalize and post closing entries.
  d. Prepare a post-closing trial balance.

3 Illustrate the financial statements prepared from a worksheet (pp. 122–23).

- An income statement, statement of owner's equity, and balance sheet may be prepared from data on the worksheet. The owner's capital account may also need to be reviewed to obtain information on owner capital contributions during the period for the statement of owner's equity.

4 Illustrate the process of journalizing and posting adjusting entries (pp. 123–26).

- End-of-year adjustments are recorded in the general journal and posted to the general ledger. Adjustments for interim financial statements are usually made only on the worksheet.

5 Describe the process of closing the temporary accounts of a sole proprietorship and a corporation (pp. 126–29).

- *Closing the books* means closing the revenue, expense, and other temporary accounts. Revenue and expense account balances are transferred to the Income Summary account. The balances of the Income Summary account and the owners' drawing accounts are closed to the owners' capital accounts. For corporations, the Income Summary account is closed to Retained Earnings.

6 Explain the nature of a post-closing trial balance (p. 129, 135).

- A post-closing trial balance contains only balance sheet accounts.

7 Summarize the complete accounting cycle (pp. 135–36).

- The first three steps in the accounting cycle—analyzing transactions, recording transactions, and posting the transaction journal entries—occur daily.
- The next three steps in the accounting cycle—preparing a trial balance, adjusting the accounts on a worksheet, and preparing financial statements—occur whenever financial statements are desired.
- The last three steps in the accounting cycle—journalizing and posting adjusting entries, journalizing and posting closing entries, and preparing a post-closing trial balance—occur at the end of the accounting period.

8 Discuss the purpose of reversing entries (pp. 135–40).

- The reversal of adjustments made for *accrued* items permits the normal recording of subsequent transactions. It safeguards against reflecting the same revenue or expense in successive periods.

KEY TERMS USED IN THIS CHAPTER

adjusted trial balance 120
closing procedures 126
interim financial statements 124
post-closing trial balance 129
reversing entries 138
worksheet 117

SELF-TEST QUESTIONS FOR REVIEW

(Answers are at the end of this chapter.)

1. Which trial balance begins a worksheet?
   (a) Post-closing trial balance.
   (b) Adjusted trial balance.
   (c) Unadjusted trial balance.
   (d) Beginning-of-year trial balance.
2. In preparing a worksheet, you have just extended the adjusted account balances to the income statement and balance sheet columns and totaled these columns. If the company is profitable this period, the total of the income statement credit column will be
   (a) Larger than the balance sheet debit column total.
   (b) Larger than the income statement debit column total.
   (c) Smaller than the income statement debit column total.
   (d) Larger than the balance sheet credit column total.
3. Closing entries
   (a) Are an optional step in the accounting cycle.
   (b) Affect only balance sheet accounts.
   (c) Permit a company to analyze routine, repetitive transactions the same way all the time.
   (d) Remove the balances from a firm's temporary accounts.
4. Which of the following closing procedures is unique to a corporation?
   (a) Close each revenue account to the Income Summary account.
   (b) Close each expense account to the Income Summary account.
   (c) Close the Income Summary account to the Retained Earnings account.
   (d) Close the owner's drawing account to the owner's capital account.
5. Assume Zee Company initially records prepayments in balance sheet accounts and makes reversing entries when appropriate. Which of the following year-end adjusting entries by Zee Company should be reversed?
   (a) The entry to record depreciation expense for the period.
   (b) The entry to record the portion of service fees received in advance that is earned by year-end.
   (c) The entry to record supplies used during the period.
   (d) The entry to record service fees earned by year-end but not yet billed.

DEMONSTRATION PROBLEM FOR REVIEW

The unadjusted trial balance of Gibbons Repair Service at the end of its first year of operations is shown below.

Gibbons Repair Service
Trial Balance
December 31, 19X1

	Debit	Credit
Cash	$ 200	
Accounts Receivable	1,500	
Prepaid Advertising	400	
Supplies on Hand	3,000	
Equipment	9,600	
Accounts Payable		$ 800
G. Gibbons, Capital		10,000
G. Gibbons, Drawing	3,600	
Service Fees Earned		14,000

Rent Expense	5,500	
Wages Expense	1,000	
	$24,800	$24,800

The following additional information is available at December 31, 19X1:

1. The prepaid advertising covers the months December, 19X1–March, 19X2.
2. Supplies on hand at December 31 are $1,300.
3. Annual depreciation on the equipment is $1,200.
4. Service fees earned but not yet billed at December 31 are $400.
5. Rent of $500 for December has not yet been paid.
6. Accrued wages at December 31 are $150.

REQUIRED

(a) Prepare a 10-column worksheet for the year ended December 31, 19X1.
(b) Prepare closing entries in general journal form.

SOLUTION TO DEMONSTRATION PROBLEM

(a)

Gibbons Repair Service
Worksheet
For the Year Ended December 31, 19X1

Description	Trial Balance Debit	Trial Balance Credit	Adjustments Debit	Adjustments Credit	Adjusted Trial Balance Debit	Adjusted Trial Balance Credit	Income Statement Debit	Income Statement Credit	Balance Sheet Debit	Balance Sheet Credit
Cash	200				200				200	
Accounts Receivable	1,500		(4) 400		1,900				1,900	
Prepaid Advertising	400			(1) 100	300				300	
Supplies on Hand	3,000			(2) 1,700	1,300				1,300	
Equipment	9,600				9,600				9,600	
Accounts Payable		800				800				800
G. Gibbons, Capital		10,000				10,000				10,000
G. Gibbons, Drawing	3,600				3,600				3,600	
Service Fees Earned		14,000		(4) 400		14,400		14,400		
Rent Expense	5,500		(5) 500		6,000		6,000			
Wages Expense	1,000		(6) 150		1,150		1,150			
	24,800	24,800								
Advertising Expense			(1) 100		100		100			
Supplies Expense			(2) 1,700		1,700		1,700			
Depreciation Expense			(3) 1,200		1,200		1,200			
Accumulated Depreciation				(3) 1,200		1,200				1,200
Rent Payable				(5) 500		500				500
Wages Payable				(6) 150		150				150
			4,050	4,050	27,050	27,050	10,150	14,400	16,900	12,650
Net Income							4,250			4,250
							14,400	14,400	16,900	16,900

			Debit	Credit
(b)	Dec. 31	Service Fees Earned	14,400	
		Income Summary		14,400
		To close the revenue account.		
	31	Income Summary	10,150	
		Rent Expense		6,000
		Wages Expense		1,150
		Advertising Expense		100
		Supplies Expense		1,700
		Depreciation Expense		1,200
		To close the expense accounts.		
	31	Income Summary	4,250	
		G. Gibbons, Capital		4,250
		To close the Income Summary account.		
	31	G. Gibbons, Capital	3,600	
		G. Gibbons, Drawing		3,600
		To close the drawing account.		

QUESTIONS

4–1 At what point in the accounting cycle is a worksheet used? What is the first accounting information placed on the worksheet?

4–2 After a worksheet is completed at the end of the accounting year, what steps remain to complete the accounting cycle?

4–3 What are the advantages of preparing a worksheet?

4–4 Identify each of the 10 amount columns of the worksheet and indicate to which columns the adjusted balances of the following accounts would be extended:

(a) Accounts Receivable
(b) Accumulated Depreciation
(c) J. Burns, Drawing
(d) Wages Payable
(e) Depreciation Expense
(f) Rent Receivable
(g) Prepaid Insurance
(h) Service Fees Earned
(i) Capital Stock
(j) Retained Earnings

4–5 Suppose the total adjusted revenue of a business is $98,000 and total adjusted expense is $76,000. (a) When the worksheet is completed, in which columns would the $22,000 difference appear? (b) If total adjusted expense amounted to $105,000, in which columns of the computed worksheet would the $7,000 difference appear?

4–6 What information is presented in a statement of owner's equity?

4–7 What is the reason why the totals of the balance sheet columns of the worksheet may differ from the total asset amount on the formal balance sheet?

4–8 When adjusted balances are extended on the worksheet, Unearned Fees of $2,000 is extended as a credit in the income statement columns and Accounts Receivable of $1,100 is extended as a debit in the income statement columns. All other extensions are properly made. (a) Does the worksheet balance? (b) How do these incorrect extensions affect the calculation of net income shown on the worksheet?

4–9 Define *interim financial statements.* Give an example of an interim financial statement.

4–10 When would adjusting entries be entered only on a worksheet and not in the accounts? Why?

4–11 A firm on a calendar-year basis prepares cumulative statements monthly, using a worksheet. Adjusting and closing entries are entered in journals and posted only on December 31. On January 1, the firm paid $1,008 for a two-year insurance policy. What worksheet adjustments for insurance should be made on (a) January 31, (b) February 28, and (c) May 31?

4–12 Which groups of accounts are closed at the end of the accounting year?

4–13 How is the Income Summary account used in closing procedures?

4–14 How do closing entries for a corporation differ from closing entries for a proprietorship?

4–15 What is the purpose of a post-closing trial balance? Which of the following accounts should not appear in the post-closing trial balance: Cash; Unearned Revenue; Jensen, Drawing; Depreciation Expense; Utilities Payable; Supplies Expense; and Retained Earnings?

4–16 Why are reversing entries made? If reversals are made, which entries would normally be reversed?

4–17 A firm accrued wages of $1,500 on December 31. On January 8, the next payday, the firm paid $3,600 in wages. The company does not make reversing entries. On January 8, the company debited Wages Expense and credited Cash for $3,600. How will this procedure affect January net income?

4–18 Since the firm in Question 4–17 did not make a reversing entry, what entry should it have made to record the January 8 payment of wages?

4–19 Assume that the firm in Question 4–17 did use reversing entry procedures. What reversing entry should the firm have made on January 1? How should the company have recorded the January 8 payment if a reversing entry had been made?

EXERCISES

Worksheet

4–20 The adjusted trial balance columns of a worksheet for Larry Hyatt, consultant, are shown below. The worksheet is prepared for the year ended December 31, 19XX.

	Adjusted Trial Balance	
	Debit	**Credit**
Cash	4,000	
Supplies on Hand	8,500	
Equipment	80,000	
Accumulated Depreciation		36,000
Accounts Payable		3,300
L. Hyatt, Capital		42,800
L. Hyatt, Drawing	11,000	
Service Fees Earned		51,700
Rent Expense	13,200	
Supplies Expense	9,100	
Depreciation Expense	8,000	
	133,800	133,800

Complete the worksheet by (a) extending these amounts to the income statement and balance sheet columns and (b) balancing the worksheet.

Income statement and balance sheet

4–21 The income statement and balance sheet columns of a worksheet for Lemon Corporation are shown below. The worksheet is prepared on December 31, 19X4, for the year ended on that date.

	Income Statement		Balance Sheet	
	Debit	Credit	Debit	Credit
Cash			2,500	
Accounts Receivable			5,400	
Office Equipment			40,000	
Accumulated Depreciation				6,000
Accounts Payable				2,100
Wages Payable				600
Capital Stock				12,000
Retained Earnings				9,000
Service Fees Earned		47,000		
Wages Expense	12,800			
Rent Expense	7,200			
Depreciation Expense	4,000			
Advertising Expense	1,600			
Income Tax Expense	3,200			
	28,800	47,000	47,900	29,700
Net Income	18,200			18,200
	47,000	47,000	47,900	47,900

Prepare an income statement and a balance sheet for Lemon Corporation.

Statement of owner's equity

4–22 On January 1, 19X2, the credit balance of the M. Rasak, Capital account was $22,000, and on December 31, 19X2, the credit balance before closing was $26,000. The M. Rasak, Drawing account had a debit balance of $8,400 on December 31, 19X2. After revenue and expense accounts were closed, the Income Summary account had a credit balance of $13,700. Prepare a 19X2 statement of owner's equity for Mary Rasak, architect.

Closing entries

4–23 The income statement columns of a worksheet prepared December 31 contain only the following accounts:

	Debit	Credit
Service Fees Earned		40,200
Rent Expense	9,900	
Salaries Expense	24,500	
Supplies Expense	3,100	
Depreciation Expense	4,200	

Included among the accounts in the balance sheet columns of the worksheet are L. Powell, Capital, $38,000 (credit), and L. Powell, Drawing, $5,000 (debit). Prepare entries to close the accounts, including the owner's drawing account. After these entries are made, what is the balance of the L. Powell, Capital account?

Closing entries

4–24 In the midst of closing procedures, Brumm Corporation's bookkeeper became ill and was hospitalized. You have volunteered to complete the closing of the books, and you find that all revenue and expense accounts have zero balances and that the Income Summary account has a single debit entry for $105,800 and a single credit entry for $127,400. The only entry in Retained Earnings this year is a debit of $9,000 for dividends, which reduced the balance to $76,000. Capital Stock has a normal balance of $200,000 and shows no entries for the year. Give the journal entry (or entries) to complete the closing procedures and calculate the total amount of the stockholders' equity.

Closing entries

4–25 Use the information in Exercise 4–20 to prepare the closing entries for Larry Hyatt, consultant, on December 31, 19XX.

Closing entries

4–26 Use the information in Exercise 4–21 to prepare the closing entries for Lemon Corporation on December 31, 19X4.

Reversing entries

4–27 Image Company closes its accounts on December 31 each year. The company works a five-day work week and pays its employees every two weeks. On December 31, 19X2, Image accrued $2,100 of salaries payable. On January 9, 19X3, the company paid salaries of $7,000 to employees. Prepare journal entries to: (a) accrue the salaries payable on December 31; (b) close the Salaries Expense account on December 31 (the account has a year-end balance of $175,000 after adjustments); (c) reverse the December 31 salary accrual on January 1; and (d) record the salary payment on January 9.

PROBLEMS

Worksheet and closing entries

4–28 Lane Cleaning Service will prepare financial statements on December 31, 19X1. The trial balance and adjustments columns of the firm's worksheet at December 31 follow.

	Trial Balance		Adjustments	
	Debit	Credit	Debit	Credit
Cash	2,500			
Accounts Receivable	4,800			
Supplies on Hand	8,000			(1) 6,400
Prepaid Insurance	1,260			(2) 420
Equipment	35,000			
Accumulated Depreciation		7,000		(3) 3,500
Accounts Payable		1,700		
B. Lane, Capital		17,880		
B. Lane, Drawing	1,800			
Cleaning Revenue		45,400		
Salaries Expense	12,400		(4) 450	
Rent Expense	5,400			
Miscellaneous Expense	820			
	71,980	71,980		
Supplies Expense			(1) 6,400	
Insurance Expense			(2) 420	
Depreciation Expense			(3) 3,500	
Salaries Payable				(4) 450
			10,770	10,770

REQUIRED

(a) Complete the worksheet.

(b) Prepare the closing entries at December 31 in general journal form.

Worksheet and financial statements

4–29 The following unadjusted trial balance was taken at March 31 of the current year:

Globe Travel Agency
Trial Balance
March 31, 19XX

	Debit	Credit
Cash	$ 1,400	
Accounts Receivable	3,000	
Supplies on Hand	1,150	
Prepaid Insurance	1,600	
Equipment	12,600	
Accumulated Depreciation		$ 2,520
Accounts Payable		340

(continued)

	Debit	Credit
Unearned Commissions		750
G. Lacy, Capital		10,000
G. Lacy, Drawing	1,000	
Commissions Earned		14,510
Salaries Expense	4,200	
Rent Expense	1,710	
Advertising Expense	900	
Utilities Expense	560	
	$28,120	$28,120

The trial balance data are cumulative for the first three months of 19XX. No adjusting entries have been made in the accounts and Gayle Lacy has not made any capital contributions during this period. The following additional information is available:

1. Depreciation for the first quarter is $315.
2. Supplies on hand at March 31 amount to $630.
3. During the quarter, $500 of the unearned commissions were earned.
4. Insurance expense for the quarter is $400.
5. Accrued salaries payable total $425 at March 31.
6. Commissions earned but not billed at March 31 are $380.

REQUIRED

(a) Enter the trial balance on a worksheet and complete the worksheet using the adjustment data given above.

(b) Prepare an income statement and a statement of owner's equity for the first quarter of the year and a balance sheet at March 31.

Adjusting entries and account classification

4–30 The first six columns of a worksheet for Custom Upholstery Service, Inc., are given below. However, only the totals of the adjustments columns are given.

Custom Upholstery Service, Inc.
Worksheet
For the Year Ended December 31, 19XX

	Trial Balance		Adjustments		Adjusted Trial Balance	
	Debit	Credit	Debit	Credit	Debit	Credit
Cash	2,500				2,500	
Accounts Receivable	4,615				4,615	
Prepaid Rent	1,875				1,250	
Supplies on Hand	12,360				5,240	
Equipment	22,000				22,000	
Accumulated Depreciation		5,250				7,875
Accounts Payable		1,300				1,300
Unearned Service Fees		800				200
Capital Stock		10,000				10,000
Retained Earnings		9,475				9,475
Service Fees Earned		32,140				32,740
Wages Expense	6,500				7,070	
Utilities Expense	2,240				2,500	
Rent Expense	6,875				7,500	
	58,965	58,965				
Supplies Expense					7,120	
Depreciation Expense					2,625	
Wages Payable						570
Utilities Payable						260
			11,800	11,800	62,420	62,420

REQUIRED
(a) Determine the adjusting entries for Custom Upholstery Service, Inc., and prepare these entries in general journal form.
(b) For each account in the adjusted trial balance, indicate whether it will appear in an income statement or in a balance sheet.

Worksheet, financial statements, and closing entries

4–31 The unadjusted trial balance shown below is for Foster Freight Service at December 31, 19X1. Brian Foster made no capital contributions during 19X1. The following data for adjustments are also available at December 31:

1. Supplies on hand amount to $1,270.
2. Prepaid insurance is $600.
3. Depreciation for the year is as follows: Equipment, $600; Trucks, $2,500.
4. Accrued wages payable are $710.
5. Estimated December utilities expense is $420; the bill has not arrived.
6. Foster has completed, but not yet billed, work amounting to $1,000.

	Debit	Credit
Cash	$ 2,200	
Accounts Receivable	3,170	
Supplies on Hand	2,760	
Prepaid Insurance	1,800	
Equipment	5,400	
Accumulated Depreciation—Equipment		$ 900
Trucks	20,000	
Accumulated Depreciation—Trucks		3,750
Notes Payable		4,000
Accounts Payable		850
B. Foster, Capital		9,250
B. Foster, Drawing	3,900	
Service Fees Earned		80,620
Rent Expense	9,000	
Salaries and Wages Expense	39,400	
Fuel Expense	8,100	
Utilities Expense	3,280	
Interest Expense	360	
	$99,370	$99,370

REQUIRED
(a) Prepare a 10-column worksheet for the year ended December 31, 19X1. Set up any additional accounts needed.
(b) Prepare an income statement and a statement of owner's equity for the year and a balance sheet at December 31, 19X1.
(c) Prepare closing entries in general journal form.

Complete accounting cycle

4–32 Ken Howard, tax consultant, began business on December 1 of the current year. December transactions were as follows:

Dec.	1	Howard invested $14,000 in the business.
	2	Paid rent for two months to Star Realty, $1,100.
	2	Purchased various supplies on account, $920.
	3	Purchased $8,000 of office equipment, paying $3,200 down with the balance due in 30 days.
	8	Paid $920 on account for supplies purchased December 2.
	13	Paid assistant's wages for two weeks, $540.
	20	Performed consulting services for cash, $1,400.
	27	Paid assistant's wages for two weeks, $540.
	30	Billed customers for December consulting services, $4,500.
	31	Howard withdrew $1,200 from the business.

REQUIRED

(a) Open the following general ledger accounts, using the account numbers shown: Cash (11); Accounts Receivable (12); Prepaid Rent (13); Supplies on Hand (14); Office Equipment (15); Accumulated Depreciation (16); Accounts Payable (21); Wages Payable (22); K. Howard, Capital (31); K. Howard, Drawing (32); Income Summary (33); Consulting Revenue (41); Supplies Expense (51); Wages Expense (52); Rent Expense (53); and Depreciation Expense (54).
(b) Journalize the December transactions, and post to the ledger.
(c) Prepare a trial balance directly on a worksheet, and complete the worksheet using the following information:
  1. Supplies on hand at December 31 are $570.
  2. Accrued wages payable at December 31 are $110.
  3. Depreciation for December is $85.
  4. Howard has spent 20 hours on an involved tax fraud case during December. When completed in January, his work will be billed at $40 per hour.
  5. Prepaid rent at December 31 is $550.
(d) Prepare a December income statement and statement of owner's equity and a December 31 balance sheet.
(e) Journalize and post adjusting and closing entries.
(f) Prepare a post-closing trial balance.
(g) Journalize and post the appropriate reversing entries.

Closing entries and corporation accounts

4–33 The last four columns of a 10-column worksheet prepared at December 31, 19XX, for Sanstar, Inc., are reproduced below.

	Income Statement		Balance Sheet	
	Debit	Credit	Debit	Credit
Cash			3,100	
Accounts Receivable			7,000	
Prepaid Insurance			4,800	
Equipment			61,000	
Accumulated Depreciation				6,600
Accounts Payable				500
Capital Stock				30,000
Retained Earnings				11,700
Service Fees Earned		84,300		
Miscellaneous Income		3,600		
Salaries Expense	39,200			
Rent Expense	10,800			
Insurance Expense	2,400			
Salaries Payable				700
Depreciation Expense	4,400			
Income Tax Expense	4,700			
	61,500	87,900	75,900	49,500
Net Income	26,400			26,400
	87,900	87,900	75,900	75,900

REQUIRED

(a) From the given information, prepare closing entries in general journal form.
(b) After the closing entries are posted, what is the balance in the Retained Earnings account?
(c) Which accounts in the worksheet would not appear if the company were organized as a sole proprietorship rather than as a corporation.

Adjusting and reversing entries

4–34 The following selected accounts appear in Corey Company's unadjusted trial balance at December 31, 19X5, the end of the fiscal year (all accounts have normal balances):

Prepaid Advertising	$ 800	Unearned Service Fees	$ 2,800
Wages Expense	30,200	Service Fees Earned	71,000
Prepaid Insurance	2,850	Rental Income	4,500

REQUIRED

(a) Make the necessary adjusting entries in general journal form at December 31, assuming the following:
   1. Prepaid advertising at December 31 is $600.
   2. Unpaid wages earned by employees in December are $725.
   3. Prepaid insurance at December 31 is $1,900.
   4. Unearned service fees at December 31 are $1,000.
   5. Rental income of $500 owed by a tenant is not recorded at December 31.

(b) Assume the company makes reversing entries. Which of the adjustments in part (a) should be reversed? Make the proper reversing entries on January 1, 19X6.

(c) Assume reversing entries have been made. Prepare the journal entries on January 4 to record (1) the payment of $1,200 in wages and (2) the receipt from the tenant of the $500 rental income.

(d) Assume reversing entries have not been made. Prepare the journal entries on January 4 to record (1) the payment of $1,200 in wages and (2) the receipt from the tenant of the $500 rental income.

ALTERNATE PROBLEMS

Worksheet and closing entries

4–28A The trial balance and adjustments columns of the worksheet for Careful Moving Service at December 31 of the current year are shown below.

	Trial Balance		Adjustments	
	Debit	Credit	Debit	Credit
Cash	3,300			
Accounts Receivable	4,620			
Supplies on Hand	2,900			(1) 2,100
Prepaid Advertising	3,000			(2) 2,000
Trucks	29,700			
Accumulated Depreciation—Trucks		7,700		(3) 3,300
Equipment	9,600			
Accumulated Depreciation—Equipment		2,700		(4) 900
Accounts Payable		1,300		
Unearned Service Fees		2,100	(5) 1,500	
F. Cary, Capital		18,360		
F. Cary, Drawing	5,200			
Service Fees Earned		62,000		(5) 1,500
Wages Expense	24,800			
Rent Expense	9,840			
Insurance Expense	1,200			
	94,160	94,160		
Supplies Expense			(1) 2,100	
Advertising Expense			(2) 2,000	
Depreciation Expense—Trucks			(3) 3,300	
Depreciation Expense—Equipment			(4) 900	
			9,800	9,800

REQUIRED
(a) Complete the worksheet.
(b) Prepare the closing entries at December 31 in general journal form.

Worksheet and financial statements

4–29A The July 31 unadjusted trial balance of Superior Outfitters, a firm renting various types of equipment to canoeists and fishermen, is shown below.

Superior Outfitters
Trial Balance
July 31, 19XX

	Debit	Credit
Cash	$ 3,250	
Supplies on Hand	6,600	
Prepaid Insurance	2,400	
Equipment	96,500	
Accumulated Depreciation		$ 12,500
Accounts Payable		3,800
Unearned Rental Fees		3,350
C. Thorp, Capital		49,100
C. Thorp, Drawing	1,600	
Rental Fees Earned		76,050
Wages Expense	27,300	
Rent Expense	3,600	
Advertising Expense	2,730	
Travel Expense	820	
	$144,800	$144,800

The trial balance data are cumulative for the first three months of the firm's fiscal year, which begins May 1. No adjusting entries have been made in the accounts during the quarter. The general ledger account for C. Thorp, Capital reveals Clark Thorp made a $10,000 capital contribution on July 1, 19XX.

1. Supplies on hand at July 31 amount to $4,300.
2. Insurance expense for the first quarter is $600.
3. Depreciation for the first quarter is $2,000.
4. The unearned rental fees consist of deposits received from customers in advance when reservations are made. During the quarter, $1,850 of the unearned rental fees were earned.
5. At July 31, unbilled revenue from rental services earned for outfitting several church groups during July amounts to $3,700.
6. Accrued wages payable for equipment handlers and guides amounts to $950 at July 31.

REQUIRED
(a) Enter the trial balance in a worksheet and complete the worksheet using the adjustment data given above.
(b) Prepare an income statement and a statement of owner's equity for the first quarter and a balance sheet at July 31.

Worksheet error corrections

4–30A Michele Linn, owner of the Linn Refinishing Service, has completed a worksheet for her business at the end of its first year of operations. She is unsure of her accounting skills, however, and asks you to review the worksheet before she prepares financial statements from it. You have reviewed the unadjusted trial balance, the adjustments, and the compilation of the adjusted trial balance columns and have found no errors. The last six columns of the worksheet are shown below (as noted, the adjusted trial balance columns are correct).

Linn Refinishing Service
Worksheet
For the Year Ended December 31, 19XX

	Adjusted Trial Balance		Income Statement		Balance Sheet	
	Debit	Credit	Debit	Credit	Debit	Credit
Cash	400				400	
Accounts Receivable	860				860	
Prepaid Rent	620				620	
Supplies on Hand	780				780	
Equipment	4,500					4,500
Accounts Payable		290			290	
M. Linn, Capital		5,300				5,300
M. Linn, Drawing	2,400				2,400	
Service Revenue		10,150		10,510		
Wages Expense	3,120		3,120			
Utilities Expense	840		840			
Rent Expense	1,500		1,500			
Supplies Expense	930		390			
Depreciation Expense	450				450	
Accumulated Depreciation		450				450
Wages Payable		120				120
Utilities Payable		90				90
	16,400	16,400	5,850	10,510	5,800	10,460
Net Income			4,660		4,660	
			10,510	10,510	10,460	10,460

REQUIRED
(a) Identify the errors contained in this partial worksheet.
(b) Prepare a correct partial worksheet (the last six columns).

Worksheet, financial statements, and closing entries

4–31A Glide and Stride, Inc., publishes magazines for skiers and hikers. The firm has the following unadjusted trial balance at December 31 of its second year of operations.

Glide and Stride, Inc.
Trial Balance
December 31, 19X2

	Debit	Credit
Cash	$ 7,400	
Accounts Receivable	10,600	
Supplies on Hand	8,500	
Prepaid Insurance	1,860	
Office Equipment	36,000	
Accumulated Depreciation—Office Equipment		$ 3,000
Building	300,000	
Accumulated Depreciation—Building		12,000
Land	40,000	
Accounts Payable		2,100
Unearned Subscription Revenue		7,200
Capital Stock		175,000
Retained Earnings		77,390
Subscription Revenue		295,100
Advertising Revenue		97,600

(continued)

	Debit	Credit
Salaries Expense	120,160	
Printing and Mailing Expense	90,600	
Advertising Expense	8,820	
Utilities Expense	4,150	
Income Tax Expense	41,300	
	$669,390	$669,390

The following information for adjusting the accounts is available at December 31:

1. Supplies on hand amount to $3,200.
2. Prepaid insurance at December 31 is $620.
3. Accrued salaries at December 31 are $1,700.
4. Of the unearned subscription revenue shown in the trial balance, $5,000 was earned during the year. The remainder will be earned next year.
5. Advertising revenue earned during the period but unbilled at December 31 is $2,300.
6. Depreciation on office equipment for the year is $3,000.
7. Depreciation on the building for the year is $12,000.

REQUIRED

(a) Prepare a 10-column worksheet for the year ended December 31, 19X2. Set up any additional accounts needed.

(b) Prepare an income statement for the year and a balance sheet at December 31.

(c) Prepare closing entries in general journal form.

Complete accounting cycle

4–32A Melissa Crane, attorney, opened her practice on December 1 of the current year. December transactions were as follows:

Dec.	1	Crane invested $8,000 in the firm.
	2	Paid rent for six months to Beyer Realty, $4,200.
	2	Purchased various supplies for cash, $650.
	3	Purchased office furniture and fixtures on account, $5,100.
	8	Paid $2,000 on account for furniture and fixtures purchased December 3.
	12	Paid assistant's salary for two weeks, $680.
	20	Performed legal services for cash, $1,000.
	26	Paid assistant's salary for two weeks, $680.
	30	Billed clients for legal work completed during the month, $3,500.
	31	Crane withdrew $400 from the business.

REQUIRED

(a) Open the following general ledger accounts, using the account numbers shown: Cash (11); Accounts Receivable (12); Prepaid Rent (13); Supplies on Hand (14); Furniture and Fixtures (15); Accumulated Depreciation (16); Accounts Payable (21); Salary Payable (22); M. Crane, Capital (31); M. Crane, Drawing (32); Income Summary (33); Professional Fees Earned (41); Supplies Expense (51); Salary Expense (52); Rent Expense (53); and Depreciation Expense (54).

(b) Journalize the December transactions, and post to the ledger.

(c) Prepare a trial balance directly on a worksheet, and complete the worksheet using the following information:

1. Supplies on hand at December 31 are $570.
2. Accrued salary payable at December 31 is $240.
3. Depreciation for December is $50.
4. Crane has spent 30 hours on an involved estate planning case during December. When completed in January, her work will be billed at $50 per hour.

5. Prepaid rent at December 31 is $3,500.

(d) Prepare a December income statement and statement of owner's equity and a December 31 balance sheet.
(e) Journalize and post adjusting and closing entries.
(f) Prepare a post-closing trial balance.
(g) Journalize and post the appropriate reversing entries.

Worksheet and financial statements

4–33A Action Engineering Services, Inc., prepares a year-to-date income statement each month. Also, a balance sheet is prepared at the end of each month. The firm makes adjusting and closing entries in its accounts only at December 31 each year. The firm's unadjusted trial balance at April 30, 19X5, is given below.

Action Engineering Services, Inc.
Trial Balance
April 30, 19X5

	Debit	Credit
Cash	$ 6,200	
Prepaid Insurance	2,340	
Supplies on Hand	8,500	
Equipment	168,000	
Accumulated Depreciation		$ 39,200
Accounts Payable		1,800
Capital Stock		60,000
Retained Earnings		48,600
Service Revenue		74,500
Salaries Expense	24,000	
Legal Fees Expense	5,600	
Rent Expense	3,500	
Utilities Expense	1,560	
Income Tax Expense	4,400	
	$224,100	$224,100

The following data for adjustments are available at April 30, 19X5:

1. Three years of insurance coverage was purchased January 1, 19X5.
2. Supplies on hand at April 30 are $4,800.
3. Monthly depreciation on equipment is $1,400.
4. Accrued salaries at April 30 are $900.
5. The firm is involved in a lawsuit with a former client. Legal fees incurred in April but not yet billed are estimated at $2,000 (credit Legal Fees Payable).

REQUIRED

(a) Record the April 30 trial balance on a 10-column worksheet. Enter the necessary adjusting entries and complete the worksheet for the four months ended April 30, 19X5.
(b) Prepare an income statement for the four months ended April 30, 19X5.
(c) Prepare a balance sheet at April 30, 19X5.

Adjusting and reversing entries

4–34A The following selected accounts appear in Quinn Company's unadjusted trial balance at December 31, 19X1, the end of the fiscal year (all accounts have normal balances):

Prepaid Maintenance	$1,800	Commission Fees Earned	$91,000
Supplies on Hand	5,400	Rent Expense	6,000
Unearned Commission Fees	6,500		

REQUIRED

(a) Make the necessary adjusting entries in general journal form at December 31, assuming the following:
 1. On September 1, 19X1, the company entered into a prepaid equipment maintenance contract. Quinn Company paid $1,800 to cover maintenance service for six months, beginning September 1, 19X1. The $1,800 payment was debited to Prepaid Maintenance.
 2. Supplies on hand at December 31 are $3,000.
 3. Unearned commission fees at December 31 are $2,000.
 4. Commission fees earned but not yet billed at December 31 are $1,500.
 5. Quinn Company's lease calls for rent of $500 per month payable on the first of each month, plus an amount equal to 1% of annual commissions earned. This additional rent is payable on January 10 of the following year. (*Note:* Be sure to use the adjusted amount of commissions earned in computing the additional rent.)

(b) Assume the company makes reversing entries. Which of the adjustments in requirement (a) should be reversed? Make the proper reversing entries on January 1, 19X2.

(c) Assume reversing entries have been made. Prepare the journal entries on January 10, 19X2, to record (1) the billing of $4,000 of commissions earned (an amount which includes the $1,500 of commissions earned but not billed at December 31) and (2) the payment of the additional rent owed for 19X1.

(d) Assume reversing entries have not been made. Prepare the journal entries on January 10, 19X2, to record (1) the billing of $4,000 of commissions earned (an amount which includes the $1,500 of commissions earned but not billed at December 31) and (2) the payment of the additional rent owed for 19X1.

BUSINESS DECISION PROBLEM

As an alternative to a summer job paying $5 per hour between her junior and senior years in college, Lynn Stowe accepted an opportunity to lease and operate the tennis court concession in a local city recreational complex during June, July, and August. Although she kept no accounting records, Lynn was careful to handle all funds related to the tennis concession through a special bank account opened for that purpose. An analysis of those deposit slips and check stubs for the three months is summarized below.

Receipts:	
Stowe's investment of personal funds	$ 1,200
Court rental fees	6,850
Tennis lesson fees	1,825
Tennis lesson fees received in advance	125
Proceeds of short-term loan from bank	800
Total receipts	$10,800
Disbursements:	
Purchase of ball-throwing machine	$ 170
Supplies purchased	850
Utilities	215
Lease payments to city	1,375
Wages to part-time assistant	1,300
Liability insurance premiums	225
Repayment of bank loan, including interest	820
Withdrawals of cash for personal expenses	780
Total disbursements	$ 5,735
Cash balance, August 31	$ 5,065

Lynn confides in you, a personal friend who happens to be studying accounting, that she is pleased with her apparent profit of $5,065 for the summer. Eager to practice your newly acquired skills, you offer to review her records and prepare an income statement for the three months and a balance sheet at the end of August. In discussions with Lynn, you learn that:

1. Some tennis lessons, paid for in advance, could not be scheduled during the summer. Lynn plans to refund these fees, which total $125.
2. Repayment to the bank included $20 of interest expense on the loan.
3. Rental receipts include all revenue earned except for $400 due from a company that rented the entire set of courts for a weekend late in August.
4. A ball-throwing machine, purchased used, turned out to be quite temperamental. After a complete breakdown in July, it was junked.
5. Supplies consisted of cans of tennis balls. Lynn gave away a free can of tennis balls for each five hours of court time rented by an individual. Supplies amounting to $100 were on hand at August 31; these may be returned for a full refund. Lynn estimates that each month during the summer, she took home $20 worth of supplies for personal use.
6. All lease payments due the city were paid except for the final amount of $250.
7. Lynn estimates that the utility bill for August, when received, will be $120.
8. The insurance premiums represent coverage for the months of June, July, and August.

REQUIRED

Prepare financial statements for Lynn's tennis concession (a sole proprietorship). You should formulate general journal entries summarizing the cash receipts and the cash disbursements and incorporating the additional data. After posting these to T accounts, you will be able to prepare the financial statements.

In further talks with Lynn, you learn that the amount she contributed had been in a savings account earning 7% interest and that she worked an average of 60 hours in each of the 13 weeks the tennis concession was operated. What observations might you offer Lynn regarding the financial success of the summer venture? What nonfinancial considerations are involved?

ANSWERS TO SELF-TEST QUESTIONS

1. (c) **2.** (b) **3.** (d) **4.** (c) **5.** (d)

5

MERCHANDISING OPERATIONS

CHAPTER OBJECTIVES

1. Describe the nature of merchandising enterprises and the steps in merchandising transactions (pp. 159–65).
2. Illustrate the accounting entries for types of merchandise transactions (pp. 165–72).
3. Illustrate the treatment of merchandise accounts in the worksheet (pp. 172–75).
4. Describe classified financial statements for a merchandise firm (pp. 175–78).
5. Illustrate adjusting and closing entries for a merchandise firm (pp. 178–81).

Everyone lives by selling something.
ROBERT LOUIS STEVENSON

Thus far in our discussion of the accounting cycle, we have used as examples firms providing services rather than those selling products. Revenue for small service enterprises such as the driving school and the television repair service consisted of fees earned for the services performed. In these firms, net income is determined simply by deducting total expenses incurred from total fees earned during a period.

Revenue for firms that sell products consists of the total amount for which the products are sold. To determine net income for such firms, we deduct from the revenue (called *sales*) for the period not only the operating expenses incurred, but also the costs of acquiring the products sold. In this chapter we will discuss the procedures followed in accounting for the costs of acquiring and selling products.

THE NATURE OF MERCHANDISING OPERATIONS

The total business segment of society is often classified into three broad types of enterprises: (1) service, (2) manufacturing, and (3) merchandising. Commercial airlines, physicians, lawyers, insurance companies, and banks are examples of service enterprises. Manufacturing enterprises convert raw materials into finished products through the application of skilled labor and machine operations. Merchandising enterprises are characterized by the basic operations of buying and selling finished products and include both wholesalers and retailers. Exhibit 5–1 illustrates the position of merchandising enterprises in the manufacturing and distribution process.

The accounting records of a merchandising firm must accommodate many transactions for the purchase of products and payment of the related accounts. Moreover, the accounting reports should indicate whether the difference between the acquisition price and the sales price to customers covers the costs of storing, displaying, advertising, selling, delivering, and collecting for the merchandise. Finally, the accounting records must reflect not only cash sales but also individual accounts receivable for a large number of customers.

INCOME STATEMENT FOR A MERCHANDISING FIRM

Exhibit 5–2 is an income statement for a merchandising firm, Madison Electronics Company. For simplicity, we have condensed the operating expenses into two amounts—selling expenses and administrative expenses. (These classifications are explained later in the chapter.)

The major difference between the income statement of a merchandising firm and that of a service business is the inclusion of an amount for the *cost of goods sold* to customers in the merchandising firm's statement. Ordinarily, this amount is deducted from the revenue figure (sales) to arrive at an intermediate amount called **gross profit on sales.** The operating expenses are then deducted from the gross profit on sales to obtain net income.

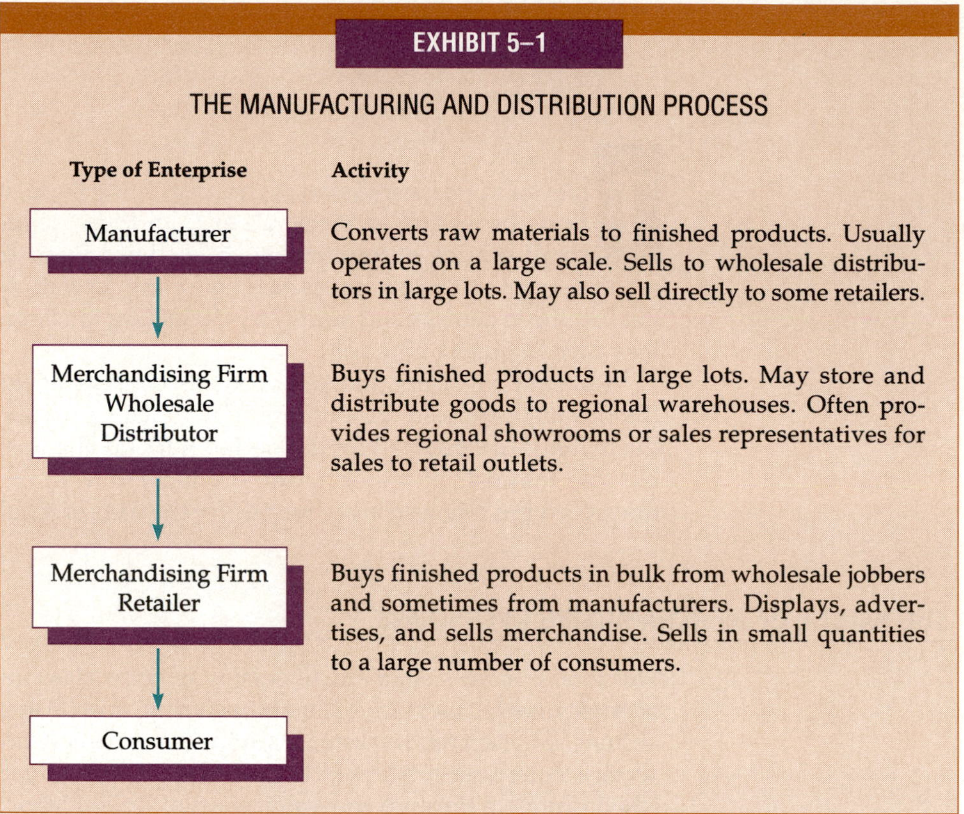

EXHIBIT 5–1
THE MANUFACTURING AND DISTRIBUTION PROCESS
Type of Enterprise
Activity
Manufacturer
Converts raw materials to finished products. Usually operates on a large scale. Sells to wholesale distributors in large lots. May also sell directly to some retailers.
Merchandising Firm Wholesale Distributor
Buys finished products in large lots. May store and distribute goods to regional warehouses. Often provides regional showrooms or sales representatives for sales to retail outlets.
Merchandising Firm Retailer
Buys finished products in bulk from wholesale jobbers and sometimes from manufacturers. Displays, advertises, and sells merchandise. Sells in small quantities to a large number of consumers.
Consumer

The gross profit on sales amount (sometimes called *gross margin*) is highly significant to management. When divided by the sales amount, it yields a **gross profit percentage** (sometimes called *average mark-up percentage on sales*), which is carefully monitored by the firm. In our illustration, the gross profit is 40% of sales ($170,000/$425,000 = 0.40 = 40%). This figure means that after 60 cents is deducted from each sales dollar to cover the cost of goods sold, 40 cents remains to cover operating expenses and provide a net income.

EXHIBIT 5–2

Madison Electronics Company
Income Statement
For the Year Ended December 31, 19XX

Sales		$425,000
Cost of Goods Sold		255,000
Gross Profit on Sales		$170,000
Operating Expenses:		
Selling Expenses	$96,200	
Administrative Expenses	48,300	
		144,500
Net Income		$ 25,500

Management usually compares its current gross profit percentage with similar calculations for prior periods or with industry averages. Such comparisons may alert management to a need to modify prices, purchasing policies or merchandise control procedures. Industry averages are usually available from such sources as trade associations or credit reporting agencies that compile statistics for various industries.

Cost of Goods Sold

To calculate the **cost of goods sold** to customers, we must consider data from a number of special merchandise accounts. We discuss the treatment of such accounts in detail later in this chapter. To provide a perspective, however, we show in condensed form in Exhibit 5–3 how cost of goods sold was calculated for the income statement in Exhibit 5–2.

At the beginning of the year, Madison Electronics had a supply of merchandise costing $115,000. During the year, the firm purchased additional merchandise with a net cost of $260,000. The sum of these two amounts is the total cost of all goods that were available for sale to customers during the year ($375,000). At the end of the year, merchandise costing $120,000 remained unsold, so we deduct this amount to arrive at the cost of goods sold, which is $255,000.

STEPS IN A MERCHANDISE TRANSACTION

Whenever a transaction for the purchase or sale of merchandise occurs, the buyer and the seller should agree on the price of the merchandise, the terms of payment, and the party to bear the cost of transportation. Owners or managers of small merchandising firms may settle the terms of the transaction informally by telephone or by discussion with the supplier's sales representative. Most large businesses, however, fill out a purchase order when ordering merchandise. A typical sequence of events for a large firm is as follows:

1. When certain items are needed or when quantities of certain merchandise fall below established reorder points, a request for a purchase, called a **purchase requisition,** is sent to the purchasing department by the person in charge of merchandise stock records. These requisitions may also be initiated by other authorized personnel, such as department heads.
2. The purchasing department then prepares a **purchase order** after consulting price lists, quotations, or suppliers' catalogs. The purchase order, addressed to the selected vendor, indicates the quantity, description, and price of the

EXHIBIT 5–3

COMPUTATION OF COST OF GOODS SOLD

Beginning Inventory, January 1	$115,000
Add: Net Cost of Purchases	260,000
Cost of Goods Available for Sale	$375,000
Less: Ending Inventory, December 31	120,000
Cost of Goods Sold	$255,000

EXHIBIT 5–4

INVOICE

MADISON ELECTRONICS COMPANY
1400 South Park St.
Madison, Wisconsin 53705

Customer's
Order No. & Date 1503
Requisition No.
Contract No.

Refer to
Invoice No. 12015
Invoice Date Nov. 20, 19XX
Vendor's Nos.

SOLD TO ABC Company
120 Weston Street
Kenosha, Wisconsin

Shipped to and Destination Same
Date Shipped Nov. 20, 19XX
Car Initials and No.
How Shipped and Route
Terms 2/10, n/30

From Madison: F.O.B. Kenosha
Prepaid or Collect: Prepaid

FOR CUSTOMER'S USE ONLY
Register No. Voucher No.
F.O.B. Checked
Terms Approved
Price Approved LNJ
Calculations Checked RSD
Transportation
Freight Bill No. Amount
Material Received
Date Signature Title
Satisfactory and Approved
Adjustments
Accounting Distribution
Audited Final Approval

QUANTITY	DESCRIPTION	UNIT PRICE	AMOUNT
7	Model E Voicemaster Tape Recorders	$70	$490

merchandise ordered. It may also indicate expected terms of payment and arrangements for transportation, including payment of freight costs.

3. After receiving the purchase order, the seller forwards an **invoice** to the purchaser upon shipment of the merchandise. The invoice—called a **sales invoice** by the seller and a **purchase invoice** by the buyer—defines the terms of the transaction. A sample invoice is shown in Exhibit 5–4.
4. Upon receiving the shipment of merchandise, the purchaser's receiving department counts and inspects the items in the shipment and makes out a **receiving report** detailing the quantities received.
5. Before approving the invoice for payment, the accounts payable department compares copies of the purchase order, invoice, and receiving report to ensure that quantities, descriptions, and prices are in agreement.

Although all of the above papers—purchase requisition, purchase order, invoice, and receiving report—are source documents, only the invoice provides the basis for recording the purchase. The other three documents are merely supporting documents. The purchaser makes no entries in the accounts until the invoice is approved for payment. The seller enters the transaction in the records when the invoice is prepared, usually upon shipment of the merchandise.

TERMS OF TRANSACTIONS

Merchandise may be purchased and sold either on credit terms or for cash on delivery. Most merchandise transactions today are made on account rather than on cash (sometimes referred to as *net cash*) terms. When goods are sold on account, a period of time called the **credit period** is allowed for payment. The length of the credit period varies among business firms and may even vary within a firm, depending on the type of product. A typical credit period for wholesalers is 30 days. Payment is expected within 30 days of the invoice date, after which the purchaser is considered delinquent. The credit period is frequently described as the *net* credit period, or *net* terms, and the notation commonly used to designate this period is "n/" followed by the length of the period in days; for example, n/30 indicates that the credit period is 30 days.

Cash Discounts

To encourage early payment of bills, many firms designate a **discount period** that is shorter than the credit period. Purchasers who remit payment during this period are entitled to deduct a **cash discount** from the total payment. Ostensibly, this discount is for prompt payment. The discount is designated by such notation as "2/10," which means that 2% may be deducted if payment is made within 10 days. For example, if a November 10 invoice for $800 carries terms of 2/10, n/30, the purchaser may deduct 2% from the invoice price if the bill is paid by November 20. The cash discount would be $16 (2% of $800), and the amount of the remittance would be $784. The full amount of the invoice, $800, would be expected if the purchaser paid between November 20 and December 10. After December 10, the amount would be overdue.

Most business firms maintain a good cash position so they can take advantage of discounts. For example, assume that a firm purchased $800 worth of merchandise on terms of 2/10, n/30. The firm has a choice of paying $784 within 10 days of the invoice date or the full amount before the end of another 20 days. Passing up the discount is essentially the same as paying 2% interest for the use of $800 for 20 days, which is equivalent to a 36% annual interest rate (360 days/20 days × 2%). Clearly, the firm would be wiser to borrow from a bank at an annual interest rate of 9–12% rather than lose a discount that amounts to a much higher rate.

Trade Discounts

Certain business firms furnish customers with price lists or catalogs showing suggested retail prices for their products. These firms, however, also include a schedule of **trade discounts** from the listed prices that enable a customer to determine the invoice price to be paid. Suppose that the Madison Electronics Company quoted a list price of $100 for each Model E tape recorder, less a discount of 30% if purchased in lots of 10 items or less and 40% if purchased in lots

IMPACT OF SALES TERMS ON PRICING

The concept of pricing is frequently confined to the identification of the price per unit charged to the customer on the sales invoice, or as listed on the company's price sheet or in its catalog. The terms and conditions of sale, often shown in fine print on the back of the invoice, are not always seen as having any direct bearing on price. In reality, they have a substantial impact on the actual price recovered, and in many instances serve to negate completely the effect of the pricing decision. Some of the sales terms are readily measurable as to the effect on price; others are not, being either hidden from view or misleading as to interpretation. In total they constitute an integral part of the pricing process, and the effects of each must be measured on a step-by-step basis to obtain the desired economic results.

One of the more obvious examples of pricing impact is the measurement of cash discounts allowed for early payment. Typical is the discount of "2% 10 days net 30." First, the discount is a direct reduction of 2% in the selling price, a reduction that will usually be taken by the customer, even beyond the 10-day period allowed. Second, the offer of a 2% reduction for payment 20 days early—in 10 days rather than 30—amounts to an annual interest rate of 36% per year, a payment for the use of money far in excess of the bank rate for funds even in times of double-digit inflation.

Taken together, these two points add up to the fact that cash discounts seldom work as intended, that in practice they routinely become nothing more than a price concession. Management is not deliberately offering 36% per annum for the use of money, but an alert customer will make the calculation properly and be quick to take advantage of it. Furthermore, the fact that many accounts take the discount well after the time allowed is evidence that customers regard it more as a price concession than a reward for early payment. Some companies attempt to charge back the unearned discount, a procedure that creates undesirable friction with their own customers, a situation the sales force would prefer to avoid.

Variations of the cash discount terms, such as "2% 10th prox," further complicate the picture by encouraging customers to bunch their orders around the first of the month to get the greatest leverage on the terms offered. This, obviously, can have the undesirable effect of creating peak work loads in order entry, shipping, and billing with consequent dry periods toward month-end.

In short, cash discounts make little economic sense as payment for the use of funds and in practice become nothing more than a reduction of price. In recent years, the great majority of companies have found it to be an awkward vehicle for price adjustment and have abandoned it in favor of net terms.

of more than 10. If the ABC Company ordered seven tape recorders, it would calculate its invoice cost as follows:

List Price ($100 × 7)	$700
Less 30%	210
Invoice Cost	$490

Trade discounts enable a supplier to vary prices for small and large purchasers and, by changing the discount schedule, to alter prices periodically without the inconvenience and expense of revising catalogs and price lists.

Trade discounts are simply a means of determining invoice prices and should not be confused with cash discounts. Trade discounts and list prices are not reflected in the accounts of either the purchaser or the seller of merchandise. In the foregoing example, both the purchaser and the seller would record only the $490 invoice amount.

RECORDING MERCHANDISE SALES

After a vendor has processed a customer's purchase order and prepared the goods for shipment, a sales invoice is prepared in several copies. The original copy is usually sent to the customer; duplicate copies are retained by the seller. The duplicates may be distributed to the shipping department to support its shipping records; to the sales department so it can analyze sales by product, territory, or sales representative; and to the accounting department so that the transaction will be recorded in the accounts.

Suppose the accounting department of Madison Electronics Company receives its copy of the November 20 invoice for the sale of the tape recorders described in the previous section. The general journal entry to record the sale would be

Nov. 20	Accounts Receivable	490	
	Sales		490
	To record the sale of seven Model E tape recorders to the ABC Company. Terms 2/10, n/30.		

The **Sales** account is used by almost all manufacturing and merchandising companies to record revenue transactions. It is the same type of account as the Instructional Fees Earned (revenue) account used by the Westgate Driving School, our example in Chapter 2. The Sales account is credited whenever credit or cash sales are made, and invariably it has a credit balance at the end of the accounting period. Only sales of merchandise held for resale are recorded in the Sales account. If a merchandising firm sold one of its delivery trucks, the credit would be made to the Delivery Equipment account, not to the Sales account. At the end of the accounting period, the Sales account is closed to the Income Summary account in the same way that the Instructional Fees account is closed. Sales is debited and Income Summary is credited for the accumulated credit balance in the Sales account.

As we mentioned earlier, the sales invoice is the document used to record credit sales. For cash sales, however, the procedure is different. For a large volume of cash sales, as in a retail merchandising establishment, cash sales are recorded and accumulated on a cash register tape as they are made.[1] At the end of each day, the amount of sales shown on the tape is recorded on a summary sheet or report. The totals on these reports are usually recorded in the Sales account for the week. Shorter or longer recording intervals may be used, depending on management's reporting needs. In general journal form, the entry to record a week's cash sales of $3,200 would be

Nov. 27	Cash	3,200	
	Sales		3,200
	To record cash sales for week of November 23–27.		

[1]Some retail firms may record sales by electronic means at the time of sale, updating records with each transaction.

RECORDING MERCHANDISE PURCHASES

When a business purchases merchandise for resale to customers, the amount is debited to the **Purchases** account. The credit is made to Accounts Payable or to Cash, depending on whether the purchase was on credit or cash terms. Assume that on November 23, the ABC Company received its shipment of seven tape recorders from the Madison Electronics Company, along with the vendor's invoice for $490. To record the credit purchase, the ABC Company makes the following entry:

Nov. 23	Purchases	490	
	Accounts Payable		490
	To record the purchase of seven Model E tape recorders from Madison Electronics Company. Terms 2/10, n/30.		

Only merchandise purchased for resale is recorded in the Purchases account. Acquisitions of such things as equipment, supplies, and investments are entered in the corresponding asset accounts rather than in Purchases.

The Purchases account normally has a debit balance at the end of the accounting period. The account is treated as an income statement account and, like the other temporary accounts, is closed at the end of the accounting year. The closing of the Purchases account is explained later in this chapter.

RETURNS AND ALLOWANCES

Sometimes a customer returns merchandise to the seller because of defects, damage in transit, or because the wrong merchandise was shipped. Upon returning merchandise, the customer requests an appropriate reduction in the original amount billed. Similar requests are made when an invoicing error has occurred. Upon receiving notification that the buyer has returned goods or has requested an allowance, the seller usually issues the customer a **credit memorandum** such as the one illustrated in Exhibit 5–5.

The credit memorandum (sometimes called *credit memo*) is a formal acknowledgment that the seller has reduced the amount owed by the customer. When the seller issues a credit memorandum, the accounting department retains a duplicate copy, which is the source document for an entry crediting the customer's account. For example, suppose two of the seven tape recorders sold to the ABC Company were returned for credit. Upon issuing a credit memo to the ABC Company, Madison Electronics Company would make the following entry:

Nov. 25	Sales Returns and Allowances	140	
	Accounts Receivable		140
	To record the issuance of credit memo No. 23 for two Model E tape recorders returned by the ABC Company.		

Upon receipt of the credit memo, the ABC Company would make the following entry:

EXHIBIT 5–5

CREDIT MEMORANDUM

MADISON ELECTRONICS COMPANY
1400 South Park St.
Madison, Wisconsin 53705

CREDIT MEMORANDUM
No. 23

TO: ABC Company
120 Weston Street
Kenosha, Wisconsin

Date Nov. 25, 19XX

We credit your account as follows:

Return of two Model E tape recorders,
our invoice No. 12015 .... $140.00

Nov. 27	Accounts Payable	140	
	Purchases Returns and Allowances		140
	To record the receipt of credit memo No. 23 for two Model E tape recorders returned to Madison Electronics Company.		

In the first entry above, Madison Electronics Company could have debited the Sales account rather than Sales Returns and Allowances. If Sales were debited, however, the account balance at the end of the accounting period would not reveal total sales made but total sales less all returns and allowances. Most companies prefer to record sales returns and allowances in a separate contra account in order to determine the aggregate amount of such items. If the amount is abnormally large, an investigation should be made to determine the reason. Returns may be caused by defective products, faulty packing or shipping, or improper billing procedures. The additional handling of goods and the additional clerical work of making adjustments can be costly, and customers may be lost in the process.

For similar reasons, the purchaser ordinarily credits the Purchases Returns and Allowances account rather than the Purchases account when a credit memorandum is received. The separate accounting permits a company to determine whether its purchasing or requisitioning procedures should be reviewed. The company may discover, for instance, that not enough care is exercised in filling out requisitions and purchase orders or in selecting reliable suppliers.

The Sales Returns and Allowances account invariably has a debit balance at the end of the accounting period. On the income statement, the amount is a deduction from the Sales amount. The Purchases Returns and Allowances account has a credit balance at the end of the accounting period, and the balance is subtracted from the Purchases amount on the income statement. Both the Sales Returns and Allowances and the Purchases Returns and Allowances accounts are closed at the end of the accounting year in a manner we shall explain shortly.

Many companies record all credit memos in the returns and allowances accounts. When the memos are issued as a result of mere clerical or arithmetical errors, however, the adjustment is best recorded in the Sales or Purchases accounts.

RECORDING RECEIPTS AND PAYMENTS

A set of merchandise transactions concludes when the seller receives the proper remittance from the purchaser and each firm makes the appropriate entries for the settlement of accounts. To illustrate, let us review the entries made thus far for Madison Electronics Company's sale of the tape recorders to the ABC Company.

Seller (Madison Electronics Company)

To Record Sale

Nov. 20	Accounts Receivable	490	
	Sales		490
	To record the sale of seven Model E tape recorders to the ABC Company. Terms 2/10, n/30.		

To Record Return of Merchandise

Nov. 25	Sales Returns and Allowances	140	
	Accounts Receivable		140
	To record the issuance of credit memo No. 23 for two Model E tape recorders returned by the ABC Company.		

Buyer (ABC Company)

To Record Purchase

Nov. 23	Purchases	490	
	Accounts Payable		490
	To record the purchase of seven Model E tape recorders from Madison Electronics Company. Terms 2/10, n/30.		

To Record Return of Merchandise

Nov. 27	Accounts Payable	140	
	Purchases Returns and Allowances		140
	To record the receipt of credit memo No. 23 for two Model E tape recorders returned to Madison Electronics Company.		

After these transactions have been posted, the seller's Accounts Receivable account and the buyer's Accounts Payable account appear as follows:

Seller (Madison Electronics Company)

Accounts Receivable

19XX		19XX	
Nov. 20	490	Nov. 25	140

Buyer (ABC Company)

Accounts Payable

19XX		19XX	
Nov. 27	140	Nov. 23	490

If the ABC Company takes advantage of the 2% discount, its remittance must be made within 10 days of the November 20 invoice date. Usually, the discount is granted if the remittance is postmarked on the last day of the discount period. The amount that the ABC Company should remit by November 30 is $343 ($350 balance owing less 2% discount of $7). Note that the discount is calculated only on the cost of the merchandise kept by the purchaser, not on the invoice price of the goods originally shipped. The entries made on the books of the seller and buyer are as follows:

	Seller (Madison Electronics Company)		
Dec. 2	Cash	343	
	Sales Discounts	7	
	Accounts Receivable		350
	To record remittance in full of account.		

	Buyer (ABC Company)		
Nov. 30	Accounts Payable	350	
	Purchases Discounts		7
	Cash		343
	To record payment of account.		

After this entry is posted, the seller's Accounts Receivable and the purchaser's Accounts Payable appear as follows:

Seller (Madison Electronics Company)

Accounts Receivable

19XX		19XX	
Nov. 20	490	Nov. 25	140
		Dec. 2	350

Buyer (ABC Company)

Accounts Payable

19XX		19XX	
Nov. 27	140	Nov. 23	490
30	350		

Note that the discount taken in this transaction is not revealed in either the seller's Accounts Receivable account or the buyer's Accounts Payable account. Discounts are accumulated in Sales Discounts on the seller's books and Purchases Discounts on the buyer's books.

The other accounts relevant to the set of transactions for the tape recorders are shown below in T-account form, after the appropriate postings have been made.

Seller (Madison Electronics Company)

Sales

		19XX	
		Nov. 20	490

Sales Returns and Allowances

19XX			
Nov. 25	140		

Sales Discounts

19XX			
Dec. 2	7		

Buyer (ABC Company)

Purchases

19XX			
Nov. 23	490		

Purchases Returns and Allowances

		19XX	
		Nov. 27	140

Purchases Discounts

		19XX	
		Nov. 30	7

From this illustration, we see that both Sales Returns and Allowances and Sales Discounts have debit balances, and the Sales account has a credit balance. This relationship always holds true, and at the close of the accounting period, the net sales for the period can be calculated by subtracting the balances of the Sales Returns and Allowances account and the Sales Discounts account from the

Sales account. The revenue section of the income statement for the year will show this calculation as follows:

Revenue		
Sales		$433,000
Less: Sales Returns and Allowances	$2,500	
Sales Discounts	5,500	8,000
Net Sales		$425,000

Similarly, Purchases Returns and Allowances and Purchases Discounts have credit balances at the close of the accounting period. On the income statement for the period, the sum of these account balances is deducted from the Purchases account balance. However, because the concept of net cost of purchases is a net *delivered* cost, we usually add another amount, *Transportation In*, to arrive at net cost of purchases. (Transportation In will be explained later in this chapter.) The calculation of net cost of purchases for Madison Electronics Company for the year appears on its income statement as follows:

Net Cost of Purchases		
Purchases		$256,500
Less: Purchases Returns and Allowances	$1,800	
Purchases Discounts	4,400	6,200
		$250,300
Add: Transportation In		9,700
Net Cost of Purchases		$260,000

This calculation appears in the cost of goods sold section of the income statement, which we shall examine more closely later in this chapter.

NET PRICE METHOD OF RECORDING PURCHASES

Some firms anticipate the cash discounts they expect to take on merchandise purchases and initially record such purchases net of the discounts. For example, if a firm purchased merchandise for $500 on terms of 2/10, n/30, the 2% discount ($10) would be deducted from the invoice cost and the entry to record the transaction would debit Purchases and credit Accounts Payable for $490. When this amount is paid during the discount period, the debit to Accounts Payable and the credit to Cash would be for the net amount, $490. No purchase discount would be recorded. When the **net price method** is used, returns and allowances are also recorded net of the related discount.

If a firm delays payment beyond the discount period, the amount of the discount not taken is debited to an account called **Discounts Lost** when the remittance is made. If the firm in our example failed to remit within the discount period, it would record the payment as a $490 debit to Accounts Payable, $10 debit to Discounts Lost, and a $500 credit to Cash.

The Discounts Lost account balance is normally added to the cost of purchases in the cost of goods sold section of the income statement. However, some firms include it with operating expenses. The principal advantage of the net price method is that it focuses attention on discounts not taken, so that management can take immediate corrective action when the aggregate amount of lost discounts becomes significant.

Illustrations of the types of entries used in the net price method are given below:

Purchase of merchandise for $500 on terms of 2/10, n/30		
Purchases	490	
Accounts Payable		490
($500 purchase, less 2% discount)		
Return of $200 merchandise		
Accounts Payable	196	
Purchases Returns and Allowances		196
($200 return, less 2% discount)		
Payment within discount period		
Accounts Payable	294	
Cash		294
($300 merchandise, less 2% discount)		
Payment after discount period		
Accounts Payable	294	
Discounts Lost	6	
Cash		300
($300 merchandise, less 2% discount lost)		

TRANSPORTATION ACCOUNTS

When merchandise is forwarded by a common carrier—a railroad, a trucking company, or an airline—the carrier prepares a *freight bill* in accordance with the instructions of the party making the transportation arrangements. (As mentioned earlier, such arrangements may be specified in the purchase order.) The freight bill designates which party bears the shipping costs and whether the shipment is *prepaid* or *collect.*

Freight bills usually show whether the shipping terms are F.O.B. shipping point or F.O.B. destination (F.O.B. is an abbreviation for "free on board"). When the freight terms are F.O.B. shipping point, the purchaser bears the shipping costs; when the terms are F.O.B. destination, the seller bears the shipping costs.

The shipping costs borne by a purchaser are debited to an account called **Transportation In.** On the firm's income statement, the balance in this account is included in the computation of net cost of purchases. Transportation costs incurred by a seller are debited to an account called **Transportation Out.** This account—sometimes called Delivery Expense—is listed with expenses on the income statement. The primary reason for such treatment is that the seller ordinarily has a number of different types of expenses directly associated with selling merchandise. Such expenses as advertising, salespersons' salaries, and insurance are frequently grouped in the income statement under the caption "Selling Expenses"; including Transportation Out with this group is logical.

Usually, the party assuming the freight cost pays the carrier. Thus, goods are shipped *freight collect* when the terms are F.O.B. shipping point and *freight prepaid* when the terms are F.O.B. destination. Sometimes, as a matter of convenience, the firm not assuming the freight cost pays the carrier. When this situation occurs, the seller and buyer simply adjust the amount of the payment for the merchandise. To illustrate, let us assume that Madison Electronics Company sells $600 worth of merchandise on account to Chicago Supply Company on terms F.O.B. shipping point, 2/10, n/30, and shipping costs of $60 are prepaid by the seller. Madison Electronics Company adds the $60 freight charge to the invoice amount, billing Chicago Supply Company for $660. On its records, Chicago Supply Company reflects the freight cost as Transportation In. The entries are as follows:

Seller (Madison Electronics Company)			**Buyer (Chicago Supply Company)**		
Accounts Receivable	660		Purchases	600	
Sales		600	Transportation In	60	
Cash		60	Accounts Payable		660

In this situation, the buyer is not entitled to a discount on the amount of freight. Thus, if Chicago Supply Company pays the invoice during the discount period, the amount to be remitted is $648 ($660 − $12 discount). The entries to record the remittance are as follows:

Seller (Madison Electronics Company)			**Buyer (Chicago Supply Company)**		
Cash	648		Accounts Payable	660	
Sales Discounts	12		Purchases Discounts		12
Accounts Receivable		660	Cash		648

On the other hand, if freight terms are F.O.B. destination, but the buyer pays the shipping charges (freight collect), the buyer deducts the freight charges from the amount owing the seller. The entries to record the shipment are:

Seller (Madison Electronics Company)			**Buyer (Chicago Supply Company)**		
Accounts Receivable	540		Purchases	600	
Transportation Out	60		Accounts Payable		540
Sales		600	Cash		60

If Chicago Supply Company pays the invoice during the discount period, the remittance is $528 ($540 − $12 discount). The entries to record the remittance are:

Seller (Madison Electronics Company)			**Buyer (Chicago Supply Company)**		
Cash	528		Accounts Payable	540	
Sales Discounts	12		Purchases Discounts		12
Accounts Receivable		540	Cash		528

WORKSHEET FOR A MERCHANDISING FIRM

We pointed out in Chapter 4 that a worksheet is prepared at the close of an accounting period to facilitate preparation of the financial statements. The structure of a worksheet for a merchandising firm is the same 10-column form used in Chapter 4 for a service firm, with pairs of columns for the trial balance, adjustments, adjusted trial balance, income statement, and balance sheet. Madison Electronics Company's worksheet in Exhibit 5–6 is prepared after all transactions for the year are recorded and posted to the accounts. The first step in preparing the worksheet is to take a trial balance of the general ledger at December 31 and record the account balances in the first two columns of the worksheet.

EXHIBIT 5–6

Madison Electronics Company
Worksheet
For the Year Ended December 31, 19XX

Description	Trial Balance		Adjustments		Adjusted Trial Balance		Income Statement		Balance Sheet	
	Debit	Credit	Debit	Credit	Debit	Credit	Debit	Credit	Debit	Credit
Cash	18,240				18,240				18,240	
Accounts Receivable	32,000				32,000				32,000	
Inventory (January 1)	115,000				115,000		115,000			
Prepaid Insurance	840			(1) 280	560				560	
Supplies on Hand	2,800			(2) 1,200	1,600				1,600	
Delivery Equipment	30,000				30,000				30,000	
Accumulated Depreciation		4,300		(3) 6,000		10,300				10,300
Accounts Payable		17,500				17,500				17,500
Long-term Notes Payable		20,000				20,000				20,000
J. Madison, Capital		134,000				134,000				134,000
J. Madison, Drawing	5,400				5,400				5,400	
Sales		433,000				433,000		433,000		
Sales Returns and Allowances	2,500				2,500		2,500			
Sales Discounts	5,500				5,500		5,500			
Purchases	256,500				256,500		256,500			
Purchases Returns and Allowances		1,800				1,800		1,800		
Purchases Discounts		4,400				4,400		4,400		
Transportation In	9,700				9,700		9,700			
Sales Salaries Expense	64,000		(4) 500		64,500		64,500			
Advertising Expense	6,170				6,170		6,170			
Delivery Expense	19,250				19,250		19,250			
Office Salaries Expense	27,500				27,500		27,500			
Rent Expense	16,500				16,500		16,500			
Utilities Expense	3,100				3,100		3,100			
	615,000	615,000								
Insurance Expense			(1) 280		280		280			
Supplies Expense			(2) 1,200		1,200		1,200			
Depreciation Expense			(3) 6,000		6,000		6,000			
Salaries Payable				(4) 500		500				500
			7,980	7,980	621,500	621,500				
Inventory (December 31)								120,000	120,000	
							533,700	559,200	207,800	182,300
Net Income							25,500			25,500
							559,200	559,200	207,800	207,800

Adjustments in the Worksheet

The second step in preparing the worksheet is to record the year-end adjusting entries in the adjustments columns. These entries, with explanations, are as follows:

1.	Dec. 31	Insurance Expense	280	
		Prepaid Insurance		280
		To charge one year's premium to expense (three-year premium, $840, paid January 1).		
2.	31	Supplies Expense	1,200	
		Supplies on Hand		1,200
		To charge to expense the supplies used during year. (Inventory of supplies is $1,600 on December 31.)		
3.	31	Depreciation Expense	6,000	
		Accumulated Depreciation		6,000
		To charge to expense one year's depreciation on delivery equipment.		
4.	31	Sales Salaries Expense	500	
		Salaries Payable		500
		To reflect the salaries earned by salespersons but not paid at December 31.		

To reflect the adjusting entries, we add the accounts not included in the trial balance to the bottom of the worksheet. After making these entries, we total the adjustments columns to confirm that debits equal credits. The trial balance amounts are combined with the adjustments to obtain the adjusted trial balance amounts; these amounts are also summed to determine the equality of the totals. We then extend the adjusted trial balance amounts into the income statement and balance sheet columns. We can see in Exhibit 5–6 that Sales, Purchases, related returns and allowances, discounts, and expense accounts are extended into the income statement columns. Assets, liabilities, and owner's equity accounts are extended into the balance sheet columns.

Inventories in the Worksheet

The inventory of a merchandising firm consists of a stock of goods that are owned by the firm and are available for sale to customers. The dollar amount of this stock of goods is carried in an asset account called **Merchandise Inventory,** or simply **Inventory.** A firm that records the acquisition of merchandise during the period in a Purchases account is using a *periodic* inventory system.[2] This system implies that the inventory account balance does not change during the period. Before the firm prepares year-end financial statements, it must determine the amount of unsold goods to be reported. The amount of this asset is usually calculated by counting and pricing individual items in stock, multiplying unit costs by number of items, then adding all amounts to obtain an aggregate measure.

In Exhibit 5–6, the inventory figure that appears in the unadjusted trial balance is the January 1 inventory. This amount still appears in the account because additions and deductions during the year have not been reflected in the

[2]Under the *perpetual* inventory system described in Chapter 9, the Inventory account is adjusted throughout the accounting period for the cost of goods purchased and sold.

account. The beginning inventory of $115,000 is extended as a debit in the income statement columns because it is combined with Purchases (less returns and allowances and discounts) and Transportation In to determine the cost of goods available for sale. The $120,000 ending inventory, recorded at the bottom of the worksheet, is a credit in the income statement columns because it is deducted from cost of goods available for sale in the calculation of cost of goods sold. In Exhibit 5–6, all the amounts comprising cost of goods sold appear in color to emphasize how cost of goods sold is reflected in the income statement columns of the worksheet. The ending inventory of $120,000 is also entered as a debit in the balance sheet columns because it is an asset at December 31.

The last step in completing the worksheet is to total the income statement and balance sheet columns and insert the balancing amount—the $25,500 net income for the year. A net income amount results in a debit in the income statement columns and a credit in the balance sheet columns. A net loss would result in a credit in the income statement columns and a debit in the balance sheet columns.

An alternative method of dealing with inventories in the worksheet and the adjusting and closing process is sometimes preferred by some accountants. This method, which removes the beginning inventory and records the ending inventory by means of adjusting entries, is explained in Appendix A.

FINANCIAL STATEMENTS OF A MERCHANDISING FIRM

Once the worksheet is completed, preparing the formal financial statements for the period is a simple matter. Exhibits 5–7 and 5–8 present the income statement for the year and the balance sheet at the end of the year for Madison Electronics Company. Both were prepared from the worksheet in Exhibit 5–6. Note that these are **classified** financial statements, meaning that accounts are separated into various categories. The income statements in previous illustrations were not classified because only a few accounts were used. A business with many accounts and transactions, however, classifies the items on the statements to facilitate analysis and interpretation of the data.

The Income Statement

The major categories of the income statement are revenue, cost of goods sold, and operating expenses. For a merchandising firm, the major revenue source is sales of goods to customers. In the revenue section, sales returns and allowances and sales discounts are deducted from gross sales to yield net sales.

We stated earlier that the cost of goods sold amount is obtained by adding the beginning inventory and net cost of purchases and deducting the ending inventory. To calculate net cost of purchases, we deduct purchases returns and allowances and purchases discounts from the purchases amount and add transportation costs of purchased goods.

A business firm's *operating expenses* relate to its primary function and appear with some regularity on the income statement. The operating expenses of a merchandising business are typically classified as selling or administrative expenses. Therefore, in our illustration, expenses resulting from sales efforts—such as salespersons' salaries, advertising, and delivery costs—are classified separately from expenses of rent, utilities, and other administrative costs. Of course, certain types of expenses may appear under both categories. For example, the insurance expense in Exhibit 5–7 is apparently on merchandise or delivery equipment,

EXHIBIT 5–7

Madison Electronics Company
Income Statement
For the Year Ended December 31, 19XX

Revenue				
Sales				$433,000
Less: Sales Returns and Allowances			$ 2,500	
Sales Discounts			5,500	8,000
Net Sales				$425,000
Cost of Goods Sold				
Inventory, January 1			$115,000	
Add: Net Cost of Purchases				
Purchases		$256,500		
Less: Purchases Returns and Allowances	$1,800			
Purchases Discounts	4,400	6,200		
		$250,300		
Add: Transportation In		9,700	260,000	
Cost of Goods Available for Sale			$375,000	
Less: Inventory, December 31			120,000	
Cost of Goods Sold				255,000
Gross Profit on Sales				$170,000
Operating Expenses				
Selling Expenses				
Sales Salaries Expense		$ 64,500		
Delivery Expense		19,250		
Advertising Expense		6,170		
Depreciation Expense		6,000		
Insurance Expense		280		
Total Selling Expenses			$ 96,200	
Administrative Expenses				
Rent Expense		$ 16,500		
Office Salaries Expense		27,500		
Utilities Expense		3,100		
Supplies Expense		1,200		
Total Administrative Expenses			48,300	
Total Operating Expenses				144,500
Net Income				$ 25,500

because it appears as a selling expense. Insurance on a company-owned office building, on the other hand, would appear with the administrative expenses.

Some business items affecting the final net income amount may not relate to the primary operating activity of the business. Interest income and interest expense, for example, may relate more to financing and investing activities than to merchandising efforts. For this reason, such items are often shown in a separate category called "Other Income and Expense" at the bottom of the income statement. Likewise, any extraordinary items (explained in Chapter 16), such as cat-

EXHIBIT 5–8

Madison Electronics Company
Balance Sheet
December 31, 19XX

ASSETS			LIABILITIES AND OWNER'S EQUITY		
Current Assets			**Current Liabilities**		
Cash	$ 18,240		Accounts Payable	$17,500	
Accounts Receivable	32,000		Salaries Payable	500	
Inventory	120,000		Total Current Liabilities		$ 18,000
Prepaid Insurance	560				
Supplies on Hand	1,600				
Total Current Assets		$172,400	**Long-term Liabilities**		
			Long-term Notes Payable		20,000
Long-term Assets			**Owner's Equity**		
Delivery Equipment	$ 30,000		J. Madison, Capital		154,100
Less: Accumulated Depreciation	10,300	19,700			
Total Assets		$192,100	Total Liabilities and Owner's Equity		$192,100

astrophic loss from an earthquake, are shown in a separate "Extraordinary Items" category before the final net income amount is figured. Madison Electronics Company had no such transactions or events to list on the income statement in Exhibit 5–7.

Because the income statement is divided into the major categories just discussed and expenses are classified into selling and administrative expenses, the reader of the statement may pick out key figures at a glance. The reader might first observe the net income figure, \$25,500, and perhaps relate it (as a percentage) to the net sales figure, \$425,000. This result, called **return on sales,** is 6% for Madison Electronics Company. Next, the reader might determine the gross margin percentage by performing the calculation

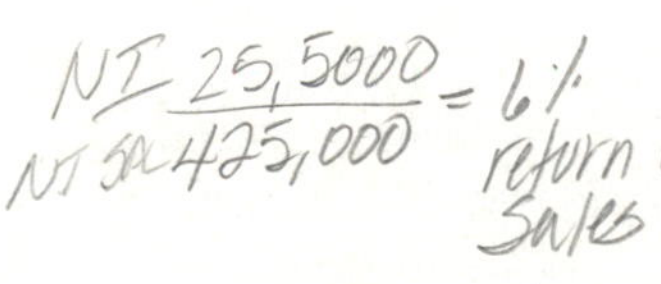

$$\frac{\$170{,}000\ (\text{gross profit})}{\$425{,}000\ (\text{net sales})} = 40\%$$

In a similar fashion, we can relate the total expenses, expense categories, or even individual expenses to net sales. We might also compare the results with those of prior periods or industry averages to determine whether the company's progress is satisfactory. A detailed treatment of such analysis appears in Chapter 20.

The Balance Sheet

The balance sheet for Madison Electronics Company at December 31 is shown in Exhibit 5–8. Note that the company's assets have been classified into *current assets* and *long-term assets*.

CURRENT ASSETS **Current assets** include cash and assets that will be converted into cash or used up during the normal operating cycle of the business or one year, whichever is longer. The *normal operating cycle* of a business is the average period required for merchandise to be bought and sold and the resulting accounts receivable to be collected. For many businesses, this period is one year or less, although certain industries—such as lumbering and distilling—may have an operating cycle of several years. Examples of current assets other than those shown in Exhibit 5–8 are notes receivable and marketable securities acquired as temporary investments. Current assets are usually listed in the order of their *liquidity*, that is, their convertibility into cash.

Prepaid expenses such as rent, insurance, and supplies are normally consumed during the operating cycle rather than converted into cash. These items are considered current assets, however, because the prepayments make cash outlays for services unnecessary during the current period.

LONG-TERM ASSETS **Long-term assets** are noncurrent, relatively long-lived assets used in operating a business. When its balance sheet was prepared, Madison Electronics Company had only one long-term asset, delivery equipment, but many firms own land, buildings, machinery, and equipment. The terms *plant assets* or *plant and equipment* are often used when such assets are extensive. Depreciable assets are normally shown at their original cost, and the accumulated depreciation to date is credited to a separate account. Other examples of long-term assets held by some firms include natural resources, intangible assets, and long-term investments. These assets are explained in later chapters.

CURRENT LIABILITIES **Current liabilities** are amounts due within the normal operating cycle or one year, whichever is longer. Examples of current liabilities are accounts payable, accrued wages and salaries payable, income or property taxes payable, and short-term notes payable. Any amounts a firm has received from customers but has not yet earned as revenue are also included in this category when they will be earned within the normal operating cycle or one year, whichever is longer. Examples include customers' deposits on future purchases and magazine subscriptions covering future periods.

LONG-TERM LIABILITIES After current liabilities, the balance sheet lists all **long-term liabilities**—amounts that are not due for a relatively long time, typically more than one year. Long-term notes, mortgages, and bonds payable are a few examples. Madison Electronics Company owed $20,000 on a long-term note when its balance sheet was compiled (Exhibit 5–8).

OWNER'S EQUITY The owner's interest in the assets of the firm appears in the owner's equity section of the balance sheet. J. Madison's capital balance at December 31 (Exhibit 5–8) is determined by adding the net income to the beginning capital balance and deducting withdrawals, as shown in Exhibit 5–9, the year-end statement of owner's equity.

ADJUSTING AND CLOSING ENTRIES

As we explained in Chapter 4, a company often will prepare monthly or quarterly financial statements directly from worksheets and not record adjusting and closing entries in the general ledger until the end of the year. Let us examine year-end procedures for Madison Electronics Company.

EXHIBIT 5–9

Madison Electronics Company
Statement of Owner's Equity
For the Year Ended December 31, 19XX

J. Madison, Capital, January 1	$134,000
Add: Net Income for 19XX	25,500
	$159,500
Less: Withdrawals for 19XX	5,400
J. Madison, Capital, December 31	$154,100

Adjusting Entries

After financial statements have been prepared from the worksheet, the adjusting entries shown on the worksheet are recorded in the general journal and posted to the accounts. These entries, given in general journal form on page 174, will not be repeated here.

Closing Entries

The closing entries follow the adjusting entries in the general journal. The procedure consists of the following steps:

1. Close the beginning inventory and all income statement accounts with *debit* balances, and debit the total to the Income Summary account.
2. Record the ending inventory, close all income statement accounts with *credit* balances, and credit the total to the Income Summary account.
3. Transfer the balance of the Income Summary account to the owner's capital account (the Retained Earnings account in a corporation).
4. Transfer the balance of the owner's drawing account to the owner's capital account.

Closing entries for Madison Electronics Company are given below:

Dec. 31	Income Summary	533,700	
	Inventory (January 1)		115,000
	Sales Returns and Allowances		2,500
	Sales Discounts		5,500
	Purchases		256,500
	Transportation In		9,700
	Sales Salaries Expense		64,500
	Advertising Expense		6,170
	Delivery Expense		19,250
	Office Salaries Expense		27,500
	Rent Expense		16,500
	Utilities Expense		3,100
	Insurance Expense		280
	Supplies Expense		1,200
	Depreciation Expense		6,000
	To close the beginning inventory and income statement accounts with debit balances.		

Dec. 31	Inventory (December 31)	120,000	
	Sales	433,000	
	Purchases Returns and Allowances	1,800	
	Purchases Discounts	4,400	
	Income Summary		559,200
	To record the ending inventory and to close income statement accounts with credit balances.		
31	Income Summary	25,500	
	J. Madison, Capital		25,500
	To close the Income Summary account and transfer net income to the owner's capital account.		
31	J. Madison, Capital	5,400	
	J. Madison, Drawing		5,400
	To close the owner's drawing account to the capital account.		

After the adjusting and closing entries have been recorded and posted, the Income Summary and J. Madison, Capital accounts appear as shown below. Although we have labeled these entries for illustrative purposes, they would ordinarily not be labeled in the actual accounts.

Income Summary

Debit		Credit	
Beginning Inventory, Purchases, Expenses, and Other Debits	533,700	Ending Inventory, Sales, and Other Credits	559,200
Net Income	25,500		
	559,200		559,200

J. Madison, Capital

Debit		Credit	
Withdrawals	5,400	Beginning Balance	134,000
Ending Balance	154,100	Net Income	25,500
	159,500		159,500
		Ending Balance	154,100

POST-CLOSING TRIAL BALANCE As we explained in Chapter 4, another trial balance of the ledger accounts is customarily taken after the books have been closed to ensure that the ledger balances and is ready for recording transactions in the next period. A December 31 post-closing trial balance for Madison Electronics Company is shown in Exhibit 5–10.

REVERSING ENTRIES If Madison Electronics Company uses reversing entries in its accounting system (see Chapter 4), it would make only one reversing entry

EXHIBIT 5–10

Madison Electronics Company
Post-closing Trial Balance
December 31, 19XX

	Debit	Credit
Cash	$ 18,240	
Accounts Receivable	32,000	
Inventory	120,000	
Prepaid Insurance	560	
Supplies on Hand	1,600	
Delivery Equipment	30,000	
Accumulated Depreciation		$ 10,300
Accounts Payable		17,500
Salaries Payable		500
Long-term Notes Payable		20,000
J. Madison, Capital		154,100
	$202,400	$202,400

on January 1. The only accrual made by the firm at the end of December was for salespersons' salaries; therefore, the entry to reverse this accrual would be

Jan. 1	Salaries Payable	500	
	Sales Salaries Expense		500
	To reverse accrual of salespersons' salaries made on December 31.		

KEY POINTS FOR CHAPTER OBJECTIVES

1 Describe the nature of merchandising enterprises and the steps in merchandising transactions (pp. 159–65).

- Merchandising enterprises are characterized by the basic operations of buying and selling finished products and include both wholesalers and retailers.
- When merchandise is needed, a purchase requisition is forwarded to the purchasing department, which sends a purchase order to the vendor. The vendor sends an invoice to the purchaser when the goods are shipped.
- The invoice, called a purchase invoice by the buyer and a sales invoice by the seller, is the basic document initiating entries for merchandise transactions.

2 Illustrate the accounting entries for types of merchandise transactions (pp. 165–72).

- When a credit merchandise transaction takes place, the purchaser debits the Purchases account and credits Accounts Payable, while the seller debits Accounts Receivable and credits Sales. The Sales account is a revenue account, while the Purchases account becomes a part of Cost of Goods Sold.
- When goods are returned to the seller, the purchaser credits Purchases Returns and Allowances (a contra account to Purchases) and the seller debits Sales Returns and Allowances (a contra account to Sales).
- When goods are paid for within the discount period, the seller debits the discount to Sales Discounts (a contra account to Sales) and the purchaser credits Purchases Discounts (a contra account to Purchases).
- Freight cost borne by the seller is debited to Transportation Out, a selling expense. Freight cost borne by the purchaser is debited to Transportation In, which is added in obtaining Net Cost of Purchases in the income statement.

3 Illustrate the treatment of merchandise accounts in the worksheet (pp. 172–75).

- Sales, Purchases, related returns and allowances, discounts, and expense accounts are extended into the income statement columns of the worksheet, with the same debit and credit positions shown in the adjusted trial balance.
- The beginning inventory balance is extended as a debit in the income statement columns, while, on the bottom of the worksheet, a line is added for the ending inventory. This amount is placed as a credit in the income statement columns and a debit in the balance sheet columns.

4 Describe classified financial statements for a merchandise firm (pp. 175–78).

- The income statement for a merchandise firm has three major sections: revenue, cost of goods sold, and operating expenses. The revenue section shows Sales, less related sales returns and allowances and discounts. In the cost of goods sold section, beginning inventory and net cost of purchases are added and ending inventory is deducted to obtain the cost of goods sold. This amount is deducted from net sales to arrive at the gross profit on sales. Operating expenses are classified functionally as selling expenses or administrative expenses.
- Both assets and liabilities in the balance sheet are classified as current or as long-term. Current assets include cash and assets that will be converted into cash or used up during the normal operating cycle of the business or one year, whichever is longer. Current liabilities are amounts due within the normal operating cycle or one year, whichever is longer. All other assets and liabilities are classified as long-term.

5 Illustrate adjusting and closing entries for a merchandise firm (pp. 178–81).

- The adjusting entries for a merchandise firm are similar to those of a service firm, studied in earlier chapters.

- Closing procedures are as follows:
  (a) Close the beginning inventory and all income statement accounts with debit balances, and debit the total to the Income Summary account.
  (b) Record the ending inventory, close all income statement accounts with credit balances, and credit the total to the Income Summary account.
  (c) Transfer the balance of the Income Summary account to the owner's capital account (the Retained Earnings account in a corporation).
  (d) Transfer the balance of the owner's drawing account to the owner's capital account.

KEY TERMS USED IN THIS CHAPTER

cash discount 163
classified financial statements 175
cost of goods sold 161
credit memorandum 166
credit period 163
current assets 178
current liabilities 178
discount period 163
discounts lost 170
gross profit on sales 159
gross profit percentage 160
inventory 174
invoice 162
long-term assets 178
long-term liabilities 178
merchandise inventory 174
net price method 170
purchases 166
purchase invoice 162
purchase order 161
purchase requisition 161
receiving report 162
return on sales 177
sales 165
sales invoice 162
trade discounts 163
transportation in 171
transportation out 171

SELF-TEST QUESTIONS FOR REVIEW

(Answers are at the end of this chapter.)

1. Which of the following documents does *not* initiate an entry to be made in the accounts?
   (a) Sales invoice.
   (b) Purchase invoice.
   (c) Purchase order.
   (d) Credit memorandum.
2. Troy, Inc., purchased merchandise from Athens, Inc., for $3,600 list price, subject to a trade discount of 25%. The goods were purchased on terms of 2/10, n/30, F.O.B. destination. Troy paid $100 transportation costs. Troy returned $400 (list price) of the merchandise to Athens and later paid the amount due Athens within the discount period. The amount paid is
   (a) $2,254 (b) $2,252 (c) $2,246 (d) $2,352
3. Bennett, Inc., which uses the net price method of recording purchases, bought merchandise for $800, terms 2/10, n/30. If Bennett returns $200 of the goods to the vendor, the entry to record the return should include a
   (a) Debit to Accounts Payable of $200.
   (b) Debit to Discounts Lost of $4.
   (c) Credit to Purchases Returns and Allowances of $196.
   (d) Debit to Purchases Returns and Allowances of $196.
4. A firm's gross profit on net sales is 40%. The firm had net sales of $500,000 and net cost of purchases of $290,000. If the beginning inventory was $60,000, the ending inventory was
   (a) $50,000 (b) $150,000 (c) $30,000 (d) $90,000

5. In preparing a 10-column worksheet for a merchandising firm,
   (a) The beginning inventory is extended as a credit in the income statement columns.
   (b) The beginning inventory is extended as a credit in the balance sheet columns.
   (c) The ending inventory is shown as a debit in the income statement columns and as a credit in the balance sheet columns.
   (d) The ending inventory is shown as a credit in the income statement columns and as a debit in the balance sheet columns.

DEMONSTRATION PROBLEM FOR REVIEW

Sportcraft, a wholesaler of sporting goods, had the following trial balance at December 31 of the current year:

Sportcraft
Trial Balance
December 31, 19XX

	Debit	Credit
Cash	$ 6,200	
Accounts Receivable	28,000	
Inventory, January 1	45,000	
Office Supplies on Hand	800	
Prepaid Insurance	2,100	
Land	34,000	
Building	82,000	
Accumulated Depreciation—Building		$ 16,000
Office Equipment	21,300	
Accumulated Depreciation—Office Equipment		5,300
Accounts Payable		19,000
J. Moran, Capital		161,200
J. Moran, Drawing	10,000	
Sales		252,000
Sales Discounts	3,500	
Purchases	151,000	
Purchases Returns and Allowances		2,400
Transportation In	8,200	
Sales Salaries Expense	27,600	
Transportation Out	7,800	
Advertising Expense	6,100	
Office Salaries Expense	22,300	
	$455,900	$455,900

The following information is available at December 31:

1. Office supplies on hand at December 31 are $250.
2. Prepaid insurance at December 31 is $1,500.
3. Depreciation for the year is building, $2,000; office equipment, $2,400.
4. Salaries payable at December 31 are sales salaries, $300; office salaries, $200.
5. Inventory at December 31 is $43,500.

REQUIRED

(a) Prepare a 10-column worksheet for the year.
(b) Prepare a classified income statement for the year. Of the insurance expense and depreciation expense on the building, 75% is treated as selling expense and 25% is treated as administrative expense.
(c) Prepare a classified balance sheet at December 31.
(d) Prepare adjusting entries in general journal form.
(e) Prepare closing entries in general journal form.

SOLUTION TO DEMONSTRATION PROBLEM

(a) See page 186.

(b)

Sportcraft
Income Statement
For the Year Ended December 31, 19XX

Revenue			
Sales		$252,000	
Less: Sales Discounts		3,500	
Net Sales			$248,500
Cost of Goods Sold			
Inventory, January 1		$ 45,000	
Add: Net Cost of Purchases			
Purchases	$151,000		
Less: Purchases Returns and Allowances	2,400		
	$148,600		
Add: Transportation In	8,200	156,800	
Cost of Goods Available for Sale		$201,800	
Less: Inventory, December 31		43,500	
Cost of Goods Sold			158,300
Gross Profit on Sales			$ 90,200
Operating Expenses			
Selling Expenses			
Sales Salaries Expense	$ 27,900		
Transportation Out	7,800		
Advertising Expense	6,100		
Insurance Expense	450		
Depreciation Expense—Building	1,500		
Total Selling Expenses		$ 43,750	
Administrative Expenses			
Office Salaries Expense	$ 22,500		
Office Supplies Expense	550		
Insurance Expense	150		
Depreciation Expense—Building	500		
Depreciation Expense—Office Equipment	2,400		
Total Administrative Expenses		26,100	
Total Operating Expenses			69,850
Net Income			$ 20,350

(c)

Sportcraft
Balance Sheet
December 31, 19XX

ASSETS

Current Assets		
Cash	$ 6,200	
Accounts Receivable	28,000	
Inventory	43,500	
Office Supplies on Hand	250	
Prepaid Insurance	1,500	
Total Current Assets		$ 79,450

(continued)

Sportcraft
Worksheet
For the Year Ended December 31, 19XX

Description	Trial Balance		Adjustments		Adjusted Trial Balance		Income Statement		Balance Sheet	
	Debit	Credit	Debit	Credit	Debit	Credit	Debit	Credit	Debit	Credit
Cash	6,200				6,200				6,200	
Accounts Receivable	28,000				28,000				28,000	
Inventory (January 1)	45,000				45,000		45,000			
Office Supplies on Hand	800			(1) 550	250				250	
Prepaid Insurance	2,100			(2) 600	1,500				1,500	
Land	34,000				34,000				34,000	
Building	82,000				82,000				82,000	
Accumulated Depreciation—Building		16,000		(3) 2,000		18,000				18,000
Office Equipment	21,300				21,300				21,300	
Accumulated Depreciation—Office Equipment		5,300		(3) 2,400		7,700				7,700
Accounts Payable		19,000				19,000				19,000
J. Moran, Capital		161,200				161,200				161,200
J. Moran, Drawing	10,000				10,000				10,000	
Sales		252,000				252,000		252,000		
Sales Discounts	3,500				3,500		3,500			
Purchases	151,000				151,000		151,000			
Purchases Returns and Allowances		2,400				2,400		2,400		
Transportation In	8,200				8,200		8,200			
Sales Salaries Expense	27,600		(4) 300		27,900		27,900			
Transportation Out	7,800				7,800		7,800			
Advertising Expense	6,100				6,100		6,100			
Office Salaries Expense	22,300		(4) 200		22,500		22,500			
	455,900	455,900								
Office Supplies Expense			(1) 550		550		550			
Insurance Expense			(2) 600		600		600			
Depreciation Expense—Building			(3) 2,000		2,000		2,000			
Depreciation Expense—Office Equipment			(3) 2,400		2,400		2,400			
Salaries Payable				(4) 500		500				500
			6,050	6,050	460,800	460,800				
Inventory (December 31)								43,500	43,500	
							277,550	297,900	226,750	206,400
Net Income							20,350			20,350
							297,900	297,900	226,750	226,750

Long-term Assets			
Land		$34,000	
Building	$82,000		
Less: Accumulated Depreciation	18,000	64,000	
Office Equipment	$21,300		
Less: Accumulated Depreciation	7,700	13,600	
Total Long-term Assets			111,600
Total Assets			$191,050

LIABILITIES AND OWNER'S EQUITY

Current Liabilities		
Accounts Payable	$19,000	
Salaries Payable	500	
Total Current Liabilities		$ 19,500
Owner's Equity		
J. Moran, Capital*		171,550
Total Liabilities and Owner's Equity		$191,050

*$161,200 Beginning Balance + $20,350 Net Income − $10,000 Withdrawals = $171,550.

(d) Adjusting entries:

Dec. 31	Office Supplies Expense	550	
	Office Supplies on Hand		550
	To reflect as expense supplies used during the year.		
31	Insurance Expense	600	
	Prepaid Insurance		600
	To reflect as expense insurance expired during the year.		
31	Depreciation Expense—Building	2,000	
	Depreciation Expense—Office Equipment	2,400	
	Accumulated Depreciation—Building		2,000
	Accumulated Depreciation—Office Equipment		2,400
	To record depreciation on building and office equipment.		
31	Sales Salaries Expense	300	
	Office Salaries Expense	200	
	Salaries Payable		500
	To reflect salaries earned by employees but unpaid at December 31.		

(e) Closing entries:

Dec. 31	Income Summary	277,550	
	Inventory (January 1)		45,000
	Sales Discounts		3,500
	Purchases		151,000
	Transportation In		8,200
	Sales Salaries Expense		27,900
	Transportation Out		7,800
	Advertising Expense		6,100
	Office Salaries Expense		22,500
	Office Supplies Expense		550

(continued)

Date	Account	Debit	Credit
	Insurance Expense		600
	Depreciation Expense—Building		2,000
	Depreciation Expense—Office Equipment		2,400
	To close the beginning inventory and income statement accounts with debit balances.		
Dec. 31	Inventory (December 31)	43,500	
	Sales	252,000	
	Purchases Returns and Allowances	2,400	
	Income Summary		297,900
	To record the ending inventory and to close income statement accounts with credit balances.		
31	Income Summary	20,350	
	J. Moran, Capital		20,350
	To close the Income Summary account and transfer net income to the owner's capital account.		
31	J. Moran, Capital	10,000	
	J. Moran, Drawing		10,000
	To close the drawing account.		

QUESTIONS

5–1 What is the most significant difference between the income statement of a service firm and that of a merchandising firm?

5–2 What is meant by *gross profit on sales,* and of what significance is this item to management?

5–3 Explain the nature, purpose, and key information appearing on each of the following forms:
(a) Purchase requisition.
(b) Purchase order.
(c) Sales invoice.
(d) Receiving report.
(e) Credit memorandum.

5–4 Differentiate between (a) credit period and discount period and (b) cash discounts and trade discounts.

5–5 For the accounts titled Sales Returns and Allowances and Purchases Returns and Allowances, indicate (a) the justification for their use; (b) their normal balances (debit or credit); and (c) their position in the financial statements.

5–6 Explain the appropriate treatment in the income statement of the accounts Transportation In and Transportation Out.

5–7 Under each of the following selling terms, who (buyer or seller) would bear the freight cost and who would *remit* to the freight company?
(a) F.O.B. shipping point, freight collect.
(b) F.O.B. destination, freight prepaid.
(c) F.O.B. shipping point, freight prepaid.
(d) F.O.B. destination, freight collect.

5–8 On April 2, Jason Company purchased $750 worth of merchandise from Lake Company, F.O.B. shipping point, freight collect, terms 2/10, n/30. On April 4, Jason Company returned $100 of the goods for credit. On April 5, Jason paid $50 freight on the shipment. If Jason settles its account with Lake Company on April 11, how much would the company remit?

5–9 How much does Jason remit in Question 5–8 if the terms are F.O.B. destination rather than F.O.B. shipping point?

5–10 A wholesale firm's gross purchases during an accounting period totaled $60,000, and Transportation In was $2,500. If the firm returned goods amounting to $1,000 and took $500 in purchases discounts during the period, what was the net purchases cost for the period?

5–11 When an unadjusted trial balance of the general ledger is taken for a merchandising firm on a periodic inventory basis, does the beginning inventory or the ending inventory appear in the trial balance? Explain.

5–12 The beginning inventory for a merchandising firm was $68,000 and the ending inventory is $62,000. If the net cost of purchases was $90,000 and net sales were $160,000, what was the gross profit?

5–13 A portion of a worksheet for a merchandising firm follows. Identify the columns—A, B, C, or D—into which the balance of any of the listed accounts should be extended.

	Income Statement		Balance Sheet	
	Debit (A)	Credit (B)	Debit (C)	Credit (D)
Inventory (Beginning)				
Sales				
Sales Returns and Allowances				
Purchases				
Purchases Returns and Allowances				
Purchases Discounts				
Transportation In				
Salaries Payable				
Inventory (Ending)				

5–14 Define (a) current assets and (b) current liabilities.

5–15 Chavez Company had net sales of $800,000, cost of goods sold of $512,000, and net income of $40,000. Compute (a) its gross profit percentage and (b) its return on sales.

5–16 A firm using the net price method of recording merchandise purchases bought goods with a price of $650, terms 2/10, n/30. What amount would be debited to the Purchases account?

EXERCISES

Trade and cash discount calculations

5–17 On April 1, Waters Company sold merchandise with a list price of $6,000. For each of the sales terms below, determine (a) the amount recorded as a sale and (b) the proper amount of cash received.

	Applicable Trade Discount (%)	Credit Terms	Date Paid
1.	30	2/10, n/30	April 8
2.	40	1/10, n/30	April 15
3.	—	2/10, n/30	April 11
4.	20	1/15, n/30	April 14
5.	40	n/30	April 28

Cash discount and remittance calculations

5–18 For each of the following Moore Company purchases, assume that credit terms are 2/10, n/30 and that any credit memorandum was issued and known before Moore Company made the payments.

	Amount	Shipping Terms	Prepaid Freight (by seller)	Credit Memorandum
1.	$ 600	F.O.B. shipping point	$ 50	$150
2.	1,200	F.O.B. destination	120	100
3.	1,400	F.O.B. shipping point	—	200
4.	2,000	F.O.B. shipping point	150	—

In each case, determine (a) the appropriate cash discount available and (b) the cash remitted if the payment is made within the discount period.

Entries for sale, return, and remittance

5–19 On June 8, Ross Company sold merchandise listing for $800 to Barr Company, terms 2/10, n/30. On June 12, $200 worth of the merchandise was returned because it was the wrong color. On June 18, Ross Company received a check for the amount due.

Record the general journal entries made by Ross Company for the above transactions.

Entries for purchase, return, and remittance

5–20 On March 10, Wild Company purchased $9,000 worth of merchandise from Evans Company, terms 1/10, n/30, F.O.B. shipping point. On March 12, Wild paid $80 freight on the shipment. On March 15, Wild returned $100 worth of the merchandise for credit. Final payment was made to Evans on March 19. Wild Company records purchases at invoice price.

(a) Give the general journal entries that Wild should make on March 12, March 15, and March 19.

(b) Give the entries that Wild should make on these three dates if the terms are F.O.B. destination.

Entries for merchandise transactions on seller's and buyer's records

5–21 The following are selected transactions of Becket, Inc.:

April 20 Sold and shipped on account to Hayes Stores merchandise listing for $1,200, terms 2/10, n/30.

27 Hayes Stores returned defective merchandise billed at $100 on April 20.

29 Received from Hayes Stores a check for full settlement of the April 20 transaction.

Record, in general journal form, the above transactions as they would appear on the books of (a) Becket, Inc., and (b) Hayes Stores. Hayes Stores records purchases at invoice price.

Net price method of recording purchases

5–22 James, Inc., uses the net price method of recording purchases. On July 1, the firm purchased merchandise for $900, terms 2/10, n/30. On July 5, the firm returned $300 of the merchandise to the seller. Payment of the account occurred on July 8.

(a) Give the general journal entries for July 1, July 5, and July 8.

(b) Assuming that the account was settled on July 14, give the entry for payment on that date.

Determination of omitted income statement data

5–23 The box below contains portions of five unrelated income statements, each with certain data omitted. Fill in the lettered blanks with the appropriate amounts.

	1	2	3	4	5
Net Sales	$60,000	$ (d)	$90,000	$70,000	$160,000
Beginning Inventory	10,000	20,000	(g)	25,000	(m)
Net Cost of Purchases	40,000	(e)	60,000	40,000	90,000
Cost of Goods Available for Sale	(a)	(f)	90,000	(j)	(n)
Ending Inventory	12,000	15,000	(h)	(k)	30,000
Cost of Goods Sold	(b)	60,000	(i)	(l)	(o)
Gross Profit	(c)	20,000	15,000	24,000	50,000

Effects of inventory errors

5–24 A company's operating figures for four consecutive periods are given below.

	Period (1)	(2)	(3)	(4)
Beginning Inventory	$25,000	$20,000	$15,000	$23,000
Net Cost of Purchases	45,000	55,000	50,000	45,000
Cost of Goods Available for Sale	$70,000	$75,000	$65,000	$68,000
Ending Inventory	20,000	15,000	23,000	16,000
Cost of Goods Sold	$50,000	$60,000	$42,000	$52,000

Assuming that the following errors were made, compute the correct cost of goods sold for each period:

Period	Error in Ending Inventory
1	Overstated $2,000
2	Understated $3,000
3	Overstated $1,000

Closing entries

5–25 A portion of the December 31 worksheet for Byrd Distributors is shown below. For simplicity, all operating expenses have been combined.

	Income Statement Debit	Income Statement Credit	Balance Sheet Debit	Balance Sheet Credit
Inventory, January 1	64,000			
Byrd, Capital				140,000
Byrd, Drawing			12,000	
Sales		500,000		
Sales Returns and Allowances	1,500			
Sales Discounts	4,500			
Purchases	330,000			
Purchases Returns and Allowances		3,000		
Purchases Discounts		6,600		
Transportation In	8,000			
Operating Expenses	125,000			
Inventory, December 31		59,000	59,000	

Using the given information, prepare the general journal entries to close the books.

Classified balance sheet

5–26 From the following accounts, listed in alphabetical order, prepare a classified balance sheet for Reilly Wholesalers at December 31, 19XX. All accounts have normal balances.

Accounts Receivable	$ 31,500	Inventory	$ 83,600
Accounts Payable	31,200	Land	32,000
Accumulated Depreciation, Building	16,500	Mortgage Payable	56,000
		Office Equipment	15,000
Accumulated Depreciation, Office Equipment	3,600	Office Supplies on Hand	1,200
		Salaries Payable	4,500
Building	65,000	T. Reilly, Capital	132,500
Cash	16,000		

PROBLEMS

Entries for merchandise transactions on seller's and buyer's records

5–27 The following transactions occurred between the Whelan Company and Mann Stores, Inc., during March of the current year.

Mar. 8 Whelan sold $3,300 worth of merchandise to Mann Stores, terms 2/10, n/30, F.O.B. shipping point.

Mar. 10 Mann Stores paid freight charges on the shipment from Whelan Company, $50.

12 Mann Stores returned $300 of the merchandise shipped on March 8. Whelan issued a credit memorandum for this amount.

17 Whelan received full payment for the net amount due from the March 8 sale.

20 Mann Stores returned goods that had been billed originally at $100. Whelan issued a check for $98.

REQUIRED

Record the above transactions in general journal form as they would appear on (a) the books of Whelan Company and (b) the books of Mann Stores, Inc. Mann Stores, Inc., records purchases at invoice price.

Entries for merchandise transactions

5–28 Melville Corporation, which began business on August 1 of the current year, sells on terms of 2/10, n/30, F.O.B. shipping point. Credit terms and freight terms for its purchases vary with the supplier. Selected transactions for August are given below. Unless noted, all transactions are on account and involve merchandise held for resale. All purchases are recorded at invoice price.

Aug. 1 Purchased merchandise from Norris, Inc., $850, terms 2/10, n/30, F.O.B. shipping point, freight collect.

4 Purchased merchandise from Cooper Company, $1,600, terms 2/10, n/30, F.O.B. destination. Freight charges of $70 were prepaid by Cooper Company.

5 Paid freight on shipment from Norris, Inc., $40.

7 Sold merchandise to Denton Corporation, $1,200.

7 Paid freight on shipment to Denton Corporation, $60, and billed Denton for the charges.

9 Returned $150 worth of the merchandise purchased August 1 from Norris, Inc., because it was defective.

9 Issued a credit memorandum to Denton Corporation for $200 worth of merchandise returned by Denton.

10 Paid Norris, Inc., the amount due.

14 Purchased from Chambers, Inc., goods with a list price of $2,000. Melville Corporation was entitled to a 25% trade discount; terms 1/10, n/30, F.O.B. shipping point, freight collect.

15 Paid freight on shipment from Chambers, Inc., $70.

17 Received the amount due from Denton Corporation.

18 Sold merchandise to Weber, Inc., $2,400.

19 Paid Cooper Company for the amount due on its August 4 invoice.

20 Paid freight on August 18 shipment to Weber, Inc., $80.

20 Received a credit memorandum of $100 from Chambers, Inc., adjusting the price charged for merchandise purchased on August 14.

24 Paid Chambers, Inc., the amount due.

28 Received the amount due from Weber, Inc.

REQUIRED

Record the transactions for Melville Corporation in general journal form.

Preparation of a worksheet

5–29 The unadjusted trial balance of Sloan Distributors on December 31 of the current year is shown on page 193.

Sloan Distributors
Trial Balance
December 31, 19XX

	Debit	Credit
Cash	$ 7,600	
Accounts Receivable	40,100	
Inventory (January 1)	69,000	
Prepaid Insurance	3,600	
Supplies on Hand	3,200	
Delivery Equipment	40,000	
Accumulated Depreciation		$ 9,500
Accounts Payable		34,800
Sloan, Capital		84,000
Sloan, Drawing	13,000	
Sales		406,000
Sales Returns and Allowances	5,800	
Sales Discounts	7,300	
Purchases	261,000	
Purchases Returns and Allowances		2,600
Purchases Discounts		5,100
Transportation In	6,400	
Salaries Expense	54,000	
Rent Expense	20,000	
Gas, Oil, and Repairs Expense	9,200	
Utilities Expense	1,800	
	$542,000	$542,000

The following data are available at December 31:

1. Prepaid insurance at December 31 is $1,200.
2. Supplies on hand at December 31 amount to $2,100.
3. Depreciation on the delivery equipment is 20% per year.
4. At December 31, the company owes its employees $600 in salaries.
5. At December 31, the company has not recorded a utility bill for $140.
6. Inventory at December 31 is $72,000.

REQUIRED

Prepare a 10-column worksheet for Sloan Distributors for 19XX.

Income statement and calculation of gross profit rate and return on sales

5–30 The following selected information is available for the Oakdale Wholesale Company for March of the current year.

Purchases	$43,000
Sales	98,500
Transportation In	2,000
Purchases Discounts	800
Inventory (March 1)	37,000
Inventory (March 31)	22,000
Purchases Returns and Allowances	700
Sales Returns and Allowances	1,500
Transportation Out	450
Rent Expense	1,600
Sales Salaries Expense	19,200
Sales Discounts	1,200
Depreciation Expense—Office Equipment	100
Office Supplies Expense	240

Office Salaries Expense	6,550
Advertising Expense	1,500
Insurance Expense (a selling expense)	160

REQUIRED
(a) Prepare the March income statement for Oakdale Wholesale Company.
(b) Calculate the ratio of gross profit to net sales and express it as a percentage.
(c) Calculate the ratio of net income to net sales and express it as a percentage.

Worksheet, financial statements, and adjusting, closing, and reversing entries

5–31 Yates Trading Company, whose accounting year ends on December 31, had the following normal balances in its general ledger at December 31 of the current year:

Cash	6,500	Sales	$320,000
Accounts Receivable	12,800	Sales Returns and Allowances	2,200
Inventory (January 1)	52,000	Sales Discounts	2,800
Prepaid Insurance	3,000	Purchases	206,000
Office Supplies on Hand	2,100	Purchases Returns and Allowances	1,900
Furniture and Fixtures	10,500	Purchases Discounts	2,100
Accumulated Depreciation—Furniture and Fixtures	2,500	Transportation In	4,500
Delivery Equipment	42,000	Sales Salaries Expense	41,000
Accumulated Depreciation—Delivery Equipment	6,000	Delivery Expense	5,400
Accounts Payable	20,500	Advertising Expense	2,800
Notes Payable (Long-term)	15,000	Rent Expense	7,200
R. Yates, Capital	68,000	Office Salaries Expense	28,000
R. Yates, Drawing	4,800	Utilities Expense	2,400

Rent expense and utilities expense are administrative expenses. During the year, the accounting department prepared monthly statements using worksheets, but no adjusting entries were made in the journals and ledgers. Data for the year-end procedures are as follows:

1. Prepaid insurance, December 31 (75% of insurance expense is classified as selling expense, and 25% is classified as administrative expense)	$ 600
2. Office supplies on hand, December 31	700
3. Depreciation expense on furniture and fixtures for the year (an administrative expense)	900
4. Depreciation expense on delivery equipment for the year	6,500
5. Salaries payable, December 31 ($900 sales salaries and $600 office salaries)	1,500
6. Inventory, December 31	56,500

REQUIRED
(a) Prepare a worksheet for the current year.
(b) Prepare a classified income statement for the year.
(c) Prepare a classified balance sheet at December 31.
(d) Record the necessary adjusting entries in general journal form.
(e) Record the closing entries in general journal form.
(f) Record any necessary reversing entries in general journal form.

Preparation of income statement from incomplete data

5–32 While on her way to the bank to negotiate a loan, Linda Evans, the treasurer of Conway, Inc., realizes that the income statement for the current year is missing from her papers. She has a December 31 balance sheet, however, and after searching through her papers, locates an unadjusted trial balance taken at December 31. She arrives at your office shortly before her appointment at the bank and asks your assistance in preparing an income statement for the year. The available data at December 31 are given on page 195.

	Unadjusted Trial Balance Debit	Unadjusted Trial Balance Credit	Balance Sheet Data
Cash	$ 39,000		$39,000
Accounts Receivable	45,500		45,500
Inventory	76,000		80,000
Office Supplies on Hand	3,100		1,400
Prepaid Insurance	3,200		2,000
Delivery Equipment	52,000		52,000
Accumulated Depreciation		$ 16,500	(24,500)
			$195,400
Accounts Payable		39,000	$ 39,000
Salaries Payable			400
Capital Stock		100,000	100,000
Retained Earnings		32,000	56,000
Sales		250,000	
Purchases	164,000		
Rent Expense	8,200		
Salaries Expense	34,000		
Advertising Expense	4,200		
Delivery Expense	8,300		
	$437,500	$437,500	$195,400

REQUIRED:
Use the given data to prepare the year's income statement for Conway, Inc., for Linda Evans. Ms. Evans informs you that the amounts shown in the unadjusted trial balance for Inventory, Office Supplies on Hand, Prepaid Insurance, and Accumulated Depreciation are the account balances at January 1 of the current year. No dividends were declared or paid during the year.

Effect of worksheet errors

5–33 The first six columns of a 10-column worksheet prepared for the Wesley Sport Shop are as follows:

	Trial Balance Debit	Trial Balance Credit	Adjustments Debit	Adjustments Credit	Adjusted Trial Balance Debit	Adjusted Trial Balance Credit
Cash	9,000				9,000	
Inventory (January 1)	36,000				36,000	
Office Supplies on Hand	1,000			600	400	
Prepaid Insurance	1,200				1,200	
Equipment	30,000				30,000	
Accumulated Depreciation		6,000		3,000		9,000
Accounts Payable		8,000				8,000
J. Wesley, Capital		48,000				48,000
J. Wesley, Drawing	5,000				5,000	
Sales		120,000				120,000
Purchases	65,000				65,000	
Transportation In	1,800				1,800	
Rent Expense	3,000				3,000	
Salaries Expense	30,000		300		30,300	
	182,000	182,000				
Depreciation Expense			3,000		3,000	
Salaries Payable				300		300
Office Supplies Expense			600		600	
			3,900	3,900	185,300	185,300
Inventory (December 31)						
Net Income						

In completing the worksheet, Wesley's accountant made the following errors:

1. The adjustment for expired insurance was omitted; premiums amounting to $900 expired during the year.
2. The $5,000 balance of Wesley's drawing account was extended as a debit in the income statement columns.
3. The $300 credit to Salaries Payable was extended as a credit in the income statement columns.
4. The January 1 Inventory balance of $36,000 was extended as a credit in the income statement columns.
5. The December 31 Inventory balance of $40,000 was recorded as a debit in the income statement columns and as a credit in the balance sheet columns.

REQUIRED

(a) Which of the errors would cause the worksheet not to balance?

(b) Without completing the worksheet, calculate the net income for the year. Assume that the accountant made no other errors and that the worksheet totals, before adding net income or net loss, were:

	Debit	Credit
Income statement	$148,700	$156,300
Balance sheet	40,600	105,000

ALTERNATE PROBLEMS

Entries for merchandise transactions on seller's and buyer's records

5–27A Fortune Distributing Company had the following transactions with Cornwall, Inc.:

Nov. 10 Fortune sold and shipped $3,000 worth of merchandise to Cornwall, terms 2/10, n/30, F.O.B. shipping point.

12 Cornwall, Inc., paid freight charges on the shipment from Fortune Company, $180.

14 Fortune issued a credit memo for $300 for merchandise returned by Cornwall.

19 Fortune received payment in full for the net amount due on the November 10 sale.

24 Cornwall returned goods that had originally been billed at $250. Fortune issued a check for $245.

REQUIRED

Record the above transactions in general journal form as they would appear (a) on the books of Fortune Distributing Company and (b) on the books of Cornwall, Inc. Cornwall, Inc., records purchases at invoice price.

Entries for merchandise transactions

5–28A The Dover Company was established on July 1 of the current year. Its sales terms are 2/10, n/30, F.O.B. destination. Credit terms for its purchases vary with the supplier. Selected transactions for the first month of operations are given below. Unless noted, all transactions are on account and involve merchandise held for resale. All purchases are recorded at invoice price.

July 1 Purchased goods from Dawson, Inc., $950; terms 1/10, n/30, F.O.B. shipping point, freight collect.

2 Purchased goods from Penn Company, $2,100, terms 2/10, n/30, F.O.B. destination. Freight charges of $80 were prepaid by Penn.

3 Paid freight on shipment from Dawson, $40.

5 Sold merchandise to Ward, Inc., $650.

5 Paid freight on shipment to Ward, Inc., $30.

July 8 Returned $150 worth of the goods purchased July 1 from Dawson, Inc., because some goods were damaged.
9 Issued credit memorandum to Ward, Inc., for $100 worth of merchandise returned.
10 Paid Dawson, Inc., the amount due.
10 Purchased goods from Dorn Company with a list price of $1,200. Dover was entitled to a $33\frac{1}{3}$% trade discount; terms 2/10, n/30, F.O.B. destination, freight collect.
11 Paid freight on shipment from Dorn Company, $65.
15 Received the amount due from Ward, Inc.
15 Sold merchandise to Colby Corporation, $1,600.
16 Mailed a check to Penn Company for the net amount due on its July 2 invoice.
17 Received a notice from Colby Corporation stating that it had paid freight of $60 on the July 15 shipment.
18 Received a credit memorandum of $50 from Dorn Company, as an allowance for defective merchandise purchased on July 10.
19 Paid Dorn Company the amount due.
25 Received the amount due from Colby Corporation.

REQUIRED
Record the transactions for Dover Company in general journal form.

Preparation of a worksheet

5–29A The unadjusted trial balance of Omaha Corporation on December 31 of the current year is shown below:

Omaha Corporation
Trial Balance
December 31, 19XX

	Debit	Credit
Cash	$ 21,500	
Accounts Receivable	32,600	
Inventory (January 1)	56,000	
Prepaid Insurance	900	
Supplies on Hand	1,700	
Furniture and Fixtures	16,000	
Accumulated Depreciation—Furniture and Fixtures		$ 1,800
Delivery Equipment	32,500	
Accumulated Depreciation—Delivery Equipment		9,500
Accounts Payable		8,700
Capital Stock		100,000
Retained Earnings		38,000
Sales		187,000
Sales Returns and Allowances	2,400	
Sales Discounts	2,000	
Purchases	110,000	
Purchases Returns and Allowances		2,800
Purchases Discounts		1,400
Transportation In	5,600	
Salaries Expense	46,000	
Rent Expense	10,400	
Delivery Expense	8,200	
Utilities Expense	3,400	
	$349,200	$349,200

The following data are available at December 31:

1. Prepaid insurance at December 31 is $180.
2. Supplies on hand at December 31 amount to $800.
3. Depreciation on the furniture and fixtures is 10% per year.
4. Depreciation on the delivery equipment is 20% per year.
5. At December 31, accrued salaries total $700.
6. Inventory at December 31 is $60,000.

REQUIRED

Prepare a 10-column worksheet for Omaha Corporation for 19XX.

Income statement and calculation of gross profit rate and return on sales

5–30A The following selected information is available for the Harper Trading Company for February of the current year.

Purchases	$ 82,000
Sales	145,000
Transportation In	1,800
Purchases Discounts	1,400
Inventory, February 1	31,500
Inventory, February 28	28,000
Purchases Returns and Allowances	1,600
Sales Returns and Allowances	900
Transportation Out	3,800
Rent Expense	6,000
Salaries Expense	30,500
Sales Discounts	1,100
Depreciation Expense	2,800

REQUIRED

(a) Prepare a February income statement for Harper Trading Company.
(b) Calculate the ratio of gross profit to net sales and express it as a percentage.
(c) Express the ratio of net profit to net sales as a percentage.

Worksheet, financial statements, and adjusting, closing, and reversing entries

5–31A Diamond Distributors, whose accounting year ends on December 31, had the following normal balances in its ledger accounts at December 31 of the current year:

Cash	$16,400	Sales	$590,000
Accounts Receivable	26,500	Sales Returns and Allowances	4,800
Inventory (January 1)	70,000	Sales Discounts	8,200
Prepaid Insurance	3,600	Purchases	395,000
Office Supplies on Hand	2,400	Purchases Returns and Allowances	1,600
Furniture and Fixtures	14,000	Purchases Discounts	4,200
Accumulated Depreciation—Furniture and Fixtures	5,400	Transportation In	17,400
Delivery Equipment	35,000	Sales Salaries Expense	54,000
Accumulated Depreciation—Delivery Equipment	12,200	Delivery Expense	18,400
Accounts Payable	34,700	Advertising Expense	13,100
Notes Payable (Long-term)	15,000	Rent Expense	15,000
L. Diamond, Capital	75,000	Office Salaries Expense	36,000
L. Diamond, Drawing	4,000	Utilities Expense	4,300

Rent expense and utilities expense are administrative expenses. During the year the accounting department prepared monthly statements using worksheets, but no adjusting entries were made in the journals and ledgers. Data for the year-end procedures are as follows:

1. Prepaid insurance, December 31 (insurance expense is classified as a selling cost)	$ 1,200
2. Office supplies on hand, December 31	900
3. Depreciation expense on furniture and fixtures for the year (an administrative expense)	1,000
4. Depreciation expense on delivery equipment for the year	5,000
5. Salaries payable, December 31 ($500 sales salaries and $300 office salaries)	800
6. Inventory, December 31	66,000

REQUIRED
(a) Prepare a worksheet for the current year.
(b) Prepare a classified income statement for the current year.
(c) Prepare a classified balance sheet at December 31.
(d) Make the necessary adjusting entries in general journal form.
(e) Make the closing entries in general journal form.
(f) Make any necessary reversing entries in general journal form.

Preparation of income statement from incomplete data

5–32A Your neighbor, James Lennon, treasurer of Nu-Art, Inc., has misplaced the firm's income statement for the current year. He needs this statement to complete a report due the next day. He comes to you with a December 31 balance sheet and an unadjusted trial balance taken at December 31 and asks if you can develop an income statement for the current year. The available data at December 31 are given below.

	Unadjusted Trial Balance		Balance Sheet Data
	Debit	Credit	
Cash	$ 28,000		$ 28,000
Accounts Receivable	42,000		42,000
Inventory	64,000		48,000
Office Supplies on Hand	900		600
Prepaid Insurance	1,500		1,000
Delivery Equipment	46,000		46,000
Accumulated Depreciation		$ 9,000	(12,000)
			$153,600
Accounts Payable		32,000	$ 32,000
Salaries Payable			1,200
Capital Stock		90,000	90,000
Retained Earnings		16,000	30,400
Sales		216,000	
Purchases	144,000		
Rent Expense	3,600		
Salaries Expense	25,000		
Advertising Expense	3,000		
Delivery Expense	5,000		
	$363,000	$363,000	$153,600

REQUIRED
Use the given data to prepare the year's income statement for Nu-Art, Inc. Mr. Lennon informs you that the amounts shown in the unadjusted trial balance for Inventory, Office Supplies on Hand, Prepaid Insurance, and Accumulated Depreciation are the account balances at January 1 of the current year. No dividends were declared or paid during the year.

Effect of worksheet errors

5–33A The first six columns of a 10-column worksheet prepared for Trent Specialty Shop are as follows:

	Trial Balance		Adjustments		Adjusted Trial Balance	
	Debit	Credit	Debit	Credit	Debit	Credit
Cash	5,600				5,600	
Inventory (January 1)	30,000				30,000	
Office Supplies on Hand	1,400				1,400	
Prepaid Insurance	600			300	300	
Equipment	25,000				25,000	
Accumulated Depreciation		4,000		2,000		6,000
Accounts Payable		10,000				10,000
L. Trent, Capital		36,000				36,000
L. Trent, Drawing	3,000				3,000	
Sales		90,000				90,000
Purchases	48,000				48,000	
Transportation In	400				400	
Rent Expense	2,000				2,000	
Salaries Expense	24,000		500		24,500	
	140,000	140,000				
Depreciation Expense			2,000		2,000	
Salaries Payable				500		500
Insurance Expense			300		300	
			2,800	2,800	142,500	142,500
Inventory (December 31)						
Net Income						

In completing the worksheet, Trent's accountant made the following errors:

1. The adjustment for Office Supplies Expense was omitted; office supplies at December 31 amounted to $600.
2. The $2,000 amount for Depreciation Expense was extended as a debit in the balance sheet columns.
3. The $500 credit to Salaries Payable was extended as a credit in the income statement columns.
4. The January 1 Inventory balance of $30,000 was extended as a credit in the income statement columns.
5. The December 31 Inventory balance of $35,000 was recorded as a debit in the income statement columns and as a credit in the balance sheet columns.

REQUIRED

(a) Which of the errors would cause the worksheet not to balance?

(b) Without completing the worksheet, calculate the net income for the year. Assume that the accountant made no other errors and that the worksheet totals, before adding net income or net loss, were:

	Debit	Credit
Income statement	$110,200	$120,500
Balance sheet	37,300	87,000

BUSINESS DECISION PROBLEM

This year's income statement for Imperial Wholesalers is given below in condensed form.

Sales	$375,000
Cost of Goods Sold	250,000
Gross Profit	$125,000
Operating Expenses	88,500
Net Income	$ 36,500

Imperial allows its customers a trade discount of 25% of list price. To arrive at the list price, Imperial adds a mark-up of 100% to its cost.

Imperial's president asks you to evaluate a proposal she has received from the sales manager to improve the company's return on sales. The memo from the sales manager states, "I suggest we permit our customers a trade discount of 30% rather than 25%. My estimates show that with the higher trade discount, we will sell 30% more units next year than this year. We can achieve this increased volume with only a 10% increase in operating expenses."

REQUIRED

(a) Compute Imperial's return on sales for this year.
(b) Compute what Imperial's return on sales will be if the sales manager's proposal is accepted and his projections are correct. Support this computation with an income statement showing the effect of the sales manager's proposal.
(c) What is your recommendation with respect to the sales manager's proposal?

ANSWERS TO SELF-TEST QUESTIONS

1. (c) **2.** (b) **3.** (c) **4.** (a) **5.** (d)

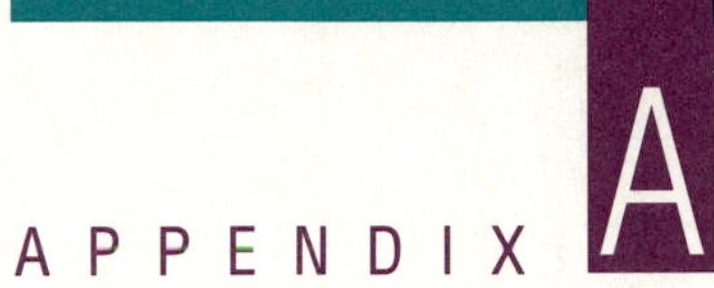

ALTERNATIVE METHOD OF RECORDING INVENTORIES

In Chapter 5, the beginning inventory of merchandise was closed and the ending inventory recorded as a part of the closing entries at the end of the accounting period. An alternative method, presented here, treats the entries for beginning and ending inventories as *adjusting* entries, rather than closing entries. To illustrate this method, we use the same data for Madison Electronics Company shown in Chapter 5.

ADJUSTING ENTRIES

Below, we repeat the four adjusting entries at year-end for Madison Electronics Company shown in Chapter 5 (page 174). In addition, we add two adjusting entries, (5) and (6), to remove the beginning inventory and to record the ending inventory. These six adjusting entries would be recorded in the journal and posted to the related ledger accounts. They would also be entered in the adjustments column of the worksheet prepared at the end of the accounting period.

1.	Dec. 31	Insurance Expense	280	
		Prepaid Insurance		280
		To charge one year's premium to expense (three-year premium, $840 paid January 1).		
2.	31	Supplies Expense	1,200	
		Supplies on Hand		1,200
		To charge to expense the supplies used during year. (Inventory of supplies is $1,600 on December 31.)		
3.	31	Depreciation Expense	6,000	
		Accumulated Depreciation		6,000
		To charge to expense one year's depreciation on delivery equipment.		
4.	31	Sales Salaries Expense	500	
		Salaries Payable		500
		To reflect the salaries earned by salespersons but not paid at December 31.		

5.	Dec. 31	Income Summary	115,000	
		Inventory		115,000
		To transfer the beginning inventory to the Income Summary account.		
6.	31	Inventory	120,000	
		Income Summary		120,000
		To record the ending inventory.		

WORKSHEET

After the adjusting entries have been entered in the worksheet (Exhibit A–1), the adjusted amounts are extended in the Adjusted Trial Balance columns. Note that the inventory adjustments have removed the $115,000 beginning inventory balance, leaving the $120,000 ending inventory amount to be extended in the adjusted trial balance. This amount is next extended as a debit in the balance sheet columns. Observe that *both* the beginning and ending inventory amounts on the income summary line in the adjustments column are extended in the adjusted trial balance columns and also in the income statement columns. The reason for extending both amounts is to have all necessary data in the income statement columns to prepare the income statement. Both inventory amounts appear in the cost of goods sold section of the statement. In Exhibit A–1 all the amounts comprising cost of goods sold appear in color to emphasize how cost of goods sold is reflected in the worksheet.

Although the alternative method yields different totals for the adjustments and adjusted trial balance columns of the worksheet, the totals of the income statement and balance sheet columns are the same as shown on page 173 of Chapter 5. The data in the financial statements is not changed in any way.

CLOSING ENTRIES

The closing entries using the alternative method of dealing with inventories are shown below. Obviously, there are no entries for inventory since these have already been transferred to the Income Summary account by means of adjusting entries.

Dec. 31	Income Summary	418,700	
	Sales Returns and Allowances		2,500
	Sales Discounts		5,500
	Purchases		256,500
	Transportation In		9,700
	Sales Salaries Expense		64,500
	Advertising Expense		6,170
	Delivery Expense		19,250
	Office Salaries Expense		27,500
	Rent Expense		16,500
	Utilities Expense		3,100
	Insurance Expense		280
	Supplies Expense		1,200
	Depreciation Expense		6,000
	To close income statement accounts with debit balances.		

EXHIBIT A–1

Madison Electronics Company
Worksheet
For the Year Ended December 31, 19XX

Description	Trial Balance Debit	Trial Balance Credit	Adjustments Debit	Adjustments Credit	Adjusted Trial Balance Debit	Adjusted Trial Balance Credit	Income Statement Debit	Income Statement Credit	Balance Sheet Debit	Balance Sheet Credit
Cash	18,240				18,240				18,240	
Accounts Receivable	32,000				32,000				32,000	
Inventory	115,000		(6) 120,000	(5) 115,000	120,000				120,000	
Prepaid Insurance	840			(1) 280	560				560	
Supplies on Hand	2,800			(2) 1,200	1,600				1,600	
Delivery Equipment	30,000				30,000				30,000	
Accumulated Depreciation		4,300		(3) 6,000		10,300				10,300
Accounts Payable		17,500				17,500				17,500
Long-term Notes Payable		20,000				20,000				20,000
J. Madison, Capital		134,000				134,000				134,000
J. Madison, Drawing	5,400				5,400				5,400	
Sales		433,000				433,000		433,000		
Sales Returns and Allowances	2,500				2,500		2,500			
Sales Discounts	5,500				5,500		5,500			
Purchases	256,500				256,500		256,500			
Purchases Returns and Allowances		1,800				1,800		1,800		
Purchases Discounts		4,400				4,400		4,400		
Transportation In	9,700				9,700		9,700			
Sales Salaries Expense	64,000		(4) 500		64,500		64,500			
Advertising Expense	6,170				6,170		6,170			
Delivery Expense	19,250				19,250		19,250			
Office Salaries Expense	27,500				27,500		27,500			
Rent Expense	16,500				16,500		16,500			
Utilities Expense	3,100				3,100		3,100			
	615,000	615,000								
Insurance Expense			(1) 280		280		280			
Supplies Expense			(2) 1,200		1,200		1,200			
Depreciation Expense			(3) 6,000		6,000		6,000			
Salaries Payable				(4) 500		500				500
Income Summary			(5) 115,000	(6) 120,000	115,000	120,000	115,000	120,000		
			242,980	242,980	741,500	741,500	533,700	559,200	207,800	182,300
Net Income							25,500			25,500
							559,200	559,200	207,800	207,800

Dec. 31	Sales	433,000	
	Purchases Returns and Allowances	1,800	
	Purchases Discounts	4,400	
	Income Summary		439,200
	To close income statement accounts with credit balances.		
31	Income Summary	25,500	
	J. Madison, Capital		25,500
	To close the Income Summary account and transfer net income to the owner's capital account.		
31	J. Madison, Capital	5,400	
	J. Madison, Drawing		5,400
	To close the owner's drawing account to the capital account.		

Both methods of treating inventories as described in Chapter 5 and in this appendix accomplish the same results. However, there are two slight advantages to the method described in Chapter 5. First, fewer entries are needed; second, the entries to the Income Summary account in the closing process can be obtained directly from the income statement column totals.

PROBLEMS

A–1 Follow the requirements in Problem 5–29, at the end of Chapter 5, using the method described in this appendix.

A–2 Follow the requirements in Problem 5–31, at the end of Chapter 5, using the method described in this appendix.

A–3 Follow the requirements in Problem 5–29A, at the end of Chapter 5, using the method described in this appendix.

A–4 Follow the requirements in Problem 5–31A, at the end of Chapter 5, using the method described in this appendix.

6

DATA PROCESSING: MANUAL AND ELECTRONIC SYSTEMS

CHAPTER OBJECTIVES

1. Describe the difference between control accounts and subsidiary ledger accounts (pp. 207–209).
2. Provide an overview of the recording process using special journals (pp. 209–11).
3. Describe and illustrate the special journals (pp. 211–16).
4. Describe the voucher system and illustrate the use of a voucher register and a check register (pp. 217–21).
5. Discuss the use of computers for processing accounting data (pp. 221–26).

Man is a tool-using animal. . . .Without tools he is nothing, with tools he is all.

THOMAS CARLYLE

In the preceding chapters, we limited our discussion of the processing of accounting transactions to recording in a general journal and posting to a general ledger. Such a system is satisfactory for introducing basic accounting procedures. However, for two reasons, this method would be inadequate for a business having even a moderate number of transactions. First, recording all transactions in the general journal would seriously curtail the number of transactions that could be processed in a day, simply because only one person at a time could make entries. Second, transactions recorded in a general journal must be posted individually, resulting in a great deal of posting labor. Therefore, even small- and moderate-sized firms use *special journals* to make their systems flexible and to reduce the amount of posting required. The use of special journals is one of the features we consider in this chapter.

Our previous illustrations were simple and contained a single Accounts Receivable account and a single Accounts Payable account. Business firms that keep accounts with individual customers and creditors find it quite burdensome to work with a general ledger containing a large number of customer and creditor accounts. Therefore, firms often use *control accounts* in the general ledger and keep separate *subsidiary ledgers* to record accounts of individual customers and creditors.

Finally, in large businesses, the sheer volume of transactions and the need for fast processing and retrieval of information call for electronic data-processing systems. In the last section of this chapter, we describe computer processing of accounting data and compare it with manual data processing.

CONTROL ACCOUNTS AND SUBSIDIARY LEDGERS

In Chapter 3, we entered all the charges to and payments from customers of Landen TV Service in a single general ledger account. The following T account illustrates these transactions:

Accounts Receivable			
Dec. 14	900	Dec. 19	500
28	2,400		

Landen TV Service cannot bill or mail statements to customers, answer inquiries about individual customer balances, or make any collection efforts if the firm has only a single record showing total claims against customers. The company needs to know each customer's name and address, transaction dates, amounts charged for services, and amounts received on account for each account receivable.

We could solve this problem by maintaining in the general ledger an individual Account Receivable for each customer. The trial balance of such a general ledger might appear as follows:

	Trial Balance	
	Debit	Credit
Cash	$13,130	
Accounts Receivable—Customer A	300	
Accounts Receivable—Customer B	700	
Accounts Receivable—Customer C	800	
Accounts Receivable—Customer D	1,000	
(All other assets)	15,350	
(All liabilities)		$ 3,550
Owner's Capital		25,000
Owner's Drawing	800	
Revenue		5,450
(All expenses)	1,920	
	$34,000	$34,000

We can easily see the limitations of this approach. The general ledger becomes unreasonably large when hundreds of customers' accounts are involved. With thousands of customers, it becomes absolutely unworkable. Alternatively, we might use one **control account** titled Accounts Receivable in the general ledger and maintain individual customer accounts in a **subsidiary ledger.** Under this approach, the general ledger is kept to a manageable size, and a detailed record of transactions with individual customers exists.

The accounts receivable subsidiary ledger, like the general ledger, may be simply a group of accounts in a binder, or it may be a file card arrangement.[1] In either case, the order is usually alphabetical by customer name. Exhibit 6–1 shows a typical form for an accounts receivable subsidiary ledger. When the three-column form is used, abnormal balances are enclosed in parentheses or shown in red. The information placed at the top of the account varies with the needs of the business and the type of customer. Often, such information concerns the granting of credit.

The following diagram shows the relationships between the Accounts Receivable control account in the general ledger and the accounts receivable subsidiary ledger.

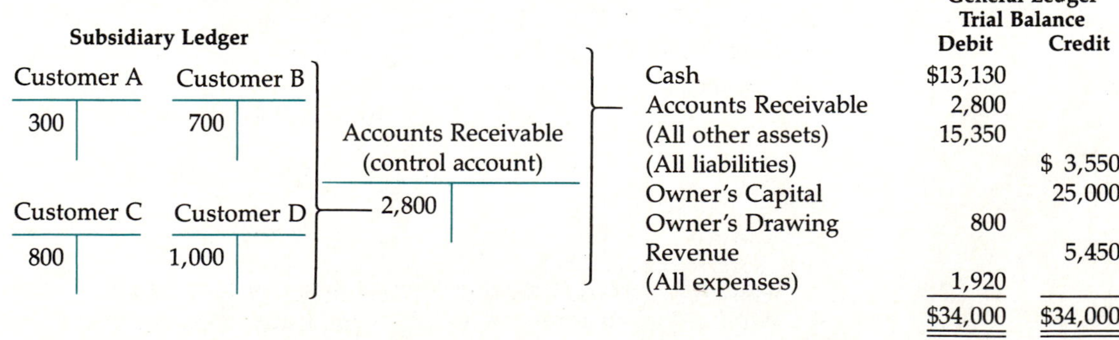

Because the total of all the balances in the accounts receivable subsidiary ledger must equal the balance in the Accounts Receivable control account in the

[1]In electronic data processing systems (discussed in the last section of this chapter), the customers' ledger might be stored on magnetic tape or disks.

EXHIBIT 6–1

CUSTOMER ACCOUNT FORM IN SUBSIDIARY LEDGER

Name ______________________

Address ______________________ Phone ______________________

Employed at ______________________ Position ______________________

Special terms ______________________ Maximum credit $ ______________________

Date		Remarks	Post Ref.	Debit	Credit	Balance

general ledger, it follows that for every amount posted to the Accounts Receivable control account, an equal amount must be posted to one or more of the customers' accounts in the accounts receivable subsidiary ledger. We will consider the specific posting procedures later in this chapter.

The control account–subsidiary ledger technique can be used to yield a detailed breakdown of many general ledger accounts, not just Accounts Receivable. Subsidiary ledgers are often used for Accounts Payable, Inventory, Buildings, and Equipment.

SPECIAL JOURNALS

Journals specifically designed in a tabular fashion to accommodate the recording of one type of transaction are called **special journals**. In addition to a general journal, most firms use at least the following special journals:

Special Journal	Specific Transactions Recorded	Posting Abbreviation
Sales journal	Sales on credit terms	S
Cash receipts journal	Receipts of cash	CR
Invoice register (purchases journal)	Purchases of merchandise and other items on credit terms	IR
Cash disbursements journal	Payments of cash	CD

Cash sales are usually recorded in the cash receipts journal rather than in the sales journal because cash is best controlled when *all* routine cash receipts are recorded in one journal. Similarly, a firm can increase control over cash disbursements by recording purchases of merchandise or other items for cash in the cash disbursements journal rather than in the purchases journal. When special journals are used, the general journal is used only for adjusting, closing, and reversing entries, and for recording transactions that do not "fit" well in any special journal. Examples of the latter include the recording of purchases and sales returns and allowances.

Posting references from the special journals are identified in the general and subsidiary ledger accounts by the letters shown above. For example, postings from page one of the Sales Journal to the general ledger and the accounts receivable subsidiary ledger are identified as "S1" (see Exhibit 6–2).

Advantages of Special Journals

A major advantage of special journals is that their use permits a division of labor. When special journals are used, the recording step in the accounting cycle can be divided among several persons, each of whom is responsible for particular types of transactions. Persons making entries in special journals do not have to be highly skilled or have a thorough knowledge of the entire accounting system.

The use of special journals often reduces recording time. Special journal transactions of a given type need no routine explanations for each entry. Also, because special column headings are used, account titles need not be repeated as is necessary in the general journal.

Probably the most significant advantage of using special journals is the time saved in posting from the journals to the ledgers. When a general journal is used, each entry must be posted separately to the general ledger. The tabular arrangement of special journals, however, often permits all entries to a given account to be added and posted as a single aggregate posting. For instance, if we entered 1,000 sales transactions in a general journal, we would make 1,000 separate credit postings to the Sales account. If we use a sales journal, however, the amounts of the 1,000 sales will appear in one money column. Therefore, we may easily obtain a total and post it as one credit to the Sales account. The sales journal has saved us the time necessary for 999 postings to the Sales account. Clearly, as more transactions are involved, more posting time is saved.

The advantages of special journals will be apparent in the examples we use on the following pages.

SALES JOURNAL

The **sales journal** of the Excel Company, shown in Exhibit 6–2, lists all credit sales for June. The information for each sale comes from a copy of the related sales invoice. Note that the tabular form of the journal is specifically designed to record sales on account.

If the same credit terms are extended to all customers, as we assume in our illustration, we need not describe them in the sales journal. When credit terms vary from customer to customer, a column can be added to the sales journal to explain the terms of each sale.

As we might expect, the posting of any journal to the general ledger must result in equal debits and credits. Also, for any posting to a control account in the general ledger, the same total amount must be posted to one or more related subsidiary ledger accounts. Exhibit 6–2 illustrates how to post the amounts in Excel Company's sales journal.

Usually, as entries are recorded in the sales journal throughout each month, they are also posted to the accounts receivable subsidiary ledger. A customer's account then reflects a transaction within a day or two of its occurrence. Con-

EXHIBIT 6–2

Sales Journal Page 1

Date		Invoice No.	Account	Post. Ref.	Amount
19XX					
June	1	101	J. Norton	✓	$ 200
	5	102	L. Ross	✓	100
	12	103	B. Travis	✓	1,000
	22	104	R. Douglas	✓	400
	29	105	M. Holton	✓	300
	30	106	E. Knight	✓	500
				12/40	$2,500

General Ledger

Accounts Receivable (12)	
6/30 S1 2,500	

Sales (40)	
	6/30 S1 2,500

Accounts Receivable Subsidiary Ledger

R. Douglas	
6/22 S1 400	

J. Norton	
6/1 S1 200	

M. Holton	
6/29 S1 300	

L. Ross	
6/5 S1 100	

E. Knight	
6/30 S1 500	

B. Travis	
6/12 S1 1,000	

sequently, the credit office can check a customer's account balance at times other than a billing date. Daily postings to the accounts receivable subsidiary ledger also allow for cycle billings (for example, billing customers whose names begin with different letters at different times of the month). The advantage of cycle billings is that statements of account can be mailed throughout the month rather than in one large group at the end of the month.

A check mark is placed in the posting reference column of the sales journal to indicate that the amount has been posted to the customer's account. At the end of the month, when all sales have been recorded and the sales journal has been totaled and ruled, the total sales figure is posted to the general ledger as a debit to the Accounts Receivable control account and as a credit to the Sales account. Note the double posting reference at the bottom of the posting reference column in the illustration; this indicates that Accounts Receivable is account No. 12 in the ledger and Sales is account No. 40. Posting of the sales journal is now complete.

Sales journals may accommodate additional information. For example, columns could be included for sales by department or by product, so that a breakdown of sales is available to management. Columns may also be provided for sales tax information, where necessary.

CASH RECEIPTS JOURNAL

All transactions involving cash receipts are recorded in a **cash receipts journal** similar to that shown in Exhibit 6–3. Because cash sales and collections from credit customers occur most often, this journal provides special columns for recording debits to Cash and to Sales Discounts and credits to Sales and Accounts Receivable. In addition, the columns on the right-hand side of the journal can be used for debits and credits to any other account.

Note that the entries on June 15 and June 30, debiting Cash and crediting Sales, record cash sales for a certain period. Actually, cash sales would be recorded daily rather than semimonthly, but we have recorded them only twice here for simplicity. The entry on June 8 records $196 received from J. Norton in payment of his June 1 purchase of $200, less the 2% cash discount taken. The entry debits Cash for $196, debits Sales Discounts for $4, and credits Accounts Receivable for $200. The entry for M. Holton on June 29 is similar. The June 21 entry illustrates the use of the Other Accounts debit column. Here, B. Travis settles her $1,000 billing of June 12 by giving a note for $500 of the debt and remitting $490 ($500 less the 2% discount) for the remainder. The debits are to Notes Receivable, $500, in the "Other Accounts" column; to Cash, $490; and to Sales Discounts, $10. The $1,000 credit to Accounts Receivable completes the entry. The entries on June 1 and June 10 represent cash received for the sale of capital stock and for a bank loan, respectively. In both cases, the "Other Accounts" credit column is used.

Before posting the cash receipts journal, we add each column and *balance* the journal to make sure that aggregate debits equal aggregate credits. (Note in our illustration that $13,480 + $20 + $500 = $1,500 + $4,500 + $8,000.) The totals of the Cash, Sales Discounts, Accounts Receivable, and Sales columns are posted to the general ledger, as noted by the posting references below these columns. Also, the individual items in the Other Accounts columns are posted to the general ledger; the totals of the Other Accounts columns are used only to balance the journal and are not posted. The individual items in the Accounts Receivable column are posted on a daily basis to the customers' subsidiary ledger to keep this ledger in balance with the Accounts Receivable control account. The postings to the customers' accounts are indicated by a check mark (√).

A **schedule** of the account balances in a subsidiary ledger is usually prepared at the end of each accounting period, to verify that the subsidiary ledger agrees with the related control account. The following schedule of Accounts Receivable for Excel Company indicates that the subsidiary ledger agrees with its control account in the general ledger.

Excel Company
Schedule of Accounts Receivable
June 30, 19XX

R. Douglas	$ 400
E. Knight	500
L. Ross	100
Total	$1,000

EXHIBIT 6–3

Cash Receipts Journal Page 1

Date		Description	Cash Debit	Sales Discounts Debit	Accounts Receivable Post. Ref.	Accounts Receivable Credit	Sales Credit	Other Accounts Account	Other Accounts Post. Ref.	Other Accounts Debit	Other Accounts Credit
19XX June	1	Sale of capital stock	$ 5,000					Capital Stock	(31)		$5,000
	8	J. Norton	196	$ 4	✓	$ 200					
	10	United Bank loan	3,000					Notes Payable	(23)		3,000
	15	Cash sales, June 1–15	2,000				$2,000				
	21	B. Travis	490	10	✓	1,000		Notes Receivable	(15)	$500	
	29	M. Holton	294	6	✓	300					
	30	Cash sales, June 16–30	2,500				2,500				
			$13,480	$20		$1,500	$4,500			$500	$8,000
			(10)	(42)		(12)	(40)			(X)	(X)

General Ledger

Cash (10)	
6/30 CR1 13,480	

Accounts Receivable (12)	
6/30 S1 2,500	6/30 CR1 1,500

Notes Receivable (15)	
6/21 CR1 500	

Sales Discounts (42)	
6/30 CR1 20	

Sales (40)	
	6/30 S1 2,500
	6/30 CR1 4,500

Capital Stock (31)	
	6/1 CR1 5,000

Notes Payable (23)	
	6/10 CR1 3,000

Accounts Receivable Subsidiary Ledger

R. Douglas	
6/22 S1 400	

M. Holton	
6/29 S1 300	6/29 CR1 300

E. Knight	
6/30 S1 500	

J. Norton	
6/1 S1 200	6/8 CR1 200

L. Ross	
6/5 S1 100	

B. Travis	
6/12 S1 1,000	6/21 CR1 1,000

INVOICE REGISTER (PURCHASES JOURNAL)

To record purchases of merchandise on account, we can use a single-column journal similar to the sales journal considered earlier (see Exhibit 6–2, page 211). We would post each entry in the journal to the individual creditors' accounts in the accounts payable subsidiary ledger. At the end of the month, we would post the total of the amount column to the general ledger as a debit to the Purchases account and as a credit to the Accounts Payable control account.

Most businesses, however, keep a multicolumn journal to record all acquisitions on account, including such items as supplies and equipment, as well as merchandise. This journal may be called a *purchases journal*, but it is usually called an **invoice register.** Exhibit 6–4 illustrates an invoice register.

The illustration shows special columns for debits to Purchases, Office Supplies on Hand, and Store Supplies on Hand, as well as for credits to Accounts Payable. A column is also provided for debits to accounts for which no special column is available.

The amounts in the Accounts Payable column are posted to the accounts payable subsidiary ledger on a daily basis. A check mark in the posting reference column indicates that this has been done. At the end of the month, the columns of the register are totaled and the journal is balanced to ensure that total debits equal total credits. (In the example, \$4,000 + \$500 + \$200 + \$1,200 = \$5,900.) The posting pattern for the invoice register is diagrammed in Exhibit 6–4.

CASH DISBURSEMENTS JOURNAL

All cash payments are recorded in a **cash disbursements journal.** Exhibit 6–5 (page 216) shows the June cash disbursements journal for Excel Company after the related transactions have been recorded and the journal balanced and posted. Note the special columns for credits to Cash and Purchases Discounts, and for debits to Accounts Payable. Ordinarily these accounts will have the most entries. Also observe that, as in the cash receipts journal, the "Other Accounts" columns are available for recording debits or credits to any other accounts.

The June 2 entry in Exhibit 6–5 recorded a check for \$2,800, which provided the cash needed to pay employees for the last part of May. The entries on June 12 and June 19 paid the accounts payable balances due Able, Inc., and Barr Company, less 2% and 1% cash discounts, respectively. Note that \$1,000 of equipment was purchased on June 15 by giving \$500 cash and a note payable for \$500; the latter amount was recorded in the "Other Accounts" credit column. Also observe that the cash purchase of merchandise for \$150 is recorded in the cash disbursements journal rather than in the purchases journal. The other entries in the journal are self-explanatory. Again, we have diagrammed the posting format for the journal.

After both the invoice register and the cash disbursements journal have been posted, the Accounts Payable control account has a \$3,300 balance (\$5,900 − \$2,600). This total agrees with the following schedule of creditors' accounts:

Excel Company
Schedule of Accounts Payable
June 30, 19XX

Echo Distributors	\$ 400
Holt, Inc.	300
Stix Supply Company	1,200
Ward Company	1,400
	\$3,300

EXHIBIT 6–4

Invoice Register Page 1

Date		Account Credited	Post. Ref.	Accounts Payable Credit	Purchases Debit	Office Supplies on Hand Debit	Store Supplies on Hand Debit	Other Debits: Account	Other Debits: Post. Ref.	Other Debits: Amount
19XX June	2	Able, Inc.	✓	$ 700	$ 700					
	9	Barr Company	✓	1,900	1,900					
	14	Stix Supply Company	✓	1,200				Office Equipment	19	$1,200
	18	Ward Company	✓	1,400	1,400					
	25	Echo Distributors	✓	400		$400				
	30	Holt, Inc.	✓	300		100	$200			
				$5,900	$4,000	$500	$200			$1,200
				(21)	(50)	(16)	(17)			(X)

Accounts Payable Subsidiary Ledger

Able, Inc.	
	6/2 IR1 700

Barr Company	
	6/9 IR1 1,900

Echo Distributors	
	6/25 IR1 400

Holt, Inc.	
	6/30 IR1 300

Stix Supply Company	
	6/14 IR1 1,200

Ward Company	
	6/18 IR1 1,400

General Ledger

Purchases (50)	
6/30 IR1 4,000	

Office Supplies on Hand (16)	
6/30 IR1 500	

Store Supplies on Hand (17)	
6/30 IR1 200	

Accounts Payable (21)	
	6/30 IR1 5,900

Office Equipment (19)	
6/14 IR1 1,200	

EXHIBIT 6–5

Cash Disbursements Journal Page 1

Date		Ck. No.	Description	Cash Credit	Purchases Discounts Credit	Accounts Payable		Other Accounts			
						Post. Ref.	Debit	Account	Post. Ref.	Debit	Credit
19XX											
June	2	101	Paid employees	$2,800				Wages Payable	27	$2,800	
	3	102	Paid June rent	600				Rent Expense	56	600	
	12	103	Able, Inc.	686	$14	✓	$ 700				
	15	104	Purchased equipment	500				Store Equipment	18	1,000	
								Notes Payable	23		$500
	19	105	Barr Company	1,881	19	✓	1,900				
	28	106	Purchased merchandise	150				Purchases	50	150	
	30	107	Insurance policy	120				Prepaid Insurance	14	120	
				$6,737	$33		$2,600			$4,670	$500
				(10)	(52)		(21)			(X)	(X)

General Ledger

Cash	(10)		
6/30 CR1	13,480	6/30 CD1	6,737

Accounts Payable	(21)		
6/30 CD1	2,600	6/30 IR1	5,900

Notes Payable	(23)		
		6/10 CR1	3,000
		6/15 CD1	500

Prepaid Insurance	(14)		
6/30 CD1	120		

Purchases	(50)		
6/28 CD1	150		
6/30 IR1	4,000		

Wages Payable	(27)		
6/2 CD1	2,800	5/31 Bal.	2,800

Store Equipment	(18)		
6/15 CD1	1,000		

Purchases Discounts	(52)		
		6/30 CD1	33

Rent Expense	(56)		
6/3 CD1	600		

Accounts Payable Subsidiary Ledger

Able, Inc.			
6/12 CD1	700	6/2 IR1	700

Barr Company			
6/19 CD1	1,900	6/9 IR1	1,900

Echo Distributors			
		6/25 IR1	400

Holt, Inc.			
		6/30 IR1	300

Stix Supply Company			
		6/14 IR1	1,200

Ward Company			
		6/18 IR1	1,400

USE OF THE GENERAL JOURNAL

When special journals are used, transactions that cannot be recorded appropriately in a special journal are recorded in the general journal. Examples include certain transactions involving notes receivable and notes payable, dispositions of plant assets, write-offs of uncollectible accounts, and merchandise returns. A special posting pattern is followed for posting to subsidiary ledgers. For example, Exhibit 6–6 demonstrates the treatment of purchases returns and allowances and sales returns and allowances. Note that whenever a posting is made to the Accounts Receivable control account or to the Accounts Payable control account from the general journal, a posting is also made to the related subsidiary ledger account. The latter posting is indicated by a check (√) in the posting reference column.

THE VOUCHER SYSTEM

Many companies control expenditures with a method that is known as the **voucher system.** Under this system, a written authorization form, called a **voucher,** is initiated for every disbursement the firm makes. Before the designated responsible official approves the voucher for payment, different employees must perform several verification steps, including the following:

1. Comparison of purchase requisition, purchase order, invoice, and receiving report for agreement of quantities, prices, types of goods, and credit terms.
2. Verification of extensions and footings (additions) on invoice.
3. Approval of account distribution (items to be debited).

Usually, each step in the verification process is listed on the face of the voucher, along with space for the signature or initials of the various employees responsible for accomplishing the procedures. The original copies of the purchase requisition, purchase order, invoice, and receiving report (if the item is merchandise) should

EXHIBIT 6–6

General Journal — Page 1

Date		Description	Post. Ref.	Debit	Credit
19XX					
July	2	Sales Returns and Allowances	41	100	
		Accounts Receivable—R. Douglas	12/√		100
		R. Douglas returned $100 merchandise for credit.			
	5	Accounts Payable—Ward Company	21/√	70	
		Purchases Returns and Allowances	51		70
		Returned $70 merchandise to Ward Company for credit.			

EXHIBIT 6–7

VOUCHER REGISTER

Voucher No.	Date	Name	Date Paid	Check No.	Vouchers Payable Credit	Purchases Debit
121	12/1	Olson Company	12/9	528	$ 350	$ 350
122	12/3	Tempo Freight	12/5	527	30	
123	12/5	Horder, Inc.	12/15	531	120	
•						
•						
•						
146	12/21	Jones Company	12/31	539	1,200	
147	12/27	Green Company			250	250
148	12/30	Dee Delivery			25	
					$18,500	$12,200
					(32)	(55)

be attached to the voucher. The voucher is then recorded in a book of original entry called the voucher register.

The Voucher Register

When a voucher system is used, the **voucher register** replaces the invoice register (or purchases journal) we discussed earlier. The voucher register provides columns for all items—merchandise, other assets, and services—for which payment must be made. Because all such items are recorded in the voucher register whether the transaction is for cash or on account, the voucher register also substitutes for part of the cash disbursements journal. Exhibit 6–7 shows one form of a simple voucher register.

Vouchers are entered in the voucher register in sequence. They should be prenumbered, of course, so they can be accounted for and referred to easily. All entries result in a credit to Vouchers Payable, which serves as the Accounts Payable control account for the company. The register has columns for those expense and asset accounts most frequently debited, such as Purchases, Transportation In, Office Supplies on Hand, and Delivery Expense. Debits to accounts for which columns are not provided are made in the "Other Accounts" section. A credit column also included in this section may be used for adjustments to vouchers and for recording purchases returns and allowances.

After vouchers have been entered in the voucher register, they are filed in an unpaid vouchers file in the order of required date of payment. In this way, the company will not miss discounts, and its credit standing will not be impaired. When a voucher is processed, the due date is usually written on the face of the voucher for filing convenience.

On the due date, the voucher is removed from the unpaid file and forwarded to the firm's disbursing officer for final approval of payment. After signing the voucher, the disbursing officer has a check drawn and mailed to the payee. The check number and payment date are recorded on the voucher, which is then

EXH 6–7 (Continued)

Transportation in Debit	Office Supplies on Hand Debit	Delivery Expense Debit	Other Accounts			
			Account	Post. Ref.	Debit	Credit
$ 30						
	$120					
			Office Equipment	15	$1,200	
		$ 25				
$850	$460	$320			$4,670	
(56)	(16)	(68)			(X)	

returned to the accounting department. To safeguard against irregularities, the voucher should not be handled again by those who prepared it, and the underlying documents should be canceled or perforated by the disbursing officer before the voucher is returned to the accounting department.

After a voucher is paid, the check number and payment date are entered in the appropriate columns of the voucher register. The total unpaid ("open") vouchers at any time may be determined by adding the items in the Vouchers Payable column for which the date paid and check number columns contain no entries. This total should, of course, agree with the total of vouchers in the unpaid file and, at the end of the month, with the amount in the Vouchers Payable account.

After these procedures have been followed, the payment is recorded in a book of original entry called the check register. Finally, the vouchers are filed in numerical sequence in a paid vouchers file.

The Check Register

In a voucher system, the **check register** replaces the cash disbursements journal. Because debits to asset, expense, and other accounts are made in the voucher register, only a few columns are required in the check register. We can see in Exhibit 6–8 that these consist of a debit column for vouchers payable and credit columns for purchases discounts and cash in bank. In addition, the check register has columns for the check number, date, and voucher number.

The check register is a company's chronological record of all check payments. Since checks are entered in the check register in numerical sequence, this record provides a convenient reference for payments when either the date or check number is known.

Under the voucher system, discounts may cause the amount of the check to differ from the gross amount of this voucher. For example, the entries for recording and paying the liability to the Olson Company for merchandise (voucher

EXHIBIT 6–8

CHECK REGISTER

Check No.	Date	Payee	Voucher No.	Vouchers Payable Debit	Purchases Discounts Credit	Cash in Bank Credit
525	12/2	Able Corporation	120	$ 250		$ 250
526	12/4	Smith Company	119	500	$ 10	490
527	12/5	Tempo Freight	122	30		30
528	12/9	Olson Company	121	350	7	343
•						
•						
•						
539	12/31	Jones Company	146	1,200		1,200
				$16,700	$120	$16,580
				(32)	(57)	(11)

No. 121, dated December 1; see Exhibit 6–7) are summarized in general journal form as follows:

Voucher Register				Check Register			
Dec. 1	Purchases	350		Dec. 9	Vouchers Payable	350	
	Vouchers Payable		350		Purchases Discounts		7
					Cash in Bank		343

Because both the gross and the net amounts of the liability are indicated on the voucher, this system should create no difficulty. Some companies, however, anticipate taking all discounts and prepare vouchers at the net amount. When this procedure is followed, only two money columns are needed in the check register—one for a debit to Vouchers Payable and one for a credit to Cash in Bank. If the company should miss a discount, an adjustment must be made in the voucher (or the original voucher must be canceled and a new one prepared). The bookkeeper must also record discounts lost in the general journal. (We explained the "net of discount" procedure and the Discounts Lost account in Chapter 5.) An alternative solution for handling lost discounts when the net price method is used is to provide a Discounts Lost column in the check register.

Recording Purchases Returns and Allowances

Companies usually handle purchases returns and allowances by canceling the original voucher and issuing a new one for the lower amount. Consider the following example.

Voucher No. 147 for $250, prepared for a merchandise purchase from the Green Company, is recorded in the voucher register on December 27. Assume that merchandise costing $50 is returned for credit and that a credit memo arrives on December 30. The original voucher for $250 is canceled and a reference made on it to a new voucher for $200. Furthermore, a note about the new voucher (No. 149) is made in the date paid column of the voucher register beside the entry for the original voucher. In recording the new voucher, the bookkeeper

EXHIBIT 6–9

VOUCHER REGISTER

Voucher No.	Date	Name	Date Paid	Check No.	Vouchers Payable Credit	Purchases ··· Debit	Other Accounts		
							Account	Debit	Credit
147	12/27	Green Company	Canceled, see #149		$250	$250			
•						···			
•									
•									
149	12/30	Green Company			200		Vouchers Payable	$250	
							Purchases Returns and Allowances		$50

credits $200 in the Vouchers Payable column. In the "Other Accounts" columns, Vouchers Payable is debited for $250 and Purchases Returns and Allowances is credited for $50. The net effect of these recording procedures is a debit of $250 to Purchases, a credit of $200 to Vouchers Payable, and a credit of $50 to Purchases Returns and Allowances (see Exhibit 6–9).

Recording Partial Payments

When installment or other partial payments are made on invoices, a separate voucher is prepared for the amount of each check issued. If a single voucher has been prepared for an invoice and the firm later decides to pay in installments, the original voucher is canceled and new vouchers are prepared. The cancelation of the original voucher and the issuance of new vouchers can be recorded in the same way that purchases returns are recorded.

MANUAL AND COMPUTER PROCESSING COMPARED

Manual Processing

We have described the manner in which data-processing functions are accomplished in a manual record-keeping system. Source documents are prepared and entered manually; classification and sorting are accomplished through columnar arrangements such as journals and ledgers; computations are often done manually; and storage is achieved by manual filing. Storage is in the form of ledger accounts, subsidiary ledgers, and various files. Retrieval and summarization are entirely manual.

Exhibit 6–10 summarizes the main procedures in the processing of accounting data for a manual record-keeping system. This exhibit does not contain all the detailed steps of the accounting process. It is presented as a basis for comparison with the processing of accounting data in a computer system.

The first step of the manual system involves the processing of source documents. This includes the manual preparation of documents generated by the firm, and the accumulation of documents from external sources. Examples of primary source documents generated by the firm are the sales invoice that is sent to a customer to request payment, the payment check that is sent to a vendor to pay for products or services acquired, and the payroll check that is given to

EXHIBIT 6–10

PROCESSING ACCOUNTING DATA IN A MANUAL SYSTEM

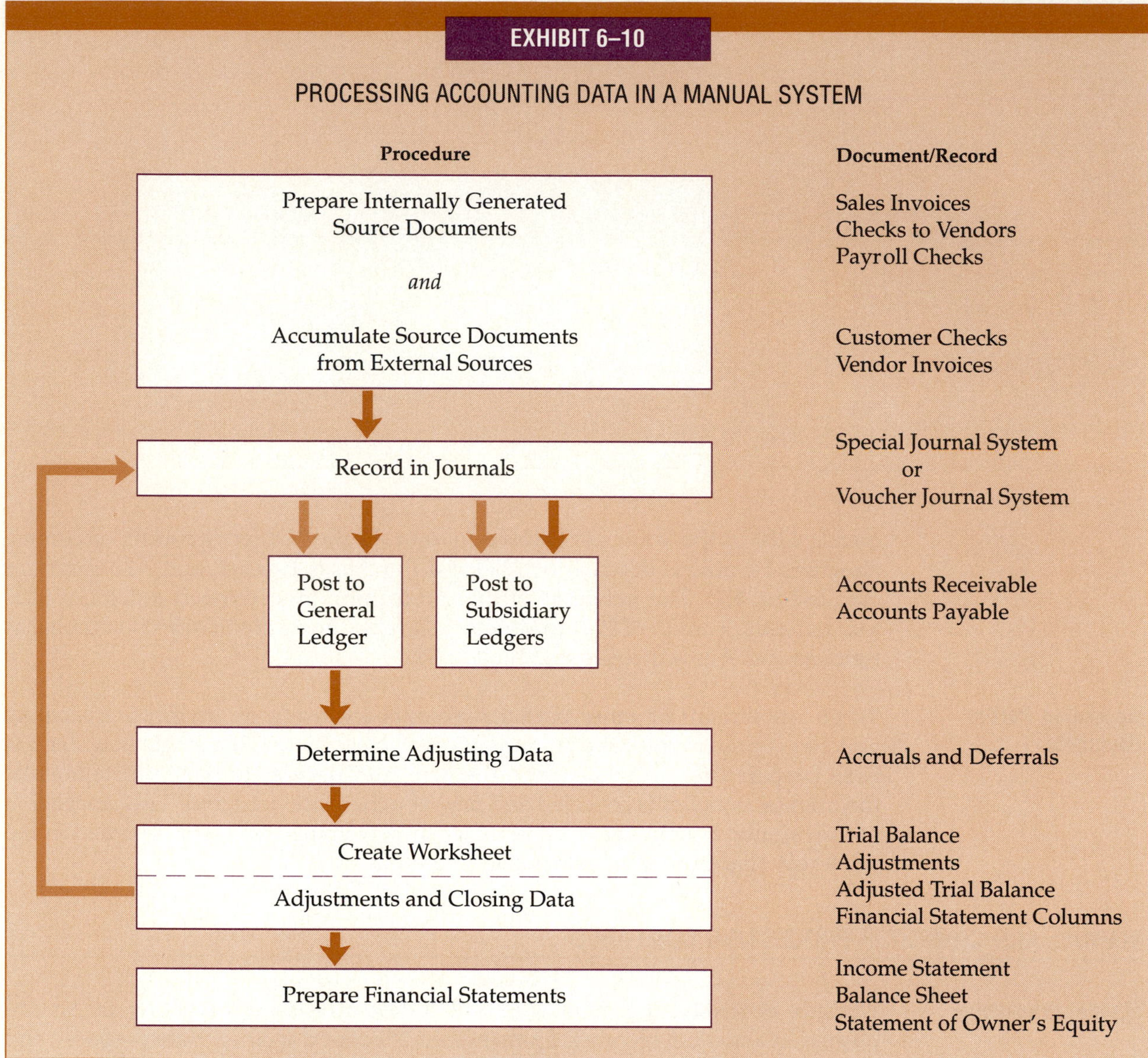

employees to compensate them for services rendered. Examples of primary documents received from external sources are customer checks and vendor invoices.

After the source documents are prepared by the firm or received from outsiders, they are analyzed and recorded in journals. Practically all firms using a manual processing system use a special journal system or a voucher system. Next, the data recorded in the various journals is manually posted to the general ledger, and, where needed, to a subsidiary ledger, such as accounts receivable or accounts payable.

At the end of an accounting period, we determine the adjustments needed and manually create a worksheet. The worksheet has the familiar pairs of columns—trial balance, adjustments, adjusted trial balance, income statement, and balance sheet. If it is the end of the accounting year, the adjusting and closing data shown on the worksheet can be recorded in the journals and then posted

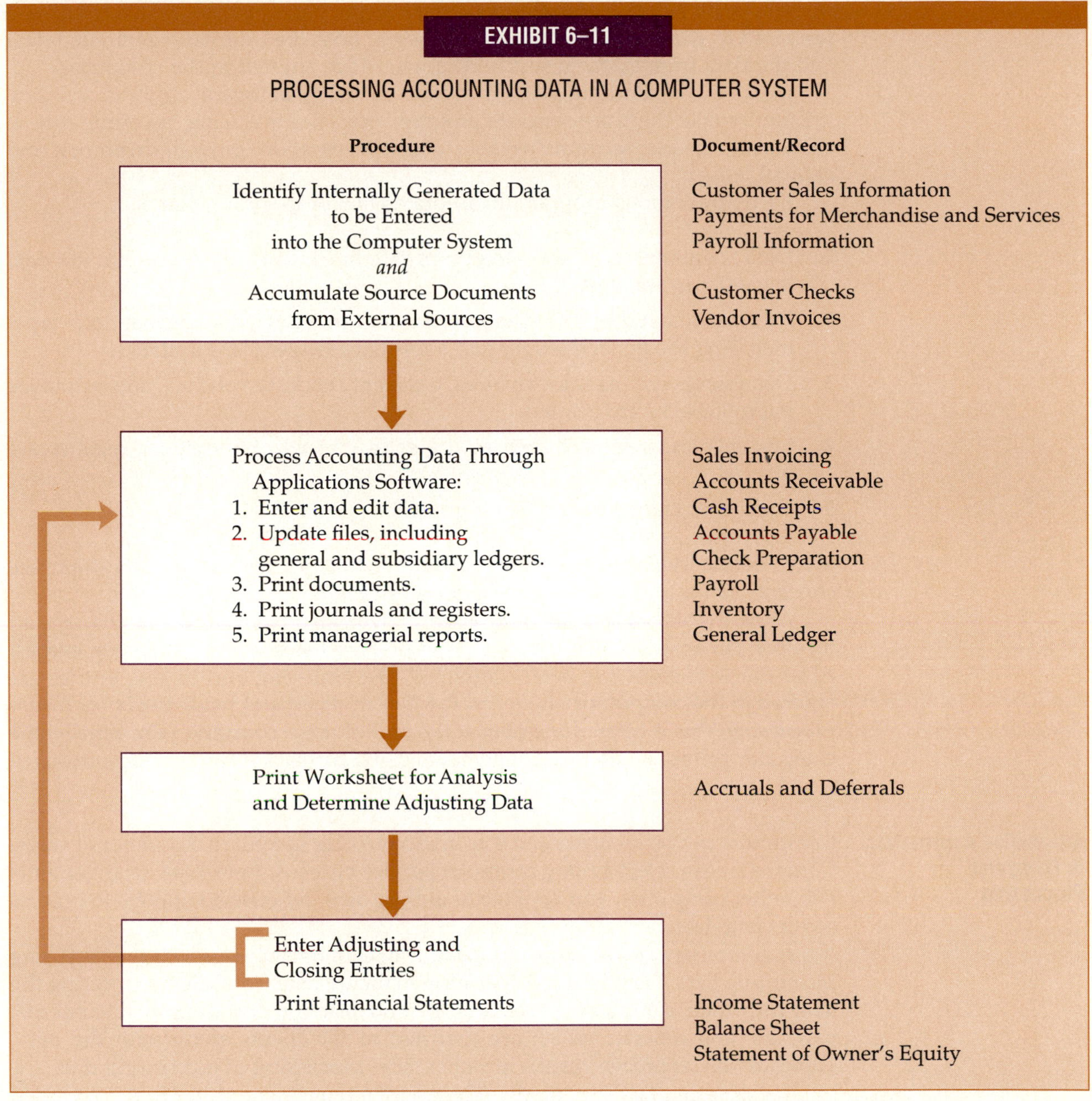

to the ledger (see light arrows in Exhibit 6–10). The financial statements are prepared using the information contained in the worksheet.

Computer Processing

Many businesses today use computers to process accounting data so that large volumes of data can be handled quickly. **Computer systems** used to process accounting data follow the logic of manual systems, but the procedures are very different.

Exhibit 6–11 outlines the processing of accounting data using a computer system. Similar to the manual system, the first step involves gathering data to be processed through the system. Internally generated data is identified, but primary source documents are usually not manually prepared. Instead, they are prepared as part of the computer processing. Both the internally generated data and the data from external source documents are entered in the computer.

Next, the accounting data is processed using software **applications programs**. Usually there are separate programs for sales invoicing, accounts receivable, cash receipts, accounts payable, check preparation, payroll, inventory, and general ledger.

Each applications program incorporates five primary functions:

1. Data is entered and processed through edit controls to ensure that the data is valid and reasonable.
2. Files maintained by the computer system on either disk or magnetic tape, including the general ledger and subsidiary ledgers, are updated.
3. Documents such as sales invoices, payment checks to vendors, and employee payroll checks are printed.
4. Journals and registers such as the sales journal or the check register are printed.
5. Various managerial reports are printed.

Many of the steps that are undertaken separately in the manual system are concentrated into this step in the computer system.

After the data has been processed, a worksheet is printed so that a staff member can analyze the trial balance and prepare the necessary adjusting entries. After the worksheet has been completed, the adjusting and closing entries are entered in the computer system and the files updated and made ready for future processing; this is often done only at the end of the accounting year. Finally, the computer prints the financial statements using formats stored in the software.

Alternative Approaches in Computer Processing

Computers can be incorporated into an accounting system in a number of ways. Companies can select among computer service bureaus, timeshare arrangements with other companies, and application of their own in-house computers to process accounting data.

A **computer service bureau** is usually an economical approach to processing accounting data. Such bureaus specialize in taking data from clients, entering the data into their computer, processing it, and printing the desired documents, journals, and reports, which are returned to the clients along with the data. Typically this approach results in rather slow processing of accounting data.

Timesharing facilities involve the use of a remote computer that is accessed through a terminal using telephone lines. Several companies can use the same computer with this approach. Each company using the system usually has its own staff members to enter data into the system, trigger the processing, and request printing through instructions entered on the terminal. Processing is significantly faster using this approach, but the cost is usually higher than that of a computer service bureau.

In-house computers are becoming increasingly popular with businesses of all sizes. Large companies, which invariably process accounting data with computers, typically use the main computer that all departments of the company use. Their accounting applications software resides in the computer system along

THE VERSATILE MICROCOMPUTER

The computing and processing capabilities of a microcomputer approach those of the largest mainframe of only 20 years ago. Ever smaller, faster, cheaper, and easier to use, the microcomputer has enjoyed spectacular sales growth. Microcomputer sales are now running over two million units per year. And the business market—as opposed to the home or hobbyist market—is now accounting for the lion's share of sales.

The small business is an obviously large market. Long closed out from the advantages of computer processing by prohibitive cost, and the need for specially trained personnel, an increasing number of small businesses now find it feasible to use microcomputers to process their basic accounting transactions, to provide ready access to necessary operating data, and to handle correspondence.

But this use—essential as it is—is only the tip of the iceberg. Microcomputers expand the options available to businesses of all sizes. Using microcomputers, management can arrange data-processing facilities with much less concern for hardware costs. A micro might be used to automate activities that for reasons of cost or confidentiality are not suitable for processing on the company's mainframe. Typical business applications include the following:

1. Forecasting, modeling, and financial statement consolidation are simplified by a microcomputer program known as an electronic spreadsheet. Once a model of relationships among a specific set of data has been established, an electronic spreadsheet program will automatically update all of the items affected by a change in one or more components. Some simple examples include the effect on the bottom line if sales double, if a division is sold, or if a union contract is settled at various possible levels.
2. Data bases may be created for the use of individual executives or departments. Once a data base file has been created in a common format, the information can be retrieved, summarized, sorted, rearranged, or used to prepare special purpose reports. The publications department might use a microcomputer to keep its mailing list current. Personnel data, meeting calendars, information on contracts with potential customers, tickler files, almost any type of data an individual or department needs to file and find for later use could become the subject of a microcomputer application. Applications that may not be cost-effective on the company's mainframe computer might well be practicable on a micro.
3. Graphics software available for microcomputers can reduce the time and cost associated with preparing illustrative charts for many types of presentations. The graphics capabilities of microcomputers are easily seen in the games run on home computers.
4. Security portfolio analysis, trend analysis, and plotting are possible with specialized programs. Arrangements can be made to use the microcomputer as a terminal to access data bases of specialized information maintained by outsiders. The Source and CompuServe are such examples available in the United States. Prestel can be accessed in the United Kingdom, and so on.

Not so long ago corporate electronic data processing was highly centralized. The high cost of the computer carried with it the need to allocate service facilities principally to priority tasks. Relatively inexpensive machines with enough processing power were simply not available. That has changed—less expensive computers have put computer power into the hands of many individuals. The power of the computer is being dispersed throughout the business organization.

Microcomputers—ever smaller and less expensive machines—are accelerating this already widespread trend. Microcomputers will not replace the mainframe computer for large-scale applications, but microcomputers are becoming so inexpensive that it is quite reasonable to automate additional activities. Distributed data processing—the use of several different computers (and now including microcomputers) in different locations all connected by transmission facilities—is becoming more and more common.

From *Microcomputers: Their Use and Misuse in Your Business*, Price Waterhouse, 1983, pages 1–2.

with the applications of the other departments. The main computer can be either a mainframe computer (such as the IBM 3090) or a mid-range computer (such as the IBM AS/400). Data can be entered either in batches (*batch processing*) or as each transaction is encountered (*interactive processing*). Many companies, such as banks and airlines, require that each transaction be entered immediately so that their files are always up to date.

The personal computer, also known as a **microcomputer,** is now being used by many smaller companies to process accounting data. A full range of applications software is available for virtually every type and brand of personal computer. Typically, there are no other users of the microcomputer when accounting data is being processed.

The various computer systems can be quite powerful and complex. The discussion above is intended only as an introduction to the use of computers for processing accounting data. A fuller discussion of manual versus computer systems can be found in *Computer Resource Guide: Principles of Accounting,* Third Edition, by John W. Wanlass, CPA, an ancillary to this text.

KEY POINTS FOR CHAPTER OBJECTIVES

1 Describe the differences between control accounts and subsidiary ledger accounts (pp. 207–209).

- Subsidiary ledgers for accounts receivable and payable enable a firm to keep track of amounts owing from specific customers and creditors.
- Control accounts showing *totals* of amounts owing from customers or to creditors simplify trial balances.

2 Provide an overview of the recording process using special journals (pp. 209–11).

- Using special journals for recording different classes of transactions permits a division of labor, reduces recording time, and reduces the number of postings to the general ledger.
- The general journal is used for adjusting, closing, and reversing entries, and for transactions that do not "fit" in special journals.

3 Describe and illustrate the special journals (pp. 211–16).

- The sales journal is used to record sales on credit terms, the invoice register (purchases journal) for purchases on credit terms, the cash receipts journal for *all* cash receipts, and the cash disbursements journal for *all* cash payments.

4 Describe the voucher system and illustrate the use of a voucher register and a check register (pp. 217–21).

- The voucher system is a control over cash disbursements. All individual requests for disbursements must be verified and approved.
- A voucher register replaces the invoice register and a check register replaces the cash disbursements journal.

5 Discuss the use of computers for processing accounting data (pp. 221–26).

- Data input in computer processing includes information from external source documents as well as the firm's own data, which enables the computer to produce the firm's primary source documents.
- Applications software programs edit entered data, update files and ledgers, print documents, print journals and registers, and print reports.
- The computer programs also are capable of preparing worksheets and financial statements.

KEY TERMS USED IN THIS CHAPTER

SELF-TEST QUESTIONS FOR REVIEW

(Answers are at the end of this chapter.)

1. If a firm uses special journals, in which journal would the sale of merchandise for cash be recorded?
   (a) Sales journal.
   (b) Cash receipts journal.
   (c) General journal.
   (d) Cash disbursements journal.
2. A firm that uses special journals acquires merchandise for $500, giving a $500 note payable. In which journal would the transaction be recorded?
   (a) Invoice register.
   (b) Sales journal.
   (c) Cash disbursements journal.
   (d) General journal.
3. A special journal contains columns for Cash, Purchases Discounts, and Accounts Payable. This journal is a(n)
   (a) Invoice register.
   (b) Sales journal.
   (c) Cash receipts journal.
   (d) Cash disbursements journal.
4. Which of the following is true of a voucher system?
   (a) All major expenditures, including cash transactions for payment of rent and utilities expense, would first be credited to Vouchers Payable before payment is made.
   (b) Transactions are first entered in the check register, and later, when payment is made, in the voucher register.
   (c) The check register replaces the cash receipts journal.
   (d) The voucher register contains a debit column for Vouchers Payable.
5. When a computer is used to process accounting data with applications software,
   (a) The general and subsidiary ledgers can be automatically updated, but related documents must always be manually prepared.
   (b) The general and subsidiary ledgers can be automatically updated and documents automatically prepared, but journals must always be prepared manually.
   (c) The general and subsidiary ledgers can be automatically updated, documents and journals automatically prepared, but managerial reports must always be prepared manually.
   (d) The general and subsidiary ledgers can be automatically updated, and documents, journals, and managerial reports can be automatically prepared.

DEMONSTRATION PROBLEM FOR REVIEW

The post-closing trial balance for Travis Distributors at December 31, 19X0, is given below:

Travis Distributors
Post-closing Trial Balance
December 31, 19X0

	Debit	Credit
Cash	$ 13,250	
Accounts Receivable	24,500	
Inventory	56,200	
Office Supplies on Hand	350	
Office Equipment	14,000	
Accumulated Depreciation		$ 3,600
Accounts Payable		21,700
J. Travis, Capital		83,000
	$108,300	$108,300

At the end of January, 19X1, the totals of the firm's special journals, before posting, are as follows:

Invoice register:	
Accounts Payable	$79,200
Purchases	74,100
Office Supplies on Hand	400
Other accounts:	
Office Equipment (Dr.)	4,700
Cash disbursements journal:	
Cash	$71,540
Purchases Discounts	960
Accounts Payable	66,400
Other accounts:	
Rent Expense (Dr.)	1,600
Salaries Expense (Dr.)	4,500

Sales journal	$93,500
Cash receipts journal:	
Cash	88,300
Sales Discounts	1,400
Accounts Receivable	79,300
Sales	6,400
Other accounts:	
J. Travis, Capital (Cr.)	4,000

REQUIRED

Prepare an unadjusted trial balance for Travis Distributors at January 31, 19X1. *Note:* A convenient method is to use a six-column worksheet, placing the post-closing trial balance in the first two columns after the account description and listing the account titles of the other accounts needed below the post-closing balance totals. The next two columns are used to record the debits and credits from the special journals, while the last two columns are used for the unadjusted trial balance at January 31.

SOLUTION TO DEMONSTRATION PROBLEM

Travis Distributors
Worksheet
January 31, 19X1

	Post-closing Trial Balance December 31, 19X0		Transactions		Trial Balance January 31, 19X1	
	Debit	Credit	Debit	Credit	Debit	Credit
Cash	13,250		(CR) 88,300	(CD) 71,540	30,010	
Accounts Receivable	24,500		(S) 93,500	(CR) 79,300	38,700	
Inventory	56,200				56,200	
Office Supplies on Hand	350		(IR) 400		750	
Office Equipment	14,000		(IR) 4,700		18,700	
Accumulated Depreciation		3,600				3,600
Accounts Payable		21,700	(CD) 66,400	(IR) 79,200		34,500
J. Travis, Capital		83,000		(CR) 4,000		87,000
	108,300	108,300				
Sales				(S) 93,500		
				(CR) 6,400		99,900
Sales Discounts			(CR) 1,400		1,400	
Purchases			(IR) 74,100		74,100	
Purchases Discounts				(CD) 960		960
Rent Expense			(CD) 1,600		1,600	
Salaries Expense			(CD) 4,500		4,500	
			334,900	334,900	225,960	225,960

QUESTIONS

6–1 What is a control account? What is a subsidiary ledger?

6–2 Criticize the following statement: "When a debit entry is made to a control account, one or more credit entries of the same aggregate total must be posted to the related subsidiary ledger."

6–3 Compare the benefits of using special journals with using only a general journal.

6–4 Explain why transactions should be posted to the subsidiary ledgers more frequently than to the general ledger.

6–5 How would you prove that a special journal "balances"?

6–6 Identify the type of transaction that would be entered in the following:
(a) A sales journal.
(b) A (single-column) purchases journal.
(c) An invoice register.
(d) A cash receipts journal.
(e) A cash disbursements journal.

6–7 A sale made on account to Mark Wells for $800 was recorded in a single-column sales journal on April 7. On April 9, Wells returned $90 worth of merchandise for credit. Where should the seller record the entry for the sales return? What entry would be made and how would it be posted?

6–8 A $560 purchase of merchandise on account from L. Meade was properly recorded in the invoice register, but was posted as $650 to Meade's subsidiary ledger account. How might this error be discovered?

6–9 Indicate how the following errors might be discovered:
(a) The total of the Accounts Payable column of the invoice register was understated by $70.
(b) The total of the single-column sales journal was understated by $50.

6–10 A retail merchandising firm recorded the sale of one of its delivery trucks in the sales journal. Why is this procedure incorrect?

6–11 John Byrd keeps an invoice register and employs the net method of recording merchandise purchases. Assume that he makes a $650 purchase from Dane Company, terms 2/10, n/30. Which journal columns would he use to record the purchase, and what debits and credits would be made?

6–12 Suppose that, in Question 6–11, Byrd made his remittance 20 days after the date of purchase. State the amounts involved, and describe how the payment would be recorded in a multicolumn cash disbursements journal.

6–13 What supporting documents are reviewed before a voucher for the purchase of merchandise is approved?

6–14 When a voucher system is used, what special journals are replaced by the voucher register and the check register?

6–15 Name three primary source documents that are manually prepared by a firm with manual processing and that could be automatically printed with computer processing.

6–16 What five primary functions are incorporated into most computer application programs?

6–17 Name and describe three alternative approaches to processing accounting data on computers.

EXERCISES

Posting special journals and general journal

6–18 Listed below are headings for the columns into which dollar amounts are entered for four special journals and a general journal. (For the sales journal, the accounts to which the single column relates are shown.) For each column heading, show where the amounts in that column should be posted, using the space provided. Use the appropriate letter (or letters) from the following key.

Key
(a) Column total posted to general ledger
(b) Column detail posted to subsidiary ledger
(c) Column detail posted to general ledger

The correct answer for the first item is given.

Sales Journal
1. Accounts Receivable ___a, b___
2. Sales ________

Invoice Register
3. Accounts Payable ________
4. Purchases ________
5. Office Supplies on Hand ________
6. Store Supplies on Hand ________
7. Other Debits ________

Cash Receipts Journal
8. Cash ________
9. Sales Discounts ________
10. Accounts Receivable ________
11. Sales ________
12. Other Accounts—Debit ________
13. Other Accounts—Credit ________

Cash Disbursements Journal
14. Cash ________
15. Purchases Discounts ________
16. Accounts Payable ________
17. Other Accounts—Debit ________
18. Other Accounts—Credit ________

General Journal
19. Debit column ________
20. Credit column ________

Recording transactions in journals

6–19 Foster Suppliers uses the four special journals illustrated in this chapter and a general journal. In which journal(s) would each of the following kinds of transactions be recorded?
(a) Owner's cash investment in business.
(b) Sale of merchandise for cash.
(c) Sale of merchandise on account.
(d) Return of merchandise sold on account.
(e) Owner's withdrawal of cash.
(f) Owner's withdrawal of merchandise for personal use.
(g) Collections from customers on account.
(h) Purchase of merchandise for cash.
(i) Purchase of merchandise on account.
(j) Return of merchandise purchased on account.
(k) Purchase of office supplies on account.
(l) Purchase of equipment for cash and a note payable.

Designing sales and purchases journals

6–20 John Lynn is a wholesaler of office supplies, vending equipment, and commercial cleaning supplies. His income statement shows sales, cost of goods sold, and gross profit amounts for each of his three product lines. He takes periodic inventories separately for each of these three departments. Design multicolumn sales and purchases journals to provide the information Lynn wants.

Errors in recording and posting

6–21 In recording transactions and posting from various journals, the bookkeeper made the following errors. In each case, state how the error might be discovered or whether discovery is unlikely.

(a) In the single-column sales journal, this month's total was underfooted (under-added) by $100.

(b) The total of the purchases column in the multicolumn invoice (purchases) register, correctly footed as $9,670, was posted to the Purchases account as $9,760.

(c) In the single-column sales journal, a sale to R. Wild was correctly recorded at $790, but posted to R. Wise's account as $970.

(d) A $600 remittance from E. Gann was correctly recorded in the cash receipts journal, but the amount was inadvertently posted to M. Gunn's account in the customers' ledger.

(e) A $620 payment to a creditor, D. Ross, was recorded in the cash disbursements journal as $520.

Recording transactions in journals

6–22 Describe how the following transactions would be recorded, indicating the journals used, the columns of each journal involved, and the way in which posting procedures are accomplished. Assume the four special journals illustrated in the chapter are available, together with a general journal.

(a) Purchased equipment for $4,000, giving $2,500 cash and a note payable for $1,500.

(b) Returned to a creditor merchandise purchased on account for $420.

(c) Owner contributed $1,200 cash and $10,000 in delivery equipment to the business.

(d) The business sold the delivery equipment in part (c) for $10,000 cash.

(e) Sent check for $60 to a customer, L. Burns, who had overpaid his account by this amount.

(f) Paid $80 freight to Acme Express Company on sale to a customer, C. Lundy. However, terms were F.O.B. shipping point, and customer was obligated to bear the freight cost.

PROBLEMS

Note: In the following problems, the journal forms used should correspond to those illustrated in the chapter.

Recording in the sales, cash receipts, and general journals

6–23 Preston Company makes all sales on terms of 2/10, n/30. Transactions for May involving sales, related returns and allowances, and cash receipts are shown below:

May 1 Sold merchandise on account to Lund, Inc., $800. Invoice No. 901.
2 Collected $392 from Grady, Inc., on account. A discount was taken by Grady.
3 Sold merchandise for cash to D. Harris, $90.
4 Issued credit memorandum to Lund, Inc., for return of $150 worth of merchandise purchased May 1.
7 Sold merchandise on account to Smart Company, $950. Invoice No. 902.
8 Received remittance from Lund, Inc., for the amount owed, less discount.
11 Sold merchandise for cash to B. Nelson, $160.
16 Sold merchandise to G. Little, receiving a note receivable for $700. Invoice No. 903.
21 Collected a non-interest-bearing note receivable from J. Boyd, $600.
22 Sold merchandise on account to Tull Company, $750. Invoice No. 904.
25 Owner H. Preston contributed cash to the business, $5,000.
28 Smart Company paid for merchandise purchased May 7.
29 Issued credit memorandum to Tull Company for $50 worth of merchandise purchased on May 22.
30 Sold merchandise on account to Young Company, $550. Invoice No. 905.

REQUIRED

(a) Record the given transactions in a single-column sales journal, a general journal, and a cash receipts journal.

(b) Open the following general ledger accounts and insert balances, when given: Cash (11) $9,000; Notes Receivable (15) $600; Accounts Receivable (16) $400; H. Preston, Capital (31) $18,000; Sales (41); Sales Returns and Allowances (42); and Sales Discounts (43). Also open a subsidiary ledger with the following customer accounts: Grady, Inc., $400; Lund, Inc.; Smart, Inc.; Tull Company; and Young Company. Only Grady's account had a beginning balance.

(c) Post all necessary amounts to the general and subsidiary ledger accounts.

(d) Prove that the Accounts Receivable control account agrees with the subsidiary ledger.

Recording in invoice register, cash disbursements journal, and general journal

6–24 Warner Company had the following transactions involving purchases, purchases returns and allowances, and cash payments during August. Warner records purchases at gross invoice price.

Aug. 1 Purchased merchandise on account from Vine Company, $1,000, terms 2/10, n/30, F.O.B. shipping point.

2 Paid Wynn Trucking, Inc., freight bill for August 1 purchase, $70. Check No. 100.

5 Paid Hahn, Inc., on account, $300. Check No. 101.

8 Purchased store supplies on account from Gem Supply Company, $450, terms n/30.

9 Owner L. Warner withdrew $800 cash from the business. Check No. 102.

11 Paid Vine Company for August 1 purchase. Check No. 103.

12 Returned $50 worth of the store supplies purchased from Gem Supply Company on August 8.

15 Purchased store supplies for cash from Rowley Wholesalers, $220. Check No. 104.

17 Purchased merchandise on account from Ford, Inc., $900, terms 2/10, n/30.

18 Paid Gem Supply Company in full of account. Check No. 105.

19 Returned $250 worth of merchandise to Ford, Inc., for credit.

22 Paid Ford, Inc., for August 17 purchase. Check No. 106.

24 Purchased office supplies on account from Hahn, Inc., $120, terms n/30.

26 Purchased delivery equipment from Long, Inc., $12,000, giving $5,000 cash and a note payable for $7,000. Check No. 107.

29 Purchased office equipment on account from Hahn, Inc., $675, terms n/30.

31 Purchased merchandise on account from Vine Company, $1,650, terms 2/10, n/30, F.O.B. shipping point.

REQUIRED

(a) Record these transactions in an invoice register (purchases journal), a cash disbursements journal, and a general journal.

(b) Open the following general ledger accounts and insert balances, when given: Cash (11) $15,000; Office Supplies on Hand (15) $450; Store Supplies on Hand (16) $320; Delivery Equipment (17) $9,000; Office Equipment (18) $6,500; Notes Payable (21); Accounts Payable (22) $300; L. Warner, Drawing (32); Purchases (51); Purchases Returns and Allowances (52); Purchases Discounts (53); and Transportation In (54). Also open a subsidiary ledger with the following creditor accounts: Ford, Inc.; Hahn, Inc., $300; Gem Supply Company; and Vine Company. Only the Hahn account had a beginning balance.

(c) Post all necessary amounts to the general and subsidiary ledger accounts.
(d) Prove that the Accounts Payable control account agrees with the subsidiary ledger.

Recording in cash receipts and cash disbursements journals

6–25 Jordan Company began business on April 1. The purchases and sales made on account during April have been recorded in the sales and purchases journals below. Purchases are recorded at gross invoice price.

Sales Journal Page 1

Date		Customer	Terms	Post. Ref.	Amount
19XX					
Apr.	5	Lane, Inc.	2/10, n/30		$700
	10	Baker Wholesalers	2/10, n/30		600
	18	Martin, Inc.	2/10, n/30		850
	21	Arden Wholesalers	2/10, n/30		650
	28	B. Hayden	2/10, n/30		800

Purchases Journal Page 1

Date		Creditor	Terms	Post. Ref.	Amount
19XX					
Apr.	2	Foster Company	2/15, n/30		$1,500
	4	Whelan Corporation	n/30		975
	12	Rowe, Inc.	2/10, n/30		500
	22	Foster Company	2/15, n/30		650
	29	Slade, Inc.	1/10, n/30		425

The April transactions to be recorded in the cash receipts and cash disbursements journals are the following:

Apr. 1 Jordan invested $20,000 cash and $15,000 worth of office equipment in the firm, a sole proprietorship. (Use two lines for entry.)
2 Paid April rent, $720. Check No. 101.
5 Received rental income for space sublet to Mann Realty, $280.
7 Purchased office supplies for cash, $370. Check No. 102.
14 Paid Foster Company for April 2 purchase. Check No. 103.
15 Cash sales were $985.
15 Received $686 from Lane, Inc., in payment of account.
18 Received $588 from Baker Wholesalers in payment of account.
21 Paid Rowe, Inc., for April 12 purchase. Check No. 104.
30 Paid office clerk's salary, $1,800. Check No. 105.
30 Cash sales were $1,295.

REQUIRED
(a) Record the April transactions in cash receipts and cash disbursements journals.
(b) Total and balance the cash receipts and cash disbursements journals.

Recording in special journals, posting, and taking a trial balance

6–26 Shannon Distributors, which sells on terms of 2/10, n/30, had the following transactions during October, the first month of the current fiscal year.

Oct. 1 Paid October rent, $500. Check No. 200.
2 Paid Sprague, Inc., $686 for merchandise purchased September 28. A 2% discount was taken. Check No. 201.

Oct. 3 Issued checks of $450 to Davis Company and $950 to Lenz Suppliers, both creditors. No discount was taken on these amounts. Checks No. 202 and No. 203.

7 Sold merchandise on account to Lyons, Inc., $550. Invoice No. 470.

8 Received checks in payment of accounts as follows: Lyons, Inc., $392; Thomas Company, $900; and White Company, $294. Discounts had been taken by Lyons, Inc., and White Company.

9 Sold merchandise on account to Thomas Company, $750. Invoice No. 471.

10 Issued check for freight to Ruan Freight, Inc., on Thomas Company shipment, $50, terms F.O.B. destination. Check No. 204.

11 Issued credit memorandum to Thomas Company for merchandise returned, $150.

14 Purchased merchandise on account from Davis Company, $800, terms 1/10, n/60.

15 Issued check for freight to Arrow Transport on purchase from Davis Company, $35, terms F.O.B. shipping point. Check No. 205.

15 Paid office salaries, $1,800. Checks No. 206 and No. 207 for $900 each for L. Voss and C. Downs.

16 Received check in payment of Cooper Company account, $650.

17 Received check from Lyons, Inc., in payment of October 7 shipment, $539.

18 Purchased store supplies, $90; equipment, $600; and office supplies, $70, on account from Lenz Suppliers, terms n/30.

21 Paid Davis Company for October 14 purchase, $792. Check No. 208.

22 Paid miscellaneous expenses, $45. Check No. 209.

24 Issued check to R. Shannon for a personal withdrawal, $500. Check No. 210.

28 Purchased merchandise on account from Sprague, Inc., $1,500, terms 2/15, n/60.

29 Returned $300 worth of merchandise to Sprague, Inc., for credit.

30 Sold merchandise on account to White Company, $1,375. Invoice No. 472.

31 Sold merchandise for cash to R. Nolan, $250.

31 Collected miscellaneous income from Dunn Advertising for use of billboard space, $350.

REQUIRED

(a) Open the following general ledger accounts, and enter the indicated October 1 balances. Number the accounts as shown.

Cash (11)	$ 5,600	Sales Discounts (43)
Accounts Receivable (12)	2,250	Miscellaneous Income (44)
Inventory (14)	28,000	Purchases (51)
Store Supplies on Hand (15)	600	Purchases Returns and Allowances (52)
Office Supplies on Hand (16)	550	Purchases Discounts (53)
Equipment (17)	24,000	Transportation In (54)
Accumulated Depreciation (18)	(6,000)	Rent Expense (61)
Accounts Payable (21)	(2,100)	Salaries Expense (62)
R. Shannon, Capital (31)	(52,900)	Transportation Out (63)
R. Shannon, Drawing (32)		Miscellaneous Expense (64)
Sales (41)		
Sales Returns and Allowances (42)		

(b) Open the following accounts in the subsidiary ledgers and enter the October 1 balances:

Customers		Creditors	
Cooper Company	$ 650	Davis Company	$ 450
Lyons, Inc.	400	Lenz Suppliers	950
Thomas Company	900	Sprague, Inc.	700
White Company	300		
	$2,250		$2,100

(c) Record the October transactions in the four special journals (sales, invoice register, cash receipts, and cash disbursements) and in the general journal. Shannon records purchases at gross invoice price.

(d) Using the forms prepared in parts (a) and (b), post all necessary amounts to the general ledger and subsidiary ledgers from the journals. Postings should be made to the subsidiary ledgers throughout the month.

(e) Prepare a trial balance of the general ledger.

(f) Prepare a schedule of accounts receivable and a schedule of accounts payable to prove control account balances.

Posting special journals and preparing a trial balance

6–27  The post-closing trial balance at December 31, 19XX, for Garret Distributors is given below:

Garret Distributors
Post-closing Trial Balance
December 31, 19XX

	Debit	Credit
Cash	$ 11,500	
Accounts Receivable	21,400	
Inventory	64,500	
Office Supplies on Hand	620	
Store Supplies on Hand	380	
Office Equipment	12,000	
Accumulated Depreciation		$ 4,500
Accounts Payable		28,300
P. Garret, Capital		77,600
	$110,400	$110,400

At the end of January, 19X1, the totals of the firm's special journals, before posting, are as follows:

Invoice register:		Sales journal	$97,200
Accounts Payable	$86,250		
Purchases	81,400	Cash receipts journal:	
Office Supplies on Hand	500	Cash	94,620
Store Supplies on Hand	850	Sales Discounts	1,360
Other accounts:		Accounts Receivable	76,500
Office Equipment (Dr.)	3,500	Sales	11,480
		Other accounts:	
		P. Garret, Capital (Cr.)	8,000

Cash disbursements journal:			
Cash	$79,430	Advertising Expense (Dr.)	850
Purchases Discounts	920	Salaries Expense (Dr.)	3,200
Accounts Payable	74,500		
Other accounts:			
Rent Expense (Dr.)	1,800		

REQUIRED
Prepare an unadjusted trial balance for Garret Distributors at January 31. *Note:* A convenient method is to use a six-column worksheet, placing the post-closing trial balance in the first two columns after the account descriptions and listing the account titles of the temporary accounts below the post-closing balance totals. The next two columns are used to record the debits and credits from the special journals, while the last two columns are used for the unadjusted trial balance at January 31. (See the demonstration problem at the end of this chapter, on page 229.)

Recording in a voucher register and check register

6–28 Century, Inc., controls its disbursements through a voucher system. The following transactions occurred during January of the current year. The firm records merchandise purchases at gross invoice price.

Jan. 1 Issued check No. 701 in payment of voucher No. 600 to Wells Company, $931. The voucher was recorded December 31 for $950. A 2% discount was taken.
1 Recorded voucher No. 601 payable to Dane Realty for January rent, $875.
2 Recorded voucher No. 602 payable to Noble Supply, Inc., for $750 worth of merchandise purchased, terms 2/10, n/30.
3 Issued check No. 702 in payment of voucher No. 601.
5 Recorded voucher No. 603 payable to Marshall Sales, Inc., for $550 worth of office supplies, terms 2/10, n/30.
7 Recorded voucher No. 604 payable to Nash Freight Company for transportation in on merchandise purchased, $65, terms F.O.B. shipping point.
10 Issued check No. 703 in payment of voucher No. 602, less discount.
12 Issued check No. 704 in payment of voucher No. 603.
15 Recorded voucher No. 605 payable to Ladd, Inc., for store equipment, $1,500, terms 2/20, n/60. (Make voucher for net amount.)
18 Issued check No. 705 in payment of voucher No. 604.
22 Recorded voucher No. 606 payable to Strang, Inc., for merchandise purchased, $840, terms 2/10, n/30.
26 Recorded voucher No. 607 payable to Union Gas and Light Company for utilities expense, $256.
26 Issued check No. 706 in payment of voucher No. 607.
28 Received credit memo for $140 from Strang, Inc., for merchandise returned to it. Canceled original voucher (No. 606) and issued voucher No. 608.
28 Issued check No. 707 in payment of voucher No. 605.
31 Recorded voucher No. 609 payable to Reeves, Inc., for merchandise purchased, $780, terms 2/10, n/30.

REQUIRED
(a) Open the following accounts and insert balances when given: Cash in Bank (11), $12,600; Office Supplies on Hand (17), $230; Store Equipment (18), $9,500; Vouchers Payable (21), $950; Purchases (51); Purchases Returns and Allowances (52); Purchases Discounts (53); Transportation In (54); Rent Expense (61); and Utilities Expense (62).
(b) Record Century's transactions in a voucher register and check register and post amounts to the accounts.
(c) List the unpaid vouchers, and compare the total with the balance of the Vouchers Payable account.

Recording in a voucher register and check register

6–29 The Bryant Company, which employs a voucher system, had the following transactions during July:

July 1 Recorded voucher No. 701 payable to L. Barr for $900 worth of merchandise purchased, terms 2/10, n/30.
2 Recorded voucher No. 702 payable to Colby Rentals for July rent, $675.
3 Issued check No. 803 in payment of voucher No. 702.
9 Recorded voucher No. 703 payable to Daly Express, Inc., for transportation in, $45, terms F.O.B. shipping point.

July 10 Issued check No. 804 in payment of voucher No. 701, less discount.
11 Issued check No. 805 in payment of voucher No. 703.
15 Recorded voucher No. 704 payable to Mason Company for $750 worth of merchandise, terms 2/10, n/30.
20 Received credit memo from Mason Company for $250 worth of the merchandise recorded on voucher No. 704. Canceled voucher No. 704 and issued voucher No. 705.
24 Recorded voucher No. 706 payable to Harris Company for $1,250 worth of merchandise, terms 2/10, n/30.
25 Issued check No. 806 in payment of voucher No. 705, less discount.

REQUIRED
Prepare a voucher register and check register, and record the transactions for the Bryant Company. The firm records merchandise purchases at gross invoice price.

ALTERNATE PROBLEMS

Note: In the following problems, the journal forms used should correspond to those illustrated in the chapter.

Recording in the sales, cash receipts, and general journals

6–23A Matson Sales Company makes all sales on terms of 2/10, n/30. Transactions for May involving sales, related returns and allowances, and cash receipts are shown below:

May 1 Collected $588 from J. Winslow on account.
1 Sold merchandise on account to Carr, Inc., $550. Invoice No. 201.
4 Sold merchandise for cash to L. Chang, $120.
5 Issued credit memorandum to Carr, Inc., for return of $100 worth of merchandise purchased May 1.
8 Sold merchandise on account to Lynch Company, $750. Invoice No. 202.
10 Received remittance from Carr, Inc., for the amount owed, less discount.
12 Sold merchandise for cash to T. Lowe, $185.
15 Sold merchandise to S. Macklin, receiving a note receivable for $900. Invoice No. 203.
18 Collected a non-interest-bearing note receivable from R. Bond, $850.
20 Owner C. Matson contributed cash to the business, $3,500.
24 Sold merchandise on account to Pearson Company, $470. Invoice No. 204.
25 Lynch Company paid for merchandise purchased on May 8.
26 Issued credit memorandum to Pearson Company for $40 worth of merchandise purchased on May 24.
30 Sold merchandise on account to M. Stone, Inc., $960. Invoice No. 205.

REQUIRED
(a) Record the given transactions in a single-column sales journal, a general journal, and a cash receipts journal.
(b) Open the following general ledger accounts and insert balances, when given: Cash (11) $7,600; Notes Receivable (15) $850; Accounts Receivable (16) $600; C. Matson, Capital (31) $32,500; Sales (41); Sales Returns and Allowances (42); Sales Discounts (43). Also open a subsidiary ledger with the following customer accounts: Carr, Inc.; Lynch Company; Pearson Company; M. Stone, Inc.; and J. Winslow, $600. Only J. Winslow's account had a beginning balance.
(c) Post all necessary amounts to the general ledger and subsidiary ledger accounts.
(d) Prove that the Accounts Receivable control account agrees with the subsidiary ledger.

Recording in invoice register, cash disbursements journal, and general journal

6–24A Domino Distributors had the following transactions involving purchases, purchases returns and allowances, and cash payments during June. Domino records purchases at gross invoice price.

June 1 Paid Beyer, Inc., on account, $520. Check No. 100.
1 Purchased merchandise on account from Gibson Company, $950, terms 2/10, n/30, F.O.B. shipping point.
2 Paid freight bill to Ruan Delivery for June 1 purchase, $40. Check No. 101.
5 Purchased store supplies on account from Cole Supply Company, $380, terms n/30.
7 Owner G. Domino withdrew cash from the business, $700. Check No. 102.
8 Purchased store supplies for cash from Wynn Wholesalers, $120. Check No. 103.
10 Paid Gibson Company amount due for June 1 purchase. Check No. 104.
11 Returned $30 worth of the store supplies purchased from Cole Supply Company on June 5.
15 Purchased merchandise on account from Ryan, Inc., $800, terms 1/10, n/30.
16 Paid Cole Supply Company in full of account. Check No. 105.
18 Returned $100 worth of merchandise to Ryan, Inc., for credit.
20 Paid Ryan, Inc., for June 15 purchase. Check No. 106.
21 Purchased office supplies on account from Beyer, Inc., $235, terms n/30.
25 Purchased delivery equipment from Austin, Inc., $8,000, giving $3,000 cash and a note payable for $5,000. Check No. 107.
30 Purchased office equipment on account from Beyer, Inc., $525, terms n/30.
30 Purchased merchandise on account from Gibson Company, $765, terms 2/10, n/30, F.O.B. shipping point.

REQUIRED

(a) Record these transactions in an invoice register (purchases journal), a cash disbursements journal, and a general journal.
(b) Open the following general ledger accounts and insert balances, when given: Cash (11) $9,500; Office Supplies on Hand (15) $340; Store Supplies on Hand (16) $460; Delivery Equipment (17) $9,000; Office Equipment (18) $3,600; Notes Payable (21); Accounts Payable (22) $520; G. Domino, Drawing (32); Purchases (51); Purchases Returns and Allowances (52); Purchases Discounts (53); and Transportation In (54). Also open a subsidiary ledger with the following creditor accounts: Beyer, Inc., $520; Cole Supply Company; Gibson Company; and Ryan, Inc. Only the Beyer, Inc., account had a beginning balance.
(c) Post all necessary amounts to the general ledger and subsidiary ledger accounts.
(d) Prove that the Accounts Payable control account agrees with the subsidiary creditors' ledger.

Recording in cash receipts and cash disbursements journals

6–25A Crane Wholesalers began business on May 1. The purchases and sales made on account during May have been recorded in the sales and purchases journals below. Purchases are recorded at gross invoice price.

Sales Journal Page 1

Date		Customer	Terms	Post. Ref.	Amount
19XX					
May	6	Temple, Inc.	2/10, n/30		$750
	9	Gray and Company	2/10, n/30		500
	17	R. D. Holmes	2/10, n/30		600
	22	Gray and Company	2/10, n/30		475
	25	F. Sanchez	2/10, n/30		230

Purchases Journal Page 1

Date		Creditor	Terms	Post. Ref.	Amount
19XX					
May	3	L. Gregg	2/10, n/30		$850
	5	Carter Corporation	n/30		430
	16	Alpine, Inc.	2/10, n/30		700
	25	L. Gregg	2/10, n/30		375
	30	G. Moss	1/10, n/30		800

The May transactions to be recorded in the cash receipts and cash disbursements journals are the following:

May 1 L. Crane invested $30,000 cash and $9,000 worth of office equipment in the firm, a sole proprietorship. (Use two lines for entry.)
2 Paid May rent, $975. Check No. 101.
3 Received rental income for space sublet to Greenleaf, Inc., $325.
4 Purchased office supplies for cash, $530. Check No. 102.
10 Paid L. Gregg for May 3 purchase. Check No. 103.
15 Cash sales were $695.
16 Received $735 from Temple, Inc., in payment of account.
19 Received $490 from Gray and Company in payment of account.
26 Paid Alpine, Inc., for May 16 purchase. Check No. 104.
31 Paid office clerk's salary, $1,750. Check No. 105.
31 Cash sales were $865.

REQUIRED

(a) Record the May transactions in cash receipts and cash disbursements journals.
(b) Total and balance the cash receipts and cash disbursements journals.

Recording in special journals, posting, and taking a trial balance

6–26A Reed Wholesalers, which sells on terms of 2/10, n/30, had the following transactions during January, the first month of the current accounting year.

Jan. 2 Paid Simon, Inc., for merchandise purchased December 28, $588. Check No. 125. Reed took a 2% discount.
3 Paid January rent, $825. Check No. 126.
5 Issued checks of $320 to Blair Company and $530 to Gabriel Suppliers, both creditors. No discount was taken on these amounts. Checks No. 127 and No. 128.
5 Sold merchandise on account to Judd, Inc., $1,450. Invoice No. 251.

Jan. 6 Received checks in payment of accounts as follows: Judd, Inc., $294; Murray Company, $630; and Rodgers Distributors, $490. Discounts had been taken by Judd, Inc., and Rodgers Distributors.

7 Sold merchandise on account to Murray Company, $2,250. Invoice No. 252.

8 Issued check for freight to Interstate, Inc., on Murray Company shipment, $60, terms F.O.B. destination. Check No. 129.

9 Issued credit memorandum to Murray Company for merchandise returned, $150.

12 Purchased merchandise on account from Blair Company, $1,200, terms 1/10, n/60.

13 Issued check for freight to Fry Freightways on purchase from Blair Company, $45, terms F.O.B. shipping point. Check No. 130.

14 Received check in payment of Birch Company account, $480.

15 Received check from Judd, Inc., in payment of January 5 shipment, $1,421.

15 Paid office salaries, $2,400. Checks No. 131 and No. 132 for $1,200 each for M. Sims and D. Ricco.

19 Purchased store supplies, $320; equipment, $950; and office supplies, $180, on account from Gabriel Suppliers, terms n/30.

20 Paid Blair Company for January 12 purchase, $1,188. Check No. 133.

21 Paid miscellaneous expense, $65. Check No. 134.

22 Owner F. Reed made a personal withdrawal, $800. Check No. 135.

26 Purchased merchandise on account from Simon, Inc., $580, terms 2/15, n/60.

27 Returned $50 worth of merchandise to Simon, Inc., for credit.

28 Sold merchandise on account to Rodgers Distributors, $2,950. Invoice No. 253.

30 Sold merchandise for cash to R. Mills, $75.

30 Collected miscellaneous income from Ward Advertising for use of billboard space, $160.

REQUIRED

(a) Open the following general ledger accounts, and enter the indicated January 1 balances. Number the accounts as shown.

Cash (11)	$12,800	Sales Discounts (43)
Accounts Receivable (12)	1,910	Miscellaneous Income (44)
Inventory (14)	32,500	Purchases (51)
Store Supplies on Hand (15)	520	Purchases Returns and Allowances (52)
Office Supplies on Hand (16)	360	Purchases Discounts (53)
Equipment (17)	24,000	Transportation In (54)
Accumulated Depreciation (18)	(4,500)	Rent Expense (61)
Accounts Payable (21)	(1,450)	Salaries Expense (62)
F. Reed, Capital (31)	(66,140)	Transportation Out (63)
F. Reed, Drawing (32)		Miscellaneous Expense (64)
Sales (41)		
Sales Returns and Allowances (42)		

(b) Open the following accounts in the subsidiary ledgers and enter the January 1 balances:

Customers		Creditors	
Birch Company	$ 480	Blair Company	$ 320
Judd, Inc.	300	Gabriel Suppliers	530
Murray Company	630	Simon, Inc.	600
Rodgers Distributors	500		
	$1,910		$1,450

(c) Record the January transactions in the four special journals (sales, invoice register, cash receipts, and cash disbursements) and in the general journal. Reed records purchases at gross invoice price.
(d) Using the forms prepared in parts (a) and (b), post all necessary amounts to the general ledger and subsidiary ledgers from the journals. Postings should be made to the subsidiary ledgers throughout the month.
(e) Prepare a trial balance of the general ledger.
(f) Prepare a schedule of accounts receivable and a schedule of accounts payable to prove control account balances.

Posting special journals and preparing a trial balance

6–27A The post-closing trial balance at December 31, 19X0, for Riggs Distributors is given below:

Riggs Distributors
Post-closing Trial Balance
December 31, 19X0

	Debit	Credit
Cash	$14,200	
Accounts Receivable	24,700	
Inventory	62,100	
Office Supplies on Hand	560	
Store Supplies on Hand	740	
Office Equipment	14,000	
Accumulated Depreciation		$ 4,800
Accounts Payable		22,900
M. Riggs, Capital		88,600
	$116,300	$116,300

At the end of January, 19X1, the totals of the firm's special journals, before posting, are as follows:

Invoice register:	
Accounts Payable	$97,650
Purchases	91,200
Office Supplies on Hand	300
Store Supplies on Hand	650
Other accounts:	
Office Equipment (Dr.)	5,500

Sales journal	$104,200

Cash receipts journal:	
Cash	97,450
Sales Discounts	1,430
Accounts Receivable	88,600
Sales	7,280
Other accounts:	
M. Riggs, Capital (Cr.)	3,000

Cash disbursements journal:	
Cash	89,200
Purchases Discounts	1,240
Accounts Payable	85,590
Other accounts:	
Rent Expense (Dr.)	1,200
Advertising Expense (Dr.)	850
Salaries Expense (Dr.)	2,800

REQUIRED
Prepare an unadjusted trial balance for Riggs Distributors at January 31. *Note:* A convenient method is to use a six-column worksheet, placing the post-closing trial balance in the first two columns after the account descriptions and listing the account titles of the temporary accounts below the post-closing balance totals. The next two columns are used to record the debits and credits from the special journals, while the last two columns are used for the unadjusted trial balance at January 31. (See the demonstration problem at the end of this chapter, on page 229.)

Recording in a voucher register and check register

6–28A Lambert, Inc., controls its disbursements through a voucher system. The following transactions occurred during January of the current year. The firm records merchandise purchases at gross invoice price.

Jan. 1 Issued check No. 505 in payment of voucher No. 400 to Ellis Company, $1,372. The voucher was recorded December 31 for $1,400. A 2% discount was taken.
1 Recorded voucher No. 401 payable to Douglas Realty for April rent, $1,500.
2 Recorded voucher No. 402 payable to Spartan Service Corporation for $850 worth of merchandise purchased, terms 2/10, n/30.
2 Issued check No. 506 in payment of voucher No. 401.
5 Recorded voucher No. 403 payable to Allied Sales, Inc., for $550 worth of office supplies, terms 2/10, n/30.
7 Recorded voucher No. 404 payable to Hill Freight Lines, Inc., for freight in on merchandise purchased, $58, terms F.O.B. shipping point.
10 Issued check No. 507 in payment of voucher No. 402, less discount.
12 Issued check No. 508 in payment of voucher No. 403.
14 Recorded voucher No. 405 payable to Verona Equipment Sales, Inc., for equipment, $2,200, terms 2/15, n/60. (Make voucher for net amount.)
18 Issued check No. 509 in payment of voucher No. 404.
21 Recorded voucher No. 406 payable to Diaz, Inc., for merchandise purchased, $675, terms 2/10, n/30.
25 Recorded voucher No. 407 payable to Capitol Gas and Light Company for utilities expense, $245.
26 Issued check No. 510 in payment of voucher No. 407.
28 Received credit memo for $75 from Diaz, Inc., for merchandise returned to it. Canceled original voucher (No. 406) and issued voucher No. 408.
28 Issued check No. 511 in payment of voucher No. 405.
31 Recorded voucher No. 409 payable to Fisher, Inc., for merchandise, $635, terms 2/10, n/30.

REQUIRED

(a) Open the following accounts and insert balances when given: Cash in Bank (11), $15,200; Office Supplies on Hand (17), $430; Store Equipment (18), $8,600; Vouchers Payable (21), $1,400; Purchases (51); Purchases Returns and Allowances (52); Purchases Discounts (53); Transportation In (54); Rent Expense (61); and Utilities Expense (62).
(b) Record Lambert's transactions in a voucher register and check register and post amounts to the accounts.
(c) List the unpaid vouchers and compare the total with the balance of the Vouchers Payable account.

Recording in a voucher register and check register

6–29A Decker Company, which uses a voucher system, had the following transactions during June:

June 1 Recorded voucher No. 601 payable to R. Long for $1,200 worth of merchandise purchased, terms 2/10, n/30.
2 Recorded voucher No. 602 payable to Anchor Rentals for June rent, $950.
3 Issued check No. 903 in payment of voucher No. 602.
9 Recorded voucher No. 603 payable to Drew Freightways for transportation in, $62, terms F.O.B. shipping point.
10 Issued check No. 904 in payment of voucher 601.
11 Issued check No. 905 in payment of voucher No. 603.
15 Recorded voucher No. 604 payable to Field Company for $825 worth of merchandise, terms 2/10, n/30.
20 Received credit memo from Field Company for $125 worth of the merchandise recorded on voucher No. 604. Canceled voucher No. 604 and issued voucher No. 605.

June 24 Recorded voucher No. 606 payable to Downey Company for $1,400 worth of merchandise, terms 2/10, n/30.
25 Issued check No. 906 in payment of voucher No. 605, less discount.

REQUIRED
Prepare a voucher register and check register, and record the transactions for Decker Company. The firm records merchandise purchases at gross invoice price.

BUSINESS DECISION PROBLEM

Camden, Inc., sells a variety of office products and supplies, including typewriters, word processing equipment, desks, chairs, filing systems, and sundry office supplies. Most sales are on account; however, many small equipment items and supplies are sold over the counter for cash.

Manager R. Sullivan asks you to provide special journals for the firm's accounting system. After discussing the matter with Sullivan, you decide to design journals for three departments: Equipment, Furniture, and Supplies. Sullivan wants the income statement to show sales, cost of goods sold, and gross profit for each of the three departments. Merchandise inventory for the three departments will be taken separately.

Practically all the firm's purchases are merchandise for resale. Most cash disbursements are payments on account to suppliers, freight on purchases (most purchases are made on terms F.O.B. shipping point), and for advertising expense. Spot advertising in local newspapers and television is paid when bills are received; no accounts payable are kept for these expenses. Employees are paid monthly.

REQUIRED
List the column headings (from left to right) that you would provide in the (a) sales journal, (b) invoice register, (c) cash receipts journal, and (d) cash disbursements journal for the three departments in Camden, Inc.

ANSWERS TO SELF-TEST QUESTIONS

1. (b) **2.** (d) **3.** (d) **4.** (a) **5.** (d)

ANNUAL REPORT PROBLEMS FOR PART 1

The following annual report problems conclude Part 1 of the text. They consist of two unrelated sections and use selected financial data from actual companies. Section I focuses on the balance sheet data of one company and section II uses income statement data from another company.

I. Balance Sheet

Following is a list, in alphabetical order, of the items included in a recent balance sheet of an actual company. The balance sheet date is as of the company's fiscal year-end, January 31, 1988.

Item	Amount (in thousands)
Accounts Payable	$ 48,129
Accounts Receivable	5,932
Accrued Liabilities (short-term)	$ 10,168
Accumulated Depreciation—Property	34,906
Cash	571
Common Stock	656
Income Taxes Payable	637
Long-term Debt	11,736
Merchandise Inventories	133,608

Notes Payable to Banks	17,000
Other Current Liabilities	349
Other Long-term Assets	680
Other Long-term Liabilities	3,887
Other Stockholders' Equity	14,488
Prepaid Expenses and Other Current Assets	4,127
Property	74,612
Retained Earnings	77,574

REQUIRED

(a) Prepare a classified balance sheet for this company. (Omit the company's name from the heading.)

(b) Following is a brief description of three companies:

Emery Air Freight Corporation—A firm providing air courier and air cargo services to cities around the world.

House of Fabrics, Inc.—A nationwide retail firm specializing in fabrics, sewing notions, sewing machines, and crafts.

Kelly Services, Inc.—A firm providing temporary help services to a diversified group of customers.

The balance sheet prepared in part (a) is the balance sheet for one of these three firms. Whose balance sheet is it? Briefly explain.

II. Income Statement

One of the most unusual and interesting companies listed on the New York Stock Exchange is Perry Drug Stores, Inc. The firm is headquartered in Pontiac, Michigan, and operates drug stores and auto parts outlets in eight midwestern states.

The firm's income statement data, taken from its annual reports for three consecutive years, are given below. The latest year is Year 3.

	Year 3	Year 2	Year 1
Sales			
Drugstore	$291,189,614*	$245,418,621	$215,865,078
Automotive	80,700,907	40,083,836	28,407,096
Total Sales	$371,890,521	$285,502,457	$244,272,174
Cost of Goods Sold	256,293,344	200,155,781	171,563,995
Gross Profit	$115,597,177	$ 85,346,676	$ 72,708,179
Operating Expenses	$101,255,916	$ 74,908,244	$ 65,469,314
Interest Expense	2,078,263	2,802,212	2,842,745
Total Expenses	$103,334,179	$ 77,710,456	$ 68,312,059
Income before Income Tax	$ 12,262,998	$ 7,636,220	$ 4,396,120
Income Tax Expense	4,613,000	3,091,000	1,528,000
Net Income	$ 7,649,998	$ 4,545,220	$ 2,868,120

REQUIRED

(a) Calculate the firm's gross profit percentage for each of the three years and comment on the change in this percentage between Year 1 and Year 3.

(b) What percent of total sales each year consisted of drugstore sales? Automotive parts sales? Which division is apparently growing faster?

(c) Based on your answers to (a) and (b), which division, drugstore or automotive parts, has the higher average mark-up percentage on sales?

(d) For each year, calculate the following as a percent of total sales: operating expenses, interest expense, income before income tax, and net income. What effect have changes in operating expenses and interest expense had on the return on sales before taxes?

*Includes $1,605,448 sales of health-care division, begun by the firm in Year 3.

PART 2

ACCOUNTING FOR ASSETS AND CURRENT LIABILITIES

7

INTERNAL CONTROL, CASH, AND SHORT-TERM INVESTMENTS

CHAPTER OBJECTIVES

1. Describe the internal control features of an accounting system (pp. 249–53).
2. Identify key controls over cash and explain the procedures for preparing a bank reconciliation (pp. 253–62).
3. Discuss the accounting for a petty cash fund (pp. 262–64).
4. Describe the accounting for short-term investments in stocks and bonds (pp. 264–69).

The use of money is all the advantage there is in having money.

BENJAMIN FRANKLIN

Management must plan, direct, and control the operations of a firm. Because accounting aids management in its various activities, accountants help develop an appropriate internal control structure for a firm. The elements of control are important to all aspects of a firm's operations, but they are particularly critical in establishing methods of handling and accounting for monetary assets. We therefore consider first the general features that are desirable in an accounting control system and then examine certain procedures that are especially important in accounting for and controlling cash transactions. The latter procedures include bank reconciliations and petty cash procedures.[1] We conclude the chapter by examining accounting for short-term investments in stocks and bonds.

INTERNAL CONTROL STRUCTURE

A firm's **internal control structure** is defined as

> the policies and procedures established to provide reasonable assurance that specific entity objectives will be achieved.[2]

Establishing an effective internal control structure is an important management responsibility. First, a firm's management is expected to provide a good *control environment*—that is, the firm's organizational structure, the functioning of the board of directors and its committees, personnel policies, and various other policies for monitoring performance. These should all be designed to foster good internal control. Second, management should provide an effective *accounting system* that will furnish complete, accurate, and timely financial data. Finally, *control procedures* should be integrated into the components of the control environment and accounting system.

The control procedures of particular concern to the accountant are those that help (1) produce accurate and reliable financial data about the firm, and (2) safeguard the firm's assets. We will use the term **accounting controls** to refer to the policies and procedures designed to promote achievement of these two objectives. We now discuss several features of a good system of accounting controls.

FEATURES OF AN ACCOUNTING CONTROL SYSTEM

Good internal accounting control includes the following requirements:

1. Competent personnel.
2. Assignment of responsibility.

---

[1]The voucher system discussed in Chapter 6 is a system of controls over cash disbursements.
[2]*Statement on Auditing Standards No. 55,* "Consideration of the Internal Control Structure in a Financial Statement Audit" (New York: American Institute of Certified Public Accountants, 1988), p. 4.

3. Division of work.
4. Separation of accountability from custodianship.
5. Adequate records and equipment.
6. Rotation of personnel.
7. Internal auditing.
8. Physical protection of assets.

Note that accounting controls may interrelate with controls in other areas. For example, hiring procedures used to identify competent accounting personnel may also be used to hire capable employees for other areas in the firm.

Competent Personnel

Employees should be carefully selected and their talents used intelligently in the operation of the accounting information system. Each person should thoroughly understand his or her function and its relationship to other functions in the system. Above all, an employee must realize the importance of following the procedures prescribed by management and should be in sympathy with the system. A well-formulated system of internal control can be destroyed by employees' lack of confidence or cooperation.

Employee cooperation is enhanced by paying employees a fair salary or wage. Poorly paid employees may feel justified in stealing from their employer or being indifferent toward their work.

Assignment of Responsibility

The plan of organization should fix responsibility for functions and confer the authority necessary to perform them. Responsibility and authority for a given function should not be shared, because this may result in duplication of effort and in jobs going undone if individuals think that another is performing the assignment. When one person is responsible for a function, praise or blame can be clearly assigned for specific results. Thus, if a plant supervisor is responsible for staying within budgeted amounts for labor costs, he or she should be given the authority to assign personnel to jobs, control overtime, and so on.

Division of Work

Division of work is one of the most important facets of a good system of controls. The duties of individuals should be defined so that no single individual has complete control over a sequence of related transactions. That is, the person who authorizes a purchase order should not also confirm receipt of the merchandise or authorize payment for the merchandise. Likewise, the person handling bank deposits and the person keeping the cash books should not receive bank statements or make bank reconciliations. Improper segregation of duties increases the possibility of fraud, carelessness, and unreliable record keeping, whereas with a proper division of duties, the work of one person or group can act as a check on work performed by another person or group. For example, when purchase orders and receiving reports are processed by different individuals, a third person can compare the order, receiving report, and vendor's invoice before approving payment. This practice reduces the likelihood of errors from carelessness as well as the possibility of fictitious purchases or fraudulent conversion of goods.

Work division is valuable not only in preventing errors and fraud, but also in providing the advantages of specialization—better performance and easier employee training.

Separation of Accountability from Custodianship

Employees who are responsible for keeping records of a firm's assets should not have custody of the assets or access to them. Separating the custody of assets from the maintenance of records is another safeguard against fraud. An employee should not be able to convert assets for personal use and cover up the conversion by falsifying the records. Periodically, an independent comparison should be made of the recorded amounts with the actual assets to determine whether there is agreement between the two amounts.

When custody of assets is adequately separated from record keeping, collusion among employees is usually necessary to perpetrate fraud. If collusion does exist, embezzlement can go undetected for a long time.

The separation feature, which should be incorporated in the system to protect all assets, is especially important in handling cash and negotiable items. For example, cash remittances from customers should be listed by personnel who have no access to accounting records. These lists can then be forwarded to the accounts receivable department for posting to customer accounts in the subsidiary ledger, while the remittances themselves are sent to the cashier for deposit. A duplicate list of remittances should also be given to the person who makes the cash receipts journal entries. This method provides several cross-checks—bank deposits must agree with the recorded cash receipts, and the Accounts Receivable control account must agree with subsidiary ledger totals. Finally, the bank should send its monthly statement to someone other than the cashier or those keeping cash-related records, so that an independent comparison of the bank statement and the company's records can be made. Exhibit 7–1 illustrates this example of separating accountability from custodianship.

Adequate Records and Equipment

Adequate records are important not only in accounting for a company's resources but also in providing management with accurate and reliable information. One of the most important features in a satisfactory record-keeping system is a comprehensive chart of accounts that classifies information in a manner best suited

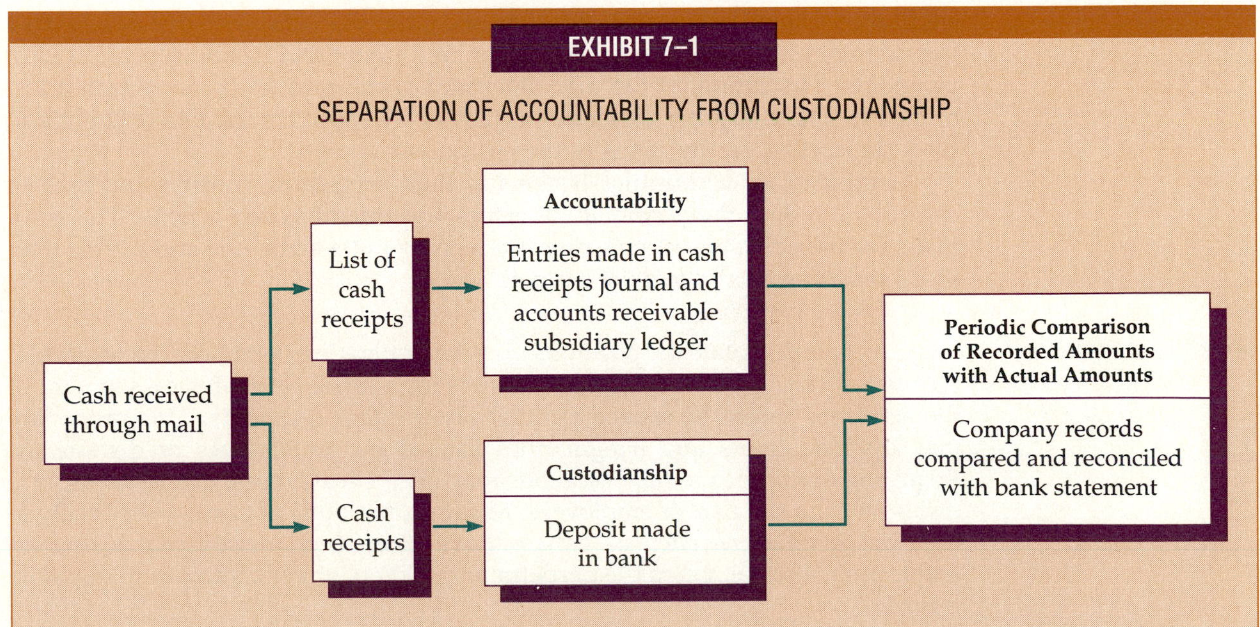

to management's needs. Control accounts and subsidiary records should be used when appropriate, so that work can be subdivided, and cross-checks may be made when the two types of accounts are reconciled. Control and subsidiary accounts can be used for such areas as accounts and notes receivable, accounts and notes payable, plant assets, and the major expense classifications of selling expense and administrative expense.

The forms used with the accounting records should promote accuracy and efficiency. If possible, individual forms should be prenumbered so that the sequence of forms used can be accounted for. Moreover, prenumbering helps a firm trace its transactions and reduces the possibility of failing to record a transaction. For example, suppose a firm issues prenumbered sales slips for each sale. A check of the number sequence would disclose any diversion of sales proceeds accomplished by destruction of the sales slip. Likewise, accounting for the sequence of prenumbered checks can detect whether unrecorded checks have been issued for unauthorized purchases.

Various types of equipment can be used with the record-keeping system to provide helpful controls. The cash registers used in retail operations, for example, have several important control features—a bell or other sound signals that the register has been opened, and a receipt allows the customer to check the transaction. Furthermore, most cash registers have a locked-in tape that accumulates and classifies transactions that have been registered. A responsible employee controlling the key can reconcile amounts shown on the tape with daily cash counts. Some registers contain separate cash drawers so that several clerks can handle the same cash register and each be accountable for his or her own operation. Another device that protects cash is the autographic register, which produces a locked-in copy of a sales invoice when the original is prepared in an over-the-counter sale. Check protectors, which perforate checks with indelible ink, are another example of a protective device for cash transactions. Checks written with such a machine cannot be altered without the change being obvious.

An electronic cash register tied in to a computer may improve control over the extension of credit to a customer using a credit card. Quick point-of-sale credit verification is possible. In a few seconds, the computer can ensure that the customer has not exceeded his or her credit limit and has been prompt with payments. The computer can also determine if the card has been reported lost or stolen. The computer either authorizes or disapproves the use of the credit card, depending on the status of the customer's account.

Computerized accounting systems include procedural controls and built-in controls to reduce the possibility of errors and unauthorized actions. The automatic features of such systems produce records more error-free and legible than those resulting from a manual system.

Rotation of Personnel

Some companies rotate the positions of certain operating personnel. For example, accounts receivable clerks, each responsible for a certain alphabetical segment of the accounts, might be rotated periodically to other segments. This procedure may disclose errors and irregularities caused by carelessness or dishonesty. Requiring employees to take vacations may also reveal lapses, carelessness, and dishonesty on the part of employees. Misappropriations of funds—especially in financial institutions such as banks—have often been discovered during an employee's absence, when the perpetrator could no longer control or manipulate records.

Internal Auditing

An important feature of the internal control structure of large companies is the internal audit function. The internal auditing department independently appraises the firm's financial and operational activities. In addition to reviewing activities for errors and irregularities, the internal audit staff determines whether prescribed policies and procedures are being followed and attempts to uncover wasteful and inefficient situations. Internal auditing is a *staff*, or advisory, function that consists of reviewing activities and making written recommendations to management. To be effective, the internal audit staff must be independent of operating (line) functions and should report to a high-ranking executive or to the firm's board of directors.

Physical Protection of Assets

Frequently, management initiates a number of physical controls to protect company property. Although some of these controls may not be closely related to the accounting system, they are almost invariably discussed in the context of internal control.

Only minimal amounts of cash or negotiable assets should be kept on the company premises, and these should be stored in a vault. A firm should keep its inventory in a secure area and maintain strict controls over issuances and physical counts of inventory. Security personnel are often engaged to protect inventories and other physical property. A company may employ outside protection services to safeguard against burglary and arson and might post gatekeepers at plant entrances and exits to observe employees and others entering and leaving the plant.

A business must be adequately insured against losses from fire, outside theft, and similar events. In addition to insuring its physical assets, a company should obtain fidelity insurance; employees having access to cash, securities, and other easily diverted assets should be bonded. For a fee, a bonding company guarantees to make good any loss from theft or embezzlement by the bonded person, up to some specified maximum amount. The bonding company investigates employees to be bonded, and anyone with a record of questionable integrity is not likely to qualify.

CASH AND CASH CONTROLS

In accounting, the term **cash** means paper money, coins, checks, and money orders—all items that are acceptable for deposit in a bank—as well as money already on deposit with a bank. IOUs, postdated checks (checks dated in the future), and uncollected customers' checks returned by the bank stamped "NSF" (not sufficient funds) are not considered cash but are normally classified as receivables. Notes sent to the bank for collection remain classified as notes receivable until notification of collection is received from the bank.

Cash in the Balance Sheet

Various ledger accounts are used to record cash transactions; some common examples are Cash on Hand, Petty Cash, and Cash in Bank. The Cash on Hand account reflects cash receipts not yet deposited in the bank, and Petty Cash represents a fund used for small disbursements. Cash in Bank usually refers to demand deposits in a checking account.

When a business firm has several checking accounts, a separate ledger account should be maintained for each account rather than one overall Cash in Bank account. Although a balance sheet prepared for management may show all

EXTERNAL EXPROPRIATIONS

A business is vulnerable to fraud not only by its employees, but also by its customers and suppliers. The following hypothetical examples show how a company can unwittingly fall prey to outside purloiners.

■ *Red flag: Open-ended contracts with suppliers.* The nature of contractual or other agreements for the supply of goods or services to a business may provide opportunities for fraud. A case in point: Central Fuel won a three-year contract to provide oil to the local school board. The contract was based on a fixed price-per-gallon for fuel oil delivered, but did not require an estimate of, nor place a limit on, the quantity of oil to be provided.

The meter in the truck that delivered the fuel was fixed so that it continued to run, even if the fuel hose had been shut off. Thus, Central Fuel was able to inflate the quantity of fuel alleged to have been delivered.

When the owner of Central Fuel was finally brought to trial, the prosecution revealed the results of an engineering study that showed that the amount of fuel that had been invoiced and allegedly delivered was considerably more than would have been required to maintain the heating system during the winter with all windows in the building wide open.

An open-ended contract also enabled Super Disposal Services, which was in the business of waste disposal, to defraud numerous customers. While SDS charged a flat fee for removal of waste bins, it also charged its customers for the cost, by weight, of the waste it disposed at local dump sites for them. Because none of the customers bothered to determine the weight of the waste removed by SDS, the company was able to defraud them by charging for inflated waste amounts. The heaviest weighbill on a given day was photocopied, and distributed to all customers, regardless of the amount of waste that each of them had had carted away.

Even when open-ended contracts are used, a business can forestall fraud by anticipating the amount of goods and services it is likely to require and comparing this with the charges. Any discrepancies will then be obvious, and will warrant immediate investigation.

■ *Red flag: An unusual increase in purchases by a customer during a brief period.* It's easy for customers to take unfair advantage of a longstanding business relationship; in fact, this often happens before a planned bankruptcy.

For example, Brittany Antiques, a company that had experienced a change in ownership and had established relationships with suppliers, was able to increase the volume of its purchases and delay payment for goods received before a planned bankruptcy. As a result it was able to acquire and dispose of large amounts of inventory without making payment—and to leave its suppliers empty-handed when the business went bankrupt.

To prevent a business from falling victim to a planned bankruptcy, it's essential to monitor customer orders on an ongoing basis and check into any sudden or unusual increases.

There are no simple, foolproof solutions to the problem of fraud. But you can provide optimum protection for your business by being alert to any red flags that exist.

From Robert J. Lindquist and James E. Baskerville, "To Catch a Thief," *World,* July–August 1985, p. 35. Reprinted by permission.

individual cash accounts, a balance sheet prepared for outsiders normally shows the combined balances of all cash accounts under a single heading, "Cash." Management is interested in the detail because it must establish policies on balances to be maintained in various bank accounts and on hand. Most outsiders, on the other hand, are interested only in the aggregated cash balance and its relationship to other items on the financial statements.

Cash amounts subject to use or withdrawal without restriction are current assets and are normally shown first in the balance sheet listing of assets. Sometimes the cash account may include an amount, called a **compensating balance,** that is not readily available for use. A compensating balance is a minimum amount that a financial institution requires a firm to maintain in its account as part of a borrowing arrangement. Compensating balances related to short-term borrowings are current assets but, if significant, should be reported separately from cash available for use without restriction. Compensating balances related to long-term borrowings should be classified among a firm's long-term assets.

Cash Control Procedures

A firm must control the handling and recording of cash because it is so susceptible to misappropriation. An adequate system of internal control over cash would include the following features:

1. Cash is handled separately from the recording of cash transactions.
2. The work and responsibilities of cash handling and recording are divided in such a way that errors are readily disclosed and the possibility of irregularities is reduced.
3. All cash receipts are deposited intact in the bank each day.
4. All major disbursements are made by check, and an imprest (fixed amount) fund is used for petty cash disbursements.

In our earlier discussion of internal control, we described and explained the desirability of the first two features. By observing the last two—depositing all receipts intact daily at the bank and making all disbursements by check—a company establishes a double record of cash transactions. One record is generated by the firm's record-keeping procedures, and the other is furnished by the bank. Comparing the two records and accounting for any differences provides control. This important procedure is called *reconciling the bank statement with the book record of cash transactions* or, simply, making a *bank reconciliation* (discussed later).

The Bank Account

When a firm opens a checking account at a bank, the members of the firm who are authorized to draw checks sign signature cards that the bank files. Occasionally, bank employees may check the signatures on these cards against the signatures on the checks.

The bank submits monthly statements to the depositor showing the beginning cash balance, all additions and deductions for the month, and the ending cash balance. In addition, the bank returns the paid (or canceled) checks for the month, together with "advice" slips indicating other charges and credits made to the account. The bank may also send copies of such advice slips individually during the month to the depositor.

To reduce handling costs, some banks do not return canceled checks to the depositor, but use a procedure called *check truncation*. The bank retains the canceled checks for a period of time (typically 90 days) and a microfilm copy of the checks for a longer period (at least one year). Should the depositor need to review a canceled check within these periods, the bank provides the check or a photocopy of it for a small fee. A bank's monthly statements to a depositor usually list paid checks in numerical sequence, so check truncation does not affect the preparation of a bank reconciliation. Further, businesses generally use a check preparation system that produces a copy of each check issued.

Exhibit 7–2 is an example of a bank statement. The left-hand section of the statement lists deposits and other credits in sequence by date. The middle section lists checks paid and other charges to the account. The checks are listed in

EXHIBIT 7–2

BANK STATEMENT

First National Bank • Madison
EAST WASHINGTON – CAPITOL SQUARE

STATEMENT OF ACCOUNT

Beta Company
101 Beltline Highway
Madison, Wisconsin
53718

ACCOUNT NUMBER
313111386

STATEMENT DATE: December 31, 19XX

Deposits/Credits		*Checks/Charges*			*Balance*	
Date	*Amount*	*No.*	*Date*	*Amount*	*Date*	*Amount*
12/01	420.00 ✓	149	12/02	125.00 ✓	12/01	6,060.30
12/02	630.00 ✓	154	12/03	56.25 ✓	12/02	6,565.30
12/07	560.80 ✓	155	12/10	135.00 ✓	12/03	6,509.05
12/10	480.25 ✓	156	12/08	315.10	12/07	6,801.19
12/14	525.00 ✓	157	12/07	233.26	12/08	6,486.09
12/17	270.25 ✓	158	12/11	27.14	12/10	6,831.34
12/21	640.20 ✓	159	12/18	275.00	12/11	6,804.20
12/26	300.00CM	160	12/15	315.37	12/14	7,329.20
12/26	475.00 ✓	161	12/17	76.40	12/15	7,013.83
12/30	440.00 ✓	162	12/21	325.60	12/17	7,207.68
		163	12/21	450.00	12/18	6,932.68
		164	12/23	239.00	12/21	6,731.58
		165	12/21	65.70	12/23	6,492.58
		166	12/28	482.43	12/26	7,262.58
		169	12/28	260.00	12/28	6,520.15
		170	12/31	122.50	12/30	6,590.04
		171	12/30	370.11	12/31	6,457.54
		RT	12/07	35.40		
		DM	12/26	5.00		
		SC	12/31	10.00		

Beginning Balance	*Deposits/Credits*		*Checks/Charges*		*Ending Balance*
	No.	*Amount*	*No.*	*Amount*	
11/30/XX 5,640.30	10	4,741.50	20	3,924.26	12/31/XX 6,457.54

Item Codes:
EC—Error Correction
SC—Service Charge
LS—List of Checks
DM—Debit Memo
OD—Overdraft
IN—Interest
CM—Credit Memo
RT—Returned Item

numerical sequence, and the payment date for each check is shown in the date column. Listing checks in numerical sequence helps the depositor identify checks written but not yet paid by the bank. The right-hand section shows the checking account balance as of the date shown in the date column. Each time a receipt or a payment occurs, a new balance is shown.

Code letters on a bank statement identify charges and credits not related to paying checks or making deposits. A legend usually appears at the bottom of the statement explaining the code letters. Although such codes are not standard from bank to bank, they are easy to understand. As we mentioned before, the depositor also receives an advice slip from the bank explaining nonroutine entries. The statement illustrated in Exhibit 7–2 uses the following codes:

EC —Error correction. Identifies transcription, arithmetic, and similar errors and corrections made by the bank.

DM—Debit memo. Identifies collection charges, repayment of bank loans, and other special charges made by the bank against the depositor's account.

CM —Credit memo. Identifies amounts collected by the bank for the depositor, such as a note receivable left at the bank by the depositor, or a loan from the bank to the depositor which is credited to the depositor's checking account.

SC —Service charge. Identifies the amount charged by the bank for servicing the account. The amount is normally based on the average balance maintained and the number of items processed during the month. Service charges are usually made on small accounts that are not otherwise profitable for the bank to handle.

OD —Overdraft. Indicates a negative, or credit, balance in the account.

RT —Returned item. Indicates items such as postdated checks or checks without proper endorsement received from customers and deposited. Sometimes NSF (not sufficient funds) checks charged back to the account are identified with these letters in the statement. NSF checks may also be identified with the letters DM (debit memo), explained earlier.

LS —List of checks. Identifies the total of a batch of checks too numerous to list separately on the statement. An adding machine tape listing the individual check amounts usually accompanies each batch of checks listed.

IN —Interest. Indicates the amount of interest added to the account. Sole proprietorships, nonprofit organizations, and individuals may open NOW (negotiable order of withdrawal) checking accounts and earn interest monthly based on the balance maintained in the account.

The Bank Reconciliation

Almost invariably, the ending balance on the bank statement differs from the balance in the company's Cash in Bank account. Some reasons for the differences are:

1. **Outstanding checks**—checks written and deducted in arriving at the book balance but not yet presented to the bank for payment.
2. Deposits not yet credited by the bank—deposits made near the end of the month and processed by the bank *after* the monthly statement has been prepared. These **deposits in transit** will appear on next month's statement.
3. Charges made by the bank but not yet reflected on the depositor's books—for example, service and collection charges, NSF checks, and repayments of the depositor's bank loans charged against the checking account.

4. Credits made by the bank but not yet reflected on the depositor's books—for example, collections of notes and drafts by the bank for the depositor and interest earned by the depositor on the checking account balance.
5. Accounting errors—errors made either by the depositor or by the bank.

The **bank reconciliation** is a schedule that accounts for any of the above differences between the bank statement balance and the company's book balance. Although we could reconcile either of these figures to the other, it is more convenient to reconcile both figures to an adjusted balance, which is the cash balance that will appear on the balance sheet. This amount could be withdrawn from the bank after all outstanding items have cleared. A convenient reconciliation form is illustrated below.

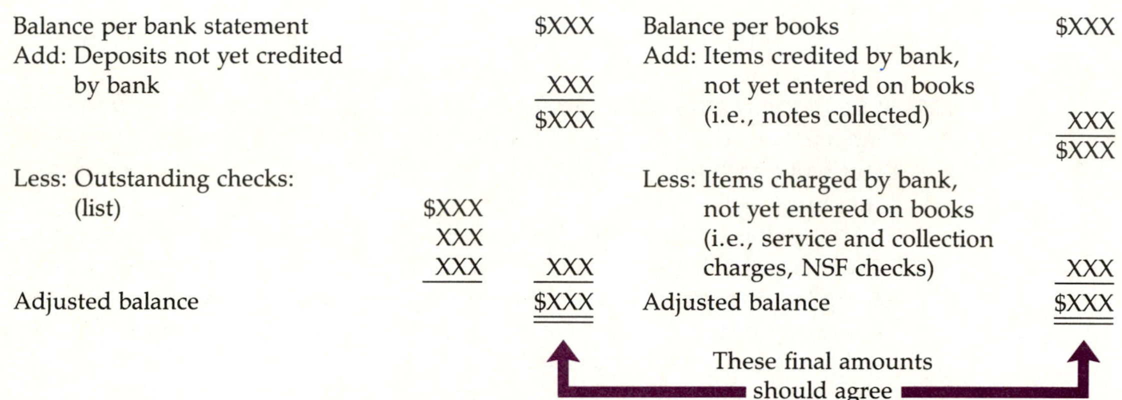

Balance per bank statement		$XXX	Balance per books	$XXX
Add: Deposits not yet credited by bank		XXX	Add: Items credited by bank, not yet entered on books (i.e., notes collected)	XXX
		$XXX		$XXX
Less: Outstanding checks: (list)	$XXX		Less: Items charged by bank, not yet entered on books (i.e., service and collection charges, NSF checks)	
	XXX			
	XXX	XXX		XXX
Adjusted balance		$XXX	Adjusted balance	$XXX

After the reconciliation is prepared, the adjusted balance per bank statement should agree with the adjusted book balance. If these amounts do not agree, we should look carefully for reconciling items omitted from the schedule or for possible errors in record keeping. The bank reconciliation may not only bring to light transactions that must be recorded, but may also detect errors or irregularities.

BANK RECONCILIATION PROCEDURE Assume that a December 31 bank reconciliation is to be prepared for the Beta Company, whose bank statement is illustrated in Exhibit 7–2. Exhibits 7–3 and 7–4 show the company's December cash receipts and cash disbursements journals, respectively, in abbreviated form. Cash receipts journals may have a column for bank deposits, as shown in Exhibit 7–3.

After the cash journals have been posted, the Cash in Bank account of the Beta Company appears as follows:

Cash in Bank (First National Bank) Account No. 11

Date		Description	Post. Ref.	Debit	Credit	Balance
19XX						
Nov.	30	Balance				5,744.05
Dec.	31		CR	4,246.50		9,990.55
	31		CD		4,699.27	5,291.28

EXHIBIT 7–3

BETA COMPANY
(PARTIAL) CASH RECEIPTS JOURNAL
DECEMBER 19XX

Date		Description	Cash Receipts	Bank Deposits
19XX				
Dec.	1	Hickman, Inc.	$ 230.00	
	2	Cash sales	400.00	$ 630.00 ✓
	4	Denton Company	410.80	
	7	Jewel and Son	150.00	560.80 ✓
	8	Benson Company (note)	300.00	
	10	Cash sales	180.25	480.25 ✓
	14	Taylor Brothers	525.00	525.00 ✓
	17	Cash sales	270.25	270.25 ✓
	18	Johnson Company	250.15	
	21	Bates Company	390.05	640.20 ✓
	26	Jordan Brothers	475.00	475.00 ✓
	30	Cash sales	440.00	440.00 ✓
	31	Johnson Company	225.00	225.00
			$4,246.50	$4,246.50

The procedures for reconciling the December 31 bank statement balance of $6,457.54 with the $5,291.28 balance on the company's books are:

1. Trace outstanding items on the previous (November) bank reconciliation to this period's statement. The November reconciliation for the Beta Company appears in Exhibit 7–5. The items identified with the ✓ mark, which were outstanding at the end of November, were all processed in December; these amounts are identified by the same mark (✓) on the bank statement in Exhibit 7–2. Any checks that have still not cleared in December should appear again on the December reconciliation.
2. Compare the record of deposits in the cash receipts journal (Exhibit 7–3) with the list of deposits on the bank statement. A check mark (✓) has been placed next to the amounts that appear in both records. Note that the $225.00 deposit made on December 31 does not appear on the bank statement. Enter this item in the December bank reconciliation as a deposit not yet credited by the bank.
3. Arrange in numerical sequence the paid checks that have been returned by the bank. Compare the record of checks written from the cash disbursements journal (Exhibit 7–4) with the checks paid by the bank and returned with the bank statement. A check mark (✓) has been placed in the cash disbursements journal next to the amount of each check paid by the bank. Since checks numbered 167, 168, 172, and 173 have not cleared the bank, enter them in the December bank reconciliation as outstanding checks. (If paid

EXHIBIT 7–4

BETA COMPANY
(PARTIAL) CASH DISBURSEMENTS JOURNAL
DECEMBER 19XX

Date		Description	Check No.	Cash Payments
19XX				
Dec.	1	Boynton Company	156	$ 315.10 ✓
	2	Meyer, Inc.	157	233.26 ✓
	4	Rapid Transit, Transportation In	158	27.14 ✓
	7	Acme Realty, December rent	159	275.00 ✓
	8	Stanton Company	160	315.37 ✓
	10	Horder, Inc., Office supplies	161	76.40 ✓
	14	A. L. Smith Company	162	325.60 ✓
	17	J. B. Adams, Office salary	163	450.00 ✓
	17	O. L. Holmes, Office salary	164	239.00 ✓
	18	Abbot Van Lines, Transportation In	165	65.70 ✓
	21	Millston, Inc.	166	482.43 ✓
	21	Odana Corporation	167	301.66
	22	R. W. Knight, Cash purchase	168	149.50
	26	W. A. Sutton	169	260.00 ✓
	29	Border and Son, Cash purchase	170	122.50 ✓
	30	R. L. Olson	171	370.11 ✓
	31	J. B. Adams, Office salary	172	450.00
	31	O. L. Holmes, Office salary	173	240.50
				$4,699.27

EXHIBIT 7–5

BETA COMPANY
BANK RECONCILIATION
NOVEMBER 30, 19XX

Balance per bank statement		$5,640.30	Balance per books	$5,754.05
Add: Deposit not credited by bank		420.00 ✓		
		$6,060.30		
Less: Outstanding checks:			Less: Bank service charge	10.00
No. 149	$125.00 ✓			
No. 154	56.25 ✓			
No. 155	135.00 ✓	316.25		
Adjusted balance		$5,744.05	Adjusted balance	$5,744.05

checks are not returned with the bank statement, compare the record of checks written from the cash disbursements journal with the numerical listing of paid checks on the bank statement.)

4. Scan the bank statement for charges and credits not yet reflected in the company's records. Note that the statement contains a charge of $35.40 for a returned item, a debit memo of $5.00, and a service charge of $10.00. Also, a credit for $300.00 appears in the deposits column on December 26. Bank advices indicate that an NSF check for $35.40 was charged against the company's account; that a $300.00 note receivable was collected on the company's behalf and a $5.00 collection charge was made; and that a $10.00 service charge was made for the month. Enter these items also in the December bank reconciliation.

After the preceding procedures have been completed, the December bank reconciliation for the Beta Company appears as shown in Exhibit 7–6.

Before financial statements are prepared for the period ended December 31, journal entries should be made to bring the Cash account balance into agreement with the adjusted balance shown on the reconciliation. The entries for Beta Company would reflect the collection of the note receivable and the related collection expense, reclassification of the NSF check as an account receivable, and the bank service charge for the month.

Cash	295.00	
Miscellaneous Expense	5.00	
Notes Receivable		300.00
To record note collected by bank, less service charge.		
Accounts Receivable	35.40	
Cash		35.40
To reclassify NSF check as an account receivable.		

EXHIBIT 7–6

BETA COMPANY
BANK RECONCILIATION
DECEMBER 31, 19XX

Balance per bank statement		$6,457.54	Balance per books		$5,291.28
Add: Deposits not credited by bank		225.00	Add: Collection of note	$300.00	
			Less: Collection charge	5.00	295.00
		$6,682.54			$5,586.28
Less: Outstanding checks:					
No. 167	$301.66				
No. 168	149.50				
No. 172	450.00		Less: NSF check	$ 35.40	
No. 173	240.50	1,141.66	Bank service charge	10.00	45.40
Adjusted balance		$5,540.88	Adjusted balance		$5,540.88

Miscellaneous Expense	10.00	
Cash		10.00
To record bank service charge for December.		

Electronic Funds Transfer

Billions of paper checks are written each year by businesses and individuals. The costs of processing this large volume of checks have motivated financial institutions to develop systems for transferring funds among parties electronically, without the need for paper checks. The exchange of cash through such a system is called **electronic funds transfer (EFT).**

A typical example of EFT is the payment of a payroll. An employer firm obtains authorizations from its employees to deposit their payroll checks directly to their checking accounts. The firm then sends to the bank a magnetic tape coded with the appropriate payroll data. The bank's computer processes the magnetic tape, deducts the total payroll amount from the firm's checking account, and adds each employee's payroll amount to his or her checking account.

EFT may also be useful for retailers in situations where customers typically pay for goods with a check at the time of purchase. Some grocery stores, for example, now use EFT. At the check-out counter, the customer uses a plastic card to activate a computer terminal connected with the bank. Funds to pay for the groceries are immediately transferred from the customer's checking account to the grocery store's account at the bank. This procedure not only eliminates the cost of processing the paper checks for the bank, but also eliminates the risk of bad checks for the grocery store.

The use of EFT will increase with the development of expanded computer networks capable of handling electronic funds transfers. The specific controls over cash transactions handled through EFT, of course, may vary from the internal control procedures under a paper check system. However, adequate controls are no less important in an electronic funds transfer system.

THE PETTY CASH FUND

Most business firms find it inconvenient and expensive to write checks for small expenditures. Therefore, small amounts of cash needed for such items as postage, delivery service, and purchases of supplies and notions are most conveniently handled by establishing a **petty cash fund.**

The size of the petty cash fund depends on the number and the amounts of minor expenditures. Of course, it is unwise to have a large amount of cash on hand because of the risk of theft or misuse. Yet, too frequent replenishment can be a nuisance. Many firms maintain funds that will last three or four weeks. The size of expenditures made from the fund is also usually limited.

Although the use of a petty cash fund technically violates the control maxim of making all expenditures by check, control can be maintained by handling the fund on an *imprest* basis and by following certain well-established procedures. In accounting, an imprest fund contains a fixed amount of cash.

Although expenditures from an imprest petty cash fund are made in currency and coin, the fund is established by writing a check against the general bank account. Replenishments are also accomplished by issuing checks—after a review of expenditures. Therefore, in the final analysis, all expenditures are actually controlled by check.

Establishing the Fund

Assume that the Beta Company establishes a petty cash fund of $100. It draws a check payable to Cash and exchanges it at the bank for currency and coin in denominations that are convenient for small expenditures. The entry reflecting establishment of the fund is:

Petty Cash	100	
Cash in Bank		100
To establish imprest petty cash fund.		

As evidence of a disbursement from the fund, the person in charge should place a prenumbered petty cash receipt in the petty cash box. At any time, the total cash on hand plus the amounts on the receipts should equal $100. Each receipt should give the date, amount, and nature of the expenditure and should be signed by the recipient of the cash. Such documents as cash register tapes and copies of invoices should be attached to the receipts.

Replenishing the Fund

When the fund must be replenished, a check is drawn to Cash in an amount that will bring the cash value of the fund back to $100. Expenditures from the fund are analyzed according to expense or other account category and recorded in the books. For example, assume that the Beta Company's fund has been drawn down to $28 and that analysis of the $72 in receipts reveals the following expenditures: Office Expense, $40; Transportation In, $27; and Postage Expense, $5. The bookkeeper makes the following entry in the cash disbursements journal (shown in general journal form):

Office Expense	40	
Transportation In	27	
Postage Expense	5	
Cash in Bank		72
To replenish petty cash fund.		

The fund cashier cashes the replenishment check at the bank and places the cash in the petty cash box.

If the imprest amount is adequate, no further entries are made to the Petty Cash account itself. Notice that replenishment results in an entry to the Cash in Bank account. Only when the prescribed amount of the imprest fund is changed will entries be made to the Petty Cash account, increasing or decreasing the amount of the fund.

One person in the firm's office should be solely responsible for custody of the fund and expenditures made from it. The replenishment checks, however, should be written by another authorized person, after review of the petty cash receipts and the expense distribution. Furthermore, this person should stamp, perforate, or otherwise mutilate the supporting receipts and documents to prevent them from being used again as a basis for reimbursement.

Cash Short and Over

Errors in making change from cash funds result in less or more cash than can be accounted for. Usually, such shortages or overages are not material in amount. An account called **Cash Short and Over** is commonly used to record these discrepancies; shortages are debited to the account, and overages are credited. For example, suppose a $100 petty cash fund contains $80 in receipts for office expense and only $16 in currency and coins. The entry to replenish the fund and to record the $4 shortage would be:

Office Expense	80	
Cash Short and Over	4	
Cash in Bank		84
To replenish petty cash fund and record shortage.		

If the fund had contained $24 in cash together with the $80 in expense receipts, the $4 overage would be credited to the Cash Short and Over account. The credit to Cash in Bank for replenishment would be $76.

The Cash Short and Over account may also be used to record cash short or over from sales when cash register tape totals do not agree with the count of cash receipts. Large discrepancies, particularly recurring shortages, should always be investigated to determine appropriate corrective steps.

A Cash Short and Over account with a debit balance at the close of an accounting period is classified as Miscellaneous Expense on the income statement. A credit balance can be classified as Other Income.

INTERNAL CONTROL IN OTHER AREAS

While it is vitally important to establish effective controls over the handling of and accounting for cash, control should also be provided for a firm's other activities. As with cash, most controls separate the authorization of a transaction, the accounting for the transaction, and the custody of any related assets. For example, the purchase and sale of securities normally require authorization by a company's board of directors, and officers who have access to the securities should not have access to the accounting records. Other personnel should record security transactions and keep a record of security certificates by certificate number and amount.

Similarly, clerks handling inventory items should not have access to inventory records, and their duties should be separated from the receiving department and the processing of accounts payable. Similar controls should be exercised over receivables, plant assets, payroll transactions, and every other facet of business activity.

The subject of internal control is quite complex. Both external and internal auditors devote a great deal of attention to internal control when analyzing an accounting system and preparing audits. The importance of internal control is underscored by the Foreign Corrupt Practices Act. Among other provisions, this law requires all corporations registering with the Securities and Exchange Commission to devise and maintain an adequate system of internal accounting controls.

SHORT-TERM INVESTMENTS

Corporate stocks and bonds may be acquired by a variety of investors, including individuals, partnerships, corporations, mutual funds, pension funds, foundations, and trusts. Shares of stock, of course, represent ownership interests in a corporation. Some corporations have more than one type of stock (discussed in Chapter 15). Investors holding a corporation's **common stock** have the most basic ownership rights. **Bonds** are long-term debt securities issued by corporations and various governmental agencies. Our discussion here focuses on short-term investments in stocks and bonds made by corporations.

A firm issuing stocks or bonds may sell directly to investors, or the securities may be sold through an underwriter. Most investments, however, do not involve original issues. In the typical investment, one investor purchases from another investor who happens to be selling at that time. Stocks and bonds are bought and sold on organized exchanges—such as the New York Stock Exchange—and through a less formal *over-the-counter market*. Both the buyer and the seller of a security normally use the services of a broker to acquire or dispose of their investments.

Many firms make temporary investments in highly marketable securities using seasonal excesses of cash. Furthermore, some firms invest in high-quality stocks and bonds as "back-up cash." Management could convert these securities to cash, if needed, without interfering with the company's normal operations. In the meantime, the investments produce dividend and interest income for the company. Both of these types of investments (investments of seasonal excesses of cash and for "back-up cash") are considered **short-term investments** and are classified as current assets on the balance sheet. They may be identified as either short-term investments or **marketable securities** on the balance sheet.

Short-term Investments in Stocks

When stock is purchased as a short-term investment, the amount initially recorded in the investment account is the stock's cost—that is, its total purchase price. The purchase price may include charges for such items as broker's commissions and transfer taxes. Suppose 100 shares of United Pride common stock are acquired as a short-term investment on October 1 at a cost of $4,290, including commissions and taxes. The investment is recorded as follows:

Oct. 1	Investment in United Pride Stock	4,290	
	Cash		4,290
	To record purchase of 100 shares of common stock for $4,290.		

DIVIDENDS A corporation's board of directors may declare a **dividend,** which is a distribution of the corporation's assets. The asset distributed is usually cash. A corporation also may distribute a **stock dividend**—shares of its own stock. For example, if a board of directors declares a 5% stock dividend, then additional shares of stock equal to 5% of the corporation's outstanding stock are distributed to the current stockholders in proportion to their current stock holdings.

Cash dividends do not accrue on shares of stock. A corporation has no legal obligation to pay a dividend until it is declared by the board of directors. A company holding stock may record the cash dividend after it has been declared by debiting Dividends Receivable and crediting Dividend Income, but ordinarily no entry is made until the dividend is received. Assuming the United Pride board of directors declares a cash dividend of $1.00 per share and dividend income is recorded when received, the entry to record the receipt of the dividend on December 29 would be:

Dec. 29	Cash	100	
	Dividend Income		100
	To record receipt of $100 dividend on investment in United Pride stock.		

The receipt of a stock dividend does not constitute income, and requires no formal journal entry. A memorandum of the number of shares received, however, should be recorded in the investment account. The recipient of the stock dividend now holds more stock without further investment, so the average cost of each share held has been reduced. If United Pride declares a 10% common stock dividend, the company holding 100 shares of United Pride would make the following notation on receipt of 10 additional shares:

> (Memorandum) Received 10 shares of United Pride common stock as stock dividend. Average cost per share of 110 shares held is now $39 ($4,290/110).

LOWER OF COST OR MARKET FOR PORTFOLIO A corporation's **stock portfolio** refers to its investment in several different stocks. At the end of an accounting period, short-term stock investments are reported on the balance sheet at the lower of the aggregate cost or market value of the portfolio. A portfolio valuation is used because firms typically view (and manage) their stock investments as collective assets (a portfolio). Should the aggregate market value drop below total cost, an unrealized loss[3] is recorded and a contra asset account (to offset short-term stock investments) is credited. To illustrate, let us assume a company has the following portfolio of short-term stock investments at the end of its first year of operations:

Stock	Cost	Market Value
United Pride Common	$ 4,290	$ 3,800
Bayou Oil Common	17,000	17,500
Swan, Inc., Common	16,500	15,200
Total	$37,790	$36,500

Because the total market value ($36,500) is less than total cost ($37,790), the following journal entry is made:

Dec. 31	Unrealized Loss on Short-term Investments	1,290	
	Allowance to Reduce Short-term Investments to Market		1,290
	To record unrealized loss on portfolio of short-term stock investments.		

The unrealized loss is reported in the current year's income statement. The credit to the contra asset account (1) permits original cost to remain in the various stock investment accounts and (2) reduces the total book value of the investments to market value on the balance sheet. The short-term stock investments would appear on the balance sheet as follows:

Short-term Stock Investments (cost)	$37,790	
Less: Allowance to Reduce Short-term Investments to Market	1,290	$36,500

[3]Unrealized losses are losses on securities still owned by the firm. For details, see *Statement of Financial Accounting Standards No. 12*, "Accounting for Certain Marketable Securities" (Stamford, CT: Financial Accounting Standards Board, 1975).

Or, the investments may be reported in condensed form:

Short-term Stock Investments, at market (cost $37,790)	$36,500

Of course, if the portfolio's market value exceeds its total cost, the investments are reported at cost and no allowance account is created.

SALE OF SHORT-TERM STOCK INVESTMENTS When a short-term stock investment is sold, a gain or loss is recorded equal to the difference between the proceeds of the sale and the stock's original cost (or the original cost adjusted for the effect of a stock dividend). For example, if all 110 shares of the United Pride stock discussed above were sold on February 1 of the next year for $3,800, the following entry would be made:

Feb. 1	Cash	3,800	
	Loss on Sale of Investments	490	
	Investment in United Pride Stock		4,290
	To record sale of stock for $3,800.		

The $490 loss is a realized loss because it relates to securities sold by the firm. Realized losses and realized gains from the sale of investments are included in the income statement in the year the securities are sold.

RECOVERY OF UNREALIZED LOSS The difference between the total cost and the market value of a short-term stock portfolio will likely change from one year-end to the next because of changes in market values or in the portfolio's composition. Thus, the contra asset account will be increased or decreased each year-end to reflect the net unrealized portfolio loss at that time. If the net unrealized loss at year-end is smaller than it was the year before, the adjusting entry records a recovery of an unrealized loss. To illustrate, let us assume that the company whose investments we have been analyzing has the following portfolio of short-term stock investments at the end of its second year of operations:

Stock	Cost	Market Value
Bayou Oil Common	$17,000	$17,600
Swan, Inc., Common	16,500	15,700
Total	$33,500	$33,300

The net unrealized loss is now $200 ($33,500 − $33,300); at the end of the preceding year, it had been $1,290. The following entry would adjust the allowance account:

Dec. 31	Allowance to Reduce Short-term Investments to Market	1,090	
	Recovery of Unrealized Loss on Short-term Investments		1,090
	To record decrease in net unrealized loss on short-term stock investments.		

The recovery of the unrealized loss is included in the current year's income statement. The $200 credit balance now in the allowance account offsets the cost of short-term investments in the year-end balance sheet.

Short-term Investments in Bonds

A short-term bond investment is initially recorded at its acquisition cost, which includes any broker's commissions and transfer taxes. Because a bond is a debt security, the bondholder receives periodic interest payments from the bond issuer. Interest accrues daily on a bond and usually is paid semiannually. On an interest payment date, a bondholder receives the full amount of interest accrued since the last payment date, regardless of when the bond was purchased. As a result, the purchase price of a bond that is sold between interest payment dates includes not only the current market price but also any interest accrued since the last interest payment date. The bond seller, therefore, receives the interest income earned up to the date of sale. The bond investor debits the accrued interest purchased to a Bond Interest Receivable account. Because the accrued interest is received with the first interest payment, it is not treated as part of the initial cost of the investment.

The **face value,** or **maturity value,** of a bond is the amount of principal to be repaid at the maturity date. The annual rate of interest payable on a bond—often called the *coupon* or *nominal* rate of interest—is stated in the bond agreement. To determine the amount of interest paid semiannually on such bonds, we multiply the face value by one-half the coupon rate of interest.

Purchasing a bond at **par** means paying an amount equal to its face value. A bond purchased at a *discount* costs less than its face value, and a bond purchased at a *premium* costs more than its face value. An investor discounts a bond when the current market rate of interest exceeds the bond's coupon interest rate; a bond sells at a premium when its coupon rate exceeds the current market interest rate. Bond prices are usually stated as a percentage of face value—for example, a bond selling at 98 costs 98% of its face value, and a bond quoted at 101 sells for 101% of its face value.

Let us assume that $10,000 face value of Anko Company 12% bonds are bought on May 1 at 97 plus accrued interest. The brokerage commission is $40. Semiannual interest is paid on January 1 and July 1. The accrued interest from January 1 to May 1 is $400 ($\$10,000 \times 0.12 \times \frac{4}{12}$), which is recorded separately in a Bond Interest Receivable account. The cost entered in the bond investment account is $9,740, including the brokerage commission. The following entry records the acquisition:

May 1	Investment in Anko Company Bonds	9,740	
	Bond Interest Receivable	400	
	Cash		10,140
	To record purchase of bonds at 97 plus commission of $40 plus four months' accrued interest.		

The entry to record the receipt of the semiannual interest payment on July 1 would be:

July 1	Cash	600	
	Bond Interest Receivable		400
	Bond Interest Income		200
	To record receipt of semiannual interest on Anko Company bonds.		

The $200 credit to interest income reflects the interest earned for the two months the bonds have been held. The other $400 is the accrued interest purchased when the bonds were acquired.

Short-term bond investments are usually sold at a gain or loss. Such gain or loss is computed by comparing the proceeds of the sale, net of any accrued interest received, to the carrying value of the investment. If the proceeds from the sale of the Anko Company bonds on October 1 were $9,800 plus accrued interest of $300 for three months, the following entry would be made:

Oct. 1	Cash	10,100	
	Investment in Anko Company Bonds		9,740
	Bond Interest Income		300
	Gain on Sale of Investments		60
	To record sale of bond investment for $9,800 plus interest of $300.		

Certificates of Deposit

In addition to marketable stocks and bonds, a corporation may invest excess cash in another type of security—a **certificate of deposit (CD).** These certificates may be purchased at banks and other financial institutions. They offer fixed rates of return on investments for specified periods (such as 90 days, six months, or one year). Generally, the fixed interest rate increases with the amount or the duration of the investment. CDs are recorded at cost and reported on the balance sheet as a current asset immediately below cash. Interest income from CDs is recorded in the period in which it is earned. These accounting guidelines apply also to short-term investments in other forms of savings certificates. The investment is recorded at its cost, and interest income is recorded in the period in which it is earned.

KEY POINTS FOR CHAPTER OBJECTIVES

1 Describe the internal control features of an accounting system (pp. 249–53).

- An internal control structure consists of the policies and procedures established to help insure that specific entity objectives are achieved.
- Accounting controls relate to the reliability of accounting data and the protection of assets.
- Accounting controls include competent personnel, assignment of responsibility, division of work, separation of accountability from custodianship, adequate records and equipment, rotation of personnel, internal auditing, and physical protection of assets.

2 Identify key controls over cash and explain the procedures for preparing a bank reconciliation (pp. 253–62).

- Depositing all receipts intact at the bank and making all major cash disbursements by check are important cash controls. These procedures provide a double record of cash—the firm's record and the bank's record.
- Neither the book balance nor the bank statement balance of cash usually represents the cash balance shown on the balance sheet. Both amounts are reconciled to a third figure—the adjusted balance—which appears on the balance sheet and is the amount that could be withdrawn after all outstanding items have cleared.

3 Discuss the accounting for a petty cash fund (pp. 262–64).

- Petty Cash is debited when an imprest fund for small expenditures is established or increased. When the fund is replenished, the individual accounts for which expenditures have been made are debited.

4 Describe the accounting for short-term investments in stocks and bonds (pp. 264–69).

- Short-term investments in stock are normally carried at the lower of cost or market value of the portfolio. Unrealized losses or recoveries of unrealized losses are included in the income statement, as are realized gains and losses from the sale of investments.
- Short-term investments in bonds are recorded at their acquisition cost. When sold, the difference between the sales proceeds (net of accrued interest) and the bond's carrying value is shown as a gain (when proceeds exceed carrying value) or as a loss (when carrying value exceeds proceeds).

KEY TERMS USED IN THIS CHAPTER

accounting controls 249
bank reconciliation 258
bond 265
cash 253
cash short and over 263
certificate of deposit (CD) 269
common stock 264
compensating balance 254
deposits in transit 257
dividend 265
electronic funds transfer (EFT) 262
face value (bond) 268
internal control structure 249
marketable securities 265
maturity value (bond) 268
outstanding checks 257
par (bond) 268
petty cash fund 262
short-term investments 265
stock dividend 265
stock portfolio 266

SELF-TEST QUESTIONS FOR REVIEW

(Answers are at the end of this chapter.)

1. A system of good internal accounting controls includes
   (a) Sharing the responsibility and authority for a given function among competent employees.
   (b) Placing one person in complete control over a sequence of related transactions.
   (c) Using checks and sales invoices that are prenumbered.
   (d) Keeping large amounts of cash on the company premises.
2. A bank reconciliation is
   (a) A formal financial statement that lists all of a firm's bank account balances.
   (b) A merger of two banks that previously were competitors.
   (c) A statement sent monthly by a bank to a depositor that lists all deposits, checks paid, and other credits and charges to the depositor's account for the month.
   (d) A schedule that accounts for differences between a firm's cash balance as shown on its bank statement and the balance shown in its general ledger Cash account.
3. An entry to debit Petty Cash is made when
   (a) A petty cash fund is established.
   (b) A petty cash fund is replenished.
   (c) A petty cash fund is established *and* when it is replenished.
   (d) A shortage in the petty cash fund is recorded.
4. Which of the following is a contra asset account?
   (a) Recovery of Unrealized Loss on Short-term Investments.
   (b) Unrealized Loss on Short-term Investments.
   (c) Loss on Sale of Investments.
   (d) Allowance to Reduce Short-term Investments to Market.
5. Finn Corporation purchased bonds with a face value of $50,000 and a 10% coupon rate at 99 plus three months' accrued interest. The brokerage commission is $50. What amount should be debited to the bond investment account?
   (a) $50,000 (c) $49,500
   (b) $49,550 (d) $50,800

DEMONSTRATION PROBLEM FOR REVIEW

At December 31 of the current year, the Cash account in Tyler Company's general ledger had a debit balance of $18,434.27. The December 31 bank statement showed a balance of $19,726.40. In reconciling the two amounts, you discover the following:

1. Bank deposits made by Tyler on December 31 amounting to $2,145.40 do not appear on the bank statement.
2. A non-interest-bearing note receivable for $2,000, left with the bank for collection, was collected by the bank near the end of December. The bank credited the proceeds, less a $5 collection charge, on the bank statement. Tyler Company has not recorded the collection.
3. Accompanying the bank statement is a debit memorandum indicating that John Miller's check for $450 was charged against Tyler's bank account on December 30 because of insufficient funds.
4. Check No. 586, written for advertising expense of $869.10, was recorded as $896.10 in Tyler Company's cash disbursements journal.

5. A comparison of the paid checks returned by the bank with the cash disbursements journal revealed the following checks still outstanding at December 31:

No. 561	$306.63	No. 591	$190.00
No. 585	440.00	No. 592	282.50
No. 588	476.40	No. 593	243.00

6. The bank mistakenly charged Tyler Company's account for check printing costs of $30.50, which should have been charged to Taylor Company.

7. The bank charged Tyler Company's account $42.50 for rental of a safe deposit box. No entry has been made in Tyler's records for this expense.

REQUIRED

(a) Prepare a bank reconciliation at December 31.

(b) Prepare any necessary journal entries at December 31.

SOLUTION TO DEMONSTRATION PROBLEM

(a)

Tyler Company
Bank Reconciliation
December 31, 19XX

Balance per bank statement		$19,726.40	Balance per books		$18,434.27
Add: Deposits not credited by bank		2,145.40	Add: Collection of note	$2,000.00	
Error by bank (Check printing charge of Taylor Co.)		30.50	Less: Collection charge	5.00	1,995.00
		$21,902.30	Error in recording check No. 586		27.00
Less: Outstanding checks:					$20,456.27
No. 561	$306.63		Less:		
No. 585	440.00		NSF check	$450.00	
No. 588	476.40		Charge for		
No. 591	190.00		safe deposit		
No. 592	282.50		box	42.50	492.50
No. 593	243.00	1,938.53			
Adjusted balance		$19,963.77	Adjusted balance		$19,963.77

(b)

Date	Account	Debit	Credit
Dec. 31	Cash	1,995.00	
	Miscellaneous Expense	5.00	
	Notes Receivable		2,000.00
	To record collection of note by bank, less collection charge.		
31	Cash	27.00	
	Advertising Expense		27.00
	To correct error in recording advertising expense.		
31	Accounts Receivable	450.00	
	Cash		450.00
	To reclassify NSF check as an account receivable.		
31	Miscellaneous Expense	42.50	
	Cash		42.50
	To record rental expense of safe deposit box.		

QUESTIONS

7–1 Define *internal control structure;* define *accounting controls.*

7–2 Name several specific features of a good system of internal accounting controls.

7–3 Why is work division an important feature of good internal accounting controls?

7–4 What internal control procedures are especially important in handling cash transactions?

7–5 Indicate whether the following statements relating to internal control structures are true or false:
(a) Under the principle of separating accountability and physical custodianship, the accounts receivable bookkeeper should not make bank deposits.
(b) When possible, the general ledger bookkeeper should also keep subsidiary records.
(c) Rotation of personnel in record-keeping duties violates the rule that responsibility should not be shared.
(d) Even with careful attention to good internal controls, guarding against embezzlements and irregularities involving collusion among employees is difficult.
(e) Internal auditing departments eliminate the need for audits by independent public accountants.

7–6 Accounting controls have two objectives. What objective is served by (a) keeping the petty cash fund in a locked desk drawer, and (b) having a comprehensive chart of accounts?

7–7 What is the purpose of a bank reconciliation?

7–8 In preparing a bank reconciliation, how should you determine (a) deposits not recorded in the bank statement and (b) outstanding checks?

7–9 Indicate whether the following bank reconciliation items should be (1) added to the bank statement balance, (2) deducted from the bank statement balance, (3) added to the ledger account balance, or (4) deducted from the ledger account balance:
(a) Bank service charge.
(b) NSF check.
(c) Deposit in transit.
(d) Outstanding check.
(e) Bank error charging company's account with another company's check.
(f) Difference of $270 in amount of check written for $410 but recorded in the cash disbursements journal for $140.

7–10 Which of the items listed in Question 7–9 require a journal entry on the company's books?

7–11 What is an imprest petty cash fund? How is such a fund established and replenished? Describe the accounting entries involved.

7–12 In preparing to replenish the $200 petty cash fund, the cashier discovers that the fund contains $186 in petty cash vouchers for office expenses and $10 in currency and coins. (a) What should be the amount of the replenishment check? (b) How should the $4 discrepancy be recorded?

7–13 Why do corporations make short-term investments in securities? Where should short-term investments be classified in the balance sheet?

7–14 Interest on bond investments is accrued, but dividends on stock investments are not accrued. Why?

7–15 What entry, if any, should be made when a corporation receives a stock dividend on a short-term stock investment? What entry should be made when a cash dividend is received on a short-term stock investment?

7–16 At what amount are short-term stock investments reported in the balance sheet? Where are unrealized losses on the short-term stock investments portfolio reported?

7–17 Loran Corporation purchased bonds with a face value of $60,000 and a 10% coupon rate at 102 plus two months' accrued interest. Calculate the total cash outlay for the bonds. What amount should be debited to the bond investment account?

7–18 What is a certificate of deposit? When should interest income on a certificate of deposit be recorded?

EXERCISES

Internal control

7–19 The following four situations occurred in Maple Corporation:

(a) The mail opener converted a check payable to Maple Corporation to his personal use. The check was included in the list of remittances sent to the accounting department. He treated the missing amount as a deposit in transit while doing the bank reconciliation.

(b) The purchasing agent used the company's purchase order form to order building materials. Later, she instructed the building supply company by telephone to deliver the materials to her home and to charge Maple Corporation's account. At month-end, she approved the invoice for payment.

(c) A vendor was paid twice for the same shipment. One payment was made on receipt of the invoice and a second payment on receipt of the monthly statement—the first remittance had arrived too late to appear on the monthly statement.

(d) The cashier pocketed cash received over the counter from certain customers paying their accounts. He then wrote off the receivables by recording a sales allowance for a billing error.

For each situation, indicate any violations of good internal control procedures, and describe the steps you would take to safeguard the system against this type of occurrence.

Internal control

7–20 Explain how each of the following unrelated procedures strengthens internal control:

(a) After preparing a check for a cash disbursement, Travis Lumber Company's treasurer cancels the supporting documentation (purchase requisition, receiving report, and invoice) with a perforator.

(b) The clerks of Wyman Department Store give each customer a cash register receipt along with the proper change.

(c) The ticket-taker of the Esquire movie theater tears each admission ticket in half and gives each patron a stub.

(d) Country Restaurant provides waiters and waitresses with prenumbered customer's checks. The servers are to void spoiled checks and issue new ones rather than make alterations or corrections on them. Voided checks must be given to the manager every day.

Bank reconciliation

7–21 Use the following information to prepare a bank reconciliation for Synden Company at June 30 of the current year.

1. Balance per Cash account, June 30, $6,042.10.
2. Balance per bank statement, June 30, $6,300.28.
3. Deposits not reflected on bank statement, $525.
4. Outstanding checks, June 30, $1,015.18.
5. Service charge on bank statement not recorded in books, $12.
6. Error by bank—Snyder Company check charged on Synden Company's bank statement, $400.
7. Check for advertising expense, $130, incorrectly recorded in books as $310.

Bank reconciliation components

7–22 Identify the amount asked for in each of the following situations.

(a) Younger Company's May 31 bank reconciliation shows deposits in transit of $1,500. The general ledger Cash in Bank account shows total cash receipts during June of $56,200. The June bank statement shows total cash deposits of $55,000 (and no credit memos). What amount of deposits in transit should appear in the June 30 bank reconciliation?

(b) Braddock Company's August 31 bank reconciliation shows outstanding checks of $1,900. The general ledger Cash in Bank account shows total cash disbursements (all by check) during September of $49,700. The September bank statement shows $48,000 of checks clearing the bank. What amount of outstanding checks should appear in the September 30 bank reconciliation?

(c) Wright Corporation's March 31 bank reconciliation shows deposits in transit of $900. The general ledger Cash in Bank account shows total cash receipts during April of $35,100. The April bank statement shows total cash deposits of $36,800 (including a credit memo for $1,100 from the collection of a note; the note collection has not yet been recorded by Wright). What amount of deposits in transit should appear in the April 30 bank reconciliation?

Petty cash

7–23 Record the following West Corporation activities in general journal form:

Apr. 1 Established a $200 petty cash fund by writing a check on the First National Bank.

17 Replenished the petty cash fund by writing a check on the First National Bank. The fund contains the following:

Currency and coins	$ 26.00
Bills and receipts:	
Delivery Expense	68.00
Contributions Expense	50.00
Office Expense	56.00
	$200.00

30 Replenished the petty cash fund and increased it to $250 by writing a check on the First National Bank. The fund contains:

Currency and coins	$ 30.00
Bills and receipts:	
Transportation In	92.00
Delivery Expense	18.00
Office Expense	60.00
	$200.00

Stock investments

7–24 During its first year of operations, Flynn, Inc., made two purchases of common stock as short-term investments. On May 20, 19X1, the firm acquired 300 shares of A Company at $28 per share plus a $150 broker's fee, and on July 16, 19X1, it purchased 200 shares of X Company at $18 per share plus a $100 broker's fee. On December 27, Flynn, Inc., received a cash dividend of $1.05 per share from A Company (Flynn records dividend income when received). The December 31 quoted market prices per share for the stock were A Company, $24, and X Company, $19. On January 26, 19X2, Flynn sold the X Company stock for $20 per share. Present journal entries to reflect (a) the stock purchases, (b) the receipt of the A Company dividend, (c) the reduction of the stock portfolio to the lower of cost or market at December 31, and (d) the sale of the X Company stock.

Stock investments

7–25 At December 31, 19X1, Mayotte Company had the following short-term stock portfolio:

Stock	Cost	Market Value
Cline, Inc., Common	$4,600	$4,850
Dwyer, Inc., Common	3,000	3,300
Total	$7,600	$8,150

On March 18, 19X2, Mayotte sold the Cline, Inc., stock for $4,700. On August 15, 19X2, Mayotte purchased Newman, Inc., common stock for $5,100. At December 31, 19X2, the common stock market values were: Dwyer, Inc., $3,100; Newman, Inc., $4,825. Prepare journal entries to reflect (a) the March 18 stock sale, (b) the August 15 stock purchase, and (c) the reduction of the stock portfolio to the lower of cost or market at December 31, 19X2.

Bond investment

7–26 As a short-term investment, Ryder Company purchased eighteen $1,000, 10% bonds at 99 plus three months' accrued interest on April 1, 19X2. The brokerage commission was $100. The bonds pay interest on June 30 and December 31. Present journal entries to reflect: (a) the purchase of the bonds for cash on April 1, 19X2; (b) the receipt of the semiannual interest payment on June 30, 19X2; and (c) the receipt of the semiannual interest payment on December 31, 19X2.

Bond investment

7–27 Present a journal entry to record the sale of the bonds described in Exercise 7–26 at 101 plus accrued interest on March 1, 19X3.

PROBLEMS

Internal control

7–28 The western branch of Wegner Distributors, Inc., handles a significant amount of credit sales, over-the-counter cash sales, and C.O.D. (cash on delivery) sales. The sales clerk prepares two copies of a sales ticket for all cash sales. One copy is given to the customer. The cashier keeps the other copy and stamps it "paid" when cash is received from an over-the-counter customer or from the delivery service. Because the sales tickets are not prenumbered, the cashier files them by the date of sale. At the end of each day, the cashier summarizes the over-the-counter cash sales and the amounts received from the delivery service for C.O.D. sales and sends the total to the bookkeeper for recording.

The branch does its own billings and collects receivables from credit customers. Mail remittances from credit customers are opened in the mailroom. Mailroom personnel make one copy of a list of remittances, which they forward to the bookkeeper together with the customers' checks. The bookkeeper verifies the cash discounts (credit sales are 2/10, n/30), records the remittances, and then sends the checks to the cashier. The cashier makes up the daily deposits for the bank, including both cash sales and remittances received on account. At the end of the month, the cashier receives the bank statement and makes the bank reconciliation. Also at month-end, the bookkeeper mails monthly statements of account to customers with outstanding balances.

REQUIRED

(a) List the irregularities that might occur with this system.
(b) Suggest improvements in the system of internal control.
(c) What feature of internal control in the current system would likely reveal that a mail clerk has converted checks received through the mail to personal use (that is, the mail clerk keeps the check and does not record it on the list of remittances)?

Internal control

7–29 Each of the following lettered paragraphs (a)–(d) briefly describes an independent situation involving some aspect of internal control.

REQUIRED

Answer the questions at the end of each paragraph or numbered section.

(a) As the office manager of a small business, Dan Gill opens all incoming mail, makes bank deposits, and keeps both the general ledger and the customers' subsidiary ledger. Two assistants write up the special journals (cash, purchases, and sales) and prepare the customers' monthly statements.

1. If Gill pocketed Customer A's $100 remittance in full of account and made no effort to conceal his embezzlement in the books, how would the misappropriation probably be discovered?
2. What routine accounting procedure would disclose Gill's $100 embezzlement in section 1, even if he destroyed Customer A's subsidiary ledger card?
3. What circumstances might disclose Gill's $100 embezzlement if he marked Customer A's account "paid in full" and set up a $100 account for fictitious Customer B with a fictitious address?
4. In section 3 above, why might Gill be anxious to open the mail himself each morning?
5. In section 3 above, why might Gill want to have the authority to write off accounts considered uncollectible?

(b) A doughnut shop uses a cash register with a locked-in tape that accumulates registered transactions. A prominently displayed sign announces a free doughnut for every customer who is not given the cash register receipt with his or her purchase. How is this procedure an internal control device for the doughnut shop?

(c) Barry Klever, a swindler, sent several business firms invoices requesting payment for office supplies that had never been delivered to the firm. A 5% discount was offered for prompt payment. What internal control procedures should prevent this swindle from being successful?

(d) Customers of The Towne Cafeteria encounter the cashier at the end of the food line. At this point, the cashier rings up the food costs, and the customer pays the bill. The customer line frequently backs up while the person paying searches for the correct amount of cash. To speed things up, the cashier often collects money from the next customer or two who have the correct change without ringing up their food costs. After the first customer finally pays, the cashier rings up the costs for those customers who have already paid.
1. What is the internal control weakness in this procedure?
2. How might the internal control over the collection of cash from the cafeteria customers be strengthened?

Bank reconciliation

7–30 On July 31, Murphy Company's Cash in Bank account had a balance of $5,620.75. On that date, the bank statement indicated a balance of $7,334.48. Comparison of returned checks and bank advices revealed the following:

1. Deposits in transit July 31 amounted to $2,415.97.
2. Outstanding checks July 31 totaled $1,129.20.
3. The bank erroneously charged a $250 check of the Murray Company against the Murphy bank account.
4. A $20 bank service charge has not yet been recorded on the books.
5. Murphy neglected to record $3,000 borrowed from the bank on a 10% six-month note. The bank statement shows the $3,000 as a deposit.
6. Included with the returned checks is a memo indicating that J. Martin's check for $490 had been returned NSF. Martin, a customer, had sent the check to pay an account of $500 less a 2% discount.
7. Murphy Company recorded an $84.50 payment for repairs as $845.

REQUIRED

(a) Prepare a bank reconciliation for Murphy Company at July 31.

(b) Prepare the general journal entry or entries necessary to bring the Cash in Bank account into agreement with the adjusted balance on the bank reconciliation.

Bank reconciliation

7–31 The bank reconciliation made by Nanco, Inc., on August 31 of the current year showed a deposit in transit of $640 and two outstanding checks, No. 597 for $415 and No. 603 for $320. The adjusted balance per books on August 31 was $7,055.

The following bank statement is available for September.

Bank Statement

TO Nanco, Inc. St. Louis, MO					September 30, 19XX STATE BANK	
Date	**Deposits**	**No.**	**Date**	**Charges**	**Date**	**Balance**
					Aug. 31	$7,150
Sept. 1	$640	597	Sept. 1	$415	Sept. 1	7,375
2	560	607	5	925	2	7,935
5	425	608	5	550	5	6,885
9	372	609	9	276	8	6,565
15	680	610	8	320	9	6,661
17	770	611	17	244	15	7,004
25	514	612	15	337	17	7,530
30	340	614	25	460	25	7,584
		NSF	29	514	29	7,070
		SC	30	18	30	7,392

A list of deposits made and checks written during September, taken from the cash receipts journal and cash disbursements journal, respectively, is shown below:

Deposits Made		**Checks Written**	
Sept. 1	$ 560	No. 607	$ 925
4	425	608	550
8	372	609	276
12	680	610	320
16	770	611	244
24	514	612	373
29	340	613	155
30	490	614	460
	$4,151	615	193
		616	210
			$3,706

The Cash in Bank account balance on September 30 was $7,500. In reviewing checks returned by the bank, the bookkeeper discovered that check No. 612, written for $337 for advertising expense, was recorded in the cash disbursements journal as $373. The NSF check for $514, which Nanco deposited on September 24, was a payment on account from customer D. Walker.

REQUIRED

(a) Prepare a bank reconciliation for Nanco, Inc., at September 30.
(b) Prepare the necessary journal entries to bring the Cash in Bank account into agreement with the adjusted balance on the bank reconciliation.

Petty cash

7–32 Ruland, Inc., established an imprest petty cash fund on July 1 of the current year. The following transactions took place during July:

July 1 Wrote check against United Bank account to establish the petty cash fund, $150.

15 Replenished the fund by check against the United Bank account for $125.50. The following bills and receipts were on hand:

Freight on C.O.D. purchase of merchandise	$ 32.50
Postage	25.00

Typewriter repair	45.00
Lunch with client (entertainment expense)	23.00
	$125.50

July 29 Replenished the fund and increased it to $250 by writing a check against the United Bank account. On this date, the fund contained $14.30 in currency and coins. Bills and receipts on hand were for postage, $28; office supplies expense, $35.60; charitable contributions, $30; and freight on C.O.D. purchase of merchandise, $40.

REQUIRED

Record the July petty cash transactions for Ruland, Inc., in general journal form.

Short-term investments

7–33 The following selected transactions relate to Rose Corporation during 19X1 and 19X2, its first two years of operations. The company closes its books on December 31.

19X1

Mar. 26 Purchased 1,500 common shares of Tower, Inc., as a short-term investment at a total cost of $23,760.

July 1 Invested $15,000 in a one-year certificate of deposit at State Bank. The annual interest rate on the certificate is 8.8%.

1 Purchased, as a short-term investment, twenty $1,000, 10% Garcia Company bonds at 102 plus $120 of commissions and taxes. The bonds pay interest on June 30 and December 31.

Sept. 7 Purchased 3,000 common shares of Miner, Inc., as a short-term investment at a total cost of $81,750.

Dec. 2 Miner, Inc., declared a cash dividend of 40 cents per common share, payable on December 29. Rose Corporation records dividend income when dividends are received.

3 Received 150 shares of Tower, Inc., common stock as a 10% stock dividend. The stock's current market price per share was $15.

29 Received cash dividend, declared December 2, from Miner, Inc.

31 Received semiannual interest payment on Garcia Company bonds.

31 Accrued interest receivable for six months on certificate of deposit. (Rose Corporation does not use reversing entries.)

31 Adjusted portfolio of short-term stock investments to lower of cost or market. Current market prices per share were Tower, Inc., $14.50, and Miner, Inc., $25.

19X2

June 30 Received $16,320 when the one-year certificate of deposit (purchased July 1, 19X1) was cashed in.

30 Received semiannual interest payment on Garcia Company bonds.

REQUIRED

(a) Record these transactions in general journal form.

(b) Assume that holdings of short-term stock investments did not change during 19X2. What entry would be made at December 31, 19X2, to adjust the portfolio to the lower of cost or market if the per share market prices at that date were Tower, Inc., $15; and Miner, Inc., $26?

Short-term investments in stocks

7–34 Tysong Corporation began operations on January 1, 19X1. The following transactions relate to Tysong Corporation's short-term investments in stocks during 19X1 and 19X2:

19X1

Feb. 15 Purchased 2,000 common shares of Leyden, Inc., at a total cost of $66,000.

April 20 Purchased 1,300 common shares of Gold Corporation at a total cost of $57,330.

June 25 Received 65 shares of Gold Corporation common stock as a 5% stock dividend. The stock's current market price per share was $46.
Aug. 6 Purchased 2,500 common shares of Archer, Inc., at a total cost of $40,000.
Sept. 3 Sold 365 Gold Corporation common shares at a price of $45 per share.
Dec. 15 Received a cash dividend of $1.10 per common share from Leyden, Inc. Leyden declared the dividend on November 20. Tysong Corporation records dividend income when dividends are received.
30 Received a cash dividend of 60 cents per common share from Archer, Inc.
31 Adjusted portfolio of short-term stock investments to lower of cost or market. Current market prices per share were Leyden, Inc., $30; Gold Corporation, $45.50; and Archer, Inc., $15.25.

19X2

Mar. 11 Sold remaining 1,000 Gold Corporation common shares at a price of $40 per share.
Dec. 15 Received a cash dividend of $1.20 per common share from Leyden, Inc.
30 Received a cash dividend of 50 cents per common share from Archer, Inc.
31 Adjusted portfolio of short-term stock investments to lower of cost or market. Current market prices per share were Leyden, Inc., $31.50; and Archer, Inc., $15.75.

REQUIRED
Record these transactions in general journal form.

ALTERNATE PROBLEMS

Internal control

7–28A Arlington Company has three clerical employees who must perform the following functions:

1. Maintain general ledger.
2. Maintain accounts payable ledger.
3. Maintain accounts receivable ledger.
4. Prepare checks for signature.
5. Maintain cash disbursements journal.
6. Issue credits on returns and allowances.
7. Reconcile the bank account.
8. Handle and deposit cash receipts.

The office manager of Arlington Company wishes to assign the above functions to the three employees in the manner that achieves the highest degree of internal control.

REQUIRED
Distribute the functions among the employees in a manner compatible with good internal control.

Internal control

7–29A The Twister amusement ride has the following system of internal control over its cash receipts. All persons pay the same price for a ride. An individual taking the ride pays the cashier and receives a ticket. The individual then walks to the ride site, hands the ticket to a ticket taker (who controls the number of people getting on each ride), and passes through a turnstile. All tickets are prenumbered. At the end of each day, the beginning ticket number is subtracted from the ending ticket number to determine the number of admissions sold. The cash is counted and compared with the number of tickets sold. The turnstile records each person that passes through it. At the end of each day, the beginning turnstile number is subtracted from the ending turnstile number to determine the number of riders that day. The number of riders is compared with the number of tickets sold.

REQUIRED

Which internal control feature would reveal each of the following irregularities?

(a) The ticket taker admits her friends without a ticket.
(b) The cashier gives his friends tickets without receiving any cash.
(c) The cashier gives too much change.
(d) The ticket taker returns the tickets she has collected to the cashier. The cashier then resells these tickets and splits the proceeds with the ticket taker.
(e) An individual sneaks into the ride line without paying the cashier.

Bank reconciliation

7–30A On May 31, the Cash in Bank account of Nahn Company, a sole proprietorship, had a balance of $3,751.24. On that date, the bank statement indicated a balance of $5,112.78. Comparison of returned checks and bank advices revealed the following:

1. Deposits in transit May 31 totaled $1,616.
2. Outstanding checks May 31 totaled $2,007.34.
3. The bank added to the account $17.20 of interest income earned by Nahn during May.
4. The bank collected a $1,500 note receivable for Nahn and charged a $10.00 collection fee. Both items appear on the bank statement.
5. Bank service charges in addition to the collection fee, not yet recorded on the books, were $14.
6. Included with the returned checks is a memo indicating that L. Dabel's check for $343 had been returned NSF. Dabel, a customer, had sent the check to pay an account of $350 less a 2% discount.
7. Nahn Company recorded the payment of an account payable as $245; the check was for $425.

REQUIRED

(a) Prepare a bank reconciliation for Nahn Company at May 31.
(b) Prepare the general journal entry or entries necessary to bring the Cash in Bank account into agreement with the adjusted balance on the bank reconciliation.

Bank reconciliation

7–31A The bank reconciliation made by Monroe Company, a sole proprietorship, on March 31 of the current year showed a deposit in transit of $550 and two outstanding checks, No. 797 for $225 and No. 804 for $445. The adjusted balance per books on March 31 was $5,860.

The following bank statement is available for April:

Bank Statement

TO Monroe Company
Fairbanks, AK

April 30, 19XX
FAIRBANKS NATIONAL BANK

Date	Deposits	No.	Date	Charges	Date	Balance
					March 31	$5,980
Apr. 1	$550	804	Apr. 2	$445	Apr. 1	6,530
3	840	807	3	365	2	6,085
7	625	808	7	570	3	6,560
13	510	809	7	419	7	6,196
18	420	810	16	520	13	6,543
23	395	811	13	163	16	6,023
27	670	813	27	270	18	6,193
30	580	814	23	300	23	6,288
30	30IN	NSF	18	250	27	6,688
		SC	30	20	30	7,278

A list of deposits made and checks written during April, taken from the cash receipts journal and cash disbursements journal, respectively, is shown below:

Deposits Made		Checks Written	
Apr. 2	$ 840	No. 807	$ 365
6	625	808	570
10	510	809	419
17	420	810	520
22	395	811	136
24	670	812	474
29	580	813	270
30	790	814	300
	$4,830	815	186
		816	460
			$3,700

The Cash in Bank account balance on April 30 was $6,990. In reviewing checks returned by the bank, the bookkeeper discovered that check No. 811, written for $163 for delivery expense, was recorded in the cash disbursements journal as $136. The NSF check for $250 was that of customer R. Koppa, deposited in April. Interest for April added to the account by the bank was $30.

REQUIRED

(a) Prepare a bank reconciliation for Monroe Company at April 30.

(b) Prepare the necessary journal entries to bring the Cash in Bank account into agreement with the adjusted balance on the bank reconciliation.

Petty cash

7–32A Towell, Inc., established an imprest petty cash fund on May 1 of the current year. The following transactions took place during May:

May 1 Wrote check against American Bank account to establish the petty cash fund, $175.

12 Replenished the fund by check against the American Bank account for $154.75. The following bills and receipts were on hand:

Charge for rush delivery of package across town	$ 28.50
Postage	32.00
Calculator repairs	38.00
Flowers sent to customer opening new office (advertising expense)	56.25
	$154.75

25 Replenished the fund and increased it to $225 by writing a check against the American Bank account. On this date, the fund contained $11.25 in currency and coins. Bills and receipts on hand were for postage, $45; office supplies expense, $58.75; and instant printing charges (advertising expense), $62.

REQUIRED

Record the May petty cash transactions for Towell, Inc., in general journal form.

Short-term investments

7–33A The following selected transactions relate to Madland Corporation during 19X1 and 19X2, its first two years of operations. The company closes its books on December 31.

19X1

Feb. 17 Purchased 1,900 common shares of Heath, Inc., as a short-term investment at a total cost of $55,100.

May 31 Purchased, as a short-term investment, sixteen $1,000, 9% Berk Company bonds at 98 plus five months' accrued interest. The brokerage commission was $80. The bonds pay interest on June 30 and December 31.

June 30 Received semiannual interest payment on Berk Company bonds.

July 1 Invested $40,000 in a one-year certificate of deposit at Hilldale Bank. The annual interest rate on the certificate is 7.5%.

Aug. 10 Purchased 1,200 common shares of Glade, Inc., as a short-term investment at a total cost of $25,200.

Dec. 1 Heath, Inc., declared a cash dividend of $1.05 per common share, payable on December 28. Madland Corporation records dividend income when dividends are received.

5 Received 60 shares of Glade, Inc., common stock as a 5% stock dividend. The stock's current market price per share was $19.

28 Received cash dividend, declared December 1, from Heath, Inc.

31 Received semiannual interest payment on Berk Company bonds.

31 Accrued interest receivable for six months on certificate of deposit. (Madland Corporation does not use reversing entries.)

31 Adjusted portfolio of short-term stock investments to lower of cost or market. Current market prices per share were Heath, Inc., $27.50, and Glade, Inc., $18.

19X2

Feb. 1 Sold Berk Company bonds for $15,920 plus accrued interest for one month.

June 30 Received $43,000 when the one-year certificate of deposit (purchased July 1, 19X1) was cashed in.

REQUIRED

(a) Record these transactions in general journal form.

(b) Assume that holdings of short-term stock investments did not change during 19X2. What entry would be made at December 31, 19X2, to adjust the portfolio to the lower of cost or market if the per share market prices at that date were Heath, Inc., $28; and Glade, Inc., $19.50?

Short-term investments

7–34A The following transactions relate to Yost Company's short-term investments in stocks and bonds during 19X5:

19X5

Jan. 10 Purchased 3,500 common shares of Pond Corporation at a total cost of $92,750.

Feb. 1 Purchased twelve $1,000, 14% Gammon Company bonds at 104 plus one month's accrued interest. The brokerage commission was $70. The bonds pay interest on January 1 and July 1.

May 28 Purchased 1,400 common shares of Edberg, Inc., at a total cost of $18,200.

June 30 Received a cash dividend of 30 cents per common share from Edberg, Inc.

July 1 Received semiannual interest payment on Gammon Company bonds.

1 Purchased fifteen $1,000, 10% Watson Company bonds at 99 plus a $90 brokerage commission. The bonds pay interest on January 1 and July 1.

Sept. 30 Received 210 shares of Pond Corporation common stock as a 6% stock dividend. The stock's current market price per share was $28.

Nov. 1 Sold the Gammon Company bonds for $12,240 plus accrued interest for four months.

17 Sold the Pond Corporation common stock for $28.50 per share.

Dec. 1 Sold the Watson Company bonds for $15,225 plus accrued interest for five months.

14 Sold the Edberg, Inc., common stock for $11.75 per share.

REQUIRED
Record these transactions in general journal form.

BUSINESS DECISION PROBLEM

On December 15 of the current year, John Galvin, who owns Galvin Company, asks you to investigate the cash-handling activities in his firm. He thinks that an employee might be stealing funds. "I have no proof," he says, "but I'm fairly certain that the November 30 undeposited receipts amounted to more than $6,000, although the November 30 bank reconciliation prepared by the cashier shows only $3,619.20. Also, the November bank reconciliation doesn't show several checks that have been outstanding for a long time. The cashier told me that these checks needn't appear on the reconciliation because he had notified the bank to stop payment on them and he had made the necessary adjustment on the books. Does that sound reasonable to you?"

At your request, Galvin shows you the following November 30 bank reconciliation prepared by the cashier:

Bank Reconciliation
November 30, 19XX

Balance per bank statement		$2,360.12	Balance per books		$5,385.22
Add: Deposits in transit		3,619.20			
		$5,979.32			
Less:			Less:		
Outstanding checks:			Bank service charge	$ 30	
No. 2351	$550.10		Unrecorded credit	600	630.00
No. 2353	289.16				
No. 2354	484.84	1,224.10			
Adjusted balance		$4,755.22	Adjusted balance		$4,755.22

You discover that the $600 unrecorded bank credit represents a note collected by the bank on Galvin's behalf; it appears in the deposits column of the November bank statement. Your investigation also reveals that the October 31 bank reconciliation showed three checks that had been outstanding longer than 10 months: No. 1432 for $300; No. 1458 for $233.45; and No. 1512 for $126.55. You also discover that these items were never added back into the Cash account in the books. In confirming that the checks shown on the cashier's November 30 bank reconciliation were outstanding on that date, you discover that check No. 2353 was actually a payment of $829.16 and had been recorded on the books for that amount.

To confirm the amount of undeposited receipts at November 30, you request a bank statement for December 1–12 (called a "cut-off" bank statement). This indeed shows a December 1 deposit of $3,619.20.

REQUIRED

(a) Calculate the amount of funds stolen by the cashier.
(b) Describe how the cashier concealed the theft.
(c) What sort of entry or entries should be made when a firm decides that checks outstanding for a long time should no longer be carried in the bank reconciliation?
(d) What suggestions would you make to Galvin about cash control procedures?

ANSWERS TO SELF-TEST QUESTIONS

1. (c) **2.** (d) **3.** (a) **4.** (d) **5.** (b)

8

TRADE ACCOUNTS AND NOTES

CHAPTER OBJECTIVES

1. Define trade receivables and payables and explain a firm's credit policies (pp. 287–88).
2. Describe the two methods that can be used to recognize losses from uncollectible accounts (pp. 288–90).
3. Illustrate the procedures for estimating and recording credit losses (pp. 290–93).
4. Describe and illustrate notes and interest calculations (pp. 293–96).
5. Illustrate the discounting of notes receivable and payable (pp. 296–303).

Short accounts make long friends.
HONORÉ DE BALZAC

Business practice today is governed by credit. Indeed, the vast daily sales of goods and services might not be made without it. In recent years, the use of credit has expanded immensely, particularly in the retail field. Millions of consumers possess and regularly use several credit cards.

The growth of credit has created a need for more elaborate and sophisticated systems for processing transactions and gathering credit information. However, the basic accounting problems of keeping track of payables and receivables have remained essentially the same.

TRADE RECEIVABLES AND PAYABLES

The terms **trade receivable** and **trade payable** usually refer to receivables and payables that arise in the regular course of a company's transactions with customers and suppliers. Payments normally are made within 30 to 60 days. Therefore, the amount of a sale of merchandise sold on account is debited to the appropriate customer's account in the subsidiary accounts receivable ledger; this amount is also debited to the Accounts Receivable control account when credit sales are posted periodically to it. The subsidiary record and the control account should reflect only trade accounts. Advances to company employees or officers should not be included here, nor should advances to affiliated companies, such as subsidiaries, be included. Such receivables should be recorded in separate accounts. In many instances, such receivables are not current, and as a result, they often appear in the balance sheet under a noncurrent heading, such as Other Assets. Advances to subsidiary companies are frequently semipermanent, and they may be found in the balance sheet under the Investments caption.

Likewise, trade accounts payable consist only of open amounts owing for the purchase of merchandise, materials, or the acquisition of services from outsiders. Separate current liability accounts contain amounts that a firm owes for salaries, wages, various types of taxes, sundry accruals, and so on.

The principal reason for separating trade accounts from other receivables and payables is to facilitate analyses by both management and outsiders. You will learn in Chapter 20 that certain techniques used in studying a company's current accounts depend on such separation.

Occasionally, individual accounts within the accounts receivable or accounts payable subsidiary ledgers may show abnormal balances. A customer may have overpaid an account, paid an advance on goods not yet shipped, or returned goods already paid for. A substantial credit balance in a customer's account is reclassified as a current liability when a balance sheet is prepared. On the other hand, if the firm itself makes advances on purchases or overpays accounts, the resulting debit balances in accounts payable are reclassified as current assets in the balance sheet.

INSTALLMENT ACCOUNTS

Many business concerns—such as mail-order houses and appliance dealers—make many of their sales on the **installment** basis. Typically, a customer of such a firm purchases merchandise by signing an installment contract in which he or she agrees to a down payment plus installment payments of a fixed amount over a period such as 24 or 36 months. Normally, the total price of the merchandise sold includes an interest charge, and the contract allows the seller to repossess merchandise if the installment payments are not made. If the installment contract conforms to the firm's normal trade practices and terms, the installment receivable is classified as a current asset.

LOSSES FROM UNCOLLECTIBLE ACCOUNTS

Few firms that extend credit to customers are immune to credit losses. Indeed, most companies anticipate them. The magnitude of such losses is often directly related to the firm's credit policy. Sometimes a company deliberately liberalizes its credit policy to obtain increased sales, fully anticipating an increase in credit losses.

Most large companies have credit departments to administer management's established credit policies. Credit personnel may set credit limits, conduct investigations of credit ratings, and follow up on unpaid accounts. They may also decide, after following established collection procedures, when a debt is uncollectible.

Credit losses, considered operating expenses of the business, are debited to an appropriately titled account such as **Uncollectible Accounts Expense.** Other account titles frequently used are *Loss from Uncollectible Accounts, Loss from Doubtful Accounts,* or *Bad Debts Expense.* Normally, the expense is classified as a selling expense on the income statement, although some companies include it with administrative expenses.

Timing of Recognition

There are two methods for recognizing losses from uncollectible accounts. One is called the direct write-off method. The other method, which is preferable, is called the allowance method.

THE DIRECT WRITE-OFF METHOD Under the **direct write-off method,** uncollectible accounts are charged to expense in the period when they are discovered to be uncollectible. Suppose that in December of last year, J. B. Stone purchased merchandise billed at $125, and that, after repeated collection attempts, the credit department decided on July 15 of the current year that the amount will never be collected. The following entry would record the loss:

July 15	Uncollectible Accounts Expense	125	
	Accounts Receivable—J. B. Stone		125
	To write off J. B. Stone's account		

This entry charges the loss to the current year's expenses and reduces the asset Accounts Receivable by $125. Also, J. B. Stone's subsidiary ledger account no longer has a balance.

The major shortcoming of the direct write-off method is that credit losses are not matched with related sales. In our example, the revenue from the sale to J. B. Stone would be reflected in last year's income statement, but the loss would appear in the current year's income statement. The use of the direct write-off method also causes the consistent overstatement of Accounts Receivable on the balance sheet. Since generally accepted accounting principles prescribe that receivables be shown at the amount the firm expects to collect, most accountants disapprove of the direct write-off method.

This method would be obviously inappropriate in certain situations. Suppose a firm liberalized its credit policy in one year, realizing a large increase in sales revenue. Much of the related uncollectible accounts expense would not appear on the income statement until the next year, because collection efforts and follow-up procedures often extend over long periods of time. Most accountants and credit people believe that the credit loss occurs at the time of sale and therefore should be reflected in the same period.

THE ALLOWANCE METHOD Most businesses employ the *matching concept* to determine net income. Therefore, they prefer to estimate the amount of uncollectible accounts expense that will eventually result from a period's sales in order to reflect the expense during the same period. This procedure, the **allowance method,** not only matches credit losses with related revenue, but also results in an estimated realizable amount for accounts receivable in the balance sheet at the end of the period. The estimate is introduced into the accounts by an adjusting entry.

Let us assume that a firm with accounts receivable of $100,000 at the end of its first business year estimates that $4,000 of these accounts will be uncollectible. The firm makes the following adjusting entry:

Dec. 31	Uncollectible Accounts Expense	4,000	
	Allowance for Uncollectible Accounts		4,000
	To record uncollectible accounts expense.		

Note that in the adjusting entry, the credit is made to an account called **Allowance for Uncollectible Accounts** rather than to Accounts Receivable. This is done for two reasons. First, when the firm makes the adjusting entry, it does not know which accounts in the subsidiary accounts receivable ledger will be uncollectible. If the Accounts Receivable control account is credited and no entries are made in the subsidiary ledger, then the two records no longer agree in total. Second, because the amount involved is only an estimate, it is preferable not to reduce Accounts Receivable directly.

The Allowance for Uncollectible Accounts is a contra asset account with a normal credit balance. To present the expected realizable amount of Accounts Receivable, we deduct the Allowance for Uncollectible Accounts from Accounts Receivable in the balance sheet as follows:

Current Assets		
Cash		$XXXXX
Accounts Receivable	$100,000	
Less: Allowance for Uncollectible Accounts	4,000	96,000
Inventory		XXXXX
Other Current Assets		XXXXX
Total Current Assets		$XXXXX

Writing Off Specific Accounts

The credit manager or other company official normally authorizes writing off a specific account. When the accounting department is notified of the action, it makes the following entry:

Jan. 5	Allowance for Uncollectible Accounts	250	
	Accounts Receivable—James Baker		250
	To write off James Baker's account.		

The credit in the above entry is made to James Baker's account in the subsidiary accounts receivable ledger as well as to the Accounts Receivable control account; therefore, these two records are still in agreement.

The entry to write off an account does not affect net income or total assets. By means of the adjusting entry, the expense is reflected in the period when the related revenue is recorded. Furthermore, because the Allowance for Uncollectible Accounts is deducted from Accounts Receivable in the balance sheet, the *net* realizable amount of accounts receivable is not changed by the write-off. After Baker's account has been written off, the Accounts Receivable and Allowance for Uncollectible Accounts ledger pages appear as follows:

Accounts Receivable Account No. 12

Date		Description	Post. Ref.	Debit	Credit	Balance
19XX						
Jan.	1	Balance				100,000
	5	Write-off, James Baker			250	99,750

Allowance for Uncollectible Accounts Account No. 13

Date		Description	Post. Ref.	Debit	Credit	Balance
19XX						
Jan.	1	Balance				4,000
	5	Write-off, James Baker		250		3,750

In these accounts, the net realizable amount of accounts receivable on January 1 is $96,000 ($100,000 − $4,000 allowance). After the January 5 write-off, the net realizable amount of accounts receivable is still $96,000 ($99,750 − $3,750 allowance). Thus, the write-off of an account does not affect the net asset balance.

Estimating Credit Losses

Estimates of credit losses are generally based on past experience, with consideration given to forecasts of sales activity, economic conditions, and planned changes in credit policy. The most commonly used calculations are related either to credit sales for the period or to the amount of accounts receivable at the close of the period.

ESTIMATES RELATED TO SALES Through experience, many companies can determine the approximate percentage of credit sales that will be uncollectible. At the end of an accounting period, the amount of the adjusting entry is determined by multiplying the total credit sales by this percentage. Suppose that credit sales for a period amount to $200,000 and that past experience indicates a loss of $1\frac{1}{2}$%. The adjusting entry for expected losses would be:

Dec. 31	Uncollectible Accounts Expense	3,000	
	Allowance for Uncollectible Accounts		3,000
	To record uncollectible accounts expense.		

Because the periodic estimates for uncollectibles under this procedure are related to sales, a firm should review its allowance account regularly to ensure a reasonable balance. Should the allowance account balance become too large or too small, the percentage used for the periodic estimates should be revised accordingly.

A company that estimates its credit losses from sales figures customarily uses credit sales only. In some cases, however, a percentage of both credit and cash sales may be calculated, as long as the proportions of the two types of sales remain relatively constant over time. Whether sales discounts or sales returns and allowances are deducted before applying a percentage to sales figures depends on how the percentage was developed; the exercises and problems in this text assume that percentages are applied to gross credit sales.

ESTIMATES RELATED TO ACCOUNTS RECEIVABLE A company's experience may show that a certain percentage of accounts receivable at the end of a period is likely to prove uncollectible. The credit balance in the allowance account should equal this amount. Therefore, the adjustment for uncollectibles is the amount needed to create the desired credit balance in the company's allowance account.

Suppose that a company estimates uncollectibles as 5% of accounts receivable and that the Accounts Receivable balance at the end of an accounting period is $50,000. Therefore, the desired credit balance in the allowance account is $2,500. If the allowance account already has a residual credit balance of $400, the amount of the adjustment is $2,100. The adjusting entry is a debit to Uncollectible Accounts Expense and a credit to Allowance for Uncollectible Accounts.

Instead of using a fixed percentage of the aggregate customers' balances, some companies determine the amount needed in the allowance account after analyzing the age structure of the account balances. These companies prepare an aging schedule similar to the one in Exhibit 8–1. An **aging schedule** is simply an analysis that shows how long customers' balances have remained unpaid. Assume that the firm whose aging schedule appears in Exhibit 8–1 sells on net

EXHIBIT 8–1

AGING SCHEDULE OF CUSTOMER BALANCES
DECEMBER 31, 19XX

			Past Due				
Customer	**Account Balance**	**Current**	**0–30 Days**	**31–60 Days**	**61–120 Days**	**121 Days –6 Mos.**	**Over 6 Mos.**
Alton, J.	$ 320	$ 320	$	$	$	$	$
Bailey, C.	400		400				
•							
•							
•							
Wall, M.	150				50	100	
Zorn, W.	210			210			
	$50,000	$42,000	$4,000	$2,000	$1,000	$800	$200

terms of 30 days. Alton's account is current, which means that the $320 billing was made within the last 30 days. Bailey's account is 0–30 days *past due*, which means that the account is from 31 to 60 days old. Wall's balance consists of a $50 billing made from 91 to 150 days ago and a $100 billing made from 151 days to seven months ago, and so on.

Companies that analyze their bad accounts experience with the aged balances may develop percentages of each stratum that are likely to prove uncollectible. At the end of each period, these percentages are applied to the totals of each age group to determine the allowance account balance. For our example, these percentages are shown below. Applying the percentages to the totals in our aging schedule, we calculate an allowance requirement of $1,560.

	Amount	Percent Doubtful	Allowance Required
Current	$42,000	2	$ 840
0–30 days past due	4,000	3	120
31–60 days past due	2,000	5	100
61–120 days past due	1,000	20	200
121 days–6 months past due	800	25	200
Over 6 months past due	200	50	100
Total Allowance Required			$1,560

Again, if the allowance account has a residual $400 credit balance, the adjustment is for $1,160. The entry would be:

Dec. 31	Uncollectible Accounts Expense	1,160	
	Allowance for Uncollectible Accounts		1,160
	To record uncollectible accounts expense.		

The adjustment brings the credit balance in the allowance account to the required amount—$1,560.

Recoveries of Accounts Written Off

Occasionally, accounts written off against the Allowance for Uncollectible Accounts later prove to be wholly or partly collectible. In such situations, a firm should reinstate the customer's account for the amount recovered before recording the collection, so that the payment is recorded in the customer's account. The entry made for the write-off is reversed to the extent of the recovery and the receipt is recorded in the usual manner. For example, assume that a company using the allowance method wrote off James Baker's $250 account on January 5 but received payment in full on April 20. The following entries (including write-off) illustrate the recovery procedure.

To write off the account

Jan. 5	Allowance for Uncollectible Accounts	250	
	Accounts Receivable—James Baker		250

To reinstate the account

Apr. 20	Accounts Receivable—James Baker	250	
	Allowance for Uncollectible Accounts		250

To record remittance

Apr. 20	Cash	250	
	Accounts Receivable—James Baker		250

These last two entries may be made even if the recovery occurs in a year after the write-off.

A business using the direct write-off method that recovers a written-off account during the year of write-off simply reverses the entry made to write off the account to the extent of the recovery and records the remittance in the usual manner. Recoveries made in years after the write-off normally require two entries also. One entry reinstates the customer's account balance, with the credit made to an income statement account titled Recoveries of Accounts Written Off. The second entry records the remittance in the usual manner.

CREDIT CARD FEES

Many retailing businesses have their credit sales handled through banks and other financial institutions that issue credit cards such as VISA and MasterCard. The issuer incurs the costs of processing and collecting the amounts charged on its credit cards and absorbs any losses from uncollectible accounts. In exchange for these services, the retail firm is charged a **fee,** usually ranging from $\frac{1}{2}$% to 5% of the amount of the credit sale. The retailer makes the credit card sale and deposits the charge slip with the financial institution, which credits the retailer's account for the amount of the sale less the credit card fee. The retailer records the transaction by debiting Cash (for the amount of the sale less the fee), debiting a Credit Card Fee Expense account (for the amount of the fee), and crediting Sales.

Credit sales may also be made to customers who use other credit cards, such as American Express and Diner's Club cards. The retailer sends the charge slip to the credit card company, then receives a check from that company for the sales amount less the credit card fee. The retailer records these sales by establishing a receivable from the credit card company (for the amount of the sale less the fee), debiting Credit Card Fee Expense (for the amount of the fee), and crediting Sales. The receivable is credited when the check is received from the credit card company.

NOTES RECEIVABLE AND PAYABLE

Promissory notes are often used in transactions when the credit period is longer than the 30 or 60 days typical for open accounts. Although promissory notes are used frequently in sales of equipment and real property, a note is sometimes exchanged for merchandise. Occasionally, a note is substituted for an open account when an extension of the usual credit period is granted. In addition, promissory notes are normally executed when loans are obtained from banks and other parties.

A **promissory note** is a written promise to pay a certain sum of money on demand or at a fixed and determinable future time. The note is signed by the **maker** and made payable to the order of either a specific **payee** or to the **bearer.** The note may be *non-interest-bearing* or *interest-bearing* at an annual rate specified on the note. An interest-bearing promissory note is illustrated in Exhibit 8–2.

EXHIBIT 8–2

A PROMISSORY NOTE

$2,000.00 Madison, Wisconsin May 3, 19XX

Sixty days after date I promise to pay to

the order of Robert Ward

Two Thousand and no/100------------------------------dollars

for value received with interest at 9%.

payable at American Exchange Bank

James Stone

A note from a debtor is called a **note receivable** by the holder and a **note payable** by the debtor. A note is usually regarded as a stronger claim against a debtor than an open account because the terms of payment are specified in writing. Although open accounts can be sold (*factored*), a note can be converted to cash more easily by discounting it at a bank. (We treat the discounting of notes later in this chapter.)

Interest on Notes

Interest on notes is commonly paid on the maturity date of the obligation, except in certain discounting transactions. Interest incurred is debited to an Interest Expense account, and interest earned is credited to an Interest Income account. When business firms distinguish between operating and other items of income and expense in their income statements, they show interest expense and interest income under the heading Other Income and Expense.

INTEREST CALCULATION The formula for determining simple interest is:

$$\text{Principal} \times \text{Rate} \times \text{Time} = \text{Interest}$$

Unless otherwise specified, we will assume that interest rates on notes are annual rates. For example, interest on a one-year note for $2,000 at 9% would be calculated as follows:

$$\$2{,}000 \times \frac{9}{100} \times 1 = \$180$$

When a note is for a certain number of months, the time is usually expressed in twelfths of a year. Thus, the interest on a six-month note for $2,000 at 9% would be calculated as follows:

$$\$2{,}000 \times \frac{9}{100} \times \frac{6}{12} = \$90$$

When the note's duration is given in days, we express the time as a fraction of a year; the number of days' duration is the numerator and 360 is the denominator. (It is general business practice to use 360 days here, although federal agencies and certain lenders may use 365 days.) Interest on a 60-day note for $2,000 at 9% would be calculated as follows:

$$\$2{,}000 \times \frac{9}{100} \times \frac{60}{360} = \$30$$

DETERMINING MATURITY DATE When a note's duration is expressed in days, we count the exact days in each calendar month to determine the **maturity date**. For example, a 90-day note dated July 21 would have an October 19 maturity date, which we determine as follows:

10	days in July (remainder of month—31 days minus 21 days)
31	days in August
30	days in September
19	days in October (number of days required to total 90)
90	

If the duration of a note is expressed in months, we find the maturity date simply by counting the months from the date of issue. For example, a two-month note dated January 31 would mature on March 31, a three-month note of the same date would mature on April 30 (the last day of the month), and a four-month note would mature on May 31.

RECORDING NOTES AND INTEREST When a note is exchanged to settle an open trade account, an entry is made to reflect the note receivable or payable and to reduce the balance of the related account receivable or payable. For example, suppose Acme Company sold $12,000 of merchandise to Bowman Company. On October 1, after the regular credit period had elapsed, Bowman Company gave Acme Company a 60-day, 9% note for $12,000. The following entries would be made by each of the parties:

Acme Company

Oct. 1	Notes Receivable	12,000	
	Accounts Receivable—Bowman Company		12,000
	Received 60-day, 9% note in payment of account.		

Bowman Company

Oct. 1	Accounts Payable—Acme Company	12,000	
	Notes Payable		12,000
	Gave 60-day, 9% note in payment of account.		

If Bowman Company pays the note on the November 30 maturity date, the following entries would be made by the parties involved:

Acme Company

Nov. 30	Cash	12,180	
	Interest Income		180
	Notes Receivable		12,000
	Collected Bowman Company note.		

Bowman Company

Nov. 30	Notes Payable	12,000	
	Interest Expense	180	
	Cash		12,180
	Paid note to Acme Company.		

Note that the interest for 60 days at 9% is reflected by the respective parties on the maturity date of the note. This would be true even if the maker defaulted on the note. If Bowman Company did not pay the note when due, Acme would debit the $12,180 to Accounts Receivable rather than to Cash. When a note receivable is dishonored at maturity, the combined principal and interest are converted to an open account. This procedure leaves only current, unmatured notes in the Notes Receivable account.

Discounting Customer Notes

Occasionally, a business may not wait until the maturity date of a note receivable to obtain cash from a customer transaction. Instead, it can endorse the note over to a bank, **discounting** the note and receiving an amount equal to the note's maturity value less the discount charged by the bank. By endorsing the note (unless it is endorsed *without recourse*), the business agrees to pay the note at the maturity date if the maker fails to pay it. Consequently, the note is the endorser's **contingent liability** (that is, the liability is contingent on the failure of the maker to pay). While the note is outstanding, the endorser discloses the contingent liability in its balance sheet. However, because a contingent liability is a potential

SPORTING ECONOMICS

As you proceed down life's highway, if you keep your eyes open, you'll find some curious types. As an example, no one can spend much time on this planet without meeting somebody who has an acute case of the frugals. It has been suggested that some people of the hunter/fisher persuasion fall into that category. It's almost inconceivable that a fisherman would be penurious when it comes to essential expenditures like a boat, motor, or boron/graphite rod. Likewise, a dedicated hunter seldom carries a shooting iron with a popple stock. Nevertheless, we have all met folks who enjoy camping, hunting and fishing and are quite snug with the buck in other ways.

Jerry Groler was an example. Jerry never married. He thought it was a dreadful waste of money. He rented his autos, too. He never loaned money to anyone because he claimed it gave them amnesia. But he owned quality guns and rifles. His fishing equipment was top shelf and he drank only the best Kentucky bourbons. He had two dogs of magnificent reputation and he loved to shoot over them. While he had an equal enjoyment for the accumulation of capital, he wouldn't think of parting with either of the animals—even at the terribly inflated amounts he had been offered.

Jerry's income was not within the nation's top twenty percent, but his expense ratios were low and that was the secret of his comfortable economic status. A conservative investor, he was dividend and interest conscious, but had the courage to sell and reinvest. So he had a nice volume of high interest securities working for him. He was also reported to keep a large amount of cash neatly tied in easy-to-count bundles stashed away in and around the leased ten acres that contained his home, a wood lot, and a stream reported to hold trout.

I always thought that story was a lot of hogwash. Jerry wouldn't keep cash when he could have it producing 10.8% for him. But the rumor persisted and, I'm sure, was accepted as gospel by many. Two of those 'many' were William Meyer and Thomas Thaves.

Meyer and Thaves were the presidents of two local competing banks. Either of them would have given an eye tooth to get Jerry's hidden cache securely reposing in his depository. Whenever either one of them met Jerry, sooner or later the conversation turned to the absolute safety of their institution, the interest rate on term deposits and such stuff like that there. But Jerry never got caught up in the spirit of the thing. He never opened an account in either bank. Until last fall, he had carefully followed the advice of Polonius and was neither a borrower nor a lender

liability rather than an actual liability, the amount is not included with the liabilities, but is disclosed in a footnote to the balance sheet. For example, the footnote may read "At December 31, 19XX, the Company was contingently liable for discounted notes receivable having a maturity value of $(amount)."

DISCOUNTING NON-INTEREST-BEARING NOTES RECEIVABLE Assume that the $12,000, 60-day note received on October 1 by Acme Company from Bowman Company is non-interest-bearing. Suppose that Acme Company discounts the note at the bank on October 31 and that the bank's discount rate is 9%.

The bank discount calculation is always based on the **maturity value** (Principal + Interest) of the note and the number of days that the bank must hold the note. Because the note in our example is non-interest-bearing, the maturity value equals the face value, $12,000. The bank must hold the note for 30 days—October 31 to November 30. (In calculating the discount period, we ignore the discount date and count the maturity date as a full day.) We calculate the proceeds as follows:

(at least as far as the local banking institutions were concerned).

As a result of all this, it was a pleasant surprise when Tom looked up one morning last September and saw Jerry Groler standing in the bank lobby—nervous and ill at ease. Tom's pulse rate increased when he came into his office and sat down. Jerry wasn't carrying a little black box, but it was clear he was there for some special purpose. After an agonizing five minutes of small talk, Jerry finally got around to wondering what interest rate he might get on a savings account. Tom began to salivate and figured the potential was good enough to kick the rate up an eighth of a point, so he said: $5\frac{5}{8}$%. (He didn't know Bill Meyer had already quoted $5\frac{3}{4}$%.) Then Jerry went back to another five minutes of small talk while Tom managed to keep control of himself. Then he wondered what the interest rate would be if he borrowed two thousand dollars. Tom shaved the rate to 12%. (This was the right thing to do, because a half hour earlier Bill Meyer had said $12\frac{1}{2}$%.)

Jerry supposed a bank would want collateral for a loan like that, but Tom said absolutely no collateral would be required from a good, fine, upstanding, honest, well-respected, honorable citizen like Jerry Groler. This apparently was a mistake because the old conservative nature of Jerry's progenitors came to the forefront. He said he didn't want any special treatment and he wasn't sure he wanted to deal with a bank that didn't insist on proper security for a loan. It might not be safe. As he got up to leave, Tom blocked his way to the door, hastened to assure him the bank usually took security, in fact, almost always took security, would be willing to take security from Jerry and why didn't he sit down and we'll discuss the arrangements now.

Once the matter was fully out in the open, Jerry came straight to the point. He had a chance to take a trip. The opportunity had developed without notice and his money was tied up in investments which wouldn't come due for a month or so. He had a dismaying choice to make—cash in and lose interest—borrow short term from a bank—or stay home. The only security he could give was his two hunting dogs—known to be worth well over $5,000.00. Tom was understanding and agreed to the loan. Jerry insisted he take the dogs as hostage for the promise to pay. The deal was struck. Jerry got the money, delivered the dogs and after an almost tearful farewell to them, he left town.

Thirty days later, Jerry returned from a long fishing vacation in Alaska. He went to Bill's bank and withdrew the same $2,000.00 he had borrowed from Tom—plus a month's interest at $5\frac{3}{4}$% ($9.58). Then he went to Tom's bank and gave him the $2,009.58—plus $10.42 of his own money—in payment of the total loan principal and interest of $2,020.00.

(And that wasn't so bad. Where else can you board two dogs for 30 days for $10.42?)

Galen Winter, "Sporting Economics," as it appeared in *Wisconsin Sportsman*, September/October 1985. Reprinted by permission.

$$\text{Maturity Value} \times \text{Discount Rate} \times \text{Discount Period} = \text{Discount}$$
$$\$12{,}000 \times 9\% \times \frac{30}{360} = \$90$$

$$\text{Maturity Value} - \text{Discount} = \text{Proceeds}$$
$$\$12{,}000 - \$90 = \$11{,}910$$

To record the discounting transaction, Acme Company makes the following entry:

Oct. 31	Cash	11,910	
	Interest Expense	90	
	Notes Receivable		12,000
	Discounted Bowman's non-interest-bearing note.		

DISCOUNTING INTEREST-BEARING NOTES RECEIVABLE We also use the procedure just described for interest-bearing notes. In this case, however, maturity value includes interest for the full term of the note. The discount computation and calculation of proceeds for a $12,000, 60-day, 9% note dated October 1 and discounted at 9% on October 31 by Acme Company is as follows:

$$\text{Maturity Value} \times \text{Discount Rate} \times \text{Discount Period} = \text{Discount}$$
$$\$12{,}180 \times 9\% \times \frac{30}{360} = \$91.35$$

$$\text{Maturity Value} - \text{Discount} = \text{Proceeds}$$
$$\$12{,}180 - \$91.35 = \$12{,}088.65$$

Acme Company records the discounting transaction as follows:

Oct. 31	Cash	12,088.65	
	Interest Income		88.65
	Notes Receivable		12,000.00
	Discounted Bowman's 60-day, 9% note at 9%.		

Note that although Acme Company and the bank each hold a note 30 days, the bank exacts an additional amount of interest. The extra $1.35 is the interest for 30 days on $180 at the 9% bank discount rate. The bank considers the transaction a loan of $12,180, the amount that must be repaid at the end of the note's term.

Normally, a firm discounting a customer's interest-bearing note at the bank earns interest income, as shown in our illustration. However, the proceeds from discounting may be less than the note's face value when the firm's holding period is fairly short and the bank's discount rate exceeds the interest rate on the note.

Suppose that Acme Company discounts the $12,000 note after holding it only six days, and the discount rate is 12%. The discount would be $\$12{,}180 \times 12\% \times \frac{54}{360} = \$219.24$. Subtracting this amount from the $12,180 maturity value yields proceeds of $11,960.76. In this case, Acme Company would record the $39.24 difference between face value and proceeds as interest expense.

Oct. 7	Cash	11,960.76	
	Interest Expense	39.24	
	Notes Receivable		12,000
	Discounted Bowman's 60-day, 9% note at 12%.		

DISCOUNTED NOTES RECEIVABLE DISHONORED When the maker of a note receivable fails to pay it (dishonors it) at maturity, the bank notifies the endorsing party and charges the full amount owed, including interest, to the endorser's bank account. In addition, the bank may also charge a small protest fee. Suppose that Bowman Company's $12,000, 60-day, 9% note, which Acme discounted on October 31, was dishonored by Bowman Company at maturity. Assume also that the bank notified Acme Company on November 30 that the maturity value of the note, $12,180, plus a $5 protest fee, was charged against Acme Company's bank account. Acme Company's entry to record paying the maturity value of the note plus the protest fee and to charge the entire amount to Accounts Receivable—Bowman Company is as follows:

Nov. 30	Accounts Receivable— Bowman Company	12,185	
	Cash		12,185
	Paid Bowman Company's note and $5 protest fee.		

Acme Company would then endeavor to collect the $12,185 from Bowman Company. If Acme fails in its efforts, it writes off the account as uncollectible, using the procedures described earlier in this chapter.

Borrowing at a Discount

When a business borrows from a bank by giving its own note, the bank often deducts the interest in advance. With this type of transaction, a business is said to be "discounting its own note." Suppose that Acme Company discounts at 12% its own $8,000, 60-day note, dated December 16, at the bank. The calculation of discount and proceeds follows the pattern used for discounting notes receivable:

$$\text{Maturity Value} \times \text{Interest Rate} \times \text{Discount Period} = \text{Discount (Interest)}$$
$$\$8{,}000 \times 12\% \times \frac{60}{360} = \$160$$

$$\text{Maturity Value} - \text{Discount (Interest)} = \text{Proceeds}$$
$$\$8{,}000 - \$160 = \$7{,}840$$

Acme records this transaction as follows:

Dec. 16	Cash	7,840	
	Discount on Notes Payable	160	
	Notes Payable		8,000
	Discounted our 60-day note at 12%.		

Note that the $160 is charged to **Discount on Notes Payable.** The balance of this contra account is subtracted from the Notes Payable amount on the balance sheet. As the period for the note elapses, the discount is reduced and charged to Interest Expense. Thus, at December 31, after 15 days have elapsed, $40 would be charged to Interest Expense and credited to Discount on Notes Payable. A complete discussion of the adjustment procedure is offered in the next section.

Because the proceeds of this type of note are less than the maturity value of the note, the *effective interest rate* for the loan is greater than the stated interest rate. The effective interest rate may be calculated by the following formula:

$$\text{Effective Interest Rate} = \frac{\text{Maturity Value of Note} \times \text{Stated Interest Rate}}{\text{Cash Proceeds from Note}}$$

Therefore, the effective interest rate on the Acme Company note is computed as follows:

$$\frac{\$8{,}000 \times 12\%}{\$7{,}840} = 12.24\%$$

Adjusting Entries for Interest

When the term of an interest-bearing note extends beyond the end of an accounting period, adjusting entries are usually necessary to reflect interest in the proper period. When material amounts are involved, year-end adjustments are normally made to accrue interest income on notes receivable and interest expense on notes payable. Often, entries are also necessary to record interest expense on a company's own discounted notes.

ACCRUED INTEREST Assume that Acme Company received a $12,000, 60-day, 10% note from Cable Company on December 16 of the current year. By the close of the accounting period on December 31, Acme Company would have earned 15 days' interest, or $50, on the note, and Cable Company would have incurred an equal amount of interest expense. The adjusting entries made by each company on December 31 are shown below:

Acme Company

Dec. 31	Interest Receivable	50	
	Interest Income		50
	To accrue interest income on Cable Company note.		

Cable Company

Dec. 31	Interest Expense	50	
	Interest Payable		50
	To accrue interest expense on note to Acme Company.		

As a result of its adjusting entry, Acme Company would report the interest earned during December in its income statement for the current year and would show the interest receivable at December 31 among the current assets in its balance sheet. Likewise, Cable Company would report the interest expense incurred during December in its income statement for the current year and the interest payable as a current liability in its December 31 balance sheet.

In Chapter 4, we mentioned that some accountants prefer to make reversing entries for most accrual adjustments, after the books have been closed and statements have been prepared. If Acme Company followed this practice, the January 1 reversing entry (debit Interest Income and credit Interest Receivable for $50) would eliminate the Interest Receivable balance and reflect a debit balance of $50 in the Interest Income account (which had no balance after closing). Collection of the note and interest on the maturity date, February 14, would be recorded in the usual manner, as follows:

Feb. 14	Cash	12,200	
	Interest Income		200
	Notes Receivable		12,000
	Collected Cable Company note and interest.		

After this collection entry has been posted to the accounts, the Interest Income account would show a net credit balance of $150—the proper amount of income earned on the note during the new year. The Interest Income account would appear as follows:

Interest Income Account No. 42

Date		Description	Post. Ref.	Debit	Credit	Balance
19XX						
Jan.	1	(reversing)		50		(50)
Feb.	14	Collection of interest			200	150

Alternatively, if Acme Company had not reversed the accrual adjustment on January 1, it would record the collection of principal and interest as follows:

Feb. 14	Cash	12,200	
	Interest Receivable		50
	Interest Income		150
	Notes Receivable		12,000
	Collected Cable Company note and interest.		

When accrual adjustments are not reversed, we must analyze the subsequent related cash transaction as we did in the above entry. This procedure accomplishes the same result with fewer entries than reversing accruals, but we must be more circumspect in recording transactions during the period after adjustment.

Obviously, our remarks also apply to accrued interest on notes payable. For example, if Cable Company reversed its accruals, the entry for payment of the note and interest would be:

Feb. 14	Notes Payable	12,000	
	Interest Expense	200	
	Cash		12,200
	Paid note and interest to Acme Company.		

If Cable Company did not follow the practice of reversing accruals, the entry at maturity date would be:

Feb. 14	Notes Payable	12,000	
	Interest Payable	50	
	Interest Expense	150	
	Cash		12,200
	Paid note and interest to Acme Company.		

DISCOUNT ON NOTES PAYABLE We pointed out earlier that when a firm discounts its own note payable, the bank deducts the interest (discount) immediately from the note's face value to obtain the proceeds. In our example, Acme Company's $8,000, 60-day note payable was discounted at 12% at the bank on December 16. Acme Company's entry is repeated below:

Dec. 16	Cash	7,840	
	Discount on Notes Payable	160	
	Notes Payable		8,000
	Discounted our 60-day note at 12%.		

At the close of the accounting period on December 31, 15 of the 60 days had elapsed, and one-fourth, or $40, of the discount was recognized as interest. Acme Company would make the following adjusting entry on December 31:

Dec. 31	Interest Expense	40	
	Discount on Notes Payable		40
	To record interest expense on our discounted note.		

In its December 31 balance sheet, Acme Company would show the remaining $120 Discount on Notes Payable as a contra liability account, subtracted from the Notes Payable amount.

When the note is paid, Acme Company would make the following entry:

Feb. 14	Notes Payable	8,000	
	Interest Expense	120	
	Discount on Notes Payable		120
	Cash		8,000
	Payment of discounted note at maturity.		

Notes and Interest in Financial Statements

A business shows short-term trade notes receivable as current assets in the balance sheet; because they can normally be converted to cash fairly easily, these notes usually are placed above trade accounts receivable. As with accounts receivable, trade notes receivable are separated from notes from officers and employees and notes representing advances to affiliated companies. If such notes are not truly short-term, they should not be classified as current assets. Interest Receivable is normally shown with Notes Receivable.

Sometimes companies with a large volume of notes receivable must provide for possible losses on notes. Frequently, the provision for credit losses also covers losses on notes as well. In such cases, the Allowance for Uncollectible Accounts is deducted from the sum of Accounts Receivable and Notes Receivable in the balance sheet.

Trade notes payable and notes payable to banks are usually shown separately in the current liabilities section of the balance sheet. Interest Payable is normally shown with Notes Payable—often as an addition, as presented in Exhibit 8–3. Discount on Notes Payable is deducted from the related Notes Payable amount. The order in which current payables appear is less important than the sequence of current assets; however, Notes Payable customarily precedes Accounts Payable.

A current section of a balance sheet is shown in Exhibit 8–3 to illustrate the presentation of items discussed in this chapter.

Because they are financial rather than operating items, we often separate Interest Expense and Interest Income from operating items in the income statement. They frequently appear under the classification *Other Income and Expense*, as shown in Exhibit 8–4. With this type of presentation, readers can make intercompany comparisons of operating results that are not influenced by the financing patterns of the companies involved (such comparisons are explained more fully in Chapter 20).

EXHIBIT 8–3

HURON COMPANY
PARTIAL BALANCE SHEET
DECEMBER 31, 19XX

Current Assets		
Cash		$ 2,000
Notes Receivable—Trade	$24,000	
Interest Receivable	300	24,300
Accounts Receivable—Trade	$50,000	
Less: Allowance for Uncollectible Accounts	1,500	48,500
Inventory		75,000
Prepaid Expenses		200
Total Current Assets		$150,000
Current Liabilities		
Notes Payable—Banks	$ 8,000	
Less: Discount on Notes Payable	60	$ 7,940
Notes Payable—Trade	$20,000	
Interest Payable	400	20,400
Accounts Payable—Trade		30,000
Other Accrued Liabilities		11,660
Total Current Liabilities		$ 70,000

EXHIBIT 8–4

HURON COMPANY
PARTIAL INCOME STATEMENT
FOR THE YEAR ENDED DECEMBER 31, 19XX

Sales		$200,000
Cost of Goods Sold		140,000
Gross Profit		$ 60,000
Operating Expenses:		
•		•
•		•
•		•
Total Operating Expenses		40,000
Net Operating Income		$ 20,000
Other Income and Expense:		
Interest Income	$1,400	
Interest Expense	800	600
Net Income		$ 20,600

KEY POINTS FOR CHAPTER OBJECTIVES

1 Define trade receivables and payables and explain a firm's credit policies (pp. 287–88).

- Trade receivables and payables refer to receivables and payables that arise in the regular course of a firm's transactions with customers and suppliers.
- A firm's credit personnel set credit limits, investigate credit ratings, follow up on unpaid accounts, and decide when a debt is uncollectible.

2 Describe the two methods that can be used to recognize losses from uncollectible accounts (pp. 288–90).

- Under the direct write-off method, credit losses are recorded when the debt is considered uncollectible, by a debit to Uncollectible Accounts Expense and a credit to Accounts Receivable.
- Under the allowance method, losses are estimated in advance of the period in which specific accounts are determined to be uncollectible. The amount of the estimate is debited to Uncollectible Accounts Expense and credited to Allowance for Uncollectible Accounts. The latter account is debited and Accounts Receivable is credited when specific accounts are determined to be uncollectible.

3 Illustrate the procedures for estimating and recording credit losses (pp. 290–93).

- Some firms determine through experience the approximate percentage of credit sales that will prove to be uncollectible. This provides the basis for the recording of Uncollectible Accounts Expense at the end of the accounting period.
- Other firms analyze (age) the accounts receivable and through experience determine the approximate percentage of each age stratum that will prove to be uncollectible. The firm can then determine the desired balance in the Allowance for Uncollectible Accounts.

4 Describe and illustrate notes and interest calculations (pp. 293–96).

- A promissory note is a written promise to pay a certain sum of money on demand or at a fixed and determinable future time.
- When a note's duration is expressed in days, we count the days in each calendar month to determine the maturity date. When the duration is expressed in months, we count the months from date of issue to find the maturity date.
- In calculating interest, we determine the product of principal × rate × duration expressed as a fraction of a year. If the duration is expressed in months, it is divided by 12; if it is expressed in days, it is divided by 360.

5 Illustrate the discounting of notes receivable and payable (pp. 296–303).

- Discount is calculated on the maturity value of a note for the period the bank must hold it. Proceeds of a note are obtained by subtracting the discount from the maturity value.
- To record the discounting of a customer's note, we debit Cash for the proceeds, and credit Notes Receivable for the face value of the note. If proceeds exceed face value, we credit the difference to Interest Income. If proceeds are less than face value, we debit the difference to Interest Expense. When a firm discounts its *own* note, Notes Payable is credited.
- If the maker of a discounted note receivable fails to pay the note at maturity, the bank notifies the endorser of the default and charges the maturity value (plus any protest fee) to the endorser's bank account. The endorser then records the payment as a debit to Accounts Receivable and a credit to Cash.
- When a firm discounts its own note, Discount on Notes Payable is debited for the difference between face value and proceeds. This contra liability account is deducted from the related Notes Payable on the balance sheet. As the term of the note expires, adjusting entries reduce the discount by charging Interest Expense.

KEY TERMS USED IN THIS CHAPTER

aging schedule 291
allowance for uncollectible accounts 289
allowance method 289
bearer 293
contingent liability 296
credit card fee 293
discount on notes payable 299
discounting 296
direct write-off method 288
installment accounts 287
maker 293
maturity date 295
maturity value 297
note payable 294
note receivable 294
payee 293
promissory note 293
trade payable 287
trade receivable 287
uncollectible accounts expense 288

SELF-TEST QUESTIONS FOR REVIEW

(Answers are at the end of this chapter.)

1. A firm on the allowance method of recording credit losses wrote off a customer's account of $500. Later, the customer paid the account. The firm reinstated the account by means of a journal entry, then recorded the collection. The result of these procedures
   (a) Increased total assets by $500.
   (b) Decreased total assets by $500.
   (c) Decreased total assets by $1,000.
   (d) Had no effect on total assets.
2. A firm has accounts receivable of $90,000 and a debit balance of $900 in Allowance for Uncollectible Accounts. Two-thirds of the accounts receivable are current and one-third is past due. The firm estimates that 2% of the current accounts and 5% of the past due accounts will prove to be uncollectible. The adjusting entry to provide for uncollectible accounts expense should be for
   (a) $2,700
   (b) $3,600
   (c) $1,800
   (d) $4,500
3. A firm discounted its own $12,000, 90-day note payable at the bank at 10%. The effective interest rate for this transaction is
   (a) 10%
   (b) 8.33%
   (c) 9.74%
   (d) 10.26%
4. A firm held an $18,000, 10%, 120-day note receivable for 20 days, then discounted the note at the bank at 12%. The entry to record the discounting of the note will show
   (a) Interest Income of $600
   (b) Interest Income of $20
   (c) Interest Expense of $20
   (d) Interest Expense of $620
5. On December 1, a firm discounted its own $9,000, 120-day note payable at the bank at 12%. The adjusting entry for interest at December 31 will show a
   (a) $90 credit to Discount on Notes Payable.
   (b) $90 debit to Discount on Notes Payable.
   (c) $90 credit to Interest Expense.
   (d) $360 debit to Interest Expense.

DEMONSTRATION PROBLEM FOR REVIEW

At December 31, 19X0, the following selected accounts appeared in Delta Company's unadjusted trial balance:

Accounts Receivable	$ 81,000	
Allowance for Uncollectible Accounts	1,200	(credit)
Notes Receivable (Jason, Inc.)	12,000	
Notes Payable (Ward, Inc.)	9,000	
Sales	250,000	

The $12,000 note receivable was a 90-day, 8% note dated December 13, 19X0, and the $9,000 note payable was a 60-day, 9% note dated December 7, 19X0. The following adjustments, reversing entries, and transactions occurred at the end of 19X0 and during the following year, 19X1:

19X0

Dec.	31	Recorded the adjusting entry for uncollectible accounts expense, at $1\frac{1}{2}\%$ of sales.
	31	Recorded the adjusting entry for interest on the $12,000 note receivable.
	31	Recorded the adjusting entry for interest on the $9,000 note payable.

19X1

Jan.	1	Recorded the reversing entry for interest on the $12,000 note receivable.
	1	Recorded the reversing entry for interest on the $9,000 note payable.
Feb.	5	Paid the $9,000 note payable to Ward, Inc., plus interest.
Mar.	13	Received payment on the $12,000 note receivable from Jason, Inc., plus interest.
Apr.	5	Wrote off the account of Abilene Company, $2,850.
July	9	Wrote off the account of Acme Suppliers, $1,450.
Sept.	5	Acme Suppliers, which is in bankruptcy proceedings, paid $450 in final settlement of the account written off on July 9.
Dec.	6	Wrote off the account of Jacobs, Inc., $1,300.
	16	Discounted the firm's own 60-day note for $7,500 at the bank at 8%.
	31	Changed from the percent-of-sales method of providing for uncollectible accounts to an estimate based on aged accounts receivable. The firm's analysis indicated a desired credit balance of $4,500 in the Allowance for Uncollectible Accounts.
	31	Made the adjusting entry for interest on the note payable dated December 16.

REQUIRED
Prepare the journal entries for the foregoing adjustments, reversals, and transactions.

SOLUTION TO DEMONSTRATION PROBLEM

19X0				
Dec.	31	Uncollectible Accounts Expense	3,750	
		Allowance for Uncollectible Accounts		3,750
		To provide for uncollectible accounts expense at $1\frac{1}{2}\%$ of sales, $250,000.		
	31	Interest Receivable	48	
		Interest Income		48
		To accrue interest on note receivable ($\$12{,}000 \times 8\% \times \frac{18}{360} = \$48$).		
	31	Interest Expense	54	
		Interest Payable		54
		To accrue interest on note payable ($\$9{,}000 \times 9\% \times \frac{24}{360} = \$54$).		
19X1				
Jan.	1	Interest Income	48	
		Interest Receivable		48
		To reverse adjusting entry to accrue interest on $12,000 note receivable.		

Date		Account	Debit	Credit
Jan.	1	Interest Payable	54	
		Interest Expense		54
		To reverse adjusting entry to accrue interest on $9,000 note payable.		
Feb.	5	Notes Payable	9,000	
		Interest Expense	135	
		Cash		9,135
		To record payment of Ward, Inc., note ($\$9,000 \times 9\% \times \frac{60}{360} = \$135$).		
Mar.	13	Cash	12,240	
		Interest Income		240
		Notes Receivable		12,000
		To record receipt of payment of Jason, Inc., note ($\$12,000 \times 8\% \times \frac{90}{360} = \$240$).		
Apr.	5	Allowance for Uncollectible Accounts	2,850	
		Accounts Receivable—Abilene Company		2,850
		To write off the account of Abilene Company as uncollectible.		
July	9	Allowance for Uncollectible Accounts	1,450	
		Accounts Receivable—Acme Suppliers		1,450
		To write off the account of Acme Suppliers as uncollectible.		
Sept.	5	Accounts Receivable—Acme Suppliers	450	
		Allowance for Uncollectible Accounts		450
		To reinstate $450 of the account of Acme Suppliers that proved collectible.		
	5	Cash	450	
		Accounts Receivable—Acme Suppliers		450
		To record payment of Acme Suppliers' account.		
Dec.	6	Allowance for Uncollectible Accounts	1,300	
		Accounts Receivable—Jacobs, Inc.		1,300
		To write off the account of Jacobs, Inc., as uncollectible.		
	16	Cash	7,400	
		Discount on Notes Payable	100	
		Notes Payable		7,500
		Discounted own $7,500 note at bank ($\$7,500 \times 8\% \times \frac{60}{360} = \$100$).		
	31	Uncollectible Accounts Expense	4,700	
		Allowance for Uncollectible Accounts		4,700
		To provide for uncollectible accounts expense ($4,500 desired balance + $200 existing debit balance = $4,700).		
	31	Interest Expense	25	
		Discount on Notes Payable		25
		To record interest expense on discounted note ($\$7,500 \times 8\% \times \frac{15}{360} = \$25$).		

QUESTIONS

8–1 What events might cause credit balances in customers' accounts and debit balances in creditors' accounts? How are such items classified in the balance sheet?

8–2 A mail-order firm regularly makes a large proportion of its sales on the installment basis, requiring a 20% down payment and monthly payments over a period of six to 24 months, depending on the type of item sold. Where should the installment receivables be classified in the balance sheet of this mail-order firm?

8–3 How do the direct write-off and allowance methods of handling credit losses differ with respect to the timing of expense recognition?

8–4 When a firm provides for credit losses under the allowance method, why is the Allowance for Uncollectible Accounts credited rather than Accounts Receivable?

8–5 Describe the two most commonly used methods of estimating uncollectible accounts expense when the allowance method is employed.

8–6 Wagner Company estimates its uncollectibles by aging its accounts and applying percentages to various strata of the aged accounts. This year, it calculated a total of $2,100 in possible losses. On December 31, the Accounts Receivable balance is $98,000 and the Allowance for Uncollectible Accounts has a credit balance of $500 before adjustment. Give the adjusting entry to provide for credit losses. Determine the net amount of Accounts Receivable added into current assets.

8–7 In June of last year, Short, Inc., sold $860 worth of merchandise to Dell Company. In November of last year, Short, Inc., wrote off Dell's account. In March of this year, Dell Company paid the account in full. Give the entries made by Short, Inc., for the write-off and the recovery, assuming that Short, Inc., uses (a) the direct write-off method, and (b) the allowance method of handling credit losses.

8–8 Wood Company sold a $750 refrigerator to a customer who charged the sale with a VISA bank credit card. Wood Company's bank charges a credit card fee of 4% of sales. What entry should Wood Company make to record the sale?

8–9 Phoenix, Inc., received a 60-day, 9% note for $12,000 on March 5 of this year.
(a) What is the maturity date of the note?
(b) What is the maturity value of the note?
(c) Assuming Phoenix, Inc., discounted the note at 9% at the bank on March 25, calculate the proceeds of the note.

8–10 On July 18 of this year, James Brown discounted at the bank his own 90-day note for $8,000 at 9%.
(a) What is the maturity date of the note?
(b) What is the maturity value of the note?
(c) What are the proceeds of the note?

8–11 Why is a discounted customer's note a contingent liability of the endorser?

8–12 The maturity value of a $7,000 customer's note discounted by Roby Company is $7,305. The customer dishonored the note, and the bank charged the $7,305 plus a $10 protest fee to Roby's bank account. What entries should Roby make to record this event?

8–13 Carr Company received a 150-day, 8% note for $15,000 on December 1. What adjusting entry is needed to accrue interest on December 31?

8–14 On December 10, Mary Reed discounted her own 90-day note for $12,000 at the bank at 8% and charged the discount to Discount on Notes Payable. What adjusting entry is necessary on December 31?

8–15 Ralph Bond gave a creditor a 90-day, 8% note for $7,200 on December 16. What adjusting entry should Bond make on December 31?

EXERCISES

Credit losses based on sales

8–16 Sims Company uses the allowance method of handling credit losses. It estimates losses at 1% of credit sales, which were $800,000 during the current year. On December 31 of the current year, the Accounts Receivable balance was $150,000, and the Allowance for Uncollectible Accounts had a credit balance of $900 before adjustment.
(a) Give the adjusting entry to record credit losses for the current year.
(b) Show how Accounts Receivable and the Allowance for Uncollectible Accounts would appear in the December 31 balance sheet.

Credit losses based on accounts receivable

8–17 Gordon, Inc., analyzed its Accounts Receivable balances at December 31 and arrived at the aged balances listed below, along with the percentages of each age group that have proven uncollectible in the past.

Age	Loss (%)	Balance
Current	1	$ 90,000
30–60 days past due	2	18,000
61–120 days past due	5	10,000
121 days–six months past due	10	8,000
Over six months past due	25	6,000
		$132,000

The company handles credit losses with the allowance method. The credit balance of the Allowance for Uncollectible Accounts is $700 on December 31 before any adjustments.
(a) Prepare the adjusting entry for estimated credit losses on December 31.
(b) Give the entry to write off Jeff Tyne's account in April of the following year, $435.

Allowance vs. direct write-off methods

8–18 On March 10 of this year, Arden, Inc., declared a $630 account receivable from Gates Company uncollectible and wrote off the account. On November 18 of this year, Arden received a $630 payment on the account from Gates.
(a) Assume Arden uses the allowance method of handling credit losses. Give the entries to record the write-off and the subsequent recovery of Gates' account.
(b) Assume Arden uses the direct write-off method of handling credit losses. Give the entries to record the write-off and the subsequent recovery of Gates' account.
(c) Assume the payment from Gates arrives on February 5 of next year rather than on November 18 of this year. Give the entries to record the write-off and subsequent recovery of Gates' account under the allowance method.
(d) Assume the payment from Gates arrives on February 5 of next year rather than on November 18 of this year. Give the entries to record the write-off and subsequent recovery of Gates' account under the direct write-off method.

Maturity dates of notes

8–19 Determine the maturity date and compute the interest for each of the following notes:

	Date of Note	Principal	Interest Rate (%)	Term
(a)	July 6	$ 7,200	9	90 days
(b)	April 10	6,000	8	120 days
(c)	May 15	5,600	$7\frac{1}{2}$	120 days
(d)	June 6	5,400	8	45 days
(e)	October 25	15,000	8	75 days

Discounting note receivable

8–20 Record the following transactions on the books of both Kenton Company and Pace, Inc.:

Oct. 1 Pace, Inc., gave Kenton Company a $12,000, 90-day, 8% note in payment of account.
21 Kenton Company discounted the note at the bank at 10%.
Nov. 30 On the maturity date of the note, Pace, Inc., paid the amount due.

Dishonored note

8–21 Suppose that, in Exercise 8–20, Pace, Inc., dishonored its note and the bank notified Kenton Company that it had charged the maturity value plus a $12 protest fee to Kenton Company's bank account. What entry should Kenton Company make on the maturity date?

e

8–22 On November 21, Tilden Company discounted its own $7,200, 60-day note at the bank at 8%.

(a) What is the maturity date of the note?
(b) What are the proceeds of the note?
(c) What amount of interest expense should be recorded as an adjustment at December 31?
(d) What will be the balance in the Discount on Notes Payable account at December 31?
(e) What is the effective interest rate on the note?

Adjusting entries for interest

8–23 The following note transactions occurred during the current year for Porter Company:

Nov. 25 Porter received a 90-day, 9% note for $6,000 from Hyatt Company.
Dec. 7 Porter discounted its own 120-day, $7,200 note at the bank at 10%, charging the discount to Discount on Notes Payable.
23 Porter gave Barr, Inc., a $9,000, 10%, 60-day note in payment of account.

Give the general journal entries necessary to adjust the interest accounts at December 31.

Computing accrued interest

8–24 Compute the interest accrued on each of the following notes receivable held by Savage, Inc., on December 31, 19X6:

Maker	Date of Note	Principal	Interest Rate (%)	Term
Barton	11/21/X6	$ 4,500	10	120 days
Lawson	12/13/X6	6,000	9	90 days
Riley	12/19/X6	15,000	8	60 days

PROBLEMS

Allowance vs. direct write-off methods

8–25 Cahill, Inc., which has been in business for three years, makes all sales on account and does not offer cash discounts. The firm's credit sales, collections from customers, and write-offs of uncollectible accounts for the three-year period are summarized below:

Year	Sales	Collections	Accounts Written Off
1	$500,000	$478,000	$3,500
2	640,000	632,000	5,600
3	700,000	678,000	6,100

REQUIRED

(a) If Cahill, Inc., had used the direct write-off method of recognizing credit losses during the three years, what amount of Accounts Receivable would appear on the firm's balance sheet at the end of the third year? What total amount of uncollectible accounts expense would have appeared on the firm's income statement during the three-year period?
(b) If Cahill, Inc., had used an allowance method of recognizing credit losses and had provided for such losses at the rate of $1\frac{1}{4}\%$ of sales, what amounts in Accounts Receivable and Allowance for Uncollectible Accounts would appear on the firm's balance sheet at the end of the third year? What total amount of uncollectible accounts expense would have appeared on the firm's income statement during the three-year period?
(c) Comment on the use of the $1\frac{1}{4}\%$ rate to provide for losses in part (b).

Entries for credit losses

8–26 At the beginning of the current year, Mason Company had the following accounts on its books:

Accounts Receivable	$94,000 (debit)
Allowance for Uncollectible Accounts	6,100 (credit)

During this year, credit sales were $820,000 and collections on account were $804,000. The following transactions, among others, occurred during the year:

Feb. 17 Wrote off R. Lowell's account, $2,800.
May 28 Wrote off G. Boyd's account, $1,850.
Oct. 13 G. Boyd, who is in bankruptcy proceedings, paid $350 in final settlement of the account written off on May 28. This amount is not included in the $804,000 collections.
Dec. 15 Wrote off K. Marshall's account, $1,150.
31 In an adjusting entry, recorded the provision for uncollectible accounts at $\frac{3}{4}$% of credit sales for the year.

REQUIRED

(a) Prepare general journal entries to record the credit sales, the collections on account, and the above transactions.
(b) Show how Accounts Receivable and the Allowance for Uncollectible Accounts would appear in the December 31 balance sheet.

Credit losses based on accounts receivable

8–27 At December 31 of the current year, Miller Company had a balance of $180,000 in its Accounts Receivable account and a credit balance of $2,100 in the Allowance for Uncollectible Accounts. The Accounts Receivable subsidiary ledger consisted of $182,500 in debit balances and $2,500 in credit balances. The company has aged its accounts as follows:

Current	$152,000
0–60 days past due	17,000
61–180 days past due	9,000
Over six months past due	4,500
	$182,500

In the past, the company has experienced losses as follows: 1% of current balances, 5% of balances 0–60 days past due, 15% of balances 61–180 days past due, and 40% of balances over six months past due. The company bases its provision for credit losses on the aging analysis.

REQUIRED

(a) Prepare the adjusting journal entry to record the provision for credit losses for the year.
(b) Show how Accounts Receivable (including the credit balances) and Allowance for Uncollectible Accounts would appear in the December 31 balance sheet.

Discounting notes payable

8–28 Fairbanks Products, Inc., had the following transactions for 19X1 and 19X2:

19X1

May 18 Discounted its own $12,000, 90-day note at the bank at 8%.
Aug. 16 Paid the bank the amount due from the May 18 note.
Oct. 2 Discounted its own $8,400, 120-day note at the bank at 9%.
Dec. 31 Made the appropriate adjusting entry for interest expense.

19X2

Jan. 30 Paid the bank the amount due from the October 2 note.

REQUIRED
(a) Record the above transactions and adjustment in general journal form.
(b) Compute the effective interest rate on the loan of:
1. May 18.
2. October 2.

Various entries for accounts and notes

8–29 Post Company had the following transactions during the current year:

Apr. 8 Received a $9,600, 75-day, 8% note from J. Dean in payment of account.
May 24 Wrote off customer P. Gunn's account against the Allowance for Uncollectible Accounts, $670.
June 22 J. Dean paid note in full.
Sept. 10 Gave a $6,400, 90-day, 9% note to M. Bolton in payment of account.
18 P. Gunn paid account written off on May 24.
Dec. 4 Discounted its own $15,000, 90-day note at the bank at 8%.
9 Paid principal and interest due on note to M. Bolton.
21 Received a $10,000, 60-day, 9% note from C. Lester on account.
23 Gave an $18,000, 60-day, 7% note to L. Shaw in payment of account.

REQUIRED
(a) Record the above transactions in general journal form.
(b) Make any necessary adjusting entries for interest at December 31.

Various entries for accounts and notes

8–30 Temple, Inc., began business on January 1 of the current year. Certain transactions for the current year are given below:

May 1 Borrowed $14,000 from the bank on a six-month, 9% note, interest to be paid at maturity.
June 8 Received a $7,500, 60-day, 8% note on account from R. Elliot.
28 Discounted Elliot's note at the bank at 9%.
Aug. 7 R. Elliot paid her note at the bank, with interest.
Sept. 1 Received a $12,000, 120-day, 9% note from B. Shore on account.
Oct. 1 Discounted Shore's note at the bank at 10%.
Nov. 1 Paid May 1 note, with interest.
21 Discounted its own $5,400, 120-day note at the bank at 9%.
Dec. 16 Received a $7,200, 45-day, 10% note from C. Judd on account.
30 The bank notified Temple, Inc., that B. Shore's note was dishonored. Maturity value of the note plus a $12 protest fee was charged against Temple's checking account at the bank.
31 Wrote off Shore's account as uncollectible. Temple, Inc., uses the allowance method of providing for credit losses.
31 Recorded expected credit losses for the year by an adjusting entry. Write-offs of accounts during this first year have created a debit balance in the Allowance for Uncollectible Accounts of $13,700. Analysis of aged receivables indicates that the desired balance of the allowance account is $11,100.
31 Made the appropriate adjusting entries for interest.

REQUIRED
Record the foregoing transactions and adjustments in general journal form.

Adjusting entries for interest

8–31 At December 31, 19X0, Sigma Corporation held one note receivable and had one note payable outstanding. At December 31, 19X1, Sigma again held one note receivable and had outstanding one note payable. The notes are described below.

	Date of Note	Principal	Interest Rate (%)	Term
December 31, 19X0				
Note Receivable	11/16/X0	$ 9,000	8%	120 days
Note Payable	12/4/X0	16,000	9%	60 days

December 31, 19X1				
Note Receivable	12/7/X1	$12,000	9%	60 days
Note Payable	12/21/X1	$18,000	10%	30 days

REQUIRED

(a) Prepare the appropriate adjusting entries for interest at December 31, 19X0.

(b) Assume that the appropriate adjusting entries were made at December 31, 19X0, but that no reversing or adjusting entries were made in 19X1. Give the journal entries to record payment of the notes that were outstanding December 31, 19X0.

(c) Assume that the appropriate adjusting entries were made at December 31, 19X0. However, no reversing or adjusting entries were made in 19X1, and the bookkeeper neglected to consider the related interest receivable and interest payable when the notes were paid in 19X1. Make the necessary adjusting entries for interest at December 31, 19X1.

ALTERNATE PROBLEMS

Allowance vs. direct write-off methods

8–25A Randwick, Inc., which has been in business for three years, makes all sales on account and does not offer cash discounts. The firm's credit sales, collections from customers, and write-offs of uncollectible accounts for the three-year period are summarized below:

Year	Sales	Collections	Accounts Written Off
1	$620,000	$605,000	$4,400
2	730,000	720,000	4,600
3	810,000	781,000	5,400

REQUIRED

(a) If Randwick, Inc., had used the direct write-off method of recognizing credit losses during the three years, what amount of Accounts Receivable would appear on the firm's balance sheet at the end of the third year? What total amount of uncollectible accounts expense would have appeared on the firm's income statements during the three-year period?

(b) If Randwick, Inc., had used an allowance method of recognizing credit losses and had provided for such losses at the rate of 1% of sales, what amounts of Accounts Receivable and Allowance for Uncollectible Accounts would appear on the firm's balance sheet at the end of the third year? What total amount of uncollectible accounts expense would have appeared on the firm's income statement during the three-year period?

(c) Comment on the use of the 1% rate to provide for losses in part (b).

Entries for credit losses

8–26A At January 1 of the current year, Spartan, Inc., had the following accounts on its books:

Accounts Receivable	$140,000 (debit)
Allowance for Uncollectible Accounts	7,600 (credit)

During this year, credit sales were $840,000 and collections on account were $822,000. The following transactions, among others, occurred during the year:

Jan.	11	Wrote off J. Wolf's account, $3,800.
Apr.	29	Wrote off B. Avery's account, $1,150.
Nov.	15	B. Avery paid debt of $1,150, written off April 29. This amount is not included in the $822,000 collections.
Dec.	5	Wrote off D. Wright's account, $2,400.
	31	In an adjusting entry, recorded the provision for uncollectible accounts at 1% of credit sales for the year.

REQUIRED

(a) Prepare general journal entries to record the credit sales, the collections on account, and the above transactions.

(b) Show how Accounts Receivable and the Allowance for Uncollectible Accounts would appear in the December 31 balance sheet.

Credit losses based on accounts receivable

8–27A At December 31 of the current year, Pyramid Company had a balance of $152,000 in its Accounts Receivable account and a credit balance of $1,400 in the Allowance for Uncollectible Accounts. The Accounts Receivable subsidiary ledger consisted of $154,800 in debit balances and $2,800 in credit balances. The company has aged its accounts as follows:

Current	$136,000
0–60 days past due	9,000
61–180 days past due	5,600
Over six months past due	4,200
	$154,800

In the past, the company has experienced losses as follows: 2% of current balances, 6% of balances 0–60 days past due, 15% of balances 61–180 days past due, and 30% of balances more than six months past due. The company bases its provision for credit losses on the aging analysis.

REQUIRED

(a) Prepare the adjusting journal entry to record the provision for credit losses for the year.

(b) Show how Accounts Receivable (including the credit balances) and Allowance for Uncollectible Accounts would appear in the December 31 balance sheet.

Discounting notes receivable

8–28A Pioneer Corporation had the following transactions for 19X3 and 19X4:

19X3

Mar. 6 Sold $7,500 worth of merchandise to E. Neal and received a $7,500, 60-day, 8% note.

21 Discounted E. Neal's note at the bank at 10%.

May 5 Neal paid the bank the amount due on the March 6 note.

Dec. 11 Received a $16,000, 60-day, 9% note from J. Banning in settlement of an open account.

31 Made the appropriate adjusting entry for interest income.

19X4

Jan. 1 Reversed the December 31 adjustment for interest income.

Feb. 9 Received payment from J. Banning on the December 11 note.

REQUIRED

(a) Record the above transactions, adjustment, and reversal in general journal form.

(b) Assume Pioneer Corporation does not make reversing entries. Give the entry to record the receipt of the note payment from J. Banning on February 9, 19X4.

Various entries for accounts and notes

8–29A Crescent Company had the following transactions during the current year:

July 15 Received a $12,500, 90-day, 8% note from L. Dobbs in payment of account.

Sept. 5 Wrote off customer D. Simon's account against the Allowance for Uncollectible Accounts, $845.
9 Gave a $9,200, 90-day, 10% note to F. Sharp in payment of account.
Oct. 13 L. Dobbs paid note in full.
21 D. Simon paid account written off on September 5.
Dec. 8 Paid principal and interest due on note to F. Sharp.
13 Discounted its own $7,000, 90-day note at the bank at 10%.
19 Received a $7,200, 60-day, 10% note from K. Brian on account.
22 Gave a $16,000, 60-day, 9% note to R. Sinclair on account.

REQUIRED
(a) Record the above transactions in general journal form.
(b) Make any necessary adjusting entries for interest at December 31.

Various entries for accounts and notes

8–30A Design, Inc., began business on January 1 of the current year. Several transactions for the current year are given below:

Mar. 1 Borrowed $30,000 from the bank on a five-month, 9% note, interest to be paid at maturity.
May 2 Received a $9,600, 60-day, 10% note on account from G. Holt.
17 Discounted G. Holt's note at the bank at 10%.
July 1 G. Holt paid his note at the bank, with interest.
1 Received a $13,500, 120-day, 10% note from B. Rich on account.
25 Discounted Rich's note at the bank at 10%.
Aug. 1 Paid March 1 note, with interest.
Oct. 30 The bank notified Design, Inc., that B. Rich's note was dishonored. Maturity value of the note plus a $10 protest fee was charged against Design's checking account at the bank.
Dec. 1 Discounted its own $18,000, 120-day note at bank at 9%.
9 Wrote off Rich's account as uncollectible. Design, Inc., uses the allowance method of providing for credit losses.
11 Received a $14,000, 90-day, 9% note from W. Maling on account.
31 Recorded expected credit losses for the year by an adjusting entry. The Allowance for Uncollectible Accounts has a debit balance of $14,200 as a result of write-offs of accounts during this first year. Analysis of aged receivables indicates that the desired balance of the allowance account is $3,600.
31 Made the appropriate adjusting entries for interest.

REQUIRED
Record the foregoing transactions and adjustments in general journal form.

Adjusting entries for interest

8–31A At December 31, 19X0, Centurion Corporation held one note receivable and had one note payable outstanding. At December 31, 19X1, Centurion again held one note receivable and had outstanding one note payable. The notes are described below.

	Date of Note	Principal	Interest Rate (%)	Term
December 31, 19X0				
Note Receivable	11/25/X0	$13,500	8%	90 days
Note Payable	12/16/X0	16,800	9%	60 days
December 31, 19X1				
Note Receivable	12/11/X1	$15,400	9%	120 days
Note Payable	12/7/X1	9,000	10%	90 days

REQUIRED
(a) Prepare the appropriate adjusting entries for interest at December 31, 19X0.
(b) Assume that the appropriate adjusting entries were made at December 31, 19X0, but that no reversing or adjusting entries were made in 19X1. Give the journal entries to record payment of the notes that were outstanding December 31, 19X0.
(c) Assume that the appropriate adjusting entries were made at December 31, 19X0. However, no reversing or adjusting entries were made in 19X1, and the bookkeeper neglected to consider the related interest receivable and interest payable when the notes were paid in 19X1. Make the necessary adjusting entries for interest at December 31, 19X1.

BUSINESS DECISION PROBLEM

The latest income statement for Ridgewood Sales, Inc., a wholesaler of electronic parts and equipment, is shown below. Company president Mark Winslow has been dissatisfied with the firm's rate of growth for several years. He believes that increasing sales promotion and liberalizing credit policies would raise gross sales substantially. Specifically, Winslow is fairly confident that gross sales would increase by 30% if the firm adopted the following plan:

1. Increase certain of the firm's trade discounts. This change would reduce the average selling price of merchandise somewhat, but it would increase sales volume.
2. Extend credit to an additional number of less creditworthy customers.

Ridgewood Sales, Inc.
Income Statement
For the Year Ended December 31, 19XX

Sales	$600,000	
Less: Sales Discounts	8,000	
Net Sales	$592,000	100%
Cost of Goods Sold	384,800	65
Gross Profit on Sales	$207,200	35%
Selling Expenses (excluding Uncollectible Accounts Expense)	$148,000	25%
Uncollectible Accounts Expense	5,920	1
Administrative Expenses	30,000	5
Total Expenses	$183,920	31%
Net Income	$ 23,280	4%

The controller for Ridgewood Sales, Inc., makes the following comments after analyzing Winslow's proposal for its likely impact on other income statement items:

1. Gross Profit on Sales—The slight decline in average selling prices of merchandise resulting from an increase in trade discounts will reduce the gross profit rate from 35% to $33\frac{1}{3}$%.
2. Sales Discounts—The firm has been selling to selected retailers on terms of 2/15, n/30, with about two-thirds of total sales subject to the discount. Even with an increased number of customers, two-thirds of total sales will still be subject to the discount.
3. Selling Expenses—Excluding uncollectible accounts expense, selling expenses will remain at 25% of net sales. Because of the expected 25% increase in sales, selling expenses, including promotion outlays, will rise accordingly.

4. Uncollectible Accounts Expense—Uncollectible accounts expense has been about 1% of net sales for several years. The proposed liberalization of credit policies will increase this expense to 2% of net sales.
5. Administrative Expenses—These expenses will remain constant even if gross sales increase.

REQUIRED
Prepare an income statement based on Winslow's proposal and the controller's comments. Based on your results, should the firm adopt Winslow's proposal?

ANSWERS TO SELF-TEST QUESTIONS

1. (d) **2.** (b) **3.** (d) **4.** (c) **5.** (a)

9

INVENTORIES

CHAPTER OBJECTIVES

1. Discuss the basic concepts of accounting for inventories (pp. 319–23).
2. Describe the pricing of inventory under a periodic inventory system using the (1) specific identification method, (2) weighted average method, (3) FIFO method, and (4) LIFO method (pp. 323–27).
3. Analyze the effects inventory pricing methods have on gross profits, income, matching of costs and revenue, and income taxes (pp. 327–30).
4. Apply the lower of cost or market rule to inventory measurements (pp. 330–31).
5. Describe the gross profit and retail inventory methods of estimating inventories (pp. 331–33).
6. Describe and illustrate the perpetual inventory system (pp. 333–36).

Good merchandise finds a ready buyer.

PLAUTUS

Inventories constitute the lifeblood of merchandising and manufacturing firms. For these firms, inventory is a significant asset, and the sale of inventory provides the major source of revenue. This chapter focuses on inventory accounting for merchandisers—firms that buy finished products to sell to their customers. Inventories of manufacturing companies are covered in a later chapter.

We have already introduced the special source documents, business transactions, and accounting techniques related to routine inventory transactions. Now we build on these facts by briefly considering the basic notions of inventories, examining and illustrating the problems of inventory determination, and comparing the consequences for periodic income determination of various inventory pricing methods.

REVIEW OF BASIC CONCEPTS

Before discussing new material, let us review some of the pertinent concepts covered earlier.

Inventory is all merchandise owned by a company and held for resale to customers in the ordinary course of business. Inventories are current assets because they typically will be sold within one year, or during a firm's normal operating cycle if it should be longer than a year. For retailing firms, inventories are often the largest or most valuable current asset.

Inventory costs are all costs necessary to acquire the merchandise and bring it to the site of sale. Inventory costs include the purchase price, plus any transportation or freight in, less purchases returns and allowances and purchases discounts.

The **cost of goods sold** is the net acquisition cost of the goods sold to customers in generating the sales revenue of an operating period. The following is a typical example of the computation of the cost of goods sold:

Beginning Inventory			$10,000
Add: Net Cost of Purchases			
Purchases		$31,000	
Less: Purchases Returns and Allowances	$2,100		
Purchases Discounts	400	2,500	
		$28,500	
Add: Transportation In		500	29,000
Cost of Goods Available for Sale			$39,000
Less: Ending Inventory			9,000
Cost of Goods Sold			$30,000

THE NEED FOR INVENTORIES

Most well-managed merchandisers find it necessary and desirable to maintain large, varied inventories. As a consumer, you have probably experienced a favorable buyer reaction to the availability of a wide assortment of colors, sizes, qualities, and types of the goods for which you shop. The prevailing affluence of our society and the related buyer habits have probably made large, varied inventories an operating necessity for most retail firms.

Other business factors can justify the existence of relatively large inventories. Clearly, a firm can sell more goods in a period than it can purchase or produce only by having beginning inventories. Beginning inventories are particularly important to seasonal industries or markets. Attractive quantity discounts may

INVENTORIES AND COMPUTERS

Behold another marketplace that is being transformed by computers.

Computers, of course, are ubiquitous in business today. But most of them are crunching numbers or processing words at ever faster speeds. Now a growing number of companies buy and sell by computer. Industries are changing as a result.

Consider the mundane business of restocking shelves at the corner drugstore. Philip Cavavetta buys merchandise for his Boston-area drugstores from two wholesalers. One of them, McKesson, is getting more of his business these days. Why? "Their computer system is so good," he says.

Not so long ago, salesmen from McKesson, as those from other wholesalers, would drop by Mr. Cavavetta's Econo Drug Marts to take orders for cough syrup, aspirin, penicillin and Valium. When the store ran short between salesmen's visits, clerks would read new orders over the phone to tape recorders at McKesson's warehouse.

Today, a clerk in Mr. Cavavetta's stores walks the aisles once a week with a McKesson-supplied computer in his palm. If the store is low on, say, bottles of cough syrup, the clerk waves a scanner over a McKesson-provided label stuck to the shelf. The computer takes note, and, when the clerk is finished, transmits the order to McKesson.

At first glance, it appears that McKesson has simply automated a costly, labor-intensive chore. But far more has happened: McKesson's computers not only dispatch the orders to a warehouse but also print price stickers that add in the precise profit margin that Mr. Cavavetta has selected and tell him monthly how profitable each of his departments is.

The electronic marketplace is spreading to so many industries that some companies have no choice but to join in. "If you're not able to do business this way, you'll be at a competitive disadvantage," says John P. Sweeney of General Motors Corp.'s Electro-Motive division.

GM and Ford Motor Co. have indicated that in the future they will do business only with suppliers who can receive and send messages electronically.

The auto companies say they need to cut inventories by arranging for parts to arrive just before they are needed on the assembly line, a cost-saving trick borrowed from the Japanese that requires quick, frequent communication with suppliers. Toward that end, Ford is electronically sending more than 700 suppliers of its Wixom, Mich., assembly plant daily updates on the parts the plants need. Previously, the information was available only once a week.

The auto industry hasn't enough experience to show how significantly inventories can be reduced, but others do. Levi Strauss, for one, says that conversing electronically with denim suppliers has helped the company reduce inventories of uncut fabrics to three days' worth or less; in the past, the company had enough fabric on hand to make a month's worth of blue jeans. Denim mills tell Levi not only how many rolls of denim are arriving on the next truck but also what shade of fabric is placed where on that truck. "This translated last year into the largest drop in days of inventory we've ever had in our history," says Thomas Tusher, Levi's executive vice president.

From David Wessel, "Computer Finds a Role in Buying and Selling, Reshaping Businesses," *The Wall Street Journal*, March 18, 1987, p. 1. Reprinted by permission of *The Wall Street Journal*,

justify a firm's buying in excess of its current sales requirements and therefore creating additional inventories. Strategic purchases offer still another reason for carrying inventories. Many firms—especially those that sell in seasonal markets—buy in excess of their needs when supply prices are favorable. They store the goods and can then maintain sales during a period of unfavorable supply prices.

Progressive firms take into account customer preferences, competitors' merchandising patterns, and favorable market situations in determining inventory size and balance, but they must also consider the cost of carrying large inventories. Often, savings obtained by purchasing in large quantities or under favorable market conditions may be more than offset by increased carrying costs. Storage and handling costs for large inventories can increase substantially. In addition, the firm may suffer losses from inventory deterioration and obsolescence. Finally, inventories tie up working capital that might be used more profitably elsewhere. These latter factors often cause merchandisers to contract inventory during recessionary periods.

INCOME DETERMINATION AND INVENTORY MEASUREMENT

Proper income determination depends on the appropriate measurement of all assets; higher asset amounts result in higher reported income amounts. Because inventories are often relatively large and their sizes fluctuate, accounting correctly for inventories is important in determining net income properly. Other things being equal, **changing the dollar amount of ending inventory changes net income dollar for dollar** (ignoring any income tax effects), as Exhibit 9–1 illustrates. Note that sales, beginning inventory, and purchases are identical in all four cases. As ending inventory increases by a given amount—$1,000 from A to B, $2,000 from B to D, for example—cost of goods sold decreases and income increases by the same amount.

Accountants must be concerned with the problems of inventory measurement because of its role in the determination of reported income. We consider these problems in the remainder of this chapter.

EXHIBIT 9–1

RELATIONSHIP OF INVENTORY MEASUREMENTS TO REPORTED INCOME

	Amounts (in Thousands of Dollars)			
Assumed Data	**A**	**B**	**C**	**D**
Sales	$25	$25	$25	$25
Beginning inventory	$ 3	$ 3	$ 3	$ 3
Net cost of purchases	20	20	20	20
Cost of goods available for sale	$23	$23	$23	$23
Ending inventory	4	5	6	7
Cost of goods sold	$19	$18	$17	$16
Reported income	$ 6	$ 7	$ 8	$ 9

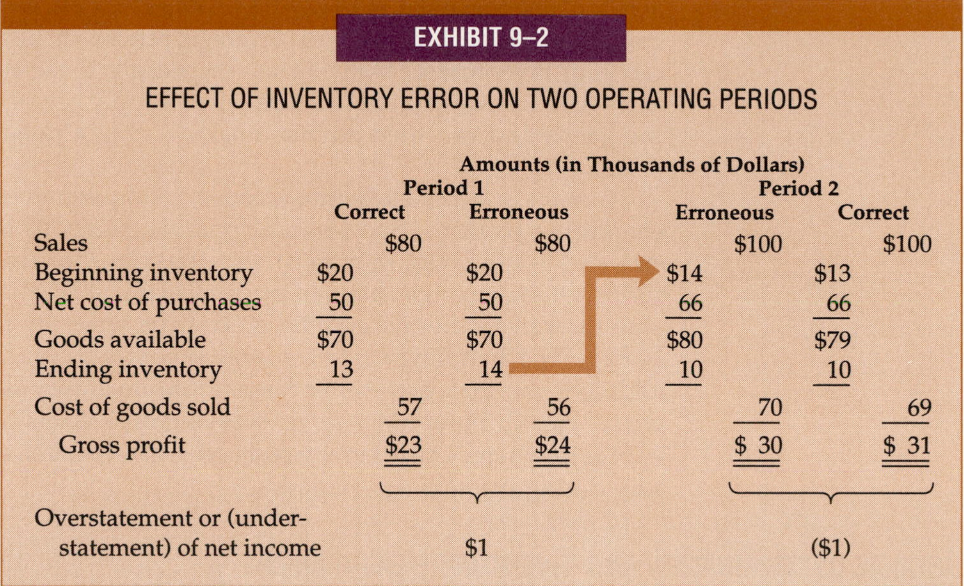

EXHIBIT 9–2

EFFECT OF INVENTORY ERROR ON TWO OPERATING PERIODS

Amounts (in Thousands of Dollars)

	Period 1				Period 2			
	Correct		Erroneous		Erroneous		Correct	
Sales		$80		$80		$100		$100
Beginning inventory	$20		$20		$14		$13	
Net cost of purchases	50		50		66		66	
Goods available	$70		$70		$80		$79	
Ending inventory	13		14		10		10	
Cost of goods sold		57		56		70		69
Gross profit		$23		$24		$ 30		$ 31
Overstatement or (understatement) of net income			$1				($1)	

THE EFFECT OF INVENTORY ERRORS

To determine the effect of inventory errors on income determination, we must consider the method for calculating cost of goods sold. We illustrate why in Exhibit 9–2, where we assume that the ending inventory of period 1 was overstated by $1,000.

Because the ending inventory in period 1 is overstated by $1,000, the cost of goods sold is understated by $1,000, and thus reported income is overstated by that amount. Because the ending inventory in period 1 is also the beginning inventory in period 2, the reported income for both periods will be misstated unless the error is corrected. Note, however, that the error in period 2 causes a misstatement of reported income that is equal in amount ($1,000) to the error in period 1 but opposite in direction (an understatement); thus, the errors in the two periods offset each other.

Therefore, uncorrected errors in ending inventories affect income determination for two periods. Overstating or understating ending inventory overstates or understates income, respectively. Regardless of the direction of the error, it will cause an offsetting error of a like amount in the second period if it is not corrected.

INVENTORY MEASUREMENT

The dollar amount of an inventory depends on two variables—quantity and price. We usually express inventories as the aggregate dollar value (Quantity × Price) of the goods on hand at a specific time. "Taking" an inventory consists of (1) counting the items involved, (2) pricing each item, and (3) summing the amounts. Exhibit 9–3 illustrates these three steps.

Inventory counts can be extremely complicated and expensive. Even moderate-sized firms may have thousands of items, hundreds of types, sizes, and qualities, purchased at a variety of unit prices, and located in dozens of ware-

EXHIBIT 9–3

THE THREE STEPS OF TAKING AN INVENTORY

1. PHYSICAL COUNT		2. PRICING	3. SUMMATION
Merchandise Item	Unit Count	Unit Price	Extension
A	30	$6	$180
B	40	7	280
C	50	8	400
			$860

houses, stores, branches, and departments. Proper planning and coordination are imperative if all items are to be counted—only once—and properly priced. Although some firms "close" for inventory-taking, many continue operations during the count and must, of course, know if counted or uncounted merchandise is sold during the inventory period.

Another problem in inventory counts is deciding what goods should be counted. Often the proper inventory is not simply "all merchandise on site." By definition, the inventory should include—and be limited to—goods *owned* by the firm and *available* for resale. Ownership transfers when title to the goods passes from the seller to the buyer. Title may pass at any time expressly agreed to by these two parties. In the absence of a specific agreement, title generally passes when the seller completes performance with regard to delivery. Therefore, a firm purchasing merchandise on terms F.O.B. shipping point may acquire title to the goods before it physically receives the goods. Such items (often called *goods in transit*) should be included in the inventory count.

Merchandise whose title has passed to customers does not belong in the inventory count, even if it has not been removed from the store or warehouse. A buyer, for example, may agree to pick up the goods at the seller's place of business. When the seller identifies the goods that fulfill the contract, title transfers to the buyer. These goods should be excluded from the seller's inventory count because they are no longer owned or available for resale. Similarly, goods held for resale on consignment from another firm are not included in the inventory count, because the goods are not owned by the firm holding them.

We see, therefore, that although a firm's ownership of merchandise often is indicated by the physical presence of goods, a firm can also own goods that it has not yet received and not own goods that it still possesses.

INVENTORY PRICING METHODS

In general, inventories are priced at their historical cost. Inventory pricing is quite simple when acquisition prices remain constant. When prices for like items change during the accounting period, however, it is not always apparent which price should be used to measure the ending inventory. Consequently, when cost prices fluctuate, we must either keep track of all costs for specific goods or make assumptions about which goods have been sold and which goods are on hand. The need for such assumptions has led to the commonly used methods of inventory pricing that we illustrate in this section. We illustrate a rising price pattern, which is the most prevalent in our economy.

Two terms are useful in considering the problems of pricing inventories under fluctuating prices. *Goods flow* describes the actual physical movement of goods in the firm's operations. Goods flow is a result of physical events. *Cost flow* is the real or *assumed* association of unit costs with goods either sold or on hand. The assumed cost flow does not always reflect the actual goods flow. Furthermore, generally accepted accounting principles permit the use of an assumed cost flow that does *not* reflect the real goods flow. There is nothing illicit about this practice; in fact, there are often compelling reasons for adopting it.

We introduce four generally accepted methods of pricing inventories: (1) specific identification; (2) weighted average; (3) first-in, first-out; and (4) last-in, first-out. Each of the four methods illustrated uses historical costs. In this section, we concentrate primarily on the computational technique of each method. A comparative evaluation is presented in the following section.

To compare more easily the four inventory methods, we illustrate all four with identical data. In each case, goods available for sale during the period are as follows:

Beginning inventory	60 units @ $10 =	$ 600
Purchases:	100 units @ 11 =	1,100
	100 units @ 13 =	1,300
	40 units @ 15 =	600
Totals	300 units	$3,600

Therefore, in each illustration:

1. Beginning inventory is priced at $600.
2. Three purchases are made during the period, as listed above.
3. Goods available for sale during the period amount to 300 units at a total cost of $3,600.

In each case, 220 units are sold during the period, leaving an ending inventory of 80 units. The four inventory methods differ in the way they assign costs to the units sold and to those remaining in inventory.

The cost of goods available for sale equals the sum of the cost of goods sold and the ending inventory (goods available for sale are either sold or are in inventory). Therefore, in assigning costs to units sold and to units on hand at period-end, we are simply allocating the cost of goods available for sale between cost of goods sold and ending inventory. We may achieve this allocation most efficiently by:

1. Calculating *either* the cost of goods sold or the ending inventory.
2. Subtracting the amount determined in step 1 from the cost of goods available for sale.
3. Assigning the residual to the element not priced in step 1.

It will usually be advantageous to calculate the ending inventory (and assign the residual amount to cost of goods sold), because the ending inventory involves fewer units than cost of goods sold. We use this approach in our illustrations.

EXHIBIT 9–4

SPECIFIC IDENTIFICATION INVENTORY PRICING

	Goods Available			Ending Inventory		
	Units	Cost	Total	Units	Cost	Total
Beginning inventory	60	@ $10 =	$ 600	20	@ $10 =	$ 200
Purchases:	100	@ 11 =	1,100	10	@ 11 =	110
	100	@ 13 =	1,300	10	@ 13 =	130
	40	@ 15 =	600	40	@ 15 =	600
	300		$3,600	80		$1,040
Cost of goods available for sale			$3,600			
Less: Ending inventory			1,040			
Cost of goods sold			$2,560			

The system of inventory accounting used in these illustrations is known as the **periodic inventory system.** Under a periodic system, no entry to record cost of goods sold is made when inventory is sold during the period. At period-end, the ending inventory is physically counted. Then, as just noted, the cost of goods available for sale is divided between the ending inventory and the cost of goods sold by using one of the four inventory pricing methods we describe. Later in the chapter, we compare the periodic system with another inventory system.

Specific Identification Method

The **specific identification method** involves (1) keeping track of the purchase price of each specific unit, (2) knowing which specific units are sold, and (3) pricing the ending inventory at the actual prices of the specific units not sold. Obviously, this approach is not practical for merchandise having large unit volumes and small unit prices. Accounting students may consider specific identification the most "precise" way of evaluating inventory because the actual unit costs are attached to a given inventory. We will see, however, that there is compelling justification for using other inventory pricing methods.

Assume that the 80 unsold units consist of 20 units from beginning inventory, 10 units from each of the first two purchases, and all 40 of the last units purchased. The costs assigned to the ending inventory and cost of goods sold are shown in Exhibit 9–4. Note that the full $3,600 cost of the goods available for sale has been assigned as either ending inventory or as cost of goods sold.

Weighted Average Method

The **weighted average method** spreads the total dollar cost of the goods available for sale equally among all units. In our illustration, this figure is $3,600/300, or $12 per unit. Exhibit 9–5 diagrams the assignment of costs under this method. Note again that the entire cost of goods available for sale has been divided between ending inventory and cost of goods sold.

It would be incorrect to use a *simple* average of the prices. The average price paid is ($10 + $11 + $13 + $15)/4 = $12.25; this figure fails to take into account the different numbers of units available at the various prices. The simple average yields the same figure as the weighted average only when the same number of units are purchased at each price.

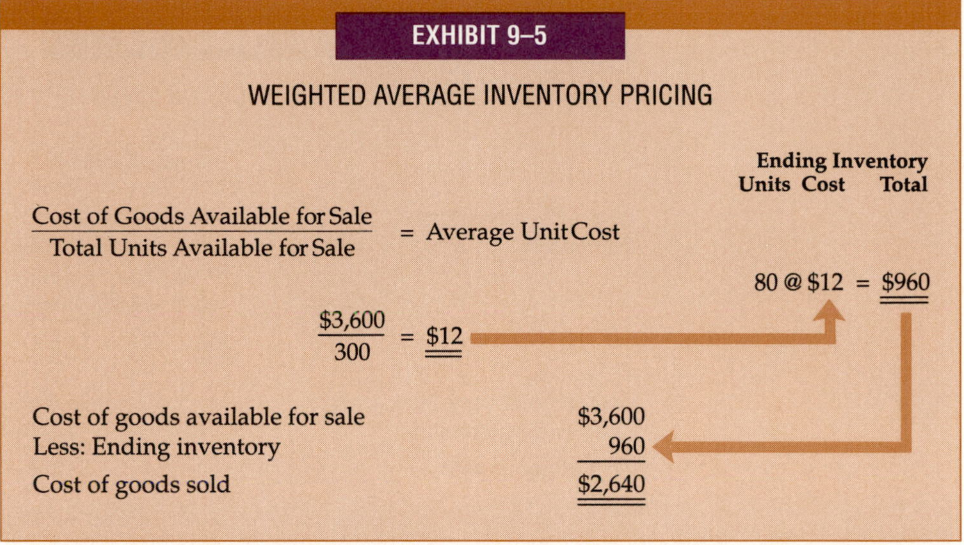

EXHIBIT 9–5

WEIGHTED AVERAGE INVENTORY PRICING

$$\frac{\text{Cost of Goods Available for Sale}}{\text{Total Units Available for Sale}} = \text{Average Unit Cost}$$

$$\frac{\$3{,}600}{300} = \$12$$

Ending Inventory Units Cost	Total
80 @ $12 =	$960

Cost of goods available for sale	$3,600
Less: Ending inventory	960
Cost of goods sold	$2,640

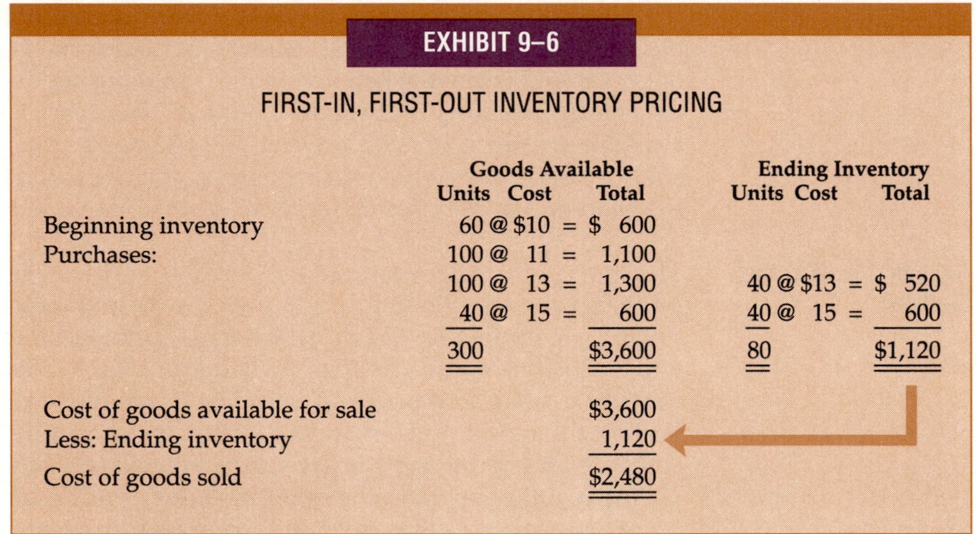

EXHIBIT 9–6

FIRST-IN, FIRST-OUT INVENTORY PRICING

	Goods Available Units Cost	Total	Ending Inventory Units Cost	Total
Beginning inventory	60 @ $10 =	$ 600		
Purchases:	100 @ 11 =	1,100		
	100 @ 13 =	1,300	40 @ $13 =	$ 520
	40 @ 15 =	600	40 @ 15 =	600
	300	$3,600	80	$1,120

Cost of goods available for sale	$3,600
Less: Ending inventory	1,120
Cost of goods sold	$2,480

First-in, First-out (FIFO) Method

First-in, first-out (FIFO) pricing assumes that the oldest goods on hand (or earliest purchased) are sold first. Thus, ending inventories are always made up of the most recent purchases. Under FIFO, goods in the beginning inventory can also be in the ending inventory only when the number of units sold is less than the number of units in the beginning inventory. A FIFO approach would result in the cost allocations as shown in Exhibit 9–6. This method assumes the first 220 units acquired are sold and the last 80 units purchased are still on hand.

Last-in, First-out (LIFO) Method

The **last-in, first-out (LIFO)** approach assumes that the most recent purchases are sold first. Thus, unless sales exceed purchases, the beginning inventory remains on hand as part of the ending inventory. Exhibit 9–7 shows how LIFO works. This method assumes the 220 units most recently purchased are sold, and the 80 oldest units available for sale (60 units from the beginning inventory and 20 units from the period's first purchase) remain on hand at the end of the period.

EXHIBIT 9–7

LAST-IN, FIRST-OUT INVENTORY PRICING

	Goods Available Units	Cost	Total	Ending Inventory Units	Cost	Total
Beginning inventory	60	@ $10 =	$ 600	60	@ $10 =	$600
Purchases:	100	@ 11 =	1,100	20	@ 11 =	220
	100	@ 13 =	1,300			
	40	@ 15 =	600			
	300		$3,600	80		$820

Cost of goods available for sale	$3,600
Less: Ending inventory	820
Cost of goods sold	$2,780

COMPARATIVE ANALYSIS OF INVENTORY PRICING METHODS

In this section, we consider the effects of and reasons for using the various inventory pricing methods just illustrated.

Variations in Income Patterns

For comparative purposes, let us assume that the 220 units in our illustration were sold for $20 each. Exhibit 9–8 shows the differences among gross profit figures resulting from each of the inventory pricing methods. Remember that these differences in reported gross profit result from assumptions made about cost flows, not from any difference in actual goods flows. Pretax income will also reflect these differences if operating expenses are equal in each case.

EXHIBIT 9–8

DIFFERENTIAL GROSS MARGINS ON SALES
BASED ON VARIOUS INVENTORY PRICING METHODS

	Inventory Pricing Method Sp. Id.	Average	FIFO	LIFO
Sales (220 units @ $20)	$4,400	$4,400	$4,400	$4,400
Beginning inventory	$ 600	$ 600	$ 600	$ 600
Total purchases	3,000	3,000	3,000	3,000
Cost of goods available for sale	$3,600	$3,600	$3,600	$3,600
Less: Ending inventory (See earlier computations)	1,040	960	1,120	820
Cost of goods sold	$2,560	$2,640	$2,480	$2,780
Gross profit on sales	$1,840	$1,760	$1,920	$1,620
Increased gross profit compared with LIFO	$220	$140	$300	

Cost Flows

The specific identification method is most appropriate for operations that involve somewhat differentiated products of relatively high unit values. New automobiles and construction equipment are good examples of merchandise that would justify the cost of maintaining the price of each inventory unit and specifically identifying each sale. Specific identification is not feasible when products have low unit values and involve large volumes.

Specific identification offers a limited potential for income manipulation. To the degree that like units of inventory are available at various cost figures, we can maximize reported income by "choosing" to sell the unit with the lowest cost. Income could be minimized by choosing to sell the unit with the highest cost.

The weighted average approach to inventory measurement is best suited to operations that store a large volume of undifferentiated goods in common areas. Liquid fuels, grains, and other commodities are good examples. To some degree, the weighted average cost represents all the various costs of accumulating the goods currently on hand. Consequently, weighted average costs typically fall between the extreme cost figures that can result from other methods.

As a matter of good business, most companies—especially those with perishable or style-affected goods—attempt to sell the oldest merchandise first. This is especially true of companies dealing in foods, certain chemicals, or drugs. In these cases, FIFO most nearly matches the cost flow to the probable goods flow.

Finding an example of a business operation in which LIFO represents the natural flow of goods is difficult. Purchases of coal or a similar commodity may all be dumped onto one pile from an overhead trestle, and sales may be taken from the top of the pile by a crane. If beginning inventories have been maintained or increased, we conclude that the firm's original purchases are still in inventory. In this case, LIFO represents the actual goods flow. Although LIFO is not the goods flow for most businesses, an estimated 50% or more of major businesses use LIFO to price some of their inventories. We explore the reasons for this choice later in this chapter.

In summary:

1. In a physical sense, specific identification best presents actual cost of goods sold.
2. Weighted average can best be associated with business operations in which like goods are commingled.
3. FIFO probably represents most accurately the actual goods flow for most firms.
4. Although LIFO represents the least plausible goods flow for most businesses, many major firms use it.

MATCHING COSTS AND REVENUE Because the use of FIFO and LIFO can result in extreme differences during times of changing prices (see Exhibit 9–8), we examine the effects of these two methods.

Consider the data below, taken from our earlier computations, which show that FIFO matches the older costs against current revenue and LIFO matches the most recent costs against current revenue. Under FIFO, therefore, the ending inventory is measured at relatively recent prices, whereas under LIFO, the ending inventory amount reflects older prices.

	Units		Cost		Total
Beginning inventory	60	@	$10	=	$ 600
Purchases:	100	@	11	=	1,100
	100	@	13	=	1,300
	40	@	15	=	600

FIFO		LIFO	
Cost of goods sold:	$2,480 (oldest 220 units)	*Cost of goods sold:*	$2,780 (latest 220 units)
Ending inventory:	1,120 (latest 80 units)	*Ending inventory:*	820 (oldest 80 units)

Most accountants agree that when prices are rising, FIFO tends to overstate income because older, lower unit costs are included in cost of goods sold and matched against current sales prices. In other words, in our example, some of the units sold are charged to costs of goods sold at unit costs of $10, $11, and $13. If our latest purchases reflect current acquisition prices, the units sold must be replaced by units costing $15 (or more if prices continue to rise). Thus, we can argue that when prices rise, LIFO better matches current costs against current revenue, because the cost of the most recent purchases constitutes cost of goods sold.

However, while LIFO associates the current, most significant, unit prices with cost of goods sold, it consequently prices the ending inventory at the older, less realistic unit prices. Because of this, the LIFO inventory figure on the balance sheet is often meaningless in terms of current prices. As we noted earlier, when inventory quantities are maintained or increased, the LIFO method prevents the older prices from appearing in the cost of goods sold. No doubt, some firms still carry LIFO inventories at unit prices that prevailed more than 25 years ago.

Phantom Profits and Income Tax Advantage

A highly simplified example will illustrate how to reduce the undesirable effects of phantom profits that result from the use of FIFO during times of rising prices. The same computations will show a related tax advantage of using LIFO during such periods.

Assume that a firm has an opening inventory of ten units costing $500 each. The firm sells the ten units for $700 each and replaces its inventory by purchasing ten more units costing $630 per unit. All transactions are for cash and, for simplicity, we also assume that operating expenses are zero and the applicable income tax rate is 35%. Exhibit 9–9 shows how FIFO produces a phantom profit that is avoided under LIFO and also shows the tax benefit of LIFO when purchase prices are rising.

Note that under FIFO, $1,300 of net income is reported, but the amount of cash from sales is only enough to replace the inventory sold and pay the income tax on the $2,000 pretax income. Thus, the net income of $1,300 is not realized in cash that can be declared as dividends or reinvested in the business; it is considered **phantom** (or **inventory**) **profit.** We can easily imagine how the phantom profit element causes problems in the planning of dividend policy and the use of net income as a source of capital investments.

When prices rise, LIFO's tax benefit is obvious. Under LIFO, inventories are measured at older (lower) prices, which causes cost of goods sold to increase and pretax income (and therefore income taxes payable) to decrease. Use of LIFO during times of *falling* prices, however, can have quite the opposite tax consequence.

EXHIBIT 9–9

FIFO–LIFO COMPARISON: PHANTOM PROFIT EFFECT AND TAX BENEFIT

	FIFO		LIFO	
	Income Statement	Cash In (Out)	Income Statement	Cash In (Out)
Sales (10 @ $700)	$ 7,000	$7,000	$ 7,000	$7,000
Cost of goods sold:				
Beginning inventory (10 @ $500)	$ 5,000		$ 5,000	
Purchases (10 @ $630)	6,300	(6,300)	6,300	(6,300)
Goods available (20 units)	$11,300		$11,300	
Ending inventory:				
10 @ FIFO	6,300			
10 @ LIFO			5,000	
Cost of goods sold	$ 5,000		$ 6,300	
Pretax income	$ 2,000		$ 700	
Income tax at 35%	700	(700)	245	(245)
Net income	$ 1,300		$ 455	
Net cash proceeds		$ 0		$ 455

Disclosure

A firm's financial statements should disclose its inventory pricing methods. This is often done in footnotes to the financial statements or parenthetically within the appropriate section of the statements.

DEPARTURES FROM COST

Inventories are generally measured at cost. The measurement may be reduced below cost, however, if there is evidence that the inventory's utility has fallen below cost. Such *inventory write-downs* may occur when (1) merchandise must be sold at reduced prices because it is damaged or otherwise not in normal salable condition, or (2) the cost of replacing items in the ending inventory has declined below their recorded cost.

Net Realizable Value

Damaged, physically deteriorated, or obsolete merchandise should be measured and reported at **net realizable value** when this value is less than cost. Net realizable value is the estimated selling price less the expected cost of disposal. For example, assume that an inventory item cost $300 but can be sold for only $200 because it is damaged. Related selling costs are an estimated $20. We should write down the item to $180 ($200 estimated selling price less $20 estimated disposal cost) and reflect a $120 loss for this period.

Lower of Cost or Market

The **lower of cost or market (LCM)** rule provides for the recognition of a loss when prices decline on new inventory items. Under this rule, the loss is reported in the period when the prices decline, rather than during a subsequent period of sale. *Market* is defined as the current replacement cost of the merchandise. This procedure assumes that decreases in replacement costs will be accompanied by proportionate decreases in selling prices. If applicable, the LCM rule simply measures inventory at the lower (replacement) market figure. Consequently, reported income decreases by the amount that the ending inventory has been written down. When the ending inventory becomes part of the cost of goods sold in a future period of lower selling prices, its reduced carrying value helps maintain normal profit margins in the period of sale.

To illustrate, let us assume an inventory item that cost $80 has been selling for $100 during the year, yielding a gross profit of 20% on sales. At year-end, the item's replacement cost has dropped to $60—a 25% decline— and a proportionate reduction in the selling price to $75 is expected. In this case, the inventory would be written down to the $60 replacement cost, reducing the current period's net income by the $20 loss. When the item is sold in a subsequent period for $75, a normal gross profit of 20% on sales will be reported ($75 − $60 = $15 gross profit).[1]

We may apply the LCM rule to (1) each inventory item, (2) the totals of major inventory classes or categories, or (3) the total inventory. The following simple illustration shows the application of these alternatives and indicates that the inventory amount obtained depends on how the rule is applied.

						Lower of Cost or Market by:		
		Per Unit		Total		Indiv.	Major	Total
Inventory Item	**Quantity**	**Cost**	**Market**	**Cost**	**Market**	**Items**	**Categories**	**Inventory**
Cameras								
Model V70	40	$80	$75	$3,200	$3,000	$3,000		
Model V85	30	60	64	1,800	1,920	1,800		
Subtotal				$5,000	$4,920		$4,920	
Calculators								
Model C20	90	13	15	$1,170	$1,350	1,170		
Model C40	50	20	17	1,000	850	850		
Subtotal				$2,170	$2,200		2,170	
Total				$7,170	$7,120	$6,820	$7,090	$7,120

If we apply LCM to the total inventory, our result is $7,120. Applied by item, however, the LCM amount is $6,820, and applied by major category, the LCM amount is $7,090. Although the item-by-item procedure is used most often, any of the three ways is acceptable. In any case, one method should be used consistently. Inventory market values appear in such sources as current price catalogs, purchase contracts with suppliers, and other forms of price quotations.

ESTIMATING INVENTORIES

Several good reasons exist for estimating inventories. When taking physical inventory counts for interim financial statements is impractical, an estimate is sufficient. The adequacy of inventory insurance coverage may be determined on the basis of an inventory estimate. Finally, an estimate may be necessary to determine the loss from merchandise destroyed by fire or other disaster. Therefore, we should examine some methods for estimating inventories.

[1]Because of the scale and complexity of modern markets, not all decreases in replacement prices are followed by proportionate reductions in selling prices. In these cases, the application of the LCM rule is modified. These modifications are covered in more advanced accounting courses.

EXHIBIT 9–10

GROSS PROFIT METHOD OF ESTIMATING INVENTORY

Beginning inventory		$20,000
Net cost of purchases		50,000
Cost of goods available for sale		$70,000
Net sales	$80,000	
Estimated gross profit (30%)	24,000	
Estimated cost of goods sold		56,000
Estimated ending inventory		$14,000

Gross Profit Method

The **gross profit method** of estimating inventories merely rearranges the cost of goods sold section of the income statement—estimated cost of goods sold is deducted from the cost of goods available for sale to derive the estimated ending inventory. Subtracting an estimated gross profit amount from sales provides the estimated cost of goods sold figure. For the gross profit method to be valid, the gross profit percentage (gross profit/net sales) used must be representative of the merchandising activities leading up to the date of the inventory estimate.

Suppose that over the past three years a company's gross profit averaged 30% of net sales. Assume also that the net sales for the current year's first interim period are $80,000; the inventory at the beginning of the period was $20,000; and net cost of purchases for the period is $50,000. Exhibit 9–10 shows how to estimate the ending inventory using the gross profit method.

Retail Method

The **retail method** represents another approach to estimating inventories. It is widely used by retail businesses, such as department stores, that keep periodic inventory records. Such firms typically mark each item of merchandise with the retail price and record purchases at both cost and retail price. A firm can estimate its ending inventory at *retail* price merely by subtracting sales from the retail price of merchandise available for sale. To determine the inventory *cost*, the firm applies a cost-to-retail price percentage, which is the ratio of cost to retail price of merchandise available for sale. In Exhibit 9–11 this ratio is 70%, which yields a cost amount of $21,000 when applied to the $30,000 retail value of the inventory.

The cost-to-retail ratio can also be used to compute the cost of a physical inventory taken at retail prices. Thus, the firm saves the considerable effort and expense of determining cost prices for each inventory item. Suppose, for example, that sales clerks count their stock and determine that the ending inventory has an aggregate retail value of $40,000. If the cost-to-retail price ratio is 70%, management could easily obtain the estimated cost of the inventory, $28,000, that is needed to prepare financial statements.

The accuracy of the retail method depends on the assumption that the ending inventory contains the same proportion of goods at the various mark-up percentages as did the original group of merchandise available for sale. To the extent that the mix of mark-up percentages does not remain constant, the accuracy of the estimate is impaired.

EXHIBIT 9–11

RETAIL METHOD OF ESTIMATING INVENTORY

	Cost	Retail Price
Beginning inventory	$14,000	$ 22,000
Net purchases	70,000	98,000
Total merchandise available for sale	$84,000	$120,000
Cost-to-retail percentage: $\frac{\$84,000}{\$120,000} = 70\%$		
Less: Sales during period		90,000
Estimated ending inventory at retail prices		$ 30,000
Applicable cost percentage		× 0.70
Estimated ending inventory at cost		$ 21,000

PERPETUAL INVENTORY PROCEDURES

Thus far in our discussion, we have assumed that all inventory situations involve a *periodic* system. This system (1) records acquisitions of merchandise as debits to a Purchases account, (2) makes no entry at the time of sale for the cost of goods sold, and (3) only periodically (hence its name) updates the Inventory account when year-end adjusting and closing entries are made. The periodic system is most suitable for businesses that have many sales transactions of relatively small unit product costs—for example, retail grocery, drug, variety, or hardware stores.

Other types of business firms, notably those with fewer sales transactions but relatively high unit product costs, may use a **perpetual inventory system.** Under the perpetual inventory system (also descriptively named), the Inventory account is "perpetually," or continually (as opposed to periodically), maintained. Perpetually updating the Inventory account requires (1) that at the time of purchase, merchandise acquisitions be recorded as debits to the Inventory account and (2) that at the time of sale, the cost of goods sold be determined and recorded by a debit to a Cost of Goods Sold account and a credit to the Inventory account. With a perpetual inventory system, Cost of Goods Sold is an actual account in the general ledger rather than merely a category on the income statement as it is with a periodic inventory system. In recent years, computerized scanning systems (scanning of product codes on merchandise sold) have extended the usage of perpetual inventory procedures.

Perpetual Inventory Entries

When a firm uses perpetual inventory procedures, the Inventory account shows the amount of inventory on hand at the end of the period—assuming that no theft, spoilage, or error has occurred. However, even if there is little chance for or suspicion of inventory discrepancy, most companies take a physical inventory count at least once a year. At that time, the account is adjusted for any inaccuracies discovered.

The following entries demonstrate the recording procedures followed under the perpetual inventory system, contrasted with the periodic system.

Journal Entries

Periodic Inventory System			Perpetual Inventory System		
1. Purchased $1,200 worth of merchandise on account, terms 2/10, n/30 (recorded at invoice price).					
Purchases	1,200		Inventory	1,200	
Accounts Payable		1,200	Accounts Payable		1,200
2. Returned $200 worth of merchandise to vendors.					
Accounts Payable	200		Accounts Payable	200	
Purchases Returns and Allowances		200	Inventory		200
3. Paid for merchandise (discount taken).					
Accounts Payable	1,000		Accounts Payable	1,000	
Purchases Discounts		20	Inventory		20
Cash		980	Cash		980
4. Sold goods costing $500 for $800 on account.					
Accounts Receivable	800		Accounts Receivable	800	
Sales		800	Sales		800
			Cost of Goods Sold	500	
			Inventory		500
5. Counted inventory at end of period, $19,800. The balance in the Inventory account under the periodic system is $25,000 (the beginning inventory). The balance in the Inventory account under the perpetual system is $20,000.					
(Closing entries for periodic inventory[2])					
Income Summary	25,000		Loss on Inventory Shrinkage	200	
Inventory		25,000	Inventory		200
Inventory	19,800				
Income Summary		19,800			

Note that under a perpetual system the Inventory account is increased by purchases and decreased by the cost of goods sold, purchases returns and allowances, and discounts. Therefore, at the end of the period, one entry brings the Inventory account balance into agreement with the amount of the physical inventory. Because we assumed the physical inventory of goods on hand amounted to $19,800, and the Inventory account had a balance of $20,000, we charged the $200 difference to Loss on Inventory Shrinkage and reduced the Inventory account balance to $19,800.

Perpetual Inventory Pricing Methods

When purchase prices for inventory items change during an accounting period, we must select a perpetual inventory pricing method so that the debit to Cost of Goods Sold for each sale may be determined. The same four methods we examined under the periodic inventory system are available—specific identification, average, FIFO, and LIFO. To illustrate these methods on a perpetual basis, we will use the following data about an inventory item:

[2] As discussed in Appendix A, an alternative method of recording inventories treats these two entries as year-end adjusting entries rather than as closing entries.

		Units	Unit Cost	Total Cost
January 1	Beginning inventory	5	$30.00	$150.00
January 15	Purchase	10	33.00	330.00
September 12	Sale	(9)		
September 29	Purchase	10	36.00	360.00

We must compute the cost of goods sold amount for the nine units sold on September 12 and determine the ending inventory on December 31.

SPECIFIC IDENTIFICATION When specific identification is used, the actual costs of the specific items sold constitute the cost of goods sold. Assuming two of the nine units sold are from the beginning inventory and the remaining seven units are from the January 15 purchase, the cost of goods sold is $291 [(2 × $30) + (7 × $33)]. Of course, the costs remaining in inventory are the actual costs of the specific items that are unsold. As shown in Exhibit 9–12, the ending inventory is $549. Specific identification gives the same results for both perpetual and periodic systems.

MOVING AVERAGE The average method under a perpetual inventory system is called the **moving average method.** Each time goods are purchased, a new average unit cost is computed for the goods on hand. Cost of goods sold for each sale is computed by multiplying the average unit cost at that time by the number of units sold. On September 12, the average unit cost is $32 ($480 total cost ÷ 15 units available for sale). Therefore, the cost of goods sold is $288 (9 × $32). On September 29, a new average unit cost of $34.50 is computed ($552 total cost ÷ 16 units available for sale). The ending inventory is $552, as shown in Exhibit 9–12.

Because unit average costs are recomputed each time a purchase occurs, the moving average method gives different answers from those obtained by using the weighted average method under a periodic inventory system.

EXHIBIT 9–12

ENDING INVENTORY UNDER PERPETUAL INVENTORY SYSTEM

	Specific Identification	Moving Average	FIFO	LIFO
Jan. 1 Beginning inventory	$150	$150	$150	$150
Jan. 15 Purchase	330	330	330	330
Sept. 12 Cost of goods sold	(291)	(288)	(282)	(297)
Sept. 29 Purchase	360	360	360	360
Dec. 31 Ending inventory	$549	$552	$558	$543

Composition of Ending Inventory	Units	Cost	Units	Cost	Units	Cost	Units	Cost
	3	$30	16	$34.50	6	$33	5	$30
	3	33			10	36	1	33
	10	36					10	36

FIRST-IN, FIRST-OUT Under the perpetual FIFO method, each time a sale is made the costs of the oldest goods on hand are charged to cost of goods sold. In our illustration, the FIFO cost of goods sold on September 12 is \$282 [(5 × \$30) + (4 × \$33)]. The ending inventory of \$558 is shown in Exhibit 9–12. The FIFO method applied on a perpetual basis results in the same total cost of goods sold amount—and the same ending inventory—as that achieved under the periodic FIFO method.

LAST-IN, FIRST-OUT When perpetual LIFO is used, each time a sale is made the costs of the most recent purchases are charged to cost of goods sold. For the September 12 sale, the most recent costs for nine units were incurred on January 15. Thus, cost of goods sold is \$297 (9 × \$33). The ending inventory is \$543, as shown in Exhibit 9–12.

Perpetual LIFO normally gives results different from periodic LIFO for both the total cost of goods sold for a period and the period's ending inventory.

Perpetual Inventory Records

When a perpetual inventory system is used, a detailed perpetual inventory record must be maintained—manually or by computer—for each inventory item. The perpetual inventory records must provide for both the inflow and outflow of merchandise as well as disclose the quantities and prices of items at any time. Although these records are continually maintained, their accuracy should be verified at least once each year by physical counts of merchandise.

Exhibit 9–13 illustrates a perpetual inventory record for an inventory item priced on the FIFO basis. At year-end, the balances on all the perpetual inventory records are added, and their total dollar amount should agree with the amount in the Inventory account, which serves as a control account.

EXHIBIT 9–13

PERPETUAL INVENTORY RECORD—FIFO BASIS

Inventory Control

Part No. 1342
Description Fastener cam (3/8")
Prime Supplier Hill Machinery Company
Location Small Parts Warehouse (Bin 32)

Maximum 16
Reorder Level 6
Reorder Quantity 10

Date		Received			Sold			Balance		
		Units	Cost/Unit	Total	Units	Cost/Unit	Total	Units	Cost/Unit	Total
19XX										
Jan.	1	Balance Fwd.						5	\$30	\$150
	15	10	\$33	\$330				5	30	
								10	33	480
Sept.	12				5	\$30	\$150			
					4	33	132	6	33	198
	29	10	36	360				6	33	
								10	36	558

KEY POINTS FOR CHAPTER OBJECTIVES

1 Discuss the basic concepts of accounting for inventories (pp. 319–23).

- Cost of goods sold under a periodic inventory system is calculated as beginning inventory plus net cost of purchases less ending inventory.
- Other things being equal, changing the dollar amount of ending inventory changes pretax income by a like amount.
- Uncorrected ending inventory errors cause the income of two periods to be misstated. The errors are equal in amount, opposite in direction, and therefore offsetting.

2 Describe the pricing of inventory under a periodic inventory system using the (1) specific identification method, (2) weighted average method, (3) FIFO method, and (4) LIFO method (pp. 323–27).

- These methods differ in the way they assume inventory costs flow through a business.

3 Analyze the effects inventory pricing methods have on gross profits, income, matching of costs and revenue, and income taxes (pp. 327–30).

- Reported income can be influenced by choosing among different inventory pricing methods.
- When prices are rising, LIFO matches current costs against revenue and results in lower reported gross profit and income than FIFO does, and thus may provide a related tax benefit.

4 Apply the lower of cost or market rule to inventory measurements (pp. 330–31).

- The lower of cost or market rule provides for losses to be recorded in the period that replacement costs of inventory items decline.
- The lower of cost or market rule may be applied to (1) each inventory item, (2) major inventory categories, or (3) the total inventory.

5 Describe the gross profit and retail methods of estimating inventories (pp. 331–33).

- The gross profit method subtracts the estimated cost of goods sold from the cost of goods available for sale. A representative gross profit percentage must be used in estimating the cost of goods sold.
- The retail method uses an appropriate cost-to-retail price percentage to reduce the ending inventory from a retail amount to a cost amount.

6 Describe and illustrate the perpetual inventory system (pp. 333–36).

- A perpetual inventory system (1) does not use a Purchases account, (2) records cost of goods sold at the time of sale, and (3) continually updates the balance in the Inventory account.
- Pricing methods under a perpetual inventory system are specific identification, moving average, FIFO, and LIFO.

KEY TERMS USED IN THIS CHAPTER

cost of goods sold 319
first-in, first-out (FIFO) method 326
gross profit method 332
inventory 319
last-in, first-out (LIFO) method 326
lower of cost or market (LCM) 330
moving average method 335
net realizable value 330
periodic inventory system 325
perpetual inventory system 333
phantom (inventory) profit 329
retail method 332
specific identification method 325
weighted average method 325

SELF-TEST QUESTIONS FOR REVIEW

(Answers are at the end of this chapter.)

1. Which inventory pricing method assumes that the goods most recently purchased are sold first?
   (a) FIFO.
   (b) Specific identification.
   (c) Weighted average.
   (d) LIFO.
2. Which inventory pricing method reflects the most recently incurred purchase costs in the ending inventory?
   (a) FIFO.
   (b) LIFO.
   (c) Retail.
   (d) Weighted average.
3. Boyer Company started 19X4 with a $140,000 inventory. Purchases totaled $300,000 during the first three months of 19X4. Sales during the same period were $500,000. Boyer's gross profit averages 45% of sales. Using the gross profit method, Boyer's March 31, 19X4, inventory is estimated at
   (a) $165,000
   (b) $275,000
   (c) $225,000
   (d) $215,000
4. Clipper, Inc., returned $600 of merchandise purchased on account. Under a perpetual inventory system, the account credited in the journal entry to record the return is
   (a) Purchases.
   (b) Purchases Returns and Allowances.
   (c) Inventory.
   (d) Accounts Payable.
5. The average inventory pricing method under a perpetual inventory system is called the
   (a) Weighted average method.
   (b) Moving average method.
   (c) Composite average method.
   (d) Simple average method.

DEMONSTRATION PROBLEM FOR REVIEW

Mackenzie, Inc., began a new fiscal year on April 1 of this year. Sales revenue for April totaled $90,000. The company uses the periodic inventory system. Its beginning inventory was $4,000, consisting of 2,000 units at $2 per unit. A summary of April purchases appears below.

April 8	5,000 units	@ $2.50 =	$12,500
19	10,000	@ 3.00 =	30,000
29	6,000	@ 3.50 =	21,000
		Total	$63,500

At the end of April, 7,000 units were on hand.

REQUIRED

(a) How much gross profit on sales would Mackenzie, Inc., report for April under (1) first-in, first-out inventory pricing, and (2) last-in, first-out inventory pricing?

(b) Calculate Mackenzie's gross profit on sales for April under (1) first-in, first-out, and (2) last-in, first-out if the April 29 purchase had been postponed until May.

(c) Calculate Mackenzie's gross profit on sales for April under (1) first-in, first-out, and (2) last-in, first-out if the April 29 purchase had been 9,000 units instead of 6,000 units.

(d) Based on your answers to parts (a), (b), and (c), what can you conclude about the impact of the timing or amount of end-of-period purchases on the gross profit on sales computed under the (1) first-in, first-out, and (2) last-in, first-out methods of inventory pricing?

SOLUTION TO DEMONSTRATION PROBLEM

(a)

		FIFO	LIFO
Sales		$90,000	$90,000
Cost of Goods Sold:			
Beginning Inventory		$ 4,000	$ 4,000
Add: Purchases		63,500	63,500
Cost of Goods Available for Sale		$67,500	$67,500
Less: Ending Inventory			
FIFO: 6,000 × $3.50 =	$21,000		
1,000 × $3.00 =	3,000	24,000	
LIFO: 2,000 × $2.00 =	$ 4,000		
5,000 × $2.50 =	12,500		16,500
Cost of Goods Sold		$43,500	$51,000
Gross Profit on Sales		$46,500	$39,000

(b) If the April 29 purchase of 6,000 units was postponed until May, the April 30 inventory would have been 1,000 units and purchases for April would have totaled $42,500 ($12,500 on April 8 + $30,000 on April 19). The gross profit on sales would then be computed as follows:

	FIFO	LIFO
Sales	$90,000	$90,000
Cost of Goods Sold:		
Beginning Inventory	$ 4,000	$ 4,000
Add: Purchases	42,500	42,500
Cost of Goods Available for Sale	$46,500	$46,500
Less: Ending Inventory		
FIFO: 1,000 × $3.00	3,000	
LIFO: 1,000 × $2.00		2,000
Cost of Goods Sold	$43,500	$44,500
Gross Profit on Sales	$46,500	$45,500

(c) If 9,000 units were purchased on April 29, then the April 30 inventory would have been 10,000 units and purchases for April would have totaled $74,000 ($12,500 on April 8 + $30,000 on April 19 + $31,500 on April 29). The gross profit on sales would then be computed as follows:

		FIFO	LIFO
Sales		$90,000	$90,000
Cost of Goods Sold:			
Beginning Inventory		$ 4,000	$ 4,000
Add: Purchases		74,000	74,000
Cost of Goods Available for Sale		$78,000	$78,000
Less: Ending Inventory			
FIFO: 9,000 × $3.50 =	$31,500		
1,000 × $3.00 =	3,000	34,500	
LIFO: 2,000 × $2.00 =	$ 4,000		
5,000 × $2.50 =	12,500		
3,000 × $3.00 =	9,000		25,500
Cost of Goods Sold		$43,500	$52,500
Gross Profit on Sales		$46,500	$37,500

(d) Gross profit on sales under the FIFO method is the same in all three cases. The gross profit is unaffected by changes in the amount or timing of end-of-period purchases.

Gross profit on sales under the LIFO method is different in each case. Gross profit is affected by changes in the amount or timing of end-of-period purchases, because—under the periodic LIFO method—the costs of the most recently purchased goods are the first costs charged to cost of goods sold.

QUESTIONS

9–1 List six factors (or cost categories) typically included in the cost of goods sold computation under a periodic inventory system and indicate whether the amount of each normally increases or decreases the cost of goods sold figure.

9–2 Define *inventory* and identify the costs that should be included as inventory costs.

9–3 Under a periodic inventory system, why is reported income affected dollar-for-dollar (disregarding income taxes) by any change in the dollar amount of ending inventory?

9–4 Thorn Company understated its 19X1 ending inventory by $15,000. Assuming the error was not discovered, what was the effect on income for 19X1? For 19X2?

9–5 For a physical inventory count, explain (a) the three steps involved, (b) why firms maintaining perpetual inventory records still take physical counts, and (c) what merchandise should be included.

9–6 What is meant by *goods flow* and *cost flow*?

9–7 Briefly describe each of the following inventory pricing methods under a periodic inventory system: (a) specific identification; (b) weighted average; (c) first-in, first-out; and (d) last-in, first-out.

9–8 Describe an appropriate operating situation (that is, goods flow corresponds with cost flow) for each of the four approaches to inventory pricing listed in Question 9–7.

9–9 Why do relatively stable purchase prices reduce the significance of the choice of an inventory pricing method?

9–10 Briefly explain the nature of *phantom profits* during periods of rising merchandise purchase prices.

9–11 If prices have been rising, which inventory pricing method—weighted average; first-in, first-out; or last-in, first-out—yields (a) the lowest inventory amount? (b) the lowest net income? (c) the largest inventory amount? (d) the largest net income?

9–12 Even though it does not represent their goods flow, why might firms adopt last-in, first-out inventory pricing during periods when prices are consistently rising?

9–13 Identify two situations in which merchandise may be inventoried at an amount less than cost.

9–14 At year-end, The Appliance Shop has a refrigerator on hand that has been used as a demonstration model. The refrigerator cost $400 and sells for $600 when new. In its present condition, the refrigerator will be sold for $390. Related selling costs are an estimated $15. At what amount should the refrigerator be carried in inventory?

9–15 Discuss the effect on reported income of applying the lower of cost or market rule.

9–16 Under what circumstances might firms estimate the dollar amount of their inventories rather than actually count them?

9–17 Contrast the accounting procedures for periodic and perpetual inventory systems.

9–18 Which inventory pricing methods give the same results (ending inventory and total cost of goods sold) when applied under a perpetual inventory system and a periodic inventory system?

EXERCISES

Periodic and perpetual systems

9–19 Hirsch Stores, Inc., uses the periodic inventory system. Its accounting records include the following balances:

Accounts Payable (all for merchandise)	$ 3,900
Delivery Expense (to customers)	2,000
Inventory	11,000
Purchases	72,000
Purchases Discounts	1,400
Purchases Returns and Allowances	1,000
Sales	99,000
Sales Discounts	1,800
Sales Returns and Allowances	1,500
Transportation In	3,200

(a) Assuming that the ending inventory, determined by physical count, is $16,000, compute the cost of goods sold.
(b) How would the above accounts differ if the firm used a perpetual inventory system?

Inventory error corrections

9–20 The following information is available for Perry Company during four consecutive operating periods:

	Amounts by Period			
	1	2	3	4
Beginning inventory	$14,000	$23,000	$17,000	$19,000
Net cost of purchases	81,000	62,000	67,000	53,000
Cost of goods available for sale	$95,000	$85,000	$84,000	$72,000
Ending inventory	23,000	17,000	19,000	16,000
Cost of goods sold	$72,000	$68,000	$65,000	$56,000

Assuming that the company made the following errors, compute the revised cost of goods sold figure for each period.

Period	Error in Ending Inventory	
1	Overstated	$2,000
2	Overstated	4,000
3	Understated	3,000

Ending inventory count

9–21 The December 31, 19XX, inventory of Lykin Company was $81,000. In arriving at this amount, the following items were considered:

1. Included in the inventory count were goods on hand costing $4,000 owned by Dunham Company but on consignment to Lykin Company.
2. Included in the inventory count were goods in transit at December 31 to Lykin Company from Tyler, Inc. These goods, costing $6,000, were shipped F.O.B. destination and arrived on January 3.
3. Excluded from the inventory count were goods sitting on Lykin Company's shipping dock on December 31. These goods, costing $2,500, were sold to Vine, Inc., on December 31 and were picked up by a Vine truck on January 2.
4. Included in the inventory count were goods in transit at December 31 to Lykin Company from Flad, Inc. The goods, costing $3,000, were shipped F.O.B. shipping point and arrived on January 2.

Compute the correct December 31, 19XX, inventory amount for Lykin Company. Lykin has no specific agreement with any party concerning the passage of title to goods bought or sold.

Inventory pricing methods—periodic

9–22 The following information is for the Saxon Company for May 19XX. Saxon sells just one product.

	Units	Unit Cost
Beginning inventory	30	$ 6
Purchases: May 11	60	7
18	40	8
23	20	11

During May, 105 units were sold, leaving an ending inventory of 45 units. Assume periodic inventory procedures and compute the ending inventory and the cost of goods sold using (a) first-in, first-out; (b) last-in, first-out; and (c) weighted average.

Inventory pricing methods—periodic

9–23 Mailer Company, which uses the periodic inventory system, has the following records for July:

	Units	Unit Cost
Beginning inventory	10	$23
Purchases: July 6	75	20
15	55	18
28	20	16

Ending inventory for July was 35 units. Compute the ending inventory and the cost of goods sold using (a) first-in, first-out; (b) weighted average; and (c) last-in, first-out.

Departures from cost

9–24 Determine the proper inventory amount for each of the following items in Vision Company's year-end inventory.

(a) Vision has 400 video games in stock. The games cost $25 each, but their year-end replacement cost is $20. Vision has been selling these games for $50, but competitors are now selling them for $40. Vision plans to drop its price to $40. Vision's normal gross profit rate on video games is 50%.

(b) Vision has 300 rolls of camera film that are past the expiration date marked on each film's box. The films cost $1.40 each and are normally sold for $2.80. New replacement films still cost $1.40. To clear out these old films, Vision will drop their selling price to $1.25. There are no related selling costs.

(c) Vision has five cameras in stock that have been used as demonstration models. The cameras cost $150 and normally sell for $225. Because these cameras are in used condition, Vision has set the selling price at $140 each. Expected selling costs are $10 per camera. New models of the camera (on order) will cost Vision $170 and will be priced to sell at $255.

Gross profit method

9–25 Over the past several years Jordan Company's gross profit has averaged 48% of net sales. During the first six months of the current year, net sales are $750,000 and net cost of purchases totals $400,000. Inventory at the beginning of the period was $60,000. The company prepares quarterly interim financial statements. Use the gross profit method to determine the estimated cost of inventory at the end of the current six-month period.

Retail method

9–26 Lodge Company's April 1 inventory had a cost of $52,000 and a retail value of $90,000. During April, Lodge's net merchandise purchases cost $69,000 and had a net retail value of $130,000. Net sales for April totaled $150,000.

(a) Compute the estimated cost of the April 30 inventory using the retail method.

(b) What key assumptions underlie the validity of this estimate of inventory cost?

Periodic and perpetual systems

9–27 Present journal entries to record the following transactions if (a) a periodic inventory system is used and (b) a perpetual inventory system is used. Purchases are recorded at invoice price.

1. Merchandise is purchased for $4,000, terms 2/10, n/30.
2. Goods originally costing $500 (in the preceding transaction) are returned to the seller before payment is made.

3. The remainder of the purchase in transaction 1 is paid for and the related discount is taken.
4. Goods costing $2,700 are sold on account for $4,300.
5. The proper balance in the Inventory account is established at the end of the period. A physical inventory at the end of the period shows goods costing $1,490 on hand. Assume that the beginning balance in this account was $800.

Inventory pricing methods—perpetual

9–28 The following are July inventory data for Maki Company, which uses perpetual inventory procedures.

July 1 Beginning inventory, 30 units @ $20 per unit.
10 Purchased 70 units @ $25 per unit.
15 Sold 80 units.
26 Purchased 50 units @ $28 per unit.

Compute the cost of goods sold for July 15 using (a) first-in, first-out; (b) last-in, first-out; and (c) moving average.

PROBLEMS

Inventory pricing methods—periodic and perpetual

9–29 Grover Sales, Inc., had a beginning inventory for May comprising 600 units that had cost $30 per unit. A summary of purchases and sales during May follows:

	Unit Cost	Units Purchased	Units Sold
May 2			300
6	$32	900	
10			700
19	36	500	
23			600
30	39	200	

REQUIRED

(a) Assuming Grover uses a periodic inventory system, calculate the amount of ending inventory and cost of goods sold under each of the following pricing methods: first-in, first-out; last-in, first-out; and weighted average.

(b) Which inventory pricing method would you choose:
1. to reflect what is probably the physical flow of goods?
2. to minimize income tax for the period?
3. To report the largest amount of income for the period?

Justify your answers.

(c) Assuming Grover uses a perpetual inventory system, calculate cost of goods sold amounts on May 2, May 10, and May 23 and the ending inventory on May 31 under each of the following pricing methods: first-in, first-out; last-in, first-out; and moving average.

Effects of FIFO and LIFO

9–30 Examine the July data below for Reed, Inc., which prices inventory on the last-in, first-out basis and uses the periodic inventory system.

Beginning inventory: 4,000 units @ $4 each

Purchases		Sales	
July 5	8,000 @ $5	July 8	7,000 @ $ 9
19	21,000 @ 6	21	20,000 @ 10
30	6,000 @ 8	28	5,000 @ 11

REQUIRED

(a) How much gross profit on sales would Reed, Inc., report for July?

(b) By what amount would Reed's reported gross profit for July change if the final merchandise purchase had been postponed for several days?

(c) How would Reed's reported gross profit differ if the final purchase had been for 13,000 units instead of for 6,000 units?
(d) Assuming Reed used the first-in, first-out method, calculate the answers to requirements (a), (b), and (c).

Income effects of inventory pricing methods

9–31 The following is a summary of Suhey Company's inventory amounts at the end of each of its first three years of operations, assuming various inventory pricing procedures.

Year-end	First-in, First-out	Last-in, First-out	Weighted Average
1	$ 7,800	$7,000	$ 7,300
2	10,400	9,400	10,000
3	9,200	8,600	8,900

REQUIRED
Answer each of the following questions, providing supporting computations or other reasoning (disregard income tax effects).
(a) For year 1, by how much could reported income change simply by choosing among the three inventory pricing methods?
(b) For year 2, which inventory pricing method would result in the *highest* reported income?
(c) For year 3, which inventory pricing method would result in the *lowest* reported income?
(d) For year 3, by how much and in what direction would reported income differ under first-in, first-out compared with weighted average?
(e) Which inventory pricing method would result in the *highest* reported income for the *three years combined*?

Lower of cost or market rule

9–32 Agase Company had the following inventory at December 31, 19X7:

	Quantity	Unit Price Cost	Unit Price Market
Fans			
Model X1	400	$15	$16
Model X2	350	22	20
Model X3	200	29	26
Heaters			
Model B7	300	21	25
Model B8	190	35	32
Model B9	100	40	38

REQUIRED
(a) Determine the ending inventory amount by applying the lower of cost or market rule to:
1. each item of inventory.
2. each major category of inventory.
3. the total inventory.
(b) Which of the LCM procedures from requirement (a) results in the lowest net income for 19X7? Explain.

Retail method

9–33 Sales clerks for Rochelle Company, a retail concern, took a year-end physical inventory at retail prices and determined that the total retail value of the ending inventory was $120,000. The following information for the year is available:

	Cost	Selling Price
Beginning inventory	$ 73,000	$110,000
Net purchases	421,000	650,000
Sales		631,000

Management estimates its inventory loss from theft and other causes by comparing its physical ending inventory at retail prices with an estimated ending inventory at retail prices (determined by subtracting sales from goods available for sale at selling prices) and reducing this difference to cost by applying the proper cost ratio.

REQUIRED

(a) Compute the estimated cost of the ending inventory using the retail method. This inventory amount will appear in the balance sheet, and the calculation should be based on the physical inventory taken at retail prices.
(b) Compute the estimated inventory loss for the year from theft and other causes.

Gross profit method

9–34 Chipper Company, an automobile parts supplier, was robbed of a portion of its inventory on the night of August 16, 19X4. The company does not keep perpetual inventory records and must, therefore, estimate the theft loss. To aid in this determination, the accounting staff compiles the following information:

Inventory, August 1, 19X4	$317,000
Inventory, August 16, 19X4 (not stolen)	145,000
Purchases, August 1–16, 19X4	97,000
Purchases returns, August 1–16, 19X4	4,000
Sales, August 1–16, 19X4	250,000
Average gross profit margin	38%

REQUIRED

Use the gross profit method to estimate the amount of the inventory theft loss.

Periodic and perpetual systems

9–35 Assume that Haslem Company had a $40,000 ending inventory balance at the close of the last period. The following sales and purchase transactions occurred during the current period:

1. Purchased merchandise on account, $19,000, terms 1/10, n/30.
2. Returned part of the above merchandise that had an original gross purchase price of $1,000.
3. Paid the balance of the purchase in time to receive the purchases discount.
4. Sold goods costing $32,000 for $50,000. Cash of $13,000 was received, with the balance due on account.

REQUIRED

(a) Record these transactions assuming that (1) a periodic inventory system is used and (2) a perpetual inventory system is used. Assume also that accounts payable are initially recorded at the full invoice price.
(b) Suppose that a physical inventory at the end of the current period shows inventory costing $24,900 to be on hand. Present the journal entries (if any) required under each inventory system to establish the proper balance in the Inventory account.
(c) Which system would best disclose any possible inventory loss in the income statement? Why?

Inventory pricing methods—perpetual

9–36 Breen Company uses a perpetual inventory system. Transactions for an inventory item during April were as follows:

April	1	Beginning inventory, 50 units @ $315 per unit.
	9	Purchased 20 units @ $350 per unit.
	14	Sold 40 units @ $550 per unit.
	23	Purchased 25 units @ $347 per unit.
	29	Sold 20 units @ $550 per unit.

REQUIRED
Record the beginning inventory, purchases, cost of goods sold, and the continuous (perpetual) inventory balance for April on an inventory control record like the one illustrated in Exhibit 9–13, page 336. Use the (a) first-in, first-out method; (b) last-in, first-out method; and (c) moving average method.

ALTERNATE PROBLEMS

Inventory pricing methods—periodic and perpetual

9–29A Singer Sales, Inc., had a beginning inventory for July comprising 1,300 units that had cost $20 per unit. A summary of purchases and sales during July follows:

	Unit Cost	Units Purchased	Units Sold
July 3			800
8	$22	1,500	
13			1,000
19	25	400	
23	28	800	
28			700

REQUIRED
(a) Assuming Singer uses a periodic inventory system, calculate the amount of ending inventory under each of the following pricing methods: first-in, first-out; last-in, first-out; and weighted average.
(b) Which inventory pricing method would you choose:
1. to reflect what is probably the physical flow of goods?
2. to minimize income tax for the period?
3. to report the largest amount of income for the period?
Justify your answers.
(c) Assuming Singer uses a perpetual inventory system, calculate cost of goods sold amounts on July 3, July 13, and July 28 and the ending inventory on July 31 under each of the following pricing methods: first-in, first-out; last-in, first-out; and moving average.

Effects of FIFO and LIFO

9–30A Examine the April data below for Winston, Inc., which prices inventory on the last-in, first-out basis and uses the periodic inventory system.

Beginning inventory: 6,000 units @ $6 each

Purchases		Sales	
Apr. 5	5,000 @ $ 8	Apr. 8	4,000 @ $10
12	8,000 @ 9	16	10,000 @ 12
21	14,000 @ 10	22	12,000 @ 13
30	7,000 @ 11	27	5,000 @ 15

REQUIRED
(a) How much gross profit on sales would Winston, Inc., report for April?
(b) By what amount would Winston's reported gross profit for April change if the final merchandise purchase had been postponed for several days?
(c) How would Winston's reported gross profit differ if the final purchase had been for 19,000 units instead of for 7,000 units?
(d) Assuming Winston used the first-in, first-out method, calculate the answers to requirements (a), (b), and (c).

Comparison of FIFO and LIFO

9–31A Selected operating data follow for Compact, Inc., a franchised distributor of compact disc players:

Beginning inventory	300 units	@ $275 each
Purchases:	600	@ 300
	200	@ 330
Sales	800	@ 550
Operating expenses	$117,500	

Compact uses the periodic inventory system priced at first-in, first-out. Assume all sales, purchases, operating expenses, and taxes are paid in cash and that a 30% income tax rate is applicable.

REQUIRED

(a) What is Compact's net income for the period?
(b) What is the net amount of cash generated by the period's activity?
(c) Why are the amounts in requirements (a) and (b) different? How would you explain this to a stockholder who expected a cash dividend equal to one-half of the reported net income?
(d) What would be your answers to requirements (a) and (b) if the firm used the last-in, first-out method to price its ending inventory?
(e) Briefly explain the nature of any phantom profit on inventory in part (a). Also, explain the nature of any tax advantage of the last-in, first-out inventory pricing in requirement (d).
(f) Contrast the ending inventory carrying values in requirements (a) and (d). Which figure is more meaningful? Why?
(g) Contrast the reported income in requirements (a) and (d). Which figure is more meaningful? Why?

Lower of cost or market rule

9–32A Appling Company had the following inventory at December 31, 19X4:

		Unit Price	
	Quantity	Cost	Market
Desks			
Model 9001	80	$200	$205
Model 9002	45	300	282
Model 9003	20	375	385
Cabinets			
Model 7001	170	60	65
Model 7002	80	90	88
Model 7003	40	120	124

REQUIRED

(a) Determine the ending inventory amount by applying the lower of cost or market rule to:
   1. each item of inventory.
   2. each major category of inventory.
   3. the total inventory.
(b) Which of the LCM procedures from requirement (a) results in the lowest net income for 19X4? Explain.

Retail method

9–33A Sales clerks for Bock Company, a retail concern, took a year-end physical inventory at retail prices and determined that the total retail value of the ending inventory was $210,000. The following information for the year is available:

	Cost	Selling Price
Beginning inventory	$158,600	$225,000
Net purchases	473,800	705,000
Sales		708,000

Management estimates its inventory loss from theft and other causes by comparing its physical ending inventory at retail prices with an estimated ending inventory at retail prices (determined by subtracting sales from goods available for sale at selling prices) and reducing this difference to cost by applying the proper cost ratio.

REQUIRED
(a) Compute the estimated cost of the ending inventory using the retail method. This inventory amount will appear in the balance sheet, and the calculation should be based on the physical inventory taken at retail prices.
(b) Compute the estimated inventory loss for the year from theft and other causes.

Gross profit method

9–34A Ladd Company, a computer supply firm, lost all of its inventory to a flood on March 15, 19X3. The company does not keep perpetual inventory records and must, therefore, estimate the flood loss for insurance purposes. To aid in this determination, the accounting staff compiles the following information:

	19X1	19X2	19X3 (to 3/15)
Net sales	$355,000	$400,000	$110,000
Beginning inventory	25,000	16,700	30,000
Purchases	225,000	260,300	55,500
Purchases returns	1,500	2,000	500
Purchases discounts	2,500	3,000	1,000
Transportation in	5,000	6,000	2,000
Ending inventory	16,700	30,000	?

REQUIRED
(a) Compute the gross profit rates for 19X1 and 19X2.
(b) Using the average of the gross profit rates for 19X1 and 19X2, use the gross profit method to estimate the amount of the flood loss on March 15, 19X3.

Periodic and perpetual systems

9–35A Assume that Corner Appliance Shop had a $14,000 ending inventory balance at the close of the last period. The following sales and purchase transactions occurred during the current period:
1. Purchased merchandise on account, $19,000, terms 2/10, n/30.
2. Returned part of the above merchandise that had an original gross purchase price of $1,500.
3. Paid the balance of the purchase in time to receive the purchases discount.
4. Sold goods costing $15,500 for $33,000. Cash of $10,000 was received, with the balance due on account.

REQUIRED
(a) Record these transactions assuming that (1) a periodic inventory system is used and (2) a perpetual inventory system is used. Assume also that accounts payable are initially recorded at the full invoice price.
(b) Suppose that a physical inventory at the end of the current period shows inventory costing $15,200 to be on hand. Present journal entries (if any) required under each inventory system to establish the proper balance in the Inventory account.
(c) Which system would best disclose any possible inventory loss in the income statement? Why?

Inventory pricing methods—perpetual

9–36A Merritt Company uses a perpetual inventory system. Transactions for an inventory item during June were as follows:

June 1 Beginning inventory, 60 units @ $70 per unit.
5 Purchased 15 units @ $80 per unit.
13 Sold 50 units @ $140 per unit.
25 Purchased 35 units @ $84 per unit.
29 Sold 20 units @ $150 per unit.

REQUIRED
Record the beginning inventory, purchases, cost of goods sold, and the continuous (perpetual) inventory balance for June on an inventory control record like the one illustrated in Exhibit 9–13, page 336. Use the (a) first-in, first-out method; (b) last-in, first-out method; and (c) moving average method.

BUSINESS DECISION PROBLEM

Redstone Company's entire inventory and many of its accounting records were destroyed by fire early in the morning of April 1, 19X3. Redstone filed an inventory loss claim of $110,000 with Worthy Insurance Company. As Worthy's representative, you must evaluate the reasonableness of Redstone's claim. You and Redstone's head bookkeeper have gathered the following information from various sources:

1. The January 1, 19X3, inventory figure of $62,500 was found on a copy of a personal property tax declaration filed with the local municipality.
2. From a statistical summary filed with a trade association, the sales and cost of goods sold for the preceding three years were as follows:

	19X0	19X1	19X2
Net sales	$650,000	$700,000	$800,000
Cost of goods sold	392,600	403,200	472,000

3. Redstone buys an estimated 80% of its merchandise from three wholesale suppliers. According to these three suppliers, Redstone's purchases for the first three months of 19X3 were as follows:

Supplier	Purchases
Hill Corporation	$47,000
Lanvin Company	72,000
Voss, Inc.	31,000

4. Redstone's sales average 5% cash and the balance on credit. Adding machine tapes totaling the accounts receivable subsidiary ledger were found and showed $36,000 and $42,000, respectively, for December 31, 19X2, and March 31, 19X3. An analysis of bank deposit slips indicates that collections from credit customers deposited in the bank in 19X3 were $92,000 for January, $88,000 for February, and $99,000 for March.

REQUIRED
Based on the preceding data, use the gross profit method to estimate Redstone Company's ending inventory destroyed by fire. Is Redstone's loss claim reasonable?

ANSWERS TO SELF-TEST QUESTIONS

1. (d) **2.** (a) **3.** (a) **4.** (c) **5.** (b)

10

PLANT ASSETS: MEASUREMENT AND DEPRECIATION

CHAPTER OBJECTIVES

1. Provide the background to understand the various problems related to the measurement of plant assets (pp. 351–52).
2. Identify the guidelines relating to the initial measurement of plant assets (pp. 352–55).
3. Discuss the nature of the depreciation process (pp. 356–57).
4. Illustrate four generally accepted methods of computing periodic depreciation (pp. 357–63).
5. Discuss the distinction between revenue and capital expenditures (pp. 363–66).

Little of all we value here
Wakes on the morn of its hundredth year.

OLIVER WENDELL HOLMES

In this chapter and Chapter 11, we discuss the accounting problems related to the acquisition, use, and disposal of assets whose benefits to a firm extend over many accounting periods. These long-term assets fall in three major balance sheet categories: *plant assets*, *natural resources*, and *intangible assets*. **Plant assets,** or **fixed assets,** refer to a firm's *property*, *plant*, and *equipment*.

The carrying values of these long-term assets are normally based on historical costs. As with other business assets, the costs related to the use of long-term assets must be properly calculated and matched against the revenue they help generate, so that periodic net income is determined correctly. Each period's expired portion of the asset's cost is called *depreciation*, *depletion*, or *amortization*, depending on the type of asset involved. All of these terms have the same meaning in accounting—that is, periodic charging to expense.

Exhibit 10–1 gives several specific examples within each asset category. The exhibit also associates the term for the periodic write-off to expense with the proper asset category. Note that site land—that is, a place on which to operate—usually has an indefinite useful life and therefore does not require any periodic write-off to expense. (Depletion and amortization are discussed more fully in Chapter 11.)

OVERVIEW OF PLANT ASSET PROBLEMS

We consider the problems associated with plant assets in the order shown in Exhibit 10–2. This exhibit is a graphic presentation of the typical accounting problems created by plant assets in relation to an asset's life cycle.

EXHIBIT 10–1

CLASSIFICATION OF LONG-TERM ASSETS
AND RELATED WRITE-OFF

Asset Category	Examples	Term for Periodic Write-off to Expense
Plant Assets	Buildings, equipment, tools, furniture, fixtures, and vehicles	Depreciation
	Land for site use	No periodic write-off; considered to have an indefinite life.
Natural Resources	Oil, timber, coal, and other mineral deposits	Depletion
Intangible Assets	Patents, copyrights, leaseholds, franchises, trademarks, and goodwill	Amortization

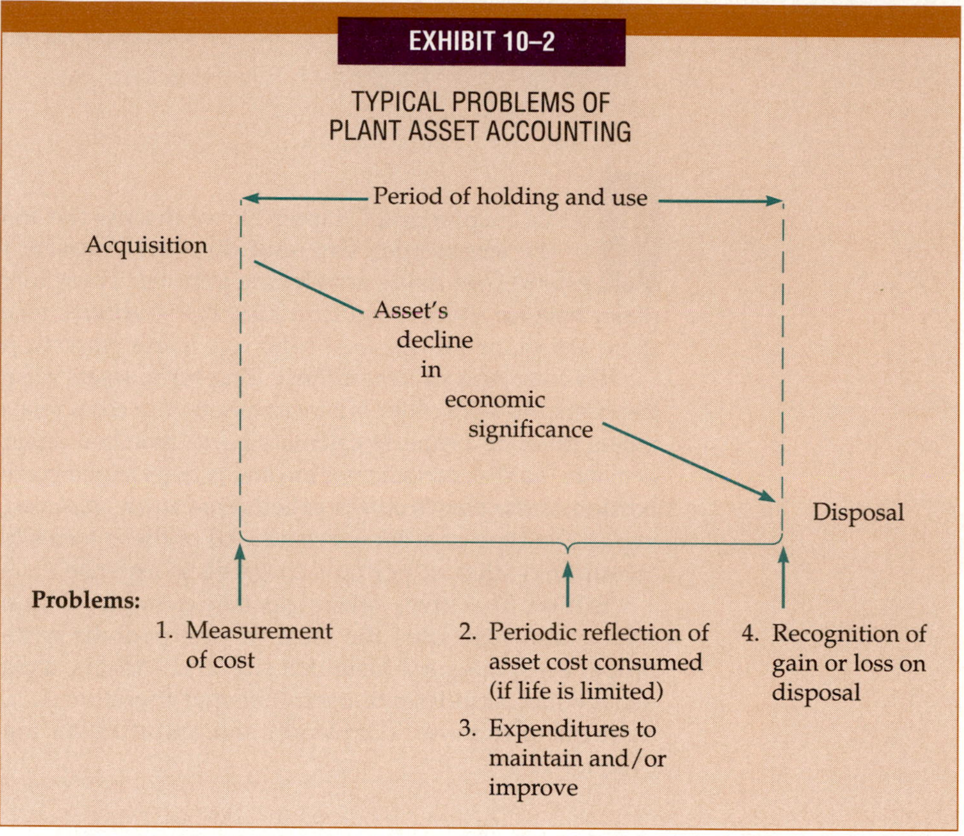

Measurement problems associated with plant assets include identifying the types and amounts of expenditures that make up the original recorded cost of the particular asset. During the use period of a limited-life asset, it is important to charge the appropriate amounts against yearly revenue to reflect the asset's consumption. This involves estimating the asset's useful life and its probable salvage value at disposal. Also during the use period, expenditures for simple maintenance (expense) must be properly differentiated from expenditures that increase the capacity or extend the life of the asset (added to asset costs). On disposal, the adjusted accounting cost of the asset must be compared with the net proceeds from disposal in order to determine any related gain or loss. We consider this last problem in Chapter 11.

ORIGINAL MEASUREMENT OF PLANT ASSETS

Plant assets are originally recorded at their cost. These measures are also called *historical costs* because they provide the basis for accounting for the assets in subsequent periods. Usually we do not attempt to reflect subsequent changes in market values for plant assets. In general, the initial cost of a plant asset is equal to the cash and/or the cash equivalent of that which is given up in order to acquire the asset *and* to prepare it for use. In other words, initial cost includes the asset's (1) implied cash price and (2) cost of preparation for use.

The expenditures to acquire and prepare the asset for use must be reasonable and necessary to be considered part of the asset's cost. Accountants do not capitalize (charge to an asset account) wasteful or inefficient expenditures. Costs of waste and inefficiency are expensed when incurred. For example, suppose equipment is damaged while it is being installed or a firm's receiving dock is damaged while equipment is being unloaded. Expenditures made to repair these damages are not part of the cost of the equipment; they are instead charged to expense.

Cash and Noncash Purchases

Often an asset's historical cost is simply the amount of cash paid when the asset is acquired and readied for use. Consider, for example, the following expenditures for a certain piece of equipment:

Purchase price factors:		
Gross invoice price	$10,000	
Less: Cash discount (1/10, n/30)	(100)	
Sales tax	500	$10,400
Related expenditures:		
Freight charges	$ 200	
Installation costs	500	
Testing of installed machine	300	1,000
Cost of equipment		$11,400

The total initial equipment cost is $11,400, consisting of a cash purchase price of $10,400 and preparation costs of $1,000. The sales tax is a necessary component of the purchase price and should not be charged to a tax expense account. Similarly, the costs of freight, installation, and testing are expenditures necessary to get the asset in condition and location for use.

If an asset's purchase price is not immediately paid in cash, we determine the cash equivalent purchase price at the acquisition date and record that amount in the asset account. Suppose we purchased the above equipment on a financing plan requiring a $1,500 cash down payment and a non-interest-bearing note for $10,000 due in one year. The implied cash price remains $10,400, even though the financing plan is used. The difference between the $10,400 and the $11,500 total disbursement under the financing plan ($1,500 down payment plus $10,000 payment on note) represents the interest cost of the financing plan. The entry to record the purchase of the asset under the financing plan would be:

Equipment	10,400	
Discount on Notes Payable	1,100	
Cash		1,500
Notes Payable		10,000
To record purchase of equipment.		

Of course, the expenditures for freight, installation, and testing are still debited to the Equipment account when they are incurred.

Capitalization of Interest

Interest cost is part of an asset's initial cost if a period of time is required to get the asset ready for use. For example, the construction of a factory building takes time to complete. Accordingly, an appropriate portion of the actual interest cost incurred during the construction period is added to the factory building's cost. We compute the amount of **interest capitalized** by multiplying the periodic interest rate times the period's average accumulated construction expenditures.

To illustrate, let us assume Miller Company borrowed $500,000 at 12% to finance the construction of a factory building. Interest of $5,000 is paid monthly. During the first month, construction expenditures total $300,000. The interest cost capitalized this first month is $1,500, computed as follows:

Average accumulated construction expenditures:		
Accumulated construction expenditures, beginning of month	$ -0-	
Accumulated construction expenditures, end of month	300,000	
Average accumulated construction expenditures for the month	$300,000 ÷ 2 =	$150,000
Monthly interest rate (1%)		0.01
Interest capitalized for the month		$ 1,500

The entry to record the first month's interest payment is

Factory Building	1,500	
Interest Expense	3,500	
Cash		5,000
To record interest payment, of which $1,500 is capitalized to factory building.		

Interest is capitalized until the factory building is completed. Of course, in subsequent months, the average accumulated construction expenditures increase, so larger amounts of interest cost are capitalized. If the average accumulated construction expenditures exceed $500,000, then additional computations based on the company's other borrowings are needed to determine the interest cost associated with the expenditures over $500,000. These computations are covered in intermediate accounting texts.

Related Expenditures

A purchase of land often raises some interesting questions about related expenditures. Suppose a firm retains a local real estate broker at a fee of $2,000 to locate an appropriate site for its new office building. The property eventually chosen has an old residence on it, which will be razed. The terms of the sale include a payment of $40,000 to the seller, with the buyer paying off an existing mortgage of $10,000 and $300 of accrued interest. In addition, the buyer agrees to pay accrued real estate taxes of $800. Other related expenditures include legal fees of $400 and a title insurance premium of $500. A local salvage company will raze the old residence, level the lot, keep all the materials, and pay the firm $200. If we apply the general plant asset measurement rule, we compute the initial cost of the land as follows:

Payment to the seller	$40,000
Commission for finding property	2,000
Payment of mortgage and interest due at time of sale	10,300
Payment of property taxes owed by seller	800
Legal fees	400
Title insurance premium	500
	$54,000
Less: Net recovery from razing	(200)
Cost of land	$53,800

Again, expenditures for the taxes, insurance, legal fees, and interest should be capitalized as part of the land, because they were necessary for its acquisition and preparation for use. Removing the old residence prepares the land for its intended use. The $200 net recovery from razing, therefore, reduces the land's cost. A net payment to remove the old building would have increased the land's cost.

When a land site is acquired in an undeveloped area, the firm may pay special assessments to the local government for such property improvements as streets, sidewalks, and sewers. These improvements are normally maintained by the local government and, accordingly, are considered relatively permanent improvements by the firm. In these circumstances, the company capitalizes the special assessments as part of the cost of the land.

The firm may make property improvements that have limited lives. Paved parking lots, driveways, private sidewalks, and fences are examples. These expenditures are charged to a separate account, **Land Improvements,** which is depreciated over the estimated lives of the improvements.

Package Purchases

Sometimes several types of assets are purchased concurrently as a package. For example, assume that a company purchased a small freight terminal including land, a building, and some loading equipment for a total price of $190,000. For accounting purposes, the total purchase price should be divided among the three asset forms because (1) they are reported in different accounts, (2) only the building and equipment are subject to depreciation, and (3) the equipment will have an estimated useful life different from that of the building.

The price of package purchases is commonly allocated on the basis of relative market or appraisal values. We assume estimated market values to illustrate this approach.

Asset	Estimated Market Value	Percent of Total	Allocation of Purchase Price	Estimated Useful Life
Land	$ 60,000	30	$ 57,000	Indefinite
Building	120,000	60	114,000	30 years
Equipment	20,000	10	19,000	8 years
Totals	$200,000	100	$190,000	

Actually, the firm may obtain realistic market values from a knowledgeable employee, a professional appraiser, or from assessed values on related property tax bills.

Nonroutine Acquisitions

Not all asset acquisitions involve specific amounts of money. Often nonmonetary assets are traded for other nonmonetary assets, and therefore the implied cash price is not readily apparent. Generally accepted accounting principles normally provide that the transaction price should be the market value of either the asset given up or the asset received, whichever is more objectively determinable. General-purpose property and equipment (standard office or factory equipment) and widely traded securities usually have more objectively determinable market values than do highly specialized buildings or equipment and securities that are new or seldom traded. In the latter instances, the accountant must exercise professional judgment.

An exception to this guideline is the exchange of a nonmonetary productive asset for a similar asset. We consider this exception in Chapter 11 in our discussion of exchanges of similar plant assets.

THE NATURE OF DEPRECIATION

With the exception of site land, the use of plant assets to generate revenue consumes their economic potential. At some point of reduced potential—usually before they are totally worthless—these assets are disposed of and possibly replaced. We can diagram the typical pattern of plant asset utilization (indicated in Exhibit 10–2) as follows:

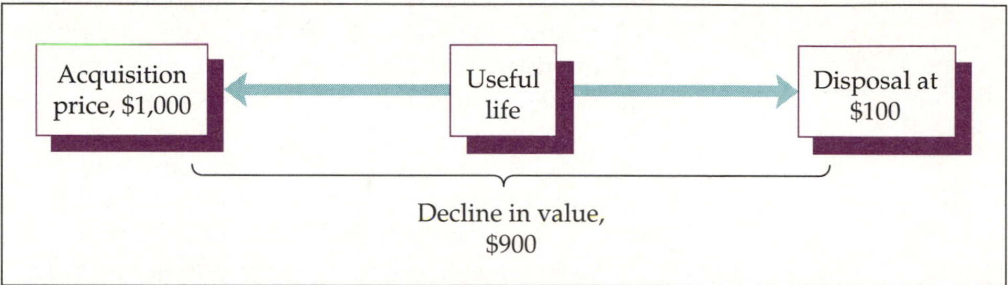

The asset is acquired for $1,000, used for several accounting periods, and then sold for $100. The $900 decline in value is, in every sense of the word, an expense of generating the revenue realized during the periods that the asset was used. Therefore, if the income figure is to be meaningful, $900 of expense must be allocated to these periods and matched against the revenue. Failure to do so would overstate income for these periods.

Note that in this process we estimate an asset's useful life and salvage value as well as properly determine its acquisition cost. **Useful life** is the expected period of economic usefulness to the current entity—the period from date of acquisition to expected date of disposal. **Salvage value** (or residual value) is the expected net recovery (Sales proceeds − Disposal costs) when the asset is sold or removed from service. When the salvage value is insignificant, it may be ignored in the depreciation process.

Allocation versus Valuation

Although the idea is theoretically appealing, accountants do not specifically base depreciation on the changes in market value or on the measured wear of assets—primarily because a reliable, objective, and practical source for such data rarely exists. Rather, **depreciation** accounting attempts to allocate in a rational and systematic manner the difference between acquisition cost and estimated salvage value over the *estimated* useful life of the asset. Depreciation accounting techniques are convenient expedients for measuring asset expirations and are therefore not precise. Though imprecise, depreciation estimates clearly provide better income determination than would result from completely expensing the asset at either the date of acquisition or the date of disposal.

Several factors are naturally related to the periodic allocation of depreciation. Depreciation can be caused by wear from use, natural deterioration through interaction of the elements, and technical obsolescence. Each factor reduces the value of the asset. To some extent maintenance (lubrication, adjustments, parts replacements, and cleaning) may partially arrest or offset wear and deterioration. Quite logically, then, when useful life and salvage values are estimated, a given level of maintenance is assumed. Therefore, the cost of using plant assets tends to be the sum of periodic maintenance expenditures plus some measure of the depreciation that occurs despite the maintenance performed. Maintenance expense normally increases toward the latter stages of most assets' lives.

How to allocate depreciation expense is just one facet of the overall problem of matching revenue and expenses. The most defensible reason for choosing one allocation pattern over another is that one pattern may better portray the pattern of services received each period from using the asset. It would be only coincidence if the book value of a particular asset were exactly equal to its market value at any time during its useful life. On the other hand, the general pattern of an asset's book value may be related to its decline in market value. Indeed, the goal is that at the end of an asset's useful life, its book value and market value (that is, salvage value) should be the same.

COMPUTATIONS OF PERIODIC DEPRECIATION

We now illustrate four widely used methods of computing periodic depreciation. For each illustration, we assume that the asset costs $1,000 and has an estimated useful life of five years. The estimated salvage value at the end of the five-year period is $100. Our computations illustrate different ways to *allocate* the amount depreciated among each of the five accounting periods in the asset's life.

Straight Line

Straight-line depreciation is probably the simplest to compute. An equal amount of depreciation expense is allocated to each full period of the asset's useful life. Using straight-line depreciation,

$$\text{Annual Depreciation} = \frac{\text{Original Cost} - \text{Salvage Value}}{\text{Periods of Useful Life}}$$

which in our example is

$$\frac{\$1{,}000 - \$100}{5\text{ years}} = \$180/\text{year}$$

The basic entry to record each period's depreciation expense is:

Depreciation Expense	180	
Accumulated Depreciation—Equipment		180
To record depreciation expense for the year.		

Like other expense accounts, Depreciation Expense is deducted from revenue in determining net income and is closed at year-end to the Income Summary account. The offsetting credit is posted to the contra account, Accumulated Depreciation, which is deducted from the related asset account on the balance sheet to compute the asset's book value, or carrying value. In this manner, the original cost of an asset is maintained in the asset account, and the cumulative balance of depreciation taken is carried in the contra account as long as the asset is in service. When an asset is disposed of, the related cost and accumulated depreciation are removed from the accounts.

For our simple illustration, the following table shows account balances and the progression of certain amounts during the asset's five-year life.

Period	Balance of Asset Account	Periodic Depreciation Expense	End-of-Period Balance Accumulated Depreciation Account	Asset's Book Value
1	$1,000	$180	$180	$820
2	1,000	180	360	640
3	1,000	180	540	460
4	1,000	180	720	280
5	1,000	180	900	100
	Total depreciation	$900		

Observe that (1) the asset account always shows the original cost of the asset, (2) each period reflects $180 of depreciation expense, (3) the Accumulated Depreciation account balance is cumulative and shows the portion of the original cost taken as depreciation to date, (4) the asset's book value is the original cost less total accumulated depreciation to date, and (5) the asset's book value at the end of five years equals the estimated salvage value. Thus, the book value decreases to the estimated salvage value as the asset is depreciated during its useful life.

The book value of the asset is shown on the balance sheet by deducting the Accumulated Depreciation account (normally a credit balance) from the asset account (normally a debit balance). At the end of the second year, for example, the asset's balance sheet presentation is as follows:

Equipment (original cost)	$1,000
Less: Accumulated Depreciation	360
Equipment (book value)	$ 640

For periods of less than one year, straight-line depreciation amounts are simply proportions of the annual amount. For example, if the asset had been acquired on April 1, depreciation for the period ended December 31 would be $\frac{9}{12} \times \$180 = \$135$. Assets acquired or disposed of during the first half of any month are usually treated as if the acquisition or disposal occurred on the first of the month. When either event occurs during the last half of any month, we assume it occurred on the first of the following month.

Straight-line allocation is best suited to an asset with a relatively uniform periodic usage and a low obsolescence factor. Examples include pipelines, storage tanks, fencing, and surface paving. These types of assets can provide approximately equal utility during all periods of their useful lives.

Units of Production

The **units-of-production method** allocates depreciation in proportion to the asset's use in operations. First, the depreciation per unit of production is computed by dividing the total expected depreciation (in our example, $900) by the asset's projected units-of-production capacity. Therefore,

$$\text{Depreciation per Unit} = \frac{\text{Original Cost} - \text{Salvage Value}}{\text{Estimated Total Units of Production}}$$

Units-of-production capacity may represent miles driven, tons hauled, hours used, or number of cuttings, drillings, or stampings of parts. Assume that our example is a drilling tool that will drill an estimated 45,000 parts during its useful life. The depreciation per unit of production is

$$\frac{\$1{,}000 - \$100}{45{,}000 \text{ parts}} = \$0.02 \text{ per part}$$

To find periodic depreciation expense, we multiply the depreciation per unit of production by the number of units produced during the period. If 8,000 units are produced during the first year, then 8,000 × $0.02 = $160 is the year's depreciation expense. If 12,000 parts are drilled the next year, that year's depreciation expense is 12,000 × $0.02 = $240.

The units-of-production approach is particularly appropriate when wear is the major cause of depreciation and the amount of use varies from period to period. Of course, if use is uniformly spread over the asset's life, the same allocation of depreciation would result from either the straight-line or units-of-production method. The units-of-production method may necessitate some extra record keeping to express the periodic use in terms of production capacity. However, this data may already be tabulated as part of a periodic production report.

Sum of the Years' Digits

The **sum-of-the-years'-digits (SYD) method** accelerates depreciation expense so that the amounts recognized in the early periods of an asset's useful life are greater than those recognized in the later periods. This type of depreciation pattern (larger amounts in early periods) identifies an **accelerated depreciation method.** The SYD is found by estimating an asset's useful life in years, assigning consecutive numbers to each year, and totaling these numbers. For n years,

$$\text{SYD} = 1 + 2 + 3 + \ldots + n$$

In our example, the SYD for a five-year asset life is 1 + 2 + 3 + 4 + 5 = 15.

NOT BAD FOR A TEN-YEAR-OLD

Carl Friedrich Gauss ranks among the greatest mathematicians of all time. Certainly, his contributions place him in the company of such mathematical giants as Archimedes and Sir Isaac Newton. Born in Brunswick, Germany, in 1777, Gauss was an infant prodigy. During his 78-year life, he made major contributions to number theory, non-Euclidean geometry, astronomy, and physics. His work in the field of magnetism led to a unit of measure being given his name—the *gauss* is the metric unit for measuring electromagnetic induction.

An episode that occurred when Gauss was ten years old relates to our study of depreciation accounting. One day during arithmetic class, the teacher assigned the students the task of finding the sum of all the numbers 1 through 100. The students did their assignments on slate tablets. As they finished an assignment, they would each place their tablet on a large table. The teacher had barely finished giving this assignment when Gauss placed his tablet on the table, exclaiming "Ligget se!" (There it is). While the other students were still busy writing and computing, the teacher finally took a look at Gauss's slate. There was only one number written on it—5,050, the correct answer!

Gauss got his answer so quickly because he noted a particular numerical relationship: if he paired the first number and the last number (1, 100), the second number and the next to last number (2, 99), the third number and the third from the last number (3, 98), and so on, the sum of each pair was the same, 101. Out of the 100 numbers, there were 50 such pairs. Thus, the sum of all the numbers is 50 × 101, or 5,050.*

This brilliantly simple solution to the problem of adding up a set of whole numbers explains the formula used in summing up an asset's years in sum-of-the-years'-digits depreciation. If we let n equal the number of years of useful life, then the number of "Gaussian" pairs is $n/2$ and the sum of each pair is $n + 1$. The sum of the numbers, therefore, is $(n/2)(n + 1)$, or, alternatively, $n(n + 1)/2$.

*This episode and other details of Gauss's life may be found in G. Waldo Dunnington, *Carl Friedrich Gauss: Titan of Science* (New York: Exposition Press, 1955).

Determining the SYD factor by simple addition can be somewhat laborious for long-lived assets. For these assets, the formula $n(n + 1)/2$, where n = the number of periods in the asset's useful life, can be applied to derive the SYD. In our example,

$$\frac{5(5+1)}{2} = \frac{30}{2} = 15$$

The yearly depreciation is then calculated by multiplying the total depreciable amount for the asset's useful life by a fraction whose numerator is the remaining useful life and whose denominator is the SYD. Thus, the formula for yearly depreciation is

$$\text{Annual Depreciation} = (\text{Original Cost} - \text{Salvage Value}) \times \frac{\text{Remaining Useful Life}}{\text{SYD}}$$

The calculations for our example are shown below:

Year of Useful Life	Fraction of Total Depreciation Taken Each Year		Original Cost Less Salvage Value		Annual Depreciation Allocation
1	$\frac{5}{15}$	×	$900	=	$300
2	$\frac{4}{15}$	×	900	=	240
3	$\frac{3}{15}$	×	900	=	180
4	$\frac{2}{15}$	×	900	=	120
5	$\frac{1}{15}$	×	900	=	60
SYD 15					Total $900

When the acquisition of an asset does not coincide with the beginning of the fiscal period, the annual depreciation amounts are allocated proportionately to the appropriate fiscal periods. For example, assume we purchased the asset on April 1. Depreciation for the period ended December 31 would be $\frac{9}{12} \times \$300 =$ $225. For the next fiscal year, a full year's depreciation would be calculated as $(\frac{3}{12} \times \$300) + (\frac{9}{12} \times \$240) = \$255$.

As an accelerated depreciation method, the SYD approach is most appropriate when the asset renders greater utility during its early life and less in its later life. Accelerated depreciation is suitable for assets with either a high technological obsolescence factor in the early life phase or a high maintenance factor in the late life phase.

Double Declining Balance

Another accelerated depreciation method is the **double declining-balance method,** which derives its name from the fact that a *constant percentage* factor of twice the straight-line rate is applied each year to the *declining balance* of the asset's book value.

The *straight-line rate* is simply the number of years in the asset's useful life divided into 100%. In our example, this would be 100%/5 = 20%. Double the straight-line rate is then 40%. In equation form,

$$\text{Double Declining-balance Rate} = \frac{100\%}{\text{Years of Useful Life}} \times 2$$

To determine the annual double declining-balance depreciation expense, we simply *multiply the asset's book value at the beginning of the period by the constant rate (or percentage)*. Remember that an asset's book value at any time is its original cost less its accumulated depreciation to date. The book value of a depreciable asset *declines* as it is depreciated. The important thing to remember is that the percentage depreciation rate remains constant; the book value—to which the percentage is applied—declines. Salvage value is not considered in the calculations, except that depreciation stops when the asset's book value equals its estimated salvage value.

Applying the general rule for double declining-balance depreciation to our example, we obtain the accelerated depreciation pattern shown in the following table (amounts to nearest dollar).

Year of Useful Life	Original Cost	Beginning Accumulated Depreciation	Beginning Book Value		Twice Straight-line Percentage		Amount of Depreciation Expense
1	$1,000	$ 0	$1,000	×	40%	=	$400
2	1,000	400	600	×	40%	=	240
3	1,000	640	360	×	40%	=	144
4	1,000	784	216	×	40%	=	86
5	1,000	870	130				30
			Total depreciation taken				$900

Observe that in the fifth year depreciation expense is only $30, the amount needed to reduce the asset's book value to the estimated salvage value of $100. Assets are not depreciated below their salvage values. If no salvage value has been estimated, the double declining-balance technique automatically provides one. When a fraction (40%, or $\frac{4}{10}$, for example) is applied to an asset's book value, the entire original cost can never be depreciated; some balance, though small, will always remain.

If an asset is purchased during the fiscal period, a pro-rata allocation of the first year's depreciation is necessary. If we acquired our asset on April 1, depreciation for the period ended December 31 would be $\frac{9}{12}$ × (40% × $1,000) = $300. In subsequent periods, the usual procedure is followed; that is, the asset's book value at the beginning of the period is multiplied by the constant rate. The next year, for example, depreciation would be 40% × ($1,000 − $300) = $280.

Because double declining-balance depreciation is also an accelerated depreciation method, it is appropriate in the same situations as the SYD method.

REVISION OF DEPRECIATION

We have stressed that depreciation allocations are based on estimates of both useful lives and salvage values. Circumstances change, however, and original estimates may be too high or too low. Once it is determined that original estimates are wrong, the computation of periodic depreciation expense for the asset's remaining useful life must be revised. We revise a depreciation estimate by allocating the revised undepreciated balance of the asset over the revised remaining useful life. To illustrate this revision procedure, we use the data from our previous examples in which an asset costing $1,000 has a five-year life and an estimated salvage value of $100.

If, based on the original estimates, straight-line depreciation of $180 has been recorded for each of the first three years, the accumulated depreciation would be 3 × $180 = $540. Now suppose that just before recording the fourth year's depreciation, circumstances indicate that the asset's life will be six years instead of five and that its salvage value at the end of the sixth year will be $40. The revised depreciation expense to be taken during the revised remaining useful life is computed as follows:

Original asset cost		$1,000
Depreciation already recorded (3 years @ $180)		540
Book value at start of fourth year		$ 460
Revised salvage value		40
Revised remaining depreciation		$ 420
Revised remaining useful life		3 years
Revised periodic depreciation expense for fourth, fifth, and sixth years	$420/3 =	$140 per year

The revision process does not change depreciation amounts recorded in earlier periods. The earlier computations utilized the best estimates available at the time. A change in an estimate, then, causes depreciation expense to be revised in the year of change and subsequent periods only.

DEPRECIATION FOR TAX PURPOSES

Depreciation expense is deducted by a business on its federal income tax return. The amount on the tax return, however, may differ substantially from the amount reported in the firm's income statement because the calculation of tax depreciation follows income tax regulations. The specific procedures for tax purposes depend on the year the asset was acquired. Assets acquired before 1981 are depreciated over their useful lives, and the acceptable methods include straight line, units of production, sum of the years' digits, and double declining balance. For property acquired from 1981 through 1986, tax depreciation is calculated under a special accelerated method called the **accelerated cost recovery system (ACRS).** The ACRS procedures are modified (and referred to as **MACRS**) for assets acquired after 1986. Both ACRS and MACRS permit firms the option of using a straight-line method. However, salvage value is ignored under ACRS, MACRS, and the straight-line options to these procedures.

ACRS and MACRS establish classes of property with prescribed write-off periods. For assets acquired after 1986, MACRS establishes eight property classes with prescribed write-off periods ranging from three years to 31.5 years. Most machinery and equipment, for example, is in a seven-year class. When acquired, property is placed in the appropriate class (per tax guidelines) and depreciated over the prescribed period following the method specified for that class. Property in the seven-year class, for example, is depreciated using double declining balance (with a switch to straight line when it gives a larger deduction).[1]

[1]MACRS assumes assets are placed in service and disposed of in the middle of the year so the write-off of property in the seven-year class is spread over eight different tax years.

ACRS was introduced into the tax law to encourage companies to invest in plant assets. Because the write-off period under ACRS and MACRS is usually shorter than an asset's useful life, these methods provide larger depreciation deductions during an asset's early years than was previously possible. In a sense, these accelerated deductions provide an interest-free loan to the firm because they allow the firm to pay less tax in the early phase of an asset's life and more in the later phase. During the intervening time, the firm can use the amount of funds equal to the postponed income tax payments.

Change and modification characterize the history of U.S. tax law. Tax depreciation guidelines will likely be modified again in the future. Keep in mind, however, that depreciation changes in the tax law do not affect the depreciation methods a firm may use in preparing its financial statements. Tax depreciation guidelines only apply to the preparation of income tax returns.

REVENUE EXPENDITURES

Revenue expenditures are expenditures relating to plant assets that are expensed when incurred. The following list identifies three common types of revenue expenditures:

1. Expenditures for ordinary maintenance and repairs of existing plant assets.
2. Expenditures to acquire low-cost items that benefit the firm for several periods.
3. Expenditures considered unnecessary or unreasonable in the circumstances.

Maintenance and Repairs

Some level of maintenance and repairs must be assumed when estimating useful lives and salvage values of property, plant, and equipment. For example, a plant asset that is not maintained or repaired will have a shorter useful life than a similar asset that is properly maintained. Periodic upkeep—such as lubrication, cleaning, and replacement of minor parts—is necessary to maintain an asset's expected level and length of usefulness. These periodic upkeep costs are charged to expense as they are incurred.

Low-cost Items

Most businesses purchase items that provide years of service at a relatively small cost, such as paperweights, ashtrays, and wastebaskets. Because of the small dollar amounts involved, establishing these items as assets and depreciating them over their expected useful lives really serves no useful purpose. The effect on the financial statements is not significant. Consequently, expensing these expenditures at the time of purchase is more efficient. The accounting for such low-cost items is thus completed in the period they are purchased. This practice of accounting for small dollar transactions in the most expedient fashion is an example of the basic principle of *materiality*. (We discuss materiality in more detail in Chapter 13.)

Unnecessary or Unreasonable Costs

As noted earlier, costs of waste and inefficiency related to the acquisition of plant assets are expensed when incurred. Because an asset's initial cost includes only necessary and reasonable expenditures, any unnecessary or unreasonable outlays are expensed. An accountant may need to exercise considerable judgment, however, in determining whether a particular expenditure is necessary and reasonable. Identical expenditures may be treated differently, depending on the circumstances. For example, assume a company pays an overtime premium to have a piece of equipment delivered on a holiday. If it is essential that the equipment be available for use on the next workday, then the overtime premium should be added to the equipment's cost as a necessary and reasonable expenditure. In contrast, if the equipment could just as well be delivered on the next workday, then the overtime premium is an unnecessary and wasteful expenditure that should be expensed.

CAPITAL EXPENDITURES

Capital expenditures increase the book value of long-term assets. To *capitalize* an amount, then, means to increase an asset's book value by that amount. Typical capital expenditures related to property, plant, and equipment are as follows:

1. Initial acquisitions and additions.
2. Betterments.
3. Extraordinary repairs.

Initial Acquisitions and Additions

Earlier in this chapter, we discussed the guidelines governing the initial measurement of plant assets. Expenditures equal to the asset's implied cash price plus the costs necessary to prepare the asset for use were debited to the asset account. These amounts were capital expenditures.

The same guidelines apply in accounting for additions to existing plant assets. Adding a new wing to a building or expanding the size of an asphalt parking lot are examples of additions. These capital expenditures should also be debited to an asset account. A separate account (and depreciation schedule) should be used for an addition when its estimated useful life differs from the remaining useful life of the existing plant asset.

Betterments

Betterments improve the quality of services rendered by a plant asset but do not necessarily extend its useful life. Examples include adding a power winch to a highway service truck or air conditioning to an automobile. In each instance, the vehicle's services are enhanced, but its useful life is not changed. Expenditures for betterments are debited to the appropriate asset account, and the subsequent periodic depreciation expense is increased to allocate the additional cost over the asset's remaining useful life.

To illustrate, let us assume Tray Service Station purchased a new service truck for $6,500 on January 2, 19X1. Its estimated useful life is six years with a salvage value of $500. Using the straight-line method, $1,000 of depreciation expense is recorded in 19X1 [($6,500 − $500)/6 = $1,000]. On January 2, 19X2, a power winch costing $700 is added to the truck. The truck's useful life does not change, but its estimated salvage value increases to $600. The January 2, 19X2, entry to record the new winch is

Truck	700	
Cash		700
To record cost of power winch added to truck.		

Annual depreciation expense of $1,120 for 19X2–19X6 is computed as follows:

Original truck cost	$6,500
Power winch cost	700
Total cost	$7,200
Depreciation recorded in 19X1	1,000
Book value after 19X2 betterment	$6,200
Revised salvage value	600
Revised remaining depreciation	$5,600
Remaining useful life	5 years
Revised periodic depreciation expense for 19X2–19X6	$5,600/5 = $1,120 per year

The December 31, 19X2, entry to record depreciation expense is

Depreciation Expense—Truck	1,120	
Accumulated Depreciation—Truck		1,120
To record 19X2 depreciation on truck.		

Betterments may involve replacing a significant asset component with an improved component. Again, the cost of the new asset component should be added to the asset account and depreciated over the asset's remaining useful life. Further, the cost and accumulated depreciation of the replaced asset component should be removed from the accounts. For example, if a building's gas furnace is replaced by a more efficient model, the cost of the new furnace is added to the Building account, and the cost and applicable depreciation on the old furnace are removed from the accounts. The book value of the old asset component may be difficult to determine if it is not accounted for separately, but a reasonable estimate frequently can be made.

Extraordinary Repairs

Extraordinary repairs are expenditures that extend an asset's expected useful life beyond the original estimate. These capital expenditures are debited to the asset's Accumulated Depreciation account (which increases the asset's book value). We charge Accumulated Depreciation because some of the previous years' depreciation presumably is recovered by the expenditures that extend the asset's useful life. Depreciation entries after an extraordinary repair should lead to the salvage value at the end of the revised (extended) useful life.

For example, assume $12,800 worth of equipment is purchased; it has an estimated useful life of eight years and a salvage value of $800. Annual straight-line depreciation expense is $1,500 [($12,800 − $800)/8]. At the beginning of the seventh year, the equipment is extensively overhauled at a cost of $2,200. The overhaul extends the equipment's useful life an estimated two years beyond the original eight, with no change in the expected salvage value. The entry to record the overhaul is

Accumulated Depreciation—Equipment	2,200	
Cash		2,200
To record cost of equipment overhaul.		

Beginning with the seventh year, annual depreciation expense is $1,300, computed as follows:

Original cost		$12,800
Less: Depreciation for six years	$9,000	
Less: Extraordinary repairs	2,200	6,800
Book value at start of seventh year		$ 6,000
Salvage value		800
Remaining depreciation		$ 5,200
Revised remaining useful life		4 years
Revised periodic depreciation expense for years 7–10	$5,200/4 =	$1,300 per year

The entry to record depreciation expense at the end of the seventh year is

Depreciation Expense—Equipment	1,300	
Accumulated Depreciation—Equipment		1,300
To record depreciation on equipment.		

In practice, the distinctions among additions, betterments, and extraordinary repairs to plant assets often become blurred. Some expenditures, for example, may improve an asset's quality of services *and* extend its useful life. Accountants must use reasonable judgment to identify (and account for) the primary effect of the transaction.

Preparation of accurate financial statements depends on maintaining the proper distinction between capital expenditures and revenue expenditures. A misclassification of expenditures results in incorrect financial statements for several periods. For example, capitalizing a revenue expenditure overstates the current period's income and understates income in subsequent periods as the amount incorrectly capitalized is depreciated. Similarly, if a capital expenditure is immediately expensed, then the current period's income is understated and income is overstated during the subsequent periods when the incorrectly expensed amount should have been depreciated. Exercising care in analyzing expenditures, of course, will minimize these undesirable effects.

KEY POINTS FOR CHAPTER OBJECTIVES

1 Provide the background to understand the various problems related to the measurement of plant assets (pp. 351–52).

- The major types of long-term assets are plant assets, natural resources, and intangible assets.
- The cost (less salvage value) of a long-term asset is periodically charged to expense over its useful life as follows:
  Plant assets: Depreciation
  Natural resources: Depletion
  Intangible assets: Amortization

2 Identify the guidelines relating to the initial measurement of plant assets (pp. 352–55).

- The initial cost of a plant asset is its implied cash price plus the expenditures necessary to prepare it for use.
- A portion of actual interest cost is included in a plant asset's initial cost if a period of time is required to get the asset ready for use.

3 Discuss the nature of the depreciation process (pp. 356–57).

- Depreciation is a cost allocation process; it allocates a plant asset's depreciable cost (acquisition cost less salvage value) in a rational and systematic manner over the asset's estimated useful life.

4 Illustrate four generally accepted methods of computing periodic depreciation (pp. 357–63).

- The most commonly used depreciation methods are straight line, units of production, sum of the years' digits, and double declining balance.
- Revisions of depreciation are accomplished by recalculating depreciation charges for current and subsequent periods.

5 Discuss the distinction between revenue and capital expenditures (pp. 363–66).

- Revenue expenditures, expensed as incurred, include the performance of ordinary repairs and maintenance, the purchase of low-cost items, and the incurrence of unnecessary or unreasonable outlays.
- Capital expenditures, which increase a plant asset's book value, include initial acquisitions, additions, betterments, and extraordinary repairs.

KEY TERMS USED IN THIS CHAPTER

SELF-TEST QUESTIONS FOR REVIEW

(Answers are at the end of this chapter.)

1. The initial cost of a plant asset is equal to the asset's implied cash price and
   (a) The interest paid on any debt incurred to finance the asset's purchase.
   (b) The market value of any noncash assets given up to acquire the plant asset.
   (c) The reasonable and necessary costs incurred to prepare the asset for use.
   (d) The asset's estimated salvage value.
2. Which of the following depreciation methods allocates equal amounts of depreciation to each full period of an asset's useful life?
   (a) Units of production.
   (b) Straight line.
   (c) Double declining balance.
   (d) Sum of the years' digits.
3. On January 1, 19X1, Rio Company purchased a delivery truck for $10,000. The company estimates the truck will be driven 80,000 miles over its eight-year useful life. The estimated salvage value is $2,000. The truck was driven 12,000 miles in 19X1. Which method results in the largest 19X1 depreciation expense?
   (a) Sum of the years' digits.
   (b) Units of production.
   (c) Straight line.
   (d) Double declining balance.
4. Which of the following statements is false?
   (a) A plant asset's useful life is the period from date of acquisition to date of disposal.
   (b) When the estimate of a plant asset's useful life is changed, depreciation amounts recorded in earlier periods are revised to reflect the new useful life.
   (c) Expenditures for extraordinary repairs are debited to an accumulated depreciation account.
   (d) Capitalizing a revenue expenditure in the current period overstates the current period's net income.
5. Which of the following expenditures is expensed when incurred?
   (a) The cost of regular monthly maintenance on a firm's copying machines.
   (b) The cost of a new table and chairs for a firm's conference room.
   (c) Interest paid that relates to the average monthly accumulated construction expenditures on a building under construction.
   (d) The cost of razing an unwanted building on newly purchased land.

DEMONSTRATION PROBLEM FOR REVIEW

Segman Company purchased a machine in 19X1 for $24,300. The machine has an expected useful life of three years and a salvage value of $900. The company expects to use the machine for 1,400 hours the first year, 2,000 hours the second year, and 1,600 hours the third year.

REQUIRED

(a) Assume the machine was purchased on January 2, 19X1. Compute each year's depreciation expense for 19X1–19X3 using each of the following depreciation methods: (1) straight line, (2) units of production (actual usage equals expected usage), (3) sum of the years' digits, and (4) double declining balance.

(b) Assume the machine was purchased June 1, 19X1. Compute each year's depreciation expense for 19X1–19X4 using each of the following depreciation methods: (1) straight line, (2) sum of the years' digits, and (3) double declining balance.

SOLUTION TO DEMONSTRATION PROBLEM

(a) 1. Straight line:

19X1: ($24,300 − $900)/3 = $7,800
19X2: ($24,300 − $900)/3 = $7,800
19X3: ($24,300 − $900)/3 = $7,800

2. Units of production:
   Depreciation per hour = ($24,300 − $900)/5,000 hours = $4.68 per hour
   19X1: 1,400 hours × $4.68 = $6,552
   19X2: 2,000 hours × $4.68 = $9,360
   19X3: 1,600 hours × $4.68 = $7,488
3. Sum of the years' digits:
   SYD = 3 + 2 + 1 = 6
   19X1: ($24,300 − $900) × 3/6 = $11,700
   19X2: ($24,300 − $900) × 2/6 = $7,800
   19X3: ($24,300 − $900) × 1/6 = $3,900
4. Double declining balance:
   Twice straight-line rate = (100%/3) × 2 = $66\frac{2}{3}\%$
   19X1: $24,300 × $66\frac{2}{3}\%$ = $16,200
   19X2: ($24,300 − $16,200) × $66\frac{2}{3}\%$ = $5,400
   19X3: ($24,300 − $21,600) × $66\frac{2}{3}\%$ = $1,800

(b) 1. Straight line (*Refer to calculations in [a]1*)
   19X1: $7,800 × $\frac{7}{12}$ = $4,550
   19X2: $7,800 (full year's depreciation)
   19X3: $7,800 (full year's depreciation)
   19X4: $7,800 × $\frac{5}{12}$ = $3,250
2. Sum of the years' digits: (*Refer to calculations in [a]3*)
   19X1: $11,700 × $\frac{7}{12}$ = $6,825
   19X2: ($11,700 × $\frac{5}{12}$) + ($7,800 × $\frac{7}{12}$) = $9,425
   19X3: ($7,800 × $\frac{5}{12}$) + ($3,900 × $\frac{7}{12}$) = $5,525
   19X4: $3,900 × $\frac{5}{12}$ = $1,625
3. Double declining balance: (*Refer to calculations in [a]4*)
   19X1: $16,200 × $\frac{7}{12}$ = $9,450
   19X2: ($24,300 − $9,450) × $66\frac{2}{3}\%$ = $9,900
   19X3: ($24,300 − $19,350) × $66\frac{2}{3}\%$ = $3,300
   19X4: $750 [This amount reduces the machine's book value to its salvage value of $900 and is the maximum depreciation expense for 19X4. ($24,300 − $22,650) × $66\frac{2}{3}\%$ = $1,100 gives an amount in excess of the maximum $750 depreciation.]

QUESTIONS

10–1 List three major types of long-term assets, present examples of each, and indicate for each type the term that denotes the periodic write-off to expense.

10–2 In what way is land different from other long-term assets?

10–3 Describe the typical sequence of transactions and related problem areas associated with plant assets.

10–4 In general, what amounts constitute the initial cost of plant assets?

10–5 Kallis Company borrowed $3,500,000 to finance the purchase of a new office building, which was ready for immediate use. May Kallis add a portion of the interest cost on the $3,500,000 to the building's cost? Explain.

10–6 Ward Company bought land with a vacant building for $850,000. Ward will use the building in its operations. Must Ward allocate the purchase price between the land and building? Why or why not? Would your answer be different if Ward intends to raze the building and build a new one? Why or why not?

10–7 Explain why the recognition of depreciation expense is necessary to match revenue and expense properly.

10–8 "Depreciation is a process of periodic reductions in a plant asset's book value to correspond with changes in the asset's market value as it ages." Do you agree? Why or why not?

10–9 How is the use of the contra account Accumulated Depreciation justified when recording depreciation?

10–10 How can we justify the use of accelerated depreciation?

10–11 Briefly describe an operational situation that lends itself naturally to each of the following depreciation methods: (a) straight line, (b) units of production, (c) sum of the years' digits, and (d) double declining balance.

10–12 How should we handle a revision of depreciation charges due to a change in an asset's estimated useful life or salvage value? Which periods—past, present, or future—are affected by the revision?

10–13 Explain the benefit of accelerating depreciation for income tax purposes when the total depreciation taken is no more than if straight-line depreciation is used.

10–14 Identify three types of revenue expenditures. What is the proper accounting for revenue expenditures?

10–15 "We cannot properly estimate an asset's useful life without first considering the level of maintenance employed." Do you agree? Why or why not?

10–16 Pierce Company purchased a $20 pencil sharpener with an estimated useful life of 20 years. How should Pierce account for this expenditure?

10–17 Identify three types of capital expenditures. What is the proper accounting for capital expenditures?

10–18 What is the difference between an ordinary repair and an extraordinary repair? What is the rationale for charging extraordinary repairs to accumulated depreciation?

EXERCISES

Initial cost of plant asset

10–19 The following data relate to a firm's purchase of a machine used in the manufacture of its product:

Invoice price	$15,000
Applicable sales tax	735
Cash discount taken for prompt payment	300
Freight paid	315
Cost of insurance coverage on machine while in transit	120
Installation costs	900
Testing and adjusting costs	425
Repair of damages to machine caused by the firm's employees	500
Prepaid maintenance contract for first year of machine's use	250

Compute the initial amount at which the machine should be carried in the firm's accounts.

Capitalization of interest

10–20 On April 1, 19X1, Kansas Company borrowed $900,000 at 9% to finance the construction of a new wing on its headquarters office building. The construction will take several months. Interest of $6,750 is paid monthly. Construction begins April 1, 19X1, and accumulated construction expenditures are $360,000 at April 30, 19X1. Determine how much interest cost should be capitalized for April.

Allocation of package purchase price

10–21 Roycet Company purchased a small established plant from one of its suppliers. The $850,000 purchase price included the land, a building, and factory machinery. Roycet also paid $3,000 in legal fees to negotiate the purchase of the plant. The property tax bill for the plant showed the following assessed values for the items purchased:

Property	Assessed Value
Land	$120,000
Building	435,000
Machinery	195,000
	$750,000

Using the assessed valuations on the property tax bill as a guide, allocate the total purchase price of the plant to the land, building, and machinery accounts in Roycet Company's records.

Depreciation methods

10–22 A delivery truck costing $10,000 is expected to have a $1,200 salvage value at the end of its useful life of four years or 110,000 miles.

(a) Assume the truck was purchased on January 2, 19X1. Compute the depreciation expense for 19X1 using each of the following depreciation methods: (1) straight line, (2) sum of the years' digits, (3) double declining balance, and (4) units of production (assume the truck was driven 30,000 miles in 19X1).

(b) Assume the truck was purchased on April 1, 19X1. Compute the depreciation expense for 19X2 using each of the following depreciation methods: (1) straight line, (2) sum of the years' digits, (3) double declining balance, and (4) units of production (assume the truck was driven 33,000 miles in 19X2).

Depreciation methods

10–23 A machine costing $36,450 was purchased January 2, 19X2. The machine should be obsolete after three years and, therefore, no longer useful to the company. The estimated salvage value is $1,350. Compute the depreciation expense for each year of the machine's useful life using each of the following depreciation methods: (a) straight line, (b) sum of the years' digits, and (c) double declining balance.

Depreciation methods

10–24 Assume the machine from Exercise 10–23 was purchased May 1, 19X2. Compute each year's depreciation expense for 19X2–19X5 using each of the following depreciation methods: (a) straight line, (b) sum of the years' digits, and (c) double declining balance.

Revision of depreciation

3

10–25 On January 2, 19X0, Lowrey, Inc., purchased new equipment for $36,000. The equipment was expected to have a $3,000 salvage value at the end of its estimated six-year useful life. Straight-line depreciation has been recorded. Before adjusting the accounts for 19X4, Lowrey decided that the useful life of the equipment should be extended by two years and the salvage value decreased to $1,500.

(a) Present a general journal entry to record depreciation expense on the equipment for 19X4.

(b) What is the book value of the equipment at the end of 19X4 (that is, after recording the depreciation expense for 19X4)?

Capital expenditure

10–26 On January 3, 19X1, Derby Company purchased a warehouse for $500,000 with an estimated useful life of 25 years and a salvage value of $50,000. Derby uses straight-line depreciation on the warehouse. In early January, 19X8, Derby spent $40,000 for the installation of a fire detection and sprinkler system in the warehouse. The useful life of the warehouse was unchanged, but its estimated salvage value increased to $54,000.

(a) Prepare the general journal entry to record the cost of the fire detection and sprinkler system.

(b) Compute the 19X8 depreciation expense on the warehouse.

(c) Prepare the general journal entry to record the warehouse's 19X8 depreciation expense.

Capital expenditure

10–27 At the end of last year, the balance sheet of Amlin Company shows a building with a cost of $926,000 and an accumulated depreciation of $354,000. The company uses the straight-line method to depreciate the building. When acquired, the building had an estimated 35-year useful life, and its salvage value was $100,000.

Early in January of the current year, Amlin made major structural repairs to the building costing $308,000. Although the capacity of the building was unchanged, the improvements will extend the useful life of the building to an estimated 45 years, rather than the original 35 years. The salvage value remains $100,000.

(a) By the end of last year, how many years had the company depreciated the building?
(b) Present the general journal entry to record the cost of the structural repairs.
(c) Present the general journal entry to record the building's depreciation expense for the current year.

Revenue and capital expenditures

10–28 Grand Company built an addition to its chemical plant. Indicate whether each of the following expenditures related to the addition is a revenue expenditure or a capital expenditure.

(a) Grand's initial application for a building permit was denied by the city as not conforming to environmental standards. Grand disagreed with the decision and spent $6,000 in attorney's fees to convince the city to reverse its position and issue the permit.
(b) Due to unanticipated sandy soil conditions, and upon the advice of construction engineers, Grand spent $30,000 to extend the footings for the addition to a greater depth than originally planned.
(c) Grand spent $5,000 to send each of the addition's subcontractors a side of beef as a thank-you gift for completing the project on schedule.
(d) Grand invited the mayor to a ribbon-cutting ceremony to open the plant addition. Grand spent $40 to purchase the ribbon and scissors.
(e) Grand spent $3,500 to have the company logo sandblasted into the concrete above the entrance to the addition.

PROBLEMS

Initial cost of plant assets

10–29 The items below represent expenditures (or receipts) related to the construction of a new home office for Chavay Company.

Cost of land site, which included an old apartment building appraised at $50,000	$140,000
Legal fees, including fee for title search	3,200
Payment of apartment building mortgage and related interest due at time of sale	6,000
Payment of delinquent property taxes assumed by the purchaser	4,000
Cost of razing the apartment building	17,000
Proceeds from sale of salvaged materials	(2,500)
Grading to establish proper drainage flow on land site	3,800
Architect's fees on new building	180,000
Proceeds from sale of excess dirt (from basement excavation) to owner of adjoining property (dirt was used to fill in a low area on property)	(900)
Payment to building contractor	3,000,000
Interest cost incurred during construction (based on average accumulated construction expenditures)	175,000
Payment of medical bills of employee accidentally injured while inspecting building construction	800
Special assessment for paving city sidewalks (paid to city)	15,000
Cost of paving driveway and parking lot	20,000
Cost of installing lights in parking lot	7,700
Premium for insurance on building during construction	6,400
Cost of open house party to celebrate opening of new building	8,000

REQUIRED
From the given data, compute the proper balances for the Land, Building, and Land Improvements accounts of Chavay Company.

Allocation of package purchase price and depreciation methods

10–30 To expand its business, Beam Company paid $475,000 for most of the property, plant, and equipment of a small trucking company that was going out of business. Before agreeing to the price, Beam hired a consultant for $5,000 to appraise the assets. The appraised values were as follows:

Land	$ 60,000
Building	240,000
Trucks	150,000
Equipment	50,000
	$500,000

Beam issued two checks totaling $480,000 to acquire the assets and pay the consultant on July 1, 19X3. Beam depreciated the assets using the straight-line method on the building, the double declining-balance method on the trucks, and the sum-of-the-years'-digits method on the equipment. Estimated useful lives and salvage values were as follows:

	Useful Life	Salvage Value
Building	20 years	$25,000
Trucks	4 years	12,000
Equipment	7 years	6,000

REQUIRED
(a) Compute the amounts allocated to the various types of plant assets acquired on July 1, 19X3.
(b) Prepare the July 1, 19X3, general journal entries to record the purchase of the assets and the payment to the consultant.
(c) Prepare the December 31, 19X3, general journal entries to record 19X3 depreciation expense on the building, trucks, and equipment.

Depreciation methods

10–31 On January 2, Winkler, Inc., purchased a laser cutting machine to be used in the fabrication of a part for one of its key products. The machine cost $80,000, and its estimated useful life was four years or 625,000 cuttings, after which it could be sold for $5,000.

REQUIRED
Compute the depreciation expense for each year of the machine's useful life under each of the following depreciation methods:
(a) Straight line.
(b) Sum of the years' digits.
(c) Double declining balance.
(d) Units of production. (Assume annual production in cuttings of 125,000; 187,500; 200,000; and 112,500.)

Comprehensive problem

10–32 During the first few days of 19X5, Cyrus Company entered into the following transactions:
1. Purchased a parcel of land with a building on it for $700,000 cash. The building, which will be used in operations, has an estimated useful life of 25 years and a residual value of $50,000. The assessed valuations for property tax purposes show the land at $90,000 and the building at $510,000.
2. Paid $25,200 for the construction of an asphalt parking lot for customers. The parking lot is expected to last 12 years and have no salvage value.
3. Paid $10,000 for the construction of a new entrance to the building.

4. Purchased store equipment, paying the invoice price (including 7% sales tax) of $53,500 in cash. The estimated useful life of the equipment is 9 years, and the salvage value is $6,000.
5. Paid $400 freight on the new store equipment.
6. Paid $1,100 to repair damages to floor caused when the store equipment was accidentally dropped as it was moved into place.
7. Paid $6,800 for four-year insurance policy on building.

REQUIRED

(a) Prepare general journal entries to record the above transactions.

(b) Prepare the December 31, 19X5, general journal entries to record the proper amounts of depreciation expense and insurance expense for the year. Sum-of-the-years'-digits depreciation is used for the equipment, and straight-line depreciation is used for the building and land improvements.

Comprehensive problem

10–33 Morgan Corporation had the following transactions related to its delivery truck:

19X1

Jan. 5 Purchased for $11,220 cash a new truck with an estimated useful life of four years and a salvage value of $1,500.

Feb. 20 Installed a new set of rear-view mirrors at a cost of $40 cash.

June 9 Paid $165 for an engine tune-up, wheel balancing, and a periodic lubrication.

Aug. 2 Paid a $375 repair bill for the uninsured portion of damages to the truck caused by Morgan's own driver.

Dec. 31 Recorded 19X1 depreciation on the truck.

19X2

May 1 Installed a set of parts bins in the truck at a cost of $880 cash. This expenditure was not expected to increase the salvage value of the truck.

Dec. 31 Recorded 19X2 depreciation on the truck.

19X3

July 1 Paid $1,870 for a major engine overhaul on the truck. The overhaul should extend the useful life of the truck an additional two years (to December 31, 19X6) with a salvage value now estimated at $1,000.

Dec. 31 Recorded 19X3 depreciation on the truck.

Morgan's depreciation policies include (1) using straight-line depreciation, (2) recording depreciation to the nearest whole month, and (3) expensing all truck expenditures of $50 or less.

REQUIRED

Present general journal entries to record these transactions.

Revision of depreciation and capital expenditure

10–34 Valley Company uses straight-line depreciation in accounting for its machines. On January 3, 19X1, Valley purchased a new machine for $48,000 cash. The machine's estimated useful life was 12 years with a $6,000 salvage value. In 19X3, the company decided its original useful life estimate should be reduced by two years. Beginning in 19X3, depreciation was based on a 10-year total useful life, and no change was made in the salvage value estimate. On January 2, 19X4, Valley added an automatic guide and a safety shield to the machine at a cost of $3,375 cash. These improvements did not change the machine's useful life, but they did increase the estimated salvage value to $6,400.

REQUIRED

(a) Prepare general journal entries to record (1) the purchase of the machine, (2) 19X1 depreciation expense, (3) 19X2 depreciation expense, (4) 19X3 depreciation expense, (5) the 19X4 improvements, and (6) 19X4 depreciation expense.

(b) Compute the book value of the machine at the end of 19X4 (that is, after recording the depreciation expense for 19X4).

Plant asset errors and corrections

10–35 During 19X2, Kirle, Inc., analyzed several transactions relating to its plant assets as described below.

Jan. 2 Paid for robotic equipment purchased and installed today. The invoice price was $150,000 and Kirle was entitled to a 2% cash discount. Entry:

Robotic Equipment	150,000	
Purchases Discounts		3,000
Cash		147,000

Feb. 6 Paid $600 for regular, annual maintenance on the firm's word processors. Entry:

Office Equipment	600	
Cash		600

June 7 Paid $3,500 to clear timber and brush from a land site purchased a few days earlier. Kirle will build a new plant on this land site. Entry:

Land Clearing Expense	3,500	
Cash		3,500

Aug. 1 Paid $30 for a wastebasket purchased today. The wastebasket has an estimated useful life of 40 years. Entry:

Office Equipment	30	
Cash		30

Dec. 30 Paid $16,170 interest on $147,000 borrowed on January 2, 19X2, to finance the purchase of the robotic equipment. Entry:

Robotic Equipment	16,170	
Cash		16,170

Dec. 31 Recorded the 19X2 straight-line depreciation on the robotic equipment purchased January 2, 19X2. The equipment has a 10-year useful life and a $9,000 expected salvage value. The Robotic Equipment account balance before depreciation was $166,170. Entry:

Depreciation Expense	15,717	
Robotic Equipment		15,717

REQUIRED

(a) Identify any errors made by Kirle, Inc., in analyzing the above transactions.

(b) Prepare journal entries at December 31, 19X2, to correct each error noted in requirement (a). The books have not been closed for 19X2.

ALTERNATE PROBLEMS

Initial cost of plant assets

10–29A The items below represent expenditures (or receipts) related to the construction of a new home office for Sweeney Investment Company.

Cost of land site, which included an abandoned railroad spur	$ 175,000
Legal fees relating to land purchase	4,500
Title insurance premiums on property	1,000
Cost of removing railroad tracks	8,000
Payment of delinquent property taxes assumed by the purchaser	6,000
Proceeds from sale of timber from walnut trees cut down to prepare site for construction	(15,000)
Proceeds from sale of salvaged railroad track	(3,500)
Grading to prepare land site for construction	5,000
Cost of basement excavation (contracted separately)	7,500
Architect's fees on new building	110,000
Payment to building contractor—original contract price	2,300,000
Cost of changes during construction to make building more energy efficient	61,000
Interest cost incurred during construction (based on average accumulated construction expenditures)	125,000
Cost of replacing windows broken by vandals	2,000
Cost of paving driveway and parking lot	25,000
Out-of-court settlement for mud slide onto adjacent property	9,000
Special assessment for paving city sidewalks (paid to city)	21,000
Cost of brick and wrought iron fence installed across front of property	8,600

REQUIRED

From the given data, compute the proper balances for the Land, Building, and Land Improvements accounts of Sweeney Investment Company.

Allocation of package purchase price and depreciation methods

10–30A In an expansion move, Berg Company paid $1,285,000 for most of the property, plant, and equipment of a small manufacturing firm that was going out of business. Before agreeing to the price, Berg hired a consultant for $15,000 to appraise the assets. The appraised values were as follows:

Land	$ 210,000
Building	518,000
Equipment	630,000
Trucks	42,000
	$1,400,000

Berg issued two checks totaling $1,300,000 to acquire the assets and pay the consultant on April 1, 19X4. Berg depreciated the assets using the straight-line method on the building, the sum-of-the-years'-digits method on the equipment, and the double declining-balance method on the trucks. Estimated useful lives and salvage values were as follows:

	Useful Life	Salvage Value
Building	15 years	$31,000
Equipment	9 years	45,000
Trucks	5 years	4,000

REQUIRED
(a) Compute the amounts allocated to the various types of plant assets acquired on April 1, 19X4.
(b) Prepare the April 1, 19X4, general journal entries to record the purchase of the assets and the payment of the consultant.
(c) Prepare the December 31, 19X4, general journal entries to record the 19X4 depreciation expense on the building, equipment, and trucks.

Depreciation methods

10–31A On January 2, 19X1, Gooden Company purchased an electroplating machine to help manufacture a part for one of its key products. The machine cost $72,900 and was estimated to have a useful life of six years or 300,000 platings, after which it could be sold for $7,800.

REQUIRED
(a) Compute each year's depreciation expense for 19X1–19X6 under each of the following depreciation methods:
1. Straight line.
2. Sum of the years' digits.
3. Double declining balance.
4. Units of production. (Assume annual production in platings of 60,000, 75,000, 50,000, 30,000, 45,000, and 40,000.)
(b) Assume the machine was purchased on July 1, 19X1. Compute each year's depreciation expense for 19X1–19X7 under each of the following depreciation methods:
1. Straight line.
2. Sum of the years' digits.
3. Double declining balance.

Comprehensive problem

10–32A During the first few days of 19X6, Walcott Company began business and entered into the following transactions:
1. Purchased a parcel of land with an old building on it for $100,000 cash. The company plans to tear the building down. The assessed valuations for property tax purposes show the land at $72,000 and the building at $18,000.
2. Demolished the old building at a cost of $23,000 cash.
3. Erected a prefabricated, modular shell building on the site in three days at a cost of $170,000 cash. The building has an estimated useful life of 18 years and an estimated salvage value of $8,000.
4. Purchased and installed equipment to enable the company to begin operations. The purchase price plus installation costs totaled $69,000 cash. The company expects to replace the equipment after eight years. Its salvage value is estimated to be $4,200.
5. Constructed a chain-link fence around the property border for security purposes. The fence cost $7,500 and is expected to last 20 years and have no salvage value. Walcott has 30 days to pay the bill for the fence.
6. Paid $10 cash to purchase a padlock for the fence gate. The padlock is expected to last 20 years.
7. Paid $3,600 cash to modify switches on the equipment to conform to federal safety standards. The switches do not extend the useful life of the equipment.

REQUIRED
(a) Prepare general journal entries to record the above transactions.
(b) Prepare the December 31, 19X6, general journal entries to record the proper amounts of depreciation expense for the year (take a full year's depreciation). Sum-of-the-years'-digits depreciation is used for the equipment, and straight-line depreciation is used for the building and land improvements.

Comprehensive problem

10–33A Quick Delivery Service had the following transactions related to its delivery truck:

19X3

Mar.	1	Purchased for $13,150 cash a new delivery truck with an estimated useful life of five years and a $1,400 salvage value.
	2	Paid $250 for painting the company name and logo on the truck.
Dec.	31	Recorded 19X3 depreciation on the truck.

19X4

July	1	Installed air conditioning in the truck at a cost of $860 cash. Although the truck's estimated useful life was not affected, its estimated salvage value was increased by $200.
Sept.	7	Paid $220 for truck tune-up and safety inspection.
Dec.	31	Recorded 19X4 depreciation on the truck.

19X5

May	2	Paid $1,100 for a major overhaul of the truck. The overhaul should extend the truck's useful life one year (to February 28, 19X9), when the revised salvage value should be $1,500.
Sept.	3	Installed a set of front and rear bumper guards at a cost of $70 cash.
Dec.	31	Recorded 19X5 depreciation on the truck.

19X6

Dec.	31	Recorded 19X6 depreciation on the truck.

Quick's depreciation policies include (1) using straight-line depreciation, (2) recording depreciation to the nearest whole month, and (3) expensing all truck expenditures of $75 or less.

REQUIRED

Present general journal entries to record these transactions.

Revision of depreciation and capital expenditure

10–34A Hirsch Company uses straight-line depreciation in accounting for its machines. On January 2, 19X1, Hirsch purchased a new machine for $57,000 cash. The machine's estimated useful life was eight years with a $7,000 salvage value. In 19X6, the company decided its original useful life estimate should be increased by three years. Beginning in 19X6, depreciation was based on an 11-year total useful life, and no change was made in the salvage value estimate. On January 3, 19X7, Hirsch added an automatic cut-off switch and a self-sharpening blade mechanism to the machine at a cost of $5,000 cash. These improvements did not change the machine's useful life, but did increase the estimated salvage value to $7,600.

REQUIRED

(a) Prepare general journal entries to record (1) the purchase of the machine, (2) 19X1 depreciation expense, (3) 19X6 depreciation expense, (4) the 19X7 improvements, and (5) 19X7 depreciation expense.

(b) Compute the book value of the machine at the end of 19X7 (that is, after recording the depreciation expense for 19X7).

Plant asset errors and corrections

10–35A On April 1, 19X1, Image Company purchased a new machine. The machine was shipped F.O.B. shipping point, freight collect. The invoice showed the following information:

Machine	$16,000
6% sales tax	960
Freight charges	240
Total due	$17,200

Image immediately paid the invoice and made the following journal entry:

Apr. 1	Machine	16,000	
	Sales Tax Expense	960	
	Transportation In	240	
	Cash		17,200

Image expects the machine to last eight years and have a salvage value of $2,000. Image uses straight-line depreciation. At year-end, Image made the following journal entry to record depreciation for 19X1 on the machine:

Dec. 31	Depreciation Expense—Machine	2,000	
	Machine		2,000
	$16,000/8 = $2,000		

REQUIRED

(a) Identify any errors made by Image Company in accounting for the machine in 19X1.

(b) Prepare journal entries at December 31, 19X1, to correct the errors noted in requirement (a). The books have not been closed for 19X1.

BUSINESS DECISION PROBLEM

Lyle Waver, president of Waver, Inc., wants you to resolve his dispute with Mia Surchum over the amount of a finder's fee due Surchum. Waver hired Surchum to locate a new plant site to expand the business. By agreement, Surchum's fee was to be 15% of the "cost of the property (excluding the finder's fee) measured according to generally accepted accounting principles."

Surchum located Site 1 and Site 2 for Waver to consider. Each site had a selling price of $175,000, and the geographic locations of both sites were equally acceptable to Waver. Waver employed an engineering firm to conduct the geological tests necessary to determine the relative quality of the two sites for construction. The tests, which cost $10,000 for each site, showed that Site 1 was superior to Site 2.

The owner of Site 1 initially gave Waver 30 days—a reasonable period—to decide whether or not to buy the property. However, Waver procrastinated in contracting the geological tests, and the results were not available by the end of the 30-day period. Waver requested a two-week extension. The Site 1 owner granted Waver the additional two weeks but charged him $5,000 for the extension (which Waver paid). Waver eventually bought Site 1.

Waver sent Surchum a fee of $27,750, which was 15% of a cost computed as follows:

Sales price, Site 1	$175,000
Geological tests, Site 1	10,000
Total	$185,000

Surchum believes she is entitled to $30,000, based on a cost computed as follows:

Sales price, Site 1	$175,000
Geological tests, Site 1	10,000
Geological tests, Site 2	10,000
Fee for time extension	5,000
Total	$200,000

REQUIRED

What fee is Surchum entitled to under the agreement? Explain.

ANSWERS TO SELF-TEST QUESTIONS

1. (c) **2.** (b) **3.** (d) **4.** (b) **5.** (a)

11

PLANT ASSET DISPOSALS, NATURAL RESOURCES, AND INTANGIBLE ASSETS

CHAPTER OBJECTIVES

1. Explain and illustrate the accounting for disposals of plant assets (pp. 381–85).
2. Identify the records used to provide control over plant assets (pp. 386, 387).
3. Discuss the nature of and the accounting for natural resources (pp. 386, 388–90).
4. Discuss the nature of and the accounting for intangible assets (pp. 390–96).
5. Identify and distinguish operating leases and capital leases (pp. 396–98).
6. Illustrate the balance sheet presentation of plant assets, natural resources, and intangible assets (pp. 398–99).

The meek shall inherit the earth,
but **not** *its mineral rights.*

J. PAUL GETTY

The preceding chapter dealt with the measurement and depreciation of plant assets. In this chapter, we examine the remaining plant asset problem area—accounting for their disposal. We then consider the accounting issues related to the acquisition and use of natural resources and intangible assets. Although plant assets, natural resources, and intangible assets are separate identifiable categories of long-term assets, the basic accounting procedures related to each category are similar.

DISPOSALS OF PLANT ASSETS

A firm may dispose of a plant asset in a variety of ways. The asset may be sold, retired, exchanged for a dissimilar asset, or traded in as partial payment for a new, similar asset. The asset's usefulness to the firm may also be ended by an unfavorable and unanticipated event—the asset may be stolen or destroyed by a natural disaster.

Depreciation must extend through an asset's total useful life to a firm. Therefore, depreciation must be recorded up to the disposal date, regardless of the manner of the asset's disposal. Should the disposal date not coincide with the end of an accounting period, a journal entry must record depreciation for a partial period (the period from the date depreciation was last recorded to the disposal date). We illustrate this partial period depreciation in two of our subsequent examples.

We use the following basic data to illustrate disposals of plant assets:

Equipment's original cost	$1,000
Estimated salvage value after five years	100
Annual straight-line depreciation	180
(Unless stated otherwise, assume that depreciation to the date of sale has been recorded.)	

Sale of Plant Assets

Firms normally sell their plant assets once they are no longer efficient or useful. Generally, the asset still has some book value and some sales value in the used market.

Most sales of plant assets involve the following related factors:

1. The sale transaction exchanges a used plant asset for cash. Because the plant asset sold is no longer on hand, the journal entry must remove from both the asset and the accumulated depreciation accounts all amounts related to that asset. These amounts reflect the asset's book value.
2. Because plant assets are most often sold for amounts either greater or less than their book values, gains or losses are produced. Sales proceeds in excess of book values create gains from the sales. Book values in excess of sales proceeds cause losses from the sales.

SOLD FOR MORE THAN BOOK VALUE Assume the equipment is sold for $230 midway through its fifth year. Depreciation was last recorded at the end of the fourth year. The related entries are

Depreciation Expense	90	
Accumulated Depreciation		90
To record depreciation expense for six months.		
Cash	230	
Accumulated Depreciation	810	
Equipment		1,000
Gain on Sale of Plant Assets		40
To record sale of equipment for $230.		

Note that recording depreciation to the date of sale adds $90 to the Accumulated Depreciation account, which totals (4 × $180) + $90 = $810. To reflect the sale properly, we must remove this entire amount of accumulated depreciation from the books. The gain is the proceeds of $230 minus the asset's book value of $190.

SOLD FOR LESS THAN BOOK VALUE Assume the equipment is sold for $30 at the end of the fifth year. The correct entry is

Cash	30	
Loss on Sale of Plant Assets	70	
Accumulated Depreciation	900	
Equipment		1,000
To record sale of equipment for $30.		

The loss equals the book value of $100 minus the sales proceeds of $30. The cash receipt is recorded, and balances from both accounts related to the asset—the asset account and its contra account—are removed from the books.

SOLD FOR BOOK VALUE Assume the equipment is sold for $280 at the end of the fourth year. The proper entry is

Cash	280	
Accumulated Depreciation	720	
Equipment		1,000
To record sale of equipment for $280.		

The equipment's book value at the end of the fourth year is $280 ($1,000 cost − $720 accumulated depreciation). The $280 sales proceeds exactly equal the book value; no gain or loss is involved. Of course, we still remove from the accounts the amounts reflecting the book value of the asset sold.

Retirement of Plant Assets

When a plant asset that has no sales value in the used market is retired from productive service, we record a loss equal to the asset's book value. Assume the equipment in our example is scrapped at the end of five years. The entry to record this event is

Loss on Retirement of Plant Assets	100	
Accumulated Depreciation	900	
Equipment		1,000
To record retirement of equipment.		

Ideally, any plant asset that will be scrapped should have a zero salvage value. Then the asset's book value is zero (accumulated depreciation equals the asset's cost) at the end of its estimated useful life. If the asset is retired on that date, no loss is recorded. The asset's cost and accumulated depreciation, of course, must still be removed from the accounts. To illustrate, let us change our example and assume a zero salvage value for the equipment. Over the equipment's five-year life, we record depreciation totaling $1,000 ($200 per year). The following entry records the equipment's retirement at the end of five years:

Accumulated Depreciation	1,000	
Equipment		1,000
To record retirement of equipment.		

Note, however, that the equipment's book value reaches zero only at the end of five years. Should the equipment be retired before that date, a loss equal to the equipment's book value will be recorded.

Exchange of Dissimilar Plant Assets

A plant asset may be exchanged for a different kind of plant asset. The seller of the new asset establishes a trade-in allowance for the used asset with the balance of the selling price due in cash. The trade-in allowance is not related to the used asset's book value. When it is applied against a legitimate cash selling price, the allowance does represent the used asset's fair value. In some exchanges, the suggested selling price may be higher than the asset's cash selling price; therefore the trade-in allowance is inflated and does not indicate the used asset's fair value.

When dissimilar plant assets are exchanged, the cash equivalent (fair) value of what is given up is not always obvious. Therefore, the new asset should be recorded at the fair value of the assets given up or the fair value of the asset received, whichever is more clearly evident. The used asset's book value, of course, is removed from the accounts. We determine any gain or loss on the transaction by comparing the fair value assigned to the new asset with the total of the used asset's book value plus any cash payment. If the new asset's fair value is larger, a gain is recorded. Should the used asset's book value plus cash paid exceed the new asset's fair value, we reflect a loss.

To illustrate, assume our equipment ($1,000 cost and $100 salvage value) is exchanged for an office desk two-thirds of the way through the second year. The desk's cash selling price is $950. The equipment receives an $800 trade-in allowance, so a $150 cash payment is required. Because equipment depreciation was last recorded at the end of the first year, the correct entries are

Depreciation Expense	120	
Accumulated Depreciation		120
To record depreciation expense for eight months.		
Office Furniture	950	
Accumulated Depreciation	300	
Equipment		1,000
Cash		150
Gain on Exchange of Plant Assets		100
To record trade of equipment for office furniture.		

The $100 gain on the transaction is the excess of the desk's fair value ($950) over the equipment's book value ($700) plus cash paid ($150).

Exchange of Similar Plant Assets

When a plant asset is traded in for a similar new asset, the accounting analysis depends upon whether a loss or a gain is implicit in the transaction. A loss will be reflected in the accounting entry, but a gain will not.

LOSS EXCHANGE Assume that the equipment in our illustration is traded in after three years (accumulated depreciation, $540) on similar new equipment that has a $1,400 cash price. A trade-in allowance of $400 is given, so a $1,000 cash payment must be made. There is a loss inherent in this exchange because the new asset's fair value ($1,400) is less than the sum of the used asset's book value plus the cash payment ($460 + $1,000 = $1,460). We analyze this exchange the same way we analyze exchanges of dissimilar plant assets. The new asset is recorded at its fair value, the used asset's book value is removed from the accounts, the cash payment is shown, and the appropriate loss is recorded. The entry to record the exchange would be:

Equipment (new)	1,400	
Loss on Exchange of Plant Assets	60	
Accumulated Depreciation	540	
Equipment (old)		1,000
Cash		1,000
To record trade of equipment.		

GAIN EXCHANGE If in the preceding exchange the company's trade-in allowance was $600 (rather than $400), then an $800 cash payment is required. Now there is a gain inherent in the exchange because the new asset's fair value ($1,400) exceeds the sum of the used asset's book value and the cash payment ($460 + $800 = $1,260).

Accounting guidelines, however, conclude that the exchange of similar productive assets is not an event that should result in an immediate gain to the company acquiring the new asset.[1] Instead, the new asset is recorded at an amount equal to the sum of the book value of the asset traded in plus any cash paid. The following entry records the exchange:

Equipment (new)	1,260	
Accumulated Depreciation	540	
Equipment (old)		1,000
Cash		800
To record trade of equipment.		

The new equipment is recorded at $1,260—the sum of the $460 book value of the old equipment and the $800 cash payment. This treatment departs from the general rule that newly acquired assets are recorded at their implied cash cost. The new equipment has a cash price of $1,400, but it is recorded at $1,260. Essentially, its book value has been reduced by the $140 gain that is not recognized in the exchange.

TRADE-IN AND TAX REGULATIONS The Internal Revenue Code specifies that any gains or losses on trade-in transactions involving similar assets are not reported

[1] *Opinions of the Accounting Principles Board, No. 29,* "Accounting for Nonmonetary Transactions" (New York: American Institute of Certified Public Accountants, 1973).

in the year of exchange. The treatment of gains parallels the analysis discussed above. Losses, however, are treated as adjustments of the carrying value of the new asset. The above loss exchange illustration would be recorded as follows under the income tax guidelines:

Equipment (new) ($1,400 + $60 loss)	1,460	
Accumulated Depreciation	540	
Equipment (old)		1,000
Cash		1,000
To record trade of equipment.		

This treatment does not recognize the loss in the year of exchange but increases the depreciation available in future years. Generally accepted accounting principles require that significant losses on trade-ins be recognized rather than deferred. Some firms, however, follow the income tax method when losses are immaterial to avoid keeping a separate record for income tax purposes.

Destruction or Theft of Plant Assets

A company's plant assets may be destroyed—by fire, flood, earthquake, tornado, or other natural disaster—or they may be stolen. If an uninsured asset is destroyed or stolen, the firm suffers a loss measured by the asset's book value. Assume the equipment in our example is uninsured and after three years is destroyed by fire. Its book value when destroyed is $460 ($1,000 cost − $540 accumulated depreciation). The proper journal entry is

Fire Loss	460	
Accumulated Depreciation	540	
Equipment		1,000
To record equipment fire loss.		

Business firms normally insure their property to eliminate, or reduce, the risk of loss by destruction or theft. When an insured asset is destroyed or stolen, a claim is filed with the insurance company. The maximum amount recoverable from the insurance company is the asset's fair market value. Because the accounting records reflect a plant asset's book value—not its fair market value—the accounting analysis of the asset's theft or destruction may show a gain or loss, even when the asset is insured. The gain or loss is the difference between the insurance settlement and the asset's book value. To illustrate, assume the equipment from the preceding example is insured and has a fair market value of $500 when destroyed by fire. The $500 insurance claim exceeds the equipment's book value, so we reflect a $40 gain from the insurance settlement in the following entry:

Receivable from Insurance Company	500	
Accumulated Depreciation	540	
Equipment		1,000
Gain on Insurance Settlement		40
To record insurance claim on equipment destroyed by fire.		

Cash is debited and Receivable from Insurance Company is credited when the $500 check settling the claim is received from the insurance company.

CONTROL OF PLANT ASSETS

Firms with a large number of plant assets use a system of control accounts and subsidiary ledgers to account for and manage these assets. The general ledger becomes unwieldy if it contains a separate account for each plant asset. Instead, plant assets are divided into functional groups and only the control accounts (asset and accumulated depreciation accounts) for each functional group appear in the general ledger. The plant asset functional groupings vary somewhat from company to company, but typical control accounts include Land Improvements, Buildings, Furniture and Fixtures, Factory Equipment, and Delivery Equipment.

A subsidiary ledger supports each plant asset control account in the general ledger. The subsidiary ledger contains a detailed record for each specific asset in the control group. The subsidiary ledger may be maintained by a manual or a computerized system. Regardless of the record's form, the following basic data are usually incorporated:

Description
Firm's assigned serial number and accounting classification
Date purchased
Assigned physical location
Insurance coverage
Person accountable
Original cost
Major modifications and repairs
Depreciation method and data
Disposition data (date, price, remarks)

Exhibit 11–1 portrays the relationship between control accounts for a plant asset functional group (Delivery Equipment) and the related subsidiary ledger. Each purchase and sale of delivery equipment is recorded in the control account and on a separate detailed record in the subsidiary ledger. In this illustration, two delivery vans were purchased in 19X1 and they represent the firm's total delivery equipment. Annual depreciation for the individual vans is noted on the subsidiary ledger records and then totaled to get the amount for the general journal entry to record the delivery equipment's annual depreciation. At the end of the accounting period, the control account balances should equal the sum of the balances of the individual assets in the subsidiary ledger (as shown in Exhibit 11–1). The detailed information in the subsidiary ledger is particularly helpful in determining (1) periodic depreciation and (2) a plant asset's book value at time of disposal.

Most firms assign a specific serial number to each plant asset when it is purchased. This is usually done by small decals, stampings, or etchings that are not easily removed or altered. Periodically, the existence and condition of these assets should be verified by a physical count.

NATURAL RESOURCES

Natural resources include such items as timber, petroleum, natural gas, coal, and other mineral deposits mined by the extractive industries. These resources are also known as **wasting assets.** As with plant assets, natural resources are initially accounted for at their cost. When known deposits are purchased, the initial measurement is quite simple. When the natural resource is discovered after

EXHIBIT 11–1

PLANT ASSET CONTROL ACCOUNTS AND SUBSIDIARY LEDGER

General Ledger Control Accounts

Delivery Equipment Account No. 164

Date		Description	Post. Ref.	Debit	Credit	Balance
19X1						
Jan.	1		J1	9,000		9,000
July	1		J8	10,400		19,400

Accumulated Depreciation—Delivery Equipment Account No. 165

Date		Description	Post. Ref.	Debit	Credit	Balance
19X1						
Dec.	31		J14		2,640	2,640

Delivery Equipment Subsidiary Ledger

Item Ford Delivery Van, Blue
Purchased From Mann Ford, Madison
Person Responsible Store 1 Manager
Service Life 5 years
Depreciation:
Method Straight line **Per Year** $1,680 **Per Mo.** $140

Account No. 164
Serial No. V280
Insurance Allgroup, #8750
Location Store 1
Salvage Value $600

Date	Descrip.	Asset			Accumulated Depreciation		
		Dr.	Cr.	Balance	Dr.	Cr.	Balance
19X1							
Jan. 1		9,000		9,000			
Dec. 31						1,680	1,680

Item Ford Delivery Van, Tan
Purchased From Mann Ford, Madison
Person Responsible Store 2 Manager
Service Life 5 years
Depreciation:
Method Straight line **Per Year** $1,920 **Per Mo.** $160

Account No. 164
Serial No. V281
Insurance Allgroup, #8750
Location Store 2
Salvage Value $800

Date	Descrip.	Asset			Accumulated Depreciation		
		Dr.	Cr.	Balance	Dr.	Cr.	Balance
19X1							
July 1		10,400		10,400			
Dec. 31						960	960

extensive exploration, however, determining its initial cost is more difficult. Because not all exploration activities are successful, we must determine which activities were necessary to discover the resource. Expenditures for these activities are capitalized as the cost of the resource, and the remaining amounts are expensed. The cost of developing the site so the natural resource may be extracted is another component of initial cost. Expenditures to remove land overburdens, build access roads, and construct mine entrances illustrate these development costs.

Depletion

The term **depletion** refers to the allocation of the cost of natural resources to the units extracted from the ground or, in the case of timberland, the board feet of timber cut. Accounting for the depletion of natural resources is comparable to units-of-production depreciation of plant assets. The average depletion cost per unit of natural resource is computed as follows:

$$\text{Depletion per Unit} = \frac{\text{Cost of Natural Resource} - \text{Residual Value}}{\text{Estimated Total Units of Resource}}$$

The unit measure used depends on the natural resource; the unit may be barrels, tons, board feet, cubic feet, or some other unit appropriate for the resource. Once depletion per unit is computed, periodic depletion is determined as follows:

$$\text{Periodic Depletion} = \text{Depletion per Unit} \times \text{Units Extracted in Current Period}$$

For example, assume that a company acquires for $520,000 a parcel of land whose major commercial value is a soft coal mine that contains an estimated 800,000 tons of extractable coal. Development costs of $100,000 are incurred to prepare the site for mining coal. The property's estimated residual value is $20,000. The coal deposit's initial cost is $620,000 ($520,000 acquisition cost + $100,000 development costs). We calculate the depletion per ton of mined coal as follows:

$$\frac{\$620{,}000 - \$20{,}000}{800{,}000 \text{ tons}} = \$0.75 \text{ per ton}$$

If, during the first period, 60,000 tons are extracted, that period's depletion charge would be 60,000 × $0.75 = $45,000. We would make the following entry:

Depletion of Coal Deposit	45,000	
Accumulated Depletion		45,000
To record depletion of coal deposit.		

In the balance sheet, Accumulated Depletion is a contra account deducted from the cost of the natural resource as follows:

Coal Deposit (original cost)	$620,000
Less: Accumulated Depletion	45,000
Coal Deposit (book value)	$575,000

This treatment is similar to handling Accumulated Depreciation accounts.

The disposition of the periodic depletion charge depends on whether the extracted units are sold or on hand at the end of the period. The depletion amount of units sold is deducted in the income statement as part of the cost of the resource sold. Units on hand at year-end, however, constitute inventory items, so their depletion charge appears in the balance sheet as part of the inventory cost. In addition to the depletion charge, the costs of extracting and processing the natural resource are part of the inventory cost.

Assume, for example, that $81,000 of extracting and processing costs are incurred the first period to mine the 60,000 tons of coal. The total cost of the 60,000 mined tons is $126,000 ($45,000 depletion + $81,000 extracting and processing costs); the average cost per ton is $2.10 ($126,000/60,000 tons). If 40,000 tons are sold during the first period, $84,000 (40,000 tons × $2.10 per ton) is expensed in the income statement as the cost of coal sold. The year-end balance sheet will show a mined coal inventory of $42,000 (20,000 tons × $2.10 per ton).

Revision of Depletion

Estimating accurately the recoverable units of a natural resource is difficult. Imagine trying to estimate the barrels of oil or the ounces of silver located underground. After extracting activities begin, better information may result in revisions of such estimates. When an estimate of recoverable units changes, a revised depletion per unit is computed. The revised depletion per unit becomes effective in the period the estimate of recoverable units changes—depletion amounts computed in prior periods are not changed. The revised depletion per unit is computed as follows:

$$\text{Revised Depletion per Unit} = \frac{\text{Book Value of Natural Resource} - \text{Residual Value}}{\text{Revised Estimate of Remaining Units of Resource}}$$

To illustrate, assume that at the beginning of the second year of our coal mining example, the estimated total amount of recoverable coal is changed to 560,000 tons. Because 60,000 tons have already been mined, an estimated 500,000 tons remain underground. The coal deposit's book value at the start of the second year is $575,000 (Cost − Accumulated Depletion). Therefore, the revised depletion per ton is $1.11, determined as follows:

$$\frac{\$575{,}000 - \$20{,}000}{500{,}000 \text{ tons}} = \$1.11 \text{ per ton}$$

Depletion for Tax Purposes

The Internal Revenue Code permits a deduction for the depletion of natural resources sold. The depletion deduction may be based on the resource's cost, using the procedures illustrated. Companies mining certain resources, however, may use **percentage depletion** if it gives a larger deduction. Under percentage depletion, the depletion deduction is a specified percentage of the gross revenue from mining activities, with certain limitations. The depletion percentages range from 5% to 22%, depending on the natural resource. Percentage depletion is not limited by the resource's cost and may, over a period of years, result in income tax depletion deductions that exceed total cost. Percentage depletion is a special income tax feature; it is not permitted under generally accepted accounting principles for financial reporting purposes.

On-site Equipment

The extraction of many natural resources requires the construction of *on-site* equipment, such as drilling and pumping devices, crushing equipment, and conveyor systems. Often in remote places, this equipment may be abandoned when the natural resource is exhausted. If the useful life of these assets expires before the resources are exhausted, ordinary depreciation techniques are appropriate. When the reverse is true—natural resources are exhausted, and the asset is abandoned before the end of its physical life—depreciation should be based on the length of the extraction period. Alternatively, we could use the units-of-production approach based on the estimated total resource to be extracted.

For example, assume coal mining equipment was acquired at a cost of $210,000 in our preceding example. The equipment has an estimated $10,000 salvage value after the coal is mined. If the units-of-production method were used, depreciation per ton for the first year would be

$$\frac{\$210,000 - \$10,000}{800,000 \text{ tons}} = \$0.25 \text{ per ton}$$

The first year's depreciation, when 60,000 tons are mined, is 60,000 × $0.25 = $15,000.

Under the units-of-production method, depreciation per unit must be revised if the estimate of extractable resource units changes. The process is similar to the depletion per unit revision discussed earlier. We compute the revised depreciation per unit by dividing the asset's book value (less any salvage value) by the revised remaining resource units. For example, at the beginning of the second year, the coal mining equipment's book value is $195,000 ($210,000 cost − $15,000 accumulated depreciation). If the coal remaining underground is now estimated at 500,000 tons, then depreciation per ton, beginning in the second year, is $0.37, computed as follows:

$$\frac{\$195,000 - \$10,000}{500,000 \text{ tons}} = \$0.37 \text{ per ton}$$

Supplemental Disclosures of Resource Reserves

Many companies in the extractive industries—especially oil- and gas-producing companies—are holding for future operations large discovered and proven reserve fields. Most often these reserves are carried at historical cost figures that may represent only a small fraction of their current values. In such cases, the financial statements may contain supplemental disclosures about reserve quantities and other data useful in estimating reserve values.[2]

INTANGIBLE ASSETS

In accounting, **intangible assets** include certain resources that benefit an enterprise's operations but lack physical substance. Several intangible assets are exclusive rights or privileges obtained from a governmental unit or by legal contract—such as patents, copyrights, franchises, trademarks, and leaseholds. Other intangible assets (1) arise from the creation of a business enterprise—namely, organization costs—or (2) reflect a firm's ability to generate above-normal earnings—that is, goodwill.

The term *intangible asset* is not used with precision in accounting literature. By convention, only certain assets are included in the intangible category. Some resources that lack physical substance—such as prepaid insurance, receivables, and investments—are not classified as intangible assets. Because intangible assets lack physical characteristics, the related accounting procedures may be more subjective and arbitrary than for tangible assets.

[2]Specific disclosure requirements have been established for oil- and gas-producing companies. For details, see *Statement of Financial Accounting Standards No. 69,* "Disclosures about Oil and Gas Producing Activities" (Stamford, CT: Financial Accounting Standards Board, 1982).

Measurement of Intangible Assets

A firm should record intangible assets acquired from outside entities initially at their cost. Similarly, some intangible assets created internally by a firm are measured at their cost. For example, the costs of forming a business are charged to an Organization Costs account, and the costs to secure a trademark—such as attorney's fees, registration fees, and design costs—are charged to a Trademarks account.

Most expenditures related to internally created intangible assets are expensed rather than capitalized. Because these intangibles are not acquired from outside entities, accountants lack an objective measure for the asset account. The accountant responds to uncertainty about an intangible asset's existence, or its proper measure, by expensing the related amounts. This situation is particularly evident in accounting for research and development costs.

RESEARCH AND DEVELOPMENT COSTS American industry annually spends billions of dollars searching for new knowledge and translating this knowledge into new or significantly improved products or processes. These **research and development costs** are important, but usually a significant uncertainty exists about the future benefits of specific research and development efforts. Only a small portion of research and development projects culminate in a new product or process, and even then commercial success is not certain. The market failure rate is high for new products. Uncertain future benefits of research and development costs influenced the Financial Accounting Standards Board's development of the following accounting guideline: *All research and development costs related to a firm's products and its production processes must be expensed when incurred.*[3]

The preceding guideline does not apply to a firm's selling and administrative activities nor to the unique exploration and development efforts of firms in the extractive industries. Also, legal costs of obtaining or defending a patent for a new product or process may be capitalized.

COMPUTER SOFTWARE The widespread use of computers has spawned an entire industry of companies that produce computer software for sale or lease. The industry's unique product and the rapidly changing computer technology caused the Financial Accounting Standards Board to consider specifically how to account for the costs of developing and producing computer software for sale or lease. The board's conclusions illustrate the application of measurement guidelines relating to research and development costs and intangible assets to a particular industry. It assigns the various development and production costs to three different categories, as follows:[4]

1. **Expensed as research and development costs.** All costs incurred to establish the software's technological feasibility are expensed as research and development costs. This covers all costs of those activities—such as planning, designing, coding, and testing—necessary to establish that the software can be produced to achieve the design specifications.

---

[3] *Statement of Financial Accounting Standards No. 2*, "Accounting for Research and Development Costs" (Stamford, CT: Financial Accounting Standards Board, 1974).

[4] *Statement of Financial Accounting Standards No. 86*, "Accounting for the Costs of Computer Software to Be Sold, Leased, or Otherwise Marketed" (Stamford, CT: Financial Accounting Standards Board, 1985).

2. **Capitalized as an intangible asset.** After technological feasibility has been established, the rest of the costs incurred to produce the product masters are capitalized as **computer software production costs,** an intangible asset. Product masters are the completed versions of the software, documentation, and training materials which are then copied to produce the items for sale or lease.
3. **Capitalized as inventory.** The costs incurred to duplicate and physically package the computer software, documentation, and training materials are capitalized in the company's inventory account.

Computer software purchased by a company to use in its selling or administrative activities may be capitalized when it clearly benefits future periods. For example, the purchase cost of a computer software package designed to serve a firm's general management information needs should be capitalized if it will be used several years. Similarly, if a firm develops its own software for internal selling or administrative uses, the development costs may be capitalized when the software will be useful for several periods. Many firms, however, follow a policy of expensing immediately all costs of developing software for internal use.

Amortization of Intangibles

The **amortization** of an intangible asset is the periodic write-off to expense of the asset's cost over the term of its expected useful life. Because salvage values are ordinarily not involved, amortization typically entails (1) determining the asset's cost, (2) estimating the period over which it benefits the firm, and (3) allocating the cost in equal amounts to each accounting period involved. Accounting principles modify this general approach by specifying that the period of amortization for intangibles should not exceed 40 years.[5] As a result, intangibles are treated as if they have a limited life—even though some, such as trademarks, may legally have indefinite lives. Straight-line amortization must be used for intangible assets unless another method is shown to be more appropriate.[6]

The amortization entry debits the appropriate amortization expense account. The entry's credit normally goes directly to the intangible asset account. An accumulated amortization account could be used for the credit, but generally there is no particular benefit to financial statement users from accumulating amortization in a separate contra asset account. In our examples, we will credit the asset account directly for its periodic amortization.

Intangible assets originally deemed to have specific useful lives should be reviewed periodically to determine if their value or their economic lives have decreased. If so, an immediate write-off or a plan of periodic amortization at an increased rate is appropriate.

Patents

A **patent** is an exclusive privilege, granted to an inventor by the federal government for a period of 17 years. The patent gives the patent holder the right to exclude others from making, using, or selling the invention. Patent laws were originated to encourage inventors by protecting them from imitators who might usurp the invention for commercial gain. Just what a patentable idea is has

[5]*Opinions of the Accounting Principles Board, No. 17,* "Accounting for Intangible Assets" (New York: American Institute of Certified Public Accountants, 1970).

[6]Annual amortization of computer software production costs, however, is to be the greater of (1) the straight-line amount or (2) an amount computed using the ratio of the current revenue for the software product to the total current and estimated future revenue for the product.

become quite complex in the modern realm of technical knowledge. Consequently, long periods of patent "searching" and, frequently, successful defense of infringement suits may precede the validation of a patent. Even though patents have a legal life of 17 years, changes in technology or consumer tastes may shorten their economic life. Because of their uncertain value, patents should probably be accounted for conservatively. When patents are purchased some time after having been granted, the buyer enjoys the privilege at most for only the remaining legal life.

To illustrate the accounting for patents, assume that, early in January, a company pays $34,000 legal costs to obtain a patent on a new product. The journal entry is

Patents	34,000	
Cash		34,000
To record legal costs of acquiring patent.		

The company expects the patent to provide benefits for 17 years. The following entry records the first year's straight-line amortization:

Amortization Expense—Patents	2,000	
Patents		2,000
To record patent amortization.		

Because an accumulated amortization account is not used, the asset account balance reflects the asset's book value. The balance sheet presentation at year-end would be

Patents (cost less amortization to date)	$32,000

Copyrights

A **copyright** protects its owner against the unauthorized reproduction of a specific written work or artwork. A copyright lasts for the life of the author plus 50 years. The purchase price of valuable copyrights can be substantial, and proper measurement and amortization are necessary for valid income determination. But even with the related legal fees, the cost of most copyrights is seldom sufficiently material to present accounting problems.

A copyright's legal life exceeds the 40-year maximum amortization period allowed for intangibles. However, copyright costs are generally amortized over periods much shorter than 40 years. Copyright costs should be amortized over the period that the copyrighted work produces revenue—for a proper matching of revenue and expense—which may be only a few years.

Franchises

Franchises most often involve exclusive rights to operate or sell a specific brand of products in a given geographical area. Franchises may be for definite or indefinite periods. Although many franchises are agreements between two private firms, various governmental units award franchises for public utility operations within their legal jurisdictions. The right to operate a Kentucky Fried Chicken restaurant or to sell Midas Mufflers in a specific area illustrates franchise agreements in the private sector.

Some franchise agreements require a substantial initial payment by the party acquiring the franchise. This amount should be debited to the intangible asset account Franchise and amortized on a straight-line basis over the franchise period or 40 years, whichever is shorter.

TRADEMARKS: PINK IS TAKEN BUT A FEW HUES ARE STILL LEFT

Companies seeking an edge in marketing their products have a new design element they can trademark: color.

Owens-Corning Fiberglas Corp., the maker of Fiberglas insulation, recently won an important trademark ruling that gives the company exclusive use of the color pink for home insulation. Trademarks—which can consist of a symbol, a word, a design, or anything else that distinguishes a product from the competition—had previously been denied when color was the sole basis for a claim.

Owens-Corning's five-year battle to obtain the ruling was difficult, and a rush of bids to trademark colors isn't likely. But the decision does reflect a gradual evolution toward more permissive trademarking. In past years, for example, shapes of bottles, stripes on running shoes and the shape and color of drug capsules have all been granted registration as trademarks.

Now that the U.S. Patent and Trademark Office has outgrown its "abhorrence of granting color trademarks," says Ken Umans, a trademark attorney, more companies will likely become aware of that evolution and its importance to their marketing strategies.

"Companies should be talking to their advertising agencies and discussing how to protect trade dress"—the combination of elements that make up a package—"even before the product is introduced," he says.

A "Muddied Area"

Color has always been an important marketing tool. "It's the first thing that grabs attention," says Charles Biondo, a New York package designer. But determining why consumers take to certain colors is difficult, says Everett R. Call, executive officer of Color Marketing Group, a Washington, D.C., marketing association of some 900 members concerned with color. Color psychology is a "muddied area with no answers," he says.

Today, the tremendous number of products on store shelves makes color increasingly important, says Richard Gerstman, a partner in the New York design firm of Gerstman & Meyers Inc. For that reason, he often recommends the broad use of a color in a product line to attract consumers. He says the Owens-Corning decision will encourage more consistent use of colors in package designs.

Owens-Corning tried to register pink as a trademark in 1980, after learning that a competitor was planning to introduce pink home insulation. "We didn't want to lose our competitive edge," says Joe Doherty, vice president for marketing communica-

Trademarks and Trade Names

Trademarks and **trade names** represent the exclusive and continuing right to use certain terms, names, or symbols, usually to identify a brand or family of products. An original trademark or trade name can be registered with the federal government at nominal cost. A company may spend considerable time and money to determine an appropriate name or symbol for a product. Also, the purchase of well-known, and thus valuable, trademarks or trade names may involve substantial amounts of funds. When the cost of a trademark or trade name is material, the amount is debited to an appropriate intangible asset account—Trademarks, for example—and amortized over the period of expected benefit (not exceeding 40 years).

Organization Costs

Expenditures incurred in launching a business (usually a corporation) are called **organization costs.** These expenditures, which may include attorney's fees, fees paid to the state, and other costs related to preparation for operations, are debited to the intangible asset account Organization Costs. Theoretically, these expenditures benefit the firm throughout its operating life, but all intangibles must be amortized over 40 years or less. Most firms amortize organization costs over a five- to 10-year period. Income tax guidelines reinforce this practice by permitting

tions. The Patent Office's Trademark Trial and Appeal Board decided that color per se was registrable as a trademark. But it withheld registration from Owens-Corning, stating that the company hadn't proved that pink was associated with the product in the minds of consumers.

Owens-Corning spent the next five years presenting evidence to the U.S. Court of Appeals to prove that when consumers think of pink insulation they think of Owens-Corning.

"Functional" Colors

"We've been making pink insulation since 1956," says Mr. Doherty. The color was originally chosen to distinguish a new, easier-to-handle insulation from an older product in light yellow, the natural color of glass fiber. So far as anyone can determine, pink was selected for no particular reason. That circumstance became important in the case because "functional" colors—such as green for a mint mouthwash—can't be trademarked.

Owens-Corning has long encouraged homeowners to "plant pink" insulation in their attics, even using a pink spokesman—the Pink Panther cartoon character—to get the message across. Consumer surveys helped the company show that its advertising over the years succeeded in identifying pink with its product.

Lawyers say trademark applicants must be prepared to make strong cases to register a color. But some companies think the Owens-Corning decision may aid their own efforts to trademark colors. Deere & Co., makers of green John Deere farm equipment, failed in its attempt to trademark green. But the company recently managed to register the yellow stripe on a green background that adorns its tractor hoods, and it has applied to trademark green machines with yellow tires.

James Fulton, a consultant design director for Owens-Corning, thinks the trademark office's decision will eventually prompt many companies to protect their product colors.

"Conventional wisdom was that there is no way to protect color," he says. But now that Owens-Corning has won its argument, he adds, designers should realize that color "can be a major advantage in making a company's product unique."

From Linda Lehrer, "Pink Is Taken; But a Few Hues Are Still Left," *The Wall Street Journal*, January 14, 1986, p. 35. Reprinted by permission of *The Wall Street Journal*,

the amortization of organization costs for tax purposes over a period of at least five years.

Goodwill

Goodwill is the value derived from a firm's ability to earn more than a normal rate of return on its specific, identifiable net assets. A firm's **net assets** are its assets minus its liabilities. The measurement of goodwill is complex, because it can stem from any factor that can make income rates high relative to investment. Examples of such factors include exceptional customer relations, advantageous location, operating efficiency, superior personnel relations, favorable financial sources, and even monopolistic position. Furthermore, goodwill cannot be severed from a firm and sold separately. Because measuring goodwill is difficult, a firm records it in the accounts only when another firm is purchased and the amount paid to acquire it exceeds the recognized value of the identifiable net assets involved. Determining the amount of goodwill often requires complex negotiations, but the agreed-on amount is almost always based on the anticipated above-normal earnings.

Accountants expense immediately all costs associated with the internal development or maintenance of goodwill. This means many firms that have created goodwill through their operations do not reflect it in the accounts because it was not purchased.

To illustrate the concept of goodwill, assume Carley Company is for sale. We know the following information about the company and the industry in which it operates:

Fair market value of Carley Company's identifiable net assets	$2,000,000
Normal rate of return on net assets for industry	× 11%
Normal earnings on $2,000,000 of identifiable net assets	$ 220,000
Average annual earnings for Carley Company (past four years)	286,000
Above-average earnings for Carley Company	$ 66,000

Carley's $66,000 of superior earnings suggests the presence of an asset—not specifically identifiable—that helps generate these excess earnings. That asset is goodwill—a combination of factors unique to Carley Company that generates the above-average rate of return on its identifiable net assets. The price paid for Carley will exceed $2,000,000 because the goodwill is also being purchased.

How much should be paid for goodwill? Although above-average earnings in the past are evidence of goodwill, the purchaser is interested in future earnings performance. Goodwill estimates are subject to uncertainty about how long the superior earnings may be sustained. A purchaser may use several methods to estimate a goodwill amount. We illustrate the following two methods:

1. Goodwill may be estimated by capitalizing the superior earnings at the normal rate of return. *Capitalizing earnings* here means dividing earnings by the rate of return; this computation for Carley Company is $66,000/0.11 = $600,000. The $600,000 represents the dollar investment that, at an 11% rate of return, will earn $66,000 each year. However, this approach implies that *every* future year will generate the $66,000 excess earnings—a tenuous assumption in a competitive environment. Sometimes excess earnings are capitalized at an above-normal rate of return in recognition of the greater risk of continued superior earnings. The higher the capitalization rate used, the lower the goodwill estimate.
2. Goodwill may be estimated as some multiple of the superior earnings. Carley's purchaser, for example, may pay five times the above-average earnings for goodwill, or 5 × $66,000 = $330,000.

Of course, the seller also estimates goodwill in determining an overall value for the firm. When the buyer and seller agree on the firm's total purchase price, we can establish the portion assignable to goodwill. The difference between the total purchase price and the fair value of the specific, identifiable net assets is the goodwill measure. For example, if Carley Company is purchased for $2,400,000, $2,000,000 is assigned to the identifiable net assets and $400,000 is assigned to goodwill.

Shown as an intangible asset in the financial statements, goodwill must be amortized over 40 years or less.

LEASES

A firm may rent property for a specified period under a contract called a **lease.** The company acquiring the right to use the property is the **lessee;** the owner of the property is the **lessor.** The rights transferred to the lessee are called a **leasehold.** Examples of leased assets are land, buildings, trucks, factory machinery, office equipment, and automobiles. A lessee's accounting treatment depends on whether a lease is an operating lease or a capital lease.

Operating Lease

The typical rental agreement illustrates an **operating lease**—the lessee pays for the use of an asset for a limited period, and the lessor retains the usual risks and rewards of owning the property. The lessee usually charges each lease payment to rent expense. Sometimes leases extending over long periods require advance payments from the lessee. The lessee debits these payments to a *Leasehold* account, then allocates the amount to rent expense over the period covered by the advance payment. For example, assume Graphic Company makes an $18,000 advance payment for the final year's rent on a 10-year lease of office space. The following entry records the advance payment:

Leasehold	18,000	
Cash		18,000
To record advance lease payment.		

The leasehold amount is an intangible asset. In this illustration, the advance payment relates specifically to year 10, so the $18,000 is classified as an intangible asset for nine years. In year 10, the $18,000 will be expensed.

Expenditures made by a lessee to alter or improve property leased under an operating lease are called **leasehold improvements.** For example, a company may construct a building on leased land or make improvements to a leased building. The improvements or alterations become part of the leased property and revert to the lessor at the end of the lease. Thus, the cost of leasehold improvements should be amortized over the life of the lease or the life of the improvements, whichever is shorter. The classification of leasehold improvements varies—some businesses classify them as intangible assets, whereas others include them in the property, plant, and equipment section of the balance sheet.

To illustrate, assume Graphic Company improves the office space leased for 10 years by adding new interior walls and built-in bookshelves. The improvements were made at the start of the lease, cost $40,000, and have an estimated life of 40 years. Graphic Company records the expenditures for the improvements as follows:

Leasehold Improvements	40,000	
Cash		40,000
To record office improvements.		

Because Graphic Company benefits from these leasehold improvements only for the 10-year lease period, it should amortize the improvements over 10 years. The following entry is made in each of the 10 years:

Amortization Expense—Leasehold Improvements	4,000	
Leasehold Improvements		4,000
To record amortization of leasehold improvements.		

Capital Lease

A **capital lease** transfers to the lessee substantially all of the benefits and risks related to the ownership of the property. A lease meeting at least one of the following criteria is a capital lease.[7]

1. The lease transfers ownership of the property to the lessee by the end of the lease term.
2. The lease contains a bargain purchase option.
3. The lease term is at least 75% of the estimated economic life of the leased property.
4. The present value of the lease payments[8] is at least 90% of the fair value of the leased property.

The economic effect of a capital lease is similar to that of an installment purchase. The lessee accounts for a capital lease by recording the leased property as an asset and establishing a liability for the lease obligation. The present value of the future lease payments determines the dollar amount of the entry. For example, assume Prescott Company leases equipment under a capital lease for 10 years at $40,000 per year, and that the proper initial valuation of this lease for accounting purposes is $226,000. Prescott Company records the capital lease as follows:

Leased Equipment	226,000	
Lease Obligation		226,000
To record 10-year capital lease.		

The leased equipment is depreciated over the period it benefits the lessee and appears among the firm's plant assets in the balance sheet. Part of each lease payment made by the lessee is charged to interest expense and the remainder reduces the lease obligation.

Lessees usually prefer to have their leases classified as operating leases rather than capital leases because it avoids showing a lease obligation among the balance sheet liabilities. Having fewer balance sheet liabilities may make it easier to borrow money from lenders. Structuring a lease so that no liability is recorded (that is, having it qualify as an operating lease) is an example of a practice known as **off-balance-sheet financing.**

We have identified the basic differences between operating and capital leases. Accounting for capital leases is quite complex. Similar complexities face lessors because they may treat some leases as sales or financing transactions rather than as typical rental agreements. These areas, which are beyond the scope of this text, are covered in intermediate accounting texts.

BALANCE SHEET PRESENTATION

Plant assets, natural resources, and intangible assets usually are presented in the balance sheet below the sections for current assets and investments. Exhibit 11–2 shows how these assets may appear on a balance sheet.

---

[7] *Statement of Financial Accounting Standards No. 13,* "Accounting for Leases" (Stamford, CT: Financial Accounting Standards Board, 1976).

[8] Present values are discussed in Appendix B, following Chapter 17.

EXHIBIT 11–2

BALANCE SHEET PRESENTATION
OF PLANT ASSETS, NATURAL RESOURCES, AND INTANGIBLE ASSETS
(IN THOUSANDS OF DOLLARS)

Plant Assets		
Land		$ 800
Buildings	$4,600	
Less: Accumulated Depreciation	1,200	3,400
Fixtures	$ 90	
Less: Accumulated Depreciation	20	70
Equipment	$1,400	
Less: Accumulated Depreciation	300	1,100
Leased Equipment	$ 226	
Less: Accumulated Depreciation	81	145
Total Plant Assets		$5,515
Natural Resources		
Timberland	$ 500	
Less: Accumulated Depletion	200	$ 300
Coal Deposit	$ 900	
Less: Accumulated Depletion	150	750
Total Natural Resources		$1,050
Intangible Assets (cost less amortization to date)		
Patents		$ 200
Goodwill		500
Organization Costs		100
Total Intangible Assets		$ 800

KEY POINTS FOR CHAPTER OBJECTIVES

1 Explain and illustrate the accounting for disposals of plant assets (pp. 381–85).

- When a firm disposes of a plant asset, depreciation must be recorded on the asset up to the disposal date.
- Gains and losses on plant asset dispositions are determined by comparing the assets' book values to their sales proceeds. Gains are not recognized on exchanges of similar productive assets, although losses on such exchanges are recognized.

2 Identify the records used to provide control over plant assets (pp. 386, 387).

- A subsidiary ledger for each plant asset control account contains the detailed information about individual plant assets.

3 Discuss the nature of and the accounting for natural resources (pp. 386, 388–90).

- Natural resources are initially measured at their cost.
- Depletion is the allocation of a natural resource's cost to the resource units as they are mined, cut, or otherwise extracted from their source.
- The units-of-production depreciation method may be appropriate for equipment used exclusively in the mining and extracting of natural resources.

4 Discuss the nature of and the accounting for intangible assets (pp. 390–96).

- Intangible assets acquired from outside entities are initially measured at their cost. Some internally created intangible assets are also measured at their cost (such as organization costs, trademarks, and computer software production costs), but most expenditures related to internally created intangible assets are expensed rather than capitalized.
- Research and development costs related to a firm's products and its production processes are expensed as incurred.
- Amortization is the periodic write-off to expense of an intangible asset's cost over the asset's useful life or 40 years, whichever is shorter.
- Goodwill reflects a firm's ability to generate above-normal earnings. Goodwill may be shown in the accounts only when it has been purchased.

5 Identify and distinguish operating leases and capital leases (pp. 396–98).

- Under an operating lease, the lessor retains the usual risks and rewards of owning the property. The lessee records no liability at the start of the lease. Each lease payment made by the lessee is charged to rent expense (unless it is an advance payment, which is initially capitalized).
- A capital lease transfers most of the usual risks and rewards of property ownership to the lessee. At the inception of the lease, the lessee records an asset (a leased asset) and a liability (a lease obligation). The asset is depreciated over its useful life to the lessee, and the liability is reduced as the periodic lease payments are made.

6 Illustrate the balance sheet presentation of plant assets, natural resources, and intangible assets (pp. 398–99).

- Plant assets, natural resources, and intangible assets usually appear in the balance sheet after current assets and investments.

KEY TERMS USED IN THIS CHAPTER

amortization 392
capital lease 398
computer software production costs 392
copyright 393
depletion 388
franchise 393

goodwill 395
intangible assets 390
lease 396
leasehold 397
leasehold improvement 397
lessee 396
lessor 397
natural resources 386
net assets 395
off-balance-sheet financing 398
operating lease 397
organization costs 394
patent 392
percentage depletion 389
research and development costs 391
trademark 394
trade name 394
wasting assets 386

SELF-TEST QUESTIONS FOR REVIEW

(Answers are at the end of this chapter.)

1. On the first day of the current year, Blakely Company sold equipment for less than its book value. Which of the following is part of the journal entry to record the sale?
   (a) A debit to Equipment.
   (b) A credit to Accumulated Depreciation.
   (c) A credit to Gain on Sale of Plant Assets.
   (d) A debit to Loss on Sale of Plant Assets.
2. Wilde Company maintains factory equipment control accounts (asset and accumulated depreciation accounts) in its general ledger, supported by a factory equipment subsidiary ledger. The annual depreciation expense on a particular piece of equipment is determined by reference to the:
   (a) Factory equipment asset control account in the general ledger.
   (b) Factory equipment accumulated depreciation control account in the general ledger.
   (c) Factory equipment subsidiary ledger.
   (d) General journal entry recording total factory equipment depreciation expense for the year.
3. Accounting for the periodic depletion of natural resources is similar to which depreciation method?
   (a) Straight line.
   (b) Units of production.
   (c) Sum of the years' digits.
   (d) Double declining balance.
4. Certain costs related to a firm's products and its production processes must be expensed when incurred. These costs are:
   (a) Research and development costs.
   (b) Computer software production costs.
   (c) Costs of forming the business (organization costs).
   (d) Legal costs to obtain a patent for a new product.
5. The value derived from a firm's ability to earn more than a normal rate of return on its specific, identifiable net assets is called:
   (a) A franchise.
   (b) Goodwill.
   (c) A patent.
   (d) Organization costs.

DEMONSTRATION PROBLEM FOR REVIEW

Rochelle Company has an office copier that originally cost $10,250 and that has an $800 expected salvage value at the end of an estimated seven-year useful life. Straight-line depreciation on the machine has been recorded for five years; the last depreciation entry was made at the end of the fifth year. Two months into the sixth year, Rochelle disposes of the copier.

REQUIRED

(a) Prepare the journal entry to record depreciation expense to the date of disposal.

(b) Prepare journal entries to record the machine's disposal in the following unrelated situations:

1. Sale of the machine for cash at its book value.
2. Sale of the machine for $3,000 cash.
3. Sale of the machine for $5,000 cash.
4. Exchange of the machine for a new office copier costing $13,000. The trade-in allowance received for the old copier is $4,200. The $8,800 balance is paid in cash. Follow generally accepted accounting principles in recording this transaction.
5. Destruction of the machine by flood. Unfortunately, Rochelle does not carry flood insurance.

SOLUTION TO DEMONSTRATION PROBLEM

(a)

	Debit	Credit
Depreciation Expense	225	
Accumulated Depreciation		225
To record depreciation expense for two months.		

Annual depreciation: $\frac{\$10,250 - \$800}{7} = \$1,350$

Two months' depreciation: $\$1,350 \times \frac{2}{12} = \$225$

(b) 1.

	Debit	Credit
Cash	3,275	
Accumulated Depreciation	6,975	
Office Equipment		10,250
To record sale of machine for book value.		

Cost		$10,250
Accumulated depreciation:		
5 years × $1,350 =	$6,750	
2 months	225	6,975
Book value		$ 3,275

2.

	Debit	Credit
Cash	3,000	
Loss on Sale of Plant Assets	275	
Accumulated Depreciation	6,975	
Office Equipment		10,250
To record sale of machine for $3,000.		

3.

	Debit	Credit
Cash	5,000	
Accumulated Depreciation	6,975	
Office Equipment		10,250
Gain on Sale of Plant Assets		1,725
To record sale of machine for $5,000.		

4.

	Debit	Credit
Office Equipment (new)	12,075	
Accumulated Depreciation	6,975	
Office Equipment (old)		10,250
Cash		8,800
To record trade of office copiers.		

5.

	Debit	Credit
Flood Loss	3,275	
Accumulated Depreciation	6,975	
Office Equipment		10,250
To record flood loss to machine.		

QUESTIONS

11–1 Identify three ways that a firm may dispose of a plant asset.

11–2 What factors determine the gain or loss on the sale of a plant asset?

11–3 Under what condition does a firm show neither a gain nor a loss from (a) the sale of a plant asset and (b) the retirement of a plant asset?

11–4 Bartels Company depreciates a piece of equipment $480 per year on a straight-line basis. After the last depreciation entry on December 31, 19X4, the equipment's book value is $2,000. On July 31, 19X5, the equipment is sold for $2,500 cash. What is the gain (or loss) on the sale of the equipment?

11–5 Caston, Inc., exchanged a used microcomputer with a $900 book value and $600 cash for office furniture having a cash selling price of $1,700. At what amount should Caston record the office furniture? What is the gain (or loss) on the exchange of assets?

11–6 Assume a company exchanged a used microcomputer with a $900 book value and $600 cash for a new microcomputer having a cash selling price of $1,700. At what amount should the company record the new microcomputer? What is the gain (or loss) on the exchange of assets?

11–7 How is the amount of loss determined when an uninsured plant asset is destroyed by flood?

11–8 Blair Company has a Buildings subsidiary ledger. Identify the general ledger control accounts which are supported by this subsidiary ledger.

11–9 Essex, Inc., has a Furniture and Fixtures subsidiary ledger. When Essex purchases furniture, should the purchase be reflected in the general ledger? The subsidiary ledger?

11–10 Define *depletion*. The total depletion charge for a period may not all be expensed in the same period. Explain.

11–11 Ryan Company installed a conveyor system that cost $66,000. The system can only be used in the excavation of gravel at a particular site. Ryan expects to excavate gravel at the site for ten years. Over how many years should the conveyor be depreciated if its physical life is estimated at (a) eight years and (b) twelve years?

11–12 Why is computing the depletion of natural resources similar to computing units-of-production depreciation?

11–13 List and briefly explain the nature of six different types of intangible assets.

11–14 How should a firm account for research and development costs related to its products and production processes?

11–15 Which costs of developing and producing computer software for sale or lease are to be capitalized as an intangible asset?

11–16 Smiley Company purchased for $7,500 computer software that is designed to process the firm's payroll, bill customers, and process customer payments. The software should be useful without significant modification for five years. What is the proper accounting for the software's cost?

11–17 What is the maximum amortization period for an intangible asset?

11–18 Briefly describe two methods for estimating the goodwill amount for a firm that is generating above-average earnings.

11–19 What is the difference between an operating lease and a capital lease?

EXERCISES

Sale of plant asset

11–20 Moon Company has a machine that originally cost $57,000. Depreciation has been recorded for five years using the straight-line method, with a $3,000 estimated salvage value at the end of an expected nine-year life. After recording depreciation at the end of the fifth year, Moon sells the machine. Prepare the journal entry to record the machine's sale for

(a) $31,000 cash.
(b) $27,000 cash.
(c) $22,000 cash.

Disposal of plant asset

11–21 On January 2, 19X1, Daley, Inc., purchased a floor maintenance machine costing $4,200. Daley estimates the machine's useful life at seven years with no salvage value. Straight-line depreciation is recorded each year on December 31. Prepare the journal entry to record the machine's disposal in the following situations:

(a) The machine is scrapped on December 31, 19X7. Assume 19X7 depreciation has been recorded.
(b) The machine is scrapped on June 30, 19X6. Prepare an entry to update depreciation before recording the machine's disposal.
(c) The machine is traded in on a lawn tractor (a dissimilar asset) on December 31, 19X5. The tractor's cash selling price is $2,500. Daley's trade-in allowance is $1,600, and it pays the remaining $900 in cash. Assume 19X5 depreciation has been recorded.

Disposal of plant asset

11–22 Refer to Exercise 11–21. Assume Daley, Inc., had estimated a $420 salvage value for the floor maintenance machine, and all other data remain the same. Prepare the journal entry to record the machine's disposal in the three situations described in Exercise 11–21.

Exchange of plant asset

11–23 Graham Company exchanges used equipment costing $48,000 (on which $32,000 of depreciation has accumulated) for similar new equipment. The new equipment's cash price, with no trade-in, is $55,000.

(a) Following generally accepted accounting principles, prepare the journal entry to record Graham's trade-in transaction when
   1. The equipment's trade-in allowance is $14,000, and the balance is paid in cash.
   2. The equipment's trade-in allowance is $19,000, and the balance is paid in cash.
(b) Following income tax guidelines, prepare the journal entry to record Graham's trade-in transaction when
   1. The equipment's trade-in allowance is $14,000, and the balance is paid in cash.
   2. The equipment's trade-in allowance is $19,000, and the balance is paid in cash.

Exchange of plant asset

11–24 Assume Harkin Company trades a used machine for a new machine with a cash price of $23,000. The old machine originally cost $19,000 and has $14,000 of accumulated depreciation. The seller allows $6,200 as a trade-in for the old machine; Harkin pays the balance in cash. Following generally accepted accounting principles, prepare the journal entry to record Harkin's trade-in transaction assuming

(a) The machines are dissimilar plant assets.
(b) The machines are similar plant assets.

Destruction of plant asset

11–25 A storage building owned by Wand Company was destroyed by flood exactly eight years after its purchase. The building, purchased for $300,000, had an estimated 20-year useful life and a $30,000 salvage value. Straight-line depreciation was up to date when the building was destroyed. Prepare the journal entry to record the destruction of the building assuming

(a) The building was not insured.
(b) The building was insured, and Wand expects a $200,000 insurance settlement.
(c) The building was insured, and Wand expects a $180,000 insurance settlement.

Computation of depletion and depreciation

11–26 Koppa Copper Company recently acquired a parcel of land containing an estimated 750,000 tons of commercial grade copper ore. Koppa paid $6,000,000 for the land and acquired extraction equipment at a cost of $780,000. Although the equipment will be worthless when the ore is depleted, Koppa estimates that the land can be sold for $450,000 after the mining operations are completed.

(a) Compute the proper depletion charge for a period during which 85,000 tons of ore are extracted and sold.

(b) Compute the proper depreciation expense on the extraction equipment, using the units-of-production method, for a period during which 85,000 tons of ore are extracted and sold.

Computation and recording of amortization expense

11–27 For each of the following unrelated situations, calculate the annual amortization expense and present a general journal entry to record the expense. Assume contra accounts are not used for accumulated amortization.

(a) A two-year-old patent was purchased for $630,000. The patent will probably be commercially exploitable for another nine years.

(b) Certain sales counter fixtures, costing $66,000, were constructed and permanently installed in a building leased from another firm. The physical life of the counters was an estimated 20 years. When the counters were installed, the operating lease had 11 years to run and contained no provision for the removal of the fixtures.

(c) A trademark is carried at a cost of $88,000, which represents the out-of-court settlement paid to another firm that has agreed to refrain from using or claiming the trademark or one similar to it. The trademark has an indefinite life.

(d) A patent was acquired on a device designed by a production worker. Although the cost of the patent to date consisted of $28,900 in legal fees for handling the patent application, the patent should be commercially valuable during its entire legal life and is currently worth approximately $272,000.

(e) A franchise granting exclusive distribution rights for a new solar water heater within a four-state area for three years was obtained at a cost of $54,000. Satisfactory sales performance over the three years permits renewal of the franchise for another three years (at an additional cost determined at renewal).

Goodwill estimation

11–28 Noble Company, which is for sale, has identifiable net assets with a fair value of $5,000,000 and no recorded goodwill. Noble's annual net income in recent years has averaged $647,000 in an industry that considers 10% a normal rate of return on net assets.

(a) Compute Noble's above-normal earnings.

(b) Estimate Noble's goodwill amount by capitalizing the above-normal earnings at the normal rate of return on net assets.

(c) How much will the goodwill estimate from part (b) change if the excess earnings are capitalized at 15%?

PROBLEMS

Disposals of plant asset

11–29 Cardex Company has a used executive charter plane that originally cost $610,000. Straight-line depreciation on the plane has been recorded for six years, with a $40,000 expected salvage value at the end of its estimated eight-year useful life. The last depreciation entry was made at the end of the sixth year. Eight months into the seventh year, Cardex disposes of the plane.

REQUIRED

Prepare journal entries to record

(a) Depreciation expense to the date of disposal.

(b) Sale of the plane for cash at its book value.

(c) Sale of the plane for $145,000 cash.

(d) Sale of the plane for $124,000 cash.
(e) Exchange of the plane for a new aircraft costing $640,000. The trade-in allowance received is $150,000, and the balance is paid in cash. Follow generally accepted accounting principles in recording this transaction.
(f) Destruction of the plane in a fire. Cardex expects a $130,000 insurance settlement.
(g) Exchange of the plane for a new yacht costing $640,000. The trade-in allowance received is $150,000, and the balance is paid in cash.

Exchange of plant assets

11–30 On July 1, 19X1, Muir Construction Company purchased a small bulldozer for $14,700. Muir estimates a six-year useful life and a $1,500 salvage value for the bulldozer. On October 1, 19X1, the company purchased a flatbed truck for $12,200. Muir estimates the truck's useful life at seven years and its salvage value at $1,000. Muir uses straight-line depreciation for all plant assets and records depreciation on December 31 each year.

On March 31, 19X6, Muir traded in the truck for a new truck. The manufacturer's "sticker" price on the new truck was $15,000, but the dealer's cash price was $14,400. After the dealer deducted the allowance for the old truck, Muir paid $9,800 cash for the new truck. Muir estimates the new truck will last five years and have a $1,200 salvage value.

On June 30, 19X6, Muir exchanged the bulldozer for a new bulldozer with a cash price of $18,000. Muir's trade-in allowance for the old bulldozer was $5,000, and the company paid $13,000 cash. The new bulldozer's estimated useful life is six years; its estimated salvage value is $1,700.

REQUIRED

Following generally accepted accounting principles, prepare journal entries to record the following events in 19X6:

Mar. 31	Update depreciation on the truck.
31	Exchange of trucks.
June 30	Update depreciation on the bulldozer.
30	Exchange of bulldozers.
Dec. 31	Depreciation for 19X6 on new truck and new bulldozer.

Depletion accounting

11–31 Pike Gravel, Inc., has just purchased a site containing an estimated 1,600,000 tons of high-grade aggregate rock. Pike makes the following expenditures before starting production:

Purchase price of property	$2,140,000
Legal fees to acquire title and secure proper zoning for operations	7,000
Removal of overburden and grading for drainage	53,000
Construction of on-site crushing, washing, and loading facilities	500,000

Once the rock deposits are no longer commercially valuable, Pike estimates the land will sell for $200,000. Certain parts of the on-site crushing, washing, and loading facilities have an estimated salvage value of $20,000 when operations are terminated.

REQUIRED

(a) Compute the total depletion charge for the first year, during which 200,000 tons of rock are extracted from the quarry.
(b) Compute the amount of depreciation on the crushing, washing, and loading facilities during the first year, in which 200,000 tons of rock are extracted. Use the units-of-production depreciation method.
(c) Compute the cost of a 25,000-ton inventory of rock at the end of the first year for which all extraction and processing costs except depletion and depreciation of crushing, washing, and loading facilities average $0.60 per ton.

(d) At the beginning of the second year, Pike estimates that only 1,000,000 tons of rock remain in the quarry. Compute the revised (1) depletion per ton of rock and (2) depreciation per ton of rock.

Accounting for intangible assets

11–32 Bluff Company owns several retail outlets. In 19X1, it expands operations and enters into the following transactions:

Jan. 2 Signed an eight-year operating lease for additional retail space for an annual rent of $27,600. Paid the first and last years' rent in advance on this date. (*Hint:* Debit the first year's rent to Prepaid Rent.)

3 Paid $12,000 to contractor for installation of new oak floor in leased facility. The oak floor's life is an estimated 50 years with no salvage value.

Mar. 1 Paid $24,000 to obtain an exclusive area franchise for five years to distribute a new line of perfume.

July 1 Paid $46,000 to LogoLab, Inc., for designing a trademark for a new line of gourmet chocolates that Bluff will distribute nationally. Bluff will use the trademark for as long as the firm (and the chocolates) remain in business. Bluff expects to be in business for at least another 50 years.

1 Paid $30,000 for advertisement in a national magazine (June issue) introducing the new line of chocolates and the trademark.

REQUIRED

(a) Prepare general journal entries to record these transactions.

(b) Prepare the necessary adjusting entries on December 31, 19X1, for these transactions. Bluff makes adjusting entries once a year. Bluff uses straight-line amortization but does not use contra accounts when amortizing intangible assets.

Accounting for plant and intangible assets

11–33 Selected 19X6 transactions and events for the Kramer Company are given below:

Jan. 2 Paid $22,000 for a four-year franchise to distribute a product line locally.

Mar. 31 Discovered a computer was stolen from the accountant's office. Kramer carries no theft insurance. The computer cost $9,500 when purchased on January 2, 19X3, and was being depreciated over six years with a $500 salvage value. Straight-line depreciation was last recorded on December 31, 19X5.

Apr. 1 Entered into a nine-year operating lease for additional warehouse space. Paid in advance the final month's rent of $2,100 when the lease was signed.

June 30 Discarded office equipment and realized no salvage value. A $400 salvage value, after a six-year useful life, had been estimated when the equipment was acquired for $4,000 on July 1, 19X0. Straight-line depreciation was last recorded on December 31, 19X5.

Aug. 1 Paid a $3,000 cash bonus to employee for designing and developing a new product.

Sept. 1 Paid a $10,800 legal services fee to obtain a new product patent, which was granted today. Kramer estimates the patent will provide effective protection from competitors for ten years.

Oct. 1 Constructed storage bins at a cost of $15,300 in the warehouse space leased April 1. The physical life of the storage bins is an estimated 15 years. The lease contains no provision for the removal of the bins; the lessor takes control of the bins at the end of the lease.

Nov. 1 Exchanged a used forklift truck for a similar new truck. The used truck cost $7,200 and had accumulated depreciation of $6,000 (through October 31, 19X6). The new truck's cash price was $9,000. Kramer's trade-in allowance was $1,500, and the company paid $7,500 cash. Kramer estimates a ten-year useful life and a $600 salvage value for the new truck.

REQUIRED

(a) Prepare general journal entries to record these transactions.

(b) Prepare the December 31, 19X6, general journal entries to record the proper amounts of depreciation and amortization expense for assets acquired during the year. Kramer uses straight-line depreciation and amortization but does not use contra accounts when amortizing intangible assets.

Preparation of balance sheet

11–34 Block Company's December 31, 19X4, post-closing trial balance contains the following normal balances:

Cash	$ 4,000
Accounts Payable	8,000
Stone Quarry	180,000
Building	195,000
Notes Payable (long term)	350,000
H. Block, Capital	430,000
Accumulated Depreciation—Equipment	80,000
Leasehold	7,000
Accumulated Depletion—Stone Quarry	64,000
Land	30,000
Accounts Receivable	9,000
Timberland	310,000
Accumulated Depreciation—Building	60,000
Wages Payable	3,000
Patent (net of amortization)	52,000
Accumulated Depletion—Timberland	90,000
Notes Payable (short term)	62,000
Inventory	95,000
Equipment	265,000

REQUIRED

Prepare a December 31, 19X4, classified balance sheet for Block Company.

ALTERNATE PROBLEMS

Disposals of plant asset

11–29A Pollard Company has a used delivery truck that originally cost $11,700. Straight-line depreciation on the truck has been recorded for three years, with a $900 expected salvage value at the end of its estimated six-year useful life. The last depreciation entry was made at the end of the third year. Four months into the fourth year, Pollard disposes of the truck.

REQUIRED

Prepare journal entries to record

(a) Depreciation expense to the date of disposal.

(b) Sale of the truck for cash at its book value.

(c) Sale of the truck for $6,400 cash.

(d) Sale of the truck for $5,300 cash.

(e) Exchange of the truck for a new truck costing $15,100. The trade-in allowance received is $5,200, and the balance is paid in cash. Follow generally accepted accounting principles in recording this transaction.

(f) Theft of the truck. Pollard carries no insurance for theft.

(g) Exchange of the truck for golf carts costing $15,100 for the company golf course. The trade-in allowance received is $6,000, and the balance is paid in cash.

Exchange of plant assets

11–30A On April 1, 19X1, Olin Excavators, Inc., purchased a tractor for $32,700. Olin estimates a nine-year useful life and a $3,000 salvage value for the tractor. On September 1, 19X1, the company paid $27,500 for a new trenching machine. Olin estimates the machine's useful life at five years and its salvage value at $2,000. Olin uses straight-line depreciation for all plant assets and records depreciation on December 31 each year.

On June 30, 19X6, Olin traded in the tractor for a new tractor with a cash price of $36,400. The dealer allowed a trade-in value of $13,400 for the old tractor, and Olin paid the remaining $23,000 in cash. Olin estimates the new tractor will last seven years and have a $3,500 salvage value.

On August 31, 19X6, Olin exchanged the trenching machine for a new trenching machine with a cash price of $30,000. Olin's trade-in allowance for the old trenching machine was $3,600, and the company paid $26,400 cash. The new machine's estimated useful life is six years; its estimated salvage value is $2,300.

REQUIRED

Following generally accepted accounting principles, prepare journal entries to record the following events in 19X6:

June 30 Update depreciation on the tractor.
30 Exchange of tractors.
Aug. 31 Update depreciation on the trenching machine.
31 Exchange of trenching machines.
Dec. 31 Depreciation for 19X6 on new tractor and new trenching machine.

Depletion accounting

11–31A Pleasant Mining Company has just purchased a site containing an estimated 1,500,000 tons of coal. Pleasant makes the following expenditures before starting operations:

Cost of land survey	$ 16,000
Purchase price of property	1,690,000
Legal fees to acquire title and secure proper zoning for operations	14,000
Construction of on-site conveyance and loading facilities	250,000

After all the coal has been extracted, Pleasant expects to sell the property for $145,000 and certain parts of the conveyance and loading facilities for $25,000.

REQUIRED

(a) Compute the total depletion charge for the first year, during which 140,000 tons of coal are extracted from the mine.
(b) Compute the amount of depreciation on the conveyance and loading facilities during the first year, in which 140,000 tons of coal are extracted. Use the units-of-production depreciation method.
(c) Compute the cost of a 30,000-ton inventory of coal at the end of the first year for which all extraction and processing costs except depletion and depreciation of conveyance and loading facilities average $1.20 per ton.
(d) At the beginning of the second year, Pleasant estimates that only 1,200,000 tons of coal remain underground. Compute the revised (1) depletion per ton of coal and (2) depreciation per ton of coal.

Accounting for intangible assets

11–32A During the first few days of 19X2, Steck Company began business and entered into the following transactions:

1. Paid $9,600 in attorney's fees and other costs related to the organization of the company.

2. Purchased an existing patent on a product for $84,000. The patent's legal protection and useful life cover 12 more years.
3. Entered into a six-year operating lease for additional office space. Paid in advance the final month's rent of $1,350 when the lease was signed.
4. Paid $7,200 to have recessed lighting installed in the leased office space. The lighting is estimated to last 20 years with no salvage value.
5. Paid $100,000 for a 20-year franchise to distribute a product line in a three-state region.
6. Spent $16,000 on the initial research for a promising new product to complement the patented product.
7. Purchased a computer software package to aid the controller's financial planning and budgeting activities. The software cost $4,400, should be useful without significant modification for four years, and has no salvage value.

REQUIRED

(a) Prepare general journal entries to record these transactions.
(b) Prepare the December 31, 19X2, general journal entries to record the proper amounts of amortization expense for the year. Organization costs are amortized over five years. Steck uses straight-line amortization but does not use contra accounts when amortizing intangible assets.

Accounting for plant and intangible assets

11–33A Selected 19X4 transactions of Worldly Publishers, Inc., are given below:

Jan. 2 Paid $50,000 to purchase copyrights to a series of romantic novels. The copyrights expire in 40 years, although Worldly expects sales of the novels to stop after 10 years.

Mar. 1 Discovered a satellite dish antenna was destroyed by lightning. The loss is covered by insurance and a claim is filed today. The antenna cost $6,880 when installed on July 1, 19X2, and was being depreciated over 12 years with a $400 salvage value. Straight-line depreciation was last recorded on December 31, 19X3. Worldly expects to receive an insurance settlement of $6,000.

Apr. 1 Leased equipment under an eight-year capital lease. The equipment will be returned to the lessor at the end of the lease. The proper initial valuation of this lease is $99,360.

July 1 Paid $120,000 to acquire a patent on a new publishing process. The patent has a remaining legal life of 15 years. Worldly estimates the new process will be utilized for 6 years before it becomes obsolete.

Oct. 1 Exchanged old printing equipment for new (similar) printing equipment. The old equipment cost $42,500 and had accumulated depreciation of $32,000 (through September 30, 19X4). The new equipment's cash price was $63,000. Worldly's trade-in allowance was $9,000 and the company paid $54,000 cash. Worldly estimates an eight-year useful life and a $7,000 salvage value for the new equipment.

Nov. 1 Paid $36,000 to obtain a four-year franchise to sell a new series of computerized do-it-yourself manuals.

REQUIRED

(a) Prepare general journal entries to record these transactions.
(b) Prepare the December 31, 19X4, general journal entries to record the proper amounts of depreciation and amortization expense for assets acquired during the year. Worldly uses straight-line depreciation and amortization but does not use contra accounts when amortizing intangible assets.

Preparation of balance sheet

11–34A Breen Company's December 31, 19X5, post-closing trial balance contains the following normal account balances:

Interest Payable	$ 24,000
Accumulated Depreciation—Equipment	130,000
Inventory	140,000
Organization Costs (net of amortization)	15,000
Copper Deposit	800,000
Notes Payable (short term)	80,000
Cash	3,000
Accumulated Depletion—Coal Deposit	125,000
Building	280,000
Accounts Receivable	19,000
Patent (net of amortization)	50,000
Equipment	265,000
C. Breen, Capital	737,000
Accumulated Depreciation—Building	70,000
Accounts Payable	14,000
Leased Equipment	140,000
Accumulated Depletion—Copper Deposit	320,000
Land	175,000
Notes Payable (long term)	822,000
Coal Deposit	600,000
Accumulated Depreciation—Leased Equipment	21,000
Lease Obligation (long term)	128,000

REQUIRED
Prepare a December 31, 19X5, classified balance sheet for Breen Company.

BUSINESS DECISION PROBLEM

Tim Garcia wants to buy Marin Company from Amy Marin. His first offer was rejected, and he seeks your advice as he prepares another offer. Your discussions with Garcia and an analysis of related data disclose the following:

1. Garcia's first offer of $1,400,000 was equal to the fair value of Marin Company's identifiable net assets. Garcia and Marin agree this amount represents the fair value of these net assets.
2. Marin rejected the first offer because she believes her company has exceptionally good supplier, customer, and employee relationships. These attributes do not appear on the balance sheet, but they are a component of the company's overall value and should be reflected in the purchase price.
3. Garcia recognizes Marin Company's favorable relationships. However, he is uncertain how long they will last when Marin leaves the company after the sale.
4. Garcia is willing to incorporate a goodwill amount in his offer and accepts a "capitalization of excess earnings" approach to estimating goodwill. In light of his uncertainty about the long-run continuation of superior earnings, however, the capitalization rate must be twice the average rate of return for the industry.
5. The industry's average rate of return on identifiable net assets is 13%.
6. Over the past several years, Marin Company's net income has averaged $271,700.

REQUIRED
Estimate a goodwill amount for Marin Company, and recommend a purchase price that Tim Garcia should offer Amy Marin.

ANSWERS TO SELF-TEST QUESTIONS

1. (d) **2.** (c) **3.** (b) **4.** (a) **5.** (b)

12

CURRENT LIABILITIES AND PAYROLL ACCOUNTING

CHAPTER OBJECTIVES

1. Define and illustrate the most common types of current and contingent liabilities (pp. 413–19).
2. Explain and illustrate the deductions made in computing net pay and the items included in employers' payroll taxes (pp. 419–29).
3. Describe and illustrate the records required in payroll accounting (pp. 429–33).

Creditors have better memories than debtors.

BENJAMIN FRANKLIN

Liabilities, one of the three elements in the accounting equation, generally represent a firm's obligations to nonowners. Total liabilities are divided into two subcategories—current liabilities and long-term liabilities. In this chapter, we focus on current liabilities, and because several liabilities are associated with a firm's payroll, we will examine payroll accounting procedures and requirements in some depth.

THE NATURE OF LIABILITIES

Liabilities are obligations resulting from past transactions or events that require the firm to pay money, provide goods, or perform services in the future. The existence of a past transaction or event is an important element in the definition of liabilities. For example, a purchase commitment is actually an agreement between a buyer and a seller to enter into a *future* transaction. The performance of the seller that will create the obligation on the part of the buyer is, at this point, a future transaction; hence, a purchase commitment is not a liability. Another example is a company's long-term salary contract with an executive. When the agreement is signed, each party is committed to perform in the future—the executive to render services and the company to pay for those services. The company does not record a liability when the contract is signed, because at this point the executive has not yet rendered any services.

Although they involve definite future cash payments, the foregoing examples are not reported as liabilities because they are related to future transactions. However, significant purchase commitments and executive compensation commitments should be disclosed in footnotes to the balance sheet.

In general, items shown as liabilities are often not legally due and payable on the balance sheet date. For example, the routine accrual of wages expense incurred but not paid during the period results in a credit balance account titled Wages Payable. In most cases, accrued wages are not legally due until several days after the balance sheet date. In the case of other accrued expenses—such as property taxes and executive bonuses—payment may not be legally due until months after the balance sheet date. Bonds payable, although shown as liabilities, may not be actually payable for several decades. These items are all reported as liabilities, however, because they are obligations resulting from past transactions that will be settled as the business continues to operate.

The determination of liabilities is basic to accounting properly for a firm's operations. For example, if a liability is omitted, then either an asset or an expense has been omitted also. If expense is involved, then income and owners' equity are misstated as well. Thus, the balance sheet or the income statement, or both, may be affected if liabilities are not reported correctly.

Most liabilities are satisfied by the eventual remittance of cash. Some may require a firm to furnish goods—for instance, a publisher obligated to provide issues of a magazine to customers who have subscribed in advance. Other liabilities may be obligations to provide services—for example, product warranties and maintenance contracts that accompany a new appliance or automobile.

Definition of Current Liabilities

For many years, **current liabilities** were considered obligations to be paid during the coming year—a simple and useful rule. The rule was subsequently made more flexible and broader in scope. The present version designates current liabilities as all obligations that will require within the coming year or the operating cycle, whichever is longer, (1) the use of existing current assets or (2) the creation of other current liabilities. We contrast the two versions of the rule by noting, for example, that a one-year note payable satisfied by the issuance of another short-term note is a current liability only under the later version of the rule. Also, the newer version has significant effects on firms in industries (for example, distilling and lumber) with operating cycles longer than one year.

Obligations that do not meet these guidelines are long-term liabilities. Two examples are mortgage notes payable and bonds payable, which we examine in Chapter 17.

Measurement of Current Liabilities

Generally speaking, current liabilities should be measured and shown in the balance sheet at the money amount necessary to satisfy the obligation. Of course, when future provision of services or goods is involved, the related dollar amount is only an estimate of the costs. The liability for product warranties, for example, may have to be estimated. Interest included in the face amount of a note payable is subtracted from the face amount when presenting the liability in the balance sheet. For example, if a company discounts its own note at the bank, the Discount on Notes Payable arising from this transaction is a contra account to the Notes Payable account.

EXAMPLES OF CURRENT LIABILITIES

In this section, we review the common types of current liabilities. Although not exhaustive, these concepts should enable you to look deeper into the accounting problems and techniques involved.

Trade Accounts and Notes Payable

In a balance sheet listing of current liabilities, amounts due to short-term creditors on open accounts or notes payable are commonly shown first. Most of the accounting procedures for accounts and notes payable are fairly routine and have been discussed in previous chapters. However, we should carefully account for transactions that occur shortly before and after the end of the accounting period. At the end of the period, recently received inventory items must be reflected as accounts payable, if unpaid, and as purchases of the period. Likewise, items that the company owns and for which a payable has been recorded must be included in inventory whether or not the items have been received. In other words, we need a proper "cut-off" of purchases, payables, and inventory for valid income determination and presentation of financial position.

Dividends Payable

Ordinary dividends are distributions of corporate earnings to stockholders. We discuss many of the accounting problems related to dividends in Chapter 16. Because the corporate board of directors determines the timing and amounts of dividends, they do not accrue as does interest expense. Instead, dividends are shown as liabilities only on formal declaration. Once declared, however, dividends are binding obligations of the corporation. Dividends are current liabilities because they are almost always paid within several weeks of the time they are declared.

Portions of Long-term Debt

The repayment of many long-term obligations is a series of installments over several years. To report liabilities involving installments properly, we should show the principal amount of the installments due within one year (or the operating cycle, if longer) as a current liability.

Sales and Excise Taxes

Many products and services are subject to sales and excise taxes. The laws governing these taxes usually require the retail (or selling) firm to collect the tax at the time of sale and to remit the collections periodically to the appropriate taxing agency. Assume that a particular product selling for $1,000 is subject to a 4% state sales tax and a 10% federal excise tax. Each tax should be figured on the basic sales price only. We record the above sale as follows:

Accounts Receivable (or Cash)	1,140	
Sales		1,000
Sales Tax Payable		40
Excise Tax Payable		100
To record sales and related taxes.		

Recording this transaction as a $1,140 sale is incorrect, because this overstates revenue and may lead to the omission of the liabilities for the taxes collected. The selling firm periodically completes a tax reporting form and remits the period's tax collections with it. The tax liability accounts are then debited and Cash is credited.

As an expedient, some firms record sales at the gross amount, including taxes collected. Then, to convert this type of revenue figure to actual sales, we divide the transaction total of $1,140 by 1.14 to yield $1,000 as the basic sales price and $140 as the total tax.

Estimated or Accrued Liabilities

Estimated or accrued liabilities are often referred to as *accrued expenses*. Generally they are the credits offsetting a series of debits to various expense accounts that are necessary for matching periodic revenue and expenses. Examples are the accrual of incurred (but unpaid) product warranty expense, various taxes, and vacation pay.

PRODUCT WARRANTIES Many firms guarantee their products for a period of time after the sale. Proper matching of revenue and expenses requires that the estimated costs of providing these **product warranties** be recognized as an expense of the period of sale rather than of a later period when the warranty costs may actually be paid.

Let us suppose that a firm sells a product for $300 per unit, which includes a 30-day warranty against defects. Past experience indicates that 3% of the units will prove defective and that the average repair cost is $40 per defective unit. Furthermore, during a particular month, product sales were $240,000, and 13 of the units sold in this month were defective and were repaired during the month. Using this information, we calculate the accrued liability for product warranties at the end of the month as follows:

Number of units sold ($240,000/$300)	800
Rate of defective units	× 0.03
Total units expected to fail	24
Less: Units failed in month of sale	13
Units expected to fail in the remainder of the warranty period	11
Average repair cost per unit	× $ 40
Estimated liability for product warranty provision at end of period	$440

This accrued liability would be recorded at the end of the period of sale as

Product Warranty Expense	440	
Estimated Liability for Product Warranty		440
To record estimated warranty expense.		

When a unit fails in a future period, the repair costs will be recorded by debiting the accrued liability, Estimated Liability for Product Warranty, and crediting Cash, Supplies, and so forth.

PROPERTY TAXES Property taxes are a primary source of revenue for city and county governments. The property taxes paid by business firms are, to some extent, the price for the many governmental services from which the firms benefit. Thus, property taxes are considered an operating expense that applies pro rata to each operating period.

Although procedures vary widely, property taxes are usually assessed annually. A typical sequence involves

1. Determination of the tax rate by relating the total revenue needed to the total value of property taxed.
2. Assessment of specific amounts of taxes against specific property parcels—at this time, the taxes are usually liens against the property.
3. Payment of taxes, usually in one or two installments.

If the taxing unit has the same accounting year as the taxpaying firm and the taxes are assessed and paid at the beginning of the year, the firm simply debits Prepaid Property Tax for the amount of the tax. At the end of each month, an adjusting entry is made debiting Property Tax Expense and crediting Prepaid Property Tax for $\frac{1}{12}$ of the annual amount.

In many cases, however, the taxing unit's accounting year differs from that of the taxpaying firm. Furthermore, assessment dates may vary widely. Often, firms do not know in advance what amount the tax will be that affects part of their accounting year. These firms must accrue an estimated amount of property tax expense (and the related liability) until they know their actual tax liability.

To illustrate, let us assume that Willetts Company, which ends its accounting year on December 31, is located in a city whose fiscal year runs from July 1 to June 30. City taxes are assessed on October 1 (for the fiscal year started the preceding July 1) and are paid by November 15. The relationship of the firm's and the city's accounting years is diagrammed as follows:

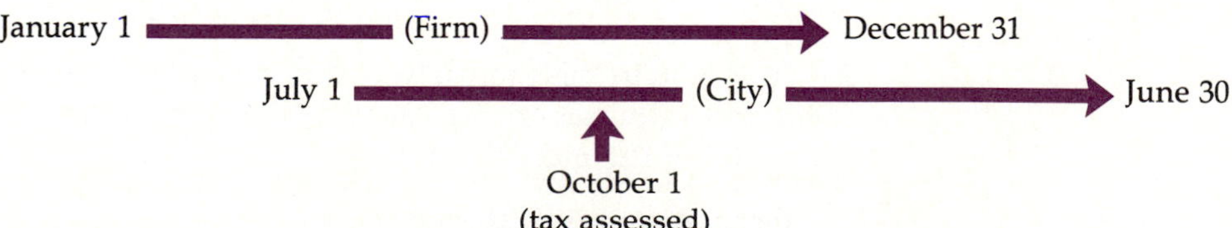

On October 1, the firm knows the amount of its property taxes for the last six months of the current calendar year and the first six months of the next calendar year. Consequently, property tax expense must be estimated for July, August, and September of each year. Willetts Company estimates in July that its property taxes for the next year will be $18,000. At the end of July, August, and September, the following entry would reflect the estimated monthly property taxes ($18,000/12 = $1,500):

Property Tax Expense	1,500	
Estimated Property Taxes Payable		1,500
To record estimated property tax expense.		

On October 1, Willetts Company receives a $19,008 property tax bill from the city. Willetts' estimate for July–September is too low by $252 ($19,008/12 = $1,584; $1,584 − $1,500 = $84; $84 × 3 months = $252). The $252 difference may be handled as an increase in the property taxes for October. The entry to record the October taxes would then be:

Property Tax Expense ($1,584 + $252)	1,836	
Estimated Property Taxes Payable		1,836
To record estimated property tax expense.		

The Estimated Property Taxes Payable account has a balance of $6,336 after the October entry. The entry on November 15 to record the property tax payment in full is:

Estimated Property Taxes Payable	6,336	
Prepaid Property Taxes	12,672	
Cash		19,008
To record payment of property taxes.		

The balance in the Prepaid Property Taxes account is amortized to Property Tax Expense from November–June—$1,584 each month.

INCOME TAXES The federal government, most states, and some municipalities levy income taxes against corporations, individuals, estates, and trusts. Sole proprietorships and partnerships are not taxable entities—their owners include the businesses' income on their personal tax returns. In the United States, income is generally reported annually on one or more income tax forms, and taxpayers compute (or assess themselves) the amount of tax due. The tax due is determined in accordance with generally accepted accounting principles, modified by the various tax laws, rulings of the taxing agencies, and many applicable court decisions. Because administration of tax laws is quite complex and many honest differences exist in their interpretation, the final tax liability for certain firms may not be settled until several years after a given tax year. Thus, the liability for income taxes is often an estimated obligation for some period of time.

Because corporations are separate taxable entities, they ordinarily incur a legal obligation for income taxes whenever corporate income is earned. Therefore, corporate financial statements are routinely adjusted for income tax liabilities. This adjustment is often recorded as follows:

Income Tax Expense	XXX	
Income Tax Payable		XXX
To record estimated income tax.		

Income Tax Expense may be included among the operating expenses in the income statement. Alternatively, to highlight the impact of income taxes, some companies derive an intermediate figure in the income statement labeled "income before income taxes." All expenses except income taxes are subtracted from revenue to derive this figure. Income taxes are then subtracted last in the income statement. Income taxes are discussed more fully in Chapter 28.

VACATION PAY Most employees enjoy vacation privileges—typically, at least two weeks per year with regular pay. Depending on the particular agreement, an employee may earn some fraction of his or her annual vacation each payroll period. Other contracts may require a full year's employment before any vacation is given. In the latter case, the proportion of employees who earn annual vacations depends on the employee turnover rate.

Generally, an employer accrues **vacation benefit expense** if the employees' vacation benefits relate to service already rendered and they vest over time, as long as payment is probable and can be estimated.[1] Assume that a firm provides an annual two-week vacation for employees who have worked 50 weeks and that with the employee turnover rate, 80% of the staff will, in fact, receive vacation benefits. These employees earn the two weeks' vacation pay during the 50 weeks worked each year, or at the rate of 4% (2 weeks vacation/50 weeks worked). The proper accrual of vacation benefits expense for a $10,000 payroll would be

$$\$10,000 \times 0.04 \times 0.8 = \$320$$

The appropriate journal entry would be

Vacation Benefits Expense	320	
Estimated Liability for Vacation Benefits		320
To record estimated vacation benefits.		

When the vacation benefits are paid, the amount would be recorded as follows:

Estimated Liability for Vacation Benefits	XXX	
Cash		XXX
To record payment of vacation benefits.		

This treatment reflects the annual vacation expense in the appropriate periods and recognizes throughout the year the accrued liability for vacation benefits.

CONTINGENT LIABILITIES

Even though a past transaction or event has taken place, the existence of some liabilities still depends on the occurrence of a future event. These types of liabilities are called **contingent liabilities.** Whether or not a contingent liability is currently recorded in the accounts depends on the likelihood of the future event occurring.

If the future event will *probably occur* and the amount of the liability can be *reasonably estimated*, the liability should be recorded in the accounts.[2] The esti-

[1] *Statement of Financial Accounting Standards No. 43*, "Accounting for Compensated Absences" (Stamford, CT: Financial Accounting Standards Board, 1980).

[2] *Statement of Financial Accounting Standards No. 5*, "Accounting for Contingencies" (Stamford, CT: Financial Accounting Standards Board, 1975).

mated liability for product warranty discussed earlier in the chapter is an example of this situation. Our analysis assumed that customers were likely to make claims under warranties for goods they had purchased and that a reasonable estimate of the amount of warranty obligation could be made.

When the future event will likely not occur or the amount of the liability cannot be reasonably estimated, contingent liabilities are not recorded in the accounts. They should, when significant, be disclosed in the financial statements either in a parenthetical note in the body of the statements or as a footnote to the balance sheet. Some common examples of contingent liabilities that typically are not recorded in the accounts are given below.

Notes receivable discounted As explained in Chapter 8, firms that discount (sell to others) notes receivable with recourse are contingently liable for their payment should the original maker fail to honor the note. We noted that this contingent liability is usually disclosed in a footnote to the balance sheet.

Credit guarantees To accommodate important but less financially secure suppliers or customers, a firm may guarantee the other company's debt by cosigning a note. Until the original debtor satisfies the obligation, the cosigning firm is contingently liable for the debt.

Lawsuits In the course of its operations, a firm may be the defendant in a lawsuit involving potential damage awards. During the time a lawsuit is pending, the firm should disclose in its financial statements the nature of the suit and any potential liability. An example of this type of disclosure, shown below, is taken from the 1987 annual report of Norfolk Southern Corporation:

> **Contingencies**
>
> Norfolk Southern's rail subsidiaries are defendants in numerous lawsuits relating to railroad operations. These subsidiaries, together with other railroads, are also defendants in several complaints filed with the Interstate Commerce Commission (ICC) challenging the reasonableness of specific freight rates in effect on October 1, 1980.
>
> While the final outcome with respect to the foregoing contingencies cannot be predicted with certainty, it is the opinion of Management, after consulting with its legal counsel, that ultimate liability will not materially affect the consolidated financial position of N[orfolk] S[outhern].

Additional income tax assessments Earlier in this chapter, we explained that many aspects of income tax laws and rulings are subject to a significant degree of interpretation. Consequently, many firms do not know their final income tax liability for a given tax period until the related return has been audited or until the applicable statute of limitations becomes effective. The federal statute of limitations for income taxes is three years. No statute of limitations exists in cases of fraud or failure to file returns. Proposed assessments for additional taxes often are contested in court for extended periods. During this time, the taxpaying firm is contingently liable for the proposed additional tax.

PAYROLL ACCOUNTING

Wages and salaries represent a major element in the cost structure of most businesses. Indeed, the largest single expense incurred by some service businesses may be the compensation paid to employees. As we examine the procedures and requirements associated with accounting for salaries and wages, we see that several different current liabilities are related to a company's payroll expense.

IMPACT OF LEGISLATION ON PAYROLL PROCEDURES

Payroll accounting procedures are influenced significantly by legislation enacted by the federal and state governments. These laws levy taxes based on payroll amounts, establish remittance and reporting requirements for employers, and set up certain minimum standards for wages and hours.

Levy of Taxes

FEDERAL INSURANCE CONTRIBUTIONS ACT In the mid-1930s, the federal government enacted a national Social Security program to provide workers with a continuing source of income during retirement. The program has been expanded several times since then, one example being the 1965 enactment of the Medicare program of hospital and medical insurance for persons 65 years of age and older. Today, in addition to health insurance benefits for eligible people, Social Security provides monthly payments to workers and their dependents when a worker retires, is disabled, or dies.

Monthly benefit payments and hospital insurance protection under Medicare are financed by taxes levied on employees, their employers, and self-employed people. Approximately 9 out of 10 employed persons in the United States currently earn Social Security protection through this process. Medical insurance under Medicare is financed by premiums paid by persons who enroll for this protection and from the general revenue of the federal government. Because we focus on payroll accounting in this chapter, we consider in more detail the financing provided by a tax on employees and their employers.

The Federal Insurance Contributions Act (FICA) establishes the tax levied on *both* employee and employer. The **FICA tax** rate for 1989 is 7.51% and for 1990 and thereafter is 7.65%. It is likely that the rates will change again during the 1990s, but at the time of this writing, no such change has been announced. Currently, the same rate of tax is imposed upon both the employee and the employer.

The FICA tax applies to wages paid to employees during a calendar year, up to a certain amount per employee. For example, in 1989 the tax is applied to the first $48,000 of an employee's wages. At a 7.51% rate, the maximum tax on any one employee in a year would be 7.51% × $48,000 = $3,604.80. The amount of earnings subject to the FICA tax is adjusted yearly for changes in the Consumers Price Index. Near the end of each year, the Social Security Administration announces the earnings base for the following year.

The employee's tax is deducted from each paycheck by the employer. The amount of tax levied on the employer and the employee is the same. At a 7.51% rate, the employer's total tax for a year would equal 0.0751 times the total amount of employees' wages subject to FICA tax during the year. For simplicity in calculations, we use a 7.5% rate in our illustrations and problems.

FEDERAL UNEMPLOYMENT TAX ACT The **Federal Unemployment Tax Act (FUTA)** is also part of the federal Social Security program. The states and the national Social Security Administration work together in a joint unemployment insurance program. FUTA raises funds to help finance the administration of the unemployment compensation programs operated by the states. Generally, funds

CHALLENGES FOR THE SOCIAL SECURITY SYSTEM

Since its founding over 50 years ago, Social Security has become the most important source of income for most elderly Americans. For example, in 1950, only 20 percent of the people over age 65 received Social Security benefits; today, well over 90 percent do. In 1950, the average monthly benefit, adjusted for inflation, was about $125 in 1980 dollars. In the early 1980s, the average benefit exceeded $300 per month.*

Since its inception, the Social Security system has been financed by payroll taxes, shared equally by employers and employees. The system is essentially a "pay-as-you-go" system, in which the aggregate tax collections from all employers and workers are used to pay benefits as they come due. Thus, Social Security can be viewed as an intergenerational transfer program, since it collects revenues from one generation (that is, workers) and passes them on to another (that is, retirees). At the inception of the program, the payroll tax amounted to 1% (2% for employer and employee combined) of the first $3,000 of earnings. In 1989, the rate exceeded $7\frac{1}{2}$% (15% combined), and the earnings base was $48,000.

In the past, the system's traditional political and social acceptance has rested on low tax rates and the belief that today's payments would assure tomorrow's benefits. However, in recent years, it has been recognized that the system is in serious financial trouble. Increased benefits, lower birth rates, longer life expectancies, and slower economic growth are some of the important factors that all add up to a vast increase in the number of retired nonworkers being supported by a decreasing proportion of workers. In 1960, for example, there were 20 Social Security beneficiaries for every 100 workers; by 1980, the rate had risen to 31 beneficiaries per 100 contributing workers. According to some estimates, this ratio is expected to rise to a range of 40 to 70 by the middle of the next century.†

The tax increases scheduled for the immediate future will undoubtedly not prove sufficient to meet the costs of Social Security as it goes into the next century. Using intermediate estimates, the Social Security Administration has estimated that, under the current structure, combined employer and employee tax rates will need to rise to 16.6% of payroll in 2010 and to 25.4% in 2030. Certain pessimistic forecasts (based on slower economic growth, lower birth rates, and substantially lower mortality rates) have the combined tax rate going to 21.4%, 36.3%, and 45.3% in 2010, 2030, and 2050, respectively. Even if more modest predictions prevail, there are serious implications for consumer purchasing power and the ability of individuals to save. In addition, higher taxes levied on employers may increase the price of goods and services and have adverse effects on employment and new investment.

Many proposals have been advanced to relieve the impending crises. Some of these, related to the present structure, include postponing eligibility for benefits to an age later than 62 or 65, taxing certain benefits of retirees above stipulated income levels, and curtailing benefit levels. The first two of these proposals are already in the process of implementation. However, many people believe that the structure of the system should be changed. A number of proposals suggest that Social Security should provide only a basic floor of retirement income for virtually all retirees, supplemented by employer pension plans with improved funding and broader coverage, and by personal saving. Many of these proposals call for income tax reform to provide more incentive for savings, such as the incentives in Individual Retirement Plans (IRAs) and Keough plans, which allow the deferral of taxes. There are also proposals to have funding, at least in part, from general tax revenues.

Clearly, Social Security is entering a new era. The combined forces of inflation, slow economic growth, demographic change, and the maturing of the system itself, have brought about the financial crises. The challenge that policy makers face is how to reshape the system so that the costs to the working generation are kept manageable and yet still fulfill the social and economic goal of providing benefits to retirees.‡

*Sylvester J. Schieber, *Social Security: Perspectives on Preserving the System* (Washington, D.C.: Employee Benefit Research Institute, 1982), p. xxii.

†Committee of the Committee for Economic Development, *Reforming Retirement Policies* (New York: Committee for Economic Development, 1981), p. 28.

‡Committee of the Committee for Economic Development, p. 29.

collected under this act are not paid out as unemployment compensation benefits, but are used to pay administrative costs at the federal and state levels. In times of high unemployment, however, the federal government may appropriate funds from its general revenue to provide extended unemployment benefits.

FUTA generates funds by a payroll tax levied only on the employer. At present, the rate is 6.2% of the first $7,000 of an employee's wages. However, the employer is entitled to a credit against this tax for unemployment taxes paid to the state. The maximum credit allowed is 5.4% of the first $7,000 of each employee's wages. Many states set their basic unemployment tax rates at this maximum credit. In these states, the effective FUTA rate on the employer is generally 0.8% (6.2% − 5.4%). Unless otherwise stated, the rates used in our illustrations and problems are 5.4% for state unemployment tax and 0.8% for the federal unemployment tax.

STATE UNEMPLOYMENT COMPENSATION TAXES Benefit payments to compensate individuals for wages lost during unemployment are handled through unemployment compensation programs administered by each state. Generally, a worker who becomes unemployed through no fault of his or her own, is able to work, and is available for work is eligible for unemployment benefits. The duration and amount of benefits typically depend on the worker's length of employment and average wage during a previous base period.

The funds for unemployment benefits are generated in most states by a payroll tax levied exclusively on *employers*. In a few states, the employee must also contribute. Because of the credit allowed against the FUTA tax, states often establish their unemployment tax rate for new employers at 5.4%. However, the rate may vary over time according to an employer's experience rating. Employers with records of stable employment may pay less than the basic rate, while employers with irregular employment records may pay more than the basic rate. An employer with a favorable experience rating who pays less than the basic rate is still entitled to the maximum 5.4% credit against the federal unemployment tax. For many years the amount of wages per employee subject to unemployment tax was the same for both state and federal unemployment compensation taxes. Recently, a number of states have increased the base beyond the $7,000 amount presently established for the federal tax, because of increases in claims. For example, the present unemployment tax base in Wisconsin is $10,500 per employee. In our examples, exercises, and problems we give the rates and amounts subject to tax for both state and federal unemployment compensation taxes.

We should remember that FICA, FUTA, and state unemployment taxes are levied on certain maximum amounts of payroll. Throughout the calendar year, employers must be alert to the fact that a greater amount of each period's wages may no longer be subject to one or more of these taxes. The following schedule indicates the possible divergence between the total payroll for a period and the payroll subject to the FICA and unemployment taxes.

Total payroll	$205,000
Wages subject to FICA tax (In 1989, for example, excludes wages in excess of $48,000 per employee)	176,000
Wages subject to state unemployment tax (excludes wages in excess of a stipulated amount per employee)	98,000
Wages subject to FUTA tax (excludes wages in excess of $7,000 per employee)	72,000

FEDERAL INCOME TAX WITHHOLDING Employers are required to withhold federal income taxes from wages and salaries paid to employees. Current withholding of income taxes facilitates the government's collection of the tax and also eliminates the possible burden on the employee of having to pay a tax on income after the income has been used for other purposes.

The amount of income tax withheld from each employee is based on the amount of the employee's wage or salary, the employee's marital status, and the number of withholding allowances to which the employee is entitled. When first employed, each employee reports his or her marital status, Social Security number, and number of withholding allowances to the employer on an **Employee's Withholding Allowance Certificate,** also known as **Form W-4** (see Exhibit 12–1). Employees file new W-4s if withholding allowances or marital status change. Employees are entitled to each of the withholding allowances for which they qualify, including one for the employee, one for his or her spouse, and one for each dependent. An employee may also claim one or more additional allowances based on expected excessive itemized deductions on his or her annual income tax return.

Employers usually use the government's wage-bracket tables to determine the amount of federal income taxes to withhold from each employee. Publication 15 of the Internal Revenue Service provides tables that indicate the amounts to be withheld at different wage levels for different numbers of withholding allowances. There are separate tables for married and single persons and for a variety of payroll periods. Exhibit 12–2 illustrates a few lines from a recent wage-bracket table.

EXHIBIT 12–1

Form **W-4** — Department of the Treasury, Internal Revenue Service

Employee's Withholding Allowance Certificate

▶ **For Privacy Act and Paperwork Reduction Act Notice, see reverse.**

OMB No. 1545-0010 — **1989**

1 Type or print your first name and middle initial — Last name: Michael R. Corrigan

2 Your social security number: 374-16-3455

Home address (number and street or rural route): 145 Canyon Drive

City or town, state, and ZIP code: Madison, WI 53711

3 Marital Status: ☐ Single ☒ Married ☐ Married, but withhold at higher Single rate.
Note: *If married, but legally separated, or spouse is a nonresident alien, check the Single box.*

4 Total number of allowances you are claiming (from line G above or from the Worksheets on back if they apply) . . . 4 | 3

5 Additional amount, if any, you want deducted from each pay . . . 5 | $

6 I claim exemption from withholding and I certify that I meet **ALL** of the following conditions for exemption:

- Last year I had a right to a refund of **ALL** Federal income tax withheld because I had **NO** tax liability; **AND**
- This year I expect a refund of **ALL** Federal income tax withheld because I expect to have **NO** tax liability; **AND**
- This year if my income exceeds $500 and includes nonwage income, another person cannot claim me as a dependent.

If you meet all of the above conditions, enter the year effective and "EXEMPT" here . . . . . ▶ 6 | 19

7 Are you a full-time student? (**Note:** *Full-time students are not automatically exempt.*) . . . 7 ☐ Yes ☐ No

Under penalties of perjury, I certify that I am entitled to the number of withholding allowances claimed on this certificate or entitled to claim exempt status.

Employee's signature ▶ Michael R. Corrigan **Date ▶** November 15, 1989

8 Employer's name and address (**Employer:** Complete 8 and 10 **only if sending to IRS**) | 9 Office code (optional) | 10 Employer identification number

EXHIBIT 12–2

WAGE-BRACKET TABLE

WEEKLY Payroll Period—Employee MARRIED												
And the wages are—		And the number of withholding allowances claimed is—										
At least	But less than	0	1	2	3	4	5	6	7	8	9	10 or more
		The amount of income tax to be withheld shall be—										
$310	$320	$38	$33	$27	$22	$16	$10	$ 5	$0	$0	$0	$0
320	330	40	34	29	23	17	12	6	1	0	0	0
330	340	41	36	30	25	19	13	8	2	0	0	0
340	350	43	37	32	26	20	15	9	4	0	0	0
350	360	44	39	33	28	22	16	11	5	0	0	0

Alternatively, employers may use the percentage method, which is especially useful when no wage-bracket tables pertain to the length of the payroll period in question. Both the wage-bracket tables and the percentage method incorporate a graduated system of withholding. That is, the withholding rates increase as the earnings subject to withholding increase.

STATE INCOME TAX WITHHOLDING Most states now have an income tax that is withheld by employers. Payroll procedures for withholding state income taxes are similar to those for withholding federal income taxes.

INCIDENCE OF PAYROLL TAXES Taxes related to payroll amounts may be levied on the employee, the employer, or both. Exhibit 12–3 summarizes the incidence of the various payroll taxes we have just discussed.

Employee versus Independent Contractor

Salaries and wages paid to employees provide the basis for withholding taxes from employees and levying payroll taxes on the employer. Independent contractors are not subject to withholding and are therefore distinguished from employees. In general, an *employee* performs services subject to the supervision and control of another party known as the employer. The following variables establish the existence of an employer–employee relationship: (1) the employer has the power to discharge the individual worker, (2) the employer sets the work hours for the individual worker, and (3) the employer furnishes a place to work. An *independent contractor,* on the other hand, may also perform services for a business firm, but that firm does not have the legal right to direct and control the methods used by this person. Independent contractors are in business for themselves; examples are certified public accountants, lawyers, and physicians.

Wages are the earnings of employees who are paid on an hourly or piecework basis. A *salary* is the compensation of employees paid on a monthly or annual basis. In practice, however, these terms are used more or less synonymously.

EXHIBIT 12–3

INCIDENCE OF TAXES RELATED TO PAYROLL AMOUNTS

Tax	Employer	Employee
Federal Insurance Contributions Act	X	X
Federal Unemployment Tax Act	X	
State Unemployment Compensation Taxes	X	In a few states
Federal Income Tax Withholding		X
State Income Tax Withholding		X

Amounts paid to independent contractors are identified as *fees*. For example, the expense account Audit Fees may be charged for the amounts paid to a certified public accountant for audit work and Legal Fees may be charged for payments to a lawyer for legal work.

Remittance and Reporting Requirements

The legislation levying various taxes on payroll amounts also specifies the procedures for remitting these taxes to the government and establishes the reports an employer must file. A sound system of payroll accounting ensures that these payments are made and reports are filed on time.

FICA TAXES AND FEDERAL INCOME TAXES WITHHELD Employer remittance and reporting requirements are the same for both employer's and employees' FICA taxes and federal income taxes withheld, because these taxes are combined for payment and reporting purposes. Generally, remittances are deposited in a Federal Reserve bank or authorized commercial bank. The specific remittance requirements vary depending on the combined dollar amount of the taxes. An employer has three banking days to make a deposit if the unpaid taxes are at least $3,000 by the 3rd, 7th, 11th, 15th, 19th, 22nd, 25th, or last day of the month. At the end of any month, undeposited taxes of $500–$3,000 must be deposited within 15 days. If the undeposited taxes are less than $500 at the end of a calendar quarter, the amount must be deposited within one month (or paid with the employer's quarterly tax return).

Each quarter, employers file an Employer's Quarterly Federal Tax Return, Form 941, with the Internal Revenue Service. On this form, the employer schedules a record of its liability for FICA taxes and withheld income taxes throughout the quarter and reports its deposits of these taxes.

By January 31, an employer must give each employee two copies of **Form W-2, Wage and Tax Statement,** which specifies the employee's total wages paid, the federal income taxes withheld, the wages subject to FICA tax, and the FICA tax withheld for the preceding calendar year (see Exhibit 12–4). The worker attaches one copy of Form W-2 to his or her federal income tax return. The employer sends a copy of each employee's Form W-2 to the Social Security Administration, which, in turn, provides the Internal Revenue Service with the income tax data that it needs from these forms.

FEDERAL UNEMPLOYMENT INSURANCE TAXES The amount due on federal unemployment insurance taxes must be reviewed quarterly. If undeposited taxes exceed

EXHIBIT 12–4

1 Control number 39-6006492W	22222	For Paperwork Reduction Act Notice, see separate instructions OMB No. 1545-0008	For Official Use Only ▶	
2 Employer's name, address, and ZIP code University of Wisconsin P.O. Box 8010 Madison, WI 53706			3 Employer's identification number 69-1360001-131	4 Employer's state I.D. number 20608
			5 Statutory employee ☒ Deceased ☐ Pension plan ☐ Legal rep. ☐ 942 emp. ☐ Subtotal ☐ Deferred compensation ☐ Void ☐	
			6 Allocated tips	7 Advance EIC payment
8 Employee's social security number 314-16-3455	9 Federal income tax withheld 14,336.20		10 Wages, tips, other compensation 64,366.00	11 Social security tax withheld 3,604.80
12 Employee's name (first, middle, last) Michael R. Corrigan			13 Social security wages 48,000.00	14 Social security tips
145 Canyon Drive Madison, WI 53711 15 Employee's address and ZIP code			16 (See Instr. for Forms W-2/W-2P)	16a Fringe benefits incl. in Box 10 366.00
			17 State income tax 3,752.80 / 18 State wages, tips, etc. 64,366.00	19 Name of state WI
			20 Local income tax / 21 Local wages, tips, etc.	22 Name of locality

Form **W-2 Wage and Tax Statement 1989**   **Copy A For Social Security Administration**   Dept. of the Treasury—IRS

$100 at the end of any of the first three quarters of a year, a deposit must be made in a Federal Reserve bank or authorized commercial bank during the first month after the quarter. If the amount due is $100 or less, no deposit is necessary. By January 31, each employer must file a Form 940, Employer's Annual Federal Unemployment Tax Return, for the preceding year. If the annual tax reported on Form 940, less deposits made, exceeds $100, the entire amount due must be deposited by January 31. If this amount is $100 or less, it may be either deposited or remitted with Form 940.

STATE UNEMPLOYMENT COMPENSATION TAXES The filing and payment requirements for unemployment compensation taxes vary among the states. Often, however, employers must pay the taxes when they file quarterly reports. Some states require payments more frequently, sometimes monthly, if the taxes owed by an employer exceed a preestablished level.

Wages and Hours

FAIR LABOR STANDARDS ACT The **Fair Labor Standards Act** establishes minimum wage, overtime pay, and equal pay standards for employees covered by the act and sets record-keeping requirements for their employers. The act's coverage has been amended several times since its passage in 1938. Its provisions now extend, with certain exemptions, to employees directly or indirectly engaged in interstate commerce and to domestic service workers. Executive, administrative, and professional employees are exempt from the act's minimum wage and overtime provisions.

At this writing, for example, the minimum wage that an employee must receive in 1989 is $3.35 per hour. Of course, employers and employees may agree to higher wages. Employers often operate under contracts negotiated with their employees' unions that provide more favorable terms to employees than the standards provided by the Fair Labor Standards Act.

A covered employee must be paid an amount equal to at least $1\frac{1}{2}$ times that employee's regular pay rate for every hour beyond 40 that he or she works in a week. The following are some examples of overtime pay computations under this standard; the examples differ by the basic method of compensating the employee.

1. Jody Green receives $5.10 per hour as her regular rate of pay. Her overtime rate of pay is $7.65 ($5.10 + $2.55) per hour. This week she worked 44 hours. Her gross earnings this week are $234.60, computed as (40 hours × $5.10/hour) + (4 hours × $7.65/hour).
2. Jack Tyler is paid on a piece rate basis. His earnings this week, before any overtime compensation, are $206.40 for 43 hours of work. For overtime pay computations, his regular hourly rate of pay is determined by dividing his weekly earnings on a piece rate basis by the number of hours worked in that week, or $206.40/43 = $4.80. For each hour worked over 40 in the week, Tyler is entitled to an overtime premium of $2.40 ($\frac{1}{2}$ of $4.80). Therefore, his total earnings this week are $206.40 + $7.20 (3 hours × $2.40) = $213.60.

   The act permits an alternative way to compute overtime for piece rate workers, if agreed upon in advance of the work. This method pays $1\frac{1}{2}$ times the piece rate for each piece produced during overtime hours.
3. Bill Jantz receives a salary of $240 for a 40-hour workweek. This week he worked 46 hours. Bill's regular rate of pay is computed at $6 per hour ($240/40); his overtime rate of pay is $6 × $1\frac{1}{2}$, or $9 per hour. Bill's gross earnings for the current 46-hour week are $240 + (6 × $9), or $294.

Again, we note that employees may negotiate overtime pay rates in excess of the minimum standard illustrated in the preceding discussion. A union contract, for example, may require double the regular pay rate for hours worked on Sundays and holidays.

Under the Fair Labor Standards Act, employers may not discriminate on the basis of sex in the rates paid to men and women employees performing equal work on jobs demanding equal skill, effort, and responsibility and having similar working conditions. The equal pay provisions also provide that employers must eliminate illegal pay differentials by a means other than reducing employee pay rates. The law does permit wage differentials between men and women when due to a job-related factor other than sex, such as a difference based on a bona fide seniority or merit system.

Employers are required under the law to maintain a detailed record of each employee's wage and hours, including the hour and day the employee's workweek begins, the regular hourly rate of pay, the total overtime pay for any week in which more than 40 hours are worked, the deductions from and additions to wages, and the employee's total wages paid each period. The law does not prescribe any particular form for these records. The payroll records maintained in a typical payroll accounting system contain much of this information, which is also needed to comply with other laws and regulations.

OTHER PAYROLL DEDUCTIONS

In addition to FICA taxes, federal income taxes, and perhaps state and local income taxes, other items may be deducted from an employee's gross earnings in arriving at the net *take-home* pay for the period. Each additional deduction must be authorized by the employee; often this is done individually, although in some instances the union contract provides the authorization needed by the employer. Examples of these items are payments for

1. Union dues.
2. Premiums on life, accident, hospital, surgical care, or major medical insurance.
3. Installment loan from employees' credit union.
4. Advance from employer.
5. U.S. savings bonds.
6. Contributions to charitable organizations.
7. Retirement plan.

NET PAY COMPUTATION FOR INDIVIDUAL EMPLOYEE

To illustrate the computation of an individual employee's net pay for a payroll period, let us assume Donald Bork's regular salary is $320 for a 40-hour work-week. He is married and claims three withholding allowances on Form W-4. He has authorized his employer to deduct $3 per week from his earnings for group hospital insurance and $2 per week as a contribution to the United Way charity. During the current week, he works 42 hours. Prior to the current week, his gross earnings for the year are $1,328. The applicable FICA tax rate is 7.5%. The amount paid to Donald Bork is shown in the following summary:

Gross earnings		$344.00
Deductions:		
FICA tax (@ 7.5%)	$25.80	
Federal income tax withheld	26.00	
Group hospital insurance	3.00	
United Way charity contribution	2.00	
Total deductions		56.80
Net earnings		$287.20

An explanation of these amounts follows:

1. Gross earnings—Bork's regular hourly pay rate is $320 ÷ 40 hours, or $8. His overtime pay rate is $1\frac{1}{2} \times$ $8, or $12 per hour. Because Bork worked two hours overtime, his overtime pay is 2 × $12 = $24. His gross pay equals his regular salary plus his overtime pay ($320 + $24 = $344).
2. FICA tax—Bork's gross earnings to date for the year ($1,672) have not yet exceeded the maximum to which the FICA tax applies. Therefore, the FICA tax on Bork's earnings is 7.5% × $344 = $25.80.
3. Federal income tax withheld—We apply the wage-bracket table of Exhibit 12–2 to this illustration. From this table, we see that the income tax withheld

from a married employee with three withholding allowances earning wages of at least $340 but less than $350 per week is $26.00.

4. Group hospital insurance and charitable contribution—Bork has specifically authorized his employer to make these deductions.

PAYROLL RECORDS

The precise nature of an enterprise's payroll records and procedures depends to a great extent on the size of the work force and the degree to which the record keeping is automated. In some form, however, two records are basic to most payroll systems—the payroll register and individual employee earnings records.

The Payroll Register

The **payroll register,** prepared each pay period, lists the company's complete payroll in detail. Each employee's earnings and deductions for the period are contained in the payroll register. Exhibit 12–5 illustrates a typical payroll register for a firm with a small number of employees. The pay period covered by this payroll register is one week.

In Exhibit 12–5, the column immediately after each employee's name shows the total hours worked by that employee during the week. Data on the hours worked are taken from time cards or similar documents maintained for each employee. In this illustration, each employee is paid a regular salary for a 40-hour work week. The regular salary is shown in the first column of the earnings section of the register. Overtime pay, computed at $1\frac{1}{2}$ times the regular hourly rate (regular weekly salary ÷ 40), is presented in the next column. The employees' gross earnings appear in the final column in the earnings section.

The 7.5% FICA tax is deducted from each employee's gross earnings. Because the payroll illustrated is early in the calendar year (the week ended February 4), no employee's earnings have exceeded the maximum amount of wages subject to the FICA tax. As discussed earlier, the federal income tax withheld is based on an employee's earnings, marital status, and number of withholding allowances. In Exhibit 12–5, for example, David Plank's relatively high federal income tax withheld is due to the fact that he is single and claims only one withholding allowance. The deductions for hospital insurance, contributions to charity, and purchases of U.S. savings bonds are specifically authorized by each employee affected by the deductions. The hospital insurance premiums vary with the number of persons covered by the plan.

An employee receives an amount equal to gross earnings less total deductions for the pay period. These net earnings are shown in the payment section of the payroll register, along with the number of the check issued by the company in payment of the wages.

In the last two columns of the payroll register, gross earnings are distributed between the office salaries and sales salaries categories. This division permits the total salaries for the period to be recorded in the proper expense accounts.

Recording the Payroll and Related Taxes

For some businesses, the payroll register is a special journal; in these cases the pertinent payroll register information is posted directly to the general ledger. Often, however, the payroll register is the basis for a general journal entry that is then posted to the general ledger. The journal entry to record the weekly payroll shown in Exhibit 12–5 follows on page 431.

EXHIBIT 12–5

PAYROLL REGISTER
FOR THE WEEK ENDED FEBRUARY 4, 19X1

		Earnings			Deductions					Payment		Distribution	
Employee	Total Hours	Regular	Overtime	Gross	FICA Tax	Federal Income Tax	Hospital Insur-ance	Other (see key)	Total Deduc-tions	Net Earnings	Check No.	Office Salaries	Sales Salaries
Donald Bork	42	320	24	344	25.80	26.00	3.00	(A) 2.00	56.80	287.20	566	344	
Jane Latt	40	280		280	21.00	22.00	2.00	(B) 5.00	50.00	230.00	567		280
Raul Lopez	44	260	37	297	22.28	22.00	3.00		47.28	249.72	568		297
David Plank	40	360		360	27.00	46.00	2.00	(B) 5.00	80.00	280.00	569		360
Myra Smiken	44	320	48	368	27.60	34.00	3.00		64.60	303.40	570		368
Fred Wells	40	280		280	21.00	22.00	2.00	(A) 2.00	47.00	233.00	571	280	
Beth White	46	320		320	24.00	27.00	2.00		53.00	267.00	572	320	
Totals		2,140	109	2,249	168.68	199.00	17.00	14.00	398.68	1,850.32		944	1,305

Key: A—United Way Charity
B—U.S. Savings Bonds

Office Salaries Expense	944.00	
Sales Salaries Expense	1,305.00	
FICA Tax Payable		168.68
Federal Income Tax Withholding Payable		199.00
Hospital Insurance Premiums Payable		17.00
United Way Contributions Payable		4.00
U.S. Savings Bond Deductions Payable		10.00
Payroll Payable		1,850.32
To record payroll for week ended February 4.		

The employer company may, when recording each payroll, also record its payroll tax liabilities. The year-to-date gross earnings for the employees in Exhibit 12–5 have not exceeded the maximum limits for either the FICA or unemployment taxes. The entry to record the employer's taxes for the week's payroll follows:

Payroll Tax Expense	308.12	
FICA Tax Payable (see preceding entry)		168.68
Federal Unemployment Tax Payable (0.8% × $2,249)		17.99
State Unemployment Tax Payable (5.4% × $2,249)		121.45
To record payroll tax expense for week ended February 4.		

Payment of the Liabilities

The various liabilities established in the entries recording the payroll and the employer's payroll taxes are settled when the employer makes payments to the appropriate parties. The issuance of the employees' payroll checks results in the following entry:

Payroll Payable	1,850.32	
Cash		1,850.32
To pay net payroll for week ended February 4.		

The FICA taxes, federal income taxes withheld, and federal unemployment insurance taxes are remitted to a depository bank in accordance with the remittance requirements discussed earlier. The state unemployment compensation taxes are remitted to the appropriate state agency, according to the state's requirements. The hospital insurance premiums are sent to the company providing the coverage, the United Way contributions are paid to that charitable organization, and the deductions for the purchase of U.S. savings bonds are remitted to the financial institution handling the acquisition of the bonds. If any of these liabilities remain unpaid when financial statements are prepared, they are classified as current liabilities in the balance sheet.

Accrual of Employer Payroll Taxes

Employer payroll taxes are based on employees' salaries and wages. A company that accrues wages and salaries with a year-end adjusting entry should also record the related employer payroll taxes as year-end adjustments. Payroll taxes are properly an expense of the period during which the related salaries and wages were earned, although the employer is *legally* obligated for these taxes in the period the salaries and wages are actually paid. This circumstance, coupled with a possibly immaterial amount of payroll taxes, leads some companies to an alternative procedure: they record the total amount of payroll taxes only in the year the payroll is paid.

Individual Employee Earnings Record

Employers maintain an **individual earnings record** for each employee. This record contains much of the information needed for the employer to comply with the various taxation and reporting requirements established by law. Exhibit 12–6 illustrates Donald Bork's individual earnings record, for the first five weeks of 19X1.

The individual earnings record contains the details on earnings and deductions shown earlier in the payroll register. In addition, the cumulative gross earnings column alerts the employer when an employee's yearly earnings have exceeded the maximum amounts to which the FICA and unemployment taxes apply.

Employers prepare Form W-2—the Wage and Tax Statement sent to every employee each year—from the individual employee earnings records. Although Form W-2 is sent only once and covers an entire year, employers typically provide employees with an earnings statement each pay period, detailing the earnings and deductions for that period. These earnings statements may be a detachable portion of the employee's paycheck or may be enclosed as a separate document with the paycheck.

PAYMENT TO EMPLOYEES

A company with a small number of employees may pay them with checks drawn on the firm's regular bank account. A company with a large number of employees usually establishes a separate bank account to pay the payroll.

Payroll Bank Account

A company with a separate payroll bank account draws a check on its regular bank account each pay period in an amount equal to the total net earnings of the employees. This check is deposited in the payroll bank account. Individual payroll checks are then drawn on this account and delivered to the employees. The issuance of the payroll checks reduces to zero the book balance in the payroll bank account.

One advantage of maintaining a separate payroll bank account is that it divides the work between the preparation and issuance of regular company checks and payroll checks. A related advantage is that it simplifies the monthly reconciliation of the regular bank account. The large number of payroll checks, many of which may be outstanding at month-end, are not run through the regular bank account. Of course, the payroll bank account must also be reconciled, but the only reconciling items for this bank account are payroll checks outstanding.

Payment in Cash

Sometimes employees are paid in currency and coin rather than by check. This may happen, for example, if the employees work in a location where it may not be convenient for them to deposit or cash checks. The company prepares and cashes its own checks for the payroll amount. Each employee's pay is delivered to the employee in an envelope. For internal control, and to have evidence of the payment, an employee signs a receipt for the payroll envelope. Often the outside of the envelope contains an itemization of the employee's gross earnings and deductions for the period.

EXHIBIT 12–6

INDIVIDUAL EMPLOYEE EARNINGS RECORD

Employee's Name	Donald Bork	Social Security No.	719-23-4866	Employee No.	6
Address	510 Many Lane	Male	X	Single	
	Archer, Florida 32600	Female		Married	X
Date of Birth	May 6, 1946	Withholding Allowances	3		
Position	Clerk-Analyst	Date of Employment	June 1, 19X0		
		Date Employment Ended			

Weekly Pay Rate $320.00

Hourly Equivalent $8.00

19X1		Earnings			Deductions					Payment		
Period Ended	Total Hours	Regular	Overtime	Gross	FICA Tax	Federal Income Tax	Hospital Insur-ance	Other: A—United Way B—Savings Bonds	Total Deduc-tions	Net Earnings	Check No.	Cumulative Gross Earnings
Jan. 7	40	320.00		320.00	24.00	22.00	3.00	A2.00	51.00	269.00	412	320.00
Jan. 14	44	320.00	48.00	368.00	27.60	28.00	3.00	A2.00	60.60	307.40	447	688.00
Jan. 21	40	320.00		320.00	24.00	22.00	3.00	A2.00	51.00	269.00	480	1,008.00
Jan. 28	40	320.00		320.00	24.00	22.00	3.00	A2.00	51.00	269.00	525	1,328.00
Feb. 4	42	320.00	24.00	344.00	25.80	26.00	3.00	A2.00	56.80	287.20	566	1,672.00

KEY POINTS FOR CHAPTER OBJECTIVES

1 Define and illustrate the most common types of current and contingent liabilities (pp. 413–19).

- Current liabilities are all obligations that will require within the coming year or the operating cycle, whichever is longer, (1) the use of existing current assets or (2) the creation of other current liabilities.
- Some common examples of current liabilities are trade accounts and notes payable, dividends payable, sales and excise taxes payable, property taxes payable, income taxes payable, and estimated liability for vacation benefits.
- Even though a past transaction or event has taken place, the existence of some liabilities, called contingent liabilities, depends on the occurrence of a future event.
- Whether or not a contingent liability is currently recorded in the accounts depends on the likelihood of the future event occurring. If the future event will *probably occur* and the amount of the liability can be *reasonably estimated,* the liability should be recorded in the accounts.

2 Explain and illustrate the deductions made in computing net pay and the items included in employers' payroll taxes (pp. 419–29).

- Deductions from employees' pay generally required by law are withheld income taxes and FICA taxes. Some deductions may be contractual, such as union dues. Others are voluntary, such as charitable contributions.
- Employers' payroll tax expenses include a matching amount (with employees) of FICA taxes, and state and federal unemployment compensation taxes. Employers may also, by contract, assume other expenses, such as a portion of health premiums.

3 Describe and illustrate the records required in payroll accounting (pp. 429–33).

- Firms with more than a few employees often prepare a payroll register, which itemizes each employee's gross earnings, deductions, and net pay. This can either be posted as a journal or used to support journal entries recording the payroll.
- Most firms must maintain an individual earnings record for each employee that contains information necessary for the employer to comply with various taxation and reporting requirements established by law.

KEY TERMS USED IN THIS CHAPTER

additional income tax assessments 419
credit guarantees 419
contingent liabilities 418
current liabilities 414
Employee's Withholding Allowance Certificate (Form W-4) 423
Fair Labor Standards Act 426
Federal Unemployment Tax Act (FUTA) 420
FICA tax 420
individual earnings record 432
lawsuits 419
liabilities 413
notes receivable discounted 419
payroll register 429
product warranties 415
vacation benefit expense 418
Wage and Tax Statement (Form W-2) 425

SELF TEST QUESTIONS FOR REVIEW

(Answers are at the end of this chapter.)

1. Which of the following is *not* considered to be a contingent liability?
   (a) Discounted notes receivable.
   (b) Notes payable.
   (c) Credit guarantees.
   (d) Lawsuit.

2. A firm sold merchandise on account for $1,840, which included a 10% excise tax and a 5% sales tax. The entry to record this sale would include
   (a) A debit of $1,600 to Accounts Receivable.
   (b) A debit of $2,116 to Accounts Receivable.
   (c) A credit of $1,600 to Sales.
   (d) A credit of $1,840 to Sales.

3. A firm sells a product for $400 per unit, which includes a 30-day warranty against defects. Experience indicates that 4% of the units will prove defective, requiring an average repair cost of $50 per unit. During the first month of business, product sales were $320,000 and 20 of the units sold were defective and repaired during the month. The accrued liability for product warranties at month-end is
   (a) $1,000 (b) $600 (c) $1,600 (d) $2,000

4. Which of the following payroll-related taxes does not represent a deduction from the employees' earnings?
   (a) FICA taxes.
   (b) Income taxes.
   (c) Federal unemployment taxes.
   (d) All of the above are deductions from employees' earnings.

5. James Sheldon, who is covered by the Fair Labor Standards Act, receives wages of $360 for a 40-hour work week. This week he worked 44 hours. Income tax withheld amounts to $42. His prior gross earnings for the year were $4,320, and the FICA tax rate is 7.5%. Sheldon's net pay is
   (a) $340.95 (b) $324.30 (c) $307.65 (d) $346.80

DEMONSTRATION PROBLEM FOR REVIEW

Archer Corporation had the following payroll data for April, 19X1:

Office salaries	$ 40,000
Sales salaries	86,000
Federal income taxes withheld	25,600
Health insurance premiums deducted	1,850
United Way contributions deducted	950
Salaries (included above):	
subject to FICA taxes	126,000
subject to federal unemployment taxes	76,000
subject to state unemployment taxes	88,000

The FICA tax rate is 7.5%, the federal unemployment compensation tax rate is 0.8%, and the state unemployment compensation tax rate is 5.4%. The amounts subject to these taxes are given above.

REQUIRED
Present general journal entries to record:
(a) Accrual of the payroll.
(b) Payment of the net payroll.
(c) Accrual of employer's payroll taxes.
(d) Payment of all liabilities related to the payroll. (Assume that all are settled at the same time.)

SOLUTION TO DEMONSTRATION PROBLEM

	Date	Account	Debit	Credit
(a)	Apr. 30	Office Salaries Expense	40,000	
		Sales Salaries Expense	86,000	
		Federal Income Tax Withholding Payable		25,600
		FICA Tax Payable		9,450
		Health Insurance Premiums Payable		1,850
		United Way Contributions Payable		950
		Payroll Payable		88,150
		To accrue payroll for April. FICA taxes: 0.075 × \$126,000 = \$9,450.		
(b)	30	Payroll Payable	88,150	
		Cash		88,150
		To pay April payroll.		
(c)	30	Payroll Tax Expense	14,810	
		FICA Tax Payable		9,450
		Federal Unemployment Tax Payable		608
		State Unemployment Tax Payable		4,752
		To record employer's payroll taxes; FICA tax = 0.075 × \$126,000 = \$9,450; federal unemployment tax = 0.008 × \$76,000 = \$608; state unemployment tax = 0.054 × \$88,000 = \$4,752		
(d)	30	Federal Income Tax Withholding Payable	25,600	
		FICA Tax Payable	18,900	
		Health Insurance Premiums Payable	1,850	
		United Way Contributions Payable	950	
		Federal Unemployment Tax Payable	608	
		State Unemployment Tax Payable	4,752	
		Cash		52,660
		To record payment of payroll-related liabilities.		

QUESTIONS

12–1 For accounting purposes, how are liabilities defined?

12–2 Present a general rule for measuring current liabilities on the balance sheet.

12–3 Define *current liabilities*.

12–4 Describe the difference between accounting for product warranties on (a) failed units repaired in the month of sale and (b) failed units repaired in a subsequent month but that are still covered by the warranty.

12–5 Under what conditions must an employer accrue employees' vacation benefits?

12–6 Define *contingent liabilities*. List three examples of contingent liabilities. When should contingent liabilities be recorded in the accounts?

12–7 On whom is the FICA tax levied? What does the FICA tax finance?

12–8 On whom are the federal and state unemployment insurance taxes levied? What do these taxes finance?

12–9 Why does an employee file a Form W-4, Employee's Withholding Allowance Certificate, with his or her employer?

12–10 What is the difference between an employee and an independent contractor?

12–11 What does Form W-2, Wage and Tax Statement, report? Who receives copies of this form?

12–12 Amos Strong is employed at $8.50 per hour. Under the Fair Labor Standards Act, how many hours in a week must he work before he is entitled to overtime pay? What is the minimum overtime rate of pay he must receive?

12–13 List at least five examples of deductions from an employee's gross earnings other than FICA taxes and federal income taxes withheld.

12–14 What is a payroll register? How does it differ from an individual employee earnings record?

12–15 If earned but unpaid wages are accrued at year-end, should employer payroll taxes on these wages be accrued at the same time? Explain.

12–16 List two advantages of maintaining a special payroll bank account for the payment of a net payroll.

EXERCISES

Current liabilities in balance sheet

12–17 For each of the following situations, indicate the amount shown as a liability on the balance sheet of Wade, Inc., at December 31, 19X2.

(a) Wade has trade accounts payable of $90,000 for merchandise included in the 19X2 ending inventory.
(b) Wade has agreed to purchase a $28,000 drill press in January 19X3.
(c) During November and December of 19X2, Wade sold products to a firm and guaranteed them against product failure for 90 days. Estimated costs of honoring this provision during 19X3 are $1,500.
(d) On December 15, 19X2, Wade declared a $60,000 cash dividend payable on January 15, 19X3, to stockholders of record on December 31, 19X2.
(e) Wade provides a profit-sharing bonus for its executives equal to 5% of the reported before-tax income for the current year. The estimated income (as defined above) for 19X2 is $540,000.

Excise and sales tax calculations

12–18 Hall Company has just billed a customer for $835.20, an amount that includes a 10% excise tax and a 6% state sales tax.

(a) What amount of revenue is recorded?
(b) Present a general journal entry to record the transaction on the books of Hall Company.

Providing for vacation benefits

12–19 Boyle, Inc.'s current vacation policy for its production workers provides four weeks paid vacation for employees who have worked 48 weeks. An analysis of the company's employee turnover rates indicates that approximately 10% of the employees will forfeit their vacation benefits.

(a) Compute the proper provision for estimated vacation benefits for a four-week period in which the total pay earned by the employee group was $324,000.

(b) Present a general journal entry to recognize the above vacation benefits.

Providing for warranty costs

12–20 Colonial Company sells an electric timer that carries a 60-day unconditional warranty against product failure. Based on a reliable statistical analysis, Colonial knows that between the sale and lapse of the product warranty, 2% of the units sold will require repair at an average cost of $40 per unit. The following data reflect Colonial's recent experience.

	October	November	December
Units sold	24,000	20,000	30,000
Known product failures from sales of:			
October	120	160	200
November		110	230
December			250

Calculate and prepare a general journal entry to record properly the estimated liability for product warranties at December 31. Assume that warranty costs of known failures have already been reflected in the records.

Payroll calculations for an employee

12–21 Ralph Kapp is an employee subject to the Fair Labor Standards Act. His regular pay rate is $8 per hour, and he is paid overtime at $1\frac{1}{2}$ times his regular pay rate. He worked 43 hours in the current week. His gross earnings prior to the current week are $9,600. He is married and claims four withholding allowances on Form W-4. No deductions other than FICA and federal income taxes are subtracted from his paycheck. Compute the following amounts related to Kapp's current week's wages:

(a) Regular earnings.

(b) Overtime earnings.

(c) FICA taxes (assume 7.5% rate).

(d) Federal income tax withheld (use wage-bracket table in Exhibit 12–2).

(e) Net earnings.

Recording payroll taxes

12–22 Gomez Company's August payroll register shows total gross earnings of $196,000. Of this amount, $16,000 is not subject to FICA taxes, $166,000 is above the maximum amount subject to federal unemployment taxes, and $140,000 is above the maximum amount subject to state unemployment taxes. Gomez Company has a favorable employment record, so its state unemployment tax rate is 2%. It is subject to a 7.5% FICA tax and a 0.8% federal unemployment tax. Prepare the general journal entry to record Gomez Company's payroll tax expense for August.

Payroll calculations for an employee

12–23 Ellen Wynn is an employee subject to the Fair Labor Standards Act who is paid on a piece rate basis. Her earnings for the current week, before any overtime compensation, are $330 for 44 hours of work. For each hour over 40 worked in a week, she receives an overtime premium of one-half her regular hourly pay rate based on the total hours worked in that week. Her gross earnings prior to the current week were $8,450. She is married and claims one withholding allowance on Form W-4. No deductions other than FICA and federal income taxes are subtracted from her paycheck. Compute the following amounts related to Wynn's current week's wages:

(a) Regular hourly pay rate.

(b) Gross earnings.

(c) FICA taxes (assume 7.5% rate).
(d) Federal income tax withheld (use wage-bracket table in Exhibit 12–2).
(e) Net earnings.

PROBLEMS

Property tax calculations

12–24 Parker Company prepares monthly financial statements and ends its accounting year on December 31. Its headquarters building is located in the city of Bayfield. City taxes are assessed on September 1 each year, are paid by October 15, and relate to the city's fiscal year which ends the next June 30 (10 months after assessment). For the city tax year 19X5–19X6, Parker paid $48,000 in property taxes on its headquarters building.

REQUIRED

(a) What amount of property tax expense should be accrued on the financial statements for July 19X6, if property taxes for 19X6–19X7 are an estimated 5% higher than the preceding year?
(b) Assume that the 19X6–19X7 tax bill received on September 1, 19X6, was for $52,800 and that the estimate in part (a) was used through August. What is the proper monthly property tax expense for September 19X6, if the deficiencies in the monthly property tax estimates through August are handled as an increase in the property tax expense for September 19X6?
(c) How does the payment of the tax bill on October 15, 19X6, affect the amount of property tax expense recognized for October?

Excise and sales tax calculations

12–25 Holland Corporation initially records its sales at amounts that include any related excise and sales taxes. During June 19XX, Holland recorded total sales of $194,040. An analysis of June sales indicated the following:

1. Three-tenths of sales were subject to both a 10% excise tax and a 6% sales tax.
2. One-half of sales were subject only to the sales tax.
3. The balance of sales were for labor charges not subject to either excise or sales tax.

REQUIRED

(a) Calculate the amount of sales revenue for June 19XX, and the related liabilities for excise and sales taxes.
(b) Prepare the necessary journal entry at June 30 to record the liabilities for excise tax payable and sales tax payable.

Recording payroll and payroll taxes

12–26 Danville Corporation had the following payroll for March 19X1:

Officers' salaries	$30,000
Sales salaries	64,000
Federal income taxes withheld	18,800
FICA taxes withheld	7,050
Hospital insurance premiums deducted	1,450
United Way contributions deducted	850
Salaries (included above) subject to federal unemployment taxes	82,000
Salaries (included above) subject to state unemployment taxes	86,000

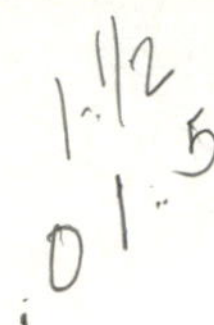

REQUIRED
Present general journal entries to record:
(a) Accrual of the payroll.
(b) Payment of the net payroll.
(c) Accrual of employer's payroll taxes. (Assume that the FICA tax matches the amount withheld, the federal unemployment tax is 0.8%, and the state unemployment tax is 5.4%.)
(d) Payment of all liabilities related to this payroll. (Assume all are settled at the same time.)

Recording payroll and payroll taxes

12–27 The following data are taken from Summers Wholesale Company's May 19X5 payroll:

Administrative salaries	$32,000
Sales salaries	48,000
Custodial salaries	6,000
Total payroll	$86,000
Salaries subject to FICA tax	$72,000
Salaries subject to FUTA unemployment taxes	14,000
Salaries subject to state unemployment taxes	20,000
Federal income taxes withheld from all salaries	19,600

Assume that (1) FICA taxes are 7.5% each for the employee and the employer and (2) the company is subject to a 2% state unemployment tax (due to a favorable experience rating) and a 0.8% federal unemployment tax on the first $7,000 paid to each employee.

REQUIRED
Record the following in general journal form:
(a) Accrual of the payroll.
(b) Payment of the net payroll.
(c) Accrual of the employer's payroll taxes.
(d) Payment of the above payroll-related liabilities. (Assume all are settled at the same time.)

Preparing payroll register and recording payroll

12–28 Racine Company employs five persons, one of whom receives a $600 salary for a 40-hour week; the other four are paid an hourly rate. All employees receive overtime pay at $1\frac{1}{2}$ times their regular pay rate. Data relating to the payroll for the week ended March 31 are given below:

Employee	Hours Worked	Pay Rate	Gross Earnings to End of Prior Week
James Allen	44	$7.50 per hour	$3,860
Paul Durango	40	$600 per week	7,800
Ann Poole	42	$7.00 per hour	3,800
John Scott	40	$7.00 per hour	3,960
Amy Thorp	40	$6.00 per hour	3,380

Additional Data:
1. Paul Durango's salary is charged to Office Salaries Expense; the gross earnings of the other employees are charged to Sales Salaries Expense.
2. All salaries and wages are subject to FICA tax; a 7.5% rate is assumed.

3. The federal unemployment tax is 0.8% of the first $7,000 of salaries and wages and the state unemployment tax is 5.4% of the first $10,500 of salaries and wages.
4. Each employee has a $3.50 per week deduction for group medical insurance.
5. Assume the federal income tax withheld the last week in March is:

Allen	$32
Durango	71
Poole	31
Scott	27
Thorp	22

REQUIRED

(a) Prepare the payroll register for the week ended March 31, using the following column headings:

	Earnings			Deductions				
Employee	Regular	Overtime	Gross	FICA Tax	Federal Income Tax	Medical Insurance	Total	Net Earnings

(b) Prepare the general journal entry to record:
   1. The week's payroll.
   2. The employer's payroll taxes for the week.
   3. The payment of the net payroll.

(c) Racine Company remits the group medical insurance premiums to the Badger Insurance Company monthly. Total premiums withheld in March were $87.50. Prepare the general journal entry to record the monthly remittance of these premiums.

(d) The March 31 balances in the FICA Tax Payable and Federal Income Tax Withholding Payable accounts—after posting the entries from part (b)—are $1,245 and $1,090, respectively. Prepare the general journal entry to record the monthly remittance of these taxes to an authorized commercial bank.

(e) Racine Company's total federal unemployment tax for the quarter ended March 31 is $174.20—after posting the entries from requirement (b). Racine Company deposits the taxes quarterly in an authorized commercial bank. Prepare the general journal entry to record this remittance.

(f) The total state unemployment tax for the quarter ended March 31 is $1,169.53—after posting the entries from requirement (b). Prepare the general journal entry to record the quarterly remittance of this tax.

ALTERNATE PROBLEMS

Property tax calculations

12–24A Denton Company prepares monthly financial statements and ends its accounting year on December 31. The company owns a factory in the city of Ashton, where city taxes are assessed on March 1 each year, are paid by May 1, and relate to the city's fiscal year which ends the next June 30 (four months after assessment). For the city tax year 19X1–19X2, Denton paid $24,000 in property taxes on its factory.

REQUIRED
(a) What amount of property tax expense should be accrued on the financial statements for July 19X2, if property taxes for 19X2–19X3 are an estimated 6% higher than they were the preceding year?
(b) Assume that the 19X2–19X3 tax bill received on March 1, 19X3, was for $26,400 and that the estimate in part (a) was used through February. What is the proper monthly property tax expense for March 19X3, if the deficiencies in the monthly property tax estimates through February are handled as an increase in the property tax expense for March 19X3?
(c) How does the payment of the tax bill on May 1, 19X3, affect the amount of property tax expense recognized for May?

Excise and sales tax calculations

12–25A Carlton Corporation initially records its sales at amounts that include any related excise and sales taxes. During May 19XX, Carlton recorded total sales of $271,360. An analysis of May sales indicated the following:
1. Two-tenths of sales were subject to both a 10% excise tax and a 5% sales tax.
2. Six-tenths of sales were subject only to the sales tax.
3. The balance of sales were for labor charges not subject to either excise or sales tax.

REQUIRED
(a) Calculate the amount of sales revenue for May 19XX, and the related liabilities for excise and sales taxes.
(b) Prepare the necessary journal entry at May 31 to record the liabilities for excise tax payable and sales tax payable.

Recording payroll and payroll taxes

12–26A Gannon, Inc., had the following payroll for March 19X8:

Officers' salaries	$38,000
Sales salaries	64,000
Federal income taxes withheld	19,800
FICA taxes withheld	7,650
Hospital insurance premiums deducted	2,100
Salaries (included above) subject to federal unemployment taxes	74,000
Salaries (included above) subject to state unemployment taxes	82,000

REQUIRED
Present general journal entries to record:
(a) Accrual of the payroll.
(b) Payment of the net payroll.
(c) Accrual of employer's payroll taxes. (Assume that the FICA tax matches the amount withheld, the federal unemployment tax is 0.8%, and the state unemployment tax is 5.4%.)
(d) Payment of all liabilities related to this payroll. (Assume all are settled at the same time.)

Recording payroll and payroll taxes

12–27A The following data are taken from Morrow Plumbing Company's March 19X4 payroll:

Administrative salaries	$28,000
Sales salaries	56,000
Custodial salaries	8,000
Total payroll	$92,000
Salaries subject to FICA tax	$92,000
Salaries subject to FUTA unemployment taxes	68,000
Salaries subject to state unemployment taxes	76,000
Federal income taxes withheld from all salaries	19,300

Assume that (1) FICA taxes are 7.5% each for the employee and the employer and (2) the company is subject to a 5.4% state unemployment tax and an 0.8% federal unemployment tax on the first $7,000 paid to each employee.

REQUIRED

Record the following in general journal form:

(a) Accrual of the payroll.
(b) Payment of the net payroll.
(c) Accrual of the employer's payroll taxes.
(d) Payment of the above payroll-related liabilities. (Assume all are settled at the same time.)

Preparing payroll register and recording payroll

12–28A 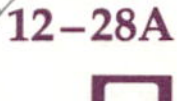 Bradford Company employs five persons, one of whom receives a $525 salary for a 40-hour week; the other four are paid an hourly rate. All employees receive overtime pay at $1\frac{1}{2}$ times their regular pay rate. Data relating to the payroll for the week ended March 31 are given below:

Employee	Hours Worked	Pay Rate	Gross Earnings to End of Prior Week
Janice Carter	43	$9.00 per hour	$4,680
Dale Farmer	40	$525 per week	6,825
George Monroe	40	$7.60 per hour	3,960
James Rider	42	$7.60 per hour	4,120
Robert Warren	40	$8.00 per hour	4,260

Additional Data:

1. Dale Farmer's salary is charged to Office Salaries Expense; the gross earnings of the other employees are charged to Sales Salaries Expense.
2. All salaries and wages are subject to FICA tax; a 7.5% rate is assumed.
3. The federal unemployment tax is 0.8% of the first $7,000 of salaries and wages and the state unemployment tax is 5.4% of the first $10,500 of salaries and wages.
4. Each employee has a $4.00 per week deduction for group medical insurance.
5. Assume the federal income tax withheld the last week in March is:

Carter	$46.00
Farmer	71.00
Monroe	37.00
Rider	34.00
Warren	34.00

REQUIRED

(a) Prepare the payroll register for the week ended March 31, using the following column headings:

Employee	Earnings			Deductions				Net Earnings
	Regular	Overtime	Gross	FICA Tax	Federal Income Tax	Medical Insurance	Total	

(b) Prepare the general journal entry to record:
   1. The week's payroll.
   2. The employer's payroll taxes for the week.
   3. The payment of the net payroll.

(c) Bradford Company remits the group medical insurance premiums to the Colonial Insurance Company monthly. Total premiums withheld in March were $100. Prepare the general journal entry to record the monthly remittance of these premiums.

(d) The March 31 balances in the FICA Tax Payable and Federal Income Tax Withholding Payable accounts—after posting the entries from part (b)—are $1,463.48 and $1,108, respectively. Prepare the general journal entry to record the monthly remittance of these taxes to an authorized commercial bank.

(e) Bradford Company's total federal unemployment tax for the quarter ended March 31 is $158.73—after posting the entries from part (b). Prepare the general journal entry to record this remittance.

(f) The total state unemployment tax for the quarter ended March 31 is $1,368.90—after posting the entries from part (b). Prepare the general journal entry to record the quarterly remittance of this tax.

BUSINESS DECISION PROBLEM

Field Enterprises manages office buildings in several Midwestern cities. The firm maintains its own janitorial staff for all buildings managed. The firm manages ten buildings in Center City, where it maintains a staff of 40 janitorial people, with a total annual payroll of $720,000. All of the staff earn more than $16,000 per year each. Only one employee's salary exceeds the maximum amount subject to FICA tax, by the amount of $2,000. Field pays a 7.5% FICA tax on its payroll and is subject to a 5.4% state unemployment tax on the first $10,000 wages earned by each employee. Its federal unemployment compensation tax rate is 0.8% of the first $7,000 earned by each employee. The firm's contribution to health insurance cost averages $60 per employee. Annual nonpayroll costs of the Center City operation are:

Supplies	$45,000
Depreciation on Equipment	28,000
Insurance	20,000
Miscellaneous	5,000
	$98,000

The firm has a high employee turnover rate and has not always kept tenants happy with the janitorial service. President George Field has been approached by Maintenance,

Inc., a commercial janitorial service chain, which has submitted a bid of $875,000 annually to provide janitorial service for the ten buildings in Center City. This firm is noted for efficiency and satisfactory service. Field estimates that hiring an outside firm would save $8,000 annually in bookkeeping costs and costs of contracting with other commercial firms for substitutes for regular help. These costs are not included in the above list of nonpayroll costs.

REQUIRED

Prepare a cost analysis for Field to help him decide whether to accept the bid of Maintenance, Inc.

ANSWERS TO SELF-TEST QUESTIONS

1. (b) **2.** (c) **3.** (b) **4.** (c) **5.** (a)

13

ACCOUNTING PRINCIPLES AND FINANCIAL STATEMENT DISCLOSURES

CHAPTER OBJECTIVES

1. Discuss the historical development of accounting principles and the nature of the conceptual framework (pp. 447–49, 450).
2. Identify the basic principles underlying accounting theory (pp. 449–58).
3. Discuss the process of revenue recognition and the matching of expenses with revenue (pp. 455–58).
4. Identify and describe the various types of financial statement disclosures (pp. 459–69).
5. Discuss the recommended disclosures concerning the impact of inflation on financial statements (pp. 464–69).

Every why hath a wherefore.
WILLIAM SHAKESPEARE

In Chapter 1, we touched briefly on the role of **generally accepted accounting principles (GAAP)** as the rules by which financial accounting statements are prepared. The phrase *generally accepted accounting principles* encompasses a wide spectrum of accounting guidelines, ranging from basic concepts and standards to detailed methods and procedures. There are principles covering almost every aspect of financial accounting and reporting. We have already discussed many of the methods and procedures within the domain of generally accepted accounting principles, such as inventory pricing methods and depreciation methods. In this chapter, we focus on the fundamental and pervasive principles of accounting, an understanding of which is indispensable to anyone who uses financial accounting data. We also consider the topic of financial statement disclosures.

HISTORICAL DEVELOPMENT

In contrast to the physical sciences, accounting has no immutable or natural laws, such as the law of gravity. The closest approximation to a law in accounting is probably the use of arithmetic functions and logic. Because no basic natural accounting law exists, accounting principles have developed on the basis of their *usefulness*. Consequently, the growth of accounting is more closely related to experience and practice than to the foundation provided by ultimate law. As such, accounting principles tend to evolve rather than be discovered, to be flexible rather than precise, and to be subject to relative evaluation rather than be ultimate or final.

Conventional accounting comprises a relatively recent body of knowledge. Although the origin of double-entry bookkeeping has been traced back to the fourteenth century, most important accounting developments have occurred in the last century.

The recent rapid development of accounting as an information system is largely explained by the economic history of the last eight to ten decades. This period included (1) the development of giant industrial firms, (2) the existence of large stockholders' groups, (3) the pronounced separation of ownership and management of large corporate firms, (4) the rapid growth of industrial and economic activity, and (5) the expansion of government regulation of industry. These factors helped create the large groups of interested parties who require a constant stream of reliable financial information concerning the economic entities they own, manage, or regulate. This information is meaningful only when prepared according to some agreed-on standards and procedures.

Accounting principles—like common law—originate from problem situations such as changes in the law, tax regulations, new business organizational arrangements, or new financing or ownership techniques. In response to the effect such problems have on financial reports, certain accounting techniques or procedures are tried. Through comparative use and analysis, one or more of these techniques are judged most suitable, obtain substantial authoritative support, and are then considered a generally accepted accounting principle.

Organizations such as the Financial Accounting Standards Board (FASB), the American Institute of Certified Public Accountants (AICPA), and the Securities and Exchange Commission (SEC) are instrumental in the development of most accounting principles.

The general acceptance of accounting principles is not determined by a formal vote or survey of practicing accountants. An accounting principle must have substantial authoritative support to qualify as generally accepted. References to a particular accounting principle in authoritative accounting literature constitute substantive evidence of its general acceptance.

Pronouncements by the FASB are the most direct evidence of whether or not a specific accounting principle is generally accepted. Organized in 1973, the FASB has issued more than 100 *Statements of Financial Accounting Standards* dealing with generally accepted accounting principles.[1] Before the creation of the FASB, pronouncements by the AICPA—many of which are still in effect—represented the most authoritative indicators of general acceptance.

During the two decades ending in 1959, the AICPA issued 51 *Accounting Research Bulletins*. These bulletins dealt with a variety of problems and, although they lacked formal legal status, they considerably influenced generally accepted practice. In 1959, the AICPA established the Accounting Principles Board (APB) to issue authoritative opinions on problems related to generally accepted accounting principles. During its existence, the APB issued 31 *Opinions of the Accounting Principles Board*. These opinions increased in importance in 1964 when the AICPA required that any departure from an APB opinion be disclosed in a footnote to the financial statements or in the accompanying auditor's report. When the FASB succeeded the APB in 1973, this requirement was extended to cover FASB pronouncements.

As a federal agency, the SEC's primary focus is to regulate the interstate sale of stocks and bonds. The SEC requires companies under its jurisdiction to submit annual audited financial statements. The SEC has the power to set the accounting principles used by these companies, but, for the most part, the SEC has relied upon the FASB (and earlier, the AICPA) to formulate accounting principles. Because of its interest in full and fair financial reporting, the SEC interacts regularly with the FASB about various accounting problems.

CONCEPTUAL FRAMEWORK

The FASB has developed an overall conceptual framework to guide the formulation of specific accounting principles. The **conceptual framework** is a cohesive set of interrelated objectives and fundamentals for external financial reporting. For business enterprises, the framework consists of (1) financial reporting objectives, (2) qualitative characteristics of accounting information, (3) financial statement elements, and (4) recognition criteria for financial statement items. A recurrent theme throughout the conceptual framework is the importance of providing information that is useful to financial statement readers.

The **financial reporting objectives** focus primarily on information useful to investors and creditors. Accordingly, financial statements should provide information that is (1) useful in making investment, credit, and similar decisions, and

[1]Paralleling the FASB structure, the Governmental Accounting Standards Board (GASB) was organized in 1984 to formulate accounting principles for state and local government financial reporting.

(2) helpful in assessing the ability of enterprises to generate future cash flows. Finally, financial statements should (3) contain information about a firm's economic resources, the claims to these resources, and the effects of events that change these resources and claims. This latter information enhances the efforts of investors and creditors to identify financial strengths and weaknesses, predict future performance, or evaluate earlier expectations.

The conceptual framework also identifies the **qualitative characteristics of accounting information** that contribute to decision usefulness. The two primary qualities are **relevance** and **reliability.** Relevant information, of course, contributes to the predictive and evaluative decisions made by investors and creditors. Reliable information contains no bias or material error, and faithfully portrays what it intends to represent.

Financial statement elements are the significant components used to put financial statements together. They include assets, liabilities, owners' equity, investments by owners, distributions to owners, revenue, expenses, gains, losses, and comprehensive income.[2] The conceptual framework identifies and defines these elements, noting that they reflect the economic resources, claims to resources, and events that are relevant to decisions made by investors and creditors.

The **recognition criteria** specify in broad terms the criteria that must be satisfied before a particular asset, liability, revenue, expense, or the like may be recorded in the accounts. Essentially, the item under consideration must meet the definition of an element and be measurable, and information about the item must achieve the two primary qualities of relevance and reliability.

Exhibit 13–1 summarizes the conceptual framework. Various pieces of this conceptual framework were already a part of the accounting discipline before their consideration by the FASB. Integrating the pieces into a cohesive framework is important, however. The FASB's intent is to solve individual accounting issues and formulate specific accounting principles within the context of the conceptual framework. Consequently, accounting principles based on this framework should form a consistent and coherent set of guidelines for financial reporting. The framework was essentially completed in the mid-1980s; it will be several years before its impact may be properly evaluated.

BASIC PRINCIPLES

The accounting principles we consider in this section are among the most important ideas in accounting theory. Though less than exhaustive, the treatment here should provide sufficient background for further accounting studies. The discussion of each principle begins with a brief description.

Accounting Entity

Each entity should be accounted for separately.

The most fundamental concept in accounting is the entity. An **accounting entity** is an economic unit with identifiable boundaries for which accountants accumulate and report financial information. Before accountants can analyze and

[2]Comprehensive income includes all changes in owners' equity during a period except investments by or distributions to owners and is a concept not yet achieved in practice. For example, prior period adjustments (discussed in Chapter 16) are not included in the income statement under current accounting principles.

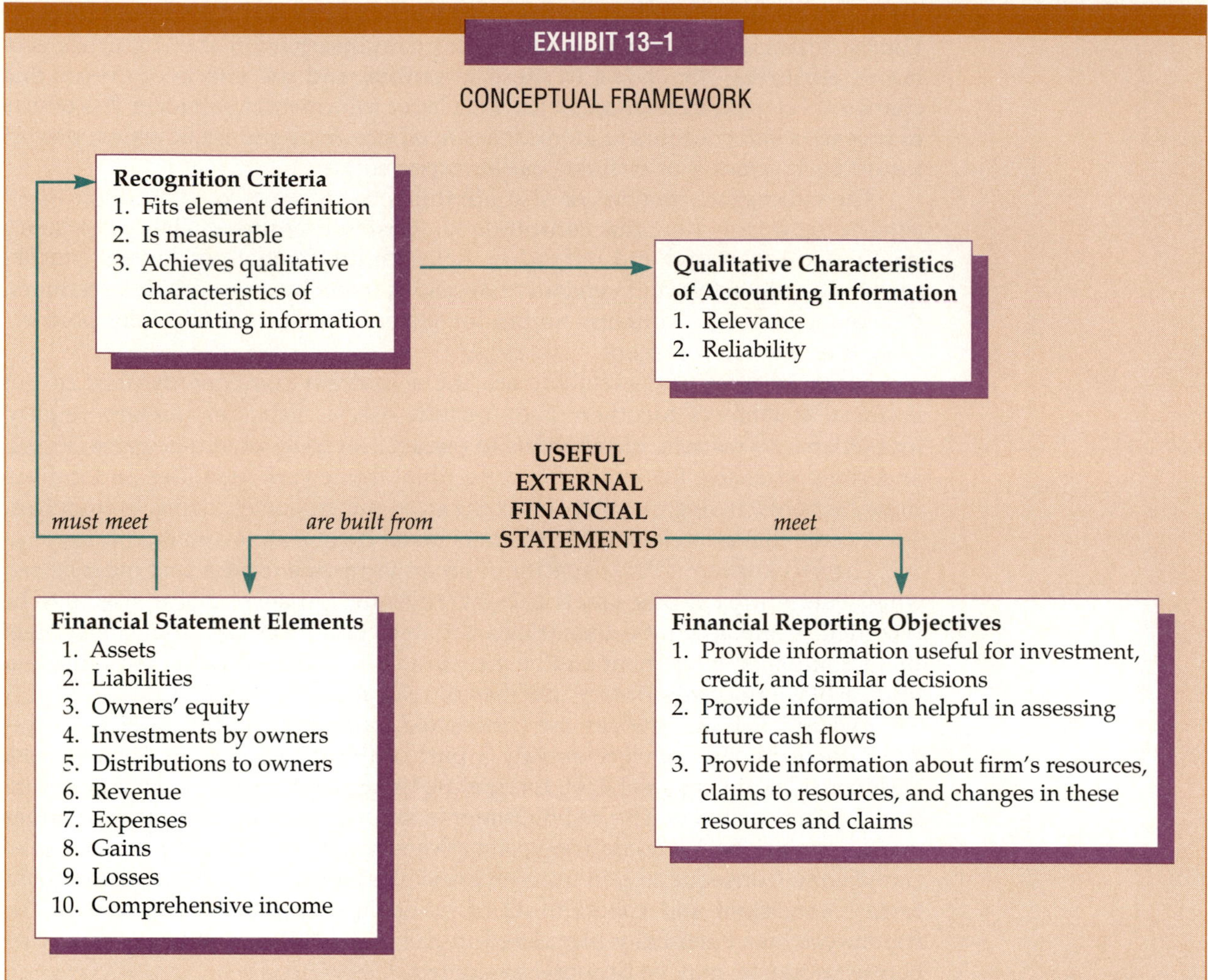

report activities, they must identify the particular entity (and its boundaries) for which they are accounting. Every financial report specifies the entity in its heading.

Each proprietorship, partnership, and corporation is a separate entity, and separate accounting records should be kept for each unit. In accumulating financial information, we must separate the activities of an accounting entity from the other economic and personal activities of its owners. For example, Matt and Lisa Cook own the Good Cook Inn restaurant as partners. The Good Cook Inn partnership is an accounting entity. Matt Cook is also an attorney whose activities constitute a proprietorship. Therefore, he keeps a set of accounting records for his legal activities separate from Good Cook Inn's records of its business activities. Lisa Cook's activities as a realtor also constitute a proprietorship. She keeps a set of accounting records for her realty activities separate from both the records of Good Cook Inn and of Matt Cook, attorney.

An accounting entity may be a unit other than a proprietorship, partnership, or corporation. Data for two or more corporations may be combined to provide financial reports for a larger economic entity. For example, a parent corporation and its wholly owned subsidiaries (corporations in their own right) may consolidate their individual financial reports into a set of consolidated statements covering the group of corporations. (This process is a topic of Chapter 18.) In contrast, internal reports to corporate management may contain financial data concerning the activities of units as small as a division, a department, a profit center, or a plant. In this type of financial reporting, the entity is the division, the department, the profit center, or the plant.

The entity concept does not negate the legal fact that an all-inclusive legal liability exists in proprietorships and partnerships. In other words, business assets are available to personal creditors, and business creditors may have legal access to both business and personal assets in these noncorporate business organizations.

Accounting Period

Accounting reports relate to specific periods—typically, one year.

The operations of most businesses are virtually continuous except for some changes associated with cyclical time periods, seasons, or dates. Thus, any division of the total life of a business into segments based on annual periods is somewhat artificial. However, the idea of **accounting periods** is useful. Many taxes are assessed on an annual basis, and comprehensive reports to corporation stockholders are made annually. In addition, many other noneconomic factors tend to consider the year a natural division of time.

For special purposes, accounting reports may cover other periods. For instance, many companies prepare *interim* financial reports for time spans of less than one year, such as quarterly (three months) or even monthly periods.

The combined effect of the entity and periodicity concepts is illustrated in Exhibit 13–2, which uses the Good Cook Inn and its two owners as an example. The shaded box isolates Good Cook Inn's activities for 19X2. Proper accounting requires that both the entity and the period be identified in financial reports.

As useful as it is, the idea of artificially "cutting off" the business at the end of a certain period presents many problems. Transactions incurred and consummated entirely within one accounting period present few problems. However, many transactions bridge two or more periods, and their total effect on the entity must often be properly allocated among these periods. Problems of *periodicity*

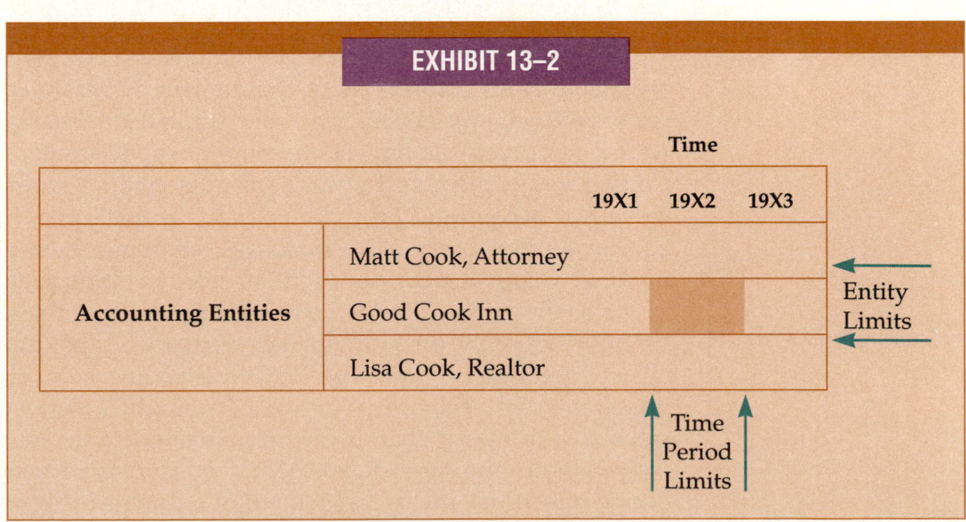

are closely related to the concept of matching revenue and expense, which is developed later in the chapter.

Materiality

Accounting transactions so insignificant that they would not affect the actions of financial statement users are recorded as is most expedient.

Sound accounting procedures require effort and cost money. When the amounts involved are too small to affect the overall picture significantly, the application of theoretically correct accounting procedures is hardly worth its cost. For example, accounting theory asserts that assets acquired and used over several accounting periods should first be recorded as assets, with systematic amounts of depreciation expense recognized in each of the periods in which the assets are used (directly or indirectly) to earn revenue. The principle of **materiality,** however, permits a firm to expense the costs of such items as small tools, pencil sharpeners, and waste paper baskets when acquired because they are "immaterial" in amount. Many firms set dollar limits—such as $25 or $100—below which the costs of all items are expensed.

The concept of materiality is relative—an immaterial amount for General Motors Corporation may be material for smaller companies. Also, the nature of the transaction should be considered. A difference of $1,000 in depreciation expense might be immaterial, but the same discrepancy in cash could be material.

The materiality of an item in a financial statement is usually judged in comparison to a related amount. For example, to determine the effect of the inclusion or omission of an income statement item, we express it as a percentage of net income; a current asset item might be expressed as a percentage of total current assets, and so on. Accounting literature is not precise about what quantitative proportions are deemed material. In specific instances, 5–15% of related amounts have been considered material, but this matter is best subject to judgment. Always remember, however, that although a given series of transactions might *each* be considered immaterial in amount, their aggregate effect could be material in certain circumstances.

Conservatism

Accounting measurements take place in a context of significant uncertainties, and possible errors in measurement of net assets and income should tend toward understatement rather than overstatement.

Accounting determinations are often based on estimates of future events and are therefore subject to a range of optimistic or pessimistic interpretations. In the early 1900s, many abuses were perpetrated on financial statement users who were given overly optimistic measurements of assets and estimates of income. Consequently, the investor was reassured when a company used the "most conservative" accounting procedures. In some instances, banks would write down handsome multistory office buildings, showing them on the balance sheet at a nominal value of $1. The intention was to emphasize the understatement of assets as evidence of conservative accounting and financial strength.

More recently, accountants have recognized that intentional understatement of net assets and income can be as misleading as overly optimistic accounting treatments. For example, stockholders might erroneously decide to sell their stock in a company that grossly understates its income through overly conservative accounting procedures. Also, a conservative treatment in one accounting period may cause the overstatement of reported income for many other periods.

For example, the bank that writes its building down to $1 is, in a sense, "over-depreciating" and therefore understating both assets and income for that period. During the building's remaining useful life, the bank's income is overstated because the related building depreciation expense is omitted from the income statements of those periods.

Today, **conservatism** is the accountant's reaction to situations in which significant uncertainties exist about the outcomes of transactions still in progress. In contrast to the intentional understatements of net assets and income, accountants follow conservative accounting procedures when they are unsure of the proper measure to use. For example, if two estimates of future amounts to be received are about equally likely, conservatism requires the less optimistic estimate be used. Thus, possible errors in measuring net assets and income should tend toward understatement rather than overstatement.

Consistency

Unless otherwise disclosed, accounting reports are prepared on a basis consistent with the preceding period.

In many instances, more than one method of applying a generally accepted accounting principle is possible. In other words, two firms that have identical operating situations might each choose a different—but equally acceptable—accounting method and report different amounts for the same types of transactions.

Changes in accounting procedures that lead to different reported values may affect the amount of reported income. Under certain circumstances, a firm could, by design, increase or decrease its reported earnings simply by changing from one generally accepted accounting principle to another that yields different values. This situation justifies the consistency principle. **Consistency** means the same accounting methods are used from one accounting period to the next. Consistency enhances the utility of financial statements when comparative data for a firm are analyzed.

Of course, there are instances when it is appropriate for a firm to change an accounting method. Indeed, progress in improving accounting data almost dictates that some changes will occur. In these cases, financial statement users should know when and to what extent reported earnings result from changes in accounting techniques. In Chapter 16, we discuss how to report the effects of changes in accounting principles.

Objectivity

Whenever possible, accounting entries must be based on objectively determined evidence.

The concept of **objectivity** requires bias-free and verifiable accounting data. Users want accounting data that are not subject to the capricious whim of either management or the accountant who prepares or audits the statements. Consequently, whenever possible, accounting determinations are based on actual invoices, documents, bank statements, and physical counts of items involved.

Not all accounting determinations can be totally objective. Periodic depreciation and estimates of the eventual collectibility of credit sales are examples of relatively subjective factors routinely incorporated into accounting reports. Several accountants required to determine independently the depreciation expense for a given period on an item of special-purpose equipment would probably come up with a range of suggested amounts. We might expect the range to be in some proportion to the degree of subjectivity involved.

Variations in accounting measurements, of course, lead to variations in reported income. Thus, the more subjective accounting records are, the greater variety there may be in reported income. Because highly subjective determinations are not readily verifiable, a user of a subjectively derived accounting report does not know where this particular statement falls in the range of reportable income figures. An even greater disadvantage is that the user has no way of knowing the motives of the individual preparing the statements. Was he or she trying to be "fair" or attempting to minimize or maximize reported income? We have no reliable source of answers to this question. For this reason, accountants—particularly independent auditors—look for objective evidence to support the accounting data in financial reports.

Going Concern

In the absence of evidence to the contrary, a business is assumed to have an indefinite life.

With few exceptions, business organizations have no anticipated termination date. Most firms operate profitably for indefinite periods and are, in fact, **going concerns.** Firms that do not succeed usually have indications of impending termination for some time before operations actually cease.

The going concern assumption has important implications for accounting procedures. It allows firms to defer costs—such as ending inventories, prepaid expenses, and undepreciated asset balances—that will be charged against the revenue of future periods. Furthermore, the going concern concept assumes the use of cost-based accounting measures rather than market-based liquidation values. Firms that expect to continue profitable operations do not ordinarily sell their operating assets; therefore, potential liquidation prices for these assets at the end of an accounting period may not be especially relevant. In this sense, the going concern assumption justifies the use of historical cost as the primary basis for accounting entries.

Measuring Unit

The unit of measure in accounting is the basic unit of money.

Although other descriptive information is often relevant, money is the common **measuring unit** for recording accounting transactions. By expressing all assets and equities in terms of money, the accountant creates a common denominator that permits addition and subtraction of all forms of assets and equities and makes possible the preparation of financial statements. Expressing all statement items in money terms also permits the comparison of (1) various elements in the financial statements of a firm, (2) different sets of statements for the same firm, and (3) the statements of two or more firms. This principle also assumes the unit of measure is stable; that is, changes in its general purchasing power are not considered sufficiently important to require adjustments to the basic financial statements.

Historical Cost

Accounting measures are primarily based on historical costs.

The dollar amounts in account balances represent the accounting measures of the items about which information is collected. Possible sources of these measures are opinions of management, professional appraisals, current market prices, and historical costs. Accountants have experimented with all of these sources at various times, but with few exceptions, they have used historical cost whenever it is available. Most practicing accountants feel that other sources are so subjective that their use should be seriously limited.

We can describe **historical cost** as an item's "historical exchange price." It represents the amount of cash, or its equivalent, paid to acquire an asset or received when a liability is incurred. Most accountants agree that no item has a single ultimate value and that for the millions of exchanges that occur daily, the exchange price probably best indicates the value of an item at the time of the transaction. Usually we do not attempt to reflect subsequent changes in market values for assets and liabilities, so the initial exchange price of an item becomes known as its historical cost.

Historical costs tend to be highly objective because under classical assumptions they are derived in the marketplace by informed, rational, and independent parties. Also, the details of the original transaction can easily be verified by consulting the documents that are customarily executed at the time of exchange (deeds, bills of sale, checks, and mortgages). An overlooked advantage of historical cost measurement is that the data are a natural byproduct of the exchange transaction itself and are therefore available at little additional cost or effort. Relative objectivity may be the primary justification for historical cost–based accounting measures, but their natural availability at negligible cost is also an important factor—especially when the historical cost method is compared with more expensive sources of values such as professional appraisals.

Matching Expenses with Revenue

To the extent feasible, all expenses related to given revenue are matched with and deducted from that revenue for the determination of periodic income.

Income determination procedures relate expenses and revenue through a matching process. **Matching expenses with revenue** occurs in the following ways:

1. Costs that relate to specific revenue are recognized as expenses whenever the related revenue is recognized. For example, cost of goods sold relates to the specific revenue from the sale of goods. Cost of goods sold is recorded, therefore, in the same accounting period as the sales revenue.
2. Costs that relate to the revenue of several accounting periods are expensed in a systematic and rational manner throughout these periods. The impact of some assets benefiting several periods cannot be traced to any specific revenue amounts. Instead, the asset's cost is matched with each period's overall revenue through appropriate depreciation and amortization procedures. The depreciation of office equipment illustrates this category of matching.
3. Costs that relate only to the current period's overall revenue are expensed immediately. Expenditures that benefit only the current accounting period, such as office salaries expense, fit this category.

The proper matching of expenses with revenue is accomplished primarily through the accrual accounting techniques illustrated throughout the text.

Revenue Recognition at Point of Sale

With limited exceptions, revenue is recognized at the point of sale.

At first, the principle of **revenue recognition at point of sale** may seem obvious. However, modern business operations are often so complicated and so extended that practical questions arise concerning the point at which revenue should be recognized. With the exceptions discussed later in this section, generally accepted accounting principles require the recognition of revenue in the accounting period in which the sale occurs. Moreover, the matching principle (explained above) dictates that we match any related expenses with this revenue in that period. Thus, the combined effect of the two principles requires the recognition of revenue and related expenses in the period of sale.

For services, the sale is deemed to occur when the service is performed. When merchandise is involved, the sale takes place when title to the goods transfers from seller to buyer. In many situations this coincides with the delivery of the merchandise. As a result, accountants usually record revenue when goods are delivered.

To understand the logic of and the exceptions to the principle of recognizing revenue at point of sale, we must consider some underlying factors. Most firms have some sort of cash-to-cash operating cycle, which is diagrammed in Exhibit 13–3. In reality, most firms are engaged in many partially overlapping operating cycles, represented by the following diagram:

For our purposes, it is sufficient to consider the isolated cycle. In Exhibit 13–3, the firm starts with $100 cash and then uses the cash to acquire, handle, store, promote, display, and finally sell the inventory. In a cash sale, inventory is immediately converted to $140 cash. If the sale is made on credit terms, the collection process must be accomplished. The $40 difference between the cash at the cycle's beginning and at its end, reduced by any applicable noncash expenses, is the income generated by the operating cycle.

EXHIBIT 13–3

TYPICAL OPERATING CYCLE FOR A FIRM

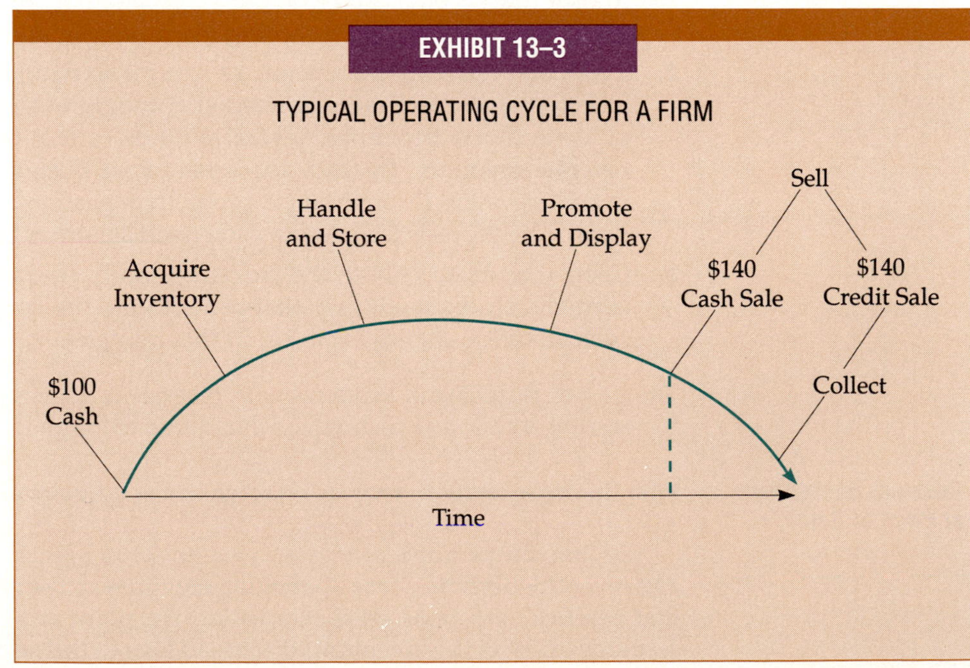

Throughout the cycle, the firm works toward the eventual sale of the goods and collection of the sales price. This cycle is the firm's **earning process** and it should be substantially complete before revenue is recorded. Also, the revenue should be realized before it is recorded in the accounts. **Realized** means that the goods (or services) are exchanged for cash or claims to cash. It is at the point of sale, then, that the two important conditions for revenue recognition are met—at that time the revenue is both (1) *earned* and (2) *realized*.[3]

Other Bases for Revenue Recognition

COLLECTION BASES For selected exceptions, revenue recognition occurs at times other than the point of sale. Methods that delay recognition until cash is collected are *collection basis methods*. These methods usually relate to installment credit sales. A conservative method, known as the **cost recovery method,** considers all cash collections a return of cost until all costs are recovered; the remaining collections are considered gross profit.

Another collection basis method is the **installment method.** The installment method takes its name from the popular sales term for purchases of moderate to large dollar amounts. In effect, the installment method treats each dollar received as part return of cost and part gross profit. The specific proportion of each is determined by the relationship between the cost and the sales price of the merchandise involved. For example, assume that on October 1, 19X7, a refrigerator costing $450 is sold for $600, with installment terms consisting of a 20% down payment and the balance due in 24 equal payments of $20 on the last day of each month. Under the installment basis, because the cost was 75% of the selling price ($450/$600), each dollar collected will be considered 75% return of cost and 25% gross profit. The resulting gross profit during the three years would be recognized as follows:

	19X7		19X8	19X9	
	Down Payment	Three $20 Payments	Twelve $20 Payments	Nine $20 Payments	Totals
Total received (100%)	$120	$60	$240	$180	$600
Considered return of cost (75%)	90	45	180	135	450
Considered gross profit (25%)	30	15	60	45	150

Collection basis methods of revenue recognition should be used when firms *cannot* reasonably estimate the extent of collectibility of the installment receivables. Companies that can reasonably predict and make accruals for future losses should not employ collection basis methods. Instead, they should recognize revenue at point of sale and match with it an appropriate estimate of uncollectible accounts. However, in some instances a firm may use the installment method on its income tax return (regardless of the method used for financial reporting purposes). A firm usually considers it desirable, when possible, to delay gross profit recognition on its income tax return.

PERCENTAGE OF COMPLETION Some operations—such as the construction of roads, dams, and large office buildings—take a long time and therefore cover several

[3] *Statement of Financial Accounting Concepts No. 5,* "Recognition and Measurement in Financial Statements of Business Enterprises" (Stamford, CT: Financial Accounting Standards Board, 1984).

accounting periods. In such situations, the point-of-sale recognition method (called the **completed contract method** when referring to long-term contract accounting) does not work very well, because the revenue (and related gross profit) from several years of construction work may be reported in the income statement of only the period in which the project was completed and sold. Consequently, another method of revenue recognition, **percentage of completion (POC),** may be used.

The POC method simply allocates the revenue on a contract among the several accounting periods involved, in proportion to the estimated percentage of the contract completed each period. To use this method, we must have a reasonably accurate and reliable procedure for estimating periodic progress on the contract. Most often, estimates of the percentage of contract completion are tied to the proportion of total costs incurred.

For example, assume that a dam is to be constructed during a two-year period beginning July 1, 19X1. The contract price is $3,000,000, and estimated total costs are $2,400,000; thus, estimated gross profit is $600,000. If the total cost incurred in 19X1 is $720,000 (that is, 30% of the estimated total), then $900,000 revenue (or 30% of the total revenue) is recognized in 19X1. Similarly, if another 50% of the total estimated costs is incurred in 19X2, then 50% of the total revenue (or $1,500,000) is recognized in 19X2. Under the POC method, the revenue is reflected among the three calendar years as follows:

	(Dollars in Thousands)			
	19X1	**19X2**	**19X3**	**Total**
Cost incurred	$720	$1,200	$480	$2,400
Percent of total costs	30%	50%	20%	100%
Revenue recognized	$900	$1,500	$600	$3,000

The periodic gross profit is equal to the revenue recognized less the costs incurred each period. In our example, the gross profit reflected each year is as follows (amounts in thousands):

	19X1	**19X2**	**19X3**	**Total**
Revenue recognized	$900	$1,500	$600	$3,000
Cost incurred	720	1,200	480	2,400
Gross profit	$180	$ 300	$120	$ 600

Clearly, in long-term construction, the POC method of revenue recognition more reasonably reflects reported revenue and gross profit as an indicator of productive effort than the completed contract basis.

Full Disclosure

All information necessary for the users' understanding of the financial statements must be disclosed.

Accounting's purpose is to provide useful information to various parties interested in a firm's financial performance and position. Often facts or conditions exist that, although not specifically part of the data in the accounts, have considerable influence on the understanding and interpretation of the financial statements. To inform users properly, a firm should disclose this additional information.

In the following section, we expand on this basic principle of **full disclosure.**

FINANCIAL STATEMENT DISCLOSURES

Disclosures related to financial statements fall into one of three categories: (1) parenthetical disclosures on the face of the financial statements, (2) notes to the financial statements, and (3) supplementary information. Most disclosures amplify or explain information contained in the financial statements. Some disclosures, however, add new kinds of information.

Parenthetical Disclosures

Parenthetical disclosures are placed next to an account title or other descriptive label in the financial statements. Their purpose is to provide succinctly some additional detail about the item. The information disclosed parenthetically could instead be disclosed by a note to the statements. The selection of the particular disclosure technique is at the discretion of individual companies. Because they are presented on the face of the financial statements, parenthetical disclosures probably stand a better chance of being noticed by statement readers than do footnote disclosures.

Several types of parenthetical disclosures follow, illustrated with examples that relate to topics we have discussed in earlier chapters.

1. A parenthetical disclosure may report contra asset amounts, such as the allowance for uncollectible accounts or accumulated depreciation.

	19X7	**19X6**
Accounts Receivable, less allowances for uncollectible accounts (19X7—$30,000; 19X6—$26,500)	$215,000	$174,000
Plant and Equipment, less accumulated depreciation (19X7—$530,000; 19X6—$450,000)	997,000	892,000

2. The measurement technique used may be revealed by a parenthetical disclosure.

	19X7	**19X6**
Inventories (at last-in, first-out cost)	$620,000	$710,000
Intangibles (cost less amortization to date)	75,000	80,000

3. An alternate financial measure for the item reported may be disclosed parenthetically.

	19X7	**19X6**
Short-term Stock Investments, at market (cost, $250,000 at December 31, 19X7, and $600,000 at December 31, 19X6)	$210,000	$525,000
Inventories (at last-in, first-out cost; cost using first-in, first-out would have been: 19X7—$1,200,000, 19X6—$1,000,000)	950,000	800,000

4. A parenthetical disclosure may report an amount that is not otherwise separately reported, such as the amount of interest capitalized during the year.

	19X7	**19X6**
Interest Expense (net of capitalized amounts of $29,000 and $11,000, respectively)	$187,000	$162,000

5. Accounts which have been combined and reported as a single figure in the financial statements may be broken down in a parenthetical disclosure.

	19X7	19X6
Cash and Cash Equivalents (including short-term investments of $300,000 and $270,000 at December 31, 19X7 and 19X6, respectively)	$540,000	$420,000

Notes to Financial Statements

Although much information is gathered, summarized, and reported in financial statements, the statements alone are limited in their ability to convey a complete picture of a firm's financial status. *Notes* are added to financial statements to help fill in the gaps. In fact, accountants have given so much attention to financial statement notes in recent years that today it is not unusual for the notes to take up more space than the statements themselves. Notes may cover a wide variety of topics. Typically, they deal with significant accounting policies, explanations of complex or special transactions, details of reported amounts, commitments, contingencies, segments, quarterly data, and subsequent events.

SIGNIFICANT ACCOUNTING POLICIES Accounting principles contain several instances where alternative procedures are acceptable. For example, there are several acceptable depreciation and inventory pricing methods, revenue on long-term construction contracts may be recognized using either the percentage-of-completion or the completed contract method, and revenue from some installment sales may be recognized using collection basis methods. The particular procedures selected obviously affect the financial data presented. Further, unique or complex events may require innovative applications of accounting principles. Knowledge of a firm's specific accounting principles and methods of applying these principles helps users understand the financial statements. Accordingly, these principles and methods are disclosed in a **summary of significant accounting policies.** The summary is either the initial note to the financial statements or immediately precedes the notes. The number of policies listed, of course, will vary from firm to firm, but the policies relating to inventory pricing methods, depreciation methods, and consolidation practices (discussed in Chapter 18) are invariably included.

For example, a recent annual report of FlightSafety International, Inc., contains the following description of its depreciation policies (FlightSafety offers training to aircraft pilots and crews of ocean-going vessels):

> Depreciation is provided on the straight-line method over estimated useful lives as follows: simulators, training equipment and spare parts, 4 to 20 years; buildings, 25 to 40 years; and furniture, fixtures and equipment, 3 to 14 years. Leasehold improvements, including buildings on leased property, are amortized over the life of the lease or the life of the improvement, whichever is shorter.
>
> Effective January 1, 1987, the Company changed the estimated useful lives of its simulators from eight to 12 years and their salvage value from zero to 10 percent of original cost, based upon historical experience and industry practices. The effect of this change was to decrease depreciation expense by approximately $11,217,000 and increase net income by $6,346,000 or 28 cents per share in 1987.

EXPLANATIONS OF COMPLEX OR SPECIAL TRANSACTIONS The complexity of certain transactions means that not all important aspects are likely to be reflected in the accounts. Financial statement notes, therefore, report the additional relevant details about such transactions. Typical examples include notes discussing financial aspects of pension plans, profit sharing plans, acquisitions of other companies, borrowing agreements, stock option and other incentive plans, and income taxes.

Transactions with related parties are special transactions requiring disclosure in the financial statement notes.[4] *Related party transactions* include transactions between a firm and its (1) principal owners, (2) members of management, (3) subsidiaries, or (4) affiliates. The transactions may be sales or purchases of property, leases, borrowings or lendings, and the like. These transactions are not arm's length transactions; that is, they are not between independent parties each acting in its own best interests (as is true in most transactions). Because of the relationships between the parties, one party may exert significant influence over the other party and the results may differ from what would occur in an arm's length transaction (for example, the interest rate for funds borrowed may be below the current market rate). A user trying to compare a firm's financial data with that of prior periods or other similar companies will find related party information useful. It may help identify and explain differences in the data.

To illustrate, a recent annual report of Patten Corporation contains the following description of a related party transaction (Patten buys, sells, and finances residential and recreational land):

> During fiscal year 1987, the Company made sales of real estate to certain officers and shareholders of Patten Corporation and a Director. Such sales of real estate amounted to $1,250,000 and had a cost of real estate sold of $318,666. Notes receivable in connection with such sales amount to $714,432 and $917,072 at April 3, 1988 and March 31, 1987, respectively, bear interest at an initial rate of 10% per annum, adjustable annually to a rate not in excess of prime plus 2%, and have a term of 15 years. The sales were approved by all of the disinterested Directors.

DETAILS OF REPORTED AMOUNTS Financial statements often summarize several groups of accounts into a single dollar amount. For example, a balance sheet may show as one asset an amount labeled "property, plant, and equipment" or it may list "long-term debt" as a single amount among the liabilities. These aggregated amounts may be sufficient for some financial statement users, but others want more detail about these items. Notes will report this detail, presenting schedules that list the types and amounts of property, plant, and equipment and long-term debt. Other items that may be summarized in the financial statements and detailed in the notes include inventories, other current assets, notes payable, accrued liabilities, owners' equity, and income tax expense.

The footnotes to Whirlpool Corporation's annual report (starting on page 1119) contain several examples of financial statement items that are detailed, including inventories (note 4), long-term debt (note 6), and income taxes (note 9).

COMMITMENTS A firm may have contractual arrangements existing at a balance sheet date where both parties to the contract still have acts to perform. If performance under these **commitments** will have a significant financial impact on the firm, the existence and nature of the commitments should be disclosed in

[4] *Statement of Financial Accounting Standards No. 57*, "Related Party Disclosures" (Stamford, CT: Financial Accounting Standards Board, 1982).

the financial statement notes. Examples of commitments reported in footnotes are commitments under operating leases, contracts to purchase materials or equipment, contracts to construct facilities, salary commitments to executives, commitments to retire or redeem stock, and commitments to deliver goods.

A recent annual report of Armco, Inc., includes the following examples of significant purchase commitments (Armco is primarily a producer of steel products):

> Armco has agreed to purchase approximately 13,200,000 tons of iron ore at competitive prices from a Brazilian iron ore company. Under this agreement, Armco will purchase its annual requirements of sinter feed ore and take annual minimum deliveries of 200,000 tons of iron ore pellets.
>
> In February, 1984, Armco contracted to purchase substantially all of its requirements of high volatile metallurgical coal for its steel operations from Peabody Coal Company. This contract provides for a minimum take of 7,454,000 tons of coal over the remaining six-year life of the contract at formula prices based on various indices to approximate market value. Armco believes its need for high volatile metallurgical coal is in excess of the minimum take amounts required to be purchased under this agreement. Armco purchased 2,477,000, 1,819,000, and 1,656,000 tons of coal from Peabody in 1987, 1986, and 1985.

CONTINGENCIES We discussed contingent liabilities in Chapter 12. As noted there, if the future event that would turn a contingency into an obligation is not likely to occur, or if the liability amount cannot be reasonably estimated, the **contingency** is disclosed parenthetically or in a note to the financial statements. Typical contingencies disclosed in notes are lawsuits, possible income tax assessments, credit guarantees, and discounted notes receivable.

Fleming Companies, a wholesale food distributor, reported the following contingency in a recent annual report:

> During 1987 the Internal Revenue Service audited the company's returns for 1983 and 1984. The service disagrees with the company's practice of excluding certain dividends received from taxable income and has advised it will propose assessments resulting in approximately $2 million additional taxes. The company believes that its position is fully supported and will vigorously oppose the assessments. In the opinion of management the ultimate resolution of this issue will have no material adverse financial effect.

SEGMENTS Many firms diversify their activities and operate in several different industries. The firms' financial statements combine information from all operations into aggregate amounts. This complicates the users' ability to analyze the statements because the interpretation of financial data is influenced by the industry in which a firm operates. Different industries face different types of risk and have different rates of profitability. In making investment and lending decisions, users evaluate risk and required rates of return. Having financial data available by industry segments is helpful to such evaluations.

The FASB recognizes the usefulness of industry data to investors and lenders. Public companies with significant operations in more than one industry must report certain information by industry **segments.** Typically, these disclosures are in the financial statement notes. The major disclosures by industry segment are revenue, operating profit or loss, and identifiable assets (the assets used by the segment).

Other types of segment data may also be disclosed. Obviously, operations in different parts of the world are subject to different risks and opportunities for growth. Thus, public firms with significant operations in foreign countries must report selected financial data by foreign geographic area. The data disclosed are revenue, operating profit or loss (or other profitability measure), and identifiable assets. Also, if a firm has export sales or sales to a single customer that are 10% or more of total revenue, the amount of such sales must be separately disclosed.

As an example of the latter type of segment disclosure, Applied Magnetics Corporation reports the following segment information in a recent annual report (Applied Magnetics manufactures magnetic heads used in disk and tape drives):

> The Company operates in one market worldwide—computer equipment, components and services.
>
> Sales of 10% or more of consolidated net sales were made to one customer in 1987 (16%), to two customers in 1986 (10% each), and to a single customer in 1985 (15%). One of these customers accounted for more than 10% of consolidated net sales in both 1987 and 1986.
>
> Net sales of the United States operations included export sales of $32,539,000, $18,144,000 and $10,970,000 in 1987, 1986 and 1985, respectively.

QUARTERLY DATA Interim financial reports cover periods shorter than one year. Companies that issue interim reports to investors and others generally do so quarterly. These reports provide users with timely information on a firm's progress and are most useful in predicting what the annual financial results will be. The SEC requires certain companies to disclose selected quarterly financial data in their annual reports to stockholders. Included among the notes, the data reported for each quarter include sales, gross profit, net income, and earnings per share. **Quarterly data** permit users to analyze such things as the seasonal nature of operations, the impact of diversification on quarterly activity, and whether the firm's activities lead or lag general economic trends.

Note 14 to Whirlpool Corporation's financial statements in its 1988 annual report (page 1128) illustrates a disclosure of quarterly data for a two-year period.

SUBSEQUENT EVENTS If a company issues a large amount of securities or suffers a casualty loss after the balance sheet date, this information should be reported in a note to the readers, even though the situation arose subsequent to the balance sheet date. Firms are responsible for disclosing any significant events that occur between the balance sheet date and the date the financial statements are issued. This guideline recognizes that it takes several weeks for financial statements to be prepared and audited before they are issued. Events occurring during this period that may have a material effect on the firm's operations are certainly of interest to readers and should be disclosed. Other examples of **subsequent events** requiring disclosure are sales of assets, significant changes in long-term debt, and acquisitions of other companies.

For example, Chyron Corporation reports the following subsequent event in its 1988 annual report (Chyron—a manufacturer of electronic titling, graphics, special effects, and editing equipment—ends its fiscal year on June 30):

> During August 1988, the Company entered into an agreement to acquire Aurora Systems (Aurora). The agreement will be incorporated in Aurora's Plan of Reorganization to be submitted to the bankruptcy court, which is subject to confirmation under Chapter 11 of the Bankruptcy Code. If confirmed, the agreement will require, among other things, an aggregate consideration, including possible contingent payments, of approximately $2,000,000, comprised of cash and the Company's common stock.

Supplementary Information

Supplementing the financial statements are several additional disclosures—management's financial discussion and analysis of the statements, selected financial data covering a five- to ten-year period, and perhaps information on the impact of inflation. These *supplementary* disclosures are either required of certain companies by the SEC or recommended (but not required) by the FASB.

MANAGEMENT'S DISCUSSION AND ANALYSIS Management may increase the usefulness of financial statements by sharing some of their knowledge about the company's financial condition and operations. This is the purpose of the disclosure devoted to management's discussion and analysis. In this supplement to the financial statements, management identifies and comments on events and trends influencing the firm's liquidity, operating results, and financial resources. Management's closeness to the company not only gives them insights unavailable to outsiders, but also may introduce certain biases into the analysis. Nonetheless, management's comments, interpretations, and explanations should contribute to a better understanding of the financial statements.

COMPARATIVE SELECTED FINANCIAL DATA The analysis of financial performance is enhanced if a firm's financial data for several years are available. By analyzing trends over time, the analyst learns much more about a company than is possible from only a single year's data. Year-to-year changes may give clues as to future growth or may highlight areas for concern. Corporate annual reports to stockholders present complete financial statements in comparative form, showing the current year and one or two preceding years. Beyond this, however, the financial statements are supplemented by a summary of selected key financial statistics for a five- or ten-year period. The financial data presented in this historical summary usually include sales, net income, dividends, earnings per share, working capital, and total assets.

INFLATION ACCOUNTING Inflation has an impact on virtually every aspect of economic affairs, including investment decisions, pricing policies, marketing strategies, and salary and wage negotiations. Persons making economic decisions utilize financial data prepared by accountants. Conventional financial statements, however, contain no explicit adjustments for the impact of inflation on the financial data. In response to this, the FASB encourages companies to disclose supplementary information about the effects of changing prices on the firm's financial data.[5]

The recommended supplementary data combine two types of adjustments for changing prices. One, **constant dollar accounting,** adjusts financial data for changes in the general purchasing power of the dollar. The other, **current cost accounting,** reflects the impact of specific price changes on a firm by incorporating current value measurements into the data. We now examine the nature of these adjustments.

Constant dollar accounting The general purchasing power of the dollar is a measure of its ability to buy goods and services. *Price-level changes* are changes in the prevailing exchange ratio between money and goods or services. Whenever a

[5] *Statement of Financial Accounting Standards No. 89,* "Financial Reporting and Changing Prices" (Stamford, CT: Financial Accounting Standards Board, 1986).

21-DIGIT INFLATION

On a few occasions in the last quarter century, the United States' annual rate of inflation has exceeded 10%. A double-digit inflation rate is considered high for the United States, but it pales before the all-time record, noted in the following excerpt.

> No, the famous hyper-inflation of the German mark in 1923 is not the world's record. That distinction is held by Hungary, whose inflation in 1946 was a *thousand* times worse. In 1939, just before World War II, one American dollar bought 3.38 Hungarian pengös. In July 1946, the same dollar was worth 500,000,000,000,000,000,000 (500 million trillion) pengös. Never before—or since—has so much been worth so little.
>
> After the war, rural Hungarians quickly abandoned money in favor of primitive barter, but people in Budapest had to cope with the monetary system. Wages were raised daily, but prices rose by the hour. Shoppers carried their money in large bags, as high-speed presses raced to turn out currency notes in ever larger denominations. Savings evaporated and the moneyed classes were wiped out. The $100,000 worth of pengös one had banked in 1939 weren't worth the trouble it took to withdraw them in 1946. Not when a haircut cost 800 trillion pengös in Budapest, and the average annual income there would buy only $50 worth of merchandise on the black market—the only place where consumer goods could be purchased.*

*From "21-Digit Inflation," Irving Wallace, David Wallechinsky, and Amy Wallace, in "Significa," *Parade* Magazine, October 18, 1981, p. 20.

rise in the general level of prices for goods and services occurs, the general purchasing power of the dollar declines; this is **inflation.** In contrast, **deflation** is an increase in the dollar's general purchasing power as the general level of prices declines. Our discussion is in the context of inflation, the prevailing price-level movement of the last several decades.

Price indexes measure price-level changes. A **price index** represents a series of measurements, stated as percentages, indicating the relationship between (a) the weighted average price of a sample of goods and services at various points in time and (b) the weighted average price of a similar sample of goods and services at a common, or base, date.

For example, assume we wish to construct a price index for a single commodity that was priced at $1.60 in December 19X2, $2 in December 19X3, and $2.50 in December 19X4. If we select December 19X3 as our base date, our price index expresses the price of this commodity in December of 19X2, 19X3, and 19X4 as a percentage of its price in December 19X3. The 19X2 price is 80% ($1.60/$2) of the 19X3 price, and the 19X4 price is 125% ($2.50/$2) of the 19X3 price. The percentage relationship on the base date is, of course, always 100%. The price index for each date is as follows (the percent sign is understood and usually not shown with index numbers):

December 19X2	80
December 19X3	100
December 19X4	125

Prominent examples of price indexes are the Consumer Price Index for All Urban Consumers and the Gross National Product Implicit Price Deflator. The FASB recommends the use of the Consumer Price Index for any general purchasing power adjustments. The monthly calculation of the Consumer Price Index is one advantage it has over the GNP Implicit Price Deflator, which is calculated quarterly.

With index numbers, amounts stated in terms of dollars of general purchasing power at a particular time may be restated in terms of dollars of different purchasing power at another time. We simply multiply the amount to be restated by the following *conversion factor:*

$$\frac{\text{Index You Are Converting TO}}{\text{Index You Are Converting FROM}}$$

For example, suppose we acquired a parcel of land for $5,000 in December 19X3, when the general price index was 100. Suppose also that the general price indexes for various times were as follows:

December 19X2	80
December 19X3	100
December 19X4	125
Average for 19X4	110

We restate the cost of the land in terms of the December 19X4 dollar by multiplying the $5,000 by the conversion factor 125/100 (December 19X4 index/December 19X3 index). The resulting measure is $6,250, the cost of the land stated in dollars of December 19X4 general purchasing power. The cost of the land in terms of the 19X4 average dollar is $5,000 × 110/100 = $5,500. The amounts $5,000, $6,250, and $5,500 each represent the cost of the land, but the cost is expressed in a different unit of measure in each case.

Current market values may also be expressed in different units of general purchasing power. Assume at December 31, 19X4, the current market value of the land is $7,500. This amount exceeds the land's historical cost adjusted for changes in the dollar's general purchasing power to December 31, 19X4 ($6,250), indicating the specific price of this land has increased more than prices in general. The land's current market value is a financial measure taken at December 31, 19X4, so it is stated in terms of the dollar's general purchasing power at that date (price index of 125). As with any dollar amount, we may restate this measure to other units of general purchasing power by using the proper conversion factor. For example, the land's December 31, 19X4, current market value restated to the 19X4 average purchasing power of the dollar is $7,500 × 110/125 = $6,600.

Generally accepted accounting principles use the dollar as a measuring unit and assume it is stable (that is, that no significant general price-level changes occur); therefore, all dollars are considered economically equal. Obviously, some single-year levels of inflation have strained the stable-dollar assumption, and certainly, some multiyear periods have invalidated it. A benefit of adjusting for changes in the general purchasing power of the dollar is that better comparisons of financial data through time are achieved.

To illustrate, assume that the average price-level indexes and Company A's sales revenue for 19X2–19X4 are as shown:

	Average Price-level Index	**Unadjusted Sales**
19X2	75	$1,500,000
19X3	88	1,650,000
19X4	110	1,900,000

Events that occur fairly evenly throughout the year, such as sales, are assumed to be initially stated in dollars of the average purchasing power for the year. The 19X2 unadjusted sales, then, are stated in dollars of 19X2 average purchasing power; 19X3 sales are measured in dollars of 19X3 average purchasing power; and 19X4 sales are stated in dollars of 19X4 average purchasing power.

The unadjusted sales figures indicate a healthy increase in sales. However, if we convert the dollars stated in the average price-level for 19X2, 19X3, and 19X4 to a common unit of general purchasing power—a dollar with the 19X4 average purchasing power—we discover the following sales levels:

	Average Price-level Index	Unadjusted Sales	Conversion Factor	Restated Sales
19X2	75	$1,500,000	110/75	$2,200,000
19X3	88	1,650,000	110/88	2,062,500
19X4	110	1,900,000	110/110	1,900,000

Adjusting the data to a common dollar indicates a decrease in sales activity rather than an increase. During periods of significant inflation, other comparative data, such as net income and dividends, may be similarly affected. Putting comparative data in the same unit of general purchasing power, then, may help users to better analyze and interpret the data.

A new item computed from constant dollar adjustments is the **purchasing power gain or loss on net monetary items.** Net monetary items are monetary assets less monetary liabilities. Monetary assets include cash and other assets—such as receivables—that represent the right to receive a fixed number of dollars in the future, regardless of price-level changes. Monetary liabilities are obligations to disburse a fixed number of dollars in the future, regardless of price-level changes. Most liabilities are monetary. By their nature, monetary items in a balance sheet are stated in dollars of current purchasing power at the balance sheet date.

Holding monetary items during a period of rising prices creates purchasing power gains and losses on these items. For example, suppose you hold $1,000 cash during a period when the general price level increases from 100 to 125. At the end of the period, your $1,000 will buy fewer goods and services than it would at the beginning of the period. This decrease in your ability to buy goods and services as a result of inflation is a *purchasing power loss on cash*. The amount of the loss, stated in end-of-year general purchasing power, is $250, calculated by multiplying the percentage increase in prices, 25%, by the $1,000 cash you held.

Assume you also had a note payable of $800 outstanding during the time the general price index increased from 100 to 125. As a result of inflation, you owe dollars whose general purchasing power at the end of the period is less than it was at the beginning of the period. The decrease in the general purchasing power of the dollars with which you will settle the liability represents a *purchasing power gain on the note payable*. The amount of the gain, stated in end-of-year general purchasing power, is $200 (25% × $800).

Combining the $250 purchasing power loss on cash and the $200 purchasing power gain on the note payable gives a $50 purchasing power loss on *net* monetary items, stated in year-end general purchasing power. Purchasing power gains and losses have no counterpart in conventional financial statements. They are computed only by making constant dollar adjustments. The net purchasing power gain or loss is one indicator of how well management handled monetary items during a period of inflation or deflation and may, therefore, be useful to financial statement readers.

Current cost accounting Current cost accounting is a system for incorporating current values into the financial data. The current cost of an asset is the estimated cost to acquire a similar asset at current prices. Under a system of current cost accounting, net income is determined by subtracting from revenue the current cost of assets used in the earning process. Assets at year-end are measured at their current cost. Changes in the current cost of an asset are reflected in the period in which the change in value occurs.

A simple example illustrates the basic concepts of current cost accounting. Assume Densmore, Inc., started business on January 1, 19X4, with the following assets:

Cash	$10,000
Inventory (7,500 units @ $10)	75,000
Land	15,000

During 19X4, Densmore, Inc., sold 5,000 inventory units at $16 each and incurred cash operating expenses of $18,000. Densmore's 19X4 historical cost income statement follows:

Historical Cost		
Sales	$80,000	(5,000 units @ $16)
Cost of Goods Sold	$50,000	(5,000 units @ $10)
Operating Expenses	18,000	
Total Expenses	$68,000	
Net Income	$12,000	

Now assume that before any inventory was sold in 19X4, its current cost increased to $11 per unit and remained there until year-end. Densmore's 19X4 income statement using current cost procedures follows:

Current Cost		
Sales	$80,000	
Cost of Goods Sold	$55,000	(5,000 units @ $11)
Operating Expenses	18,000	
Total Expenses	$73,000	
Net Income	$ 7,000	

The $7,000 current cost net income shows earnings after first providing for the replacement of assets used in operations. Expenses are measured at their current costs when incurred. Current cost net income, therefore, indicates the profitability of operations at the company's current level of operating costs. It also represents the maximum dividend the company could pay and still maintain its present level of operations.

Changes in the specific prices of assets held during the year are identified using current cost procedures. To continue our Densmore, Inc., illustration, assume the replacement cost of land increased to $19,000 by year-end. Current cost procedures will show a 19X4 increase of $11,500 in the current cost of inventory and land held during the year, computed as follows:

Inventory: Increase from $10 to $11 on 7,500 units	$ 7,500
Land: Increase from $15,000 to $19,000	4,000
Increase in current cost during 19X4	$11,500

Note the current cost increase includes $5,000 that relates to the inventory units sold during 19X4. The increase in their replacement cost occurred before they were sold so the increase does belong as part of the value change that occurred while Densmore held the assets.

One issue in current cost accounting is whether the changes in the current costs of assets held should be included as part of net income or handled separately. The disclosures encouraged by the FASB use the latter treatment.

FASB disclosures From December 25, 1979, through December 2, 1986, the FASB required large, publicly held companies to disclose supplementary inflation information. During this time, the FASB experimented with, and evaluated, various constant dollar and current cost disclosures. By the end of 1986, the inflation rate was low enough that the disclosures were made voluntary. Most of the disclosures encouraged by the FASB are current cost amounts stated in a constant unit of general purchasing power. It believes that this combination encompasses the best aspects of both constant dollar and current cost accounting. Constant dollar adjustments stabilize the purchasing power of the unit of measure and reveal the purchasing power gain or loss on net monetary items, while current cost calculations show the impact of specific price changes during the period.

The disclosures encouraged by the FASB consist of a five-year schedule of selected data (all stated in the same unit of general purchasing power) and a few additional current year disclosures. Included in the five-year schedule are such items as net sales, net income[6] computed using current cost accounting, the purchasing power gain or loss on net monetary items, and the increase or decrease in the current cost of inventory and plant assets. Included among the additional current year disclosures are the year-end current costs of inventory and plant assets.

Because there is a cost to compiling constant dollar and current cost data, few companies are voluntarily making these supplementary disclosures. Should the future rate of inflation increase to the point where disclosures are again required, the current recommended disclosures will be the likely starting point for the development of the required disclosures.

Concluding Remarks

The preceding catalogue of parenthetical disclosures, notes, and supplementary information demonstrates the breadth and detail of data that accompanies a set of financial statements. To some, the vast and increasing array of financial statement disclosures threatens to turn a wealth of information into an information "overload." Whether there is too much information, of course, depends on the needs and financial sophistication of users. Nonetheless, it is obvious that much may be learned by reading these disclosures.

[6]If a company reports extraordinary items or discontinued operations, then income from continuing operations rather than net income is reported on a current cost basis. We discuss extraordinary items, discontinued operations, and income from continuing operations in Chapter 16.

KEY POINTS FOR CHAPTER OBJECTIVES

1. Discuss the historical development of accounting principles and the nature of the conceptual framework (pp. 447–49, 450).
   - The FASB, the AICPA, and the SEC have been instrumental in the development of generally accepted accounting principles.
   - The conceptual framework is a cohesive set of interrelated objectives and fundamentals for external financial reporting.
2. Identify the basic principles underlying accounting theory (pp. 449–58).
   - Each of the following is an important basic accounting principle:

accounting entity	going concern
accounting period	measuring unit
materiality	historical cost
conservatism	matching expenses with revenue
consistency	revenue recognition at point of sale
objectivity	full disclosure

3. Discuss the process of revenue recognition and the matching of expenses with revenue (pp. 455–58).
   - Revenue is usually recognized at point of sale because it is then both earned and realized.
   - The installment method of revenue recognition treats each dollar received as part return of cost and part gross profit.
   - The percentage of completion method recognizes revenue in proportion to the amount of the total contract completed in the period.
4. Identify and describe the various types of financial statement disclosures (pp. 459–69).
   - Financial statement disclosures provide additional information about financial performance and position and appear as parenthetical disclosures, notes, or supplementary information.
5. Discuss the recommended disclosures concerning the impact of inflation on financial statements (pp. 464–69).
   - Recommended inflation disclosures combine constant dollar adjustments and current cost adjustments.
   - Constant dollar adjustments restate financial data to dollars of the same general purchasing power.
   - Current cost adjustments reflect operating expenses at their current costs and measure assets at current costs.

KEY TERMS USED IN THIS CHAPTER

accounting entity 449
accounting period 451
commitments 461
completed contract method 458
conceptual framework 448
conservatism 453
consistency 453
constant dollar accounting 464
contingencies 462
cost recovery method 457
current cost accounting 464
deflation 465
earning process 457
financial reporting objectives 448
financial statement elements 449
full disclosure 458
generally accepted accounting principles (GAAP) 447
going concern 454
historical cost 455
inflation 465
installment method 457

matching expenses with revenue 455
materiality 452
measuring unit 454
objectivity 453
percentage of completion (POC) method 458
price index 465
purchasing power gain or loss on net monetary items 467
qualitative characteristics of accounting information 449
quarterly data 463
realized 457
recognition criteria 449
relevance 449
reliability 449
revenue recognition at point of sale 455
segments 462
subsequent events 463
summary of significant accounting policies 460

SELF-TEST QUESTIONS FOR REVIEW

(Answers are at the end of this chapter.)

1. Which of the following is not included in the overall conceptual framework for business enterprises?
   (a) Financial reporting objectives.
   (b) Financial statement elements.
   (c) Inflation accounting disclosures.
   (d) Qualitative characteristics of accounting information.
2. Plant assets are depreciated over their useful lives. Which basic principle of accounting does this procedure reflect?
   (a) Historical cost. (c) Consistency.
   (b) Matching expenses with revenue. (d) Objectivity.
3. On August 1, 19X5, Perry Company sold a computer costing $3,500 for $5,000. The customer paid 25% down with the balance due in 30 equal monthly payments of $125 starting September 1, 19X5. Using the installment method, how much gross profit is recognized in 19X5?
   (a) $525 (b) $1,500 (c) $150 (d) $1,225
4. During 19X5, Switzer Company made interest-free loans totaling $2,500,000 to certain of its officers. The money is used to finance construction of a special facility which will then be leased to Switzer. Switzer discloses this situation in a note to its 19X5 financial statements. This note is an example of a
   (a) Contingency disclosure.
   (b) Significant accounting policy disclosure.
   (c) Related party disclosure.
   (d) Subsequent event disclosure.
5. Assume constant dollar adjustments are made. Which of the following items will generate a purchasing power loss if held by a company during an inflationary period?
   (a) Accounts payable. (c) Wages payable.
   (b) Land. (d) Accounts receivable.

DEMONSTRATION PROBLEM FOR REVIEW

On November 1, 19X7, Dent Company sold a sofa for $900 on terms of 20% down on the purchase date, and 18 equal monthly payments of $40 beginning December 1, 19X7. The sofa cost $540. Compute the amount of gross profit shown in each calendar year involved using the following revenue recognition methods:

(a) Point-of-sale method.
(b) Installment method.
(c) Cost recovery method.

SOLUTION TO DEMONSTRATION PROBLEM

(a) Under the point-of-sale method, all of the revenue and gross profit would be recognized in November, 19X7, as follows:

Sales	$900
Cost of Goods Sold	540
Gross Profit	$360

(b) Under the installment method, the gross profit percentage is $360/$900 = 40%. Cash collected is treated as 60% cost recovery and 40% gross profit.

	19X7	19X8	19X9
Cash collected			
19X7: Down payment ($180) + one $40 monthly payment	$220		
19X8: Twelve $40 monthly payments		$480	
19X9: Five $40 monthly payments			$200
Considered return of cost (60%)	132	288	120
Considered gross profit (40%)	88	192	80

(c) Under the cost recovery method, no gross profit is recorded until the cost of the item sold ($540) has been collected in cash; all cash collected after the cost has been recovered is gross profit.

	19X7	19X8	19X9
Cash collected	$220	$480	$200
Considered return of cost (first $540)	220	320	0
Considered gross profit (last $360)	0	160	200

QUESTIONS

13–1 How would you determine whether a particular accounting procedure is a generally accepted accounting principle?

13–2 Discuss the origin of accounting principles.

13–3 Why has the FASB developed a conceptual framework?

13–4 Identify two primary qualities of accounting information that contribute to decision usefulness.

13–5 In one sentence, describe each of the following accounting principles:

accounting entity	going concern
accounting period	measuring unit
materiality	historical cost
conservatism	matching expenses with revenue
consistency	revenue recognition at point of sale
objectivity	full disclosure

13–6 Why is the accounting entity the most fundamental accounting concept?

13–7 Why do accounting principles emphasize historical cost as a basis for measuring assets?

13–8 How do accountants justify using the point of sale for revenue recognition?

13–9 Explain the procedures and justification for using the following methods of revenue recognition: (a) the installment method and (b) the percentage-of-completion method.

13–10 Identify the three categories of financial statement disclosures.

13–11 Morris Knudsen Corporation owns the largest shipbuilding company on the west coast. Where in Morris Knudsen's financial report should you look to determine the method it uses to recognize revenue on new ship construction and on ship repair contracts?

13–12 The Tribune Company operates principally in four industries: newspaper publishing, newsprint manufacturing, broadcasting, and entertainment production. What financial information about these industry activities should be available in the Tribune financial report? Where and why is this information disclosed?

13–13 Identify and briefly explain two types of adjustments to financial data to reflect the impact of changing prices.

13–14 Explain how price-level indexes can be used to convert the dollars of one year to those of another year.

13–15 Define *inflation*. What difficulty does inflation cause for financial accounting?

13–16 Define *monetary assets* and *monetary liabilities*. Give examples of each.

13–17 What is a purchasing power loss on net monetary items?

13–18 How is net income computed in a current cost accounting system?

13–19 In its recommended supplementary inflation disclosures, does the FASB include in current cost net income the changes in the current cost of inventory and plant assets held?

EXERCISES

Basic principles

13–20 Indicate the basic principle or principles of accounting that underlie each of the following independent situations:

(a) Dr. Koppa is a practicing pediatrician. Over the years, she has accumulated a personal investment portfolio of securities, virtually all of which have been purchased from her earnings as a pediatrician. The investment portfolio is not reflected in the accounting records of her medical practice.

(b) A company purchases a desk tape dispenser for use by the office secretary. The tape dispenser cost $14 and has an estimated useful life of 25 years. The purchase is debited to the Office Supplies Expense account.

(c) A company sells a product that has a two-year warranty covering parts and labor. In the same period that sales are recorded, an estimate of future warranty costs is debited to the Product Warranty Expense account.

(d) A company pays $60,000 for a patent that has an estimated useful life of 12 years and no salvage value. The amount, debited to the Patent account, is amortized over a 12-year period.

(e) A company purchased a parcel of land several years ago for $40,000. The land's estimated current market value is $55,000. The Land account balance is not increased, but remains at $40,000.

(f) A company has a calendar-year accounting period. On January 8, 19X2, a tornado destroyed its largest warehouse, causing a $700,000 loss. This information is reported in a footnote to the 19X1 financial statements.

Revenue recognition

13–21 For each of the following independent situations, determine how much revenue should be reported in the current period and how much should be deferred to a future period. If a collection basis method applies, determine the appropriate gross profit amounts under both the installment method and the cost recovery method.

(a) Purchased merchandise for $28,000 that will be sold early in the next period for $42,000.

(b) Took a special order for merchandise that is both acquired and delivered to the customer during the next period. The merchandise costs $6,300 and sells for $8,600.

(c) Began work on a long-term construction contract with a price of $950,000. Expected costs total $675,000, of which $162,000 were incurred this period.
(d) Sold undeveloped real estate lots for $80,000 on installment terms. Of the $80,000, 30% was collected during this period. No reasonable estimate of the collectibility of the remaining balances is possible. The cost of the property sold is $52,000.
(e) Accomplished 55% of the work on an order of machinery that will be completed during the first month of the next period and sold for $85,000. Total estimated cost for the machinery when completed is $59,500.

Revenue recognition

13–22 On October 1, 19X2, Beckett Appliance Company sold a combination refrigerator–freezer for $800 on terms of 10% down on the purchase date, and 16 equal monthly payments of $45 beginning November 1, 19X2. The appliance cost $560. Compute the amount of gross profit shown in each calendar year involved using the following revenue recognition methods:
(a) The cost recovery method.
(b) The installment method.
(c) The point-of-sale method.

Financial statement notes

13–23 Notes to financial statements present information on significant accounting policies, complex or special transactions, details of reported amounts, commitments, contingencies, segments, quarterly data, and subsequent events. Indicate which type of note disclosure is illustrated by each of the following notes.
(a) The company has an option to purchase eight British Aerospace Jetstream 31 aircraft for an aggregate purchase price of $21,200,000. A refundable $25,000 deposit for all eight aircraft was made in April of the current year. Tentative delivery dates are between the second and fourth quarter of next year.
(b) The company has deferred certain costs related to major accounting and information systems enhancements which are anticipated to benefit future years. Upon completion, the related cost is amortized over a period not exceeding five years.
(c) The company has guaranteed loans and leases of independent distributors approximating $26,800,000 as of December 31 of the current year.
(d) Sales to an airline company accounted for approximately 43% of the company's net sales in the current year.
(e) An officer of the company is also a director of a major raw material supplier of the company. The amount of raw material purchases from this supplier approximated $365,000 in the current year.
(f) The company's product liability insurance coverage with respect to insured events occurring after January 1 of the current year is substantially less than the amount of that insurance available in the recent past. The company is now predominantly self-insured in this area. The reduction in insurance coverage reflects trends in the liability insurance field generally and is not unique to the company.

Constant dollar accounting

13–24 In 19X1, Weber Company purchased a parcel of land for $60,000 when the general price-level index was 120. By the end of 19X5, the land's current market value was $94,000. General price-level indexes for 19X2–19X5 follow:

December 19X2	132
December 19X3	150
December 19X4	156
December 19X5	180
Average for 19X5	171

(a) Restate the land's cost in terms of the dollar's general purchasing power at (1) December 19X2, (2) December 19X3, (3) December 19X4, (4) December 19X5, and (5) for the year 19X5 (average for 19X5).
(b) Restate the land's December 19X5 market value in terms of the dollar's average purchasing power for 19X5.

Constant dollar accounting

13–25 Penn Corporation has reported sales revenue for the past three years as follows:

19X5	$3,500,000
19X6	4,400,000
19X7	5,500,000

The average general price-level indexes for these three years are as follows: 19X5, 120; 19X6, 150; and 19X7, 180. The price-level index at the end of 19X7 is 198. Prepare a schedule of sales revenue for 19X5–19X7 stated in the general purchasing power of the dollar (a) at the end of 19X7, and (b) for the year 19X7 (average for 19X7).

Purchasing power gain or loss on monetary items

13–26 Listed below are the year-end monetary assets and liabilities of Jenkins Company and the general price-level index on the date each account balance was established.

	Balance	Price-level Index
Cash	$30,000	256
Accounts Receivable	80,000	250
Notes Receivable	24,000	300
Accounts Payable	30,750	246
Notes Payable	18,000	240

The year-end price index is 320. Assume the balance of each monetary item has not changed since it was established.

(a) Compute the purchasing power gain or loss on each monetary item, stated in terms of the year-end purchasing power of the dollar.

(b) What is the purchasing power gain or loss on net monetary items?

Current cost accounting

13–27 On January 2, 19X5, Lobeck Company started business and bought 7,000 inventory items at $50 each. On January 3, the unit purchase price increased to $53 and remained there until year-end. During 19X5, Lobeck sold 4,800 of these items (and made no more purchases). If Lobeck followed current cost accounting procedures, what would be the amount of (a) the 19X5 cost of goods sold expense, and (b) the increase in the current cost of inventory during 19X5?

PROBLEMS

Basic principles

13–28 The following are certain unrelated accounting situations and the accounting treatment, in general journal form, that has been followed in each firm's records.

1. Girard Company mounts a $300,000, year-long advertising campaign on a new national cable television network. The television network required full payment in December at the beginning of the campaign. Accounting treatment is

Advertising Expense	300,000	
Cash		300,000

2. Because of a local bankruptcy, machinery worth $100,000 was acquired at a "bargain" purchase price of $84,000. Accounting treatment is

Machinery	84,000	
Cash		84,000

3. Gary Esse, a consultant operating a sole proprietorship, withdrew $9,000 from the business and purchased securities as a gift to his wife. Accounting treatment is

Investments	9,000	
Cash		9,000

4. The Secure State Bank, by action of the board of directors, wrote down the book value of its home office building to a nominal amount of $100. The objective was to bolster its customers' confidence in the bank's financial strength by obviously understating bank assets. Accounting treatment is

Retained Earnings	2,499,900	
Buildings		2,499,900

5. Hanby, Inc., ends its fiscal year on June 30. Financial statements for the year just ended are prepared on July 10. During the July 4 holiday weekend, a fire destroyed most of the inventories of the company. Because the company may have violated local fire regulations, the loss may not be covered by insurance. This possible loss is reflected in the financial statements for the year just ended. Accounting treatment is

Fire Loss	328,000	
Merchandise Inventory		328,000

6. Wahl Company received a firm offer of $76,000 for a parcel of land it owns which cost $53,000 two years ago. The offer was refused, but the indicated gain was recorded in the accounts. Accounting treatment is

Land	23,000	
Income from Increase in Value of Land		23,000

7. In December, 19X1, Akron Company adopted a policy of paying its salespersons a 6% commission on sales made, payable in the month following the sale. Sales during December, 19X1, were $150,000. Accounting treatment at December 31, 19X1, is

Sales Commissions Expense	9,000	
Sales Commissions Payable		9,000

REQUIRED

(a) In each of the given situations, indicate which generally accepted accounting principles apply and whether they have been used appropriately.

(b) If you decide the accounting treatment is not generally accepted, discuss the effect of the departure on the balance sheet and the income statement.

Installment method

13–29 During December, 19X7, Browning Realty Company sold several residential lots on an installment basis. The sales totaled $325,000. Terms were 30% down on the date of purchase, and 20 equal monthly payments beginning January 2, 19X8. The cost of property sold on the installment basis was $182,000. Browning Realty Company elects the installment method to report the gross profit from these sales on its income tax return. On its books, the company recognizes the revenue and related cost of property sold when the sale is made.

REQUIRED

(a) Comment on why Browning Realty Company would elect the installment method to report the gross profit on its income tax return.

(b) Assuming all installment payments are collected as scheduled, how much gross profit from these December installment sales will Browning Realty Company report on its income tax return for (1) 19X7, (2) 19X8, and (3) 19X9?

(c) Assuming all installment payments are collected as scheduled, how much gross profit from these December installment sales will Browning Realty Company report on its books for (1) 19X7, (2) 19X8, and (3) 19X9?

Percentage of completion accounting

13–30 On December 1, 19X1, Unicom, Inc., signed a contract to build a communications satellite. Completion and sale of the satellite were scheduled for November 19X3. The total contract price for the satellite was $44,000,000, and total estimated cost was $35,000,000. The contract specified the following cash payments by the buyer:

$11,000,000 on signing the contract;
$17,600,000 when the satellite is considered one-half completed;
$13,200,000 when the satellite is completed; and
$2,200,000 90 days after completion.

The degree of completion is considered equal to the proportion of estimated total cost incurred by the builder. Unicom accounts for operations on a calendar-year basis. Costs for the satellite were incurred and paid as follows:

December 19X1	$ 6,300,000
19X2	18,900,000
19X3	9,800,000

The satellite was finished and the sale was consummated November 8, 19X3.

REQUIRED
(a) Calculate the gross profit (or loss) that would be reported each year if a cash basis of accounting (cash receipts less cash disbursements) were used.
(b) Calculate the gross profit that would be reported each year on an accrual basis of accounting using (1) the completed contract (point-of-sale) method of revenue recognition; and (2) the percentage-of-completion method of revenue recognition.
(c) Comment on the relative usefulness of these approaches to periodic income determination.

Financial statement notes—quarterly data

13–31 Actual recent quarterly data are presented below for Company A and Company B. One of these companies is Gibson Greetings, Inc., which manufactures and sells greeting cards. The other company is Hon Industries Inc., which manufactures and sells office furniture. Both companies are on a calendar-year basis.

	First Quarter	Second Quarter	Third Quarter	Fourth Quarter	Year
			(Amounts in thousands)		
Company A:					
Net sales	$137,507	$131,603	$141,880	$144,383	$555,373
Gross profit	41,561	37,715	43,579	43,588	166,443
Net income	6,154	4,227	7,365	7,020	24,766
Company B:					
Net sales	$ 55,758	$ 51,049	$106,303	$144,917	$358,027
Gross profit	35,851	33,297	52,350	63,748	185,246
Net income	3,199	1,806	7,816	11,279	24,100

REQUIRED
(a) Compute the percent of annual net sales generated each quarter by Company A. Round to the nearest percent.
(b) Compute the percent of annual net sales generated each quarter by Company B. Round to the nearest percent.
(c) Which company has the most seasonal business? Briefly explain.
(d) Which company is Gibson Greetings, Inc.? Hon Industries Inc.? Briefly explain.
(e) Which company's interim quarterly data is probably most useful for predicting annual results? Briefly explain.

Constant dollar accounting

13–32 Appearing below are the 19X2 year-end asset accounts of Sage Company under historical cost accounting and the general price-level index that reflects the purchasing power of the dollar used to measure each asset.

	Balance	Price-level Index
Cash	$ 40,000	150
Notes Receivable	60,000	150
Supplies on Hand	20,000	125
Building (net of accumulated depreciation)	700,000	60
Equipment (net of accumulated depreciation)	180,000	80
Total Assets	$1,000,000	

The average general price-level index for 19X2 is 135, while the year-end index is 150.

REQUIRED

(a) Restate each asset balance to a constant unit of general purchasing power—the 19X2 *year-end* purchasing power of the dollar—and compute the total assets.

(b) Restate each asset balance to a constant unit of general purchasing power—the 19X2 *average* purchasing power of the dollar—and compute the total assets.

(c) Prepare a schedule showing the percent of total assets each asset represents using (1) historical cost measures, (2) constant dollar (end-of-year dollar) measures, and (3) constant dollar (average-for-the-year dollar) measures. Round answers to the nearest percent.

(d) Based on your answers to (c), does changing the unit of measure from one constant dollar to another constant dollar alter the relationships among assets?

Current cost accounting

13–33 Hofstad Corporation began operations on January 2, 19X2, with the following assets:

Cash	$ 35,000
Inventory (12,000 units @ $20)	240,000
Land	90,000

During 19X2, Hofstad sold 7,000 inventory units at $35 each and incurred cash operating expenses of $55,000. Hofstad's historical cost income statement for 19X2 was as follows:

Sales		$245,000
Cost of Goods Sold	$140,000	
Operating Expenses	55,000	
Total Expenses		195,000
Net Income		$ 50,000

Hofstad did not purchase any inventory units after January 2, 19X2. Before any inventory was sold, its current cost increased to $22 per unit and remained there until year-end. The current cost of the land at December 31, 19X2, was $107,000.

REQUIRED
(a) Prepare a schedule showing Hofstad's 19X2 net income using current cost accounting procedures.
(b) Prepare a schedule showing the year-end current cost of inventory and land, and a schedule showing the year-end historical cost of inventory and land.
(c) Prepare a schedule showing the increase in the current cost of inventory and land that occurred during 19X2.
(d) How much of the increase computed in (c) relates to inventory units sold during 19X2 and how much relates to assets on hand at year-end?

ALTERNATE PROBLEMS

Basic principles

13–28A The following are several unrelated accounting practices:

1. A recession has caused slow business and low profits for Swiss Company. Consequently, the firm takes no depreciation on its plant assets this year.
2. Shawn Williams, a consultant operating a sole proprietorship, used his business car for a personal, month-long vacation. A full year's depreciation on the car is charged to the firm's depreciation expense account.
3. Birch Company purchased a new $21 snow shovel that is expected to last six years. The shovel is used to clear the firm's front steps during the winter months. The shovel's cost is debited to the Snow Shovel asset account and will be depreciated over six years.
4. Temple Corporation has been named as the defendant in a $25,000,000 pollution lawsuit. Because the lawsuit will take several years to resolve and the outcome is uncertain, Temple's management decides not to mention the lawsuit in the current year financial statements.
5. Axel Corporation's portfolio of short-term stock investments has an aggregate market value below cost. Management believes that stock prices will rise soon and, therefore, does not write down the portfolio at year-end to its lower market value amount.
6. The management of Derrin Corporation prefers the financial results using constant dollar adjustments and issues financial statements in constant dollars (rather than the conventional statements) to stockholders.

REQUIRED
(a) For each of the given practices, indicate which generally accepted accounting principles apply and whether they have been used appropriately.
(b) For each inappropriate accounting practice, indicate the proper accounting procedure.

Installment method

13–29A Shelby Company sells residential building lots and makes all sales on an installment basis. Selected financial data for its first three years of operations are shown below.

	19X1	19X2	19X3
Sales	$200,000	$350,000	$500,000
Cost of Property Sold	124,000	210,000	275,000
Gross Profit	$ 76,000	$140,000	$225,000
Cash collections from 19X1 sales	$ 90,000	$ 80,000	$ 30,000
Cash collections from 19X2 sales		150,000	140,000
Cash collections from 19X3 sales			210,000

Shelby Company elects the installment method to report the gross profit from its installment sales on its income tax return. On its books, the company recognizes the revenue and related cost of property sold when the sale is made.

REQUIRED

(a) What is the gross profit percentage on sales for 19X1, 19X2, and 19X3?
(b) How much gross profit will Shelby report on its income tax returns in 19X1, 19X2, and 19X3?
(c) For the three year period 19X1–19X3, how much less gross profit will Shelby have reported on its income tax returns compared with the gross profit recorded on its books?

Percentage of completion accounting

13–30A On November 1, 19X2, Vessels, Inc., signed a contract to build a large seagoing oil tanker. Completion and sale of the ship were scheduled for October 19X4. The total contract price for the ship was $24,000,000 and the total estimated cost was $18,000,000. The contract specified the following cash payments by the buyer:

$2,000,000 on signing the contract;
$12,000,000 when the ship is considered one-half completed;
$8,000,000 when the ship is completed;
$2,000,000 90 days after completion.

The degree of completion is considered equal to the proportion of estimated total cost incurred by the builder. The company accounts for operations on a calendar-year basis. Costs for the ship were incurred and paid as follows:

November and December, 19X2	$2,160,000
19X3	9,720,000
19X4	6,120,000

The ship was finished and the sale was consummated October 20, 19X4.

REQUIRED

(a) Calculate the gross profit (or loss) that would be reported each year if a cash basis of accounting (cash receipts less cash disbursements) were used.
(b) Calculate the gross profit that would be reported each year on an accrual basis of accounting using (1) the completed contract (point-of-sale) method of revenue recognition; and (2) the percentage-of-completion method of revenue recognition.
(c) Comment on the relative usefulness of these approaches to periodic income determination.

Financial statement notes—quarterly data

13–31A Actual recent quarterly data are presented below for Company C and Company D. One of these companies is Fedders Corporation, a manufacturer of room air conditioners. The other company is Guardsman Products, Inc. Guardsman produces various consumer cleaning products and industrial custom coatings. Both companies are on a calendar-year basis.

	First Quarter	Second Quarter	Third Quarter	Fourth Quarter	Year
		(Amounts in thousands)			
Company C:					
Net sales	$27,934	$31,313	$35,501	$32,811	$127,559
Gross profit	9,406	9,820	9,822	9,404	38,452
Net income	1,172	1,354	1,440	1,244	5,210
Company D:					
Net sales	$34,974	$41,104	$22,996	$29,585	$128,659
Gross profit	7,183	7,749	5,904	7,605	28,441
Net income	3,268	4,559	2,801	3,354	13,982

REQUIRED

(a) Compute the percent of annual net sales generated each quarter by Company C. Round to the nearest percent.

(b) Compute the percent of annual net sales generated each quarter by Company D. Round to the nearest percent.

(c) Which company has the most seasonal business? Briefly explain.

(d) Which company is Fedders Corporation? Guardsman Products, Inc.? Briefly explain.

(e) Company D's quarterly sales dropped by 44% from the second quarter to the third quarter. Should this drop be of significant concern to a potential investor? Suppose Company C's quarterly sales dropped by 44% from the second quarter to the third quarter. Should this drop be of significant concern to a potential investor?

Constant dollar accounting

13–32A Appearing below are Roth Company's sales for three years under historical cost accounting and the average general price-level index for each year.

	Sales	Average Price-level Index
19X6	$4,500,000	120
19X7	5,850,000	144
19X8	8,190,000	160

The 19X8 year-end general price-level index is 180.

REQUIRED

(a) Restate each year's sales amount to a constant unit of general purchasing power—the 19X8 *year-end* purchasing power of the dollar.

(b) Restate each year's sales amount to a constant unit of general purchasing power—the 19X8 *average* purchasing power of the dollar.

(c) Prepare a schedule showing the percent of sales increase from 19X6 to 19X7, and from 19X7 to 19X8 using (1) historical cost measures, (2) constant dollar (end-of-year dollar) measures, and (3) constant dollar (average-for-the-year dollar) measures. Round to the nearest percent.

(d) Based on your answers to (c), does changing the unit of measure from one constant dollar to another constant dollar change the year-to-year relationships between sales amounts?

Current cost accounting

13–33A Fryar Corporation began operations on January 2, 19X5, with the following assets:

Cash	$ 25,000
Inventory (8,000 units @ $16)	128,000
Land	60,000

During 19X5, Fryar sold 5,500 inventory units at $28 each and incurred cash operating expenses of $17,000. Fryar's historical cost income statement for 19X5 was as follows:

Sales		$154,000
Cost of Goods Sold	$88,000	
Operating Expenses	17,000	
Total Expenses		105,000
Net Income		$ 49,000

Before any inventory was sold, its current cost increased to $19 per unit. After the last sale in 19X5, Fryar's supplier announced a year-end price increase to $20 per unit. The current cost of the land at December 31, 19X5, was $67,000.

REQUIRED

(a) Prepare a schedule showing Fryar's 19X5 net income using current cost accounting procedures.

(b) Prepare a schedule showing the year-end current cost of inventory and land, and a schedule showing the year-end historical cost of inventory and land.

(c) Prepare a schedule showing the increase in the current cost of inventory and land that occurred during 19X5.

(d) How much of the increase computed in (c) relates to inventory units sold during 19X5 and how much relates to assets on hand at year-end?

BUSINESS DECISION PROBLEM

Copterific, Inc., started operations on January 1, 19X1. Its primary assets are two helicopters, which are used in the following ways:

1. For carrying passengers between a major air terminal and a downtown heliport. As a new business promotion, the company sold 700 booklets of one-way tickets. Each booklet contained ten tickets and was priced at $180. During 19X1, purchasers of the booklets used 4,500 tickets.
2. For passenger charter flights. A local corporation charters a helicopter to transport executives to and from an island conference facility. A deposit of 25% of the charter fee is required when a charter flight is booked. On December 31, 19X1, the company had deposits of $2,500 for scheduled charter flights. The company received a total of $24,000 for charter flights flown during 19X1.
3. For construction material and equipment transportation. Building contractors rent a helicopter for $150 per hour for moving material and equipment to and from construction sites. Contractors used the helicopters a total of 210 hours during 19X1. Of this total, 20 hours occurred in December, for which the company has not yet received payment.
4. For "Save a Life" efforts during holidays. The state rents a helicopter for $100 per hour on holiday weekends to carry a medical team to accident locations. The state used the helicopters a total of 260 hours in 19X1. The company has not yet collected for 40 hours of use in December.

Copterific's bookkeeper has prepared the following schedule of revenue for 19X1:

One-way ticket booklets (700 @ $180)	$126,000
Charter flights made	24,000
Deposits on charter flights scheduled	2,500
Contractors (190 hours @ $150)	28,500
"Save a Life" program (220 hours @ $100)	22,000
Total Revenue	$203,000

The president of Copterific, Inc., has asked you to evaluate whether the bookkeeper has correctly determined the 19X1 revenue in accordance with generally accepted accounting principles.

REQUIRED
Has the bookkeeper correctly determined the 19X1 revenue? If not, prepare a revised 19X1 revenue schedule. Give reasons for any changes you make from the bookkeeper's schedule.

ANSWERS TO SELF-TEST QUESTIONS

1. (c) **2.** (b) **3.** (a) **4.** (c) **5.** (d)

ANNUAL REPORT PROBLEMS FOR PART 2

The following annual report problems conclude Part 2 of the text. They consist of three unrelated sections and use selected financial statement disclosure data from actual companies. In each case, we give a brief profile of the company and selected disclosure data from a recent annual report to stockholders, followed by questions relating to certain accounting principles and practices discussed thus far in the text.

I. Nature's Sunshine Products, Inc.

PROFILE Nature's Sunshine Products, Inc., manufactures a variety of nutritional and personal care products, including encapsulated herbs, vitamins, food supplements, grooming aids, cosmetics, a water purifier, and a weight loss program. These products are sold directly to consumers by means of an independent sales force situated throughout the United States, Canada, Australia, New Zealand, and Japan. At the end of 1987, total assets were $14.6 million and sales revenue exceeded $38 million for 1987.

DISCLOSURE DATA (*from* note on significant accounting policies in 1987 annual report)

Revenue Recognition
The Company generally receives its product sales price in cash accompanying orders from independent sales force members. A volume incentive payment related to product orders is made in the month following the sale. Sales and related volume incentives are generally recorded when the merchandise is shipped. Cash received for unshipped merchandise is recorded as a liability.

Selling Expenses
Independent sales force members may earn Company-paid attendance at conventions by achieving the required levels of product purchases within the qualification period. The paid attendance costs and expenses are accrued over the qualification period as they are earned.

REQUIRED

(a) Why doesn't Nature's Sunshine Products, Inc., record revenue when it receives the sales orders and cash from its sales force members? Why does it wait until the merchandise is shipped?

(b) The volume incentives are part of the firm's direct sales marketing program and represent compensation paid to independent sales force members for reaching certain levels of sales performance and organizational development. In 1987, volume incentives amounted to $18,144,910 (47.5% of sales). What accounting principle underlies the firm's procedure of recording volume incentives as an expense when merchandise is shipped?

(c) The firm's December 31, 1987, balance sheet shows Accrued Volume Incentives of $1,509,068 as a current liability. Why is this item classified as a current liability?

(d) What accounting principle underlies the firm's procedure of accruing company-paid convention attendance costs and expenses over the qualification period rather than expensing these amounts when they are paid at the time of the convention?

II. Bush Industries

PROFILE Bush Industries manufactures quality ready-to-assemble (R-T-A) furniture. The firm, which is located in Jamestown, New York, went public in 1984 and made *Forbes'* list of the "200 Best Small Companies in America" in 1987. The firm was ranked 37 based on a five-year average return on equity of 27.9%. In 1987 the firm's sales were $93.5 million and its assets were $53.4 million.

DISCLOSURE DATA (*from* notes to financial statements in 1987 annual report)

Commitments The Company operates in various owned and leased facilities. Rent expense for the year ended December 25, 1987, was $296,000 for real estate and $716,000 for equipment. Equipment rental consists of payments made for transportation, computer, and manufacturing equipment. Minimum future obligations under all operating leases in effect at December 25, 1987, are summarized as follows:

1988	$656,000	1991	$552,000
1989	610,000	1992	413,000
1990	629,000		

REQUIRED

(a) Would you expect a long-term liability for lease commitments to appear on the firm's December 25, 1987, balance sheet relating to the rentals shown in the foregoing schedule? Why or why not?

(b) The firm shows $188,294 for leasehold improvements on its December 25, 1987, balance sheet. Generally, how should this asset be amortized? What is the longest period over which any of the leasehold improvements now on the balance sheet should be amortized?

III. Pfizer, Inc.

PROFILE Pfizer, Inc., is a research-based firm that develops, manufactures, and sells health care, agricultural, chemical, and other products in 140 countries. In 1987, the firm's total sales were $4,919.8 million and total assets were $6,922.6 million.

DISCLOSURE DATA (*from* yearly sales summary in 1987 annual report)

	1987	1986	1985	1984	1983	1982	1981	1980
Sales (in millions)	$4,919.8	$4,476.0	$4,024.5	$3,875.9	$3,764.7	$3,496.0	$3,280.9	$3,054.3

REQUIRED

(a) Calculate, as a percentage of 1980 sales, the sales of each year for the period 1980–1987. (Example: for 1981, the percentage is calculated as $3,280.9/$3,054.3 = 107.4%.)

(b) Restate the sales figures for each year of the period in terms of 1987 purchasing power, using the following average consumer price index for the period:

	1987	**1986**	**1985**	**1984**	**1983**	**1982**	**1981**	**1980**
Consumer price index, 1967 = 100	340.4	328.4	322.2	311.1	298.4	289.1	272.4	246.8

(Example: for 1980, restated sales are $3,054.3 × 340.4/246.8 = $4,212.7.)

(c) Recalculate, as a percentage of 1980 restated sales, the restated sales of each year for the period 1980–1987. Compare these percentages with those calculated in requirement (a) and comment on the differences.

advantageous form of organization for tax purposes requires careful analysis of existing tax laws and the tax status of the persons going into business.

CAPITAL, DRAWING, AND LOAN ACCOUNTS

Accounting for partnerships is similar in most respects to accounting for sole proprietorships. Each partner has a capital account and a drawing account that serve the same functions as the related accounts for a sole proprietor. A partner's capital account is credited for his or her investments, and each individual drawing account is debited to reflect assets withdrawn from the partnership. At the end of each accounting period, the balances in the drawing accounts are closed to the related capital accounts.

Occasionally a partner may advance amounts to the partnership beyond the intended permanent investment. These advances should be credited to the partner's loan account and classified among the liabilities, separate from liabilities to outsiders. By the same token, if a partner withdraws money with the intention of repaying it, the debit should go to the partner's advance (or loan receivable) account and be classified separately among the partnership's receivables.

The formation of partnerships, the division of profits and losses, the admission and retirement of partners, and the liquidation of partnerships represent areas of particular interest in accounting for these entities. We focus on these issues in the remainder of the chapter.

FORMATION OF A PARTNERSHIP

A partnership's books are opened with an entry reflecting the net contribution of each partner to the firm. Asset accounts are debited for assets invested in the partnership, liability accounts are credited for any liabilities assumed by the partnership, and a separate capital account is credited for the amount of each partner's net investment (Assets − Liabilities).

Assume that Earl Ames, a sole proprietor, and John Baker form a partnership. Ames invests $8,000 cash, office equipment with a current fair value of $25,000, and office supplies worth $2,000. The partnership agrees to assume the $5,000 balance on a note issued by Ames when he acquired the equipment. Baker invests $10,000 cash. The following opening entries on the books of the partnership record the investments of Ames and Baker:

Cash	8,000	
Office Equipment	25,000	
Office Supplies on Hand	2,000	
Notes Payable		5,000
E. Ames, Capital		30,000
To record Ames' investment in the partnership of Ames and Baker.		
Cash	10,000	
J. Baker, Capital		10,000
To record Baker's investment in the partnership of Ames and Baker.		

Assets invested in the partnership should be recorded at their current fair values. These assets (less any liabilities assumed by the partnership) determine the opening capital balances for each partner. If the assets are not recorded initially at their fair values, inequities develop among the partners in terms of their respective capital balances.

For example, assume the office equipment invested by Ames was recorded incorrectly at $22,000 (its book value from his proprietorship records). If the partnership immediately sold the equipment for its current fair value of $25,000, the resulting $3,000 gain, on closing, would increase the capital balances of both Ames and Baker. This is not equitable. The $3,000 "gain" was not added to the asset by the operations of the partnership. Baker should not be credited with any part of this amount. A similar inequity develops if the equipment is used in operations rather than sold. Owing to a lower total depreciation over the life of the equipment, income would be $3,000 greater over the same period. To avoid such inequities, the partnership records the office equipment initially at $25,000. The values assigned to assets invested in a partnership are important and should be agreeable to all partners.

DIVISION OF PARTNERSHIP PROFITS AND LOSSES

In the absence of a profit and loss sharing agreement, partnership profits and losses are divided equally. Partners who do not wish to share profits equally must specify, preferably in a formal written agreement, the manner in which profit and loss distributions are made. Such arrangements may specify a fixed ratio (such as $\frac{2}{3}$ to $\frac{1}{3}$, 60% to 40%, or 5:3) or a sharing formula of some kind based on the relative financial participation of the partners, the services performed by the partners, or both. Any arrangement can be made, and losses may be shared differently from profits. If an agreement specifies the manner of sharing profits but is silent on the sharing of losses, losses will be divided in the same fashion as profits. In the following sections, we discuss several common arrangements.

Capital Ratios

When the services performed or skills provided by the various partners are considered equal, profits and losses may be divided according to the partners' relative investments in the firm. Assume that the Ames and Baker partnership had a profit of $18,000 for the year and that the partners' capital balances before any profit distribution at year-end were as follows:

E. Ames, Capital		
	19XX	
	Jan. 1	30,000

J. Baker, Capital		
	19XX	
	Jan. 1	10,000
	July 1	10,000

The $18,000 profit might be divided according to the beginning capital investment ratio or the average capital investment ratio for the year.

BEGINNING CAPITAL RATIO At the beginning of the year, the total capital investment in the firm was $40,000—$30,000 for Ames and $10,000 for Baker. If they shared according to the ratio of *beginning* capital balances, the profit distribution would be 3:1, or $13,500 for Ames and $4,500 for Baker, computed as follows:

	Beginning Capital	Percent of Total	Division of Profit
Ames	$30,000	75	$13,500
Baker	10,000	25	4,500
	$40,000	100	$18,000

The following entry would be made to distribute the balance in the Income Summary account:

Income Summary	18,000	
E. Ames, Capital		13,500
J. Baker, Capital		4,500
To close the Income Summary account.		

AVERAGE CAPITAL RATIO Because partners' investments may change during the year, the partners may decide that using *average* capital balances rather than beginning capital balances provides a more equitable division of profits. Under this scheme, investment balances are *weighted* by multiplying the amount of the investment by the portion of the year that these funds were invested. Because Baker invested an additional $10,000 on July 1, his average capital would be based on a $10,000 investment for the first six months and a $20,000 investment for the last six months. The computation might be as follows:

		Dollars × Months		Average Investment
Ames				
$30,000 × 12 months		$360,000	÷ 12 =	$30,000
Baker				
$10,000 × 6 months	$ 60,000			
$20,000 × 6 months	120,000	180,000	÷ 12 =	15,000
		$540,000		$45,000

Profit Distribution

$$\text{Ames: } \frac{\$30,000}{\$45,000} \times \$18,000 = \$12,000$$

$$\text{Baker: } \frac{\$15,000}{\$45,000} \times \$18,000 = 6,000$$

$$\$18,000$$

The entry to close the Income Summary account would credit E. Ames, Capital with $12,000 and J. Baker, Capital with $6,000.

Salary and Interest Allowances

A sharing agreement may provide for variations in the personal services contributed by partners and in their relative investments. **Salary allowances** provide for differences in personal services; **allowances for interest** on capital balances provide for differences in the financial participation of partners.

The terms *salary allowances* and *allowances for interest* describe only the process of dividing net income among partners. These terms should not be confused with any salary expense and interest expense appearing in the firm's records or with any cash withdrawals the partners make. For example, the partnership agreement may provide that partners may make withdrawals equal to their salary allowances. These withdrawals would be debited to each partner's drawing account, which is eventually closed to his or her capital account. The cash withdrawals in no way affect the division of net income among partners—the division of net income is governed by the sharing agreement.

SALARY ALLOWANCE Suppose Ames and Baker render different degrees of personal services and therefore specify a salary allowance in their sharing agreement—$6,000 for Ames and $4,000 for Baker. The remainder of net income is divided equally. The division of the $18,000 net income is as follows:

	Ames	Baker	Total
Earnings to be divided			$18,000
Salary allowances:			
Ames	$ 6,000		
Baker		$4,000	10,000
Remainder			$ 8,000
Remainder ($8,000) divided equally	4,000	4,000	
Partner's shares	$10,000	$8,000	

The $18,000 balance in the Income Summary account would be closed by crediting E. Ames, Capital for $10,000 and J. Baker, Capital for $8,000.

SALARY AND INTEREST ALLOWANCES Next, assume that Ames and Baker wish to acknowledge the differences in their financial involvement as well as in their personal services. They have the following sharing agreement: salaries of $6,000 to Ames and $4,000 to Baker; 8% interest on *average* capital balances; and the remainder divided equally. We computed average investments for Ames and Baker earlier at $30,000 and $15,000, respectively. The $18,000 net income would therefore be divided as follows:

	Ames	Baker	Total
Earnings to be divided			$18,000
Salary allowances:			
Ames	$ 6,000		
Baker		$4,000	10,000
			$ 8,000
Allowance for interest on average capital:			
Ames ($30,000 × 0.08)	2,400		
Baker ($15,000 × 0.08)		1,200	3,600
Remainder			$ 4,400
Remainder ($4,400) divided equally	2,200	2,200	
Partners' shares	$10,600	$7,400	

The entry closing the $18,000 net income in the Income Summary account would credit E. Ames, Capital for $10,600 and J. Baker, Capital for $7,400.

If Ames and Baker had withdrawn cash equal to their salary allowances, their drawing accounts at the end of the year would contain debit balances of $6,000 and $4,000, respectively. The entry to close the drawing accounts would be

E. Ames, Capital	6,000	
J. Baker, Capital	4,000	
E. Ames, Drawing		6,000
J. Baker, Drawing		4,000
To close the partners' drawing accounts.		

ALLOWANCES EXCEED EARNINGS Unless a special provision is included in the sharing agreement, the same allocation procedures apply in the event of a loss or of earnings insufficient to cover allowances for salary and interest. For example, assume that net income for the year was only $8,000. After salary and interest allowances are allocated, a *sharing agreement loss* of $5,600 would be divided equally between the partners to fulfill their agreement. The computations are shown below:

	Ames	Baker	Total
Earnings to be divided			$ 8,000
Salary allowances	$6,000	$4,000	
Interest allowances	2,400	1,200	
Total salary and interest	$8,400	$5,200	13,600
Remainder (sharing agreement loss)			($ 5,600)
Remainder divided equally	(2,800)	(2,800)	
Partners' shares	$5,600	$2,400	

The entry closing the $8,000 net income in the Income Summary account would credit E. Ames, Capital with $5,600 and J. Baker, Capital with $2,400.

PARTNERSHIP FINANCIAL STATEMENTS

A few unique features of partnership financial statements arise because a partnership consists of co-owners. The partnership income statement may show, at the bottom, how the net income is divided among the partners. A capital account for each partner appears in the owners' equity section of the balance sheet. The statement of partners' (or owners') capital portrays the changes in the capital balances of each partner, as shown in Exhibit 14–1.

ADMISSION OF A PARTNER

New partners may be admitted to a partnership either by purchasing an interest from current members or by investing in the firm. When a person buys an interest from one or more of the current partners, the assets of the firm are not affected. Payment is made personally to the member or members from whom

EXHIBIT 14–1

Ames and Baker
Statement of Partners' Capital
For the Year Ended December 31, 19XX

	Ames	Baker	Total
Capital Balances, January 1, 19XX	$30,000	$10,000	$40,000
Add: Additional Contributions		10,000	10,000
Net Income for 19XX	10,600	7,400	18,000
Totals	$40,600	$27,400	$68,000
Less: Withdrawals	6,000	4,000	10,000
Capital Balances, December 31, 19XX	$34,600	$23,400	$58,000

the interest is obtained, resulting in merely a transfer among capital accounts. When an investment is made in the firm, however, total assets increase by the amount contributed.

Economic circumstances usually dictate a new partner's mode of entry. A firm with sufficient capital may seek the skills and services of a particular new partner. Or, current partners may wish to liquidate part of their interests and scale down their individual investments. In these situations, the firm may sell an interest in the current partnership. On the other hand, if additional capital is needed, adding a partner who will contribute assets may be a proper solution.

For the benefit of the existing partners, the net assets of the current partnership should reflect their current fair values when a new partner is admitted. This may require a revaluation of certain assets. The resultant gain or loss would be apportioned to the current partners in their profit and loss sharing ratio. If the net assets do not reflect their fair values, the new partner may share in gains and losses that developed before admission to the firm. In the following examples of new partner admissions, we assume that the recorded book values of the current partnership's assets do not require restatement.

Purchase of an Interest

Suppose that Ames and Baker have capital balances of $30,000 and $10,000, respectively, and that Ames sells one-half of his interest to Susan Carter. For Carter to become a partner, both Ames and Baker must consent to the sale. The entry to record Carter's admission would be

E. Ames, Capital	15,000	
S. Carter, Capital		15,000
To record admission of Carter.		

The actual cash amount paid to Ames is entirely a personal matter between the two persons and is not relevant in recording Carter's admission. Whether an interest is purchased from one partner or several, a transfer of capital is made only for the amounts of the interests purchased without regard to the payment made. Suppose that Carter purchased a one-fourth interest in the firm by obtaining one-fourth of each partner's current share. One-fourth interest would amount to $10,000 (one-fourth of $40,000 present capital). The entry for Carter's admission would be

E. Ames, Capital	7,500	
J. Baker, Capital	2,500	
S. Carter, Capital		10,000
To record admission of Carter.		

Admission by Investment

Clearly, if an incoming partner contributes assets to the firm, total capital increases. If the current partners' capital balances are realistically stated, the new partner simply contributes assets equal to the desired proportionate interest in the total capital of the new firm. In our example, present capital is $40,000—$30,000 for Ames and $10,000 for Baker. Carter wants to contribute enough cash to obtain one-third interest in the new firm. The current partners' capital of $40,000 represents two-thirds of the new firm's capital; therefore, Carter should contribute $20,000. The entry for admission would be

Cash	20,000	
S. Carter, Capital		20,000
To record admission of Carter.		

BONUS TO CURRENT PARTNERS If a partnership interest is especially attractive because of a superior earnings record or the promise of exceptional future earnings, the current partners may require the new partner to pay an additional amount as a **bonus** for admission. Suppose that Ames and Baker required a $35,000 payment for a one-third interest in the new firm. The total capital of the new firm would then be $75,000, of which a one-third interest would be $25,000, as follows:

E. Ames, Capital	$30,000
J. Baker, Capital	10,000
Present Capital	$40,000
Contribution of Carter	35,000
Capital of New Firm	$75,000
One-third Interest	$25,000

The $10,000 difference between Carter's payment of $35,000 and her interest of $25,000 is a bonus to the former partners, to be divided according to their profit and loss sharing ratio. If the agreement provides for equal sharing, the entry to admit Carter is

Cash	35,000	
E. Ames, Capital		5,000
J. Baker, Capital		5,000
S. Carter, Capital		25,000
To record admission of Carter.		

BONUS TO NEW PARTNER A firm eager to add a partner who has ready cash or unique skills, management potential, or other desirable characteristics may award the new partner a larger interest than would be warranted by his or her contribution. Because the capital of the new partner will be greater than his or her asset contribution, the current partners must make up the difference (bonus to new partner) by reducing their capital balances. Assume that Carter receives a one-third interest by contributing only $14,000 to the new firm. The capital of the new firm increases to $54,000 ($40,000 + $14,000), of which a one-third interest is $18,000, as shown below:

E. Ames, Capital	$30,000
J. Baker, Capital	10,000
Present Capital	$40,000
Contribution of Carter	14,000
Capital of New Firm	$54,000
One-third Interest	$18,000

The $4,000 difference between Carter's $14,000 contribution and her $18,000 interest is a bonus to Carter. Ames and Baker reduce their capital balances accordingly, with amounts based on the profit and loss sharing ratio. With equal sharing, the entry to admit Carter as a partner in the firm is

Cash	14,000	
E. Ames, Capital	2,000	
J. Baker, Capital	2,000	
S. Carter, Capital		18,000
To record admission of Carter.		

RETIREMENT OF A PARTNER

A retiring partner may (1) sell his or her interest to an outsider, (2) sell that interest to one or more of the remaining partners, or (3) receive payment for the interest from partnership funds.

Sale of Partnership Interest

INTEREST SOLD TO NEW PARTNER The procedure for recording the sale of a retiring partner's interest to an outsider is similar to that illustrated earlier for the purchase of an interest. Suppose that retiring partner Baker, with the firm's approval, sells his $10,000 interest to Stan Dodge. Regardless of the personally determined amount of Dodge's actual payment to Baker, the entry to record Dodge's admission and Baker's departure is

J. Baker, Capital	10,000	
S. Dodge, Capital		10,000
To record Dodge's purchase of Baker's interest.		

INTEREST SOLD TO REMAINING PARTNERS This transaction is a personal one between Baker and his partners. If Baker sells his interest to remaining partners Ames and Carter, Baker's interest is merely transferred to their capital accounts, regardless of the actual amount of the payments. If Baker sells equal portions of his interest to the remaining partners, the entry is

J. Baker, Capital	10,000	
E. Ames, Capital		5,000
S. Carter, Capital		5,000
To record sale of Baker's interest to Ames and Carter.		

Payment from Partnership Funds

SETTLEMENT EXCEEDS CAPITAL BALANCE A partner's retirement may be an occasion for reviewing partners' capital balances. Because of such factors as appreciation of assets or an exceptional partnership performance record, the capital balances may not provide a realistic basis for determining the value of partnership interests. In such situations, the partners may recognize any amount by which the current fair value of the retiring partner's partnership interest exceeds his or her capital balance by paying a bonus to the retiring partner.

If the retiring partner receives funds from the partnership for his or her interest, any difference between the amount of this interest and the sum paid affects the capital balances of the remaining partners. For example, assume that the capital balances of Ames, Baker, and Carter are $35,000, $15,000, and $25,000, respectively, when Baker retires and that the firm pays $20,000 for Baker's interest. Baker's $5,000 bonus is divided by the other partners according to their profit and loss sharing ratio (assumed here to be equal). The entry would be:

E. Ames, Capital	2,500	
S. Carter, Capital	2,500	
J. Baker, Capital	15,000	
Cash		20,000
To record Baker's withdrawal from the partnership.		

When the fair value of a retiring partner's interest exceeds his or her related capital balance, the remaining partners might revalue total partnership assets proportionately upward, distribute the increase to all partners in their profit and loss sharing ratio, and then pay the retiring partner an amount equal to his or her new capital balance. Such an approach, however, obviously departs from the principle of historical cost. Although the increased value of the partnership interest is properly considered in settling with the retiring partner, revaluing total partnership assets above their historical cost is not acceptable.

CAPITAL BALANCE EXCEEDS SETTLEMENT In certain circumstances, a retiring partner may accept a settlement less than his or her capital balance. Examples include a history of poor partnership earnings or recognition of operating disadvantages resulting from the partner's retirement. In such cases, the excess of the retiring partner's capital balance over the settlement constitutes a bonus to the remaining partners. Assume that Baker, who has a capital balance of $15,000, accepts $11,000 rather than $20,000 for his interest. The $4,000 bonus is allocated to the remaining partners in their profit and loss sharing ratio (assumed here to be equal). The entry to record this bonus is

J. Baker, Capital	15,000	
E. Ames, Capital		2,000
S. Carter, Capital		2,000
Cash		11,000
To record Baker's withdrawal from the partnership.		

LIQUIDATION OF A PARTNERSHIP

The situations that arise during partnership liquidations can be quite complex. Because liquidations are treated comprehensively in advanced accounting texts, we will provide only a basic approach to them here. When a business partnership is discontinued, the assets are sold, liabilities are paid, and the remaining cash is distributed to the partners. The conversion of the partnership assets into cash (by selling the assets) is called **realization.** Essentially, gains and losses realized in selling assets are carried to the partners' capital accounts (in the established profit and loss sharing ratio), and each partner eventually receives the balance remaining in his or her capital account.

Let us suppose that Ames, Baker, and Carter share profits and losses in the ratio of 40%, 40%, and 20%, respectively, and that before liquidation the partnership's balance sheet can be summarized as follows (assume that for the final operating period, the partnership books have been adjusted and closed and the profit or loss allocated to each partner):

Cash	$ 15,000	Liabilities	$ 40,000
Other Assets (net)	100,000	E. Ames, Capital	35,000
		J. Baker, Capital	15,000
		S. Carter, Capital	25,000
	$115,000		$115,000

Capital Balances Exceed Losses

If the noncash assets in the balance sheet in our example are sold for $80,000, the firm sustains a $20,000 loss. Because the partners share the loss, their capital balances are ultimately reduced by the following amounts: Ames, $8,000; Baker, $8,000; and Carter, $4,000. The appropriate entries might be as follows:

Cash	80,000	
Loss on Realization of Assets	20,000	
Other Assets (net)		100,000
To record loss on sale of other assets.		
E. Ames, Capital	8,000	
J. Baker, Capital	8,000	
S. Carter, Capital	4,000	
Loss on Realization of Assets		20,000
To distribute loss on sale of other assets.		

After these entries have been recorded, the firm's balance sheet accounts would be as follows:

Cash	$95,000	Liabilities	$40,000
		E. Ames, Capital	27,000
		J. Baker, Capital	7,000
		S. Carter, Capital	21,000
	$95,000		$95,000

Finally, the entries to pay the liabilities and distribute the remaining cash to the partners would be:

Liabilities	40,000	
Cash		40,000
To record payment of liabilities.		
E. Ames, Capital	27,000	
J. Baker, Capital	7,000	
S. Carter, Capital	21,000	
Cash		55,000
To record cash distribution to partners.		

Observe that *only gains and losses* on liquidation are shared in the profit and loss sharing ratio—not the residual cash. Remaining funds are distributed to partners *in the amounts of their capital balances* after all gains and losses have been shared.

Losses Exceed Partner's Capital

When liquidation losses occur, a partner's share of losses may exceed his or her capital balance. That partner will be expected to contribute cash to the partnership to offset the capital account debit balance. For example, suppose that in our illustration the $100,000 of other assets are sold for only $60,000. The resulting $40,000 loss on realization of assets is recorded and then distributed in the 40%:40%:20% sharing ratio, reducing partners' capital accounts as follows: Ames, $16,000; Baker, $16,000; and Carter, $8,000. Entries to record and distribute the loss and to pay the liabilities are

Cash	60,000	
Loss on Realization of Assets	40,000	
Other Assets (net)		100,000
To record loss on sale of other assets.		

E. Ames, Capital	16,000	
J. Baker, Capital	16,000	
S. Carter, Capital	8,000	
Loss on Realization of Assets		40,000
To distribute loss on sale of other assets.		
Liabilities	40,000	
Cash		40,000
To record payment of liabilities.		

After recording and distributing the loss on the sale of other assets and payment of the liabilities, the following account balances remain:

Cash	$35,000	E. Ames, Capital	$19,000
		J. Baker, Capital (debit)	(1,000)
		S. Carter, Capital	17,000
	$35,000		$35,000

Note that Baker's $16,000 share of the loss on realization of the other assets absorbs his $15,000 capital balance and leaves a $1,000 capital deficit (debit balance) in his capital account.

If Baker pays the firm $1,000 to make up his deficit, the resulting $36,000 cash balance is the amount distributed to Ames ($19,000) and Carter ($17,000). If Baker cannot make the contribution, the $1,000 is treated as a loss distributed to Ames and Carter in their profit and loss sharing ratio. Because the ratio of their respective shares is 40:20, Ames sustains 40/60, or two-thirds, of the $1,000 loss and Carter, 20/60, or one-third. The entry to redistribute Baker's debit balance would be

E. Ames, Capital	667	
S. Carter, Capital	333	
J. Baker, Capital		1,000
To record distribution of Baker's capital deficit to Ames and Carter.		

The $35,000 cash is then paid to Ames and Carter in the amounts of their final capital balances.

E. Ames, Capital	18,333	
S. Carter, Capital	16,667	
Cash		35,000
To record cash distribution to partners.		

Sometimes a partner with a capital account deficit may be uncertain about making up the deficit. At the same time, the other partners may want to distribute whatever cash is available after creditors have been paid. In our illustration, if Ames and Carter had doubts about receiving $1,000 from Baker, cash might be distributed as shown in the last entry—$18,333 to Ames and $16,667 to Carter. This would leave sufficient amounts in their capital accounts—$667 for Ames and $333 for Carter—to absorb a $1,000 loss in the sharing ratio if Baker defaults on payment. If he does contribute the amount needed, the other partners will be paid the balances of their capital accounts.

Statement of Partnership Liquidation

Liquidation of a partnership can continue over an extended period. To provide interested parties with a comprehensive report of the initial assets and liabilities, the sale of noncash assets, the payment of liabilities, and the final distribution of cash to the partners, the partnership may prepare a **statement of partnership liquidation.** Using data from our illustration, Exhibit 14–2 presents a statement of liquidation for the Ames, Baker, and Carter partnership. We assume that noncash assets are sold for $60,000 and that Baker does not cover his $1,000 capital deficit.

Observe the following about the statement of partnership liquidation:

1. The statement is dated to reflect the period during which the liquidation took place.
2. The initial numbers on the statement reflect the partnership balance sheet at the beginning of the liquidation (see page 500 in our illustration).
3. Each line that reflects a step in the liquidation (sale of noncash assets, allocation of loss, payment of liabilities, allocation of partner's capital deficit, and final cash distribution) matches related journal entries in the illustration (see pages 501–502).
4. The statement shows how each step affects the liquidation and is therefore an excellent vehicle for analysis.

EXHIBIT 14–2

Ames, Baker, and Carter (Partnership)
Statement of Partnership Liquidation
From January 1 to March 31, 19XX

	Cash	Noncash Assets	Liabilities	E. Ames, Capital (40%)	J. Baker, Capital (40%)	S. Carter, Capital (20%)	Realization Gain (Loss)
Beginning Balances	$15,000	$100,000	$40,000	$35,000	$15,000	$25,000	
Sale of Noncash Assets	60,000	(100,000)					($40,000)
	$75,000	$ -0-	$40,000	$35,000	$15,000	$25,000	($40,000)
Allocation of Loss to Partners				(16,000)	(16,000)	(8,000)	40,000
	$75,000		$40,000	$19,000	$ (1,000)	$17,000	$ -0-
Payment of Liabilities	(40,000)		(40,000)				
	$35,000		$ -0-	$19,000	$ (1,000)	$17,000	
Allocation of Baker's Capital Deficit				(667)	1,000	(333)	
	$35,000			$18,333	$ -0-	$16,667	
Final Distribution of Cash	(35,000)			(18,333)		(16,667)	
	$ -0-			$ -0-		$ -0-	

KEY POINTS FOR CHAPTER OBJECTIVES

1 Describe the partnership form of organization and the formation of a partnership (pp. 489–93).

- A partnership is a voluntary association of persons who agree to become joint owners of a business. Each general partner is an agent for the partnership, has unlimited liability for partnership debts, and co-owns firm property with all partners. A partnership is a nontaxable entity and may be dissolved by any membership change or by court decree.
- Partnership assets should be recorded initially at their current fair values, which precludes future inequities in partners' capital balances resulting from the use of these assets.

2 Illustrate various methods for the division of profits and losses (pp. 493–96).

- Partnership profits and losses are divided among partners according to their sharing agreement. If no sharing agreement exists, profits and losses are divided equally.
- Besides using ratios and percents in allocating profits and losses, agreements may include salary allowances and interest on capital investments. In certain cases, some partners may receive an increase in capital, while others may suffer a decrease, when profits and losses are allocated.

3 Describe the methods for admitting a new partner (pp. 496–98).

- When all or part of a partner's interest is purchased by another party, there is merely a transfer of capital from the selling partner to the other party. Total capital remains unchanged.
- When an incoming partner contributes assets to the firm, he or she may be credited with the amount of the investment if there is no bonus arrangement. If the incoming partner is credited with less than the investment, the bonus is accorded current partners in their profit and loss sharing ratio. If the incoming partner is credited with more than the investment, current partners absorb the bonus in their profit and loss sharing ratio.

4 Describe the alternatives when a partner retires (pp. 499–500).

- When a retiring partner sells his or her interest to a new partner or current partners, there is merely a transfer of recorded capital, regardless of the amount paid.
- When payment is made from partnership funds, however, a bonus may be involved. If the settlement exceeds the retiring partner's capital balance, the bonus is absorbed by the remaining partners in their profit and loss sharing ratio. If the capital balance exceeds the settlement, the bonus is accorded the remaining partners in their profit and loss sharing ratio.

5 Explain how partnerships are liquidated (pp. 500–503).

- The following steps are followed in a typical partnership liquidation: (1) Noncash assets are sold and any gain or loss on sale is distributed to the partners' capital accounts; (2) liabilities are paid; and (3) partners are paid the amounts in their capital accounts.
- If step 1 above results in a deficit for any partner(s) who are unable to make up the deficit, such deficit should be distributed to partners having credit balances in their capital accounts, in their profit and loss sharing ratio, before any cash distributions are made to partners.

KEY TERMS USED IN THIS CHAPTER

allowance for interest 494
articles of co-partnership 489
bonus 498
general partnership 489

SELF-TEST QUESTIONS FOR REVIEW

(Answers are at the end of this chapter.)

1. Partners A and B have beginning investments of $40,000 and $60,000, respectively. Profit and loss sharing is as follows: interest at 20% on beginning capital balances, salaries to A and B of $10,000 and $5,000, respectively, and the remainder shared in the ratio 2:3. How much of $30,000 net income would be distributed to A?
(a) $18,000 (b) $16,000 (c) $15,500 (d) $14,000

2. Partners Hill and Dale have capital balances of $50,000 and $30,000, respectively, and share profits and losses equally. Brown purchases one-half of Hill's interest for $28,000. The entry for Brown's admission is:

(a)	Hill, Capital	28,000	
	Brown, Capital		28,000
(b)	Cash	28,000	
	Brown, Capital		28,000
(c)	Hill, Capital	25,000	
	Brown, Capital		25,000
(d)	Hill, Capital	26,500	
	Dale, Capital	1,500	
	Brown, Capital		28,000

3. Byrd and Carr have capital balances of $80,000 and $70,000, respectively, and share profits and losses equally. Drumm invests an amount to give him exactly a one-third interest in the firm. No bonuses are to be awarded to any partners.
(a) Drumm should invest $75,000 and be credited with $75,000.
(b) Drumm should invest $50,000 and be credited with $50,000
(c) Drumm should invest $50,000 and be credited with $75,000.
(d) Drumm should invest $75,000 and be credited with $50,000.

4. Partners Doyle, Farr, and Gibbs have capital balances of $50,000, $60,000, and $70,000, respectively, and share profits and losses in the ratio 3:2:1. Doyle retires and is paid $56,000 with partnership funds. The entry to record Doyle's retirement will include a
(a) Debit to Doyle, Capital for $56,000.
(b) Debit to Farr, Capital for $3,000.
(c) Credit to Farr, Capital for $4,000.
(d) Debit to Gibbs, Capital for $2,000.

5. Partners Hughes, Judd, and King share profits and losses in the ratio 3:5:2. Just before liquidation, the partnership has the following balance sheet:

Cash	$ 20,000	Hughes, Capital	$ 60,000
Other Assets	140,000	Judd, Capital	20,000
		King, Capital	80,000
	$160,000		$160,000

Other Assets are sold for $80,000. Assuming that none of the partners can make up any resulting capital deficit, the final cash distribution to partner King is
(a) $68,000 (b) $64,000 (c) $20,000 (d) $72,000

DEMONSTRATION PROBLEM FOR REVIEW

J. Porter and M. Kantor have been partners for several years, operating Fast Moves, a moving business. The business has had its ups and downs, but overall has been quite successful. In recognition of Porter's administrative responsibilities, the profit and loss sharing agreement allows him a salary of $5,000, with the remainder shared equally.

On January 1, 19X1, Porter and Kantor had capital balances of $14,000 and $9,000, respectively. During 19X1, Porter withdrew $4,000 cash from the partnership, and 19X1 net income was $11,000. On December 31, 19X1, the partnership had the following assets and liabilities: Cash, $4,000; Other Assets, $29,000; and Accounts Payable, $3,000.

Porter and Kantor liquidate the partnership on January 1, 19X2. On that date, other assets are sold for $35,000, creditors are paid, and the partners receive the remaining cash.

REQUIRED

(a) Prepare a schedule showing how the $11,000 net income for 19X1 should be divided between Porter and Kantor.

(b) Prepare a statement of partners' capital for 19X1.

(c) Prepare a balance sheet at December 31, 19X1.

(d) Give the January 1, 19X2, journal entries to record the sale of other assets and recognition of any related gain or loss, the distribution of any gain or loss to partners' capital accounts, the payment of liabilities, and the distribution of cash to the partners.

SOLUTION TO DEMONSTRATION PROBLEM

(a)

	Porter	Kantor	Total
Earnings to be divided			$11,000
Salary allowance	$5,000		5,000
Remainder			$ 6,000
Remainder divided equally	3,000	$3,000	
Partners' shares	$8,000	$3,000	

(b)

Fast Moves
Statement of Partners' Capital
For the Year 19X1

	Porter	Kantor	Total
Capital Balances, January 1, 19X1	$14,000	$ 9,000	$23,000
Add: Net Income for 19X1	8,000	3,000	11,000
Totals	$22,000	$12,000	$34,000
Less: Withdrawals	4,000		4,000
Capital Balances, December 31, 19X1	$18,000	$12,000	$30,000

(c)

Fast Moves
Balance Sheet
December 31, 19X1

Assets		Liabilities		
Cash	$ 4,000	Accounts Payable		$ 3,000
Other Assets	29,000			
		Owners' Equity		
		J. Porter, Capital	$18,000	
		M. Kantor, Capital	12,000	30,000
Total Assets	$33,000	Total Liabilities and Owners' Equity		$33,000

(d) **19X2**

		Debit	Credit
Jan. 1	Cash	35,000	
	Other Assets		29,000
	Gain on Realization of Assets		6,000
	To record sale of other assets.		
1	Gain on Realization of Assets	6,000	
	J. Porter, Capital		3,000
	M. Kantor, Capital		3,000
	To distribute gain on sale of other assets.		
1	Accounts Payable	3,000	
	Cash		3,000
	To record payment of liabilities.		
1	J. Porter, Capital	21,000	
	M. Kantor, Capital	15,000	
	Cash		36,000
	To record cash distribution to partners.		

QUESTIONS

14–1 What is meant by *mutual agency*? By *unlimited liability*?

14–2 A corporation is said to have continuity of existence, whereas a partnership is characterized by a limited life. Name several events that may cause the dissolution of a partnership.

14–3 Porter understands that a partnership is a nontaxable entity and believes that if she does not withdraw any assets from the firm this year, she will not have any taxable income from her partnership activities. Is Porter correct? Why or why not?

14–4 Yates invests in his partnership a machine that originally cost him $20,000. At the time of the investment, his personal records carry it at a book value of $9,000. Its current market value is $12,000. At what amount should the partnership record the machine? Why?

14–5 What factors should persons going into partnership consider in deciding how to share profits and losses?

14–6 If a partnership agreement is silent on the sharing of profits and losses, how will they be divided? What if the agreement indicates the method of sharing profits, but states nothing about the sharing of losses?

14–7 What are salary allowances? What is the difference between a salary allowance and a salary expense?

14–8 In what ways do the financial statements of a partnership differ from those of a sole proprietorship? What is the purpose of a statement of partners' capital?

14–9 Distinguish between the admission of a partner by the purchase of an interest and by investment in the firm.

14–10 What circumstances might cause (a) current partners to receive a bonus when admitting a new partner and (b) an incoming partner to receive a bonus?

14–11 Boyd and Hill, who share profits and losses equally, admit Lowe as a new partner. Lowe contributes $80,000 for a one-fourth interest in the new firm. The entry to admit Lowe shows a $15,000 bonus each to Boyd and Hill. What is the apparent total capital of the new partnership?

14–12 When a partner retires, are the assets and capital of the partnership reduced? Explain.

14–13 When a partnership liquidates, how do accountants handle the gains and losses realized in selling the assets?

14–14 In a partnership liquidation, the residual cash is distributed to partners in the amounts of their capital balances just prior to the distribution. Why is this the proper distribution procedure?

14–15 Assume that during liquidation a debit balance arises in a partner's capital account and the partner is unable to contribute any more assets to the partnership. How does the partnership dispose of the debit balance in the capital account?

14–16 How is a statement of partnership liquidation dated and what accounting information does this statement contain?

EXERCISES

Partnership formation

14–17 Clark and Egan form a partnership on May 1. Clark contributes $75,000 cash and Egan contributes the following items from a separate business:

Marketable securities—cost of $12,000; current fair value of $15,000
Equipment—cost of $50,000; accumulated depreciation of $20,000, current fair value of $25,000
Land—cost of $40,000; current fair value of $55,000
Note payable (secured by equipment)—$15,000 assumed by partnership

Give the opening general journal entries of the partnership to record the investments of Clark and Egan.

Profit and loss sharing

14–18 Benson and Ward are partners whose profit and loss sharing agreement gives salary allowances of $24,000 to Benson and $16,000 to Ward, with the remainder divided equally.

(a) Net income for the year is $60,000. Give the general journal entry to distribute the income to Benson and Ward.
(b) Assume a $20,000 net loss for the year. Give the general journal entry to distribute the loss to Benson and Ward.

Statement of partners' capital

14–19 Use the following data to prepare a 19XX statement of partners' capital for Baker and Ross, who share profits and losses in the ratio of 60% to Baker and 40% to Ross.

Baker, Capital, January 1, 19XX	$90,000
Ross, Capital, January 1, 19XX	50,000
Baker, Drawing	20,000
Ross, Drawing	18,000
Additional investments by Baker	5,000
Net income for 19XX	40,000

Admission of a partner

14–20 Cole and Davis are partners with capital balances of $80,000 and $60,000, respectively. They share profits and losses in the ratio of 60% to Cole and 40% to Davis. Mann receives a one-fourth interest in the firm by investing $60,000 cash on May 4.

(a) Give the general journal entry to record Mann's admission assuming a bonus is allowed Cole and Davis.
(b) Briefly explain circumstances that might cause existing partners to receive a bonus when admitting a new partner.

Retirement of a partner

14–21 Berg, Dane, and Ebert are partners sharing profits and losses in the ratio 5:3:2, respectively. Their capital balances are Berg, $40,000; Dane, $60,000; and Ebert, $60,000. Berg retires from the firm on June 30 and is paid $50,000 from partnership funds.
(a) Give the general journal entry to record Berg's retirement, assuming that Dane and Ebert absorb the bonus paid Berg.
(b) Briefly explain circumstances that might cause a retiring partner to receive a bonus.

Partnership liquidation

14–22 In the liquidation of the ABC Partnership, noncash assets were sold for $30,000 and the related gain or loss on realization resulted in debits to the capital accounts of partners A, B, and C for $8,000, $6,000, and $6,000, respectively.
(a) Were the noncash assets sold at a gain or a loss? How do you know? How much was the gain or the loss?
(b) What is the partners' apparent profit and loss sharing ratio?
(c) What was the apparent book value of the noncash assets sold?

Partnership liquidation

14–23 Just before liquidation, the balance sheet of Budd and Jason, who share profits and losses equally, appeared as follows:

Cash	$ 36,000	Liabilities	$ 10,000
Other Assets	64,000	Budd, Capital	60,000
		Jason, Capital	30,000
	$100,000		$100,000

(a) If other assets are sold for $60,000, what amounts will Budd and Jason receive as the final cash distribution?
(b) If other assets are sold for $70,000, what amounts will Budd and Jason receive as the final cash distribution?
(c) If Budd receives $51,000 and Jason receives $21,000 as the final (and only) cash distribution, what amount was received from the sale of the other assets?

Partnership liquidation

14–24 Case, Frye, Hahn, and Gordon are liquidating their partnership. All assets have been converted to cash, and all liabilities have been paid. At this point, the capital accounts show the following: Case, $10,000 credit balance; Frye, $16,000 credit balance; Hahn, $9,000 debit balance; and Gordon, $11,000 credit balance. Profits and losses are shared equally.
(a) How much cash is available to distribute to partners?
(b) If there is doubt concerning Hahn's ability to make up the $9,000 deficit, how should the available cash be distributed.

Partnership liquidation

14–25 The following is a summary of a statement of partnership liquidation. Each numbered line represents some aspect of the liquidation. Amounts in parentheses represent decreases or losses. Briefly describe what each numbered line represents, indicating the apparent partners' sharing ratio when appropriate.

	Cash	Noncash Assets	Liabilities	A, Capital	B, Capital	Gain or Loss on Realization
1.	$30,000	$70,000	$22,000	$50,000	$28,000	
2.	50,000	($70,000)				($20,000)
3.	(22,000)		($22,000)			
4.				(15,000)	(5,000)	$20,000
5.	($58,000)			($35,000)	($23,000)	

PROBLEMS

Profit and loss sharing

14–26 Grove and Fraser form a partnership and invest $70,000 and $50,000, respectively. During its first year, the partnership earned a $24,000 net income.

REQUIRED

(a) Give the entry to close the Income Summary account and distribute the $24,000 net income under each of the following independent assumptions:
   1. The partnership agreement is silent on the sharing of profits and losses.
   2. Profits and losses are shared in the ratio of beginning capital investments.
   3. Profits and losses are shared by allowing 10% interest on beginning capital investments, with the remainder divided equally.

(b) Assume the partnership had a $12,000 loss in its first year. Give the entry to close the Income Summary account and distribute the $12,000 loss under each of the foregoing assumptions.

Profit and loss sharing

14–27 The capital accounts and the Income Summary account of the Hayes, Kean, and Ladd partnership appear below. None of the partners withdrew capital during the year.

Hayes, Capital

	19XX	
	Jan. 1	24,000
	July 1	32,000

Kean, Capital

	19XX	
	Jan. 1	32,000
	Oct. 1	32,000

Ladd, Capital

	19XX	
	Jan. 1	80,000

Income Summary

	19XX	
	Dec. 31	60,000

REQUIRED

(a) Give the entry to distribute the $60,000 net income if Hayes, Kean, and Ladd share profits and losses:
   1. Equally.
   2. In the ratio 5:3:2, respectively.
   3. In the ratio of *average* capital balances for the year.
   4. Under an agreement allowing $20,000 salary to Ladd, 10% interest on *beginning* investments, with the remainder shared equally.

(b) Assume that net income was $21,000 rather than $60,000. Give the entry to distribute the $21,000 earnings if the agreement allows $20,000 salary to Ladd, 10% interest on beginning investments, with the remainder shared equally.

Admission of a partner

14–28 Bower and Daly are partners with capital balances of $40,000 and $32,000, respectively. Profits and losses are shared equally.

REQUIRED
Give the entries to record the admission of a new partner, Mack, under each of the following separate circumstances:
(a) Mack purchases one-half of Daly's interest, paying Daly $18,000 personally.
(b) Mack invests sufficient funds to receive exactly one-fourth interest in the new partnership. (No bonuses are recorded.)
(c) Mack invests $23,000 for a one-fifth interest, with any bonus distributed to the capital accounts of Bower and Daly.
(d) Mack invests $16,000 for a one-fourth interest, with any bonus credited to Mack's capital account.
(e) In requirements (c) and (d) above, what do the terms of admission imply regarding the relative negotiating positions of the new partner and the old partners?

Retirement of a partner

14–29 Hope, Lucas, and Reece are partners with capital balances of $70,000, $40,000, and $50,000, respectively. Profits and losses are shared equally. Reece retires from the firm.

REQUIRED
Record the entries for Reece's retirement in each of the following separate circumstances:
(a) Reece's interest is sold to Winston, a new partner, for $58,000.
(b) Hope and Lucas each acquire one-half of Reece's interest for $28,000 apiece.
(c) Reece receives $58,000 of partnership funds for his interest. The remaining partners absorb the bonus paid Reece.
(d) The partners agree that Reece's abrupt retirement presents operating disadvantages and therefore Reece should receive only $46,000 for his interest. Payment is from partnership funds, with any bonuses going to Hope and Lucas.

Sharing of loss, admission and withdrawal of partners

14–30 Bolt and Drew formed a partnership on January 1, 19X1, with capital investments of $31,000 and $62,000, respectively. The profit and loss sharing agreement allowed Bolt a salary of $8,000, with the remainder divided equally. During the year, Drew made withdrawals of $5,000; no other investments or withdrawals were made in 19X1. The partnership incurred a net loss of $10,000 in 19X1.

On January 1, 19X2, Kiley was admitted to the partnership. Kiley purchased one-third of Drew's interest, paying $15,000 directly to Drew. Bolt, Drew, and Kiley agreed to share profits and losses in the ratio 3:5:2, respectively. No provision was made for salaries. The partnership earned a net income of $60,000 in 19X2.

On January 1, 19X3, Drew withdrew from the partnership. Drew received $65,000 of partnership funds for her interest. Bolt and Kiley absorbed the bonus paid Drew.

REQUIRED

(a) Give the December 31, 19X1, entry to close the Income Summary account and distribute the $10,000 loss for 19X1.
(b) Compute the capital balances of Bolt and Drew at December 31, 19X1.
(c) Give the entry to record the admission of Kiley on January 1, 19X2.
(d) Give the December 31, 19X2, entry to close the Income Summary account and distribute the $60,000 income for 19X2.
(e) Compute the December 31, 19X2, capital balances of Bolt, Drew, and Kiley.
(f) Give the January 1, 19X3, entry to record Drew's withdrawal.

Statement of partners' capital

14–31 Judd and Karl formed a partnership in 19X1, agreeing to share profits and losses equally. On December 31, 19X1, their capital balances were: Judd, $80,000; Karl, $48,000.

On January 1, 19X2, Moran was admitted to a one-fourth interest in the firm by investing $48,000 cash. Moran's admission was recorded by according bonuses to Judd and Karl. The profit and loss sharing agreement of the new partnership allowed salaries of $16,000 to Judd and $20,000 to Moran, with the remainder divided in the ratio 3:3:2 among Judd, Karl, and Moran, respectively.

Net income for 19X2 was $84,000. Judd and Moran withdrew cash during the year equal to their salary allowances. Immediately after the net income had been closed to the partners' capital accounts, Moran retired from the firm. Moran received $70,000 of partnership funds for his interest, and the remaining partners absorbed the bonus paid Moran.

REQUIRED

Prepare a statement of partners' capital for 19X2.

Partnership liquidation

14–32 Carr, Hawk, and Lund are partners who share profits and losses in the ratio of 5:3:2, respectively. Just before the partnership's liquidation, its balance sheet accounts appear as follows:

Cash	$ 50,000	Accounts Payable	$ 60,000
Other Assets	150,000	Carr, Capital	30,000
		Hawk, Capital	60,000
		Lund, Capital	50,000
	$200,000		$200,000

REQUIRED

(a) Assuming that other assets are sold for $120,000, give the entries to record the sale of the other assets and distribute the related loss, pay liabilities, and distribute the remaining cash to the partners.
(b) Assuming that other assets are sold for $80,000, give the entries to record the sale of the other assets and distribute the related loss, pay liabilities, apportion any partner's deficit among the other partners (assuming any such deficit is not made up by the partner involved), and distribute the remaining cash to the appropriate partners.
(c) Assuming that liquidation procedures occurred between January 1 and February 15, 19X4, prepare a statement of partnership liquidation using the data in requirement (b).

Sharing of loss and partnership liquidation

14–33 Abner, Boyd, Case, and Dunn are partners who share profits and losses in the ratio of 4:3:2:1, respectively. Their partnership agreement provides for annual interest at 20% on partners' beginning capital balances and annual salaries of $12,000 and $4,000 to Abner and Case, respectively.

Due to a history of modest earnings, they liquidate their partnership at December 31, 19X4. Just prior to completing the closing of the partnership books for 19X4, the trial balance is summarized as follows:

Cash	$ 74,000	Liabilities	$ 60,000
Noncash Assets (net)	110,000	Abner, Capital	30,000
Abner, Drawing	12,000	Boyd, Capital	70,000
Case, Drawing	4,000	Case, Capital	20,000
Income Summary (loss)	30,000	Dunn, Capital	50,000
	$230,000		$230,000

REQUIRED

(a) Assuming that none of the partners made any capital contributions during the year, prepare journal entries to complete the closing of the books at December 31, 19X4. During the year, Abner and Case withdrew amounts equal to their salary allowances.

(b) Starting with the partnership post-closing trial balance at December 31, 19X4, prepare a statement of partnership liquidation assuming that

1. Noncash assets were sold for $70,000 cash.
2. All liabilities were paid in cash.
3. Any partner experiencing a capital deficit would be unable to make up the deficit to the partnership.
4. The final distribution of cash to partners was made on February 20, 19X5.

ALTERNATE PROBLEMS

Profit and loss sharing

14–26A Arden and Bolton form a partnership and invest $60,000 and $30,000, respectively. During its first year, the partnership earned $21,000 net income.

REQUIRED

(a) Give the entry to close the Income Summary account and distribute the $21,000 net income under each of the following independent assumptions:
1. The partnership agreement is silent on the sharing of profits and losses.
2. Profits and losses are shared in the ratio of beginning capital investments.
3. Profits and losses are shared by allowing 10% interest on beginning capital investments with the remainder divided equally.

(b) Assume the partnership had a $12,000 loss in its first year. Give the entry to close the Income Summary account and distribute the $12,000 loss under each of the foregoing assumptions.

Profit and loss sharing

14–27A The capital accounts and the Income Summary account of the Dean, Hagen, and Owen partnership appear below. None of the partners withdrew capital during the year.

Dean, Capital

	19XX	
	Jan. 1	60,000
	Sept. 1	60,000

Hagen, Capital

	19XX	
	Jan. 1	30,000
	July 1	20,000

Owen, Capital			Income Summary	
	19XX			19XX
	Jan. 1 24,000			Dec. 31 36,000

REQUIRED
(a) Give the entry to distribute the $36,000 net income if Dean, Hagen, and Owen share profits and losses:
1. Equally.
2. In the ratio 3:2:1, respectively.
3. In the ratio of *average* capital balances for the year.
4. Under an agreement allowing $18,000 salary to Dean, 10% interest on *beginning* investments, with the remainder shared equally.

(b) Assume that net income was $24,000 rather than $36,000. Give the entry to distribute the $24,000 earnings if the agreement allows $18,000 salary to Dean, 10% interest on beginning investments, with the remainder shared equally.

Admission of a partner

14–28A Ford and Gibson are partners with capital balances of $60,000 and $36,000, respectively. Profits and losses are shared equally.

REQUIRED
Give the entries to record the admission of a new partner, Hanley, under each of the following separate circumstances:
(a) Hanley purchases one-half of Gibson's interest, paying Gibson $22,000 personally.
(b) Hanley invests sufficient funds to receive exactly one-fourth interest in the new partnership. (No bonuses are recorded.)
(c) Hanley invests $34,000 for a one-fifth interest, with any bonus distributed to the capital accounts of Ford and Gibson.
(d) Hanley invests $28,000 for a one-fourth interest, with any bonus credited to Hanley's capital account.
(e) In requirements (c) and (d) above, what do the terms of admission imply regarding the relative negotiating positions of the new partner and the old partners?

Retirement of a partner

14–29A Baker, Egan, and Lynn are partners with capital balances of $60,000, $50,000, and $40,000, respectively. Profits and losses are shared equally. Lynn retires from the firm.

REQUIRED
Record the entries for Lynn's retirement in each of the following separate circumstances:
(a) Lynn's interest is sold to Hines, a new partner, for $45,000.
(b) One-half of Lynn's interest is sold to each of the remaining partners for $22,000 apiece.
(c) Lynn receives $46,000 of partnership funds for his interest. The remaining partners absorb the bonus paid to Lynn.
(d) The partners agree that Lynn's abrupt retirement presents operating disadvantages and therefore Lynn should receive only $36,000 for his interest. Payment is from partnership funds, with any bonuses going to Baker and Egan.

Sharing of loss, admission and withdrawal of partners

14–30A Casey and Kohl formed a partnership on January 1, 19X1, with capital investments of $41,000 and $65,000, respectively. The profit and loss sharing agreement allowed Casey a salary of $10,000 with the remainder divided equally. During the year, Kohl made withdrawals of $9,000; no other investments or withdrawals were made in 19X1. The partnership incurred a net loss of $12,000 in 19X1.

On January 1, 19X2, Mackey was admitted to the partnership. Mackey purchased one-third of Kohl's interest, paying $18,000 directly to Kohl. Casey, Kohl, and Mackey agreed to share profits and losses in the ratio 5:3:2, respectively. No provision was made for salaries. The partnership earned a net income of $50,000 in 19X2.

On January 1, 19X3, Kohl withdrew from the partnership. Kohl received $52,000 of partnership funds for his interest. Casey and Mackey absorbed the bonus paid Kohl.

REQUIRED

(a) Give the December 31, 19X1, entry to close the Income Summary account and distribute the $12,000 loss for 19X1.
(b) Compute the capital balances of Casey and Kohl at December 31, 19X1.
(c) Give the entry to record the admission of Mackey on January 1, 19X2.
(d) Give the December 31, 19X2, entry to close the Income Summary account and distribute the $50,000 income for 19X2.
(e) Compute the December 31, 19X2, capital balances of Casey, Kohl, and Mackey.
(f) Give the January 1, 19X3, entry to record Kohl's withdrawal.

Statement of partners' capital

14–31A Lucas and Brown formed a partnership in 19X1, agreeing to share profits and losses equally. On December 31, 19X1, their capital balances were: Lucas, $70,000; Brown, $54,000.

On January 1, 19X2, Carter was admitted to a one-fourth interest in the firm by investing $56,000 cash. Carter's admission was recorded by according bonuses to Lucas and Brown. The profit and loss sharing agreement of the new partnership allowed salaries of $14,000 to Lucas and $16,000 to Carter, with the remainder divided in the ratio 4:3:3 among Lucas, Brown, and Carter, respectively.

Net income for 19X2 was $72,000. Lucas and Carter withdrew cash during the year equal to their salary allowances. Immediately after net income had been closed to the partners' capital accounts, Carter retired from the firm. Carter received $59,000 for his interest, and the remaining partners absorbed the bonus paid Carter.

REQUIRED

Prepare a statement of partners' capital for 19X2.

Partnership liquidation

14–32A Cody, Lyon, and Parker are partners who share profits and losses in the ratio of 5:3:2, respectively. Just before the partnership's liquidation, its balance sheet appears as follows:

Cash	$ 30,000	Accounts Payable	$ 20,000
Other Assets (net)	80,000	Cody, Capital	16,000
		Lyon, Capital	30,000
		Parker, Capital	44,000
	$110,000		$110,000

REQUIRED

(a) Assuming that other assets are sold for $65,000, give the entries to record the sale of the other assets and distribute the related loss, pay liabilities, and distribute the remaining cash to the partners.

(b) Assuming that other assets are sold for $44,000, give the entries to record the sale of the other assets and distribute the related loss, pay liabilities, apportion any partner's deficit among the other partners (assuming any such deficit is not made up by the partner involved), and distribute the remaining cash to the appropriate partners.

(c) Assuming that liquidation procedures occurred between January 1 and February 8, 19X5, prepare a statement of partnership liquidation using the data in requirement (b).

Sharing of loss and partnership liquidation

14–33A Beard, Dale, Gregg, and Ritt are partners who share profits and losses in the ratio of 5:3:1:1, respectively. Their partnership agreement provides for annual interest at 20% on partners' beginning capital balances and annual salaries of $5,000 and $10,000 to Beard and Dale, respectively.

Due to a history of modest earnings, they liquidate their partnership on December 31, 19X5. Just prior to completing the closing of the partnership books for 19X5, the trial balance is summarized as follows:

Cash	$ 27,000	Liabilities	$ 17,000
Noncash Assets (net)	80,000	Beard, Capital	25,000
Beard, Drawing	10,000	Dale, Capital	20,000
Dale, Drawing	15,000	Gregg, Capital	50,000
Income Summary	10,000	Ritt, Capital	30,000
	$142,000		$142,000

REQUIRED

(a) Assuming that none of the partners made any capital contributions during the year, prepare journal entries to complete the closing of the books at December 31, 19X5.

(b) Starting with the partnership post-closing trial balance at December 31, 19X5, prepare a statement of partnership liquidation assuming that
   1. Noncash assets were sold for $60,000 cash.
   2. All liabilities were paid in cash.
   3. Any partner experiencing a capital deficit would be unable to make up the deficit to the partnership.
   4. The final distribution of cash to partners was made on January 31, 19X6.

BUSINESS DECISION PROBLEM

Thomas and Wood were in business for several years, sharing profits and losses equally. Because of Wood's poor health, they liquidated the partnership. Thomas managed the liquidation because Wood was in the hospital. Just before liquidation, the partnership balance sheet contained the following information:

Cash	$ 80,000	Liabilities	$ 50,000
Other Assets	220,000	Thomas, Capital	100,000
		Wood, Capital	150,000
	$300,000		$300,000

Thomas (1) sold the other assets at the best prices obtainable, (2) paid off all the creditors, and (3) divided the remaining cash between Wood and himself equally, according to their profit and loss sharing ratio.

Wood received a note from Thomas that read "Good news—sold other assets for $250,000. Have $140,000 check waiting for you. Get well soon." Because he will not be released from the hospital for several days, Wood asks you to review Thomas's liquidation and cash distribution procedures.

REQUIRED

Do you approve of Thomas's liquidation and cash distribution procedures? Explain. If you believe Thomas erred, what amount of final cash settlement should Wood receive?

ANSWERS TO SELF-TEST QUESTIONS

1. (b) **2.** (c) **3.** (a) **4.** (d) **5.** (b)

15

CORPORATIONS: ORGANIZATION AND CAPITAL STOCK

CHAPTER OBJECTIVES

1. Define and discuss the corporate form of organization (pp. 519–22).
2. Explain the difference between par and no-par value stock (p. 522).
3. Identify and discuss the types of stock and their basic rights (pp. 522–26).
4. Describe the accounting for issuances of stock for cash, by subscription, and for noncash assets (pp. 526–29).
5. Define and discuss stock splits (p. 530).
6. Explain the accounting for treasury stock and donated capital (pp. 530–32).
7. Define and discuss the terms *book value, market value,* and *liquidation value per share* of stock (pp. 532–35).

The genius of the industrial system lies in its organized use of capital and technology.

JOHN KENNETH GALBRAITH

Without a doubt, the modern corporation dominates the national and international economic landscape. In the United States, corporations generate well over three-fourths of the combined business receipts of corporations, partnerships, and proprietorships, even though fewer than one of every five businesses is organized as a corporation. The corporate form of organization is used for a variety of business efforts—from the large, multinational corporation with more than a million owners operating in countries all over the world to the small, family-owned business in a single community.

In this and the next three chapters, we consider various aspects of accounting for the corporation. In this chapter, we emphasize the organization of the corporation and the accounting procedures for its capital stock transactions.

NATURE AND FORMATION OF A CORPORATION

A **corporation** is a legal entity—an artificial legal "person"—created on the approval of the appropriate governmental authority. The right to conduct business as a corporation is a privilege granted by the state in which the corporation is formed. All states have laws specifying the requirements for creating a corporation. In some instances, such as the formation of a national bank, the federal government must approve the creation of a corporation.

To form a corporation, the incorporators (often at least three are required) must apply for a charter. The incorporators prepare and file the **articles of incorporation,** which delineate the basic structure of the corporation, including the purposes for which it is formed, the amount of capital stock to be authorized, and the number of shares into which the stock is to be divided. If the incorporators meet the requirements of the law, the government issues a charter or certificate of incorporation. After the charter has been granted, the incorporators (or, in some states, the subscribers to the corporation's capital stock) hold an organization meeting to elect the first board of directors and adopt the corporation's bylaws.

Because assets are essential to corporate operations, the corporation issues *certificates of capital stock* to obtain the necessary funds. As owners of the corporation, *stockholders*, or *shareholders*, are entitled to a voice in the control and management of the company. Stockholders with voting stock may vote at the annual meeting and participate in the election of the board of directors. The board of directors is responsible for the overall management of the corporation. Normally, the board selects such corporate officers as a president, one or more vice-presidents, a controller, a treasurer, and a secretary. The officers implement the policies of the board of directors and actively manage the day-to-day affairs of the corporation.

Creating a corporation is more costly than organizing a proprietorship or partnership. The expenditures incurred to organize a corporation are charged to Organization Costs, an intangible asset account. These costs include attorney's fees, fees paid to the state, and costs of promoting the enterprise. As we discussed in Chapter 11, organization costs typically are amortized over a period of five to ten years.

CHARACTERISTICS OF CORPORATIONS

Separate Legal Entity

A business with a corporate charter is empowered to conduct business affairs apart from its owners. The corporation, as a legal entity, may acquire assets, incur debt, enter into contracts, sue, and be sued—all in its own name. The owners, or stockholders, of the corporation receive stock certificates as evidence of their ownership interests; the stockholders, however, are separate and distinct from the corporation. This characteristic contrasts with proprietorships and partnerships, which are accounting entities but not legal entities apart from their owners. Owners of proprietorships and partnerships can be held responsible separately and collectively for unsatisfied obligations of the business.

Limited Liability

The liability of shareholders with respect to company affairs is usually limited to their investment in the corporation. Because of this limited liability, state laws restrict distributions to shareholders. Most of these laws have fairly elaborate provisions that define the various forms of owners' equity and describe distribution conditions. To protect creditors, the state controls the distribution of contributed capital. Distributions of retained earnings (undistributed profits) are not legal unless the board of directors formally declares a dividend. Because of the legal delineation of owner capital available for distribution, corporations must maintain careful distinctions in the accounts to identify the different elements of stockholders' equity.

Transferability of Ownership

Shares in a corporation may be routinely transferred without affecting the company's operations. The corporation merely notes such transfers of ownership in the stockholder records (ledger). Although a corporation must have stockholder records to notify shareholders of meetings and to pay dividends, the price at which shares transfer between owners is not recognized in the corporation's accounts.

Continuity of Existence

Because routine transfers of ownership do not affect a corporation's affairs, the corporation is said to have continuity of existence. In this respect, a corporation is completely different from a partnership. In a partnership, any change in ownership technically results in discontinuance of the old partnership and formation of a new one. (Many large professional service partnerships, however, follow procedures that provide for continuity with changes in ownership.)

In a partnership, the individual partners' capital accounts indicate their relative interests in the business. The stockholders' equity section of a corporate balance sheet does not present individual stockholder accounts. A shareholder, however, can easily compute his or her interest in the corporation by calculating the proportion of the total shares outstanding that his or her shares represent. For example, if only one class of stock is outstanding and it totals 1,000 shares, an individual owning 200 shares has a 20% interest in the corporation's total stockholders' equity, which includes all contributed capital and retained earnings. The dollar amount of this interest, however, is a book amount, rarely coinciding with the market value. A stockholder who liquidates his or her investment would sell it at a price negotiated with a buyer or, if the stock is traded on a stock exchange, at the exchange's quoted market price.

Capital-raising Capability

The limited liability of stockholders and the ease with which shares of stock may be transferred from one investor to another are attractive features to potential stockholders. These characteristics enhance the ability of the corporation to raise large amounts of capital by issuing shares of stock. Because both large and small investors may acquire ownership interests in a corporation, a wide spectrum of potential investors exists. Corporations with thousands of stockholders are not uncommon. The ability to accumulate and use tremendous amounts of capital makes the corporation the dominant form of business organization in the U.S. economy.

Taxation

As legal entities, corporations are subject to federal income taxes on their earnings, whether distributed or not. In addition, shareholders must pay income taxes on earnings received as dividends. In many small corporations in which the shareholders themselves manage the business affairs, large salaries may reduce earnings to a point where the double taxation feature is not onerous. However, the firm may have to justify the reasonableness of such salaries to the Internal Revenue Service. Under certain circumstances, a corporation with 35 or fewer shareholders may elect partnership treatment for tax purposes. Although partnerships must submit "information" tax returns, an income tax is not imposed on their earnings. Instead, the partners report their respective shares of partnership earnings on their individual income tax returns.

Usually, corporations are subject to state income taxes in the states in which they are incorporated or are doing business. They may also be subject to real estate, personal property, and franchise taxes.

Regulation and Supervision

Corporations are subject to greater degrees of regulation and supervision than are proprietorships and partnerships. Each state has the right to regulate the corporations it charters. State laws limit the powers a corporation may exercise, identify reports that must be filed, and define the rights and liabilities of stockholders. If stock is issued to the public, the corporation must comply with the laws governing the sale of corporate securities. Furthermore, corporations whose stock is listed and traded on organized security exchanges—such as the New York Stock Exchange—are subject to the various reporting and disclosure requirements of these exchanges.

OWNERS' EQUITY AND ORGANIZATIONAL FORMS

Differences arise between accounting for the owners' equity of a corporation and for that of a sole proprietorship or partnership. In a sole proprietorship, only a single owner's capital account is needed to reflect increases from capital contributions and net earnings as well as decreases from withdrawals and net losses. In practice, as explained in Chapter 2, many sole proprietors keep a separate drawing account to record withdrawals of cash and other business assets. This separate record is kept only for convenience, however; no subdivision of the owner's capital account is required either by law or by accounting principles.

A similar situation exists in most partnerships, which customarily maintain capital and drawing accounts for each partner. A partnership is simply an association of two or more persons who agree to become joint owners of a business. Because more than one individual is involved in the business, a written agreement should govern the financial participation and business responsibilities of the partners. However, no legal or accounting requirement demands that a distinction be maintained between contributed capital and undistributed earnings.

A corporation, on the other hand, is subject to certain legal restrictions imposed by the government approving its creation. These restrictions focus on the distinction between contributed capital and retained earnings and make accounting for the owners' equity somewhat more complex for corporations than for other types of business organizations. Note that much of the accounting for corporate owners' equity is actually a polyglot of legal prescription and accounting convention. The detailed reporting of stockholders' equity transactions, however, provides analytical information that is often useful and, in many instances, required by law.

PAR AND NO-PAR VALUE STOCK

The corporate charter may specify a face value, or **par value,** for each share of a stock of any class. In the early days of corporate stock issuances, par value represented the market value of the stock when it was issued. In this century, however, par values have typically been set at amounts well below the stock's market value at date of issue. Par value today, therefore, has no economic significance.

Par value may have legal implications.[1] In some states, par value may represent the minimum amount that must be paid in per share of stock. If stock is issued at a *discount* (that is, at less than par value), the stockholder may have a liability for the discount should creditor claims remain unsatisfied after the company's liquidation. Issuing stock at a discount has been a rare event in this century, though, because boards of directors have generally established par values below market values at time of issue.

Par value may also be used in some states to define a corporation's legal capital. The *legal capital* is the minimum amount of contributed capital that must remain in the corporation as a margin of protection for creditors. A distribution of assets to stockholders would not be allowed if it reduced stockholders' equity below the amount of legal capital. Given the role that par value may play in defining legal capital, accountants carefully segregate and record the par value of stock transactions in an appropriate capital stock account.

Most states permit the issuance of stock without a par value—that is, **no-par stock.** The company's board of directors usually sets a **stated value** for the no-par stock. In such cases, the stated value will determine the corporation's legal capital. Again, the stated value figure is usually set well below market value at time of issue, but in contrast to par value, the stated value is not printed on the stock certificate. For accounting purposes, stated value amounts are treated in a fashion similar to par value amounts. In the absence of a stated value, the entire proceeds from the issuance of no-par stock will likely establish the corporation's legal capital.

TYPES OF STOCK

The amounts and kinds of stock that a corporation may issue are enumerated in the company's charter. Providing for several classes of stock permits the company

[1]For a more complete discussion of the legal implications of par value stock, see Philip McGough, "The Legal Significance of the Par Value of Common Stock: What Accounting Educators Should Know," *Issues in Accounting Education*, Fall 1988, pp. 330–50.

to raise capital from different types of investors. The charter also specifies the corporation's **authorized stock**—the maximum number of shares of each class of stock that may be issued. A corporation that wishes to issue more shares than its authorized number must first amend its charter. Shares that have been sold and issued to stockholders constitute the **issued stock** of the corporation. Some of this stock may be repurchased by the corporation. Shares actually held by stockholders are called **outstanding stock,** whereas those reacquired by the corporation (and not retired) are *treasury stock.* We discuss treasury stock later in the chapter.

Common Stock

When only one class of stock is issued, it is called **common stock.** Common shareholders compose the basic ownership class. They have rights to vote, to share in earnings, to participate in additional issues of stock, and—in the case of liquidation—to share in assets after prior claims on the corporation have been settled. We now consider each of these rights.

As the owners of a corporation, the common shareholders elect the board of directors and vote on other matters requiring the approval of owners. Common shareholders are entitled to one vote for each share of stock they own. Owners who do not attend the annual stockholders' meetings may vote by proxy (this may be the case for most stockholders in large corporations).

A common stockholder has the right to a proportionate share of the corporation's earnings that are distributed as dividends. All earnings belong to the corporation, however, until the board of directors formally declares a dividend.

Each shareholder of a corporation has a **preemptive right** to maintain his or her proportionate interest in the corporation. If the company issues additional shares of stock, current owners of that type of stock receive the first opportunity to acquire, on a pro-rata basis, the new shares. In certain situations, management may request shareholders to waive their preemptive rights. For example, the corporation may wish to issue additional stock to acquire another company. Further, stockholders of firms incorporated in some states do not receive preemptive rights.

A liquidating corporation converts its assets to a form suitable for distribution, usually cash, which it then distributes to parties having claims on the corporate assets. Any assets remaining after all claims have been satisfied belong to the residual ownership interest in the corporation—the common stockholders. These owners are entitled to the final distribution of the balance of the assets.

A company may occasionally use *classified* common stock; that is, it may issue more than one class of common stock. Two classes of common stock issued are identified as Class A and Class B. The two classes usually differ in either their respective dividend rights or their respective voting powers. Usually, classified common stock is issued when the organizers of the corporation wish to acquire funds from the public while retaining voting control. To illustrate, let us assume 10,000 shares of Class A stock are issued to the public at $40 per share, while 20,000 shares of Class B stock are issued to the organizers at $5 per share. If each shareholder receives one vote per share of stock, the Class B stockholders have twice as many votes as the Class A stockholders. Yet the total investment of Class B stockholders is significantly less than that of the Class A stockholders. To offset the difference in the voting power per dollar of investment, the Class A stockholders may have better dividend rights, such as being entitled to dividends in early years, while the Class B stockholders may not receive dividends until a certain level of earning power is reached.

Preferred Stock

Preferred stock is a class of stock with various characteristics that distinguish it from common stock. Preferred stock has one or more preferences over common stock, usually with reference to (1) dividends and (2) assets when the corporation liquidates. To determine the features of a particular issue, we must examine the stock contract. The majority of preferred issues, however, have certain typical features, which we discuss below.

DIVIDEND PREFERENCE When the board of directors declares a distribution of earnings, preferred stockholders are entitled to a certain annual amount of dividends before common stockholders receive any distribution. The amount is usually specified in the preferred stock contract as a percentage of the par value of the stock or in dollars per share if the stock does not have a par value. Thus, if the preferred stock has a $100 par value and a 6% dividend rate, the preferred shareholders receive $6 per share in dividends. However, the amount is owed to the stockholders only if declared.

Preferred dividends are usually **cumulative**—that is, regular dividends to preferred stockholders omitted in past years must be paid in addition to the current year's dividend before any distribution is made to common shareholders. For example, a dividend may not be declared in an unprofitable year. If the $6 preferred stock dividend mentioned above is one year in arrears and a dividend is declared in the current year, preferred shareholders would receive $12 per share before common shareholders received anything. If a preferred stock is noncumulative, omitted dividends do not carry forward. Because investors normally consider the noncumulative feature unattractive, noncumulative preferred stock is rarely issued.

Dividends in arrears (that is, omitted in past years) on cumulative preferred stock are not an accounting liability and do not appear in the liability section of the balance sheet. They do not become an obligation of the corporation until the board of directors formally declares such dividends. Any arrearages are typically disclosed to investors in a footnote to the balance sheet.

Ordinarily, preferred stockholders receive a fixed amount and do not participate further in distributions made by the corporation. Occasionally, however, the stock contract may make the preferred a **participating** stock. To illustrate the participating feature, let us assume that a company had outstanding 1,000 shares of $100 par value, 6% *fully participating* cumulative preferred stock and 10,000 shares of $20 par value common stock. Assume also that the company declared total dividends of $27,000 and that no preferred dividends were in arrears. The distribution would be made as follows:

	Preferred	Common	Total
Outstanding stock (total par value)	$100,000	$200,000	$300,000
Preferred dividends in arrears	$ -0-		$ -0-
Regular dividend (6%) and matching rate to common (6%)	6,000	$ 12,000	18,000
Remainder of $9,000 ($27,000 − $18,000) divided to give each class the same rate: $9,000/$300,000 = 3%	3,000	6,000	9,000
Total distribution	$ 9,000	$ 18,000	$ 27,000
Rate of distribution (based on total par value)	9%	9%	

Note that, after the preferred stock is accorded its regular 6% dividend, a like rate of 6% ($12,000) is allocated to the common stock. The remaining $9,000 is then apportioned so both classes of stock receive the same *rate* of distribution. This rate is determined by dividing the remainder to be distributed by the total par value of both classes of stock ($300,000). It is important to note that the preferred stock does not participate until the common stock is accorded an amount corresponding to the regular preferred dividend rate.

Preferred stock may also be *partially* participating. For example, suppose that the preferred shares participate to 8%. They would then be entitled only to an additional 2% over their regular 6% dividend, and any remaining amount would be accorded to the common shares.

Any arrearage on cumulative preferred stock must first be awarded to the preferred shareholders. Therefore, had there been one year's arrearage on the fully participating stock in the foregoing example, $12,000 ($6,000 dividends in arrears and $6,000 current dividends) would have been allocated to the preferred stock and then the normal 6%, or $12,000, to the common stock. Of the remaining $3,000, $1,000 would be assigned to the preferred stock and $2,000 to the common stock.

Of course, if either the common stock or the preferred stock is no-par value stock, preferred stock participation is determined on some basis other than total par values. For example, the participation may be achieved by allocating dividends of equal dollar amounts per share to each class of stock.

ASSET DISTRIBUTION PREFERENCE Preferred stockholders normally have a preference over common stockholders as to the receipt of assets when a corporation liquidates. As the corporation goes out of business, the claims of creditors are settled first. Then preferred stockholders have the right to receive assets equal to the par value of their stock or a larger stated liquidation value per share before any assets are distributed to common stockholders. The preferred stockholders' preference to assets in liquidation also includes any dividends in arrears.

OTHER FEATURES Although preferred shareholders do not ordinarily have the right to vote in the election of directors, this right can be accorded by contract. Some state laws require that all stock issued by a corporation be given voting rights. Sometimes, a preferred stock contract confers full or partial voting rights under certain conditions—for example, when dividends have not been paid for a specified period.

Preferred stock contracts may contain features that cause the stock to resemble the common stock equity at one end of a spectrum or a debt obligation at the other end. The stock may, for example, be *convertible* into common stock at some specified rate. With this feature, the market price of the preferred often moves with that of the common. When the price of the common stock rises, the value of the conversion feature is enhanced. Preferred stock may also be convertible into long-term debt securities (bonds).

Preferred stock may be *callable,* which means the corporation can redeem the stock after a length of time and at a price specified in the contract. The call feature makes the stock similar to a bond, which frequently is callable or has a limited life. Most preferred stocks are callable, with the call or redemption price set slightly above the original issuance price.

To be successful in selling its preferred stock, a corporation often must cater to current market vogues. Features are added or omitted, depending on market conditions and the desires of the investor group the corporation wishes to attract. Management must balance market requirements with its own goals. Sometimes management must compromise and issue securities that it hopes to change over time, perhaps through conversion or refinancing, to arrive at the desired financial plan.

Preferred stocks appeal to investors who want a steady rate of return that is normally somewhat higher than that on bonds. These investors often feel that preferred stock entails less risk than common stock, although the common will pay off more if the company does well.

From both the legal and the accounting standpoint, preferred stock is part of stockholders' equity. Dividends are distributions of earnings and, unlike interest on bonds, are not shown as expenses on the income statement. Also, because of the legal classification of preferred stock as stockholders' equity, the company cannot deduct dividends as expenses for income tax purposes, whereas interest on debt can be deducted as an expense.

STOCK ISSUANCES FOR CASH

In issuing its stock, a corporation may use the services of an investment banker, a specialist in marketing securities to investors. The investment banker may *underwrite* a stock issue—that is, the banker buys the stock from the corporation and resells it to investors. The corporation does not risk being unable to sell its stock. The underwriter bears this risk in return for the profits generated by selling the stock to investors at a price higher than that paid the corporation. An investment banker who is unwilling to underwrite a stock issue may handle it on a *best efforts* basis. In this case, the investment banker agrees to sell as many shares as possible at a set price, but the corporation bears the risk of unsold stock.

When capital stock is issued, the appropriate capital stock account is always credited with the par value of the shares, or if the stock is no-par, with its stated value, if any. The asset received for the stock (usually cash) is debited, and any difference is placed in an appropriately named account.

To illustrate the journal entries to record various stock issuances for cash, let us assume that in its first year of operations a corporation issued three different types of stock, as follows:

1. Issued 1,000 shares of $100 par value, 9% preferred stock at $107 cash per share.

Cash	107,000	
9% Preferred Stock		100,000
Paid-in Capital in Excess of Par Value		7,000

In this transaction, the preferred stock is issued at a *premium* (that is, at more than par value). The par value of the preferred stock issued is credited to the 9% Preferred Stock account and the $7,000 premium is credited to Paid-in Capital in Excess of Par Value. If there is more than one class of par value stock, the account title may indicate the class of stock to which the premium relates, in this case Paid-in Capital in Excess of Par Value—9% Preferred Stock. An alternative account title for the $7,000 premium is Premium on

Preferred Stock. The account title used in the journal entry, however, is more typical.

2. Issued 1,000 shares of $100 par value, 6% preferred stock at $98 cash per share.

Cash	98,000	
Excess of Par Value over Amount Paid In	2,000	
6% Preferred Stock		100,000

This preferred stock is issued at a discount. Again, a capital stock account (in this case, 6% Preferred Stock) is credited for the par value of the shares issued. The account Excess of Par Value over Amount Paid In (or, alternatively, Discount on Preferred Stock) is debited for the $2,000 discount.

3. Issued 5,000 shares of no-par common stock, stated value $20, at $30 cash per share.

Cash	150,000	
Common Stock		100,000
Paid-in Capital in Excess of Stated Value		50,000

When no-par stock has a stated value, as in entry 3, the stated value of the total shares issued is credited to the proper capital stock account and any additional amount received is credited to an account called Paid-in Capital in Excess of Stated Value. If no stated value for no-par stock exists, the entire proceeds should be credited to the appropriate capital stock account. In entry 3, if the common stock had no stated value, the entire $150,000 amount would have been credited to the Common Stock account.

These three stock issuances are reflected in Exhibit 15–1, which presents the stockholders' equity section in the company's year-end balance sheet. (Retained earnings are assumed to be $25,000.) The stockholders' equity section is divided into two major categories—paid-in capital and retained earnings. **Paid-in capital** is the amount of capital contributed to the corporation by various transactions, such as by issuances of preferred stock and common stock. The capital contributed by owners through the issuance of stock is broken down between the legal capital (par or stated value of the stock) and amounts received in excess of the legal capital (or, in rare instances, the discount below legal capital). Later in this chapter we discuss other events (treasury stock transactions and donations) that may increase a corporation's paid-in capital. *Retained earnings*, of course, represent the cumulative net earnings and losses of the company that have not been distributed to owners as dividends. We discuss retained earnings in more detail in Chapter 16.

In Exhibit 15–1, we assume that all authorized amounts of both classes of preferred stock and half of the 10,000 shares of common stock authorized have been issued. Note that both the premium on the 9% preferred stock and the excess received over stated value of the no-par common stock are added to the par and stated values, respectively. On the other hand, the $2,000 discount on the 6% preferred stock is deducted from par value to show the amount received for this class. All the accounts in the illustration have credit balances in the general ledger, except Excess of Par Value over Amount Paid In on the 6% preferred stock, which has a $2,000 debit balance.

EXHIBIT 15–1

STOCKHOLDERS' EQUITY SECTION

Paid-in Capital:		
9% Preferred Stock, $100 Par Value, 1,000 shares authorized, issued, and outstanding	$100,000	
Paid-in Capital in Excess of Par Value	7,000	$107,000
6% Preferred Stock, $100 Par Value, 1,000 shares authorized, issued, and outstanding	$100,000	
Excess of Par Value over Amount Paid In	(2,000)	98,000
No-par Common Stock, Stated Value $20, 10,000 shares authorized; 5,000 shares issued and outstanding	$100,000	
Paid-in Capital in Excess of Stated Value	50,000	150,000
Total Paid-in Capital		$355,000
Retained Earnings		25,000
Total Stockholders' Equity		$380,000

STOCK SUBSCRIPTIONS

Sometimes a corporation sells stock directly to investors rather than through an investment banker. The corporation may obtain signatures of prospective purchasers on *subscription contracts* prior to issuing shares. Frequently, such contracts provide for installment payments. When subscriptions are obtained, the corporation debits a receivable account, Stock Subscriptions Receivable. Instead of crediting the regular Common Stock account for the par or stated value of the subscribed shares, the firm credits a temporary paid-in capital account called Common Stock Subscribed. The use of a temporary account signifies that the shares have not yet been fully paid for or issued. Until the shares are issued, the account is shown immediately after the regular Common Stock account in the stockholders' equity section of the balance sheet. If the subscription price exceeds the stock's par or stated value, the excess is credited to the usual paid-in capital account for such excess amounts. After all payments have been received and the stock is issued, the corporation debits the temporary account, Common Stock Subscribed, and credits the regular account, Common Stock.

To illustrate the journal entries for stock subscription transactions, let us assume that 5,000 shares of $10 par value common stock were sold on subscription for $12 a share, paid in installments of $4 and $8. The entries would be:

To record receipt of subscriptions

Stock Subscriptions Receivable—Common	60,000	
Common Stock Subscribed		50,000
Paid-in Capital in Excess of Par Value		10,000
Received subscriptions for 5,000 shares at $12 per share.		

To record collection of first installment

Cash	20,000	
Stock Subscriptions Receivable—Common		20,000
Collected first installment of $4 per share.		

To record collection of final installment and issuance of shares

Cash	40,000	
Stock Subscriptions Receivable—Common		40,000
Collected final installment of $8 per share.		
Common Stock Subscribed	50,000	
Common Stock		50,000
To record issuance of 5,000 shares.		

STOCK ISSUANCES FOR ASSETS OTHER THAN CASH

When stock is issued for property other than cash or for services, the accountant must carefully determine the amount recorded. We should not assume that the par or stated value of the shares issued automatically sets a value for the property or services received. In the early years of U.S. corporations, such an assumption frequently resulted in the recording and reporting of excessive asset valuations.

Property or services acquired should be recorded at their current fair value or at the fair value of the stock issued, whichever is more clearly determinable. If the stock is actively traded on a securities exchange, the market price of the stock issued may indicate an appropriate value. For example, if the current market price is $14 per share and 5,000 shares are issued for a parcel of land, this land may be valued, in the absence of other price indicators, at $70,000. An effort should be made, however, to determine a fair value for the property. Certainly, all aspects of the transaction should be carefully scrutinized to ascertain that the number of shares issued was objectively determined. If no market value for the stock is available, we would seek an independently determined value for the property or services received.

Let us suppose the stock issued for the land is $10 par value common stock and its market value is the best indicator of the property's fair value. The entry to record the transaction would be

Land	70,000	
Common Stock		50,000
Paid-in Capital in Excess of Par Value		20,000
To record issuance of 5,000 shares of common stock for land valued at $70,000.		

STOCK SPLITS

Occasionally, a corporation reduces the par or stated value of its common stock and issues additional shares to its stockholders. This type of transaction, called a **stock split,** does not change the balances of the stockholders' equity accounts—only a memorandum entry is made in the records to show the altered par or stated value of the stock. For example, if a company that has 10,000 shares outstanding of $10 par value common stock announced a 2-for-1 stock split, it would simply reduce the par value of its stock to $5 per share. After the stock split, each shareholder would have twice the number of shares held before the split.

The major reason for a stock split is to reduce the market price of the stock. Some companies like their stock to sell within a certain price range. They may feel that higher prices narrow the breadth of their market, because investors often prefer to buy 100-share lots (purchases of fewer shares are odd-lot purchases and may be subject to higher brokers' fees), and obviously, many small investors cannot purchase high-priced stocks in 100-share lots.

When shares are selling below the desired price, a *reverse split* can be accomplished by increasing the par value of the shares and reducing the number outstanding. Such transactions are encountered less frequently than stock splits.

TREASURY STOCK

When a corporation reacquires its own outstanding shares for a purpose other than retiring them, the reacquired shares are called **treasury stock.** Treasury stock may be purchased for a variety of reasons, which include reissuing them to officers and employees in profit-sharing schemes or stock-option plans. Whatever the purpose, the corporation is reducing owner capital for a period of time. Consequently, treasury stock is not regarded as an asset. The shares do not carry voting privileges or preemptive rights, are not paid dividends, and do not receive assets on the corporation's liquidation.

Because treasury stock is stock that has been issued before, it differs in one significant way from unissued stock. If the treasury stock was fully paid for when first issued (that is, it was initially issued for an amount equal to or more than its par value), then it may be reissued at less than par value without any discount liability attaching to it. As we mentioned earlier, some states may attach a liability to shares initially issued at a discount, whereas other states do not even permit such issuances.

Accountants commonly record treasury stock at cost, debiting a Treasury Stock account. The aggregate cost is deducted from total stockholders' equity in the balance sheet. Suppose a corporation had outstanding 20,000 shares of $10 par value common stock and then repurchased 1,000 shares at $12 per share. The entry for the repurchase would be

Treasury Stock	12,000	
Cash		12,000
To record purchase of 1,000 shares of treasury stock at $12 per share.		

The corporation may accept any price for the reissue of treasury stock. Treasury stock transactions are not part of a firm's normal operating activities, and any additional capital obtained from reissuing such shares at more than cost is not regarded as earnings and is not added to retained earnings. The corporation should regard any additional amounts paid by subsequent purchasers as paid-in capital. Therefore, increases in capital from the reissue of purchased treasury shares are credited to a paid-in capital account such as Paid-in Capital from Treasury Stock. Decreases on reissue of treasury stock at less than cost offset previously recorded paid-in capital from treasury stock transactions or, if that is not possible, retained earnings.

Let us assume that 500 shares of the treasury stock reacquired are resold by the corporation at $13 per share. The entry to record the reissue would be

Cash	6,500	
Treasury Stock		6,000
Paid-in Capital from Treasury Stock		500
To record sale of 500 shares of treasury stock at $13 per share.		

Observe that Treasury Stock is credited at the cost price of $12 per share, a basis consistent with the original debit to the account. The excess over cost is credited to Paid-in Capital from Treasury Stock. If a balance sheet is prepared after this transaction, the stockholders' equity section would appear as shown below (assuming retained earnings of $40,000):

Stockholders' Equity

Paid-in Capital:	
Common Stock, $10 Par Value, authorized and issued 20,000 shares; 500 shares in treasury, 19,500 shares outstanding	$200,000
Paid-in Capital from Treasury Stock	500
Total Paid-in Capital	$200,500
Retained Earnings	40,000
	$240,500
Less: Treasury Stock (500 shares) at Cost	6,000
Total Stockholders' Equity	$234,500

Note that the $200,000 par value of all *issued* stock is shown, although 500 shares are no longer outstanding. The total cost of the 500 shares, however, is later deducted from total stockholders' equity.

In the above owners' equity situation, the corporation apparently has $40,000 retained earnings unfettered by any legal restrictions; the entire amount might be distributed as dividends if the corporation's cash position permits. In some states, however, the corporation must restrict (reduce) the retained earnings available for declaration of dividends by the cost of any treasury stock held. Then, in our illustration, only $34,000 in retained earnings would be available for dividends, and the reason would be disclosed in the stockholders' equity section. Methods of disclosing retained earnings restrictions are discussed in Chapter 16. The statutory restriction exists because a corporation that reduces its paid-in capital by repurchasing shares must protect creditors by "buffering" the reduced capital with its retained earnings in an amount equal to resources expended.

DONATED CAPITAL

Occasionally, a corporation may acquire treasury stock by a shareholder's donating shares to the corporation. Perhaps the donor received the shares in exchange for a patent on a product and now wishes the corporation to raise additional capital to promote and market the product. As noted, because treasury shares represent stock that has been issued once, they can be reissued at any price. Thus, the corporation may find it easier to market these shares than to sell unissued shares, especially if investors have shown little interest in the venture and the unissued shares could be sold only at a discount.

The reacquisition of treasury shares by donation, whatever the reason, is usually not recorded—except for a memorandum entry—at the time of reacquisition. When such shares are subsequently sold, the amount received is credited to **Donated Capital,** a form of paid-in capital. To illustrate, suppose a stockholder donates 500 shares of common stock to a corporation, which then resells the shares at $25 per share. The entries for these transactions would be

To record receipt of donated treasury shares

(Memorandum) Received 500 shares of donated common stock.

To record sale of donated treasury shares

Cash	12,500	
Donated Capital		12,500
To record sale of 500 donated shares at $25 per share.		

The Donated Capital account may also be credited for the fair market value of any property donated to the corporation, assuming that a value can be determined objectively. For example, communities wanting to attract industry have donated land sites to corporations. If fair values can be established by appraisal or by study of prices for similar local property, the amount may be recorded.

Assume that a city donates a plant site to a corporation. An independent appraiser values the land at $26,000, which is accepted by the board of directors as an appropriate valuation. The entry to record the donation would be

Land	26,000	
Donated Capital		26,000
To record receipt of donated land valued at $26,000.		

Exhibit 15–2 illustrates the presentation of donated capital in stockholders' equity, along with examples of other paid-in capital items that we have discussed in this chapter.

BOOK VALUE PER SHARE

Book value per share is often calculated for a class of stock, particularly common stock. **Book value per share,** which is the dollar amount of net assets represented

EXHIBIT 15–2

STOCKHOLDERS' EQUITY SECTION

Paid-in Capital:		
6% Preferred Stock, $100 Par Value, 2,000 shares authorized, issued, and outstanding	$100,000	
Paid-in Capital in Excess of Par Value—Preferred Stock	30,000	$230,000
Common Stock, $1 Par Value, 250,000 shares authorized; 150,000 shares issued; 5,000 shares subscribed; and 3,000 shares in the treasury	$150,000	
Common Stock Subscribed, 5,000 shares	5,000	
Paid-in Capital in Excess of Par Value—Common Stock	455,000	610,000
Paid-in Capital from Treasury Stock		4,000
Donated Capital		26,000
Total Paid-in Capital		$870,000
Retained Earnings		115,000
		$985,000
Less: Treasury Stock (3,000) at Cost		15,000
Total Stockholders' Equity		$970,000

by one share of stock, is computed by dividing the amount of stockholders' equity associated with a class of stock by the number of outstanding shares in that class. The computation uses stockholders' equity, because a corporation's net assets (Assets − Liabilities) equals its stockholders' equity. The measure is based on amounts recorded in the books and presented in the balance sheet—hence, the term *book* value per share.

For example, assume the following stockholders' equity section of a balance sheet:

Stockholders' Equity

Paid-in Capital:	
Common Stock, $50 Par Value, 5,000 shares authorized, issued, and outstanding	$250,000
Paid-in Capital in Excess of Par Value	100,000
Total Paid-in Capital	$350,000
Retained Earnings	80,000
Total Stockholders' Equity	$430,000

Because this corporation has only one class of stock, the book value per share is the total stockholders' equity divided by the shares outstanding—that is, $430,000/5,000 = $86. Note that the divisor is shares outstanding; it does not include shares of unissued common stock or treasury stock.

ANOTHER USE FOR BOOK VALUE PER SHARE

Investment fads come and go, but many successful investors still swear by one of the oldest and easiest ways to buy stocks.

Year in and year out, in bull markets and bear markets, they say, the best way to find undervalued companies and possible takeover candidates is to buy stocks that are selling below their book value.

"If I had to limit my stock selection to only one thing, I'd choose book value," says Charles Allmon, manager of Growth Stock Outlook Trust, Chevy Chase, Md. "I don't care if a company is selling dirty diapers or clean diapers. If the price is right, I'll buy it."

Book value is generally defined as a company's net worth, its assets minus its liabilities. Those who use the buy-below-book strategy typically focus on "tangible" book value. This excludes such intangibles as patents and goodwill, which is a monetary value commonly placed on things such as a reputation when one company acquires another.

Companies publish their book value per share in their annual reports. Investors can also look up a company's book value in Standard & Poor's stock guide or the Value Line Investment Survey. A. G. Edwards & Sons publishes "Value Investing Update," a periodic listing of stocks selling below their book value.

But while buying below book has proved to be a successful strategy over the long term, it can also be a trap. Some stocks sell below book merely because they are out of favor, but others may be genuinely troubled. For example, 227 of 1,550 New York Stock Exchange companies are selling below book, but many of these were selling at less than $5 a share and were having serious difficulties.

"A price below book value is a beginning tool in the hunt for bargain stocks, not an end in itself," says Mark Keller, vice president of securities research at A. G. Edwards. For example, he says, "If you buy a company that sells below book value yet has a high debt, it may never recover."

Some of the biggest proponents of buying below book are followers of Benjamin Graham, the late Columbia University professor generally considered the father of modern portfolio analysis. Successful investors such as Warren Buffet, chairman of Berkshire Hathaway Inc., and William Ruane of Sequoia Fund have credited much of their good fortune to the value investing advocated by Mr. Graham.

In Mr. Graham's view, investors should concentrate on buying stocks below or close to their book value, or no more than 30% above that figure. "The greater the premium above the book value, the less certain the basis for determining intrinsic value, and the more this value depends on the changing moods and measurements of the stock market," Mr. Graham wrote in his 1949 book, *The Intelligent Investor*.

Historically, the book value approach has worked out well. A prime example was steel company stocks in 1986, says Mr. Keller. Battered by Japanese competition, Bethlehem Steel and Inland Steel appeared to have a gloomy future. Their stock prices plunged way below book. Analysts couldn't foresee how a change in their cost structure and a decline in the value of the dollar could make them competitive once again. Today they trade over book. Investors who bought them when they were below book have done well.

From Earl C. Gottschalk Jr., "Picking Stocks by the Book Is a Standby Some Swear By," *The Wall Street Journal*, November 3, 1988, p. C1.

To compute book values per share when more than one class of stock is outstanding, we must determine the portion of stockholders' equity attributable to each class of stock. Preferred stocks are assigned the amounts their owners would receive if the corporation liquidated—that is, the liquidation preference of preferred stock plus any dividend arrearages on cumulative stock. The common shares receive the remainder of the stockholders' equity. For example, assume the following stockholders' equity section:

Stockholders' Equity

Paid-in Capital:	
9% Preferred Stock, $100 Par Value, 1,000 shares authorized, issued, and outstanding	$100,000
Paid-in Capital in Excess of Par Value—Preferred Stock	5,000
No-par Common Stock, Stated Value $40, 3,000 shares authorized, issued, and outstanding	120,000
Paid-in Capital in Excess of Stated Value—Common Stock	6,000
Total Paid-in Capital	$231,000
Retained Earnings	73,000
Total Stockholders' Equity	$304,000

If the stated liquidation preference is $103 per share for the preferred stock (with no dividends in arrears), then the book value per share for the preferred stock is also $103. The computation for the common stock follows:

Total Stockholders' Equity	$304,000
Less: Equity Applicable to Preferred Stock	103,000
Equity Allocated to Common Stock	$201,000
Shares of Common Stock Outstanding	3,000
Book Value per Share of Common Stock ($201,000/3,000)	$67

The book value per share of common stock may be used in many ways. Management may include the book value per share—and any changes in it for the year—in the annual report to stockholders. Two corporations negotiating a merger through an exchange of stock may find their respective book values per share to be one of several factors influencing the final exchange ratio. Or an individual may acquire an option to buy stock in the future, with the purchase price related to the future book value of the stock.

MARKET VALUE AND LIQUIDATION VALUE

The book value of common stock is different from its market value and its liquidation value. The **market value per share** is the current price at which the stock may be bought or sold. This price reflects such things as the earnings potential of the company, dividends, book values, capital structure, and general economic conditions. Because book value is only one of several variables influencing market price (and usually not the most significant one at that), market values and book values rarely coincide.

The **liquidation value per share** of common stock is the amount that would be received if the corporation liquidated. The amounts recorded in the books do not portray liquidation proceeds, so no correlation exists between liquidation values and book values of common stocks. Liquidation values may not be easy to determine, but corporate managements must be alert to the relationship between the market value and the approximate liquidation value of their common stock. A corporation whose liquidation value exceeds its market value may be the object of a "raid." A raider acquires control of a corporation (by buying stock at market values) and then liquidates the business (at liquidation values), keeping the difference as a gain.

KEY POINTS FOR CHAPTER OBJECTIVES

1 Define and discuss the corporate form of organization (pp. 519–22).

- A corporation is a separate legal entity chartered by the state in which it is formed or, in some cases, by the federal government.
- The liability of corporate shareholders is usually limited to their ownership investment, whereas claims against partners and sole proprietors may extend to their personal resources.
- Unlike proprietorships and partnerships, corporations must report paid-in capital separately from the accumulated balance of retained earnings. Distributions to shareholders are limited by the amount of retained earnings and other capital as specified by state law.

2 Explain the difference between par and no-par value stock (p. 522).

- Par value is the face value printed on a stock certificate. It has no economic significance but may have legal significance.
- No-par stock has no face value printed on the stock certificate, although generally the board of directors sets a stated value for the stock.

3 Identify and discuss the types of stock and their basic rights (pp. 522–26).

- Common stock represents a corporation's basic ownership class of stock.
- Preferred stocks may differ from common stock in any of several characteristics. Typically, preferred stocks have some type of dividend preference and a prior claim to assets in liquidation.

4 Describe the accounting for issuances of stock for cash, by subscription, and for noncash assets (pp. 526–29).

- When capital stock is issued, the appropriate capital stock account is credited with the par or stated value of the shares issued; the asset received for the stock is debited; and any difference is placed in an appropriately named account.

5 Define and discuss stock splits (p. 530).

- Stock splits change the par or stated value of stock and affect the number of shares outstanding. Only a memorandum notation records stock splits.

6 Explain the accounting for treasury stock and donated capital (pp. 530–32).

- Treasury stock represents repurchased shares of the firm's own stock. It is commonly recorded at cost and deducted from total stockholders' equity in the balance sheet.
- Donated capital results from gifts to the corporation that, if feasible, should be recorded at fair market value.

7 Define and discuss the terms *book value, market value,* and *liquidation value per share* of stock (pp. 532–35).

- The book value per share of common stock indicates the net assets, based on recorded amounts, associated with a share of common stock. Common stock book values are different from market values or liquidation values.

KEY TERMS USED IN THIS CHAPTER

articles of incorporation 519
authorized stock 523
book value per share 532
common stock 523
corporation 519
cumulative preferred stock 524
donated capital 532
issued stock 523
liquidation value per share 535
market value per share 535

no-par stock 522
outstanding stock 523
paid-in capital 527
participating preferred stock 524
par value stock 522
preemptive right 523
preferred stock 524
stated value 522
stock split 530
treasury stock 530

SELF-TEST QUESTIONS FOR REVIEW

(Answers are at the end of this chapter.)

1. The liability of stockholders for corporation actions is usually
   (a) Unlimited.
   (b) Limited to the par or stated value of the stock they hold.
   (c) Limited to the amount of their investment in the corporation.
   (d) Limited to the amount of the corporation's retained earnings.
2. Which type of stock may have dividends in arrears?
   (a) Cumulative preferred stock.
   (b) Common stock.
   (c) Noncumulative preferred stock.
   (d) Treasury stock.
3. Wyler Company issues 20,000 shares of $10 par value common stock in exchange for a building with a current fair value of $1,000,000. In recording this transaction, what amount should be credited to Paid-in Capital in Excess of Par Value?
   (a) $1,000,000
   (b) $200,000
   (c) $800,000
   (d) $980,000
4. Which of the following accounts has a normal debit balance?
   (a) Common Stock Subscribed.
   (b) Paid-in Capital in Excess of Stated Value.
   (c) Donated Capital.
   (d) Treasury Stock.
5. Caffey Corporation has a total stockholders' equity of $1,860,000. Caffey has 20,000 shares of $25 par value, 6% preferred stock issued and outstanding, and 60,000 shares of $10 par value common stock issued and outstanding. The preferred stock has a liquidation preference of $27 per share and no dividends in arrears. What is the book value per share of common stock?
   (a) $31.00
   (b) $22.00
   (c) $22.67
   (d) $10.00

DEMONSTRATION PROBLEM FOR REVIEW

Goodwin Corporation has outstanding 6,000 shares of $50 par value, 5% preferred stock and 30,000 shares of $30 par value common stock. This year the company declares and pays a total cash dividend of $90,000.

REQUIRED
For each of the following independent cases, calculate the total dividends paid to each class of stock.

(a) The preferred stock is noncumulative and nonparticipating.
(b) The preferred stock is cumulative and nonparticipating; dividends are in arrears one year.
(c) The preferred stock is cumulative and participating to 7%; there is no dividend arrearage.
(d) The preferred stock is cumulative and fully participating; there is no dividend arrearage.
(e) The preferred stock is cumulative and fully participating; dividends are in arrears three years.

SOLUTION TO DEMONSTRATION PROBLEM

	Preferred	Common	Total
Outstanding stock (total par value)	$300,000	$900,000	$1,200,000
(a) Regular preferred dividend (5%)	$15,000		$15,000
Remainder to common		$75,000	75,000
Total distribution	$15,000	$75,000	$90,000
(b) Dividend in arrears one year (5%)	$15,000		$15,000
Regular preferred dividend (5%)	15,000		15,000
Remainder to common		$60,000	60,000
Total distribution	$30,000	$60,000	$90,000
(c) Regular preferred dividend (5%) and matching rate to common (5%)	$15,000	$45,000	$60,000
Preferred participation dividend (2%) and matching rate to common (2%)	6,000	18,000	24,000
Remainder to common		6,000	6,000
Total distribution	$21,000	$69,000	$90,000
(d) Regular preferred dividend (5%) and matching rate to common (5%)	$15,000	$45,000	$60,000
Remainder of $30,000 divided to give each class the same rate: $30,000/$1,200,000 = 2.5%	7,500	22,500	30,000
Total distribution	$22,500	$67,500	$90,000
(e) Dividends in arrears three years (3 × 5% = 15%)	$45,000		$45,000
Regular preferred dividend (5%)	15,000		15,000
Remainder to common (not enough to achieve a 5% rate)		$30,000	30,000
Total distribution	$60,000	$30,000	$90,000

QUESTIONS

15–1 Explain the meaning of each of the following terms and, when appropriate, how they interrelate: *corporation, articles of incorporation, corporate charter, board of directors, corporate officers,* and *organization costs.*

15–2 What is meant by the limited liability of a shareholder? Does this characteristic enhance or reduce a corporation's ability to raise capital?

15–3 Contrast the federal income taxation of corporations with that of sole proprietorships and partnerships. Which of the three types of organizations must file a federal income tax return?

15–4 Define *par value stock.* What is the significance of a stock's par value?

15–5 What is the preemptive right of a shareholder?

15–6 What are the basic differences between preferred stock and common stock? What are the typical features of preferred stock?

15–7 What features make preferred stock similar to debt? Similar to common stock?

15–8 What is meant by dividend arrearage on preferred stock? If dividends are two years in arrears on $250,000 of 7% preferred stock and dividends are declared this year, what amount of total dividends must preferred shareholders receive before any distributions can be made to common shareholders?

15–9 What is fully participating preferred stock? Partially participating preferred stock?

15–10 Distinguish between authorized stock and issued stock. Why might the number of shares issued be greater than the number of shares outstanding?

15–11 Distinguish between premium and discount on stock. Where do such amounts appear in the balance sheet?

15–12 A company acquired machines with a fair market value of $75,000 in exchange for 12,000 shares of $5 par value common stock. How should this transaction be recorded in the accounts?

15–13 Define *stock split*. What is the major reason for a stock split?

15–14 Define *treasury stock*. Why might a corporation acquire treasury stock? How is treasury stock shown in the balance sheet?

15–15 If a corporation purchases 500 shares of its own common stock at $20 per share and resells it at $30 per share, where would the $5,000 increase in capital appear in the financial statements? Why is no gain reported?

15–16 A corporation has total stockholders' equity of $496,000 and one class of $10 par value common stock. The company has issued 16,000 shares and currently holds 500 shares as treasury stock. What is the book value per share?

15–17 A corporation has total stockholders' equity of $3,600,000 and one class of $20 par value common stock. The corporation has 200,000 shares authorized; 100,000 shares issued; 90,000 shares outstanding; and 10,000 shares as treasury stock. What is the book value per share?

15–18 Define and contrast the terms *book value*, *market value*, and *liquidation value per share* of common stock.

EXERCISES

Dividend distribution

15–19 Bayshore Company has outstanding 5,000 shares of $40 par value, 7% cumulative preferred stock and 25,000 shares of $10 par value common stock. The company declared cash dividends amounting to $81,000.

(a) If no arrearage on the preferred stock exists, how much in total dividends, and in dividends per share, is paid to each class of stock?

(b) If one year's dividend arrearage on the preferred stock exists, how much in total dividends, and in dividends per share, is paid to each class of stock?

(c) Assume that no arrearage on the preferred stock exists but that the stock is fully participating. How much in total dividends, and in dividends per share, is paid to each class of stock?

Stock issuances for cash

15–20 On June 1, Blough, Inc., issued 4,000 shares of $25 par value preferred stock at $37 per share and 7,000 shares of no-par common stock at $19 per share. The common stock has no stated value. All issuances were for cash.

(a) Give the general journal entries to record the issuances.

(b) Give the entry for the issuance of the common stock, assuming it had a stated value of $10 per share.

(c) Give the entry for the issuance of the common stock, assuming it had a par value of $5 per share.

Stock subscriptions

15–21 On May 1, Gentry Company received subscriptions for 3,000 shares of $10 par value common stock at $38 per share, paid as follows: 50% on May 30, 30% on June 15, and 20% on July 1. All payments were received on schedule, and the shares were issued on July 1. Give the general journal entries made on May 1, May 30, June 15, and July 1.

Noncash stock issuances

15–22 Piper Corporation was organized in 19X4. The company's charter authorizes 100,000 shares of $15 par value common stock. The attorney who helped organize the corporation billed Piper $6,000 for services rendered. On August 1, 19X4, the attorney accepted 250 shares of Piper common stock in settlement of the bill. On October 15, 19X4, Piper issued 1,500 common shares to acquire a vacant land site appraised at $42,000. Give the general journal entries to record the stock issuances on August 1 and October 15.

Stock split

15–23 On March 1 of the current year, Monitor Corporation has 150,000 shares of $15 par value common stock that are issued and outstanding. The general ledger shows the following account balances relating to the common stock:

Common Stock	$2,250,000
Paid-in Capital in Excess of Par Value	1,650,000

On March 2, Monitor Corporation splits its stock 3 for 1 and reduces the par value to $5 per share.

(a) How many shares of common stock are issued and outstanding immediately after the stock split?
(b) What is the balance in the Common Stock account immediately after the stock split?
(c) What is the balance in the Paid-in Capital in Excess of Par Value account immediately after the stock split?
(d) Is a general journal entry required to record the stock split? If yes, what is the entry?

Treasury stock

15–24 Thorn Corporation issued 10,000 shares of $10 par value common stock at $22 per share and 2,000 shares of $50 par value, 8% preferred stock at $68 per share. Later, the company repurchased 3,000 shares of common stock at $25 per share.

(a) Give the general journal entries to record the stock issuances and the repurchase of the common shares.
(b) Assume that Thorn resold 1,900 shares of the treasury stock at $29 per share. Give the general journal entry to record the resale of this treasury stock.
(c) Assume that Thorn resold the remaining 1,100 shares of treasury stock at $23 per share. Give the general journal entry to record the resale of this treasury stock.

Stock issuance and treasury stock

15–25 Rand, Inc., recorded certain capital stock transactions shown in the following respective journal entries: (1) issuance of common stock for $46 cash per share; (2) subsequent repurchase of some shares at $48 per share; and (3) reissuance of some of the reacquired shares.

(1) Cash	828,000	
Common Stock		270,000
Paid-in Capital in Excess of Par Value		558,000
(2) Treasury Stock	124,800	
Cash		124,800
(3) Cash	72,800	
Treasury Stock		67,200
Paid-in Capital from Treasury Stock		5,600

(a) How many shares were originally issued?
(b) What was the par value of the shares issued?
(c) How many shares of treasury stock were reacquired?
(d) How many shares of treasury stock were reissued?
(e) At what price per share was the treasury stock reissued?

Donated capital

15–26 Cardex Company has 9,000 shares of $5 par value common stock outstanding. Prepare the general journal entries (if required) to record the following transactions:

Aug. 12 The community in which Cardex Company is building a new plant donated the land site to the company. The appraised value of the land is $56,000.

Oct. 7 Shareholders donated 500 shares to the corporation.

22 The company sold the donated shares for $31 cash per share.

Book value per share

15–27 The stockholders' equity section of Morgan Company appears as follows:

Paid-in Capital:		
8% Cumulative Preferred Stock, $50 Par Value, 8,000 shares authorized, issued, and outstanding	$400,000	
Paid-in Capital in Excess of Par Value—Preferred Stock	88,000	$ 488,000
No-par Common Stock, $5 Stated Value, 60,000 shares authorized, issued, and outstanding	$300,000	
Paid-in Capital in Excess of Stated Value—Common Stock	480,000	780,000
Paid-in Capital from Treasury Stock		22,000
Total Paid-in Capital		$1,290,000
Retained Earnings		260,000
Total Stockholders' Equity		$1,550,000

The preferred stock has a liquidation preference of $52 per share, and no dividends are in arrears. Compute the book value per share of the common stock.

PROBLEMS

Stockholders' equity—transactions and balance sheet presentation

15–28 Oaktree Corporation was organized on April 1 of the current year with an authorization of 20,000 shares of 7%, $50 par value preferred stock and 100,000 shares of $10 par value common stock. During April, the following transactions affecting stockholders' equity occurred:

Apr. 1 Issued 9,000 shares of preferred stock for $76 cash per share and 60,000 shares of common stock at $16 cash per share.

3 Issued 750 shares of common stock to attorneys and promoters in exchange for their services in organizing the corporation. The services were valued at $12,000.

8 Issued 1,000 shares of preferred stock in exchange for equipment with a fair market value of $77,000.

17 Received land valued at $45,000 as a donation from the city to attract Oaktree to its present location. The land will allow Oaktree to have adequate parking for its operations.

20 Issued 5,000 shares of common stock for cash at $18 per share.

30 Closed the $36,000 net income for April from the Income Summary account to Retained Earnings.

REQUIRED

(a) Prepare general journal entries to record the foregoing transactions.

(b) Prepare the stockholders' equity section of the balance sheet at April 30.

Dividend distribution

15–29 Plano Corporation has outstanding 20,000 shares of $75 par value, 8%, cumulative preferred stock and 75,000 shares of $10 par value common stock. The company has declared cash dividends of $495,000.

REQUIRED

(a) Calculate the total dividends and the dividends per share paid to each class of stock. There are no dividend arrearages.

(b) Assuming that one year's dividend arrearage exists on the preferred stock, calculate the total dividends and the dividends per share paid to each class of stock.

(c) Assuming that the 8% preferred stock is participating only to 10% (and no dividend arrearges exist), calculate the total dividends and the dividends per share paid to each class of stock.

(d) Assuming that the 8% preferred stock is fully participating (and no dividend arrearages exist), calculate the total dividends and the dividends per share paid to each class of stock.

Stockholders' equity—transactions, balance sheet presentation, and book value per share

15–30 The stockholders' equity of Ingram Corporation at January 1 of the current year appears below:

6% Preferred Stock, $25 Par Value, 15,000 shares authorized; 4,800 shares issued and outstanding	$120,000
Paid-in Capital in Excess of Par Value—Preferred Stock	96,000
Common Stock, $10 Par Value, 200,000 shares authorized; 50,000 shares issued and outstanding	500,000
Paid-in Capital in Excess of Par Value—Common Stock	200,000
Retained Earnings	270,000

During the current year, the following transactions occurred:

Jan. 10 Issued 12,000 shares of common stock for $16 cash per share.
23 Repurchased 5,000 shares of common stock for the treasury at $18 per share.
Mar. 2 Shareholders donated 2,000 shares of common stock to the corporation.
14 Sold one-half of the treasury shares acquired January 23 for $20 per share.
14 Sold the donated shares at $20 per share.
July 15 Issued 2,200 shares of preferred stock to acquire special equipment with a fair market value of $110,000.
Sept. 15 Received subscriptions to 15,000 shares of common stock at $24 per share.
Oct. 15 Received cash payment for one-third of the common stock subscription price.
Nov. 15 Received the balance due on the September 15 stock subscriptions in cash, and issued the stock certificates.
Dec. 31 Closed the net income of $99,200 from the Income Summary account to Retained Earnings.

REQUIRED

(a) Set up T accounts for the stockholders' equity accounts at the beginning of the year, and enter January 1 balances.

(b) Prepare general journal entries to record the foregoing transactions, and post to T accounts (set up any additional T accounts needed). Determine the ending balances for the stockholders' equity accounts.

(c) Prepare the December 31 stockholders' equity section of the balance sheet.

(d) Assume the preferred stock has a liquidation preference of $27 per share. No dividends are in arrears. Compute the book value per share of common stock at December 31.

Stockholders' equity—information and entries from comparative data

15–31 Comparative stockholders' equity sections from two successive years' balance sheets of Whistler, Inc., are as follows:

	Dec. 31, 19X2	Dec. 31, 19X1
Paid-in Capital:		
8% Preferred Stock, $50 Par Value, authorized 10,000 shares; issued and outstanding, 19X1: 7,500 shares; 19X2: 9,000 shares	$ 450,000	$ 375,000
Paid-in Capital in Excess of Par Value—Preferred Stock	222,000	180,000
Common Stock, No-par Value, $10 Stated Value, authorized 50,000 shares; outstanding, 19X1: 30,000 shares (4,000 shares in treasury); 19X2: 41,000 shares.	410,000	340,000
Common Stock Subscribed, 19X1: 2,000 shares		20,000
Paid-in Capital in Excess of Stated Value—Common Stock	330,000	270,000
Paid-in Capital from Treasury Stock	12,000	
Donated Capital	75,000	
Retained Earnings	280,000	215,000
		$1,400,000
Less: Treasury Stock (4,000 shares common) at Cost		80,000
Total Stockholders' Equity	$1,779,000	$1,320,000

No dividends were declared or paid during 19X2. The company received a donated parcel of land from the city in 19X2.

REQUIRED

Prepare the general journal entries for the transactions affecting stockholders' equity that evidently occurred during 19X2.

Book value per share

15–32 Sabin Corporation has the following stockholders' equity section in its balance sheet:

Paid-in Capital:		
6% Preferred Stock, $100 Par Value, 8,000 shares authorized, issued, and outstanding	$ 800,000	
Paid-in Capital in Excess of Par Value—Preferred Stock	104,000	
Common Stock, $5 Par Value, 100,000 shares authorized; 80,000 shares issued and outstanding	400,000	
Paid-in Capital in Excess of Par Value—Common Stock	560,000	
Paid-in Capital from Treasury Stock	26,000	$1,890,000
Retained Earnings		326,000
Total Stockholders' Equity		$2,216,000

REQUIRED

For each of the following independent cases, compute the book value per share for the preferred stock and the common stock.

(a) The preferred stock is noncumulative, nonparticipating, and has a liquidation preference of $102 per share.

(b) The preferred stock is cumulative, nonparticipating, and has a liquidation preference per share equal to par value plus dividends in arrears. No dividends are in arrears.

(c) The preferred stock is cumulative, nonparticipating, and has a liquidation preference of $101 per share plus dividends in arrears. Dividends are three years in arrears.

Stockholders' equity—transactions and balance sheet presentation

15–33 The stockholders' equity of Macklin Corporation at January 1 of the current year is shown below:

7% Preferred Stock, $100 Par Value, 10,000 shares authorized; 4,000 shares issued and outstanding	$ 400,000
Paid-in Capital in Excess of Par Value—Preferred Stock	12,000
Common Stock, $10 Par Value, 100,000 shares authorized; 60,000 shares issued and outstanding	600,000
Paid-in Capital in Excess of Par Value—Common Stock	480,000
Retained Earnings	325,000
Total Stockholders' Equity	$1,817,000

The following transactions, among others, occurred during the year:

Jan.	12	Announced a 2-for-1 common stock split, reducing the par value of the common stock to $5 per share. The authorization was increased to 200,000 shares.
	20	Received subscriptions for the sale of 18,000 shares of common stock at $12 per share.
	29	Received one-half of the January 20 subscription price in cash.
Feb.	9	Received the remainder of payment for the shares subscribed on January 20 in cash, and issued the stock certificates.
Apr.	14	Received a plant site valued at $120,000 as a gift from the city.
June	1	Acquired equipment with a fair market value of $53,000 in exchange for 500 shares of preferred stock.
Sept.	1	Reacquired 3,000 shares of common stock for cash at $15 per share.
Oct.	12	Resold 300 treasury shares at $17 per share.
Dec.	21	Received subscriptions for the sale of 10,000 shares of common stock at $15 per share.
Dec.	28	Resold 700 of the remaining treasury shares at $14 per share.
	31	Closed the Income Summary account, with net earnings of $85,000, to Retained Earnings.

REQUIRED

(a) Set up T accounts for the stockholders' equity accounts at the beginning of the year and enter January 1 balances.

(b) Prepare general journal entries for the given transactions, and post them to the T accounts (set up any additional T accounts needed). Determine the ending balances for the stockholders' equity accounts.

(c) Prepare the stockholders' equity section of the balance sheet at December 31 of the current year.

ALTERNATE PROBLEMS

Stockholders' equity—transactions and balance sheet presentation

15–28A Dylan Corporation was organized on July 1 of the current year with an authorization of 25,000 shares of $4 no-par value preferred stock ($4 is the annual dividend) and 50,000 shares of $20 par value common stock. During July, the following transactions affecting stockholders' equity occurred:

July 1 Issued 8,000 shares of preferred stock for $65 cash per share and 22,000 shares of common stock at $35 cash per share.
5 The local municipality donated a vacant building to the corporation as an inducement to operate the business in the community. The fair market value of the building was $450,000.
12 Issued 2,000 shares of common stock in exchange for equipment with a fair market value of $75,000.
15 Issued 1,000 shares of preferred stock for cash at $63 per share.
16 Received subscriptions for 5,000 shares of common stock at $38 per share.
31 Received a 25% cash payment on the common stock subscriptions. The balance of the subscription price is due on August 31.
31 Closed the $44,000 net income for July from the Income Summary account to Retained Earnings.

REQUIRED
(a) Prepare general journal entries to record the foregoing transactions.
(b) Prepare the stockholders' equity section of the balance sheet at July 31.

Dividend distribution

15–29A Busch Corporation has outstanding 8,000 shares of $50 par value, 7%, cumulative preferred stock and 40,000 shares of $15 par value common stock. The company has declared cash dividends of $134,000.

REQUIRED
(a) Calculate the total dividends and the dividends per share paid to each class of stock. There are no dividend arrearages.
(b) Assuming that two years' dividend arrearages exist on the preferred stock, calculate the total dividends and the dividends per share paid to each class of stock.
(c) Assuming that the 7% preferred stock is participating only to 10% (and no dividend arrearages exist), calculate the total dividends and the dividends per share paid to each class of stock.
(d) Assuming that the 7% preferred stock is fully participating (and no dividend arrearages exist), calculate the total dividends and the dividends per share paid to each class of stock.

Stockholders' equity—transactions, balance sheet presentation, and book value per share

15–30A The stockholders' equity of Stork Corporation at January 1 of the current year appears below:

Common Stock, $20 Par Value, 80,000 shares authorized; 40,000 shares issued and outstanding	$800,000
Paid-in Capital in Excess of Par Value—Common Stock	580,000
Retained Earnings	353,000

During the current year, the following transactions occurred:

Jan. 5 Issued 6,000 shares of common stock for $28 cash per share.
18 Repurchased 2,000 shares of common stock for the treasury at $29 per share.
Mar. 10 Shareholders donated 1,500 shares to the corporation.
12 Sold one-half of the treasury shares acquired January 18 for $30 per share.
12 Sold the donated shares at $30 per share.

July 17	Sold 400 shares of the remaining treasury stock for $27 per share.
Sept. 20	Received subscriptions to 4,000 shares of common stock at $31 per share.
Oct. 20	Received cash payment for one-fourth of the common stock subscription price.
Nov. 25	Received the balance due on the September 20 stock subscription in cash, and issued the stock certificates.
Dec. 31	Closed the net income of $46,700 from the Income Summary account to Retained Earnings.

REQUIRED
(a) Set up T accounts for the stockholders' equity accounts at the beginning of the year, and enter January 1 balances.
(b) Prepare general journal entries to record the foregoing transactions, and post to T accounts (set up any additional T accounts needed). Determine the ending balances for the stockholders' equity accounts.
(c) Prepare the December 31 stockholders' equity section of the balance sheet.
(d) Compute the book value per share of common stock at December 31.

Stockholder's equity—transaction descriptions from account data

15–31A The T accounts below contain keyed entries representing seven transactions involving the stockholders' equity of Dawkins, Inc.

Cash

(1)	31,500	(4)	3,600
(2)	30,000		
(6)	2,940		

Stock Subscriptions Receivable—Common

(7)	34,000		

Land

(3)	45,000		
(5)	35,000		

Preferred Stock, $25 Par

		(1)	22,500

Paid-in Capital in Excess of Par Value—Preferred Stock

		(1)	9,000

Common Stock, $10 Par

		(2)	30,000
		(3)	40,000

Common Stock Subscribed

		(7)	20,000

Paid-in Capital in Excess of Par Value—Common Stock

		(3)	5,000
		(7)	14,000

Treasury Stock

(4) (300 shares of common)	3,600	(6)	2,520

Paid-in Capital from Treasury Stock

		(6)	420

Donated Capital

		(5)	35,000

REQUIRED
Using this information, give detailed descriptions, including number of shares and price per share when applicable, for each of the seven transactions.

Book value per share

15–32A Mannheim, Inc., has the following stockholders' equity section in its balance sheet:

Paid-in Capital:		
7% Preferred Stock, $50 Par Value, 10,000 shares authorized, issued, and outstanding	$500,000	
Paid-in Capital in Excess of Par Value—Preferred Stock	100,000	
Common Stock, $1 Par Value, 750,000 shares authorized; 400,000 shares issued and outstanding	400,000	
Paid-in Capital in Excess of Par Value—Common Stock	900,000	
Donated Capital	80,000	$1,980,000
Retained Earnings		220,000
Total Stockholders' Equity		$2,200,000

REQUIRED
For each of the following independent cases, compute the book value per share for the preferred stock and the common stock.
(a) The preferred stock is noncumulative, nonparticipating, and has a liquidation preference of $52 per share.
(b) The preferred stock is cumulative, nonparticipating, and has a liquidation preference per share equal to par value plus dividends in arrears. No dividends are in arrears.
(c) The preferred stock is cumulative, nonparticipating, and has a liquidation preference of $53 per share plus dividends in arrears. Dividends are two years in arrears.

Stockholders' equity—transactions and balance sheet presentation

15–33A The following is the stockholders' equity of Cloud Corporation at January 1 of the current year:

8% Preferred Stock, $50 Par Value, 5,000 shares authorized; 4,000 shares issued and outstanding	$ 200,000
Paid-in Capital in Excess of Par Value—Preferred Stock	28,000
Common Stock, $30 Par Value, 50,000 shares authorized; 25,000 shares issued and outstanding	750,000
Paid-in Capital in Excess of Par Value—Common Stock	250,000
Retained Earnings	290,000
Total Stockholders' Equity	$1,518,000

The following transactions, among others, occurred during the year:

Jan. 12 Issued 1,000 shares of preferred stock for $62 cash per share.
20 Received subscriptions for the sale of 6,000 shares of common stock at $48 per share.
30 Received one-third of the January 20 subscription price in cash.
Feb. 9 Received the remainder of payment for the shares subscribed on January 20 in cash, and issued the stock certificates.
Mar. 10 Received a vacant school building valued at $425,000 as a gift from the city. The company plans to remodel the building for additional office space.

May	18	Announced a 3-for-1 common stock split, reducing the par value of the common stock to $10 per share. The authorization was increased to 150,000 shares.
June	1	Acquired equipment with a fair market value of $48,000 in exchange for 3,000 shares of common stock.
Sept.	1	Reacquired 2,500 shares of common stock for cash at $18 per share.
Oct.	12	Resold 500 treasury shares at $19 per share.
Dec.	22	Received subscriptions for the sale of 8,000 shares of common stock at $17 per share.
	28	Resold 1,000 of the remaining treasury shares at $17 per share.
	31	Closed the Income Summary account, with net earnings of $60,000, to Retained Earnings.

REQUIRED

(a) Set up T accounts for the stockholders' equity accounts at the beginning of the year and enter January 1 balances.

(b) Prepare general journal entries for the given transactions, and post them to the T accounts (set up any additional T accounts needed). Determine the ending balances for the stockholders' equity accounts.

(c) Prepare the stockholders' equity section of the balance sheet at December 31 of the current year.

BUSINESS DECISION PROBLEM

Walter Lamm has operated Lamm's Hardware very successfully as a sole proprietorship. He feels that the continued growth and success of his business depends on increasing its scale of operations, which requires additional working capital. He also wishes to relocate his store from its rented quarters to a new retail shopping area. After exploring several opportunities that would result in large personal debts, Lamm incorporates his business, taking in as stockholders Dr. Alec Turner, who invests cash, and Ms. Ruth Brady, a real estate developer who owns land and a suitable vacant building in the desired shopping area.

As an initial step, Lamm and his attorney secure a corporate charter for Hardware City, Inc., authorizing it to issue 50,000 shares of $10 par value common stock. On June 1 of the current year, the date of incorporation, the post-closing trial balance of Lamm's Hardware is as follows:

	Debit	Credit
Cash	$ 3,500	
Accounts Receivable	10,400	
Allowance for Uncollectible Accounts		$ 100
Merchandise Inventory	150,000	
Store Equipment	68,000	
Accumulated Depreciation—Store Equipment		41,000
Accounts Payable		7,300
Note Payable (due two years hence)		20,000
W. Lamm, Capital		163,500
	$231,900	$231,900

Other details of the agreement follow:

1. After a detailed review of the accounts of Lamm's Hardware, the new stockholders agree that:
   (a) The allowance for uncollectible accounts should increase by $400.
   (b) Because of damaged and obsolete goods, the merchandise inventory should be written down by $15,000.

(c) The store equipment will be recorded in the corporate accounts at its fair market value of $30,000 with no accumulated depreciation.
(d) The new corporation assumes at face value the recorded liabilities of the proprietorship.

2. Lamm has agreed to accept shares in the new corporation at par value in exchange for his adjusted equity in the assets of the proprietorship. He will purchase for cash at par value any additional shares necessary to bring his total holdings to the next even 100 shares.
3. The total value of Brady's building and land is agreed to be $162,000, of which $22,000 is associated with the land. Brady has agreed to accept stock at $12 per share for her land and building.
4. In an effort to stimulate local business, the Business Development Commission of the local city government has deeded to the corporation, for a token fee of $600, a small strip of land that will provide better delivery access to the rear of Brady's building. The fair value of the parcel is $6,000.
5. Turner has agreed to purchase for cash 5,000 shares at $12 per share. He will subscribe to an additional 500 shares at $14 per share, paying the subscription price in two equal installments, 90 and 180 days later.
6. Legal and accounting costs of $7,500 associated with acquiring the corporate charter and issuing the stock are paid from corporate funds. (Treat these as the asset, Organization Costs.)

REQUIRED

(a) As Lamm's accountant, you must prepare a balance sheet for the new corporation reflecting the shares issued, the stock subscription received, the parcel of land received from the city, and payment of legal and accounting costs. (*Hint:* You may wish to prepare a worksheet with the following headings:

	Lamm's Hardware Trial Balance		Adjustments and Organizational Transactions		Hardware City, Inc. Trial Balance	
Accounts	**Dr.**	**Cr.**	**Dr.**	**Cr.**	**Dr.**	**Cr.**

Properly combining and extending the amounts in the first two pairs of columns provide amounts for the trial balance of Hardware City, Inc. When recording the Lamm's Hardware trial balance, leave extra lines for the several transactions that will affect the Cash and W. Lamm, Capital accounts. Also, leave extra lines when entering the Common Stock and Paid-in Capital in Excess of Par Value accounts on the worksheet. For purposes of review, you may wish to key your adjustments and transactions to the letters and numbers used in the problem data.)

(b) In contrast to what they contributed to the corporation, what specifically do Lamm and Brady "own" after the incorporation?

(c) From Lamm's viewpoint, what are the advantages and disadvantages of incorporating the variety store?

ANSWERS TO SELF-TEST QUESTIONS

1. (c) **2.** (a) **3.** (c) **4.** (d) **5.** (b)

16

CORPORATIONS: DIVIDENDS, RETAINED EARNINGS, AND EARNINGS DISCLOSURE

CHAPTER OBJECTIVES

1. Identify and distinguish between cash dividends and stock dividends (pp. 551–55).
2. Illustrate a retained earnings statement and a statement of stockholders' equity (pp. 555–56).
3. Discuss the accounting for prior period adjustments and the process of appropriating retained earnings (pp. 556–58).
4. Identify and discuss the income statement sections used to report certain types of transactions (pp. 558–65).
5. Identify and illustrate the computation and disclosure of earnings per share (pp. 565–68).

All things have their place, knew we how to place them.

GEORGE HERBERT

The two major components of stockholders' equity are paid-in capital and retained earnings. The preceding chapter focused on events affecting paid-in capital; in this chapter we emphasize retained earnings and its components.

Retained earnings represents the stockholders' equity arising from the corporation's retention of assets generated from profit-directed activities. At the end of an accounting period, the Retained Earnings account is credited with the corporation's net income (when the Income Summary account is closed to it) or debited with a net loss. A debit balance in the Retained Earnings account resulting from accumulated losses is called a **deficit.** The board of directors may decide, based on the income performance of the corporation, to declare a dividend. The dividend declaration reduces retained earnings.

Profits (or net income) cause retained earnings to increase. Profits play a significant role in the organization and functioning of economic activity in the United States. A corporation's profitability is vitally important both to its owners and to potential investors. For this reason, data reported in the income statement are usually considered the most important financial information presented by corporations. Because of the importance of income data, accountants have developed several guidelines for their disclosure. After discussing the accounting for dividends and retained earnings, we will discuss the guidelines for reporting income data.

DIVIDENDS

Dividends are distributions of assets or stock from a corporation to its stockholders. A corporation can distribute dividends to shareholders only after its board of directors has formally declared a distribution. Dividends are usually paid in cash but may also be property or additional shares of stock in the firm. Legally, declared dividends are an obligation of the firm, and an entry to record the dividend obligation is made on the *declaration date.* Cash and property dividends payable are carried as liabilities, and stock dividends to be issued are shown in the stockholders' equity section of the balance sheet. At the declaration, a *record date* and *payment date* are established. For example, on April 25 (declaration date), the board of directors might declare a dividend payable June 1 (payment date) to those who own stock on May 15 (record date). Stockholders owning stock on the record date receive the dividend even if they dispose of their shares before the payment date. Therefore, shares sold between the record date and payment date are sold *ex-dividend* (without right to the dividend).

Most dividend declarations reduce retained earnings; under certain conditions, however, state laws may permit distributions from paid-in capital. Shareholders should be informed of the source of such dividends, because, in a sense, they are a return of capital rather than a distribution of earnings.

Cash Dividends

The majority of dividends distributed by corporations are paid in cash. Although companies may pay such dividends annually, many large firms pay quarterly dividends. Some companies occasionally pay an extra dividend at year-end.

DIVIDEND REINVESTMENT PLANS OPEN THE DOOR

Over the past year or two, Kay Feldman, a former kindergarten teacher in West Houston, Texas, has bought shares of Walt Disney Co., McDonald's Corp., Xerox Corp., International Business Machines Corp., Browning-Ferris Industries and Aetna Life & Casualty Co.—all without paying a penny in brokerage fees.

Ms. Feldman, who recently became a financial planner, uses a relatively little-known stock-purchase technique called optional cash investment. "I'm just a do-it-yourself type of person," she says.

More than 900 companies offer such plans, which allow individuals to buy shares directly with no service charge, or for a low fee, according to Sumie Kinoshita, editor of the Directory of Companies Offering Dividend Reinvestment Plans, published by Evergreen Enterprises in Laurel, Md. Many plans also allow those shares to be sold for fees far below usual brokerage commissions.

Brokerage costs can loom large as a percentage of a modest-sized transaction. Say an investor starts with $500 and buys 50 shares of stock at $10 each. Over the next year, the stock rises 10% to $11—not bad. But minimum commissions of many brokerage houses on the purchase, $30 for example, and another one on the sale would more than wipe out the $50 gain.

Optional cash investment can be a way around the commission problem. To participate, an investor must first own at least one share of a company's stock and then enroll in the company's dividend-reinvestment plan. This means all dividends the investor receives will automatically be used to buy more stock. Most of the companies also allow participants to buy additional shares using their own cash.

In most cases, the purchases are commission-free. In some cases, a commission is charged, but because the company buys and sells shares in bulk, it passes along a far lower cost per-share than an individual could obtain from a broker. Most company fees are about $3 per transaction. And a few companies even give a 3% to 5% discount off the stock price.

Optional cash investing does have some drawbacks. More than 7,000 stocks actively trade on the nation's major exchanges and in the national system of the National Association of Securities Dealers. Among those eliminated are stocks that don't pay dividends, which include some fast-growing concerns that are plowing all available money into expansion.

Lack of control over the timing of purchases or sales can also be a headache. The company determines the transaction date, often monthly on a preset schedule. Investors, having already sent in money to purchase stock, get the number of shares the sum will buy at that day's price.

The loss of control could be especially troublesome when investors decide to sell. One way to mitigate that problem is to request that the company send stock certificates from time to time. Once in possession of the certificates, individuals can sell the shares independently through a brokerage firm, although they would incur a brokerage fee on the sale.

Companies also limit the amount an individual can invest through optional cash investment programs, but the limits are fairly generous. Often, the maximum is $1,000 a month or $5,000 a quarter. At a few companies (including Coca-Cola Co., Exxon Corp. and General Electric Co.), it's as high as $50,000 to $100,000 a year.

Despite the disadvantages, optional cash investment can be attractive for many people.

From John R. Dorfman, "Certain Stocks Offer Trading at Little Cost," *The Wall Street Journal*, January 13, 1988, p. 25.

Usually this is done when the company wishes to increase the total annual distribution without departing from a standard quarterly amount that was established by custom or announced in advance.

In declaring cash dividends, a company must have both an appropriate amount of retained earnings and the necessary amount of cash. Uninformed investors often believe that a large Retained Earnings balance automatically permits generous dividend distributions. A company, however, may successfully accumulate earnings and at the same time not be sufficiently liquid to pay large dividends. Many companies, especially new firms in the so-called growth industries, use retained earnings for expansion and pay out only a small portion, or perhaps none, of their earnings.

Cash dividends are based on the number of shares of stock outstanding. When a company's directors declare a cash dividend, an entry is made debiting Retained Earnings and crediting Dividends Payable, a current liability account. Assume, for example, that a company has outstanding 1,000 shares of $100 par value, 6% preferred stock and 6,000 shares of $10 par value common stock. If the company declares the regular $6 dividend on the preferred stock and a $2 dividend on the common stock, the dividend payment totals $18,000. The following entry is made at the declaration date:

Retained Earnings	18,000	
Dividends Payable—Preferred Stock		6,000
Dividends Payable—Common Stock		12,000
To record declaration of $6 dividend on preferred stock and $2 dividend on common stock.		

Unpaid cash dividends are carried as a current liability on the balance sheet. On the payment date, the following entry is made:

Dividends Payable—Preferred Stock	6,000	
Dividends Payable—Common Stock	12,000	
Cash		18,000
To record payment of dividends on preferred and common stocks.		

Some companies, especially those paying quarterly dividends, debit an account called Dividends on the declaration date. Dividends is a contra account to Retained Earnings until it is closed by a debit to Retained Earnings at year-end.

Stock Dividends

Companies frequently distribute shares of their own stock as dividends to shareholders in lieu of, or in addition to, cash dividends. A company may issue **stock dividends** when it does not wish to deplete its working capital by paying a cash dividend. Distribution of a stock dividend may also signify management's desire to "plough back" earnings into the company. The distribution transfers a portion of retained earnings to the paid-in capital accounts. The so-called permanent capital is thereby increased although no new assets are acquired. Young and growing companies often issue stock dividends, inasmuch as earnings are needed to acquire new facilities and to expand. The use of stock dividends is by no means confined to such companies, however.

Although stock dividends may take a number of forms, usually common shares are distributed to common shareholders. We limit our discussion to this type of distribution.

For small stock dividends—additional shares issued are fewer than 20–25% of the number previously outstanding—an amount equal to the market value of the shares issued is transferred from Retained Earnings to Paid-in Capital. In some respects, the issuance of new shares in the form of a dividend can be viewed as a transaction that avoids the test of the marketplace. If the shareholders receive cash and immediately purchase additional shares of the firm's stock, the purchases are made at market value. Thus, the number of shares issued in exchange for a given amount of retained earnings should be related to the market value of the shares.

To illustrate the entries reflecting a declaration of a stock dividend, we assume that the stockholders' equity of a company is as follows before declaration of a 10% stock dividend:

Common Stock, $5 Par Value, 20,000 shares issued and outstanding	$100,000
Paid-in Capital in Excess of Par Value	20,000
Retained Earnings	65,000
Total Stockholders' Equity	$185,000

With 20,000 shares outstanding, declaration of a 10% stock dividend requires the issuance of an additional 2,000 shares. Let us assume that the market price per share is $11. The amount transferred from Retained Earnings is $22,000, of which $10,000 (par value of the shares) is credited to the Stock Dividend to Be Issued account. The premium of $6 per share, or $12,000, is credited to Paid-in Capital in Excess of Par Value.

Retained Earnings	22,000	
Stock Dividend to Be Issued		10,000
Paid-in Capital in Excess of Par Value		12,000
To record declaration of 10% stock dividend on common shares.		

When the stock is distributed, the following entry is made:

Stock Dividend to Be Issued	10,000	
Common Stock		10,000
To record issuance of stock dividend on common shares.		

After the stock dividend is distributed, the stockholders' equity appears as follows:

Common Stock, $5 Par Value, 22,000 shares issued and outstanding	$110,000
Paid-in Capital in Excess of Par Value	32,000
Retained Earnings	43,000
Total Stockholders' Equity	$185,000

If a balance sheet is prepared between the declaration date and the distribution date of a stock dividend, the Stock Dividend to Be Issued account is shown in stockholders' equity immediately after the Common Stock account.

The relative position of a common shareholder is not altered by the receipt of a common stock dividend. If a 10% stock dividend is distributed, all shareholders increase their proportionate holdings by 10%, while the total stock outstanding is increased in the same proportion. No income is realized by the shareholders. If the stock dividend distributed is not large in relation to the outstanding shares, little or no change may occur in the market value of the stock. If the market value does not decrease and the company continues the same cash dividends per share, shareholders have benefited by the distribution.

EXHIBIT 16–1

Geyser Corporation
Retained Earnings Statement
For the Year Ended December 31, 19X1

Retained Earnings, January 1, 19X1	$48,000
Add: Net Income	32,000
	$80,000
Less: Cash Dividends Declared	19,000
Retained Earnings, December 31, 19X1	$61,000

When the number of shares issued as a stock dividend is large enough to reduce materially the per-share market value, the shareholders may not perceive the same benefits as they do for small stock dividends. Accordingly, the accounting analysis is different for large stock dividends (those over 20–25%). The journal entry to record the declaration of a large stock dividend debits Retained Earnings and credits Stock Dividend to Be Issued for the minimum increase in paid-in capital required by law for the issuance of new shares. Usually this amount is the par or stated value of the stock. Once the stock is issued, the increase in paid-in capital is reflected in the Common Stock account.[1]

RETAINED EARNINGS STATEMENT

A **retained earnings statement** presents an analysis of the Retained Earnings account for the accounting period. The statement begins with the retained earnings balance at the beginning of the period, shows the items that caused retained earnings to change during the period, and ends with the period-end retained earnings balance. An example of a retained earnings statement is shown in Exhibit 16–1.

STATEMENT OF STOCKHOLDERS' EQUITY

Rather than reporting a retained earnings statement, corporations often integrate information about retained earnings into a more comprehensive statement called a **statement of stockholders' equity.** This statement presents an analysis of all components of stockholders' equity for the accounting period. The statement begins with the beginning balances of the various stockholders' equity components, reports the items causing changes in these components, and ends with the period-end balances.

[1]A large stock dividend is similar in many respects to a stock split (discussed in Chapter 15). A stock's par or stated value per share is not changed by a stock dividend, however, while a stock split reduces the par or stated value in proportion to the increase in shares of stock. This difference leads to a difference in analysis—only a memorandum entry is made for a stock split, while a large stock dividend requires a journal entry to transfer the legal capital of shares to be issued from retained earnings to paid-in capital.

EXHIBIT 16–2

Geyser Corporation
Statement of Stockholders' Equity
For the Year Ended December 31, 19X1

	Common Stock	Paid-in Capital in Excess of Par Value	Paid-in Capital from Treasury Stock	Retained Earnings	Treasury Stock	Total
Balance, January 1, 19X1	$200,000	$120,000	$18,000	$48,000	($14,000)	$372,000
6,000 common shares issued	30,000	24,000				54,000
500 treasury shares issued			2,000		3,500	5,500
Net income				32,000		32,000
Cash dividend declared				(19,000)		(19,000)
200 treasury shares acquired					(2,000)	(2,000)
Balance, December 31, 19X1	$230,000	$144,000	$20,000	$61,000	($12,500)	$442,500

Exhibit 16–2 presents a statement of stockholders' equity for Geyser Corporation. This statement reveals all of the events affecting Geyser's stockholders' equity during 19X1. These events are the issuance of common stock, the issuance of treasury stock, the earning of net income, the declaration of cash dividends, and the acquisition of treasury stock. Note that the information in the retained earnings column contains the same information as a retained earnings statement.

PRIOR PERIOD ADJUSTMENTS

Essentially, **prior period adjustments** correct errors made in financial statements of prior periods.[2] Errors may result from mathematical mistakes, oversights, incorrect applications of accounting principles, or improper analyses of existing facts when the financial statements are prepared.

Prior period adjustments are not included in the current year's income statement. Instead, corrections of material errors of past periods are charged or credited directly to Retained Earnings and are reported as adjustments to the beginning balance of Retained Earnings in the current year's retained earnings statement. The prior period adjustment should be shown net of any related income tax effects.

For example, assume Geyser Corporation discovered in 19X2 that several mathematical errors caused its December 31, 19X1, inventory to be understated by $10,000. Assuming an applicable income tax rate of 30%, the company reports the $7,000 prior period adjustment in the 19X2 retained earnings statement, as follows:

Retained Earnings, January 1, 19X2	$61,000
Add: Correction of Prior Period Inventory Error (net of $3,000 income taxes)	7,000
Retained Earnings Adjusted Balance, January 1, 19X2	$68,000

[2] *Statement of Financial Accounting Standards No. 16*, "Prior Period Adjustments" (Stamford, CT: Financial Accounting Standards Board, 1977). The correction of a current period error does not require a prior period adjustment. The correction of current period errors is discussed in Chapter 3.

APPROPRIATIONS OF RETAINED EARNINGS

Portions of the Retained Earnings balance are often restricted so that these amounts cannot be paid out as dividends. The amounts so segregated are called **retained earnings appropriations,** or *retained earnings reserves.*

In some instances, appropriations of retained earnings may be entirely *voluntary*—the board of directors may restrict dividends to use corporate funds for a specific internal purpose. For example, the company may want to enlarge its plant or establish a buffer against possible adversity. By appropriating retained earnings, the directors inform the shareholders of the need to restrict dividend payments.

Other types of retained earnings appropriations may be *statutory* or *contractual.* In Chapter 15, we mentioned a statutory appropriation in connection with treasury stock purchases—some states require that retained earnings be restricted in an amount equal to the cost of treasury stock purchased by the corporation. A contractual restriction may result from agreements made when a company issues long-term debt. The debt agreement may limit the amount of dividends the company may pay until the debt is settled. Such an agreement helps protect the availability of the company's working capital for debt payment purposes.

Retained earnings may be appropriated by making an entry in the company's records. For example, assume that the board of directors of Holmes Corporation appropriates $60,000 for plant expansion in 19X2. The following entry is made:

Retained Earnings	60,000	
Retained Earnings Appropriated for Plant Expansion		60,000
To record retained earnings appropriation for plant expansion.		

Exhibit 16–3 shows the presentation of the $60,000 appropriation in Holmes Corporation's 19X2 retained earnings statement (assuming $40,000 had been appropriated before 19X2). The appropriated amount is presented in the December 31, 19X2, balance sheet as follows:

Retained Earnings	
Appropriated for Plant Expansion	$100,000
Unappropriated	90,000
Total Retained Earnings	$190,000

Note that Holmes has total retained earnings of $190,000, of which only $90,000 is available for the declaration of dividends.

Certain points should be emphasized regarding the appropriation of retained earnings. First, segregating retained earnings for a particular objective only restricts dividend amounts. The procedure does not ensure that funds will be available for the avowed objective, because a company may have a large Retained Earnings balance without having an ample amount of liquid assets. When a company appropriates retained earnings for plant expansion, for example, management may also *fund* the appropriation. This is accomplished by setting aside funds, as they become available, in a special asset account to permit eventual *spending* for plant expansion.

Second, expenditures are never charged against retained earnings appropriations. When the purpose is accomplished or the event transpires for which

EXHIBIT 16–3

Holmes Corporation
Retained Earnings Statement
For the Year Ended December 31, 19X2

Appropriated			
Appropriated for Plant Expansion:			
Balance, January 1, 19X2		$ 40,000	
Appropriated in 19X2		60,000	$100,000
Unappropriated			
Balance, January 1, 19X2		$130,000	
Add: Net Income		35,000	
		$165,000	
Less: Dividends Declared	$15,000		
Appropriation for Plant Expansion (see above)	60,000	75,000	90,000
Total Retained Earnings, December 31, 19X2			$190,000

the appropriation was made, the restricted amount is returned, intact, to unappropriated retained earnings. For example, suppose that Holmes Corporation implemented its expansion plans in 19X3, spending $95,000 for new plant equipment. After recording the purchase by debiting Plant Equipment and crediting Cash for the amount spent, the company returns the total appropriation to unappropriated retained earnings with the following entry (in this illustration, a total of $100,000 was appropriated):

Retained Earnings Appropriated for Plant Expansion	100,000	
Retained Earnings		100,000
To return appropriation to Retained Earnings.		

As an alternative to segregating retained earnings formally, a note to the balance sheet may inform shareholders of restrictions on retained earnings. The following note from an annual report of Georgia-Pacific Corporation illustrates this type of disclosure:

> Certain insurance company loan agreements place limitations on cash dividends that can be paid. The amount of retained earnings available for cash dividends under the most restrictive covenants of these agreements is approximately $1.1 billion. In addition, the agreements require the Corporation to maintain a minimum of $250 million of consolidated working capital and impose certain limitations on additional borrowings.

INCOME STATEMENT SECTIONS

Accountants believe that the usefulness of the income statement is enhanced if certain types of transactions and events are reported in separate sections. For this reason, information about extraordinary items, discontinued operations, and effects of changes in accounting principles are disclosed separately in an income statement. Segregating these categories of information from the results of ordinary, continuing operations should make it easier for financial statement users to estimate the future earnings performance of the company.

The creation of several sections in the income statement, however, complicates the reporting of income tax expense. Items affecting the overall amount of income tax expense may appear in more than one section. If this is the case, accountants allocate the income tax expense among those sections of the statement in which the items affecting the tax expense appear.

The income statement's usefulness is also enhanced if it contains information on earnings per share. Accordingly, earnings per share are reported in the income statement immediately after the net income amount.

We now examine these areas in more detail.

EXTRAORDINARY ITEMS

Extraordinary items are transactions and events that are *unusual in nature* and *occur infrequently.*[3] An item that is unusual in nature is highly abnormal and significantly different from the firm's ordinary and typical activities. To determine a firm's ordinary and typical activities, we must consider such things as the types of operations, lines of business, operating policies, and the environment in which the firm operates. The operating environment includes the characteristics of the industry, the geographic location of the firm's facilities, and the type of government regulations imposed. A transaction or event is considered to occur infrequently if the firm does not expect it to recur in the foreseeable future.

The two criteria—unusual nature and infrequent occurrence—considerably restrict the events and transactions that qualify as extraordinary items. For example, suppose a tobacco grower suffers crop loss from a flood, which normally happens every few years in this area. The history of floods creates a reasonable expectation that another flood will occur in the foreseeable future. The loss, therefore, does not meet the criteria for an extraordinary item. Now consider a different tobacco grower who suffers flood damage to his crop for the first time from a broken dam. The dam is repaired and is not expected to fail in the foreseeable future. The flood loss in this circumstance is an extraordinary item.

Other events that may generate extraordinary losses are earthquakes, expropriation of property, and prohibitions under newly enacted laws (such as a government ban on a product currently marketed). An extraordinary gain may result from a nonrecurring sale of an asset never used in operations. Assume a manufacturing company acquired land several years ago for future use but then changed its plans and held the land for appreciation. If this is the only land the company owns and it will not speculate in land in the foreseeable future, any gain from the sale of the land is considered extraordinary.

One exception to the criteria defining extraordinary items relates to gains and losses incurred when a company extinguishes its own debt. These gains and

[3]*Opinions of the Accounting Principles Board, No. 30,* "Reporting the Results of Operations—Reporting the Effects of Disposal of a Segment of a Business, and Extraordinary, Unusual and Infrequently Occurring Events and Transactions" (New York: American Institute of Certified Public Accountants, 1973).

EXHIBIT 16–4

Pacific Corporation
Income Statement
For the Year Ended December 31, 19XX

Sales		$700,000
Cost of Goods Sold		360,000
Gross Profit on Sales		$340,000
Less: Selling Expenses	$90,000	
Administrative Expenses	80,000	
Loss from Plant Strike	45,000	215,000
Income before Taxes and Extraordinary Item		$125,000
Less: Income Taxes		37,500
Income before Extraordinary Item		$ 87,500
Extraordinary Item:		
Gain from Sale of Z Company Stock	$80,000	
Less: Income Taxes	24,000	56,000
Net Income		$143,500
Earnings per Common Share:		
Income before Extraordinary Item		$1.75
Extraordinary Gain		1.12
Net Income		$2.87

losses are aggregated and, if material, classified as extraordinary items.[4] An example of a debt extinguishment loss is presented in Chapter 17.

Exhibit 16–4 is an income statement for a corporation with an extraordinary item. During 19XX Pacific Corporation, a manufacturing concern, sold a block of common stock of Z Company, a publicly traded company, at a gain of $80,000. The shares of stock were the only security investment the company had ever owned, and it does not plan to acquire other stocks in the foreseeable future. For Pacific Corporation, this gain is unusual, infrequent, and properly considered an extraordinary item. The gain is reported net of $24,000 of income taxes on the gain, as shown in Exhibit 16–4.

UNUSUAL OR NONRECURRING ITEMS

Events and transactions that are unusual *or* nonrecurring, but not both, are not extraordinary items. *Accounting Principles Board Opinion No. 30* notes several examples of gains and losses that are not extraordinary either because they are typical or because they may recur as a result of continuing business activities. Examples of such items are gains and losses from (a) the write-down or write-

[4]Unless the gains or losses result from extinguishments of debt made to satisfy sinking-fund requirements that must be met within one year. See *Statement of Financial Accounting Standards No. 64,* "Extinguishments of Debt Made to Satisfy Sinking-fund Requirements" (Stamford, CT: Financial Accounting Standards Board, 1982).

off of receivables, inventories, and intangible assets; (b) the exchange or translation of foreign currencies; (c) the sale or abandonment of property, plant, or equipment used in the business; (d) the effects of a strike; and (e) the adjustments of long-term contract accruals. An unusual or infrequently occurring item of a material amount should be reported as a separate component of income before extraordinary items.

Assume that during 19XX Pacific Corporation incurred a $45,000 loss because of a labor strike at one of its plants. The strike was not part of the company's ordinary activities, but Pacific Corporation has a history of labor difficulties. Therefore, even though the strike loss was unusual, it was not infrequent because it will likely happen again in the foreseeable future. Because it did not qualify as an extraordinary item, the before-tax amount of the strike loss was reported as a separate item among the ordinary expenses, as shown in Exhibit 16–4.

TAX ALLOCATION WITHIN A PERIOD

Note that the extraordinary gain in Exhibit 16–4 is shown net of applicable income taxes. Pacific Corporation's total income tax expense of $61,500 has been allocated to two parts of the income statement: $37,500 deducted in deriving income before extraordinary items, and $24,000 deducted in the extraordinary items section. This process, known as **tax allocation within a period,** reports the tax effect of an extraordinary item in the same section of the income statement as the item itself. By the same token, the income taxes deducted in the income before extraordinary items section relate only to the revenue and expenses disclosed in that section. Thus tax allocation within a period portrays normal relationships within the income statement between income taxes and the items affecting their calculation.

A tax reduction due to an extraordinary loss would be deducted from the loss in the extraordinary items section. Suppose that instead of the $80,000 gain, Pacific Corporation incurred an extraordinary flood loss of $30,000, which reduced income subject to a 30% tax rate. The lower portion of the company's income statement, after tax allocation, would appear as follows:

Income before Taxes and Extraordinary Item		$125,000
Less: Income Taxes		37,500
Income before Extraordinary Item		$ 87,500
Extraordinary Item:		
Flood Loss	$30,000	
Less: Tax Reduction from Flood Loss	9,000	21,000
Net Income		$ 66,500

An alternative way of reporting the tax effects of extraordinary items is to disclose them parenthetically. Using this procedure, the extraordinary gain would be shown as

Gain from Sale of Z Company Stock (net of $24,000 of income taxes)	$56,000

The extraordinary loss would be reported as follows:

Flood Loss (net of $9,000 reduction of income taxes)	$21,000

DISCONTINUED OPERATIONS

When a company sells, abandons, or otherwise disposes of a segment of its operations, a **discontinued operations** section of the income statement reports information about the discontinued segment. The discontinued operations section presents two categories of information:

1. The income or loss from the segment's operations for the portion of the year before its discontinuance.
2. The gain or loss from the disposal of the segment.

The section is placed after information about ordinary, continuing operations and before any extraordinary items.

A *segment* of a business is a unit—such as a department or a division—whose activities constitute a separate major line of business or serve a particular class of customer. The assets and operating results of the segment must be clearly distinguishable from the rest of the company. For example, a furniture manufacturing division of a diversified manufacturing company is a segment of the business.

To illustrate the reporting of discontinued operations, we assume that on July 1 of the current year, Atlantic Corporation sold its Division Y. From January 1 through June 30, Division Y had operated at a loss, net of taxes, of $26,000 ($40,000 operating loss less a $14,000 reduction in income taxes caused by the operating loss). The loss, net of taxes, from the sale of the division was $65,000 ($100,000 loss on the sale less a $35,000 reduction in income taxes caused by the loss). Exhibit 16–5 illustrates the income statement for Atlantic Corporation, including the information about Division Y in the discontinued operations section. Note that when there is a discontinued operations section, the difference between the ordinary revenue and expenses is labeled "income from continuing operations."

CHANGES IN ACCOUNTING PRINCIPLES

Occasionally a company may implement a **change in accounting principle**—that is, switch from one generally accepted principle to another. Examples include a change in inventory pricing method—such as from FIFO to weighted average—or a change in depreciation method—such as from double declining balance to straight line. Because the comparability of financial data through time is enhanced by the consistent use of accounting principles, a company should change principles only when it can demonstrate that the new principle is preferable.

Almost all changes in accounting principles introduce a new item into the income statement—the **cumulative effect of a change in principle.** This item represents the total difference in the cumulative income for all prior years had the new principle been used in those years. It is equal to the difference between (a) the retained earnings at the beginning of the year and (b) the retained earnings amount at the beginning of the year had the new principle been used in all years in which the previous principle was followed for the items in question. The cumulative effect is disclosed immediately before the net income figure.

To illustrate the reporting of the cumulative effect of a change in principle, we assume that Atlantic Corporation in Exhibit 16–5 changed its method of depreciating plant equipment in 19XX, switching from an accelerated method to

EXHIBIT 16–5

Atlantic Corporation
Income Statement
For the Year Ended December 31, 19XX

Sales		$1,900,000
Expenses:		
Cost of Goods Sold	$1,100,000	
Selling Expenses	200,000	
Administrative Expenses	180,000	
Interest Expense	20,000	
Income Tax Expense	140,000	
Total Expenses		1,640,000
Income from Continuing Operations		$ 260,000
Discontinued Operations:		
Loss from Operations of Discontinued Division Y (net of $14,000 reduction of income taxes)	$ 26,000	
Loss on Disposal of Division Y (net of $35,000 reduction of income taxes)	65,000	91,000
Income before Cumulative Effect of a Change in Accounting Principle		$ 169,000
Cumulative Effect on Prior Years of Changing to a Different Depreciation Method (net of $7,000 income taxes)		13,000
Net Income		$ 182,000
Earnings per Common Share:		
Income from Continuing Operations		$ 3.71
Discontinued Operations		(1.30)
Income before Cumulative Effect of a Change in Accounting Principle		$ 2.41
Cumulative Effect on Prior Years of Changing to a Different Depreciation Method		.19
Net Income		$ 2.60

the straight-line method. Cumulative income before income taxes for years prior to 19XX would have been $20,000 greater if the straight-line method had been used to depreciate the plant equipment in those years. If we assume an income tax rate of 35%, the $13,000 after-tax amount of the effect of the change in principle would be reported on Atlantic Corporation's income statement as shown in Exhibit 16–5.

In addition to reporting the cumulative effect, the company should, in a note to the financial statements, justify the change and disclose the effect of the change on the current year's income exclusive of the cumulative adjustment. The effect of the change on earnings per share should also be reported.

Annual financial reports often include financial statements for prior periods for comparative purposes. These prior period statements are not revised to reflect the new principle adopted this period. For each period reported, however, the net income and the related earnings per share are recomputed as if the new principle had been in effect in that period.[5] Each period's income statement will disclose these recomputed amounts.

The above disclosure requirements accommodate two conflicting positions on the appropriate method of disclosing a change in accounting principle. One position stresses the possible dilution of public confidence in financial statements if previously reported statements are revised to reflect a new principle—hence, the inclusion of a cumulative effect on prior years' income in the current year's income statement with no revision of prior period statements. The other position emphasizes the importance of consistency in the use of accounting principles for comparative analysis of data—hence, the disclosure of selected, significant pieces of information, recomputed using the new principle, for all periods presented in the financial statements.

CHANGES IN ACCOUNTING ESTIMATES

Estimates play an integral part in accounting. In preparing periodic financial statements, we estimate the effects of transactions continuing in the future. For example, we must estimate uncollectible accounts, useful lives of plant and intangible assets, salvage values of plant assets, and product warranty costs. As a normal consequence of such estimates, new information, changed conditions, or more experience may require the revision of previous estimates.

The effect of a **change in accounting estimate** should be reflected in the income statements of *current and future periods* to the extent appropriate in each case. The estimated amounts reported in prior period financial statements are not changed. Presumably, the previous estimates were the best possible, given the information then available.

The total impact of some changes in estimates is included in the current year's income statement. A revision of an estimated liability recorded in prior periods is one example. Assume that unanticipated cost increases have caused a company to underestimate its liability for product warranty carried into the current year by $900. The estimated liability is revised as follows:

Product Warranty Expense	900	
Estimated Liability for Product Warranty		900
To record change in estimated warranty liability.		

An estimate revision may affect both the period of change and future periods. If so, the effect of the revision should be accounted for over the current and future periods. The revision of depreciation discussed on page 361 illustrates this type of change.

SINGLE-STEP AND MULTIPLE-STEP INCOME STATEMENTS

Exhibit 16–5 (page 563) illustrates a **single-step income statement,** in which the ordinary, continuing income of the business is derived in one step—by subtract-

[5]If an extraordinary item is reported, the income before extraordinary item and the related per-share amount must also be recomputed using the new principle.

ing total expenses from total revenue. In Exhibit 16–5, all the expenses, totaling $1,640,000, are combined and then subtracted from the total revenue of $1,900,000. The single-step statement is a popular reporting format.

Exhibit 16–4 (page 560) is an example of a **multiple-step income statement,** in which one or more intermediate amounts are derived before the ordinary, continuing income is reported. In Exhibit 16–4, "gross profit on sales" and "income before taxes and extraordinary item" are intermediate amounts presented before the "income before extraordinary item" figure. Both the multiple-step and the single-step formats are acceptable procedures.

EARNINGS PER SHARE

A financial statistic of great interest to corporation shareholders and potential investors is the **earnings per share** of common stock. Consequently, earnings per share data are widely disseminated, reaching interested persons through such channels as annual stockholder reports, financial newspapers, and financial statistical services. Because this financial information is so important, accounting guidelines require the disclosure of earnings per share data on the income statement.[6]

In determining the presentation of earnings per share data, accountants distinguish between corporations with simple capital structures and those with complex capital structures. A **simple capital structure** contains no securities that, if exercised or converted, reduce (dilute) earnings per share of common stock. Convertible debt, convertible preferred stock, stock options, and stock warrants are examples of potentially dilutive securities, because if they are exercised or converted, the number of outstanding shares of common stock increases. A **complex capital structure** contains one or more potentially dilutive securities. Corporations with simple capital structures make a single presentation of earnings per share, while corporations with complex capital structures make a dual presentation.

Simple Capital Structure

Corporations with simple capital structures calculate earnings per share by dividing net income by a weighted average of the shares of common stock outstanding during the year. If preferred stock also is outstanding, its dividend requirements are first subtracted from net income to derive earnings available to common stockholders.

Suppose that Owens Corporation has a net income of $39,000 for 19XX. On January 1, 19XX, 10,000 shares of common stock were outstanding. An additional 6,000 shares were issued on July 1. The company has no preferred stock. The company's 19XX earnings per share is $3.00, computed as follows:

$$\text{Earnings per Share} = \frac{\text{Net Income}}{\text{Weighted Average of Common Shares Outstanding}}$$

$$= \frac{\$39{,}000}{13{,}000} = \underline{\underline{\$3.00}}$$

The weighted average of the shares of common stock outstanding during the year is computed as follows:

[6] *Opinions of the Accounting Principles Board, No. 15,* "Earnings Per Share" (New York: American Institute of Certified Public Accountants, 1969).

Shares		Months Outstanding		Share Months
10,000	×	6	=	60,000
16,000	×	6	=	96,000
		12		156,000

$$\text{Weighted Average of Common Shares Outstanding} = \frac{156{,}000}{12} = 13{,}000$$

Complex Capital Structure

The dual presentation for corporations with complex capital structures consists of a primary earnings per share and a fully diluted earnings per share. The computation of **primary earnings per share** considers the common stock outstanding during the year plus any potentially dilutive securities that are equivalent to common stock. (Accounting guidelines contain criteria for determining when a potentially dilutive security is a common stock equivalent.) The calculation of **fully diluted earnings per share** is based on the *assumption* that all dilutive securities are converted into common stock. The difference between the two per-share amounts shows the maximum possible dilution in earnings per share from any outstanding dilutive securities that are not common stock equivalents.

To illustrate the computation of primary and fully diluted earnings per share, let us suppose Bodeen Company had a net income of $90,000 for the current year. All year the company had 40,000 shares of common stock and 5,000 shares of convertible preferred stock outstanding. The annual dividend on the convertible preferred stock is 80 cents per share, and each share is convertible into one share of common stock. The convertible preferred stock is a potentially dilutive security; we assume it is not a common stock equivalent. The company's primary earnings per share is $2.15 and its fully diluted earnings per share is $2.00, computed as follows:

Primary Earnings per Share

$$\text{Primary Earnings per Share} = \frac{\text{Net Income} - \text{Preferred Stock Dividend}}{\text{Weighted Average of Common Shares Outstanding}}$$

$$= \frac{\$90{,}000 - \$4{,}000}{40{,}000} = \$2.15$$

Fully Diluted Earnings per Share (Assumes all preferred stock is converted into common stock at the beginning of the year.)

$$\text{Fully Diluted Earnings per Share} = \frac{\text{Net Income} - \text{Preferred Stock Dividend}}{\text{Weighted Average of Common Shares Outstanding}}$$

$$= \frac{\$90{,}000 - \$0^{*}}{45{,}000^{\dagger}} = \$2.00$$

*Under the assumption of preferred stock conversion into common stock, there would be no preferred stock dividend.

†Under the assumption of preferred stock conversion into common stock, there would be an additional 5,000 shares of common stock outstanding (40,000 actual common shares outstanding + 5,000 assumed additional common shares outstanding = 45,000 weighted average of common shares outstanding).

The variety of potentially dilutive securities and of events that affect outstanding common stock can make the computations of earnings per share quite complex. The analysis required for such computations is covered in advanced courses.

Additional per-Share Disclosures

The form in which earnings per share are disclosed should correspond to the income statement contents. Thus if a firm reports extraordinary gains or losses, earnings per share should be disclosed for income before extraordinary items as well as for net income. Companies may also disclose the per-share effect of each extraordinary item, although this disclosure is optional. Exhibit 16–4 (page 560) illustrates an earnings per share presentation with an extraordinary item.

Similarly, if a firm reports discontinued operations, earnings per share should be reported for income from continuing operations. At the company's option, the per-share effect of discontinued operations may also be shown. If a firm reports a cumulative effect of a change in an accounting principle, earnings per share should be disclosed for income before cumulative effect of a change in accounting principle. Accounting standards also require the disclosure of the per-share amount of the cumulative effect of the accounting change. Exhibit 16–5 (page 563) illustrates the earnings per share presentation for an income statement that contains both discontinued operations and a change in an accounting principle.

SUMMARY OF THE INCOME STATEMENT

Reporting the income of a corporation with the variety of items discussed in this chapter can be complex. Exhibit 16–6 summarizes these items and indicates their placement on the income statement, the order in which they are normally reported, and whether each is reported before or net of its income tax effect. Each of these items on the statement is keyed with the number of its related explanation.

Note that changes in accounting estimates and unusual *or* nonrecurring items are reported without any related income tax amounts because they are included in the computation of income from continuing operations. Income tax expense in this section relates to all preceding items of revenue and expense. All items below income from continuing operations are reported at amounts net of their income tax effects. The income statement in Exhibit 16–6 is a single-step income statement. Income from continuing operations is computed in one step, subtracting total expenses from sales. Of course, a single-step statement may include sections other than income from continuing operations.

Note also that when the income statement contains special sections, the number of per-share disclosures increases. In Exhibit 16–6, the required earnings per share disclosures are per-share amounts for income from continuing operations, income before extraordinary items and cumulative effect of a change in accounting principle, cumulative effect of change in accounting principle, and net income.

EXHIBIT 16–6

SUMMARY OF INCOME STATEMENT FORMAT

EXPLANATIONS

1 Changes in Accounting Estimates
Before-tax amounts are reported as part of related ordinary expenses.

2 Unusual or Nonrecurring Items
Before-tax amounts are separate items listed among the ordinary expenses.

3 Income Tax Expense
The initial allocation of income taxes applies to the net of all preceding revenue and expense items. All items appearing below income from continuing operations are reported net of income taxes.

4 Discontinued Operations
Involves reporting separately for the discontinued segment:
(a) Gain or loss from operations net of income taxes.
(b) Gain or loss on disposal net of income taxes.

5 Extraordinary Items
Reported net of income taxes.

6 Cumulative Effect of Change in Accounting Principle
Reported net of income taxes as the last item before net income on the income statement.

7 Earnings per Share
Items in color type are required disclosures; others are optional. Complex capital structures require reporting of primary and fully diluted earnings per share amounts.

ABC Corporation
Income Statement
For the Year Ended December 31, 19XX

	Sales		$XXX
	Expenses:		
1	Ordinary Expenses (including effects of changes in accounting estimates)	$XX	
2	Unusual or Nonrecurring Items	XX	
3	Income Tax Expense	XX	
	Total Expenses		XXX
	Income from Continuing Operations		$XXX
4	Discontinued Operations:		
	Gain or Loss from Operations (net of income taxes)	$XX	
	Gain or Loss on Disposal (net of income taxes)	XX	XX
	Income before Extraordinary Items and Cumulative Effect of a Change in Accounting Principle		$XXX
5	Extraordinary Items (net of income taxes)		XX
6	Cumulative Effect on Prior Years of Change in Accounting Principle (net of income taxes)		XX
	Net Income		$XXX
7	Earnings per Common Share:		
	Income from Continuing Operations		$X
	Discontinued Operations		X
	Income before Extraordinary Items and Cumulative Effect of a Change in Accounting Principle		$X
	Extraordinary Item		X
	Cumulative Effect of Change in Accounting Principle		X
	Net Income		$X

KEY POINTS FOR CHAPTER OBJECTIVES

1 Identify and distinguish between cash dividends and stock dividends (pp. 551–55).

- Cash dividends reduce retained earnings and are a current liability when declared.
- Stock dividends are accounted for by a transfer of retained earnings to the appropriate stock and paid-in capital accounts at the market value of the shares for small stock dividends and at the legal minimum for large stock dividends.

2 Illustrate a retained earnings statement and a statement of stockholders' equity (pp. 555–56).

- A retained earnings statement presents the events causing retained earnings to change during an accounting period.
- A statement of stockholders' equity presents the events causing each component of stockholders' equity (including retained earnings) to change during an accounting period.

3 Discuss the accounting for prior period adjustments and the process of appropriating retained earnings (pp. 556–58).

- Prior period adjustments are corrections of material errors made in previous periods. They are charged or credited directly to Retained Earnings.
- Retained earnings appropriations are restrictions placed on retained earnings that reduce the amount of retained earnings available for dividends.

4 Identify and discuss the income statement sections used to report certain types of transactions (pp. 558–65).

- Extraordinary items are both unusual *and* nonrecurring; they are reported in a separate section of the income statement. Unusual *or* nonrecurring items are not reported in a separate section, but they may be separately identified in the first section of the income statement reporting data on ordinary and continuing operations.
- Tax allocation within a period improves the reporting of income taxes by disclosing both the tax effect and the item causing that effect in the same location in financial statements.
- Gains and losses from discontinued operations are reported in a special income statement section immediately following income from continuing operations.
- The cumulative effects of most changes in accounting principles are disclosed in the income statement in a special section immediately preceding net income.
- The effects of changes in accounting estimates are spread over the appropriate current and future periods.
- The ordinary, continuing income may be reported in a single-step format or in a multiple-step format.

5 Discuss and illustrate the computation and disclosure of earnings per share (pp. 565–68).

- Corporations with complex capital structures present data on both primary and fully diluted earnings per share. A single presentation of earnings per share is appropriate for a corporation with a simple capital structure.
- Per-share amounts in addition to net income per share are reported when there are special sections in the income statement.

KEY TERMS USED IN THIS CHAPTER

change in accounting estimate 564
change in accounting principle 562
complex capital structure 565
cumulative effect of a change in principle 562
deficit 551

discontinued operations **562**
dividends **551**
earnings per share **565**
extraordinary items **559**
fully diluted earnings per share **566**
multiple-step income statement **565**
primary earnings per share **566**
prior period adjustments **556**
retained earnings **551**
retained earnings appropriations **557**
retained earnings statement **555**
simple capital structure **565**
single-step income statement **564**
statement of stockholders' equity **555**
stock dividends **553**
tax allocation within a period **561**

SELF-TEST QUESTIONS FOR REVIEW

(Answers are at the end of this chapter.)

1. Which of the following events decreases a corporation's stockholders' equity?
   (a) A payment of a previously declared cash dividend.
   (b) A declaration of a 6% stock dividend.
   (c) A $100,000 retained earnings appropriation.
   (d) A declaration of a $1.00 cash dividend per share of preferred stock.
2. In 19X3, Corliss, Inc., discovered an arithmetic error had been made in 19X2, causing 19X2's depreciation expense to be overstated. Corliss corrected the error in 19X3 with a journal entry that included a credit to Retained Earnings. This situation illustrates a:
   (a) Prior period adjustment.
   (b) Change in an accounting estimate.
   (c) Change in an accounting principle.
   (d) Restriction on retained earnings.
3. Assume an income statement contains each of the four sections listed below. Which will be the last section in the income statement?
   (a) Extraordinary item.
   (b) Cumulative effect of a change in accounting principle.
   (c) Income from continuing operations.
   (d) Discontinued operations.
4. A corporation will make a dual presentation of earnings per share (primary and fully diluted earnings per share) when it
   (a) Has two classes of stock outstanding (preferred and common stock).
   (b) Uses a multiple-step income statement format.
   (c) Has a capital structure that contains at least one potentially dilutive security (a complex capital structure).
   (d) Has restrictions on the amount of earnings that may be paid out as dividends.
5. Which of the following items will appear in either a single-step or a multiple-step income statement for a merchandising firm?
   (a) Appropriation of retained earnings.
   (b) Gross profit on sales.
   (c) Income before extraordinary item.
   (d) Prior period adjustment.

DEMONSTRATION PROBLEM FOR REVIEW

Information related to the income and retained earnings of Alpha, Inc., for 19X1 is listed below. For simplicity, amounts are limited to three digits. Using these data, prepare a single-step income statement and a retained earnings statement for Alpha, Inc., for 19X1. Assume that all changes in income are subject to a 30% income tax rate. Disregard earnings per share disclosures.

Additional uncollectible accounts expense due to revised estimate of percentage of anticipated uncollectible accounts (considered a selling expense)	$ 20
Cost of goods sold	420
Cash dividends declared	70
Overstatement of 19X0 ending inventory (caused by error)	10
Gain on condemnation of property (considered unusual and infrequent)	40
Gain on disposal of discontinued Beta Division	80
Increase in prior years' reported income before income taxes due to change in depreciation method	$ 20
Loss from labor strike (considered unusual but recurring)	40
Loss from operations of discontinued Beta Division	50
Other operating expenses	230
Retained earnings balance at end of 19X0	454
Sales	980
Selling and administrative expenses (before revised estimate of uncollectible accounts)	170

SOLUTION TO DEMONSTRATION PROBLEM (Selected computations appear as notes to the financial statements.)

Alpha, Inc.
Income Statement
For the Year Ended December 31, 19X1

Sales		$980
Expenses:		
Cost of Goods Sold	$420	
Other Operating Expenses	230	
Selling and Administrative Expenses (Note A)	190	
Loss from Labor Strike	40	
Income Tax Expense (Note B)	30	
Total Expenses		910
Income from Continuing Operations		$ 70
Discontinued Operations:		
Loss from Operations of Discontinued Beta Division (net of $15 reduction of income taxes) (Note C)	($ 35)	
Gain on Disposal of Discontinued Beta Division (net of $24 income taxes) (Note D)	56	21
Income before Extraordinary Item and Cumulative Effect of a Change in Accounting Principle		$ 91
Extraordinary Item:		
Gain on Condemnation of Property (net of $12 income taxes) (Note E)		28
Cumulative Effect on Prior Years of Changing to a Different Depreciation Method (net of $6 income taxes) (Note F)		14
Net Income		$133

Alpha, Inc.
Retained Earnings Statement
For the Year Ended December 31, 19X1

Retained Earnings, January 1, 19X1	$454
Less: Correction of Prior Period Inventory Error (net of $3 reduction of income taxes) (Note G)	7
Retained Earnings Adjusted Balance, January 1, 19X1	$447
Add: Net Income	133
	$580
Less: Cash Dividends Declared	70
Retained Earnings, December 31, 19X1	$510

Notes to financial statements:
(A) $170 + $20 = $190
(B) 30% [$980 − ($420 + $230 + $190 + $40)] = $30
(C) $50 − [0.3($50)] = $35
(D) $80 − [0.3($80)] = $56
(E) $40 − [0.3($40)] = $28
(F) $20 − [0.3($20)] = $14
(G) $10 − [0.3($10)] = $7

QUESTIONS

16–1 What is a stock dividend? How does a common stock dividend paid to common shareholders affect their respective ownership interests?

16–2 Distinguish between the accounting for a small stock dividend and the accounting for a large stock dividend.

16–3 What information is presented in a retained earnings statement? a statement of stockholders' equity?

16–4 Hosket Company discovered this year that a significant portion of its inventory was overlooked during its inventory count at the end of last year. How should the correction of this error be disclosed in the financial statements?

16–5 What is an *appropriation* of retained earnings? Why and by whom are such appropriations made?

16–6 Where do the following accounts (and their balances) appear in the balance sheet?
(a) Dividends Payable—Common Stock
(b) Stock Dividend to Be Issued
(c) Retained Earnings Appropriated for Contingencies

16–7 Define *extraordinary items*. How are extraordinary items shown in the income statement?

16–8 A manufacturing plant of Loren Corporation was destroyed by an earthquake, which is rare in the region where the plant was located. Where should this loss be classified in the income statement?

16–9 A Florida citrus grower incurs substantial frost damage to crops. Frost damage typically is experienced every few years. How should the loss on the crops be shown in the income statement?

16–10 What is meant by *tax allocation within a period*? What is the purpose of this type of tax allocation?

16–11 What is a business *segment*? Why are gains and losses from a discontinued segment reported in a separate section of the income statement?

16–12 This year, Walcott Company switched from the FIFO method of inventory pricing to the weighted average method. Cumulative income before income taxes for previous years would have been $80,000 lower if the weighted average method had been used.

(a) Assuming a 35% income tax rate, how should the effect of this inventory pricing change be shown in the income statement?

(b) If a comparative income statement is presented in the annual report, should Walcott revise last year's income statement using the weighted average method?

16–13 Distinguish between an error and a change in accounting estimate. How is reporting corrections of errors different from reporting changes in accounting estimates?

16–14 What is the difference between a single-step income statement and a multiple-step income statement?

16–15 Which one of the following amounts would appear only in a multiple-step income statement?

Income from continuing operations
Income before extraordinary item
Gross profit on sales
Net income

16–16 Distinguish between corporations with simple capital structures and those with complex capital structures. What does the type of capital structure imply regarding the presentation of earnings per share data?

16–17 In 19XX, Haven Company earned a net income of $121,600. The company, which has a simple capital structure, started the year with 18,000 shares of common stock outstanding and issued an additional 3,000 shares on September 1. What is Haven Company's 19XX earnings per share?

16–18 What assumption underlies the computation of fully diluted earnings per share? What does the difference between the amounts of primary earnings per share and fully diluted earnings per share reveal?

EXERCISES

Cash and stock dividends

16–19 Scallon Corporation has 9,000 shares of $10 par value common stock outstanding and retained earnings of $128,000. The company declares a cash dividend of $1.25 per share and a 5% stock dividend. The market price of the stock at the declaration date is $24 per share.

(a) Give the general journal entries for (1) the declaration of dividends and (2) the payment (or issuance) of the dividends.

(b) Assume that the company declares a 40% stock dividend rather than a 5% stock dividend. Give the general journal entries for (1) the declaration of the stock dividend and (2) the issuance of the stock dividend.

Large stock dividend and stock split

16–20 Key Corporation has 15,000 shares of $20 par value common stock outstanding and retained earnings of $620,000. The company declares a 100% stock dividend. The market price at the declaration date is $28 per share.

(a) Give the general journal entries for (1) the declaration of the dividend and (2) the issuance of the dividend.

(b) Assume that the company splits its stock two shares for one share and reduces the par value from $20 to $10 rather than declaring a 100% stock dividend. How does the accounting for the stock split differ from the accounting for the 100% stock dividend?

Retained earnings appropriation

16–21 In both 19X3 and 19X4, Kurl Construction Company appropriated $70,000 of retained earnings for a future truck crane acquisition. In 19X5, the company acquired the truck crane for $134,000 cash. Prepare general journal entries to record the appropriations of retained earnings in 19X3 and 19X4, the purchase of the truck crane in 19X5, and the disposition of the balance in the appropriated retained earnings account after the purchase.

Stockholders' equity section

16–22 Use the following data to prepare the stockholders' equity section of Devine Corporation's balance sheet. All account balances are normal.

Unappropriated Retained Earnings	$308,000
Paid-in Capital in Excess of Par Value—Common Stock	320,000
Paid-in Capital in Excess of Par Value—Preferred Stock	70,000
Retained Earnings Appropriated—Treasury Stock Purchases	12,000
6% Preferred Stock, $50 Par Value, 7,000 shares outstanding	350,000
Common Stock, $5 Par Value, 80,000 shares issued	400,000
Treasury Stock (Common), 1,000 shares (at cost)	12,000
Retained Earnings Appropriated—Plant Expansion	250,000

Retained earnings statement

16–23 Use the following data to prepare a retained earnings statement for Sandy Corporation for 19X2. Assume a 30% tax rate.

Total retained earnings originally reported at December 31, 19X1, of which $200,000 is appropriated for future plant expansion	$430,000
Cash dividends declared in 19X2	60,000
Net income reported for 19X2	196,000
Additional appropriation of retained earnings in 19X2 for future plant expansion	50,000
Understatement of 19X1 ending inventory discovered late in 19X2 (caused by arithmetic errors)	20,000

Income statement sections

16–24 During the current year, Polk Corporation incurred an extraordinary tornado loss of $250,000 and sold a segment of its business at a gain of $140,000. Until it was sold, the segment had a current period operating loss of $75,000. Also, the company discovered that an error caused last year's ending inventory to be understated by $15,000 (a material amount). The company had $500,000 income from continuing operations for the current year. Prepare the lower part of the income statement, beginning with the $500,000 income from continuing operations. Follow tax allocation procedures, assuming all changes in income are subject to a 40% income tax rate. Disregard earnings per share disclosures.

Accounting changes and prior period adjustment

16–25 For each of the following current year events for Carmel, Inc., (1) identify the type of accounting change or other category of event involved; (2) indicate where each would be reported on the current year's income or retained earnings statement; and (3) illustrate how each would be disclosed including the relevant dollar amounts. Assume all changes in income are subject to a 30% income tax rate.

(a) The company changed from the sum-of-the-years'-digits to the straight-line method of depreciating its equipment. Cumulative income before income taxes for prior years would have been $80,000 higher under the straight-line method.

(b) The company discovered that, because of a new employee's oversight, depreciation of $30,000 on an addition to the plant had been omitted last year. The amount is material.

(c) A patent acquired at a cost of $75,000 five years ago (including the current year) has been amortized under the straight-line method using an estimated useful life of 15 years. In reviewing accounts for the year-end adjustments, the company revised its estimate of the total useful life to 12 years.

Earnings per share

16–26 The Palace Corporation began the year with a simple capital structure consisting of 54,000 shares of common stock outstanding. On April 1, 9,000 additional shares were issued, and another 3,000 shares were issued on August 1. The company had a net income for the year of $403,000.

(a) Compute the earnings per share of common stock.

(b) Assume that the company also had 31,000 shares of 8%, $50 par value cumulative preferred stock outstanding throughout the year. Compute the earnings per share of common stock.

Earnings per share

16–27 During 19X3, Coral Corporation had 50,000 shares of $10 par value common stock and 10,000 shares of 7%, $50 par value convertible preferred stock outstanding. The preferred stock is not a common stock equivalent. Each share of preferred stock may be converted into two shares of common stock. Coral Corporation's 19X3 net income was $224,000.

(a) Compute the primary earnings per share for 19X3.

(b) Compute the fully diluted earnings per share for 19X3.

Earnings per share

16–28 Guthrie, Inc., discloses earnings per share amounts for extraordinary items. Use the following summarized income data for the current year to prepare earnings per share disclosures for the company, assuming that a 40% income tax rate is applicable and that 25,000 shares of common stock were outstanding during the year. The company elects to show the per-share effect of the extraordinary loss.

Sales	$970,000
Total operating expenses (excluding income taxes)	650,000
Extraordinary flood loss	100,000

PROBLEMS

Retained earnings—transactions and statement

16–29 The stockholders' equity of Checker Corporation at January 1, 19X2, appears below:

Common Stock, $20 Par Value, 100,000 shares authorized; 40,000 shares issued and outstanding	$800,000
Paid-in Capital in Excess of Par Value—Common Stock	244,000
Unappropriated Retained Earnings	363,000

During 19X2, the following transactions occurred:

June 7	The board of directors appropriated $125,000 of retained earnings for future land acquisition.
Dec. 10	Declared a cash dividend of $1.30 per share and a 5% stock dividend. Market value of the common stock was $31 per share.
31	Closed the net income of $183,000 from the Income Summary account to Retained Earnings.

REQUIRED

(a) Prepare general journal entries to record the foregoing transactions.

(b) Prepare a retained earnings statement for 19X2.

(c) The cash dividend was paid and the stock dividend was issued on January 17, 19X3. Make the necessary journal entries.

(d) The board of directors dropped its plan to acquire land in the future and on January 25, 19X3, eliminated the appropriation for future land acquisition. Make the necessary journal entry.

Retained earnings—transactions and statement

16–30 The stockholders' equity of Basin Corporation at January 1, 19X4, follows.

6% Preferred Stock, $25 Par Value, 10,000 shares authorized; 8,000 shares issued and outstanding	$ 200,000
Common Stock, $5 Par Value, 200,000 shares authorized; 120,000 shares issued and outstanding	600,000
Paid-in Capital in Excess of Par Value—Common Stock	480,000
Retained Earnings Appropriated for Plant Expansion	360,000
Unappropriated Retained Earnings	410,000
Total Stockholders' Equity	$2,050,000

The following transactions, among others, occurred during 19X4:

Feb. 10 Discovered the bookkeeper overlooked a 19X3 adjusting entry for $4,000 of goodwill amortization. Goodwill amortization is not deductible for tax purposes, so this error has no income tax effect.

June 18 Declared a 6% stock dividend on all outstanding shares of common stock. The market value of the stock was $12 per share.

July 1 Issued the stock dividend declared on June 18.

Sept. 8 The board of directors appropriated an additional $90,000 of retained earnings for plant expansion.

Dec. 20 Declared the annual cash dividend on the preferred stock and a cash dividend of $1.15 per share of common stock, payable on January 20 to stockholders of record on December 28.

Dec. 31 Closed the Income Summary account, with net earnings of $352,000, to Retained Earnings.

REQUIRED

(a) Prepare general journal entries to record the foregoing transactions.
(b) Prepare a retained earnings statement for 19X4.

Retained earnings—transactions and financial statement presentations

16–31 The stockholders' equity of Mauer Corporation at January 1, 19X2, is shown below:

8% Preferred Stock, $60 Par Value, 8,000 shares authorized; 5,000 shares issued and outstanding	$ 300,000
Paid-in Capital in Excess of Par Value—Preferred Stock	45,000
Common Stock, $5 Par Value, 100,000 shares authorized; 36,000 shares issued and outstanding	180,000
Paid-in Capital in Excess of Par Value—Common Stock	288,000
Unappropriated Retained Earnings	387,000
Total Stockholders' Equity	$1,200,000

The following transactions, among others, occurred during 19X2:

Jan. 15 Mauer Corporation carries life insurance on its key officers (with the corporation as beneficiary), and in 19X1 it paid insurance premiums of $8,000 covering 19X1 and 19X2. Today the company discovered that the full $8,000 had been charged to Insurance Expense in 19X1. These premiums are not deductible for tax purposes, so this error has no tax effect.

May 1 Declared a 50% stock dividend on all outstanding shares of common stock. The market value of the stock was $18 per share.

15 Issued the stock dividend declared on May 1.

Sept. 1 Reacquired 4,000 shares of common stock for cash at $14 per share.

2 Appropriated an amount of retained earnings equal to the cost of the treasury shares acquired September 1.

Dec. 5 Declared a 5% stock dividend on all outstanding shares of common stock. The market value of the stock was $16 per share.
15 Issued the stock dividend declared on December 5.
16 Declared the annual cash dividend on the preferred stock and a cash dividend of $1.40 per common share, payable on January 10 to stockholders of record on December 30.
31 Closed the Income Summary account, with net earnings of $204,000, to Retained Earnings.

REQUIRED
(a) Prepare general journal entries to record the foregoing transactions.
(b) Prepare a retained earnings statement for 19X2.
(c) Prepare the stockholders' equity section of the balance sheet at December 31, 19X2.

Stockholders' equity—transactions and statement

16–32 The stockholders' equity section of Munn Corporation at December 31, 19X1, follows:

Common Stock, $10 Par Value, 100,000 shares authorized, 25,000 shares issued, 3,000 shares are in the treasury	$250,000
Paid-in Capital in Excess of Par Value	150,000
Paid-in Capital from Treasury Stock	11,000
Retained Earnings (see Note)	98,000
	$509,000
Less: Treasury Stock (3,000 shares) at Cost	54,000
Total Stockholders' Equity	$455,000

Note: The availability of retained earnings for cash dividends is restricted by $54,000 due to the purchase of treasury stock.

The following transactions affecting stockholders' equity occurred during 19X2:
Jan. 8 Issued 8,000 shares of previously unissued common stock for $20 cash per share.
Mar. 12 Sold all of the treasury shares for $21 cash per share.
June 30 Declared a 6% stock dividend on all outstanding shares of common stock. The market value of the stock was $24 per share.
July 10 Issued the stock dividend declared on June 30.
Oct. 7 Acquired 1,000 shares of common stock for the treasury at $22 cash per share.
Dec. 18 Declared a cash dividend of 75 cents per outstanding common share, payable on January 9 to stockholders of record on December 31.
31 Closed the Income Summary account, with net income of $74,000, to Retained Earnings.

REQUIRED
(a) Prepare general journal entries to record the foregoing transactions.
(b) Prepare a statement of stockholders' equity for 19X2.

Income statement format

16–33 The following information from Sycamore Company's 19X1 operations is available:

Net Income $57,400

Administrative expenses	$ 70,000
Cost of goods sold	512,000
Sales	835,000
Flood loss (considered unusual and infrequent)	28,000
Selling expenses	105,000
Interest expense	8,000

Loss from operations of discontinued segment	$ 80,000
Gain on disposal of discontinued segment	50,000
Income taxes:	
Amount applicable to ordinary operations	42,000
Reduction applicable to flood loss	8,400
Reduction applicable to loss from operations of discontinued segment	24,000
Amount applicable to gain on disposal of discontinued segment	15,000

REQUIRED

(a) Prepare a multiple-step income statement for 19X1.
(b) Prepare a single-step income statement for 19X1.

Earnings per share

16–34 Genoa Corporation began 19XX with 66,000 shares of common stock and 5,000 shares of convertible preferred stock outstanding. On March 1 an additional 5,000 shares of common stock were issued. On August 1, another 2,000 shares of common stock were issued. On November 1, 6,000 shares of common stock were reacquired for the treasury. The preferred stock has a $1.40 per-share dividend rate, and each share may be converted into one share of common. The preferred stock is not a common stock equivalent. Genoa Corporation's 19XX net income is $262,500.

REQUIRED

(a) Compute primary earnings per share for 19XX.
(b) Compute fully diluted earnings per share for 19XX.
(c) If the preferred stock were not convertible, Genoa Corporation would have a simple capital structure. What would be its earnings per share for 19XX?

Earnings per share and multiple-step income statement

16–35 Faircrest Corporation discloses earnings per share amounts for extraordinary items. The following summarized data relate to the company's 19X3 operations:

Sales	$790,000
Cost of goods sold	470,000
Selling expenses	61,000
Administrative expenses	74,000
Loss from earthquake damages (considered unusual and infrequent)	42,000
Loss on sale of equipment	5,000

Shares of common stock:	
Outstanding at January 1, 19X3	25,000 shares
Additional issued at May 1, 19X3	4,000 shares
Additional issued at November 1, 19X3	2,000 shares

REQUIRED

Prepare a multiple-step income statement for Faircrest Corporation for 19X3. Assume a 30% income tax rate. Include earnings per share disclosures for 19X3 at the bottom of the income statement.

ALTERNATE PROBLEMS

Retained earnings—transactions and statement

16–29A The stockholders' equity of Penn Corporation at January 1, 19X8, appears below:

Common Stock, $10 Par Value, 80,000 shares authorized; 50,000 shares issued and outstanding	$500,000
Paid-in Capital in Excess of Par Value—Common Stock	250,000
Unappropriated Retained Earnings	295,000

During 19X8, the following transactions occurred:

May 12 Fearing a strike early next year, the board of directors appropriated $75,000 of retained earnings for contingencies.

Dec. 5 Declared a cash dividend of 80 cents per share and a 7% stock dividend. Market value of the common stock was $18 per share on this date.

31 Closed the net income of $149,000 from the Income Summary account to Retained Earnings.

REQUIRED

(a) Prepare general journal entries to record the foregoing transactions.
(b) Prepare a retained earnings statement for 19X8.
(c) The cash dividend was paid and the stock dividend was issued on January 20 of the following year. Make the necessary journal entries.
(d) The expected employee strike did not materialize, and the board of directors on January 22 eliminated the appropriation for contingencies. Make the necessary journal entry.

Retained earnings—transactions and statement

16–30A The stockholders' equity of Avenue Corporation at January 1, 19X5, appears below:

6% Preferred Stock, $50 Par Value, 6,000 shares authorized, issued, and outstanding	$ 300,000
Common Stock, $30 Par Value, 40,000 shares authorized; 25,000 shares issued and outstanding	750,000
Paid-in Capital in Excess of Par Value—Common Stock	185,000
Retained Earnings Appropriated for Future Litigation	100,000
Unappropriated Retained Earnings	380,000
Total Stockholders' Equity	$1,715,000

The following transactions, among others, occurred during 19X5:

Jan. 22 Discovered the bookkeeper made an arithmetic error in 19X4 causing a $14,000 overstatement of goodwill amortization for that year. Goodwill amortization is not deductible for tax purposes, so this error has no income tax effect.

Aug. 10 Declared a 4% stock dividend on all outstanding shares of common stock. The market value of the stock was $43 per share.

26 The board of directors appropriated an additional $50,000 of retained earnings for possible future litigation.

Sept. 5 Issued the stock dividend declared on August 10.

Dec. 5 Declared the annual cash dividend on the preferred stock and a cash dividend of $2.20 per share of common stock, payable on January 25 to stockholders of record on December 27.

30 Appropriated $40,000 of retained earnings for general contingencies.

31 Closed the Income Summary account, with net earnings of $194,000, to Retained Earnings.

REQUIRED

(a) Prepare general journal entries to record the foregoing transactions.
(b) Prepare a retained earnings statement for 19X5.

Retained earnings—transactions and financial statement presentations

16–31A The stockholders' equity of Dover Corporation at January 1, 19X4, is shown below:

5% Preferred Stock, $100 Par Value, 10,000 shares authorized; 4,000 shares issued and outstanding	$ 400,000
Paid-in Capital in Excess of Par Value—Preferred Stock	40,000
Common Stock, $5 Par Value, 200,000 shares authorized; 80,000 shares issued and outstanding	400,000
Paid-in Capital in Excess of Par Value—Common Stock	320,000
Unappropriated Retained Earnings	521,000
Total Stockholders' Equity	$1,681,000

The following transactions, among others, occurred during 19X4:

Feb. 12 Dover Corporation carries life insurance on its key officers (with the corporation as beneficiary), and in 19X3 it paid insurance premiums of $10,800 covering the three-year period 19X3–19X5. Today the company discovered that none of the $10,800 had been charged to Insurance Expense in 19X3 (it all remained in Prepaid Insurance). These premiums are not deductible for tax purposes, so this error has no tax effect.

Apr. 1 Declared a 100% stock dividend on all outstanding shares of common stock. The market value of the stock was $16 per share.

15 Issued the stock dividend declared on April 1.

Aug. 11 Reacquired 6,000 shares of common stock for cash at $10 per share.

12 Appropriated an amount of retained earnings equal to the cost of the treasury shares acquired August 11.

Dec. 7 Declared a 3% stock dividend on all outstanding shares of common stock. The market value of the stock was $11 per share.

17 Issued the stock dividend declared on December 7.

20 Declared the annual cash dividend on the preferred stock and a cash dividend of $1.00 per common share, payable on January 15 to stockholders of record on December 31.

31 Closed the Income Summary account, with net earnings of $286,000, to Retained Earnings.

REQUIRED

(a) Prepare general journal entries to record the foregoing transactions.

(b) Prepare a retained earnings statement for 19X4.

(c) Prepare the stockholders' equity section of the balance sheet at December 31, 19X4.

Income statement and dividend relationships

16–32A Savard Company presented the following earnings per share data:

Earnings per Share of Common Stock:	
Income before Extraordinary Item	$5.46
Extraordinary Gain (net of tax)	1.04
Net Income	$6.50

The company, which has a simple capital structure, began the year with 38,000 shares of $10 par value common stock and 6,500 shares of 5%, $40 par value preferred stock outstanding. On September 1, an additional 6,000 shares of common stock were issued. Cash dividends were distributed to both preferred and common stockholders.

REQUIRED
(a) What is the annual preferred stock dividend requirement?
(b) What was the net income for the current year for Savard Company?
(c) What was the amount of the extraordinary gain, net of the tax effect? What was the amount of the gain before the tax effect, assuming a 35% tax rate on the gain?
(d) If the tax rate on ordinary income is 35%, what amount of income tax expense was reported in the income before extraordinary item section of the income statement?

Single-step income statement and retained earnings statement

16–33A The information listed below is related to Galley Corporation's 19X3 income and retained earnings.

Administrative expenses	$ 47,000
Appropriation of retained earnings in 19X3 for plant expansion	150,000
Cash dividends declared	83,000
Cost of goods sold	488,000
Understatement of 19X2 depreciation expense (caused by an error)	20,000
Increase in prior years' income before income taxes due to change in inventory pricing method (from weighted average to FIFO)	50,000
Loss from uninsured portion of brushfire damages (considered unusual but recurring)	32,000
Loss from expropriation of property by foreign government (considered unusual and infrequent)	90,000
Retained earnings appropriated for plant expansion (balance at December 31, 19X2)	300,000
Unappropriated retained earnings (balance at December 31, 19X2)	495,000
Sales	946,000
Selling expenses	59,000
Income taxes:	
Amount applicable to ordinary operations	112,000
Reduction applicable to loss from expropriation of property	31,500
Amount applicable to increase in prior years' income before income taxes due to change in inventory pricing method	17,500
Reduction applicable to 19X2 depreciation expense error	7,000

REQUIRED
(a) Prepare a single-step income statement for Galley Corporation for 19X3.
(b) Prepare a retained earnings statement for Galley Corporation for 19X3.

Earnings per share

16–34A Midland Corporation began the year 19XX with 18,000 shares of common stock and 2,500 shares of convertible preferred stock outstanding. On May 1, an additional 12,000 shares of common stock were issued. On July 1, 6,000 shares of common stock were reacquired for the treasury. On September 1, the 6,000 treasury shares of common stock were reissued. The preferred stock has a $2.40 per-share dividend rate, and each share may be converted into two shares of common. The preferred stock is not a common stock equivalent. Midland Corporation's 19XX net income is $102,000.

REQUIRED
(a) Compute primary earnings per share for 19XX.
(b) Compute fully diluted earnings per share for 19XX.
(c) If the preferred stock were not convertible, Midland Corporation would have a simple capital structure. What would be its earnings per share for 19XX?

Earnings per share and multiple-step income statement

16–35A Hilltop Corporation discloses earnings per share amounts for extraordinary items. The following summarized data are related to the company's 19X2 operations:

Sales	$1,970,000
Cost of goods sold	1,080,000
Selling expenses	160,000
Administrative expenses	115,000
Gain from expropriation of property by foreign government (negotiated settlement; considered unusual and infrequent)	160,000
Loss from plant strike	75,000
Shares of common stock:	
Outstanding at January 1, 19X2	66,000 shares
Additional issued at April 1, 19X2	17,000 shares
Additional issued at August 1, 19X2	3,000 shares

REQUIRED

Prepare a multiple-step income statement for Hilltop Corporation for 19X2. Assume a 40% income tax rate. Include earnings per share disclosures for 19X2 at the bottom of the income statement.

BUSINESS DECISION PROBLEM

The stockholders' equity section of Silver Corporation's comparative balance sheet at the end of 19X7 and 19X8—part of the financial data just reviewed at a stockholders' meeting—is presented below:

	December 31, 19X8	December 31, 19X7
Common Stock, $10 Par Value, 600,000 shares authorized; issued at December 31, 19X8, 345,000 shares; 19X7, 300,000 shares	$3,450,000	$3,000,000
Paid-in Capital in Excess of Par Value	3,930,000	3,300,000
Retained Earnings:		
Appropriated for Plant Expansion	1,000,000	800,000
Unappropriated	866,000	1,660,000
Total Stockholders' Equity	$9,246,000	$8,760,000

The following items were also disclosed at the stockholders' meeting: net income for 19X8 was $900,000; a 15% stock dividend was issued December 14, 19X8; when the stock dividend was declared, the market value was $24 per share; the market value per share at December 31, 19X8, was $22; management plans to borrow $250,000 to help finance a new plant addition, which is expected to cost a total of $1,150,000; and the customary $1.38 per share cash dividend had been revised to $1.20 when declared and issued the last week of December, 19X8.

As part of its investor relations program, during the stockholders' meeting management asked stockholders to write any questions they might have concerning the firm's operations or finances. As assistant controller, you are given the stockholders' questions.

REQUIRED

Prepare brief but reasonably complete answers to the following questions:

(a) What did Silver do with the cash proceeds from the stock dividend issued in December?
(b) What was my book value per share at the end of 19X7 and 19X8?

(c) I owned 6,000 shares of Silver in 19X7 and have not sold any shares. How much more or less of the corporation do I own at December 31, 19X8, and what happened to the market value of my interest in the company?
(d) I heard someone say that stock dividends don't give me anything I didn't already have. Why did you issue one? Are you trying to fool us?
(e) Instead of a stock dividend, why didn't you declare a cash dividend and let us buy the new shares that were issued?
(f) Why are you cutting back on the dividends I receive?
(g) If you have $1,000,000 put aside for the new plant addition, which will cost $1,150,000, why are you borrowing $250,000 instead of just the $150,000 needed?

ANSWERS TO SELF-TEST QUESTIONS

1. (d) **2.** (a) **3.** (b) **4.** (c) **5.** (c)

17

LONG-TERM LIABILITIES AND BOND INVESTMENTS

CHAPTER OBJECTIVES

1. Describe mortgages and various kinds of bonds (pp. 585–87).
2. Discuss the relationship of bond prices to interest rates, and illustrate accounting for bond issuance, interest, and amortization (pp. 587–96).
3. Illustrate the classification of bonds payable, premium, and discount on the balance sheet (pp. 592–93).
4. Illustrate the retirement and conversion of bonds and the use of sinking funds (pp. 596–99).
5. Describe and illustrate accounting for long-term bond investments (pp. 599–601).
6. Describe the basic ideas of pension accounting (p. 601).
7. Describe and illustrate deferred income taxes (pp. 602–605).

In investing money the amount of interest you want should depend on whether you want to eat well or sleep well.

J. K. MORLEY

Some of the most frequently encountered or significant long-term liabilities of business firms are mortgage notes payable, bonds payable, employee pension liability, deferred income taxes payable, and capital lease liabilities. We discuss the accounting treatment of the first four of these long-term liabilities in this chapter; accounting for capital leases, a direct method of financing plant and equipment, was discussed in Chapter 11. Because accounting for long-term bond investments is similar to that for bonds payable, this chapter also includes a discussion of such investments.

MORTGAGE NOTES AND BONDS PAYABLE

At various times in the course of business operations, particularly during phases of expansion, firms must secure additional long-term funds. Often they choose long-term borrowing, rather than issue additional capital stock, to avoid diluting the ownership interests or because the borrowed funds may have a lower net cost to current stockholders.[1] The interest cost of long-term debt has identifiable limits; that is, creditors do not receive an increased return on investment if profits grow. Furthermore, the borrowing firm may deduct interest payments on debt for tax purposes, but it may not deduct dividend distributions to owners.

Not all aspects of long-term debt are necessarily desirable for the borrowing company. In contrast with dividends on common stock, interest on debt represents a fixed periodic expenditure that the firm is contractually obligated to make. Fixed interest charges can be a financial burden when operations do not develop as favorably as expected. Because long-term debt normally has a definite maturity date, the firm must also provide for repayment of the obligation. Finally, a long-term borrowing agreement may restrict the company's financial policies while the debt is outstanding.

Mortgage Notes Payable

A firm may borrow long-term funds by issuing a **mortgage note,** which is actually two related agreements. The note is an agreement to repay the principal and to pay specified interest amounts on certain dates; the mortgage is a legal agreement pledging certain property of the borrower as security for repayment of the note. Usually, a mortgage note is used when all the funds are borrowed from one lender. Sometimes a firm finds it more strategic or even necessary to borrow large amounts of funds from several lenders. In these latter cases, issuing bonds is more practical.

Bonds Payable

Bonds are, in essence, notes payable. Their special characteristics are dictated by the specific objectives of a given borrowing situation. Because a complete

[1]The concept of investment leverage is explained in Chapter 20.

discussion of the wide variety of bonds is beyond the scope of this text, only the more significant characteristics of bonds are described below.

Bonds are used most often when a borrower receives funds from a large number of lenders contributing various amounts. Consequently, bonds are usually drawn up to be negotiable. Because many parties are involved, the borrower should select a **trustee**—often a large bank—to represent the group of bondholders. As a third party to the transaction, the trustee may take security title to any pledged property and is likely to initiate any action necessitated by failure to meet the terms of the bond agreement.

If the borrower fails to meet the provisions of the bond agreement, the bondholders, represented by the trustee, may institute a variety of actions. Examples of less significant actions are enforcing agreements restricting dividend payments, prescribing minimum cash balances or financial operating ratios, placing restrictions on additional financing, and electing new members to the board of directors. The ultimate action, of course, is to bring foreclosure proceedings. The trustee may also maintain a record of current bond owners and may act as disbursing agent for the interest and principal payments.

CHARACTERISTICS OF BONDS Bond agreements may be formulated to capitalize on certain lending situations, appeal to special investor groups, or provide special repayment patterns. We now list some common bond characteristics.

Secured bonds pledge some specific property as security for meeting the terms of the bond agreement. The specific title of the bonds may indicate the type of property pledged—for example, real estate mortgage bonds (land or buildings), chattel mortgage bonds (machinery or equipment), and collateral trust bonds (negotiable securities). If property is subject to two or more mortgages, the relative priority of each mortgage is denoted by its identification as a "first," "second," or even "third" mortgage.

Bonds that have no specific property pledged as security for their repayment are **debenture bonds.** Holders of such bonds rely on the borrower's general credit reputation. Because the lender's risk is usually greater than with secured bonds, the sale of unsecured bonds may require offering a higher interest rate.

The maturity dates of **serial bonds** are staggered over a series of years. For example, a serial bond issue of $15 million may provide for $1 million of the bonds to mature each year for 15 years. An advantage of serial bonds is that lenders can choose bonds with maturity dates that correspond with their desired length of investment.

The issuing corporation (or its trustee) maintains a record of the owners of **registered bonds.** At appropriate times, interest payments are mailed to the registered owners. Interest on **coupon bonds** is paid in a different manner. A coupon for interest payable to the bearer is attached to the bond for each interest period. Whenever interest is due, the bondholder detaches a coupon and deposits it with his or her bank for collection.

Callable bonds allow the borrower to *call in* (retire) the bonds and pay them off after a stated date. Usually, an extra amount or premium must be paid to the holders of the called bonds. Callable bonds offer borrowers an additional flexibility that may be significant if funds become available at interest rates substantially lower than those being paid on the bonds. To some degree, borrowers can in effect "call" any of their bonds by buying them in the open market.

Convertible bonds grant the holder the right to convert them to capital stock at some specific exchange ratio. This provision gives an investor the security of a creditor during a certain stage of a firm's life, with the option of becoming a stockholder if the firm becomes sufficiently profitable.

BOND PRICES Most bonds are sold in units of $1,000 face (maturity) value, and the market price is expressed as a percentage of face value. For example, a $1,000 face value bond quoted at 98 sells for $980, and a bond quoted at 103 sells for $1,030. Generally, bond prices fluctuate in response to changes in market interest rates, which are determined by government monetary policies (managing the demand and supply of money) and economic expectations. Obviously, they are also affected by the outlook for the issuing firm. Market prices are quoted in the financial news at the nearest $\frac{1}{8}$% of the true market price.

RECORDING BOND ISSUES Firms often authorize more bonds than they actually anticipate issuing at one time. Authorization of bonds usually includes (1) formal action by the board of directors, (2) application to and approval of some government agency, (3) retention of a trustee, and (4) all the attendant negotiations and legalities. For secured bonds, the total value of the bonds authorized is typically some fraction of the value of the property pledged. The difference between the dollar amount of the bonds issued and the value of the pledged property represents a margin of safety to bondholders.

Because individual bond issues may have widely varying characteristics, separate accounts with reasonably descriptive titles should be used for each bond issue. When the bonds are authorized, an account is opened in the general ledger, and a memorandum entry may be made in the account stating the total amount of bonds authorized.

The *face value* of a bond is the amount of principal to be repaid at the maturity date. Interest on bonds is usually paid semiannually, with the payments six months apart (such as January 1 and July 1). The annual rate of interest—also called the *coupon* or *nominal* rate of interest—payable on a bond is stated in the bond agreement. The amount of interest paid semiannually on such bonds is the face value multiplied by one-half the nominal rate of interest. If financial statements are prepared between interest payment dates, the periodic interest expense and the related liability for interest payable are accrued to the date of the statements.

To provide a simple illustration, we use informal account titles and an unrealistically short bond life. Assume that on January 1, Reid, Inc., issues at face value ten $10,000, 10% bonds that mature in four years with interest paid on June 30 and December 31. The following entry records the bond issue:

Jan. 1	Cash	100,000	
	Bonds Payable		100,000
	To record issuance of bonds.		

Interest of $5,000 ($100,000 $\times$ 0.10 $\times$ $\frac{6}{12}$) will be paid on each of the eight payment dates (four years, semiannual payments). For example, the entry on June 30, the first interest payment date, is

June 30	Bond Interest Expense	5,000	
	Cash		5,000
	To record payment of semiannual interest on bonds payable.		

When the bonds mature, Reid, Inc., records their retirement in the following manner:

(final year)			
Dec. 31	Bonds Payable	100,000	
	Cash		100,000
	To record retirement of bonds.		

BOND PRICES AND INTEREST RATES In our illustration, we assume that the Reid, Inc., bonds are issued at par or face value. Often, the issue price differs from the face value because the market rate of interest for the bonds differs from the **nominal** or **contract** rate on the bond certificate. The nominal rate dictates the amount of interest paid each period, whereas the **market** rate—sometimes called the **effective** rate—is the rate of return investors expect on their investment. Market rates of interest fluctuate constantly.

When the market rate of interest on the bonds exceeds the nominal rate, investors expect the bonds to sell at a *discount* (Face Value − Price). When the market rate falls below the nominal rate, investors expect to pay a *premium* (Price − Face Value).

Since bonds are usually printed and sold at different times, the two interest rates often differ. Also, a firm may desire a nominal rate expressed in even percents or in easily recognized fractions of a percent (that is, 10% or $9\frac{1}{2}$%), whereas the market rate for a particular bond issue may be expressed in a more complex fraction or decimal amount.

Bonds issued at a discount If the nominal rate of interest on the bonds issued is less than the current market rate of interest for the type and quality of the bonds, they can be sold only at a price less than their face value. In such cases, investors "discount" the bonds to earn the amount of interest reflected in the current money market. For example, assume that Reid, Inc.'s $100,000 issue of 10%, four-year bonds are sold on January 1 at 98—98% of their face value—because the applicable market rate exceeds the 10% nominal rate. The following entry records the issue of these bonds:

Jan. 1	Cash	98,000	
	Bond Discount	2,000	
	Bonds Payable		100,000
	To record issuance of bonds at 98.		

The $2,000 discount is not an immediate loss or expense to Reid, Inc. Rather, it represents an adjustment of interest expense over the life of the bonds. We illustrate this by comparing the funds Reid, Inc., receives with the funds it must pay to the bondholders. Regardless of their selling price, the bonds are an agreement to pay $140,000 to the bondholders ($100,000 principal plus eight semiannual interest payments of $5,000 each).

Total funds paid to bondholders	$140,000
Total funds received from bond sale	98,000
Difference equals total interest paid	$ 42,000
Average expense per year ($42,000/4)	$ 10,500

Although Reid, Inc., makes only two $5,000 interest payments—a total of $10,000—each year, its full annual interest expense on the bonds exceeds that amount. To reflect the larger periodic interest expense, the bond discount is *amortized*. Amortization of bond discount means that periodically an amount is transferred from bond discount to interest expense.

Basically, there are two methods of amortization—the straight-line method and the effective interest method. Under the *straight-line method*, equal amounts are transferred from bond discount to interest expense for equal periods of time. For Reid, Inc., this amount is $250 every six months ($2,000 total bond discount ÷ 8 semiannual interest periods). Some companies may amortize the discount annually rather than semiannually; the annual amortization for Reid, Inc., is $500. The more complex *effective interest method* reflects a constant rate of interest over the life of the bonds. The effective interest method is discussed later in this chapter.

Assuming the straight-line method of amortization, the journal entries each year to record interest expense for Reid, Inc., are as follows. (We assume that the bond sale is already recorded as illustrated above and that the bonds were issued on the day they are dated.)

June 30	Bond Interest Expense	5,000	
	Cash		5,000
	To record first semiannual interest payment.		
30	Bond Interest Expense	250	
	Bond Discount		250
	To record semiannual amortization of bond discount.		
Dec. 31	Bond Interest Expense	5,000	
	Cash		5,000
	To record second semiannual interest payment.		
31	Bond Interest Expense	250	
	Bond Discount		250
	To record semiannual amortization of bond discount.		

These entries result in four debits to the Bond Interest Expense account each year, a total of $10,500 annual interest expense. Amortizing the bond discount over the four-year life of the bonds at $250 every six months leaves a zero balance in the Bond Discount account at the maturity date of the bonds. The retirement of the bonds is then recorded by debiting Bonds Payable and crediting Cash for $100,000, the amount of their face value.

Bonds issued at a premium If the market rate of interest had been below the 10% offered by Reid, Inc.'s bonds, investors would have been willing to pay a premium for them. Like a bond discount, a bond premium is considered an adjustment of interest expense over the life of the bonds. We just saw that bond discount increases interest expense; now we see that bond premium reduces interest expense. The following entries illustrate the sale of Reid, Inc., bonds at 104 (104% of face value), the payments of interest, the amortization of bond premium, and the retirement of the bonds at maturity:

Date	Account	Debit	Credit
Jan. 1	Cash	104,000	
	Bonds Payable		100,000
	Bond Premium		4,000
	To record sale of bonds at a premium.		
June 30	Bond Interest Expense	5,000	
	Cash		5,000
	To record first semiannual interest payment.		
	Bond Premium	500	
	Bond Interest Expense		500
	To record semiannual amortization of bond premium.		
Dec. 31	Bond Interest Expense	5,000	
	Cash		5,000
	To record second semiannual interest payment.		
31	Bond Premium	500	
	Bond Interest Expense		500
	To record semiannual amortization of bond premium.		
(final year) Dec. 31	Bonds Payable	100,000	
	Cash		100,000
	To retire bonds at maturity.		

The eight semiannual $500 debit entries to the Bond Premium account leave it with a zero balance when the bonds mature. We can verify the $9,000 total annual interest expense reflected by the above entries as follows:

Total funds paid to bondholders	$140,000
Total funds received from bondholders	104,000
Difference equals total interest paid	$ 36,000
Average interest expense per year ($36,000/4)	$ 9,000

The related interest expense account would have a balance of $9,000, shown in the following T account:

Bond Interest Expense

First semiannual interest payment	5,000	First semiannual amortization of bond premium	500
Second semiannual interest payment	5,000	Second semiannual amortization of bond premium	500

Year-end or interim adjustments When a periodic interest payment date does not correspond with year-end, adjustment of the general ledger accounts should include an entry reflecting the amount of interest expense incurred but not paid and an entry reflecting a pro-rata amortization of bond discount or bond premium for the portion of the year involved. Similar adjustments are appropriate when interim financial statements are prepared and the interim date does not correspond with an interest payment date.

Assume the bonds issued by Reid, Inc., at 98 were dated and issued April 1 and had interest payment dates on April 1 and October 1. At December 31 of each year, the following entries would be made:

Dec. 31	Bond Interest Expense	2,500	
	Bond Interest Payable		2,500
	To accrue interest expense for three months ($100,000 × 0.10 × $\frac{3}{12}$).		
31	Bond Interest Expense	125	
	Bond Discount		125
	To amortize bond discount for three months ($500 annual amortization/4).		

If the bonds were issued at a premium rather than at a discount, an entry would amortize the bond premium for three months. The Bond Interest Payable account is classified as a current liability in the balance sheet.

Issuance between interest dates Not all bonds are sold on the exact day on which their interest begins to accumulate (the date on the bond certificates). For example, issuance may be delayed in anticipation of a more favorable bond market. Investors who buy bonds after the interest begins to accrue are expected to "buy" the accrued interest. Such bonds are said to be sold at some price "plus accrued interest." To illustrate, let us assume that Reid, Inc., sold its $100,000, 10%, four-year bonds at 104 on April 1 instead of on January 1, the date on the bond certificates. The entry would be

Apr. 1	Cash	106,500	
	Bonds Payable		100,000
	Bond Premium		4,000
	Bond Interest Payable		2,500
	To record bond issuance at 104 plus three months' accrued interest.		

The interest accrued on the bonds on April 1 is $2,500 ($100,000 × 0.10 × $\frac{3}{12}$). On the first interest payment date, June 30, Reid, Inc., would make the following entry:

June 30	Bond Interest Payable	2,500	
	Bond Interest Expense	2,500	
	Cash		5,000
	To record payment of semiannual interest on bonds payable.		

This entry records interest expense of $2,500, the appropriate amount for the three months the bonds have been outstanding. The other $2,500 represents the return of the accrued interest collected from the bond purchasers on April 1.

In this situation, the $4,000 bond premium would be amortized over the period the bonds are outstanding, or 45 months. Therefore, on June 30, the amount of the premium to be amortized is $266.67 [($4,000/45) × 3 months, rounded]. The entry would be

June 30	Bond Premium	266.67	
	Bond Interest Expense		266.67
	To amortize bond premium for three months [($4,000/45) × 3].		

Thus, the bond interest expense for the three months ended June 30 consists of the $2,500 net interest paid, less the $266.67 amortization of premium, or $2,233.33.

A similar treatment would be used if the bonds had been sold at a discount. In other words, the amortization period for premium or discount extends from the date of sale to the maturity date of the bonds.

BONDS PAYABLE ON THE BALANCE SHEET In this section, we use the data relating to Reid, Inc., bonds with interest payment dates of June 30 and December 31 and straight-line amortization. Exhibit 17–1 shows that regardless of whether bond premium or bond discount is involved, the book value of bonds progresses toward and equals their face value at the time of maturity.

Assume that Reid, Inc., issued bonds on January 1, 19X1, corresponding to each of the examples above. At the end of the second year, the firm's trial balance would include the following accounts:

	Debit	Credit
Bond Discount, Second Mortgage Series	$1,000	
Bonds Payable, 10%, 19X4, First Mortgage Series		$100,000
Bonds Payable, 10%, 19X4, Second Mortgage Series		100,000
Bond Premium, First Mortgage Series		2,000

EXHIBIT 17–1

AMORTIZATION SCHEDULE

	Reid, Inc., Bonds Sold at 104 (Premium) (Straight-line Amortization)			Reid, Inc., Bonds Sold at 98 (Discount) (Straight-line Amortization)		
	Balances			Balances		
At Year-end	Bonds Payable (Credit)	Bond Premium (Credit)	Book Value	Bonds Payable (Credit)	Bond Discount (Debit)	Book Value
At issue	$100,000	$4,000	$104,000	$100,000	$2,000	$ 98,000
19X1	100,000	3,000	103,000	100,000	1,500	98,500
19X2	100,000	2,000	102,000	100,000	1,000	99,000
19X3	100,000	1,000	101,000	100,000	500	99,500
19X4	100,000	0	100,000	100,000	0	100,000

The Bond Premium and Bond Discount accounts are classified properly as an addition to and as a deduction from, respectively, the face value of the bonds in the balance sheet, as follows:

Long-term Liabilities:		
Bonds Payable, 10%, 19X4, First Mortgage Series	$100,000	
Add: Unamortized Premium	2,000	$102,000
Bonds Payable, 10%, 19X4, Second Mortgage Series	$100,000	
Less: Unamortized Discount	1,000	99,000

Bonds payable maturing within the next year should be classified as a current liability. An exception to this guideline arises when a bond sinking fund, a noncurrent asset, is used to retire the bonds. In that case, because a current asset is not utilized to retire the bonds, the bonds payable may be classified as long-term liabilities.

EFFECTIVE INTEREST METHOD OF AMORTIZATION Many business firms use the straight-line method of amortizing bond discount and premium because of its simplicity. This method recognizes equal amounts of interest expense each year. However, because the **book value** (**carrying value**) of the bonds changes each year (see Exhibit 17–1), the interest, expressed as a percentage of the book value, changes over the life of the bonds. Theoretically, this percentage should be constant; otherwise, the firm's borrowing rate appears to change each year. The **effective interest method** of amortization corrects this deficiency. With this method, a constant percentage of the book value of the bonds is recognized as interest expense each year, resulting in unequal recorded amounts of interest expense. In *APB Opinion No. 21*, the Accounting Principles Board recommends the use of the effective interest method whenever the two methods yield materially different results.

To obtain a period's interest expense under the effective interest method, we multiply the bonds' book value at the beginning of each period by the effective interest rate. The difference between this amount and the amount of interest paid (Nominal Interest Rate × Face Value of Bonds) is the amount of discount or premium amortized. When using the effective interest method of amortization, accountants often prepare an amortization schedule similar to Exhibit 17–2, explained in the following example.

Bonds issued at a discount Assume that on April 1, 19X1, a firm issues four-year bonds of $100,000 face value with an 8% annual interest rate and interest dates of April 1 and October 1. Also assume that the bonds are dated April 1, 19X1, so that there is no accrued interest at the time of sale, and that the maturity date is four years from the date of sale. The selling price is $93,552, which provides an effective interest rate of 10%.[2] Exhibit 17–2 gives an amortization schedule for the life of the bonds, with amounts rounded to the nearest dollar.

The schedule shows six-month interest periods; therefore, the interest rates shown in columns A and B are one-half the annual rates. Column A lists the constant amounts of interest paid each six months, that is, the nominal interest rate times face value (4% × $100,000). The amounts in column B are obtained

[2]See Appendix B at the end of this chapter (pp. 620–31) for a discussion of effective interest rates and the determination of issue prices.

EXHIBIT 17–2

BONDS SOLD AT A DISCOUNT:
PERIODIC INTEREST EXPENSE, AMORTIZATION,
AND BOOK VALUE OF BONDS

Year	Interest Period	(A) Interest Paid (4% of face value)	(B) Interest Expense (5% of bond book value)	(C) Periodic Amortization (B – A)	(D) Balance of Unamortized Discount (D – C)	(E) Book Value of Bonds, End of Period ($100,000 – D)
(at issue)					$6,448	$ 93,552
1	1	$4,000	$4,678	$678	5,770	94,230
	2	4,000	4,712	712	5,058	94,942
2	3	4,000	4,747	747	4,311	95,689
	4	4,000	4,784	784	3,527	96,473
3	5	4,000	4,824	824	2,703	97,297
	6	4,000	4,865	865	1,838	98,162
4	7	4,000	4,908	908	930	99,070
	8	4,000	4,930*	930	0	100,000

*Adjusted for cumulative rounding error of $24.

by multiplying the book value at the beginning of each period (column E) by the 5% effective interest rate. For example, the $4,678 interest expense for the first period is 5% of $93,552; for the second period, it is 5% of $94,230, or $4,712, and so on. Note that the amount changes each period. For discounted bonds, the amount increases each period because the book value increases over the life of the bonds until it reaches face value at the maturity date. The amount of discount amortization for each period, given in column C, is the difference between the corresponding amounts in columns A and B. Column D lists the amount of unamortized discount at the end of each period.

The amounts recorded for the issuance of the bonds and each interest payment can be read directly from the amortization schedule. The following entry records the issuance:

Apr. 1	Cash	93,552	
	Bond Discount	6,448	
	Bonds Payable		100,000
	To record issuance of bonds.		

The following entry records interest expense and discount amortization on October 1, 19X1:

Oct. 1	Bond Interest Expense	4,678	
	Bond Discount		678
	Cash		4,000
	To record semiannual interest expense and discount amortization.		

Bonds issued at a premium Suppose that the bonds in our illustration carried an 8% nominal interest rate but that the effective interest rate was 6%. These bonds would be issued at $106,980 (for computations, see Appendix B). The amortization schedule for the bond issue is given in Exhibit 17–3. The nominal interest rate of 4% in column A and the effective interest rate of 3% in column B are one-half the annual rates for the bonds, because the calculations are for six-month periods. The issuance of the bonds is recorded as follows:

Apr. 1	Cash	106,980	
	Bonds Payable		100,000
	Bond Premium		6,980
	To record issuance of bonds.		

The entry to record interest expense and premium amortization on October 1, 19X1, is

Oct. 1	Bond Interest Expense	3,209	
	Bond Premium	791	
	Cash		4,000
	To record semiannual interest expense and premium amortization.		

Year-end adjusting entries We record interest and amortization of the discount or premium on the bonds in our two examples on April 1 and October 1. Therefore,

EXHIBIT 17–3

BONDS SOLD AT A PREMIUM:
PERIODIC INTEREST EXPENSE, AMORTIZATION,
AND BOOK VALUE OF BONDS

Year	Interest Period	(A) Interest Paid (4% of face value)	(B) Interest Expense (3% of bond book value)	(C) Periodic Amortization (A – B)	(D) Balance of Unamortized Premium (D – C)	(E) Book Value of Bonds, End of Period ($100,000 + D)
(at issue)					$6,980	$106,980
1	1	$4,000	$3,209	$791	6,189	106,189
	2	4,000	3,186	814	5,375	105,375
2	3	4,000	3,161	839	4,536	104,536
	4	4,000	3,136	864	3,672	103,672
3	5	4,000	3,110	890	2,782	102,782
	6	4,000	3,083	917	1,865	101,865
4	7	4,000	3,056	944	921	100,921
	8	4,000	3,079*	921	0	100,000

*Adjusted for cumulative rounding error of $51.

at December 31, adjustments are needed to accrue interest and amortize the discount or premium for three months.

The amounts can be computed from those shown for the second interest period in the amortization schedules. For our earlier example (bonds issued at a discount), one-half of the amount shown for the second interest period in Exhibit 17–2, column A, [($4,000/2) = $2,000] is the interest payable. Similarly, from column B, [($4,712/2) = $2,356] is the interest expense, and from column C, [($712/2) = $356] is the discount amortization. The year-end adjusting entry is

Dec. 31	Bond Interest Expense	2,356	
	Bond Discount		356
	Bond Interest Payable		2,000
	To accrue interest for three months and amortize one-half of the discount for the interest period.		

For our second example (bonds issued at a premium), we follow the same procedure, using the second interest period in Exhibit 17–3. Again we use one half of the amounts shown to derive the amounts for our year-end adjusting entry:

Dec. 31	Bond Interest Expense	1,593	
	Bond Premium	407	
	Bond Interest Payable		2,000
	To accrue interest for three months and amortize one-half of the premium for the interest period.		

Retirement of Bonds before Maturity

Bonds are usually retired at their maturity dates with an entry debiting Bonds Payable and crediting Cash for the amount of the face value of the bonds. However, bonds may be retired before maturity—for example, to take advantage of more attractive financing terms.

In accounting for the retirement of bonds before maturity, the following factors should be considered:

1. Amortization of any related premium or discount as of the retirement date.
2. Removal of both the bond liability account and any related Bond Premium or Bond Discount accounts.
3. Recognition of any gain or loss on the retirement of the bonds.

For this example, assume that the Reid, Inc., bonds issued at 104 were called for retirement at 105 plus accrued interest on April 1 of their fourth and final year. Also assume that the bond premium has been amortized using the straight-line method. Exhibit 17–1 shows that the related account balances at the end of their third year are

Bonds Payable	$100,000
Bond Premium	1,000

If interest is paid semiannually on June 30 and December 31, and financial statements are prepared annually, no premium amortization entry has been made since the end of the third year. Thus, the following entries properly reflect the retirement of the bonds on April 1:

Apr. 1	Bond Premium	250	
	Bond Interest Expense		250
	To amortize bond premium for three months ($1000/4).		
1	Bonds Payable	100,000	
	Bond Premium	750	
	Bond Interest Expense	2,500	
	Loss on Bond Retirement	4,250	
	Cash		107,500
	To retire bonds at 105 plus interest and record the loss on retirement.		

The loss on retirement is the difference between the retirement amount ($105,000) and the book value of the bonds at retirement ($100,750). The amount of interest paid at retirement ($2,500) does not affect the gain or loss on retirement. The gain or loss, if material, should be classified as an extraordinary item on the income statement.

Conversion of Bonds

Few convertible bonds are redeemed for cash, since at some point these bonds are usually converted into common stock. Because, as noted earlier, the conversion feature is attractive to potential investors, a company may issue convertible bonds at a lower interest rate than it would pay without the conversion feature.

A company may also issue convertible bonds to reduce the dilutive effect that a common stock issue would have on earnings per share. This occurs because the conversion price is higher than the current market price of the stock when the convertible bonds are issued. For example, suppose a company that needs $100,000 of funds could issue additional common stock at $20 per share. The company needs to issue 5,000 shares to obtain $100,000. Alternatively, the firm may issue $100,000 of convertible bonds and establish a conversion price of $25 per share. When the bonds are converted into stock (and the company expects this to happen), the number of common shares issued will be 4,000 ($100,000/$25). The fewer number of common shares associated with the convertible bonds produces higher earnings per share than if common stock had been issued initially.

Convertible bonds include a call feature. When the market value of the stock to be received on conversion is significantly higher than the call price on the bond, a company may force conversion by calling in the bonds. Of course, one of the risks of issuing convertible bonds is that the market price of the stock may not increase in the future. Bondholders may then decide it is not to their advantage to convert the bonds, and the company cannot force conversion by exercising the call feature.

The entry to record a bond conversion transfers the book value of the bonds to the common stock accounts. For example, assume that the Reid, Inc., bonds issued at 98 were convertible into 4,000 shares of $20 par value common stock. All the bonds were converted into stock on January 1 of the third year. Exhibit 17–1 shows that the book value of the bonds at the end of the second year is $99,000. The following entry records the conversion:

Jan. 1	Bonds Payable	100,000	
	Bond Discount		1,000
	Common Stock		80,000
	Paid-in Capital in Excess of Par Value		19,000
	To record conversion of bonds into 4,000 shares of $20 par value common stock.		

BOND SINKING FUNDS

As additional security to bondholders, some bond agreements require the borrower to make periodic cash deposits to a **bond sinking fund,** which is used to retire the bonds. The fund is often controlled by a trustee—usually a bank or a trust company. The trustee invests the cash deposited periodically in the sinking fund in income-producing securities. The objective is to accumulate investments and investment income sufficient to retire the bonds at their maturity.

We now illustrate typical transactions for a simple bond sinking fund managed by a trustee. Assume that Reid, Inc., establishes such a fund to retire its $100,000 bond issue, which matures in four years. Reid, Inc., makes equal annual deposits to the sinking fund at the end of each of the four years.

Periodic Deposit of Cash to the Fund

The amount of the equal periodic contributions is determined by compound interest tables and assumes an average annual rate of net investment income.[3] If the trustee estimates that the sinking-fund securities will earn 8% annually, Reid, Inc.'s annual cash payment to the trustee should be $22,192. Earning 8% annually, the fund will grow to $100,000 after four years, as follows:

Year	Annual Cash Deposit	8% Annual Interest	Fund Balance at Year-end
1	$22,192	—	$ 22,192
2	22,192	$1,775	46,159
3	22,192	3,693	72,044
4	22,192	5,764	100,000

The entry to record the annual cash deposit is

Bond Sinking Fund	22,192	
Cash		22,192

Income Reported on Sinking-fund Securities

Reid, Inc., records on its books the trustee's periodic reports on the earnings of the sinking-fund securities. For example, if the fund earned $1,775 during the second year, Reid, Inc., makes the following journal entry:

Bond Sinking Fund	1,775	
Bond Sinking-fund Income		1,775

[3]An example showing how such periodic contributions are determined is given in Appendix B at the end of this chapter.

Retirement of Bonds

Usually, the trustee sells the sinking-fund securities and pays the bondholders with the proceeds. Reid, Inc., then records the retirement of the bonds as follows:

Bonds Payable	100,000	
Bond Sinking Fund		100,000

Any deficit in the sinking fund needed to retire the bonds requires an additional cash payment from Reid, Inc. Any surplus is transferred to the Cash account in closing out the sinking fund.

The Bond Sinking Fund is classified in the balance sheet as an investment. Bond Sinking-fund Income is reported under Other Income and Expenses in the income statement.

LONG-TERM BOND INVESTMENTS

Corporate bonds may be acquired by a variety of investors, including individuals, partnerships, corporations, mutual funds, pension funds, foundations, and trusts. Our discussion focuses on bond investments by corporations.

Bonds may be purchased when they are originally issued or at some time thereafter from an investor. Bond investments are recorded by the purchaser at cost plus any brokerage commission. Because bonds acquired as a long-term investment may be held for extended periods, the related premium or discount is usually amortized to interest income. The straight-line method of amortization is commonly used; however, as we mentioned earlier, the effective interest method should be used when the two methods yield materially different results. In our example, we use the straight-line method.

Assume that a firm purchases ten National Telephone $10,000, 8% bonds at 98 on a semiannual interest date (January 1) ten years prior to maturity. Brokerage commission is $200. Because the bonds will have a maturity value of $100,000 in ten years, the bond discount is $1,800, which is amortized (using the straight-line method) at a rate of $90 at the end of each of the 20 remaining semiannual interest periods ($1,800/20 = $90). The following entry records the purchase:

Jan. 1	National Telephone Bonds	98,200	
	Cash		98,200
	To record purchase of ten bonds at 98 on interest date plus commission of $200.		

Note that although the bond discount is amortized, no Bond Discount account is established. The investment is initially recorded at cost, and the discount amortization entry is made directly to the asset account. For example, on the next interest date, the following entries record the receipt of interest and amortization of discount:

July 1	Cash	4,000	
	Bond Interest Income		4,000
	To record receipt of semiannual interest on National Telephone bonds.		
1	National Telephone Bonds	90	
	Bond Interest Income		90
	To record semiannual amortization of discount on National Telephone bonds.		

BOND INVESTMENTS AND THEIR RATINGS

Investments in bonds generally provide less risk than stock investments. Bond prices do not fluctuate as much as stock prices, and they always have some value as long as the issuing firm can pay interest. On the other hand, stock prices can plummet drastically when a firm has a sustained period of losses and pays no dividends. Also, when a firm goes bankrupt, bondholders' claims to assets have priority over those of stockholders.

The quality of bonds varies a great deal. Investors who want to know the relative quality of a particular bond issue can consult a bond rating service. Four companies provide bond ratings: Standard and Poor's, Moody's, Fitch's, and Dun and Bradstreet. For example, Standard and Poor's rates bonds as AAA, AA, A, BBB, BB, and so on, down to D, which means "defaulted." The diagram shows the relationship between the ratings and the degree of risk, using Standard and Poor's bond ratings system as an example.

At one time, top-quality (AAA) bonds were referred to as "gilt edge" investments, but one rarely hears that term anymore. *The Wall Street Journal* defines "junk bonds" as bonds with a BB rating or lower.* These are bonds of dubious quality, some of which have been featured in "leveraged buyout" takeovers in recent years (see boxed insert, p. 647). The cautious investor usually buys bonds rated A or higher.

Generally bonds with poor ratings offer higher interest rates than highly rated bonds. However, bond interest rates are affected by many other factors, such as the type of bond, the general level of interest rates, the state of the stock market, and length of time to maturity.

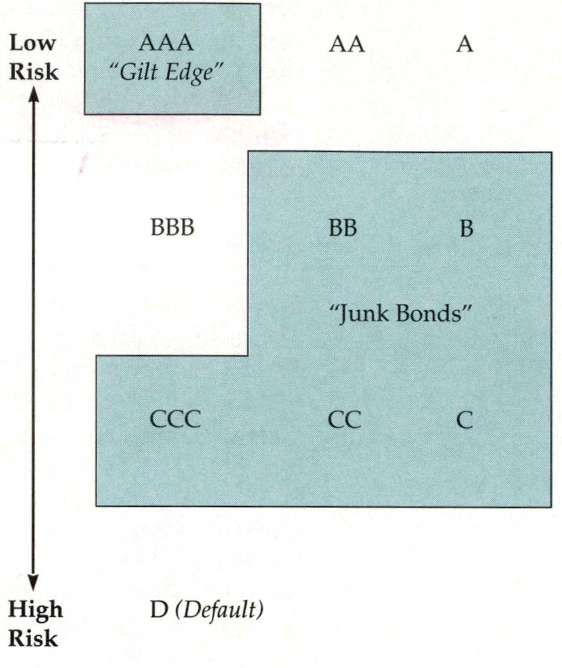

Standard and Poor's Bond Ratings

**The Wall Street Journal*, 1987/88 Educational Edition, p. 12.

As in the case of Bonds Payable on the books of borrowers, the carrying value of the bonds increases until they reach their maturity value on their maturity date.

When the purchase price of a bond exceeds its maturity value, the bond is still recorded at cost and the related premium amortization entry is a debit to Bond Interest Income and a credit to the Investment account. Thus, the carrying value of bonds acquired at a premium progresses downward toward maturity value. Also, the net amount of interest income reported is less (by the amount of premium amortized) than the cash received as interest income each period.

Bonds may be sold before they reach maturity. Assume that on January 1, five years after they were purchased, the National Telephone bonds were sold at

$99\frac{1}{2}$ less a $150 commission. Discount amortization over the ten semiannual interest periods during which the bonds were held would have raised their carrying value to $99,100 [$98,200 + (10 × $90) = $99,100]. Again, we figure the accounting gain by comparing the book value of the asset to the net proceeds from the sale. The sale is recorded as follows:

Jan. 1	Cash	99,350	
	National Telephone Bonds		99,100
	Gain on Sale of Investments		250
	To record sale of bond investment at $99\frac{1}{2}$ less a commission of $150.		

PENSION PLANS

Many companies have established plans to pay benefits to their employees after they retire. The cost of these **pension plans** may be paid entirely by the employer. Sometimes, the employees pay part of the cost through deductions from their salaries and wages. The employer and employee contributions are usually paid into a pension fund which is managed by another company. Retirement benefits are paid from the assets in the pension fund.

The employer's pension plan cost must be expensed during the years the employees work for the company. For some plans, this accounting analysis is fairly simple; for other plans, it is not. In a *defined contribution* plan, for example, the employer's responsibility is to contribute a certain defined amount to the pension fund each year (a percentage of employee salaries, perhaps). The assets available in the pension fund, then, determine the size of the retirement benefits. The employer's pension accounting analysis is straightforward—when the required contribution is made, Pension Expense is debited and Cash is credited.

The analysis becomes more complex in *defined benefit* plans. These plans specify the retirement benefits to be received in the future; typically, the retirement benefits are a function of the number of years an employee works for the company and the salary or wage level at or near retirement. One complexity under such plans is the determination of the periodic pension expense and contribution amounts. These amounts are influenced by such factors as employee turnover, employee life expectancies, future salary and wage levels, and pension fund investment performance. Actuaries are used to make the required pension estimates.

When a defined benefit plan is first adopted, the company usually gives employees credit for their years of employment prior to the plan's adoption. The cost of providing the retirement benefits earned by this earlier service is called **prior service cost.** Prior service cost may be quite sizeable and the company may take many years to fund it. A similar situation may develop when a company amends a plan to increase benefit levels. Another complexity in a defined benefit plan, then, is that the accumulated pension retirement benefits may exceed the assets in the pension fund. In such cases, the FASB requires companies to record a liability equal to the excess amount.[4] This liability may run into the millions or hundreds of millions of dollars for some companies.

[4] *Statement of Financial Accounting Standards No. 87*, "Employers' Accounting for Pensions" (Stamford, CT: Financial Accounting Standards Board, 1985).

DEFERRED INCOME TAXES

Corporations pay income taxes based on the amount of taxable income they report on their income tax returns. Most of the revenues and expenses used to compute taxable income are exactly the same as the firm reports in its income statement. There are several areas, however, in which the tax law either requires or permits a firm to report revenues and expenses in a different pattern on the tax return than on the income statement.

Deferred Tax Liabilities

Following are two examples of differences between when a transaction affects taxable income and when it affects the income statement:

1. A company prepays an expense (such as rent, insurance, or advertising) in the current year. In its current year financial statements, the company sets up a prepaid asset that will be allocated to expense in the future. On the current year tax return, the company immediately expenses the prepayment.
2. A company purchases a plant asset in the current year and depreciates it in its financial statements using the straight-line method with no expected salvage value. On the tax return, the company depreciates the asset using the *modified accelerated cost recovery system (MACRS).* (See Chapter 10.) The first year's MACRS depreciation exceeds the straight-line amount.

Both transactions create a situation in which, at the end of the current year, the book value of the related asset (prepaid expense and plant asset) exceeds the asset's tax basis (that is, the remaining amount that can be expensed on future tax returns). The difference is only temporary, however, because eventually both the asset's book value and its tax basis will be zero (as the expensing of the asset is completed in the financial statements and on the tax return). Further, in the future year(s) when the temporary difference (excess of book value over tax basis) is expensed in the financial statements, the company will owe income taxes on that amount (because there will not be any corresponding expense in that year's tax return). These future income taxes payable represent a deferred tax consequence, therefore, from a situation in which an asset's book value temporarily exceeds its tax basis.

Accounting standards require that a **deferred tax liability** be recorded for the deferred tax consequences of temporary differences.[5] In other words, an accounting liability must be recognized when a temporary difference between an asset's book value and its tax basis will result in future taxable amounts. The deferred tax liability is an appropriate liability to report in the balance sheet—it represents an estimate of future income taxes payable resulting from an already existing temporary difference. The deferred tax liability is computed by applying the proper income tax rate to the future taxable amount.

[5]*Statement of Financial Accounting Standards No. 96,* "Accounting for Income Taxes" (Stamford, CT: Financial Accounting Standards Board, 1987). The FASB uses the term "temporary differences" rather than "timing differences" (a term used in a previous standard). Temporary differences encompass timing differences as well as other differences that are beyond the scope of this text.

To illustrate, assume that in December, 19X1, Lenscape, Inc., enters into a contract to rent warehouse space for 19X2 from another company. In December 19X1, Lenscape prepays the 19X2 rent of $12,000 and debits the $12,000 cash outlay to Prepaid Rent. On its 19X1 income tax return, however, Lenscape deducts the $12,000 prepayment as rent expense (the tax law permits this). In 19X2, Lenscape recognizes the $12,000 as Rent Expense in its financial statements. This is the only difference between Lenscape's financial statements and tax returns. The income tax rate is 35% for 19X1 and 19X2.

Assume Lenscape's income before rent expense and income taxes is $50,000 in 19X1 and $70,000 in 19X2. Lenscape's pretax financial income and taxable income for 19X1 and 19X2 will then be as follows:

	19X1		19X2	
	Financial Income	Taxable Income	Financial Income	Taxable Income
Income before rent expense and income taxes	$50,000	$50,000	$70,000	$70,000
Rent expense	-0-	12,000	12,000	-0-
Pretax financial income	$50,000		$58,000	
Taxable income		$38,000		$70,000

The book value and tax basis of prepaid rent at December 31, 19X1, and December 31, 19X2, are as follows:

	December 31, 19X1		December 31, 19X2	
	Book Value	Tax Basis	Book Value	Tax Basis
Prepaid rent	$12,000	-0-	-0-	-0-

The following observations may be drawn from Lenscape's handling of the rent prepayment.

1. Deducting the prepayment on 19X1's tax return causes a $12,000 difference between the book value and tax basis of prepaid rent at December 31, 19X1.
2. The $12,000 difference at December 31, 19X1, between prepaid rent's book value and its tax basis is temporary. It is eliminated in 19X2.
3. The elimination of the $12,000 temporary difference in 19X2 causes taxable income that year to be $12,000 greater than pretax financial income. Lenscape, therefore, will pay an income tax on the $12,000 in 19X2 of $4,200 (35% × $12,000). This is the liability that must be recognized at December 31, 19X1, as a deferred tax liability.

The journal entry to record income taxes at December 31, 19X1, is

19X1			
Dec. 31	Income Tax Expense	17,500	
	Income Tax Payable		13,300
	Deferred Tax Liability		4,200
	To record 19X1 income taxes.		

The entry to Deferred Tax Liability is the amount necessary to establish the proper year-end account balance. At December 31, 19X1, there should be a Deferred Tax Liability of $4,200 (35% × $12,000). Lenscape has no previous balance in this account so the credit entry is for the full $4,200. The entry to Income Tax Payable reflects the income taxes currently due to the government—it is computed by multiplying the 19X1 taxable income by the 19X1 tax rate ($38,000 × 35% = $13,300). The debit to Income Tax Expense is the balancing amount in the journal entry; in this case, it is determined by combining the income tax payable and deferred tax liability amounts.

The journal entry to record income taxes at December 31, 19X2 is:

19X2			
Dec. 31	Income Tax Expense	20,300	
	Deferred Tax Liability	4,200	
	Income Tax Payable		24,500
	To record 19X2 income taxes.		

The $4,200 debit to Deferred Tax Liability brings this account balance to zero. This is the correct balance at December 31, 19X2, because the temporary difference is eliminated in 19X2. The $24,500 credit to Income Tax Payable correctly records the 19X2 income tax owed to the government ($70,000 × 35% = $24,500). The balancing debit to Income Tax Expense is determined by netting the income tax payable and deferred tax liability amounts.

Income Tax Rate

The proper income tax rate to use in determining a deferred tax liability is the tax rate scheduled to be in effect when the future taxable amount occurs. If a new tax rate has been enacted into law for the future year, then that tax rate is used. To illustrate using the Lenscape, Inc., example, assume that the tax rates enacted into law are 35% for 19X1 and 40% for 19X2. The journal entries to record income taxes for 19X1 and 19X2 would then be as follows:

19X1			
Dec. 31	Income Tax Expense	18,100	
	Income Tax Payable		13,300
	Deferred Tax Liability		4,800
	To record 19X1 income taxes: Deferred tax liability: $12,000 × 40% = $4,800; Income tax payable: $38,000 × 35% = $13,300; Income tax expense: $4,800 + $13,300 = $18,100.		

19X2			
Dec. 31	Income Tax Expense	23,200	
	Deferred Tax Liability	4,800	
	Income Tax Payable		28,000
	To record 19X2 income taxes: Deferred tax liability: to eliminate account balance; Income tax payable: $70,000 × 40% = $28,000; Income tax expense: $28,000 − $4,800 = $23,200.		

If tax rates are changed after a deferred tax liability has been recorded, a journal entry will be necessary to revise the account balance to its proper amount (with an offsetting debit or credit to Income Tax Expense).

Balance Sheet Presentation

Deferred tax liabilities are presented among the liabilities in a firm's balance sheet, properly divided between current and long-term liabilities. The current portion is the amount that will become payable within the next year. In our Lenscape, Inc., illustration, all of the deferred tax liability at the end of 19X1 would be classified as a current liability in the December 31, 19X1, balance sheet.

The amounts reported as deferred tax liabilities in actual balance sheets may be quite large, often millions of dollars for major corporations. The deferred income taxes shown among Whirlpool Corporation's liabilities at December 31, 1988, for example, total $139,300,000 (see page 1115).

Other Temporary Differences

Differences in the accounting for revenue may also create temporary differences that will result in deferred tax liabilities. These situations include (1) a contractor who accounts for long-term contracts by using the percentage-of-completion method in its financial statements and the completed contract method on the tax return, and (2) a company that recognizes revenue from installment sales at point of sale in its financial statements and uses the installment method for tax purposes.[6]

Some temporary differences cause an asset's book value to be *less* than its tax basis. For example, a firm may use the allowance method in its financial statements to account for uncollectible accounts expense and use the direct write-off method for tax purposes. Also, some temporary differences may create a liability with a book value larger than its tax basis. For example, a company may receive an advance payment for future services to be performed (crediting a liability account for the advance payment) but include the payment in taxable income in the year it is received. These temporary differences have the potential to create a deferred tax asset (future reduction or refund of income taxes). The guidelines for recognizing deferred tax assets, however, are much more restrictive and complex than those that apply to deferred tax liabilities and are beyond the scope of this text.

CORPORATION BALANCE SHEET

Exhibit 17–4 is a comprehensive illustration of a corporation's balance sheet that contains many of the items discussed in this chapter and in Chapters 15 and 16.

[6]These topics are discussed in Chapter 13. At this writing, the tax law permits firms with less than $10 million revenue to use the completed contract method for long-term contracts. Other firms may use the completed contract method for only 10% of a long-term contract. Legislation is pending in Congress, however, to repeal the completed contract method for tax purposes. The tax law also permits the installment method to be used for installment sales of residential lots, timeshare units, and property used in the trade or business of farming.

EXHIBIT 17–4

Superior Corporation
Balance Sheet
December 31, 19XX

ASSETS

Current Assets				
Cash			$ 20,000	
Short-term Investments (at lower of cost or market)			10,000	
Accounts Receivable		$65,000		
Less: Allowance for Uncollectible Accounts		5,000	60,000	
Inventories (at lower of cost or market)			120,000	
Prepaid Expenses			10,000	
Total Current Assets				$220,000
Investments				
Sinking Fund for Bond Retirement			$ 20,400	
Long-term Bond Investments			29,600	
Total Investments				50,000
Plant Assets	**Cost**	**Accumulated Depreciation**	**Book Value**	
Land	$ 30,000	—	$ 30,000	
Buildings	100,000	$20,000	80,000	
Machinery and Equipment	170,000	30,000	140,000	
Total Plant Assets				250,000
Intangible Assets (cost less amortization to date)				
Goodwill			$ 28,000	
Patents			12,000	
Total Intangible Assets				40,000
Total Assets				$560,000

EXH 17–4 (Continued)

Superior Corporation
Balance Sheet
December 31, 19XX (continued)

LIABILITIES		
Current Liabilities		
Accounts Payable	$ 45,000	
Income Tax Payable	18,000	
Dividends Payable	15,000	
Accrued Payables	2,000	
Total Current Liabilities		$ 80,000
Long-term Liabilities		
First Mortgage, 9% Bonds Payable (due 1996)	$100,000	
Premium on First Mortgage Bonds	6,000	
	$106,000	
Deferred Tax Liability	30,000	
Total Long-term Liabilities		136,000
Total Liabilities		$216,000
STOCKHOLDERS' EQUITY		
Paid-in Capital		
Common Stock, $100 Par Value, authorized and issued 2,000 shares; 50 shares in treasury	$200,000	
Paid-in Capital in Excess of Par Value	20,000	
Total Paid-in Capital		$220,000
Retained Earnings		
Appropriated for Plant Expansion	$ 44,000	
Appropriated for Treasury Stock	6,000	
Unappropriated	80,000	
Total Retained Earnings		130,000
		$350,000
Less: Treasury Stock (50 shares) at Cost		6,000
Total Stockholders' Equity		$344,000
Total Liabilities and Stockholders' Equity		$560,000

KEY POINTS FOR CHAPTER OBJECTIVES

1 Describe mortgages and various kinds of bonds (pp. 585–87).

- Mortgages involve an agreement, evidenced by a note, to repay the principal amount borrowed and to pay interest on certain dates, and an agreement to pledge certain property as security for repayment of the note.
- Bonds are long-term notes payable and permit borrowing from a large number of investors, who are usually represented by a trustee. Bonds may be secured or unsecured (debenture bonds). Bonds may all come due at the same time or may have staggered maturities (serial bonds). For registered bonds, the issuer keeps records of owners and mails them interest payments. Owners of coupon bonds detach the interest coupons when due and deposit them in a bank. Bonds may be callable after a certain date, and some bonds are convertible into the firm's stock at a specified exchange ratio.

2 Discuss the relationship of bond prices to interest rates, and illustrate accounting for bond issuance, interest, and amortization (pp. 587–96).

- Bond prices are expressed as a percentage of face value, which is usually $1,000.
- The nominal rate of interest, stated on the bond certificate, dictates the amount of interest paid each period. The effective, or market, rate of interest is the rate investors expect to receive on their investment.
- When the market interest rate exceeds the nominal rate on bonds, they are sold at a discount; when the nominal rate exceeds the market rate, the bonds are sold at a premium. Discounts and premiums are recorded when the bonds are issued.
- Discounts and premiums are amortized each interest date usually by adding a pro-rata share to interest expense for discounts, or deducting a pro-rata share for premiums.
- In certain cases the *effective interest* method is used instead of the pro-rata method. The effective interest method results in a constant rate of interest on the bond book value throughout the life of the bonds.

3 Illustrate the classification of bonds payable, premium, and discount on the balance sheet (pp. 592–93).

- Bonds payable are shown in the long-term liabilities section of the balance sheet, with unamortized premium added or unamortized discount deducted.

4 Illustrate the retirement and conversion of bonds and the use of sinking funds (pp. 596–99).

- The entry for retirement of bonds removes both the Bonds Payable account and any related Bond Premium or Bond Discount account at the date of retirement and recognizes any gain or loss on retirement.
- The entry for bond conversion into common stock removes both the appropriate portion of the Bonds Payable account and any related Bond Premium or Bond Discount at the date of conversion. The par value of common stock issued is recorded, together with the appropriate amount of paid-in capital in excess of par value.
- Some bond agreements require the borrower to make periodic payments to a sinking fund controlled by a trustee, who invests the amounts. The invested amounts plus accumulated income is used to retire the bonds at maturity.

5 Describe and illustrate accounting for long-term bond investments (pp. 599–601).

- Long-term bond investments are recorded at cost, including brokerage commissions.
- Discounts or premiums are amortized each interest date by deducting a pro-rata share of premiums from interest income or adding a pro-rata share for discounts.

The investment account is debited for amortized discounts or credited for amortized premiums.

- When sold, the book value of bond investments is removed as of the sale date, and any gain or loss is recorded.

6 Describe the basic ideas of pension accounting (p. 601).

- In a defined contribution plan, the employer contributes a defined amount to the pension fund each year, debiting Pension Expense and crediting Cash. The fund assets determine the size of benefits.
- Defined benefit plans specify retirement benefits to be received in the future. They are often a function of years worked and the salary or wage level at retirement. Pension expense and contributions are influenced by such variables as employee turnover, life expectancies, and future salary and wage levels, and actuaries are needed to make estimates.

7 Describe and illustrate deferred income taxes (pp. 602–605).

- When a difference in tax accounting and financial reporting results in the related asset having a book value in excess of its tax basis, a deferred tax liability results.
- The deferred tax liability is phased out as the difference in book value and tax basis disappears.

KEY TERMS USED IN THIS CHAPTER

bonds 585
bond sinking fund 598
book value 593
callable bonds 586
carrying value 593
contract rate 588
convertible bonds 586
coupon bonds 586
debenture bonds 586
deferred tax liability 602
effective interest method 593
effective rate 588
market rate 588
mortgage note 585
nominal rate 588
pension plans 601
prior service cost 601
registered bonds 586
secured bonds 586
serial bonds 586
trustee 586

SELF-TEST QUESTIONS

(Answers are at the end of this chapter.)

1. On May 1 of the current year, a firm issued $400,000, 12-year, 12% bonds payable at $96\frac{1}{2}$ plus accrued interest. The bonds are dated January 1 of the current year, and interest is payable on January 1 and July 1 of each year. The amount the firm receives on May 1 is
   (a) $370,000 (b) $402,000 (c) $430,000 (d) $398,000
2. The amount of discount on the bonds in question 1 to be amortized (straight line) on July 1 of the current year is
   (a) $200 (b) $194.44 (c) $600 (d) $583.33
3. A firm issued $500,000, 10-year, 12% bonds payable on January 1 of the current year for $562,360, yielding an effective rate of 10%. Interest is payable on January 1 and July 1 each year. The firm records amortization on each interest date. Bond interest expense for the first six months of this year, using effective interest amortization, is
   (a) $30,000 (b) $33,741.60 (c) $28,118 (d) $26,882

4. A firm purchased $20,000, 10-year, 9% bonds as an investment at 96 on January 1, 19X1, 10 years before maturity. The firm records interest and amortization on interest dates. On January 1, three years from the purchase date, the firm sold the bonds at 98. The gain or loss to be recorded on the date of sale is
(a) $160 loss (b) $160 gain (c) $240 loss (d) $240 gain

5. A firm deducted a $10,000 expense on its tax return in 19X1, but reported it in its income statement in 19X2. The firm's pretax financial income was $100,000 in 19X1 and $90,000 in 19X2 (after deducting the $10,000 item). The income tax rate is 40%. At the end of 19X1, the Deferred Tax Liability account has a balance of
(a) $6,000 credit (b) $10,000 debit (c) $4,000 debit (d) $4,000 credit

DEMONSTRATION PROBLEM FOR REVIEW

The following are selected transactions of Tyler, Inc., for 19X1 and 19X2. The firm closes its books on December 31.

19X1

Jan.	1	Issued $500,000 of 9%, 10-year convertible bonds at 103. Interest is payable January 1 and July 1. The holder of each $1,000 bond may convert it into 90 shares of $10 par value Tyler, Inc., common stock.
July	1	Paid semiannual interest and recorded semiannual premium amortization (straight line) on bonds.
	1	Purchased, as a long-term investment, $40,000, 8% Martin Company bonds at 98. The bonds pay interest on July 1 and January 1 and mature in ten years.
Dec.	31	Recorded accrued interest payable and semiannual premium amortization on convertible bonds and accrued interest receivable and semiannual discount amortization on Martin Company bonds. (Tyler, Inc., does not use reversing entries.) Straight-line amortization is used both for bonds payable and bond investments.

19X2

Jan.	1	Paid semiannual interest on convertible bonds and received semiannual interest on Martin Company bonds.
	2	Converted $50,000 of convertible bonds to common stock.

REQUIRED
Record these transactions in general journal form.

SOLUTION TO DEMONSTRATION PROBLEM

19X1

			Debit	Credit
Jan.	1	Cash	515,000	
		Bond Premium		15,000
		Bonds Payable		500,000
		Issued $500,000 of 9%, 10-year convertible bonds at 103.		
July	1	Bond Interest Expense	22,500	
		Cash		22,500
		Paid semiannual interest on convertible bonds ($500,000 × 0.09 × $\frac{6}{12}$ = $22,500).		

Date		Account and Explanation	Debit	Credit
July	1	Bond Premium	750	
		Bond Interest Expense		750
		Semiannual amortization of convertible bond premium ($15,000/20 periods = $750).		
	1	Martin Company Bonds	39,200	
		Cash		39,200
		Purchased $40,000 of Martin Company bonds at 98.		
Dec.	31	Bond Interest Expense	22,500	
		Bond Interest Payable		22,500
		Accrual of six months' bond interest ($500,000 × 0.09 × $\frac{6}{12}$).		
	31	Bond Premium	750	
		Bond Interest Expense		750
		Semiannual amortization of convertible bond premium.		
	31	Bond Interest Receivable	1,600	
		Bond Interest Income		1,600
		Accrued interest receivable for six months ($40,000 × 0.08 × $\frac{6}{12}$ = $1,600).		
	31	Martin Company Bonds	40	
		Bond Interest Income		40
		Semiannual amortization of discount on Martin Company bonds ($800/20 interest periods = $40).		
19X2				
Jan.	1	Bond Interest Payable	22,500	
		Cash		22,500
		Paid semiannual interest on convertible bonds, accrued on December 31, 19X1.		
	1	Cash	1,600	
		Bond Interest Receivable		1,600
		Received semiannual interest on Martin Company bonds.		
	2	Bonds Payable	50,000	
		Bond Premium	1,350	
		Common Stock		45,000
		Paid-in Capital in Excess of Par Value – Common Stock		6,350
		Conversion of $50,000 convertible bonds into 4,500 shares of $10 par value common stock.		

Book value of bonds converted:

Face amount	$50,000
Add: Premium (10% of total premium)	1,350
Book Value	$51,350

QUESTIONS

17–1 Define the following terms:

(a) mortgage notes	(g) convertible bonds
(b) bonds payable	(h) face value
(c) trustee	(i) nominal interest rate
(d) secured bonds	(j) bond discount
(e) serial bonds	(k) bond premium
(f) callable bonds	(l) amortization of bond premium or discount

17–2 Explain how issuing bonds at a premium or discount "adjusts the nominal rate to the applicable market rate of interest."

17–3 A $1,000,000 issue of 10-year, 9% bonds was sold at 96 plus accrued interest three months after the bonds were dated. What net amount of cash is received?

17–4 Regardless of whether premium or discount is involved, what generalization can be made about the change in the book value of bonds payable during the period in which they are outstanding?

17–5 How should premium and discount on bonds payable be presented in the balance sheet?

17–6 On April 30, 19X5, eight months before maturity, Western Company retired $100,000 of 9% bonds payable at 101 plus accrued interest. The book value of the bonds on April 30 was $98,500. Bond interest was last paid on December 31, 19X4. What is the gain or loss on the retirement of the bonds?

17–7 Give reasons why a convertible bond may be attractive to both an investor and the issuing company. Why do corporations typically include a call feature in a convertible bond?

17–8 What is the purpose of a bond sinking fund? Where is the bond sinking fund classified in the balance sheet?

17–9 Under what conditions should the effective interest method be used to amortize discount or premium on bonds payable and on long-term bond investments?

17–10 If the effective interest amortization method is used for bonds payable, how does the periodic interest expense change over the life of the bonds when they are issued (a) at a discount and (b) at a premium?

17–11 Lowell Company invested in bonds at a premium on a long-term basis. Should the bond premium be amortized? Where should the bond investment be classified in the balance sheet?

17–12 In employee pension plans, what does the term *prior service cost* mean?

17–13 What accounting analysis is required when the accumulated retirement benefits under a firm's pension plan exceed the assets in the pension fund?

17–14 Give three examples of temporary differences that will result in the recognition of deferred tax liabilities.

17–15 On January 1, 19X4, Vycan, Inc., paid $10,000 cash for two years (19X4 and 19X5) of insurance coverage. Vycan deducted all $10,000 as insurance expense on its 19X4 income tax return. The tax rate is 30% for 19X4 and 19X5. What amount of deferred tax liability related to the insurance prepayment should appear in Vycan's December 31, 19X4, balance sheet?

17–16 A firm records an outlay as prepaid expense in 19X1 but deducts the outlay as an expense on its 19X1 income tax return. In 19X2 the entire amount will be expensed for financial reporting. In 19X1, tax rates enacted into law were 35% for 19X1 and 40% for 19X2. Which rate is used in determining the deferred tax liability at December 31, 19X1? Explain.

17–17 When are deferred tax liabilities classified as current liabilities? as long-term liabilities?

EXERCISES

Bonds payable entries; conversion

17–18 On January 1, Martin Company issued $200,000 of 10-year, 10% convertible bonds at 103. Interest is payable semiannually on June 30 and December 31. Each $1,000 bond may be converted into 40 shares of $25 par value common stock. Present journal entries to reflect (a) the issuance of the bonds, (b) the payment of interest for the first six months, (c) the premium amortization for the first six months (straight-line), and (d) the conversion of $100,000 face amount of bonds into stock exactly five years after the issuance of the bonds.

Bonds payable entries; retirement

17–19 Tillson Company issued $500,000 of 10-year, 9% bonds at 97. The bonds were issued on March 1, 19X1, with interest payable semiannually on March 1 and September 1. Present journal entries to reflect (a) the issuance of the bonds, (b) the payment of interest for the first six months, (c) the discount amortization for the first six months (straight line), and (d) the retirement of the bonds at 101 plus accrued interest on June 1, 19X5.

Bonds payable on balance sheet

17–20 The adjusted trial balance for the Lancer Corporation at the end of the current year contains the following accounts:

Bond Interest Payable	$ 31,600
9% Bonds Payable	750,000
10% Bonds Payable	600,000
Discount on 9% Bonds Payable	5,000
Premium on 10% Bonds Payable	2,000
Sinking Fund for Bond Retirement	150,000
Long-term Bond Investment	92,600

Prepare the long-term liabilities section of the balance sheet. Indicate the proper balance sheet classification for accounts listed above that do not belong in the long-term liabilities section.

Effective interest amortization

17–21 Walker, Inc., issued $400,000 of 10-year, 9% bonds payable on January 1, 19X1. The bonds were sold for $375,116, yielding an effective interest rate of 10%. Semiannual interest is payable on January 1 and July 1, and the effective interest method is used to amortize the discount.

(a) Prepare an amortization schedule showing the necessary information for the first two interest periods. Round amounts to the nearest dollar.

(b) Give the entries to record interest expense and discount amortization on July 1 and December 31.

Effective interest amortization

17–22 Refer to Exhibit 17–3 on page 595 of this chapter. The $100,000, 8% bonds in the example were issued on April 1, 19X1, and sold at a premium. Interest payment dates were April 1 and October 1. Give the adjusting entry to record interest expense and premium amortization on December 31, 19X2.

Bond investment entries

17–23 As a long-term investment, eight 10-year, $1,000, 10% bonds were purchased at 104 on the first day of their first semiannual interest period. Present journal entries to record (a) their purchase for cash, (b) the receipt of the first two semiannual interest payments, (c) the semiannual amortizations of bond premium for the first year (straight line), and (d) the sale of the bonds at 101 two years after they were purchased.

Bond investment entries

17–24 Assume that the bonds in Exercise 17–23 were purchased at 96 on the first day of their first semiannual interest period. Present journal entries to record (a) their purchase for cash, (b) the receipt of the first two semiannual interest payments, (c) the semiannual amortizations of bond discount for the first year (straight line), and (d) the sale of the bonds at 98 two years after they were purchased.

Deferred income taxes

17–25 Bearsly, Inc., purchased $100,000 of special manufacturing tools on January 1, 19X1. The tools are being depreciated on a straight-line basis over five years with no expected salvage value. MACRS depreciation is being used on the firm's tax returns. At December 31, 19X2, the tools' book value is $60,000 and their tax basis is $22,000 (this is Bearsly's only temporary difference). Over the next three years, straight-line depreciation will exceed MACRS depreciation by $5,000 in 19X3, $13,000 in 19X4, and $20,000 in 19X5. The income tax rate in effect for all years is 30%.

(a) What amount of deferred tax liability should appear in Bearsly's December 31, 19X2, balance sheet? How much should be classified as a current liability and as a long-term liability?
(b) What amount of deferred tax liability should appear in Bearsly's December 31, 19X3, balance sheet? How much should be classified as a current liability and as a long-term liability?
(c) What amount of deferred tax liability should appear in Bearsly's December 31, 19X4, balance sheet? How much should be classified as a current liability and as a long-term liability?

PROBLEMS

Bonds payable entries

17–26 On January 1, 19X4, Baker, Inc., sold at 96 a $300,000 issue of 8% bonds that mature in ten years. Bond interest is payable on June 30 and December 31. Baker's accounting year ends on December 31. The firm uses the straight-line method of amortization.

REQUIRED
(a) Show all entries pertaining to the bonds for 19X4.
(b) Present the entries necessary to record properly the retirement of one-half the bonds at 98 plus accrued interest on March 1, 19X7.

Bonds payable entries

17–27 Wade, Inc., which closes its books on December 31, is authorized to issue $800,000 of 9%, 12-year bonds dated April 1, 19X1, with interest payments on October 1 and April 1.

REQUIRED
Present general journal entries to record the following events, assuming the bonds were (a) sold at 97 on April 1, 19X1; and (b) sold at $103\frac{1}{2}$ plus accrued interest on August 1, 19X1.

1. The bond issue.
2. Payment of the first semiannual period's interest and amortization on that date of any related bond premium or discount (straight-line).
3. Accrual of bond interest expense and any related bond premium or discount amortization at December 31, 19X1.
4. Retirement of $200,000 of the bonds at 101 on April 1, 19X7.

Effective interest amortization

17–28 On January 1, 19X5, Lewis, Inc., issued $700,000 face value, 8%, 10-year bonds for $612,836, yielding an effective interest rate of 10%. Semiannual interest is payable on January 1 and July 1 each year. The firm uses the effective interest method to amortize the discount.

REQUIRED
(a) Prepare an amortization schedule showing the necessary information for the first two interest periods. Round amounts to the nearest dollar.
(b) Prepare the journal entry for the bond issuance on January 1, 19X5.
(c) Prepare the entry to record bond interest expense and discount amortization at July 1, 19X5.
(d) Prepare the adjusting entry to record interest expense and discount amortization at December 31, 19X5, the close of the firm's accounting year.

Effective interest amortization

17–29 On April 1, 19X5, Regal, Inc., issued $600,000 face value 10%, 10-year bonds for $681,300, yielding an effective interest rate of 8%. Semiannual interest is payable on April 1 and October 1 each year. The firm uses the effective interest method to amortize the premium.

REQUIRED

(a) Prepare an amortization schedule showing the necessary information for the first two interest periods. Round amounts to the nearest dollar.
(b) Prepare the journal entry for the bond issuance on April 1, 19X5.
(c) Prepare the entry to record bond interest expense and premium amortization at October 1, 19X5.
(d) Prepare the adjusting entry to record interest expense and premium amortization at December 31, 19X5, the close of the firm's accounting year.

Sinking-fund entries

17–30 Elko, Inc., issued $450,000 of bonds and is required by its bond agreement to maintain a bond sinking fund managed by a trustee. The following transactions relate to the fund at various times in its life.

(1) Elko remits a periodic cash deposit of $24,750 to the fund.
(2) The trustee reports sinking fund earnings of $5,760 during the period.
(3) The trustee reports the sale of sinking-fund securities and the retirement of the $450,000 of outstanding bonds. Just before this report, the Bond Sinking Fund account for Elko, Inc., showed a balance of $450,000. The trustee also reports the sale of the securities generated an unexpected gain of $6,250, and a check for this amount accompanies the trustee's report (credit to Bond Sinking-fund Income).

REQUIRED

Present general journal entries for these sinking-fund transactions.

Bonds payable and bond investment entries

17–31 The following are selected transactions of Atlas Corporation for 19X1 and 19X2. The company closes its books on December 31.

19X1

Jan. 1 Issued $600,000 of 9%, 10-year convertible bonds at 97. Interest is payable on January 1 and July 1. The holder of each $1,000 bond may convert it into 90 shares of $10 par value Atlas Corporation common stock.

July 1 Paid semiannual interest and recorded semiannual discount amortization (straight line) on convertible bonds.

1 Purchased, as a long-term investment, 60 $1,000, 8% Hunt Company bonds at 104. The bonds pay interest on July 1 and January 1 and mature in ten years.

Dec. 31 Recorded accrued interest payable and semiannual discount amortization on convertible bonds and accrued interest receivable and semiannual premium amortization on Hunt Company bonds. (Atlas Corporation does not use reversing entries.) Straight-line amortization is used both for bonds payable and bond investments.

19X2

Jan. 1 Paid semiannual interest on convertible bonds and received semiannual interest on Hunt Company bonds.

2 Converted $60,000 of convertible bonds to common stock.

Apr. 1 Sold one-half of the Hunt Company bonds at 102 plus accrued interest.

REQUIRED

Record these transactions in general journal form.

Bond investment entries

17–32 The following transactions relate to certain bonds acquired by Baxter Corporation as a long-term investment.

19X2

Mar. 1 Purchased $200,000 face value of Graham, Inc., 20-year, 9% bonds dated January 1, 19X2, directly from the issuing company for $207,140 plus accrued interest. Interest is paid January 1 and July 1.

July 1 Received semiannual interest on Graham, Inc., bonds and amortized the related bond premium. The straight-line method of amortization is used.

Dec. 31 Accrued interest receivable on Graham, Inc., bonds and amortized the related bond premium. (Baxter Corporation does not use reversing entries.)

19X4

Jan. 2 Received semiannual interest on Graham, Inc., bonds.

May 1 Sold the Graham, Inc., bonds at 101 plus accrued interest. A selling commission of $600 was deducted from the proceeds. Amortized bond premium to date of sale.

REQUIRED

Record these transactions in general journal form.

Deferred income taxes

17–33 During December 19X5, Zaleski, Inc., paid a $26,000 insurance premium for new insurance coverage during 19X6 (the company was self-insured and had no insurance expense during 19X5). When the cash payment was made, Zaleski debited Prepaid Insurance. The prepaid insurance was allocated to Insurance Expense during 19X6. Zaleski deducted the entire $26,000 as an expense on its 19X5 income tax return. The insurance premium represented the only difference between Zaleski's financial statements and income tax returns. Zaleski's income before insurance expense and income taxes was $176,000 in 19X5 and $216,000 in 19X6. Tax rates enacted into law at December 31, 19X5, were 30% for both 19X5 and 19X6.

REQUIRED

(a) What amount of deferred tax liability should be reported in Zaleski's year-end balance sheets for 19X5 and 19X6?
(b) Prepare journal entries to record income taxes at December 31, 19X5, and December 31, 19X6.
(c) Assume the tax rates enacted into law at December 31, 19X5, were 30% for 19X5 and 35% for 19X6. Prepare journal entries to record income taxes at December 31, 19X5, and December 31, 19X6.

ALTERNATE PROBLEMS

Bonds payable entries

17–26A On January 1, 19X6, Knight, Inc., sold at 102 a $300,000 issue of 10% bonds that mature in 20 years. Bond interest is payable on June 30 and December 31. Knight's accounting year ends on December 31. The firm uses the straight-line method of amortization.

REQUIRED

(a) Show all entries pertaining to the bonds for 19X6.
(b) Present the entries necessary to record properly the retirement of one-half of the bonds at 101 plus accrued interest on May 1, 19X9.

Bonds payable entries

17–27A Penn, Inc., which closes its books on December 31, is authorized to issue $400,000 of 9%, 20-year bonds dated March 1, 1989, with interest payments on March 1 and September 1.

REQUIRED
Present general journal entries to record the following events, assuming the bonds were (a) sold for $388,000 on March 1, 1989; and (b) sold for $408,260 plus accrued interest on July 1, 1989.

1. The bond issue.
2. Payment of the first semiannual period's interest and amortization on that date of any related bond premium or discount (straight-line).
3. Accrual of bond interest expense and any related bond premium or discount amortization at December 31, 1989 (compute to the nearest dollar).
4. Retirement of $100,000 of the bonds at 101 on March 1, 1999.

Effective interest amortization

17–28A On April 1, 19X6, Hayes, Inc., issued $500,000 face value, 9%, 10-year bonds for $468,895, yielding an effective interest rate of 10%. Semiannual interest is payable on April 1 and October 1 each year. The firm uses the effective interest method to amortize the discount.

REQUIRED
(a) Prepare an amortization schedule showing the necessary information for the first two interest periods. Round amounts to the nearest dollar.
(b) Prepare the journal entry for the bond issuance on April 1, 19X6.
(c) Prepare the entry to record bond interest expense and discount amortization at October 1, 19X6.
(d) Prepare the adjusting entry to record interest expense and discount amortization at December 31, 19X6, the close of the firm's accounting year.

Effective interest amortization

17–29A Complete the requirements of Problem 17–28A assuming that the bonds were issued for $533,775, yielding an effective interest rate of 8%. The firm uses the effective interest method to amortize the premium.

Sinking-fund entries

17–30A Holt, Inc., issued $350,000 of bonds and is required by its bond agreement to maintain a bond sinking fund managed by a trustee. The following transactions relate to the fund at various times in its life.
(1) Holt remits a periodic cash deposit of $18,250 to the fund.
(2) The trustee reports sinking-fund earnings of $5,760 during the period.
(3) The trustee reports the sale of sinking-fund securities and the retirement of the $350,000 of outstanding bonds. Just before this report, the Bond Sinking Fund account for Holt, Inc., showed a balance of $350,000. The trustee also reports the sale of the securities generated an unexpected gain of $5,450, and a check for this amount accompanies the trustee's report (credit to Bond Sinking-fund Income).

REQUIRED
Present general journal entries for these sinking-fund transactions.

Bonds payable and bond investment entries

17–31A The following are selected transactions of Hudson Corporation for 19X7 and 19X8. The company closes its books on December 31.

19X7

Jan. 1 Issued $360,000 of 10%, 20-year bonds payable at 102. Interest is payable on January 1 and July 1.

June 30 Purchased, as a long-term investment, 80 $1,000, 9% Gem Company bonds at 97. The bonds pay interest on June 30 and December 31 and mature in ten years.

July 1 Paid semiannual interest and recorded semiannual discount amortization (straight line) on bonds payable.

Dec. 31 Received semiannual interest on Gem Company bonds.
31 Recorded accrued interest payable and semiannual premium amortization on bonds payable and discount amortization on Gem Company bonds. (Hudson Corporation does not use reversing entries.) Straight-line amortization is used both for bonds payable and bond investments.

19X8

Jan. 1 Paid semiannual interest on bonds payable.
2 Retired $180,000 of bonds payable at 101.
Apr. 1 Sold Gem Company bonds at 99 plus accrued interest.

REQUIRED
Record these transactions in general journal form.

Bond investment entries

17–32A The following transactions relate to certain bonds acquired by Ross Corporation as a long-term investment.

19X4

Feb. 1 Purchased $1,000,000 face value of Manly, Inc., 20-year, 9% bonds dated January 1, 19X4, directly from the issuing company for $990,440 plus accrued interest. Interest is paid January 1 and July 1.
July 1 Received semiannual interest on Manly, Inc., bonds and amortized the related bond discount. The straight-line method of amortization is used.
Dec. 31 Accrued interest receivable on Manly, Inc., bonds and amortized the related bond discount. (Ross Corporation does not use reversing entries.)

19X6

Jan. 2 Received semiannual interest on Manly, Inc., bonds.
May 1 Sold the Manly, Inc., bonds at 99 plus accrued interest. A selling commission of $1,400 was deducted from the proceeds. Amortized bond discount to date of sale.

REQUIRED
Record these transactions in general journal form.

Deferred income taxes

17–33A During December 19X1, Lasar Company prepaid $100,000 for an advertising campaign that was going to run in 19X2 and 19X3. In 19X1, Lasar debited the $100,000 to Prepaid Advertising. The prepayment was allocated to Advertising Expense equally in 19X2 and 19X3 (Lasar had no advertising expense for 19X1). Lasar deducted the entire $100,000 as an expense on its 19X1 income tax return. This represented the only difference between Lasar's financial statements and income tax returns. Lasar's income before advertising expense and income taxes was $200,000 in 19X1, $290,000 in 19X2, and $350,000 in 19X3. Tax rates enacted into law at December 31, 19X1 were 35% for 19X1, 35% for 19X2, and 40% for 19X3.

REQUIRED
(a) What is the book value of prepaid advertising at December 31, 19X1; December 31, 19X2; and December 31, 19X3?
(b) What is the tax basis of prepaid advertising at December 31, 19X1; December 31, 19X2; and December 31, 19X3?
(c) What amount of deferred tax liability should be reported in the year-end balance sheets for 19X1, 19X2, and 19X3?
(d) Prepare journal entries to record income taxes at December 31, 19X1; December 31, 19X2; and December 31, 19X3.

BUSINESS DECISION PROBLEM

Allendale Corporation has total assets of $6,000,000 and has been earning an average of $600,000 before income tax the past several years. The firm is planning to expand plant facilities to manufacture a new product and needs an additional $2,000,000 in funds, on which it expects to earn 16% before income tax. The income tax rate is expected to be 35% for the next several years. The firm has no long-term debt outstanding and presently has 60,000 shares of common stock outstanding. The firm is considering three alternatives:

1. Obtain the $2,000,000 by issuing 20,000 shares of common stock at $100 per share.
2. Obtain the $2,000,000 by issuing $1,000,000, 10%, 20-year bonds at face value and 10,000 shares of common stock at $100 per share.
3. Obtain the $2,000,000 by issuing $2,000,000, 10%, 20-year bonds at face value.

REQUIRED

As a stockholder of Allendale Corporation, which alternative would you prefer, if your main concern is enhancing the firm's earnings per share?

ANSWERS TO SELF-TEST QUESTIONS

1. (b) **2.** (a) **3.** (c) **4.** (b) **5.** (d)

APPENDIX B

PRESENT VALUES AND EFFECTIVE INTEREST AMORTIZATION

In this appendix, we explain the concept of present value and the techniques of bond valuation to expand on the subject of effective interest amortization, which was introduced in Chapter 17.

PRESENT VALUES

Concept of Present Value

Would you rather receive a dollar now or a dollar one year from now? Most persons would answer, "a dollar now." Intuition tells us that a dollar received now is more valuable than the same amount received sometime in the future. Sound reasons exist for choosing the earlier dollar, the most obvious of which concerns risk. Because the future is always uncertain, some event may prevent us from receiving the dollar at the later date. To avoid this risk, we choose the earlier date.

A second reason for choosing the earlier date is that the dollar received now could be invested; one year from now, we could have not only the dollar, but also the interest income for the period. Using these risk and interest factors, we can generalize that (1) the right to receive an amount of money now—its **present value**—is normally worth more than the right to receive the same amount later—its future value; (2) the longer we must wait to receive an amount, the less attractive the receipt is; and (3) the difference between the present value of an amount and its future value is a function of interest (Principal × Interest Rate × Time). The more risk associated with any situation, the higher the appropriate interest rate.

We support these generalizations with an illustration. What amount could we accept now that would be as valuable as receiving $100 one year from now if the appropriate interest rate is 10%? We recognize intuitively that with a 10% interest rate, we should accept less than $100, or approximately $91. We base this estimate on the realization that the $100 received in the future must equal the present value (100%) plus 10% interest on the present value. Thus, in our example, the $100 future receipt must be 1.10 times the present value. Dividing ($100/1.10), we obtain a present value of $90.90. In other words, under the given conditions we would do as well to accept $90.90 now as to wait one year and receive \$100. To confirm the equality of a \$90.90 receipt now to a \$100 receipt one year later, we calculate the future value of \$90.90 at 10% for one year as follows:

$$\$90.90 \times 1.10 \times 1 \text{ year} = \$100 \text{ (rounded)}$$

Thus, we compute the present value of a future receipt by discounting (deducting an interest factor) the future receipt back to the present at an appropriate interest rate. We present this schematically below:

Present value, \$90.90 ← Discounted for one year at 10% ← Future value, \$100

If either the time period or the interest rate were increased, the resulting present value would decrease. If more than one time period is involved, compound interest computations are appropriate.

Use of Present Value Tables

Because present value tables, such as Table I on page 628 are widely available, we need not present here the various formulas for interest computations. Table I can be used to compute the present value amounts in the illustrations and problem materials that follow. Simply stated, present value tables provide a multiplier for many combinations of time periods and interest rates that, when applied to the dollar amount of a future receipt, determines its present value.

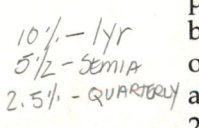

Present value tables are used as follows. First, determine the number of interest compounding periods involved (three years compounded annually is three periods, three years compounded semiannually is six periods, three years compounded quarterly is 12 periods, and so on). The extreme left-hand column indicates the number of periods covered in the table.

Next, determine the interest rate per compounding period. Note that interest rates are usually quoted on a *per year* basis. Therefore, only in the case of annual compoundings is the quoted interest rate the interest rate per compounding period. In other cases, the rate per compounding period is the annual rate divided by the number of compounding periods in a year. For example, an interest rate of 10% per year would be 10% for one compounding period if compounded annually, 5% for two compounding periods if compounded semiannually, and $2\frac{1}{2}$% for four compounding periods if compounded quarterly.

Locate the factor that is to the right of the appropriate number of compounding periods and beneath the appropriate interest rate per compounding period. Multiply this factor by the number of dollars involved.

Note the logical progressions among multipliers in Table I. All values are less than 1.0 because the present value is always smaller than the \$1 future amount if the interest rate is greater than zero. Also, as the interest rate increases (moving from left to right in the table) or the number of periods increases (moving from top to bottom), the multipliers become smaller.

EXAMPLE 1 Compute the present value of \$100 one year hence, at 10% interest compounded annually.

Number of periods (one year, annually) = 1
Rate per period (10%/1) = 10%
Multiplier = 0.909
Present value = \$100.00 × 0.909 = \$90.90
(Note that this agrees with our earlier illustration.)

EXAMPLE 2 Compute the present value of $116.99 two years hence, at 8% compounded semiannually.

Number of periods (two years, semiannually) = 4
Rate per period (8%/2) = 4%
Multiplier = 0.855
Present value = $116.99 × 0.855 = $100 (rounded)

Annuity Form of Cash Flows

Using present value tables like Table I, we can compute the present value of any single future receipt or series of future receipts. One frequent pattern of cash receipts, however, is subject to a more convenient treatment. This pattern, known as the **annuity form,** can be described as *equal amounts equally spaced over a period.*

For example, $100 is to be received at the end of each of the next three years as an annuity. As shown below, the present value of this annuity can be computed from Table I by computing the present value of each of the three individual receipts and summing them (assuming 5% annual interest).

Future Receipts (annuity) Yr. 1	Yr. 2	Yr. 3		PV Multiplier (Table I)		Present Value
$100			×	0.952	=	$ 95.20
	$100		×	0.907	=	90.70
		$100	×	0.864	=	$ 86.40
				Total present value		$272.30

Table II (page 629) provides a single multiplier for computing the present value of a series of future cash receipts in the annuity form. Referring to Table II in the "3 periods" row and the 5% column, we see that the multiplier is 2.723. When applied to the $100 annuity amount, the multiplier gives a present value of $272.30. Of course, the same present value is derived from the several multipliers of Table I. For annuities of 5, 10, or 20 years, the computations avoided by using annuity tables are considerable.

Bond Valuations

In Chapter 17, we explained that (1) the essence of a bond investment is lending money; (2) the amount received by the lender consists of a series (usually semiannual) of interest income amounts and a single lump-sum repayment of the bond principal; and (3) bonds are sold at premiums or discounts to adjust their effective interest rates to the prevailing market rate when they are issued.

Because of the role of interest in bond investments, the selling price (or valuation) of a bond that is necessary to yield a specific rate can be determined as follows:

1. Use Table I to compute the present value of the future principal repayment at the desired (or effective) rate of interest.
2. Use Table II to compute the present value of the future series of interest receipts at the desired (or effective) rate of interest.
3. Add the present values obtained in steps 1 and 2.

We illustrate in Exhibit B–1 the valuation of a $100,000 issue of 8%, four-year bonds paying interest semiannually and sold on the date of issue to yield 8%.

EXHIBIT B–1

VALUATION OF A BOND ISSUE USING PRESENT VALUE TABLES

Future Cash Receipts	Multiplier (Table I)	Multiplier (Table II)	Present Values
Principal repayment, $100,000 (a single amount received eight semiannual periods hence)	0.731		$ 73,100
Interest receipts, $4,000 at end of each of eight semiannual interest periods		6.733	26,900 (rounded)
Total present value (or issue price) of bond			$100,000

We use the 4% column in both tables because the interest rate is 8% compounded semiannually (8%/2 = 4% per compounding period), and we use the eight periods hence line because there are eight semiannual periods in four years. The multiplier from Table I is applied to the $100,000 because the principal repayment is a single sum. Because the eight semiannual interest receipts are in the annuity form, we use the multiplier from Table II to compute their present value. Note that the computation in Exhibit B–1 confirms the observation that the price of 8% bonds sold to yield 8% should be face (or par) value.

EFFECTIVE INTEREST AMORTIZATION

Most bonds sell at more or less than their face value, and therefore accounting for them involves amortizing bond premium or bond discount. For the remainder of this illustration, we show (1) how the $100,000, 8% bond issue used earlier would be valued if it were sold to yield either 6% or 10% compounded semiannually, and (2) how the bond discount and premium amounts would be determined under the effective interest method of amortization.

We calculate the amount of discount and premium in the illustration as follows:

	Bonds Sold at Discount (to yield 10%)		Bonds Sold at Premium (to yield 6%)	
Future Cash Receipts	Present Value Multiplier	Present Value	Present Value Multiplier	Present Value
Principal receipt of $100,000 (eight semiannual periods hence, factors from Table I)	0.677	$67,700	0.789	$ 78,900
Interest receipts of $4,000 each (a series of eight in annuity form, factors from Table II)	6.463	25,852	7.020	28,080
Selling price of bond issues		$93,552		$106,980
Amount of bond discount or premium		$ 6,448		$ 6,980

According to these results, an investor wishing to earn 10%, compounded semiannually, must discount the bonds by $6,448 (that is, pay only $93,552 for them). An investor paying as much as a $6,980 premium for the bonds would still earn 6%, compounded semiannually, on the investment.

As we explained in Chapter 17, the book value of bonds consists of their face value plus any unamortized premium or less any unamortized discount. Thus, at issuance, the book value of the bonds is equal to their selling price. To calculate the periodic amount of amortization using the effective interest method:

1. Determine the period's interest expense by multiplying the bonds' book value at the beginning of the period involved by the desired (or effective) interest rate.
2. Determine the period's amortization by comparing the period's interest expense (step 1 above) to the amount of interest actually paid. If the interest expense is greater than the amount of interest paid, the difference is discount amortization; if the expense is less than the interest paid, the difference is premium amortization.

Face value of bonds	$100,000
Less: Discount	6,448
Book value of bonds at beginning of period	$ 93,552
Multiply by the interest rate per interest period (10%/2 = 5%)	× 0.05
Interest expense for first period (rounded)	$ 4,678
Actual interest paid ($100,000 × 0.08 × $\frac{6}{12}$)	4,000
First period's discount amortization	$ 678

Exhibits B–2 and B–3 summarize the calculations, related account balances, and the general progressions involved in the other periods of our illustration. These amortization schedules also appear in Chapter 17 and are explained there. We repeat them here for your convenience.

The effective interest method of amortization is often justified as being more precise than the straight-line method. This contention probably rests on the fact that, by incorporating a changing amount of total interest expense, the effective interest method results in a uniform interest rate throughout the life of the bonds. Obviously, this increased precision is offset by the added complexity and the fact that the difference between the two methods is often considered immaterial.

Future Value of a Single Amount

The **future value** of a single sum is the amount a specified investment will be worth at a future date if invested at a given rate of compound interest. Suppose we decide to invest $6,000 in a savings account that pays 6% annual interest, and that we intend to leave the principal and interest in the account for five years. We assume that interest is credited to the account at the end of each year. The balance in the account at the end of five years is determined using Table III, on page 630, which furnishes the future value of a dollar after a given number of time periods, as follows:

Principal	×	**Factor**	=	**Future Value**
$6,000	×	1.338	=	$8,028

The factor 1.338 is found on the line for five periods and the column for 6%.

EXHIBIT B–2

BONDS SOLD AT A DISCOUNT: PERIODIC INTEREST EXPENSE, AMORTIZATION, AND BOOK VALUE OF BONDS

Year	Interest Period	(A) Interest Paid (4% of face value)	(B) Interest Expense (5% of bond book value)	(C) Periodic Amortization (B – A)	(D) Balance of Unamortized Discount (D – C)	(E) Book Value of Bonds, End of Period ($100,000 – D)
(at issue)					$6,448	$ 93,552
1	1	$4,000	$4,678	$678	5,770	94,230
	2	4,000	4,712	712	5,058	94,942
2	3	4,000	4,747	747	4,311	95,689
	4	4,000	4,784	784	3,527	96,473
3	5	4,000	4,824	824	2,703	97,297
	6	4,000	4,865	865	1,838	98,162
4	7	4,000	4,908	908	930	99,070
	8	4,000	4,930*	930	0	100,000

*Adjusted for cumulative rounding error of $24.

EXHIBIT B–3

BONDS SOLD AT A PREMIUM: PERIODIC INTEREST EXPENSE, AMORTIZATION, AND BOOK VALUE OF BONDS

Year	Interest Period	(A) Interest Paid (4% of face value)	(B) Interest Expense (3% of bond book value)	(C) Periodic Amortization (A – B)	(D) Balance of Unamortized Premium (D – C)	(E) Book Value of Bonds, End of Period ($100,000 + D)
(at issue)					$6,980	$106,980
1	1	$4,000	$3,209	$791	6,189	106,189
	2	4,000	3,186	814	5,375	105,375
2	3	4,000	3,161	839	4,536	104,536
	4	4,000	3,136	864	3,672	103,672
3	5	4,000	3,110	890	2,782	102,782
	6	4,000	3,083	917	1,865	101,865
4	7	4,000	3,056	944	921	100,921
	8	4,000	3,079*	921	0	100,000

*Adjusted for cumulative rounding error of $51.

Suppose the interest is credited to the account semiannually, rather than annually. In this situation, there are ten compounding periods, and we use a 3% rate (one-half the annual rate). The future value calculation is as follows:

Principal	× Factor	= Future Value
$6,000	× 1.344	= $8,064

Future Value of an Annuity

If, instead of investing a single amount at the beginning of a series of periods, we invest a specified amount each period, we are investing in the annuity form. Suppose we decide to invest $2,000 at the end of each year for five years at an 8% annual rate of return. To determine the accumulated amount of principal and interest, we refer to Table IV, on page 631, which furnishes the future value of a dollar paid at the end of each period. The factor 5.867 is found on the line for five periods and the column for 8%, and the calculation is as follows:

Periodic Payment	× Factor	= Future Value
$2,000	× 5.867	= $11,734

If we decide to make payments of $1,000 at the end of each six months for five years at an 8% annual rate of return, we would use the factor for ten periods at 4%, as follows:

Periodic Payment	× Factor	= Future Value
$1,000	× 12.01	= $12,010

When the future value is some desired amount and the periodic payment is to be calculated, you need only to *divide* the future value by the factor to determine the periodic payment.

For example, a corporation issued $100,000, 10-year bonds payable and agreed to contribute the necessary amounts to a sinking fund at the end of each year in order to retire the bonds in 10 years. It is expected that the bonds will earn a 12% average rate of return over the period. The factor for 10 periods at 12%, taken from Table IV, is 17.55. The annual contribution to the sinking fund is:

Future Value	÷ Factor	= Periodic Payment
$100,000	÷ 17.55	= $5,698.01 (rounded)

PROBLEMS

Note: Use Tables I–IV (pages 628–31) to solve the following problems.

Computing various present values

B–1 Compute the present value of each of the following:

(a) $80,000 ten years hence if the annual interest rate is:
1. 8% compounded annually.
2. 8% compounded semiannually.
3. 8% compounded quarterly.

(b) $500 received at the end of each year for the next eight years if money is worth 12% per year compounded annually.

(c) $300 received at the end of each six months for the next nine years if the interest rate is 10% per year compounded semiannually.

(d) $200,000 inheritance ten years hence if money is worth 10% per year compounded annually.

(e) $1,000 received each half-year for the next ten years plus a single sum of $50,000 at the end of ten years if the interest rate is 8% per year compounded semiannually.

Computing present value of annuity

B–2 Using Table II, calculate the present value of a five-year, $8,000 annuity if the interest rate is 8% per year compounded annually. Verify your answer by using Table I. Briefly explain how these tables are related.

Determining bond purchase price

B–3 You have an opportunity to purchase a bond issued by a local hospital. The bond has a face value of $50,000, will pay 8% interest per year in semiannual payments, and will mature in five years. How much should you pay for the bond if you want to earn 10% interest per year compounded semiannually on your investment?

Determining bond selling price

B–4 Sharpe, Inc., plans to issue $400,000 of 10% bonds that will pay interest semiannually and mature in five years. Assume that the effective interest rate is 12% per year compounded semiannually.
(a) Compute the selling price of the bonds.
(b) Construct a table similar to Exhibit B–2 for the first two years of the bonds' life. Round amounts to the nearest dollar.

Determining bond selling price

B–5 Complete the requirements of Problem B–4 assuming the effective interest rate is 8% per year compounded semiannually. For requirement (b), construct a table similar to Exhibit B–3.

Determining sinking fund contributions

B–6 A firm issued $300,000 of 10-year bonds payable. The bond agreement requires annual contributions to a sinking fund at the end of each year, in order to accumulate $300,000 to retire the bonds at maturity.
(a) Using Table IV, calculate the amount of the annual contribution to the sinking fund if a 10% rate of return is expected.
(b) Calculate the balance in the sinking fund at the end of the second year.
(c) Prepare the journal entry to record the sinking fund income at the end of the second year.

Calculating future value of a single amount

B–7 Using Table III, calculate the following:
(a) Future value of a single amount of $4,000 invested for eight years at 10% compounded annually.
(b) Future value of a single amount of $4,000 invested for eight years at 10% compounded semiannually.

Calculating future value of an annuity paid

B–8 Using Table IV, calculate the following:
(a) Future value of an annuity of $12,000 paid at the end of each year for nine years at an annual rate of 10%.
(b) Future value of an annuity of $6,000 paid at the end of each six months for nine years at an annual rate of 10%.

PRESENT VALUE TABLES

TABLE I

PRESENT VALUE OF $1 RECEIVED IN THE FUTURE

Periods Hence	Rate per Compounding Period									
	2%	3%	4%	5%	6%	8%	10%	12%	15%	20%
1	0.980	0.971	0.962	0.952	0.943	0.926	0.909	0.893	0.870	0.833
2	0.961	0.943	0.925	0.907	0.890	0.857	0.826	0.797	0.756	0.694
3	0.942	0.915	0.889	0.864	0.840	0.794	0.751	0.712	0.658	0.579
4	0.924	0.889	0.855	0.823	0.792	0.735	0.683	0.636	0.572	0.482
5	0.906	0.863	0.822	0.784	0.747	0.681	0.621	0.567	0.497	0.402
6	0.888	0.838	0.790	0.746	0.705	0.630	0.564	0.507	0.432	0.335
7	0.871	0.813	0.760	0.711	0.665	0.583	0.513	0.452	0.376	0.279
8	0.854	0.789	0.731	0.677	0.627	0.540	0.467	0.404	0.327	0.233
9	0.837	0.766	0.703	0.645	0.592	0.500	0.424	0.361	0.284	0.194
10	0.821	0.744	0.676	0.614	0.558	0.463	0.386	0.322	0.247	0.162
11	0.804	0.722	0.650	0.585	0.527	0.429	0.350	0.287	0.215	0.135
12	0.789	0.701	0.625	0.557	0.497	0.397	0.319	0.257	0.187	0.112
13	0.773	0.681	0.601	0.530	0.469	0.368	0.290	0.229	0.163	0.093
14	0.758	0.661	0.577	0.505	0.442	0.340	0.263	0.205	0.141	0.078
15	0.743	0.642	0.555	0.481	0.417	0.315	0.239	0.183	0.123	0.065
16	0.728	0.623	0.534	0.458	0.394	0.292	0.218	0.163	0.107	0.054
17	0.714	0.605	0.513	0.436	0.371	0.270	0.198	0.146	0.093	0.045
18	0.700	0.587	0.494	0.416	0.350	0.250	0.180	0.130	0.081	0.038
19	0.686	0.570	0.475	0.396	0.331	0.232	0.164	0.116	0.070	0.031
20	0.673	0.554	0.456	0.377	0.312	0.215	0.149	0.104	0.061	0.026
30	0.552	0.412	0.308	0.231	0.174	0.099	0.057	0.033	0.015	0.004
40	0.453	0.307	0.208	0.142	0.097	0.046	0.022	0.011	0.004	0.001
50	0.372	0.228	0.141	0.087	0.054	0.021	0.009	0.003	0.001	—

TABLE II

PRESENT VALUE OF $1 ANNUITY RECEIVED AT END OF EACH PERIOD

Periods Hence	Rate per Compounding Period									
	2%	3%	4%	5%	6%	8%	10%	12%	15%	20%
1	0.980	0.971	0.962	0.952	0.943	0.926	0.909	0.893	0.870	0.833
2	1.942	1.914	1.886	1.859	1.833	1.783	1.736	1.690	1.626	1.528
3	2.884	2.829	2.775	2.723	2.673	2.577	2.487	2.402	2.283	2.106
4	3.808	3.717	3.630	3.546	3.465	3.312	3.170	3.037	2.855	2.589
5	4.714	4.580	4.452	4.330	4.212	3.993	3.791	3.605	3.352	2.991
6	5.601	5.417	5.242	5.076	4.917	4.623	4.355	4.111	3.784	3.326
7	6.472	6.230	6.002	5.786	5.582	5.206	4.868	4.564	4.160	3.605
8	7.326	7.020	6.733	6.463	6.210	5.747	5.335	4.968	4.487	3.837
9	8.162	7.786	7.435	7.108	6.802	6.247	5.760	5.328	4.772	4.031
10	8.983	8.530	8.111	7.722	7.360	6.710	6.145	5.650	5.019	4.192
11	9.787	9.253	8.761	8.306	7.887	7.139	6.495	5.988	5.234	4.327
12	10.575	9.954	9.385	8.863	8.384	7.536	6.814	6.194	5.421	4.439
13	11.348	10.635	9.986	9.394	8.853	7.904	7.103	6.424	5.583	4.533
14	12.106	11.296	10.563	9.899	9.295	8.244	7.367	6.628	5.724	4.611
15	12.849	11.938	11.118	10.380	9.712	8.560	7.606	6.811	5.847	4.675
16	13.578	12.561	11.652	10.838	10.106	8.851	7.824	6.974	5.954	4.730
17	14.292	13.166	12.166	11.274	10.477	9.122	8.022	7.120	6.047	4.775
18	14.992	13.754	12.659	11.690	10.828	9.372	8.201	7.250	6.128	4.812
19	15.679	14.324	13.134	12.085	11.158	9.604	8.365	7.366	6.198	4.844
20	16.351	14.878	13.590	12.462	11.470	9.818	8.514	7.469	6.259	4.870
30	22.397	19.600	17.292	15.373	13.765	11.258	9.427	8.055	6.566	4.979
40	27.356	23.115	19.793	17.159	15.046	11.925	9.779	8.244	6.642	4.997
50	31.424	25.730	21.482	18.256	15.762	12.234	9.915	8.304	6.661	4.999

FUTURE VALUE TABLES

TABLE III

FUTURE VALUE OF $1
AFTER A GIVEN NUMBER OF TIME PERIODS

Periods Hence	Rate per Compounding Period									
	2%	3%	4%	5%	6%	8%	10%	12%	15%	20%
1	1.020	1.030	1.040	1.050	1.060	1.080	1.100	1.120	1.150	1.200
2	1.040	1.061	1.082	1.103	1.124	1.166	1.210	1.254	1.323	1.440
3	1.061	1.093	1.125	1.158	1.191	1.260	1.331	1.405	1.521	1.728
4	1.082	1.126	1.170	1.216	1.262	1.360	1.464	1.574	1.749	2.074
5	1.104	1.159	1.217	1.276	1.338	1.469	1.611	1.762	2.011	2.488
6	1.126	1.194	1.265	1.340	1.419	1.587	1.772	1.974	2.313	2.986
7	1.149	1.230	1.316	1.407	1.504	1.714	1.949	2.211	2.660	3.583
8	1.172	1.267	1.369	1.477	1.594	1.851	2.144	2.476	3.059	4.300
9	1.195	1.305	1.423	1.551	1.689	1.999	2.358	2.773	3.518	5.160
10	1.219	1.344	1.480	1.629	1.791	2.159	2.594	3.106	4.046	6.192
11	1.243	1.384	1.539	1.710	1.898	2.332	2.853	3.479	4.652	7.430
12	1.268	1.426	1.601	1.796	2.012	2.518	3.138	3.896	5.350	8.916
13	1.294	1.469	1.665	1.886	2.133	2.720	3.452	4.363	6.153	10.699
14	1.319	1.513	1.732	1.980	2.261	2.937	3.798	4.887	7.076	12.839
15	1.346	1.558	1.801	2.079	2.397	3.172	4.177	5.474	8.137	15.407
16	1.373	1.605	1.873	2.183	2.540	3.426	4.595	6.130	9.358	18.488
17	1.400	1.653	1.948	2.292	2.693	3.700	5.054	6.866	10.761	22.186
18	1.428	1.702	2.026	2.407	2.854	3.996	5.560	7.690	12.375	26.623
19	1.457	1.754	2.107	2.527	3.026	4.316	6.116	8.613	14.232	31.948
20	1.486	1.806	2.191	2.653	3.207	4.661	6.728	9.646	16.367	38.338
30	1.811	2.427	3.243	4.322	5.743	10.06	17.45	29.96	66.212	237.376
40	2.208	3.262	4.801	7.040	10.29	21.72	45.26	93.05	267.864	1,469.772
50	2.692	4.384	7.107	11.47	18.42	46.90	117.4	289.0	1,083.657	9,100.438

TABLE IV

FUTURE VALUE OF $1 ANNUITY PAID EACH PERIOD FOR A NUMBER OF TIME PERIODS

Periods Hence	Rate per Compounding Period 2%	3%	4%	5%	6%	8%	10%	12%	15%	20%
1	1.000	1.000	1.000	1.000	1.000	1.000	1.000	1.000	1.000	1.000
2	2.020	2.030	2.040	2.050	2.060	2.080	2.100	2.120	2.150	2.200
3	3.060	3.091	3.122	3.153	3.184	3.246	3.310	3.374	3.473	3.640
4	4.122	4.184	4.246	4.310	4.375	4.506	4.641	4.779	4.993	5.368
5	5.204	5.309	5.416	5.526	5.637	5.867	6.105	6.353	6.742	7.442
6	6.308	6.468	6.633	6.802	6.975	7.336	7.716	8.115	8.754	9.930
7	7.434	7.662	7.898	8.142	8.394	8.923	9.487	10.09	11.07	12.92
8	8.583	8.892	9.214	9.549	9.897	10.64	11.44	12.30	13.73	16.50
9	9.755	10.16	10.58	11.03	11.49	12.49	13.58	14.78	16.79	20.80
10	10.95	11.46	12.01	12.58	13.18	14.49	15.94	17.55	20.30	25.96
11	12.17	12.81	13.49	14.21	14.97	16.65	18.53	20.65	24.35	32.15
12	13.41	14.19	15.03	15.92	16.87	18.98	21.38	24.13	29.00	39.58
13	14.68	15.62	16.63	17.71	18.88	21.50	24.52	28.03	34.35	48.50
14	15.97	17.09	18.29	19.60	21.02	24.21	27.98	32.39	40.50	59.20
15	17.29	18.60	20.02	21.58	23.28	27.15	31.77	37.28	47.58	72.04
16	18.64	20.16	21.82	23.66	25.67	30.32	35.95	42.75	55.72	87.44
17	20.01	21.76	23.70	25.84	28.21	33.75	40.54	48.88	65.08	105.9
18	21.41	23.41	25.65	28.13	30.91	37.45	45.60	55.75	75.84	128.1
19	22.84	25.12	27.67	30.54	33.76	41.45	51.16	63.44	88.21	154.7
20	24.30	26.87	29.78	33.07	36.79	45.76	57.28	72.05	102.4	186.7
30	40.57	47.58	56.08	66.44	79.06	113.3	164.5	241.3	434.7	1,181.2
40	60.40	75.40	95.03	120.8	154.8	259.1	442.6	767.1	1,779	7,343.
50	84.58	112.8	152.7	209.3	290.3	573.8	1,164	2,400	7,218	45,497.

18

LONG-TERM STOCK INVESTMENTS AND CONSOLIDATED FINANCIAL STATEMENTS

CHAPTER OBJECTIVES

1. Describe the various kinds of long-term stock investments and the accounting for them (pp. 633–36).
2. Define parent–subsidiary relationships and illustrate how their balance sheet data are consolidated (pp. 636–46).
3. Discuss the treatment of acquisitions when cost exceeds the book value acquired in a subsidiary (pp. 646–48).
4. Explain and illustrate the consolidation of parent and subsidiary income statements (pp. 648–52).
5. Provide an overview of accounting for acquisitions under the "pooling of interests" method (pp. 652–53).

A man is known by the company he merges.

LEONARD LOUIS LEVINSON

In previous chapters, we have discussed the nature and accounting treatment of short-term investments and long-term bond investments. Now we examine the nature and accounting treatment of long-term stock investments.

Firms purchase the shares of other companies on a long-term basis for a variety of reasons. Sometimes modest investments are made simply because the shares promise a good yield or an increase in value over time. Sizeable long-term stock investments—particularly controlling interests in other firms—are more often made for such economic reasons as growth, product diversification, market penetration, assurance of raw material supplies, and tax savings. Most business combinations today are achieved by stock acquisitions. Practically all of the corporations listed on the organized stock exchanges own all or a majority of the voting stock of other companies. Accounting for such business combinations is treated later in this chapter.

TYPES OF OWNERSHIP INTEREST

Although all long-term investments in stock are first entered in the accounts at cost, the subsequent accounting procedures differ according to the circumstances. Basically, the accounting treatment used depends on whether the ownership interest acquired is a controlling interest—that is, an interest that permits the investor company to exercise significant influence over the company whose stock is held—or an interest that is neither controlling nor influential.

Noncontrolling and Noninfluential Interest

Long-term investments of less than 20% of a corporation's voting stock are considered small enough to preclude the investor company from significantly influencing the policies of the company whose stock is acquired. Such investments are initially recorded at cost, and, depending on company policy, cash dividends are recorded as income either when declared or received. These procedures are known as the **cost method** of accounting for investments. On the balance sheet, however, these investments are carried at the lower of cost or market value of the portfolio, determined at the balance sheet date. Thus, like temporary stock investments, their carrying value may increase or decrease from period to period (but never above cost). Unlike temporary stock investments, however, any unrealized losses or recoveries of unrealized losses are not shown in the income statement; instead, the net unrealized loss on the portfolio of long-term stock investments is reported separately as a contra stockholders' equity account in the balance sheet.

The journal entries for noncontrolling and noninfluential investments are similar to those for temporary stock investments, shown in Chapter 7. For convenience, we review certain typical entries here.

Suppose 100 shares of Hytex, Inc., common stock are acquired on October 1 at a cost of $6,600, including commissions and taxes. The investment is recorded as follows:

Oct. 1	Investment in Hytex Stock	6,600	
	Cash		6,600
	To record purchase of 100 shares of common stock for $6,600.		

DIVIDENDS As in the case of temporary investments, cash dividends received are credited to a Dividend Income account, whereas a memorandum entry records any stock dividends received, since they do not constitute income. The entry for the stock dividend reveals the new average cost of the stock held. Assume that on December 10, Hytex, Inc., paid a cash dividend of $2 per share and a stock dividend of 10%. The following entries record the cash and stock dividends:

Dec. 10	Cash	200	
	Dividend Income		200
	To record receipt of $200 dividend on Hytex, Inc., stock.		

(Memorandum) Received ten shares of Hytex, Inc., common stock as stock dividend. Average cost per share of 110 shares held is now $60 ($6,600/110).

LOWER OF COST OR MARKET FOR PORTFOLIO All of a company's noncontrolling and noninfluential investments in long-term stocks constitute a portfolio. At the end of the accounting period, they are reported on the balance sheet at the lower of the aggregate cost or market value of the portfolio. Should the aggregate market value drop below total cost, an unrealized loss is recorded and a contra asset account (to offset long-term stock investments) is credited. To illustrate, assume a company has the following portfolio of long-term stock investments at the end of its first year of operations:

Stock	Cost	Market Value
Hytex, Inc., Common	$ 6,600	$ 4,800
Intersouth, Inc., Common	20,000	21,500
Wade Corporation Common	15,400	12,000
Total	$42,000	$38,300

Because the total market value ($38,300) is less than total cost ($42,000), the company makes the following journal entry:

Dec. 31	Unrealized Loss on Long-term Investments	3,700	
	Allowance to Reduce Long-term Investments to Market		3,700
	To record unrealized losses on portfolio of long-term stock investments.		

The unrealized loss on long-term investments is considered temporary and is therefore reported separately as a contra stockholders' equity account in the balance sheet (thereby reducing total stockholders' equity). On the balance sheet, the Allowance to Reduce Long-term Investments to Market account balance is deducted from the cost of long-term investments or the investment is shown in the following condensed form:

Long-term Stock Investments, at market (cost $42,000)	$38,300

If the portfolio's market value exceeds its total cost, the investments are reported at cost and no allowance is created.

SALE OF LONG-TERM INVESTMENTS When a long-term stock investment is sold, a gain or loss is recorded equal to the difference between the sale proceeds and the stock's original cost (or the original cost adjusted for the effect of a stock dividend). For example, if all 110 shares of Hytex, Inc., stock discussed above were sold on March 1 of the next year for $4,800, the following entry would be made:

Mar. 1	Cash	4,800	
	Loss on Sale of Investments	1,800	
	Investment in Hytex Stock		6,600
	To record sale of stock for $4,800.		

RECOVERY OF UNREALIZED LOSS The difference between the total cost and market value of a stock portfolio will likely change from one year-end to the next because of changes in market values or in the portfolio's composition. Thus, the contra asset account increases or decreases each year-end to reflect the net unrealized portfolio loss at that time. If the net unrealized loss at year-end is smaller than it was the year before, the adjusting entry records a recovery of an unrealized loss. Assume the company whose investments we have been analyzing has the following portfolio of long-term stock investments at the end of its second year of operations:

Stock	Cost	Market Value
Intersouth, Inc., Common	$20,000	$22,100
Wade Corporation Common	15,400	12,800
Total	$35,400	$34,900

The net unrealized loss is now $500 ($35,400 − $34,900); at the end of the preceding year, it had been $3,700. The following entry would adjust the allowance account:

Dec. 31	Allowance to Reduce Long-term Investments to Market	3,200	
	Unrealized Loss on Long-term Investments		3,200
	To record decrease in net unrealized loss on long-term stock investments.		

On the year-end balance sheet, the contra amount to stockholders' equity is only $500, and the long-term investments would be shown at market value ($35,400 cost − $500 allowance).

Influential but Noncontrolling Interest

A corporation that owns 20% or more of another corporation's voting stock may exert a significant influence on the operating or financial decisions of that company. However, if 50% or less of the total voting stock is owned, the investment will not usually represent a controlling interest. Investments in the 20–50% ownership range may therefore be considered influential but noncontrolling interests. The **equity method** of accounting is appropriate for investments in this category.

Under the equity method, the investor company records as income or loss each period its proportionate share of the income or loss reported for that period by the company whose stock is held. For example, if Warner Company owns 30% of Rose Corporation's voting stock and Rose Corporation reports earnings of $20,000 for the current year, Warner Company makes the following entry:

Investment in Rose Corporation Stock	6,000	
Income from Investment in Rose Corporation Stock		6,000
To record as income 30% of Rose Corporation's current year earnings of $20,000.		

As this entry shows, when the investor company records its share of the other corporation's income, the investment amount also increases. When cash dividends are received, however, the investor company reports no income. The receipt of a dividend is treated as a reduction of the investment balance. To ilustrate, assume Rose Corporation declared and paid a $7,000 dividend for the current year. Warner Company's entry on receipt of its share of the dividend is

Cash	2,100	
Investment in Rose Corporation Stock		2,100
To record receipt of $2,100 dividend from Rose Corporation.		

Controlling Interest

A company holding more than 50% of another corporation's stock owns a controlling interest. In some cases—such as by agreement with other stockholders—control may exist with a lesser percentage of stock ownership. The financial data of controlled corporations are usually *consolidated* (combined) with the data of the investor company in **consolidated financial statements.** Either the cost or equity method may be used for investments in these controlled corporations; in either case, the application of consolidation procedures yields the same result.

PARENT–SUBSIDIARY RELATIONSHIP

A corporation that controls the policies and operations of other corporations through ownership of their stock commonly presents financial statements of the combined group in published reports. Such consolidated statements portray the financial position and operating results of affiliated companies as a single economic unit. The company holding all or a majority of the stock of the others is the **parent company,** and the wholly owned or majority-held companies are **subsidiaries.** It is important to observe that the individual companies of a group

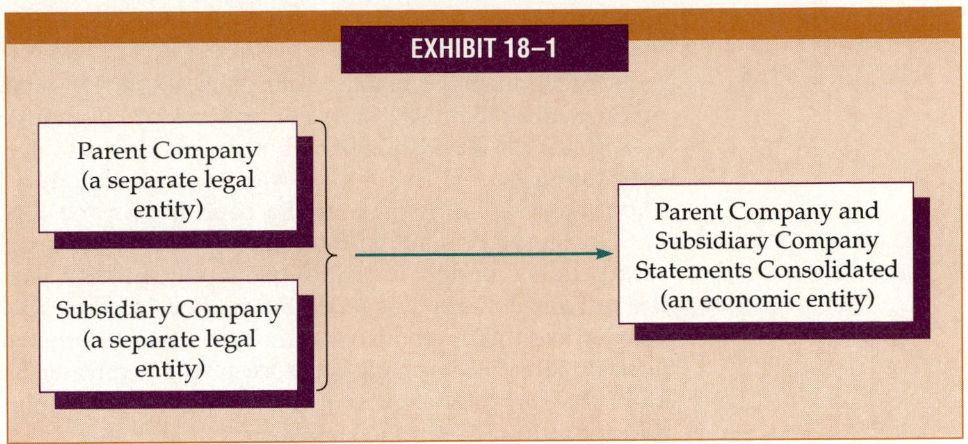

are *legal entities*, each with separate financial statements. When the financial data of these legal entities are combined, the resulting statements portray the group as an *economic entity*, as shown in Exhibit 18–1.

Consolidated financial statements present both the total resources controlled by a parent company and the aggregate results of the group's operations that are difficult to perceive when viewing only the separate reports of the individual companies. Consolidated statements are particularly valuable to the managers and stockholders of the parent company. In addition, creditors, government agencies, and the general public are informed of the magnitude and scope of an economic enterprise through consolidated statements.

Practically all companies prepare consolidated statements when they hold more than 50% of the subsidiary's stock. With this kind of control, the parent can usually direct the policies and activities of the subsidiary. For many years, the accounts of majority-held and wholly owned subsidiaries engaged in activities completely unrelated to those of the parent and other affiliates were routinely excluded from consolidated financial statements. Thus firms such as Sears Company excluded its insurance subsidiary, Allstate, and Ford, General Motors, and FMC Corporation excluded their wholly owned finance and insurance companies. It was felt that the economic operations and accounts of such firms were not compatible in financial statements with merchandising and manufacturing operations. In recent years, however, there has been huge growth and diversity in conglomerate firms, and most of these firms have been consolidating nonhomogenous subsidiaries. For this reason, and because past practice permitted omission of significant amounts of assets, liabilities, revenues and expenses, the exclusion of nonhomogenous subsidiaries is no longer permitted.[1] At present, the major exceptions to the rule are subsidiaries in bankruptcy and foreign subsidiaries with severe exchange restrictions.

Whenever a majority-held or wholly owned subsidiary's accounts are excluded from the consolidated financial statements, the parent company's investment is shown in the consolidated balance sheet as Investment in Unconsolidated Subsidiary.[2] Because the viability of excluded subsidiaries is often in doubt, they should be carried at cost.

---

[1] *Statement of Financial Accounting Standards No. 94*, "Consolidation of All Majority-owned S[illegible]es" (Stamford, CT: Financial Accounting Standards Board, 1987).

[2] Often firms report condensed financial statements of unconsolidated subsidiaries [illegible] the consolidated balance sheet.

ACQUISITION OF SUBSIDIARIES

A corporation may obtain a subsidiary either by establishing a new firm and holding more than 50% of its voting stock or by acquiring more than 50% of the voting stock of an existing firm. Both methods have been extensively used. When an existing firm is acquired, however, the method of acquisition may play an important role in the manner of accounting for the subsidiary.

One common method of acquiring an existing firm is to give up cash, other assets, notes, or debt securities. Generally, this is a *purchase* of a subsidiary, and the **purchase method** of reporting is used in consolidated financial statements. We discuss this method of acquisition first. Another method, called *pooling of interests,* involves exchanging stock of the acquiring company for substantially all of the shares of another firm. We discuss the pooling method of accounting and reporting later in the chapter.

WHOLLY OWNED SUBSIDIARIES—CONSOLIDATION AT ACQUISITION DATE

Creating a Subsidiary Company

Let us assume that, on January 1, 19XX, P Company established a new, wholly owned subsidiary, S Company, to market P Company's products. P Company acquired all of S Company's common stock for $100,000 cash. To record this transaction, P Company debits Investment in S Company and credits Cash for $100,000. In its records, S Company debits Cash and credits Common Stock for $100,000. Condensed balance sheets before and after the creation of the subsidiary are given in Exhibit 18–2.

Notice that the only change in P Company's balance sheet is a shift of $100,000 from Cash and Other Assets to Investment in S Company. The latter represents the 100% ownership of S Company common stock, giving P Company control over the resources of S Company ($100,000 cash). Thus, the $100,000 Investment in S Company on P Company's balance sheet and the $100,000 stockholders' equity (Common Stock) on the subsidiary's balance sheet are reciprocal items. If

EXHIBIT 18–2

Before Creating S Company		After Creating S Company			
P Company Balance Sheet January 1, 19XX		**P Company Balance Sheet January 1, 19XX**		**S Company Balance Sheet January 1, 19XX**	
Cash and Other Assets	$750,000	Cash and Other Assets	$650,000	Cash	$100,000
		Investment in S Company	100,000		
	$750,000		$750,000		$100,000
Liabilities	$200,000	Liabilities	$200,000	Liabilities	$ —
Common Stock	400,000	Common Stock	400,000	Common Stock	100,000
Retained Earnings	150,000	Retained Earnings	150,000	Retained Earnings	—
	$750,000		$750,000		$100,000

Reciprocal Items

EXHIBIT 18–3

P and S Companies
Consolidated Balance Sheet Worksheet
January 1, 19XX

	P Company	S Company	Eliminations Debit	Eliminations Credit	Consolidated Balance Sheet
Cash and Other Assets	650,000	100,000			750,000
Investment in S Company	100,000	—		100,000	—
	750,000	100,000			750,000
Liabilities	200,000	—			200,000
Common Stock					
P Company	400,000				400,000
S Company		100,000	100,000		—
Retained Earnings					
P Company	150,000				150,000
	750,000	100,000	100,000	100,000	750,000

we combine (consolidate) the accounts on the balance sheets of the two companies at January 1, the reciprocal items must be eliminated; otherwise, assets and stockholders' equity would be "double-counted." The eliminating entry made in a consolidated worksheet debits Common Stock (S Company) for $100,000 and credits Investment in S Company for $100,000. Exhibit 18–3 is the worksheet showing how the balance sheets are consolidated. Note that after eliminating the reciprocal elements, the consolidated balance sheet (the right-hand column in Exhibit 18–3) is identical with that of P Company before the creation of the subsidiary. This is logical because P Company commands no more resources than it did formerly. Also, observe that the stockholders' equity on the consolidated balance sheet is the parent company's—that is, *outside* shareholders. *The intercompany equity existing on the balance sheets is always eliminated.*

Acquisition of an Existing Firm

The general concept of consolidating affiliated companies is always the same, whether a subsidiary is created or an existing firm is acquired. Intercompany items—such as intercompany stockholders' equity—are eliminated so that the consolidated statements show only the interests of outsiders. (Later we discuss the elimination of other intercompany items.)

Suppose that P Company, instead of creating a new firm, purchased 100% of the common stock of an existing firm, Z Company, for $100,000. In this case, we assume that Z Company *already has* $100,000 in Cash and Other Assets and no liabilities. The only difference from our previous example is that Z Company's $100,000 of stockholders' equity is composed of $80,000 of Common Stock and $20,000 of Retained Earnings.

The entry on P Company's books to record the acquisition debits Investment in Z Company for $100,000 and credits Cash for $100,000. Z Company makes no entry because payment is made directly to current shareholders of Z Company. Therefore, the balance sheets of the two companies *immediately after the acquisition* are as shown in Exhibit 18–4.

EXHIBIT 18–4

P Company
Balance Sheet
January 1, 19XX

Cash and Other Assets	$650,000
Investment in Z Company	100,000
	$750,000
Liabilities	$200,000
Common Stock	400,000
Retained Earnings	150,000
	$750,000

Z Company
Balance Sheet
January 1, 19XX

Cash and Other Assets	$100,000
	—
	$100,000
	—
Common Stock	$ 80,000
Retained Earnings	20,000
	$100,000

Reciprocal Items

The only significant difference between the balance sheets in Exhibit 18–4 and the balance sheets after acquisition in Exhibit 18–2 is that the stockholders' equity of Z Company consists of $80,000 Common Stock and $20,000 Retained Earnings rather than $100,000 Common Stock. In this case, the reciprocal items are the $100,000 Investment in Z Company on P Company's balance sheet and the Common Stock and Retained Earnings ($80,000 + $20,000) on Z Company's balance sheet. To avoid double-counting assets and stockholders' equity, we must eliminate these items when consolidating the accounts of the two firms. The worksheet entry debits Common Stock (Z Company) for $80,000, debits Retained Earnings (Z Company) for $20,000, and credits Investment in Z Company for $100,000. The worksheet to prepare the consolidated balance sheet is shown in Exhibit 18–5.

EXHIBIT 18–5

P and Z Companies
Consolidated Balance Sheet Worksheet
January 1, 19XX

	P Company	Z Company	Eliminations Debit	Eliminations Credit	Consolidated Balance Sheet
Cash and Other Assets	650,000	100,000			750,000
Investment in Z Company	100,000	—		100,000	—
	750,000	100,000			750,000
Liabilities	200,000	—			200,000
Common Stock					
P Company	400,000				400,000
Z Company		80,000	80,000		—
Retained Earnings					
P Company	150,000				150,000
Z Company		20,000	20,000		—
	750,000	100,000	100,000	100,000	750,000

WHOLLY OWNED SUBSIDIARIES—CONSOLIDATION AFTER ACQUISITION DATE

In accounting periods following a parent–subsidiary affiliation, the parent company may account for its investment in the subsidiary by either the cost or the equity method. In all of our examples and problems, we use the equity method, because it is easier to understand.[3] Recall that under this method, the parent periodically reflects on its own records its share (100% in our example) of the subsidiary's earnings by debiting the Investment in Subsidiary account and crediting Income from Investment in Subsidiary. The latter item eventually increases the parent company's retained earnings. (If the subsidiary has a loss, the entry would be a debit to Loss from Investment in Subsidiary and a credit to Investment in Subsidiary, the debit eventually reducing the parent's retained earnings.) Whenever the subsidiary pays dividends, the parent company debits Cash and credits the Investment in Subsidiary account for the amount received.

To illustrate, let us return to the example (Exhibit 18–2) in which P Company created a subsidiary by purchasing 100% of S Company's stock for $100,000 cash. We assume that during the year following acquisition, P Company earned $40,000 *before* adding its earnings from S Company and paid no dividends. We also assume that S Company earned $20,000, paying $10,000 in dividends.

To record its share of S Company's earnings and to record the dividends received, P Company makes the following entries *in its own records:*

Investment in S Company	20,000	
Income from Investment in S Company (Retained Earnings)		20,000
To record 100% of S Company's earnings for the current year.		
Cash	10,000	
Investment in S Company		10,000
To record dividends received from S Company.		

The balance sheets of P Company and S Company at December 31, 19XX, are given in Exhibit 18–6.

Let us review the changes that have occurred in these two balance sheets since the date of acquisition. P Company's Cash and Other Assets has increased $50,000. This increase consists of P Company's own net income of $40,000 plus $10,000 in dividends received from S Company. (For simplicity, we assume that all of P Company's net income increases Cash and Other Assets, with liabilities remaining unchanged.) The Investment in S Company has increased $10,000 ($20,000 S Company earnings less $10,000 dividends received). P Company's Retained Earnings has increased $60,000 ($40,000 of its own net income plus $20,000 S Company net income).

For S Company, Cash and Other Assets has increased $15,000, along with a $5,000 increase in liabilities. Thus, net assets have increased $10,000. The corresponding $10,000 increase in Retained Earnings resulted from $20,000 net income less $10,000 dividends declared and paid. Exhibit 18–7 shows a worksheet to prepare a consolidated balance sheet at December 31, 19XX.

---

[3]As we mentioned earlier in this chapter, both methods yield the same results when appropriate procedures are used. Consolidation procedures for both methods are taught in advanced accounting courses.

EXHIBIT 18–6

P Company
Balance Sheet
December 31, 19XX

Cash and Other Assets	$700,000
Investment in S Company	110,000
	$810,000
Liabilities	$200,000
Common Stock	400,000
Retained Earnings	210,000
	$810,000

S Company
Balance Sheet
December 31, 19XX

Cash and Other Assets	$115,000
	—
	$115,000
Liabilities	$ 5,000
Common Stock	100,000
Retained Earnings	10,000
	$115,000

Whenever consolidated statements are prepared after the acquisition date, the worksheet entries eliminate the intercompany equity existing *at the date of the consolidated statements.* P Company's 100% interest in S Company includes all of the subsidiary's common stock and retained earnings. Therefore, the eliminating entry on the worksheet debits Common Stock (S Company) for $100,000, debits Retained Earnings (S Company) for $10,000, and credits Investment in S Company for $110,000.

A formal consolidated balance sheet is given in Exhibit 18–8. Note that the Cash and Other Assets of both firms have been combined, as well as the liabilities. The intercompany equity—100% of S Company stockholders' equity—has been eliminated; therefore, the stockholders' equity is that of the parent company.

EXHIBIT 18–7

P and S Companies
Consolidated Balance Sheet Worksheet
December 31, 19XX

			Eliminations		Consolidated
	P Company	S Company	Debit	Credit	Balance Sheet
Cash and Other Assets	700,000	115,000			815,000
Investment in S Company	110,000	—		110,000	—
	810,000	115,000			815,000
Liabilities	200,000	5,000			205,000
Common Stock					
P Company	400,000				400,000
S Company		100,000	100,000		—
Retained Earnings					
P Company	210,000				210,000
S Company		10,000	10,000		—
	810,000	115,000	110,000	110,000	815,000

EXHIBIT 18-8

P and S Companies
Consolidated Balance Sheet
December 31, 19XX

Cash and Other Assets	$815,000	Liabilities	$205,000
		Common Stock	400,000
		Retained Earnings	210,000
	$815,000		$815,000

MAJORITY-HELD SUBSIDIARIES—CONSOLIDATION AT ACQUISITION DATE

When a firm owns more than a 50% but less than a 100% interest in another firm, the parent company's interest is a **majority interest.** The interest of the other (outside) stockholders of the subsidiary company is called the **minority interest.** In preparing a consolidated balance sheet for a parent company and a majority-held subsidiary, the assets and liabilities of the affiliated companies are combined in the usual way to show their total resources and liabilities. The parent company's equity in the subsidiary at the date of the consolidated statements is eliminated as before, but in this case, the equity represents less than 100% of the subsidiary's common stock and retained earnings. The amount of the subsidiary's common stock and retained earnings not eliminated, which represents the minority interest in the subsidiary, will appear on the consolidated balance sheet.

For example, assume that P Company purchased 80% of Q Company's voting stock on January 1, 19XX, for $160,000. After the acquisition, the separate balance sheets of the two firms appeared as shown in Exhibit 18–9.

Note that Q Company's stockholders' equity is $200,000 ($150,000 Common Stock and $50,000 Retained Earnings). The equity acquired by P Company is therefore $160,000 (80% of $200,000), which is the amount P Company paid for

EXHIBIT 18-9

P and Q Companies
Balance Sheets
January 1, 19XX

	P Company	Q Company
Cash and Other Assets	$590,000	$220,000
Investment in Q Company	160,000	—
	$750,000	$220,000
Liabilities	$200,000	$ 20,000
Common Stock	400,000	150,000
Retained Earnings	150,000	50,000
	$750,000	$220,000

its interest. This intercompany equity at the date of the consolidated statements is eliminated. The remaining 20% minority interest, however, must be shown in the consolidated balance sheet. In other words, the minority, or outside, shareholders have a $40,000 interest in the stockholders' equity of Q Company (20% of $200,000). The worksheet entry to eliminate the intercompany equity and to reflect the minority interest debits Common Stock (Q Company) for $150,000, debits Retained Earnings (Q Company) for $50,000, credits Investment in Q Company for $160,000, and credits Minority Interest for $40,000. The worksheet to prepare the consolidated balance sheet is given in Exhibit 18–10.

A formal consolidated balance sheet for the two companies, prepared from the right-hand column of the worksheet, is given in Exhibit 18–11. Note that the total consolidated stockholders' equity of $590,000 consists of the parent com-

EXHIBIT 18–10

P and Q Companies
Consolidated Balance Sheet Worksheet
January 1, 19XX

	P Company	Q Company	Eliminations Debit	Eliminations Credit	Consolidated Balance Sheet
Cash and Other Assets	590,000	220,000			810,000
Investment in Q Company	160,000	—		160,000	—
	750,000	220,000			810,000
Liabilities	200,000	20,000			220,000
Minority Interest				40,000	40,000
Common Stock					
P Company	400,000				400,000
Q Company		150,000	150,000		—
Retained Earnings					
P Company	150,000				150,000
Q Company		50,000	50,000		—
	750,000	220,000	200,000	200,000	810,000

EXHIBIT 18–11

P and Q Companies
Consolidated Balance Sheet
January 1, 19XX

Cash and Other Assets	$810,000	Liabilities		$220,000
		Stockholders' Equity:		
		Minority Interest	$ 40,000	
		Common Stock	400,000	
		Retained Earnings	150,000	590,000
	$810,000			$810,000

pany's common stock and retained earnings (totaling $550,000) and the $40,000 minority interest. Thus the interests of outside shareholders (the parent firm's shareholders and the subsidiary's minority shareholders) are portrayed in the consolidated balance sheet. Sometimes, in formal consolidated balance sheets, the minority interest amount is shown between the liabilities and the stockholders' equity. Most financial analysts, however, consider the minority interest part of stockholders' equity, and it is probably a better practice to classify it with the stockholders' equity.

MAJORITY-HELD SUBSIDIARIES—CONSOLIDATION AFTER ACQUISITION DATE

Assume that the separate balance sheets of P Company and Q Company (of our previous example) one year after the acquisition date are as shown in the first two columns of Exhibit 18–12. During the year following acquisition, Q Company earned $25,000 net income and paid $5,000 in dividends. Therefore, its Retained Earnings increased by $20,000, to $70,000. Since P Company would reflect 80% of the increase in its Investment in Q Company under the equity method, the balance of this account at year-end would be $176,000 ($160,000 + $16,000). As shown in Exhibit 18–12, this amount would be eliminated in preparing a consolidated balance sheet. Likewise, the Common Stock and Retained Earnings of Q Company would be eliminated, and 20% of the $220,000 total stockholders' equity of Q Company would be established as minority interest, $44,000. Note that the $4,000 increase in this amount consists of 20% of the increase in Q Company's retained earnings since acquisition. The formal consolidated balance sheet taken from the last column of the worksheet is shown in Exhibit 18–13.

EXHIBIT 18–12

P and Q Companies
Consolidated Balance Sheet Worksheet
December 31, 19XX

	P Company	Q Company	Eliminations Debit	Eliminations Credit	Consolidated Balance Sheet
Cash and Other Assets	624,000	250,000			874,000
Investment in Q Company	176,000	—		176,000	—
	800,000	250,000			874,000
Liabilities	210,000	30,000			240,000
Minority Interest				44,000	44,000
Common Stock					
P Company	400,000				400,000
Q Company		150,000	150,000		—
Retained Earnings					
P Company	190,000				190,000
Q Company		70,000	70,000		—
	800,000	250,000	220,000	220,000	874,000

from consolidation[4] appears as an intangible asset on the consolidated balance sheet. In the consolidated statements of subsequent years, the amount paid in excess of the equity acquired in the subsidiary is amortized over the life of the assets to which the amount has been assigned. In the case of goodwill, the period cannot exceed 40 years.

We rarely encounter a situation in which the parent company pays less than the equity acquired for a particular interest in a subsidiary company. If this situation occurs, an analogous treatment is used to prepare a consolidated balance sheet. If the difference is attributed to an overvaluation of subsidiary assets, the eliminating entry on the worksheet credits such assets. On the other hand, if the difference is attributed to the subsidiary's poor earnings record, an account called Excess of Book Value of Investment in Subsidiary over Cost of Equity Acquired is credited. In a consolidated balance sheet, such an amount is probably best subtracted from total consolidated assets.

CONSOLIDATED INCOME STATEMENT

So far we have dealt only with consolidated balance sheets. Now we look at the problem of consolidating the income statements of affiliated firms. If we wish to show the scope of operations of affiliated companies as an entity, combining the revenue, cost of goods sold, and expenses of the several companies is logical. In preparing a consolidated income statement, however, we should present only the results of transactions with firms and individuals *outside* the entity. Any intercompany transactions—such as intercompany sales and purchases—should be eliminated. Likewise, revenue and expense amounts representing services rendered by one firm to an affiliated firm should be eliminated. Otherwise, the consolidated income statement would distort the extent of the group's operations.

For example, if a single company has two divisions—one manufacturing products and another marketing them—transfers of products from the manufacturing division to the marketing division are not regarded as sales transactions. Only sales by the marketing division are reflected in the firm's income statement. The same situation exists when two separate firms make up one consolidated entity.

To illustrate the procedures for preparing a consolidated income statement, we use Exhibit 18–15, the separate income statements of P Company and its 75%-held subsidiary, S Company. For simplicity, we assume that P Company has not yet reflected its 75% share of S Company's net income in its own income statement.[5]

We have indicated in the income statements that $30,000 of S Company's sales were to P Company. Assume that P Company, in turn, sold all of this merchandise to outsiders. In preparing a consolidated income statement, we must eliminate $30,000 from the sales reported by S Company and from the purchases (in cost of goods sold) reported by P Company. The worksheet to prepare a consolidated income statement for the two firms is given in Exhibit 18–16.

[4]Often this is called Excess of Cost over Book Value of Investment in Subsidiary. Many accountants and financial analysts, however, prefer to call it Goodwill from Consolidation.

[5]If P Company had already included its share of S Company's earnings in its own income statement, this amount would have to be eliminated to avoid double-counting when the revenue and expenses of the two firms are consolidated.

EXHIBIT 18–15

P Company Income Statement For the Year Ended December 31, 19XX		S Company Income Statement For the Year Ended December 31, 19XX	
Sales	$500,000	Sales (including $30,000 sold to P Company)	$200,000
Cost of Goods Sold (including $30,000 of purchases from S Company)	300,000	Cost of Goods Sold	140,000
Gross Profit	$200,000	Gross Profit	$ 60,000
Operating Expenses (including income taxes)	160,000	Operating Expenses (including income taxes)	40,000
Net Income	$ 40,000	Net Income	$ 20,000

EXHIBIT 18–16

P and S Companies
Consolidated Income Statement Worksheet
For the Year Ended December 31, 19XX

			Eliminations		Consolidated
	P Company	S Company	Debit	Credit	Income Statement
Sales	500,000	200,000	30,000		670,000
Cost of Goods Sold	300,000	140,000		30,000	410,000
Gross Profit	200,000	60,000			260,000
Expenses (including income taxes)	160,000	40,000			200,000
Net Income	40,000	20,000			60,000
Minority Interest in Net Income of S Company (25% of $20,000)					(5,000)
Consolidated Net Income					55,000

In Exhibit 18–16, the $30,000 in S Company's sales and the reciprocal amount in P Company's cost of goods sold have been eliminated so that only sales to outsiders are reflected in the consolidated income statement. Notice that this elimination does not affect consolidated net income, because the same amount is excluded from both sales and cost of goods sold. It does, however, avoid distorting the sales volume and costs of the group. Of the $60,000 aggregate net income of the two firms, the $5,000 minority interest (25% of S Company's net income) is deducted, so the consolidated net income of the affiliated firms is $55,000. Thus, the $55,000 consolidated net income consists of $40,000 (the parent's net income from its own operations) plus $15,000 (the parent's 75% interest in the $20,000 subsidiary net income). The consolidated net income statement, shown in Exhibit 18–17, is prepared directly from the last column of the worksheet.

EXHIBIT 18–17

P and S Companies
Consolidated Income Statement
For the Year Ended December 31, 19XX

Sales	$670,000
Cost of Goods Sold	410,000
Gross Profit	$260,000
Expenses (including income taxes)	200,000
Net Income before Minority Interest	$ 60,000
Less: Minority Interest in Net Income of S Company	5,000
Consolidated Net Income	$ 55,000

CONSOLIDATED RETAINED EARNINGS STATEMENT

Preparation of a consolidated retained earnings statement for affiliated firms is a relatively simple task, and worksheets are rarely required. Using our previous example, assume that the January 1, 19XX, balance of consolidated retained earnings for P and S companies amounted to $260,000 and that P Company declared cash dividends of $25,000 during 19XX. The 19XX consolidated retained earnings statement for the two companies is given in Exhibit 18–18.

Observe that the consolidated retained earnings balance is increased by consolidated net income, which consisted of P Company's earnings plus its 75% share of S Company's earnings ($40,000 + $15,000 = $55,000). P Company enters the $15,000 income from S Company on its books by increasing the Investment in S Company account. Only dividends declared by the parent company appear in the consolidated retained earnings statement. We pointed out earlier that dividends received by the parent company from the subsidiary are credited to the Investment in Subsidiary account. Dividends paid by the subsidiary to the minority shareholders reduce the minority interest in the consolidated balance sheet.

EXHIBIT 18–18

P and S Companies
Consolidated Retained Earnings Statement
For the Year Ended December 31, 19XX

Consolidated Retained Earnings, January 1	$260,000
Add: Consolidated Net Income for the Year	55,000
	$315,000
Less: Dividends Declared (by P Company)	25,000
Consolidated Retained Earnings, December 31	$290,000

OTHER INTERCOMPANY ACCOUNTS

Because affiliated companies often engage in a variety of intercompany transactions, treating the resulting amounts in consolidated statements can be fairly complex. For example, transactions may include intercompany loans, intercompany bond and preferred stockholdings, or plant and equipment transfers. Because this chapter is only an introduction to consolidated statements, we discuss here only some of the most commonly encountered relationships—intercompany receivables and payables and intercompany profit in assets.

Intercompany Receivables and Payables

In our example of the preparation of a consolidated income statement (Exhibit 18–16), S Company, a 75%-held subsidiary, sold merchandise to P Company for $30,000 during the year. Suppose that at year-end, P Company still owed $15,000 to S Company for some of the merchandise. P Company therefore had an account payable to S Company for $15,000 in its balance sheet at year-end, and S Company showed a receivable from P Company for the same amount. The consolidated balance sheet should show receivables and payables only with *outsiders;* otherwise both total receivables and payables of the consolidated entity are overstated. Therefore, the reciprocal receivable and payable of $15,000 must be eliminated in preparing the consolidated balance sheet, as shown in the following partial worksheet:

			Eliminations		Consolidated
Assets	**P Company**	**S Company**	**Debit**	**Credit**	**Balance Sheet**
Accounts Receivable	80,000	60,000		15,000	125,000
⋮					
Liabilities					
Accounts Payable	45,000	40,000	15,000		70,000
⋮					

Unrealized Intercompany Profit in Assets

In the above example, when S Company sold P Company $30,000 worth of merchandise, we assumed that P Company in turn sold all of it to outside parties. As far as the entity is concerned, a profit was *realized* on *all* of the merchandise. If the merchandise had cost S Company $22,000, and P Company eventually sold all of it to outsiders for $36,000, the entity would have made a profit of $14,000 on the merchandise. Remember that the only elimination necessary to avoid double-counting was excluding $30,000 from S Company sales and $30,000 from P Company's cost of goods sold.

Suppose, however, that P Company still had $10,000 worth of the merchandise in its inventory at year-end. Also assume that S Company's cost for the remaining $10,000 worth of merchandise had been $8,000. In this situation, the $2,000 of S Company profit residing in P Company's inventory is *unrealized* from the standpoint of the entity. In a consolidated balance sheet, the $2,000 is eliminated from P Company's inventory amount and from S Company's retained earnings. This elimination is made in addition to the $30,000 elimination from S Company's sales and P Company's cost of goods sold.

In addition to merchandise, a firm may sell an affiliate such assets as securities, plant, and equipment. Following our general rule, any intercompany profit residing in the assets of the entity must be eliminated in preparing consolidated financial statements; only profits earned in dealing with outsiders can be reflected in consolidated net income and in consolidated retained earnings statements.

The technical procedures for handling these detailed adjustments in preparing consolidated financial statements are somewhat complex; they are explored in detail in advanced accounting courses.

CONSOLIDATED STATEMENTS—POOLING METHOD (Read only)

In all of the foregoing examples, we assumed that an acquiring company *purchased* a controlling interest in the shares of another firm by issuing cash, other assets, or debt. Thus, a purchase and sale transaction occurred, and we used the *purchase method* to prepare consolidated statements.

On the other hand, if the acquiring company obtains substantially all (90% or more) of a subsidiary company's shares by *issuing its own shares* (and by meeting certain other criteria[6]), a **pooling of interests** has occurred. In a pooling of interests, stockholders of the subsidiary company become stockholders of the parent company. Basically, two sets of interests "unite" rather than have a purchase and sale transaction take place.

If a combination is a pooling of interests, the parent's investment and the consolidated financial statements are prepared according to the **pooling method** of accounting. In a consolidated balance sheet prepared under the pooling method, the *book values* of the affiliated companies are combined. Of course, the market values of each firm's stock play an important part in determining the number of shares exchanged for the subsidiary's shares. However, once the negotiations are completed, the market values of the shares play no role in recording the parent's investment or in preparing consolidated financial statements.

Because the consolidated statements under the pooling method reflect the book values of the subsidiary's assets, we do not revalue these assets, nor does any goodwill (excess of cost over equity acquired) emerge from the consolidation. On the other hand, under the purchase method, the subsidiary's assets are revalued (almost invariably upward during periods of rising prices), and goodwill often appears in the consolidated balance sheet. Also, the increase in tangible assets and any goodwill are amortized over future periods. Consequently, future yearly consolidated earnings are less under the purchase method than under the pooling method.

Another facet of the pooling method is that the subsidiary's and the parent's net incomes for the entire period of the acquisition year can be combined regardless of the date of acquisition. For example, suppose a parent company earned $500,000 net income in the year that it used the pooling method to acquire a 100% interest in a subsidiary that earned $400,000. The acquisition occurred October 1, and the subsidiary's earnings for the last quarter were $100,000. The pooling method combines the subsidiary's entire $400,000 with the parent's earnings, for a total consolidated net income of $900,000. With the purchase method, only the last quarter's earnings of the subsidiary ($100,000) are combined with the parent's $500,000 earnings, for a net income of $600,000.

[6]The criteria for determining whether a pooling has occurred are set forth in *Opinions of the Accounting Principles Board, No. 16,* "Business Combinations" (New York: American Institute of Certified Public Accountants, 1970), page 297.

We summarize the pooling method as follows:

1. With the pooling method, total consolidated assets do not increase, because book values of each firm are combined. With the purchase method, asset revaluation and goodwill (excess of cost over equity acquired) often increase total consolidated assets.
2. Without amortization of revaluation increases or goodwill, the pooling method results in higher future earnings than the purchase method.
3. When pooling is used, parent company and subsidiary earnings for the entire year are combined in the year of acquisition. With the purchase method, only the subsidiary's earnings after the acquisition date are included with parent company earnings.

Combination by pooling was widely used in the 1960s, because this method enabled companies to show an immediate (often synthetic) improvement in their earnings records *purely as a result of the combination* rather than through improved operations. Combining firms were allowed wide latitude in their methods of recording and consolidation, regardless of the nature of the exchange, with the result that the pooling method was selected for most combinations. In 1970, however, the Accounting Principles Board issued *Opinion No. 16*, "Business Combinations," which curtailed certain abuses by specifying more restrictive criteria that combining firms must meet to use the pooling method of accounting.

USEFULNESS OF CONSOLIDATED STATEMENTS

Consolidated statements present an integrated report of an economic unit comprising a number of business enterprises related through stock ownership. In fact, no other way can depict, fairly concisely, the extent of resources and scope of operations of many companies subject to common control.

The statements do have certain limitations, however. The status or performance of weak constituents in a group can be "masked" through consolidation with successful units. Rates of return, ratios, and trend percentages calculated from consolidated statements may sometimes prove deceptive because they are really composite calculations. Shareholders and creditors of controlled companies who are interested in their legal rights and prerogatives should examine the separate financial statements of the relevant constituent companies.

In recent years, supplemental disclosures have improved the quality of consolidated statements, particularly those of *conglomerates*—entities with diversified lines of business. Both the Financial Accounting Standards Board and the Securities and Exchange Commission have stipulated that certain firms disclose information regarding revenue, income from operations, and identifiable assets for various business segments.

KEY POINTS FOR CHAPTER OBJECTIVES

1 Describe the various kinds of long-term stock investments and the accounting for them (pp. 633–36).

- Long-term stock investments are of three types:
  1. Noncontrolling and noninfluential interest—that is, interest amounting to less than 20% of the investee's voting stock. Such investments are recorded at cost, and the portfolio is valued at the lower of total cost or market at each year-end. Unrealized losses are shown contra to stockholders' equity.
  2. Influential but noncontrolling interest—that is, interest amounting to 20–50% of the investee's voting stock. Such investments are recorded at cost, then adjusted periodically according to the equity method. The firm's share of the investee's earnings is added to and the dividends are deducted from the investment's carrying value.
  3. Controlling interest—that is, interest amounting to over 50% of the investee's voting stock. The investment may be carried on either the cost or equity basis; the application of consolidation procedures results in the same consolidated statements under either method.

2 Define parent–subsidiary relationships and illustrate how their balance sheet data are consolidated (pp. 636–46).

- With few exceptions, all wholly owned or majority-held subsidiaries are consolidated with the parent firm.
- A parent company that carries its investment in a subsidiary under the equity method—as illustrated in this chapter—uses the following accounting procedures:
  1. The parent periodically debits Investment in Subsidiary and credits Income from Subsidiary for its share of subsidiary earnings. Dividends received from the subsidiary are debited to Cash and credited to Investment in Subsidiary.
  2. The parent eliminates its equity in the subsidiary existing when the consolidated balance sheet is prepared.
  3. If a subsidiary is majority-held, the portion of the subsidiary's stockholders' equity not eliminated in procedure 2 above is presented as minority interest.
  4. Any amounts owing between the parent and subsidiaries are eliminated in preparing consolidated statements.

3 Discuss the treatment of acquisitions when cost exceeds the book value acquired in a subsidiary (pp. 646–48).

- In a purchase combination, the acquiring company initially records its investment at cost. In preparing consolidated statements, any amount in excess of the book value acquired in the subsidiary is allocated among specific assets when possible. Any unallocated amount is goodwill, which must be amortized over a period of years.

4 Explain and illustrate the consolidation of parent and subsidiary income statements (pp. 648–52).

- A consolidated income statement presents only the results of transactions with firms and individuals outside the entity. Any intercompany transactions, such as intercompany sales and purchases, are eliminated from sales and cost of goods sold.
- After revenues, cost of goods sold, and expenses are combined and a combined net income is determined, any minority interest in the subsidiary's earnings are deducted to determine consolidated net income.

5 Provide an overview of accounting for acquisitions under the "pooling of interests" method (pp. 652–53).

- When an acquiring firm obtains 90% or more of another firm's shares by issuing its own shares, the transaction may be treated as a pooling of interests.

- In a pooling combination, the parent firm records its investment in accordance with the book value of the acquired firm's net assets. Cost (as measured by the market value of shares exchanged) is ignored. The acquired firm's retained earnings at acquisition date are added to those of the acquiring firm in preparing consolidated statements. Earnings of both firms are likewise combined for the period when the acquisition occurred.

KEY TERMS USED IN THIS CHAPTER

consolidated financial statements 636
cost method 633
equity method 636
goodwill 646
majority interest 643
minority interest 643
parent company 636
pooling of interests 652
pooling method 652
purchase method 638
subsidiaries 636

SELF-TEST QUESTIONS FOR REVIEW

(Answers are at the end of this chapter.)

1. A firm purchased noncontrolling and noninfluential long-term stock investments that cost $65,000. At the close of the year, the portfolio had a market value of $60,000. The entry to adjust the carrying value of the investments at the end of the year includes a
   (a) Credit of $5,000 to Unrealized Loss on Long-term Investments.
   (b) Debit of $5,000 to Long-term Stock Investments.
   (c) Credit of $5,000 to Allowance to Reduce Long-term Investments to Market.
   (d) Debit of $60,000 to Long-term Stock Investments.
2. Artway Company purchased 30% of the voting stock of Barton Company for $60,000 on January 1 of the current year. During the year, Barton Company earned $50,000 net income and paid $15,000 in dividends. At the end of the year, Artway Company's account, Investment in Barton Company, should have a balance of
   (a) $110,000 (b) $70,500 (c) $95,000 (d) $60,000
3. X Company purchased an 80% interest in Y Company for $225,000 at the beginning of the current year. At that time, X Company had $500,000 common stock and $150,000 retained earnings, and Y Company had $200,000 common stock and $60,000 retained earnings. On the consolidated balance sheet prepared at the time of the acquisition, consolidated retained earnings should be
   (a) $150,000 (b) $210,000 (c) $198,000 (d) $48,000
4. Suppose that Y Company, in question 3 above, earned $40,000 net income and paid $10,000 dividends during the year following acquisition. The minority interest to be shown on a consolidated balance sheet prepared at the end of the year should be
   (a) $232,000 (b) $60,000 (c) $18,000 (d) $58,000
5. Brown Company, which owns 70% of Greene Company's voting stock, sold merchandise during the year to Greene Company for $60,000. The merchandise had cost Brown Company $40,000. Greene Company sold all of the merchandise to outsiders during the year. The eliminating entry to prepare a consolidated income statement for the year should reduce the sales amount and the cost of goods sold amount by
   (a) $60,000 (b) $40,000 (c) $20,000 (d) $28,000

DEMONSTRATION PROBLEM FOR REVIEW

On January 1, 19XX, Montana Company purchased 75% of the common stock of Utah Company for $180,000. On that date, the stockholders' equity of Utah Company consisted of $200,000 of common stock and $40,000 in retained earnings. Separate balance sheets of the two firms at December 31, 19XX, follow.

Montana and Utah Companies
Balance Sheets
December 31, 19XX

Assets	**Montana**	**Utah**
Investment in Utah	$195,000	—
Other Assets	305,000	$300,000
	$500,000	$300,000
Liabilities and Stockholders' Equity		
Liabilities	$100,000	$ 40,000
Common Stock	300,000	200,000
Retained Earnings	100,000	60,000
	$500,000	$300,000

Neither firm declared or paid dividends during the year. At year-end, Utah Company owed $7,000 to Montana Company on a loan made during the year.

REQUIRED
Prepare a consolidated balance sheet worksheet at December 31, 19XX.

SOLUTION TO DEMONSTRATION PROBLEM

Montana and Utah Companies
Consolidated Balance Sheet Worksheet
December 31, 19XX

			Eliminations		Consolidated
	Montana	**Utah**	**Debit**	**Credit**	**Balance Sheet**
Investment in Utah	195,000	—		(1) 195,000	—
Other Assets	305,000	300,000		(2) 7,000	598,000
	500,000	300,000			598,000
Liabilities	100,000	40,000	(2) 7,000		133,000
Minority Interest				(1) 65,000	65,000
Common Stock					
Montana Company	300,000				300,000
Utah Company		200,000	(1) 200,000		—
Retained Earnings					
Montana Company	100,000				100,000
Utah Company		60,000	(1) 60,000		—
	500,000	300,000	267,000	267,000	598,000

Utah Company had earnings of $20,000 during the year, because its retained earnings increased from $40,000 to $60,000 and no dividends were declared. At December 31, Montana Company's $195,000 investment consisted of the $180,000 originally paid plus $15,000—its 75% share of Utah Company's earnings. At December 31, the minority interest is $65,000—25% of the total stockholders' equity of Utah Company (25% of $260,000).

QUESTIONS

18–1 What is a noncontrolling and noninfluential long-term stock investment?

18–2 How are noncontrolling and noninfluential long-term stock investments reported in the balance sheet? Where are unrealized losses on the portfolio of such investments reported?

18–3 Describe the accounting procedures used when a stock investment represents 20–50% of the voting stock.

18–4 Describe the accounting procedures used when a stock investment represents over 50% of the voting stock.

18–5 What is the purpose of consolidated financial statements?

18–6 In a recent annual report, FMC Corporation's consolidated financial statements showed an amount under Investments that included a 50% interest in Ketchikan Pulp Corporation and its subsidiaries. The latter investment represents a 50/50 joint venture with Louisiana Pacific Corporation. Explain why the accounts of this firm were not consolidated with the accounts of FMC and its other subsidiaries. On what accounting basis is the investment in this unconsolidated subsidiary carried?

18–7 What is the difference between a purchase acquisition and a pooling of interests?

18–8 P Company purchases all of the common stock of S Company for $600,000 when S Company has $500,000 of common stock and $100,000 of retained earnings. If a consolidated balance sheet is prepared immediately after the acquisition, what amounts are eliminated in preparing it?

18–9 Suppose, in Question 18–8, that P Company acquires only 75% of S Company's common stock by paying $450,000. If a consolidated balance sheet is prepared immediately after the acquisition, what amounts are eliminated in preparing this statement? What amount of minority interest appears in the consolidated balance sheet?

18–10 Explain the entries made in a parent company's records under the equity method of accounting to (a) reflect its share of the subsidiary's net income for the period and (b) record the receipt of dividends from the subsidiary.

18–11 On January 1 of the current year, P Company purchased 70% of the common stock of S Company for $560,000. During the year, S Company had $90,000 of net income and paid $40,000 in cash dividends. At year-end, what amount appears in P Company's balance sheet as Investment in S Company under the equity method?

18–12 Danton Company purchased an interest in West Company for $370,000 when West Company had $300,000 of common stock and $60,000 of retained earnings.
(a) If Danton Company had acquired a 100% interest in West Company, what amount of Goodwill from Consolidation would appear on the consolidated balance sheet? (Assume that West's assets are fairly valued.)
(b) If Danton had acquired only a 90% interest in West Company, what amount of Goodwill from Consolidation would appear?

18–13 Crown Company purchased a 70% interest in Wells Company on January 1 of the current year. Crown Company had $300,000 net income for the current year before reflecting its share of Wells Company's net income. If Wells Company had net income of $90,000 for the year, what is the consolidated net income for the year?

18–14 Ricci Company, which owns 80% of Hall Company, sold merchandise during the year to Hall Company for $60,000. The merchandise cost Ricci Company $40,000. If Hall Company in turn sold all of the merchandise to outsiders for $90,000, what eliminating entry related to these transactions does Ricci make in preparing a consolidated income statement for the year?

18–15 Suppose, in Question 18–14, that Hall Company still owed Ricci Company $25,000 for the merchandise acquired during the year. What eliminating entry is made for this item in preparing a consolidated balance sheet at year-end?

18–16 P Company acquired 100% of S Company on September 1 of the current year. Explain why the consolidated earnings of the two firms for the current year might be greater if the transaction is treated as a pooling of interests rather than as a purchase.

18–17 What are the inherent limitations of consolidated financial statements?

EXERCISES

Entries for a noncontrolling and noninfluential investment

18–18 As a long-term investment, 5,000 shares of Puritan Company common stock were acquired on March 10, 19X1, at a total cost of $172,400. The investment represented 15% of the company's voting stock. On December 28, 19X1, Puritan Company declared a cash dividend of $1.25 per share, which was received on January 15, 19X2. Dividend income is recorded when received. Present the necessary journal entries to reflect (a) the purchase of the stock and (b) the receipt of the cash dividend.

Entries for an influential but noncontrolling investment

18–19 Assume the 5,000 shares purchased in Exercise 18–18 represent 25% of Puritan Company's voting stock. Puritan Company's 19X1 net income was $80,000. Using the equity method, present the journal entries to reflect (a) the purchase of the stock, (b) the proportionate share of Puritan Company's 19X1 net income (dated December 31, 19X1), and (c) the receipt of the cash dividend.

Calculating unrealized loss in investment portfolio

18–20 During its first year of operations, a firm purchased the following noncontrolling and noninfluential long-term investments:

2,000 shares of A Company stock at $40 per share
4,000 shares of B Company stock at $50 per share

At year-end, the market value of the A Company stock was $35 per share, and the market value of the B Company stock was $51 per share. What was the unrealized loss at year-end, and where does it appear in the firm's financial statements?

Eliminating entry and stockholders' equity in consolidation

18–21 On January 1 of the current year, Brill Company purchased all of the common shares of Wilson Company for $360,000 cash. On this date, the stockholders' equity of Brill Company consisted of $500,000 in common stock and $90,000 in retained earnings. Wilson Company had $300,000 in common stock and $60,000 in retained earnings.

(a) Give the worksheet eliminating entry to prepare a consolidated balance sheet on the acquisition date.
(b) What amount of total stockholders' equity appears on the consolidated balance sheet?

Stockholders' equity in consolidated balance sheet

18–22 Kirk Company purchased 75% of the common stock of Reed Company for $360,000 in cash and notes when the stockholders' equity of Reed Company consisted of $400,000 in common stock and $80,000 in retained earnings. On the acquisition date, the stockholders' equity of Kirk Company consisted of $600,000 in common stock and $140,000 in retained earnings. Present the stockholders' equity section in the consolidated balance sheet prepared on the acquisition date.

Eliminating entry including asset revaluation and goodwill

18–23 On January 1 of the current year, Gem Company purchased all of the common shares of Sterling Company for $500,000 cash and notes. Balance sheets of the two firms immediately after the acquisition were as follows:

	Gem	Sterling
Current Assets	$1,500,000	$170,000
Investment in Sterling Company	500,000	—
Plant and Equipment	3,000,000	380,000
	$5,000,000	$550,000
Liabilities	$ 700,000	$ 90,000
Common Stock	3,500,000	400,000
Retained Earnings	800,000	60,000
	$5,000,000	$550,000

During the negotiations for the purchase, Sterling's plant and equipment were appraised at $390,000. Furthermore, Gem concluded that an additional $30,000 demanded by Sterling's shareholders was warranted because Sterling's earning power was somewhat better than the industry average. Give the worksheet eliminating entry to prepare a consolidated balance sheet on the acquisition date.

Determining investment balance using the equity method

18–24 Carver Company purchased a 70% interest in Devlin Company for $520,000 cash on January 1 of the current year. During the year, Devlin Company earned $60,000 net income and declared and paid half its earnings in dividends. Carver Company carries its investment in Devlin Company on the equity method. What is the carrying value of Carver Company's Investment in Devlin Company account at year-end?

Eliminating entry for intercompany sales

18–25 Foster Company has an 80% interest in Hobson Company. During the current year, Hobson Company sold merchandise costing $32,000 to Foster company for $50,000. Assuming that Foster Company sold all of the merchandise to outsiders, what worksheet eliminating entry should be made in preparing a consolidated income statement for the period?

Calculating amounts on consolidated statements

18–26 On January 1, 19XX, Knight Company purchased for $360,000 cash a 90% stock interest in Jackson, Inc., which then had common stock of $300,000 and retained earnings of $80,000. On December 31, 19XX, after Knight had taken up its share of Jackson's earnings, the balance sheets of the two companies were as follows:

	Knight	Jackson, Inc.
Investment in Jackson, Inc. (at equity)	$396,000	—
Other Assets	504,000	$480,000
	$900,000	$480,000
Liabilities	$ 50,000	$ 60,000
Common Stock	700,000	300,000
Retained Earnings	150,000	120,000
	$900,000	$480,000

Jackson, Inc., did not declare or pay dividends during the year.
(a) What was the net income of Jackson, Inc., for the year?

(b) The consolidated balance sheet prepared December 31, 19XX, would show
   1. What amount of common stock?
   2. What amount of retained earnings?
   3. What amount of minority interest?

(c) Assuming that Jackson, Inc., assets are properly stated, what amount of goodwill from consolidation is reported?

PROBLEMS

Entries for noninfluential and noncontrolling investments

18–27 The following selected transactions and information are for the Alpine Corporation for 19X1 and 19X2.

19X1

July 1 Purchased, as a long-term investment, 1,000 shares of Lincoln, Inc., common stock at a total cost of $62,500. This interest is noninfluential and noncontrolling.

Oct. 1 Purchased, as a long-term investment, 2,000 shares of Mead, Inc., common stock at a total cost of $84,600, and 2,000 shares of Scott, Inc., common stock at a total cost of $72,000. Both investments are noninfluential and noncontrolling interests.

Nov. 9 Received a cash dividend of 80 cents per share on the Mead, Inc., stock.

Dec. 31 The Lincoln, Inc., shares have a market value of $60 per share; the Mead, Inc., shares have a market value of $41 per share; and the Scott, Inc., shares have a market value of $37 per share. (An entry should be made to adjust the carrying value of the portfolio to the lower of cost or market.)

19X2

Feb. 1 Sold the Mead, Inc., stock for $39 per share less a $50 commission fee.

Dec. 31 The market value of the long-term stock investment portfolio is as follows: Lincoln, Inc., $62 per share; Scott, Inc., $35.50 per share. (An entry should be made to adjust the carrying value of the investments and the unrealized loss account.)

REQUIRED

Give the journal entries to record these transactions and adjustments.

Contrasting entries for influential and noninfluential investments

18–28 On January 2, 19X1, Mohawk Corporation purchased, as a long-term investment, 8,000 shares of Dover Company common stock for $26 per share, including commissions and taxes. On December 31, 19X1, Dover Company announced a net income of $56,000 for the year and a dividend of $1.25 per share, payable January 20, 19X2, to stockholders of record on January 10, 19X2. Mohawk Corporation received its dividend on January 23, 19X2.

REQUIRED

(a) Assume the stock acquired by Mohawk Corporation represents 15% of Dover Company's voting stock. Prepare all journal entries appropriate for this investment, beginning with the purchase on January 2, 19X1, and ending with the receipt of the dividend on January 23, 19X2. (Mohawk Corporation recognizes dividend income when received.)

(b) Assume the stock acquired by Mohawk Corporation represents 25% of Dover Company's voting stock. Prepare all journal entries appropriate for this investment, beginning with the purchase on January 2, 19X1, and ending with the receipt of the dividend on January 23, 19X2.

Determining eliminations and consolidated data on date of acquisition (wholly owned subsidiary)

18–29 Syntex Company purchased all of Lee Company's common stock for cash on January 1, 19XX, after which the separate balance sheets of the two corporations appeared as follows:

Syntex and Lee Companies
Balance Sheets
January 1, 19XX

	Syntex	Lee
Investment in Lee Company	$ 650,000	—
Other Assets	2,350,000	$700,000
	$3,000,000	$700,000
Liabilities	$ 900,000	$120,000
Common Stock	1,500,000	500,000
Retained Earnings	600,000	80,000
	$3,000,000	$700,000

During the negotiations for the purchase, Syntex Company determined that the appraised value of Lee Company's Other Assets amounted to $750,000.

REQUIRED

(a) Give the worksheet entry to eliminate the intercompany equity and to reflect the appraised value of Lee Company's assets.

(b) What amount of total assets should appear on a January 1 consolidated balance sheet?

(c) What amount of total stockholders' equity should appear on a January 1 consolidated balance sheet?

Determining intercompany data one year after acquisition (wholly owned subsidiary)

18–30 On January 1, 19XX, Kansas Company purchased all of the common stock of Topeka Company for $350,000 cash. The stockholders' equity of Topeka consisted of $300,000 in common stock and $50,000 in retained earnings. On December 31, 19XX, the separate balance sheets of the two firms were as follows:

Kansas and Topeka Companies
Balance Sheets
December 31, 19XX

	Kansas	Topeka
Cash	$ 75,000	$ 60,000
Accounts Receivable	95,000	90,000
Investment in Topeka Company (at equity)	380,000	—
Other Assets	350,000	300,000
	$900,000	$450,000
Accounts Payable	$ 50,000	$ 70,000
Common Stock	700,000	300,000
Retained Earnings	150,000	80,000
	$900,000	$450,000

During the year, Topeka Company had net income of $40,000. At December 31, Topeka owed Kansas $20,000 on account for merchandise.

REQUIRED

(a) What amount of dividends did Topeka Company declare and pay during the year?

(b) Give Kansas Company's journal entries for 19XX that affect the Investment in Topeka Company account.

(c) What amount of total assets would appear in a December 31, 19XX, consolidated balance sheet?

Preparing consolidated balance sheet worksheet on acquisition date

18–31 On January 1, 19XX, Bradford Company purchased 75% of the common stock of Summit Company for $570,000 cash, after which the separate balance sheets of the two firms were as follows:

Bradford and Summit Companies
Balance Sheets
January 1, 19XX

	Bradford	Summit
Investment in Summit Company	$ 570,000	—
Other Assets	1,230,000	$800,000
	$1,800,000	$800,000
Liabilities	$ 500,000	$ 80,000
Common Stock	1,000,000	600,000
Retained Earnings	300,000	120,000
	$1,800,000	$800,000

REQUIRED

Prepare a consolidated balance sheet worksheet at January 1, 19XX. Assume that any amount paid by Bradford Company in excess of the equity acquired in Summit Company's net assets is attributable to goodwill.

Preparing consolidated income statement worksheet

18–32 Gibson Company owns 70% of the common stock of Todd Company. The income statements of the two companies for the current year are shown below. In its income statement, Gibson Company has not recorded its share of Todd Company's net income.

Gibson and Todd Companies
Income Statements
For the Current Year

	Gibson	Todd
Sales	$560,000	$240,000
Cost of Goods Sold	364,000	150,000
Gross Profit	$196,000	$ 90,000
Expenses (including income taxes)	130,000	52,000
Net Income	$ 66,000	$ 38,000

During the year, Gibson Company sold Todd Company merchandise for $40,000, which had cost Gibson $25,000. Todd Company sold all of this merchandise to outsiders.

REQUIRED

Prepare a consolidated income statement worksheet for the current year.

Analyzing data from statements consolidated a year after acquisition

18–33 On January 1, 19XX, Crest Company acquired an interest in Easton Company for $240,000, consisting of $120,000 cash and $120,000 in notes payable. The following information is available about the two companies at December 31, 19XX:

Assets	Crest	Easton	Consolidated
Cash	$ 50,000	$ 30,000	$ 80,000
Accounts Receivable	70,000	50,000	100,000
Inventory	100,000	70,000	170,000
Investment in Easton (at equity)	280,000	—	
Other Assets	270,000	200,000	470,000
Excess of Cost over Equity Acquired in Easton			30,000
Total Assets	$770,000	$350,000	$850,000
Liabilities and Stockholders' Equity			
Accounts Payable	$ 70,000	$ 60,000	$110,000
Notes Payable	130,000	40,000	170,000
Common Stock	400,000	200,000	400,000
Retained Earnings	170,000	50,000	170,000
Total Liabilities and Stockholders' Equity	$770,000	$350,000	$850,000

REQUIRED

(a) Is the acquisition of Easton Company by Crest Company a purchase or a pooling of interests? Explain.

(b) What ownership percentage of Easton Company did Crest Company acquire?

(c) What were Easton Company's 19XX earnings? Easton declared and paid no dividends in 19XX.

(d) How much of Easton Company's retained earnings is included in the consolidated retained earnings?

(e) What were the amounts of intercompany receivables and payables at December 31?

Parent's entries for acquisition, income, and dividends of majority-held subsidiary

18–34 On January 1, 19XX, Oxford Company purchased 80% of the common shares of Kirby Company for $550,000 cash. At that time, the stockholders' equity of Kirby Company consisted of $500,000 of common stock and $150,000 of retained earnings. At December 31, 19XX, the separate balance sheets of the two firms were as follows:

Oxford and Kirby Companies
Balance Sheets
December 31, 19XX

	Oxford	Kirby
Investment in Kirby (at equity)	$ 590,000	—
Other Assets	2,410,000	$1,000,000
	$3,000,000	$1,000,000
Liabilities	$ 650,000	300,000
Common Stock	2,000,000	500,000
Retained Earnings	350,000	200,000
	$3,000,000	$1,000,000

REQUIRED

(a) Give Oxford Company's general journal entry to record the purchase of Kirby Company's shares on January 1, 19XX.

(b) Kirby Company's 19XX net income was $70,000. Kirby declared and paid $20,000 in dividends near the end of 19XX.
   1. Give Oxford Company's general journal entry to record its share of Kirby's net income for the year.
   2. Give Oxford Company's general journal entry to record the receipt of dividends from Kirby Company.

(c) Prepare a consolidated balance sheet worksheet for the two firms at December 31, 19XX. Assume that two-thirds of any amount paid by Oxford Company in excess of the equity acquired in Kirby's net assets at January 1 is goodwill. The remaining one-third represents an appraisal increase of Kirby's Other Assets. At December 31, Kirby Company owed $60,000 to Oxford Company for a loan made during the year.

ALTERNATE PROBLEMS

Entries for noninfluential and noncontrolling investments

18–27A The following selected transactions and information are for Barlow Corporation for 19X1 and 19X2.

19X1

Aug.	1	Purchased, as a long-term investment, 2,500 shares of York, Inc., common stock at a total cost of $87,500. This interest is noninfluential and noncontrolling.
Nov.	3	Purchased, as a long-term investment, 4,000 shares of Harmon, Inc., common stock at a total cost of $224,000, and 2,000 shares of Baxter, Inc., common stock at a total cost of $48,000. Both investments are noninfluential and noncontrolling interests.
	21	Received a cash dividend of $2 per share on the Harmon, Inc., stock.
Dec.	31	The York, Inc., shares have a market value of $32 per share; the Harmon, Inc., shares have a market value of $54 per share; and the Baxter, Inc., shares have a market value of $26 per share. (An entry should be made to adjust the carrying value of the portfolio to the lower of cost or market.)

19X2

Jan.	15	Sold the Harmon, Inc., stock for $52 per share less a $150 commission fee.
Dec.	31	The market value of the long-term investment portfolio is as follows: York, Inc., $34 per share; Baxter, Inc., $24 per share. (An entry should be made to adjust the carrying value of the investments and the unrealized loss account.)

REQUIRED

Give the journal entries to record these transactions and adjustments.

Contrasting entries for influential and noninfluential investments

18–28A On January 2, 19X1, Clinton, Inc., purchased, as a long-term investment, 10,000 shares of Owen, Inc., common stock for $54 per share, including commissions and taxes. On December 31, 19X1, Owen, Inc., announced a net income of $120,000 for the year and a dividend of 90 cents per share, payable January 15, 19X2, to stockholders of record on January 5, 19X2. Clinton, Inc., received its dividend on January 18, 19X2.

REQUIRED

(a) Assume the stock acquired by Clinton, Inc., represents 16% of Owen, Inc.'s voting stock. Prepare all journal entries appropriate for this investment, beginning with the purchase on January 2, 19X1, and ending with the receipt of the dividend on January 18, 19X2. (Clinton, Inc., recognizes dividend income when received.)

(b) Assume the stock acquired by Clinton, Inc., represents 30% of Owen, Inc.'s voting stock. Prepare all journal entries appropriate for this investment, beginning with the purchase on January 2, 19X1, and ending with the receipt of the dividend on January 18, 19X2.

Determining eliminations and consolidated data on date of acquisition (majority-held subsidiary)

18–29A Niles Company purchased 70% of Troy Company's voting stock on January 1, 19XX, after which the separate balance sheets of the two companies appeared as follows:

Niles and Troy Companies
Balance Sheets
January 1, 19XX

	Niles	Troy
Investment in Troy Company	$ 500,000	—
Other Assets	1,000,000	$800,000
	$1,500,000	$800,000
Liabilities	$ 200,000	$120,000
Common Stock	900,000	500,000
Retained Earnings	400,000	180,000
	$1,500,000	$800,000

In purchasing Troy Company's shares, Niles Company attributed the excess of the amount paid over the equity acquired in Troy entirely to that company's superior earning potential.

REQUIRED

(a) Give the worksheet entry to eliminate the intercompany equity and to reflect the goodwill.

(b) What amount of total assets should appear on a January 1 consolidated balance sheet?

(c) What amount of total stockholders' equity should appear on a January 1 consolidated balance sheet?

Determining intercompany data one year after acquisition (wholly owned subsidiary)

18–30A On January 1, 19XX, Lockport Company purchased all of the common stock of Grant Company for $440,000 cash. The stockholders' equity of Grant Company consisted of $350,000 of common stock and $65,000 of retained earnings. On December 31, 19XX, the separate balance sheets of the two firms were as follows:

Lockport and Grant Companies
Balance Sheets
December 31, 19XX

	Lockport	Grant
Cash	$ 50,000	$ 40,000
Accounts Receivable	90,000	80,000
Investment in Grant Company (at equity)	475,000	—
Other Assets	585,000	380,000
	$1,200,000	$500,000
Accounts Payable	$ 120,000	$ 50,000
Common Stock	800,000	350,000
Retained Earnings	280,000	100,000
	$1,200,000	$500,000

During the year, Grant Company had net income of $50,000. At December 31, Grant owed Lockport $12,000 on account for merchandise.

REQUIRED
(a) What amount of dividends did Grant Company declare and pay during the year?
(b) Give Lockport Company's journal entries for 19XX that affect the Investment in Grant Company account.
(c) What amount of total assets would appear in a December 31, 19XX, consolidated balance sheet?

Preparing consolidated balance sheet worksheet one year after acquisition

18–31A On January 1, 19XX, Valley, Inc. purchased 75% of the voting stock of Layton, Inc., for $420,000. At that date, Layton had $450,000 in common stock outstanding and $90,000 in retained earnings. On December 31, 19XX, the separate balance sheets of the two companies were as follows:

Valley, Inc., and Layton, Inc.
Balance Sheets
December 31, 19XX

	Valley	Layton
Investment in Layton, Inc. (at equity)	$ 450,000	—
Other Assets	950,000	$700,000
	$1,400,000	$700,000
Liabilities	$ 240,000	$120,000
Common Stock	800,000	450,000
Retained Earnings	360,000	130,000
	$1,400,000	$700,000

During the year, Layton, Inc., paid $24,000 in dividends.

REQUIRED
Prepare a consolidated balance sheet worksheet at December 31, 19XX. Assume that any amount paid by Valley in excess of the equity acquired in Layton is attributable to goodwill.

Preparing consolidated income statement worksheet

18–32A Hunter Company purchased a 60% interest in Mills Company on January 1, 19XX. The income statements for the two companies for 19XX are given below. Hunter Company has not yet recorded its share of Mills Company's net income.

Hunter and Mills Companies
Income Statements
For the Year Ended December 31, 19XX

	Hunter	Mills
Sales	$960,000	$520,000
Cost of Goods Sold	620,000	312,000
Gross Profit	$340,000	$208,000
Operating Expenses (including income taxes)	256,000	162,000
Net Income	$ 84,000	$ 46,000

Mills Company did not pay any dividends in 19XX. During the year, Hunter sold merchandise costing $56,000 to Mills for $90,000, all of which Mills sold to outsiders.

REQUIRED
Prepare a consolidated income statement worksheet for 19XX.

Analyzing data from statements consolidated at acquisition date

18–33A On January 1, 19XX, Peters Company acquired an interest in Sargent Company by issuing to Sargent Company stockholders 1,500 shares of its own $100 par value common stock. At the time of the acquisition, Peters Company shares had a market value of $220 per share. The separate balance sheets of the two firms and a consolidated balance sheet at the date of acquisition are shown below:

	Peters	Sargent	Consolidated
Investment in Sargent	$240,000	—	
Other Assets	500,000	$265,000	$765,000
	$740,000	$265,000	$765,000
Liabilities	$ 50,000	$ 25,000	$ 75,000
Common Stock	500,000	200,000	500,000
Paid-in Capital from Acquisition	90,000	—	50,000
Retained Earnings	100,000	40,000	140,000
	$740,000	$265,000	$765,000

REQUIRED

(a) Is the acquisition of Sargent Company by Peters Company treated as a purchase or a pooling of interests? Explain.

(b) What ownership percentage of Sargent Company did Peters Company acquire? Explain.

(c) If Peters Company issued 1,500 shares of its own stock worth $220 per share, why doesn't goodwill from consolidation appear on the consolidated balance sheet?

Parent's entries for acquisition, income, and dividends of majority-held subsidiary

18–34A On January 1, 19XX, Olson Company purchased 70% of the common shares of Sinclair Company for $450,000 cash. At that time, the stockholders' equity of Sinclair Company consisted of $400,000 common stock and $220,000 retained earnings. At December 31, 19XX, the separate balance sheets of the two firms were as follows:

Olson and Sinclair Companies
Balance Sheets
December 31, 19XX

	Olson	Sinclair
Investment in Sinclair (at equity)	$ 471,000	—
Other Assets	1,049,000	$750,000
	$1,520,000	$750,000
Liabilities	$ 250,000	$100,000
Common Stock	950,000	400,000
Retained Earnings	320,000	250,000
	$1,520,000	$750,000

REQUIRED

(a) Give Olson Company's general journal entry to record the purchase of Sinclair Company's shares on January 1, 19XX.

(b) Sinclair Company's 19XX net income was $40,000. Sinclair declared and paid $10,000 in dividends near the end of 19XX.

  1. Give Olson Company's general journal entry to record its share of Sinclair's net income for the year.

2. Give Olson Company's general journal entry to record the receipt of dividends from Sinclair Company.

(c) Prepare a consolidated balance sheet worksheet for the two firms at December 31, 19XX. Assume that any amount paid by Olson Company in excess of the equity acquired is goodwill. At December 31, Sinclair Company owed Olson Company $25,000 for merchandise.

BUSINESS DECISION PROBLEM

Ace, Inc., manufactures heating and cooling systems. It has a 75% interest in Guardall Company, which manufactures thermostats, switches, and other controls for heating and cooling products. It also has a 100% interest in Ace Finance Company, created by the parent company to finance sales of its products to contractors and other consumers. The parent company's only other investment is a 15% interest in the common stock of Wizard, Inc., which produces certain circuits used by Ace, Inc. A condensed consolidated balance sheet of the entity for the current year is given below:

Ace, Inc., and Subsidiaries
Consolidated Balance Sheet
December 31, 19XX

Assets		
Current Assets		$25,400,000
Investment in Stock of Wizard, Inc. (15%) at Cost		3,200,000
Other Assets		67,600,000
Excess of Cost over Equity Acquired in Net Assets of Guardall Company		1,800,000
Total Assets		$98,000,000
Liabilities and Stockholders' Equity		
Current Liabilities		$11,300,000
Long-term Liabilities		15,000,000
Stockholders' Equity:		
Minority Interest	$ 4,600,000	
Common Stock	50,000,000	
Retained Earnings	17,100,000	71,700,000
Total Liabilities and Stockholders' Equity		$98,000,000

This balance sheet, along with other financial statements, was furnished to shareholders before their annual meeting, and all shareholders were invited to submit questions to be answered at the meeting. As chief financial officer of Ace, Inc., you have been appointed to respond to the questions at the meeting.

REQUIRED

Answer the following stockholder questions:

(a) What is meant by *consolidated* financial statements?

(b) Why is the investment in Wizard, Inc., shown on the consolidated balance sheet, while the investments in Guardall Company and Ace Finance Company are omitted?

(c) Explain the meaning of the asset Excess of Cost over Equity Acquired in Net Assets of Guardall Company.

(d) What is meant by *minority interest* and to what company is this account related?

ANSWERS TO SELF-TEST QUESTIONS

1. (c) **2.** (b) **3.** (a) **4.** (d) **5.** (a)

ANNUAL REPORT PROBLEMS FOR PART 3

The following problems conclude Part 3 of the text. These problems use the financial statement disclosure data of actual companies. In each case, we give a brief profile of the company and selected disclosure data from a recent annual report to stockholders, followed by questions relating to certain accounting principles and practices discussed thus far in the text.

I. A. Schulman, Inc.

PROFILE A. Shulman, Inc., is a leading supplier of high-quality plastics and resins, which are produced at its seven manufacturing facilities in North America and Europe. The firm, based in Akron, Ohio, had sales of $597.7 million and total assets of $240.5 million for the year ended August 31, 1988.

DISCLOSURE DATA (*from* consolidated statement of stockholders' equity)

	Common Stock		Retained Earnings
	Shares	Amount	Amount
Three-for-two stock split paid as a 50% stock dividend	2,975,956	$2,976,000	($2,976,000)

REQUIRED

(a) Aside from selling additional shares, there are two ways a corporation may increase its outstanding common stock by 50%: (1) implement a formal three-for-two stock split or (2) declare and distribute a 50% stock dividend. What is the difference in the accounting analysis for a formal three-for-two stock split compared with the analysis for a 50% stock dividend?

(b) Was A. Schulman, Inc.'s, increase of 50% in shares treated as a stock split or as a 50% stock dividend?

(c) What is the par or stated value of A. Schulman, Inc.'s, common stock?

II. Fay's Drug Company, Inc.

PROFILE Fay's Drug Company, Inc., operates the largest chain of super drug stores in the northeast, comprising 155 stores in New York, Pennsylvania, Connecticut, and Massachusetts. For the year ended January 31, 1988, sales were $500.4 million and total assets were $166.2 million.

DISCLOSURE DATA (*from* consolidated statements of stockholders' equity *and* notes to consolidated financial statements)

The consolidated statements of stockholders' equity for the three years ended January 31, 1988, showed a $131,411 deduction from Retained Earnings in the year ended January 31, 1986, for "Provision for unrealized loss on long-term investments." For the year ended January 31, 1987, there appeared a $234,585 addition to Retained Earnings for "Decrease in valuation allowance on long-term investments." For the year ended January 31, 1988, no adjustment for the valuation of long-term investments appeared.

In a note to the consolidated financial statements, the following information was given:

	January 31,	
	1988*	1987
Investments, at cost	$909,811	$7,003,596
Investments, at market	909,811	7,022,920

*$6,093,785 long-term investments were sold in 1988.

REQUIRED

(a) How are long-term stock investments valued in the year-end balance sheet according to generally accepted accounting principles?

(b) Give the entries that were made by Fay's Drug Company, Inc., for the $131,411 unrealized loss for the year ended January 31, 1986, and for the $234,585 decrease in the valuation allowance on long-term investments for the year ended January 31, 1987.

(c) Why did no entry appear for revaluation of long-term investments for the year ended January 31, 1988?

III. Pfizer, Inc.

PROFILE Pfizer, Inc., is a research-based firm that develops, manufactures, and sells health care, agricultural, chemical, and other products in 140 countries. In 1987, the firm's total sales were $4,919.8 million and total assets were $6,922.6 million.

DISCLOSURE DATA (*from* notes to consolidated financial statements)

The consolidated financial statements include the accounts of Pfizer, Inc., and all significant subsidiaries. Material intercompany transactions are eliminated.

In 1987, the Company adopted the provisions of *Statement of Financial Accounting Standards (SFAS) No. 94,* "Consolidation of All Majority-owned Subsidiaries." By implementing this accounting standard, the financial operations of its wholly owned, offshore banking subsidiary, as well as a small captive offshore insurance company, are consolidated. These companies were previously presented as unconsolidated subsidiaries accounted for under the equity method of accounting. Prior year financial statements have been restated to reflect this change.

REQUIRED

For many years, before the issuance of *Statement of Financial Accounting Standards (SFAS) No. 94,* firms did not include the accounts of certain nonhomogenous affiliates in consolidated financial statements. For example, the accounts of finance, insurance, and banking affiliates were routinely excluded from consolidated statements, with the investments in such firms carried according to the equity method of acounting.

(a) In the past, what reasons were usually given for excluding such affiliate accounts from the consolidated statements?

(b) What accounting procedures were followed in using the equity method of carrying an investment in a majority-owned affiliate?

(c) Why has the Financial Accounting Standards Board changed consolidation practice to include the accounts of virtually all majority-owned subsidiaries in consolidated financial statements?

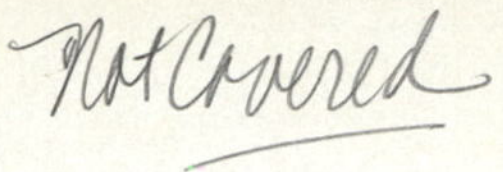

APPENDIX C

ACCOUNTING FOR BRANCHES

Many business firms expand by opening new outlets, or **branches,** at different locations. The development of suburban shopping centers has provided the impetus for branch marketing of goods and services by many firms, especially retail stores, banks, and savings and loan companies. Both wholesale and retail merchandising companies have expanded their marketing territories through widespread branch operations.

Typically, the various branches offer the same goods or services and follow fairly standardized operations. A manager appointed for each branch normally is responsible for that outlet's profitability. From a managerial viewpoint, each branch is an accounting entity, even though branches are usually segments of a single legal entity—a corporation, partnership, or sole proprietorship. The principal outlet, from which the firm's activities are normally directed, is often referred to as the **home office.**

Generally, merchandising policies, advertising, and promotion are directed or heavily influenced by the home office. Although branches may be given some latitude in acquiring merchandise, often the major portion of goods is purchased centrally.

The accounting system for branch operations should furnish management with complete and timely information to measure branch profitability. The size and complexity of branch operations, geographic location, and degree of autonomy, among other things, may influence the type of accounting system adopted. Most systems, however, are variations of two basic schemes—centralized accounting by the home office and decentralized accounting by the branch.

CENTRALIZED BRANCH RECORDS

Under a **centralized** accounting system, the home office maintains most of the records needed to account for branch operations. Thus separate asset, liability, revenue, and expense records for each branch are maintained at the home office. Typically, cash is transferred to the branch to establish a working fund for small disbursements. This fund is ordinarily kept on an imprest basis (like a petty cash fund) and replenished regularly by the home office on the basis of expense vouchers or summaries submitted by the branch. A branch that collects any amounts in its operations must often deposit such amounts in a home office bank account and transmit deposit slips and lists of the remittances to the home office for recording. The branch also transmits other documents such as copies of sales invoices and credit memos to the home office for recording. The data needed to record branch transactions may be transmitted by a telecommunication or similar device, with the documents forwarded periodically. In some cases, the documents may be filed at the branch, with periodic audits by either home office auditors or independent accountants.

DECENTRALIZED BRANCH RECORDS

Under a **decentralized** accounting system, each branch ordinarily maintains a comprehensive set of accounting records for its operations and forwards periodic financial statements to the home office. Normally, the forms of the records and statements are standardized for all branches, so that they may be conveniently analyzed by the home office and integrated into the financial reports of the whole organization. Emphasis is often placed on the operating, or income statement, accounts. Also, the branch may keep accounts for current assets—such as cash, accounts receivable, and inventory—but the home office may retain the accounts for equipment, fixtures, and accumulated depreciation.

In place of owners' equity accounts, the branch has an account called **Home Office,** which represents amounts of advances or assets received from the home office plus accumulated branch earnings not transferred to the home office. A reciprocal account called **Branch Office** is maintained in the ledger of the home office. When both accounts are posted and up to date, the dollar balances should be identical.

From the branch's viewpoint, the Home Office account may be regarded as either a capital account or a liability. Likewise, the Branch Office balance on the books of the home office may be viewed either as an investment or as a receivable. The classification of these accounts is not especially important; the branch is only an accounting segment, and when its accounts are combined with those of the home office, the balances of these two accounts offset each other and do not appear in the combined financial statements.

ILLUSTRATION OF DECENTRALIZED ACCOUNTING

Assume that on May 1 of the current year Foto-Art Company, retailer of photographic equipment, opened its Western Branch in another city, leasing the store facilities and fixtures. The home office transferred $20,000 cash and $40,000 in merchandise to the branch to begin operations. The following entries record the transfer establishing the branch:

Home Office Records			Western Branch Records		
Western Branch	60,000		Cash	20,000	
Cash		20,000	Shipments from Home Office	40,000	
Shipments to Western Branch		40,000	Home Office		60,000

This entry established the investment in the branch (or receivable from the branch) for the amount of cash and merchandise advanced to the new outlet. The $60,000 amount shown in Western Branch's reciprocal account equals the amount of capital received from the home office.

Generally, merchandise shipped from the home office to the branch should be differentiated from branch acquisitions purchased from outsiders. Therefore, a Shipments to Branch account is credited on the home office records, and a Shipments from Home Office account is debited on the branch records whenever the home office transfers merchandise to the branch. On the home office records, the Shipments to Branch account can be considered a contra account to the Purchases account. On the branch records, the Shipments from Home Office debit balance can be considered a purchases amount. When the branch closes its books, it closes the Shipments from Home Office account to the Income Summary account. Likewise, the home office closes the Shipments to Branch balance to its own Income Summary account.

The following transactions, including the asset transfer establishing the branch, are shown in summary form:

Summary of May Transactions	**Home Office Records**			**Western Branch Records**		
1. Home office opened Western Branch, transferring $20,000 cash and $40,000 merchandise.	Western Branch	60,000		Cash	20,000	
	Cash		20,000	Shipments from Home Office	40,000	
	Shipments to Western Branch		40,000	Home Office		60,000
2. Purchased $15,000 merchandise from outsiders.				Purchases	15,000	
				Accounts Payable		15,000
3. Sold merchandise on account for $30,000.				Accounts Receivable	30,000	
				Sales		30,000
4. Incurred $5,000 selling expenses and $3,000 general expenses; of the total, $2,000 was on account.				Selling Expenses	5,000	
				General Expenses	3,000	
				Cash		6,000
				Accounts Payable		2,000
5. Collected $24,000 on account from customers.				Cash	24,000	
				Accounts Receivable		24,000
6. Paid $12,000 to creditors on account.				Accounts Payable	12,000	
				Cash		12,000
7. Sent $10,000 cash to home office.	Cash	10,000		Home Office	10,000	
	Western Branch		10,000	Cash		10,000
8. Attributed $1,000 home office general expenses to Western Branch.	Western Branch	1,000		General Expenses	1,000	
	General Expenses		1,000	Home Office		1,000

After the foregoing entries have been posted to Western Branch's ledger, the trial balance for the branch would appear as shown in Exhibit C–1.

Western Branch next records any necessary end-of-period adjustments in the usual fashion. For the sake of simplicity, we assume that none are needed.

BRANCH FINANCIAL STATEMENTS

After the branch has recorded any necessary adjusting entries, financial statements can be prepared. Exhibits C–2 and C–3 show the May income statement

EXHIBIT C–1

Foto-Art Company
Western Branch
Trial Balance
May 31, 19XX

	Debit	Credit
Cash	$16,000	
Accounts Receivable	6,000	
Home Office		$51,000
Accounts Payable		5,000
Sales		30,000
Purchases	15,000	
Shipments from Home Office	40,000	
Selling Expenses	5,000	
General Expenses	4,000	
	$86,000	$86,000

and the May 31 balance sheet for Western Branch. Note in the balance sheet that the net income for the period is added to the balance of the Home Office account. Actually, the branch's net income would be closed to the Home Office account at the end of the accounting period, as shown later in the closing entries.

EXHIBIT C–2

Foto-Art Company
Western Branch
Income Statement
For the Month of May, 19XX

Sales		$30,000
Cost of Goods Sold:		
Beginning Inventory	—	
Purchases	$15,000	
Shipment from Home Office	40,000	
Goods Available for Sale	$55,000	
Less: Ending Inventory	37,000	
Cost of Goods Sold		18,000
Gross Profit on Sales		$12,000
Operating Expenses:		
Selling Expenses	$ 5,000	
General Expenses	4,000	
Total Operating Expenses		9,000
Net Income		$ 3,000

EXHIBIT C–3

Foto-Art Company
Western Branch
Balance Sheet
May 31, 19XX

Assets		Liabilities and Home Office Equity		
Cash	$16,000	Accounts Payable		$ 5,000
Accounts Receivable	6,000	Home Office	$51,000	
Inventory	37,000	Net Income	3,000	54,000
	$59,000			$59,000

COMBINED FINANCIAL STATEMENTS

At the end of the accounting period, the various branches submit their financial statements (or alternatively, adjusted trial balances) to the home office, which combines the data into a single set of statements for the whole enterprise. The worksheets in Exhibit C–4 provide a convenient vehicle for compiling and integrating the data for the company. In the illustration, the data for home office operations are assumed. Note that the reciprocal amounts of $40,000 representing shipments from the home office to the branch are eliminated and the accounts do not appear in the combined income statement. Likewise, the home office and branch office accounts, with $54,000 balances, are eliminated when the combined balance sheet is prepared.

CLOSING ENTRIES

After financial statements are prepared, the following closing entries are recorded by the branch:

May 31	Income Summary	64,000	
	Purchases		15,000
	Shipments from Home Office		40,000
	Selling Expenses		5,000
	General Expenses		4,000
	To close income statement accounts with debit balances.		
31	Inventory	37,000	
	Sales	30,000	
	Income Summary		67,000
	To record the ending inventory and to close income statement account with credit balance.		
31	Income Summary	3,000	
	Home Office		3,000
	To close the Income Summary account to the Home Office account.		

EXHIBIT C–4

Foto-Art Company
Home Office and Western Branch
Income Statement Worksheet
For the Month of May, 19XX

	Home Office	Western Branch	Eliminations	Combined Income Statement
Sales	65,000	30,000		95,000
Cost of Goods Sold:				
Inventory, May 1	38,000	—		38,000
Purchases	70,000	15,000		85,000
Shipments to Branch	(40,000)		40,000	
Shipments from Home Office		40,000	(40,000)	
Goods Available for Sale	68,000	55,000		123,000
Less: Inventory, May 31	28,000	37,000		65,000
Cost of Goods Sold	40,000	18,000		58,000
Gross Profit on Sales	25,000	12,000		37,000
Operating Expenses:				
Selling Expenses	9,000	5,000		14,000
General Expenses	7,000	4,000		11,000
Total Operating Expenses	16,000	9,000		25,000
Net Income	9,000	3,000		12,000

Foto-Art Company
Home Office and Western Branch
Balance Sheet Worksheet
May 31, 19XX

Assets	Home Office	Western Branch	Eliminations	Combined Balance Sheet
Cash	20,000	16,000		36,000
Accounts Receivable	36,000	6,000		42,000
Inventory	28,000	37,000		65,000
Western Branch	54,000		(54,000)	
Plant Assets, Net of Accumulated Depreciation	80,000			80,000
Total Assets	218,000	59,000	(54,000)	223,000
Liabilities and Stockholders' Equity				
Accounts Payable	18,000	5,000		23,000
Accrued Liabilities	2,000			2,000
Home Office		54,000	(54,000)	
Common Stock	150,000			150,000
Retained Earnings	48,000			48,000
Total Liabilities and Stockholders' Equity	218,000	59,000	(54,000)	223,000

On May 31, the home office reflects the branch net income by making a corollary entry to the last entry shown above:

May 31	Western Branch	3,000	
	Net Income—Western Branch		3,000
	To reflect net income of Western Branch.		

In closing its records, the home office closes the Net Income—Western Branch account to its Income Summary account.

PROBLEMS

Entries to Home Office account by branch

C–1 Eastgate Branch had a beginning balance of $56,000 in its Home Office account. During the current month, Eastgate received $38,000 in merchandise shipments from the home office. At month-end, the branch's share of home office general expenses was $4,200. After closing its records, Eastgate Branch determined its net income as $22,600. The branch then sent $20,000 cash to the home office.

REQUIRED

(a) Give the branch's journal entry made on receiving the $38,000 in merchandise from the home office.

(b) What amount would be in the Home Office account after all entries were posted for the current month?

Entries on branch and home office records

C–2 Verona Branch of Elkin Tax Service, which has decentralized accounting records, opened on July 1 of the current year and had the following July transactions:

July 1 The home office transferred $10,000 cash and $25,000 in equipment to the branch.
15 The branch collected $12,000 tax service fees.
20 The branch paid $6,400 in operating expenses.
30 The home office allocated $2,600 of home office general expenses to the branch. (Debit Operating Expenses for branch.)
31 The branch collected $7,500 tax service fees and sent $10,000 cash to the home office.
31 The branch recorded depreciation on equipment, $200. (Debit Operating Expenses.)
31 The branch made the appropriate entries to close the books at the end of July. The branch has one revenue account (Fee Revenue) and one expense account (Operating Expenses).
31 The branch reported its net income of $10,300 to the home office.

REQUIRED

Journalize the foregoing entries on the branch books and on the home office books.

Entries on branch and home office records

C–3 Mayer, Inc., which operates a large music store in Chicago, arranged in May of the current year to open a branch in Rockford. Record keeping for the branch is decentralized. A summary of the branch's transactions for May is given below:

May 1 The Chicago store transferred $60,000 cash and $120,000 in merchandise to the Rockford branch.
3 Purchased $60,000 in merchandise on account from various dealers.
10 Paid $25,000 on accounts payable.
15 Sales to date: cash, $18,000; on account $26,000.
18 Collected $12,500 on account from customers.
20 Selling expenses for the branch were $11,000 and general expenses were $6,500; of the total, $2,500 was on account and the remainder paid in cash.
25 Sent $20,000 cash to the Chicago store.
30 Sales during the last half of the month: cash, $16,000; on account, $29,000.

TRANSLATION OF FOREIGN CURRENCY TRANSACTIONS

Transactions a U.S. business may have with a foreign entity include the purchase or sale of goods and the borrowing or lending of funds. A transaction is a **foreign currency transaction** if it is *denominated* in a foreign currency; that is, if its terms are fixed in the amount of foreign currency to be paid or received. A steel purchase from a Japanese firm requiring payment of a fixed number of yen is a foreign currency transaction. Similarly, an export sale to an English enterprise that requires settlement in a fixed number of British pounds is a foreign currency transaction.

Accounting at Transaction Date

A U.S. firm keeps its financial records in U.S. dollars. All foreign currency transactions, therefore, must be translated into U.S. dollars so they may be properly recorded. When journalized, each transaction component is translated into U.S. dollars using the exchange rate at the transaction date.

To illustrate, assume a U.S. firm purchases merchandise on account from a Canadian firm on June 1, 19X1. The cost is 10,000 Canadian dollars (C$). Payment is due in 30 days. The exchange rate for Canadian dollars on June 1 is $0.85. Using the June 1 exchange rate, the U.S. firm translates the C$10,000 to $8,500 (C$10,000 × $0.85) and makes the following entry:

June 1	Purchases	8,500	
	Accounts Payable		8,500
	To record purchase of merchandise on account (C$10,000 × $0.85 = $8,500).		

Accounting at Settlement Date

Exchange rates may change before the settlement date for a foreign currency payable or receivable. Should this occur, a **foreign exchange gain or loss** is recorded at the settlement date. The foreign exchange gain or loss measures the change in the U.S. dollar equivalent required to settle the transaction. Foreign exchange gains and losses are reported in the income statement. A company experiencing both foreign exchange gains and foreign exchange losses during the same period may combine them and report a net foreign exchange gain or loss in its income statement.

We continue our previous example. Assume that on July 1 the U.S. company settles its account payable with the Canadian firm. The exchange rate on July 1 is $0.83. On July 1, it costs the U.S. firm $8,300 to purchase the 10,000 Canadian dollars needed to settle the account. The exchange rate decline creates a $200 foreign exchange gain ($8,500 − $8,300) for the U.S. firm. The July 1 settlement is recorded as follows:

July 1	Accounts Payable	8,500	
	Cash		8,300
	Foreign Exchange Gain		200
	To record payment of account payable (C$10,000 × $0.83 = $8,300) and foreign exchange gain.		

Unsettled Foreign Currency Transactions

Foreign currency receivables and payables that are not settled at a balance sheet date are adjusted to reflect the exchange rate at that date. Such adjustments place foreign exchange gains and losses in the period when exchange rates change. Any foreign exchange gain or loss at the settlement date, then, relates only to exchange rate changes since the latest balance sheet date.

To illustrate, assume that on December 15, 19X1, our U.S. firm purchases more merchandise on 30-day account from the Canadian firm. The merchandise costs 15,000 Canadian dollars. The U.S. firm's accounting period ends on December 31, 19X1. The account payable is settled on January 14, 19X2. Exchange rates for the Canadian dollar are:

December 15	$0.82
December 31	0.84
January 14	0.81

The U.S. firm accounts for this foreign currency transaction as follows:

Date	Account	Debit	Credit
Dec. 15	Purchases	12,300	
	Accounts Payable		12,300
	To record purchase of merchandise on account (C$15,000 × $0.82 = $12,300).		
31	Foreign Exchange Loss	300	
	Accounts Payable		300
	To adjust accounts payable to current exchange rate (C$15,000 × $0.84 = $12,600; $12,600 − $12,300 = $300) and record foreign exchange loss.		
Jan. 14	Accounts Payable	12,600	
	Cash		12,150
	Foreign Exchange Gain		450
	To record payment of account payable (C$15,000 × $0.81 = $12,150) and foreign exchange gain.		

On December 31, 19X1, a $300 foreign exchange loss is recorded to reflect the impact of the strengthening of the Canadian dollar between December 15 and December 31. Because the account payable is not settled on this date, the loss is unrealized. It is included, however, in the 19X1 income statement. The account payable is settled on January 14, 19X2. The Canadian dollar has weakened since December 31, 19X1, so a $450 foreign exchange gain is recorded and included in the 19X2 income statement.

Transactions Denominated in U.S. Currency

A U.S. firm's transactions with foreign entities that are denominated in U.S. dollars are *not* foreign currency transactions. No translation is required (the transaction is initially stated in U.S. dollars) and no foreign exchange gains or losses develop. For example, assume a U.S. firm sells merchandise to a Swiss firm on account. The sales price is $6,000 U.S. dollars, due in 30 days. Because the transaction is denominated in U.S. dollars, the U.S. firm accounts for the transaction no differently than if the customer was in the United States. The Swiss firm, in contrast, must translate its foreign currency transaction into Swiss francs and faces gains and losses from exchange rate changes.

CONVERSION OF FOREIGN CURRENCY FINANCIAL STATEMENTS

U.S. multinational corporations frequently use foreign subsidiary companies to conduct their foreign activities. If the foreign subsidiary is more than 50% owned, its financial statements are usually consolidated with the U.S. parent's statements. Of course, when the subsidiary's accounting records are kept in the foreign currency, its financial statements must be converted to U.S. dollars before consolidation can occur.

There are two different procedures that may be used to convert foreign financial statements to U.S. dollars:

1. Translation procedures.
2. Remeasurement procedures.

The **functional currency** of a foreign subsidiary determines which of these two procedures is used. As defined by the Financial Accounting Standards Board:

> An entity's functional currency is the currency of the primary economic environment in which the entity operates; normally, that is the currency of the environment in which an entity primarily generates and expends cash.[2]

Depending on the circumstances, the functional currency may be either the foreign currency or the U.S. dollar. For example, a West German subsidiary manufactures and sells its own products. Its expenses as well as cash generated by its operations are primarily in deutsche marks and have little impact on its parent's cash flows. This subsidiary's operations are well integrated with the West German economy. Thus, its functional currency is the foreign currency (deutsche mark). In contrast, consider a West German subsidiary that is a sales outlet for its U.S. parent's goods. The subsidiary takes orders, bills and collects the invoice price, warehouses the goods to facilitate delivery, and remits its net cash flows primarily to the parent. This subsidiary is essentially an agent for the parent company. Its functional currency would be the U.S. dollar.

The functional currency is also the U.S. dollar for foreign subsidiaries that operate in highly inflationary economies (economies whose cumulative inflation over a three-year period is approximately 100 percent or more). The U.S. dollar is deemed the functional currency because it is the more stable currency; the foreign currency is too unstable. Argentina and Mexico are recent examples of countries whose three-year cumulative inflation exceeds 100 percent.

Once the functional currency is determined, the specific conversion procedures are selected as follows:

1. *Foreign currency is functional currency:* Use translation procedures.
2. *U.S. dollar is functional currency:* Use remeasurement procedures.

To illustrate these two procedures for converting foreign financial statements to U.S. dollars, we assume Wyso Company was organized in West Germany on January 1, 19X1, as a wholly owned subsidiary of Minor Corporation, a U.S. company. Wyso's opening balance sheet, in West German deutsche marks (DM), consisted of the following assets and stockholders' equity:

---

[2] *Statement of Financial Accounting Standards No. 52,* "Foreign Currency Translation" (Stamford, CT: Financial Accounting Standards Board, 1981), p. 3.

Assets		Stockholders' Equity	
Cash	DM 40,000	Common Stock	DM800,000
Inventory	160,000		
Plant Assets	600,000		
Total	DM800,000		

Wyso's 19X1 income statement and December 31, 19X1, balance sheet, in deutsche marks, follow.

Wyso Company
Income Statement
For the Year Ended December 31, 19X1

Sales		DM750,000
Cost of Goods Sold	DM500,000	
Depreciation Expense	30,000	
Other Expenses	70,000	
Total Expenses		600,000
Net Income		DM150,000

Wyso Company
Balance Sheet
December 31, 19X1

Assets		Liabilities		
Cash	DM 60,000	Accounts Payable		DM 30,000
Accounts Receivable (net)	140,000	**Stockholders' Equity**		
Inventory	210,000	Common Stock	DM800,000	
Plant Assets (net)	570,000	Retained Earnings	150,000	950,000
Total Assets	DM980,000	Total Liabilities and Stockholders' Equity		DM980,000

Exchange rates for the deutsche mark are:

January 1, 19X1	$0.54
Average for 19X1	0.50
December 31, 19X1	0.46

Translation Procedures

Assume that Wyso Company's operations are fully integrated with West Germany's economy. Thus its functional currency is the deutsche mark and translation procedures are used. **Translation procedures** convert foreign financial statements to U.S. dollars as follows:

1. All asset and liability accounts are converted using the exchange rate at the balance sheet date (current rate).
2. Capital stock accounts are converted using the exchange rate on the date the stock was issued (historical rate).
3. All revenue and expense accounts are converted using the exchange rate at the date these items were recognized. If revenue and expenses are generated

in a relatively uniform pattern during the year, an average exchange rate for the year may be used (average rate).

The purpose of these translation procedures is to retain, in the converted data, the financial results and relationships among assets and liabilities that were created by the subsidiary's operation in its foreign environment.

Exhibit D–3 shows these translation procedures applied to Wyso Company's financial statements. Note the $70,000 **translation adjustment** in the exhibit, shown as a reduction of stockholders' equity in U.S. dollars. Translation procedures create a translation adjustment. The translation adjustment balances the balance sheet and arises because the same exchange rate is not used to convert all accounts. The $70,000 may be calculated as:

Common stock × (historical rate − current rate)	
DM800,000 × ($0.54 − $0.46) =	$64,000
Net income × (average rate − current rate)	
DM150,000 × ($0.50 − $0.46) =	6,000
Translation adjustment	$70,000

The translation adjustment is reported as a separate component of stockholders' equity. Depending on the direction of exchange rate changes, it may reduce stockholders' equity (as in our illustration) or increase stockholders' equity.

EXHIBIT D–3

TRANSLATION OF WYSO COMPANY FINANCIAL STATEMENTS
DECEMBER 31, 19X1
DEUTSCHE MARK = FUNCTIONAL CURRENCY

	Deutsche Marks	Exchange Rate	U.S. Dollars
Balance Sheet			
Cash	DM 60,000	$0.46	$ 27,600
Accounts Receivable (net)	140,000	0.46	64,400
Inventory	210,000	0.46	96,600
Plant Assets (net)	570,000	0.46	262,200
Total	DM980,000		$450,800
Accounts Payable	DM 30,000	0.46	$ 13,800
Common Stock	800,000	0.54	432,000
Retained Earnings	150,000	See Net Income	75,000
Translation Adjustment			(70,000)
Total	DM980,000		$450,800
Income Statement			
Sales	DM750,000	0.50	$375,000
Cost of Goods Sold	DM500,000	0.50	$250,000
Depreciation Expense	30,000	0.50	15,000
Other Expenses	70,000	0.50	35,000
Total Expenses	DM600,000		$300,000
Net Income	DM150,000		$ 75,000

Remeasurement Procedures

Now assume Wyso Company's operations are essentially a direct extension of Minor Corporation's (the parent) activities. In this circumstance, Wyso's functional currency is the U.S. dollar and remeasurement procedures are used. **Remeasurement procedures** convert foreign financial statements to U.S. dollars as follows:

1. Monetary asset and liability accounts (basically all cash, receivables, and payables) are converted using the exchange rate at the balance sheet date (current rate).
2. All other balance sheet accounts are converted using the exchange rate in effect when the item was initially recorded on the books (historical rate).
3. Revenue and expense accounts are converted using the exchange rate related to the transaction. Generally, the average exchange rate for the period is used. However, expenses that relate to assets converted at historical rates are converted at the appropriate historical rate. Depreciation expense and cost of goods sold are in this latter category.

The objective of these remeasurement procedures is to produce the same U.S. dollar financial statements as if the foreign entity's accounting records had been initially maintained in the U.S. dollar.

Exhibit D–4 shows these remeasurement procedures applied to Wyso Company's financial statements. Schedule A in the exhibit details the remeasurement of cost of goods sold, which requires converting the beginning inventory, purchases, and ending inventory at historical exchange rates. The average rate for the year ($0.50) applies to the purchases of DM550,000 while a rate of $0.48 applies to the ending inventory (the average exchange rate during the latter part of the year when the ending inventory was acquired). Also, note the $8,400 foreign exchange loss among the income statement expenses in U.S. dollars.[3] Remeasurement procedures produce foreign exchange gains or losses—the effects on assets and liabilities of exchange rate changes. These foreign exchange gains and losses are included in net income.

Generally Accepted Accounting Principles

At present, there are no international accounting principles that are broadly accepted and enforced. Accounting principles vary among countries because legal, economic, and regulatory systems differ, just as social values and traditions do. Foreign company financial statements, therefore, may vary in some respects from U.S. generally accepted accounting principles. If they do, the statements must be changed to conform to U.S. generally accepted accounting principles *before* the conversion to U.S. dollars may occur.

PROBLEMS

Translation of foreign currency transactions

D–1 On June 18, 19X3, Eagle, Inc., a U.S. company, purchased merchandise on account from Bourne Company, a French firm. The merchandise cost was 90,000 French

[3]The $8,400 foreign exchange loss is the amount needed to obtain a $54,800 net income. When transferred to retained earnings, the $54,800 balances the balance sheet.

EXHIBIT D–4

REMEASUREMENT OF WYSO COMPANY FINANCIAL STATEMENTS
DECEMBER 31, 19X1
U.S. DOLLAR = FUNCTIONAL CURRENCY

	Deutsche Marks	Exchange Rate	U.S. Dollars
Balance Sheet			
Cash	DM 60,000	$0.46	$ 27,600
Accounts Receivable (net)	140,000	0.46	64,400
Inventory	210,000	0.48	100,800
Plant Assets (net)	570,000	0.54	307,800
Total	DM980,000		$500,600
Accounts Payable	DM 30,000	0.46	$ 13,800
Common Stock	800,000	0.54	432,000
Retained Earnings	150,000	See Net Income	54,800
Total	DM980,000		$500,600
Income Statement			
Sales	DM750,000	0.50	$375,000
Cost of Goods Sold	DM500,000	See Schedule A	$260,600
Depreciation Expense	30,000	0.54	16,200
Other Expenses	70,000	0.50	35,000
Foreign Exchange Loss			8,400
Total Expenses	DM600,000		$320,200
Net Income	DM150,000		$ 54,800
Schedule A			
Inventory (beginning)	DM160,000	0.54	$ 86,400
Purchases	550,000	0.50	275,000
	DM710,000		$361,400
Inventory (ending)	210,000	0.48	100,800
Cost of Goods Sold	DM500,000		$260,600

francs. Eagle paid the amount due (in francs) on July 10, 19X3. Eagle's fiscal year ends on June 30. Exchange rates for the French franc were:

June 18, 19X3	$0.16
June 30, 19X3	0.14
July 10, 19X3	0.13

REQUIRED

(a) Prepare the journal entries to account for the Bourne Company transaction on Eagle's records for June 18, 19X3, June 30, 19X3, and July 10, 19X3.

(b) Assume Eagle's accounting year ends December 31 rather than June 30. Prepare the necessary journal entries on Eagle's records in 19X3 to account for the foreign currency transaction with Bourne Company.

(c) Assume Eagle's accounting year ends June 30 and the exchange rates for the French franc were:

June 18, 19X3	$0.13
June 30, 19X3	0.15
July 10, 19X3	0.12

Prepare the journal entries to account for the Bourne Company transaction on Eagle's records for June 18, 19X3, June 30, 19X3, and July 10, 19X3.

Translation of foreign currency transactions

D–2 On December 20, 19X5, Bedrock, Inc., a U.S. firm, sold merchandise on account to Soytan Company, a Japanese company. The sales price was 5,000,000 yen. Bedrock received the amount due (in yen) on January 18, 19X6. Bedrock ends its accounting year on December 31. Exchange rates for the Japanese yen were:

December 20, 19X5	$0.0068
December 31, 19X5	0.0075
January 18, 19X6	0.0078

REQUIRED

(a) Prepare the journal entries to account for the Soytan Company transaction on Bedrock's records for December 20, 19X5, December 31, 19X5, and January 18, 19X6.

(b) Assume Bedrock's accounting year ends October 31 rather than December 31. Prepare the necessary journal entries on Bedrock's records in 19X5 and 19X6 to account for the foreign currency transaction with Soytan Company.

(c) Assume Bedrock's accounting year ends December 31 and the exchange rates for the Japanese yen were:

December 20, 19X5	$0.0079
December 31, 19X5	0.0074
January 18, 19X6	0.0071

Prepare the journal entries to account for the Soytan Company transaction on Bedrock's records for December 20, 19X5, December 31, 19X5, and January 18, 19X6.

Translation of foreign currency transactions

D–3 Listed below are selected 19X1 transactions and adjustments of Richter, Inc., a U.S. company.

Oct. 7 Purchased merchandise on account from Lafayette Company, a French firm. The merchandise cost 65,000 French francs and payment is due within 30 days. The exchange rate today for the French franc is $0.15.

19 Sold merchandise for 17,000 deutsche marks on account to Neumann Company, a West German firm. Payment is due within 30 days. The exchange rate today for the deutsche mark is $0.54.

Nov. 5 Paid French francs to settle the account payable with Lafayette Company (see October 7 transaction). The exchange rate today for the French franc is $0.16.

16 Received full payment on account, in deutsche marks, from Neumann Company (see October 19 transaction). The exchange rate today for the deutsche mark is $0.52.

Dec. 8 Sold merchandise for 35,000 guilders on account to Brinker Company, a Dutch firm. Payment is due within 30 days. The exchange rate today for the Dutch guilder is $0.48.

10 Purchased merchandise on account from Regal Company, an English firm. The merchandise cost 14,000 British pounds and payment is due within 30 days. The exchange rate today for the British pound is $1.7705.

31 Adjusted the account receivable with Brinker Company (see December 8 transaction) and the account payable with Regal Company (see December 10 transaction) to reflect current exchange rates. The exchange rate today is $0.49 for the Dutch guilder and $1.7585 for the British pound.

REQUIRED
Prepare journal entries to record the above transactions and adjustments of Richter, Inc.

Conversion of foreign currency financial statements—translation procedures

D–4 Geneva Company was organized in Switzerland on January 1, 19X1, as a wholly owned subsidiary of Flagg, Inc., a U.S. company. Geneva's opening balance sheet, in Swiss francs (SF), consisted of the following assets and stockholders' equity:

Assets		Stockholders' Equity	
Cash	SF 10,000	Common Stock	SF650,000
Inventory	140,000		
Plant Assets	500,000		
Total	SF650,000		

Geneva's 19X1 income statement and December 31, 19X1, balance sheet, in Swiss francs, follow.

Geneva Company
Income Statement
For the Year Ended December 31, 19X1

Sales		SF700,000
Cost of Goods Sold	SF400,000	
Depreciation Expense	40,000	
Other Expenses	60,000	
Total Expenses		500,000
Net Income		SF200,000

Geneva Company
Balance Sheet
December 31, 19X1

Assets		Liabilities		
Cash	SF 70,000	Accounts Payable		SF 20,000
Accounts Receivable (net)	100,000	**Stockholders' Equity**		
Inventory	240,000	Common Stock	SF650,000	
Plant Assets (net)	460,000	Retained Earnings	200,000	850,000
Total Assets	SF870,000	Total Liabilities and Stockholders' Equity		SF870,000

Exchange rates for the Swiss franc are:

January 1, 19X1	$0.64
Average for 19X1	0.61
December 31, 19X1	0.58

REQUIRED
Assume the functional currency for Geneva Company is the Swiss franc. Use translation procedures to convert Geneva's 19X1 income statement and December 31, 19X1, balance sheet to U.S. dollars. Follow the format of Exhibit D–3.

Conversion of foreign currency financial statements—remeasurement procedures

D–5 Refer to the data given for the Geneva Company in Problem D–4. In addition, the historical exchange rate applicable to the ending inventory is $0.59 and the historical exchange rate applicable to the 19X1 purchases of SF500,000 is $0.61.

REQUIRED

Assume the functional currency for Geneva Company is the U.S. dollar. Use remeasurement procedures to convert Geneva's 19X1 income statement and December 31, 19X1, balance sheet to U.S. dollars. There is a 19X1 foreign exchange loss of $4,800 from the remeasurement procedures. Follow the format of Exhibit D–4.

19

STATEMENT OF CASH FLOWS

CHAPTER OBJECTIVES

1. Provide a basis for understanding a statement of cash flows (pp. 695–99).
2. Compare and contrast the direct and indirect methods of determining net cash flow from operating activities (pp. 699–708).
3. Illustrate a worksheet approach to preparing a statement of cash flows using the direct method (pp. 708–15).
4. Illustrate a worksheet approach to preparing a statement of cash flows using the indirect method (pp. 715–21).

Happiness is . . . Positive Cash Flow.

FREDERICK R. ADLER

The **statement of cash flows** is a basic financial statement that summarizes information about the flow of cash into and out of a company. The statement of cash flows complements the balance sheet and the income statement. The balance sheet reports the company's financial position at a point in time (the end of each period) while the statement of cash flows explains the change in one component of financial position—cash—from one balance sheet date to the next. The income statement reveals the results of the company's operating activities for the period, and these operating activities are a major contributor to the change in cash reported in the statement of cash flows.

The statement of cash flows replaces the statement of changes in financial position. The statement of changes in financial position was a required financial statement for over fifteen years and presented information on a firm's sources and uses of funds. When preparing the statement of changes in financial position, firms had the option of defining funds as either working capital (current assets less current liabilities) or cash. Initially, most companies prepared the statement with a focus on working capital. Dissatisfaction with this format by various users caused many firms to switch to a cash format. By the mid-1980s, most firms were using the cash format. When prepared in a cash format, the statement of changes in financial position bore many similarities to the statement of cash flows discussed in this chapter. Replacing the statement of changes in financial position with the statement of cash flows, in essence, completed the transition from a working capital to a cash focus.

CASH AND CASH EQUIVALENTS

Even though it is called a statement of cash flows, the statement actually encompasses a somewhat broader concept than just cash. More precisely, the statement is to explain the change in a firm's cash and cash equivalents. **Cash equivalents** are short-term, highly liquid investments that firms acquire with cash in excess of their immediate needs. To qualify as a cash equivalent, an investment must (1) be easily convertible into a known cash amount, and (2) be close enough to maturity so that its market value is not sensitive to interest rate changes (generally, investments with initial maturities of three months or less).[1] Not all investments that qualify as cash equivalents must be so classified. Each firm must set, and disclose, a policy for deciding which qualifying investments are treated as cash equivalents. Typical examples of cash equivalents are Treasury bills, commercial paper (short-term notes issued by corporations), and money market funds.

When preparing a statement of cash flows, the cash and cash equivalents are added together and treated as a single sum. This is done because the purchase and sale of investments in cash equivalents are considered to be part of a firm's overall management of cash rather than a source or use of cash. As statement users evaluate and project cash flows, for example, it may matter very little to

[1] *Statement of Financial Accounting Standards No. 95*, "Statement of Cash Flows" (Stamford, CT: Financial Accounting Standards Board, 1987), par. 8.

them whether the cash is on hand, deposited in a bank account, or invested in cash equivalents. Transfers back and forth between a firm's cash account and its investments in cash equivalents, therefore, are not treated as cash inflows and cash outflows in a statement of cash flows.

The period-end cash and cash equivalents reported in a statement of cash flows must agree with the amount of cash and cash equivalents reported in the firm's balance sheet. Items treated as cash equivalents, therefore, are distinct from assets classified in the balance sheet as short-term investments or marketable securities. Purchases and sales of these latter items do create cash outflows and cash inflows that are reported in the statement of cash flows.

When discussing the statement of cash flows, accountants generally use the word *cash* rather than the term *cash and cash equivalents*. We will follow the same practice in this chapter.

CLASSIFICATIONS IN THE STATEMENT OF CASH FLOWS

A statement of cash flows classifies cash receipts and payments into three major categories: operating activities, investing activities, and financing activities. Grouping cash flows into these categories identifies the effects on cash of each of the major activities of a firm. The combined effects on cash of all three categories explain the net change in cash for the period. The period's net change in cash is then reconciled with the beginning and ending amounts of cash. Exhibit 19–1 illustrates the basic format for a statement of cash flows.

Operating Activities

A company's income statement reflects the transactions and events that constitute its operating activities. Generally, the cash effects of these transactions and events are what determine the net cash flow from operating activities. The usual

EXHIBIT 19–1

FORMAT FOR THE STATEMENT OF CASH FLOWS

Sample Company
Statement of Cash Flows
For the Year Ended December 31, 19XX

Cash Flows from Operating Activities		
(Details of individual cash inflows and outflows)	$XXX	
Net Cash Provided (Used) by Operating Activities		$XXX
Cash Flows from Investing Activities		
(Details of individual cash inflows and outflows)	$XXX	
Net Cash Provided (Used) by Investing Activities		XXX
Cash Flows from Financing Activities		
(Details of individual cash inflows and outflows)	$XXX	
Net Cash Provided (Used) by Financing Activities		XXX
Net Increase (Decrease) in Cash		$XXX
Cash at Beginning of Year		XXX
Cash at End of Year		$XXX

focus of a firm's operating activities is on the selling of goods or the rendering of services. Cash flows from **operating activities** are defined broadly enough, however, to encompass any cash receipts or payments that are not classified as investing or financing activities. For example, cash received as lawsuit or insurance settlements and cash payments to charity are treated as cash flows from operating activities. Examples of cash inflows and outflows relating to operating activities are listed below.

Operating Activities

Cash Inflows

1. Receipts from customers for sales made or services rendered.
2. Receipts of interest and dividends.
3. Other receipts that are not related to investing or financing activities, such as lawsuit and insurance settlements received.

Cash Outflows

1. Payments to suppliers.
2. Payments to employees.
3. Payments of interest to creditors.
4. Payments of taxes to government.
5. Other payments that are not related to investing or financing activities, such as contributions to charity.

Investing Activities

A firm's transactions involving (1) the acquisition and disposal of plant assets and intangible assets, (2) the purchase and sale of stocks, bonds, and other securities (that are not cash equivalents), and (3) the lending and subsequent collection of money constitute the basic components of its **investing activities**.[2] The related cash receipts and payments appear in the investing activities section of the statement of cash flows. Examples of these cash flows are listed below.

Investing Activities

Cash Inflows

1. Receipts from sales of plant assets and intangible assets.
2. Receipts from sales of investments in stocks, bonds, and other securities (other than cash equivalents).
3. Receipts from repayments of loans by borrowers.

Cash Outflows

1. Payments to purchase plant assets and intangible assets.
2. Payments to purchase stocks, bonds, and other securities (other than cash equivalents).
3. Payments made to lend money to borrowers.

Financing Activities

A firm engages in **financing activities** when it obtains resources from owners, returns resources to owners, borrows resources from creditors, and repays amounts borrowed. Cash flows related to these events are reported in the financing activities section of the statement of cash flows. Examples of these cash flows are listed below.

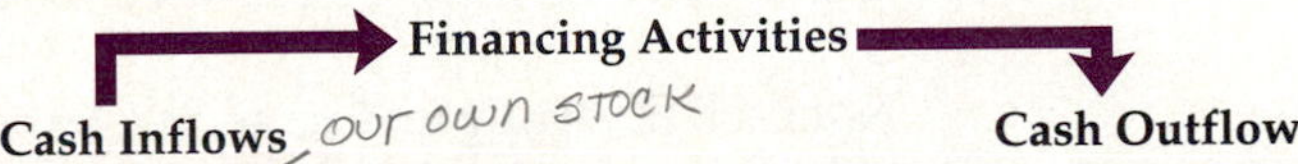

Cash Inflows

1. Receipts from issuing common stock and preferred stock.
2. Receipts from issuing bonds payable, mortgage notes payable, and other notes payable.

Cash Outflows

1. Payments to reacquire treasury stock.
2. Payments of dividends.
3. Payments to settle outstanding bonds payable, mortgage notes payable, and other notes payable.

---

[2]There are exceptions to the classification of these events as investing activities. For example, the purchase and sale of mortgage loans by a mortgage banker and the purchase and sale of securities in the trading account of a broker and dealer in securities represent operating activities for these businesses.

Observe that paying cash to settle such obligations as accounts payable, wages payable, interest payable, and income tax payable are operating activities, not financing activities.

The classification of cash flows into three categories of activities helps financial statement users interpret cash flow data. To illustrate, assume companies D, E, and F are similar companies operating in the same industry. Each company showed a $100,000 cash increase during the current year. Information from their current-year statements of cash flows is summarized below.

	D	E	F
Net Cash Provided by Operating Activities	$100,000	$ –0–	$ –0–
Cash Flows from Investing Activities:			
Sale of Plant Assets	–0–	100,000	–0–
Cash Flows from Financing Activities:			
Issuance of Notes Payable	–0–	–0–	100,000
Net Increase in Cash	$100,000	$100,000	$100,000

Although each company's cash increase was the same, the source of the increase varied by company. This variation affects the analysis of the cash flow data, particularly for potential short-term creditors who must evaluate the likelihood of obtaining repayment in the future for any funds loaned to the company. Based only on this cash flow data, a potential creditor would feel more comfortable lending money to D than to either E or F. D's cash increase came from its operating activities, while both E and F could only break even on their cash flows from operations. E's cash increase came from the sale of plant assets, and this is not a source that is likely to recur regularly. F's cash increase came entirely from borrowed funds. F faces additional cash burdens in the future when the interest and principal payments on the note payable become due.

NONCASH INVESTING AND FINANCING ACTIVITIES

A secondary objective of cash flow reporting is to present summary information about a firm's investing and financing activities. Of course, many of these activities affect cash and are therefore already included in the investing and financing sections of the statement of cash flows. Some significant investing and financing events, however, do not affect current cash flows. Examples of **noncash investing and financing activities** are the issuance of stocks or bonds in exchange for plant assets or intangible assets, the exchange of long-term assets for other long-term assets, and the conversion of long-term debt into common stock. Information about these events must be reported as a supplement to the statement of cash flows.

Noncash investing and financing transactions generally do affect future cash flows, however. Issuing bonds payable to acquire equipment, for example, requires future cash payments for interest and principal on the bonds. On the other hand, converting bonds payable into common stock eliminates future cash payments related to the bonds. Knowledge of these types of events, therefore, should be helpful to users of cash flow data who wish to assess a firm's future cash flows.

The information on noncash investing and financing transactions is disclosed in a schedule that is separate from the statement of cash flows. The separate schedule may be placed immediately below the statement of cash flows or it may be placed among the notes to the financial statements.

USEFULNESS OF THE STATEMENT OF CASH FLOWS

The Financial Accounting Standards Board believes that one objective of financial reporting is to help external users assess the amount, timing, and uncertainty of future cash flows to the enterprise.[3] These assessments, in turn, help users evaluate their own prospective cash receipts from their investments in, or loans to, the firm. Although statements of cash flows report past cash flows, these statements should be useful for assessing the future cash flows of firms.

A statement of cash flows shows the periodic cash effects of a firm's operating, investing, and financing activities. Distinguishing among these different categories of cash flows helps users compare, evaluate, and predict cash flows. With cash flow information, creditors and investors are better able to assess a firm's ability to settle its liabilities and pay its dividends. A firm's need for outside financing may also be better evaluated. Over time, the statement of cash flows permits users to observe and analyze management's investing and financing policies.

A statement of cash flows also provides information useful in evaluating a firm's financial flexibility. *Financial flexibility* is a firm's ability to generate sufficient amounts of cash to respond to unanticipated needs and opportunities. Information about past cash flows, particularly cash flows from operations, helps in assessing financial flexibility. An evaluation of a firm's ability to survive an unexpected drop in demand, for example, may include a review of its past cash flows from operations. The larger these cash flows, the greater will be the firm's ability to withstand adverse changes in economic conditions. Other financial statements, particularly the balance sheet and its notes, also contain information useful for judging financial flexibility.

Some investors and creditors find the statement of cash flows useful in evaluating the "quality" of a firm's income. As we know, determining income under accrual accounting procedures requires many accruals, deferrals, allocations, and valuations. These adjustment and measurement procedures introduce more subjectivity into income determination than some financial statement users prefer. These users will relate a more objective performance measure—cash flow from operations—to net income. To these users, the higher this ratio is, the higher is the quality of the income.

NET CASH FLOW FROM OPERATING ACTIVITIES

In Chapter 1 we defined a cash basis system of accounting. Such a system records revenue when cash is received and expenses when cash is disbursed. This system is particularly relevant when we focus on a firm's cash flows from operating activities. Essentially, a firm's net cash flow from operating activities is equal to its income computed on a cash basis.

Of course, most business firms compute income using accrual accounting, not cash basis accounting. To calculate the net cash flow from operating activities,

[3]*Statement of Financial Accounting Concepts No. 1,* "Objectives of Financial Reporting by Business Enterprises" (Stamford, CT: Financial Accounting Standards Board, 1978), p. 18. The FASB also believes information should be reported about earnings. It notes that earnings measured by accrual accounting are a better indicator of periodic financial performance than information about current cash receipts and payments.

then, it is often necessary to convert amounts computed using accrual accounting to the corresponding cash basis amounts. To better understand the process of converting from accrual measures to cash amounts, let us consider the following financial data for Bennett Company:

Balance Sheet at December 31, 19X1

Cash	$ 10,000	Note Payable	$ 50,000
Accounts Receivable	34,000	Accounts Payable	19,000
Inventory	60,000	Interest Payable	2,000
Prepaid Insurance	4,000	Income Tax Payable	3,500
Plant Assets	200,000	Common Stock	140,000
Accumulated Depreciation	(40,000)	Retained Earnings	53,500
Total Assets	$268,000	Total Liabilities and Stockholders' Equity	$268,000

Transactions During 19X2
(colored numbers identify cash transactions)

1. Made sales on account of $250,000.
2. Collected accounts receivable of $245,000.
3. Purchased merchandise on account of $134,000.
4. Determined cost of goods sold was $140,000.
5. Paid accounts payable (for merchandise purchased) of $143,000.
6. Paid wages to employees of $47,500.
7. Paid insurance premium of $18,000 to extend coverage for three years.
8. Allocated $5,000 of prepaid insurance to insurance expense.
9. Paid interest on note of $4,000.
10. Accrued interest expense (and interest payable) of $2,500 at December 31, 19X2 (the note was renewed during the year at a higher interest rate).
11. Paid income taxes to government of $12,500 (paid final portion of 19X1 taxes and initial installments of 19X2 taxes).
12. Recorded 19X2's total income tax expense (and income tax payable) of $11,000.

As a result of these transactions, Bennett's 19X2 income statement and December 31, 19X2, balance sheet appear as shown in Exhibit 19–2 (the 19X1 year-end balance sheet is also included for comparative purposes).

Direct Method

First, we will determine and present Bennett's 19X2 net cash flow from operating activities using the direct method. The **direct method** shows the major categories of operating cash receipts and payments and is, in essence, a cash basis income statement. Using the direct method, we may determine the cash amounts for the various categories either by (1) reviewing and classifying the firm's cash transactions or (2) converting the firm's accrual basis revenues and expenses to corresponding cash amounts.

REVIEW AND CLASSIFY CASH TRANSACTIONS A review of Bennett's 19X2 transactions shows that transactions 2, 5, 6, 7, 9, and 11 reflect the cash receipts and disbursements from its operating activities. The direct method presents the net cash flow from operating activities by reporting these cash receipts and payments as follows:

EXHIBIT 19–2

Bennett Company
Balance Sheets

Assets	Dec. 31, 19X2	Dec. 31, 19X1	Liabilities and Stockholders' Equity	Dec. 31, 19X2	Dec. 31, 19X1
Cash	$ 30,000	$ 10,000	Note Payable	$ 50,000	$ 50,000
Accounts Receivable	39,000	34,000	Accounts Payable	10,000	19,000
Inventory	54,000	60,000	Interest Payable	2,500	2,000
Prepaid Insurance	17,000	4,000	Income Tax Payable	2,000	3,500
Plant Assets	200,000	200,000	Common Stock	140,000	140,000
Accumulated Depreciation	(50,000)	(40,000)	Retained Earnings	85,500	53,500
Total Assets	$290,000	$268,000	Total Liabilities and Stockholders' Equity	$290,000	$268,000

Bennett Company
Income Statement
For the Year Ended December 31, 19X2

Sales		$250,000
Cost of Goods Sold	$140,000	
Wages Expense	47,500	
Insurance Expense	5,000	
Depreciation Expense	10,000	
Interest Expense	4,500	
Income Tax Expense	11,000	
Total Expenses		218,000
Net Income		$ 32,000

Cash Received from Customers		$245,000
Cash Paid for Merchandise Purchased	$143,000	
Cash Paid to Employees	47,500	
Cash Paid for Insurance	18,000	
Cash Paid for Interest	4,000	
Cash Paid for Income Taxes	12,500	225,000
Net Cash Provided by Operating Activities		$ 20,000

Most businesses experience a volume of cash transactions that makes their review and classification an impractical way to determine operating cash flows. A more efficient procedure is to begin with amounts that are already available in the records—the accrual basis revenues and expenses.

CONVERT REVENUES AND EXPENSES Bennett's major categories of operating cash receipts and payments may be determined by starting with its revenues and expenses from operating activities and converting them to the corresponding cash amounts. We will now explain and illustrate these conversion procedures.

Convert sales to cash received from customers During 19X2, accounts receivable increased $5,000. This increase means that during 19X2 cash collections on account (which decrease accounts receivable) were less than credit sales (which increase accounts receivable). We compute cash received from customers, then, as follows:[4]

Sales	$250,000
+ Beginning Accounts Receivable	34,000
− Ending Accounts Receivable	(39,000)
= Cash Received from Customers	$245,000

Convert cost of goods sold to cash paid for merchandise purchased The conversion of cost of goods sold to cash paid for merchandise purchased is a two-step process. First, cost of goods sold is adjusted for the change in inventory to determine the amount of purchases during the year. Then the purchases amount is adjusted for the change in accounts payable to derive the cash paid for merchandise purchased.

Inventory decreased from $60,000 to $54,000 during 19X2. This $6,000 decrease indicates that the cost of goods sold exceeded the cost of goods purchased during the year. The year's purchases amount is computed as:

Cost of Goods Sold	$140,000
+ Ending Inventory	54,000
− Beginning Inventory	(60,000)
= Purchases	$134,000

During 19X2, accounts payable decreased $9,000. This decrease reflects the fact that cash payments for merchandise purchased on account (which decrease accounts payable) exceeded purchases on account (which increase accounts payable). The cash paid for merchandise purchased, therefore, is computed as:

Purchases	$134,000
+ Beginning Accounts Payable	19,000
− Ending Accounts Payable	(10,000)
= Cash Paid for Merchandise Purchased	$143,000

Convert wages expense to cash paid to employees No adjustment to wages expense is needed. The absence of any beginning or ending accrued liability for wages payable means that wages expense and cash paid to employees as wages are the same amount—$47,500.

Convert insurance expense to cash paid for insurance Prepaid insurance increased $13,000 during 19X2. The $13,000 increase reflects the excess of cash paid for insurance during 19X2 (which increases prepaid insurance) over the year's insurance expense (which decreases prepaid insurance). Starting with insurance expense, then, the cash paid for insurance is computed as:

[4]This computation assumes no accounts were written off as uncollectible during the period. The impact on the computation of an allowance account and uncollectible accounts expense is beyond the scope of this discussion.

Insurance Expense	$ 5,000
+ Ending Prepaid Insurance	17,000
− Beginning Prepaid Insurance	(4,000)
= Cash Paid for Insurance	$18,000

Eliminate depreciation expense and other noncash operating expenses Depreciation expense is a noncash expense. Because it does not represent a cash payment, depreciation expense is completely eliminated as we convert accrual expense amounts to the corresponding amounts of cash payments. If Bennett Company had any amortization expense or depletion expense, they also would be eliminated for the same reason. The amortization of an intangible asset and the depletion of a natural resource are entirely noncash expenses.

Convert interest expense to cash paid for interest Interest payable increased from $2,000 at December 31, 19X1, to $2,500 at December 31, 19X2. This $500 increase means that cash paid for interest in 19X2 (which includes $2,000 charged to expense in 19X1) is less than 19X2's interest expense (which includes $2,500 accrued but not paid at year-end). This change in interest payable is used to convert interest expense to cash paid for interest, as follows:

Interest Expense	$4,500
+ Beginning Interest Payable	2,000
− Ending Interest Payable	(2,500)
= Cash Paid for Interest	$4,000

Convert income tax expense to cash paid for income taxes The decrease in income tax payable from $3,500 at December 31, 19X1, to $2,000 at December 31, 19X2, means that 19X2's income tax expense (which increases income tax payable) was $1,500 less than 19X2's tax payments (which decrease income tax payable). If we start with income tax expense, then we calculate cash paid for income taxes in the following manner:

Income Tax Expense	$11,000
+ Beginning Income Tax Payable	3,500
− Ending Income Tax Payable	(2,000)
= Cash Paid for Income Taxes	$12,500

We have now applied the proper adjustments to convert each accrual basis revenue and expense amount to the corresponding cash amount. Note that the computed cash receipts and cash payments are exactly the same amounts as identified in transactions 2, 5, 6, 7, 9, and 11 for Bennett Company.

Exhibit 19–3 summarizes the procedures for converting individual revenues and expenses from operating activities to a cash basis. To be more efficient, just the changes in the balance sheet accounts during the period (increases or decreases) are used rather than both the beginning and ending account balances.

Indirect Method

A second method of determining and presenting net cash flow from operating activities is the **indirect** (or *reconciliation*) **method.** The indirect method begins with the accrual basis net income and applies a series of adjustments to convert the net income to a cash basis. In contrast to the direct method, the indirect method does not show categories of cash receipts and payments.

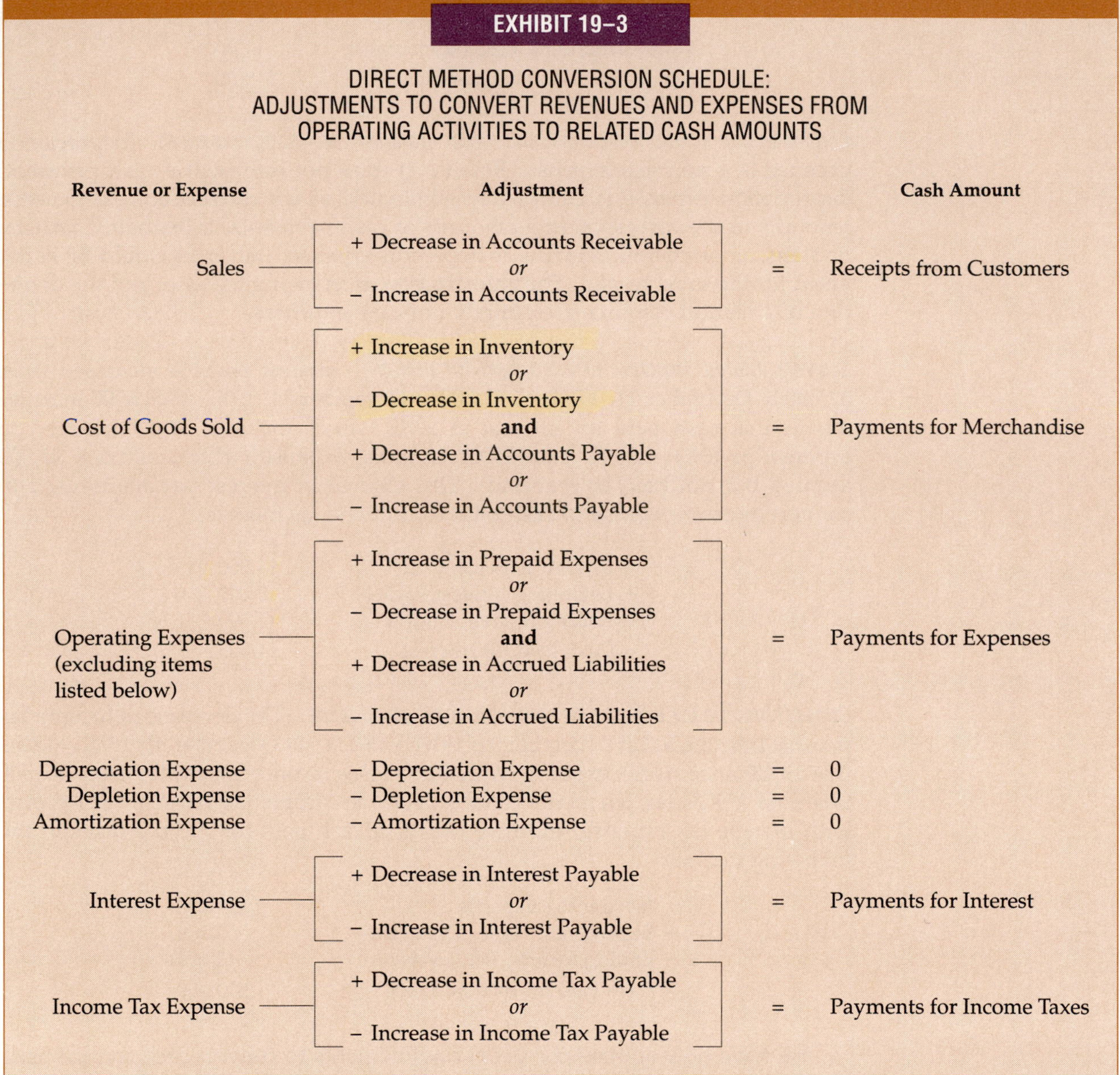

EXHIBIT 19–3

DIRECT METHOD CONVERSION SCHEDULE:
ADJUSTMENTS TO CONVERT REVENUES AND EXPENSES FROM OPERATING ACTIVITIES TO RELATED CASH AMOUNTS

Revenue or Expense	Adjustment		Cash Amount
Sales	+ Decrease in Accounts Receivable *or* − Increase in Accounts Receivable	=	Receipts from Customers
Cost of Goods Sold	+ Increase in Inventory *or* − Decrease in Inventory **and** + Decrease in Accounts Payable *or* − Increase in Accounts Payable	=	Payments for Merchandise
Operating Expenses (excluding items listed below)	+ Increase in Prepaid Expenses *or* − Decrease in Prepaid Expenses **and** + Decrease in Accrued Liabilities *or* − Increase in Accrued Liabilities	=	Payments for Expenses
Depreciation Expense	− Depreciation Expense	=	0
Depletion Expense	− Depletion Expense	=	0
Amortization Expense	− Amortization Expense	=	0
Interest Expense	+ Decrease in Interest Payable *or* − Increase in Interest Payable	=	Payments for Interest
Income Tax Expense	+ Decrease in Income Tax Payable *or* − Increase in Income Tax Payable	=	Payments for Income Taxes

The adjustments to net income consist primarily of the adjustments we just reviewed in converting individual revenue and expense amounts to a cash basis. However, the adjustments are applied to net income rather than to individual operating revenues and expenses. Further, because the starting point *is* net income, additional adjustments are necessary to eliminate the effects on net income of any gains or losses from investing and financing transactions. Examples are gains and losses from sales of plant assets and retirements of bonds payable. The cash effects of these transactions are reported in the investing and financing sections of the statement of cash flows. The related gains and losses are included in net income and must be eliminated from net income as we compute the net cash flow from operating activities. We eliminate the gains and losses by adding the losses to net income and deducting the gains from net income.

Under the indirect method, then, noncash expenses such as depreciation, amortization, and depletion are added to net income to eliminate the effect they had on net income. Also eliminated are the effects on net income of the investing and financing gains and losses. Changes during the year in accounts receivable, inventory, prepaid expenses, accounts payable, accrued liabilities, interest payable, and income tax payable are either added to or subtracted from net income, depending on which account we are analyzing and whether the change was an increase or a decrease. Exhibit 19–4 presents a conversion schedule for the indirect method that summarizes the treatment of these adjustments.

Applying the adjustments from Exhibit 19–4 to the data in our illustration, we present Bennett Company's net cash flow operating activities under the indirect method as follows:

Net Income	$32,000
Add (Deduct) Items to Convert Net Income to Cash Basis:	
Depreciation	10,000
Accounts Receivable Increase	(5,000)
Inventory Decrease	6,000
Prepaid Insurance Increase	(13,000)
Accounts Payable Decrease	(9,000)
Interest Payable Increase	500
Income Tax Payable Decrease	(1,500)
Net Cash Provided by Operating Activities	$20,000

If there is a net loss for the period, the indirect method begins with the net loss. It is possible, of course, for the net amount of add-backs to exceed the loss so that there is a positive net cash flow from operating activities even when there is an accrual basis net loss.

EXHIBIT 19–4

INDIRECT METHOD CONVERSION SCHEDULE: ADJUSTMENTS TO CONVERT NET INCOME TO NET CASH FLOW FROM OPERATING ACTIVITIES

Add to Net Income	Deduct from Net Income
Depreciation Expense	
Amortization Expense	
Depletion Expense	
Losses (investing/financing)	Gains (investing/financing)
Decrease in Accounts Receivable	Increase in Accounts Receivable
Decrease in Inventory	Increase in Inventory
Decrease in Prepaid Expenses	Increase in Prepaid Expenses
Increase in Accounts Payable	Decrease in Accounts Payable
Increase in Accrued Liabilities	Decrease in Accrued Liabilities
Increase in Interest Payable	Decrease in Interest Payable
Increase in Income Tax Payable	Decrease in Income Tax Payable

Comparison of Methods

Exhibit 19–5 presents Bennett Company's net cash flow from operating activities under both the direct method and the indirect method. Although both methods show the same final net cash provided by operating activities, the financial presentation deriving the final amount is quite different. The direct method shows the specific sources and uses of cash from operations. The indirect method shows the adjustments to convert net income to a cash basis amount.

Both the direct and indirect methods have strengths and weaknesses. One advantage of the direct method is its understandability for financial statement users. A presentation of cash flow from operations as the difference between operating cash receipts and cash payments is a simple and easily understood presentation. In contrast, the rationale for the additions to and deductions from net income under the indirect method may not be clear to the users of cash flow data.

Because it begins with net income, an advantage of the indirect method is that it provides a direct linkage with the income statement. The direct method does not provide any income statement linkage—no cash flow component under the direct method necessarily agrees with any amount in the income statement. All other things being equal, accountants prefer to have their various financial statements articulate, or tie together, as much as possible.

The Financial Accounting Standards Board encourages companies to use the direct method but permits the use of the indirect method. Interestingly, the FASB's guidelines require the disclosure of some information from both methods. Firms must disclose (1) the reconciliation of net income to the net cash flow from operating activities, (2) cash paid for interest (net of amount capitalized), and (3) cash paid for income taxes. Thus a firm using the direct method will disclose cash paid for interest and cash paid for income taxes as part of its presentation of cash flows from operating activities; the firm will make a supplemental disclosure reconciling net income to the net cash flow from operating activities (which is the entire

EXHIBIT 19–5

Bennett Company
Net Cash Flow from Operating Activities for 19X2

Direct Method

Cash Received from Customers		$245,000
Cash Paid for Merchandise Purchased	$143,000	
Cash Paid to Employees	47,500	
Cash Paid for Insurance	18,000	
Cash Paid for Interest	4,000	
Cash Paid for Income Taxes	12,500	225,000
Net Cash Provided by Operating Activities		$ 20,000

Indirect Method

Net Income	$32,000
Add (Deduct) Items to Convert Net Income to Cash Basis:	
Depreciation	10,000
Accounts Receivable Increase	(5,000)
Inventory Decrease	6,000
Prepaid Insurance Increase	(13,000)
Accounts Payable Decrease	(9,000)
Interest Payable Increase	500
Income Tax Payable Decrease	(1,500)
Net Cash Provided by Operating Activities	$20,000

A LOOK AT THE FASB'S DECISION-MAKING PROCESS

How does the FASB weigh the often competing interests of different segments of its constituency? Chairman Dennis Beresford used the Board's recently published statement on cash flows to explain . . . some of the inner workings of the FASB.

The Board and staff spent nine months on the project, and received 450 comment letters, Beresford explained. On eight occasions, the Board met to discuss cash flow reporting issues, and three times it held meetings with knowledgeable outsiders on the more controversial issues. One meeting was on the direct/indirect method. By the time the process had concluded, two Board members had changed the position on the direct/indirect issue that they had taken in the exposure draft. The swing vote in the final four-to-three tally depended on, he said, "a tradeoff between requiring the direct method or changing the status of other issues that that Board member considered more important."

The majority of comment letters came from bank lending officers, said Beresford, as a result of an effort by Robert Morris Associates to encourage comments. "Many of those letters made eloquent arguments in favor of requiring the use of the direct method of reporting operating cash flows." Preparers, on the other hand, had little incentive to argue against this issue, he added, because the exposure draft allowed either the direct or the indirect method.

As part of the process, Beresford said, a researcher was engaged to determine whether the cost to provide the direct method information would be excessive. "The limited study showed," he said, "that most companies could not obtain amounts of gross operating cash receipts and payments directly from their accounting system. But it also showed that information about those major classes might be determined indirectly by adjusting revenue and expense amounts for the change during the period in related asset and liability accounts."

The direct method was not required in the final statement, Beresford said, "but the users' preference for separately reporting noncash items was adopted. Furthermore, the final statement strongly encourages the use of the direct method for reporting cash flows from operating activities."

And while most preparers agreed with the final decision on the direct/indirect method, Beresford said, "I'm sure that preparers weren't happy with several other parts of the standard, such as including the reporting currency equivalent of foreign currency cash flows, and requiring that all banks and other financial institutions prepare a cash flow statement."

From "Technically Speaking," *Financial Executive,* March/April 1988, pp. 60–61. Reprinted by permission of Financial Executives Institute.

indirect method). And a firm using the indirect method will reconcile net income to the net cash flow from operating activities as the way it initially reports the net cash flow from operating activities; this firm will make a supplemental disclosure of the cash paid for interest and the cash paid for income taxes (which are components of the direct method).

A firm using the direct method must, at a minimum, disclose the following categories of operating cash receipts and payments:

1. Cash received from customers.
2. Cash received as dividends and interest.
3. Cash received from other operating activities, if any.
4. Cash paid to employees and other suppliers of goods and services, including suppliers of insurance, advertising, and the like.
5. Cash paid for interest.

6. Cash paid for income taxes.
7. Cash paid for other operating activities, if any.[5]

These are the categories we will use in the remaining illustrations of statements of cash flows that are prepared using the direct method.

PREPARING THE STATEMENT OF CASH FLOWS

Preparing a statement of cash flows and the related separate disclosures involves four steps:

1. Compute the net increase or decrease in cash during the year.
2. Prepare a worksheet to identify the cash flows for the year.
3. Prepare the statement of cash flows using information from the worksheet.
4. Determine the information for the required separate disclosures.

To demonstrate these four steps, we use the financial data of Superior Corporation. Exhibit 19–6 shows comparative balance sheets for 19X1 and 19X2, and Exhibit 19–7 presents the income statement for 19X2. Assume that during 19X2 the following transactions took place, in addition to routine transactions:

1. Sold equipment having a book value of $4,000 ($10,000 cost − $6,000 accumulated depreciation) for $20,000 cash.
2. Purchased new equipment for $65,000 cash.
3. Retired $80,000 of bonds payable for $89,000 cash.
4. Acquired equipment worth $30,000 by issuing 3,000 shares of common stock.
5. Issued additional common stock at par value for $120,000 cash.
6. Declared and paid cash dividends of $11,000.

We will illustrate the four steps to construct a statement of cash flows and prepare the related separate disclosures under both the direct and indirect methods.

Direct Method

STEP 1 Determine the net increase or decrease in cash during the year by comparing the cash balances on the comparative balance sheets. Superior Corporation's cash increased $12,000 (from $13,000 to $25,000) during 19X2.

STEP 2 Prepare a *worksheet* to analyze the changes in all the noncash balance sheet accounts and identify, by type of activity, the cash inflows and outflows for the period. We review all noncash balance sheet accounts for two reasons:

1. Because of the basic accounting equation (Assets = Liabilities + Owners' Equity), the net change in cash during a period must equal the net change in all other balance sheet accounts. By analyzing the changes in all noncash balance sheet accounts, we will be able to identify all events affecting cash flows.

[5] *Statement of Financial Accounting Standards No. 95*, "Statement of Cash Flows" (Stamford, CT: Financial Accounting Standards Board, 1987), par. 27.

EXHIBIT 19–6

Superior Corporation
Balance Sheets

ASSETS	Dec. 31, 19X2	Dec. 31, 19X1	Increase (Decrease)
Current Assets			
Cash	$ 25,000	$ 13,000	$ 12,000
Accounts Receivable (net)	55,000	60,000	(5,000)
Inventory	94,000	80,000	14,000
Prepaid Expenses	13,000	10,000	3,000
Total Current Assets	$187,000	$163,000	$ 24,000
Plant Assets			
Building and Equipment	$418,000	$333,000	$ 85,000
Accumulated Depreciation	(75,000)	(68,000)	7,000
Total Plant Assets	$343,000	$265,000	$ 78,000
Total Assets	$530,000	$428,000	$102,000
LIABILITIES AND STOCKHOLDERS' EQUITY			
Current Liabilities			
Accounts Payable	$ 32,000	$ 42,000	($10,000)
Interest Payable	1,000	3,000	(2,000)
Income Tax Payable	2,000	1,000	1,000
Total Current Liabilities	$ 35,000	$ 46,000	($11,000)
Long-term Debt			
Bonds Payable	$ 40,000	$120,000	($80,000)
Stockholders' Equity			
Common Stock ($10 par value)	$350,000	$200,000	$150,000
Retained Earnings	105,000	62,000	43,000
Total Stockholders' Equity	$455,000	$262,000	$193,000
Total Liabilities and Stockholders' Equity	$530,000	$428,000	$102,000

2. A required disclosure accompanying the statement of cash flows is a presentation of all noncash investing and financing activities. An analysis of the changes in all noncash balance sheet accounts will permit us to identify these events also.

Exhibit 19–8 (page 711) shows the worksheet for Superior Corporation under the direct method.

Worksheet heading and form The worksheet heading includes the name of the company, an identification of the statement the worksheet deals with, and the period covered by the analysis.

The worksheet form illustrated in Exhibit 19–8 has a description column and four money columns. Each of the two headings, "Changes in Noncash Accounts" and "Analyzing Entries," has a debit and credit column.

EXHIBIT 19–7

Superior Corporation
Income Statement
For the Year Ended December 31, 19X2

Sales		$360,000
Cost of Goods Sold	$200,000	
Wages and Other Operating Expenses	78,000	
Depreciation Expense	13,000	
Interest Expense	10,000	
Income Tax Expense	12,000	
Gain on Sale of Equipment	(16,000)	
Loss on Bond Retirement*	9,000	306,000
Net Income		$ 54,000

*If material, this loss is extraordinary. Separate disclosure of cash flows relating to extraordinary items is not required. For simplicity, a separate extraordinary section is not used here.

Changes in noncash balance sheet accounts The content of the worksheet focuses on the company's noncash balance sheet accounts.

1. First, a list of all noncash balance sheet accounts is entered in the description column. The debit or credit change in each account balance for the period is entered in the appropriate column under the "Changes in Noncash Accounts" heading. Accounts Receivable, for example, decreased from $60,000 at December 31, 19X1, to $55,000 at December 31, 19X2; the $5,000 decrease is entered in the credit column. Inventory, Prepaid Expenses, and Building and Equipment increased during 19X2 and their increases are entered in the debit column. During 19X2, Accumulated Depreciation increased from $68,000 to $75,000; the $7,000 increase is entered in the credit column. The 19X2 increases in Income Tax Payable, Common Stock, and Retained Earnings are also entered in the credit column. The decreases in Accounts Payable, Interest Payable, and Bonds Payable are entered in the debit column.
2. After the changes for all noncash balance sheet accounts are entered, the two columns are totaled. The difference between the column totals equals the cash change calculated in step 1. The cash change is entered on the worksheet—an increase in the debit column, a decrease in the credit column—and the two columns are totaled and double ruled to show their equality. Exhibit 19–8 shows the $12,000 cash increase for Superior Corporation in the debit column.
3. At this point, the label "cash flows from operating activities" is written in the description column. Beneath this, labels for the appropriate categories of operating cash flows are entered, leaving several lines for each category. Because revenues and expenses are the starting points for calculating the various operating cash flows under the direct method, we review the income statement to establish which of the minimum categories required by the FASB are present. At the same time, we also identify if there are any gains or losses

EXHIBIT 19–8

Superior Corporation
Worksheet for Statement of Cash Flows (Direct Method)
For the Year Ended December 31, 19X2

Description	Changes in Noncash Accounts		Analyzing Entries	
	Debit	Credit	Debit	Credit
Accounts Receivable		5,000		(2) 5,000
Inventory	14,000		(3) 14,000	
Prepaid Expenses	3,000		(3) 3,000	
Building and Equipment	85,000		(9) 65,000	(7) 10,000
			(10)* 30,000	
Accumulated Depreciation		7,000	(7) 6,000	(4) 13,000
Accounts Payable	10,000		(3) 10,000	
Interest Payable	2,000		(5) 2,000	
Income Tax Payable		1,000		(6) 1,000
Bonds Payable	80,000		(8) 80,000	
Common Stock		150,000		(10)* 30,000
				(11) 120,000
Retained Earnings		43,000	(8) 9,000	(1) 47,000
			(12) 11,000	(7) 16,000
	194,000	206,000		
Increase in Cash	12,000			
	206,000	206,000		
Cash Flows from Operating Activities				
Cash Received from Customers				
Sales			(1) 360,000	
Add: Accounts Receivable Decrease			(2) 5,000	
Cash Paid to Employees and Suppliers				
Employee and Supplier Expenses				(1) 291,000
Add: Combined changes in Inventory, Prepaid Expenses, and Accounts Payable				(3) 27,000
Less: Depreciation			(4) 13,000	
Cash Paid for Interest				
Interest Expense				(1) 10,000
Add: Interest Payable Decrease				(5) 2,000
Cash Paid for Income Taxes				
Income Tax Expense				(1) 12,000
Less: Income Tax Payable Increase			(6) 1,000	
Cash Flows from Investing Activities				
Sale of Equipment			(7) 20,000	
Purchase of Equipment				(9) 65,000
Cash Flows from Financing Activities				
Retirement of Bonds Payable				(8) 89,000
Issuance of Common Stock			(11) 120,000	
Payment of Dividends				(12) 11,000
			749,000	749,000

present that relate to investing or financing activities. The classification of the items in Superior Corporation's 19X2 income statement follows:

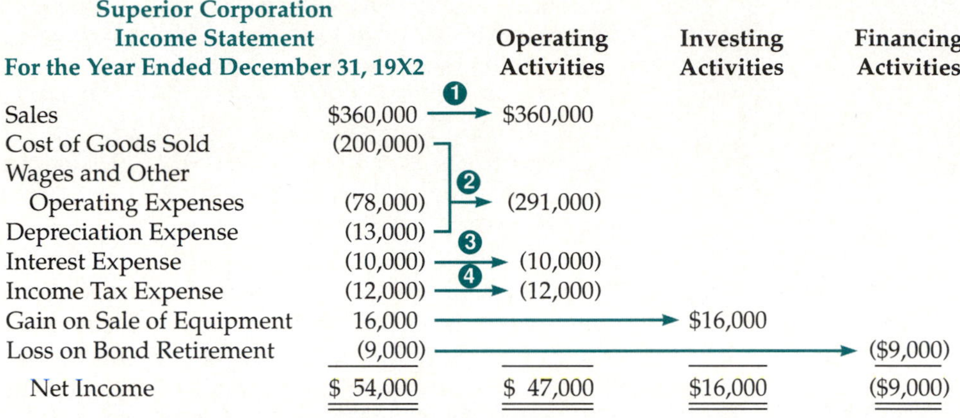

Superior Corporation Income Statement For the Year Ended December 31, 19X2		Operating Activities	Investing Activities	Financing Activities
Sales	$360,000	❶ $360,000		
Cost of Goods Sold	(200,000)			
Wages and Other Operating Expenses	(78,000)	❷ (291,000)		
Depreciation Expense	(13,000)			
Interest Expense	(10,000)	❸ (10,000)		
Income Tax Expense	(12,000)	❹ (12,000)		
Gain on Sale of Equipment	16,000		$16,000	
Loss on Bond Retirement	(9,000)			($9,000)
Net Income	$ 54,000	$ 47,000	$16,000	($9,000)

Superior has the following categories of operating cash receipts and payments:

❶ Cash received from customers—this amount will be computed by starting with the sales revenue of $360,000.

❷ Cash paid to employees and suppliers—this amount will be computed by starting with the $291,000 combined expenses of cost of goods sold, wages and other operating expenses, and depreciation expense (we label these combined expenses "employee and supplier expenses"). Generally, we combine all expenses other than interest expense and income tax expense to obtain the starting point for this category of operating cash outflow. Note that noncash expenses such as depreciation, amortization, and depletion are included in this starting point; they will subsequently be eliminated.

❸ Cash paid for interest—this amount will be computed by starting with the $10,000 of interest expense.

❹ Cash paid for income taxes—this amount will be computed by starting with the $12,000 of income tax expense.

Labels and spacing for these four categories of operating cash flows are entered on the worksheet. Next, the label "cash flows from investing activities" is written in the description column. Several lines are skipped and the label "cash flows from financing activities" is entered in the column. The worksheet is now ready for the analyzing entries.

Analyzing entries Analyzing entries explain the changes that occurred in the noncash accounts during the period. If the change affected cash flows, we enter the appropriate amount on the worksheet in the proper cash flow category. When all changes in noncash accounts have been explained, our analysis is complete.

Essentially, the analysis consists of two sets of analyzing entries. The initial set determines the various operating cash flows. The second set completes the analysis and identifies any investing or financing cash flows.

Analyzing entries for operating cash flows

1. The first analyzing entry places on the worksheet the revenue and expense amounts that are the starting points for calculating operating cash flows and also shows their net effect on retained earnings (because net income has been closed to retained earnings). The entry debits Sales for $360,000 under cash received from customers, credits Employee and Supplier Expenses for $291,000 under cash paid to employees and suppliers, credits Interest Expense for $10,000 under cash paid for interest, credits Income Tax Expense for $12,000 under cash paid for income taxes, and credits Retained Earnings for $47,000.

The remaining entries in this set reflect the adjustments needed to convert revenues and expenses to cash amounts. As discussed earlier, changes in accounts receivable, inventory, prepaid expenses, accounts payable, accrued liabilities, interest payable, and income tax payable affect these conversions. Changes in these accounts are *added* to revenues or expenses if the change means the cash flow exceeds the accrual amount; the changes are *deducted* if the change means the cash flow is smaller than the accrual amount. We also must eliminate any noncash expenses such as depreciation, amortization, and depletion from accrual expenses; we accomplish this by deducting the noncash expense from the accrual expense amount. (These adjustments are summarized in Exhibit 19–3 on page 704.)

2. The $5,000 decrease in accounts receivable must be added to sales to obtain the cash received from customers. Entry 2 does this with a debit to cash received from customers and a credit to Accounts Receivable for $5,000.
3. Entry 3 reflects the impact of changes in inventory, prepaid expenses, and accounts payable in converting the combined expenses of $291,000 to a cash amount. Changes in all three accounts cause the related cash outflows to be larger than the accrual amounts. The entry debits Inventory for $14,000, debits Prepaid Expenses for $3,000, debits Accounts Payable for $10,000 and credits cash paid to employees and suppliers for the combined effect of $27,000.
4. Entry 4 eliminates depreciation expense by debiting cash paid to employees and suppliers and crediting Accumulated Depreciation for $13,000.
5. Entry 5 adjusts interest expense for the change in interest payable during the period. The $2,000 decrease in interest payable is debited to Interest Payable and credited to cash paid for interest.
6. Entry 6 adjusts income tax expense for the change in income tax payable during the period. The $1,000 increase in income tax payable is debited to cash paid for taxes and credited to Income Tax Payable.

Analyzing entries to complete the analysis The second set of analyzing entries explains the changes in the noncash balance sheet accounts that were not analyzed in determining the operating cash flows. This set of entries derives any cash flows from investing or financing activities and also identifies the noncash investing and financing transactions. We begin this set of entries by reconstructing on the worksheet the investing or financing transactions whose related gains or losses appear in the income statement. Superior Corporation has a $16,000 gain related to an investing transaction and a $9,000 loss related to a financing transaction.

7. Entry 7 reconstructs the entry for the sale of equipment at a gain. The transaction generated a cash inflow of $20,000, which is debited to cash flows from investing activities. The $6,000 accumulated depreciation is debited to Accumulated Depreciation, the equipment's $10,000 cost is credited to Building and Equipment, and the $16,000 gain is credited to Retained Earnings (to reflect the impact of the gain on retained earnings).
8. Entry 8 reconstructs the entry for the retirement of bonds payable at a loss. The transaction caused a cash outflow of $89,000. The entry debits Bonds Payable for $80,000, debits Retained Earnings for $9,000 (to reflect the impact of the loss on retained earnings), and credits the $89,000 cash payment to cash flows from financing activities.

At this point, we review each noncash balance sheet account whose change has not been fully explained by our previous analyzing entries and reconstruct the entries, in summary form, to explain these remaining changes. Any effects of these transactions on cash are entered in the worksheet's lower portion as either a cash inflow or a cash outflow. Cash inflows are entered as debits and cash outflows as credits. Not every analyzing entry will necessarily affect cash. An analyzing entry that does not affect cash, however, may reflect a noncash investing and financing transaction that must be separately disclosed. Analyzing entries 9–12 explain the remaining changes in the noncash balance sheet accounts.

9. The cash purchase of equipment for $65,000 was an investing transaction. Entry 9 debits the $65,000 to Building and Equipment and credits the $65,000 purchase to cash flows from investing activities.
10. Entry 10 reconstructs the entry for the acquisition of equipment in exchange for common stock. The entry debits Building and Equipment and credits Common Stock for $30,000. This event is a noncash investing and financing transaction that must be disclosed in a supplementary schedule. We highlight the analyzing entry with an asterisk (*) to identify it as an event requiring special disclosure treatment.
11. The issuance of common stock for cash was a financing event that caused a $120,000 cash inflow. Entry 11 debits this $120,000 event to cash flows from financing activities and credits Common Stock for $120,000.
12. The dividend of $11,000 declared and paid in 19X2 was a financing event that reduced cash. Entry 12 reconstructs the effect of the dividend by debiting $11,000 to Retained Earnings and crediting the $11,000 outflow to cash flows from financing activities.

For each noncash account, the debit or credit balance of the analyzing entries now equals the change shown in the first two columns. Our analysis is complete, and we total and double rule the last two columns to complete the worksheet. The analyzing entries help us compile information for a statement of cash flows; they are not recorded in the accounts.

STEP 3 Prepare the statement of cash flows from the information in the worksheet. The worksheet already classifies cash flows in the proper categories for the statement of cash flows. For each category of cash flow related to operating activities, combine the debit and credit entries into a single amount. For Superior Corporation, cash received from customers is \$360,000 + \$5,000 = \$365,000; cash paid to employees and suppliers is \$291,000 + \$27,000 − \$13,000 = \$305,000; cash paid for interest is \$10,000 + \$2,000 = \$12,000; and cash paid for income taxes is \$12,000 − \$1,000 = \$11,000.

The sum of the cash flows from the operating, investing, and financing activities will equal the change in cash calculated in Step 1. In the statement of cash flows, the period's change in cash is reconciled with the beginning and ending cash balances. The statement of cash flows for Superior Corporation, using the direct method, is shown in Exhibit 19–9.

Cash inflows and outflows from similar areas of investing and financing activities are reported separately (rather than reporting only the net difference). For example, in Exhibit 19–9, proceeds from the sale of equipment are reported separately from outlays made to acquire equipment. Similarly, funds borrowed would be reported separately from debt repayments, and proceeds from issuing stock would be reported separately from outlays to acquire treasury stock.

STEP 4 Determine the information for the required separate disclosures. The required disclosures for firms using the direct method in the statement of cash flows are (1) a reconciliation of net income to net cash flow from operating activities, (2) all noncash investing and financing transactions, and (3) the policy for determining which highly liquid, short-term investments are treated as cash equivalents.

The required reconciliation is the indirect method of computing the net cash flow from operating activities. We discussed earlier the necessary adjustments to net income to achieve this reconciliation (the adjustments are summarized in Exhibit 19–4 on page 705). The required reconciliation will contain these adjustments. Exhibit 19–9 presents the required reconciliation for Superior Corporation in a separate schedule to the statement of cash flows.

The noncash investing and financing transactions are identified in the worksheet for the statement of cash flows (the analyzing entries containing an asterisk identify these events). Exhibit 19–9 shows the supplemental disclosure of Superior Corporation's one noncash investing and financing transaction.

Superior Corporation has no short-term investments, so a separate disclosure to indicate which highly liquid, short-term investments are treated as cash equivalents is not needed.

Indirect Method

The procedures to prepare a statement of cash flows using the indirect method are quite similar to the procedures under the direct method. The differences relate to determining and reporting the net cash flow from operating activities. We will review the steps for the indirect method, emphasizing the differences from the direct method.

STEP 1 Determine the net increase or decrease in cash during the year. This step is the same as under the direct method. Superior Corporation's cash balance increased \$12,000 during 19X2.

STEP 2 Prepare a worksheet to identify the cash flows for the year. The basic worksheet approach under the indirect method is the same as under the direct method. The changes in the noncash balance sheet accounts are analyzed to

EXHIBIT 19–9

STATEMENT OF CASH FLOWS—DIRECT METHOD
WITH SUPPLEMENTARY DISCLOSURES

Superior Corporation
Statement of Cash Flows
For the Year Ended December 31, 19X2

Cash Flows from Operating Activities		
Cash Received from Customers		$365,000
Cash Paid to Employees and Suppliers	$305,000	
Cash Paid for Interest	12,000	
Cash Paid for Income Taxes	11,000	328,000
Net Cash Provided by Operating Activities		$ 37,000
Cash Flows from Investing Activities		
Sale of Equipment	$ 20,000	
Purchase of Equipment	(65,000)	
Net Cash Used by Investing Activities		(45,000)
Cash Flows from Financing Activities		
Issuance of Common Stock	$120,000	
Retirement of Bonds Payable	(89,000)	
Payment of Dividends	(11,000)	
Net Cash Provided by Financing Activities		20,000
Net Increase in Cash		$ 12,000
Cash at Beginning of Year		13,000
Cash at End of Year		$ 25,000

Reconciliation of Net Income to Net Cash Flow from Operating Activities:	
Net Income	$54,000
Add (Deduct) Items to Convert Net Income to Cash Basis:	
Depreciation	13,000
Gain on Sale of Equipment	(16,000)
Loss on Bond Retirement	9,000
Accounts Receivable Decrease	5,000
Inventory Increase	(14,000)
Prepaid Expenses Increase	(3,000)
Accounts Payable Decrease	(10,000)
Interest Payable Decrease	(2,000)
Income Tax Payable Increase	1,000
Net Cash Provided by Operating Activities	$37,000
Schedule of Noncash Investing and Financing Activities:	
Issuance of Common Stock to Acquire Equipment	$30,000

identify, by area of activity, the cash inflows and outflows. The worksheet heading, description column, and money columns are identical to the format under the direct method. Exhibit 19–10 shows the worksheet for Superior Corporation using the indirect method.

Changes in noncash balance sheet accounts As under the direct method, we begin the worksheet by listing all noncash balance sheet accounts and their account

EXHIBIT 19–10

Superior Corporation
Worksheet for Statement of Cash Flows (Indirect Method)
For the Year Ended December 31, 19X2

Description	Changes in Noncash Accounts		Analyzing Entries	
	Debit	Credit	Debit	Credit
Accounts Receivable		5,000		(5) 5,000
Inventory	14,000		(6) 14,000	
Prepaid Expenses	3,000		(7) 3,000	
Building and Equipment	85,000		(11) 65,000	(3) 10,000
			(12)* 30,000	
Accumulated Depreciation		7,000	(3) 6,000	(2) 13,000
Accounts Payable	10,000		(8) 10,000	
Interest Payable	2,000		(9) 2,000	
Income Tax Payable		1,000		(10) 1,000
Bonds Payable	80,000		(4) 80,000	
Common Stock		150,000		(12)* 30,000
				(13) 120,000
Retained Earnings		43,000	(14) 11,000	(1) 54,000
	194,000	206,000		
Increase in Cash	12,000			
	206,000	206,000		
Net Cash Flow from Operating Activities				
Net Income			(1) 54,000	
Add: Depreciation			(2) 13,000	
Less: Gain on Sale of Equipment				(3) 16,000
Add: Loss on Bond Retirement			(4) 9,000	
Add: Accounts Receivable Decrease			(5) 5,000	
Less: Inventory Increase				(6) 14,000
Less: Prepaid Expenses Increase				(7) 3,000
Less: Accounts Payable Decrease				(8) 10,000
Less: Interest Payable Decrease				(9) 2,000
Add: Income Tax Payable Increase			(10) 1,000	
Cash Flows from Investing Activities				
Sale of Equipment			(3) 20,000	
Purchase of Equipment				(11) 65,000
Cash Flows from Financing Activities				
Retirement of Bonds Payable				(4) 89,000
Issuance of Common Stock			(13) 120,000	
Payment of Dividends				(14) 11,000
			443,000	443,000

balance changes in the proper columns. We total the two columns showing these changes in the noncash accounts and then enter the change in cash as a balancing amount.

At this point we enter the labels for the cash flow categories in the description column. Under the indirect method, only one label relating to operating cash flows is entered: "net cash flow from operating activities." Several lines are skipped to allow for the determination of the net cash flow from operating activities. The remaining two labels entered in the description column are the same as for the direct method: "cash flows from investing activities" and "cash flows from financing activities."

Analyzing entries The analyzing entries have the same purpose as under the direct method. All changes in the noncash balance sheet accounts are analyzed for their impact on the determination of cash flows. Under the indirect method, the analysis consists of two sets of analyzing entries. The initial set determines the net cash flow from operating activities using the indirect method. The second set completes the analysis of the noncash account changes.

Analyzing entries to compute net cash flow from operating activities

1. The first analyzing entry establishes the starting point for computing the net cash flow from operating activities—accrual basis net income. On the worksheet, Superior Corporation's $54,000 net income is debited to net cash flow from operating activities and credited to Retained Earnings.

The remaining entries in this set reflect the adjustments needed to convert net income to a cash amount. These adjustments have been discussed earlier (and are summarized in Exhibit 19–4 on page 705). When these adjustments reflect gains and losses related to investing or financing activities, the analyzing entry will present the entire transaction. As a result, some investing and financing cash flows may be identified in this set of analyzing entries.

2. Entry 2 adds depreciation expense to net income (thus eliminating its effect on net income). The entry debits $13,000 to net cash flow from operating activities and credits $13,000 to Accumulated Depreciation.
3. Entry 3 eliminates the effect of the gain on sale of equipment from net income (and, therefore, from the net operating cash flow). The equipment sale was an investing event resulting in a $20,000 cash inflow. The entry debits $20,000 to cash flows from investing activities, debits the equipment's $6,000 of accumulated depreciation to Accumulated Depreciation, credits the equipment's $10,000 cost to Building and Equipment, and credits the $16,000 gain to net cash flow from operating activities (to eliminate the effect of the gain on net income).
4. Entry 4 eliminates the effect of the loss on bond retirement from net income (and, therefore, from the net operating cash flow). The bond retirement was a financing event resulting in an $89,000 cash outflow. The entry debits Bonds Payable for $80,000, debits net cash flow from operating activities for $9,000 (to eliminate the effect of the loss on net income), and credits cash flows from financing activities for $89,000.
5. Entry 5 adds the decrease in accounts receivable to net income with a debit to net cash flow from operating activities and a credit to Accounts Receivable for $5,000.
6. Entry 6 subtracts the inventory increase from net income by debiting Inventory and crediting net cash flow from operating activities for $14,000.

7. Entry 7 subtracts the increase in prepaid expenses from net income by debiting Prepaid Expenses and crediting net cash flow from operating activities for $3,000.
8. Entry 8 subtracts the decrease in accounts payable from net income with a debit of $10,000 to Accounts Payable and a credit of $10,000 to net cash flow from operating activities.
9. Entry 9 subtracts the decrease in interest payable from net income with a $2,000 debit to Interest Payable and a $2,000 credit to net cash flow from operating activities.
10. Entry 10 adds the increase in income tax payable to net income by debiting net cash flow from operating activities and crediting Income Tax Payable for $1,000.

Analyzing entries to complete the analysis At this point, we review each noncash balance sheet account whose change has not been fully explained by our previous analyzing entries and reconstruct the entries, in summary form, to explain these remaining changes. Any effects of these transactions on cash are entered in the worksheet's lower portion as either a cash inflow (entered as a debit) or a cash outflow (entered as a credit). Not every analyzing entry necessarily affects cash. An analyzing entry that does not affect cash, however, may reflect a noncash investing and financing transaction that must be separately disclosed. Analyzing entries 11–14 explain the remaining changes in the noncash balance sheet accounts. (They are exactly the same as analyzing entries 9–12 under the direct method.)

11. The $65,000 cash purchase of equipment was an investing transaction. Entry 11 debits the $65,000 to Building and Equipment and credits the $65,000 purchase to cash flows from investing activities.
12. Entry 12 reconstructs the entry for the acquisition of equipment in exchange for common stock. The entry debits Building and Equipment and credits Common Stock for $30,000. This event is a noncash investing and financing transaction that must be disclosed in a supplementary schedule. We highlight the analyzing entry with an asterisk (*) to identify it as an event requiring special disclosure treatment.
13. The issuance of common stock for cash was a financing activity that caused a $120,000 cash inflow. Entry 13 analyzes this event with a $120,000 debit to cash flows from financing activities and a $120,000 credit to Common Stock.
14. The dividend of $11,000 declared and paid in 19X2 was a financing event that reduced cash. Entry 14 reconstructs the effect of the dividend by debiting $11,000 to Retained Earnings and crediting the $11,000 outflow to cash flows from financing activities.

For each noncash account, the debit or credit balance of the analyzing entries now equals the change shown in the first two columns. Our analysis is complete, and we total and double rule the last two columns to complete the worksheet. The analyzing entries help us compile information for a statement of cash flows; they are not recorded in the accounts.

STEP 3 Prepare the statement of cash flows from the information on the worksheet. The worksheet provides the adjustments necessary to reconcile net income to the net cash flow from operating activities (the indirect method). The worksheet also provides the various cash flows from the investing activities and the financing activities. The sum of the operating, investing, and financing cash flows equals the change in cash calculated in Step 1. In the statement of cash flows, the period's change in cash is reconciled with the beginning and ending cash balances. The statement of cash flows for Superior Corporation, using the indirect method, is presented in Exhibit 19–11.

EXHIBIT 19–11

STATEMENT OF CASH FLOWS—INDIRECT METHOD
WITH SUPPLEMENTARY DISCLOSURES

Superior Corporation
Statement of Cash Flows
For the Year Ended December 31, 19X2

Net Cash Flow from Operating Activities		
Net Income	$ 54,000	
Add (Deduct) Items to Convert Net Income to Cash Basis:		
Depreciation	13,000	
Gain on Sale of Equipment	(16,000)	
Loss on Bond Retirement	9,000	
Accounts Receivable Decrease	5,000	
Inventory Increase	(14,000)	
Prepaid Expenses Increase	(3,000)	
Accounts Payable Decrease	(10,000)	
Interest Payable Decrease	(2,000)	
Income Tax Payable Increase	1,000	
Net Cash Provided by Operating Activities		$37,000
Cash Flows from Investing Activities		
Sale of Equipment	$ 20,000	
Purchase of Equipment	(65,000)	
Net Cash Used by Investing Activities		(45,000)
Cash Flows from Financing Activities		
Issuance of Common Stock	$120,000	
Retirement of Bonds Payable	(89,000)	
Payment of Dividends	(11,000)	
Net Cash Provided by Financing Activities		20,000
Net Increase in Cash		$12,000
Cash at Beginning of Year		13,000
Cash at End of Year		$25,000
Supplemental Cash Flow Disclosures:		
Cash Paid for Interest		$12,000
Cash Paid for Income Taxes		11,000
Schedule of Noncash Investing and Financing Activities:		
Issuance of Common Stock to Acquire Equipment		$30,000

STEP 4 Determine the information for the required separate disclosures. The required disclosures for firms using the indirect method in the statement of cash flows are (1) cash paid during the year for interest (net of amount capitalized) and for income taxes, (2) all noncash investing and financing transactions, and (3) the policy for determining which highly liquid, short-term investments are treated as cash equivalents.

Cash paid for interest is computed by adjusting interest expense for the change during the year in interest payable. Superior Corporation's 19X2 cash paid for interest is $12,000 ($10,000 + $2,000). Cash paid for income taxes is computed by adjusting income tax expense for the change during the year in income tax payable. Superior Corporation's 19X2 cash paid for income taxes is $11,000 ($12,000 − $1,000). Exhibit 19–11 shows these amounts as supplemental disclosures to the statement of cash flows.

The noncash investing and financing transactions are identified in the worksheet for the statement of cash flows (the analyzing entries containing an asterisk identify these events). Exhibit 19–11 shows the supplemental disclosure of Superior Corporation's one noncash investing and financing transaction.

Superior Corporation has no short-term investments, so a separate disclosure to indicate which highly liquid, short-term investments are treated as cash equivalents is not needed.

KEY POINTS FOR CHAPTER OBJECTIVES

1 Provide a basis for understanding a statement of cash flows (pp. 695–99).

- A statement of cash flows explains the net increase or decrease in cash and cash equivalents during the period.
- A statement of cash flows separates cash flows into operating, investing, and financing categories.
- A secondary objective of cash flow reporting is to provide information about a firm's investing and financing activities. A required supplemental disclosure reports noncash investing and financing activities.
- A statement of cash flows should help users compare, evaluate, and predict a firm's cash flows and also help evaluate its financial flexibility.

2 Compare and contrast the direct and indirect methods of determining net cash flow from operating activities (pp. 699–708).

- The direct method shows the major categories of operating cash receipts and payments.
- The indirect method reconciles net income to net cash flow from operating activities.
- The FASB encourages use of the direct method, but permits use of either the direct or the indirect method.
- A firm using the direct method must separately disclose the reconciliation of net income to net cash flow from operating activities.
- A firm using the indirect method must separately disclose the cash paid for interest (net of amount capitalized) and the cash paid for income taxes.

3 Illustrate a worksheet approach to preparing a statement of cash flows using the direct method (pp. 708–15).

- The worksheet contains entries analyzing the changes in all noncash balance sheet accounts to determine their effects, if any, on cash flows. The analyzing entries that determine operating cash flows convert operating revenues and expenses to the related cash amounts.
- The worksheet also identifies noncash investing and financing transactions.

4 Illustrate a worksheet approach to preparing a statement of cash flows using the indirect method (pp. 715–21).

- The worksheet contains entries analyzing the changes in all noncash balance sheet accounts to determine their effects, if any, on cash flows. The analyzing entries that relate to cash flow from operating activities reconcile net income to net cash flow from operating activities.
- The worksheet also identifies noncash investing and financing transactions.

KEY TERMS USED IN THIS CHAPTER

cash equivalents 695
direct method 700
financing activities 697
indirect method 703
investing activities 697
noncash investing and financing activities 698
operating activities 697
statement of cash flows 695

SELF-TEST QUESTIONS FOR REVIEW

(Answers are at the end of this chapter.)

1. Which of the following is not disclosed in a statement of cash flows?
   (a) A transfer of cash to a cash equivalent investment.
   (b) The amount of cash on hand at year-end.
   (c) Cash outflows from investing activities during the period.
   (d) Cash inflows from financing activities during the period.
2. Which of the following events will appear in the cash flows from financing activities section of the statement of cash flows?
   (a) Cash purchase of equipment.
   (b) Cash purchase of bonds issued by another company.
   (c) Cash received as repayment for funds loaned.
   (d) Cash purchase of treasury stock.
3. Which of the following methods will disclose the cash paid to employees and suppliers in the statement of cash flows?
   (a) Indirect method. (c) Direct method.
   (b) Reconciliation method. (d) Both direct and indirect methods.
4. Tyler Company has a net income of $49,000 and the following related items:

Depreciation expense	$ 5,000
Accounts receivable increase	2,000
Inventory decrease	10,000
Accounts payable decrease	4,000

   Using the indirect method, what is Tyler's cash flow from operations?
   (a) $42,000 (b) $46,000 (c) $58,000 (d) $38,000
5. A worksheet for a statement of cash flows analyzes the changes in
   (a) Each of the firm's bank accounts.
   (b) All of the firm's noncash balance sheet accounts.
   (c) The firm's working capital accounts only.
   (d) The firm's noncurrent balance sheet accounts only.

DEMONSTRATION PROBLEM FOR REVIEW

Terry Company's 19X1 income statement and comparative balance sheets at December 31 of 19X1 and 19X0 are shown below.

Terry Company
Income Statement
For the Year Ended December 31, 19X1

Sales		$385,000
Dividend Income		5,000
		$390,000
Cost of Goods Sold	$233,000	
Wages and Other Operating Expenses	89,000	
Depreciation Expense	11,000	
Franchise Amortization Expense	3,000	
Income Tax Expense	17,000	
Loss on Sale of Investments	2,000	355,000
Net Income		$ 35,000

Terry Company
Balance Sheets

Assets	Dec. 31, 19X1	Dec. 31, 19X0
Cash	$ 8,000	$ 12,000
Accounts Receivable	22,000	28,000
Inventory	94,000	64,000
Prepaid Expenses	12,000	8,000
Long-term Investments	30,000	41,000
Plant Assets	168,000	120,000
Accumulated Depreciation	(72,000)	(61,000)
Franchise	10,000	13,000
Total Assets	$272,000	$225,000

Liabilities and Stockholders' Equity		
Accounts Payable	$ 27,000	$ 14,000
Accrued Liabilities	6,000	2,500
Income Tax Payable	3,000	4,500
Common Stock	139,000	125,000
Retained Earnings	97,000	79,000
Total Liabilities and Stockholders' Equity	$272,000	$225,000

Cash dividends of $17,000 were declared and paid during 19X1. Plant assets were purchased for cash, and later in the year, additional common stock was issued for cash. Investments costing $11,000 were sold for cash at a $2,000 loss.

REQUIRED

(a) Prepare a worksheet for a statement of cash flows using the direct method.
(b) Prepare a 19X1 statement of cash flows using the direct method.
(c) Prepare a reconciliation of net income to net cash flow from operating activities.

SOLUTION TO DEMONSTRATION PROBLEM

(a)

Terry Corporation
Worksheet for Statement of Cash Flows
For the Year Ended December 31, 19X1

	Changes in Noncash Accounts		Analyzing Entries	
Description	Debit	Credit	Debit	Credit
Accounts Receivable		6,000		(2) 6,000
Inventory	30,000		(3) 30,000	
Prepaid Expenses	4,000		(3) 4,000	
Long-term Investments		11,000		(7) 11,000
Plant Assets	48,000		(8) 48,000	
Accumulated Depreciation		11,000		(4) 11,000
Franchise		3,000		(5) 3,000
Accounts Payable		13,000		(3) 13,000
Accrued Liabilities		3,500		(3) 3,500
Income Tax Payable	1,500		(6) 1,500	

(continued)

Description	Changes in Noncash Accounts Debit	Changes in Noncash Accounts Credit	Analyzing Entries Debit	Analyzing Entries Credit
Common Stock		14,000		(9) 14,000
Retained Earnings		18,000	(7) 2,000	(1) 37,000
			(10) 17,000	
	83,500	79,500		
Decrease in Cash		4,000		
	83,500	83,500		
Cash Flows from Operating Activities				
Cash Received from Customers				
Sales			(1) 385,000	
Add: Accounts Receivable Decrease			(2) 6,000	
Cash Received as Dividends				
Dividend Income			(1) 5,000	
Cash Paid to Employees and Suppliers				
Employee and Supplier Expenses				(1) 336,000
Add: Combined changes in Inventory, Prepaid Expenses, Accounts Payable, and Accrued Liabilities				(3) 17,500
Less: Depreciation			(4) 11,000	
Less: Franchise Amortization			(5) 3,000	
Cash Paid for Income Taxes				
Income Tax Expense				(1) 17,000
Add: Income Tax Payable Decrease				(6) 1,500
Cash Flows from Investing Activities				
Sale of Investments			(7) 9,000	
Purchase of Plant Assets				(8) 48,000
Cash Flows from Financing Activities				
Issuance of Common Stock			(9) 14,000	
Payment of Dividends				(10) 17,000
			535,500	535,500

Explanation of Analyzing Entries:

(1) Places revenues and expenses related to operating activities on the worksheet: Sales, Dividend Income, Employee and Supplier Expenses (the sum of Cost of Goods Sold, Wages and Other Operating Expenses, Depreciation Expense, and Franchise Amortization Expense), and Income Tax Expense. The credit to Retained Earnings is the net difference between these revenues and expenses.

(2) Adjustment to sales for decrease in accounts receivable.

(3) Adjustment to employee and supplier expenses for changes in inventory, prepaid expenses, accounts payable, and accrued liabilities.

(4) Elimination of depreciation expense.

(5) Elimination of franchise amortization expense.

(6) Adjustment to income tax expense for decrease in income tax payable.

(7) Entry for sale of investments for $9,000; the $2,000 loss is debited to Retained Earnings.

(8) Entry for purchase of plant assets for $48,000.
(9) Entry for issuance of common stock for $14,000.
(10) Entry for payment of dividends of $17,000.

(b)

Terry Corporation
Statement of Cash Flows
For the Year Ended December 31, 19X1

Cash Flows from Operating Activities		
Cash Received from Customers	$391,000	
Cash Received as Dividends	5,000	$396,000
Cash Paid to Employees and Suppliers	$339,500	
Cash Paid for Income Taxes	18,500	358,000
Net Cash Provided by Operating Activities		$ 38,000
Cash Flows from Investing Activities		
Sale of Investments	$ 9,000	
Purchase of Plant Assets	(48,000)	
Net Cash Used by Investing Activities		(39,000)
Cash Flows from Financing Activities		
Issuance of Common Stock	$ 14,000	
Payment of Dividends	(17,000)	
Net Cash Used by Financing Activities		(3,000)
Net Decrease in Cash		$ 4,000
Cash at Beginning of Year		12,000
Cash at End of Year		$ 8,000

(c) Reconciliation of Net Income to Net Cash Flow from Operating Activities:

Net Income	$ 35,000
Add (Deduct) Items to Convert Net Income to Cash Basis:	
Depreciation	11,000
Franchise Amortization	3,000
Loss on Sale of Investments	2,000
Accounts Receivable Decrease	6,000
Inventory Increase	(30,000)
Prepaid Expenses Increase	(4,000)
Accounts Payable Increase	13,000
Accrued Liabilities Increase	3,500
Income Tax Payable Decrease	(1,500)
Net Cash Provided by Operating Activities	$ 38,000

QUESTIONS

19–1 Define *cash equivalents.* Give three examples of cash equivalents.

19–2 Why are cash equivalents included with cash in a statement of cash flows?

19–3 Identify the three major types of activities classified on a statement of cash flows and give an example of a cash inflow and a cash outflow in each classification.

19–4 Identify in which of the three activity categories of a statement of cash flows each of the following items would appear, and indicate for each item whether it represents a cash inflow or a cash outflow:
(a) Cash purchase of equipment
(b) Cash collections on loans

(c) Cash dividends paid
(d) Cash dividends received
(e) Cash proceeds from issuing stock
(f) Cash receipts from customers
(g) Cash interest paid
(h) Cash interest received

19–5 Hunt Company acquired a $1,000,000 building by issuing $1,000,000 worth of bonds payable. In terms of cash flow reporting, what type of transaction is this? What special disclosure requirements apply to a transaction of this type?

19–6 Why are noncash investing and financing transactions disclosed as supplemental information to a statement of cash flows?

19–7 Why is a statement of cash flows a useful financial statement?

19–8 Distinguish between the direct method and the indirect (reconciliation) method of presenting net cash flow from operating activities.

19–9 A firm is converting its accrual basis revenues and expenses to corresponding cash amounts using the direct method. Sales on the income statement are $835,000. Beginning and ending accounts receivable on the balance sheet are $74,000 and $67,000, respectively. What is the amount of cash received from customers?

19–10 A firm reports $180,000 cost of goods sold in its income statement. Beginning and ending inventories are $45,000 and $41,000, respectively, and beginning and ending accounts payable (for merchandise purchased) are $22,000 and $15,000, respectively. What is the amount of cash paid for merchandise purchased?

19–11 A firm reports $90,000 wages expense in its income statement. If beginning and ending wages payable are $2,800 and $1,800, respectively, what is the amount of cash paid to employees?

19–12 A firm reports $33,000 advertising expense in its income statement. If beginning and ending prepaid advertising are $9,000 and $12,000, respectively, what is the amount of cash paid for advertising?

19–13 A firm uses the indirect method of presenting net cash flow from operating activities. Calculate this net cash flow using the following information:

Net Income	$25,000
Accounts receivable decrease	8,000
Inventory increase	7,000
Accounts payable decrease	3,500
Income tax payable increase	1,000
Depreciation expense	6,000

19–14 In determining net cash flow from operating activities using the indirect method, why must we add depreciation back to net income? Give an example of another item that is added back to net income under the indirect method.

19–15 Scott Company sold equipment for $2,800 cash that had cost $22,000 and had $18,600 of accumulated depreciation. Describe how this event is handled in a statement of cash flows using (a) the direct method, and (b) the indirect method.

19–16 Bueno Company sold for $37,000 cash long-term investments originally costing $25,000. The company recorded a gain on the sale of $12,000. Describe how this event is handled in a statement of cash flows using (a) the direct method, and (b) the indirect method.

19–17 If a business had a net loss for the year, under what circumstances would the statement of cash flows show a positive net cash flow from operating activities?

19–18 What is the purpose of the analyzing entries on a worksheet for a statement of cash flows?

19–19 What separate disclosures are required for a company that reports a statement of cash flows using the direct method?

19–20 What separate disclosures are required for a company that reports a statement of cash flows using the indirect method?

EXERCISES

Classification of cash flows

19–21 For each of the items below, indicate in which of the three categories—cash flows from operating activities (direct method), cash flows from investing activities, or cash flows from financing activities—the item should appear.

(a) Cash receipts from customers for services rendered.
(b) Sale of long-term investments for cash.
(c) Acquisition of plant assets for cash.
(d) Payment of income taxes.
(e) Bonds payable issued for cash.
(f) Payment of cash dividends declared in previous year.
(g) Purchase of short-term investments (not cash equivalents) for cash.
(h) Cash loaned to borrowers.
(i) Preferred stock issued for cash.
(j) Payment of interest.

Classification of cash flows

19–22 For each of the items below, indicate whether it is: (1) a cash flow from an operating activity; (2) a cash flow from an investing activity; (3) a cash flow from a financing activity; (4) a noncash investing and financing activity; or (5) none of the above.

(a) Retired bonds payable at a loss.
(b) Received cash as settlement of a lawsuit.
(c) Acquired a patent in exchange for common stock.
(d) Received advance payments from customers on orders for custom-made goods.
(e) Gave large cash contribution to local university.
(f) Exchanged, at a gain, stock held as an investment for a parcel of land.
(g) Invested cash in a money market fund (cash may be easily withdrawn from the fund).
(h) Loaned cash to help finance the start of a new biotechnology firm.

Statement of cash flows—direct method

19–23 Use the following information about the 19X1 cash flows of Mazur Corporation to prepare a statement of cash flows using the direct method.

Cash balance, end of 19X1	$ 18,000
Cash paid to employees and suppliers	131,000
Cash received from sale of land	15,000
Cash paid to acquire treasury stock	5,000
Cash balance, beginning of 19X1	26,000
Cash received as interest	6,000
Cash paid as income taxes	10,000
Cash paid to purchase equipment	51,000
Cash received from customers	150,000
Cash received from issuing bonds payable	25,000
Cash paid as dividends	7,000

Statement of cash flows—indirect method

19–24 Use the following information about Lindquist Corporation for 19X2 to prepare a statement of cost flows using the indirect method.

Accounts payable increase	$ 6,000
Accounts receivable increase	2,000
Accrued liabilities decrease	1,000
Amortization expense	4,000

Cash balance, beginning of 19X2	31,000
Cash balance, end of 19X2	37,000
Cash paid as dividends	15,000
Cash paid to purchase land	57,000
Cash paid to retire bonds payable	25,000
Cash received from issuance of common stock	18,000
Cash received from sale of equipment	8,000
Depreciation expense	24,000
Income tax payable decrease	2,000
Inventory decrease	7,000
Net income	42,000
Prepaid expenses increase	1,000

Operating cash flows

19–25 Powell Company's current year income statement contains the following data:

Sales	$820,000
Cost of Goods Sold	530,000
Gross Profit	$290,000

Powell's comparative balance sheets show the following data (accounts payable relate to merchandise purchases):

	End of Year	Beginning of Year
Accounts Receivable	$ 34,000	$42,000
Inventory	110,000	97,000
Prepaid Expenses	7,000	10,000
Accounts Payable	32,000	36,000

Compute Powell's current-year cash received from customers and cash paid for merchandise purchased.

Net cash flow from operating activities—direct method

19–26 The Landfall Company, a sole proprietorship that owns no plant assets, had the following income statement for the current year:

Sales		$480,000
Cost of Goods Sold	$310,000	
Wages Expense	70,000	
Rent Expense	30,000	
Insurance Expense	12,000	422,000
Net Income		$ 58,000

Additional information about the company follows:

	End of Year	Beginning of Year
Accounts Receivable	$37,000	$32,000
Inventory	66,000	76,000
Prepaid Insurance	5,000	4,000
Accounts Payable	28,000	21,000
Wages Payable	5,000	8,000

Use the preceding information to calculate the net cash flow from operating activities using the direct method. Show a related cash flow for each revenue and expense.

Net cash flow from operating activities—indirect method

19–27 Refer to the information in Exercise 19–26. Calculate the net cash flow from operating activities using the indirect method.

Operating cash flows

19–28 Calculate the cash flow asked for in each of the following cases.

(a) Calculate cash paid for advertising:

Advertising expense	$37,000
Prepaid advertising, January 1	16,000
Prepaid advertising, December 31	20,000

(b) Calculate cash paid for income taxes:

Income tax expense	$19,000
Income tax payable, January 1	5,500
Income tax payable, December 31	3,600

(c) Calculate cash paid for merchandise purchased:

Cost of goods sold	$99,000
Inventory, January 1	26,000
Inventory, December 31	21,000
Accounts payable, January 1	10,000
Accounts payable, December 31	13,000

(d) Calculate cash received as interest:

Interest income	$11,000
Interest receivable, January 1	2,400
Interest receivable, December 31	3,200

Net cash flow from operating activities—indirect method

19–29 The following information was obtained from Moline Company's comparative balance sheets.

	Dec. 31, 19X1	Dec. 31, 19X0
Cash	$ 5,000	$ 9,000
Accounts Receivable	35,000	26,000
Inventory	51,000	38,000
Prepaid Rent	2,000	3,000
Long-term Investments	8,000	20,000
Plant Assets	126,000	88,000
Accumulated Depreciation	(23,000)	(18,000)
Accounts Payable	18,000	14,000
Income Tax Payable	1,000	4,000
Common Stock	105,000	95,000
Retained Earnings	80,000	53,000

Assume Moline Company's 19X1 income statement showed depreciation expense of $5,000, a gain on sale of investments of $3,000, and a net income of $35,000. Calculate the net cash flow from operating activities using the indirect method.

Investing and financing cash flows

19–30 Refer to the information in Exercise 19–29. During 19X1 Moline Company purchased plant assets for cash, sold investments for cash, and issued common stock for cash. The firm also declared and paid cash dividends in 19X1. What items and amounts will appear in the (a) cash flows from investing activities and the (b) cash flows from financing activities sections of a 19X1 statement of cash flows?

Net cash flow from operating activities—indirect method

19–31 Tunic Company had a $12,000 net loss from operations for 19X2. Depreciation expense for 19X2 was $5,500 and a 19X2 dividend of $4,000 was declared and paid. Balances of the current asset and current liability accounts at the beginning and end of 19X2 are as follows:

	End	Beginning
Cash	$ 4,000	$ 9,000
Accounts Receivable	10,000	18,000
Inventory	38,000	39,000
Prepaid Expenses	2,500	4,000
Accounts Payable	8,500	6,000
Accrued Liabilities	2,000	4,000

Did Tunic Company's 19X2 operating activities provide or use cash? Use the indirect method to determine your answer.

PROBLEMS

Statement of cash flows—direct method

19–32 Alpine Company's 19X1 income statement and comparative balance sheets at December 31 of 19X1 and 19X0 are shown below.

Alpine Company
Income Statement
For the Year Ended December 31, 19X1

Sales		$410,000
Cost of Goods Sold	$285,000	
Wages and Other Operating Expenses	63,000	
Depreciation Expense	10,000	
Interest Expense	7,000	
Income Tax Expense	15,000	380,000
Net Income		$ 30,000

Alpine Company
Balance Sheets

Assets	Dec. 31, 19X1	Dec. 31, 19X0
Cash	$ 11,000	$ 6,000
Accounts Receivable	28,000	20,000
Inventory	60,000	38,000
Prepaid Expenses	2,000	5,000
Plant Assets	165,000	120,000
Accumulated Depreciation	(42,000)	(32,000)
Total Assets	$224,000	$157,000
Liabilities and Stockholders' Equity		
Accounts Payable	$ 8,000	$ 12,000
Accrued Liabilities	5,000	3,000
Income Tax Payable	3,000	4,000
Bonds Payable	90,000	40,000
Common Stock	70,000	70,000
Retained Earnings	48,000	28,000
Total Liabilities and Stockholders' Equity	$224,000	$157,000

Cash dividends of $10,000 were declared and paid during 19X1. Plant assets were purchased for cash and bonds payable were issued for cash. Bond interest is paid semiannually on June 30 and December 31.

REQUIRED

(a) Prepare a worksheet for a 19X1 statement of cash flows using the direct method.

(b) Prepare a 19X1 statement of cash flows using the direct method.
(c) Prepare a separate reconciliation of 19X1 net income to net cash flow from operating activities.

Statement of cash flows—direct method

19–33 Winn Company's income statement for the current year and comparative balance sheet at December 31 of this year and last year are presented below.

Winn Company
Income Statement
For the Current Year

Sales		$584,000
Cost of Goods Sold	$370,000	
Wages and Other Operating Expenses	79,000	
Depreciation Expense	18,000	
Goodwill Amortization Expense	6,000	
Interest Expense	9,000	
Income Tax Expense	30,000	
Loss on Bond Retirement	4,000	516,000
Net Income		$ 68,000

Winn Company
Balance Sheets

Assets	**Dec. 31, This Year**	**Dec. 31, Last Year**
Cash	$ 23,000	$ 15,000
Accounts Receivable	44,000	40,000
Inventory	86,000	92,000
Prepaid Expenses	10,000	8,000
Plant Assets	300,000	280,000
Accumulated Depreciation	(72,000)	(70,000)
Goodwill	36,000	42,000
Total Assets	$427,000	$407,000
Liabilities and Stockholders' Equity		
Accounts Payable	$ 27,000	$ 22,000
Interest Payable	3,000	6,000
Income Tax Payable	5,000	7,000
Bonds Payable	50,000	100,000
Common Stock	210,000	190,000
Retained Earnings	132,000	82,000
Total Liabilities and Stockholders' Equity	$427,000	$407,000

During the year, the company sold for $14,000 old equipment that had cost $30,000 and had $16,000 accumulated depreciation. New equipment worth $50,000 was acquired in exchange for $50,000 of bonds payable. Bonds payable of $100,000 were retired for cash at a loss. An $18,000 cash dividend was declared and paid this year. All stock issuances were for cash.

REQUIRED

(a) Prepare a worksheet for a statement of cash flows for this year using the direct method.
(b) Prepare a statement of cash flows for this year using the direct method.
(c) Prepare separate schedules showing (1) a reconciliation of net income to net cash flow from operating activities, and (2) noncash investing and financing transactions.

Statement of cash flows—direct method

19–34 Baylor Company's income statement for the current year and comparative balance sheets at December 31 of this year and last year are shown below.

Baylor Company
Income Statement
For the Current Year

Sales		$750,000
Dividend Income		15,000
		$765,000
Cost of Goods Sold	$440,000	
Wages and Other Operating Expenses	130,000	
Depreciation Expense	38,000	
Patent Amortization Expense	8,000	
Interest Expense	12,000	
Income Tax Expense	44,000	
Loss on Sale of Equipment	5,000	
Gain on Sale of Investments	(10,000)	667,000
Net Income		$ 98,000

Baylor Company
Balance Sheets

Assets	**Dec. 31, This Year**	**Dec. 31, Last Year**
Cash and Cash Equivalents	$ 21,000	$ 24,000
Accounts Receivable	40,000	31,000
Inventory	97,000	77,000
Prepaid Expenses	10,000	7,000
Long-term Investments	30,000	80,000
Land	190,000	100,000
Buildings	445,000	350,000
Accumulated Depreciation—Buildings	(91,000)	(75,000)
Equipment	179,000	225,000
Accumulated Depreciation—Equipment	(41,000)	(46,000)
Patents	54,000	32,000
Total Assets	$934,000	$805,000
Liabilities and Stockholders' Equity		
Accounts Payable	$ 25,000	$ 16,000
Interest Payable	6,000	5,000
Income Tax Payable	8,000	10,000
Bonds Payable	150,000	125,000
Preferred Stock ($100 par value)	100,000	70,000
Common Stock ($5 par value)	410,000	400,000
Paid-in Capital in Excess of Par Value—Common	130,000	124,000
Retained Earnings	105,000	55,000
Total Liabilities and Stockholders' Equity	$934,000	$805,000

During the year, the following transactions occurred:

1. Purchased land for cash.
2. Sold long-term investments costing $50,000 for $60,000 cash.
3. Capitalized an expenditure of $95,000 made to improve the building.
4. Sold equipment for $14,000 cash that originally cost $46,000 and had $27,000 accumulated depreciation.
5. Issued bonds payable at face value for cash.

6. Acquired a patent with a fair value of $30,000 by issuing 300 shares of preferred stock at par value.
7. Declared and paid a $48,000 cash dividend.
8. Issued 2,000 shares of common stock for cash at $8 per share.
9. Recorded depreciation of $16,000 on buildings and $22,000 on equipment.

REQUIRED
(a) Prepare a worksheet for a statement of cash flows for this year using the direct method.
(b) Prepare a statement of cash flows for this year using the direct method.
(c) Prepare separate schedules showing (1) a reconciliation of net income to net cash flow from operating activities, and (2) noncash investing and financing transactions.

Statement of cash flows—direct method

19–35 March Company's 19X1 income statement and comparative balance sheets at December 31 of 19X1 and 19X0 are shown below.

March Company
Income Statement
For the Year Ended December 31, 19X1

Sales		$260,000
Cost of Goods Sold	$195,000	
Wages and Other Operating Expenses	76,000	
Depreciation Expense	8,000	
Interest Expense	6,000	
Gain on Sale of Land	(9,000)	276,000
Net Loss		$ 16,000

March Company
Balance Sheets

Assets	Dec. 31, 19X1	Dec. 31, 19X0
Cash	$ 21,000	$ 10,000
Accounts Receivable	15,000	18,000
Inventory	39,000	41,000
Prepaid Expenses	3,000	4,000
Plant Assets	129,000	75,000
Accumulated Depreciation	(28,000)	(20,000)
Total Assets	$179,000	$128,000
Liabilities and Stockholders' Equity		
Accounts Payable	$ 6,000	$ 11,000
Interest Payable	2,000	—
Bonds Payable	80,000	—
Common Stock	90,000	90,000
Retained Earnings	11,000	27,000
Treasury Stock	(10,000)	—
Total Liabilities and Stockholders' Equity	$179,000	$128,000

During 19X1, March sold land for $25,000 that had originally cost $16,000. March also purchased equipment for cash, reacquired treasury stock for cash, and issued bonds payable for cash.

REQUIRED
(a) Prepare a worksheet for a 19X1 statement of cash flows using the direct method.
(b) Prepare a 19X1 statement of cash flows using the direct method.
(c) Prepare a separate reconciliation of 19X1 net loss to net cash flow from operating activities.

Statement of cash flows—indirect method

19–36 Refer to the data given for Alpine Company in Problem 19–32.

REQUIRED
(a) Prepare a worksheet for a 19X1 statement of cash flows using the indirect method.
(b) Prepare a 19X1 statement of cash flows using the indirect method.
(c) Prepare a supplemental disclosure showing cash paid for interest and for income taxes.

Statement of cash flows—indirect method

19–37 Refer to the data given for Winn Company in Problem 19–33.

REQUIRED
(a) Prepare a worksheet for a statement of cash flows for this year using the indirect method.
(b) Prepare a statement of cash flows for this year using the indirect method.
(c) Prepare separate schedules showing (1) cash paid for interest and for income taxes, and (2) noncash investing and financing transactions.

Statement of cash flows—indirect method

19–38 Refer to the data given for Baylor Company in Problem 19–34.

REQUIRED
(a) Prepare a worksheet for a statement of cash flows for this year using the indirect method.
(b) Prepare a statement of cash flows for this year using the indirect method.
(c) Prepare separate schedules showing (1) cash paid for interest and for income taxes, and (2) noncash investing and financing transactions.

Statement of cash flows—indirect method

19–39 Refer to the data given for March Company in Problem 19–35.

REQUIRED
(a) Prepare a worksheet for a 19X1 statement of cash flows using the indirect method.
(b) Prepare a 19X1 statement of cash flows using the indirect method.
(c) Prepare a supplemental disclosure showing cash paid for interest.

ALTERNATE PROBLEMS

Statement of cash flows—direct method

19–32A Tower Company's 19X1 income statement and comparative balance sheets at December 31 of 19X1 and 19X0 are shown below.

Tower Company
Income Statement
For the Year Ended December 31, 19X1

Sales		$375,000
Cost of Goods Sold	$220,000	
Wages Expense	68,000	
Depreciation Expense	12,000	
Other Operating Expenses	17,000	
Income Tax Expense	18,000	335,000
Net Income		$ 40,000

Tower Company
Balance Sheets

Assets	Dec. 31, 19X1	Dec. 31, 19X0
Cash	$ 12,000	$ 22,000
Accounts Receivable	31,000	36,000
Inventory	110,000	84,000
Prepaid Expenses	11,000	7,000
Plant Assets	220,000	160,000
Accumulated Depreciation	(76,000)	(64,000)
Total Assets	$308,000	$245,000
Liabilities and Stockholders' Equity		
Accounts Payable	$ 17,000	$ 10,000
Accrued Liabilities	7,000	4,000
Income Tax Payable	3,000	5,000
Common Stock	175,000	150,000
Paid-in Capital in Excess of Par Value	43,000	34,000
Retained Earnings	63,000	42,000
Total Liabilities and Stockholders' Equity	$308,000	$245,000

Cash dividends of $19,000 were declared and paid during 19X1. Plant assets were purchased for cash and additional common stock was issued for cash.

REQUIRED
(a) Prepare a worksheet for a 19X1 statement of cash flows using the direct method.
(b) Prepare a 19X1 statement of cash flows using the direct method.
(c) Prepare a separate reconciliation of 19X1 net income to net cash flow from operating activities.

Statement of cash flows—direct method

19–33A Sugar Company's income statement for the current year and comparative balance sheets at December 31 of this year and last year are presented below.

Sugar Company
Income Statement
For the Current Year

Sales		$485,000
Cost of Goods Sold	$260,000	
Wages and Other Operating Expenses	111,000	
Depreciation Expense	31,000	
Interest Expense	5,000	
Income Tax Expense	29,000	
Gain on Sale of Equipment	(8,000)	428,000
Net Income		$ 57,000

Sugar Company
Balance Sheets

Assets	Dec. 31, This Year	Dec. 31, Last Year
Cash	$ 12,000	$ 16,000
Accounts Receivable	35,000	22,000
Inventory	104,000	78,000
Prepaid Expenses	5,000	6,000
Plant Assets	455,000	382,000
Accumulated Depreciation	(97,000)	(90,000)
Total Assets	$514,000	$414,000

Liabilities and Stockholders' Equity		
Accounts Payable	$ 20,000	$ 14,000
Interest Payable	3,000	—
Income Tax Payable	6,000	8,000
Bonds Payable	75,000	40,000
Common Stock	340,000	300,000
Retained Earnings	95,000	52,000
Treasury Stock	(25,000)	—
Total Liabilities and Stockholders' Equity	$514,000	$414,000

During the year, Sugar Company sold equipment for $13,000 cash that originally cost $29,000 and had $24,000 accumulated depreciation. New equipment was purchased for cash. Bonds payable outstanding at the beginning of the year were converted into common stock with a total par value equal to the bond's book value. During the year, other bonds payable were issued for cash. Cash dividends of $14,000 were declared and paid this year. At the end of the year, shares of treasury stock were purchased for cash.

REQUIRED
(a) Prepare a worksheet for a statement of cash flows for this year using the direct method.
(b) Prepare a statement of cash flows for this year using the direct method.
(c) Prepare separate schedules showing (1) a reconciliation of net income to net cash flow from operating activities, and (2) noncash investing and financing transactions.

Statement of cash flows—direct method

19–34A Hub Company's income statement for the current year and comparative balance sheets at December 31 of this year and last year are presented below.

Hub Company
Income Statement
For the Current Year

Service Fees Earned		$200,000
Dividend and Interest Income		21,000
		$221,000
Wages and Other Operating Expenses	$187,000	
Depreciation Expense	34,000	
Franchise Amortization Expense	7,000	
Loss on Sale of Equipment	8,000	
Gain on Sale of Investments	(11,000)	225,000
Net Loss		$ 4,000

Hub Company
Balance Sheets

Assets	Dec. 31, This Year	Dec. 31, Last Year
Cash	$ 28,000	$ 25,000
Accounts Receivable	9,000	12,000
Interest Receivable	3,000	2,000
Prepaid Expenses	8,000	6,000
Long-term Investments	125,000	180,000
Plant Assets	302,000	336,000
Accumulated Depreciation	(118,000)	(94,000)
Franchise	58,000	14,000
Total Assets	$415,000	$481,000

Liabilities and Stockholders' Equity		
Accrued Liabilities	$ 8,000	$ 12,000
Note Payable	—	20,000
Common Stock	400,000	400,000
Retained Earnings	36,000	49,000
Treasury Stock	(29,000)	—
Total Liabilities and Stockholders' Equity	$415,000	$481,000

During the year, the following transactions occurred:

1. Sold equipment for $16,000 cash that originally cost $34,000 and had $10,000 accumulated depreciation.
2. Sold long-term investments that had cost $55,000 for cash.
3. Paid cash to extend the company's exclusive franchise for another three years.
4. Paid off a note payable at the bank on January 1.
5. Declared and paid a $9,000 dividend.
6. Purchased treasury stock for cash.

REQUIRED

(a) Prepare a worksheet for a statement of cash flows for this year using the direct method.
(b) Prepare a statement of cash flows for this year using the direct method.
(c) Prepare a separate reconciliation of net loss to net cash flow from operating activities.

Statement of cash flows—direct method

19–35A Holt Company's 19X2 income statement and comparative balance sheets at December 31 of 19X2 and 19X1 are shown below.

Holt Company
Income Statement
For the Year Ended December 31, 19X2

Sales		$450,000
Cost of Goods Sold	$300,000	
Wages and Other Operating Expenses	96,000	
Depreciation Expense	15,000	
Patent Amortization Expense	3,000	
Interest Expense	10,000	
Income Tax Expense	14,000	
Gain on Exchange of Land for Patent	(20,000)	418,000
Net Income		$ 32,000

Holt Company
Balance Sheets

Assets	Dec. 31, 19X2	Dec. 31, 19X1
Cash	$ 19,000	$ 9,000
Accounts Receivable	31,000	28,000
Inventory	47,000	35,000
Land	60,000	90,000
Building and Equipment	250,000	200,000
Accumulated Depreciation	(66,000)	(55,000)
Patent	47,000	—
Total Assets	$388,000	$307,000

Liabilities and Stockholders' Equity		
Accounts Payable	$ 20,000	$ 14,000
Interest Payable	7,000	3,000
Income Tax Payable	4,000	7,000
Bonds Payable	100,000	40,000
Common Stock	200,000	200,000
Retained Earnings	57,000	43,000
Total Liabilities and Stockholders' Equity	$388,000	$307,000

During 19X2, $18,000 of cash dividends were declared and paid. A patent valued at $50,000 was obtained in exchange for land. Equipment that originally cost $10,000 and had $4,000 accumulated depreciation was sold for $6,000 cash. Bonds payable were sold for cash and cash was used to pay for structural improvements to the building.

REQUIRED

(a) Prepare a worksheet for a 19X2 statement of cash flows using the direct method.
(b) Prepare a 19X2 statement of cash flows using the direct method.
(c) Prepare separate schedules showing (1) a reconciliation of net income to net cash flow from operating activities, and (2) noncash investing and financing transactions.

Statement of cash flows—indirect method

19–36A Refer to the data given for Tower Company in Problem 19–32A.

REQUIRED

(a) Prepare a worksheet for a 19X1 statement of cash flows using the indirect method.
(b) Prepare a 19X1 statement of cash flows using the indirect method.
(c) Prepare a supplemental disclosure showing cash paid for income taxes.

Statement of cash flows—indirect method

19–37A Refer to the data given for Sugar Company in Problem 19–33A.

REQUIRED

(a) Prepare a worksheet for a statement of cash flows for this year using the indirect method.
(b) Prepare a statement of cash flows for this year using the indirect method.
(c) Prepare separate schedules showing (1) cash paid for interest and for income taxes, and (2) noncash investing and financing transactions.

Statement of cash flows—indirect method

19–38A Refer to the data given for Hub Company in Problem 19–34A.

REQUIRED

(a) Prepare a worksheet for a statement of cash flows for this year using the indirect method.
(b) Prepare a statement of cash flows for this year using the indirect method.

Statement of cash flows—indirect method

19–39A Refer to the data given for Holt Company in Problem 19–35A.

REQUIRED

(a) Prepare a worksheet for a 19X2 statement of cash flows using the indirect method.
(b) Prepare a 19X2 statement of cash flows using the indirect method.
(c) Prepare separate schedules showing (1) cash paid for interest and for income taxes, and (2) noncash investing and financing transactions.

BUSINESS DECISION PROBLEM

Recently hired as assistant controller for Media, Inc., you are sitting next to the controller as she responds to questions at the annual stockholders' meeting. The firm's financial statements contain a statement of cash flows prepared using the indirect method. A stockholder raises his hand.

Stockholder: "I notice depreciation expense is shown as an addition in the calculation of the net cash flow from operating activities."

Controller: "That's correct."

Stockholder: "What depreciation method do you use?"

Controller: "We use the straight-line method for all plant assets."

Stockholder: "Well, why don't you switch to an accelerated depreciation method, such as double declining balance, increase the annual depreciation amount, and thus increase the net cash flow from operating activities?"

The controller pauses, turns to you, and replies: "My assistant will answer your question."

REQUIRED

Prepare an answer to the stockholder's question.

ANSWERS TO SELF-TEST QUESTIONS

1. (a) **2.** (d) **3.** (c) **4.** (c) **5.** (b)

APPENDIX E

T-ACCOUNT APPROACH TO PREPARING THE STATEMENT OF CASH FLOWS

Some accountants prefer to use a T-account approach to accumulate the information needed for a statement of cash flows. Although the basic analysis is similar to the worksheet approach discussed in Chapter 19, the T-account method may be faster to set up and complete when the situation is not too complicated. In this appendix we explain the T-account approach for a statement of cash flows prepared using the indirect method.

FIVE STEPS IN THE T-ACCOUNT APPROACH—INDIRECT METHOD

Preparing a statement of cash flows (indirect method) and the related separate disclosures using a T-account approach involves five steps:

1. Set up a large T account for Cash showing the net change in cash that occurred during the year.
2. Set up T accounts for all other balance sheet accounts showing the net change in each account that occurred during the year.
3. Record entries in the T accounts to account for and explain the net change that occurred in each account.
4. Prepare the statement of cash flows using information from the Cash T account.
5. Determine the information for the required separate disclosures.

ILLUSTRATION OF T-ACCOUNT APPROACH

We will illustrate the T-account approach for the indirect method using the data for Superior Corporation presented in the chapter (pages 708–10).

STEP 1 Set up a large T account labeled Cash and enter the period's net change in cash in the account—a cash increase is entered on the debit side and a cash decrease is entered on the credit side. Superior Corporation's cash increased $12,000 during 19X2, so $12,000 is entered on the debit side and identified as "Net Change." Place a single rule beneath this entry to separate it from the analyzing entries that will be reflected in the account.

Divide the T account into the following six categories, leaving space for entries in each category:

Debit Side	**Credit Side**
Operating Activities—Increases	Operating Activities—Decreases
Investing Activities—Increases	Investing Activities—Decreases
Financing Activities—Increases	Financing Activities—Decreases

STEP 2 Set up T accounts for each remaining balance sheet account and enter the period's net change on the appropriate side of each account. During 19X2, Superior Corporation's accounts receivable decreased $5,000, so $5,000 is entered on the credit side of the Accounts Receivable T account; inventory increased $14,000, so $14,000 is entered on the debit side of the Inventory T account; and so on. Place a single rule beneath the net change entered in each account.

Exhibit E–1 shows the T accounts for Superior Corporation after all the net changes have been entered and ruled. The net change for each account is the *target number* for that account. Our objective is to analyze all changes in the noncash balance sheet accounts to determine the events affecting cash flows. Entries recorded in each account will eventually equal that account's target number. Our analysis is complete when the target numbers in all T accounts are equalled by the entries in the T accounts.

STEP 3 Record entries in the T accounts to account for and explain the net changes in the accounts. These entries are placed directly into the T accounts; for ease of study, we also present them in a general journal format. Entries to the Cash T account need a descriptive label because this account provides the data for the statement of cash flows.

The T-account entries are divided into two sets. The *first set* of entries determines the net cash flow from operating activities using the indirect method. The indirect method begins with net income (or net loss) and applies a series of adjustments to convert the net income (or net loss) to a cash amount. (These adjustments are summarized in Exhibit 19–4 on page 705.) When these adjustments deal with gains and losses related to investing and financing activities, the T-account entry will present the entire transaction. The *second set* of entries explains the remaining changes in the T accounts.

Entries 1–10 comprise the first set of entries and determine the net cash flow from operating activities for Superior Corporation. (You should trace each entry into the completed T-account analysis shown in Exhibit E–2 on page 747.)

		Debit	Credit
1.	Cash—Operating Activities (Net Income)	54,000	
	Retained Earnings		54,000

This entry establishes net income as the starting point for computing the net cash flow from operating activities and shows the increase in retained earnings caused by the period's net income.

		Debit	Credit
2.	Cash—Operating Activities (Depreciation)	13,000	
	Accumulated Depreciation		13,000

The period's depreciation expense is added to net income in computing the net cash flow from operating activities. Depreciation expense also increased accumulated depreciation.

EXHIBIT E-1

Cash

Net Change	12,000		
Operating Activities—Increases		**Operating Activities—Decreases**	
Investing Activities—Increases		**Investing Activities—Decreases**	
Financing Activities—Increases		**Financing Activities—Decreases**	

Accounts Receivable

		Net Change	5,000

Inventory

Net Change	14,000		

Prepaid Expenses

Net Change	3,000		

Building and Equipment

Net Change	85,000		

Accumulated Depreciation

		Net Change	7,000

Accounts Payable

Net Change	10,000		

Interest Payable

Net Change	2,000		

Income Tax Payable

		Net Change	1,000

Bonds Payable

Net Change	80,000		

Common Stock

		Net Change	150,000

Retained Earnings

		Net Change	43,000

14. Retained Earnings	11,000	
Cash—Financing Activities (Payment of Dividends)		11,000

The $11,000 dividend declared and paid in 19X2 reduced retained earnings and used cash for a financing activity.

After these fourteen entries, the T-account entries equal the target amounts for all of the noncash balance sheet accounts. The entries in the Cash T account should also equal the target amount; we total the debit entries and credit entries to confirm this. The totals show:

Cash debit entries	$222,000
Cash credit entries	210,000
Cash target amount—debit	$ 12,000

Exhibit E–2 shows the T accounts with all of the entries recorded in the accounts. We are now ready to prepare the statement of cash flows.

STEP 4 Prepare the statement of cash flows from the information in the Cash T account. This T account provides the adjustments necessary to reconcile net income to the net cash flow from operating activities. It also provides the various cash inflows and outflows from the investing activities and the financing activities. The sum of the operating, investing, and financing cash flows will equal the period's change in cash. In the statement of cash flows, the change in cash is reconciled with the beginning and ending cash balances. The statement of cash flows for Superior Corporation, using the indirect method, is shown in Exhibit 19–11 (page 720).

STEP 5 Determine the information for the required separate disclosures. The required disclosures for firms using the indirect method in the statement of cash flows are (1) cash paid during the year for interest (net of amount capitalized) and for income taxes, (2) all noncash investing and financing transactions, and (3) the policy for determining which highly liquid, short-term investments are treated as cash equivalents.

Cash paid for interest is computed by adjusting interest expense for the change during the year in interest payable. Superior Corporation's 19X2 cash paid for interest is $12,000 ($10,000 + $2,000). Cash paid for income taxes is computed by adjusting income tax expense for the change during the year in income tax payable. Superior Corporation's 19X2 cash paid for income taxes is $11,000 ($12,000 − $1,000). Exhibit 19–11 shows these amounts as supplemental disclosures to the statement of cash flows.

The noncash investing and financing transactions are identified in the T accounts (the entries containing an asterisk identify these events). Exhibit 19–11 shows the supplemental disclosure of Superior Corporation's one noncash investing and financing transaction—the $30,000 issuance of common stock to acquire equipment.

Superior Corporation has no short-term investments, so a separate disclosure to indicate which highly liquid, short-term investments are treated as cash equivalents is not needed.

EXHIBIT E–2

Cash

Net Change	12,000		
Operating Activities—Increases		**Operating Activities—Decreases**	
(1) Net Income	54,000	(3) Gain on Sale of Equipment	16,000
(2) Depreciation	13,000	(6) Inventory Increase	14,000
(4) Loss on Bond Retirement	9,000	(7) Prepaid Expenses Increase	3,000
(5) Accounts Receivable Decrease	5,000	(8) Accounts Payable Decrease	10,000
(10) Income Tax Payable Increase	1,000	(9) Interest Payable Decrease	2,000
Investing Activities—Increases		**Investing Activities—Decreases**	
(3) Sale of Equipment	20,000	(11) Purchase of Equipment	65,000
Financing Activities—Increases		**Financing Activities—Decreases**	
(13) Issuance of Common Stock	120,000	(4) Retirement of Bonds Payable	89,000
	222,000	(14) Payment of Dividends	11,000
			210,000

Accounts Receivable

		Net Change	5,000
		(5)	5,000

Inventory

Net Change	14,000		
(6)	14,000		

Prepaid Expenses

Net Change	3,000		
(7)	3,000		

Building and Equipment

Net Change	85,000		
(11)	65,000	(3)	10,000
(12)*	30,000		

Accumulated Depreciation

		Net Change	7,000
(3)	6,000	(2)	13,000

Accounts Payable

Net Change	10,000		
(8)	10,000		

Interest Payable

Net Change	2,000		
(9)	2,000		

Income Tax Payable

		Net Change	1,000
		(10)	1,000

Bonds Payable

Net Change	80,000		
(4)	80,000		

Common Stock

		Net Change	150,000
		(12)*	30,000
		(13)	120,000

Retained Earnings

		Net Change	43,000
(14)	11,000	(1)	54,000

PROBLEMS

Statement of cash flows—T-account approach

E–1 Refer to the data given for Alpine Company in Problem 19–32.

REQUIRED
(a) Use the T-account approach to compile data for a 19X1 statement of cash flows using the indirect method.
(b) Prepare a 19X1 statement of cash flows using the indirect method.
(c) Prepare a supplemental disclosure showing cash paid for interest and for income taxes.

Statement of cash flows—T-account approach

E–2 Refer to the data given for Winn Company in Problem 19–33.

REQUIRED
(a) Use the T-account approach to compile data for a statement of cash flows for this year using the indirect method.
(b) Prepare a statement of cash flows for this year using the indirect method.
(c) Prepare separate schedules showing (1) cash paid for interest and for income taxes, and (2) noncash investing and financing transactions.

Statement of cash flows—T-account approach

E–3 Refer to the data given for Baylor Company in Problem 19–34.

REQUIRED
(a) Use the T-account approach to compile data for a statement of cash flows for this year using the indirect method.
(b) Prepare a statement of cash flows for this year using the indirect method.
(c) Prepare separate schedules showing (1) cash paid for interest and for income taxes, and (2) noncash investing and financing transactions.

Statement of cash flows—T-account approach

E–4 Refer to the data given for March Company in Problem 19–35.

REQUIRED
(a) Use the T-account approach to compile data for a 19X1 statement of cash flows using the indirect method.
(b) Prepare a 19X1 statement of cash flows using the indirect method.
(c) Prepare a supplemental disclosure showing cash paid for interest.

Statement of cash flows—T-account approach

E–5 Refer to the data given for Tower Company in Problem 19–32A.

REQUIRED
(a) Use the T-account approach to compile data for a 19X1 statement of cash flows using the indirect method.
(b) Prepare a 19X1 statement of cash flows using the indirect method.
(c) Prepare a supplemental disclosure showing cash paid for income taxes.

Statement of cash flows—T-account approach

E–6 Refer to the data given for Sugar Company in Problem 19–33A.

REQUIRED
(a) Use the T-account approach to compile data for a statement of cash flows for this year using the indirect method.
(b) Prepare a statement of cash flows for this year using the indirect method.
(c) Prepare separate schedules showing (1) cash paid for interest and for income taxes, and (2) noncash investing and financing transactions.

Statement of cash flows—T-account approach

E–7 Refer to the data given for Hub Company in Problem 19–34A.

REQUIRED

(a) Use the T-account approach to compile data for a statement of cash flows for this year using the indirect method.
(b) Prepare a statement of cash flows for this year using the indirect method.

Statement of cash flows—T-account approach

E–8 Refer to the data given for Holt Company in Problem 19–35A.

REQUIRED

(a) Use the T-account approach to compile data for a 19X2 statement of cash flows using the indirect method.
(b) Prepare a 19X2 statement of cash flows using the indirect method.
(c) Prepare separate schedules showing (1) cash paid for interest and for income taxes, and (2) noncash investing and financing transactions.

20

ANALYSIS AND INTERPRETATION OF FINANCIAL STATEMENTS

CHAPTER OBJECTIVES

1. Describe and illustrate horizontal analysis of financial statements (pp. 752–56).
2. Describe and illustrate vertical analysis of financial statements (pp. 757–58).
3. Explain measures for evaluating operating performance (pp. 758–62).
4. Discuss the use of earnings per share, price–earnings ratios, and dividend yields in evaluating a firm (pp. 762–63).
5. Define and illustrate *trading on the equity* (pp. 764–66).
6. Explain measures for evaluating financial strength (pp. 766–71).
7. Discuss the limitations of financial analysis (pp. 771–72).

The best prophet of the future is the past.
LORD BYRON

Many individuals and groups are interested in the data appearing in a firm's financial statements, including managers, owners, prospective investors, creditors, labor unions, governmental agencies, and the public. These parties are usually interested in the profitability and financial strength of the firm in question, although such factors as size, growth, and the firm's efforts to meet its social responsibilities may also be of interest. Managers, owners, and prospective investors may ask the following questions: How do profits compare with those of previous years? How do profits compare with those of other firms in the industry? Creditors may ask: Will our debt be repaid on time? Will the interest payments be met? Unions may ask: How can we show that the firm can support a particular wage increase? Regulatory agencies may ask: What rate of return should the firm be permitted? Is the firm enjoying windfall profits? These kinds of questions can be answered by interpreting the data in financial reports.

Various techniques are used to analyze and interpret financial statement data. In the following pages, we concentrate on some widely used methods of evaluation. In many cases, management may profitably use these techniques to plan and control its own operations, but in this discussion our viewpoint is primarily that of an outsider.

SOURCES OF INFORMATION

Except for closely held companies, business firms publish financial statements at least annually, and most large companies also issue them quarterly. Normally, annual statements are attested to by certified public accountants, and the careful analyst reads the accountants' opinion to determine the reliability of the given data. Companies listed on stock exchanges submit annual statements to the Securities and Exchange Commission. These statements, which are available to any interested parties, are generally more useful than annual reports because they furnish a greater amount of detail. Even more detail can be found in prospectuses submitted to the SEC by certain companies issuing large amounts of new securities.

For data not provided by the financial statements, a trained analyst has a number of sources: personal interviews with company management, contacts with research organizations, trade association data, and subscriptions to financial services that periodically publish analytical data for many firms. The analyst also can obtain useful information from financial newspapers, such as *The Wall Street Journal* and *Barron's*, and from magazines devoted to financial and economic reporting, such as *Business Week* and *Forbes*. Data on industry norms, average ratios, and other relationships are available from such agencies as Dun & Bradstreet and Robert Morris and Associates. The analyst may want to compare the performance of a particular firm with that of the industry. Both Dun & Bradstreet and Robert Morris and Associates compile industry statistics for a variety of manufacturers, wholesalers, and retailers. In addition, the Dun & Bradstreet statistics report not only median performance, but the performance of firms in the upper and the lower quartiles of the industry. Robert Morris and Associates reports statistics by size of organization.

ANALYTICAL TECHNIQUES

Absolute dollar amounts of profits, sales, assets, and other key data are not meaningful when studied individually. For example, knowing that a company's annual earnings are $1 million is of little value unless these earnings can be related to other data. A $1 million profit might represent excellent performance for a company with less than $10 million in invested capital. On the other hand, such earnings would be meager for a firm that has several hundred million dollars in invested capital. Thus, the most significant information derived in analysis concerns the relationships between two or more variables, such as earnings to assets, earnings to sales, and earnings to stockholders' investment. To describe these relationships clearly and to make comparisons easy, the analyst states these relationships in terms of ratios and percentages.

For example, we might express the relationship of $15,000 in earnings to $150,000 in sales as a 10% ($15,000/$150,000) rate of earnings on sales. To describe the relationship between sales of $150,000 and inventory of $20,000, we might use a ratio or a percentage; ($150,000/$20,000) may be expressed as 7.5, 7.5:1, or 750%.

Changes in selected items compared in successive financial statements are often expressed as percentages. For example, if a firm's earnings increased from $40,000 last year to $48,000 this year, the $8,000 increase related to the base year is expressed as a 20% increase ($8,000/$40,000). To express a dollar increase or decrease as a percentage, however, the analyst must make the base year amount a positive figure. If, for example, a firm had a net loss of $4,000 in one year and earnings of $20,000 in the next, the $24,000 increase cannot be expressed as a percentage. Similarly, if a firm showed no marketable securities in last year's balance sheet but showed $15,000 of such securities in this year's statement, the $15,000 increase cannot be expressed as a percentage.

When evaluating a firm's financial statements for two or more years, analysts often use **horizontal analysis.** This type of analysis is useful in detecting improvement or deterioration in a firm's performance and in spotting trends. The term **vertical analysis** describes the study of a single year's financial statements.

Horizontal Analysis

COMPARATIVE FINANCIAL STATEMENTS The form of horizontal analysis encountered most often is **comparative financial statements** for two or more years, showing dollar and percentage changes for important items and classification totals. Dollar increases and decreases are divided by the earliest year's data to obtain percentage changes. The 19X4 and 19X5 financial statements of Alliance Company, an electronic components and accessories manufacturer, are shown in Exhibits 20–1, 20–2, and 20–3. We use the data in these statements throughout this chapter to illustrate various analytical techniques.

When examining financial statements, the analyst focuses immediate attention on significant items only. Large percentage changes frequently occur in items whose dollar amounts may not be significant compared with other items on the statements. For example, although a large percentage change in Alliance Company's balance sheet occurred in Prepaid Expenses, the analyst would scarcely notice this item in an initial examination of changes. Instead, attention would be directed first to changes in totals—current assets, long-term assets, total assets, current liabilities, and so on. Next, changes in significant individual items, such as receivables and inventory, would be examined. These changes may be related to certain changes in income statement items to determine whether they are favorable.

EXHIBIT 20–1

Alliance Company
Comparative Balance Sheets
(Thousands of Dollars)

Assets	Dec. 31, 19X5	Dec. 31, 19X4	Increase (Decrease)	Percent Change
Current Assets:				
Cash	$ 5,500	$ 4,200	$ 1,300	31.0
Marketable Securities	1,500	2,400	(900)	(37.5)
Accounts Receivable (less allowance for uncollectible accounts of $2,400 in 19X5 and $2,000 in 19X4)	61,600	52,000	9,600	18.5
Inventory [lower of cost (first-in, first-out) or market]	76,000	63,000	13,000	20.6
Prepaid Expenses	900	600	300	50.0
Total Current Assets	$145,500	$122,200	$23,300	19.1
Long-term Assets:				
Property, Plant, and Equipment (net of accumulated depreciation)	$ 45,000	$ 40,000	$ 5,000	12.5
Investments	1,800	1,600	200	12.5
Total Long-term Assets	$ 46,800	$ 41,600	$ 5,200	12.5
Total Assets	$192,300	$163,800	$28,500	17.4
Liabilities and Stockholders' Equity				
Liabilities				
Current Liabilities:				
Notes Payable	$ 5,700	$ 3,000	$ 2,700	90.0
Accounts Payable	22,000	24,100	(2,100)	(8.7)
Accrued Liabilities	30,000	27,300	2,700	9.9
Total Current Liabilities	$ 57,700	$ 54,400	$ 3,300	6.1
Long-term Liabilities:				
12% Debenture Bonds Payable	$ 25,000	$ 20,000	$ 5,000	25.0
Total Liabilities	$ 82,700	$ 74,400	$ 8,300	11.2
Stockholders' Equity				
10% Preferred Stock, $100 Par Value	$ 8,000	$ 8,000	$ —	—
Common Stock, $5 Par Value	20,000	14,000	6,000	42.9
Paid-in Capital in Excess of Par Value	7,500	5,500	2,000	36.4
Retained Earnings	74,100	61,900	12,200	19.7
Total Stockholders' Equity	$109,600	$ 89,400	$20,200	22.6
Total Liabilities and Stockholders' Equity	$192,300	$163,800	$28,500	17.4

EXHIBIT 20–2

Alliance Company
Comparative Income Statements
(Thousands of Dollars)

	Year Ended Dec. 31, 19X5	Year Ended Dec. 31, 19X4	Increase (Decrease)	Percent Change
Net Sales	$415,000	$320,000	$95,000	29.7
Cost of Goods Sold	290,000	230,000	60,000	26.1
Gross Profit	$125,000	$ 90,000	$35,000	38.9
Selling and Administrative Expenses:				
Selling Expenses	$ 39,500	$ 27,300	$12,200	44.7
Administrative Expenses	49,640	32,600	17,040	52.3
Total	$ 89,140	$ 59,900	$29,240	48.8
Income before Interest Expense and Income Taxes	$ 35,860	$ 30,100	$ 5,760	19.1
Interest Expense	3,000	2,400	600	25.0
Income before Income Taxes	$ 32,860	$ 27,700	$ 5,160	18.6
Income Tax Expense	14,100	12,300	1,800	14.6
Net Income	$ 18,760	$ 15,400	$ 3,360	21.8
Earnings per Share	$5.28	$5.21		
Dividends per Share	1.44	0.81		

For example, Alliance Company's total assets increased 17.4% (Exhibit 20–1), and sales increased 29.7% (Exhibit 20–2). A fairly large percentage increase in sales was supported by a much smaller rate of increase in assets. Furthermore, the 20.6% increase in inventory was also considerably less than the increase in sales. These results reflect quite favorably on the firm's performance. In addition, the 29.7% increase in sales was accompanied by an increase in accounts receivable of only 18.5%; on the surface, the company's sales growth was not associated with a relaxation in credit policy.

We see on the income statement that the 38.9% gross profit increase outstripped the rate of increase in sales, indicating a higher mark-up rate in the latest year. Net income, however, increased only 21.8%; therefore, expenses must have grown disproportionately. Indeed, selling and administrative expenses increased 44.7% and 52.3%, respectively.

From this limited analysis of comparative financial statements, an analyst would conclude that operating performance for the latest year appeared favorable. Further analysis using some of the techniques described later in the chapter, however, might cause the analyst to modify that opinion. The foregoing analysis has revealed one reservation—expenses, particularly administrative expenses, have increased at a fairly high rate. Many selling expenses—such as sales salaries, commissions, and advertising—should rise somewhat proportionately with sales, but administrative expenses should not. An investigation of the reasons for the large increase in the latter expense might be indicated.

TREND ANALYSIS To observe percentage changes over time in selected data, analysts compute **trend percentages.** Most companies provide summaries of data

EXHIBIT 20-3

Alliance Company
Comparative Retained Earnings Statements
(Thousands of Dollars)

	Year Ended Dec. 31, 19X5	Year Ended Dec. 31, 19X4	Increase (Decrease)	Percent Change
Retained Earnings, Jan. 1	$61,900	$49,580	$12,320	24.8
Net Income	18,760	15,400	3,360	21.8
Total	$80,660	$64,980	$15,680	24.1
Dividends:				
On Preferred Stock	$ 800	$ 800	$ —	—
On Common Stock	5,760	2,280	3,480	152.6
Total	$ 6,560	$ 3,080	$ 3,480	113.0
Retained Earnings, Dec. 31	$74,100	$61,900	$12,200	19.7

for the past five or ten years in their annual reports. With such information, the analyst may examine changes over a period longer than two years. For example, suppose you were interested in sales and earnings trends for Alliance Company for the past five years. The dollar data, taken from the company's published annual report in the fifth year (19X5) of the period, are shown below:

Alliance Company
Annual Performance (Millions of Dollars)

	Year 1	Year 2	Year 3	Year 4	Year 5
Sales	$202.0	$215.0	$243.0	$320.0	$415.0
Net Earnings	10.9	11.7	13.5	15.4	18.8

The above data suggests a fairly healthy growth pattern for this company, but we can determine the pattern of change from year to year more precisely by calculating trend percentages. To do this, we select a base year and then divide the data for each of the other years by the base-year data. The resultant figures are actually indexes of the changes occurring throughout the period. If we choose year 1 as the base year, all data for years 2 through 5 will be related to year 1, which is represented as 100%.

To create the following table, we divided each year's sales—from year 2 through year 5—by $202, the year 1 sales in millions of dollars. Similarly, the net earnings for years 2 through 5 were divided by $10.9, the year 1 net earnings in millions of dollars.

Annual Performance (Percentage of Base Year)

	Year 1	Year 2	Year 3	Year 4	Year 5
Sales	100	106	120	158	205
Net Earnings	100	107	124	141	172

The trend percentages reveal that the growth in earnings outstripped the growth in sales for years 2 and 3, then fell below the sales growth in the last two years. We saw in our analysis of comparative statements that a disproportionate increase in operating expenses emerged in 19X5 (year 5). We might therefore analyze the 19X4 data to determine if net income was affected for the same reason or if the reduced growth was caused by other factors.

We must exercise care in interpreting trend percentages. Remember that all index percentages are related to the *base year.* Therefore, the change between the year 2 sales index (106%) and the year 3 sales index (120%) represents a 14% increase in terms of *base year* dollars. To express the increase as a percentage of year 2 dollars, we divide the 14% increase by the 106% year 2 sales index, to obtain an increase of 13%. We must also be careful to select a *representative* base year. For example, consider the following sales and earnings data during the identical period for a competing company (which we call Century Company):

Century Company
Annual Performance

	Year 1	Year 2	Year 3	Year 4	Year 5
Sales (millions of dollars)	$192.3	$204.4	$225.0	$299.0	$414.6
(Percentage of base year)	100	106	117	155	216
Net Earnings (millions of dollars)	$ 1.9	$ 3.0	$ 4.0	$ 6.5	$ 10.0
(Percentage of base year)	100	158	210	342	526

Note that Century Company's sales growth pattern is similar to Alliance Company's. When judged from trend percentages, however, the net earnings growth is over three times that of Alliance Company. Using an unrepresentative base year for Century Company—when earnings were depressed—makes the earnings trend misleading. In year 1, Century Company earned less than 1% of sales ($1.9/$192.3). But in the later years of the period, a more normal relationship between earnings and sales prevailed, and earnings were roughly $2–2\frac{1}{2}\%$ of sales. The earnings/sales relationship for Alliance Company was relatively normal in year 1.

Other data that the analyst may relate to sales and earnings over a period of years include total assets, plant investment, and expenditures for research and development.

EFFECT OF INFLATION As we saw in Chapter 13, financial information reported on a historical cost basis during a period of inflation may not portray economic reality. Comparisons made for a firm over time and with other firms may be deceptive. In the foregoing analysis, for example, sales and net earnings growth for Alliance Company would be considerably less if the data were adjusted for the effects of inflation. Many other relationships would likewise be distorted unless adjusted for inflation. Relationships between income statement items—such as sales—and balance sheet items may be distorted because the sales figure is expressed in current-year dollars, and inventories (especially LIFO inventories) and plant and equipment include dollar amounts of earlier price levels.

The financial analyst should therefore attempt to determine the effect of inflation on the data being examined. Certain inflation-adjusted operating data will be available for some companies because the FASB encourages its disclosure in supplementary form (see Chapter 13). When analyzing the financial reports of firms not making these disclosures, the analyst must make the necessary inquiries and estimates of the effects of inflation on the data.

Vertical Analysis

The relative importance of various items in financial statements for a single year can be highlighted by showing them as percentages of a key figure or total. Calculation of such percentages is particularly useful in presenting income statement data. For example, each item on the income statement may be shown as a percentage of the sales figure as illustrated in Exhibit 20–4 for Alliance Company's 19X5 income statement.

COMMON-SIZE STATEMENTS **Common-size financial statements,** prepared by the analyst, contain the percentages of a key figure alone, without the corresponding dollar figures. Common-size income statements for Alliance Company are compared with Century Company's in Exhibit 20–5.

We see from Exhibit 20–5 that Century Company has a smaller gross profit margin percentage than does Alliance Company. The disparity might be due either to lower sales prices or to higher production costs for Century Company. Selling and administrative expenses as a percentage of sales are fairly comparable, except that, combined, they are a higher percentage of the sales dollar for Alliance Company than for Century Company in 19X5. The interest expense as a percentage of sales in 19X5 is somewhat higher for Century Company than for Alliance Company. If we consider Century Company's low rate of net income to net sales (2.2% in 19X5), the interest percentage is significant. Yet Alliance Company's higher rate of return on sales (about double that of Century Company) is due mainly to its better gross profit margin.

We may also use common-size percentages to analyze balance sheet data, although less successfully than with income statement data. For example, if for a period of several years we state current assets and long-term assets as a percentage of total assets, we can determine whether a company is becoming more or less liquid. By determining each current asset's percentage of total current assets, we may observe any changes in these ingredients of working capital.

EXHIBIT 20–4

Alliance Company
Income Statement
For the Year Ended December 31, 19X5
(Thousands of Dollars)

Net Sales	$415,000	100.0%
Cost of Goods Sold	290,000	69.9
Gross Profit	$125,000	30.1%
Selling and Administrative Expenses:		
Selling Expenses	$ 39,500	9.5%
Administrative Expenses	49,640	12.0
Total	$ 89,140	21.5%
Income before Interest and Taxes	$ 35,860	8.6%
Interest Expense	3,000	0.7
Income before Income Taxes	$ 32,860	7.9%
Income Tax Expense	14,100	3.4
Net Income	$ 18,760	4.5%

EXHIBIT 20–5

Alliance and Century Companies
Common-size Income Statements
(Percentage of Net Sales)

	Alliance Company		Century Company	
	Year Ended Dec. 31, 19X5	Year Ended Dec. 31, 19X4	Year Ended Dec. 31, 19X5	Year Ended Dec. 31, 19X4
Net Sales	100.0%	100.0%	100.0%	100.0%
Cost of Goods Sold	69.9	71.9	73.8	74.9
Gross Profit	30.1%	28.1%	26.2%	25.1%
Selling and Administrative Expenses:				
Selling Expenses	9.5%	8.5%	8.6%	8.2%
Administrative Expenses	12.0	10.2	12.3	11.4
Total	21.5%	18.7%	20.9%	19.6%
Income before Interest and Taxes	8.6%	9.4%	5.3%	5.5%
Interest Expense	0.7	0.8	1.0	0.8
Income before Income Taxes	7.9%	8.6%	4.3%	4.7%
Income Tax Expense	3.4	3.8	2.1	2.3
Net Income	4.5%	4.8%	2.2%	2.4%

The best use of common-size statements with balance sheet data is probably with the sources of capital (equities). The proportions of the total capital supplied by short-term creditors, long-term creditors, preferred stockholders, and common stockholders of Alliance Company are shown below for 19X5:

	Amount (Millions of Dollars)	Common-size Percentage
Current debt	$ 57.7	30
Long-term debt	25.0	13
Preferred stock equity	8.0	4
Common stock equity	101.6	53
	$192.3	100

These percentages reveal that 53% of Alliance Company's capital is supplied by the common shareholders and 47% by preferred stockholders and creditors. We will discover shortly that such percentages are useful in appraising the financial structure of a firm.

ANALYSIS OF OPERATING PERFORMANCE

In evaluating the operating performance of a firm, the analyst invariably uses **rate of return** analysis. This analysis, which deals with the firm's profitability, relates either the income before interest expense and income taxes or the net income to some base, such as average total assets, average stockholders' equity, or the year's sales. The resultant percentage can be compared with similar rates for the firm in past years or to other firms. The most important relationships are

1. Return on assets.
2. Return on common stockholders' equity.
3. Return on sales.

Return on Assets

The rate of return on the total assets, generally called *return on assets*, is probably one of the most useful measures of the firm's profitability and efficiency. It is calculated by dividing the year's income before deducting interest expense and income tax expense by the average total assets used during the year.

$$\text{Rate of Return on Assets} = \frac{\text{Income before Interest Expense and Income Taxes}}{\text{Average Total Assets}}$$

Because the return for a year is earned on assets used throughout the year and assets may vary during that time, we compute the return on the *average* amount of assets. We obtain the approximate average by summing the beginning and ending asset totals and dividing by two.

If the percentage is a true index of productivity and accomplishment, it should not be influenced by the manner in which the company is financed. Therefore, we use income before interest charges and tax expense as a measure of the dollar return in the numerator. As a result, we may compare the return for a company having a relatively high proportion of debt with that of a company using mostly owners' equity to finance its assets.

For example, assume that Company X and Company Y each have $5,000,000 in average total assets and that each has income of $700,000 before interest expense and taxes. Suppose that Company X has no interest-bearing debt but Company Y has $2,000,000 of 10% bonds payable outstanding. The bottom portions of the income statements of these two companies (rearranged to highlight the effect of interest and taxes) are shown in Exhibit 20–6 (for simplicity, we assume a 40% effective income tax rate).

Company X and Company Y earn the same percentage return—14%—on their assets ($700,000 income before interest and taxes divided by $5,000,000 average total assets). Company Y, however, is financed partially by bonds. Thus,

EXHIBIT 20–6

Partial Income Statements

	Company X	Company Y
Income before Interest Expense and Income Tax Expense	$700,000	$700,000
Interest Expense (10% of $2,000,000)	—	200,000
	$700,000	$500,000
Income Tax Expense (40%)	280,000	200,000
Net Income	$420,000	$300,000

its interest expense of $200,000 less a 40% tax benefit of $80,000 makes its final net income $120,000 less than that of Company X. This difference is due solely to the manner in which the two companies are financed and is unrelated to their *operational accomplishment*. For this reason, the return on assets is normally measured before interest and income taxes. We demonstrate later that judicious use of debt in financing may benefit the owners of a business.

The return on assets, sometimes called the **productivity ratio,** is useful for comparing similar companies operating in the same industry. It also aids management in gauging the effectiveness of its use of assets. When we consider this ratio along with such relationships as return on stockholders' equity and return on sales (explained below), we gain much insight about a firm's operating performance.

Alliance Company's return on assets for 19X5 and 19X4 is calculated below:

		19X5	19X4
Income before Interest Expense and Income Taxes		$ 35,860	$ 30,100
Total Assets:			
Beginning of Year	(a)	$163,800	$142,500
End of Year	(b)	192,300	163,800
Average [(a + b)/2]		178,050	153,150
Rate of Return on Average Assets		20.1%	19.7%

Return on Common Stockholders' Equity

The *rate of return on common shareholders' equity* is calculated using net income less preferred stock dividend requirements. This ratio measures the ultimate profitability of the investment to the common stockholders. Although the ratio can be figured before taxes, it is commonly done after taxes as follows:

$$\text{Rate of Return on Common Stockholders' Equity} = \frac{\text{Net Income} - \text{Preferred Dividend Requirements}}{\text{Average Common Stockholders' Equity}}$$

The return is earned on the stockholders' equity invested *throughout* the year. Because this amount varies during the year, we commonly approximate the average investment by summing the beginning and ending balances and dividing by two.

This rate of return for Alliance Company in 19X5 and 19X4 is calculated below:

		19X5	19X4
Net Income		$ 18,760	$15,400
Less: Preferred Dividend Requirements (10% of $8,000)		800	800
Common Stock Earnings		$ 17,960	$14,600
Common Stockholders' Equity:			
Beginning of Year	(a)	$ 81,400	$63,500
End of Year	(b)	101,600	81,400
Average [(a + b)/2]		91,500	72,450
Rate of Return on Common Stockholders' Equity		19.6%	20.2%

Return on Sales

Another important measure of operating performance is the *rate of return on the net sales* of a firm. The most commonly used version of this ratio is **net income to net sales.** When common-size percentages, or component percentages, are available with the income statement, return on sales equals the net income percentage, calculated as follows:

$$\text{Rate of Return on Sales} = \frac{\text{Net Income}}{\text{Net Sales}}$$

The calculations for Alliance Company are given below:

	19X5	19X4
Net Income	$ 18,760	$ 15,400
Net Sales	415,000	320,000
Rate of Return on Sales	4.5%	4.8%

Net income to net sales percentages are performance indexes used solely when studying similar companies in the same industry or when comparing different periods for the same company. The rate of return on sales varies widely from industry to industry. Some industries are characterized by low profit margins and high turnover of principal assets. (The ratio of net sales to average total assets is called *asset turnover.*) For example, meat processing companies and supermarkets seldom have a net income to net sales ratio exceeding 2%. They have huge sales volumes, however, and turn over their assets (especially inventory) many times. In contrast, a company manufacturing and selling fine grand pianos might have an extremely high net income to net sales ratio. Because production capabilities of making pianos are inherently limited, turnover of assets is low. As a general rule, firms that deal in slow-moving products involving fairly long production periods require higher profit margins for a respectable rate of return on assets and on the owners' investments.

USING THE NET INCOME FIGURE

When analyzing the operating performance of a company, intelligent analysts make their own evaluations of a firm's reported net income. Because they are interested in the prospects for future income, they analyze carefully the factors influencing the net income figure. If possible, they wish to determine which segments of the business contribute the most to net income and what the future prospects are for these segments. In this respect, the analysts' inquiries frequently lead to information sources other than the financial statements. However, an analyst can usually determine from the statements themselves (1) how representative the net income figure is and (2) whether it was determined by conservative accounting principles.

The analyst scrutinizes a firm's income statement to determine whether its net income is representative of its earning capability. Often, any unusual or nonrecurring items included in the determination of net income are eliminated for analytical purposes. Such items as gains and losses on sales of plant assets or securities, casualty losses, and the like, are either omitted or apportioned to a number of years' income calculations.

The analyst also examines such factors as inventory pricing techniques and depreciation methods (and rates) to determine their effect on net income. The analyst wants to know whether the company's net income falls in the low (conservative) or high side of the spectrum of possible amounts. Once this is determined, the analyst may develop a more informed evaluation of a company's operating performance, stock values, growth potential, and so on.

Earnings per Share

Because stock market prices are quoted on a per-share basis, it is useful to calculate a firm's earnings on the same basis. *Earnings per share* for common stock are usually prominent in reports because both analysts and investors consider the relationship of prices and earnings to be quite important. An independent public accountant computing earnings per share for reporting purposes should follow procedures described in Accounting Principles Board *Opinion No. 15*, "Earnings Per Share." We discussed these procedures in Chapter 16.

Analysts may use the earnings-per-share figures that are available in annual reports—if they find such computations meaningful—or they may compute their own figures. We compute earnings per share by dividing common stock earnings (net income less any preferred dividend requirements) by the average number of shares outstanding during the year, as follows:[1]

$$\text{Earnings per Share} = \frac{\text{Net Income} - \text{Preferred Dividend Requirements}}{\text{Average Number of Common Shares Outstanding}}$$

The following calculations are made for Alliance Company:

		19X5	19X4
Net Income		$18,760	$15,400
Less: Preferred Dividend Requirements (10% of $8,000)		800	800
Common Stock Earnings		$17,960	$14,600
Common Shares Outstanding:			
Beginning of Year	(a)	2,800	2,800
End of Year	(b)	4,000	2,800
Average [(a + b)/2]		3,400	2,800
Earnings per Share		$5.28	$5.21

Alliance Company's earnings per share increased only slightly in 19X5 because a large number of additional shares were issued during the year.

Price–Earnings Ratio

The **price–earnings ratio** is the result of dividing the market price of a share of stock by the earnings per share. For many analysts and investors, this ratio is an important tool in assessing stock values. For example, after evaluating the strong and weak points of several companies in an industry, the analyst may compare price–earnings ratios to determine the "best buy."

When determining the price–earnings ratio, we customarily use the latest market price and the common stock earnings for the last four quarters of a company's operations. In our calculation for Alliance Company, we use 19X5 common stock earnings and the market price at year-end, $37.50.

$$\text{Price–Earnings Ratio} = \frac{\text{Market Price per Common Share}}{\text{Common Stock Earnings per Share}} = \frac{\$37.50}{\$5.28} = 7.1$$

[1] Analysts usually use the number of shares outstanding at year-end in this calculation. However, the average number of shares outstanding during the year is a more meaningful figure. The Accounting Principles Board suggests the use of a weighted average that takes into account the periods during which various amounts of stock were outstanding.

In other words, the market price of a share of Alliance Company common stock was approximately seven times the amount that share earned for the year. By itself, this multiplier is not particularly meaningful, although price–earnings ratios well below 10 often indicate a depressed market price. A prospective investor might compare this ratio with that of Century Company or with the average for the (electronic accessories) industry. Coupled with a fair evaluation of the strengths and weaknesses of several investment prospects and some knowledge of the industry itself, the price–earnings ratio might indicate whether the stock is overvalued in the market or an attractive investment.

Yield and Dividend Payout

Investors' expectations vary a great deal with personal economic circumstances and with the overall economic outlook. Some investors are more interested in the price appreciation of a stock investment than in present income in the form of dividends. When shares are disposed of in the future, only part of the gains may be taxed under the capital gains provision of the income tax laws, whereas dividends are fully taxable. Other investors are more concerned with dividends than with price appreciation. Such investors desire a high **yield**—or dividend rate of return—on their investments. Yield is normally calculated by dividing the current annual dividends per share by the current price of the stock. For Alliance Company, we use the 19X5 dividends and the year-end price per share to calculate yield, as follows:

$$\text{Dividend Yield} = \frac{\text{Common Dividends per Share}}{\text{Market Price per Share}} = \frac{\$1.44}{\$37.50} = 3.8\%$$

Investors who emphasize the yield on their investments may also be interested in a firm's **dividend payout ratio,** which is the percentage of the common stock earnings paid out in dividends. The payout ratio indicates whether a firm has a conservative or a liberal dividend policy and may also indicate whether the firm is conserving funds for internal financing of growth. For Alliance Company, we calculate the payout ratio for 19X5 as follows:

$$\text{Dividend Payout Ratio} = \frac{\text{Common Dividends per Share}}{\text{Common Stock Earnings per Share}} = \frac{\$1.44}{\$5.28} = 27.3\%$$

Both the yield and the dividend payout ratio for the common shares of Alliance Company were relatively low in 19X5. The firm has embarked on an expansion program and is conserving funds to finance acquisitions internally.

Low payout ratios can have a depressing effect on the market price of a stock, and reducing the payout ratio may have a dramatic effect on the stock price. For example, General Motors once reduced its payout ratio by cutting its year-end dividend, and within two weeks the common stock price skidded down 10%.

Payout ratios for typical, seasoned industrial corporations vary between 40% and 60%. Many corporations, however, need funds for internal financing of growth and pay out little or nothing in dividends. At the other extreme, some companies—principally utility companies—may pay out as much as 80% or 90% of their earnings. Utilities have less need of retaining funds for growth because the bulk of their financing is through long-term debt. They are said to "trade on the equity" to a large extent. We discuss this idea in greater detail in the next section.

RAIDERS HELP PUT SPOTLIGHT ON STOCK-PICKING METHOD

Thanks partly to corporate raiders, an obscure stock-picking tool is getting increased attention.

Known as the price–sales ratio, or PSR, it is a company's stock price divided by its sales revenue per share. If a company's stock is trading at $35 a share and the company's sales revenue per share works out to $50, the PSR is 0.70.

The people who use the ratio are bargain hunters. They seek low PSR companies that are (temporarily, they hope) unpopular. In general, a ratio of 0.50 or less is considered potential bargain material, and 1.00 or more is considered high. But what's low for an aerospace company would be high for a supermarket.

Companies often have low PSRs because of anemic profit margins—earnings as a percent of sales. But a potential acquirer may figure it can "clean [the company] up a little bit and increase the bottom line," says Norman Weinger, director of special research at Oppenheimer & Co.

"People like [Donald] Trump, the Bass brothers, the Tisches or the Pritzkers have always looked" for companies whose stock market valuation was small compared to their sales, says Mr. Weinger. He thinks the PSR is "more important now than it was before" because the stock market is increasingly dominated by takeover activity.

Besides being raider bait, low PSR companies are possible turnaround candidates. Those two factors may help explain why several academic studies have suggested that low PSR stocks outperform others.

In Search of Bargains

Stocks with lowest price–sales ratios* in selected industries

Airlines	
NWA	0.5
Delta Air Lines	0.6
Texas Air	0.6
Auto and Truck	
Chrysler	0.3
Ford Motor	0.4
General Motors	0.4
Department Stores	
Sears Roebuck	0.5
May Dept. Stores	0.6
J.C. Penney	0.7
Grocery Stores	
Great A&P	0.2
Winn-Dixie	0.2
Kroger	0.2
Life Insurance	
Travelers	0.2
Aetna Life & Casualty	0.3
Lincoln National	0.3
Oil	
Texaco	0.4
Ashland Oil	0.5
Mobil	0.5

*Stock price plus debt per share, divided by sales per share. Foreign stocks are excluded. Source: Portfolio Strategy, Oppenheimer & Co., Aug. 10, 1988.

TRADING ON THE EQUITY

The expression **trading on the equity** designates the use of borrowed funds, particularly long-term debt, in the capital structure of a firm. Trading *profitably* on the equity means that the borrowed funds generate a higher rate of return than the interest rate paid for the use of the funds. The excess, of course, accrues to the benefit of the common shareholders because it magnifies, or increases, their earnings. To illustrate, let us return to the example in Exhibit 20–6, in which both companies X and Y have assets of $5,000,000. Company X has its entire capital in common stockholders' equity, while Company Y has $2,000,000 in 10% bonds payable and $3,000,000 in common stockholders' equity. Both firms have $700,000 income before interest and taxes. For clarity, we repeat the net

In a study by Edwin Hansen and John Plotnicki at Colorado State University, about 1,000 stocks were analyzed over the period from 1967 to 1985. The 10% of stocks with the lowest PSRs provided superior performance in 13 of the 19 years. Their compound annual return was 30%, compared with 18% for the average stock studied.

Kenneth L. Fisher, a San Francisco money manager, began to popularize the use of PSRs about four years ago. He argues that they're superior in several ways to the more familiar price–earnings ratios published daily in newspaper stock tables.

For one thing, sales are less susceptible than earnings to accounting tricks. For another, many stocks don't have meaningful price–earnings ratios because they have scant or nonexistent earnings.

Mr. Fisher uses PSRs as the first step in picking stocks. "We're looking for a company that's not making the money now that it should be making, but is basically a good company," he says. "We see the world as looking for needles in haystacks. It takes a lot of time. We want to get rid of 95% of the haystack quickly." The PSR, he says, "tells you what not to buy."

Mr. Fisher's current favorites, selected partly for their low PSRs, include General Motors Corp., Sears, Roebuck & Co., Honeywell Inc., Fleetwood Enterprises Inc., Fieldcrest Cannon Inc. and American President Cos. "All [the PSR] does is measure popularity," Mr. Fisher says. "All I'm trying to do is buy unpopular stocks of good companies."

Al Frank, editor of the Prudent Speculator, a stock market newsletter, is also a fan of PSRs. But his process is the reverse of Mr. Fisher's: He looks at other variables first, then uses the PSR to help make up his mind. Among Mr. Frank's current selections are Computer Horizons Corp. with a PSR of 0.26, Integrated Resources Inc., 0.10, and Hofmann Industries Inc., 0.16.

Not all money managers endorse PSRs. One who has doubts is James Owen, managing director of NWQ Investment Management Co. in Los Angeles. Money managers today "depend too much on formula investing" and "computer-driven approaches," he says. Mr. Owen says picking stocks is an "art form" in which judgment is the most important factor. He distrusts any system that puts heavy reliance on a single variable. "Guys in our business have a need to find the keys to the kingdom," he says.

For his part, Mr. Weinger cautions that the ratio should only be used to compare stocks in the same industry. Supermarkets, for example, always have low profit margins and therefore low PSRs.

He also thinks it's vital to adjust the ratios for debt levels. Using the basic ratio alone, he says, Texas Air Corp. would look like a screaming bargain. Its stock sells for about eight cents for each dollar of sales.

But a potential acquirer would have to assume the airline's Texas-sized debt. Adjusted for that, the PSR becomes about 0.6, no better than Delta Air Lines Inc. and not as good as NWA Inc.

From John R. Dorfman, "Raiders Help Put Spotlight on Stock-Picking Method," *The Wall Street Journal*, October 20, 1988, p. C1. Reprinted by permission of *The Wall Street Journal*,

income calculation below, together with percentages earned on assets and on stockholders' equity.

	Company X	Company Y
Income before interest expense and income taxes	$700,000	$700,000
Interest expense (10% of $2,000,000)	—	200,000
	$700,000	$500,000
Income tax expense (40%)	280,000	200,000
Net income	$420,000	$300,000
Return on assets:		
For both companies: $700,000/$5,000,000 =	14%	14%
Return on stockholders' equity:		
For Company X: $420,000/$5,000,000 =	8.4%	
For Company Y: $300,000/$3,000,000 =		10%

Note that Company Y achieved a higher return on its stockholders' investment than did Company X. We account for this additional 1.6% on stockholders' equity as follows:

14% earned on $2,000,000 borrowed	$280,000
10% interest paid for use of funds	200,000
Trading on equity gain before income tax	$ 80,000
Less: 40% income tax	32,000
Trading on equity gain after taxes	48,000
$48,000 gain ÷ $3,000,000 stockholders' equity =	1.6%

Because Company Y earned 14% on its assets (including the $2,000,000 borrowed) and paid only 10% on the money borrowed, it had an $80,000 gain before income taxes. After deducting 40% for taxes, the gain was $48,000. The after-tax gain of $48,000 is a 1.6% return on the stockholders' equity of $3,000,000. Magnifying gains for the shareholders in this manner is sometimes referred to as the use of **leverage.**

Leverage in the capital structure must be used judiciously because some risk is involved. Leverage can also magnify losses. Suppose that income before interest expense and taxes had been only $300,000, representing a 6% return on the assets of $5,000,000. The after-tax return for Company Y would be only $60,000 [$300,000 − ($200,000 interest + $40,000 taxes)]. The return on stockholders' equity would then be only 2% ($60,000/$3,000,000) compared with a return of 3.6% for Company X ($300,000 − $120,000 taxes = $180,000; $180,000/$5,000,000 = 3.6%).

In general, companies with stable earnings can afford more debt in their capital structure than those with fluctuating earnings. Because of their stable earnings, utility companies may have as much as 70% of their financial structure in debt, whereas most industrial companies rarely have more than 50% debt financing.

ANALYSIS OF FINANCIAL STRENGTH

Because the ultimate source of any company's financial strength is its earning power, our discussion has stressed the operating performance and earning power of the business firm. However, certain other relationships in the financial statements give the analyst insight into the financial strength of a company. The first of these relationships concerns the company's financial structure and its fixed charges. The second relates to the company's working capital position.

Equity Ratio

To determine the manner in which a company is financed, we calculate the **equity ratio,** which is the common stockholders' equity divided by the company's total assets.

$$\text{Equity Ratio} = \frac{\text{Common Stockholders' Equity}}{\text{Total Assets}}$$

We commonly use year-end balances for the elements in this ratio rather than averages because we are interested in the capital structure at a particular point in time. The calculations for Alliance Company are as follows:

	19X5	19X4
Common Stockholders' Equity	$101,600	$ 81,400
Total Assets	$192,300	$163,800
Equity Ratio	53.0%	49.7%

The equity ratio is readily available in common-size percentages calculated from the balance sheet (see page 758). At the close of 19X5, 53% of Alliance Company's capital was provided by common shareholders and 47% by debtors and preferred shareholders. Because the analyst's concern is whether the company may be trading on the equity too heavily, the equity ratio indicates the extent of the firm's borrowing in relation to its assets.

When we analyze a firm's leverage, we may question the treatment of any preferred stock outstanding. Remember that the dividends on ordinary preferred stock are not a fixed charge, such as bond interest, but a contingent charge—contingent on a declaration by the firm's board of directors. Despite this fact, most analysts treat regular preferred stock as debt when examining a company's long-term position. They evidently feel that preferred dividends should be treated as a fixed charge, because ordinarily such dividends must be paid before distributions are made to common shareholders. Usually, preferred stock is included with stockholders' equity *for analytical purposes* only when the preferred stock is convertible into common and is likely to be converted in the near future.

Although no explicit rules of thumb or standards exist for equity ratios, the analyst may have a general idea of what a company's financial structure should be. An equity ratio that falls outside the analyst's subjective range of percentages will be investigated further.

Bond Interest Coverage

To evaluate further the size of a company's debt, an analyst may observe the relationship of interest charges to earnings. For example, an extremely low equity ratio for a company may indicate heavy borrowing. However, if its earnings are sufficient, even in poor years, to meet the interest charges on the debt several times over, the analyst may regard the situation quite favorably.

Analysts, particularly long-term creditors, almost always calculate the **bond interest coverage,** sometimes called **times interest earned.** This ratio is determined by dividing the income before bond interest and income taxes by the annual bond interest:

$$\text{Bond Interest Coverage} = \frac{\text{Income before Interest Expense and Income Taxes}}{\text{Annual Bond Interest}}$$

The computations for Alliance Company are as follows:

	19X5	19X4
Income before Interest Expense and Income Taxes	$35,860	$30,100
Annual Bond Interest (12% of Bonds Payable)	$ 3,000	$ 2,400
Times Interest Earned	12.0	12.5

In other words, Alliance Company's income available to meet interest charges each year was approximately 12 times the amount of its interest expense. Obviously, Alliance Company has an exceptionally good margin of safety. Generally speaking, a company that earns its interest several times before taxes in its poor years is regarded as a satisfactory risk by long-term creditors.

Preferred Dividend Coverage

Quite naturally, preferred stockholders would like some assurance that dividends will continue to be paid. They may therefore wish to calculate the **preferred dividend coverage.** To compute the number of times preferred dividends are earned, we divide income before interest and income taxes by the sum of the annual bond interest and preferred dividend requirements, as follows:

$$\text{Preferred Dividend Coverage} = \frac{\text{Income before Interest Expense and Income Taxes}}{\text{Annual Bond Interest} + \text{Preferred Dividend Requirements}}$$

The following calculations for Alliance Company show ample protection for the preferred dividends:

	19X5	19X4
Income before Interest Expense and Income Taxes	$35,860	$30,100
Annual Bond Interest	$ 3,000	$ 2,400
Preferred Dividend Requirements	800	800
	$ 3,800	$ 3,200
Times Preferred Dividends Earned	9.4	9.4

The preferred dividend requirement is combined with the bond interest in the calculations because bond interest is a prior charge against earnings—that is, it must be paid before any preferred dividends are distributed.[2] An inexperienced analyst may calculate the preferred dividend coverage by dividing net income after income taxes by the dividend requirement. If we did this for Alliance Company in 19X5, the result would be a coverage of 23.5 times ($18,760/$800). This result is obviously absurd, since the bond interest coverage is only 12 times. Inasmuch as bond interest is a prior charge, the protection for dividends on a junior security such as preferred stock cannot be better than the protection for the bond interest.

Analysis of Working Capital Position

A firm's *working capital* is the difference between its current assets and current liabilities. Adequate working capital enables a firm to meet its current obligations on time and take advantage of available discounts. Shortages of working capital can sometimes force a company into disadvantageous borrowing at inopportune times and unfavorable interest rates and can also affect its ability to pay interest and dividends. Many long-term debt contracts contain provisions that require the borrowing firm to maintain an adequate (or *defensive*) working capital position.

Analysis of a firm's working capital, or *current position,* involves looking at the firm's current assets and current liabilities and relating various elements to other accounts, such as sales and cost of goods sold. In the remainder of this chapter we examine the current position of Alliance Company, whose working capital in 19X5 (in thousands of dollars) was $87,800 ($145,500 current assets − $57,700 current liabilities).

---

[2]Because bond interest is tax deductible and preferred dividends are not, some analysts place the dividends on the same basis as the interest by dividing them by (1 − tax rate). With a 40% tax rate, the dividends would be $1,333. We have ignored this technicality in our discussion.

The adequacy of a firm's working capital is indicated in its relation to sales and in the ratio between current assets and current debt. Compare the following sets of 19X5 data for Alliance Company and Century Company:

	(Thousands of Dollars)	
	Alliance	**Century**
Current Assets	$145,500	$139,549
Current Liabilities	57,700	90,136
Working Capital	$ 87,800	$ 49,413
Sales	$415,000	$414,644

In this example, the ratio of sales to working capital (called **working capital turnover**) is 4.7 for Alliance ($415,000/$87,800) and 8.4 for Century ($414,644/$49,413). We might wonder about this disparity. How much working capital should support a given amount of sales? We can determine which of the two companies has a better defensive position by calculating the current ratio.

CURRENT RATIO The **current ratio** is simply the current assets divided by the current liabilities.

$$\text{Current Ratio} = \frac{\text{Current Assets}}{\text{Current Liabilities}}$$

This ratio is a measure of a firm's ability to meet its current obligations on time and to have funds readily available for current operations. The calculations below show that Alliance Company improved its position in 19X5 and has a current ratio of 252%.

	19X5	**19X4**
Current Assets	$145,500	$122,200
Current Liabilities	$ 57,700	$ 54,400
Current Ratio	2.52	2.25

This represents a better current position than that of Century Company, which had a ratio of only 155% ($139,549/$90,136). Century Company's working capital may be too small to support its volume of sales.

For many years, some short-term creditors have relied on a rule of thumb that the current ratio for industrial companies should exceed 200%. This arbitrary guideline probably developed from the premise that, because inventories frequently amount to as much as one-half of current assets, the remaining, more liquid current assets should at least equal the current debt. The rule is not completely reliable, since many companies have operated successfully with lower current ratios. Nonetheless, the 200% can be used as a general guide. When a company's current ratio is low, the analyst should attempt to determine if the situation is temporary and if the company has access to a line of credit so that refinancing can be accomplished easily in the event of difficulty.

QUICK RATIO Sometimes analysts calculate the ratio between the liquid, or *quick*, current assets and the current liabilities, called the **quick ratio.** Quick current assets are cash, marketable securities, and receivables. Compared with the current ratio, the main item omitted is inventory. Prepaid items are also omitted, but they are usually not material in amount. The quick ratio may give a better picture than the current ratio of a company's ability to meet current debts and to take advantage of discounts offered by creditors. The quick ratio and the current ratio together indicate the influence of the inventory figure in the company's working capital position. For example, a company might have an acceptable current ratio, but if its quick ratio falls much below 100%, the analyst might be uneasy about the size of the inventory and analyze the inventory position more carefully. Again, the 100% rule of thumb for the quick ratio is an arbitrary standard used only to alert the analyst to the need for further scrutiny.

We calculate the quick ratio for Alliance Company as follows:

$$\text{Quick Ratio} = \frac{\text{Cash} + \text{Marketable Securities} + \text{Receivables}}{\text{Current Liabilities}}$$

	19X5	19X4
Cash, Marketable Securities, and Receivables	$68,600	$58,600
Current Liabilities	$57,700	$54,400
Quick Ratio	1.19	1.08

INVENTORY TURNOVER An analyst concerned about a company's inventory position may compute the company's average **inventory turnover.** This figure indicates whether the inventory amount is disproportionate to the amount of sales. Excessive inventories not only tie up company funds and increase storage costs but may also lead to subsequent losses if the goods become outdated or unsaleable. The computation always involves dividing some measure of sales volume by a measure of the typical inventory level. Most accountants use cost of goods sold as a measure of sales volume and the average inventory for the year as a measure of the typical inventory level, as follows:

$$\text{Inventory Turnover} = \frac{\text{Cost of Goods Sold}}{\text{Average Inventory}}$$

Using this measure for Alliance Company gives the following results:

		19X5	19X4
Cost of Goods Sold		$290,000	$230,000
Beginning Inventory	(a)	$ 63,000	$ 48,000
Ending Inventory	(b)	76,000	63,000
Average Inventory [(a + b)/2]		69,500	55,500
Inventory Turnover		4.17	4.14

We use cost of goods sold in the calculation because the inventory measure in the denominator is a *cost* figure; we should therefore use a cost figure in the numerator. However, many credit agencies and analysts commonly use the sales amount instead of cost of goods sold to calculate inventory turnover. Calculated in this manner, Alliance Company's turnover is 5.97 times in 19X5. Analysts who compare a firm's inventory turnover with industry averages computed in this manner should use the sales figure in the calculations.

Usually, the average inventory is obtained by adding the year's beginning and ending inventories and dividing by two. Since inventories taken at the beginning and end of the year are likely to be lower than the typical inventory, an unrealistically high turnover ratio may result. We should use a 12-month average if monthly inventory figures are available. Furthermore, we should be careful in calculating inventory turnover ratios for companies that use last-in, first-out inventory measurement methods. In calculating inventory turnover, company management may restate the inventories at current prices using price indexes or other available data. Outside analysts may not be able to make such adjustments and may have to make some subjective allowance for overstatement of turnover.

A low inventory turnover can, of course, result from an overextended inventory position or from inadequate sales volume. For this reason, appraisal of inventory turnover should be accompanied by scrutiny of the quick ratio and analysis of trends in both inventory and sales. Inventory turnover figures vary considerably from industry to industry, and analysts frequently compare a firm's experience with industry averages.

AVERAGE COLLECTION PERIOD We can measure the average quality of a firm's trade receivables by calculating the **average collection period.** This calculation, sometimes called *day's sales outstanding*, is made as follows:

$$\text{Average Collection Period} = \frac{\text{Trade Accounts Receivable}}{\text{Year's Sales}} \times 365$$

Note that this equation results from first calculating the average day's sales (Sales/365) and then dividing this figure into the accounts receivable balance to determine how many average days' sales are uncollected. In the computation, the numerator should be the year-end receivables before deducting the allowance for uncollectible accounts, and only credit sales should be in the denominator. In the following calculations, we assume that all of Alliance Company's sales were credit sales.

		19X5	19X4
Year-end Receivables (before allowance for uncollectible accounts)	(a)	$ 64,000	$ 54,000
Net Credit Sales	(b)	415,000	320,000
Average Collection Period [(a/b) × 365]		56 days	62 days

Analysts calculate the average collection period to discover whether the accounts receivable are slow or overdue. A rough rule of thumb sometimes used by credit agencies is that the average collection period should not exceed $1\frac{1}{3}$ times the net credit period. For example, the average collection period of a firm selling on 30-day net terms should probably not exceed 40 days.

LIMITATIONS OF FINANCIAL ANALYSIS

The ratios, percentages, and other relationships we have described in this chapter are merely the result of analytical techniques. They may only isolate areas requiring further investigation. Moreover, we must interpret them with due consideration to general economic conditions, conditions of the industry in which the companies operate, and the positions of individual companies within the industry.

We should also be aware of the inherent limitations of financial statement data. Problems of comparability are frequently encountered. Companies otherwise similar may use different accounting methods, which can cause problems in comparing certain key relationships. For instance, inventory turnover is different for a company using LIFO than for one using FIFO inventory costing. Inflation may distort certain computations, especially those resulting from horizontal analysis. For example, trend percentages calculated from unadjusted data may be deceptive. Sometimes, gains over time in sales, earnings, and other key figures disappear when the underlying data are adjusted for changes in price levels.

We must be careful even when comparing companies in a particular industry. Such factors as size, diversity of product, and mode of operations can make the firms completely dissimilar. Some firms, particularly conglomerates, are difficult to classify by industry. If segment information—particularly product-line data—is available, the analyst may compare the statistics for several industries. Often, trade associations such as the American Meat Institute prepare industry statistics that are stratified by size of firm or type of product, making analysis easier.

KEY POINTS FOR CHAPTER OBJECTIVES

1 Describe and illustrate horizontal analysis of financial statements (pp. 752–56).

- A common form of horizontal analysis is inspecting dollar and percentage changes in comparative financial statements for two or more years.
- Analyzing trend percentages of key figures, such as net sales, net income, and total assets for a number of years, related to a base year, is often useful.

2 Describe and illustrate vertical analysis of financial statements (pp. 756–58).

- Vertical analysis deals with the relationships of financial statement data for a single year.
- Common-size statements express items on a financial statement as a percentage of a key item, such as expressing income statement items as a percentage of net sales.

3 Explain measures for evaluating operating performance (pp. 758–61).

- *Return on assets:* Net income before interest and income tax expenses divided by average total assets for the year.
- *Return on common stockholders' equity:* Net income (less preferred dividends) divided by average common stockholders' equity for the year.
- *Return on sales:* Net income divided by net sales.

4 Discuss the use of earnings per share, price–earnings ratios, and dividend yields in evaluating a firm (pp. 761–64).

- *Earnings per share:* Common stock earnings divided by the year's average number of common shares outstanding.
- *Price–earnings ratio:* Year-end common stock price divided by earnings per share of common stock.
- *Dividend yield:* Common stock dividends per share divided by the year-end common stock price.

5 Define and illustrate *trading on the equity* (pp. 764–66).

- Trading on the equity refers to the use of borrowed capital and capital from preferred stock at lower rates than are generated by such capital, with the excess accruing to the common stockholders.

6 Explain measures for evaluating financial strength (pp. 766–71).

- Financial strength is measured by the *equity ratio* (common stockholders' equity divided by total assets), *bond interest coverage* (income before bond interest and tax expenses divided by bond interest expense), *preferred dividend coverage* (income before interest expense and income taxes divided by the sum of annual bond interest and preferred dividend requirements), and by the firm's current position.
- Current position is measured by the current ratio (current assets divided by current liabilities), *quick ratio* (the sum of cash, short-term investments, and receivables divided by current liabilities), *inventory turnover* (cost of goods sold divided by average inventory), and *average collection period for receivables* (year-end accounts receivable divided by year's sales times 365).

7 Discuss the limitations of financial analysis (pp. 771–72).

- When analyzing statements, one must be aware of the firm's accounting methods, the effects of inflation, and the difficulty of identifying a firm's industry classification.

KEY TERMS USED IN THIS CHAPTER

SELF-TEST QUESTIONS FOR REVIEW

(Answers are at the end of this chapter.)

All of the self-test questions are based on the following data:

Thermo Company
Balance Sheet
December 31, 19XX

Cash	$ 40,000	Current Liabilities	$ 80,000
Accounts Receivable (net of $2,000 Allowance for Uncollectible Accounts	80,000	10% Bonds Payable	120,000
Inventory	130,000	Common Stock	200,000
Plant and Equipment	250,000	Retained Earnings	100,000
	$500,000		$500,000

Net sales for the year were $800,000, gross profit was $320,000, and net income was $36,000. The income tax rate was 40%. A year ago inventory was $110,000, and common stockholders' equity was $260,000. The bonds payable were outstanding all year.

1. The current ratio of Thermo Company at 12/31, calculated from the above data, was 3.125, and the working capital was $170,000. If the firm paid $20,000 of its current liabilities, immediately after this transaction,
   (a) Both the current ratio and the working capital would decrease.
   (b) Both the current ratio and the working capital would increase.
   (c) The current ratio would increase, but the working capital would remain the same.
   (d) The current ratio would increase, but the working capital would decrease.
2. The firm's inventory turnover for the year is
   (a) 6.67 times (b) 4 times (c) 6 times (d) 3.69 times
3. The firm's return on common stockholders' equity was
   (a) 25.71% (b) 12.86% (c) 17.14% (d) 21.43%
4. The firm's average collection period for receivables was
   (a) 36.5 days (b) 37.41 days (c) 35.59 days (d) 18.25 days
5. The firm's bond interest coverage for the year was
   (a) 4 times (b) 3 times (c) 5 times (d) 6 times

DEMONSTRATION PROBLEM FOR REVIEW

Knox Instruments, Inc., is a manufacturer of various medical and dental instruments. Financial statement data for the firm are given below.

	(Thousands of Dollars)
This Year:	
Net Sales	$200,000
Net Income (after income taxes)	9,750
Dividends	4,000
Interest Expense	2,000
Income Taxes	5,250

Knox Instruments, Inc.
Balance Sheets
(Thousands of Dollars)

Assets	Dec. 31, This Year	Dec. 31, Last Year
Cash	$ 3,200	$ 3,000
Accounts Receivable (net of allowance for uncollectible accounts of $1,100 last year and $1,200 this year)	26,800	27,700
Inventory	55,000	32,000
Total Current Assets	$ 85,000	$62,700
Long-term Assets	35,000	29,300
Total Assets	$120,000	$92,000
Liabilities and Stockholders' Equity		
Current Liabilities	$ 35,000	$28,750
10% Bonds Payable	20,000	14,000
Total Liabilities	$ 55,000	$42,750
Common Stock, $100 Par Value	$ 41,000	$31,000
Retained Earnings	24,000	18,250
Total Stockholders' Equity	$ 65,000	$49,250
Total Liabilities and Stockholders' Equity	$120,000	$92,000

REQUIRED

(a) Using the given data, Calculate items 1 through 8 for this year. Compare the performance of Knox Instruments, Inc., with the industry averages given below and comment on its operations.

	Median Ratios for the Industry
1. Current ratio.	3.03
2. Quick ratio.	1.20
3. Average collection period.	59 days
4. Net sales to ending inventory.	4.9 times
5. Equity ratio.	52.0%
6. Return on assets.	18.6%
7. Return on stockholders' equity.	10.9%
8. Return on sales.	4.2%

(b) Calculate the dividends paid per share of common stock. (Use average number of shares outstanding during the year.) What was the payout ratio?

(c) If the most recent price per share of common stock is $150, what is (1) the price–earnings ratio? (2) the dividend yield?

SOLUTION TO DEMONSTRATION PROBLEM

(a) 1. Current Ratio $= \dfrac{\$85{,}000}{\$35{,}000} = 2.43$

2. Quick Ratio $= \dfrac{\$30{,}000}{\$35{,}000} = 0.86$

3. Average Collection Period $= \dfrac{\$28{,}000^*}{\$200{,}000} \times 365 = 51.1$ days

*$26,800 + $1,200

4. Net Sales to Ending Inventory $= \dfrac{\$200{,}000}{\$55{,}000} = 3.64$ times

(Note: This formula for inventory turnover is used because the median industry turnover figure was calculated in this manner.)

5. Equity Ratio $= \dfrac{\$65{,}000}{\$120{,}000} = 54.17\%$

6. Return on Assets $= \dfrac{\$9{,}750 + \$2{,}000 + \$5{,}250}{(\$120{,}000 + \$92{,}000)/2} = 16.04\%$

7. Return on Stockholders' Equity $= \dfrac{\$9{,}750}{(\$65{,}000 + \$49{,}250)/2} = 17.07\%$

8. Return on Sales $= \dfrac{\$9{,}750}{\$200{,}000} = 4.88\%$

Although the firm's current ratio, 2.43, is below the industry median, it is still acceptable. However, the quick ratio, 0.86%, is far below the industry median. This indicates that the inventory (which is omitted from this calculation) is excessive; this is borne out by the firm's inventory turnover of 3.64 times, which compares with the industry median of 4.9 times. The firm's return on assets is slightly below the industry median, but the return on stockholders' equity is far higher than the industry median. Also, the firm's return on sales, 4.88%, is better than the industry median, as is the average collection period.

(b) Average number of shares outstanding = (410,000 + 310,000)/2 = 360,000 shares.
$4,000,000 dividends/360,000 shares = $11.11 dividends per average share.
Payout ratio = $4,000,000 dividends/$9,750,000 net income = 41.03%.

(c) Earnings per share = $9,750,000/360,000 shares = $27.08.
Price–earnings ratio = $150/$27.08 = 5.54.
Dividend yield = $11.11/$150 = 7.41%.

QUESTIONS

20–1 What are trend percentages, and how are they calculated? What pitfalls must an analyst avoid when preparing trend percentages?

20–2 Distinguish between horizontal analysis and vertical analysis of financial statements.

20–3 The following data are taken from the income statements of the Mason Company. Using year 1 as the base year, calculate trend percentages.

	Year 1	Year 2	Year 3	Year 4
Sales	$600,000	$680,000	$720,000	$750,000
Earnings	25,000	28,100	30,200	34,300

20–4 During the past year, Woods Company had net income of $3 million, and Collins Company had net income of $7 million. Both companies manufacture electrical components for the building trade. What additional information would you need to compare the profitability of the two companies? Discuss your answer.

20–5 Under what circumstances can return on sales be used to appraise the profitability of a company? Can this ratio be used to compare the profitability of companies from different industries? Explain.

20–6 Why do we calculate the rate of return on assets? Give reasons why the income measure used in this calculation is not reduced for interest or income taxes.

20–7 What does the rate of return on common stockholders' equity measure? Why are interest expense and income taxes deducted from the income measure in this ratio?

20–8 What are common-size percentages, and how are they used?

20–9 Verity, Inc., earned $7.50 per share of common stock in the current year and paid dividends of $3.00 per share. The most recent market price of the common stock is $48 per share. Calculate (a) the price–earnings ratio, (b) the dividend yield, and (c) the dividend payout ratio.

20–10 Explain, by giving an example, what is meant by *trading on the equity*.

20–11 Why is it dangerous for a company with unstable earnings to trade heavily on the equity?

20–12 Discuss the significance of the equity ratio, and explain how it is computed.

20–13 Why do we determine bond interest coverage, and how is it calculated?

20–14 List three important ratios for evaluating the current position of a firm, and state how they are used.

20–15 What is meant by the *yield* on a common stock investment? Give an example of a computation of yield.

20–16 Utility companies have a high "payout" ratio compared with industrial companies. What is meant by a *payout ratio*? Why would utility companies continue high payout ratios?

EXERCISES

In the following exercises, inventory turnover is calculated using cost of goods sold in the numerator.

Comparative and common-size statements

20–17 Consider the following income statement data from the Arrow Company for this year and last year:

	This Year	Last Year
Sales	$640,000	$520,000
Cost of Goods Sold	403,200	317,200
Selling Expenses	121,600	104,000
General Expenses	70,400	67,600
Income Tax Expense	6,720	5,100

(a) Prepare a comparative income statement, showing increases and decreases in dollars and in percentages.
(b) Prepare common-size income statements for each year.
(c) Comment briefly on the changes between the two years.

Current ratio and working capital

20–18 Bryant Company has a current ratio of 240% (2.4:1) on December 31 of the current year. On that date its current assets are as follows:

Cash		$ 65,000
Accounts Receivable	$123,000	
Less: Allowance for Uncollectible Accounts	8,000	115,000
Merchandise Inventory		170,000
Prepaid Expenses		10,000
		$360,000

(a) What is the firm's working capital on December 31?
(b) What is the quick ratio on December 31?

(c) If the company pays a current note payable of $30,000 immediately after December 31, how does the transaction affect the current ratio? Working capital?

Collection of receivables and inventory turnover

20–19 Bryant Company, whose current assets are shown in Exercise 20–18, had net sales of $980,000 during the current year. The beginning inventory for the year was $150,000. Cost of goods sold for the year amounted to $560,000.

(a) What was the average collection period for receivables?

(b) What was the average inventory turnover for the year?

Current ratio and working capital

20–20 The following data are taken from a recent quarterly report of Dow Jones & Company, Inc., publishers of *The Wall Street Journal* and *Barron's*. Calculate the working capital and the current ratio.

Current Assets	$248,791,000
Current Liabilities:	
Accounts Payable and Accrued Liabilities	$153,173,000
Income Taxes Payable	36,116,000
Unexpired Subscriptions	153,870,000
Total Current Liabilities	$343,159,000

Does any of this data suggest a modification of the normal way in which the working capital and the current ratio are calculated?

Earnings and dividend ratios

20–21 Kirk Corporation pays a quarterly dividend of $2.50 per share of common stock. Its earnings after taxes during the past four quarters of operation were $3,200,000. The company has 200,000 shares of $100 par value common stock and 40,000 shares of $50 par value, 10% preferred stock outstanding. The current market price of the common shares is $123.

(a) Calculate the earnings per share for the common stock.

(b) Calculate the price–earnings ratio for the common stock.

(c) What is the current dividend yield on the common stock?

Long-term debt vs. stock financing

20–22 Nuline Company has total assets of $3,000,000 and earns an average of $300,000 before income taxes. Currently, the company has no long-term debt outstanding. The company needs an additional $1,000,000 in funds on which it plans to earn 18% before income taxes. It can borrow the money at 10% or issue additional common stock. The effective tax rate is 35%. The company has 20,000 shares of common stock outstanding. Calculate the earnings per share expected (a) if the additional funds are borrowed and (b) if an additional 8,000 shares are sold at $125 per share.

Various ratios

20–23 The following information is available for Baylor Company:

	Dec. 31, This Year	Dec. 31, Last Year
Total Assets	$6,000,000	$5,400,000
Current Liabilities	$1,200,000	$ 900,000
10% Bonds Payable	1,500,000	1,500,000
Common Stock ($100 Par Value)	2,500,000	2,500,000
Retained Earnings	800,000	500,000
	$6,000,000	$5,400,000

For this year, net sales amounted to $8,200,000, and net income was $455,000. The income tax rate was 35%. Calculate the following for this year:

(a) Return on assets.

(b) Return on common stockholders' equity.

(c) Return on sales.

(d) Bond interest coverage.

(e) Equity ratio.

PROBLEMS

Note: Unless otherwise indicated, inventory turnover is calculated using cost of goods sold in the numerator in the following problems.

Trend percentages

20–24 Net sales, net income, and total asset figures for Spectrum Paint, Inc., for five consecutive years are given below:

	Annual Amounts (Thousands of Dollars)				
	Year 1	**Year 2**	**Year 3**	**Year 4**	**Year 5**
Net Sales	$61,500	$67,350	$76,080	$82,780	$91,520
Net Income	2,780	2,983	3,542	4,305	4,668
Total Assets	37,700	39,440	43,580	46,860	49,800

REQUIRED

(a) Calculate trend percentages, using year 1 as the base year.

(b) Calculate the return on sales for each year. (Rates above 3.5% are considered good for paint and varnish companies; rates above 5% are considered very good.)

(c) Comment on the results of your analysis.

Changes in various ratios

20–25 Selected information follows for Bravo Company, taken from the current year's and last year's financial statements:

	This Year	**Last Year**
Net Sales	$720,000	$640,000
Cost of Goods Sold	460,000	416,000
Bond Interest Expense	15,000	15,000
Income Tax Expense	10,000	8,000
Net Income (after income taxes)	40,000	32,000
Accounts Receivable, December 31 (before allowance for uncollectible accounts)	96,000	82,000
Inventory, December 31	170,000	150,000
Common Stockholders' Equity	340,000	320,000
Total Assets	560,000	480,000

REQUIRED

(a) Calculate the following ratios and relationships for this year. Last year's results are given for comparative purposes.

	Last Year
1. Return on assets.	12.2%
2. Return on sales.	5.0%
3. Return on common stockholders' equity (no preferred stock was outstanding).	10.5%
4. Average collection period.	46.8 days
5. Inventory turnover.	2.97 times
6. Bond interest coverage.	3.67 times

(b) Comment on the changes between the two years.

Ratios from comparative and common-size data

20–26 Consider the following financial statements for Delta Company for the past two years.

During the year just ended, management obtained additional bond financing to enlarge its production facilities. The company faced higher production costs during the year for such things as fuel, materials, and freight. Because of temporary government price controls, a planned price increase on products was delayed several months.

As a holder of both common and preferred stock, you analyze the financial statements for the past two years.

Delta Company
Balance Sheets
(Thousands of Dollars)

	Dec. 31, This Year	Dec. 31, Last Year
Assets		
Cash	$ 13,000	$ 9,000
Accounts Receivable (net of allowance for uncollectible accounts)	38,000	28,000
Inventory	74,000	70,000
Prepaid Expenses	15,000	8,000
Plant and Other Assets (net)	315,000	272,000
	$455,000	$387,000
Liabilities and Stockholders' Equity		
Current Liabilities	$ 52,000	$ 49,000
10% Bonds Payable	150,000	100,000
9% Preferred Stock, $50 Par Value	50,000	50,000
Common Stock, $10 Par Value	150,000	150,000
Retained Earnings	53,000	38,000
	$455,000	$387,000

Delta Company
Income Statements
(Thousands of Dollars)

	This Year	Last Year
Sales	$540,000	$450,000
Cost of Goods Sold	356,400	288,000
Gross Profit	$183,600	$162,000
Selling and Administrative Expenses	115,600	101,250
Income before Interest Expense and Income Taxes	$ 68,000	$ 60,750
Bond Interest Expense	15,000	10,000
Income before Income Taxes	$ 53,000	$ 50,750
Income Tax Expense	15,500	11,750
Net Income	$ 37,500	$ 39,000

REQUIRED

(a) Calculate the following for each year: current ratio, quick ratio, inventory turnover (inventory was $66,000,000 two years ago), equity ratio, times interest earned, preferred dividend coverage, return on assets (total assets were $300,000,000 two years ago), and return on common stockholders' equity (common stock equity was $180,000,000 two years ago).

(b) Calculate common-size percentages for each year's income statement.

(c) Calculate the apparent amount of common dividends per share paid during the year just ended. (Use number of shares at year-end.)

(d) Comment on the results of your analysis.

Ratios compared with industry averages

20–27 Because you own both preferred and common stock of Kilgore Corporation, a manufacturer of paints and varnishes, you are analyzing the firm's performance for the most recent year. The following data are taken from the firm's last annual report.

	Dec. 31, This Year	Dec. 31, Last Year
Total Assets	$3,200,000	$2,800,000
Current Liabilities	$ 350,000	$ 300,000
12% Bonds Payable	800,000	800,000
10% Preferred Stock, $100 Par Value	250,000	250,000
Common Stock, $50 Par Value	1,500,000	1,200,000
Retained Earnings	300,000	250,000
Total Liabilities and Stockholders' Equity	$3,200,000	$2,800,000

For this year, net sales amount to $7,600,000, and net income is $370,500. The income tax rate is 35%.

REQUIRED

(a) Calculate the following for this year:
   1. Return on sales.
   2. Return on assets.
   3. Return on common stockholders' equity.
   4. Equity ratio.
   5. Bond interest coverage.
   6. Preferred dividend coverage.

(b) Trade association statistics and information provided by credit agencies reveal the following data on industry norms:

	Median	Upper Quartile
Return on sales	3.5%	5.7%
Return on assets	15.6	20.5
Return on stockholders' equity	11.2	20.5
Equity ratio	50.0	62.0

Compare Kilgore Corporation's performance with industry performance.

Constructing statements from ratio data

20–28 The following are the 19X8 financial statements for Alpha Company, with almost all dollar amounts missing.

Alpha Company
Balance Sheet
December 31, 19X8

Cash	$?	Current Liabilities	$?
Accounts Receivable (net of allowance for uncollectible accounts)	?	8% Bonds Payable	?
Inventory	?	Common Stock	?
Equipment (net)	?	Retained Earnings	280,000
Total Assets	$1,800,000	Total Liabilities and Stockholders' Equity	$1,800,000

Alpha Company
Income Statement
For the Year Ended December 31, 19X8

Net Sales	$?
Cost of Goods Sold	?
Gross Profit	?
Selling and Administrative Expenses	?
Income before Interest Expense and Income Taxes	?
Bond Interest Expense	?
Income before Income Taxes	?
Income Tax Expense (35%)	?
Net Income	$195,000

The following information is available about Alpha Company's 19X8 financial statements:

1. Quick ratio, 1.5:1.
2. Inventory turnover (inventory at January 1, 19X8 was $610,000), 4 times.
3. Return on sales, 5%.
4. Average collection period, 46.795 days. Allowance balance is $20,000. (Round Accounts Receivable balance to nearest $1,000.)
5. Gross profit rate, 30%.
6. Return on assets (total assets at January 1, 19X8 were $1,400,000), 20%.
7. Equity ratio, 60%.
8. The interest expense relates to the bonds payable that were outstanding all year.

REQUIRED
Compute the missing amounts, and complete the financial statements of Alpha Company. *Hint:* Complete the income statement first.

Ratios compared with industry averages

20–29 Stacey Plastics, Inc., manufactures various plastic and synthetic products. Financial statement data for the firm are as follows:

	(Thousands of Dollars)
This Year:	
Net Sales	$720,000
Net Income (after income taxes)	42,000
Dividends	15,000
Interest Expense	8,000
Income Tax Expense	23,000

Stacey Plastics, Inc.
Balance Sheets
(Thousands of Dollars)

	Dec. 31, This Year	Dec. 31, Last Year
Assets		
Cash	$ 18,500	$ 7,000
Accounts Receivable (net of allowance for uncollectible accounts of $3,200 last year and $4,000 this year)	86,500	52,000
Inventory	215,000	171,000
Total Current Assets	$320,000	$230,000
Plant Assets (net)	154,000	142,000
Other Assets	6,000	8,000
Total Assets	$480,000	$380,000

Liabilities and Stockholders' Equity		
Notes Payable—Banks	$ 3,000	$ 5,000
Accounts Payable	75,500	62,400
Income Tax Payable	7,400	5,600
Accrued Liabilities	34,600	24,500
Total Current Liabilities	$120,500	$ 97,500
Long-term Debt (10% Bonds Payable)	80,000	80,000
Total Liabilities	$200,500	$177,500
Common Stock, $100 Par Value	$200,000	$150,000
Retained Earnings	79,500	52,500
Total Stockholders' Equity	$279,500	$202,500
Total Liabilities and Stockholders' Equity	$480,000	$380,000

REQUIRED

(a) Using the given data, calculate items 1 through 8 below for this year. Compare the performance of Stacey Plastics, Inc., with industry averages (below, right), and comment on its operations.

	Median Ratios for Manufacturers of Plastic and Synthetic Products
1. Current ratio.	3.42
2. Quick ratio.	1.30
3. Average collection period.	51 days
4. Net sales to ending inventory.	5.3 times
5. Equity ratio.	52.6%
6. Return on assets.	19.1%
7. Return on stockholders' equity.	11.8%
8. Return on sales.	3.4%

(b) Calculate the dividends paid per share of common stock. (Use average number of shares outstanding during the year.) What was the payout ratio?

(c) If the most recent price per share of common stock is $152.50, what is the price–earnings ratio? The dividend yield?

ALTERNATE PROBLEMS

Note: Unless otherwise indicated, inventory turnover is calculated using cost of goods sold in the numerator in the following problems.

Trend percentages

20–24A Net sales, net income, and total asset figures for Monroe Meat Processing, Inc. for five consecutive years are given below:

	Annual Amounts (Thousands of Dollars)				
	Year 1	**Year 2**	**Year 3**	**Year 4**	**Year 5**
Net Sales	$560,000	$572,000	$621,000	$715,000	$754,000
Net Income	8,300	12,000	15,100	14,800	16,100
Total Assets	120,000	125,000	138,000	146,000	152,000

REQUIRED

(a) Calculate trend percentages, using year 1 as the base year.

(b) Calculate the return on sales for each year. (Rates above 1% are considered good for meat processing companies; rates above 1.5% are considered very good.)

(c) Comment on the results of your analysis.

Various ratios

20–25A Selected information follows for the Clayton Company, taken from the current year's and last year's financial statements:

	This Year	Last Year
Net Sales	$810,000	$720,000
Cost of Goods Sold	480,000	430,000
Bond Interest Expense	10,000	8,000
Income Tax Expense	11,500	9,000
Net Income (after income taxes)	45,000	36,000
Accounts Receivable, December 31 (before allowance for uncollectible accounts)	95,000	77,500
Inventory, December 31	126,000	110,000
Common Stockholders' Equity	280,000	240,000
Total Assets	480,000	390,000

REQUIRED

Calculate the following for this year:

(a) Return on assets.
(b) Return on sales.
(c) Return on common stockholders' equity (no preferred stock was outstanding).
(d) Average collection period.
(e) Inventory turnover.
(f) Bond interest coverage.

Ratios from comparative and common-size data

20–26A Consider the following financial statements for the Weston Company for the past two years.

During the year just ended, management obtained additional bond financing to enlarge its production facilities. The plant addition would produce a new high-margin product, which is supposed to improve the average rates of gross profit and return on sales.

As a holder of both common and preferred stock, you analyze the financial statements for the past two years.

Weston Company
Balance Sheets
(Thousands of Dollars)

	Dec. 31, This Year	Dec. 31, Last Year
Assets		
Cash	$ 21,000	$ 18,000
Accounts Receivable (net of allowance for uncollectible accounts)	29,000	14,000
Inventory	88,000	60,000
Prepaid Expenses	2,000	3,000
Plant and Other Assets (net)	385,000	355,000
	$525,000	$450,000
Liabilities and Stockholders' Equity		
Current Liabilities	$ 74,000	$ 38,000
10% Bonds Payable	150,000	125,000
8% Preferred Stock, $50 Par Value	50,000	50,000
Common Stock, $10 Par Value	200,000	200,000
Retained Earnings	51,000	37,000
	$525,000	$450,000

Weston Company
Income Statements
(Thousands of Dollars)

	This Year	Last Year
Sales	$700,000	$580,000
Cost of Goods Sold	448,000	388,600
Gross Profit	$252,000	$191,400
Selling and Administrative Expenses	192,000	147,400
Income before Interest Expense and Income Taxes	$ 60,000	$ 44,000
Bond Interest Expense	15,000	12,500
Income before Income Taxes	$ 45,000	$ 31,500
Income Tax Expense	15,000	10,500
Net Income	$ 30,000	$ 21,000

REQUIRED
(a) Calculate the following for each year: current ratio, quick ratio, inventory turnover (inventory was $56 million two years ago), equity ratio, times interest earned, preferred dividend coverage, return on assets (total assets were $410 million two years ago), and return on common stockholders' equity (common stock equity was $197 million two years ago).
(b) Calculate common-size percentages for each year's income statement.
(c) Calculate the apparent amount of common dividends per share paid during the year just ended.
(d) Comment on the results of your analysis.

Ratios compared with industry averages

20–27A You are analyzing the performance of Merrill Corporation for the most recent year. The following data are taken from the firm's last annual report.

	Dec. 31, This Year	Dec. 31, Last Year
Total Assets	$6,000,000	$5,250,000
Current Liabilities	$ 750,000	$ 600,000
10% Bonds Payable	1,500,000	1,500,000
10% Preferred Stock	750,000	750,000
Common Stock, $50 Par Value	2,500,000	2,225,000
Retained Earnings	500,000	175,000
Total Liabilities and Stockholders' Equity	$6,000,000	$5,250,000

For this year, net sales amount to $12,500,000, and net income is $637,000. The income tax rate is 35%.

REQUIRED
(a) Calculate the following for this year:
1. Return on sales.
2. Return on assets.
3. Return on common stockholders' equity.
4. Equity ratio.
5. Bond interest coverage.
6. Preferred dividend coverage.

(b) Trade association statistics and information provided by credit agencies reveal the following data on industry norms:

	Median	Upper Quartile
Return on sales	4.5%	6.09%
Return on assets	16.2	21.3
Return on stockholders' equity	12.5	19.4
Equity ratio	52.0	61.0

Compare Merrill Corporation's performance with industry performance.

Constructing statements from ratio data

20–28A The following are the 19X8 financial statements for Rhodes Company, with almost all dollar amounts missing:

Rhodes Company
Balance Sheet
December 31, 19X8

Cash	$?	Current Liabilities	$?
Accounts Receivable (net of allowance for uncollectible accounts)	?	10% Bonds Payable	?
Inventory	?	Common Stock	?
Equipment (net)	?	Retained Earnings	260,000
Total Assets	$2,000,000	Total Liabilities and Stockholders' Equity	$2,000,000

Rhodes Company
Income Statement
For the Year Ended December 31, 19X8

Net Sales	$?
Cost of Goods Sold	?
Gross Profit	?
Selling and Administrative Expenses	?
Income before Interest Expense and Taxes	?
Bond Interest Expense	?
Income before Income Taxes	?
Income Tax Expense (35%)	?
Net Income	$156,000

The following information is available about Rhodes Company's 19X8 financial statements:

1. Quick ratio, 1.2:1.
2. Inventory turnover (inventory at January 1, 19X8, was $480,000), 5.2 times.
3. Return on sales, 3.9%.
4. Average collection period, 39.97 days. Allowance balance is $10,000. (Round Accounts Receivable balance to nearest $1,000.)
5. Gross profit rate, 35%.

6. Return on assets (total assets at January 1, 19X8 were $1,600,000), 15%.
7. Equity ratio, 63%.
8. The interest expense relates to the bonds payable that were outstanding all year.

REQUIRED
Compute the missing amounts, and complete the financial statements of Rhodes Company. *Hint:* Complete the income statement first.

Ratios compared with industry averages

20–29A Amherst Instruments, Inc., is a manufacturer of various measuring and controlling instruments. Financial statement data for the firm are as follows:

	(Thousands of Dollars)
This Year:	
Net Sales	$190,000
Net Income (after income taxes)	9,100
Dividends	3,300
Interest Expense	2,000
Income Tax Expense	4,900

Amherst Instruments Inc.
Balance Sheets
(Thousands of Dollars)

	Dec. 31, This Year	Dec. 31, Last Year
Assets		
Cash	$ 2,200	$ 2,000
Accounts Receivable (net of allowance for uncollectible accounts of $1,300 last year and $1,200 this year)	24,800	27,700
Inventory	52,000	32,000
Total Current Assets	$ 79,000	$ 61,700
Long Term Assets (net)	29,700	28,300
Other Assets	1,300	1,000
Total Assets	$110,000	$ 91,000
Liabilities and Stockholders' Equity		
Notes Payable—Banks	$ 5,500	$ 4,000
Accounts Payable	16,000	12,000
Income Taxes Payable	1,900	1,000
Accrued Liabilities	10,500	10,800
Total Current Liabilities	$ 33,900	$ 27,800
Long-term Debt	21,100	14,000
Total Liabilities	$ 55,000	$ 41,800
Common Stock, $25 Par Value	$ 11,000	$ 11,000
Retained Earnings	44,000	38,200
Total Stockholders' Equity	$ 55,000	$ 49,200
Total Liabilities and Stockholders' Equity	$110,000	$ 91,000

REQUIRED
(a) Using the given data, calculate items 1 through 8 for this year. Compare the performance of Amherst Instruments, Inc., with industry averages (given below), and comment on its operations.

	Median Ratios for Manufacturers of Measuring and Controlling Instruments
1. Current ratio.	2.83
2. Quick ratio.	1.20
3. Average collection period.	64 days
4. Net sales to ending inventory.	4.1 times
5. Equity ratio.	47%
6. Return on assets.	12%
7. Return on stockholders' equity.	10.3%
8. Return on sales.	4%

(b) Calculate the dividends paid per share of common stock. What was the payout ratio?

(c) If the most recent price per share of common stock is $145, what is the price–earnings ratio? The dividend yield?

BUSINESS DECISION PROBLEM

Crown Lighting, Inc., which manufactures electric lighting and wiring equipment, has been in business five years. The company has had modest profits and has experienced few operating difficulties until this year, when president John Stone discusses his company's working capital problems with you, a loan officer at Empire Bank. Stone explains that expanding his firm has created difficulties in meeting obligations when they come due and in taking advantage of cash discounts offered by manufacturers for timely payment. He would like to borrow $75,000 from Empire Bank. At your request, Stone submits the following financial data for the past two years:

	This Year	Last Year
Net Sales	$1,500,000	$1,200,000
Net Income (after income taxes)	47,500	42,000
Dividends	20,000	15,000
Interest Expense	27,000	21,000
Income Tax Expense	12,000	10,500
Total Assets Two Years Ago		720,000
Total Stockholders' Equity Two Years Ago		320,000

Crown Lighting, Inc.
Balance Sheets

	Dec. 31, This Year	Dec. 31, Last Year
Assets		
Cash	$ 50,000	$ 30,500
Accounts Receivable (net of allowance for uncollectible accounts of $5,000 last year and $7,000 this year)	230,000	167,500
Inventory	420,000	297,500
Prepaid Expenses	10,000	5,000
Total Current Assets	$ 710,000	$500,500
Plant Assets (net)	360,000	349,500
Total Assets	$1,070,000	$850,000

Liabilities and Stockholders' Equity		
Notes Payable—Banks	$ 60,000	$ 35,000
Accounts Payable	252,000	195,000
Income Tax Payable	3,000	2,500
Accrued Liabilities	65,000	45,000
Total Current Liabilities	$ 380,000	$277,500
10% Mortgage Payable	220,000	180,000
Total Liabilities	$ 600,000	$457,500
Common Stock	$ 400,000	$350,000
Retained Earnings	70,000	42,500
Total Stockholders' Equity	$ 470,000	$392,500
Total Liabilities and Stockholders' Equity	$1,070,000	$850,000

You calculate the following items for both years from the given data and compare them with the typical ratios for electric lighting and wiring equipment manufacturers provided by a commercial credit firm:

	Typical Ratios for Electric Lighting and Wiring Equipment Manufacturers
(a) Current ratio.	2.66
(b) Quick ratio.	1.3
(c) Average collection period.	46 days
(d) Net sales to ending inventory.	4.8 times
(e) Equity ratio.	49%
(f) Return on assets.	13.1%
(g) Return on stockholders' equity.	11.9%
(h) Return on sales.	4.08%

REQUIRED
Based on your analysis, decide whether and under what circumstances you would grant Stone's request for a loan. Explain the reasons for your decision.

ANSWERS TO SELF-TEST QUESTIONS

1. (c) **2.** (b) **3.** (b) **4.** (b) **5.** (d)

ANNUAL REPORT PROBLEMS FOR PART 4

The following problems conclude Part 4 of the text. They use the financial statement disclosure data of actual companies. In each case, we give a brief profile of the company and selected disclosure data from a recent annual report to stockholders, which is followed by questions relating to certain accounting principles and practices discussed thus far in the text.

I. J. P. Industries, Inc.

PROFILE J. P. Industries, Inc., is a global manufacturer involved in transportation products and plumbing products. Sales for the year ended September 30, 1987, were $386.5 million and total assets were $366.8 million.

DISCLOSURE DATA (*from* 1987 annual report to stockholders)
Selected financial data (all amounts in thousands):

	1987	1986	1985
For the Year			
Net sales	$386,516	$233,654	$133,252
Cost of sales	293,578	180,977	101,809
Income before interest expense and income taxes	35,939	21,999	13,550
Net income	14,773	10,812	6,405
At Year-end			
Current assets	197,112	111,343	
Quick current assets	80,664	48,535	
Inventories	109,011	58,961	19,852
Total assets	366,815	169,975	86,686
Current liabilities	62,446	30,638	
Long-term debt	183,007	45,895	22,082
Common stockholders' equity	108,548	91,337	41,500
Weighted average shares outstanding	11,221	10,012	7,352

REQUIRED

(a) Compute the following ratios for J. P. Industries, Inc., for 1987 and 1986:
1. Rate of return on assets
2. Rate of return on common stockholders' equity (there is no outstanding preferred stock)
3. Rate of return on sales
4. Equity ratio
5. Current ratio
6. Quick ratio
7. Inventory turnover
8. Earnings per share

(b) Based on the ratios computed above, comment on the firm's financial performance and strength during 1987 and 1986.

(c) What ratio exhibited the most startling change between 1986 and 1987? What happened in 1987 to cause the change?

(d) The earnings per share of J. P. Industries, Inc., for the years 1982 through 1985 were:

1982	1983	1984	1985
$.32	$.59	$.63	$.87

The first page of the company's 1987 annual report states that the firm has provided "an average earnings per share growth of 35 percent per year over the past five years." Using the per-share earnings data given above and the per-share earnings computed by you in requirement (a) for 1986 and 1987, show how this growth rate of 35% was computed. What was the average earnings per share growth rate per year over the past *four* years? Comment on this growth rate.

II. Tubby's, Inc., and Subsidiaries

PROFILE Tubby's, Inc., and Subsidiaries franchises fast food restaurants under the trade names "Tubby's Sub Shops" and "Ricky's Dairy Bar & Luxury Grill." As of November 30, 1987, 60 franchised restaurants were operated in the metropolitan areas of Detroit, Michigan; Atlanta, Georgia; Murray, Kentucky; and Largo, Florida. Revenues for 1987 were $1.06 million and total assets were $1.6 million.

DISCLOSURE DATA (*from* 1987 annual report to stockholders)

Tubby's, Inc., and Subsidiaries
Consolidated Statement of Changes in Financial Position
For the Year Ended November 30, 1987

Sources of Working Capital:		
Operations:		
Net Income	$103,418	
Charges Against Operations Not Involving Working Capital in the Current Period:		
Depreciation	32,658	
Deferred Income Taxes, Noncurrent Portion	26,339	
Working Capital Provided from Operations	$162,415	
Increase in Long-term Debt	237,892	
Total Sources of Working Capital		$400,307
Applications of Working Capital:		
Purchase of Property and Equipment	$ 71,458	
Current Maturities and Repayment of Long-Term Debt	270,003	
Increase in Notes Receivable (Noncurrent)	4,486	
Increase in Other Assets	18,876	
Total Applications of Working Capital		364,823
Increase in Working Capital		$ 35,484
Changes in Components of Working Capital:		
Increase in Current Assets:		
Cash	$ 6,777	
Refundable Federal Income Taxes	25,397	
Accounts and Notes Receivable	20,654	
Prepaid Expenses and Other Current Assets	12,601	
	$ 65,429	
Increase (Decrease) in Current Liabilities:		
Accounts Payable	$ 83,866	
Accrued Liabilities	(13,209)	
Deferred Revenue	18,750	
Deferred Income Taxes	(7,339)	
Long-term Debt Due within One Year	(52,123)	
	$ 29,945	
Increase in Working Capital		$ 35,484

REQUIRED

In November 1987, the Financial Accounting Standards Board issued *Statement No. 95*, "Statements of Cash Flows," which requries firms having a fiscal year ending after July 15, 1988, to present a statement of cash flows in their annual reports, rather than a statement of changes in financial position. The basic format of cash flow statements was presented in Chapter 19. Using the data in the Tubby's, Inc., statement of changes in financial position for the period ended November 30, 1987, prepare a statement of cash flows using the indirect method. Tubby's cash balance was $64,222 at November 30, 1986, and $70,999 at November 30, 1987.

PART 5

ACCOUNTING IN MANUFACTURING COMPANIES

21

ACCOUNTING FOR MANUFACTURING OPERATIONS

CHAPTER OBJECTIVES

1. Identify the key differences between a merchandising firm and a manufacturing firm (p. 795).
2. Explain the basic concepts of accounting for manufacturing operations (pp. 795–97).
3. Describe the financial statement features unique to manufacturing accounting (pp. 797–98).
4. Introduce the special accounts used in manufacturing accounting (pp. 798–803).
5. Outline end-of-period accounting procedures for a manufacturing firm (pp. 804–12).

Man is made to create,
from the poet to the potter.

BENJAMIN DISRAELI

So far, our discussion of accounting systems and procedures has related mainly to merchandising firms and service firms. Another important segment of industry comprises manufacturing firms.

Although the accounting principles and techniques described earlier apply to manufacturing firms, accounting for manufacturing operations is usually more complex because more activities are involved in producing a product than in simply purchasing a product, as in a merchandising firm. Because specific purchase prices are known, the cost of goods purchased for resale is relatively easy to determine. In manufacturing operations, however, the costs of all inputs must be accumulated and allocated to calculate the cost of the units produced. In addition, manufacturers must account for the buying, selling, and administrative activities that are common to other types of firms.

Manufacturing operations vary widely in complexity. In this chapter, a general accounting system is adapted to a relatively simple manufacturing operation using the periodic inventory method. No specific product costing system is involved. The two primary cost accounting systems—*job order costing* and *process costing*—are considered in Chapters 22 and 23.

KEY CONCEPTS IN MANUFACTURING ACCOUNTING

Cost of Goods Manufactured

The major difference between merchandising and manufacturing firms is that merchandising firms *buy* finished products to sell whereas manufacturers *make* the products they sell. This difference is apparent in the following comparative illustration of cost of goods sold for each:

Merchandising Firm	
Beginning Merchandise Inventory	$ 80
Add: Net Cost of Merchandise Purchases	620
Cost of Goods Available for Sale	$700
Less: Ending Merchandise Inventory	100
Cost of Goods Sold	$600

Manufacturing Firm	
Beginning Finished Goods Inventory	$ 80
Add: Cost of Goods Manufactured	620
Cost of Goods Available for Sale	$700
Less: Ending Finished Goods Inventory	100
Cost of Goods Sold	$600

Note on the manufacturing firm's statement that cost of goods manufactured corresponds to net cost of merchandise purchases on the merchandising firm's statement. In both cases, these amounts represent costs of finished goods ready for sale.

Product and Period Costs

Product costs are all costs necessary to bring a manufactured product to completion. Thus all the costs of factory materials and labor, as well as such other factory costs as utilities, depreciation, insurance, and repairs, are incorporated into the total cost of the products manufactured.

When accounting for service and merchandising organizations, we immediately expense such items as wages, salaries, depreciation, and utilities. In manufacturing accounting, however, all such costs for the factory are product costs and thus are initially taken into inventory. They will be expensed (as cost of goods sold) in the period in which the related products are sold to customers.

Period costs are charged to expense in the period incurred. The benefits associated with such costs are considered to expire in that period rather than relate to whatever product may have been produced in that period. Traditionally, selling expenses and nonfactory administrative expenses are considered period costs. Some functions in a manufacturing firm—such as a personnel department and a company security department—may benefit both factory and nonfactory activities. The costs of such functions are partly product cost and partly period cost.

Based on the above concepts, income statements for manufacturing firms have the following form:

Sales		$900
Cost of Goods Sold (product costs of units sold)		600
Gross Profit on Sales		$300
Operating Expenses (period costs):		
Selling Expenses	$160	
Nonfactory Administrative Expenses	80	240
Net Income		$ 60

Multiple Inventory Accounts

At any point in time, manufacturing operations typically have units of products at various stages of completion. Consequently, three **inventory** accounts are usually maintained:

1. The **Materials Inventory** account reflects factory materials that have been acquired but not yet placed into production. (Even though these items may be finished products for the supplying firm, they are raw materials for the using firm.) Materials are accounted for at their net delivered cost.
2. The **Work in Process Inventory** account reflects all factory costs associated with units of product started but not completed on the date the firm's financial statements are prepared.
3. The **Finished Goods Inventory** account reflects all factory costs associated with the units of product completed but not yet sold.

All three inventory accounts represent current assets.

Manufacturing Cost Categories

Manufacturing costs are usually accounted for in the following three categories:

1. **Direct material** includes all of the important materials or component parts that physically comprise the product. Examples are sheets of steel, electric motors, and microprocessors. Incidental material items—such as glue and fasteners—are considered indirect materials and are included in factory overhead. Supply items—such as cleaning supplies and lubricants—are considered factory supplies and are included in factory overhead.
2. **Direct labor** includes the salary and wage costs of factory employees who work directly on the product. Machine operators, assemblers, and painters are examples of such workers. The salary and wage costs of factory employees who work indirectly on the product—such as supervisors, inspectors,

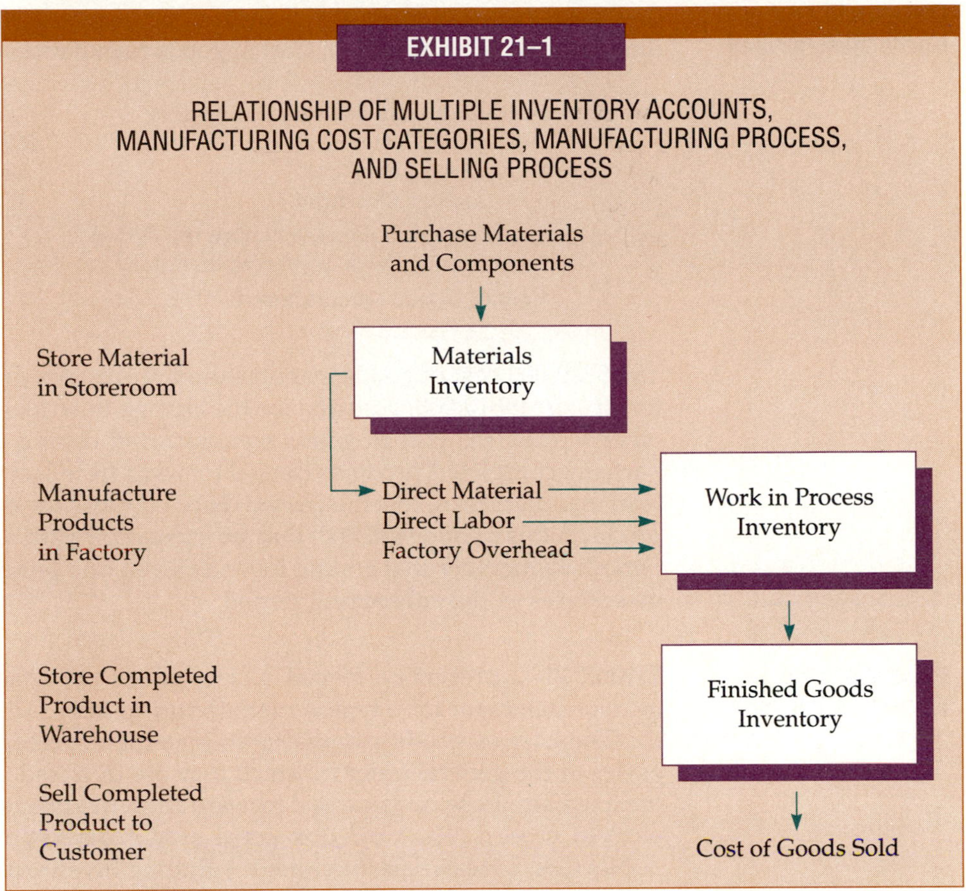

material handlers, and maintenance workers—are considered indirect labor costs and are included in factory overhead.

3. **Factory overhead,** sometimes called manufacturing overhead or factory burden, includes all other manufacturing costs not included in direct material or direct labor. Examples of items included in factory overhead are indirect material, factory supplies used, indirect labor, factory payroll taxes and fringe benefits, factory utilities (natural gas and electricity), factory building and equipment costs (insurance, property taxes, repairs and maintenance, and depreciation), and other factory costs.

Factory overhead specifically excludes selling expenses and nonfactory administrative expenses, since these are not incurred in the manufacturing process.

Exhibit 21–1 illustrates the relationship of the multiple inventory accounts, the manufacturing cost categories, the manufacturing process, and the selling process. Materials are purchased and placed in the Materials Inventory. Direct material, direct labor, and factory overhead are combined to create products. Completed products are stored until they are sold to customers.

FINANCIAL STATEMENT FEATURES UNIQUE TO MANUFACTURING ACCOUNTING

Financial statement features unique to manufacturing accounting are concentrated in the cost of goods manufactured statement and the income statement.

Calculating Cost of Goods Manufactured

Cost of goods manufactured is the cost of goods whose manufacture is completed during the accounting period. Cost of goods manufactured is calculated as follows:

Beginning Work in Process Inventory		$ 30,000
Add: Direct Material Used	$190,000	
Direct Labor	240,000	
Factory Overhead	180,000	610,000
Cost of Work in Process During the Period		$640,000
Less: Ending Work in Process Inventory		20,000
Cost of Goods Manufactured		$620,000

The $620,000 cost of goods manufactured represents this period's total manufacturing cost ($610,000) adjusted for the change in work in process inventories. In other words, the cost of goods manufactured during this period is the cost of partially completed products carried forward from last period ($30,000) plus the total manufacturing cost this period ($610,000) less the cost of partially completed products this period ($20,000) that are carried forward and completed in the next period. Remember that ending inventories of one period become the beginning inventories of the subsequent period.

Illustrations of Financial Statements

Exhibit 21–2 presents a formal cost of goods manufactured statement and an income statement for a typical manufacturing firm. All amounts are assumed.

The cost of goods manufactured statement presents the several cost categories in the general order in which they are incurred. In a sense, the first costs incurred are those costs carried forward from the preceding period as beginning work in process. Next, direct material used is determined (Beginning Inventory + Net Cost of Materials Purchased − Ending Inventory). The cost of direct labor follows, usually shown as a single figure. Factory overhead—a list of all factory costs other than direct material and direct labor—is then added. If the list of overhead costs is extensive, only the total factory overhead may be shown with a reference to a supporting schedule of factory overhead costs. Beginning work in process, direct material used, direct labor, and factory overhead are added to determine total cost of work in process. Finally, the ending work in process is deducted to derive cost of goods manufactured.

On the income statement of a manufacturing firm, the cost of goods sold and gross profit are determined in much the same manner as for a merchandising concern—except that cost of goods manufactured, rather than merchandise purchases, is added to the beginning finished goods inventory. Selling expense and nonfactory administrative expense are deducted from gross profit to determine net income. Income taxes are omitted.

SPECIAL ACCOUNTS FOR MANUFACTURING

Many accounts appearing in a manufacturing firm's ledger—such as Cash, Accounts Receivable, and Sales—are similar to those of service and merchandising firms. The unique aspects of manufacturing, however, have led to the use of several special accounts, particularly Materials Inventory, Materials Purchases, Materials Returns and Allowances, Work in Process Inventory, Finished Goods Inventory, and Manufacturing Summary accounts.

EXHIBIT 21–2

A Manufacturing Company
Cost of Goods Manufactured Statement
For the Year Ended December 31, 19XX

Beginning Work in Process Inventory		$ 30,000
Direct Material Used:		
Beginning Materials Inventory	$ 50,000	
Net Cost of Materials Purchased	250,000	
Cost of Materials Available	$300,000	
Less: Ending Materials Inventory	110,000	
Direct Material		190,000
Direct Labor		240,000
Factory Overhead:		
Depreciation	$ 25,000	
Utilities	34,000	
Insurance	15,000	
Property Taxes	28,000	
Indirect Labor	39,000	
Factory Supplies Used	21,000	
Other Factory Overhead	18,000	
Total Factory Overhead		180,000
Total Cost of Work in Process During 19XX		$640,000
Less: Ending Work in Process Inventory		20,000
Cost of Goods Manufactured		$620,000

A Manufacturing Company
Income Statement
For the Year Ended December 31, 19XX

Net Sales		$900,000
Cost of Goods Sold:		
Beginning Finished Goods Inventory	$ 80,000	
Cost of Goods Manufactured	620,000	
Cost of Goods Available for Sale	$700,000	
Less: Ending Finished Goods Inventory	100,000	
Cost of Goods Sold		600,000
Gross Profit on Sales		$300,000
Operating Expenses:		
Selling Expenses	$160,000	
Administrative Expenses	80,000	240,000
Net Income		$ 60,000
Earnings per Share of Common Stock		$3

Accounts Related to Materials

When the periodic inventory method is used, accounting for the acquisition and use of materials is similar to the accounting for merchandise purchases by a retailer. The manufacturer uses separate accounts to record purchases of materials (Material Purchases), related returns and adjustments (Material Returns and Allowances), and costs of transporting material purchases to the factory (Transportation In). At the end of the accounting period, the balances of these accounts are used to calculate the net cost of materials purchased and are closed to the Manufacturing Summary account.

Entries in the Materials Inventory account are made only when the end-of-period physical inventory count is taken. During the period, the transfer of material into production is not recorded. Determining the ending materials inventory involves counting all units on hand, identifying an appropriate cost price per unit (perhaps from a recent purchase invoice or supply catalog), multiplying quantity by price, and combining all items for a total inventory figure.

Work in Process Inventory Account

The Work in Process Inventory account reflects the costs of products that have been begun but are not completed at the end of the accounting period. All or part of direct material may have been added, but portions of direct labor and factory overhead have not. In a general accounting system using periodic inventory procedures, the amount of work in process is estimated at the end of the period, usually by a production supervisor or someone familiar with the manufacturing process. An illustrative calculation of estimated work in process inventory using assumed amounts appears below:

	Estimated Cost per Finished Unit of Product	Average Proportion Applied	
Direct Material:			
Material A (wood)	$2	100%	$ 2
Material B (paint)	4	25	1
Direct Labor	8	50	4
Factory Overhead	6	50	3
			$ 10
Number of Units in Ending Work in Process			× 2,000
Estimated Cost of Ending Work in Process			$20,000

Estimating the ending work in process inventory typically involves (1) estimating the amount of each manufacturing cost element associated with a finished unit of product, (2) multiplying each cost by an appropriate estimate of the average proportion applied, (3) summing the estimated costs for the various factors, and (4) multiplying by the number of units in the ending inventory. This new work in process figure is the recorded amount of work in process for the end of the current period. Both the beginning and ending balances of work in process are used to calculate the cost of goods manufactured for the period.

Finished Goods Inventory

The balance in the Finished Goods Inventory account represents the cost of finished products awaiting sale to customers. In a periodic inventory system, the ending finished goods inventory is determined by (1) estimating the average cost per finished unit of product for each manufacturing cost element, (2) making a physical count of the unsold finished units of product on hand, (3) multiplying the units by the estimated total cost per unit, and (4) aggregating the total finished goods inventory cost. An illustrative calculation of finished goods inventory costing using assumed amounts follows:

Product	Direct Material A	Direct Material B	Direct Labor	Factory Overhead	Total Unit Cost	Units on Hand	Total Cost of Inventory
101	$3	$0	$ 4	$3	$10	2,500	$ 25,000
102	4	2	8	6	20	3,000	60,000
103	3	1	12	9	25	600	15,000
Totals						6,100	$100,000

Notice that different amounts of each manufacturing cost may be applied to various products. Entries to the Finished Goods Inventory account occur only at the end of the accounting period when a new balance is determined. Both the beginning and ending balances of Finished Goods Inventory are involved in computing the cost of goods sold for the period.

Determining both work in process and finished goods inventories requires a knowledge of product design specifications and cost data relating to various production inputs. The cost of direct material and direct labor is reasonably estimated as some normal or average quantity of materials or direct labor multiplied by some normal or average cost or rate for each factor. Factory overhead, however, can only be related *indirectly* to units of product. The appropriate amounts per unit of product for such costs as factory supervision, depreciation, utilities, and property taxes are not readily apparent. Most firms therefore assume that the amount of factory overhead assigned to products is in proportion to some other known and important production variable such as direct labor hours or direct labor costs.

A *factory overhead rate* is determined by dividing the total overhead cost by the total of the base used to assign overhead. For example, the cost of goods manufactured statement in Exhibit 21–2 shows total direct labor costs of $240,000 and total factory overhead of $180,000. Thus this firm might compute its factory overhead rate as:

$$\text{Factory Overhead Rate} = \frac{\text{Total Factory Overhead}}{\text{Total Direct Labor Costs}} = \frac{\$180{,}000}{\$240{,}000} = 75\% \text{ of Direct Labor Costs}$$

Using this factory overhead rate, an ending work in process inventory that included $5,000 of direct labor would be assigned $3,750 ($0.75 \times \$5{,}000$) of factory overhead.

Manufacturing Summary Account

Manufacturing firms use both a Manufacturing Summary account and an Income Summary account. As its name implies, the **Manufacturing Summary** account summarizes the total manufacturing costs for the period and determines the cost of goods manufactured. As is true for the Income Summary account, entries are made only during the closing procedures, after which the account itself is closed. Stated simply, the balance of the Manufacturing Summary account equals the cost of goods manufactured for the period when (1) all accounts for factory costs are closed to the Manufacturing Summary account, and (2) the Materials Inventory and Work in Process Inventory accounts are closed to the Manufacturing Summary account (beginning balances debited and ending balances credited).

EXHIBIT 21–3

Manufacturing Summary

19XX			19XX		
Dec. 31	Work in Process Inventory (Beginning)	30,000	Dec. 31	Work in Process Inventory (Ending)	20,000
31	Materials Inventory (Beginning)	50,000	31	Materials Inventory (Ending)	110,000
31	Materials Purchases	250,000	31	(To close to Income Summary)	620,000
31	Direct Labor	240,000			
31	Factory Overhead (total)	180,000			
		750,000			750,000

Income Summary

19XX			19XX		
Dec. 31	Finished Goods Inventory (Beginning)	80,000	Dec. 31	Sales	900,000
31	Cost of Goods Manufactured	620,000	31	Finished Goods Inventory (Ending)	100,000
31	Selling Expenses (total)	160,000			
31	Administrative Expenses (total)	80,000			
31	(To close to Retained Earnings)	60,000			
		1,000,000			1,000,000

The Manufacturing Summary and Income Summary accounts are illustrated in Exhibit 21–3 in T-account form, using the data from Exhibit 21–2.

The balance of the Manufacturing Summary account comprises a series of entries reflecting (1) debits for the manufacturing costs carried forward to this period as beginning materials and work in process inventories, and the other manufacturing costs incurred during this period—such as materials purchases, transportation in, direct labor, and factory overhead—and (2) credits representing the ending materials and work in process inventories. In effect, we deduct these latter amounts because they are carried forward as costs of the subsequent manufacturing period. Had materials returns and allowances been involved in this illustration, the debit for purchases would have included the gross amount of purchases, and an additional credit would appear in the Manufacturing Summary account for materials returns and allowances. In turn, the Manufacturing Summary account is closed to Income Summary, therefore becoming an important factor in determining the period's net income.

Notice that the finished goods inventory is not part of the cost of goods manufactured. Rather, the beginning and ending finished goods inventory amounts are closed to and appear, respectively, as a debit and a credit in the Income Summary account. This procedure combines the cost of goods manufactured, the beginning finished goods inventory, and the ending finished goods inventory, so that the cost of goods sold can be determined.

MAJOR TRENDS IN MANUFACTURING

Dramatic changes have been taking place in factories across the United States. Traditional manufacturing methods and procedures are being restructured or replaced by new methods and procedures that allow manufacturers to be more competitive, especially with foreign manufacturers. The companies adopting these new methods and procedures are referred to as world-class manufacturers.

World-class manufacturers in the U.S. have been adopting techniques that were developed locally and abroad. Six major trends are reflected in these techniques: higher quality, lower inventories, flexible flow lines, automation, product line organization, and effective use of information.*

Higher product quality is now viewed as consistent with lower production cost. Many foreign competitors proved this to be true, forcing U.S. producers to change from competition based primarily on average quality and low selling price. In fact, many U.S. manufacturers are now convinced that lower-quality manufacturing causes higher levels of cost. For example, low-quality raw materials, improperly trained workers, and poorly maintained equipment will increase costs related to excess scrap, reworking faulty products, equipment breakdowns, and product warranty claims.

Lower inventory levels are generating very significant cost reductions for many manufacturers. Reduction of inventory levels decreases financing and carrying costs associated with inventories (often 20–25% of the product cost) and frees cash for investment in productive assets. *Just-in-time* (JIT) inventory techniques have been adopted to ensure that material is available only when needed and in the amount needed, thus minimizing inventory carrying costs. Vendors of material are monitored for material quality and delivery performance; poor vendors are replaced. Computerized production scheduling and statistical process control also facilitate lower inventory levels.

Traditional factories have a functional plant layout, with similar types of machines grouped together. For example, all the drill presses would be located in the same area of the plant. The functional layout causes a lengthy flow line (the physical path that a product follows through a manufacturing facility), which usually results in high material handling time and costs. World-class manufacturers are changing to *flexible flow lines* to shorten the length of time needed to produce a product and decrease cost. Flexible flow lines incorporate multiple lines with different types of machines brought together for each line. These lines often become factories within the factory.

Automation is the most recognized of the trends. *Stand-alone automation* incorporates a computer-controlled machine or robot into an existing manufacturing process. Stand-alone automation usually results in lower material and labor costs as well as higher product quality. *Flexible-manufacturing-systems automation* involves a series of electronically interlocked machines that perform an entire set of prescribed operations controlled by a computer. This type of automated system produces the product from start to finish. Many U.S. companies have realized a substantial competitive advantage from automation.

Product line organization reorganizes the service and support personnel of the factory, reassigning them directly to product lines. Centralized departments are dispersed to the individual lines to form small, separate organizations that concentrate on a small number of products. These small suborganizations typically outperform larger, traditional organizations. Many of the operational problems of U.S. manufacturers during the last decade can be traced to managers of large factories who rarely set foot on the factory floor.

Effective use of information is closely coupled with the other trends. Managements of world-class manufacturers have set a goal of developing and maintaining *integrated information systems*, which use a single data base that is maintained on a real-time basis. Different information needed for operation control, managerial reports, and external financial statements would all be facilitated. Computers are essential to implementing this type of information system.

These trends are working together to reduce direct labor and to increase factory overhead, with an overall reduction in manufacturing costs and an increase in product quality. The changes are allowing U.S. manufacturers to truly become world-class competitors.

*Robert A. Howell and Stephen R. Soucy, "The New Manufacturing Environment: Major Trends for Management Accounting," *Management Accounting*, July 1987, pp. 21–27.

END-OF-PERIOD PROCEDURES FOR A MANUFACTURING FIRM

Most end-of-period procedures for manufacturing firms are similar to those presented for other types of firms in Chapters 4 and 5. In the remainder of this chapter, we present a comprehensive illustration of these procedures for a manufacturing firm, including preparation and use of the worksheet to adjust the general ledger accounts, preparation of financial statements from worksheet data, and procedures for closing the temporary accounts at year-end. The illustration highlights the unique aspects of manufacturing accounting.

Worksheet for a Manufacturing Firm

Remember from Chapter 4 that a **worksheet** facilitates adjusting the general ledger accounts and preparing financial statements because:

1. It places in one location the debit and credit balances of all general ledger accounts.
2. It makes apparent the effects of any adjustment.
3. It groups all adjusted account balances involved in preparing each financial statement.

Worksheets for manufacturing firms differ from those presented in Chapters 4 and 5. An additional set of columns is provided for the accounts contained in the cost of goods manufactured statement, and three, rather than one, inventory accounts are involved. Also, note that the adjusted trial balance columns have been omitted. Instead, the adjusted amounts are computed and placed directly in the proper financial statement column. This more efficient procedure is considered appropriate at this stage of your study. The following basic aspects of the worksheet are similar for all firms:

1. The unadjusted trial balance is transcribed from the general ledger to the first set of money columns.
2. Appropriate adjustments are formulated in the second set of money columns.
3. Unadjusted account balances and any related adjustments are combined to derive adjusted balances for all accounts, which are then extended to the appropriate set of columns representing the cost of goods manufactured, the income statement, and the balance sheet.
4. Each set of statement columns is balanced in turn, to check the arithmetical accuracy of the worksheet.

Exhibit 21–4 (pages 805–806) presents the worksheet for Lollar Manufacturing, Inc., for an accounting year ended December 31, 19XX. Remember that in preparing monthly or quarterly financial statements, worksheet adjustments are not recorded and posted to the general ledger. When annual statements are prepared, however, both adjusting and closing entries are recorded in the general journal and posted to the general ledger.

Adjusting entry data for our year-end illustration are as follows:

1. Unexpired insurance at year-end on factory machinery, $1,000.
2. Unpaid wages and salaries at year-end (by category): direct labor, $4,000; indirect labor, $3,000; office salaries, $1,000; and sales salaries, $2,000.
3. Depreciation on factory machinery, $6,000.

EXHIBIT 21–4

Lollar Manufacturing, Inc.
Manufacturing Worksheet
For the Year Ended December 31, 19XX

Description	Trial Balance		Adjustments		Cost of Goods Manufactured		Income Statement		Balance Sheet	
	Debit	Credit	Debit	Credit	Debit	Credit	Debit	Credit	Debit	Credit
Cash	13,000								13,000	
Accounts Receivable	45,000								45,000	
Allowance for Uncollectible Accounts		1,000		(5) 9,000						10,000
Materials Inventory (January 1)	10,000				10,000					
Work in Process Inventory (January 1)	6,000				6,000					
Finished Goods Inventory (January 1)	20,000						20,000			
Factory Supplies on Hand	17,000			(6) 13,000					4,000	
Office Supplies on Hand	5,000			(7) 3,000					2,000	
Prepaid Insurance	4,000			(1) 3,000					1,000	
Factory Machinery	90,000								90,000	
Accumulated Depreciation—Factory Machinery		20,000		(3) 6,000						26,000
Accounts Payable		7,000								7,000
Long-term Notes Payable—10%		40,000								40,000
Common Stock—$10 Par Value		50,000								50,000
Retained Earnings		20,000								20,000
Dividends	4,000								4,000	
Sales		450,000						450,000		
Materials Purchases	114,000				114,000					
Transportation In	2,000				2,000					
Direct Labor	77,000		(2) 4,000		81,000					
Indirect Labor	43,000		(2) 3,000		46,000					

(continued)

4. Accrued interest payable at year-end, $1,000.
5. Uncollectible accounts expense is an estimated 2% of sales.
6. Factory supplies on hand, $4,000.
7. Office supplies on hand, $2,000.
8. Estimated income taxes, $17,000.

Because these adjustments are routine and parallel those of other firms, related journal entries with explanations are not presented here. Related amounts in the adjustments columns of the worksheet in Exhibit 21–4 are keyed to the numbers of these data items.

EXH 21–4 (Continued)

Lollar Manufacturing, Inc.
Manufacturing Worksheet
For the Year Ended December 31, 19XX

Description	Trial Balance Debit	Trial Balance Credit	Adjustments Debit	Adjustments Credit	Cost of Goods Manufactured Debit	Cost of Goods Manufactured Credit	Income Statement Debit	Income Statement Credit	Balance Sheet Debit	Balance Sheet Credit
Factory Utilities	20,000				20,000					
Factory Repairs	10,000				10,000					
Factory Rent	40,000				40,000					
Administrative Rent Expense	7,000						7,000			
Sales Rent Expense	23,000						23,000			
Office Salaries Expense	12,000		(2) 1,000				13,000			
Sales Salaries Expense	16,000		(2) 2,000				18,000			
Advertising Expense	7,000						7,000			
Interest Expense	3,000		(4) 1,000				4,000			
	588,000	588,000								
Factory Insurance			(1) 3,000		3,000					
Wages Payable				(2) 10,000						10,000
Factory Depreciation—Machinery			(3) 6,000		6,000					
Interest Payable				(4) 1,000						1,000
Uncollectible Accounts Expense			(5) 9,000				9,000			
Factory Supplies Used			(6) 13,000		13,000					
Office Supplies Expense			(7) 3,000				3,000			
Income Tax Expense			(8) 17,000				17,000			
Income Tax Payable				(8) 17,000						17,000
Materials Inventory (December 31)						18,000			18,000	
Work in Process Inventory (December 31)						8,000			8,000	
Finished Goods Inventory (December 31)								26,000	26,000	
			62,000	62,000	351,000	26,000				
Cost of Goods Manufactured						325,000	325,000			
					351,000	351,000	446,000	476,000	211,000	181,000
Net Income							30,000			30,000
							476,000	476,000	211,000	211,000

MANUFACTURING INVENTORIES IN THE WORKSHEET As noted in Chapter 5, there are two approaches to handling inventories on a worksheet when a periodic inventory system is used. The first approach, described in Chapter 5, treats the entries related to inventories as closing entries at the end of the accounting period. This approach is used in the following paragraphs and the illustrations in this chapter. The second approach, described in Appendix A (following Chapter 5), treats the entries related to inventories as adjusting entries at the end of the accounting period. This alternative approach is used in Appendix F (following this chapter).

Inventory amounts in the trial balance of a manufacturing firm using a periodic inventory system are debits representing the beginning balances for the inventories. Remember that only materials and work in process inventories (not finished goods inventory) are involved in determining cost of goods manufactured. Finished goods inventory is used in determining cost of goods sold on the income statement.

The worksheet inventory procedures result in (1) beginning inventory balances being added to—and ending inventory balances being deducted from—other related net debit amounts for determining cost of goods manufactured and cost of goods sold, and (2) the ending balances of all three inventories being reflected as current assets on the balance sheet. These procedures are as follows:

1. Extend the beginning balances of materials and work in process inventories as debits in the cost of goods manufactured columns.
2. Extend the beginning finished goods inventory as a debit in the income statement columns.
3. At the bottom of the worksheet, record all three inventory account titles and record the ending balances of materials and work in process inventories as credits in the cost of goods manufactured columns, and the ending balance of finished goods inventory as a credit in the income statement columns.
4. On the same respective lines used in step 3, record the ending balance of each inventory account as a debit in the balance sheet columns.

We represent these procedures schematically in the chart below. The plus (+) and minus (−) signs indicate the respective effects on cost of goods manufactured, cost of goods sold, and total assets on the balance sheet.

	Cost of Goods Manufactured		Income Statement		Balance Sheet	
	Debit	Credit	Debit	Credit	Debit	Credit
Extension of Beginning Balances:						
Materials inventory	+					
Work in process inventory	+					
Finished goods inventory			+			
Recording Ending Balances at Bottom of Worksheet:						
Materials inventory		−			+	
Work in process inventory		−			+	
Finished goods inventory				−	+	

Review of Exhibit 21–4 shows the effects of these procedures in the worksheet illustrated there.

TOTALING AND BALANCING THE WORKSHEET After all other relevant amounts are extended, the cost of goods manufactured columns are added; the amount needed to balance them (a credit of $325,000) is the cost of goods manufactured figure for this period. The $325,000 credit needed to balance the cost of goods manufactured columns is then extended as a debit to the income statement columns. The $30,000 debit needed to balance these columns represents net income for the period. The $30,000 is then extended as a credit to balance the balance sheet columns. When operating losses occur, the *credit* needed to balance the income statement columns is extended as a debit to balance the balance sheet columns. This completes the worksheet.

Preparation of Financial Statements

Properly completed, the worksheet contains all the data necessary to prepare the cost of goods manufactured statement, the income statement, the retained earnings statement, and the balance sheet. Exhibit 21–5 presents those statements for Lollar Manufacturing, Inc., prepared from the data on the worksheet in Exhibit 21–4. Observe that the key income statement figures—cost of goods manufactured and net income—agree with the amounts that balance the related worksheet columns.

EXHIBIT 21–5

FINANCIAL STATEMENTS OF LOLLAR MANUFACTURING, INC.

Lollar Manufacturing, Inc.
Cost of Goods Manufactured Statement
For the Year Ended December 31, 19XX

Beginning Work in Process Inventory		$ 6,000
Direct Material Used:		
Beginning Materials Inventory	$ 10,000	
Materials Purchases	114,000	
Transportation In	2,000	
Cost of Materials Available	$126,000	
Less: Ending Materials Inventory	18,000	
Direct Material		108,000
Direct Labor		81,000
Factory Overhead:		
Indirect Labor	$ 46,000	
Factory Utilities	20,000	
Factory Repairs	10,000	
Factory Rent	40,000	
Factory Supplies Used	13,000	
Factory Insurance	3,000	
Factory Depreciation—Machinery	6,000	
Total Factory Overhead		138,000
Total Cost of Work in Process During 19XX		$333,000
Less: Ending Work in Process Inventory		8,000
Cost of Goods Manufactured		$325,000

Closing Entries

Recall that closing procedures occur only at the end of the operating year. The worksheet provides all the data necessary to prepare closing entries for manufacturing cost accounts and expense accounts and to record inventory changes at year-end. Using compound journal entries when appropriate, we use the following closing procedures:

1. Close the beginning Materials and Work in Process inventory accounts and all manufacturing cost accounts with *debit* balances and debit the total to the Manufacturing Summary account.
2. Record (as debits) the ending materials and work in process inventories, close any manufacturing cost accounts with *credit* balances, and credit the total to the Manufacturing Summary account. (The balance of the

EXH 21–5 (Continued)

FINANCIAL STATEMENTS OF LOLLAR MANUFACTURING, INC.

Lollar Manufacturing, Inc.
Income Statement
For the Year Ended December 31, 19XX

Net Sales			$450,000
Cost of Goods Sold:			
Beginning Finished Goods Inventory		$ 20,000	
Cost of Goods Manufactured		325,000	
Cost of Goods Available for Sale		$345,000	
Less: Ending Finished Goods Inventory		26,000	
Cost of Goods Sold			319,000
Gross Profit on Sales			$131,000
Operating Expenses:			
Selling Expenses:			
Sales Rent Expense	$23,000		
Sales Salaries Expense	18,000		
Advertising Expense	7,000		
Total Selling Expenses		$ 48,000	
Administrative Expenses:			
Administrative Rent Expense	$ 7,000		
Office Salaries Expense	13,000		
Uncollectible Accounts Expense	9,000		
Office Supplies Expense	3,000		
Total Administrative Expenses		32,000	
Total Operating Expenses			80,000
Income from Operations			$ 51,000
Less: Interest Expense			4,000
Income before Income Taxes			$ 47,000
Less: Income Tax Expense			17,000
Net Income			$ 30,000
Earnings per Share of Common Stock			$6

(continued)

EXH 21–5 (Continued)

FINANCIAL STATEMENTS OF LOLLAR MANUFACTURING, INC.

Lollar Manufacturing, Inc.
Balance Sheet
December 31, 19XX

ASSETS		
Current Assets		
Cash		$ 13,000
Accounts Receivable	$45,000	
Less: Allowance for Uncollectible Accounts	10,000	35,000
Inventories:		
Materials	$18,000	
Work in Process	8,000	
Finished Goods	26,000	52,000
Prepaid Expenses:		
Factory Supplies on Hand	$ 4,000	
Office Supplies on Hand	2,000	
Prepaid Insurance	1,000	7,000
Total Current Assets		$107,000
Plant Assets		
Machinery and Equipment	$90,000	
Less: Accumulated Depreciation	26,000	64,000
Total Assets		$171,000
LIABILITIES AND STOCKHOLDERS' EQUITY		
Current Liabilities		
Accounts Payable		$ 7,000
Wages Payable		10,000
Interest Payable		1,000
Income Tax Payable		17,000
Total Current Liabilities		$ 35,000
Long-term Notes Payable (10%, due 5 years hence)		40,000
Total Liabilities		$ 75,000
Stockholders' Equity		
Common Stock, $10 Par Value, 5,000 Shares Authorized, Issued, and Outstanding	$50,000	
Retained Earnings	46,000	96,000
Total Liabilities and Stockholders' Equity		$171,000

Lollar Manufacturing, Inc.
Retained Earnings Statement
For the Year Ended December 31, 19XX

Retained Earnings, January 1	$20,000
Add: Net Income for 19XX	30,000
	$50,000
Less: Dividends Declared	4,000
Retained Earnings, December 31	$46,000

Manufacturing Summary account should now equal the total cost of goods manufactured.)

3. Close the beginning Finished Goods Inventory account, the Manufacturing Summary account, and all other income statement accounts with *debit* balances, and debit the total to the Income Summary account.
4. Record (as a debit) the ending finished goods inventory, close any income statement account with a *credit* balance, and credit the total to the Income Summary account. (The balance of the Income Summary account should now equal net income.)
5. Close the Income Summary account to Retained Earnings.
6. Close the Dividends account to Retained Earnings.

The closing entries for Lollar Manufacturing, Inc., follow (entries are numbered to indicate the related closing step involved):

1.	Manufacturing Summary	351,000	
	Materials Inventory (beginning)		10,000
	Work in Process Inventory (beginning)		6,000
	Materials Purchases		114,000
	Transportation In		2,000
	Direct Labor		81,000
	Indirect Labor		46,000
	Factory Utilities		20,000
	Factory Repairs		10,000
	Factory Rent		40,000
	Factory Supplies Used		13,000
	Factory Insurance		3,000
	Factory Depreciation—Machinery		6,000
	To close beginning Materials and Work in Process accounts and manufacturing cost accounts having debit balances to the Manufacturing Summary account.		
2.	Materials Inventory (ending)	18,000	
	Work in Process Inventory (ending)	8,000	
	Manufacturing Summary		26,000
	To record the ending materials and work in process inventories.		
3.	Income Summary	446,000	
	Finished Goods Inventory (beginning)		20,000
	Administrative Rent Expense		7,000
	Sales Rent Expense		23,000
	Office Salaries Expense		13,000
	Office Supplies Expense		3,000
	Sales Salaries Expense		18,000
	Advertising Expense		7,000
	Interest Expense		4,000
	Uncollectible Accounts Expense		9,000
	Income Tax Expense		17,000
	Manufacturing Summary		325,000

(entry continued)

		Debit	Credit
	To close the beginning finished goods inventory, all expense accounts, and the Manufacturing Summary account to the Income Summary account.		
4.	Finished Goods Inventory (ending)	26,000	
	Sales	450,000	
	Income Summary		476,000
	To record the ending finished goods inventory and close Sales to the Income Summary account.		
5.	Income Summary	30,000	
	Retained Earnings		30,000
	To close the Income Summary account to Retained Earnings.		
6.	Retained Earnings	4,000	
	Dividends		4,000
	To close the Dividends account to Retained Earnings.		

After the closing entries are recorded and posted, the general ledger reflects only the balances of those assets, liabilities, and stockholders' equity accounts that are carried forward as beginning balances for the next year.

In manufacturing accounting, a general accounting system using the periodic inventory method may be satisfactory for small, stable, single-product firms. The limitations of this approach are critical, however, in more complex, multiproduct manufacturing operations. When periodic inventory procedures are used, the amounts of materials used and cost of goods sold are merely residual figures that offer little opportunity for management control. Also, periodic inventory procedures permit accurate income determination only at the end of the period, when ending inventories are taken. However, management may need reliable current product cost data on a day-to-day basis. Because multiple products may involve widely varying types and amounts of materials, different production techniques, and a variety of production routines in a series of departments, product cost accounting requires a more sophisticated approach. Therefore, cost accounting systems using perpetual inventories have been developed. Cost accounting systems are discussed in Chapters 22 and 23.

KEY POINTS FOR CHAPTER OBJECTIVES

1 Identify the key differences between a merchandising firm and a manufacturing firm (p. 795).

- A merchandising firm has merchandise inventory while a manufacturing firm has finished goods inventory.
- A merchandising firm's income statement includes Net Cost of Merchandise Purchases while a manufacturing firm's income statement includes Cost of Goods Manufactured.

2 Explain the basic concepts of manufacturing accounting (pp. 795–97).

- Product costs include all costs necessary to bring the manufactured product to completion.
- Manufacturers have three inventory accounts—Materials, Work in Process, and Finished Goods.
- Manufacturing costs are accounted for in three categories: (1) direct material; (2) direct labor; and (3) factory overhead, which includes all manufacturing costs other than direct material and direct labor.
- In manufacturing accounting, all product costs—direct material, direct labor, and factory overhead—are capitalized; that is, they become the cost of goods sold.

3 Describe the financial statement features unique to manufacturing accounting (pp. 797–98).

- Cost of goods manufactured equals the total of all manufacturing costs incurred adjusted for the change in work in process inventory.
- Cost of goods sold equals cost of goods manufactured adjusted for the change in finished goods inventory.
- Neither cost of goods manufactured nor cost of goods sold includes selling expenses or nonfactory administrative expenses.

4 Introduce the special accounts used in manufacturing accounting (pp. 798–802).

- Special accounts related to material include Materials Inventory, Materials Purchases, and Materials Returns and Allowances.
- Special accounts are also maintained for Work in Process Inventory and Finished Goods Inventory.
- The Manufacturing Summary account summarizes the total manufacturing costs for the period and determines the cost of goods manufactured. It is closed to the Income Summary account.

5 Outline end-of-period accounting procedures for a manufacturing firm (pp. 804–12).

- Worksheets for manufacturing firms have an additional set of columns for cost of goods manufactured.
- Closing procedures for manufacturers incorporate a Manufacturing Summary account to which beginning Materials and Work in Process Inventory account balances and all accounts related to the cost of goods manufactured are closed. Ending Materials and Work in Process Inventory account balances are recorded as credits in the Manufacturing Summary account and as debits in the related balance sheet asset accounts. Beginning Finished Goods Inventory, the Manufacturing Summary account, and all income statement accounts are closed to the Income Summary account. Ending Finished Goods Inventory is recorded as a credit in the Income Summary account and as a debit in the related balance sheet asset account.

KEY TERMS USED IN CHAPTER

direct labor 796
direct material 796
factory overhead 797
finished goods inventory 796
inventory 796
manufacturing costs 796
manufacturing summary 801
materials inventory 796
period costs (expenses) 796
product costs 795
work in process inventory 796
worksheet 804

SELF-TEST QUESTIONS FOR REVIEW

(Answers are at the end of this chapter.)

1. Which of the following is not an element of factory overhead?
   (a) Factory office salaries.
   (b) Plant manager's salary.
   (c) Product inspector's salary.
   (d) President's salary.
2. Which of the following is never an element of product cost?
   (a) Insurance.
   (b) Advertising.
   (c) Utilities.
   (d) Supplies.
3. Which of the following is extended to the Income Statement columns on a manufacturing worksheet?
   (a) Beginning materials inventory.
   (b) Beginning work in process inventory.
   (c) Beginning finished goods inventory.
   (d) Dividends.
4. Which of the following would typically not be a factor in determining an overhead rate?
   (a) Pounds of material.
   (b) Direct labor hours.
   (c) Total overhead costs.
   (d) Direct labor cost.
5. Under the periodic inventory method, entries are made in the materials inventory:
   (a) When materials are purchased.
   (b) When materials are used.
   (c) At the end of the accounting period.
   (d) All of the above.

DEMONSTRATION PROBLEM FOR REVIEW

Perez Manufacturing Corporation completed its fiscal year on December 31, 19XX. The following account balances are available from Perez's general ledger:

	January 1, 19XX	December 31, 19XX
Materials Inventory	$ 80,000	$ 60,000
Work in Process Inventory	100,000	140,000
Finished Goods Inventory	120,000	110,000
Direct Labor		280,000
Materials Purchases		180,000
Indirect Labor		90,000
Depreciation—Factory		30,000
Factory Supplies Used		16,000
Repairs and Maintenance—Factory		22,000
Selling Expenses		64,000
Administrative Expenses—Nonfactory		58,000

REQUIRED
Prepare a cost of goods manufactured statement for the year ended December 31, 19XX.

SOLUTION TO DEMONSTRATION PROBLEM

Perez Manufacturing Corporation
Cost of Goods Manufactured Statement
For the Year Ended December 31, 19XX

Beginning Work in Process Inventory		$100,000
Direct Material Used:		
Beginning Materials Inventory	$ 80,000	
Materials Purchases	180,000	
Cost of Materials Available	$260,000	
Less: Ending Materials Inventory	60,000	
Direct Material		200,000
Direct Labor		280,000
Factory Overhead:		
Indirect Labor	$ 90,000	
Depreciation—Factory	30,000	
Factory Supplies Used	16,000	
Repairs and Maintenance—Factory	22,000	
Total Factory Overhead		158,000
Total Cost of Work in Process During 19XX		$738,000
Less: Ending Work in Process Inventory		140,000
Cost of Goods Manufactured		$598,000

QUESTIONS

21–1 In what two important ways is accounting for a manufacturing firm more complex than accounting for a merchandising firm?

21–2 How are product costs accounted for differently from period costs? Give examples of each.

21–3 What is the basic format of the income statement of a manufacturing firm?

21–4 Name the three inventory accounts maintained by manufacturing firms and briefly describe the nature of each.

21–5 Name and briefly describe the three major categories used to account for manufacturing costs.

21–6 List six examples of factory overhead costs.

21–7 In what way is the total manufacturing cost during the year different from cost of goods manufactured?

21–8 If cost of work in process during the year is $450,000 and ending work in process inventory is $40,000, what is the amount of cost of goods manufactured?

21–9 If beginning and ending finished goods inventories are $60,000 and $40,000, respectively, and the cost of goods sold is $380,000, what is the cost of goods manufactured?

21–10 Identify and briefly describe the normal balances and typical entries in the four accounts usually maintained for the purchase and use of materials.

21–11 What information is necessary to estimate the ending work in process inventory? The ending finished goods inventory?

21–12 Briefly describe the nature and timing of the entries expected in the Manufacturing Summary account.

21–13 Briefly outline a typical worksheet format for a manufacturing company. What four steps are followed to prepare such a worksheet?

21–14 "Preparation of a worksheet does not specifically affect the general ledger." Do you agree or disagree with this statement? Why?

21–15 Briefly explain the year-end closing procedures for a manufacturing firm.

21–16 In what important way is the assignment of factory overhead to the work in process and finished goods inventories different from the assignment of direct material and direct labor costs? Briefly explain the approach that is widely used to assign factory overhead.

EXERCISES

Cost of goods manufactured statement

21–17 The following account balances are available from the Richards Manufacturing Company ledger:

	Beginning of Year	End of Year
Materials Inventory	$30,000	$ 20,000
Work in Process Inventory	40,000	60,000
Finished Goods Inventory	70,000	60,000
Direct Labor		120,000
Materials Purchases		100,000
Indirect Labor		45,000
Depreciation—Factory		25,000
Factory Supplies Used		10,000
Repairs and Maintenance—Factory		15,000
Selling Expenses (total)		34,000
Nonfactory Administrative Expenses (total)		31,000

Prepare a cost of goods manufactured statement for the current year.

Income statement

21–18 Richards Manufacturing Company (see Exercise 21–17) sold 15,000 units of product for $28 each during the current year. During the year, 5,000 shares of common stock were outstanding. Prepare an income statement for the year.

Cost of goods manufactured and cost of goods sold

21–19 For each of the following unrelated columns of data, compute the cost of goods manufactured and the cost of goods sold:

	A	B	C
Selling Expenses	$ 480	$ 792	$ 576
Factory Insurance	240	192	336
Nonfactory Administrative Expenses	216	384	264
Ending Finished Goods Inventory	1,080	2,400	3,120
Factory Taxes	312	240	216
Materials Inventory (beginning)	480	768	288
Direct Labor	2,400	1,920	5,040

	A	B	C
Factory Maintenance	$ 192	$ 288	$ 456
Materials Purchased	1,080	1,560	1,200
Beginning Finished Goods Inventory	720	2,880	2,640
Increase (Decrease) in Work in Process	240	0	(648)
Factory Utilities	216	720	1,728
Depreciation—Factory	480	2,160	1,440
Indirect Labor	744	504	2,640
Factory Supplies Used	312	408	912
Materials Inventory (ending)	408	600	216

Factory overhead rate and assigning overhead

21–20 During the current year, Thompson Factories, Inc., recorded the following costs and expenses:

Direct Material	$ 54,000
Direct Labor	120,000
Factory Supplies Used	28,000
Indirect Labor	41,000
Sales Commissions	12,000
Factory Supervision	16,000
Nonfactory Administrative Expenses	17,000
Other Factory Overhead	11,000

Assume that Thompson assigns factory overhead on the basis of direct labor costs.

(a) Compute the factory overhead rate.

(b) Indicate the total cost of the ending work in process inventory that has been assigned $6,000 of direct material cost and $11,000 of direct labor cost.

Estimated cost of inventories

21–21 Benton Manufacturing Company's accounting department has estimated that each completed unit of its product involves an average of two pounds of direct material costing $4 per pound and five hours of direct labor costing $10 per hour. Factory overhead is assigned on the basis of total direct labor cost incurred, which for the current year are $204,000 and $240,000, respectively.

(a) Determine the proper cost of an ending finished goods inventory that comprises 4,000 units.

(b) Determine the proper cost of an ending work in process inventory that involves 800 units, to which all direct material has been added but for which only 60% of the direct labor has been assigned.

Assigning overhead and estimated cost of inventories

21–22 The only product of Gregg Manufacturers, Inc., is produced in a continuous process. At the end of the current year, the ending inventories of work in process and finished goods were as follows:

	Estimated Amounts Assigned per Unit		
	Direct Material	Direct Labor	Total Units
Work in Process	$ 8	$ 9	5,000
Finished Goods	10	12	7,000

Assuming that factory overhead is assigned at the rate of 80% of direct labor cost, compute the cost of the ending work in process and finished goods inventories.

Recording changes in inventory and closing entries

21–23 Using the following summarized data, prepare the compound journal entries (similar to those illustrated in the chapter) to record the changes in inventories and to close the manufacturing accounts at year-end to Manufacturing Summary and, in turn, to close Manufacturing Summary to Income Summary.

	Beginning of Year	End of Year
Materials Inventory	$ 13,000	$14,000
Work in Process Inventory	7,000	10,000
Materials Purchases	85,000	
Direct Labor	105,000	
Factory Overhead (total)	80,000	
Selling Expenses (total)	20,000	
Nonfactory Administrative Expenses (total)	40,000	

Cost of goods manufactured statement

21–24 The following cost of goods manufactured columns are from a Howard Manufacturing, Inc., worksheet for the year ended December 31, 19X1. Simple, summarized data are used.

	Cost of Goods Manufactured Debit	Cost of Goods Manufactured Credit
Materials Inventory (beginning)	10	
Work in Process Inventory (beginning)	13	
Materials Purchases	91	
Direct Labor	65	
Transportation In—Purchases	15	
Indirect Labor	36	
Factory Supervision	22	
Factory Utilities	14	
Factory Supplies Used	7	
Depreciation—Equipment	18	
Depreciation—Factory Building	20	
Other Factory Overhead	27	
Ending Inventories:		
Materials Inventory		12
Work in Process Inventory		9
	338	21
Cost of Goods Manufactured		317
	338	338

Using these data, prepare a cost of goods manufactured statement for the year ended December 31, 19X1.

PROBLEMS

Cost of goods manufactured statement and income statement

21–25 Selected account balances from the completed year-end worksheet of the Paulson Manufacturing Company appear below:

Administrative Salaries (Nonfactory)	69,000	Work in Process Inventory (Jan. 1)	15,000
Advertising and Promotion Expense	42,000	Finished Goods Inventory (Jan. 1)	63,000

Depreciation—Machinery	27,000
Depreciation—Equipment (Nonfactory Administrative)	21,000
Depreciation—Sales Fixtures	18,000
Direct Labor	210,000
Factory Rent	18,000
Factory Supervision	30,000
Factory Supplies Used	24,000
Indirect Labor	21,000
Materials Inventory (Jan. 1)	12,000
Materials Inventory (Dec. 31)	18,000
Work in Process Inventory (Dec. 31)	36,000
Finished Goods Inventory (Dec. 31)	51,000
Maintenance—Machinery	15,000
Nonfactory Administrative Rent	36,000
Other Factory Overhead	33,000
Other Selling Expenses	27,000
Purchases—Materials	93,000
Sales	840,000
Sales Salaries Expense	75,000
Transportation In	9,000

REQUIRED
Using the above data, prepare a cost of goods manufactured statement and an income statement for the current year (disregard income tax and earnings per share considerations).

Cost of goods manufactured statement

21–26 The following journal entries recorded the changes in inventories and closed the manufacturing accounts of Glendale Factory, Inc., at year-end:

Manufacturing Summary	577,000	
Materials Inventory (beginning)		21,000
Work in Process Inventory (beginning)		13,000
Direct Labor		154,000
Indirect Labor		77,000
Transportation In		9,000
Depreciation—Factory		25,000
Depreciation—Equipment		22,000
Factory Repairs and Maintenance		17,000
Factory Supplies Used		10,000
Other Factory Overhead		33,000
Materials Purchases		196,000
To close the beginning materials and work in process inventories and the manufacturing cost accounts having debit balances to the Manufacturing Summary account.		
Materials Inventory (ending)	28,000	
Work in Process Inventory (ending)	15,000	
Manufacturing Summary		43,000
To record the ending materials and work in process inventories.		

REQUIRED
Using the above information, prepare a cost of goods manufactured statement for the current year for Glendale Factory, Inc.

Cost of goods manufactured and sold

21–27 The data on page 820 relate to three independent production periods of Riverside Manufacturing Company. Missing data are indicated by question marks.

	A	B	C
Materials:			
Beginning Inventory	$ 52	$ 164	$110
Purchases	?	700	500
Ending Inventory	74	100	?
Direct Material	330	?	440
Direct Labor	580	960	800
Factory Overhead:			
Factory Supplies Used	96	?	120
Indirect Labor	160	150	350
Other	?	200	340
Total Factory Overhead	520	480	?
Work in Process Inventories:			
Beginning	?	90	260
Ending	70	?	100
Finished Goods Inventories:			
Beginning	?	400	80
Ending	330	120	330
Cost of Goods Manufactured	1,480	?	?
Cost of Goods Sold	1,440	2,000	?

REQUIRED

Using the above data, calculate the cost of goods manufactured and cost of goods sold. (You should list in order the items appearing on the cost of goods manufactured statement and the cost of goods sold computation, fill in the known data, and calculate the missing amounts.)

Cost per unit and inventory costing

21–28 The following data relate to estimating the ending work in process and finished goods inventories of Bishop Manufacturing Company:

	Estimated Cost of Completed Unit of Product	Estimated Proportions Assigned to Work in Process
Direct Material: A	6 lb @ $8/lb	100%
B	5 lb @ $9/lb	60%
Direct Labor: Cutting	1 hr @ $11/hr	70%
Assembly	2 hr @ $10/hr	40%

For the manufacturing period, total direct labor was $400,000, and total factory overhead was $360,000. Factory overhead is assigned to products on the basis of direct labor cost.

REQUIRED

Using the above data, calculate the cost of an ending finished goods inventory of 900 units and an ending work in process inventory of 700 units.

Statements and journal entries

21–29 The following balances appear in the cost of goods manufactured and the income statement columns of a December 31 worksheet for the current year's operations of Taylor Corporation.

	Cost of Goods Manufactured		Income Statement	
	Debit	Credit	Debit	Credit
Materials Inventory (beginning)	80,000			
Work in Process Inventory (beginning)	48,000			
Finished Goods Inventory (beginning)			120,000	

(continued)

	Cost of Goods Manufactured Debit	Cost of Goods Manufactured Credit	Income Statement Debit	Income Statement Credit
Sales				1,320,000
Materials Purchases	320,000			
Transportation In	12,800			
Direct Labor	380,000			
Indirect Labor	96,000			
Utilities	6,000			
Repairs and Maintenance	10,000			
Depreciation—Machinery	10,800			
Insurance	12,400			
Property Taxes	13,200			
Selling Expenses			144,000	
Administrative Expenses			112,000	
Income Tax Expense			30,000	
Ending Inventories:				
Materials Inventory		60,000		
Work in Process Inventory		56,000		
Finished Goods Inventory				92,000
	989,200	116,000		
Cost of Goods Manufactured		873,200	873,200	
	989,200	989,200	1,279,200	1,412,000
Net Income			132,800	
			1,412,000	1,412,000

REQUIRED

(a) Prepare a cost of goods manufactured statement and an income statement for Taylor Corporation. Assume that 8,000 shares of common stock were outstanding during the year.

(b) Prepare general journal entries to reflect the changes in inventories and to close the manufacturing accounts, the Manufacturing Summary account, the revenue and expense accounts, and the Income Summary account.

Cost of goods manufactured and income statements

21–30 Two inventors, organized as Innovation, Inc., consult you regarding a planned new product. They have estimates of the costs of materials, labor, overhead, and other expenses involved but need to know how much to charge for each unit to earn a profit in the first year equal to 15% of their estimated total long-term investment of $400,000 (ignore income taxes).

Their plans indicate that each unit of the new product requires:

Direct Material

4 lb of a material costing $5/lb

Direct Labor

2 hr of a metal former's time at $11/hr
0.6 hr of an assembler's time at $8/hr

Major items of production overhead would be annual rent of $46,460 for a factory building and $28,660 for machinery. Other production overhead is an estimated 80% of total direct labor costs. Selling expenses are an estimated 30% of total sales while nonfactory administrative expenses are 20% of total sales.

The consensus at Innovation is that during the first year 10,000 units of product should be produced for selling and another 2,000 units for the next year's beginning inventory. Also, an extra 3,000 pounds of material will be purchased as beginning inventory for the next year. Because of the nature of the manufacturing process, all units started must be completed, so work in process inventories are negligible.

REQUIRED
(a) Incorporate the above data into an estimated cost of goods manufactured statement and compute the unit production cost.
(b) Prepare an estimated income statement that would provide the target amount of profit.
(c) What unit sales price should Innovation charge for the new product?

Worksheet, financial statements, and closing entries

21–31 The trial balance for Newton Manufacturing Corporation at the end of the current year follows:

	Debit	Credit
Cash	$ 40,000	
Accounts Receivable	248,000	
Allowance for Uncollectible Accounts		$ 5,600
Materials Inventory (January 1)	164,000	
Work in Process Inventory (January 1)	72,000	
Finished Goods Inventory (January 1)	92,000	
Land	140,000	
Factory Buildings	800,000	
Accumulated Depreciation—Factory Buildings		184,000
Factory Equipment	700,000	
Accumulated Depreciation—Factory Equipment		68,000
Accounts Payable		144,000
Long-term Notes Payable—8%		224,000
Common Stock, $400 Par Value (all outstanding)		1,120,000
Retained Earnings		228,000
Sales		1,680,000
Materials Purchases	380,000	
Direct Labor	504,000	
Indirect Labor	124,000	
Factory Utilities	19,600	
Repairs and Maintenance	16,000	
Factory Property Taxes	18,000	
Selling Expenses	192,000	
Administrative Expenses	144,000	
	$3,653,600	$3,653,600

The following information is available for adjusting and closing the accounts:
1. December 31 inventories are: materials, $136,000; work in process, $80,000; and finished goods, $64,000.
2. Accrued wages and salaries at December 31 are: direct labor, $8,400; indirect labor, $2,800; and sales salaries, $11,200.
3. Annual amounts of depreciation are: factory buildings, $44,000; factory equipment, $28,000.
4. Accrued utilities payable at December 31, $2,000.
5. Uncollectible accounts expense, $\frac{1}{2}$% of sales. (Debit this expense to Selling Expenses.)
6. Estimated income taxes, $38,880.

REQUIRED
(a) Prepare a manufacturing worksheet for the year.
(b) Prepare a cost of goods manufactured statement and an income statement.
(c) Prepare a balance sheet.
(d) Prepare closing entries.

Worksheet, financial statements, and closing entries

21–32 The trial balance of Hyde Company at December 31 of the current year is given below, together with the worksheet adjustments.

	Trial Balance		Adjustments	
	Debit	Credit	Debit	Credit
Cash	28,000			
Materials Inventory (Jan. 1)	36,000			
Work in Process Inventory (Jan. 1)	27,800			
Finished Goods Inventory (Jan. 1)	42,000			
Prepaid Insurance	2,800			(1) 1,400
Factory Machinery	240,000			
Accumulated Depreciation—Factory Machinery		50,000		(2) 17,000
Unamortized Cost of Patents	40,800			(3) 3,200
Accounts Payable		61,200		
Common Stock, $170 Par Value		170,000		
Retained Earnings		45,800		
Dividends	20,400			
Sales		620,000		
Materials Purchases	142,800			
Direct Labor	176,800		(4) 4,000	
Indirect Labor	60,000		(4) 1,000	
Factory Utilities	8,200			
Repairs and Maintenance—Factory	4,400			
Factory Buildings Rent	18,000			
Sales Salaries Expense	52,000			
Advertising Expense	13,600			
Nonfactory Administrative Expenses	33,400			
	947,000	947,000		
Insurance—Factory			(1) 1,400	
Depreciation—Factory Machinery			(2) 17,000	
Amortization of Patents			(3) 3,200	
Wages Payable				(4) 5,000
Income Tax Expense			(5) 20,000	
Income Tax Payable				(5) 20,000
			46,600	46,600

Additional information:
1. December 31 inventories are: materials, $52,000; work in process, $30,000; and finished goods, $42,000.
2. Patent amortization applies to factory operations.

REQUIRED
(a) Complete the manufacturing worksheet.
(b) Prepare a cost of goods manufactured statement and an income statement.
(c) Prepare closing entries.

ALTERNATE PROBLEMS

Cost of goods manufactured statement and income statement

21–25A Selected account balances from the completed year-end worksheet of the Porter Manufacturing Company appear below in alphabetical order:

Administrative Salaries*	60,000
Advertising and Promotion Expense	63,000
Depreciation—Machinery	39,000
Depreciation—Office Equipment*	30,000
Depreciation—Sales Fixtures	18,000
Direct Labor	268,000
Factory Rent	46,000
Factory Supervision	26,000
Factory Supplies Used	12,000
Indirect Labor	32,000
Materials Inventory (Jan. 1)	18,000
Work in Process Inventory (Jan. 1)	$22,000
Finished Goods Inventory (Jan. 1)	82,000
Materials Inventory (Dec. 31)	48,000
Work in Process Inventory (Dec. 31)	36,000
Finished Goods Inventory (Dec. 31)	44,000
Maintenance—Machinery	24,000
Materials Purchases	174,000
Nonfactory Area Rent*	38,000
Other Factory Overhead	19,000
Other Selling Expenses	20,000
Sales	900,000
Sales Salaries Expense	48,000
Transportation In	8,000

REQUIRED
Using the above data, prepare a cost of goods manufactured statement and an income statement for the current year (disregard income tax and earnings per share considerations).

Cost of goods manufactured statement

21–26A The following journal entries recorded the changes in inventories and closed the manufacturing accounts of Golden Gate Factory, Inc., at year-end:

Manufacturing Summary	896,000	
Materials Inventory (beginning)		32,000
Work in Process Inventory (beginning)		19,000
		(entry continues)

*These amounts relate to nonfactory administration.

Direct Labor		240,000
Indirect Labor		115,000
Transportation In		13,000
Depreciation—Factory Building		42,000
Depreciation—Machinery		34,000
Factory Repairs and Maintenance		26,000
Factory Supplies Used		14,000
Other Factory Overhead		51,000
Materials Purchases		310,000
To close the beginning materials and work in process inventories and the manufacturing cost accounts having debit balances to the Manufacturing Summary account.		
Materials Inventory (ending)	43,000	
Work in Process Inventory (ending)	22,000	
Manufacturing Summary		65,000
To record the ending materials and work in process inventories.		

REQUIRED
Using the above information, prepare a cost of goods manufactured statement for the current year for Golden Gate Factory, Inc.

Cost of goods manufactured and sold

21–27A The data below relate to three independent production periods of Randolph Manufacturing Company. Missing data are indicated by question marks.

	A	B	C
Materials:			
Beginning Inventory	$ 78	$ 410	$ 220
Purchases	?	1,750	1,000
Ending Inventory	111	250	?
Direct Material	495	?	880
Direct Labor	870	2,400	1,600
Factory Overhead:			
Factory Supplies Used	144	?	240
Indirect Labor	240	375	700
Other	?	500	680
Total Factory Overhead	780	1,200	?
Work in Process Inventories:			
Beginning	?	225	520
Ending	105	?	200
Finished Goods Inventories:			
Beginning	?	1,000	160
Ending	495	300	660
Cost of Goods Manufactured	2,220	?	?
Cost of Goods Sold	2,160	5,000	?

REQUIRED
Using the above data, calculate the cost of goods manufactured and cost of goods sold. (You should list in order the items appearing on the cost of goods

manufactured statement and the cost of goods sold computation, fill in the known data, and calculate the missing amounts.)

Cost per unit and inventory costing

21–28A The following data relate to estimating the ending work in process and finished goods inventories of Bourne Manufacturing Company:

	Estimated Cost of Completed Unit of Product	Estimated Proportions Assigned to Work in Process
Direct Material:		
A	4 lb @ $6/lb	100%
B	3 lb @ $7/lb	70%
Direct Labor:		
Machining	3 hr @ $9/hr	60%
Assembly	2 hr @ $8/hr	30%

For the manufacturing period, total direct labor was $400,000 and total factory overhead was $480,000. Factory overhead is assigned to products on the basis of direct labor cost.

REQUIRED

Using the above data, calculate the cost of (a) an ending finished goods inventory of 1,000 units and (b) an ending work in process inventory of 800 units.

Statements and journal entries

21–29A The following balances appear in the cost of goods manufactured and the income statement columns of a December 31 worksheet for the current year's operations of Tempe Corporation.

	Cost of Goods Manufactured		Income Statement	
	Debit	Credit	Debit	Credit
Materials Inventory (beginning)	46,000			
Work in Process Inventory (beginning)	32,000			
Finished Goods Inventory (beginning)			124,000	
Sales				1,680,000
Materials Purchases	484,000			
Transportation In	34,000			
Direct Labor	300,000			
Indirect Labor	132,000			
Factory Utilities	18,000			
Factory Repairs and Maintenance	22,000			
Depreciation—Equipment	10,000			
Factory Insurance	6,000			
Factory Property Taxes	14,000			
Selling Expenses			106,000	
Administrative Expenses			74,000	
Income Tax Expense			128,000	

(continued)

	Cost of Goods Manufactured Debit	Cost of Goods Manufactured Credit	Income Statement Debit	Income Statement Credit
Ending Inventories:				
Materials Inventory		64,000		
Work in Process Inventory		24,000		
Finished Goods Inventory				72,000
	1,098,000	88,000		
Cost of Goods Manufactured		1,010,000	1,010,000	
	1,098,000	1,098,000	1,442,000	1,752,000
Net Income			310,000	
			1,752,000	1,752,000

REQUIRED
(a) Prepare a cost of goods manufactured statement and an income statement for Tempe Corporation. Assume that 40,000 shares of common stock were outstanding during the year.
(b) Prepare general journal entries to reflect the changes in inventories and to close the manufacturing accounts, the Manufacturing Summary account, the revenue and expense accounts, and the Income Summary account.

Cost of goods manufactured and income statements

21–30A You are consulted by Investors, Inc., a group of investors planning a new product. They have estimates of the costs of materials, labor, overhead, and other expenses involved but need to know how much to charge for each unit of the new product to earn a profit in the first year equal to 10% of their estimated investment of $500,000 (ignore income taxes).

Their plans indicate that each unit of the new product requires:

Direct Material
4 lb of a material costing $6/lb

Direct Labor
3 hr of a die cutter's time at $9/hr
2 hr of an assembler's time at $8/hr

Major items of production overhead would be annual rent of $61,000 on the factory building and $25,000 on machinery. Other production overhead is an estimated 60% of total direct labor costs. Selling expenses are an estimated 20% of total sales while nonfactory administrative expenses are 10% of total sales.

The consensus at Investors is that during the first year 4,000 units of product should be produced for selling and another 1,000 units for the next year's beginning inventory. Also, an extra 6,000 pounds of material will be purchased as beginning inventory for the next year. Because of the nature of the manufacturing process, all units started must be completed, so work in process inventories are negligible.

REQUIRED
(a) Incorporate the above data into an estimated cost of goods manufactured statement and compute the unit production cost.
(b) Prepare an estimated income statement that would provide the target amount of profit.
(c) Rounded to the nearest dollar, what unit sales price should Investors charge for the new product?

Worksheet, financial statements, and closing entries

21–31A The trial balance for the Niagara Boatbuilders Corporation at the end of the current year follows:

	Debit	Credit
Cash	$ 40,000	
Accounts Receivable	151,200	
Allowance for Uncollectible Accounts		$ 7,200
Materials Inventory (January 1)	64,000	
Work in Process Inventory (January 1)	32,000	
Finished Goods Inventory (January 1)	80,000	
Land	104,000	
Factory Buildings	550,000	
Accumulated Depreciation—Factory Buildings		148,000
Factory Machinery	740,000	
Accumulated Depreciation—Factory Machinery		108,000
Accounts Payable		116,000
Long-term Notes Payable—9%		216,000
Common Stock—$100 Par Value (all outstanding)		360,000
Retained Earnings		510,000
Sales		1,476,000
Materials Purchases	416,000	
Direct Labor	296,000	
Indirect Labor	110,000	
Factory Utilities	30,000	
Repairs and Maintenance	18,000	
Property Taxes	24,000	
Selling Expenses	172,000	
Administrative Expenses	114,000	
	$2,941,200	$2,941,200

The following information is available for adjusting and closing the accounts:

1. December 31 inventories are: materials, $50,000; work in process, $44,000; and finished goods, $54,000.
2. Accrued wages and salaries at December 31 are: direct labor, $6,000; indirect labor, $1,000; and sales salaries, $3,600.
3. Annual amounts of depreciation are: factory buildings, $32,000; factory machinery, $26,000.
4. Accrued utilities payable at December 31, $1,800.
5. Uncollectible accounts expense, 1% of sales. (Debit this expense to Selling Expenses.)
6. Estimated income taxes, $73,136.

REQUIRED

(a) Prepare a manufacturing worksheet for the year.
(b) Prepare a cost of goods manufactured statement and an income statement.
(c) Prepare a balance sheet.
(d) Prepare closing entries.

Worksheet, financial statements, and closing entries

21–32A The trial balance of Hunter Company at December 31 of the current year is given below, together with the worksheet adjustments.

	Trial Balance Debit	Trial Balance Credit	Adjustments Debit		Adjustments Credit	
Cash	34,000					
Materials Inventory (Jan. 1)	68,000					
Work in Process Inventory (Jan. 1)	50,000					
Finished Goods Inventory (Jan. 1)	84,000					
Prepaid Insurance	10,000				(1)	5,000
Factory Machinery	570,000					
Accumulated Depreciation—Factory Machinery		48,000			(2)	22,400
Unamortized Cost of Copyright	98,000				(3)	6,000
Accounts Payable		134,000				
Common Stock—$200 Par Value		224,000				
Retained Earnings		188,000				
Dividends	32,000					
Sales		1,900,000				
Materials Purchases	504,000					
Direct Labor	476,000		(4)	14,000		
Indirect Labor	180,000		(4)	6,000		
Factory Utilities	26,000					
Repairs and Maintenance—Factory	12,000					
Factory Building Rent	30,000					
Sales Salaries Expense	134,000					
Advertising Expense	62,000					
Administrative Expenses	124,000					
	2,494,000	2,494,000				
Insurance—Factory			(1)	5,000		

(continued)

	Trial Balance		Adjustments			
	Debit	Credit		Debit		Credit
Depreciation—Machinery			(2)	22,400		
Amortization of Patents			(3)	6,000		
Wages Payable					(4)	20,000
Income Tax Expense			(5)	106,000		
Income Tax Payable					(5)	106,000
				159,400		159,400

Additional information:

1. December 31 inventories are: materials, $78,000; work in process, $34,000; and finished goods, $66,000.
2. Copyright amortization applies to factory operations.

REQUIRED

(a) Complete the manufacturing worksheet.
(b) Prepare a cost of goods manufactured statement and an income statement.
(c) Prepare closing entries.

BUSINESS DECISION PROBLEM

William Martin, an engineer, needs some accounting advice. In their spare time during the past year, Martin and his college-aged son, Robert, have manufactured a small weed-trimming sickle in a rented building near their home. Robert, who has had one accounting course in college, keeps the books.

Martin is pleased about the results of their first year's operations. He asks you to look over the following income report prepared by Robert before they leave on a well-deserved vacation to Hawaii, after which they plan to expand their business significantly.

Sales (34,000 units at $10 each)		$340,000
Costs of producing 35,000 units:		
Materials:		
Precast blades at $1.50 each	$ 57,000	
Preturned handles at $1 each	40,000	
Labor costs of hired assemblers	26,600	
Labor costs of hired painters	33,000	
Rent on building	15,700	
Rent on machinery	6,300	
Utilities for production	8,000	
Other production costs	11,900	
Advertising expense	27,800	
Sales commissions	34,250	
Delivery of products to customers	14,200	
Total costs	$274,750	
Less: Ending inventory of 1,000 units at average production costs of $7.85 (or $274,750/35,000 units)	7,850	
Cost of sales		266,900
Net Income		$ 73,100

After you examine the income report, Martin responds to your questions and assures you that (1) no theft or spoilage of materials has occurred, (2) no partially completed units are involved, and (3) he and his son have averaged 30 hours each per week in the business for 50 weeks, and (4) he is in approximately the 40% income tax bracket (before considering the sickle venture).

REQUIRED

(a) Identify any apparent discrepancy in the income report in the cost of materials used.
(b) Recalculate the cost of goods manufactured, the average cost per unit produced, and the net income for the year, including a provision for estimated income taxes on the earnings.
(c) What factors should Martin consider regarding the profitability of his venture before deciding to expand it significantly?

ANSWERS TO SELF-TEST QUESTIONS

1. (d) **2.** (b) **3.** (c) **4.** (a) **5.** (c)

APPENDIX F

ALTERNATIVE METHOD OF RECORDING MANUFACTURING INVENTORIES

In Chapter 21, the beginning inventories (material, work in process, and finished goods) were closed and the ending inventories recorded as part of the closing process at the end of the accounting period. An alternative method, presented in this appendix, treats the entries for the beginning and ending inventories as adjusting entries at the end of the accounting period.

ADJUSTING ENTRIES

To illustrate this method, we use the same data presented in chapter 21 for Lollar Manufacturing, Inc. Adjusting entry data for Lollar Manufacturing, Inc., for the year-end illustration were:

1. Unexpired insurance at year-end on factory machinery, $1,000.
2. Unpaid wages and salaries at year-end (by category): direct labor, $4,000; indirect labor, $3,000; office salaries, $1,000; and sales salaries, $2,000.
3. Depreciation on factory machinery, $6,000.
4. Accrued interest payable at year-end, $1,000.
5. Uncollectible accounts expense is an estimated 2% of sales.
6. Factory supplies on hand, $4,000.
7. Office supplies on hand, $2,000.
8. Estimated income taxes, $17,000.

An adjusting journal entry will be required for each item listed above. In addition, adjusting journal entries will be required for each of the three manufacturing inventories:

	January 1 Balances	December 31 Balances
Materials Inventory	$10,000	$18,000
Work in Process Inventory	6,000	8,000
Finished Goods Inventory	17,000	26,000

WORKSHEET

Exhibit F–1 presents the worksheet for Lollar Manufacturing, Inc., when the alternative method (adjusting entries) for handling manufacturing inventories on the worksheet is used. The first eight adjusting entries listed above are entered in the adjustments columns of the worksheet using the same procedures described in Chapters 4 and 5 (see items 1 through 8 in the adjustments column of Exhibit F–1).

The procedure for entering the manufacturing inventories on the worksheet in Exhibit F–1 consists of five steps:

1. Remove the beginning inventory balances by making the following entries in the adjustments columns of the worksheet:

Manufacturing Summary	10,000	
Materials Inventory	10,000	
To transfer the beginning Materials Inventory balance to the Manufacturing Summary account. *(Adjustment 9 on the worksheet)*		
Manufacturing Summary	6,000	
Work in Process Inventory		6,000
To transfer the beginning Work in Process Inventory balance to the Manufacturing Summary account. *(Adjustment 10 on the worksheet)*		
Income Summary	20,000	
Finished Goods Inventory		20,000
To transfer the beginning Finished Goods Inventory balance to the Income Summary account. *(Adjustment 11 on the worksheet)*		

2. Set up the ending balances of the inventories by making the following entries in the adjustments columns of the worksheet:

Materials Inventory	18,000	
Manufacturing Summary		18,000
To record the ending Materials Inventory balance. *(Adjustment 12 on the worksheet)*		
Work in Process Inventory	8,000	
Manufacturing Summary		8,000
To record the ending Work in Process Inventory balance. *(Adjustment 13 on the worksheet)*		
Finished Goods Inventory	26,000	
Income Summary		26,000
To record the ending Finished Goods Inventory balance. *(Adjustment 14 on the worksheet)*		

EXHIBIT F–1

Lollar Manufacturing, Inc.
Manufacturing Worksheet
For the Year Ended December 31, 19XX

Description	Trial Balance Debit	Trial Balance Credit	Adjustments Debit	Adjustments Credit	Cost of Goods Manufactured Debit	Cost of Goods Manufactured Credit	Income Statement Debit	Income Statement Credit	Balance Sheet Debit	Balance Sheet Credit
Cash	13,000								13,000	
Accounts Receivable	45,000								45,000	
Allowance for Uncollectible Accounts		1,000		(5) 9,000						10,000
Materials Inventory	10,000		(12) 18,000	(9) 10,000					18,000	
Work in Process Inventory	6,000		(13) 8,000	(10) 6,000					8,000	
Finished Goods Inventory	20,000		(14) 26,000	(11) 20,000					26,000	
Factory Supplies on Hand	17,000			(6) 13,000					4,000	
Office Supplies on Hand	5,000			(7) 3,000					2,000	
Prepaid Insurance	4,000			(1) 3,000					1,000	
Factory Machinery	90,000								90,000	
Accumulated Depreciation—Factory Machinery		20,000		(3) 6,000						26,000
Accounts Payable		7,000								7,000
Long-term Notes Payable—10%		40,000								40,000
Common Stock—$10 Par Value		50,000								50,000
Retained Earnings		20,000								20,000
Dividends	4,000								4,000	
Sales		450,000						450,000		
Materials Purchases	114,000				114,000					
Transportation In	2,000				2,000					
Direct Labor	77,000		(2) 4,000		81,000					
Indirect Labor	43,000		(2) 3,000		46,000					

(continued)

3. Extend the balances of the inventory accounts on the worksheet by placing the net amount for each inventory in the debit column of the balance sheet columns:

   Materials = $10,000 + $18,000 − $10,000 = $18,000
   Work in Process = $ 6,000 + $ 8,000 − $ 6,000 = $ 8,000
   Finished Goods = $20,000 + $26,000 − $20,000 = $26,000

4. Extend both the debit amount (beginning balance) and the credit amount (ending balance) of both lines of the Manufacturing Summary into the cost of goods manufactured columns, the debit amounts into the debit column and the credit amounts into the credit column. All four amounts will be needed to prepare the cost of goods manufactured statement.

EXH F–1 (Continued)

Lollar Manufacturing, Inc.
Manufacturing Worksheet
For the Year Ended December 31, 19XX

Description	Trial Balance Debit	Trial Balance Credit	Adjustments Debit	Adjustments Credit	Cost of Goods Manufactured Debit	Cost of Goods Manufactured Credit	Income Statement Debit	Income Statement Credit	Balance Sheet Debit	Balance Sheet Credit
Factory Utilities	20,000				20,000					
Factory Repairs	10,000				10,000					
Factory Rent	40,000				40,000					
Administrative Rent Expense	7,000						7,000			
Sales Rent Expense	23,000						23,000			
Office Salaries Expense	12,000		(2) 1,000				13,000			
Sales Salaries Expense	16,000		(2) 2,000				18,000			
Advertising Expense	7,000						7,000			
Interest Expense	3,000		(4) 1,000				4,000			
	588,000	588,000								
Factory Insurance			(1) 3,000		3,000					
Wages Payable				(2) 10,000						10,000
Factory Depreciation—Machinery			(3) 6,000		6,000					
Interest Payable				(4) 1,000						1,000
Uncollectible Accounts Expense			(5) 9,000				9,000			
Factory Supplies Used			(6) 13,000		13,000					
Office Supplies Expense			(7) 3,000				3,000			
Income Tax Expense			(8) 17,000				17,000			
Income Tax Payable				(8) 17,000						17,000
Manufacturing Summary:										
Materials			(9) 10,000	(12) 18,000	10,000	18,000				
Work in Process			(10) 6,000	(13) 8,000	6,000	8,000				
Income Summary			(11) 20,000	(14) 26,000			20,000	26,000		
			150,000	150,000	351,000	26,000				
Cost of Goods Manufactured						325,000	325,000			
					351,000	351,000	446,000	476,000	211,000	181,000
Net Income							30,000			30,000
							476,000	476,000	211,000	211,000

5. Extend both the debit amount (beginning balance) and the credit amount (ending balance) of the Income Summary into the income statement columns, the debit amount into the debit column and the credit amount into the credit column. These two amounts, representing the beginning and ending balances of finished goods, will be used when the income statement is prepared.

Although this alternative method yields different totals for the adjustments columns of the worksheet, the totals for the income statement columns and the balance sheet columns will be the same as the illustration in Chapter 21. Further, the information in the financial statements and the formats of the financial statements will be exactly the same as the illustration in Chapter 21.

CLOSING ENTRIES

Closing journal entries will be required at the end of the year. The worksheet provides all the data needed to prepare the closing entries. The alternative method used in this appendix will cause the closing entries to be different than those in the illustration in Chapter 21. The closing entries for Lollar Manufacturing, Inc., are listed below:

Manufacturing Summary	335,000	
Materials Purchases		114,000
Transportation In		2,000
Direct Labor		81,000
Indirect Labor		46,000
Factory Utilities		20,000
Factory Repairs		10,000
Factory Rent		40,000
Factory Supplies Used		13,000
Factory Insurance		3,000
Factory Depreciation—Machinery		6,000
To close manufacturing cost accounts to the Manufacturing Summary account.		
Income Summary	426,000	
Administrative Rent Expense		7,000
Sales Rent Expense		23,000
Office Salaries Expense		13,000
Office Supplies Expense		3,000
Sales Salaries Expense		18,000
Advertising Expense		7,000
Interest Expense		4,000
Uncollectible Accounts Expense		9,000
Income Tax Expense		17,000
Manufacturing Summary		325,000
To close all expense accounts and the Manufacturing Summary account (which had a balance of $10,000 credit as a result of the inventory adjusting entries) to the Income Summary account.		
Sales	450,000	
Income Summary		450,000
To close the Sales account to the Income Summary account.		

Income Summary	30,000	
Retained Earnings		30,000
To close the Income Summary account to the Retained Earnings account. (The Income Summary account had a $6,000 credit from the inventory adjusting entries, a $426,000 debit from the second closing entry, and a $450,000 credit from the third closing entry.)		
Retained Earnings	4,000	
Dividends		4,000
To close the Dividends account to Retained Earnings.		

PROBLEMS

Worksheet, financial statements, and closing entries

F–1 Follow the requirements of Problems 21–31 at the end of Chapter 21, using the method described in this appendix.

Worksheet, financial statements, and closing entries

F–2 Follow the requirements of Problem 21–31A at the end of Chapter 21, using the method described in this appendix.

Worksheet, financial statements, and closing entries

F–3 Follow the requirements of Problem 21–32 at the end of Chapter 21, using the method described in this appendix.

Worksheet, financial statements, and closing entries

F–4 Follow the requirements of Problem 21–32A at the end of Chapter 21, using the method described in this appendix.

22

COST ACCOUNTING SYSTEMS: JOB ORDER COSTING

CHAPTER OBJECTIVES

1. Discuss the limitations of cost determinations (pp. 839–40).
2. Describe the use of perpetual inventories and explain the need for timely product costing (pp. 840–41).
3. Introduce the calculation and use of predetermined overhead rates (pp. 841–42).
4. Describe the accumulation and tracing of product costs through a cost accounting system (pp. 842–46).
5. Present the documents and procedures used in a job order costing system (pp. 847–51).
6. Outline the journal entries needed in a job order costing system (pp. 851–58).
7. Illustrate the use of general ledger control accounts and subsidiary ledger accounts in a job order costing system (pp. 847–58).

So soon as we begin to count the cost, the cost begins.
HENRY DAVID THOREAU

In Chapter 21, we introduced the concepts of multiple manufacturing inventories, cost of goods manufactured, and financial statements for a manufacturing concern. Our approach presented a general accounting system for a simple manufacturing operation using periodic inventory procedures. The limitations of that system justify the development of specialized cost accounting systems and the use of perpetual inventories to provide cost data that are more meaningful for managerial decision making. In this and the following chapter, we introduce important aspects of cost accounting and illustrate two important types of cost accounting systems for manufacturing firms.

LIMITATIONS OF COST DETERMINATIONS

There are inherent limitations in most cost determinations. Misconceptions prevail that accounting cost figures are exact and that a precise cost can be assigned to any asset, product, or unit of activity. Although an exhaustive consideration of these issues is beyond the scope of this chapter, a review of several examples should provide a realistic perspective.

We determine cost basically by accumulating the total costs incurred in doing something and then allocating these costs among the various units of accomplishment. Any unit of activity, service rendered, or product manufactured may be involved. Accounting procedures for both the accumulation and the allocation of costs may necessarily involve somewhat arbitrary choices. Often no single cost measurement or allocation scheme is demonstrably better than any other. Therefore, the accountant must choose from among a group of equally defensible approaches to cost measurement and allocation. Following are several examples, the first two of which were mentioned in previous chapters.

Assumed Cost Flows

The purchase prices of materials often vary throughout the year. Assigning costs to cost of goods sold and ending inventories may involve arbitrarily assuming a cost flow such as FIFO, LIFO, or some form of average cost.

Depreciation Estimates

The service potential of plant assets is utilized over many operating periods. No method can determine the precise amount of the asset's cost to be allocated to a given period. Instead, periodic depreciation expense is based on estimates of useful life and salvage value as well as on an often arbitrary choice among several depreciation methods.

Allocated Joint Costs

Joint costs are common to two or more products or manufacturing processes. Costs of materials, supervisors' salaries, and service department costs are often joint costs. In a lumbering mill operation, for example, no single precise method can allocate the cost of a whole log to the several wood products that result—prime clear boards used for furniture, rough construction-grade boards, the bark sold as mulch to landscapers, and the sawdust used for paper. Joint product costs are often allocated arbitrarily on the basis of the relative sales value, weights, or volumes of each joint product. In Chapter 23, we illustrate accepted allocation techniques for joint products and service departments.

Realistically then, *the* cost of something is actually determined by our choices from among a series of perhaps equally valid assumptions.

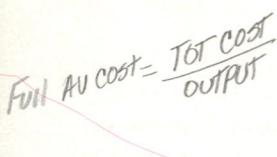

Another aspect of the limitations of cost determination is that the concept of cost varies and different versions may be useful for different purposes. Ordinarily, cost systems provide *full average cost,* or the total of all costs divided by all output. For example, if costs of $100,000 are incurred in producing 80,000 units of product, the average unit cost is $1.25 ($100,000/80,000). Suppose that in evaluating the opportunity to accept an additional overseas order for 10,000 units, production engineers advise that producing the additional 10,000 units would raise total costs to $108,000. In its decision to accept or reject the offer, management could consider the new average unit cost of $1.20 ($108,000/90,000 units) or the incremental unit cost of 80 cents (the $8,000 increase in cost divided by the 10,000 unit increase in production). Neither of these costs is wrong, nor the other right. Rather, depending on certain management decision situations, either one may be defended as more appropriate. This and other instances of management's use of "different cost for different purposes" are illustrated in subsequent chapters.

It is important to realize that, as necessary and useful as cost data are, they are complex and have inherent limitations. Users of cost data must be aware of the specific assumptions made, the costing procedures used, and the proper application of the variations of cost data.

THE NATURE AND ADVANTAGES OF COST ACCOUNTING SYSTEMS

Any orderly method of developing cost information constitutes cost accounting. Typically, some amount of cost is accumulated and related to some unit of activity or accomplishment. Examples include accumulating the costs of cutting or forming materials, assembling parts, and the painting and finishing that might result in a completed unit of product such as a lawnmower, a computer, or a custom-designed executive jet aircraft. Although a cost system could be maintained independently of a firm's formal accounting records, most comprehensive cost systems are integrated into the formal accounting system.

Cost accounting systems are usually illustrated in the context of a manufacturing situation involving unit product costs. Remember, however, that reliable cost-per-unit-of-accomplishment data are vital to decision makers in all economic endeavors. For example, a municipality may need to know the cost per ton of snow removal; a hospital, the cost per patient of providing various surgical or diagnostic services; and an insurance company, the cost of providing various combinations of homeowner protection to specific groups of policyholders. Many of the costing concepts and techniques used in manufacturing costing systems also apply to nonmanufacturing situations.

Use of Perpetual Inventories

The inherent weaknesses of using periodic inventory procedures for manufacturing operations were discussed in Chapter 21. Cost of materials used and cost of goods sold tend to be residual (or *plug*) figures when periodic inventory procedures are used. Also, relatively current cost data are available only at end-of-period intervals, and many significant departmental cost details are not readily apparent.

Cost accounting systems usually incorporate perpetual inventory procedures. That is, additions to and deductions from all inventory accounts—materials, work in process, and finished goods—are recorded as they occur. The more current cost information and greater cost controls justify the additional bookkeeping costs of perpetually maintaining the inventory accounts.

Perpetual inventory records are customarily verified by physical inventory counts at least once a year. Necessary adjustments for errors and unrecorded inventory shrinkages can then be made. The flow of product costs—direct material, direct labor, and factory overhead—through the various perpetual inventory accounts of a cost accounting system should be apparent in both the simple and more comprehensive illustrations appearing in this chapter.

Timely Product Costing

A cost accounting system must provide for the timely determination of product costs. Product costs are needed to arrive at inventory amounts for work in process and for finished goods; these amounts are required in the preparation of financial statements. Obviously, to determine income properly, we must have some method of identifying costs with the products sold and the products that remain on hand in a finished or unfinished state.

Management uses engineering studies and cost analyses to establish cost standards and budgets. Only by knowing product costs can management compare actual costs with standards and budgets and take necessary remedial action.

Management also needs product cost data to establish price lists and to submit bids on special orders for its products. Although many factors, including marketing and legal constraints, affect pricing decisions, unit product costs are often an important determinant. Furthermore, once prices are established, knowledge of costs enables management to determine profit margins and to direct its efforts intelligently to the promotion of its more profitable items.

To identify costs with a product or a group of products, a manufacturer must trace factory costs—direct material, direct labor, and factory overhead—to lots or batches of product. Tracing material and labor costs to products is relatively easy. To account for material used, a company may keep track of the costs of material requisitioned for production. Labor costs can similarly be accounted for by time-keeping methods or by identifying the product with the payroll costs of personnel in those operations or departments that produce the product. A firm cannot directly determine the amount of factory overhead that should be identified with different products or groups of products. Consequently, a firm typically assigns overhead costs to products throughout the production period by using a predetermined overhead rate.

Use of Predetermined Overhead Rates

Many of the concepts and procedures underlying the use of **predetermined overhead rates** are extensive and complex. In this chapter, we present only a basic treatment, sufficient to convey a general understanding of the use of these rates in product costing.

Before the beginning of an accounting period, management normally prepares budgets. Sales forecasts are translated into production budgets, which in turn permit estimates of plant use in terms of a common measure of activity. This common measure is typically direct labor hours, direct labor costs, or machine hours. Using historical data and projected activity levels, management can estimate the total factory overhead cost to be incurred. The overhead rate is computed by dividing the estimated total factory overhead cost by the selected measure of activity. Calculations of predetermined overhead rates are usually based on year-long production periods.

Assume that the number of direct labor hours used is the most appropriate measure of activity for applying overhead in a given situation. If the estimated number of direct labor hours is 100,000 and the estimated total factory overhead is \$150,000, the overhead rate may be calculated as follows:

$$\text{Overhead Rate} = \frac{\text{Estimated Factory Overhead for the Year}}{\text{Estimated Direct Labor Hours for the Year}}$$
$$= \frac{\$150{,}000}{100{,}000 \text{ hours}}$$
$$= \$1.50/\text{direct labor hour}$$

If, during the accounting period, a particular product requires 50 direct labor hours of production time, \$75 of overhead (50 × \$1.50) is charged to this product.

Before selecting the basis for applying overhead to products, a firm should analyze carefully the relationship between overhead incurred and various alternative measures of activity. Direct labor hours or direct labor costs would be used as the measure of activity in a factory that has labor-intensive manufacturing. However, in a factory where automation has replaced many of the production workers, machine-hours may be a more appropriate measure.

Using a predetermined overhead rate, management can estimate the overhead costs of any job at any stage of production, computing "costs to date" both for control purposes and for inventory costing. This method also eliminates wide fluctuations in unit costs that might result if actual recorded overhead costs were assigned to products during short interim periods when production departed markedly from average levels.

For example, assume that normal production is 100,000 direct labor hours per year and that production fluctuates seasonally throughout the year. Suppose also that a large share of actual factory overhead cost is spread fairly evenly over the year. (Such costs as depreciation, maintenance, utilities, and supervisory costs remain fairly constant from month to month.) Exhibit 22–1 illustrates the possible differences between assigned overhead costs based on actual monthly overhead rates and those based on an annual overhead rate. The estimated annual rate in this example is \$1.50 per direct labor hour (\$150,000/100,000 direct labor hours). The actual monthly rates vary from \$3.10 in February to \$1.10 in July, with only the months of April, September, and October even approaching the annual average of \$1.50 per direct labor hour. Using actual monthly rates and assuming that a particular unit of product requires three direct labor hours, a unit produced in July when production activity was highest would be assigned overhead costs of \$3.30 (3 × \$1.10). In contrast, a unit produced in February when production activity was lowest would be assigned overhead costs of \$9.30 (3 × \$3.10). The \$6 difference is hardly defensible, especially when the two units of product may be virtually indistinguishable physically. Clearly, basing product costs on allocations of actual monthly overhead amounts is unrealistic. The use of a predetermined overhead rate employing a yearly average produces more meaningful unit cost figures.

Flow of Product Costs

The simple illustration on the next few pages introduces the basic ideas of cost accounting systems. The final part of this chapter presents a more detailed example for assigning costs to manufactured products. The simple illustration below identifies a first phase of accumulating product costs and a second phase of tracing these costs as they become sequentially (1) work in process, during man-

EXHIBIT 22–1

COMPARISON OF ACTUAL MONTHLY AND ESTIMATED ANNUAL OVERHEAD RATES

	Factory Overhead Costs Incurred Each Month*	Direct Labor Hours Worked Each Month	Actual Monthly Overhead Rates	Estimated Annual Overhead Rate
January	$ 9,900	4,000	$2.48	$1.50
February	9,300	3,000	3.10	1.50
March	10,500	5,000	2.10	1.50
April	12,300	8,000	1.54	1.50
May	14,100	11,000	1.28	1.50
June	14,700	12,000	1.23	1.50
July	16,500	15,000	1.10	1.50
August	15,300	13,000	1.18	1.50
September	13,500	10,000	1.35	1.50
October	12,300	8,000	1.54	1.50
November	11,100	6,000	1.85	1.50
December	10,500	5,000	2.10	1.50
Annual Amounts	$150,000	100,000		

*Assumed to be $7,500 each month plus 60 cents per direct labor hour.

ufacturing operations; (2) finished goods, when completed; and (3) costs of goods sold, when sold. Remember in this illustration that all product costs are capitalized (accounted for as assets).

ACCUMULATING PRODUCT COSTS The basic relationships in this illustration underlie all cost accounting systems, although the account titles used vary in practice. For simplicity in presenting these basic concepts, we assume no beginning inventory. Each entry is explained and its effect keyed to related accounts shown here in T-account form.

❶ Recording Acquisition of Materials

	Debit	Credit
Materials Inventory	1,000	
Accounts Payable		1,000

Materials Inventory	
❶ 1,000	

Accounts Payable	
	❶ 1,000

The perpetual inventory procedures for purchasing merchandise explained in Chapter 9 are used to derive this entry.

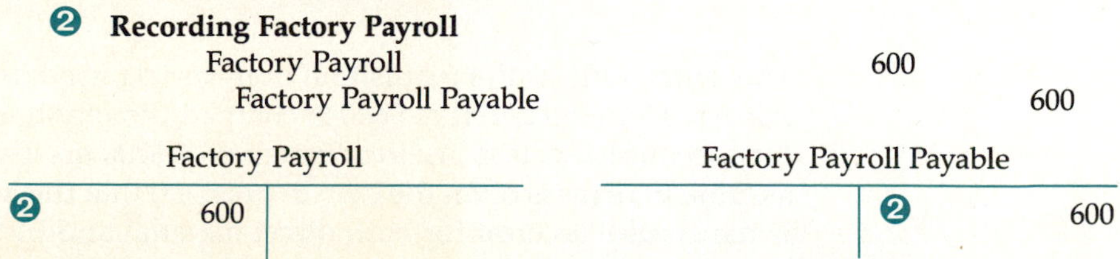

❷ Recording Factory Payroll

	Debit	Credit
Factory Payroll	600	
Factory Payroll Payable		600

Factory Payroll	
❷ 600	

Factory Payroll Payable	
	❷ 600

Here, the total factory payroll includes both direct and indirect labor. Later, these two items will be handled separately. Data for this entry would come from a detailed analysis of factory payroll records.

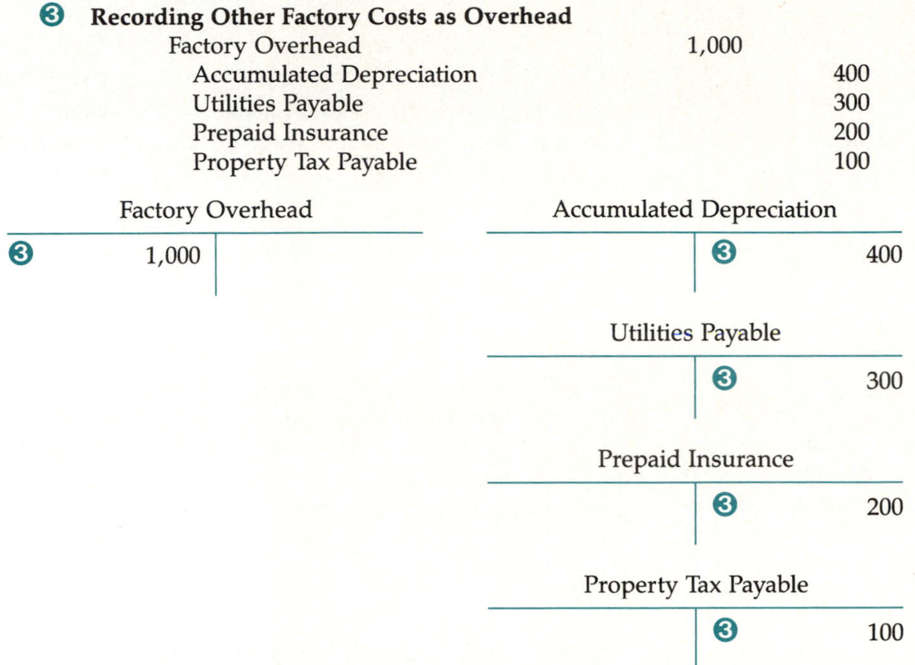

Realistically, factory overhead includes many more items than are shown here. We chose these particular items to illustrate depreciation, accruals, and the write-off of prepaid items.

At this point, all product costs have been accumulated into debit balances in the Materials Inventory, Factory Payroll, and Factory Overhead accounts. We now trace these costs through to Cost of Goods Sold.

TRACING PRODUCT COSTS In this phase of our illustration, we show how the product costs accumulated earlier are transferred sequentially through the Work in Process Inventory and Finished Goods Inventory accounts to the Cost of Goods Sold account. Descriptions, journal entries, and explanations for each step are keyed to the cost flow diagram in Exhibit 22–2. As you read the material, trace each entry in the cost flow diagram.

❹ **Recording Requisitions of Direct Material and Indirect Material**

	Debit	Credit
Work in Process Inventory	600	
Factory Overhead	200	
Materials Inventory		800

This entry reflects the requisition of materials used in production by the various parties. Direct material of $600 is charged directly to the Work in Process Inventory account. Costs of indirect material of $200 are part of factory overhead. We assume here (as is often the case in practice) that the Materials Inventory account is the control account for both direct material and indirect material.

❺ **Recording Distribution of Factory Payroll**		
Work in Process Inventory	500	
Factory Overhead	100	
Factory Payroll		600

Work in Process Inventory is debited for $500 of direct labor, and Factory Overhead is debited for $100 of indirect labor. Observe that the total factory payroll is distributed, leaving a zero balance in the Factory Payroll account. The division of total factory payroll into direct and indirect labor is based on a detailed analysis of each employee's job description, wage rates, and hours worked.

❻ **Recording Application of Factory Overhead**		
Work in Process Inventory	1,200	
Factory Overhead		1,200

This entry adds the third and final category of factory costs to work in process. Note that the amount of this entry is not equal to the $1,300 of actual factory overhead incurred to date. As explained earlier, most firms do *not* apply the actual amount of overhead incurred each period to the goods manufactured during that period. Instead, they apply a predetermined overhead rate that reflects estimates of total annual production volume and total annual overhead costs.

❼ **Recording Completed Production**		
Finished Goods Inventory	2,000	
Work in Process Inventory		2,000

This entry assigns costs to completed production and transfers those costs from Work in Process Inventory to Finished Goods Inventory. As explained later, the amount of this entry is derived from production records, the details of which vary with the firm's particular product costing system. The balance remaining in the Work in Process Inventory account represents the costs assigned to the ending work in process inventory.

❽ **Recording Cost of Goods Sold**		
Cost of Goods Sold	1,400	
Finished Goods Inventory		1,400

This entry transfers the cost of finished products sold to the Cost of Goods Sold account. The balance remaining in the Finished Goods Inventory account reflects costs assigned to the ending inventory of finished goods.

Exhibit 22–2 diagrams the results of the foregoing entries as the various product costs move through the manufacturing accounts. The following list summarizes these entries:

1. Entries ❶–❸ accumulate factory costs into three accounts—Materials Inventory, Factory Payroll, and Factory Overhead.
2. Entry ❹ reflects the requisition of both direct material and indirect material.
3. Entry ❺ distributes the total factory payroll to direct labor and indirect labor.

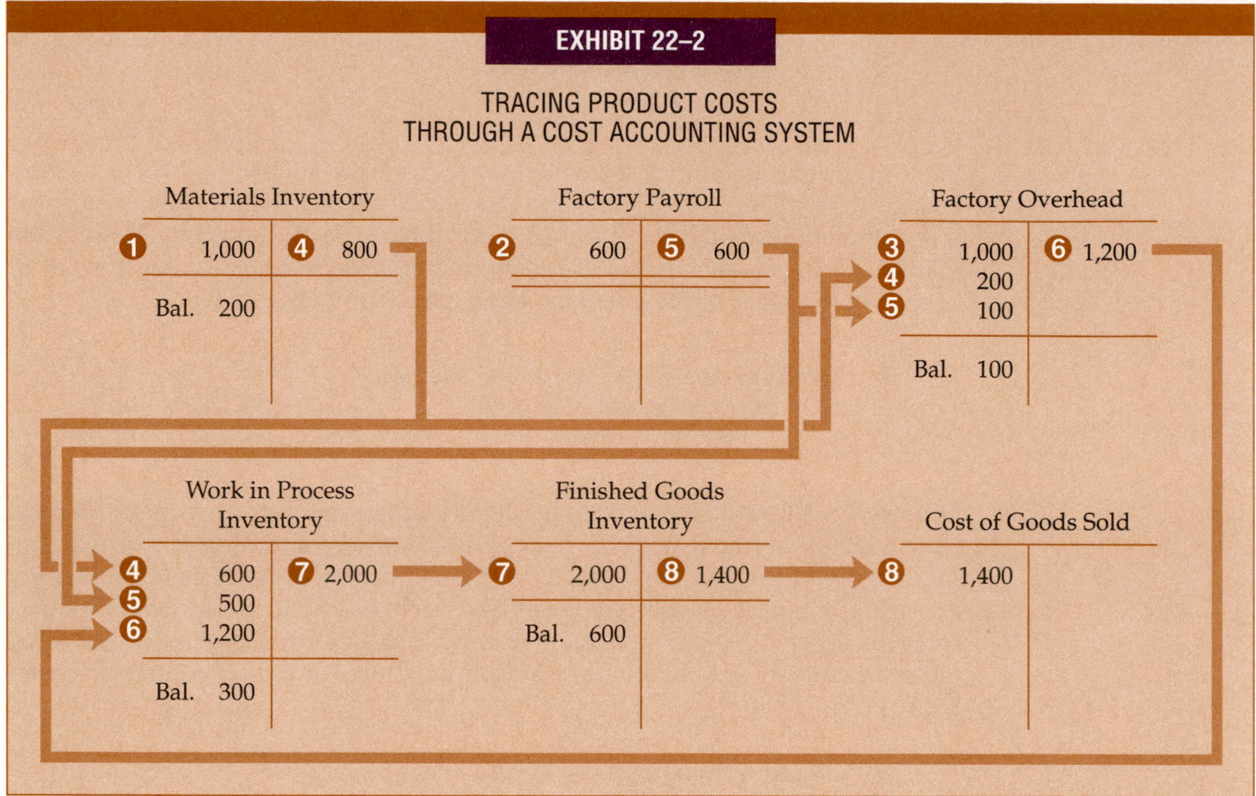

At this point, debits in the Factory Overhead account reflect the actual factory overhead incurred.

4. Entry ❻ applies an amount of factory overhead based on a predetermined annual overhead rate. The $100 balance in the Factory Overhead account represents an amount of actual overhead incurred but not yet applied to work in process, the nature and disposition of which are explained later in the chapter. After entry ❻ the Work in Process Inventory account has been charged for all three categories of product cost—direct material, direct labor, and applied factory overhead.
5. Entry ❼ transfers to Finished Goods Inventory the costs assigned to completed production. The $300 balance in the Work in Process Inventory account is the cost assigned to the goods that are only partially completed at this point.
6. Entry ❽ transfers to Cost of Goods Sold the costs of the finished goods sold. The balance in the Finished Goods Inventory account represents the cost assigned to the goods that are finished but not yet sold.

So far, we have presented the important aspects of cost accounting systems including the use of perpetual inventory procedures, the provision of timely product costs, the use of predetermined overhead rates, and an illustration of the flow of product costs through a cost accounting system. We now turn to an illustration of the widely used *job order* cost accounting system.

JOB ORDER COSTING SYSTEMS

The two basic types of cost accounting systems are job order cost accounting and process cost accounting. **Job order cost accounting** (sometimes called *specific order* costing) is appropriate when production is characterized by a series of different products or jobs undertaken either to fill specific orders from customers or to produce a general stock of products from which future orders are filled. This type of costing is widely used in construction, printing, and machine shop operations. Often the products or batches of products vary in their material components and manner of production. In contrast, *process cost accounting* lends itself most readily to the production of a large volume of products manufactured in a "continuous flow" operation, such as distillation of fuels or manufacture of paint, chemicals, wire, and similar items. Essentially the same ingredients and operations are involved during each period of manufacture.

Both systems allocate manufacturing costs primarily to products to determine unit costs. In a job order system, costs are identified with specific jobs to determine the cost of products manufactured. In a process system, costs are identified with production processes and averaged over the products made during the period. This chapter describes a job order costing system; the basic concepts of process costing are presented in Chapter 23.

Exhibits 22–3 through 22–7 show some of the important accounting forms used in a manual job order costing system. Each of the three inventory accounts—Materials Inventory, Work in Process Inventory, and Finished Goods Inventory—

EXHIBIT 22–3

MATERIALS LEDGER CARD

Materials Ledger Card

Stock No. 32
Description 1/8" Steel Wire — Reorder Quantity 4,000 ft.
Supplier Steel Supply Corp. — Minimum Quantity 1,000 ft.

	Received				Issued				Balance		
Date	Rec'g. Report No.	Units	Price	Total Price	Mat'l. Req'n. No.	Units	Price	Total Price	Units	Price	Total Price
19XX											
8/1	320	4,000	0.20	800.00					4,000	0.20	800.00
8/5					567	700	0.20	140.00	3,300	0.20	660.00
8/9	332	4,000	0.21	840.00					3,300	0.20	660.00
									4,000	0.21	840.00

EXHIBIT 22–4

MATERIALS REQUISITION FORM

Materials Requisition

Date 8/5/XX Job. No. 372 Requisition No. 567

Item	Quantity		Unit Price	Amount
	Authorized	Issued		
Stock No. 32 (1/8" wire)	700 ft.	700 ft.	0.20	$140
Total				$140

Authorized by: G.E.K. Issued by: G.A.P. Received by: F.W.E.

has a subsidiary ledger in which unit costs are accounted for. **Materials ledger cards** (Exhibit 22–3) for each type of direct material or indirect material used make up the subsidiary ledger for the Materials Inventory account; the cards show quantities received, issued, and on hand, unit costs, and total amounts. **Materials requisition forms** (Exhibit 22–4) authorize the issuance of direct material for various jobs or of indirect material. **Time tickets** (Exhibit 22–5) document the amount of time spent and the individual employee labor cost incurred as direct labor for individual jobs or as a part of factory overhead.

Job cost sheets (Exhibit 22–6) comprise the subsidiary ledger for the Work in Process Inventory account. For each job in process, the sheet indicates the cost of direct material, direct labor, and applied overhead identified with the job. When a job is completed, the total cost is divided by the number of units in the lot to obtain a unit cost. The job's cost sheet is then removed from the Work in Process subsidiary ledger and an entry is made on a **finished goods ledger card** (Exhibit 22–7). These cards comprise the subsidiary ledger for Finished Goods Inventory. The cards in this last ledger identify the stock number and name of the product and show quantities, unit costs, and total costs of the various lots of product awaiting sale.

We now turn to the comprehensive illustration of job order costing, which shows how to use these forms. In this illustration, we make the following three assumptions:

1. Bradley Company uses materials A and B to produce products Y and Z.
2. Bradley also uses material C, which is classified as indirect material.
3. Bradley uses a predetermined overhead rate based on annual direct labor hours to assign factory overhead to products.

EXHIBIT 22-5

TIME TICKET

Time Ticket

Employee Name Robert Smith Employee No. 42
Skill Specification Machine Operator Payroll Period Ending 8/16/XX

Time Started	Time Stopped	Total Time	Hourly Labor Rate	Department	Job No.	Total Cost
8:00	12:00	4.0	$8.00	B	372	$32.00
1:00	2:00	1.0	8.00	B	372	8.00
Total		5.0				$40.00

Approved by: R. L. T.

Accounting for Materials

A materials clerk records the amounts of materials received and increases the balances on the appropriate materials ledger cards. Purchases are also posted to the Materials Inventory account in the general ledger. The amount added to this account equals the amounts added to the materials ledger cards during the period.

When direct material (A and B, in this case) is requisitioned for specific orders or jobs, the materials clerk records the reductions on the appropriate materials ledger cards. Cost clerks then enter these amounts in the materials section of the job cost sheets for the specific jobs in which the material is used. Amounts on requisitions representing indirect material (material C) are handled by the materials clerk in the same fashion as amounts for direct material. The amounts, however, are charged to the Factory Overhead account in the general ledger.

For example, assume the following:

1. Bradley Company purchased $2,500 of material A, $1,500 of material B, and $500 of material C during its first month of operations. (Total: $4,500.)
2. $1,700 of materials were requisitioned: $1,000 of material A for job 1; $500 of material B for job 2; and $200 of material C for general factory use.

The effect of these transactions is shown in Exhibit 22–8. Notice that for each subsidiary ledger, *matching* postings (debits for debits and credits for credits) totaling each entry are made to the related general ledger control account.

Accounting for Labor

To identify labor costs with specific jobs, firms use time tickets to accumulate the hours spent on various jobs by each employee. Hourly wage rates can then be

EXHIBIT 22–6

JOB COST SHEET

Job Cost Sheet

Customer Gordon Sales Company | Job No. 372
Product Bracket-H3 | Date Promised 9/1/XX
Quantity 200 | Dates: Started 8/1/XX Completed 8/20/XX

Direct Material		Direct Labor			Cost Summary	
Mat'l. Req'n. No.	**Amount**	**Payroll Summary Dated**	**Dept.**	**Amount**		
567	140.00	8/2	A	70.00	**Direct Material**	700.00
573	180.00	8/9	A	240.00	**Direct Labor**	600.00
591	200.00	8/16	B	190.00	**Factory Overhead (applied at):**	
603	180.00	8/23	B	100.00	150% of direct labor cost	900.00
					Total Cost	2,200.00
Totals	700.00			600.00	**Units Finished** 200 **Unit Cost**	11.00

used to compute the labor costs for the various jobs. Periodically, the direct labor amounts are posted to the job cost sheets. To continue our example, we assume the following:

3. Total direct labor hours used and charges incurred during the period ($2,400):
   Job 1—200 hours, $1,600 total direct labor
   Job 2—100 hours, $800 total direct labor
4. Indirect labor payroll for the period, $1,000.

The effect of these transactions is shown in Exhibit 22–9, where we use the Work in Process Inventory account, its subsidiary ledger (the job cost sheets), the Factory Overhead account, and the Factory Payroll account. We do not show the Factory Payroll account debit entry that would be part of the entry to record the factory payroll liability.

Accounting for Overhead

Exhibits 22–8 and 22–9 demonstrate how indirect material and indirect labor costs for the period are introduced into the accounts. In our example, the cost of indirect material amounted to $200 and the indirect labor costs were $1,000. Other

EXHIBIT 22–7

FINISHED GOODS LEDGER CARD

Finished Goods Ledger Card

Stock No. H3
Item Bracket-H3 Minimum Quantity 50

Manufactured			Sales			Balance			
Job No.	Quantity	Total Cost	Invoice No.	Quantity	Total Cost	Date	Quantity	Unit Cost	Total Cost
372	200	2,200.00				8/20	200	11.00	2,200.00
			123	100	1,100.00	8/25	100	11.00	1,100.00

overhead costs are charged to the Factory Overhead account as incurred or through adjusting entries at the end of the accounting period. For instance, assume that in addition to the indirect material and indirect labor costs, the following overhead costs were incurred during the period: utilities, \$50; repairs, \$60; depreciation, \$180; and insurance, \$40. The general journal entry to record these items is given below:

		Debit	Credit
5.	Factory Overhead—Utilities	50	
	Factory Overhead—Repairs	60	
	Factory Overhead—Depreciation	180	
	Factory Overhead—Insurance	40	
	Cash (*or* Accounts Payable)		110
	Accumulated Depreciation		180
	Prepaid Insurance		40

The debits in entry 5 are shown as they would appear in the Factory Overhead account (see Exhibit 22–10). The accounts credited in the entry—Cash, Accumulated Depreciation, and Prepaid Insurance—are omitted from the exhibit.

As explained earlier, actual overhead is not identified directly with specific jobs. Instead, through the use of a predetermined overhead rate, the Work in Process Inventory account is charged with overhead applied. We assume that Bradley Company charges overhead to jobs on the basis of direct labor hours. Its forecasting and budgeting process has determined an overhead rate of \$5 per direct labor hour. Because job 1 accumulated 200 hours, Bradley applies \$1,000 of overhead cost to this job, while job 2, requiring 100 hours, receives \$500 of overhead cost. The general journal entry to charge work in process inventory with applied overhead would be as follows at the top of page 854.

EXHIBIT 22–8

ENTRIES FOR PURCHASE AND REQUISITION OF MATERIALS

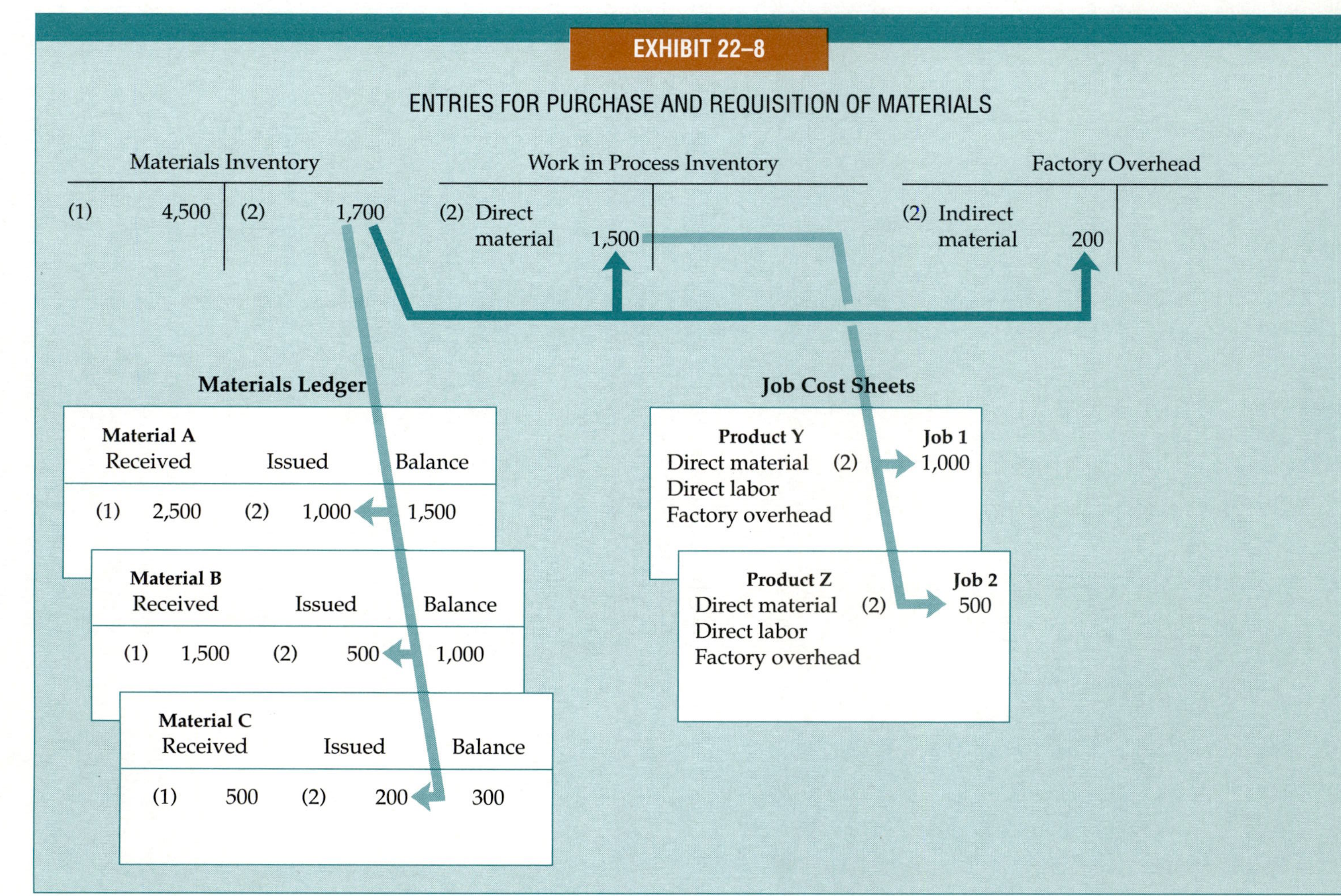

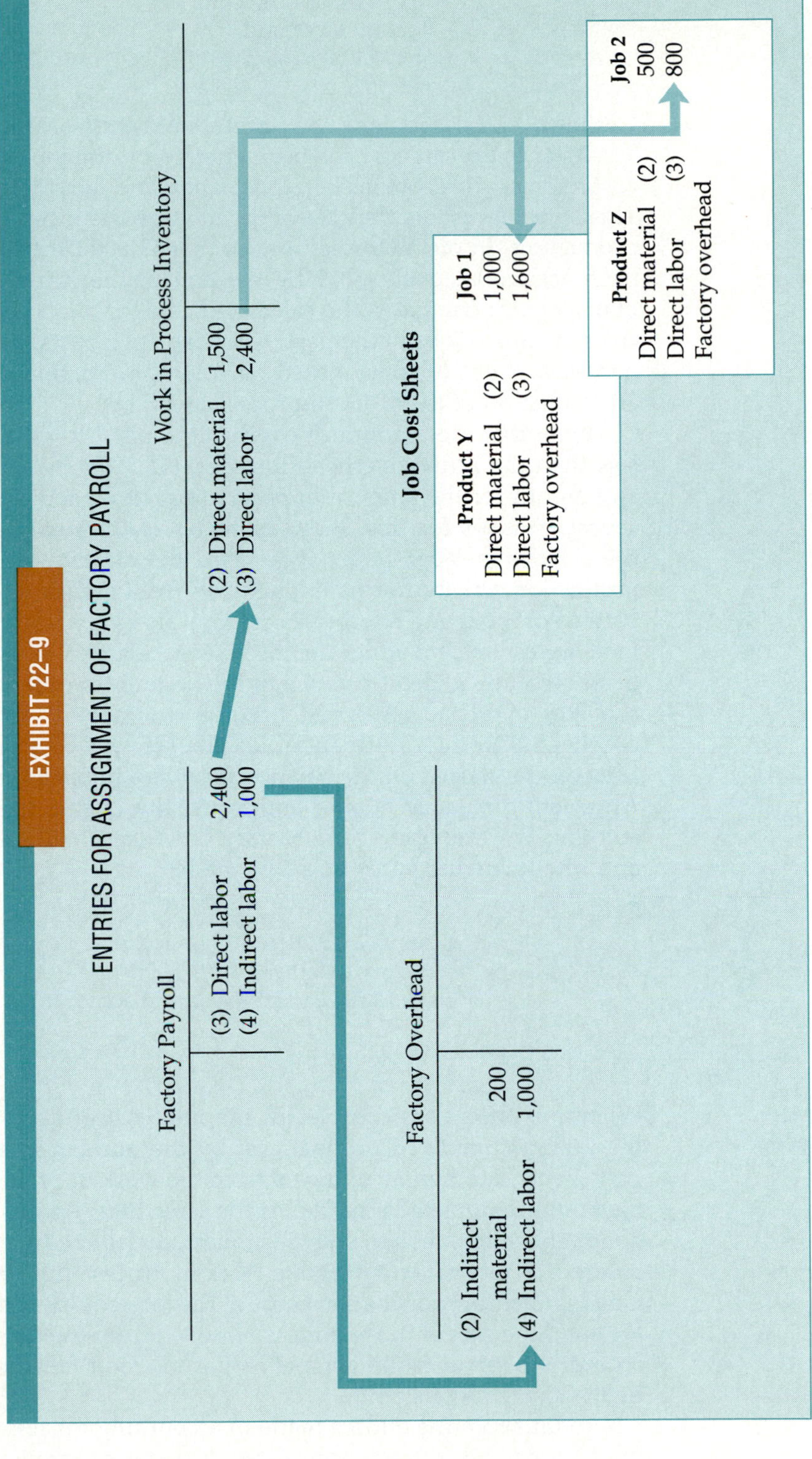
EXHIBIT 22–9
ENTRIES FOR ASSIGNMENT OF FACTORY PAYROLL
Factory Payroll
(3) Direct labor 2,400
(4) Indirect labor 1,000
Work in Process Inventory
(2) Direct material 1,500
(3) Direct labor 2,400
Factory Overhead
(2) Indirect material 200
(4) Indirect labor 1,000
Job Cost Sheets
Product Y
Job 1
Direct material (2) 1,000
Direct labor (3) 1,600
Factory overhead
Product Z
Job 2
Direct material (2) 500
Direct labor (3) 800
Factory overhead

6.	Work in Process Inventory	1,500	
	Factory Overhead		1,500
	(Job 1, $1,000; job 2, $500)		

Exhibit 22–10 shows how the accounts reflect overhead items.

After overhead cost has been entered on the job cost sheets, all elements of cost to date—direct material, direct labor, and factory overhead—can be totaled. This sum represents the cost of the job from its inception to its present stage of production. In our example, we see that $3,600 ($1,000 + $1,600 + $1,000) has been accumulated on job 1 by the end of the accounting period. Frequently, management compares the calculated cost for a job not yet completed with the costs of similar jobs in the past. Knowing such costs, management may take any necessary steps to control costs. In addition, accumulating cost by jobs permits an evaluation of the work in process inventory.

Note that the amount of overhead applied to jobs during the period is $30 less than the actual overhead incurred ($1,530). In fact, it would be unusual in any month for the amount applied to equal the actual overhead cost. There are several reasons for this. First, estimates of the total annual overhead cost and the activity in labor hours were used to calculate the overhead rate. Second, production activity normally fluctuates from month to month. Third, the actual pattern of incurring overhead cost may also vary from month to month. Therefore, we can expect either debit or credit balances monthly in the Factory Overhead account. A debit balance in the account is called **underapplied** (or *underabsorbed*) overhead. A credit balance would be **overapplied** (or *overabsorbed*) overhead. On interim financial statements, the Factory Overhead account balance can be shown on the balance sheet as a deferred debit or a deferred credit. An existing balance at year-end is usually closed to the Cost of Goods Sold account. For example, if the Factory Overhead had a $30 debit balance at year-end, the following entry might be made:

Cost of Goods Sold	30	
Factory Overhead		
To close the Factory Overhead account.		30

Accounting for Finished Goods

When job orders are completed, the unit cost of items is obtained by dividing the total accumulated product cost by the number of units produced. The job cost sheets can then be removed from the work in process subsidiary ledger and filed in the completed jobs file. At the same time, entries are made in the finished goods subsidiary ledger, showing quantities, unit cost, and total cost of the items entered. A journal entry credits Work in Process Inventory and debits Finished Goods Inventory for the total cost of the jobs completed. When units of product are sold, the cost of those units is removed from the finished goods ledger cards; an entry is made in the general ledger to credit Finished Goods Inventory and debit Cost of Goods Sold.

To illustrate the entries made in accounting for finished goods, assume that job 1, costing $3,600, was completed during the current period, resulting in 1,000 units of product Y, and that 400 units of product Y were sold for $6 each. Job 2 was still in process at the end of the period. The following entries record the

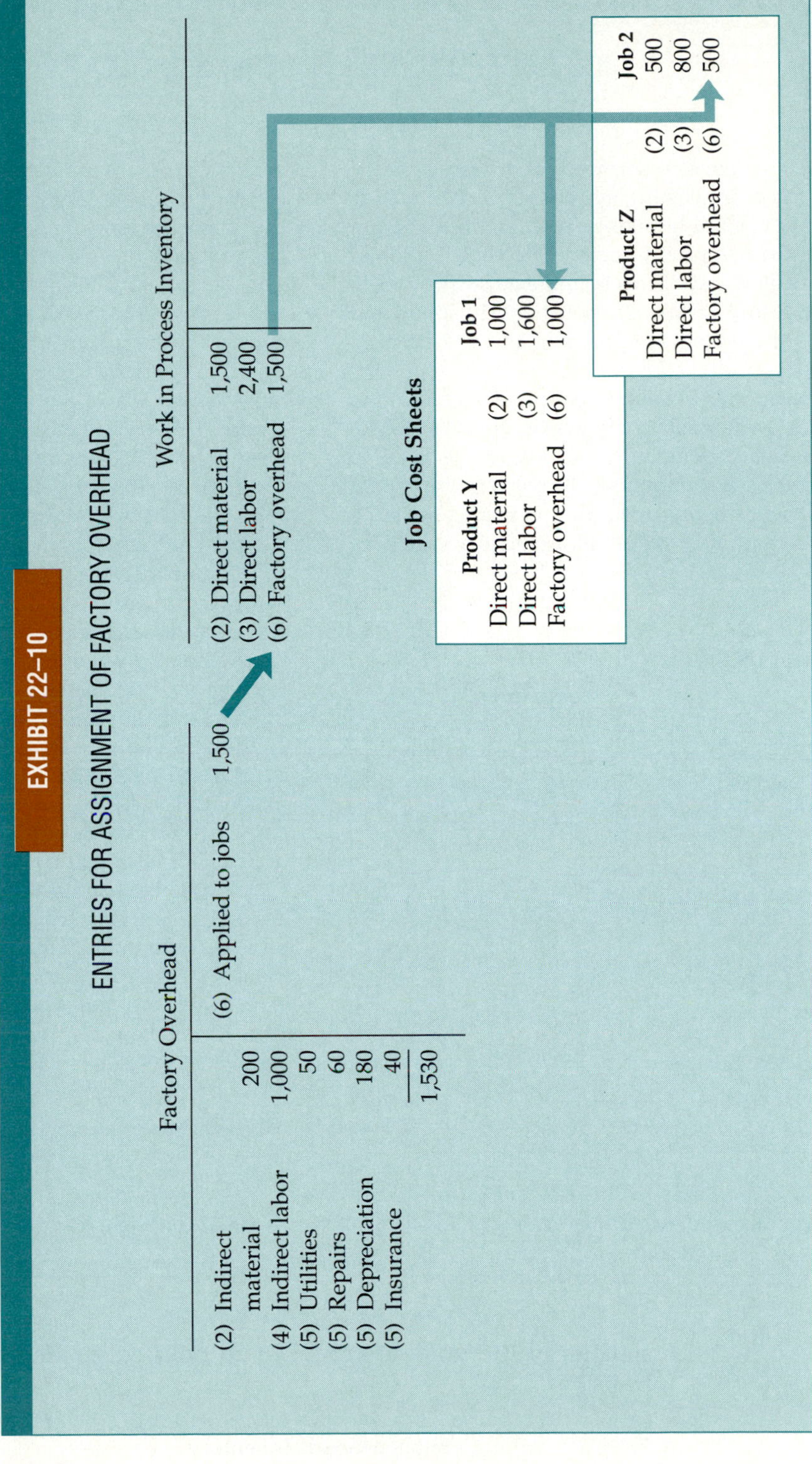

Factory Overhead
(2) Indirect material 200
(4) Indirect labor 1,000
(5) Utilities 50
(5) Repairs 60
(5) Depreciation 180
(5) Insurance 40
1,530
(6) Applied to jobs 1,500
Work in Process Inventory
(2) Direct material 1,500
(3) Direct labor 2,400
(6) Factory overhead 1,500
Job Cost Sheets
Product Y
Job 1
Direct material (2) 1,000
Direct labor (3) 1,600
Factory overhead (6) 1,000
Product Z
Job 2
Direct material (2) 500
Direct labor (3) 800
Factory overhead (6) 500

EXHIBIT 22–10

ENTRIES FOR ASSIGNMENT OF FACTORY OVERHEAD

JOB ORDER COSTING IN SERVICE INDUSTRIES

Many firms in service industries use variations of job order costing systems for accumulating costs and developing billings to customers. Manufacturing firms typically accumulate costs by job or product while service firms accumulate costs by client (accounting and law firms), by patient (hospitals and clinics), or by project (engineering and architectural firms).

For example, hospitals use patient accounting systems to accumulate the costs of all services provided to each patient during a stay in the hospital and to develop the amounts to be billed to the patient or the patient's health insurance company for each service. A typical hospital bill includes a variety of items:

EXAMPLE HOSPITAL

September 30, 19XX

John R. Thatcher
1620 Adams Street
Lansing, Minnesota 98203

INVOICE for hospital stay:
9/10/XX through 9/14/XX

X-rays	$ 80
Room supplies	42
Surgeon's fee	875
Private duty nurse	440
Room charge	1,250
TOTAL	$2,687

Each of the items in this bill can be related to the job costing framework. X-rays were taken by a separate group of radiologists that billed the hospital $80 for the x-rays. They were billed to the patient at the same amount. The room supplies were taken from the hospital's material inventory. They had an original cost of $30 but were billed to the patient at $42, incorporating a $12 gross profit. X-rays and room supplies represent material charges.

Two types of labor charges are included in the bill—the surgeon's fee and the private duty nurse charge. The $875 surgeon's fee was based on 2.5 hours of surgery at $350 per hour, a direct parallel to factory direct labor. The private duty nurse charge represents four shifts of eight hours. The nurses are paid $85 per shift while each shift is billed to the patient at $110, incorporating a total gross profit of $100.

Many other costs cannot be directly identified with each patient in an efficient manner. These overhead-type cost items (such as staff interns, general nursing care, food service, building depreciation, and utilities) are allocated to individual patients using a daily room charge. This charge is primarily a predetermined overhead rate, but also incorporates a gross profit. The bill for Mr. Thatcher includes five days of room charge at $250 per day, which consists of $1,050 of allocated cost and $200 of gross profit.

The patient accounting system accumulates these charges in an account the equivalent of work in process, with subsidiary records by patient. When the billing is prepared for a patient, the billed amount is removed from the work in process account. There is no equivalent of finished goods inventory in a hospital system.*

*For further discussion of cost accounting in hospitals, see James D. Suver and Bruce R. Neumann, *Management Accounting for Healthcare Organizations*, Revised Edition (Chicago: Pluribus Press, Inc., and Oakbrook, Illinois: Healthcare Financial Management Association, 1986).

transfer of the units of product Y to finished goods and reflect the sale of 400 units:

7.	Finished Goods Inventory	3,600	
	Work in Process Inventory		3,600
	Job 1 completed, producing 1,000 units of product Y at $3.60 per unit.		

		Debit	Credit
8.	Cost of Goods Sold	1,440	
	Finished Goods Inventory		1,440
	Cost of 400 units of product Y at $3.60 each.		
9.	Accounts Receivable	2,400	
	Sales		2,400
	Sold 400 units of product Y at $6 per unit.		

After transactions 7–9 are entered, the relevant accounts and subsidiary records would appear as shown in Exhibit 22–11. Note three points: (1) an obvious parallel exists between the physical flow of goods and the related accounting

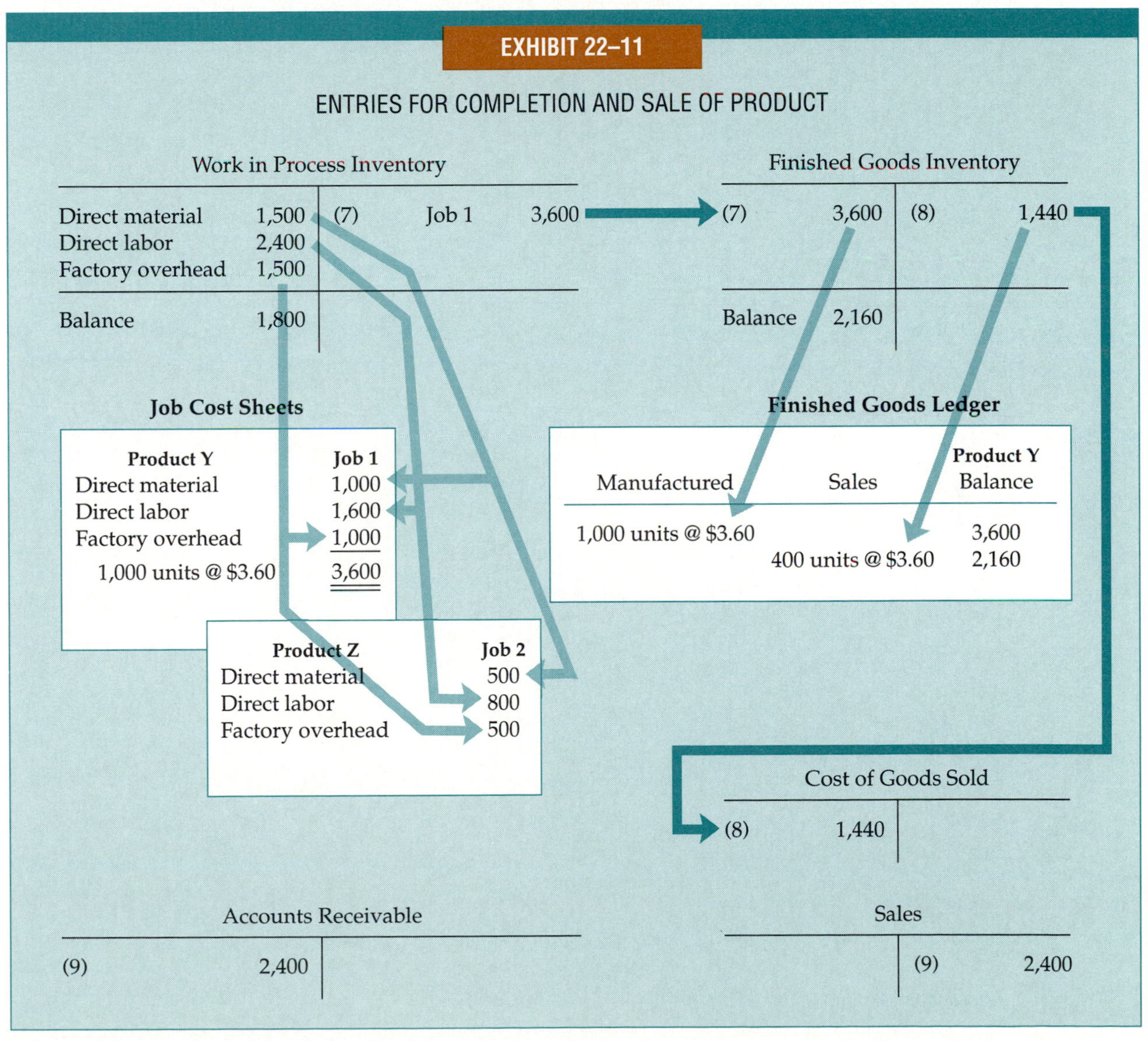

entries; (2) the various subsidiary ledgers contain a detailed analysis of the aggregate amounts in their related general ledger control accounts; and (3) the sale of finished goods involves entries at both the selling price and the related cost amount.

COST ACCOUNTING SYSTEMS AND FINANCIAL STATEMENTS

When perpetual inventory procedures are used in cost accounting systems, the ending balances of all three inventory accounts reflect the period's routine transactions that increase and decrease inventories. These ending balances are adjusted only if a discrepancy appears in year-end physical inventory counts. Note also that the cost of goods sold figure has been accumulated throughout the year in a general ledger account and can be placed directly on the income statement. Detailed information is available in the related accounts for preparing analyses of cost of goods manufactured and cost of goods sold. The format of financial statements for firms using cost accounting systems is similar to that illustrated in Chapter 21.

KEY POINTS FOR CHAPTER OBJECTIVES

1 Discuss the limitations of cost determinations (pp. 839–40).

- The basic concept of cost accounting is the accumulation and allocation of cost to some unit of activity or accomplishment.
- Virtually all cost data are based on assumptions about—and relatively arbitrary choices among—equally defensible accounting procedures. Users of cost data should be aware of the variations inherent in cost data and any resulting limitations to the data used.

2 Describe the use of perpetual inventories and explain the need for timely product costing (pp. 840–41).

- Perpetual inventory procedures are used with all three manufacturing inventories—materials, work in process, and finished goods.
- All additions to and deductions from inventories are recorded when they occur in a perpetual inventory system.

3 Introduce the calculation and use of predetermined overhead rates (pp. 841–43).

- Predetermined overhead rates are computed by dividing estimated annual overhead cost by estimated annual plant use in terms of a common measure of activity—direct labor hours, direct labor cost, or machine hours.
- Use of predetermined overhead rates along with perpetual inventories enables timely product costing.

4 Describe the accumulation and tracing of product costs through a cost accounting system (pp. 843–46).

- A cost accounting system is basically a method of accumulating the costs of direct material, direct labor, and factory overhead and allocating them sequentially to work in process, finished goods, and cost of goods sold.

5 Present the documents and procedures used in a job order costing system (pp. 847–48).

- Job order costing is used with production of a series of different jobs or products while process costing is used with continuous flow production.
- Materials requisition forms authorize the issuance of material, which is recorded in the materials subsidiary ledger along with all purchases.
- Time tickets document the labor time by job number.
- The job cost sheet summarizes the product costs for one job—direct material (from materials requisitions), direct labor (from time tickets), and factory overhead applied, using the predetermined overhead rate.

6 Outline the journal entries needed in a job order costing system (pp. 848–57).

- Actual overhead items are posted as debits to Factory Overhead while overhead applied is posted as a credit to Factory Overhead.
- Under- or overapplied overhead is shown as a deferred debit or a deferred credit on interim financial statements; at year-end, the balance is closed to Cost of Goods Sold.

7 Illustrate the use of general ledger control accounts and subsidiary ledger accounts in a job order costing system (pp. 857–58).

- Materials ledger cards, job cost sheets, and finished goods ledger cards are subsidiary ledgers for Materials Inventory, Work in Process Inventory, and Finished Goods Inventory, respectively.

KEY TERMS USED IN THIS CHAPTER

finished goods ledger card 848
job cost sheets 848
job order cost accounting 847
materials ledger card 848
materials requisition form 848
overapplied overhead 854
predetermined overhead rates 841
time ticket 848
underapplied overhead 854

SELF-TEST QUESTIONS FOR REVIEW

(Answers are at the end of this chapter.)

1. Which of the following statements is true about perpetual inventories?
   (a) Cost of materials used and cost of goods sold tend to be residual (or plug) figures.
   (b) Relatively current cost data are available only at end-of-period intervals.
   (c) Additions to and deductions from inventory accounts are recorded as they occur.
   (d) Physical inventory counts are not needed.
2. Predetermined overhead rates should be:
   (a) Greater than actual overhead rates.
   (b) Less than actual overhead rates.
   (c) Based on monthly budgets.
   (d) Based on annual budgets.
3. Which account is debited to record the issuance of material to production for incorporation into the product?
   (a) Direct material.
   (b) Materials inventory.
   (c) Work in process inventory.
   (d) Factory supplies.
4. Which of the following is usually not found on a Job Cost Sheet?
   (a) Factory overhead applied.
   (b) Finished units currently on hand.
   (c) Direct material.
   (d) Unit cost.
5. When should the balance of the Factory Overhead account be zero?
   (a) At the end of each month.
   (b) Only after year-end closing.
   (c) Never.
   (d) Each time a job is completed.

DEMONSTRATION PROBLEM FOR REVIEW

The annual budget for Diamond Corporation for 19XX included the following costs and expenses:

Direct Material	$ 30,000
Direct Labor ($8 per hour)	120,000
Sales Commissions	28,000
Factory Supervision	16,000
Indirect Labor	27,000
Factory Depreciation	25,000
Factory Taxes	7,000
Factory Insurance	6,000
Factory Utilities	9,000

REQUIRED

(a) Compute the predetermined factory overhead rate for 19XX using direct labor hours as the activity measure.

(b) Determine the amount of factory overhead that would be applied to jobs during March 19XX, when 1,100 direct labor hours were actually incurred.

SOLUTION TO DEMONSTRATION PROBLEM

(a) Budgeted factory overhead:

Factory supervision	$16,000
Indirect labor	27,000
Factory depreciation	25,000
Factory taxes	7,000
Factory insurance	6,000
Factory utilities	9,000
Budgeted factory overhead	$90,000

Budgeted direct labor hours:

$$\frac{\$120{,}000}{\$8/\text{hour}} = 15{,}000 \text{ Budgeted Direct Labor Hours}$$

Predetermined overhead rate:

$$\frac{\text{Budgeted Factory Overhead}}{\text{Budgeted Direct Labor Hours}} = \frac{\$90{,}000}{15{,}000} = \$6 \text{ per Direct Labor Hour}$$

(b) 1,100 hours × $6 = $6,600 applied factory overhead

QUESTIONS

22–1 What are the two primary objectives of cost accounting systems?

22–2 What are the limitations of most cost determinations?

22–3 In a manufacturing operation, what important advantages do perpetual inventory procedures have over periodic inventory procedures?

22–4 Identify several important uses of unit product costs. Why might management need unit product costs before the operating year-end?

22–5 What is a predetermined factory overhead rate, and how, in general, is it determined?

22–6 Briefly justify the use of an annual predetermined factory overhead rate as opposed to actual monthly factory overhead.

22–7 Marshall Manufacturing, Inc., employs an overhead rate of 140% of direct labor cost. The job 301 cost sheet shows that $6,000 in direct material has been used and that $9,000 in direct labor has been incurred. If 1,000 units of product have been produced on job 301, what is the unit cost of the product?

22–8 Briefly explain the sequential flow of product costs through a cost accounting system.

22–9 For what types of manufacturing activities are job order costing systems most appropriate? For what types are process costing systems most appropriate?

22–10 What type of records would be used or maintained for the following manufacturing activities?
(a) Determining the amount of a specific material on hand.
(b) Issuing direct material for production.
(c) Assigning the direct labor costs for a particular worker.
(d) Accumulating the cost of a particular product or batch of products.
(e) Determining the amounts and cost of completed products on hand.

22–11 Explain the general format and give examples of the data that would appear on (a) a materials ledger card, (b) a job cost sheet, and (c) a finished goods ledger card.

22–12 Briefly explain (a) the concept of a control account and a subsidiary ledger, (b) the three inventory accounts in a manufacturing cost system that are often control accounts, (c) the name of the subsidiary ledger record for each account in part (b), and (d) how to determine that a control account and subsidiary ledger agree.

22–13 Why can we say that the sale of a manufactured product is recorded at two different amounts?

22–14 Weber Company records both actual overhead and applied overhead in a single Factory Overhead account. On January 31, the account has a credit balance. Has overhead been underapplied or overapplied during January? What is the significance of this balance, and how should it be treated in the January financial statements?

22–15 Outline the disposition of an amount of underapplied overhead, assuming it exists either at the end of an interim accounting period or at year-end.

22–16 Greene Manufacturing Company applies factory overhead at the rate of 150% of direct labor cost. During the current period, Johnson incurred $82,000 of direct labor costs and $118,000 of factory overhead costs. What is the amount of over- or underapplied factory overhead?

EXERCISES

Calculate and use overhead rate

22–17 Selected data for the fabrication department of Tulsa Manufacturing, Inc., are presented below:

Estimated factory overhead cost for the year	$202,500
Estimated direct labor cost for the year (@ $9/hr)	162,000
Actual factory overhead cost for January	13,000
Actual direct labor cost for January (1,200 hours)	11,000

Assuming that direct labor cost is the basis for applying factory overhead:
(a) Calculate the predetermined overhead rate.
(b) Present a journal entry that applies factory overhead for January.
(c) By what amount is factory overhead over- or underapplied in January?
(d) How would the amount in part (c) be reflected in January's financial statements?

Calculate and use overhead rate

22–18 Using the data in Exercise 22–17, but assuming that the basis for applying factory overhead is direct labor *hours*, complete requirements (a) through (d).

Calculate and use overhead rate

22–19 During the coming accounting year, Kane Manufacturing, Inc., anticipates the following costs, expenses, and operating data:

Direct Material (16,000 lb)	$40,000
Direct Labor (@ $10/hr)	70,000
Indirect Material	6,000
Indirect Labor	11,000
Sales Commissions	17,000
Factory Administration	8,000
Nonfactory Administrative Expenses	10,000
Other Factory Overhead*	24,000

*Provides for operating 35,000 machine hours.

(a) Calculate the predetermined overhead rate for the coming year for each of the following application bases: (1) direct labor hours, (2) direct labor costs, and (3) machine hours.
(b) For each case in part (a), determine the proper application of factory overhead to job No. 63, to which 8 direct labor hours, $70 of direct labor cost, and 45 machine hours have been charged.

Applied vs. actual overhead

22–20 Quinn Manufacturing Corporation applies factory overhead on the basis of 110% of direct labor cost. An analysis of the related accounts and job cost sheets indicates that during the year total factory overhead incurred was $210,400 and that at year-end Work in Process Inventory, Finished Goods Inventory, and Cost of Goods Sold included $12,000, $40,000, and $130,000, respectively, of direct labor charges incurred during the current year.

(a) Determine the amount of over- or underapplied overhead at year-end.
(b) Prepare a journal entry to close the Factory Overhead account at year-end.

Flow of product costs through accounts

22–21 Assuming a routine manufacturing activity, present journal entries (account titles only) for each of the following transactions:

(a) Purchased direct material on account.
(b) Recorded factory payroll earned but not paid.
(c) Requisitioned both direct material and indirect material.
(d) Assigned direct and indirect factory payroll costs.
(e) Recorded factory depreciation, property tax expense, and insurance expense.
(f) Applied factory overhead to production.
(g) Completed monthly production.
(h) Sold finished goods.

Flow of product costs through accounts

22–22 The following is a cost flow diagram similar to Exhibit 22–2 in which all or part of typical manufacturing transactions (or account entries) are indicated by parenthetical letters on the debit or credit side of each account.

Materials Inventory	
(a)	(c)

Factory Payroll	
(b)	(d)

Factory Overhead	
(c)	(f)
(d)	
(e)	

Work in Process Inventory	
(c)	(g)
(d)	
(f)	

Finished Goods Inventory	
(g)	(h)

Cost of Goods Sold	
(h)	

For each parenthetical letter, present a general journal entry indicating the apparent transaction or procedure that has occurred (disregard amounts).

Job cost records

22–23 For each of the manufacturing transactions or activities indicated by the parenthetical letters in the cost flow diagram in Exercise 22–22, briefly identify the detailed forms, records, or documents (if any) that would probably underlie each journal entry.

Perpetual inventories

22–24 The following summary data are from the job cost sheets of Barnes Company:

	Dates				
Job No.	**Started**	**Finished**	**Shipped**	**Total Costs Assigned at April 30**	**Total Production Costs Added in May**
1	4/10	4/20	5/9	$5,600	
2	4/18	4/30	5/20	4,100	
3	4/24	5/10	5/25	2,200	$4,400
4	4/28	5/20	6/3	2,800	3,600
5	5/15	6/10	6/20		2,000
6	5/22	6/18	6/28		3,000

Using the above data, compute (a) the finished goods inventory at May 1 and May 31, (b) the work in process inventory at May 1 and May 31, and (c) the cost of goods sold for May.

Finished goods and cost of goods sold

22–25 Before the completed production for June is recorded, the Work in Process Inventory account for Franklin Company appears as follows:

Work in Process Inventory

Balance, June 1	9,000		
Direct material	25,000		
Direct labor	21,000		
Factory overhead	16,000		

Assume that completed production for June includes jobs 107, 108, and 109 with total costs of $14,000, $30,000, and $17,000, respectively.

(a) Determine the cost of unfinished jobs at June 30 and prepare a journal entry recording completed production.

(b) Using general journal entries, record the sale of job 107 for $20,000 on account.

Job cost sheet

22–26 Carter Manufacturing Company has the following account in its cost records:

Work in Process Inventory

Direct material	40,000	To finished goods	98,400
Direct labor	32,000		
Factory overhead	38,400		

Carter applies overhead to production at a predetermined rate based on direct labor costs. Assume that Carter uses a job order costing system and that job 110, the only job in process at the end of the period, has been charged with direct material of $3,200. Complete the following cost sheet for job 110.

Cost Sheet—Job 110 (in process)

Direct material	______
Direct labor	______
Factory overhead	______
Total cost	______

PROBLEMS

Note: In all problems and alternate problems, assume perpetual inventory procedures, a single Factory Overhead account, first-in, first-out costing of inventories, and that the Materials Inventory account is the control account for both direct material and indirect material.

Determine and use overhead rate

22–27 Butler Manufacturing, Inc., expects the following costs and expenses during the coming year:

Direct Material	$ 45,000
Direct Labor (@ $9/hr)	153,000
Sales Commissions	34,000
Factory Supervision	22,500
Indirect Labor	42,000
Factory Depreciation	32,000
Factory Taxes	7,500
Factory Insurance	9,000
Factory Supplies Used	8,000
Factory Utilities	15,000

REQUIRED

(a) Compute a predetermined factory overhead rate applied on the basis of direct labor hours.
(b) Present a general journal entry to apply factory overhead during an interim period when 1,400 direct labor hours were worked.
(c) What amount of overhead would be assigned to job 466, to which $180 in direct labor had been charged?

Determine and use overhead rate

22–28 The following selected ledger accounts of Dalton Company are for February (the second month of its accounting year):

Materials Inventory

Feb. 1 bal.	30,000	February credits	112,500
February debits	102,000		

Factory Overhead

February debits	136,500	Feb. 1 bal.	10,500
		February credits	135,000

Work in Process Inventory

Feb. 1 bal.	21,000	February credits	345,000
February debits:			
Direct material	91,500		
Direct labor	150,000		
Factory overhead	135,000		

Factory Payroll Payable

February debits	193,500	Feb. 1 bal.	45,000
		February credits	175,500

Finished Goods Inventory

Feb. 1 bal.	76,500	February credits	382,500
February debits	345,000		

REQUIRED

(a) Determine the amount of indirect material requisitioned for production during February.
(b) How much indirect labor cost was apparently incurred during February?
(c) Calculate the factory overhead rate based on direct labor cost.
(d) Was factory overhead for February under- or overapplied, and by what amount?
(e) Was factory overhead for the first two months of the year under- or overapplied, and by what amount?
(f) What is the cost of production completed in February?
(g) What is the cost of goods sold in February?

Job cost journal entries

22–29 Fulton Manufacturing had the following inventories at the end of its last fiscal year:

Materials inventory	29,000
Work in process inventory	12,000
Finished goods inventory	22,000

During the first month of the current year, the following transactions occurred:

1. Purchased materials on account, $52,000.
2. Incurred factory payroll, $103,000.
3. Requisitioned direct material of $48,000 and indirect material of $20,000.
4. Assigned total factory payroll, of which $17,000 was considered indirect labor.
5. Incurred other factory overhead, $33,000. (Credit Accounts Payable.)
6. Applied factory overhead on the basis of 70% of direct labor costs.
7. Determined completed production, $160,000.
8. Determined cost of goods sold, $137,000.

REQUIRED

(a) Prepare general journal entries to record these transactions.

(b) If the above transactions covered a full year's operations, present a journal entry to dispose of the overhead account balance.

Job cost journal entries

22–30 At the beginning of the current year, Modern Company estimated that it would incur $108,800 of factory overhead cost during the year, using 16,000 direct labor hours to produce the desired volume of goods. On January 1 of the current year, beginning balances of Materials Inventory, Work in Process Inventory, and Finished Goods Inventory were $20,000, $–0–, and $31,000, respectively.

REQUIRED

Prepare general journal entries to record the following transactions for the current year:

(a) Purchased materials on account, $28,000.

(b) Of the total dollar value of materials used, $22,000 represented direct material and $8,000 were indirect material.

(c) Determined total factory labor, $127,500 (15,000 hours at $8.50/hr).

(d) Of the factory labor, 80% was direct and 20% indirect.

(e) Applied factory overhead based on direct labor hours to work in process.

(f) Determined actual factory overhead other than those items already recorded, $39,000. (Credit Accounts Payable.)

(g) Ending inventories of work in process and finished goods were $23,000 and $42,000, respectively. (Make separate entries.)

(h) Closed the balance in Factory Overhead to Cost of Goods Sold.

Job cost journal entries and T accounts

22–31 Following are certain operating data for Allied Manufacturing Company during its first month of the current year's operations.

	Materials Inventory	Work in Process Inventory	Finished Goods Inventory
Beginning Inventory	$38,000	$16,000	$50,000
Ending Inventory	22,000	27,000	32,000

Total sales were $1,200,000, on which the company earned a 40% gross profit. Allied uses a predetermined factory overhead rate of 120% of direct labor costs. Factory overhead applied was $240,000. Exclusive of indirect material used, total factory overhead incurred was $162,000; it was overapplied by $15,000.

REQUIRED

Compute the following items. (Set up the T accounts involved in the manufacturing cost flows as in Exhibit 22–2, fill in the known amounts, and then use the normal relationships among the various accounts to compute the unknown amounts.)

(a) Cost of goods sold.

(b) Cost of goods manufactured.

(c) Direct labor incurred.

(d) Direct material used.

(e) Indirect material used.

(f) Total materials purchased.

Determine overhead rate and analyze accounts

22–32 The following summary of job cost sheets relates to the production of Statz Manufacturing, Inc., during the first month of the current operating year. Statz uses the same overhead rate for all jobs.

Job No.	Direct Material	Direct Labor	Factory Overhead
109	$ 800	$ 600	$ 900
110	1,100	900	1,350
111	2,200	2,600	3,900
112	1,500	1,600	2,400
113	1,200	1,000	1,500

Job 109 was in process at the end of the preceding year, when it had incurred direct labor charges of $400 and total charges of $1,450. Job 113 is the current month's ending work in process.

REQUIRED

(a) What is the apparent factory overhead rate?
(b) Determine the total direct material requisitioned in the current month.
(c) What is the total direct labor incurred in the current month?
(d) If factory overhead is underapplied by $850 at the end of the current month, what is the total factory overhead incurred during the month?
(e) If finished goods inventory decreased during the month by $1,800, what is the cost of goods sold for the month?

Job cost journal entries and T accounts

22–33 Summarized data for the first month's operations of Lawrence Welding Foundry are presented below. A job order costing system is used.

1. Materials purchased on account, $29,000.
2. Amounts of materials requisitioned and foundry labor used:

Job No.	Materials	Foundry Labor
1	$2,200	$1,300
2	3,500	2,500
3	1,600	1,200
4	6,000	2,300
5	2,400	1,400
6	700	600
Indirect material	3,100	
Indirect labor		1,700

3. Foundry overhead is applied at the rate of 200% of direct labor costs.
4. Miscellaneous foundry overhead incurred:

Prepaid foundry insurance written off	$ 740
Property taxes on foundry building accrued	1,180
Foundry utilities payable accrued	2,640
Depreciation on foundry equipment	3,720
Other costs incurred on account	5,160

5. Ending work in process consisted of jobs 4 and 6.
6. Jobs 1 and 3 and one-half of job 2 were sold on account for $10,000, $8,700, and $7,200, respectively.

REQUIRED

(a) Open general ledger T accounts for Materials Inventory, Foundry Payroll, Foundry Overhead, Work in Process Inventory, Finished Goods Inventory, and Cost of Goods Sold. Also set up subsidiary T accounts as job cost sheets for each job.

(b) Prepare general journal entries to record the summarized transactions for the month, and post appropriate entries to any accounts listed in requirement (a). Key each entry parenthetically to the related number in the problem data.

(c) Determine the balances of any accounts necessary and prepare schedules of jobs in ending work in process and jobs in ending finished goods to confirm that they agree with the related control accounts.

Complex job cost journal entries and analysis

22–34 During June, its first month of operations, Madison Manufacturing Company completed the transactions listed below. Madison uses a simple job order costing system. Materials requisitions and the factory payroll summary are analyzed on the fifteenth and the last day of each month, and charges for direct material and direct labor are entered directly on specific job cost sheets. Factory overhead at the rate of 140% of direct labor costs is recorded on individual job cost sheets when a job is completed and at month-end for any job then in process. At month-end, entries to the general ledger accounts summarize materials requisitions, distribution of factory payroll costs, and the application of factory overhead for the month. All other entries to general ledger accounts are made as they occur.

1. Purchased materials on account, $65,000.
2. Paid miscellaneous factory overhead costs, $16,300.
3. Paid the semimonthly factory payroll, $49,500.
4. An analysis of materials requisitions and the factory payroll summary for June 1–15 indicates the following cost distribution:

Job No.	Materials	Factory Labor
1	$10,800	$18,400
2	5,200	8,000
3	2,200	5,400
Indirect material	3,800	
Indirect labor		17,700
	$22,000	$49,500

5. Jobs 1 and 2 were completed on June 15 and transferred to Finished Goods Inventory on the next day. (Enter the appropriate factory overhead amounts on the job cost sheets, mark them completed, and make a general journal entry transferring the appropriate amount of cost to the Finished Goods Inventory account.)
6. Paid miscellaneous factory overhead costs, $11,700.
7. Sold job 1 on account, $92,800 (recognized its cost of sales in the general journal).
8. Paid the semimonthly factory payroll, $48,100.
9. An analysis of materials requisitions and factory payroll summary for June 16–30 indicates the following cost distribution:

Job No.	Materials	Factory Labor
3	$11,400	$ 8,400
4	9,000	16,200
5	3,900	6,500
6	1,500	2,300
Indirect material	3,400	
Indirect labor		14,700
	$29,200	$48,100

10. Jobs 3 and 4 were completed on June 30 and transferred to Finished Goods Inventory on the same day. (See transaction 5.)

11. Sold job 3 on account, $77,800 (recognized its cost of sales in the general journal).
12. Recorded the following additional factory overhead:

Depreciation on factory building	$13,000
Depreciation on factory equipment	7,600
Expiration of prepaid factory insurance	2,100
Accrual of factory taxes payable	3,500
	$26,200

13. Recorded monthly general journal entry for the costs of all materials used.
14. Recorded monthly general journal entry for the distribution of factory payroll costs.
15. Recorded factory overhead on the job cost sheets for jobs in ending work in process and in the general journal for all factory overhead applied during the month.

REQUIRED

(a) Set up the following general ledger T accounts: Materials Inventory, Factory Payroll Summary, Factory Overhead, Work in Process Inventory, Finished Goods Inventory, Cost of Goods Sold, and Sales.

(b) Set up subsidiary ledger T accounts for each of jobs 1–6 as job cost sheets.

(c) Noting the accounting procedures described in the first paragraph of the problem, do the following:
   1. Record general journal entries for all transactions. Note that general journal entries are *not* required in transactions 4 and 9. Post only those portions of these entries affecting the general ledger accounts set up in requirement (a).
   2. Enter the applicable amounts directly on the appropriate job cost sheets for transactions 4, 5, 9, 10, and 15. Note parenthetically the nature of each amount entered.

(d) Present a brief analysis showing that the general ledger accounts for Work in Process Inventory and for Finished Goods Inventory agree with the related job cost sheets.

(e) Explain in one sentence each what the balance of each general ledger account established in requirement (a) represents.

ALTERNATE PROBLEMS

Determine and use overhead rate

22–27A Beamon Manufacturing, Inc., expects the following costs and expenses during the coming year:

Direct Material	$ 78,000
Direct Labor (@ $7/hr)	287,000
Sales Commissions	46,000
Factory Supervision	75,000
Indirect Labor	144,000
Factory Depreciation	62,000
Indirect Material	30,000
Factory Taxes	18,000
Factory Insurance	14,000
Factory Utilities	26,000

REQUIRED

(a) Compute a predetermined factory overhead rate applied on the basis of direct labor hours.

(b) Present a general journal entry to apply factory overhead during an interim period when 3,400 direct labor hours were worked.
(c) What amount of overhead would be assigned to job 325, to which $280 in direct labor had been charged?

Determine and use overhead rate

22–28A The following selected ledger accounts of the Dearst Company are for May (the fifth month of its accounting year):

Materials Inventory

May 1 bal.	40,000	May credits	150,000
May debits	136,000		

Factory Overhead

May debits	182,000	May 1 bal.	14,000
		May credits	160,000

Work in Process Inventory

May 1 bal.	28,000	May credits	460,000
May debits:			
Direct material	122,000		
Direct labor	200,000		
Factory overhead	160,000		

Factory Payroll Payable

May debits	258,000	May 1 bal.	60,000
		May credits	234,000

Finished Goods Inventory

May 1 bal.	102,000	May credits	510,000
May debits	460,000		

REQUIRED

(a) Determine the amount of indirect material requisitioned for production during May.
(b) How much indirect labor cost was apparently incurred during May?
(c) Calculate the factory overhead rate based on direct labor cost.
(d) Was factory overhead for May under- or overapplied, and by what amount?
(e) Was factory overhead for the first five months of the year under- or overapplied, and by what amount?
(f) What is the cost of production completed in May?
(g) What is the cost of goods sold in May?

Job cost journal entries

22–29A Ferris Manufacturing had the following inventories at the end of its last fiscal year:

Materials inventory	$26,000
Work in process inventory	22,000
Finished goods inventory	40,000

During the first month of the current year, the following transactions occurred:

1. Purchased materials on account, $88,000.
2. Incurred factory payroll, $140,000.

3. Requisitioned total materials of $80,000, of which $14,000 was considered indirect material.
4. Assigned total factory payroll, of which $20,000 was considered indirect labor.
5. Incurred other factory overhead, $52,000. (Credit Accounts Payable.)
6. Applied factory overhead on the basis of 80% of direct labor costs.
7. Determined ending work in process, $40,000.
8. Determined ending finished goods, $70,000.

REQUIRED

(a) Prepare general journal entries to record these transactions.
(b) If the above transactions covered a full year's operations, present a journal entry to dispose of the overhead account balance.

Job cost journal entries

22–30A At the beginning of the current year, the Manchester Company estimated that it would incur $153,000 of factory overhead cost during the year, using 34,000 direct labor hours to produce the desired volume of goods. On January 1 of the current year, beginning balances of Materials Inventory, Work in Process Inventory, and Finished Goods Inventory were $48,000, $–0–, and $87,000, respectively.

REQUIRED

Prepare general journal entries to record the following transactions for the current year:

(a) Purchased materials on account, $123,000.
(b) Of the total dollar value of materials used, $102,000 represented direct material and $24,000 were indirect material.
(c) Determined total factory labor, $378,000 (36,000 hours @ $10.50/hr).
(d) Of the factory labor, 75% was direct and 25% indirect.
(e) Applied factory overhead based on direct labor hours to work in process.
(f) Determined actual factory overhead other than those items already recorded, $28,200. (Credit Accounts Payable.)
(g) Ending inventories of work in process and finished goods were $57,000 and $117,000, respectively. (Make separate entries.)
(h) Closed the balance in Factory Overhead to Cost of Goods Sold.

Job cost journal entries and T accounts

22–31A Following are certain operating data for Anchor Manufacturing Company during its first month of the current year's operations.

	Materials Inventory	Work in Process Inventory	Finished Goods Inventory
Beginning Inventory	$20,000	$25,000	$40,000
Ending Inventory	35,000	30,000	28,000

Total sales were $1,000,000, on which the company earned a 40% gross profit. Anchor uses a predetermined factory overhead rate of 110% of direct labor costs. Factory overhead applied was $198,000. Exclusive of indirect material used, total factory overhead incurred was $150,000; it was overapplied by $12,000.

REQUIRED

Compute the following items. (Set up the T accounts involved in the manufacturing cost flows as in Exhibit 22–2, fill in the known amounts, and then use the normal relationships among the various accounts to compute the unknown amounts.)

(a) Cost of goods sold.
(b) Cost of goods manufactured.
(c) Direct labor incurred.
(d) Direct material used.
(e) Indirect material used.
(f) Total materials purchased.

Determine overhead rate and analyze accounts

22–32A The following summary of job cost sheets relates to the production of Simpson Manufacturing, Inc., during the first month of the current operating year. Simpson uses the same overhead rate for all jobs.

Job No.	Direct Material	Direct Labor	Factory Overhead
109	$2,000	$2,400	$1,680
110	3,600	1,800	1,260
111	9,000	7,600	5,320
112	6,000	4,600	3,220
113	2,600	2,200	1,540

Job 109 was in process at the end of the preceding year, when it had incurred direct labor charges of $700 and total charges of $2,240. Job 113 is the current month's ending work in process.

REQUIRED

(a) What is the apparent factory overhead rate?

(b) Determine the total direct material requisitioned in the current month.

(c) What is the total direct labor incurred in the current month?

(d) If factory overhead is overapplied by $2,000 at the end of the current month, what is the total factory overhead incurred during the month?

(e) If finished goods inventory increased during the month by $3,000, what is the cost of goods sold for the month?

Job cost journal entries and T accounts

22–33A Summarized data for the first month's operations of Lubbock Foundry are presented below. A job order costing system is used.

1. Materials purchased on account, $44,000.
2. Amounts of materials requisitioned and foundry labor used:

Job No.	Materials	Foundry Labor
1	$2,300	$1,800
2	2,600	3,000
3	1,900	4,400
4	6,700	6,000
5	3,200	3,600
6	2,000	1,000
Indirect material	5,500	
Indirect labor		9,000

3. Foundry overhead is applied at the rate of 150% of direct labor costs.
4. Miscellaneous foundry overhead incurred:

Prepaid foundry insurance written off	$ 940
Property taxes on foundry building accrued	1,880
Foundry utilities payable accrued	2,200
Depreciation on foundry equipment	4,200
Other costs incurred on account	7,320

5. Ending work in process consisted of jobs 4 and 6.
6. Jobs 1 and 3 and one-half of job 2 were sold on account for $12,600, $15,800, and $9,460, respectively.

REQUIRED

(a) Open general ledger T accounts for Materials Inventory, Foundry Payroll, Foundry Overhead, Work in Process Inventory, Finished Goods Inventory, and Cost of Goods Sold. Also set up subsidiary T accounts as job cost sheets for each job.

(b) Prepare general journal entries to record the summarized transactions for the month, and post appropriate entries to any accounts listed in requirement (a). Key each entry parenthetically to the related number in the problem data.

(c) Determine the balances of any accounts necessary and prepare schedules of jobs in ending work in process and jobs in ending finished goods to confirm that they agree with the related control accounts.

Complex job cost journal entries and analysis

22–34A During June, its first month of operations, Morton Manufacturing Company completed the transactions listed below. Morton uses a simple job order costing system. Materials requisitions and the factory payroll summary are analyzed on the fifteenth and the last day of each month, and charges for direct material and direct labor are entered directly on specific job cost sheets. Factory overhead at the rate of 160% of direct labor costs is recorded on individual job cost sheets when a job is completed and at month-end for any job then in process. At month-end, entries to the general ledger accounts summarize materials requisitions, distribution of factory payroll costs, and the application of factory overhead for the month. All other entries to general ledger accounts are made as they occur.

1. Purchased materials on account, $105,000.
2. Paid miscellaneous factory overhead costs, $26,000.
3. Paid the semimonthly factory payroll, $80,000.
4. An analysis of materials requisitions and the factory payroll summary for June 1–15 indicates the following cost distribution:

Job No.	Materials	Factory Labor
1	$17,000	$30,000
2	8,000	13,000
3	4,000	9,000
Indirect material	7,000	
Indirect labor		28,000
	$36,000	$80,000

5. Jobs 1 and 2 were completed on June 15 and transferred to Finished Goods Inventory on the next day. (Enter the appropriate factory overhead amounts on the job cost sheets, mark them completed, and make a general journal entry transferring the appropriate amount of cost to the Finished Goods Inventory account.)
6. Paid miscellaneous factory overhead costs, $19,000.
7. Sold job 1 on account, $150,000 (recognized its cost of sales in the general journal).
8. Paid the semimonthly factory payroll, $78,000.
9. An analysis of materials requisitions and factory payroll summary for June 16–30 indicates the following cost distribution:

Job No.	Materials	Factory Labor
3	$18,000	$14,000
4	15,000	27,000
5	6,000	10,000
6	3,000	4,000
Indirect material	5,000	
Indirect labor		23,000
	$47,000	$78,000

10. Jobs 3 and 4 were completed on June 30 and transferred to Finished Goods Inventory on the same day. (See transaction 5.)
11. Sold job 3 on account, $125,000 (recognized its cost of sales in the general journal).
12. Recorded the following additional factory overhead:

Depreciation on factory building	$21,000
Depreciation on factory equipment	12,000
Expiration of prepaid factory insurance	3,500
Accrual of factory taxes payable	6,500
	$43,000

13. Recorded monthly general journal entry for the costs of all materials used.
14. Recorded monthly general journal entry for the distribution of factory payroll costs.
15. Recorded factory overhead on the job cost sheets for jobs in ending work in process and in the general journal for all factory overhead applied during the month.

REQUIRED

(a) Set up the following general ledger T accounts: Materials Inventory, Factory Payroll Summary, Factory Overhead, Work in Process Inventory, Finished Goods Inventory, Cost of Goods Sold, and Sales.

(b) Set up subsidiary ledger T accounts for each of jobs 1–6 as job cost sheets.

(c) Noting the accounting procedures described in the first paragraph of the problem, do the following:
   1. Record general journal entries for all transactions. Note that general journal entries are *not* required in transactions 4 and 9. Post only those portions of these entries affecting the general ledger accounts set up in requirement (a).
   2. Enter the applicable amounts directly on the appropriate job cost sheets for transactions 4, 5, 9, 10, and 15. Note parenthetically the nature of each amount entered.

(d) Present a brief analysis showing that the general ledger accounts for Work in Process Inventory and for Finished Goods Inventory agree with the related job cost sheets.

(e) Explain in one sentence each what the balance of each general ledger account established in requirement (a) represents.

BUSINESS DECISION PROBLEM

Conway Manufacturing Company plans to make and sell a newly designed fuel director valve for use in small aircraft manufactured by other companies. If made with traditional materials, the valve would require the following materials and labor:

Materials	
A	5 lb @ $3 each
B	6 lb @ $8 each
C	4 lb @ $14 each
Labor	
Casting	3 hr @ $7/hr
Finishing	3 hr @ $9/hr
Assembling	2 hr @ $8/hr

Overhead costs in these departments should be $15 per direct labor hour.

Management may also use a new synthetic material, D, perfected in space technology. Making the body of the valve out of material D would alter the cost and manufacturing procedures as follows: Eight pounds of D, costing $12 per pound, would replace both materials A and B. Casting and finishing labor time would be reduced by 50%. However, each valve would require four hours of machining labor costing $10 per hour and performed on a highly specialized, partially automated machine. Factory overhead in the machining department is applied at the rate of $13 per machine hour.

Conway's marketing department advises management that the valve made of traditional materials would sell for 150% of the company's cost and that aircraft manufacturers would pay 170% of the company's cost for the valve made of the new lightweight material D.

REQUIRED

Present an analysis showing the gross profit per unit for each manufacturing alternative. Based on this analysis, recommend whether or not the new material should be used.

ANSWERS TO SELF-TEST QUESTIONS

1. (c) **2.** (d) **3.** (c) **4.** (b) **5.** (b)

23

COST ACCOUNTING SYSTEMS: PROCESS COSTING

CHAPTER OBJECTIVES

1. Compare and contrast job order costing and process costing (pp. 877–78).
2. Describe the basic concepts of process costing (pp. 878–79).
3. Explain techniques for determining unit costs when process costing is used (pp. 879–82).
4. Illustrate the journal entries used with process costing (pp. 882–84).
5. Describe the calculation of equivalent units and costs per equivalent unit using the FIFO method in a multiple department process costing system (pp. 884–85, 887–88).
6. Explain the procedures used to prepare the production cost report using the FIFO method in a process costing system (pp. 886–87, 889).
7. Identify the journal entries to transfer product cost from work in process to finished goods to cost of goods sold (pp. 887, 890).
8. Describe the procedures for cost allocation for service departments (pp. 891–94).
9. Identify joint product costs and byproduct costs and describe techniques to account for them (pp. 894–96).

For which of you, desiring to build a tower, does not first sit down and count the cost . . . ?

LUKE 14:28

The early sections of this chapter explain and illustrate the concepts and procedures typical of a process costing system that involves more than one processing department. The concluding sections of the chapter deal with accounting for the costs of service departments, joint products, and byproducts.

JOB ORDER COSTING AND PROCESS COSTING

In Chapter 22, we introduced and discussed the concepts used in job order costing. Exhibit 23–1 presents the typical flow of product cost in a job order costing system. Direct material and direct labor are accumulated, by job or product, in the work in process inventory. Overhead cost is applied to the work in process inventory using an annual predetermined overhead rate.

Actual overhead costs, including indirect material and indirect labor, are accumulated in the factory overhead account as debits while the applied overhead is recorded in the same account as a credit. Perpetual inventory techniques are

EXHIBIT 23–1

PRODUCT COST FLOWS IN A JOB ORDER COSTING SYSTEM

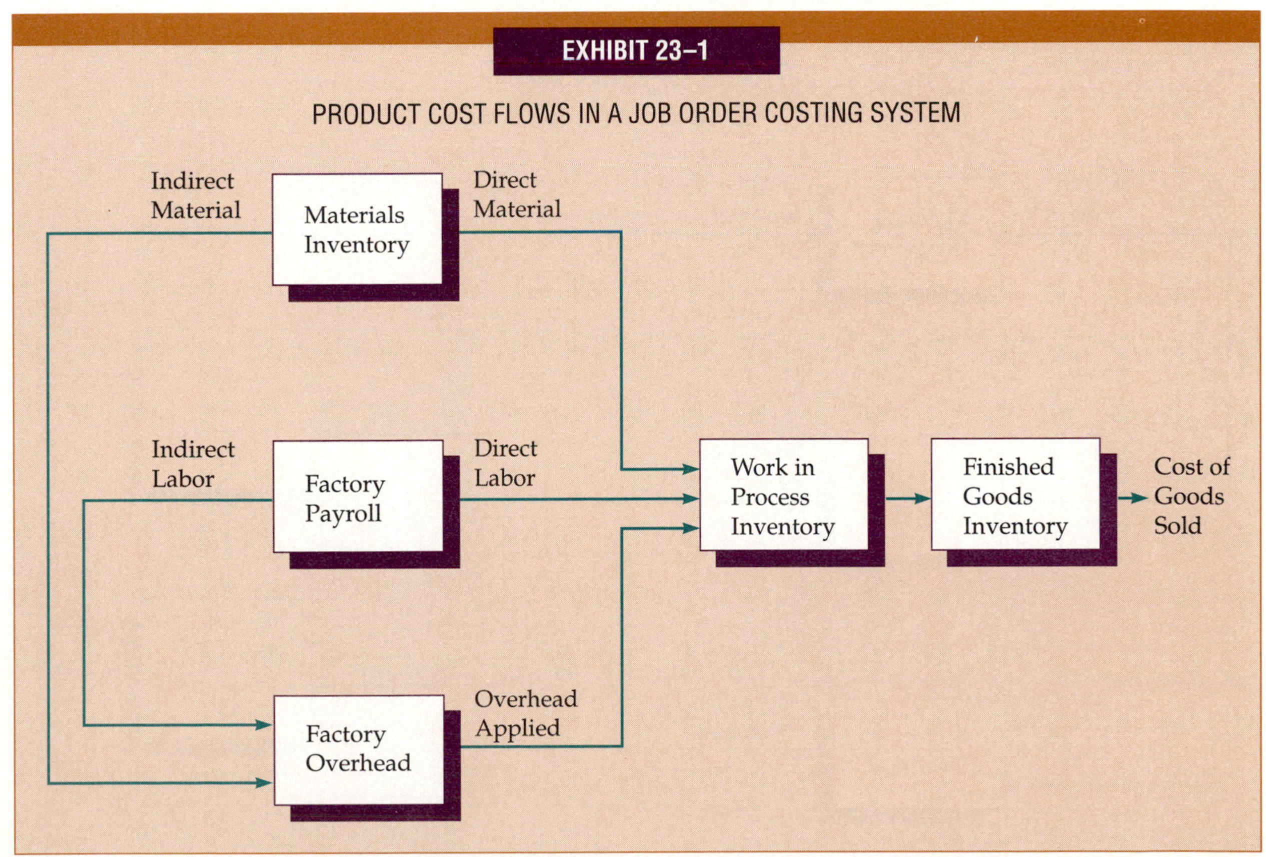

used to move product cost from the work in process inventory to the finished goods inventory and finally to cost of goods sold.

Job order costing is adopted whenever production is characterized by a series of different products or jobs undertaken either to fill specific orders from customers or to produce a stock of products from which future orders can be filled. **Process costing,** however, is used when large volumes of product are manufactured in a continuous flow operation, such as the production of fuels, chemicals, small appliances, building materials, and electricity. With process costing, product costs are accumulated by department, not by job or product.

Characteristics of Process Costing

Exhibit 23–2 presents the typical flow of product cost in a process costing system. The following characteristics of process costing are evident in Exhibit 23–1 and Exhibit 23–2:

1. There is a separate work in process inventory for each manufacturing department when process costing is used, while there is only one work in process account when job order costing is used. In Exhibit 23–2, there are two work in process inventories since there are two manufacturing departments.
2. Direct material, direct labor, and factory overhead costs can be added to the work in process inventory in each department. Exhibit 23–2 shows all three elements of product cost being added to both work in process inventories.

EXHIBIT 23–2

PRODUCT COST FLOWS IN A PROCESS COSTING SYSTEM

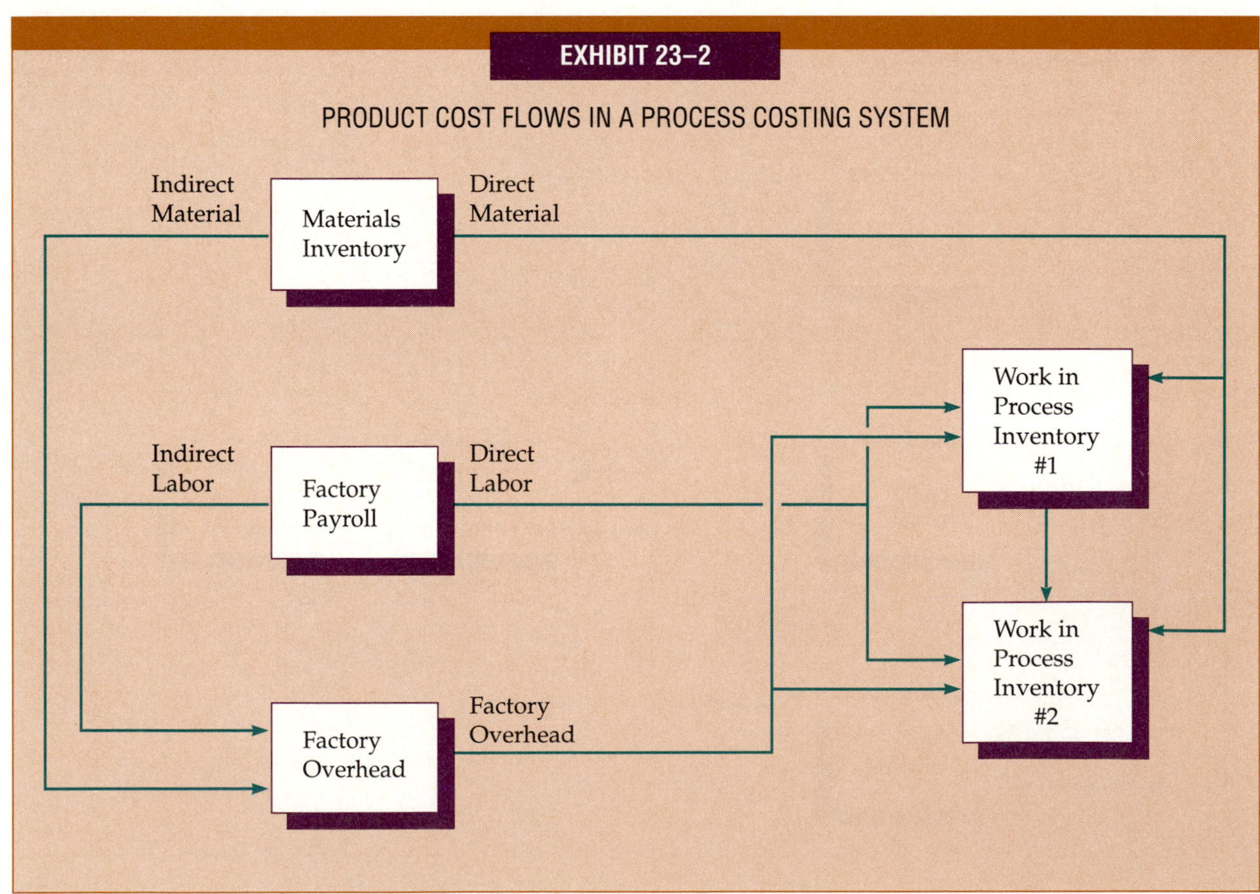

EXHIBIT 23–3

SEQUENTIAL PRODUCT PROCESSING

Work in Process Inventory #1 → Work in Process Inventory #2 → Work in Process Inventory #3 → Finished Goods Inventory → **Cost of Goods Sold**

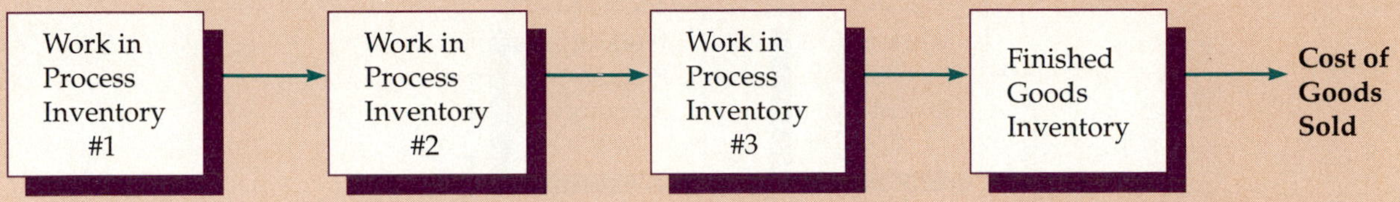

3. Perpetual inventory techniques are not used to flow product costs from one work in process inventory to another when process costing is used. Nor are perpetual inventory techniques used to flow product cost to the finished goods inventory (or to cost of goods sold) during the accounting period when process costing is used. The accounting techniques introduced in this chapter will provide a means of transferring product cost, at the end of the accounting period, from one work in process inventory to the next work in process inventory, from the final work in process inventory to the finished goods inventory, and from the finished goods inventory to cost of goods sold.

Manufacturing Departments

Typically, multiple manufacturing departments are identified when process costing is used. Products will flow through these departments at different stages of the manufacturing process. For example, a consumer product might be processed through three departments—machining, painting, and assembling. In any particular manufacturing plant, some products may go through many departments while other products may go through only a few departments, depending on the nature of the work to be done. Regardless, the work in any department must be performed uniformly on all units and the output of the department must be uniform in nature.

Basic Processing Patterns

There are two basic patterns for arranging the departments in a process costing situation—sequential and parallel. Exhibit 23–3 presents a sequential product processing pattern. With sequential processing, there is a single path through the manufacturing process. Exhibit 23–4 presents a simple example of parallel product processing. There are numerous possible variations of parallel processing. The process costing techniques described in this chapter can be used regardless of which pattern a particular manufacturing process follows.

DETERMINING UNIT COSTS

The techniques described in this chapter require the calculation of *unit costs* to facilitate the end-of-period transfer of product cost from one work in process inventory to another, from the final work in process inventory to the finished goods inventory, and from the finished goods inventory to cost of goods sold. With process costing, unit costs are usually calculated on a monthly basis. These unit costs can be compared to unit costs of prior accounting periods to determine when additional cost control measures are necessary.

EXHIBIT 23–4

PARALLEL PRODUCT PROCESSING

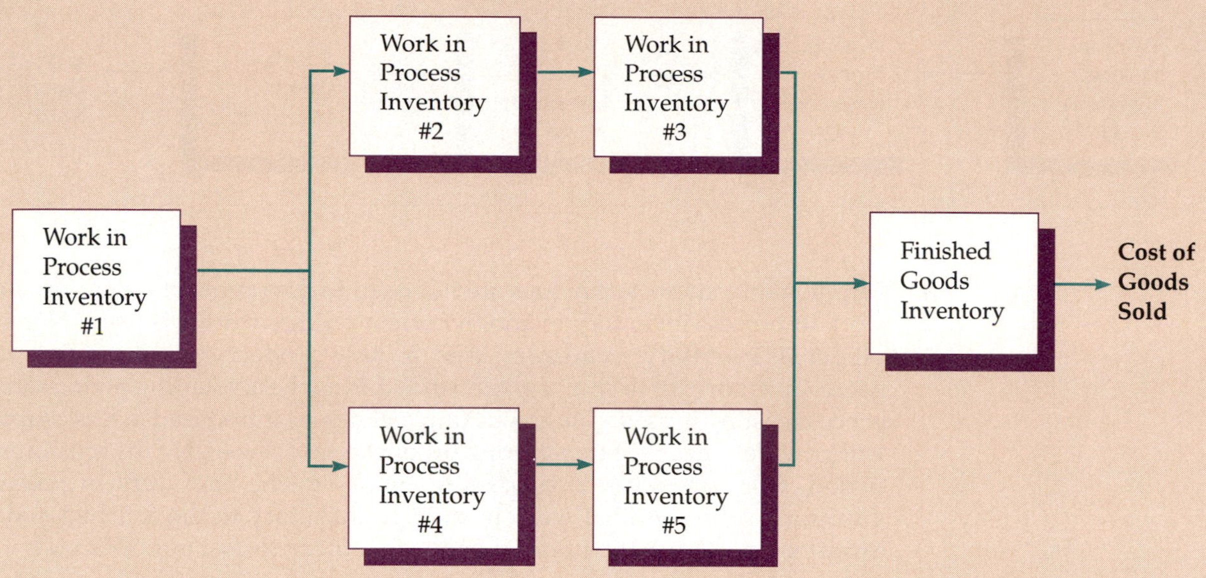

Equivalent Units

Assume that department 1 of Bower Company uses process costing and that it had the following results for January:

Direct material added	$1,400
Direct labor incurred	2,000
Factory overhead cost	800
Total Costs	$4,200

Units in process at January 1 (20% complete) = 200 units
Units started and finished during January = 500 units
Units in process at January 31 (40% complete) = 100 units

In order to properly determine unit costs, we need to calculate the amount of work completed during the month of January, which, in turn, will require the calculation of the number of equivalent units of completed work during the month. **Equivalent units** are the smaller number of full measures of work accomplished that is the equivalent of a larger number of partially accomplished units of work. Using the data for department 1 of Bower Company, we can calculate the number of equivalent units for January as follows:

	Units Involved		Proportion Completed This Month		Equivalent Units
Beginning inventory	200	×	80%	=	160
Started and finished during January	500	×	100%	=	500
Ending inventory	100	×	40%	=	40
	800				700

The units in the beginning inventory are assumed to be completed during January. Therefore, the percent complete went from 20% at the beginning of the month to 100% by the end of the month. Therefore, 80% of the work was accomplished during the month. If we assume that material, labor, and overhead are added gradually throughout processing, the unit cost for department 1 for January would be:

$$\frac{\text{Total Costs for January}}{\text{Equivalent Units Processed}} = \frac{\$4{,}200}{700 \text{ gallons}} = \$6 \text{ per gallon}$$

In process cost systems, unit cost calculations may be complicated by the fact that materials are added at a different rate or at a different time than are labor and overhead, which are usually grouped together and called **conversion costs.** For example, materials may be added at the beginning of the process, while conversion costs are added evenly throughout the process. In this case, the number of equivalent units used to calculate the unit cost of materials is different from the number of equivalent units used to compute the unit cost of conversion.

Exhibit 23–5 graphically presents the revised computation of equivalent units when all materials are added initially and conversion costs are incurred evenly throughout the process. Because all materials for beginning work in process were added during the previous period (when these units were started), this batch has no equivalent units for materials in this period. However, any unit of product started this period has all materials added this period, so the 500 units started

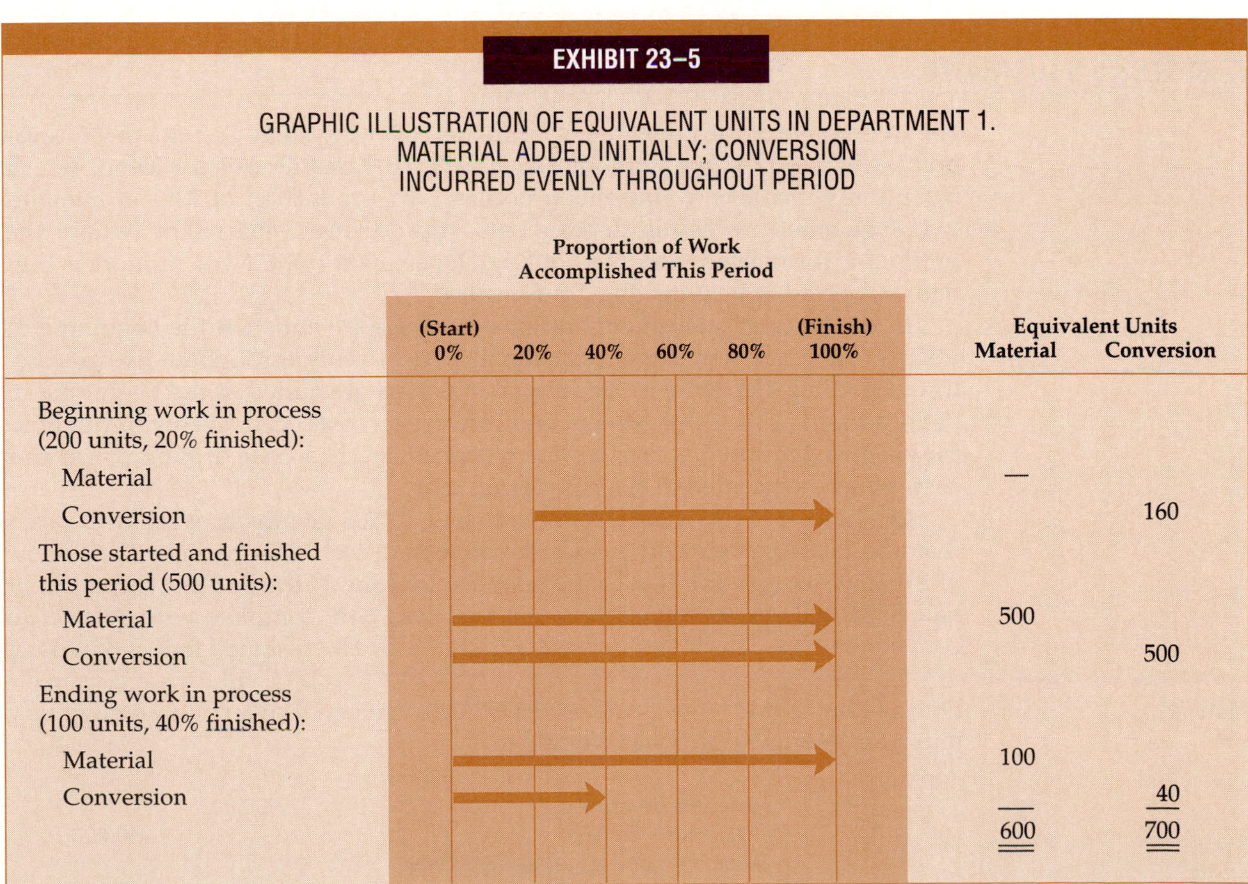

and finished and the 100 units only started (ending work in process) are assigned full equivalent units for materials. For conversion costs, (1) the 200 units in beginning work in process represent only 160 (80% × 200) equivalent units because only the final 80% of processing occurred this period; (2) each of the 500 units of product started and finished this period equals one equivalent unit because all conversion was accomplished this period; and (3) the 100 units in ending work in process equal only 40 (40% × 100) equivalent units because only 40% of their processing was accomplished this period. Under these assumptions, the number of equivalent units completed for the period is not the same for material as for conversion costs. Consequently, the computation of cost per equivalent unit requires separate calculations for the two cost components, which are then totaled. In our illustration, these are:

$$\frac{\text{Material Cost}}{\text{Equivalent Units}} = \frac{\$1{,}400}{600} = \$2.333 \text{ for material}$$

$$\frac{\text{Conversion Costs}}{\text{Equivalent Units}} = \frac{\$2{,}000 + \$800}{700} = 4.000 \text{ for conversion}$$

$$\text{Total cost for a unit processed this period} \quad \underline{\underline{\$6.333}}$$

Note again that equivalent unit costs for a specific period are derived by dividing the total costs for the period by the related amount of work accomplished during that period.

COST FLOWS ILLUSTRATED

For an example of the operation of a process costing system, assume that Northbrook Chemical Company produces an industrial cleaner called Kleeno, which Northbrook markets in one-gallon bottles. The production of Kleeno involves two sequential processing departments—the Mixing Department (where the product is formulated) and the Bottling Department (where the product is bottled, subjected to heat treating, and inspected).

In the Mixing Department, various materials are added at the beginning of the process while conversion costs are incurred evenly throughout the process. In the Bottling Department, additional materials are added at the beginning of the processing in this department and conversion costs occur evenly throughout the process. Northbrook uses a predetermined overhead rate to assign overhead cost, which is included in the conversion cost.

On June 1, the Mixing Department had 10,000 gallons in work in process that was 25% complete with respect to conversion cost. This inventory had a cost of $106,500 assigned to it at that date. Also on June 1, the Bottling Department had 8,000 gallons in work in process that was 30% complete with respect to conversion cost. This inventory had a cost of $184,880 assigned to it at that date.

Material

During June, Northbrook purchased $950,000 of material on account. A summary entry for the June purchases would be:

Materials Inventory	950,000	
Accounts Payable		950,000
To record June material purchases.		

The direct material requisitioned during June for each processing department and the indirect material for general factory use are shown in the following summary entry:

Work in Process—Mixing Department	704,000	
Work in Process—Bottling Department	240,000	
Factory Overhead	42,000	
Materials Inventory		966,000
To record direct and indirect material used during June.		

Labor

During June, Northbrook accrued $587,200 of factory payroll. A summary entry to record this payroll would be:

Factory Payroll	587,200	
[Other accounts]		587,200
To record the factory payroll for June.		

The factory payroll for June was made up of $298,400 of direct labor for the Mixing Department and $186,500 of direct labor for the Bottling Department. Indirect labor costs amounted to $102,300. The following summary entry distributes these costs:

Work in Process—Mixing Department	298,400	
Work in Process—Bottling Department	186,500	
Factory Overhead	102,300	
Factory Payroll		587,200
To distribute the June factory payroll.		

Factory Overhead

At this point, we have recorded $42,000 of indirect material and $102,300 of indirect labor in the Factory Overhead account. Assume that other overhead costs (such as maintenance, depreciation, and utilities) total $467,500. To record these amounts, we normally would credit various accounts such as Accumulated Depreciation, Accounts Payable, and Prepaid Expenses. For simplicity in this example, we will credit these other accounts in the following summary entry:

Factory Overhead	467,500	
[Other accounts]		467,500
To record various factory overhead costs.		

Northbrook applies overhead to work in process using predetermined overhead rates. The following entry records the amount of applied factory overhead for the two processing departments:

Work in Process—Mixing Department	486,800	
Work in Process—Bottling Department	123,900	
Factory Overhead		610,700
To apply factory overhead to work in process inventories.		

Actual costs charged to the Factory Overhead account total $611,800 ($42,000 + $102,300 + $467,500). The previous entry assigned only $610,700 to the inventory accounts, resulting in $1,100 of underapplied overhead. Recall that underapplied factory overhead can be carried as a deferred balance sheet charge until year-end and then closed to Cost of Goods Sold.

As a result of the journal entries recorded during the month, the two work in process accounts contain the following balances as of the end of the month:

	Mixing Department	Bottling Department
Beginning balance	$ 106,500	$184,880
Direct material	704,000	240,000
Direct labor	298,400	186,500
Factory overhead	486,800	123,900
	$1,595,700	$735,280

At the end of the month, additional journal entries are needed to reflect the costs transferred from the Mixing Department to the Bottling Department, from the Bottling Department to finished goods, and from finished goods to cost of goods sold.

FIFO METHOD FOR PROCESS COSTING

We have explained how material and conversion costs are charged to work in process accounts for each processing department during the month. At the end of each month, we must calculate the cost of goods transferred out and the cost of goods remaining uncompleted for each department. Calculations can be performed using either the first-in first-out (FIFO) accounting method or the weighted average accounting method. We illustrate the FIFO method in this chapter and the weighted average method in Appendix G.

Exhibit 23–6 shows the June **production report** for the two processing departments. Note the following key observations regarding the production report:

1. All unit figures are in whole gallons rather than in equivalent units.
2. In the Mixing Department, the beginning work in process (10,000) plus units started (80,000) constitute the total number of units to be accounted for (90,000).

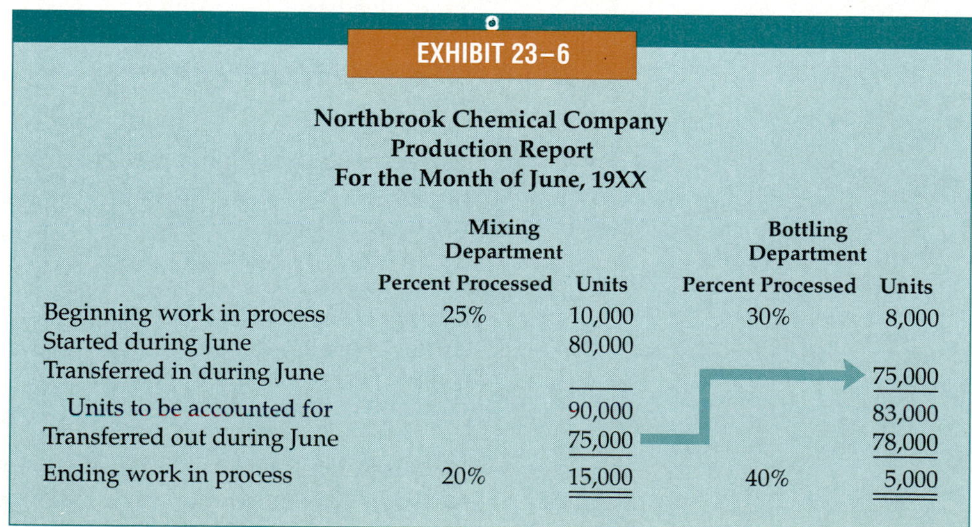

EXHIBIT 23–6

Northbrook Chemical Company
Production Report
For the Month of June, 19XX

	Mixing Department Percent Processed	Mixing Department Units	Bottling Department Percent Processed	Bottling Department Units
Beginning work in process	25%	10,000	30%	8,000
Started during June		80,000		
Transferred in during June				75,000
Units to be accounted for		90,000		83,000
Transferred out during June		75,000		78,000
Ending work in process	20%	15,000	40%	5,000

The 90,000 units are accounted for as units transferred out (75,000) plus units in ending work in process (15,000) of the Mixing Department.

3. For the Bottling Department, the beginning work in process (8,000) plus units transferred in from the Mixing Department (75,000) constitute the total number of units to be accounted for (83,000). The 83,000 units are accounted for as units transferred out to finished goods (78,000) plus units in ending work in process (5,000) of the Bottling Department.
4. The number of units transferred out of the Mixing Department (75,000) is equal to the number of units transferred into the Bottling Department (75,000).

We now examine how costs are allocated to the various units, beginning with the Mixing Department.

Mixing Department

Remember that in the Mixing Department, materials are added at the start of the mixing process, but conversion costs are incurred evenly throughout the process. Therefore, we must calculate equivalent units and cost per equivalent unit separately for material and conversion costs. Exhibit 23–7 presents these calculations in a cost per equivalent unit report. It is important to note that, with the FIFO method, only current-month equivalent units and current-month costs are included in the cost per equivalent unit calculations.

In allocating costs to various units of product, three batches of Kleeno are considered: (1) units finished from the June 1 inventory, (2) units started and

EXHIBIT 23–7

Northbrook Chemical Company
Mixing Department
Cost per Equivalent Unit Report
For the Month of June, 19XX

FIFO Method:	Units Involved	Conversion Completed This Month	Materials (added initially)	Conversion (added throughout)
Current equivalent units:				
Transferred out:				
Beginning work in process (25%)	10,000	75%	–0–	7,500
Started and finished this month	65,000	100%	65,000	65,000
Units transferred out this month	75,000			
Ending work in process (20%)	15,000	20%	15,000	3,000
Units accounted for	90,000			
Current equivalent units			80,000	75,500
Current costs:				
Direct material			$704,000	
Direct labor				$298,400
Factory overhead				486,800
Current costs			$704,000	$785,200
Current cost per current equivalent unit			$8.80	$10.40

finished in June, and (3) units started but not finished in June. The composition of costs for the three batches of product handled by the Mixing Department is explained below and in the production cost report shown in Exhibit 23–8:

1. **Beginning inventory** The 10,000 gallons in the beginning inventory had all the material and 25% of the required conversion work added in May, for a $106,500 total cost in that month. The remaining 75% of the conversion work was completed in June. We multiply the conversion cost of a full unit ($10.40) by the equivalent units (7,500 gallons) to obtain the $78,000 cost to finish this batch. Thus, this batch cost $184,500.
2. **Started and finished in June** During June, all required material and conversion work were applied to the 65,000 gallons started and finished. The material added this month at $8.80 per gallon and the conversion work completed at $10.40 per unit are applied to each of the 65,000 units. The total cost of the 75,000 gallons in the two batches transferred to the Bottling

EXHIBIT 23–8

Northbrook Chemical Company
Mixing Department
Production Cost Report
For the Month of June, 19XX

FIFO Method:	Total Cost	Unit Cost
Costs to be accounted for:		
Prior month costs	$ 106,500	
Direct material	704,000	
Direct labor	298,400	
Factory overhead	486,800	
Total costs to be accounted for	$1,595,700	
Costs accounted for:		
Transferred out:		
Beginning work in process:		
Prior month	$ 106,500	
Materials (0 × $8.80)	0	
Conversion (7,500 × $10.40)	78,000	
	$ 184,500	
Started and finished:		
Materials (65,000 × $8.80)	572,000	
Conversion (65,000 × $10.40)	676,000	
Total costs transferred out	$1,432,500	$19.10
Ending work in process:		
Materials (15,000 × $8.80)	$ 132,000	
Conversion (3,000 × $10.40)	31,200	
Ending work in process	$ 163,200	
Total costs accounted for	$1,595,700	

Department amounts to $1,432,500, and the average cost of the two batches is $19.10 per gallon ($1,432,500/75,000).

3. **Ending inventory** The 15,000 units started but not finished in June contain all required material but only 20% of the needed conversion work. Therefore, we multiply the per-unit material cost of $8.80 by 15,000 gallons to obtain the 132,000 material cost. We then multiply the $10.40 conversion cost by the 3,000 equivalent units of conversion work performed to obtain the $31,200 conversion cost.

Notice that the production cost report fully accounts for both the 90,000 units of product involved and the total costs of $1,595,700 charged to the Mixing Department.

The following entry transfers the cost of the work completed in the Mixing Department during June to the Bottling Department:

Work in Process—Bottling Department	1,432,500	
Work in Process—Mixing Department		1,432,500
To transfer cost of completed work from Mixing to Bottling.		

The Work in Process account for the Mixing Department would now appear as follows:

Work in Process—Mixing Department

June 1 (beginning balance)	106,500	Transferred to Bottling Department	1,432,500
Direct material	704,000		
Direct labor	298,400		
Factory overhead	486,800		
June 30 (ending balance)	163,200		

Note that all costs charged to this account have been accounted for as either transferred out or as ending inventory.

Bottling Department

In the Bottling Department, materials are added at the start of the process, while conversion costs are incurred evenly throughout the process. The units handled during June include 8,000 units from the beginning work in process inventory of the Bottling Department and the 75,000 units transferred in from the Mixing Department. The 8,000 units in the beginning inventory had $184,880 of product cost assigned to them in the prior month. The 75,000 units had $1,432,500 assigned to them in the Mixing Department prior to being transferred to the Bottling Department.

Again, we must convert the work performed into equivalent units and obtain costs per equivalent unit. Exhibit 23–9 presents the cost per equivalent unit report for the Bottling Department and Exhibit 23–10 presents the production cost report for the Bottling Department.

The cost per equivalent unit report for the Bottling Department differs from the same report for the Mixing Department in that transferred-in costs must be accounted for in the Bottling Department. As a result, there is a "Transferred In"

EXHIBIT 23–9

Northbrook Chemical Company
Bottling Department
Cost per Equivalent Unit Report
For the Month of June, 19XX

FIFO Method:	Units Involved	Conversion Completed This Month	Transferred In	Materials (added initially)	Conversion (added throughout)
Current equivalent units:					
Transferred out:					
Beginning work in process (30%)	8,000	70%	–0–	–0–	5,600
Transferred in and finished	70,000	100%	70,000	70,000	70,000
Units transferred out this month	78,000				
Ending work in process (40%)	5,000	40%	5,000	5,000	2,000
Units accounted for	83,000				
Current equivalent units			75,000	75,000	77,600
Current costs:					
Costs transferred in from Mixing Department			$1,432,500		
Direct material				$240,000	
Direct labor					$186,500
Factory overhead					123,900
Current costs			$1,432,500	$240,000	$310,400
Current cost per current equivalent unit			$19.10	$3.20	$4.00

column added to the cost per equivalent unit report for the Bottling Department. As Exhibit 23–9 demonstrates, three cost per equivalent unit amounts are calculated—transferred in, material, and conversion.

The percentages of conversion completed this month in Exhibit 23–9 are calculated the same as before. Since the beginning work in process inventory in the Bottling Department was 30% complete, and since we assume these units were finished during June, then the percentage of conversion work completed during June was 70% (100% – 30%).

It should be noted that the transferred-in cost per equivalent unit on Exhibit 23–9 is the same as the transferred-out unit cost on Exhibit 23–8. When the FIFO method is used, this relationship is always true, since the transferred-in column in the cost per equivalent unit report contains units and costs transferred in during the current month only.

There are three groups of cost to be accounted for on the production cost report in Exhibit 23–10: (1) prior month costs (beginning work in process for the Bottling Department), (2) transferred in this month (transferred into the Bottling Department from the Mixing Department), and (3) direct material, direct labor, and factory overhead (current month costs incurred in the Bottling Department). All of these costs are accounted for either as transferred out (to finished goods) or ending work in process (for the Bottling Department).

EXHIBIT 23–10

Northbrook Chemical Company
Bottling Department
Production Cost Report
For the Month of June, 19XX

FIFO Method:	Total Cost	Unit Cost
Costs to be accounted for:		
Prior month costs	$ 184,880	
Transferred in this month	1,432,500	
Direct material	240,000	
Direct labor	186,500	
Factory overhead	123,900	
Total costs to be accounted for	$2,167,780	
Costs accounted for:		
Transferred out:		
Beginning work in process:		
Prior month	$ 184,880	
Transferred in (0 × $19.10)	0	
Materials (0 × $3.20)	0	
Conversion (5,600 × $4.00)	22,400	
	$ 207,280	
Transferred in and finished:		
Transferred in (70,000 × $19.10)	1,337,000	
Materials (70,000 × $3.20)	224,000	
Conversion (70,000 × $4.00)	280,000	
Total costs transferred out	$2,048,280	$26.26
Ending work in process:		
Transferred in (5,000 × $19.10)	$ 95,500	
Materials (5,000 × $3.20)	16,000	
Conversion (2,000 × $4.00)	8,000	
Ending work in process	$ 119,500	
Total costs accounted for	$2,167,780	

All prior month costs ($184,880) are included with the beginning work in process in the transferred-out section. No additional transferred-in costs or materials costs are assigned to the beginning work in process since they were assigned in the prior month. Since 5,600 equivalent units of conversion work were added during June, $22,400 of conversion cost is added (5,600 × $4.00). Therefore, the total cost assigned to the units that were in the beginning work in process is $207,280.

The transferred in and finished section and the ending work in process section are handled the same way the started and finished section and the ending work in process section were handled in the Mixing Department. As a result of the calculations of Exhibit 23–10, $2,048,280 representing 78,000 units were

2. $$\begin{matrix}\text{Allocation} \\ \text{Rate}\end{matrix} \times \begin{matrix}\text{Amount of Allocation Base} \\ \text{Related to Department}\end{matrix} = \begin{matrix}\text{Specific Amount} \\ \text{Allocated}\end{matrix}$$

$$\$200 \times 15 \text{ employees} = \$3{,}000 \text{ (for mixing)}$$

$$\$200 \times 25 \text{ employees} = \$5{,}000 \text{ (for bottling)}$$

As a final step, we should check allocations and verify that the sum of allocated amounts equals the total amount allocated.

Exhibit 23–12 illustrates a worksheet often used to accumulate and allocate factory overhead in a multidepartment factory operation that includes service departments. Note the following:

1. Three categories of costs are involved:
   (a) Those directly identifiable with departments.
   (b) Those requiring allocations to production and service departments.
   (c) Service department costs allocated to production departments.
2. A total overhead amount is first accumulated for each service department and each production department.
3. After service department costs are allocated, the total overhead is assigned to the production departments only.
4. The final amounts assigned to each production department are used to calculate departmental overhead rates. (See the footnotes to Exhibit 23–12).

The amounts, proportions, and variety of costs shown in Exhibit 23–12 have been chosen for simplicity of presentation to stress the basic concepts.

Obviously, we might ask why service department costs are not allocated to other service departments. More sophisticated allocation techniques may involve allocations of some service department costs to other service departments and even mutual assignment of all of one or more service departments' costs to all other service departments. In many instances, these refinements do not result in materially different allocations; such detailed discussions are beyond our present objectives.

JOINT PRODUCTS

Often, the processing of direct material results in two or more products of significant commercial value. Such products derived from a common input are **joint products,** and the related cost of the direct material is a **joint product cost.** An obvious example of a direct material whose processing results in joint products is crude oil, from which a variety of fuels, solvents, lubricants, and residual petrochemical pitches are derived. Cattle, from which the meat packer obtains many cuts and grades of meat, hides, and other products, are another example.

It is impossible to allocate a joint product cost among joint products in such a way that management can decide whether to continue production or what price to charge for a joint product. To decide to produce one joint product is to decide to produce all related joint products, even if some are discarded. Therefore, to make informed decisions about joint products, management must compare the total revenue generated by all joint products with their total production costs.

The primary reason for allocating a joint product cost among two or more products is to assign cost to the ending inventories of joint products when determining periodic income. The most popular method of allocating joint product costs for inventory costing purposes is the **relative sales value** method. Like the

EXHIBIT 23–12

Overhead Distribution Worksheet
For the Year Ended December 31, 19XX

	Totals	Service Departments: Building Maintenance	Service Departments: Machine Repairs	Production Departments: Mixing	Production Departments: Bottling	Allocation Base
Directly identifiable with departments:						
Indirect labor	85,000	8,000	20,000	38,500	18,500	Factory payroll analysis
Factory supplies used	24,000	3,000	2,000	9,000	10,000	Requisition forms
Allocated to production and service departments:						
Building depreciation	6,000	600	1,200	3,000	1,200	Square feet of floor space
Personal property taxes	4,000	400	800	1,500	1,300	Assessed value of equipment used
Total cost to be allocated	119,000	12,000	24,000	52,000	31,000	
Allocation of service departments:						
Building maintenance (assumed as $\frac{2}{3}$ for mixing and $\frac{1}{3}$ for bottling)		(12,000)		8,000	4,000	Square feet of factory area used
Machinery repairs (assumed as $\frac{1}{6}$ for mixing and $\frac{5}{6}$ for bottling)			(24,000)	4,000	20,000	Machine hours
Totals	119,000	–0–	–0–	64,000*	55,000†	

*Assuming a factory overhead allocation base of 20,000 machine hours, the overhead rate for the Mixing Department is $3.20 per machine hour ($64,000/20,000 machine hours).
†Assuming a factory overhead allocation base of $110,000 direct labor, the overhead rate for the Bottling Department is 50 cents per direct labor dollar ($55,000/$110,000 direct labor).

cost allocations explained earlier, this approach uses arithmetic proportions. The total joint product cost is allocated to the several joint products in the proportions of their individual sales values to the total sales value of all joint products at the *split-off point*—that is, where physical separation takes place. For example, assume that 50,000 55-gallon barrels of crude oil costing $1,200,000 are processed into 800,000 gallons of fuel selling for 75 cents per gallon; 400,000 gallons of lubricants selling for $2 per gallon; and 1,000,000 gallons of petrochemical residues selling for 20 cents per gallon. The following calculations illustrate the joint product cost allocation using the relative sales value approach:

Joint Products	Quantity Produced (gallons)		Unit Sales Value		Product Sales Value	Proportion of Total Sales Value
Fuel	800,000	×	$0.75	=	$ 600,000	6/16
Lubricants	400,000	×	2.00	=	800,000	8/16
Residues	1,000,000	×	0.20	=	200,000	2/16
Total sales value					$1,600,000	16/16

Allocations of joint product costs would be undertaken as follows:

	Proportion of Materials Cost	Allocated Cost		Quantity Produced		Cost per Unit
Fuel	6/16 × $1,200,000	$ 450,000	÷	800,000	=	$0.5625 per gallon
Lubricants	8/16 × $1,200,000	600,000	÷	400,000	=	$1.50 per gallon
Residues	2/16 × $1,200,000	150,000	÷	1,000,000	=	$0.15 per gallon
		$1,200,000				

Note that the relative sales value approach results in assigned unit costs that are the same percentage of the selling price for each product. In our illustration, the cost per unit equals 75% of the sales value per unit.

BYPRODUCTS

Byproducts have relatively little sales value compared with the other products derived from a particular process. Byproducts are considered incidental to the manufacture of the more important products. For example, the sawdust and shavings generated in a lumber planing mill or in a furniture factory's cutting department are byproducts.

We may account for byproducts by assigning them a cost equal to their sales value less any disposal costs. This net amount is charged to an inventory account for the byproduct and credited to the work in process account that was charged with the original materials. For example, consider a furniture factory in which walnut boards are processed through a cutting and shaping department. In processing $40,000 worth of lumber, 800 bushels of sawdust and shavings are generated, which, after treatment costing $80, can be sold for $1 per bushel. The following accounts illustrate the amounts and entries involved:

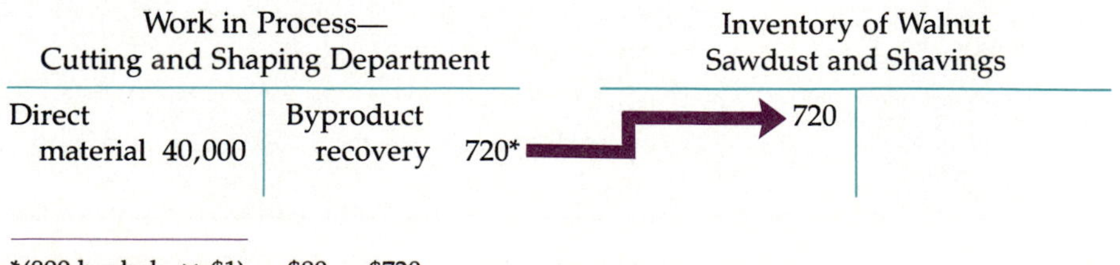

*(800 bushels × $1) − $80 = $720

This procedure reduces the costs of the main products by the net amount recovered from byproducts.

KEY POINTS FOR CHAPTER OBJECTIVES

1 Compare and contrast job order costing and process costing (pp. 877–78).

- Job order costing is used when production consists of a variety of different products or customer orders while process costing is used when production consists of a large volume of the same product produced in a continuous flow.

2 Describe the basic concepts of process costing (pp. 878–79).

- There is a separate work in process account for each department with process costing, whereas there is only one work in process account with job order costing.
- Perpetual inventory techniques flow product cost from work in process to finished goods to cost of goods sold during the accounting period when job order costing is used; end of the period entries are required to flow product cost from work in process to finished goods to cost of goods sold when process costing is used.
- Products flow through multiple departments which are arranged in either a sequential pattern or a parallel pattern.

3 Explain techniques for determining unit costs when process costing is used (pp. 879–82).

- When work in process inventories exist at the beginning and the end of the accounting period, the measurement of work accomplished requires that partially finished units be converted to equivalent units.
- When materials are added at a different rate than conversion work is accomplished, equivalent units must be computed separately for material and conversion.

4 Illustrate the journal entries used with process costing (pp. 882–84).

- Product cost flows and the related journal entries during the accounting period are similar for process costing and job order costing except for the transfer of product cost to finished goods and cost of goods sold.

5 Describe the calculation of equivalent units and costs per equivalent unit using the FIFO method in a multiple department process costing system (pp. 884–85, 887–88).

- In assigning manufacturing costs, three batches of product are considered: units from beginning work in process, units started and finished this period, and units remaining in the ending work in process.
- Under the FIFO method, costs per equivalent unit are calculated by dividing current costs by current equivalent units; prior period costs and equivalent units are excluded from these calculations but included in the total costs to be accounted for.

6 Explain the procedures used to prepare the production cost report using the FIFO method in a process costing system (pp. 886–87, 889).

- The total cost accounted for in any particular department includes costs associated with units transferred in from prior departments.
- Costs associated with the prior accounting period are included as part of the cost of the units transferred out.

7 Identify the journal entries to transfer product cost from work in process to finished goods to cost of goods sold (pp. 887, 890).

8 Describe the procedures for cost allocation for service departments (pp. 891–94).

- Service department costs are overhead costs that are allocated to production departments and eventually assigned to products as part of the production department's overhead.
- Each different service cost may be allocated using a different allocation base.

9 Identify joint product costs and byproduct costs and describe techniques to account for them (pp. 894–96).

- Joint products are products of significant value originating from a common direct material or process. Joint product costs are allocated among joint products primarily for inventory costing purposes.
- Byproducts have relatively insignificant sales values and are assigned costs equal to their net recoverable value, which is removed from the related work in process account and charged to an appropriate inventory account.

KEY TERMS USED IN THIS CHAPTER

byproducts 896
conversion costs 881
cost per equivalent unit report 885
equivalent units 880
joint product cost 894
joint products 894
process costing 878
production report 884
production cost report 886
relative sales value 894
service departments 891

SELF-TEST QUESTIONS FOR REVIEW

(Answers are at the end of this chapter.)

1. Which of the following costs will not be part of product cost when using a process costing system?
(a) Prior department cost.
(b) Conversion cost.
(c) Byproduct cost.
(d) Material cost.

2. For which of the following account titles will there be multiple accounts in the general ledger when using process costing?
(a) Finished Goods.
(b) Work in Process.
(c) Materials.
(d) Factory Payroll.

3. Which of the following will be excluded from the calculation of equivalent units when FIFO is used?
(a) Prior department units transferred in.
(b) Ending inventory units.
(c) Beginning inventory units.
(d) Units sold.

4. Which of the following is not one of the categories of cost involved in the allocation of service department costs?
(a) Service department costs allocated to production departments.
(b) Costs directly identifiable with departments.
(c) Costs requiring allocation to departments.
(d) Selling department costs.

5. What basis should be used to allocate joint product costs to the individual products?
(a) Quantity sold × unit sales price.
(b) Quantity produced × unit sales price.
(c) Quantity sold × unit cost.
(d) Quantity produced × unit cost.

DEMONSTRATION PROBLEM FOR REVIEW

Arlington Manufacturing, Inc., produces a liquid polish in two sequential processes organized as the Mixing Department and the Bottling Department. Direct material is added initially in the Mixing Department and evenly throughout the Bottling Department. All conversion cost in both departments is added evenly throughout the process. The following are cost data for May:

	Mixing Department	Bottling Department
Beginning work in process inventory	$ 42,360	$126,100
Operating costs for May:		
Direct material	360,000	242,900
Direct labor	211,200	109,200
Factory overhead	316,800	203,100
	$930,360	$681,300

Beginning work in process consisted of 20,000 gallons (30% complete) in the Mixing Department and 25,000 gallons (20% complete) in the Bottling Department. 180,000 gallons were started in the Mixing Department during May. Ending work in process consisted of 30,000 gallons (40% complete) in the Mixing Department and 22,000 gallons (25% complete) in the Bottling Department. Assume that Arlington uses the FIFO method for process costing.

REQUIRED

(a) Prepare a production report for May for the two departments.

(b) For the Mixing Department:
1. Prepare a cost per equivalent unit report for May.
2. Prepare a production cost report for May.
3. Prepare journal entries to record the transfer of completed units.

(c) For the Bottling Department:
1. Prepare a cost per equivalent unit report for May.
2. Prepare a production cost report for May.
3. Prepare journal entries to record the transfer of completed units.

SOLUTION TO DEMONSTRATION PROBLEM

(a)

Arlington Manufacturing, Inc.
Production Report
For the Month of May, 19XX

	Mixing Department Percent Processed	Mixing Department Units	Bottling Department Percent Processed	Bottling Department Units
Beginning work in process	30%	20,000	20%	25,000
Started during May		180,000		
Transferred in during May				170,000
Units to be accounted for		200,000		195,000
Transferred out during May		170,000		173,000
Ending work in process	40%	30,000	25%	22,000

FIFO Method:	Total Cost	Unit Cost
Costs accounted for:		
Transferred out:		
Beginning work in process:		
Prior month	$ 126,100	
Transferred in (0 × $4.908)	0	
Materials (20,000 × $1.40)	28,000	
Conversion (20,000 × $1.80)	36,000	
	$ 190,100	
Transferred in and finished:		
Transferred in (148,000 × $4.908)	726,384	
Materials (148,000 × $1.40)	207,200	
Conversion (148,000 × $1.80)	266,400	
Total costs transferred out	$1,390,084	$8.035
Ending work in process:		
Transferred in (22,000 × $4.908)	$ 107,976	
Materials (5,500 × $1.40)	7,700	
Conversion (5,500 × $1.80)	9,900	
Ending work in process	$ 125,576	
Total costs accounted for	$1,515,660	

(c) 3.			
	Finished Goods Inventory	1,390,084	
	Work in Process—Bottling Department		1,390,084
	To record completion of 173,000 units at a cost of $8.035 per unit and their transfer to finished goods inventory.		

QUESTIONS

23–1 What are the important differences between job order and process costing systems? Give two examples of industries that might use each system.

23–2 How are all manufacturing costs for a series of processing departments accumulated as finished goods inventory?

23–3 Why do unit cost computations in a manufacturing process require equivalent unit computations?

23–4 Why do we say that process cost accounting is basically an averaging computation?

23–5 What is meant by the term *equivalent unit*?

23–6 Why must we sometimes compute equivalent units separately for materials and for conversion costs?

23–7 Describe the three batches of products that are typically involved in a period's production under the FIFO accounting method. In what special situation are there only two batches?

23–8 What is meant by the expression that in each department's Work in Process account all charges must be accounted for, either as being transferred out or as ending work in process inventory?

23–9 Contrast service departments with production departments. Give three examples of service departments.

23–10 Why might service departments be treated as cost centers?

23–11 Explain what each of the following statements means:
(a) Service departments do not work directly on products.

(b) Service department costs are factory overhead costs.
(c) Overhead rates are not used for service departments.
(d) In spite of part (c), service department costs become part of product costs.

23–12 How do we choose a base for allocating a cost to several departments?

23–13 How is an allocation rate calculated? How is the specific amount allocated to a department calculated?

23–14 Briefly describe the general format, data, and calculations that would appear on an overhead distribution worksheet for a company with a number of production and service departments.

23–15 Define *joint product*, and give two examples of industries that have joint products because of the nature of the materials used.

23–16 If allocated joint product costs are irrelevant for management decisions, how do we justify allocating joint costs among joint products?

23–17 Define *byproduct*, and briefly describe an accepted procedure in accounting for them.

EXERCISES

Product report and equivalent units

23–18 Jonathon Corporation makes a powdered rug shampoo concentrate in two sequential departments, Compounding and Drying. Materials are added initially in the Compounding Department. All other costs are added evenly throughout each process. The FIFO method is used for process costing. In the Compounding Department, beginning work in process was 4,000 pounds (70% processed), 35,000 pounds were started in process, 34,000 pounds transferred out, and ending work in process was 60% processed. In the Drying Department, beginning work in process was 2,000 pounds (25% processed), 30,000 pounds were transferred out, and the ending work in process was 40% processed. Prepare a production report for the current month, and calculate the relevant amounts of equivalent units for each department.

Cost flows through journal entries

23–19 The Mixing Department performs the last of a series of processes in which a fluid chemical is emulsified. Records indicate that the Mixing Department has been charged with $90,000 of transferred-in costs from the Compounding Department and $32,000 of direct labor costs. The factory overhead rate is 150% of direct labor costs. Beginning work in process was $22,000, and ending work in process totaled $17,000. One-half of this period's completed product is sold on account at a price equal to 160% of its cost. Prepare journal entries to record: (1) various costs charged to the Mixing Department this period, (2) transfer of this period's completed product, and (3) sale of one-half of this period's production.

Equivalent units calculations

23–20 The following are selected operating data for the Blending Department for April. Tinting and packaging operations are carried out subsequently in other departments.

Beginning inventory	8,000 units, 60% complete
Units both begun and completed	50,000 units
Ending inventory	9,000 units, 30% complete

Calculate the equivalent units accomplished using the FIFO method, assuming that:

(a) All materials are added and conversion accomplished evenly throughout the process.
(b) The materials are added initially and conversion costs are incurred evenly throughout.

Assume all manufacturing costs are incurred evenly throughout each process, that 80% of July's production was sold on account at a price equal to 150% of its cost, and that the FIFO method was used.

REQUIRED

(a) Briefly explain the July 31 status of the units started in process during July.
(b) For each department, prepare a cost per equivalent unit report for July.
(c) Prepare journal entries to record the completion and transfer of products from each department and the sale of 80% of July's production.

Calculate units, costs, and transferred costs

23–28 Madison Manufacturing, Inc., operates a plant that produces its own regionally marketed Spicy Steak Sauce. The sauce is produced in two processes, blending and bottling. In the Blending Department, all materials are added at the start of the process, and labor and overhead are incurred evenly throughout the process. Madison uses the FIFO method. The Work in Process—Blending Department account for January follows:

Work in Process—Blending Department

January 1 inventory (5,000 gallons, 60% processed)	16,954	Transferred to Bottling Department (61,000 gallons)	______
January charges:			
Direct material (62,000 gallons)	161,200		
Direct labor	70,900		
Factory overhead	53,500		
January 31 inventory (______ gallons, 70% processed)	______		

REQUIRED

Calculate the following amounts for the Blending Department:

(a) Number of units in the January 31 inventory.
(b) Equivalent units for materials cost and conversion cost.
(c) January cost per equivalent unit for conversion.
(d) Cost of the units transferred to the Bottling Department.
(e) Cost of the incomplete units in the January 31 inventory.

Calculate units, costs, and transferred costs

23–29 Sterling Company processes a food seasoning powder through a Compounding Department and a Packaging Department. In the Packaging Department, costs of direct material, direct labor, and factory overhead are incurred evenly throughout the process. Sterling uses the FIFO method. Costs in the Packaging Department for August were:

Inventory, August 1 (2,000 units, 40% complete)	$ 5,510
Transferred in from Compounding Department (30,000 units)	75,000
Direct material	11,640
Direct labor	32,815
Factory overhead	26,840
	$151,805

At August 31, 3,000 units were in process, 30% finished.

REQUIRED
Calculate the following for the Packaging Department:
(a) Equivalent units during August.
(b) Costs per equivalent unit.
(c) Total cost of units transferred to finished goods inventory.
(d) Inventory cost at August 31.

Journal entries with supporting calculations

23–30 Davis Laboratories, Inc., produces one of its products in two successive departments. All materials are added at the beginning of the process in Department 1; no materials are used in Department 2. Conversion costs are incurred evenly in both departments. Davis uses the FIFO method for process costing. January 1 inventory account balances are as follows:

Materials Inventory	$30,000
Work in Process—Department 1 (2,000 units, 35% complete)	16,140
Work in Process—Department 2 (2,500 units, 40% complete)	42,100
Finished Goods Inventory (2,000 units @ $20.40)	40,800

During January, the following transactions occurred:
1. Purchased materials on account, $60,000.
2. Placed 20,000 units of materials at $3.30 per unit into process in Department 1.
3. Distributed total payroll costs—$151,200 of direct labor to Department 1, $45,300 of direct labor to Department 2, and $42,000 of indirect labor to Factory Overhead.
4. Incurred other actual factory overhead costs, $58,000. (Credit Other Accounts.)
5. Applied overhead to the two processing departments—$75,600 to Department 1 and $30,200 to Department 2.
6. Transferred 19,000 completed units from Department 1 to Department 2. The 3,000 units remaining in Department 1 were 20% completed with respect to conversion costs.
7. Transferred 15,000 completed units from Department 2 to Finished Goods Inventory. The 6,500 units remaining in Department 2 were 75% completed with respect to conversion costs.
8. Sold 6,000 units on account at $27 per unit. Davis uses FIFO inventory costing procedures for the finished goods inventory.

REQUIRED
(a) Record the January transactions in general journal form.
(b) State the balances remaining in Materials Inventory, in each work in process account, and in Finished Goods Inventory.

Production cost report

23–31 Grand Manufacturing Corporation produces a cosmetic product in three consecutive processes. The costs of Department 2 for May were as follows:

Cost of beginning inventory		$ 75,270
Cost from Department 1		532,000
Costs added in Department 2:		
Direct material	$66,470	
Direct labor	72,650	
Factory overhead	36,830	175,950

Department 2 handled the following units during May:

Units in process, May 1	5,000
Units transferred in from Department 1	38,000
Units transferred to Department 3	37,000
Units in process, May 31	6,000

On average, the May 1 units were 30% complete while the May 31 units were 60% complete. Both materials and conversion costs occur evenly throughout the process in Department 2. Grand uses the FIFO method for process costing.

REQUIRED

Prepare the production cost report for Department 2 for May.

Overhead distribution worksheet

23–32 The following are selected operating data for the production and service departments of Princeton Company for the current operating period.

	Departments			
	Service		Production	
	1	2	1	2
Overhead costs (identified by department)				
Indirect material	$48,000	$ 80,400	$254,400	$ 516,000
Indirect labor	$97,200	$144,000	$324,000	$1,440,000
Square feet of building floor space used	4,800	7,200	12,000	24,000
Assessed value of equipment used	$21,000	$ 63,000	$126,000	$ 210,000
Cubic yards of factory space used			88,000	132,000
Machine hours			51,200	204,800
Direct labor			$187,500	$ 375,000

Building depreciation of $192,000 is allocated on the basis of square feet of floor space. Personal property taxes of $72,000 are allocated on the basis of assessed values of equipment used. Costs for Service Departments 1 and 2 are allocated to production departments on the basis of cubic yards of factory space and machine hours, respectively.

REQUIRED

(a) Prepare an overhead distribution worksheet similar to Exhibit 23–12.

(b) Compute the factory overhead rates for Production Departments 1 and 2 using machine hours and direct labor costs, respectively, for allocation bases.

Allocating joint product costs

23–33 Harrison Company produces joint products A and B and byproduct B-1 from a common material and manufacturing process involving sequential processing departments for blending and distilling. After distilling, the three products are separable and considered finished goods.

Because of the nature of the operation, no beginning or ending work in process inventories exist. For the current period, charges to Work in Process—Distilling Department were

Transferred in from Blending Department	$116,900
Direct labor	29,400
Factory overhead	47,500
	$193,800

REQUIRED

Assume that the following quantities and sales prices are available when the products are separable:

Product	Quantity (pounds)	Unit Price
A	20,000	$ 5.00
B	30,000	10.00
B-1	5,000	2.00*

*Special freight charges of $800 are incurred in selling product B-1 for this price.

(a) Allocate the joint product costs to each joint product on the basis of relative sales value.

(b) Prepare journal entries to record the current period's product completion in and transfer from the Distilling Department to Finished Goods Inventory.

ALTERNATE PROBLEMS

Calculate units started and equivalent units

23–26A Venice Corporation manufactures decorated planters in three consecutive processing departments: Construction, Painting, and Packaging. The following information is taken from September's unit product reports:

	Units in Beginning Inventory	Percent Complete	Units Started in September	Units in Ending Inventory	Percent Complete
Construction Department	13,000	40	75,000	16,000	30
Painting Department	15,000	60	?	14,000	70
Packaging Department	12,000	20	?	11,000	40

Materials are added at the start of the process in the Construction Department and evenly throughout processing in the Packaging Department. No materials are used in the Painting Department. Conversion costs are incurred evenly in all processing departments. The FIFO method is used to compute equivalent units and cost inventories.

REQUIRED

(a) Calculate the number of units started or transferred in during September in the Painting and Packaging Departments.

(b) Calculate the equivalent units relating to materials and conversion costs in each department.

Calculate equivalent units and costs; journal entries

23–27A Columbia, Inc., produces a shoe polish in two sequential processes designated Phase I and Phase II. Columbia shut down during August, when all employees took their annual vacations. Production began again on September 1. The following operating data apply to September:

	Phase I	Phase II
Units started in process	120,000	
Units transferred in from Phase I		110,000
Units in ending work in process (on the average, 40% processed)	10,000	15,000
Costs charged to departments:		
Direct material	$102,600	$171,700
Direct labor	237,100	231,500
Factory overhead	127,700	152,300

Assume all manufacturing costs are incurred evenly throughout each process, that three-fourths of September production was sold on account at a price equal to 140% of its cost, and that the FIFO method was used.

REQUIRED

(a) Briefly explain the September 30 status of the units started in process during September.
(b) For each department, prepare a cost per equivalent unit report for September.
(c) Prepare journal entries to record the finishing and transfer of products from each department and the sale of three-fourths of September's production.

Calculate units, costs, and transferred costs

23–28A Morton Manufacturing, Inc., operates a plant that produces its own regionally marketed Super Salad Dressing. The dressing is produced in two processes, blending and bottling. In the Blending Department, all materials are added at the start of the process, and labor and overhead are incurred evenly throughout the process. Morton uses the FIFO method. The Work in Process—Blending Department account for January follows:

Work in Process—Blending Department

January 1 inventory (4,000 gallons, 75% finished)	41,580	Transferred to Bottling Department (73,000 gallons)	_____
January charges:			
Direct material (75,000 gallons)	525,000		
Direct labor	261,300		
Factory overhead	143,500		
January 31 inventory (_____ gallons, 60% finished)	_____		

REQUIRED

Calculate the following amounts for the Blending Department:

(a) Number of units in the January 31 inventory.
(b) Equivalent units for materials cost and conversion cost.
(c) January cost per equivalent unit for conversion.
(d) Cost of the units transferred to the Bottling Department.
(e) Cost of the incomplete units in the January 31 inventory.

Calculate units, costs, and transferred costs

23–29A Superior Company processes a scouring powder through a Compounding Department and a Packaging Department. In the Packaging Department, costs of direct material, direct labor, and factory overhead are incurred evenly throughout the process. Superior uses the FIFO method. Costs charged to the Packaging Department in October were:

Inventory, October 1 (5,000 units, 25% complete)	$ 8,410
Transferred in from Compounding Department (80,000 units)	144,000
Direct material	47,730
Direct labor	42,600
Factory overhead	21,040
	$263,780

At October 31, 7,000 units were in process, 40% completed.

REQUIRED
Calculate the following for the Packaging Department:
(a) Equivalent units during October.
(b) Costs per equivalent unit.
(c) Total cost of units transferred to finished goods inventory.
(d) Inventory cost at October 31.

Journal entries with supporting calculations

23–30A Davenport Laboratories, Inc., produces one of its products in two successive departments. All materials are added at the beginning of the process in Department 1; no materials are used in Department 2. Conversion costs are incurred evenly in both departments. August 1 inventory account balances are as follows:

Materials Inventory	$15,000
Work in Process—Department 1 (6,000 units, 25% finished)	19,300
Work in Process—Department 2 (4,000 units, 35% finished)	37,630
Finished Goods Inventory (4,000 units @ $9.90)	39,600

During August, the following transactions occurred:
1. Purchased materials on account, $51,000.
2. Placed 16,000 units of materials at $3.75 per unit into process in Department 1.
3. Distributed total payroll costs—$82,700 of direct labor to Department 1, $41,280 of direct labor to Department 2, and $18,500 of indirect labor to Factory Overhead.
4. Incurred other actual factory overhead costs, $16,100. (Credit Other Accounts.)
5. Applied overhead to the two processing departments: Department 1, $16,620, Department 2, $13,760.
6. Transferred 20,000 completed units from Department 1 to Department 2. The 2,000 units remaining in Department 1 were 30% completed with respect to conversion costs.
7. Transferred 15,000 completed units from Department 2 to Finished Goods Inventory. The 9,000 units remaining in Department 2 were 40% completed with respect to conversion costs.
8. Sold 9,000 units on account at $21 per unit. Davenport uses FIFO inventory costing for finished goods inventory.

REQUIRED
(a) Record the August transactions in general journal form.
(b) State the balances remaining in Materials Inventory, in each work in process account, and in Finished Goods Inventory.

Production cost report

23–31A Grafton Manufacturing Corporation produces a dandruff shampoo in three consecutive processes. The costs of Department 2 for June were as follows:

Cost of beginning inventory		$ 25,840
Cost from Department 1		504,000
Costs added in Department 2:		
Direct material	$52,125	
Direct labor	90,240	
Factory overhead	34,860	177,225

Department 2 handled the following units during June:

Units in process, June 1	2,000
Units transferred in from Department 1	42,000
Units transferred to Department 3	39,000
Units in process, June 30	5,000

On average, the June 1 units were 40% complete while the June 30 units were 70% complete. Both materials and conversion costs occur evenly throughout the process in Department 2. Grafton uses the FIFO method for process costing.

REQUIRED
Prepare the production cost report for Department 2 for June.

Overhead distribution worksheet

23–32A The following are selected operating data for the production and service departments of Paulson Company for the current operating period.

	Departments			
	Service		Production	
	1	2	1	2
Overhead costs (identified by department)				
Factory supplies used	$ 64,000	$107,200	$339,200	$ 688,000
Indirect labor	$129,600	$192,000	$432,000	$1,920,000
Square feet of building floor space used	7,200	10,800	18,000	36,000
Assessed value of equipment used	$ 28,000	$ 84,000	$168,000	$ 280,000
Cubic yards of factory space used			132,000	198,000
Machine hours			76,800	307,200
Direct labor ($10 per hour)			$250,000	$ 500,000

Building depreciation of $256,000 is allocated on the basis of square feet of floor space. Personal property taxes of $96,000 are allocated on the basis of assessed values of equipment used. Costs for Service Departments 1 and 2 are allocated to production departments on the basis of cubic yards of factory space and machine hours, respectively.

REQUIRED
(a) Prepare an overhead distribution worksheet similar to Exhibit 23–12.
(b) Compute the factory overhead rates for Production Departments 1 and 2 using machine hours and direct labor hours, respectively, for allocation bases.

Allocating joint product costs

23–33A Hallstrom Company produces joint products R and S and byproduct T from a common material and manufacturing process involving two sequential processing departments. After the second process, the three products are separable and considered finished goods.

Because of the nature of the operation, no beginning or ending work in process inventories exist. For the current period, charges to Work in Process—Department 2 were

Transferred in from Department 1	$52,100
Direct labor	13,700
Factory overhead	20,600
	$86,400

REQUIRED
Assume that the following quantities and sales prices are available when the products are separable:

Product	Quantity (pounds)	Unit Price
R	15,000	$4.00
S	12,000	7.50
T	5,000	1.00*

*Special freight charges of $600 are incurred in selling product T for this price.

(a) Allocate the joint product costs to each joint product on the basis of relative sales value.

(b) Prepare journal entries to record the current period's product completion in and transfer from Department 2 to finished goods inventory.

BUSINESS DECISION PROBLEM

Adams Corporation makes a new high-tech adhesive in a single process that blends and bottles the product, which currently sells for $20 per gallon. Market demand for the product seems good, but management is not satisfied with the product's seemingly low profit margin and has sought your advice.

Because of its concern, management has allocated a $55,000 fund for a program of product promotion or cost reduction, or both. Members of the firm's controller's office and marketing staff have identified the following three possible plans:

1. Plan A: Devote all funds to product promotion, which allows all costs and the sales volume to remain the same, but permits a $3.50 per gallon sales price increase.
2. Plan B: Spend $30,000 on product promotion and $25,000 on cost reduction techniques, which maintains sales volume, permits a price increase of $2 per gallon, and reduces conversion costs by 10% per gallon.
3. Plan C: Devote all funds to cost reduction efforts. Sales volume and price do not change. For each gallon produced, however, direct material cost decreases 10%, and conversion cost decreases 20%.

The controller's office also provides you with the following operating data for a typical period (all materials are added initially; conversion costs occur evenly throughout the process; the FIFO method is used for process costing):

Beginning work in process (4,500 gallons, 60% processed)	$ 60,495
Units started in process (33,000 gallons)	
Ending work in process (7,500 gallons, 60% processed)	
Costs charged to the department:	
Direct material	257,400
Direct labor	218,180
Factory overhead	95,050
	$631,125

Using the data from this representative production period, analyze the apparent relative benefits derived from each plan and make a recommendation supported by relevant calculations. Assume sales will equal units completed.

ANSWERS TO SELF-TEST QUESTIONS

1. (c) **2.** (b) **3.** (d) **4.** (d) **5.** (b)

ACCOUNTING PRACTICE PROBLEM FOR PART 5

The managerial accounting system used by a firm of certified public accountants (CPAs) incorporates many of the aspects of job order costing used by manufacturing firms.

A. Each client is accounted for as a separate job.
B. The individual client accounts collectively represent the detailed subsidiary ledger for the work in process inventory.
C. A variation of normal product costing is typically used to accumulate product cost (plus gross profit) by client in the work in process inventory.
   1. Items such as postage, photocopies, and travel expense are charged to client accounts as direct material.
   2. The time spent by the professional accountants and the clerical staff working on clients' projects is charged to client accounts as direct labor. Direct labor is the first component of the predetermined billing rates.
   3. Other expenses such as rent, utilities, management, training, and depreciation are charged to client accounts as overhead. Overhead is the second component of the predetermined billing rates.
   4. Gross profit is also charged to client accounts. Gross profit is the third component of the predetermined billing rates.

The managerial accounting system for a CPA firm is often named the *client accounting system*, which consists of two major subsystems—*client work in process* and *client accounts receivable*.

MARTIN & TAYLOR, CPAs The basic input record for client work in process is the *employee timesheet*. Two employees of Martin & Taylor, CPAs, have completed their timesheets for March 20, 19XX, as follows:

Employee name: Mary J. Albertson **Employee number:** 109

Billable Time				Nonbillable Time		
Date	**Client**	**Description**	**Hours**	**Date**	**Description**	**Hours**
3/20	Clark	Meeting with banker	1.5	3/20	Training	2.0
3/20	Jensen	Tax return	3.0			
3/20	Smith	Projection	2.0			

Employee name: Jonathon Frank **Employee number:** 216

Billable Time				Nonbillable Time		
Date	**Client**	**Description**	**Hours**	**Date**	**Description**	**Hours**
3/20	Jensen	Tax return	1.0	3/20	Meeting	2.5
3/20	Smith	Tax return	4.0			
3/20	Smith	Meeting to explain taxes	1.5			

An employee timesheet is completed by each professional accountant and clerical employee of the CPA firm. The left side of the form accumulates time that will be billable to clients (direct labor) while the right side of the form accumulates the time that will not be billable to clients (overhead).

Billable time is posted to client work in process using the time recorded on the employee timesheets and the predetermined billing rates for the appropriate employees. The amount posted represents direct labor, overhead, and gross profit.

REQUIRED

(a) Calculate the billing rates for Mary (a junior accountant) and Jonathon (a senior accountant), using the formula that billing rate equals 2.5 times rate of pay. Mary is paid $14 per hour while Jonathon is paid $18 per hour.
(b) Post the time for clients Clark, Jensen, and Smith in the client work in process subsidiary ledger accounts, which have the following column headings: date, employee number, hours, billable amount, amount billed, and balance to be billed.
(c) Post the expenses specifically incurred for the clients in the client work in process subsidiary ledger accounts, using March 31 as the date and employee number 900 to identify the item as an expense. The expenses are: Clark = $32; Jensen = $105, and Smith = $51.

MONTHLY BILLING At the end of each month, the management of the CPA firm will typically review the balance to be billed for each client and determine whether to bill the client and how much to bill. The amount billed is posted in the amount billed column and deducted from the balance to be billed column of the client work in process subsidiary ledger accounts. The amount is also set up in the client accounts receivable subsidiary ledger accounts.

(d) Post the March 31 amount billed in the client work in process subsidiary ledger accounts, assuming that Clark and Smith were billed for their entire balances while the billing for Jensen was deferred until the next month.
(e) Prepare general journal entries to reflect the transactions described in (b), (c), and (d) above and payment in full by Clark on April 10, 19XX. Assume Martin & Taylor uses accrual accounting and has general ledger control accounts for client work in process and client accounts receivable.

The balance of the general ledger control account for client work in process will equal the sum of the individual client work in process account balances, while the balance of the general ledger control account for client accounts receivable will equal the sum of all the client accounts receivable account balances. There is no account equivalent to finished goods.

Many managerial reports can be prepared from the work in process and accounts receivable files, including (1) aging of accounts receivable, (2) aging of balance to be billed, (3) percent of total time that is billable with detail by employee, and (4) time spent on each client during the year with detail by employee. The client accounting system not only keeps track of amounts billable to and collectible from each client but also provides the management of the CPA firm with valuable information about the firm's practice.

WEIGHTED AVERAGE METHOD FOR PROCESS COSTING

Chapter 23 illustrates the concept of equivalent units, the cost flows and journal entries in process costing, and the FIFO method of assigning product cost to the goods transferred out of processing departments as well as the ending work in process accounts of the processing departments. Appendix G illustrates the use of the weighted average method to assign product cost to the goods transferred out and to the ending work in process inventories.

In this appendix, we will continue the Northbrook Chemical Company example introduced in Chapter 23. Recall that, as a result of the journal entries recorded during the month, the work in process accounts at the end of June contained the following balances:

	Mixing Department	Bottling Department
Beginning balance	$ 106,500	$184,880
Direct material	704,000	240,000
Direct labor	298,400	186,500
Factory overhead	486,800	123,900
	$1,595,700	$735,280

Exhibit G–1 shows the June production report for the two processing departments. Note the following key observations about the production report:

1. All unit figures are in whole gallons rather than in equivalent units.
2. In the Mixing Department, the beginning work in process (10,000) plus units started (80,000) constitute the total number of units to be accounted for (90,000). The 90,000 units are accounted for as units transferred out (75,000) plus units in ending work in process (15,000) of the Mixing Department.
3. For the Bottling Department, the beginning work in process (8,000) plus units transferred in from the Mixing Department (75,000) constitute the total number of units to be accounted for (83,000). The 83,000 units are accounted for as units transferred out to finished goods (78,000) plus units in ending work in process (5,000) of the Bottling Department.
4. The number of units transferred out of the Mixing Department (75,000) is equal to the number of units transferred into the Bottling Department (75,000).

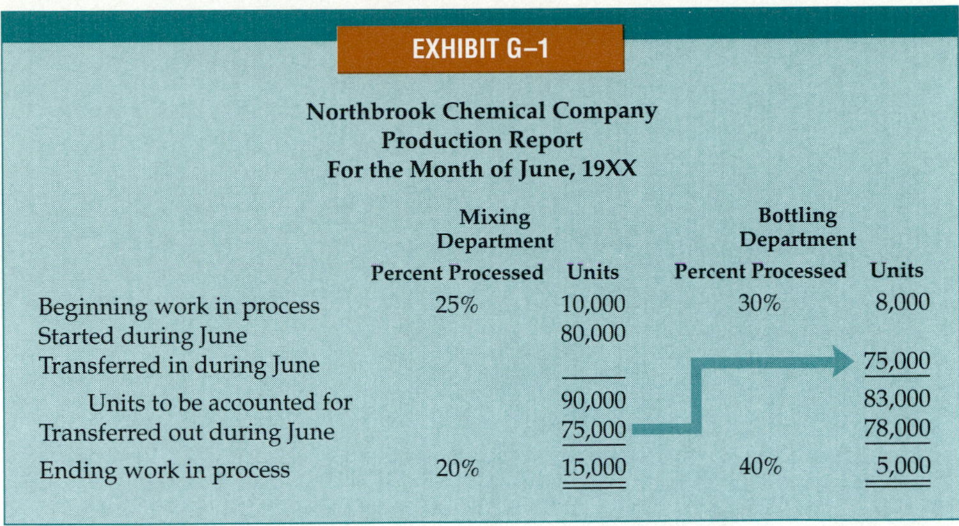

EXHIBIT G–1

Northbrook Chemical Company
Production Report
For the Month of June, 19XX

	Mixing Department		Bottling Department	
	Percent Processed	Units	Percent Processed	Units
Beginning work in process	25%	10,000	30%	8,000
Started during June		80,000		
Transferred in during June				75,000
Units to be accounted for		90,000		83,000
Transferred out during June		75,000		78,000
Ending work in process	20%	15,000	40%	5,000

We now examine how costs are allocated to the various units, beginning with the Mixing Department.

Mixing Department

In the Mixing Department, materials are added at the start of the mixing process, while conversion costs are incurred evenly throughout the process. Therefore, we must calculate equivalent units and cost per equivalent unit separately for material and conversion costs. Exhibit G–2 presents these calculations in a cost per equivalent unit report. It is important to note that, with the weighted average method, total equivalent units and total costs are included in the cost per equivalent unit calculations. "Total" means that both prior month and current month amounts are included.

In allocating costs to various units of product, three batches of Kleeno are considered: (1) units finished from the June 1 inventory, (2) units started and finished in June, and (3) units started but not finished in June. The composition of costs for the three batches of product handled by the Mixing Department is explained below and in the production cost report in Exhibit G–3:

1. **Beginning inventory** The 10,000 gallons in the beginning inventory had all the material ($84,400 cost) and 25% of the required conversion work ($22,100 cost) added in May, for a $106,500 total cost in that month. The remaining 75% of the conversion work was completed in June. All of the costs, both current month and prior month, were included in the costs per equivalent unit. Therefore, we multiply the equivalent units of material (10,000) by the cost per equivalent unit for material ($8.76) and the equivalent units of conversion (10,000) by the cost per equivalent unit for conversion ($10.35) to obtain the cost assigned to the units in the beginning work in process ($191,100).
2. **Started and finished in June** During June, all required material and conversion work were applied to the 65,000 gallons started and finished. The material added this month at $8.76 per gallon and the conversion work completed at $10.35 are applied to each of the 65,000 gallons. The total cost of the 75,000 gallons in the two batches transferred to the Bottling Department amounts to $1,433,250, and the average cost of the two batches is $19.11 per gallon ($1,433,250/75,000).

EXHIBIT G–2

Northbrook Chemical Company
Mixing Department
Cost per Equivalent Unit Report
For the Month of June, 19XX

Weighted Average Method:	Units Involved	Total Conversion Completed	Materials (added initially)	Conversion (added throughout)
Total equivalent units:				
Transferred out:				
Beginning work in process (25%)	10,000	100%	10,000	10,000
Started and finished this month	65,000	100%	65,000	65,000
Units transferred out this month	75,000			
Ending work in process (20%)	15,000	20%	15,000	3,000
Units accounted for	90,000			
Total equivalent units			90,000	78,000
Total costs:				
Prior month			$ 84,400	$ 22,100
Direct material			704,000	
Direct labor				298,400
Factory overhead				486,800
Total costs			$788,400	$807,300
Total cost per total equivalent unit			$8.76	$10.35

3. **Ending inventory** The 15,000 units started but not finished in June contain all required material but only 20% of the needed conversion work. Therefore, we multiply the per-unit material cost of $8.76 by 15,000 gallons to obtain the $131,400 material cost. We then multiply the $10.35 conversion cost by the 3,000 equivalent units of conversion to obtain the $31,050 conversion cost.

Notice that the production cost report fully accounts for both the 90,000 units of product involved and the total costs of $1,595,700 charged to the Mixing Department.

The following entry transfers the cost of the work completed in the Mixing Department during June to the Bottling Department:

Work In Process—Bottling Department	1,433,250	
Work In Process—Mixing Department		1,433,250
To transfer cost of completed work from Mixing to Bottling.		

The work in process account for the Mixing Department would now appear as follows:

EXHIBIT G-3

Northbrook Chemical Company
Mixing Department
Production Cost Report
For the Month of June, 19XX

Weighted Average Method:	**Total Cost**	**Unit Cost**
Costs to be accounted for:		
Prior month costs	$ 106,500	
Direct material	704,000	
Direct labor	298,400	
Factory overhead	486,800	
Total costs to be accounted for	$1,595,700	
Costs accounted for:		
Transferred out:		
Beginning work in process:		
Materials (10,000 × $8.76)	$ 87,600	
Conversion (10,000 × $10.35)	103,500	
	$ 191,100	
Started and finished:		
Materials (65,000 × $8.76)	569,400	
Conversion (65,000 × $10.35)	672,750	
Total costs transferred out	$1,433,250	$19.11
Ending work in process:		
Materials (15,000 × $8.76)	$ 131,400	
Conversion (3,000 × $10.35)	31,050	
Ending work in process	$ 162,450	
Total costs accounted for	$1,595,700	

Work in Process—Mixing Department

June 1 (beginning balance)	106,500	Transferred to Bottling Department	1,433,250
Direct material	704,000		
Direct labor	298,400		
Factory overhead	486,800		
June 30 (ending balance)	162,450		

Note that all costs charged to this account have been accounted for either as transferred out or as ending inventory.

Bottling Department

In the Bottling Department, materials are added at the start of the process, while conversion costs are incurred evenly throughout the process. The units handled during June include 8,000 units from the beginning work in process inventory of the Bottling Department and the 75,000 units transferred in from the Mixing

Department. The 8,000 units in the beginning inventory had $184,880 of product cost assigned to them in the prior month. The 75,000 units had $1,433,250 assigned to them in the Mixing Department prior to being transferred to the Bottling Department.

Again, we must convert the work performed into equivalent units and obtain costs per equivalent unit. Exhibit G–4 presents the cost per equivalent unit report for the Bottling Department and Exhibit G–5 presents the production cost report for the Bottling Department.

The cost per equivalent unit report for the Bottling Department differs from the same report for the Mixing Department in that transferred-in costs must be accounted for in the Bottling Department. As a result, there is a "Transferred In" column added to the cost per equivalent unit report for the Bottling Department. As Exhibit G–4 demonstrates, three cost per equivalent unit amounts are calculated—transferred in, material, and conversion.

The percentages of conversion completed this month in Exhibit G–4 are calculated the same as before. Since the beginning work in process inventory in the Bottling Department was 30% finished, and since we assume these units were finished during June, then the percentage of conversion work finished during June was 70% (100% – 30%).

EXHIBIT G–4

Northbrook Chemical Company
Bottling Department
Cost per Equivalent Unit Report
For the Month of June, 19XX

Weighted Average Method:	Units Involved	Total Conversion Completed	Transferred In	Materials (added initially)	Conversion (added throughout)
Total equivalent units:					
Transferred out:					
Beginning work in process (30%)	8,000	100%	8,000	8,000	8,000
Transferred in and finished	70,000	100%	70,000	70,000	70,000
Units transferred out this month	78,000				
Ending work in process (40%)	5,000	40%	5,000	5,000	2,000
Units accounted for	83,000				
Total equivalent units			83,000	83,000	80,000
Total costs:					
Prior month (detail from prior month)			$ 154,540	$ 23,940	$ 6,400
Costs transferred in from Mixing Department			1,433,250		
Direct material				240,000	
Direct labor					186,500
Factory overhead					123,900
Total costs			$1,587,790	$263,940	$316,800
Total cost per total equivalent unit			$19.13	$3.18	$3.96

EXHIBIT G–5

Northbrook Chemical Company
Bottling Department
Production Cost Report
For the Month of June, 19XX

Weighted Average Method:	Total Cost	Unit Cost
Costs to be accounted for:		
Prior month costs	$ 184,880	
Transferred in from Mixing Department	1,433,250	
Direct material	240,000	
Direct labor	186,500	
Factory overhead	123,900	
Total costs to be accounted for	$2,168,530	
Costs accounted for:		
Transferred out:		
Beginning work in process:		
Transferred in (8,000 × $19.13)	$ 153,040	
Materials (8,000 × $3.18)	25,440	
Conversion (8,000 × $3.96)	31,680	
	$ 210,160	
Transferred in and finished:		
Transferred in (70,000 × $19.13)	1,339,100	
Materials (70,000 × $3.18)	222,600	
Conversion (70,000 × $3.96)	277,200	
Total costs transferred out	$2,049,060	$26.27
Ending work in process:		
Transferred in (5,000 × $19.13)	$ 95,650	
Materials (5,000 × $3.18)	15,900	
Conversion (2,000 × $3.96)	7,920	
Ending work in process	$ 119,470	
Total costs accounted for	$2,168,530	

It should be noted that the transferred-in cost per equivalent unit in Exhibit G–4 is not the same as the transferred-out unit cost in Exhibit G–3. When the weighted average method is used, the two amounts usually are not the same, since the calculation for the Bottling Department's transferred-in cost per equivalent unit includes both the cost transferred in during the current month and the cost transferred in during the prior month.

There are three groups of cost to be accounted for on the production cost report in Exhibit G–5: (1) prior month costs (beginning work in process for the Bottling Department); (2) costs transferred in this month (transferred into the Bottling Department from the Mixing Department); and (3) direct material, direct labor, and factory overhead (current month costs incurred in the Bottling Department). All of these costs are accounted for as either transferred out (to finished goods) or as ending work in process (for the Bottling Department).

All prior month costs ($184,880) are included in the costs per equivalent unit. Therefore, cost is assigned to the units in the beginning work in process by multiplying the 8,000 total equivalent units by the cost per equivalent unit for transferred in ($19.13), material ($3.18), and conversion cost ($3.96). The resulting total cost assigned to the units that were in the beginning work in process is $210,160.

The transferred in and finished section and the ending work in process section are handled the same way the started and finished section and the ending work in process section were handled in the Mixing Department for the weighted average method. As a result of the calculations of Exhibit G–5, $2,049,060 representing 78,000 units were transferred from the Bottling Department work in process inventory to the finished goods inventory with a unit cost of $26.27.

The following entry transfers the cost of completed work in the Bottling Department during June:

Finished Goods Inventory	2,049,060	
Work In Process—Bottling Department		2,049,060
To transfer cost of completed work from the Bottling Department to finished goods inventory.		

The Work in Process account for the Bottling Department would now appear as follows:

Work in Process—Bottling Department

June 1 (beginning balance)	184,880	Transferred to finished goods	2,049,060
Transferred in from Mixing Department	1,433,250		
Direct material	240,000		
Direct labor	186,500		
Factory overhead	123,900		
June 30 (ending balance)	119,470		

Again, note that all costs accumulated to this point have been accounted for.

Finished Goods and Cost of Goods Sold

In the cost flows for a process costing system, the journal entries to record sales are similar to those made in a job order costing system. We assume that during June Northbrook sold goods costing $1,800,000 for $2,400,000. In summary form, the following entries reflect the sales:

Accounts Receivable	2,400,000	
Sales		2,400,000
To record June sales.		
Cost of Goods Sold	1,800,000	
Finished Goods Inventory		1,800,000
To record cost of goods sold during June.		

PROBLEMS

Production report, cost per equivalent unit report, production report, and journal entries

G–1 Using the data for Arlington Manufacturing, Inc., that is presented in the demonstration problem in this chapter (page 899), assume that Arlington Manufacturing, Inc., uses the weighted average method for process costing. The beginning work in process inventories include the following costs:

	Mixing Department	Bottling Department
Material cost	$28,000	$3,430
Conversion cost	14,360	5,430

REQUIRED

(a) Prepare a production report for May for the two departments.
(b) For the Mixing Department:
  1. Prepare a cost per equivalent unit report for May.
  2. Prepare a production cost report for May.
  3. Prepare journal entries to record the transfer of completed units.
(c) For the Bottling Department:
  1. Prepare a cost per equivalent unit report for May.
  2. Prepare a production cost report for May.
  3. Prepare journal entries to record the transfer of completed units.

Calculate units started and equivalent units

G–2 Using the data in Problem 23–26, assume that Verona Corporation uses the weighted average method for process costing.

REQUIRED

(a) Calculate the number of units started or transferred in during July in the Printing and Packaging Departments.
(b) Calculate the equivalent units relating to transferred in, materials, and conversion costs in each department.

Calculate units, costs, and transferred costs

G–3 Using the data in Problem 23–28, assume that Madison Manufacturing, Inc., uses the weighted average method for process costing. The beginning work in process cost includes $9,650 of material and $7,304 of conversion cost.

REQUIRED

Calculate the following amounts for the Blending Department:
(a) Number of units in the January 31 inventory.
(b) Equivalent units for materials and conversion cost.
(c) January cost per equivalent unit of conversion.
(d) Cost of the units transferred to the Bottling Department.
(e) Cost of the incomplete units in the January 31 inventory.

Production cost report

G–4 Shorewood Manufacturing Company uses the weighted average method for process costing. Shorewood produces processed food products that pass through three sequential departments. The costs for Department 2 for September were as follows:

Cost of beginning inventory:		
Transferred in from Department 1	$71,600	
Material	5,120	
Conversion	4,960	$ 81,680
Cost from Department 1 during September		600,000
Costs added in Department 2 during September:		
Direct material	$64,000	
Direct labor	70,000	
Factory overhead	46,000	180,000

Department 2 handled the following units during September:

Units in process, September 1	5,000
Units transferred in from Department 1	41,000
Units transferred out to Department 3	39,000
Units in process, September 30	7,000

On average, the September 1 units were 30% complete while the September 30 units were 60% complete. Both materials and conversion costs occur evenly throughout the process in Department 2.

REQUIRED
Prepare the production cost report for September for Department 2.

Production report, cost per equivalent unit report, and production cost report

G–5 Warner Manufacturing Corporation produces chemical products using a continuous process. The weighted average method is used for process costing. All manufacturing is accomplished in one department. Material is added initially while conversion costs are incurred evenly throughout the process.

The work in process inventory at the beginning of February consisted of 10,000 units that were 20% complete. The work in process at the end of February consisted of 15,000 units which were 40% complete. 195,000 units were transferred to finished goods during February.

The beginning inventory contained $45,000 of material cost and $15,000 of conversion cost. Product costs incurred during February consisted of $1,005,000 of material and $1,593,000 of conversion.

REQUIRED
Prepare the production report, cost per equivalent unit report, and production cost report for Warner Manufacturing Corporation for the month of February.

PART 6

PLANNING, CONTROL, AND DECISION MAKING

24

COST–VOLUME–PROFIT RELATIONSHIPS

CHAPTER OBJECTIVES

1. Develop an understanding of how specific types of costs change in response to volume changes (pp. 927–31).
2. Define the concept of relevant range (pp. 931–32).
3. Outline the approach to developing cost formulas (pp. 932–34).
4. Present a discussion of and a formula for calculating the break-even point (pp. 934–36).
5. Define contribution margin and contribution margin ratio (pp. 936–37).
6. Present alternate break-even formulas and examples of their application (p. 937).
7. Discuss approaches to planning net income using cost–volume–profit analyses (pp. 937–41).

We lose money on every sale—but make it up on volume.
ANONYMOUS

Management must study a number of factors when planning the future course for an organization. One of the most important factors is the relationship of sales (revenue), costs (expenses), and profit (net income). Cost–volume–profit analysis is used to study this relationship.

Cost–volume–profit analysis is appropriately used by for-profit organizations as well as not-for-profit organizations. The latter type of organization uses the analysis with a target profit of zero. All of the relationships studied in the analysis are equally valid for both types of organizations.

COST BEHAVIOR ANALYSIS

Cost behavior analysis is the study of the ways in which specific costs respond to changes in the volume of business activity. Each specific cost incurred by an organization may be affected differently by changes in the volume of business activity. Some costs will increase proportionately as volume increases, some costs will change disproportionately, and some costs will remain the same. Other factors besides volume can also cause changes in specific costs; an increase in the assessment rate, for example, can raise property tax expense, whereas a decrease in electricity rates can lower utility expense. These types of changes, however, are not typically caused by fluctuation in the volume of business activity.

The Activity Base

For meaningful managerial analysis, costs must be related to some measure of volume of business activity. In a manufacturing operation, such measures include units of product, direct labor hours, machine hours, and percent of capacity. The cost analyst must consider the use of the analysis when selecting the most relevant and useful activity base to which costs can be related. For example, if management uses the analysis for control purposes and for establishing responsibility for costs, the analyst selects measures that are meaningful to those responsible for incurring costs. We may use several bases, depending on the objectives of the analysis.

Cost–Volume Graphs

One of the most useful analytic tools for relating cost changes to volume changes is the *cost–volume graph*. Exhibits 24–1 and 24–2 are examples of cost–volume graphs. In these two exhibits, costs (in thousands of dollars) are measured on the vertical axis, and volume (in thousands of units) is measured on the horizontal axis. Point A in Exhibit 24–1 shows that at a volume level of 30,000 units the associated cost is $20,000. Similarly, point B in Exhibit 24–1 represents a cost of $30,000 for a volume level of 50,000 units.

Cost–volume graphs are particularly valuable when available cost–volume data are plotted on the same graph and other cost–volume relationships are estimated by fitting a line to the known points. In Exhibit 24–2, for example, we use three known data points (a greater number of known data points should be

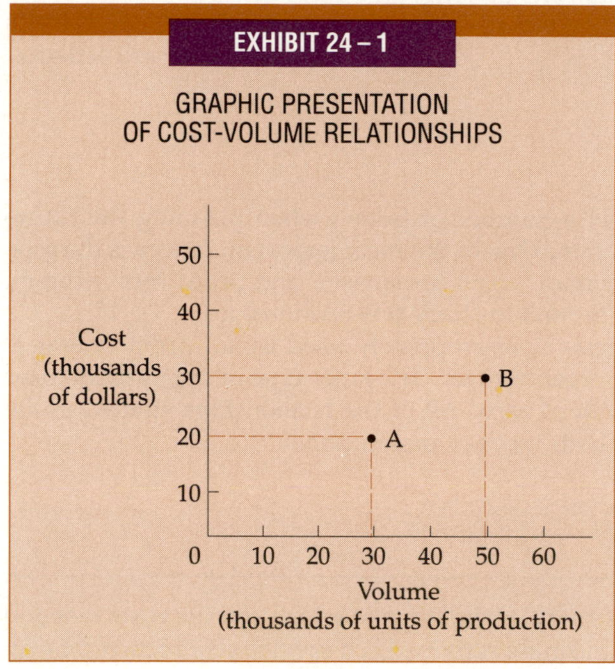

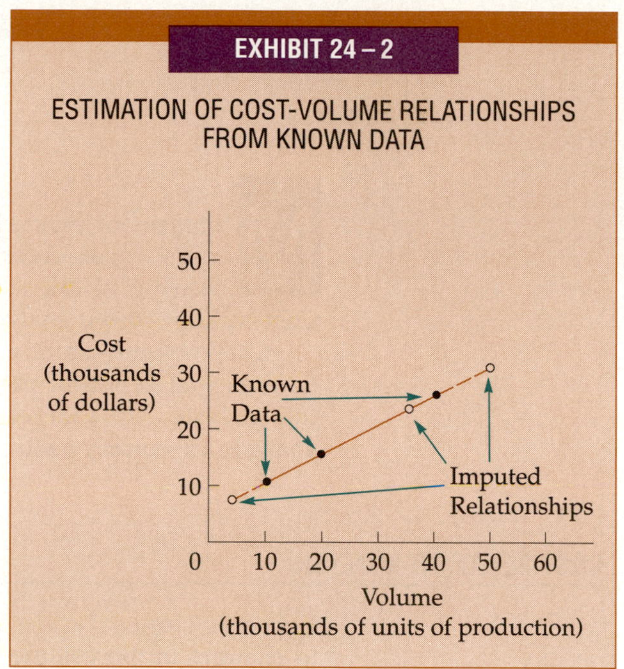

used to develop a reliable graph). The known data points, represented by solid points, are:

Volume (units)	Cost (dollars)
10,000	10,000
20,000	15,000
40,000	25,000

By connecting the known data points with a straight line, we may impute the costs associated with other levels of volume. For example, the open points indicate that for volumes of 5,000, 35,000, and 50,000 units, the related costs would be $7,500, $22,500, and $30,000, respectively. Some important limitations to the validity of this type of imputed cost–volume relationship are discussed later in the chapter.

Classifications of Cost Behavior Patterns

For purposes of analyzing their behavior patterns, costs are usually classified as *variable*, *fixed*, or *semivariable*. However, the classification of costs into these distinct groups is seldom a simple matter.

Despite the difficulties of classification, the study of approximate cost behavior patterns can aid in planning and analyzing operations. Let us examine the ways in which cost–volume graphs vary among the three cost classifications.

Variable costs change proportionately with changes in the volume of activity. Direct material cost and direct labor cost, for example, are variable costs.

Exhibit 24–3 is a typical variable cost graph. As illustrated here, a purely variable cost pattern always passes through the origin, because zero cost is associated with zero volume. Also, because variable costs respond in direct proportion to changes in volume, a variable cost line always slopes upward to the right. The steepness of the slope depends on the amount of cost associated with each unit of volume; the greater the unit cost, the steeper the slope. In Exhibit 24–3,

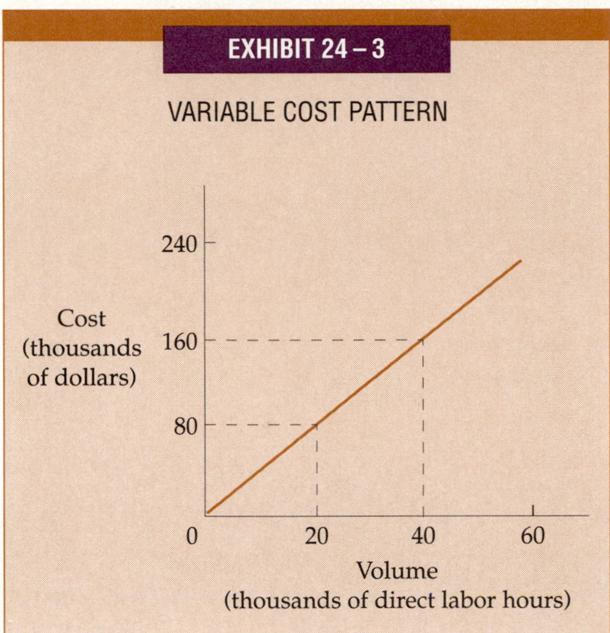

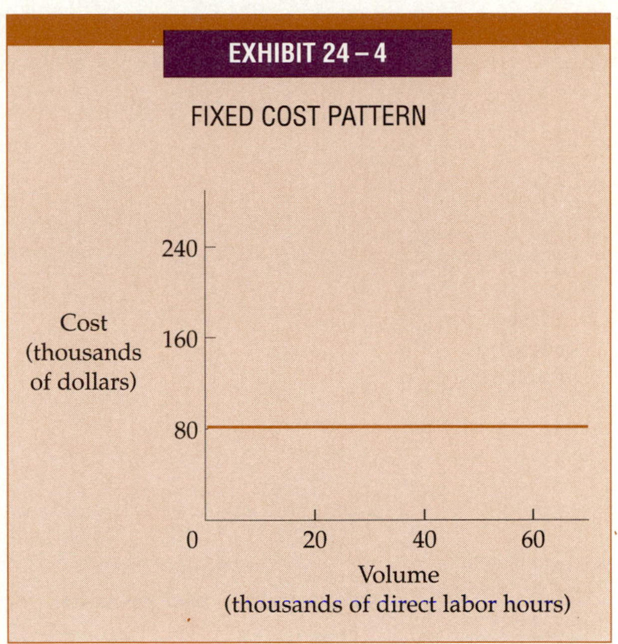

volume is measured in direct labor hours, and the total variable dollar cost is twice as great at 40,000 hours as at 20,000 hours, as expected.

Fixed costs do not change when the volume of activity changes. Examples are depreciation on buildings and property taxes.

Since fixed costs do not respond to changes in volume, they are represented by horizontal lines on a cost–volume graph. In Exhibit 24–4, fixed costs are $80,000 regardless of the volume level considered.

Semivariable costs—sometimes called *mixed costs*—can be described analytically as having both fixed and variable components. A semivariable cost changes linearly with changes in activity, but is some positive amount at zero activity, as shown in Exhibit 24–5. Changes in total semivariable costs are therefore not proportional to changes in operating volume.

As an example of a semivariable cost, consider a firm's utility expense. Even if the firm shuts down production for one period, it typically must pay a minimum amount for utilities. When production resumes, the costs of heat, light, and power increase as production increases.

For purposes of cost analysis, a semivariable cost is divided into its fixed and variable components. We accomplish this by any one of several approaches that vary in their degree of sophistication. One simple method entails plotting on a graph the amount of cost experienced at several levels of volume. If cost behavior in actual situations were perfectly correlated, the observations (points) would form a straight line. More realistically, however, we expect only a discernible pattern as shown in Exhibit 24–6.

The line in Exhibit 24–6 has been subjectively determined to approximate the pattern of data points. Extending this line to the vertical axis indicates a $1,000 fixed portion. We subtract this $1,000 fixed cost from the total $4,000 cost at 60,000 direct labor hours to find a total variable portion of $3,000. Therefore, the rate of variation is $3,000/60,000, or 5 cents, per direct labor hour. Hence, we could describe this semivariable cost as $1,000 plus 5 cents per direct labor hour.

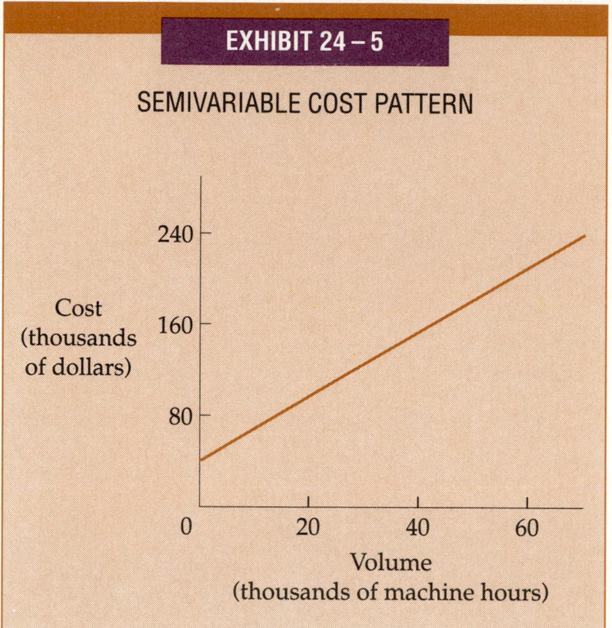

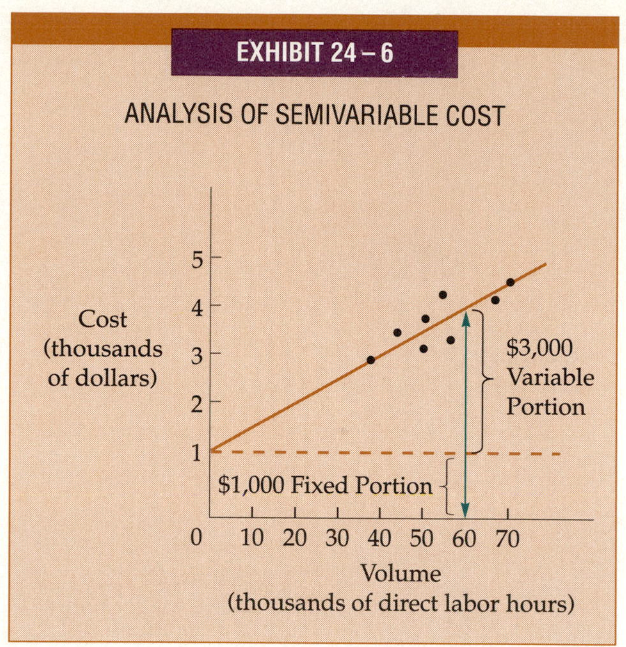

We can obtain a better approximation by fitting the line to the cost observation pattern (data points) by the method of least squares. That technique, which is beyond the scope of this text, is illustrated in most introductory statistics texts.

High–Low Method

When too few cost observations are available to plot a graph, or when the analyst wishes to avoid fitting lines to data, the **high–low method** can be used to approximate the position and slope of the cost line. This relatively simple method compares costs at the highest and lowest levels of activity for which representative cost data are available. The variable cost per activity unit (here, per direct labor hour) is determined by dividing the difference in costs at these two levels by the difference in activity. The fixed element of cost is then isolated by multiplying the variable cost per unit by either the top or bottom level of activity and then subtracting the resulting product from the total cost at the selected activity level.

For example, assume that the lowest and highest levels of activity are 40,000 and 60,000 direct labor hours, respectively, and that total costs for these two levels are shown below:

	Level of Activity	Total Cost
High	60,000 direct labor hours	$4,200
Low	40,000 direct labor hours	3,000
Difference	20,000 (increase)	$1,200 (increase)

Because an increase of 20,000 direct labor hours causes a $1,200 increase in total cost (and only the variable portion of the cost could increase), the variable portion of the total semivariable cost must be $1,200/20,000 direct labor hours, or 6 cents per direct labor hour. Subtracting the total variable portion from the total semivariable cost at the high and low activity levels gives us the fixed portion of total cost as follows:

	Volume Levels	
	Low	High
Total semivariable cost	$3,000	$4,200
Less variable portions:		
$0.06 × 40,000 direct labor hours	2,400	
$0.06 × 60,000 direct labor hours		3,600
Fixed portion of total cost	$ 600	$ 600

The high–low analysis tells us that any volume level has $600 of fixed cost plus a variable portion of 6 cents per direct labor hour, which can be formulated as:

$$\text{Total Cost} = \$600 + (\$0.06 \times \text{Direct Labor Hours})$$

In other words, we can now easily compute the total cost for varying levels of direct labor hours. Obviously, if either the high or low value used in this method is not representative of the actual cost behavior, the resulting cost formula is inexact.

Relevant Range

The foregoing illustrations of cost behavior are oversimplified because they portray linear cost behavior over the entire range of possible activity. Actually, plotting costs against volume may not always produce a single straight line. For example, certain costs may increase abruptly at intervals in a "step" pattern; others may exhibit a curvilinear pattern when plotted over a wide range of activity. Examples of these cost patterns are shown graphically in Exhibit 24–7.

Clearly, an assumption of linear costs over the entire scale on either axis in these two cases causes some degree of error. The significance of this error is often minimized by the fact that many of the firm's decisions involve relatively small changes in volume around some relevant range of activity. The actual cost pattern at extremely low- or high-volume levels is not relevant to the firm's

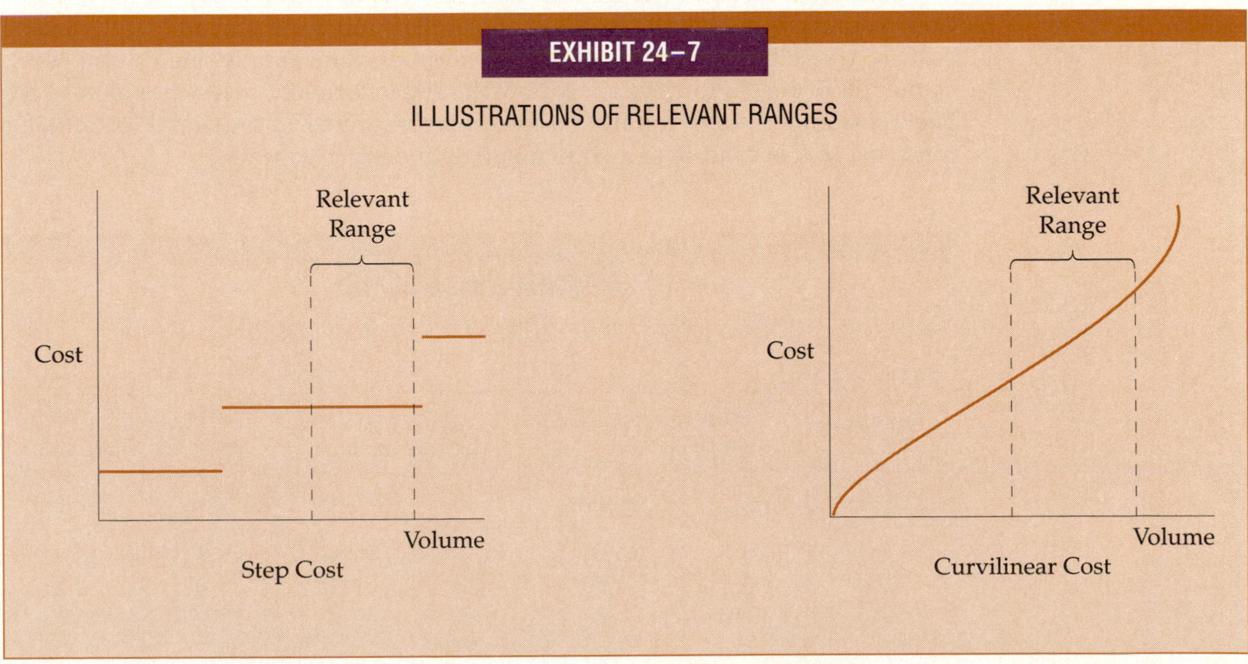

decisions. The cost pattern need only be reasonably linear within the **relevant range** of activity.

Total Versus Per-unit Costs

The cost–volume relationships for fixed cost, variable cost, and semivariable cost typically remain the same for only one range of activity and for only one time period (frequently one year). Fixed, variable, and semivariable costs are assumed to react only to changes in volume within the relevant range during the given time period. The cost relationships, however, may change when moving to a different range of activity or a different time period. For example, a higher level of activity (above the current relevant range) could require a higher level of supervisory personnel, which would result in a higher level of fixed salary expense. Similarly, next year could have a higher fixed property tax expense due to a higher property tax assessment rate.

It is important for many forms of managerial analysis to fully understand the behavior patterns of total fixed and variable costs and per-unit fixed and variable costs. Exhibit 24–8 presents an example of total and per-unit cost behavior for a relevant range of 200 to 1,000 units.

An analysis of Exhibit 24–8 reveals that:

1. Total variable cost increases proportionately with increases in volume, while per-unit variable cost remains constant.
2. Total fixed cost remains constant with increases in volume, while per-unit fixed cost decreases proportionately.
3. Total variable plus fixed cost increases with increases in volume (but not proportionately), while per-unit variable plus fixed cost decreases (but not proportionately).

These patterns hold true for all feasible relevant ranges and are summarized in Exhibit 24–9.

Total fixed cost and per-unit variable cost are *stable* cost expressions, because they remain constant as volume is changed. Per-unit fixed cost and total variable cost are *unstable* cost expressions because they are valid at only one volume level. In the following section, we show how the stable forms of cost expression—*total* fixed cost and *per-unit* variable cost—are incorporated in a general formula for total cost that is valid over a wide range of operating volumes.

EXHIBIT 24–8

ANALYSIS OF TOTAL AND PER-UNIT COSTS

Activity Level	Variable Cost ($1.00 per unit)		Fixed Cost ($600 per month)		Total Cost ($600 + $1.00 per unit)	
Units	Total	Per-unit	Total	Per-unit	Total	Per-unit
200	$ 200	$1.00	$600	$3.00	$ 800	$4.00
600	600	1.00	600	1.00	1,200	2.00
1,000	1,000	1.00	600	0.60	1,600	1.60

EXHIBIT 24–9

PATTERNS OF TOTAL AND PER-UNIT COSTS AS VOLUME INCREASES

Cost Category	Total Cost	Per-unit Cost
Variable	Increases proportionately	Remains constant
Fixed	Remains constant	Decreases proportionately
Variable Plus Fixed	Increases, but not proportionately	Decreases, but not proportionately

Planning Total Costs

Budgeting for a business firm, which is treated in detail in Chapter 26, is usually a financial plan that reflects anticipated or planned amounts of such items as revenue, costs, cash balances, and net income. Underlying most aspects of budgeting is some assumed number of units or dollars of sales, as well as an analysis of the total cost incurred for that level of operation.

As stated previously, all costs are variable, semivariable, or fixed. For most cost analyses, semivariable costs are separated into their two components, fixed and variable, with the variable component added to the variable costs and the fixed component added to the fixed costs. The following formula and example use this approach.

For an example, we assume that total fixed cost is $10,000, semivariable cost has a fixed portion of $5,000 and a variable portion of $2 per unit, and that variable costs are $4 per unit. The formulation for planning or budgeting a total cost, using the stable forms of cost expression, is:

$$\text{Total Cost} = \text{Total Fixed Cost} + \left(\begin{matrix}\text{Variable}\\ \text{Cost}\\ \text{per Unit}\end{matrix} \times \begin{matrix}\text{Number of}\\ \text{Units}\end{matrix}\right)$$

In our example:

$$\text{Total cost} = \$15{,}000 + (\$6 \times \text{Units})$$

Therefore, at zero units total cost is $15,000, or the total of all fixed costs. At 5,000 units total cost is $45,000, or [$15,000 + ($6 × 5,000)]. At 10,000 units, total cost is $75,000, or [$15,000 + ($6 × 10,000)]. Notice that when the number of units doubles from 5,000 to 10,000, total cost responds, but less than proportionately.

By using this formula, a firm can forecast costs at different levels of activity. In Exhibit 24–10, each type of cost behavior pattern is considered in the formula. The dollar amounts have been chosen for ease of manipulation, and the 10,000-unit activity level is incorporated for illustrative purposes.

We see from Exhibit 24–10 that by combining the various cost factors into the aggregate formula, we determine expected costs not only at the 10,000-unit level but also at other levels simply by inserting the appropriate volume figure in the final formula. For example, total planned cost at 8,000 units is [$15,000 + ($6 × 8,000) = $63,000]; at 12,000 units, it is [$15,000 + ($6 × 12,000) = $87,000].

EXHIBIT 24 – 10

COST FACTORS IN A FORMULA
FOR TOTAL COST AT 10,000 UNITS

Type of Cost	Total Cost	=	Total Fixed Cost	+	(Variable Cost per Unit	×	Number of Units)
Direct Material (variable)	$20,000	=			($2.00	×	10,000 units)
Direct Labor (variable)	25,000	=			(2.50	×	10,000 units)
Factory Overhead:							
Factory Supplies (variable)	10,000	=			(1.00	×	10,000 units)
Property Taxes (fixed)	4,000	=	$ 4,000				
Maintenance (semivariable)	7,000	=	5,000	+	(0.20	×	10,000 units)
Selling and Administrative Expense (semivariable)	9,000	=	6,000	+	(0.30	×	10,000 units)
Total Cost	$75,000	=	$15,000	+	($6.00	×	10,000 units)

A word of caution is appropriate here. Because the cost formula relies so heavily on cost analysis, all the limitations of the latter (assumed linearity, relevant ranges, and so on) apply. Also, we repeat, analyzing many costs into fixed and variable components is often quite complex and inexact. All these limitations to some degree affect the potential contribution of managerial accounting. In many cases, the analytical approach presented here is the best available.

COST–VOLUME–PROFIT ANALYSIS

For purposes of illustration, we use the following data for Johnson Company throughout the next several sections.

Johnson Company
Condensed Income Statement

Sales (10,000 units @ $20)		$200,000
Costs:		
Variable Cost (10,000 units @ $12)	$120,000	
Fixed Cost	60,000	
Total Cost		180,000
Net Income		$ 20,000

This information assumes that any semivariable costs have been divided into their fixed and variable components and combined with the fixed and variable cost elements. We now examine some of the uses of this information.

Break-even Analysis

Management frequently wants to know the level of revenue or number of units of sales at which there is no net income or loss. The level at which total revenue equals total cost or expense is the **break-even point.** Typically it is expressed in dollars or in units of sales. Let us calculate Johnson Company's break-even point, using the above condensed income statement data.

THE BREAK-EVEN CHART For the break-even chart we use the same basic graph employed earlier to explain and portray cost behavior patterns. In Exhibit 24–11 the vertical axis measures both total revenue and total cost. As before, volume is measured along the horizontal axis. For the Johnson Company, the activity base is units of product. Total revenue and total cost are measured in thousands of dollars along the vertical axis.

With zero revenue for zero sales, the graph of total revenue always passes through the origin, which is one point on the line. In general, then, we draw the total revenue line by connecting the origin with any other point that represents total revenue for some volume amount. For Johnson Company, total revenue for 10,000 units is $200,000—point A in Exhibit 24–11. To construct the total revenue line, we simply draw a straight line from the origin to point A and extend it beyond point A.

We now construct the total cost line in the same manner. With fixed costs of $60,000, the total cost line must intersect the vertical axis at $60,000. For Johnson Company, we are given total cost of $180,000 for 10,000 units. From this we can plot point B and draw the total cost line for Johnson Company as shown in Exhibit 24–11.

Extending the dashed lines as indicated from the point of intersection of the two graphed lines to the two axes, we find Johnson Company's break-even point (where total revenue equals total cost) to be 7,500 units of production, or $150,000 of total sales revenue. Note that all points lying below the break-even point indicate a loss, and points above the break-even level represent profit. The profit and loss areas are shaded on our graph. The amount of profit or loss at any volume level is determined by measuring the vertical distance between the total

EXHIBIT 24–11

BREAK-EVEN CHART

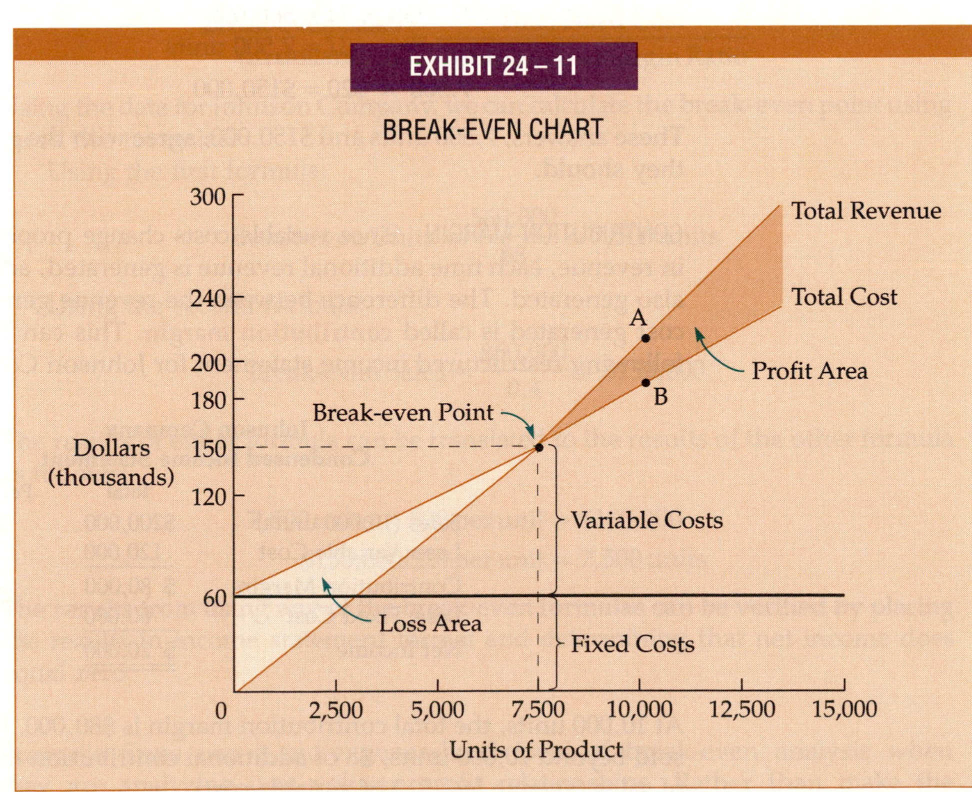

COST–VOLUME–PROFIT ANALYSIS FOR RESTAURANTS

Most retailing industries have developed relationships between product cost and retail price that need to be maintained in order to be profitable. Each segment of each industry has its own ideal relationship. For example, a men's clothing store would typically have a lower ratio of retail price to product cost than a retail furrier, while a downhill ski shop would typically have a higher ratio than a department store.

Many restaurants strive to have the price of their meals set at 2.5 times the cost of the food used in the meal. Portion control is a key element in applying this ratio. For each food item or ingredient to be included in one portion or meal, a standard quantity (weight or volume) is established. This standard recipe can be used to determine the food cost of a meal. For example, 8 ounces of ingredient A costing 35 cents per ounce plus 2 ounces of ingredient B costing 25 cents per ounce would yield a food cost of \$3.30 per portion and a target price of \$8.25.

Retail establishments also have variable staffing levels. The number of employees on duty will vary, depending on the time of day. For example, a restaurant might have 2 cooks and 5 waiters working from 11:00 am to 2:00 pm, 1 cook and 2 waiters working from 2:00 pm to 5:00 pm, and 2 cooks and 5 waiters working from 5:00 pm to 9:00 pm. The number and type of employees to have on duty has to be predetermined. Therefore, the cost of these employees is fixed. They are typically paid the same amount regardless of how many meals are served. Customer tips (which are not an expense of the restaurant) would vary, depending in part on the number of meals served.

These concepts have to be incorporated into cost–volume–profit analysis for a restaurant. If a restaurant serves only three types of meals with food costs per meal of \$5.00, \$4.00, and \$3.00, then the related prices should be \$12.50, \$10.00, and \$7.50 if the 2.5 ratio is used. If 20% of the meals sold were sold for \$12.50, 50% were sold for \$10.00, and 30% were sold for \$7.50, then the average revenue per meal sold would be \$9.75 and the average food cost would be \$3.90:

\$12.50 × 0.20 = \$2.50	\$5.00 × 0.20 = \$1.00
\$10.00 × 0.50 = 5.00	\$4.00 × 0.50 = \$2.00
\$ 7.50 × 0.30 = 2.25	\$3.00 × 0.30 = \$0.90
\$9.75	\$3.90

The weighted average unit contribution margin, therefore, is \$9.75 − \$3.90 = \$5.85.

If the total fixed costs, including personnel, are \$64,350 for a typical 30-day month when the restaurant is open every day for the scheduled hours, the break-even volume would be calculated as follows:

$$\frac{\$64{,}350}{\$5.85} = 11{,}000 \text{ meals per month}$$

a net income of \$42,000 and if the income tax rate is 30%, what would the impact be on desired units sold of installing robots?

$$\text{Desired Units} = \frac{\text{Fixed Cost} + \text{Desired Net Income Before Income Tax}}{\text{Unit Contribution Margin}}$$

Without robots:

$$\text{Desired Units} = \frac{\$60{,}000 + \dfrac{\$42{,}000}{1 - 0.3}}{\$20 - \$12} = 15{,}000 \text{ units}$$

With robots:

$$\text{Desired Units} = \frac{\$83{,}000 + \dfrac{\$42{,}000}{1 - 0.3}}{\$20 - \$9} = 13{,}000 \text{ units}$$

The installation of robots would decrease the desired volume from 15,000 units to 13,000 units. As a result, Johnson Company would be able to sell 2,000 fewer units at the same price and still attain the same desired net income.

Break-even Analysis and Multiple Products

As indicated earlier, we must assume in break-even analysis that only one product is involved or that the product mix (the ratio of units of each product sold to the total units sold) is constant. Break-even sales can be computed for a sales mix of two or more products by calculating the weighted average unit contribution margin.

Assume that a company sells products A and B, has a product sales mix of 75% A and 25% B, and has fixed costs of $88,000. Also assume that the following relationships between selling price and variable cost exist:

	A	B
Unit selling price	$14.00	$7.00
Unit variable cost	8.00	3.00
Unit contribution margin	$ 6.00	$4.00

The weighted average unit contribution margin can be calculated as follows:

$$\begin{aligned} \text{Product A: } \$6.00 \times 0.75 &= \$4.50 \\ \text{Product B: } \$4.00 \times 0.25 &= \underline{1.00} \\ & \$5.50 \end{aligned}$$

The break-even volume can then be calculated:

$$\text{Break-even Units} = \frac{\text{Fixed Cost}}{\text{Weighted Average Unit Contribution Margin}} = \frac{\$88{,}000}{\$5.50} = 16{,}000 \text{ units}$$

The 16,000 units are comprised of units of A and units of B. The exact mix and related contribution margin are calculated as follows:

Product	Product Mix	Units Sold	Unit Contribution Margin	Total Contribution Margin
A	.75	12,000	$6.00	$72,000
B	.25	4,000	4.00	16,000
Total		16,000		$88,000

These concepts could be applied to any product mix or number of products.

A Perspective on Cost Analysis

Managing costs is a prevailing concern of management. The concepts introduced in this chapter underlie most efforts to analyze and project cost in a variety of decision situations. In practice, because projections of future costs are subject to many complicating factors, for most companies they are *estimates of probable costs* rather than precise determinations. Properly used—with full recognition of their limitations—cost behavior analyses can be highly useful to management.

KEY POINTS FOR CHAPTER OBJECTIVES

1 Develop an understanding of how specific types of costs change in response to volume changes (pp. 927–31).

- Behavior of total cost in response to volume changes are divided into three basic categories within a relevant range:
  (a) Variable, which responds proportionately, with zero cost at zero volume.
  (b) Fixed, which is constant.
  (c) Semivariable, which responds, but less than proportionately, due to the fixed component.
- Total cost for most entities is best represented by the semivariable cost pattern.
- Semivariable costs may be divided into fixed and variable subelements using graphic plottings, the high–low method, or statistical methods.

2 Define the concept of relevant range (pp. 931–32).

- We can assume linearity of cost because it is approximately true within the range of volume relevant to the analysis.
- Within the relevant range, per-unit costs behave as follows when volume is increased:
  (a) Variable costs remain constant.
  (b) Fixed costs decrease proportionately.
  (c) Variable plus fixed cost decreases, but not proportionately.

3 Outline the approach to developing cost formulas (pp. 932–34).

- A general formula for planning total cost is:
  Total Cost = Total Fixed Cost + (Variable Cost per Unit × Number of Units)

4 Present a discussion of and a formula for calculating the break-even point (pp. 934–36).

- The break-even point (where Revenues = Costs) can be derived by graph, formula, or contribution margin analysis.
- Assumptions underlying break-even analysis include:
  (a) Total fixed cost and per-unit variable cost are constant over the entire relevant range.
  (b) Selling price per unit remains the same regardless of the volume of sales.
  (c) When more than one product is involved and sales volume varies, each product's percent of total sales (sales mix) does not change.

5 Define *contribution margin* and *contribution margin ratio* (pp. 936–37).

- Contribution Margin = Revenue − Variable Cost.
- $\text{Contribution Margin ratio} = \dfrac{\text{Contribution Margin}}{\text{Sales}}$

  or

  $\text{Contribution Margin Ratio} = \dfrac{\text{Unit Contribution Margin}}{\text{Unit Selling Price}}$

6 Present alternate break-even formulas and examples of their application (p. 937).

- Formulas used in break-even analysis include:
  (a) $\text{Break-even Units} = \dfrac{\text{Total Fixed Cost}}{\text{Unit Contribution Margin}}$
  (b) $\text{Break-even Sales} = \dfrac{\text{Total Fixed Cost}}{\text{Contribution Margin Ratio}}$

7 Discuss approaches to planning net income using cost–volume–profit analyses (pp. 937–41).

- Formulas used in planning net income include:
  (a) Desired Sales = Variable Cost + Fixed Cost + Desired Net Income Before Income Tax

(b) $\text{Desired Units} = \dfrac{\text{Fixed Cost} + \text{Desired Net Income Before Tax}}{\text{Unit Contribution Margin}}$

(c) $\text{Desired Sales} = \dfrac{\text{Fixed Cost} + \text{Desired Net Income Before Tax}}{\text{Contribution Margin Ratio}}$

- The relationship between net income before income tax and net income is demonstrated by the formula:

  $\text{Net Income Before Tax} = \dfrac{\text{Net Income}}{1 - \text{Tax Rate}}$

- Margin of Safety = Actual Sales − Break-even Sales
- Break-even and net income planning computations involving multiple products incorporate the concept of weighted average unit contribution margin.

KEY TERMS USED IN THIS CHAPTER

break-even point 934
contribution margin 936
contribution margin ratio 937
cost behavior analysis 927
fixed costs 929
high–low method 930
margin of safety 939
relevant range 932
semivariable costs 929
variable costs 928

SELF-TEST QUESTIONS

(Answers are at the end of this chapter.)

1. When moving from the low end of a relevant range to the high end, straight-line depreciation expense per unit:
   (a) Increases.
   (b) Decreases.
   (c) Remains the same.
   (d) Changes unpredictably.
2. In a typical cost formula:
   (a) Fixed costs are per unit and variable costs are per unit.
   (b) Fixed costs are per unit and variable costs are in total.
   (c) Fixed costs are in total and variable costs are in total.
   (d) Fixed costs are in total and variable costs are per unit.
3. At the break-even point:
   (a) Contribution margin = fixed costs.
   (b) Variable costs = fixed costs.
   (c) Sales = contribution margin.
   (d) Contribution margin = 0.
4. Contribution margin ratio is:
   (a) Unit sales price/unit contribution margin.
   (b) 1/margin of safety.
   (c) Total contribution margin/sales.
   (d) Variable cost/fixed cost.
5. Net income before tax is:
   (a) Net income/1 − tax rate.
   (b) Tax rate/net income.
   (c) Net income + contribution margin.
   (d) Net income/tax rate.

DEMONSTRATION PROBLEM FOR REVIEW

Maricopa Corporation has developed the budget for its next year of operations. The budget included:

Sales of 100,000 units at $5.	
Units sold will equal units produced.	
Variable costs for 100,000 units:	
Direct material	$125,000
Direct labor	100,000
Variable overhead	30,000
Selling and administrative expense	45,000
Total fixed costs	120,000
Income tax rate of 30%.	

REQUIRED

(a) What is Maricopa's break-even point, in units and in dollars, for next year?
(b) Demonstrate that the units amount reconciles with the dollar amount.
(c) What amount of sales revenue would Maricopa need to realize next year so they could generate a net income of $63,000?
(d) Demonstrate the correctness of the calculations in part (c) by constructing an income statement.

SOLUTION TO DEMONSTRATION PROBLEM

(a) Variable costs:

Direct material	$125,000
Direct labor	100,000
Variable overhead	30,000
Selling and administrative	45,000
Total at 100,000 units	$300,000

$300,000/100,000 units = $3 per unit

Unit Contribution Margin = $5 − $3 = $2

$$\text{Contribution Margin Ratio} = \frac{\$2}{\$5} = 0.4$$

$$\text{Break-even Units} = \frac{\text{Total Fixed Cost}}{\text{Unit Contribution Margin}} = \frac{\$120{,}000}{\$2} = 60{,}000 \text{ units}$$

$$\text{Break-even Sales} = \frac{\text{Total Fixed Cost}}{\text{Contribution Margin Ratio}} = \frac{\$120{,}000}{0.4} = \$300{,}000$$

(b) 60,000 units × $5 unit selling price = $300,000

(c) Desired Sales $= \dfrac{\text{Fixed Cost} + \dfrac{\text{Net Income}}{1 - \text{Tax Rate}}}{\text{Contribution Margin Ratio}}$

$= \dfrac{\$120{,}000 + \dfrac{\$63{,}000}{1 - 0.3}}{0.4}$

$= \$525{,}000$

(d)		
Sales		$525,000
Variable Cost (1 − 0.4)($525,000)		315,000
Contribution Margin		$210,000
Fixed Cost		120,000
Net Income Before Tax		$ 90,000
Income Tax at 30%		27,000
Net Income		$ 63,000

QUESTIONS

24–1 Define the terms *cost behavior* and *relevant range.*

24–2 Identify some common activity bases in terms of which the volume of a manufacturing operation might be stated. What general criterion might be used in choosing a base?

24–3 Name, define, and plot on a graph the three most widely recognized cost behavior patterns. Plot activity horizontally and cost vertically.

24–4 Explain (a) how a semivariable cost can be considered "partly fixed and partly variable," and (b) why a firm's total cost is best represented by the semivariable cost pattern.

24–5 Briefly describe two techniques for dividing a semivariable cost into its fixed and variable components.

24–6 "Actual costs often behave in a nonlinear fashion. Therefore, assumptions of linearity invalidate most cost behavior analyses." Do you agree or disagree with this statement? Briefly defend your position.

24–7 Describe how fixed and variable costs per unit respond to volume increases.

24–8 Present a formula based on units for planning total costs, and explain how semivariable costs are incorporated into the formula.

24–9 Define and briefly explain three approaches to break-even analysis.

24–10 Mary's Bakery Shop has fixed costs per month of $1,800, and variable costs are 55% of sales. What amount of monthly sales allows the shop to break even?

24–11 Quality Car Wash has fixed costs per month of $8,400, and variable costs are 20% of sales. The average amount collected per car serviced during the past year has been $5. How many cars must be serviced per month to break even?

24–12 You have graphed the cost–volume–profit relationships for a company on a break-even chart, after being informed of certain assumptions. Explain how the lines on the chart would change (a) if fixed costs increased over the entire range of activity, (b) if selling price per unit decreased, and (c) if variable costs per unit increased.

24–13 Define *contribution margin.* Is it best expressed as a total amount or as a per-unit amount? In what way is the term descriptive of the concept?

24–14 Explain the approach to break-even analysis that is used for a mix of two or more products.

24–15 Explain how break-even formulas can provide income-planning analyses.

24–16 In planning net income, how can net income be incorporated into the planning formula?

EXERCISES

Cost–volume graph

24–17 Set up a cost–volume graph similar to those presented in the chapter. Volume should range from zero to 24,000 units (in 4,000-unit increments) and cost should range from zero to $24,000 (in $4,000 increments). Plot each of the following groups of cost data using different marks for each group. After completing the graph, indicate the type of cost behavior exhibited by each group.

Volume (applicable to each group)	Group A Costs	Group B Costs	Group C Costs
2,000	$ 6,600	$ 2,400	$8,000
6,000	9,800	7,200	8,000
10,000	13,000	12,000	8,000
20,000	21,000	24,000	8,000

High–low method

24–18 Apply the high–low method of cost analysis to the three cost data groups in Exercise 24–17. What cost behavior patterns are apparent? Express each as a cost formula.

High–low method

24–19 The highest and lowest levels of activity for the Analog Company were 54,000 direct labor hours and 36,000 direct labor hours, respectively. If maintenance costs were $276,000 at the 54,000-hour level and $204,000 at the 36,000-hour level, what cost might we expect at an operating level of 40,000 direct labor hours?

High–low method

24–20 During the past year, Phoenix, Inc., operated within the relevant range of its fixed costs. Monthly production volume during the year ranged from 40,000 to 60,000 units of product and corresponding average manufacturing costs ranged from $3.30 to $3.60 per unit. Determine the total cost behavior pattern experienced by Phoenix, Inc.

High–low method

24–21 The following selected data relate to the major cost categories experienced by Nolden Company at varying levels of operating volumes. Assuming that all operating volumes are within the relevant range, calculate the appropriate costs in each column where blanks appear:

	Total Cost (at 3,000 units)	Total Cost (at 4,000 units)	Variable Cost per Unit	Fixed Cost	Total Cost (at 5,000 units)
Direct labor (variable)	$30,000	$40,000	_____	_____	_____
Factory supervision (semivariable)	25,000	32,500	_____	_____	_____
Factory depreciation (fixed)	15,000	15,000	_____	_____	_____

Cost formula

24–22 Midvale Company has analyzed its overhead costs and derived a general formula for their behavior: $30,000 + $7 per direct labor hour employed. The company expects to use 50,000 direct labor hours during the next accounting period. What overhead rate per direct labor hour should be applied to jobs worked during the period?

Cost formula

24–23 The following amounts of various cost categories are experienced by Thomas Factories in producing and selling its only product:

Direct material	$5 per unit of product
Direct labor	$10 per direct labor hour*
Factory overhead	$10,000 + $6 per direct labor hour
Selling expenses	$14,000 + $2 per unit of product
Administrative expenses	$7,000 + $0.50 per unit of product

*Each unit of product requires one-half direct labor hour.

Combine the various cost factors into a general total cost formula for Thomas Factories, and determine the total cost for producing and selling 12,000 units.

Break-even chart

24–24 Set up a break-even chart similar to Exhibit 24–11 with proportional scales from zero to $72,000 (in $12,000 increments) on the vertical axis and from zero to 12,000 units of production (in 2,000-unit increments) on the horizontal axis. Prepare the break-even chart for Delton Company, assuming total fixed costs of $18,000 and unit selling price and unit variable cost for the company's one product of $6 and $4, respectively.

Break-even calculations

24–25 Compute the break-even point in units for each of the following independent situations. Confirm each answer using contribution margin ratio analysis.

	Unit Selling Price	Unit Variable Cost	Total Fixed Cost
(a)	$20	$14	$ 90,000
(b)	24	18	144,000
(c)	10	6	54,000

Net income planning

24–26 In each of the three situations presented in Exercise 24–25, what unit sales volume is necessary to earn the following related amounts of net income before income taxes? (a) $18,000; (b) $27,000; and (c) equal to 20% of sales revenue.

Cost–volume–profit analysis

24–27 Wright Company sells a single product for $20 per unit. Variable costs are $12 per unit and fixed costs are $52,000 at an operating level of 10,000 units.

(a) What is Wright Company's break-even point in units?
(b) How many units must be sold to earn $20,000 before income taxes?
(c) How many units must be sold to earn $35,000 after income taxes, assuming a 30% tax rate?

Multiple product break-even

24–28 Bryant Company has $155,000 total fixed costs and sells products A and B with a product mix of 40% A and 60% B. Selling prices and variable costs for A and B result in contribution margins per unit of $8 and $5, respectively. Compute the break-even point.

Net income planning

24–29 Gates Corporation earned a net income of $240,000 last year. Fixed costs were $880,000. The selling price per unit of its product was $175, of which $50 was a contribution to fixed cost and net income. The income tax rate was 40%.
(a) How many units of product were sold last year?
(b) What was the break-even point in units last year?
(c) The company wishes to increase its net income by 20% this year. If selling prices and the income tax rate remain unchanged, how many units must be sold?

Cost patterns

24–30 The graphs below represent approximations of cost behavior patterns. The horizontal axis of each graph represents units while the vertical axis represents dollars of total cost.

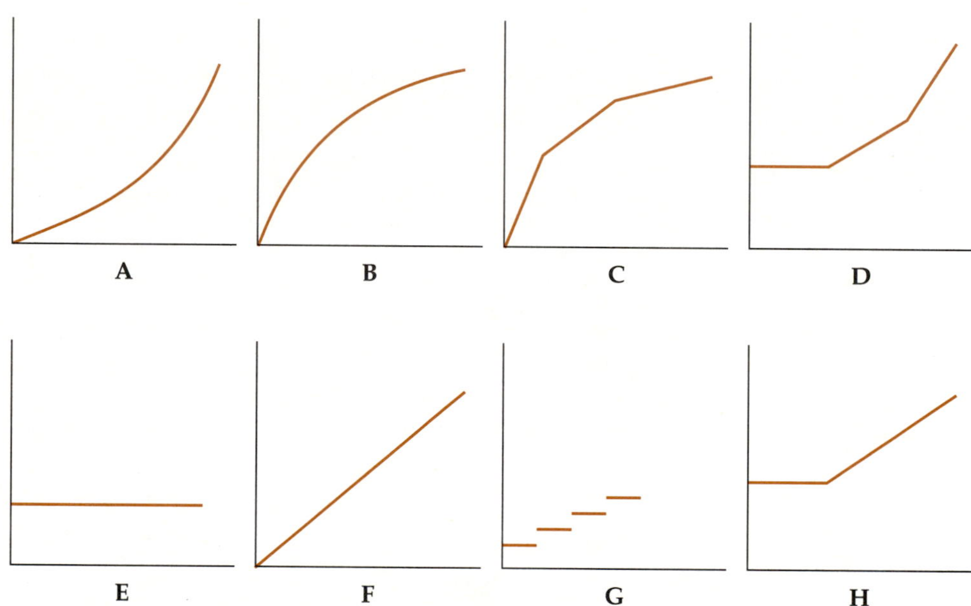

Select the graph that best matches each of the situations described below. Each graph may be selected more than once.
(a) Straight-line depreciation of a factory building.
(b) Utility bill for electricity that includes a fixed charge per month plus a constant usage rate per hour for hours in excess of 100.
(c) Cost of microchip incorporated into a product.
(d) Labor cost of machine operators who become more productive as they gain experience.
(e) Water bill that includes a flat fee for the first 10,000 gallons used plus an increasing usage charge for each additional 10,000 gallons used.
(f) Cost of factory supplies, where increasing quantities bring cost discounts as each price break level is attained.
(g) Salaries of quality inspectors, where one additional inspector is hired for each 20,000 units produced.
(h) Cost of an advertising campaign.

Cost patterns

24–31 The following graph depicts cost–volume relations for Glendale Company:

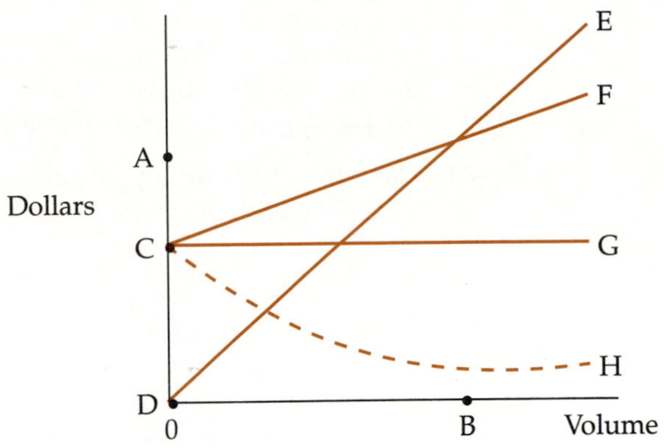

Choose a labeled point *or* line on the graph that *best* represents the behavior of each of the following items as operating volume is increased. Answers may be the same for more than one item. Answer each item independently.

(a) Total sales revenue
(b) Total cost for the firm
(c) Variable cost per unit
(d) Total variable cost
(e) Total fixed cost
(f) Fixed cost per unit
(g) Total semivariable cost
(h) Break-even point

PROBLEMS

Net income planning

24–32 Selected operating data for Batavia Company in four independent situations are shown below:

	A	B	C	D
Sales	$288,000	$______	$______	$240,000
Variable expense	$______	$ 72,000	$______	$ ______
Fixed expense	$______	$ 36,000	$ 43,200	$124,800
Net income before tax (loss)	$ 24,000	$ 24,000	$ 28,800	($ 28,800)
Units sold	20,000	______		
Unit contribution margin	$4.80	$6.00		
Contribution margin ratio			0.40	______

REQUIRED

Fill in the blanks for each independent situation. Show your calculations.

Graphing semivariable cost

24–33 During a recent six-month period, Carson Corporation has the following monthly volume of production and total monthly maintenance expense:

	Units Produced	Maintenance Expense
Mar.	21,000	$140,800
Apr.	15,000	112,000
May	30,000	184,000
June	27,500	172,000
July	35,000	208,000
Aug.	25,000	160,000

REQUIRED

Assume that all volumes are in the relevant range.

(a) Explain why the data indicate that the maintenance expense is neither a fixed nor a variable expense.
(b) Construct a graph similar to Exhibit 24–6 and plot the above cost observations.
(c) Fit a line (by sight) to the cost observation points and estimate the cost formula.
(d) Confirm your answer in requirement (c) with high–low analysis.

Cost formulas

24–34 Dayton Manufacturing produces a single product requiring the following direct material and direct labor:

Description	Cost per Unit of Input	Required Amount per Unit of Product
Material A	$16/lb	10 oz
Material B	10/lb	8 oz
Material C	40/gal	0.3 gal
Cutting labor	18/hr	30 min
Shaping labor	22/hr	15 min
Finishing labor	24/hr	45 min

Factory overhead consists of indirect material, $1.20 per unit of product; indirect labor, $2,000 per month plus $1.40 per unit of product; factory maintenance, $28,000 per year plus $1.10 per unit of product; factory depreciation, $30,000 per year; and annual factory property taxes, $16,000. Selling and administrative expenses include the salaries of a sales manager, $60,000 per year; an office manager, $36,000 per year; and two salespersons, each of whom is paid a base salary of $22,000 per year and a commission of $6 per unit sold. Advertising and promotion of the product are done through a year-round media package program costing $2,000 per week.

REQUIRED

(a) Analyze all cost and expense factors to determine a general formula (based on units of production) for total cost.
(b) Assuming a relevant range of 10,000 to 20,000 units, what is the estimated unit cost for producing and selling 10,000 units? 20,000 units? Explain the variation in unit cost at the two levels of production.
(c) If 15,000 units are produced and sold in a year, what selling price results in a net income before taxes of $120,000?

High–low and cost formula

24–35 Elgin Company has accumulated the following total factory overhead costs for two levels of activity (within the relevant range):

	Low	High
Activity (direct labor hours)	80,000	120,000
Total factory overhead	$234,000	$302,000

The total overhead costs include variable, fixed, and semivariable (mixed) costs. At 120,000 direct labor hours, the total cost breakdown is as follows:

Variable costs	$132,000
Fixed costs	80,000
Semivariable costs	90,000

REQUIRED

(a) Using the high–low method of cost analysis, determine the variable portion of the semivariable costs per direct labor hour. Determine the total fixed cost component of the semivariable cost.
(b) What should the total planned overhead cost be at 100,000 direct labor hours?

Cost formula

24–36 The following total cost data are for Ralston Manufacturing Company, which has a normal capacity per period of 25,000 units of product that sell for $20 each. For the foreseeable future, sales volume should equal normal capacity of production.

Direct material	$147,500
Direct labor	82,500
Variable overhead	42,500
Fixed overhead (Note 1)	70,000
Selling expense (Note 2)	40,000
Administrative expense (fixed)	28,000
	$410,500

1. Beyond normal capacity, fixed overhead costs increase $3,175 for each 1,000 units *or fraction thereof* until a maximum capacity of 30,000 units is reached.
2. Selling expenses are a 5% sales commission plus shipping costs of 60 cents per unit.

REQUIRED
(a) Using the information available, prepare a formula to estimate Ralston's total costs at various production volumes up to normal capacity.
(b) Prove your answer in requirement (a) against the above total cost figure at 25,000 units.
(c) Calculate the planned total cost at 20,000 units, and explain why total cost did not decrease in proportion to the reduced volume.
(d) If Ralston were operating at normal capacity and accepted an order for 500 more units, what would it have to charge for the order to earn a net income before tax of $4 per unit on the new sale?

Net income planning

24–37 Woodfield Corporation sells a single product for $30 per unit, of which $18 is contribution margin. Total fixed costs are $36,000 and net income before tax is $14,400.

REQUIRED
Determine the following (show key computations):
(a) The present sales volume in dollars.
(b) The break-even point in units.
(c) The sales volume in units necessary to attain a net income before tax of $19,800.
(d) The sales volume in units necessary to attain a net income before tax equal to 20% of sales revenue.
(e) The sales volume in units necessary to attain a net income of $21,600 if the tax rate is 40%.

Break-even and net income planning

24–38 The controller of Miller Company is preparing data for a conference concerning certain *independent* aspects of its operations.

REQUIRED
Prepare answers to the following questions for the controller:
(a) Total fixed costs are $720,000 and a unit of product is sold for $6 in excess of its unit variable cost. What is break-even unit sales volume?

(b) The company will sell 60,000 units of product—each having a unit variable cost of $11—at a price that will enable the product to absorb $300,000 of fixed cost. What minimum unit sales price must be charged to break even?
(c) Net income before taxes of $160,000 is desired after covering $600,000 of fixed cost. What minimum contribution margin ratio must be maintained if total sales revenue is to be $1,900,000?
(d) Net income before taxes is 10% of sales revenue, the contribution margin ratio is 30%, and the break-even dollar sales volume is $320,000. What is the amount of total revenue?
(e) Total fixed costs are $500,000, variable cost per unit is $15, and unit sales price is $40. What dollar sales volume will generate a net income of $42,000 when the income tax rate is 40%?

Break-even and net income planning

24–39 Jensen Company has recently leased facilities for the manufacture of a new product. Based on studies made by its accounting personnel, the following data are available:

Estimated annual sales: 40,000 units

Estimated Costs	Amount	Unit Cost
Direct material	$348,000	$ 8.70
Direct labor	292,000	7.30
Factory overhead	188,000	4.70
Administrative expenses	93,600	2.34
	$921,600	$23.04

Selling expenses are expected to be 10% of sales, and the selling price is $32 per unit. Ignore income taxes in this problem.

REQUIRED
(a) Compute a break-even point in dollars and in units. Assume that factory overhead and administrative expenses are fixed but that other costs are variable.
(b) What would net income before tax be if 30,000 units were sold?
(c) How many units must be sold to earn a net income before tax of 10% of sales?

Break-even and net income planning

24–40 Kenton Company manufactures and sells the three products below:

	Economy	Standard	Deluxe
Unit sales	10,000	6,000	4,000
Unit sales price	$24	$28	$34
Unit variable cost	$15	$16	$18

REQUIRED
Assume that total fixed costs are $169,500.
(a) Compute the net income before income tax based on the sales volumes shown above.
(b) Compute the break-even point in total dollars of revenue and in units for each product.
(c) Prove your break-even calculations by computing the total contribution margin related to your answer in requirement (b).

ALTERNATE PROBLEMS

Net income planning

24–32A Selected operating data for Bingham Company in four independent situations are shown below:

	A	B	C	D
Sales	$640,000	$_____	$_____	$560,000
Variable expense	$_____	$ 96,000	$_____	_____
Fixed expense	$_____	$112,000	$240,000	$240,000
Net income before tax (loss)	$ 80,000	$ 32,000	$ 96,000	($ 16,000)
Units sold	7,000	_____		
Unit contribution margin	$40.00	$18.00		
Contribution margin ratio			0.70	_____

REQUIRED
Fill in the blanks for each independent situation. Show your calculations.

Graphing semivariable cost

24–33A During the past operating year, Chandler Corporation had the following monthly volume of production and total monthly maintenance expense:

	Units Produced	Maintenance Expense		Units Produced	Maintenance Expense
Jan.	120,000	$22,400	July	124,000	$22,800
Feb.	144,000	25,400	Aug.	154,000	26,600
Mar.	156,000	26,800	Sept.	128,000	23,400
Apr.	130,000	23,200	Oct.	160,000	27,200
May	140,000	25,000	Nov.	152,000	26,400
June	150,000	26,400	Dec.	156,000	26,800

REQUIRED
Assume all volumes are in the relevant range.

(a) Explain why the data indicate that the maintenance expense is neither a fixed nor a variable expense.
(b) Construct a graph similar to Exhibit 24–6 and plot the above cost observations.
(c) Fit a line (by sight) to the cost observation points, and estimate the cost formula.
(d) Confirm your answer in requirement (c) with high–low analysis.

Cost formulas

24–34A Delta Manufacturing produces a single product requiring the following direct material and direct labor:

Description	Cost per Unit of Input	Required Amount per Unit of Product
Material A	$18/lb	24 oz
Material B	12/lb	12 oz
Material C	24/gal	0.5 gal
Cutting labor	20/hr	45 min
Shaping labor	24/hr	15 min
Finishing labor	22/hr	30 min

Factory overhead consists of indirect materials, $1.60 per unit of product; indirect labor, $20,000 per year plus $2.40 per unit of product; factory maintenance, $2,000 per month plus $1.20 per unit of product; factory depreciation, $44,000 per year; and annual factory property taxes, $40,000. Selling and administrative expenses include the salaries of a sales manager, $60,000 per year, an office manager, $36,000 per year, and two salespersons, each of whom is paid a base salary of $24,000 per year and a commission of $8 per unit sold. Advertising and promotion of the product are done through a year-round media package program costing $1,200 per week.

REQUIRED

(a) Analyze all cost and expense factors to determine a general formula (based on units of production) for total cost.
(b) Assuming a relevant range of 20,000 to 40,000 units, which is the estimated unit cost for producing and selling 20,000 units? 40,000 units? Explain the variation in unit cost at the two levels of production.
(c) If 35,000 units are produced and sold in a year, what selling price results in a net income before taxes of $113,600?

High–low and cost formula

24–35A Eastside Company has accumulated the following total factory overhead costs for two levels of activity (within the relevant range):

	Low	High
Activity (direct labor hours)	30,000	50,000
Total factory overhead	$135,000	$181,000

The total overhead costs include variable, fixed, and semivariable (mixed) costs. At 50,000 direct labor hours, the total cost breakdown is as follows:

Variable costs	$100,000
Fixed costs	45,000
Semivariable costs	36,000

REQUIRED

(a) Using the high–low method of cost analysis, determine the variable portion of the semivariable costs per direct labor hour. Determine the total fixed cost component of the semivariable cost.
(b) What should the total planned overhead cost be at 40,000 direct labor hours?

Cost formula

24–36A The following total cost data are for Richmond Manufacturing Company, which has a normal capacity per period of 40,000 units of product that sell for $30 each. For the foreseeable future, sales volume should equal normal capacity of production.

Direct material	$320,000
Direct labor	200,000
Variable overhead	100,000
Fixed overhead (Note 1)	108,000
Selling expense (Note 2)	140,000
Administrative expense (fixed)	44,000
	$912,000

1. Beyond normal capacity, fixed overhead costs increase $3,120 for each 2,000 units *or fraction thereof* until a maximum capacity of 50,000 units is reached.
2. Selling expenses are a 10% sales commission plus shipping costs of 50 cents per unit.

REQUIRED

(a) Using the information available, prepare a formula to estimate Richmond's total costs at various production volumes up to normal capacity.

(b) Prove your answer in requirement (a) against the above total cost figure at 40,000 units.
(c) Calculate the planned total cost at 30,000 units, and explain why total cost did not decrease in proportion to the reduced volume.
(d) If Richmond were operating at normal capacity and accepted an order for 600 more units, what would it have to charge for the order to earn a net income before tax of $4 per unit on the new sale?

Net income planning

24–37A Worthington Corporation sells a single product for $50 per unit, of which $20 is contribution margin. Total fixed costs are $60,000 and net income before tax is $24,000.

REQUIRED
Determine the following (show key computations):
(a) The present sales volume in dollars.
(b) The break-even point in units.
(c) The sales volume in units necessary to attain a net income before tax of $30,000.
(d) The sales volume in units necessary to attain a net income before tax equal to 10% of sales revenue.
(e) The sales volume in units necessary to attain a net income of $27,000 if the tax rate is 40%.

Break-even and net income planning

24–38A The controller of Mauston Company is preparing data for a conference concerning certain *independent* aspects of its operations.

REQUIRED
Prepare answers to the following questions for the controller:
(a) Total fixed costs are $360,000, and a unit of product is sold for $5.00 in excess of its unit variable cost. What is break-even unit sales volume?
(b) The company will sell 30,000 units of product—each having a unit variable cost of $7—at a price that will enable the product to absorb $180,000 of fixed cost. What minimum unit sales price must be charged to break even?
(c) Net income before taxes of $75,000 is desired after covering $205,000 of fixed cost. What minimum contribution margin ratio must be maintained if total sales revenue is to be $800,000?
(d) Net income before taxes is 20% of sales revenue, the contribution margin ratio is 60%, and the break-even dollar sales volume is $100,000. What is the amount of total revenue?
(e) Total fixed costs are $175,000, variable cost per unit is $13, and unit sales price is $28. What dollar sales volume will generate a net income of $30,000 when the income tax rate is 40%?

Break-even and net income planning

24–39A Jerold Company has recently leased facilities for the manufacture of a new product. Based on studies made by its accounting personnel, the following data are available:

Estimated annual sales: 60,000 units

Estimated Costs	Amount	Unit Cost
Direct material	$333,000	$ 5.55
Direct labor	234,000	3.90
Factory overhead	270,000	4.50
Administrative expenses	145,800	2.43
	$982,800	$16.38

Selling expenses are expected to be 10% of sales, and the selling price is $21 per unit. Ignore income taxes in this problem.

REQUIRED

(a) Compute a break-even point in dollars and in units. Assume that factory overhead and administrative expenses are fixed but that other costs are variable.
(b) What would net income before tax be if 50,000 units were sold?
(c) How many units must be sold to earn a net income before tax of 10% of sales?

Break-even and net income planning

24–40A Kirscher Company manufactures and sells the three products below:

	Red	Blue	Green
Unit sales	20,000	30,000	50,000
Unit sales price	$15	$31	$9
Unit variable cost	$ 9	$19	$7

REQUIRED

Assume that total fixed costs are $162,400. Ignore income taxes in this problem.

(a) Compute the net income based on the sales volumes shown above.
(b) Compute the break-even point in total dollars of revenue and in specific unit sales volume for each product.
(c) Prove your break-even calculations by computing the total contribution margin related to your answer in requirement (b).

BUSINESS DECISION PROBLEM

The following total cost data are for Midwest Manufacturing Company, which has a normal capacity per period of 400,000 units of product that sell for $9 each. For the foreseeable future, regular sales volume should continue at normal capacity of production.

Direct material	$ 860,000
Direct labor	560,000
Variable overhead	280,000
Fixed overhead (Note 1)	440,000
Selling expense (Note 2)	360,000
Administrative expense (fixed)	100,000
	$2,600,000

1. Beyond normal capacity, fixed overhead costs increase $15,000 for each 20,000 units *or fraction thereof* until a maximum capacity of 640,000 units is reached.
2. Selling expenses are a 10% sales commission plus shipping costs of 30 cents per unit. Midwest pays only one-half of the regular sales commission rate on any sale of 20,000 or more units.

Midwest's sales manager has received a special order for 48,000 units from a large discount chain at a special price of $8 each, F.O.B. factory. The controller's office has furnished the following additional cost data related to the special order:

1. Changes in the product's construction will reduce direct material $0.90 per unit.
2. Special processing will add 25% to the per-unit direct labor costs.

3. Variable overhead will continue at the same proportion of direct labor costs.
4. Other costs should not be affected.

REQUIRED

(a) Present an analysis supporting a decision to accept or reject the special order. Assume Midwest's regular sales are not affected by this special order.
(b) What is the lowest unit sales price Midwest could receive and still make a before-tax profit of $19,800 on the special order?

ANSWERS TO SELF-TEST QUESTIONS

1. (b) **2.** (d) **3.** (a) **4.** (c) **5.** (a)

25

SPECIAL ANALYSES FOR MANAGEMENT

CHAPTER OBJECTIVES

1. Describe management's use of accounting information in the decision-making process (pp. 959–61).
2. Present an overview of reporting operations for segments of a business (pp. 961–62).
3. Introduce the concept of multiple-level performance reporting (pp. 962–63).
4. Outline the procedures for reporting revenue and expense by department and for allocating indirect expenses (pp. 963–68).
5. Discuss variable costing and the differences between variable costing and absorption costing (pp. 968–72).
6. Describe the use of differential analysis (pp. 972–74).
7. Provide examples of the use of differential analysis in managerial decision-making (pp. 974–79).

The traditional measurement is not the right measurement; if it were, there would be no need for decisions.

PETER DRUCKER

A well-developed accounting system is a continuing source of operational information for management. The quality of information available to management will influence the success of the operating decisions based on that information. In this chapter, we consider the management decision-making process and some cost concepts that are used in managerial analyses.

MANAGEMENT AND THE DECISION-MAKING PROCESS

There are many definitions of *management*. In the broad sense, anyone who directs the activities of others is a manager. For a typical manufacturing firm, this includes shop supervisors, department heads, plant supervisors, division managers, and the company president. A large, complex firm has many management levels.

As depicted in Exhibit 25–1, top management is responsible for establishing long-range goals and policies, including major financial arrangements, expansion into foreign markets, and mergers with other firms. Middle-level management may deal with the strategies and tactics related to the automation of a department, the establishment of new product lines, and the direction of the merchandising plan. Such matters as daily production quotas, compliance with planned costs, and other detailed operating concerns are the responsibility of lower-level management. To varying degrees, therefore, all levels of management are involved in decision making.

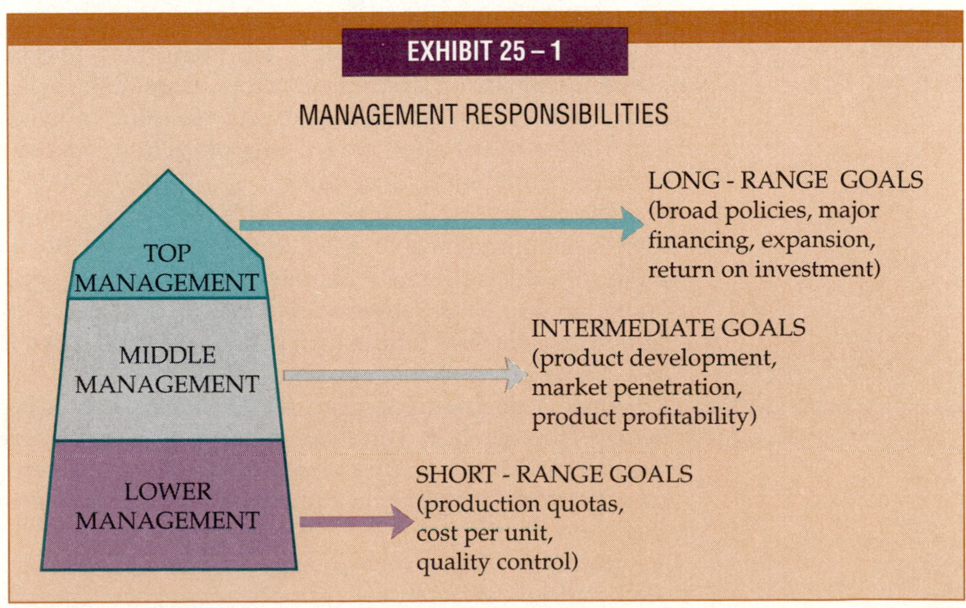

Decision making requires that a choice be made among alternatives. The business decision process is analogous to the play of a well-organized football team. Virtually all the elements of decision making are present in football—the awareness of the objectives and goals that lead to winning; the balancing of such short-run goals as first downs with the long-run goals of winning games and conference championships; the presence of organization, strategy, and tactics in a "hostile" environment where inaction and poor performance result in losses; the development of plays with the hope of achieving particular results; the moment of commitment in the huddle, immediately followed by the period of execution; and finally, the informal evaluation of performance on the field followed by a formal evaluation when game films are analyzed.

Phases of Decision Making

Decision making may be divided roughly into a planning phase, an execution phase, and an evaluation phase incorporating some form of remedial feedback. The following diagram illustrates the sequential nature of the elements of most decision processes:

The **planning phase** begins with *goal identification,* the specification of objectives to be sought or accomplished. One of the most common business goals is the long-run optimization of net income. Other goals include target growth rates in sales revenue or total assets and target shares in various markets. Still other goals—such as leadership in product research, innovation, and quality—are difficult to measure. Probably the most widely recognized goal is a specified return on assets.

The next steps in planning are identifying feasible alternative courses of action for achieving desired goals and estimating their qualitative and quantitative effects on the specified goals. All planning involves the future. As a result, data related to the alternative courses of action must be estimated and projected in an environment of uncertainty.

The **execution phase** begins with the actual moment of decision—management's commitment to a specific plan of action. Because of the complexity of modern industry, some elaborate plans may need lead times of several years. Poor planning, or the absence of planning, may lead to operating crises that carry significant penalties for the firm in terms of extra costs, lost opportunities, and—in extreme cases—bankruptcy.

Once a decision has been made, the plan is implemented, which usually involves the acquisition and commitment of materials, labor, and long-lived assets such as machinery and buildings. Management is kept informed through periodic accounting reports on the acquisition and use of these facilities during the execution phase.

In the **evaluation phase,** steps are taken to control the outcome of a specific plan of action. Virtually every important aspect of business—costs, product quality, inventory levels, and sales revenue—must be reasonably well controlled if a firm is to operate successfully. Measuring performance is an essential element of control. Performance measurement must compare current operations with desired operations to allow management to take remedial action when significant unfavorable variations exist. **Managerial accounting** data and reports play a key role in informing management about performance in various areas during the evaluation phase of decision making.

Decision processes do not, however, fall into three neatly divided phases. Changes in competition, technology, and customer demand must be considered. Furthermore, most management teams are engaged in all three decision-making phases at any given time. They may be planning decisions in one area, executing them in a second, and evaluating them in a third.

BUSINESS SEGMENTS

Many business entities are very complex, with diverse divisions and departments in multiple locations. Management of this type of entity finds it useful to divide the entity into *segments* to enhance managerial planning and control. Segments usually are based on organizational units (divisions or departments) or areas of economic activity (geographic regions or product lines). Many large companies have found that segmentation by organizational unit is the approach that proves most useful. It is important that the managerial accounting systems and procedures that develop information for planning and control decisions be structured to reflect the segmentation.

In Chapter 13 we discussed certain segment disclosures that public companies must include in financial reports to stockholders and other outside parties. Now we focus on the internal reporting of segment data, including departmental operations.

INTERNAL REPORTING OF SEGMENT OPERATIONS

Internal reporting of segment operations deals primarily with the measurement of operating performance. As a result, segmented reports usually take the format of an income statement or a portion of an income statement. These statements may provide information to answer the following types of questions:

1. What amount does each segment contribute to sales and operating income of the entity as a whole?
2. How do revenues and expenses for each segment compare to planned or budgeted amounts?
3. What is the rate of profitability of each segment? Should any segment be expanded, reduced, or eliminated?
4. Which areas need corrective action and what should be done?
5. Where should promotional effort be directed?

Segments such as divisions or departments are usually classified as either cost centers or profit centers. The manager of a **cost center** is responsible only for the costs and expenses of that segment of the business. There is no responsibility for revenue generation. An example of a cost center would be the machining department of a manufacturer of consumer products. The output of this department is only a part or an intermediate product that is not sold to consumers outside the company. As a result, no revenue is generated directly by this department.

The manager of a **profit center** is responsible for revenue generation as well as for cost and expense control. An example of a profit center would be a division that completely produces a product and sells it to consumers outside the company.

Managerial reports that measure the operating performance of a business entity and its segments reflect whether the segments are profit centers or cost centers. Revenue, expenses, and profitability are reported for segments that are profit centers; only expenses are reported for cost centers. The examples in this chapter are profit centers.

A common principle of segment reporting is that costs are classified as either controllable or noncontrollable. Under this principle, segment managers should be held responsible only for costs and expenses that they control. Frequently costs are considered controllable at one level of management but not at other levels. For example, the vice president of marketing may be responsible for decisions related to advertising. Even though the cost of advertising is incurred at the division level, the manager of the division should not be held responsible for that expense if a higher-level manager makes all the decisions relative to that cost or expense.

PERFORMANCE REPORTING

Performance reports are usually constructed periodically for each profit center and cost center. They contain different levels of detail for different levels of management. In general, top managers need highly summarized information while lower-level managers need specialized reports with greater detail.

Exhibit 25–2 presents three performance reports for three successively higher levels of management. The arrows show how the totals from the lower-level reports flow to and are included in the higher-level reports. While not all performance reports have the exact format of Exhibit 25–2, most will include a comparison of budgeted performance to actual performance.

DEPARTMENTAL OPERATIONS

Departmentalization is a common and logical type of segmentation for many firms. In manufacturing and merchandising firms, departments are generally classified by product sold. The very term "department store" signifies a type of merchandising by product. Food stores are also commonly departmentalized by product groups such as meat, produce, groceries, delicatessen, and so forth. Sometimes departments are also classified by type of customer. For example, firms selling such products as floor coverings, lighting fixtures, and heating and air conditioning units may separate commercial sales operations from residential sales operations.

The methods of accounting and reporting for departmental operating activity depend on the performance measures used and the degree of analysis desired by management. Some firms may desire only to identify gross profit by department. In others, management may wish to determine a net income figure for each department. Still others may adopt an intermediate performance measure, such as gross profit less only those expenses directly incurred by the department.

EXHIBIT 25 – 2

Performance Report—Supervisor of Drilling Department
For the Month of August, 19XX

	Budgeted Cost	Actual Cost	Over (Under)
Direct Material	$16,000	$15,800	$(200)
Direct Labor	18,000	16,700	(1,300)
Factory Overhead:			
(listed in detail)	6,200	6,500	300
	$40,200	$39,000	$(1,200)

Performance Report—Manager of Machining Operations
For the Month of August, 19XX

	Budgeted Cost	Actual Cost	Over (Under)
Lathe Department	$ 56,200	$ 51,000	$(5,200)
Drilling Department	40,200	39,000	(1,200)
Finishing Department	25,900	30,000	4,100
	$122,300	$120,000	$(2,300)

Performance Report—Vice-president of Production
For the Month of August, 19XX

	Budgeted Cost	Actual Cost	Over (Under)
Administration	$ 14,700	$ 19,100	$ 4,400
Machining Operations	122,300	120,000	(2,300)
Fabricating Operations	118,600	122,300	3,700
Assembly Operations	118,400	118,600	200
	$374,000	$380,000	$ 6,000

Departmental Gross Profit

The main reason for analyzing gross profit by department is that it permits management to review pricing policies and supplier costs. Comparisons can be made among departments to determine areas with high gross profit and in which areas major promotional efforts should be made. Comparisons can also be made with gross profit achieved in other periods, or with average percentage statistics for other firms selling the same lines. (These statistics may be obtained from trade association publications and credit agencies.) Often, very low gross profit signals a need to investigate purchasing policies or to revise prices.

EXHIBIT 25–3

Decorator Lighting Company
Departmental Income Statement
For the Year Ended December 31, 19XX

	Residential Department	Commercial Department	Total
Sales	$330,000	$220,000	$550,000
Less: Sales Returns and Allowances	(4,000)	(5,500)	(9,500)
Sales Discounts	(6,000)	(4,500)	(10,500)
Net Sales	$320,000	$210,000	$530,000
Cost of Goods Sold:			
Inventory, Jan. 1	$ 88,000	$ 42,000	$130,000
Purchases	194,000	144,000	338,000
Less: Purchases Returns	(4,500)	(2,000)	(6,500)
Purchases Discounts	(3,500)	(3,000)	(6,500)
Transportation In	6,000	4,000	10,000
Cost of Goods Available for Sale	$280,000	$185,000	$465,000
Less: Inventory, Dec. 31	72,000	38,000	110,000
Cost of Goods Sold	$208,000	$147,000	$355,000
Gross Profit	$112,000	$ 63,000	$175,000
Operating Expenses:			
Selling Expenses			$ 70,000
Administrative Expenses			60,000
Total Operating Expenses			$130,000
Income before Tax			$ 45,000
Income Tax Expense			15,100
Net Income			$ 29,900

To obtain gross profit figures by department, a firm customarily keeps separate departmental accounts for sales, purchases, inventory, discounts, returns, and allowances related to sales and purchases transactions. Transportation costs on purchases must also be segregated. Because firms frequently receive incoming shipments for a number of departments, it is often easier to analyze freight costs by department at the end of the accounting period than by individual freight bills being received and recorded throughout the accounting period.

Exhibit 25–3 is a departmental income statement for Decorator Lighting Company, which accumulates gross profit data by department. This firm, segmented into two departments—residential and commercial—sells lighting fixtures in a large retail outlet for retail residential customers and for individual builders who purchase fixtures for single-home construction. In addition, the company sells in a market that supplies lighting fixtures for large-scale contractors engaged in the construction of office buildings, motels, and other commercial installations.

Departmental Net Income

Ordinarily, it is not difficult to maintain an accounting system in which departmental reporting is carried only to the point of measuring gross profit. A firm that desires a more refined measure of operating performance, however, is faced with the problem of assigning or allocating operating expenses to the departments. If a measure of departmental net income is desired, it is necessary to trace *all* expenses to departments.

Some expenses may be readily identified with the operation of particular departments, while others cannot be. To identify expenses with departments, it is helpful to classify them into the following two general categories:

Direct expenses or costs: Those operating expenses or costs traceable to and incurred for the benefit of a single department and thus ordinarily controllable by the department.
Indirect expenses or costs: Those operating expenses or costs incurred for the benefit of multiple departments and thus neither traceable to nor controllable by a specific department.

For example, payroll expense related to personnel who work exclusively in one department is a direct expense of that department. Payroll expense related to administrative personnel whose work benefits all departments is an indirect expense of the operating departments. A firm usually has many indirect expenses, incurred for the benefit of more than one department. Some examples are heat, light, maintenance, depreciation, and other occupancy expenses, office salaries, executive salaries, and a variety of other administrative expenses. These expenses must be fairly allocated to the operating departments if the measure of departmental net income is to be meaningful. Because it is difficult and cumbersome to allocate indirect expenses at the time they are incurred, they are usually analyzed and allocated to departments at the end of the accounting period.[1]

Assume that the $130,000 operating expenses for Decorator Lighting Company in Exhibit 25–3 consisted of the following:

Sales Salaries Expense	$ 45,000
Advertising Expense	15,000
Delivery Expense	10,000
Insurance Expense (on merchandise)	6,000
Occupancy Expense	16,000
Uncollectible Accounts Expense	3,000
Office Salaries Expense	20,000
Other Administrative Expense	15,000
	$130,000

In preparing a departmental income statement, Decorator Lighting might analyze and allocate these expenses and the income tax expense of $15,100 as follows:

Sales Salaries Expense. The sales force for the residential department is separate from that of the commercial department. Therefore, the sales salaries for each department can be directly determined from payroll records, which show $25,000 for the residential department and $20,000 for the commercial department.

Advertising Expense. Of the company's $15,000 advertising expense, $7,000 was spent on newspaper and television advertising of residential lighting products,

[1]This approach is consistent with allocation approaches presented in Chapter 10 (package purchase) and in Chapter 23 (service department costs and joint product cost).

$3,000 on producing illustrated brochures with price lists for commercial customers, and $5,000 on general newspaper advertising directed at both markets. The latter amount was allocated on the basis of relative sales. ($330,000/$550,000 = 60% residential; $220,000/$550,000 = 40% commercial.)

	Residential	Commercial	Total
Direct advertising	$ 7,000	$3,000	$10,000
Indirect advertising	3,000	2,000	5,000
	$10,000	$5,000	$15,000

Delivery Expense. Products are delivered to all commercial customers via Ace Trucking Service at a cost of $2,000. All residential deliveries are made with the company's own truck or via United Delivery Service and total $8,000. Thus departmental delivery costs can be determined directly.

Insurance Expense (on merchandise). The cost of insurance is based on the average inventories of the two departments:

Residential ($88,000 + $72,000)/2 =	$ 80,000	80/120 × $6,000 =	$4,000
Commercial ($42,000 + $38,000)/2 =	$ 40,000	40/120 × $6,000 =	2,000
	$120,000		$6,000

Occupancy Expense. Rent, maintenance, and utility expenses are included in this item, which is allocated on the basis of square feet of floor space used by each department. Of the total floor space, $\frac{5}{8}$ is occupied by the residential department and $\frac{3}{8}$ by the commercial department. Of the $16,000 total cost, $10,000 is allocated to the residential department and $6,000 to the commercial department.

Uncollectible Accounts Expense. The firm maintains a separate customers' ledger for each department and determines its expense from uncollectible accounts by aging the accounts. Estimated uncollectible accounts totaled $1,600 for residential customers and $1,400 for commercial customers.

Office Salaries and Other Administrative Expense. Often, salaries of office personnel and other administrative expenses are allocated to departments on the basis of the relative sales of each department, since a good share of this cost is related to billings, collections, and customer inquiries. The alternative is to attempt an analysis of time spent by office employees on the affairs of each department and to estimate administrative supplies used, correspondence, and other office expenses by department. Such analysis is liable to be costly and time-consuming, and it may not provide much additional accuracy. Decorator Lighting uses relative sales as a basis, allocating 60% of the expenses to the residential department and 40% to the commercial department:

	Residential 60%	Commercial 40%	Total
Office Salaries Expense	$12,000	$ 8,000	$20,000
Other Administrative Expense	9,000	6,000	15,000
	$21,000	$14,000	$35,000

Income Tax Expense. Because Decorator Lighting Company is a corporation, it must pay federal income taxes at the appropriate rates on various portions of its taxable income. Here we assume that the total tax on $45,000 income is $15,100. The only realistic way to allocate the tax expense is on the basis of income before taxes. These amounts must be calculated by department (see Exhibit 25–4) before income tax expense can be allocated to the departments. Thus $32,400/$45,000 × $15,100 = $10,872 tax expense for the residential department, and $12,600/$45,000 × $15,100 = $4,228 tax expense for the commercial department. Some accountants believe that because departments are not taxable entities, allocation of tax expense among them does not result in meaningful performance measures; they would extend the departmental figures only to income before taxes.

A summary of the operating expenses and income tax expense, giving the direct expenses and allocated indirect expenses of each department, follows.

	Residential Department			Commercial Department		
	Direct	Indirect	Total	Direct	Indirect	Total
Sales Salaries Expense	$25,000		$25,000	$20,000		$20,000
Advertising Expense	7,000	$ 3,000	10,000	3,000	$ 2,000	5,000
Delivery Expense	8,000		8,000	2,000		2,000
Insurance Expense (on merchandise)	4,000		4,000	2,000		2,000
Occupancy Expense		10,000	10,000		6,000	6,000
Uncollectible Accounts Expense	1,600		1,600	1,400		1,400
Office Salaries Expense		12,000	12,000		8,000	8,000
Other Administrative Expense		9,000	9,000		6,000	6,000
	$45,600	$34,000	$79,600	$28,400	$22,000	$50,400
Income Tax Expense		$10,872			$ 4,228	

This departmental expense distribution was used to prepare the income statement for Decorator Lighting Company shown in Exhibit 25–4, which extends the departmental operating results through net income.

Departmental Contribution to Indirect Expenses

Operating statements that extend departmental results to net income measures are often criticized on the grounds that the indirect or common expenses are not controllable at the departmental level and therefore should not be assigned to departments when measuring performance. A further criticism is that the bases for assignment of indirect expenses are frequently arbitrary.

Some accountants favor an intermediate type of performance measure as a means of appraising departmental operating results. The **departmental contribution to indirect expenses** is obtained by deducting the direct departmental expenses from departmental gross profit. The resulting amount is a measure of the department's contribution to the firm's pool of common or indirect expenses incurred for the benefit of all operating units. Using this measure eliminates the need for allocating the indirect expenses. Although this approach emphasizes direct expenses, it should not be assumed that all aspects of direct expenses are controllable at the departmental level. Higher management may direct that a certain amount of expense be incurred by a department. The expense is properly

EXHIBIT 25–4

Decorator Lighting Company
Departmental Income Statement
For the Year Ended December 31, 19XX

	Residential Department	Commercial Department	Total
Net Sales	$320,000	$210,000	$530,000
Cost of Goods Sold	208,000	147,000	355,000
Gross Profit	$112,000	$ 63,000	$175,000
Operating Expenses:			
Sales Salaries Expense	$ 25,000	$ 20,000	$ 45,000
Advertising Expense	10,000	5,000	15,000
Delivery Expense	8,000	2,000	10,000
Insurance Expense (on merchandise)	4,000	2,000	6,000
Occupancy Expense	10,000	6,000	16,000
Uncollectible Accounts Expense	1,600	1,400	3,000
Office Salaries Expense	12,000	8,000	20,000
Other Administrative Expense	9,000	6,000	15,000
Total Operating Expenses	$ 79,600	$ 50,400	$130,000
Income before Tax	$ 32,400	$ 12,600	$ 45,000
Income Tax Expense	10,872	4,228	15,100
Net Income	$ 21,528	$ 8,372	$ 29,900

described as direct and no allocation is required, but to say it is fully controllable at the departmental level would be incorrect. A departmental income statement showing departmental contributions appears in Exhibit 25–5.

VARIABLE COSTING

use this as a reference

In Chapter 21, we defined product costs as all factory costs—direct material, direct labor, and factory overhead. These costs were capitalized as inventory during the production period and recognized as expense (cost of goods sold) only when the related merchandise was sold. This method of attaching all factory costs to the product is known as **absorption costing.**

In contrast, some firms use **variable costing** to determine the cost of their manufactured products.[2] Under variable costing, only variable manufacturing costs are capitalized as inventory. Any fixed manufacturing costs are expensed in the period incurred. Exhibit 25–6 contrasts the two approaches to costing. The only difference between absorption and variable costing is that fixed factory overhead is capitalized under absorption costing and expensed under variable costing.

[2]Variable costing is also referred to as *direct costing*. The latter is a misnomer, however, because *variable* costs—not *direct* costs—are capitalized under *direct* costing. This distinction is readily apparent in Exhibit 25–6.

MEASUREMENT AND CONTROL OF DIVISIONAL PERFORMANCE

To measure divisional performance by means of a profit figure arrived at after deducting items which are neither controllable at divisional level nor directly related to divisional activity is to use a measure which is arbitrary to the extent that the allocations are arbitrary. It is not independent of conditions outside the division, and may lead divisions into courses of action detrimental to the company. It could, moreover, mislead head office executives into thinking that a division was making a loss or a very small profit, and that therefore it should be liquidated. This could happen even though the facts were that, while the division was failing to make an adequate contribution to the head office expenses and profit, it was making *some* contribution, sufficient perhaps to keep it operating in the hope of eventual recovery.

Most company executives are aware of these arguments against expense allocations but are not always convinced by them. The counterargument most commonly used is that divisions must be made aware that there are nondivisional costs to be covered out of their earnings before the company as a whole can show a profit. Unless this awareness is sharpened by showing the central expense allocations on the divisional profit statements each month, the division may, in pricing policies and other marketing decisions, plan to contribute less than its due share of the company's net income. Moreover, it is argued, if the division were an independent company it would have a top administration of its own.

These counterarguments are not convincing. It is true that some methods of overhead allocation (e.g., allocations based on divisional sales) create possibilities for a division to diminish its contribution to the company's over-all profitability while increasing its own apparent net profit. But such aberrations result simply from the fact of allocation itself. Apart from such allocation practices, *so long as corporate (i.e., non-divisional) expenses are independent of divisional activity,* whatever policies maximize divisional net profits will also maximize divisional contributions to corporate profits before the allocation of corporate expenses. In the general case, in other words, corporate net profits will not suffer if corporate fixed expenses are left unallocated.

SOURCE: David Solomons, *Divisional Performance: Measurement and Control,* Financial Executives Research Foundation, Inc., New York, 1965. Reprinted by permission.

In general, variable costing (carrying only variable costs in the inventory accounts) is considered a departure from financial accounting standards. These standards require that published financial reports attested to by CPAs be prepared on an absorption costing basis. In these reports, all factory costs should be attributed to products and inventories of work in process and finished goods should contain their allocable shares of factory costs, both fixed and variable. Likewise, the Internal Revenue Service has generally insisted on the use of absorption costing in determining net income for tax purposes, with some adjustments.

Although variable costing should not be used to prepare financial statements for external use, management may use variable costing statements for internal analytical purposes. A principal benefit is that variable costing usually causes net income figures to move in the same direction as sales. With absorption costing, net income may increase in periods when production volume outstrips sales and decrease when the company outsells production and thus reduces inventory levels.

In Exhibit 25–7, a comparison of partial income statements for Elway Company for three periods, using both absorption costing and variable costing, demonstrates the effects just discussed. For this simple illustration, we assume that

EXHIBIT 25 – 5

Decorator Lighting Company
Departmental Income Statement
Showing Contributions to Indirect Expenses
For the Year Ended December 31, 19XX

	Residential Department	Commercial Department	Total
Net Sales	$320,000	$210,000	$530,000
Cost of Goods Sold	208,000	147,000	355,000
Gross Profit	$112,000	$ 63,000	$175,000
Direct Operating Expenses:			
Sales Salaries Expense	$ 25,000	$ 20,000	$ 45,000
Advertising Expense	7,000	3,000	10,000
Delivery Expense	8,000	2,000	10,000
Insurance Expense (on merchandise)	4,000	2,000	6,000
Uncollectible Accounts Expense	1,600	1,400	3,000
Total Direct Expenses	$ 45,600	$ 28,400	$ 74,000
Contribution to Indirect Expenses	$ 66,400	$ 34,600	$101,000
Indirect Operating Expenses:			
Advertising Expense			$ 5,000
Occupancy Expense			16,000
Office Salaries Expense			20,000
Other Administrative Expense			15,000
Total Indirect Expenses			$ 56,000
Income before Tax			$ 45,000
Income Tax Expense			15,100
Net Income			$ 29,900

EXHIBIT 25 – 6

COMPARISON OF ABSORPTION AND VARIABLE COSTING

		Absorption Costing		Variable Costing	
Typical Manufacturing Cost (or Expense)	**Typical Behavior Pattern**	**Product Cost**	**Period Cost**	**Product Cost**	**Period Cost**
Direct Costs:					
Direct Material	Variable	X		X	
Direct Labor	Variable	X		X	
Indirect Costs:					
Variable Factory Overhead	Variable	X		X	
Fixed Factory Overhead	Fixed	X			X
Other Expenses:					
Selling	Semivariable		X		X
Nonfactory Administrative	Semivariable		X		X

EXHIBIT 25–7

Elway Company
Partial Income Statements

ABSORPTION COSTING

	Period 1		Period 2		Period 3	
Sales (100 units @ $5)		$500		$500		$500
Cost of Goods Sold:						
Beginning Inventory	$ 0		$ 0		$150	
Cost of Goods Manufactured	400		450		350	
	$400		$450		$500	
Ending Inventory	0		150		0	
Cost of Goods Sold		400		300		500
Gross Profit		$100		$200		$ 0

VARIABLE COSTING

	Period 1		Period 2		Period 3	
Sales (100 units @ $5)		$500		$500		$500
Cost of Goods Sold:						
Beginning Inventory	$ 0		$ 0		$ 50	
Variable Cost of Goods Manufactured	100		150		50	
	$100		$150		$100	
Ending Inventory	0		50		0	
Variable Cost of Goods Sold		100		100		100
		$400		$400		$400
Fixed Manufacturing Costs		300		300		300
Gross Profit		$100		$100		$100

a single item is sold for $5 per unit, that variable product costs are $1 per unit, and that fixed manufacturing costs are $300 per period. The following sales and production figures, in units, are given for the three periods:

	Period 1	Period 2	Period 3	Total
Sales (in units)	100	100	100	300
Production (in units)	100	150	50	300

Elway Company normally produces and sells 100 units per period. Note, however, that in period 2 the company produced an additional 50 units for inventory that are sold in period 3 together with the 50 units produced in period 3.

In the absorption costing statement shown in the top half of Exhibit 25–7, the cost of goods manufactured includes fixed product costs of $300 per period and variable product costs of $1 per unit produced. The $150 inventory shown at the end of period 2 consists of $50 variable costs (50 units × $1) and $100 fixed costs. (Because one-third of the units produced remain in inventory, one-third of the $300 fixed costs is assigned to the inventory.)

In the variable costing statement shown in the lower half of Exhibit 25–7, the cost of goods manufactured includes only variable product costs at $1 per unit produced. Likewise, the inventory at the end of period 2 consists only of $1 variable product cost times the 50 units in the inventory.

A total of $300 gross profit is reported for the three periods under both methods. However, the variable costing method shows the same gross profit figures each period, which are correlated with the constant sales volume over the three periods. On the other hand, under the absorption costing method, gross profit moves up and down with production. The reason, of course, is that the fixed costs are added to the inventory when production outstrips sales and released when the company sells its entire inventory.

To highlight the effect of variable costing on inventories and income in the foregoing illustration, we considered only manufacturing costs. When detailed income statements are prepared under the variable costing method, fixed and variable costs of all types—including selling and administrative expenses—must be properly segregated. An example of a detailed income statement prepared in accordance with the variable costing concept is shown in Exhibit 25–8, page 974.

The term **manufacturing margin,** which appears in Exhibit 25–8, describes the difference between revenue and variable cost of goods sold. Then contribution margin is obtained by deducting variable selling and administrative expenses from the manufacturing margin. Finally, all types of fixed costs and expenses—manufacturing, selling, and administrative—are deducted to arrive at net income.

The following advantages and disadvantages of using variable costing originate in the fact that under variable costing no fixed overhead costs are assigned to inventory carrying values.

Advantages of Variable Costing

1. Management may be more aware of cost behavior in the firm's operations and may be likely to use this information in short-term decision situations in which contribution margin analysis is most appropriate.
2. Reported net income tends to follow sales volume. (This may not be true under absorption costing.)
3. Cost–volume–profit relationships are more easily discerned from variable costing income statements than from conventional absorption costing statements.

Disadvantages of Variable Costing

1. Accounting measures derived under variable costing are not in accord with generally accepted accounting principles, nor are they acceptable for reporting purposes under the Internal Revenue Code.
2. Inventories (and therefore working capital and owners' equity) tend to be understated.
3. Carrying inventories at only their variable costs may lead to long-run pricing decisions that provide for recovery of variable cost only rather than total cost, and thus does not produce net income in the long run.

DIFFERENTIAL ANALYSIS

Differential analysis is based on the widely accepted decision rule that *only the aspects of a choice that differ among alternatives are relevant to a decision*. For example, when you are deciding which theater to attend, the admission price is irrelevant if both theaters charge the same price. However, if the taxi fare is $4 to one and

$3 to the other, then the $1 differential cost is relevant to the choice. The decision process is simplified by concentrating only on the factors that are different.

Suppose a firm may use certain facilities to produce and sell either product A or product B. The decision is to be in favor of the product promising the greater net income based on the following estimated operating data:

	Alternatives	
	Product A	**Product B**
Units that can be produced and sold	12,000	18,000
Unit selling price	$8	$6
Manufacturing costs:		
Variable (per unit)	$3	$2
Fixed (total)	$32,000	$32,000
Selling and administrative expenses:		
Variable (per unit)	$1.50	$1.50
Fixed (total)	$6,000	$6,000

We may compare the alternatives by preparing comparative income statements which would appear as follows:

	Alternatives		
	Product A	**Product B**	**Difference**
Revenue			
(12,000 units @ $8)	$96,000		
(18,000 units @ $6)		$108,000	$12,000
Cost of goods sold (manufacturing costs):			
Variable (12,000 @ $3 per unit)	$36,000		
(18,000 @ $2 per unit)		$ 36,000	$ –0–
Fixed (total)	32,000	32,000	–0–
Selling and administrative expenses:			
Variable (@ $1.50 per unit)	18,000	27,000	9,000
Fixed (total)	6,000	6,000	–0–
Total expenses	$92,000	$101,000	$ 9,000
Net income	$ 4,000	$ 7,000	$ 3,000

This analysis shows a $3,000 increase in net income associated with alternative B as a result of a $12,000 increase in total revenue that is partially offset by a $9,000 increase in variable selling and administrative expenses.

Differential analysis of the same situation is illustrated below, where consideration is limited to the revenue and expense factors that differ if product B is produced rather than product A.

Differential revenue:	
Revenue foregone on first 12,000 units, ($8 − $6) × 12,000	($24,000)
Additional revenue from increased sales volume, $6 × 6,000 units	36,000
Net additional revenue	$12,000
Differential costs:	
Increase in variable selling and administrative expenses, 6,000 units at $1.50	9,000
Net differential income in favor of product B	$ 3,000

Clearly, the differential approach shows the same net advantage for alternative B as the income statements, but does so more concisely. For this reason, management often uses differential analysis in decision making.

EXHIBIT 25 – 8

Rogers Company
Variable Costing Income Statement
For the Year Ended December 31, 19XX

Sales (20,000 units @ $5)		$100,000
Variable Cost of Goods Sold:		
Beginning Inventory (12,000 units @ $3)	$36,000	
Cost of Goods Manufactured (18,000 units @ $3)	54,000	
Goods Available for Sale	$90,000	
Ending Inventory (10,000 units @ $3)	30,000	60,000
Manufacturing Margin		$ 40,000
Variable Selling and Administrative Expenses:		
Variable Selling Expense	$ 8,000	
Variable Administrative Expense	4,000	12,000
Contribution Margin		$ 28,000
Fixed Costs and Expenses:		
Fixed Manufacturing Cost	$12,000	
Fixed Selling Expense	5,000	
Fixed Administrative Expense	3,000	20,000
Net Income		$ 8,000

ILLUSTRATIONS OF DIFFERENTIAL ANALYSIS

The Special Order

Business firms occasionally receive special orders from purchasers who wish a price concession. The prospective purchaser may suggest a price or ask for a bid. Sometimes the buyer may request that the firm produce a special version of a product to be identified with the buyer's private brand. As long as no overriding qualitative considerations exist, management should evaluate such propositions fully and be receptive to their profit potential.

Assume that Company A makes a nationally advertised automobile accessory, which it sells to distributors for $16. A discount firm has proposed that the company supply 2,000 units of the accessory for $14 per unit. The accessory would carry the brand name of the discount firm. If Company A were to accept the order, a special machine attachment would be needed to differentiate the product and imprint the private brand. This attachment, which costs $1,500, would be discarded after the order was processed. Also assume that Company A has unused production capacity, and thus anticipates no change in fixed capacity costs. The following unit cost data are available for the regular production of the item:

Direct material	$ 5
Direct labor	4
Variable factory overhead	2
Fixed factory overhead (allocated)	3
Total cost per unit	$14

At first glance, the proposal seems unprofitable because the unit cost figure shown here is $14, the same as the buyer's offered price, and an additional cost of $1,500 must be incurred to process the order. However, the fixed overhead of $3 included in the $14 total unit cost is not relevant to the decision and should not be considered, because Company A's total fixed costs will be incurred whether the special order is accepted or not. The following differential cost and revenue analysis reveals that the special order should be accepted:

Increase in revenue (2,000 units × $14)			$28,000
Increase in costs:			
Direct material	$ 5 per unit		
Direct labor	4 per unit		
Variable factory overhead	2 per unit		
	$11 × 2,000 units	$22,000	
Cost of special attachment		1,500	
Total differential cost			23,500
Net advantage in accepting special order			$ 4,500

The differential costs of accepting the order consist of the variable production costs and the additional cost of the attachment needed to differentiate the product. Actually, with any price higher than $11.75 ($23,500 total differential costs ÷ 2,000 units), the company would earn a profit on the order.

Note that excess production capacity is significant to the special order decision. Without sufficient excess capacity, the additional production would probably cause additional amounts of fixed costs to be incurred. Also observe that although the $1,500 special attachment in this example is a fixed cost, it is relevant to this decision.

Specific qualitative factors that should be considered here include ascertaining (1) that the special price does not constitute unfair price discrimination prohibited under the Robinson–Patman Act, (2) that regular sales at regular prices are not unfavorably affected by the sales of the discount store, and (3) that the long-run price structure for the product is not adversely affected by the special order. Significant concern in any of these areas might be a basis for rejecting the special order despite the potential $4,500 profit.

Make or Buy?

Many manufacturing situations require the assembly of large numbers of specially designed components and subassemblies. Usually, the manufacturer must choose between making these components and subassemblies or buying them from outside suppliers. In each situation, management should evaluate the relative costs of the two choices. Because making a component uses some portion of the firm's manufacturing capacity, we assume that no more attractive use of that capacity is available.

To illustrate the make-or-buy decision, we assume that a company has made 10,000 units of a necessary component at the following costs:

Direct material	$10,000
Direct labor	12,000
Variable factory overhead	4,000
Fixed factory overhead	24,000
Total costs	$50,000
Cost per unit ($50,000/10,000)	$5

Investigations by the purchasing department indicate that a comparable component can be purchased in sufficient quantities at a unit price of $4.50, an indicated savings of 50 cents per unit. At first glance, the opportunity to purchase seems most attractive. The analysis of differential costs, however, shows quite the contrary.

A review of operations indicates that by purchasing the component, the firm can reduce fixed overhead associated with producing the component from $24,000 to $8,000. A differential analysis follows:

	Make Part	Buy Part	Increase (Decrease) in Cost if Part Is Bought
Cost of 10,000 units:			
Direct material	$10,000		($10,000)
Direct labor	12,000		(12,000)
Variable factory overhead	4,000		(4,000)
Fixed factory overhead	24,000	$ 8,000	(16,000)
Purchase price of components		45,000	45,000
	$50,000	$53,000	$ 3,000

The following approach to this analysis confirms the more comprehensive one above.

Cost to purchase component (10,000 × $4.50)		$45,000
Less costs avoided by purchasing:		
Direct material	$10,000	
Direct labor	12,000	
Variable factory overhead	4,000	
Fixed factory overhead	16,000	42,000
Increase in acquisition cost by purchasing		$ 3,000

These analyses assume that the manufacturing capacity released by the decision to purchase would not be used. However, should an opportunity arise to use this capacity to generate more than $3,000 of contribution margin, then the opportunity to purchase the components would be attractive.

Dropping Unprofitable Segments

Assume that the condensed income statement in Exhibit 25–9 reflects last year's operations of Martin Company. It might seem that the firm's total income could be raised to $125,000 by discontinuing Department C and avoiding that segment's $25,000 operating loss. The following differential analysis, however, indicates that the firm's overall income would decrease, rather than increase, by discontinuing Department C (assume fixed manufacturing costs would decrease by $20,000):

Decrease in revenue		$300,000
Decrease in costs and expenses:		
Variable cost of goods sold	$175,000	
Variable operating expenses	70,000	
Fixed manufacturing costs	20,000	265,000
Decrease in total contribution margin (and net income) from discontinuing Department C		$ 35,000

EXHIBIT 25 – 9

Martin Company
Condensed Income Statement
For the Year Ended June 30, 19XX
(Thousands of Dollars)

	Total	A	B	C
Sales	$1,400	$700	$400	$300
Variable Costs:				
Manufacturing	$ 600	$300	$125	$175
Operating	130	40	20	70
Total Variable Costs	$ 730	$340	$145	$245
Contribution Margin	$ 670	$360	$255	$ 55
Fixed Costs:				
Manufacturing	$ 400	$200	$150	$ 50
Operating	170	80	60	30
Total Fixed Costs	$ 570	$280	$210	$ 80
Net Income	$ 100	$ 80	$ 45	$ (25)

Even though Department C reports a $25,000 annual loss, it does generate a contribution margin of $55,000 toward the absorption of fixed costs and expenses. If Department C is discontinued, there would be no contribution margin while $60,000 of fixed cost would remain. This would result in a loss of $60,000, which is $35,000 worse than the current $25,000 loss.

Management must often consider other factors in decisions of this type. Among these are (1) the potential termination of employees and subsequent effects on employee morale and (2) the possible effects on customer patronage (for example, customers of Departments A and B may go to other firms for all their purchases if Department C's products are no longer available from the same source).

Sell or Process Further?

Firms sometimes face the decision of either selling products at one point in the production sequence or processing them further and selling them at a higher price. Examples are finished versus unfinished furniture, regular versus high-test gasoline, and unassembled kits versus assembled units of product. These process-further decision situations present another opportunity to apply differential analysis.

Assume that Company B makes and sells 50,000 unfinished telephone stands with the following operating figures per unit:

Current sales price		$12.00
Costs:		
Direct material	$4.00	
Direct labor	2.00	
Variable factory overhead	1.50	
Fixed factory overhead*	1.00	8.50
Gross margin per unit		$ 3.50

*Applied at 50% of direct labor costs (total fixed factory overhead is $60,000).

The company now has excess productive capacity, which should remain available in the foreseeable future. Consequently, management believes that part of this excess capacity could be used to paint and decorate the telephone stands and sell them at $15 per unit in the finished furniture market. A study carried out by the company's production department indicates that the additional processing will add $1.30 to the direct material cost and 80 cents to the direct labor cost of each unit and that variable overhead will continue to be incurred at 75% of direct labor cost.

The following differential analysis supports the proposal to process further:

		Per Unit	Totals for 50,000 Units
Differential revenue ($15 − $12)		$3.00	$150,000
Differential costs:			
Direct material	$1.30		$ 65,000
Direct labor	0.80		40,000
Variable factory overhead (75% of $0.80)	0.60		30,000
Fixed factory overhead	0		0
Total differential costs		2.70	$135,000
Excess of differential revenue over differential costs		$0.30	$ 15,000

Both the per-unit and total differential analyses indicate the advantage of processing further.

Product Emphasis

Because most firms produce several products, management must continually examine operating data and decide which combination of products offers the greatest total long-run profit potential. The decisions related to product emphasis are seldom as simple as determining the most profitable product and confining production to that one product. Typically, management faces such operational constraints as limited demand for the most profitable products, the competitive necessity of offering a line of products with a variety of qualities and capacities, and, in seeking better utilization of existing capacity, the need to produce other, less profitable products.

In product emphasis analysis, an important and widely accepted generalization is that *the firm optimizes its income when it maximizes the contribution margin earned per unit of constraining resource*. The concept of constraining resource stems from the realization that as a firm increases its volume, some resource is eventually exhausted and thus constrains, or limits, the continued expansion of the firm. Which resources are constraining depends on the firm, the operating conditions, and even the products under consideration. Typical examples are key materials, labor skills, machine capacities, and factory floor space or storage space. Simply stated, management has optimized the firm's product mix when it maximizes the contribution margin earned on each unit of the particular resource that limits increased production.

To illustrate product emphasis decisions, assume that Beta Company produces products X, Y, and Z, and that factory machine capacity is its constraining resource. Beta Company operates at 90% capacity, and management wants to devote the unused capacity to one of the products. The following data represent Beta Company's current operations:

	Products		
	X	Y	Z
Per-unit data:			
Sales price	$20	$22	$6
Variable costs	8	16	2
Contribution margin	$12	$ 6	$4
Fixed costs*	6	2	1
Net income	$ 6	$ 4	$3

*Allocated on basis of machine hours at $1 per hour.

Intuition suggests that the extra capacity should be devoted either to product Y, which has the highest sales price, or to product X, which has the highest per-unit contribution margin and net income. However, an analysis of the *contribution margin of each product per unit of constraining factor* reveals that product Z should receive the added capacity.

Note that fixed costs are allocated among products on the basis of machine hours—the constraining resource in our example. Furthermore, the unit allocations of fixed costs, above, indicate that product X requires three times as many machine hours as product Y and six times as many as product Z. The contribution per unit of machine capacity for each product follows:

	Products		
	X	Y	Z
Contribution margin per unit	$12	$6	$4
Divided by units of machine capacity required	6	2	1
Contribution margin per unit of machine capacity (the constraining resource)	$ 2	$3	$4

Use of the remaining capacity generates a greater contribution margin if devoted to product Z. As this simple example illustrates, in deciding product emphasis, management should use contribution margin per unit of constraining resource, rather than the relative sales prices, unit contribution margins, or even unit profit of various products.

KEY POINTS FOR CHAPTER OBJECTIVES

1 Describe management's use of accounting information in the decision-making process (pp. 959–61).

- Top management establishes long-range goals, middle management deals with intermediate goals, and lower management focuses on short-range goals.
- Decision making, which is essentially choosing among alternatives, usually comprises three phases: planning, execution, and evaluation.

2 Present an overview of reporting operations for segments of a business (pp. 961–62).

- Business segments may consist of organizational units (departments or divisions) or areas of economic activity (product lines or markets).
- A business segment may be a profit center (where management is responsible for both revenues and expenses) or a cost center (where management is responsible for expenses only).
- Accounting and reporting by business segment are indispensible to management and very important to external groups such as investors and creditors.

3 Introduce the concept of multiple-level performance reporting (pp. 962–63).

- A performance report is usually prepared each accounting period for each profit center and each cost center.
- Total amounts from lower-level reports flow to and are included in higher-level reports.

4 Outline the procedures for reporting revenue and expense by department and for allocating indirect expenses (pp. 963–68).

- Expenses incurred by, or for the benefit of, one business segment are called direct expenses. Expenses incurred for more than one business segment are called indirect expenses and are allocated to segments using appropriate bases of allocation.
- Reporting for segments of a firm is typically extended to one of three operating measures: gross profit, contribution to indirect expenses, or net income. When net income is used, both direct and indirect expenses are deducted from gross profit. When contribution to indirect expenses is used, only direct expenses are deducted.

5 Discuss variable costing and the differences between variable costing and absorption costing (pp. 968–72).

- Variable costing does not assign fixed factory overhead as a product cost, but expenses it in the period incurred.
- Manufacturing margin describes the difference between revenue and variable cost of goods sold.
- Accounting measures derived under variable costing are not in accord with generally acceptable accounting principles, nor are they acceptable for tax reporting.

6 Describe the use of differential analysis (pp. 972–74).

- Differential analysis is the study of those amounts that are expected to differ among alternatives.

7 Provide illustrations of the use of differential analysis in managerial decision making (pp. 974–79).

- The special order at a special price.
- Make or buy needed components for products.
- Dropping unprofitable business segments.
- Sell or process further.
- Product emphasis.

KEY TERMS USED IN THIS CHAPTER

absorption costing 968
cost center 961
decision making 960
departmental contribution to indirect expenses 967
differential analysis 972
direct expenses or costs 965
evaluation phase 960
execution phase 960
indirect expenses or costs 965
managerial accounting 961
manufacturing margin 972
performance reports 962
planning phase 960
profit center 962
variable costing 968
variable costs 969

SELF-TEST QUESTIONS FOR REVIEW

(Answers are at the end of this chapter.)

1. The manager of which of the following segments of a business is responsible for revenue generation as well as for cost and expense control?
   (a) Cost center.
   (b) Accounting department.
   (c) Profit center.
   (d) Assembly line.
2. Which of the following is not considered in determining contribution to indirect expenses?
   (a) Income taxes.
   (b) Cost of goods sold.
   (c) Direct expenses.
   (d) Net sales.
3. In performance reporting, where budgeted cost is compared to actual cost, which performance report must be prepared first?
   (a) Division, consisting of five departments.
   (b) Region, consisting of three divisions.
   (c) Department, consisting of four cost centers.
   (d) Company, consisting of two regions.
4. When using differential analysis to analyze two alternatives to the current operation, what factors should not be considered?
   (a) Direct material costs which are different.
   (b) Direct labor costs that exist only for one alternative.
   (c) Overhead costs that are the same for both alternatives.
   (d) Sales commissions which apply to only one alternative.
5. In determining inventory costs, which of the following cost elements is included when using absorption costing but excluded when using variable costing?
   (a) Selling costs.
   (b) Direct labor cost.
   (c) Nonfactory administrative costs.
   (d) Fixed overhead.

DEMONSTRATION PROBLEM FOR REVIEW

Tuttle Manufacturing Company produces only one product, which sells for $50. Product costs at the normal level of manufacturing operations (10,000 units) are:

Direct material	$14 per unit
Direct labor	$12 per unit
Variable overhead	$ 4 per unit
Fixed overhead	$49,500

Selling expenses (100% variable) are $3 per unit while administrative expenses (100% fixed) are $30,000. During the year, Tuttle produced 11,000 units and sold 9,000 units. Tuttle had no beginning inventory of product.

REQUIRED
Determine net income (ignoring income taxes) using:
1. Absorption costing.
2. Variable costing.

SOLUTION TO DEMONSTRATION PROBLEM

Absorption Costing		
Sales (9,000 units × $50)		$450,000
Cost of Goods Sold:		
Direct Material (11,000 × $14)	$154,000	
Direct Labor (11,000 × $12)	132,000	
Variable Overhead (11,000 × $4)	44,000	
Fixed Overhead	49,500	
	$379,500	
Less: Ending Inventory [($379,500/11,000) × 2,000]	69,000	
Cost of Goods Sold		310,500
Gross Profit		$139,500
Selling Expense (9,000 units × $3)	$ 27,000	
Administrative Expense	30,000	
		57,000
Net Income		$ 82,500

Variable Costing		
Sales (9,000 units × $50)		$450,000
Variable Expenses:		
Direct Material (11,000 × $14)	$154,000	
Direct Labor (11,000 × $12)	132,000	
Variable Overhead (11,000 × $4)	44,000	
	$330,000	
Less: Ending Inventory [($330,000/11,000) × 2,000]	60,000	
Variable Cost of Goods Sold		270,000
Manufacturing Margin		$180,000
Less: Variable Selling Expense (9,000 × $3)		27,000
Contribution Margin		$153,000
Fixed Expenses:		
Fixed Overhead	$ 49,500	
Administrative Expense	30,000	
		79,500
Net Income		$ 73,500

Comparison	
Absorption costing net income	$ 82,500
Variable costing net income	73,500
Difference (explained below)	$ 9,000

The amount of fixed overhead contained in the absorption costing ending inventory is:

$$[(\$49{,}500/11{,}000) \times 2{,}000] = \$9{,}000$$

The amount of fixed overhead contained in the variable costing ending inventory is 0. The different treatment of fixed overhead fully explains the difference.

QUESTIONS

25–1 Give examples of segments for business firms segmented by (a) organizational unit and (b) economic activity.

25–2 Identify three phases of decision making and briefly discuss the role of each phase in the decision process.

25–3 Distinguish between a profit center and a cost center.

25–4 Distinguish between *direct expenses* and *indirect expenses*. Which are more likely to be controllable at the department level?

25–5 When a firm wishes to measure gross profit by department, what basic modifications are needed in the chart of accounts?

25–6 Suggest an allocation basis for each of the following common expenses of a departmentalized firm that uses a net income measure to determine the profitability of departments:
(a) Janitorial expense.
(b) Plant manager's salary.
(c) Utilities (heat, light, and air conditioning).
(d) Sales salaries.
(e) Uncollectible accounts.
(f) Property taxes.

25–7 What is meant by departmental contribution to indirect expenses? What advantages does this measure have over net income in measuring departmental performance?

25–8 "The higher the management level receiving reports, the more detailed the reports should be." Comment.

25–9 Although separate phases of decision making are identifiable, management is usually involved in all phases at the same time. Explain.

25–10 List several common aspects of decision making that are often not subject to quantification.

25–11 What is variable costing? List its advantages and disadvantages.

25–12 What generalizations can be made about the difference in income reported under variable and absorption costing?

25–13 Explain what is meant by the term *differential analysis*.

25–14 Explain how differential analysis can be applied to the following types of decisions:
(a) Accepting special orders.
(b) Making or buying product components.
(c) Dropping unprofitable segments of the firm.
(d) Selling or processing further.
(e) Product emphasis.

25–15 Department B of a discount store shows a contribution to indirect expenses of \$14,000 and a net loss of \$8,000 (before taxes). The firm believes that discontinuance of Department B will not affect sales, gross profit, or direct expenses of other departments. If total indirect expenses remain unchanged, what effect will discontinuance of Department B have on the income before taxes of the firm?

25–16 Department 2 of a firm has a gross profit of $80,000, representing 40% of net departmental sales. Direct departmental expenses are $60,000. Management believes that an increase of $6,000 in advertising, coupled with a 5% average increase in sales prices, will permit the physical volume of products sold to remain the same next period but will improve the department's contribution to indirect expenses. If management's expectations are correct, what will be the effect on this contribution?

25–17 Department A of a firm has a gross profit of $70,000, representing 35% of net departmental sales. Management believes that an increase of $18,000 in advertising will increase volume of product sold by 20%. Other direct departmental expenses are $32,000. What effect will this decision have on Department A's contribution to indirect expenses?

25–18 Operating at 80% capacity, Thornton Company produces and sells 16,000 units of its only product for $30. Per-unit costs are direct material, $6; direct labor, $8; variable factory overhead, $4; and fixed factory overhead, $5. A special order is received for 1,000 units. Based on this information, what price should Thornton charge to make a $3,000 gross profit on the special order?

25–19 Carbondale Company produces unassembled picture frames at the following average per-unit costs: direct material, $X; direct labor, $Y; and factory overhead, $Z. Carbondale can assemble the frames at a unit cost of $1.25 and raise the selling price from $5.50 to $7.50. What is the apparent advantage or disadvantage of assembling the frames?

25–20 Explain the concept of *constraining resource,* and present a general rule for optimizing product mixes.

25–21 "In differential analysis, we can generally count on variable cost being relevant and fixed cost being irrelevant." Comment.

25–22 If both approaches to a decision lead to the same conclusion, why might differential analysis be considered superior to a comprehensive analysis that reflects all revenue and costs?

EXERCISES

Allocating indirect expenses

25–23 Selected data for the Larson Company, which operates three departments, are given below.

	Department A	Department B	Department C
Inventory	$ 40,000	$144,000	$ 56,000
Equipment (average cost)	360,000	216,000	144,000
Payroll	405,000	360,000	135,000
Square feet of floor space	18,000	9,000	3,000

During the year, the company's indirect expenses included the following:

Depreciation on equipment	$40,000
Real estate taxes	12,000
Personal property taxes (on inventory and equipment)	19,200
Personnel department expenses	20,000

Using the most causally related bases, prepare a schedule allocating the indirect expenses to the three departments.

Dropping unprofitable department

25–24 Sumner Corporation has four departments, all of which appear to be profitable except Department 4. Operating data for the current year are as follows:

	Total	Departments 1–3	Department 4
Sales	$950,000	$800,000	$150,000
Cost of Goods Sold	631,000	520,000	111,000
Gross Profit	$319,000	$280,000	$ 39,000
Direct Expenses	$145,000	$120,000	$ 25,000
Indirect Expenses	123,000	105,000	18,000
Total Expenses	$268,000	$225,000	$ 43,000
Net Income (Loss)	$ 51,000	$ 55,000	($ 4,000)

(a) Calculate the gross profit percentage for Departments 1–3 combined and for Department 4.

(b) Assuming that the operating data for next year will be the same as for the current year, what effect would elimination of Department 4 have on total firm net income? (Ignore the effect of income taxes.)

Analyzing operational changes

25–25 Operating results for Department B of the Karel Company during the current year are as follows:

Sales	$360,000
Cost of Goods Sold	252,000
Gross Profit	$108,000
Direct Expenses	80,000
Indirect Expenses	44,000
Total Expenses	$124,000
Net Loss	($ 16,000)

If Department B could maintain the same physical volume of product sold, while raising selling prices an average of 15% and making an additional advertising expenditure of $30,000, what would be the effect on the department's net income or net loss? (Ignore income taxes in your calculations.)

Analyzing operational changes

25–26 Suppose that Department B in Exercise 25–25 could increase physical volume of product sold by 10% if it spent an additional $12,000 on advertising while leaving selling prices unchanged. What effect would this have on the department's net income or net loss? (Ignore income taxes in your calculations.)

Differential analysis

25–27 In each of four independent cases, the amount of differential revenue or differential cost is as follows (parentheses indicate decreases):

	1	2	3	4
Increases (decreases) in:				
Revenue	$36,000	$–0–	?	?
Costs	?	?	($24,000)	$–0–

For each case, determine the missing amount that would be necessary for the net differential amount to be:

(a) $20,000 favorable.

(b) $12,000 unfavorable.

Indicate whether your answers reflect increases or decreases.

Special order

25–28 Stillwell Manufacturing, Inc., sells a single product for $35 per unit. At an operating level of 8,000 units, variable costs are $16 per unit and fixed costs $8 per unit.

Stillwell has been offered a price of $18 per unit on a special order of 2,000 units by Big Mart Discount Stores, which would use its own brand name on the item. If Stillwell accepts the order, material cost will be $2 less per unit than for regular production. However, special stamping equipment costing $5,000 would be needed to process the order; it would then be discarded.

Assuming that volume remains within the relevant range, prepare an analysis of differential revenue and costs to determine whether Stillwell should accept the special order.

Special order

25–29 Berkley Company regularly sells its only product for $32 per unit and has a 25% profit on each sale. The company has accepted a special order for a number of units, the production of which would use part of its unused capacity. The special order sales price is 50% of the normal price, while the profit margin is only 60% of the regular dollar profit. What, apparently, is:

(a) Berkley's profit per unit on the special order?
(b) Berkley's variable cost per unit?
(c) Berkley's average fixed cost per unit on regular sales?

Make or buy

25–30 Perkins Company incurs a total cost of $135,000 in producing 10,000 units of a component needed in the assembly of its major product. The component can be purchased from an outside supplier for $12 per unit. A related cost study indicates that the total cost of the component includes fixed costs equal to 50% of the variable costs involved.

(a) Should Perkins buy the component if it cannot otherwise use the released capacity? Present your answer in the form of differential analysis.
(b) What would be your answer to requirement (a) if the released capacity could be used in a project that would generate $40,000 of contribution margin?

Sell or process further

25–31 Platt Manufacturing Company makes a partially completed assembly unit that it sells for $32 per unit. Normally, 42,000 units are sold each year. Variable unit cost data on the assembly are as follows:

Direct material	$10
Direct labor	8
Variable factory overhead	4

The company is now using only 70% of its normal capacity; it could fully use its normal capacity by processing the assembly further and selling it for $40 per unit. If the company does this, material and labor costs will each increase by $2 per unit and variable overhead will go up by $1 per unit. Fixed costs will increase from the current level of $160,000 to $215,000.

Prepare an analysis showing whether Platt should process the assemblies further.

Product emphasis

25–32 The following analysis of selected data is for each of the two products Walsh Corporation produces.

	Product A	**Product B**
Per-unit Data at 10,000 Units		
Sales price	$26	$16
Production costs:		
Variable	9	7
Fixed	6	4
Selling and administrative expenses:		
Variable	5	2
Fixed	3	1

In Walsh's operation, machine capacity is the company's constraining resource. Each unit of A requires 3 hours of machine time while each unit of B requires 1 hour of machine time. Assuming that all production can be sold at a normal price, prepare an analysis showing which of the two products should be produced with any unused productive capacity that Walsh might have.

Variable and absorption costing

25–33 McMahon Company sells its product for $50 per unit. Variable manufacturing costs per unit are $20, and fixed manufacturing costs at the normal operating level of 12,000 units are $120,000. Variable selling expenses are $8 per unit sold. Fixed administrative expenses total $52,000. McMahon had no beginning inventory in 19X1. During 19X1, the company produced 12,000 units and sold 9,000. Would net income for McMahon Company in 19X1 be higher if calculated using variable costing or using absorption costing? Indicate reported income using each method.

Variable and absorption costing

25–34 During its first year, Westra, Inc., showed a $10.50 per unit profit under absorption costing but would have reported a total profit $8,400 less under variable costing. If production exceeded sales by 700 units and an average contribution margin of 60% was maintained, what is the apparent

(a) Fixed cost per unit?
(b) Variable cost per unit?
(c) Sales price per unit?
(d) Unit sales volume if total profit under absorption costing was $94,500?

PROBLEMS

Departmental income statement

25–35 Janesville Flooring Company sells floor coverings through two departments, Carpeting and Hard Covering (tile and linoleum). Operating information for the current year appears below.

	Carpeting Department	Hard Covering Department
Inventory, January 1	$ 30,000	$ 13,000
Inventory, December 31	25,000	15,000
Net Sales	390,000	240,000
Purchases	242,000	181,000
Purchases Returns	14,000	4,000
Purchases Discounts	8,000	2,000
Transportation In	9,000	7,000
Direct Departmental Expenses	54,000	28,000

Indirect operating expenses of the firm were $60,000.

REQUIRED

(a) Prepare a departmental income statement showing departmental contribution to indirect expenses and net income of the firm. Assume an overall effective income tax rate of 30%.
(b) Calculate the gross profit percentage for each department.
(c) If the indirect expenses were allocated 60% to the Carpeting Department and 40% to the Hard Covering Department, what would the net income be for each department?

Allocate indirect expenses

25–36 The following information was obtained from the ledger of Baxter Candies, Inc., at the end of the current year:

Baxter Candies, Inc.
Trial Balance
December 31, 19XX

	Debit	Credit
Cash	$ 28,000	
Accounts Receivable (net)	104,000	
Inventory, December 31	120,000	
Equipment and Fixtures (net)	360,000	
Accounts Payable		$ 72,000
Common Stock		300,000
Retained Earnings		120,000
Sales—Department X		560,000
Sales—Department Y		240,000
Cost of Goods Sold—Department X	280,000	
Cost of Goods Sold—Department Y	144,000	
Sales Salaries Expense	128,000	
Advertising Expense	28,000	
Insurance Expense	16,000	
Uncollectible Accounts Expense	6,000	
Occupancy Expense	24,000	
Office and Other Administrative Expense	54,000	
	$1,292,000	$1,292,000

Baxter analyzes its operating expenses at the end of each period in order to prepare an income statement that will exhibit net income by department. From payroll records, advertising copy, and other records, the following tabulation was obtained:

	Direct Expense		Indirect	Allocation Basis for Indirect
	Dept. X	Dept. Y	Expense	Expense
Sales Salaries Expense	$98,000	$30,000		
Advertising Expense	12,000	4,000	$12,000	Relative sales
Insurance Expense	10,000	6,000		
Uncollectible Accounts Expense	4,000	2,000		
Occupancy Expense			24,000	Floor space
Office and Other Administrative Expense	8,000	6,000	40,000	6-to-4 ratio (X to Y)

Department X occupies 10,000 square feet of floor space and Department Y, 5,000 square feet. Indirect expenses should be allocated to departments as indicated above.

REQUIRED
Prepare a departmental income statement for Baxter Candies, Inc., showing net income by department, assuming an overall income tax rate of 35%.

Analyze operational changes

25–37 Lancaster's is a retail store with eight departments, including a garden department that has been operating at a loss. The following condensed income statement gives the latest year's operating results:

	Garden Department	All Other Departments
Sales	$672,000	$4,800,000
Cost of Goods Sold	403,200	3,120,000
Gross Profit	$268,800	$1,680,000

(continued)

	Garden Department	All Other Departments
Direct Expenses	$216,000	$ 546,000
Indirect Expenses	96,000	624,000
Total Expenses	$312,000	$1,170,000
Net Income (Loss)	($ 43,200)	$ 510,000

REQUIRED

(a) Calculate the gross profit percentage for the garden department and for the other departments as a group.

(b) Suppose that if the garden department were discontinued, the space occupied could be rented to an outside firm for $36,000 per year, and the indirect expenses of the firm would be reduced by $9,000. What effect would this action have on Lancaster's net income? (Ignore income taxes in your calculations.)

(c) It is estimated that if an additional $12,000 were spent on advertising, prices in the garden center could be raised an average of 5% without a change in physical volume of products sold. What effect would this have on operating results of the garden department? (Again, ignore income taxes in your calculations.)

Departmental contribution to indirect expenses

25–38 Certain operating information is shown below for Delwood Department Store:

	Department A	Department B	All Other Departments
Sales	$400,000	$600,000	$1,400,000
Direct expenses	70,000	110,000	400,000
Indirect expenses	60,000	80,000	200,000
Gross profit percentage	30%	40%	50%

The managers are disappointed with the operating results of Department A. They do not believe that competition will permit raising prices; however, they believe that spending $14,000 more for promoting this department's products will increase the physical volume of products sold by 20%.

An alternative is to discontinue Department A and use the space to expand Department B. It is believed that Department B's physical volume of products sold can thus be increased 37.5%. Special sales personnel are needed, however, and Department B's direct expenses would increase by $60,000. Neither alternative would appreciably affect the total indirect departmental expense.

REQUIRED

(a) Calculate the contribution now being made to indirect expenses by Department A, by Department B, and by the combination of other departments.

(b) Which of the two alternatives should management choose: increase promotional outlays for Department A, or discontinue Department A and expand Department B? Support your answer with calculations.

Special order

25–39 Total cost data follow for Concord Manufacturing Company, which has a normal capacity per period of 8,000 units of product that sell for $30 each. For the foreseeable future, regular sales volume should continue to equal normal capacity.

Direct material	$ 50,400
Direct labor	31,200
Variable factory overhead	23,400
Fixed factory overhead (Note 1)	19,200
Selling expense (Note 2)	17,600
Administrative expense (fixed)	7,500
	$149,300

1. Beyond normal capacity, fixed overhead costs increase $900 for each 500 units *or fraction thereof* until a maximum capacity of 10,000 units is reached.
2. Selling expenses consist of a 6% sales commission and shipping costs of 40 cents per unit. Concord pays only three-fourths of the regular sales commission rate on sales totaling 501 to 1,000 units and only two-thirds the regular commission on sales totaling 1,000 units or more.

Concord's sales manager has received a special order for 1,200 units from a large discount chain at a price of $18 each, F.O.B. factory. The controller's office has furnished the following additional cost data related to the special order:

1. Changes in the product's design will reduce direct material costs 75 cents per unit.
2. Special processing will add 20% to the per-unit direct labor costs.
3. Variable overhead will continue at the same proportion of direct labor costs.
4. Other costs should not be affected.

REQUIRED

(a) Present an analysis supporting a decision to accept or reject the special order. (Round computations to nearest cent.)

(b) What is the lowest price Concord could receive and still make an $1,800 profit before income taxes on the special order?

(c) What general qualitative factors should Concord consider?

Make or buy

25–40 Harper Corporation currently makes the nylon convertible top for its main product, a fiberglass boat designed especially for water skiing. The costs of producing the 1,500 tops needed each year are:

Nylon fabric	$135,000
Aluminum tubing	48,000
Frame fittings	12,000
Direct labor	81,000
Variable factory overhead	15,000
Fixed factory overhead	76,000

Dustin Company, a specialty fabricator of synthetic materials, can make the needed tops of comparable quality for $200 each, F.O.B. shipping point. Harper would furnish its own trademark insignia at a unit cost of $8. Transportation in would be $14 per unit, paid by Harper Corporation.

Harper's chief accountant has prepared a cost analysis, which shows that only 20% of fixed overhead could be avoided if the tops are purchased. The tops have been made in a remote section of Harper's factory building, using equipment for which no alternate use is apparent in the foreseeable future.

REQUIRED

(a) Prepare a differential analysis showing whether or not you would recommend that the convertible tops be purchased from Dustin Company.

(b) Assuming that the production capacity released by purchasing the tops could be devoted to a subcontracting job for another company that netted a contribution margin of $20,800, what maximum purchase price could Harper Corporation pay for the tops?

(c) Identify two important qualitative factors that Harper Corporation should consider in deciding whether to purchase the needed tops.

Dropping unprofitable division

25–41 Based on the following analysis of last year's operations of Rockville, Inc., a financial vice president of the company believes that the firm's total net income could be increased by $100,000 if its Soft Goods Division were discontinued. (Amounts are given in thousands of dollars.)

	Totals	All Other Divisions	Soft Goods Division
Sales	$5,600	$4,000	$1,600
Cost of Goods Sold:			
Variable	(1,940)	(1,300)	(640)
Fixed	(1,060)	(700)	(360)
Gross Profit	$2,600	$2,000	$ 600
Operating Expenses:			
Variable	(1,500)	(1,000)	(500)
Fixed	(800)	(600)	(200)
Net Income (Loss)	$ 300	$ 400	($ 100)

REQUIRED

Provide answers for each of the following independent situations:

(a) Assuming that fixed costs and expenses would not be affected by discontinuing the Soft Goods Division, prepare an analysis showing why you agree or disagree with the vice president.

(b) Assume that discontinuance of the Soft Goods Division will enable the company to avoid 20% of the fixed portion of cost of goods sold and 25% of the fixed operating expenses allocated to the Soft Goods Division. Calculate the resulting effect on net income.

(c) Assume that in addition to the cost avoidance in requirement (b), the production capacity released by discontinuance of the Soft Goods Division can be used to produce 6,000 units of a new product that would have a variable cost per unit of $18 and would require additional fixed costs totaling $34,000. At what unit price must the new product be sold if Rockville is to increase its total net income by $60,000?

Product emphasis

25–42 Northern Corporation manufactures both a deluxe and a standard model of a household food blender. Because of limited demand, for several years production has been at 80% of estimated capacity, which is thought to be limited by the number of machine hours available. At current operation levels, a profit analysis for each product line shows the following:

	Per-unit Data			
	Deluxe		Standard	
Sales price		$432		$168
Production costs:				
Direct material	$178		$ 24	
Direct labor	72		46	
Variable factory overhead	30		22	
Fixed factory overhead*	50	$330	20	$112
Variable operating expenses		36		20
Fixed operating expenses		16		10
Total costs		$382		$142
Operating income		$ 50		$ 26

*Assigned on the basis of machine hours at normal capacity.

Management wants to utilize the company's current excess capacity by increasing production.

REQUIRED

(a) What general decision guideline applies in this situation?

(b) Assuming that sufficient units of either product can be sold at current prices to use existing capacity fully and that fixed costs will not be affected, prepare an analysis showing which product line should be emphasized if net income for the firm is the decision basis.

Variable and absorption costing

25–43 Turner Manufacturing makes a product with total unit manufacturing costs of $27, of which $18 is variable. No units were on hand at the beginning of 19X0. During 19X0 and 19X1, the only product manufactured was sold for $42 per unit, and the cost structure did not change. Turner uses the first-in, first-out inventory method and has the following production and sales for 19X0 and 19X1:

	Units Manufactured	Units Sold
19X0	120,000	90,000
19X1	120,000	130,000

REQUIRED

(a) Prepare gross profit computations for 19X0 and 19X1 using absorption costing.
(b) Prepare gross profit computations for 19X0 and 19X1 using variable costing.
(c) Explain how your answers illustrate the impact of differences between production and sales volumes on the gross profits reported each year under absorption and variable costing.

Variable and absorption costing

25–44 Summarized data for the first year's operations of Shaw Products, Inc., follow:

Sales (75,000 units)	$1,500,000
Production costs (80,000 units):	
Direct material	440,000
Direct labor	360,000
Factory overhead:	
Variable	272,000
Fixed	160,000
Operating expenses:	
Variable	84,000
Fixed	120,000

REQUIRED

(a) Prepare an income statement based on full absorption costing.
(b) Prepare an income statement based on variable costing.
(c) Assume you must decide quickly whether to accept a special one-time order for 1,000 units for $15 per unit. Which income statement presents the most relevant data? Determine the apparent profit or loss on the special order based solely on this data.
(d) If the ending inventory is destroyed by fire, which costing approach would you use as a basis for filing an insurance claim for the fire loss? Why?

ALTERNATE PROBLEMS

Departmental income statement

25–35A Jackson Appliance & Furniture Company has two departments, Appliances and Furniture. Operating information for the current year appears below.

	Appliance Department	Furniture Department
Inventory, January 1	$ 240,000	$ 180,000
Inventory, December 31	151,200	96,000
Net Sales	2,240,000	1,520,000
Purchases	1,280,000	960,000
Purchases Discounts	16,000	12,000
Transportation In	36,000	32,000
Direct Departmental Expenses	399,200	164,000

Indirect operating expenses of the firm were $360,000.

REQUIRED

(a) Prepare a departmental income statement showing departmental contribution to indirect expenses and net income of the firm. Assume an overall effective income tax rate of 40%.

(b) Calculate the gross profit percentage for each department.

(c) If the indirect expenses were allocated 70% to the Appliance Department and 30% to the Furniture Department, what would the net income be for each department?

Allocate indirect expenses

25–36A The following information was obtained from the ledger of Bayview Emporium, Inc., at the end of the current year:

Bayview Emporium, Inc.
Trial Balance
December 31, 19XX

	Debit	Credit
Cash	$ 36,000	
Accounts Receivable (net)	140,000	
Inventory, December 31	90,000	
Equipment and Fixtures (net)	194,000	
Accounts Payable		$ 68,000
Common Stock		240,000
Retained Earnings		60,000
Sales—Department A		720,000
Sales—Department B		280,000
Cost of Goods Sold—Department A	432,000	
Cost of Goods Sold—Department B	140,000	
Sales Salaries Expense	148,000	
Advertising Expense	62,000	
Insurance Expense (on merchandise)	20,000	
Uncollectible Accounts Expense	6,000	
Occupancy Expense	32,000	
Office and Other Administrative Expense	68,000	
	$1,368,000	$1,368,000

Bayview analyzes its operating expenses at the end of each period in order to prepare an income statement that will exhibit net income by department. From payroll records, advertising copy, and other records, the following tabulation was obtained:

	Direct Expense Dept. A	Direct Expense Dept. B	Indirect Expense	Allocation Basis for Indirect Expenses
Sales Salaries Expense	$96,000	$40,000	$12,000	Equally
Advertising Expense	30,000	12,000	20,000	Relative sales
Insurance Expense	16,000	4,000		
Occupancy Expense			32,000	Floor space
Uncollectible Accounts Expense	4,000	2,000		
Office and Other Administrative Expense	34,000	18,000	16,000	3-to-1 ratio (A to B)

Department A occupies 5,000 square feet of floor space, while Department B has 3,000 square feet. Indirect expenses should be allocated to departments as indicated above.

REQUIRED
Prepare a departmental income statement for Bayview Emporium, Inc., showing net income by department. Assume an overall income tax rate of 30%.

Analyze operational changes

25–37A The management of Luddington's Department Store is concerned about the operation of its sporting goods department, which has not been very successful. The following condensed income statement gives the latest year's results:

	Sporting Goods Department	All Other Departments
Sales	$320,000	$1,600,000
Cost of Goods Sold	240,000	1,040,000
Gross Profit	$ 80,000	$ 560,000
Direct Expenses	$ 45,000	$ 224,000
Indirect Expenses	32,000	160,000
Total Expenses	$ 77,000	$ 384,000
Net Income	$ 3,000	$ 176,000

REQUIRED
(a) Calculate the gross profit percentage for the Sporting Goods department and for the other departments as a group.
(b) It is estimated that if an additional $7,000 were spent on promotion of sporting goods, average prices can be raised 5% without affecting physical volume of goods sold. What effect would this have on the operating results of the Sporting Goods department? (Ignore the effect of income taxes.)
(c) Alternatively, it is estimated that physical volume of goods sold could be increased 8% if an additional $10,000 were spent on promotion of sporting goods and prices were not increased. Assuming that operating expenses remain the same, what effect would this have on the operating results of the Sporting Goods department? (Ignore the effect of income taxes.)

Departmental contribution to indirect expenses

25–38A Certain operating information is shown below for Dakota Department Store:

	Department R	Department S	All Other Departments
Sales	$160,000	$240,000	$560,000
Direct expenses	28,000	44,000	160,000
Indirect expenses	24,000	32,000	80,000
Gross profit percentage	30%	40%	50%

The managers are disappointed with the operating results of Department R. They do not believe that competition will permit raising prices; however, they believe that spending $5,000 more for promoting this department's products will increase the physical volume of products sold by 20%.

An alternative is to discontinue Department R and use the space to expand Department S. It is believed that Department S's physical volume of products sold can thus be increased 35%. Special sales personnel are needed, however, and Department S's direct expenses would increase by $24,000. Neither alternative would appreciably affect the total indirect departmental expense.

REQUIRED
(a) Calculate the contribution now being made to indirect expenses by Department R, by Department S, and by the combination of other departments.

(b) Which of the two alternatives should management choose: increase promotional outlays for Department R, or discontinue Department R and expand Department S? Support your answer with calculations.

Special order

25–39A Total cost data follows for Clearwater Manufacturing Company, which has a normal capacity per period of 20,000 units of product that sell for $27 each. For the foreseeable future, regular sales volume should continue to equal normal capacity.

Direct material	$133,400
Direct labor	100,000
Variable factory overhead	76,000
Fixed factory overhead (Note 1)	59,400
Selling expense (Note 2)	64,800
Administrative expense (fixed)	25,000
	$458,600

1. Beyond normal capacity, fixed overhead costs increase $2,250 for each 1,000 units *or fraction thereof* until a maximum capacity of 24,000 units is reached.
2. Selling expenses consist of a 10% sales commission and shipping costs of $0.50 per unit. Clearwater pays only one-half of the regular sales commission rate on any sale amounting to $1,500 or more.

Clearwater's sales manager has received a special order for 2,500 units from a large discount chain at a price of $22 each, F.O.B. factory. The controller's office has furnished the following additional cost data related to the special order:

1. Changes in the product's design will reduce direct material $2 per unit.
2. Special processing will add 10% to the per-unit direct labor costs.
3. Variable overhead will continue at the same proportion of direct labor costs.
4. Other costs should not be affected.

REQUIRED

(a) Present an analysis supporting a decision to accept or reject the special order.

(b) What is the lowest price Clearwater could receive and still make a profit of $2,500 before income taxes on the special order?

(c) What general qualitative factors should Clearwater consider?

Make or buy

25–40A Hubbard Corporation currently makes the nylon mooring cover for its main product, a fiberglass boat designed for tournament bass fishing. The costs of producing the 2,000 covers needed each year are:

Nylon fabric	$160,000
Wood battens	32,000
Brass fittings	16,000
Direct labor	64,000
Variable factory overhead	48,000
Fixed factory overhead	80,000

Calvin Company, a specialty fabricator of synthetic materials, can make the needed covers of comparable quality for $160 each, F.O.B. shipping point. Hubbard would furnish its own trademark insignia at a unit cost of $10. Transportation in would be $8 per unit, paid by Hubbard Corporation.

Hubbard's chief accountant has prepared a cost analysis, which shows that only 30% of fixed overhead could be avoided if the covers are purchased. The covers have been made in a remote section of Hubbard's factory building, using equipment for which no alternate use is apparent in the foreseeable future.

REQUIRED

(a) Prepare a differential analysis showing whether or not you would recommend that the mooring covers be purchased from Calvin Company.
(b) Assuming that the production capacity released by purchasing the covers could be devoted to a subcontracting job for another company that netted a contribution margin of $32,000, what maximum purchase price could Hubbard pay for the covers?
(c) Identify two important qualitative factors that Hubbard Corporation should consider in deciding whether to purchase the needed covers.

Dropping unprofitable division

25–41A Based on the following analysis of last year's operations of Redwood, Inc., a financial vice president of the company believes that the firm's total net income could be increased by $80,000 if its Soft Goods Division were discontinued. (Amounts are given in thousands of dollars.)

	Totals	All Other Divisions	Soft Goods Division
Sales	$9,400	$7,200	$2,200
Cost of Goods Sold:			
Variable	(3,800)	(2,800)	(1,000)
Fixed	(2,400)	(2,000)	(400)
Gross Profit	$3,200	$2,400	$ 800
Operating Expenses:			
Variable	(1,680)	(1,000)	(680)
Fixed	(800)	(600)	(200)
Net Income (Loss)	$ 720	$ 800	($ 80)

REQUIRED

Provide answers for each of the following independent situations:

(a) Assuming that fixed costs and expenses would not be affected by discontinuing the Soft Goods Division, prepare an analysis showing why you agree or disagree with the vice president.
(b) Assume that discontinuance of the Soft Goods Division will enable the company to avoid 30% of the fixed portion of cost of goods sold and 40% of the fixed operating expenses allocated to the Soft Goods Division. Calculate the resulting effect on net income.
(c) Assume that in addition to the cost avoidance in requirement (b), the production capacity released by discontinuance of the Soft Goods Division can be used to produce 6,000 units of a new product that would have a variable cost per unit of $30 and require additional fixed costs totaling $34,000. At what unit price must the new product be sold if Redwood is to increase its total net income by $90,000?

Product emphasis

25–42A Nichols Corporation manufactures both automatic and manual residential water softeners. Because of limited demand, for several years production has been at 90% of estimated capacity, which is thought to be limited by the number of machine hours available. At current operation levels, a profit analysis for each product line shows the following:

	Per-unit Data			
	Automatic		Manual	
Sales price		$400		$208
Production costs:				
Direct material	$72		$40	
Direct labor	64		32	
Variable factory overhead	32		16	
Fixed factory overhead*	72	$240	36	$124
Variable operating expenses		40		8
Fixed operating expenses		72		48
Total costs		$352		$180
Operating income		$ 48		$ 28

*Assigned on the basis of machine hours at normal capacity.

Management wants to utilize the company's current excess capacity by increasing production.

REQUIRED

(a) What general decision guideline applies in this situation?

(b) Assuming that sufficient units of either product can be sold at current prices to use existing capacity fully and that fixed costs will not be affected, prepare an analysis showing which product line should be emphasized if net income for the firm is the decision basis.

Variable and absorption costing

25–43A Thomas Manufacturing makes a product with total unit manufacturing costs of $32, of which $18 is variable. No units were on hand at the beginning of 19X0. During 19X0 and 19X1, the only product manufactured was sold for $48 per unit, and the cost structure did not change. Thomas uses the first-in, first-out inventory method and has the following production and sales for 19X0 and 19X1:

	Units Manufactured	Units Sold
19X0	100,000	70,000
19X1	100,000	120,000

REQUIRED

(a) Prepare gross profit computations for 19X0 and 19X1 using absorption costing.

(b) Prepare gross profit computations for 19X0 and 19X1 using variable costing.

(c) Explain how your answers illustrate the impact of differences between production and sales volumes on the gross profits reported each year under absorption and variable costing.

Variable and absorption costing

25–44A Summarized data for the first year's operations of Scott Products, Inc., are as follows:

Sales (200,000 units)	$4,000,000
Production costs (210,000 units):	
Direct material	1,050,000
Direct labor	840,000
Factory overhead:	
Variable	630,000
Fixed	525,000
Operating expenses:	
Variable	280,000
Fixed	320,000

REQUIRED

(a) Prepare an income statement based on full absorption costing.

(b) Prepare an income statement based on variable costing.

(c) Assume you must decide quickly whether to accept a special one-time order for 1,000 units for $14 per unit. Which income statement presents the most relevant data? Determine the apparent profit or loss on the special order based solely on this data.

(d) If the ending inventory is destroyed by fire, which costing approach would you use as a basis for filing an insurance claim for the fire loss? Why?

BUSINESS DECISION PROBLEM

Harris Corporation manufactures both an automatic and a manual household dehumidifier. Because of limited demand, for several years production has been at 80% of estimated capacity, which is thought to be limited by the number of machine hours available. At current operation levels, a profit analysis for each product line shows the following:

	Per-unit Data			
	Automatic		Manual	
Sales price		$370		$140
Production costs:				
Direct material	$75		$22	
Direct labor	45		25	
Variable factory overhead	68		16	
Fixed factory overhead	50	$238	18	$ 81
Variable operating expenses		52		21
Fixed operating expenses		30		13
Total costs		$320		$115
Operating income		$ 50		$ 25

Management wants to make use of the company's current excess capacity by increasing production. Each unit of the automatic model requires 2.5 machine hours, while the manual model requires 1 machine hour per unit.

REQUIRED

Present answers for the following questions in each independent situation:

(a) Assume that sufficient units of either product can be sold at current prices to utilize existing capacity fully and that fixed costs will not be affected.
   1. To which product should the excess capacity be devoted if the decision basis is maximization of sales revenue?
   2. What would be your answer to question 1 if the decision were based on contribution margin per unit of product?
   3. Prepare an analysis showing which product line should be emphasized if the firm's net income is the decision basis.
   4. What general decision guideline applies in this situation?

(b) Suppose the excess capacity represents 10,000 machine hours, which can be used to make 4,000 automatic units or 10,000 manual units or any proportionate combination. The only market available for these extra units is a foreign market in which the sales prices must be reduced by 20% and in which no more than 6,000 units of either model can be sold. All costs will remain the same except that the selling commission of 10% (included in variable operating expenses) will be avoided. Prepare an analysis showing which product should be emphasized and the effect on the firm's net income.

(c) Assume that the excess capacity can be used as indicated in requirement (b), and that the firm's market research department believes that the production available from using the excess capacity exclusively on either model can be sold in the domestic market at regular prices if a promotion campaign costing $220,000 is undertaken for the automatic model or $240,000 for the manual model. Prepare an analysis indicating for which product the campaign should be undertaken.

ANSWERS TO SELF-TEST QUESTIONS

1. (c) **2.** (a) **3.** (c) **4.** (c) **5.** (d)

26

BUDGETING AND STANDARD COSTS

CHAPTER OBJECTIVES

1. Describe the budgeting process used by business and other entities (pp. 1001–1002).
2. Present an illustration of the development of a master budget by a business entity (pp. 1003–10).
3. Define *standard costs* and describe their use in standard cost accounting (pp. 1010–11).
4. Develop an understanding of the determination of standard costs for direct material, direct labor, variable overhead, and fixed overhead (pp. 1011–13).
5. Outline the procedures for determining cost variances for direct material, direct labor, variable overhead, and fixed overhead (pp. 1014–20).
6. Describe the procedures for calculating total overhead variances (pp. 1020–22).
7. Present and illustrate the use of standard costs in financial statements (pp. 1022–23).

Fortune is the arbiter of half our actions,
but she still leaves the control of the other half to us.

MACHIAVELLI

Management has a basic responsibility to plan, control, measure performance, and make decisions. In order to carry out this responsibility, management must plan revenues and expenses, compare actual results to planned results, evaluate differences between actual and planned results, and make decisions and take corrective action based on the evaluations. Budgeting and standard costs are two concepts that facilitate this process.

BUDGETING

A *budget* is a formal, written, financial plan that presents management's planned actions and the projected financial effects of these plans. **Budgeting** incorporates many of the accounting concepts discussed in previous chapters. The budget usually presents the financial plan in financial statement format, including income statement, balance sheet, and statement of cash flows.

All types of entities can derive benefits from the budgeting process—manufacturing firms, retail businesses, governmental agencies, private clubs, sole proprietorships, churches, trade associations. The format of the budget document differs among the different types of entities, but the basic concepts of budgeting are the same.

ADVANTAGES OF BUDGETING

A Plan for Accomplishing Objectives

The annual planning process forces management to step back from the daily operations of the entity and methodically examine the entity as a whole and the direction in which it is moving. Management must carefully consider anticipated market demand and recent trends, changes in productive capacity, availability of new technologies, anticipated actions of competitors, performance of outside suppliers, and many other factors. Long-term goals should be reevaluated, and all short-term goals should be reviewed during the planning process.

The budget should then be developed in concert with the goals and objectives that management wants the entity to achieve. The budgeting process will therefore project some of the current operations as they exist and plan for changes in others.

Control of Operations

The budget provides the planned basis to which actual results can be compared to test whether remedial action is necessary. Reasonably frequent comparison of budgeted and actual operating data is a sound operating procedure. This provides a natural base for the application of management by exception principles.

A Basis of Performance Measurement

A firm is successful because its key personnel do their jobs efficiently, reliably, and with general adherence to plans. For all major aspects of a firm's operation, a well-developed budget includes criteria for a high level of performance. Therefore, *properly used,* a budget can be a significant motivational force because managers at various levels know that their actual performance is evaluated by comparison with a desired level of performance.

BUDGET PREPARATION

Even though specific budgeting procedures vary widely among firms, all business enterprises engaged in comprehensive budgeting should consider the following elements of budget preparation: the budget committee, the budget period, and the master budget.

Budget Committee

A *budget committee* generally consists of representatives from all major areas of a firm—such as sales, production, and finance—and is frequently headed by the firm's controller. The committee must coordinate preparation of the budget, initiate budget procedures, collect and integrate data from various organizational units, supervise the review and modification of original estimates, and direct the implementation of the budget. All departments should participate in formulating the budget, so it will be accepted as a reasonable standard of performance. In the absence of such participation, the budget may be viewed as an unreasonable goal imposed by outsiders who do not fully understand the department's operations.

Budget Period

The period covered by a budget varies according to the nature of the specific activity involved. Cash budgets may cover a week or a month, production budgets a month or a calendar quarter, general operating budgets a calendar quarter or year, and budgets for acquisition of plant assets several years. In **continuous budgeting,** an interesting extension of period-by-period budgeting, the coming year is dealt with in terms of quarterly periods. At any given time, the firm has four sequential quarterly budgets, and it adds a new quarterly budget as each quarter expires. With this system, regardless of the time of the year, the current budget always covers the current calendar quarter plus the next three quarters. Continuous budgeting can also be carried out in monthly periods.

Master Budget

The **master budget** is a comprehensive document that integrates all the detailed budgets for the firm's various activities. The master budget contains the projected financial statements for the budget period as well as the related data and schedules needed to develop the financial statements. Typically, all amounts in the master budget are based on the expected level of operations.

The details of a master budget vary according to whether the firm's operations are manufacturing, merchandising, or service oriented. In this chapter, we illustrate budgeting for a small manufacturing operation, Baker Corporation. The following key components constitute Baker Corporation's master budget:

Sales budget Units of production budget Direct material budget Direct labor budget Factory overhead budget Operating expense budget	Provide a basis for the projected income statement
Capital expenditures budget Cash budget	Provide a basis for the projected balance sheet

ZERO-BASE BUDGETING

Traditional budgeting procedures often start with the preceding year's budget or the preceding year's actual expenditures. In many instances, the budgeting process simply results in last year's figures plus a percentage. Although some adjustments may be made, too often this approach automatically justifies the amounts budgeted or expended last year and limits thorough analysis and justification procedures to the "new money," or the incremental portion of the total budget. The obvious defect in this approach is that portions of last year's expenditures may not deserve continued justification. The firm may want to take funds from existing operations and devote them to more attractive new operations.

Zero-base budgeting (ZBB) avoids the problem in traditional budgeting described above. In general, ZBB requires each of the firm's budgetary units to justify *all* of its expenditures as if the unit's operations were just starting. Hence, the label *zero-base* budgeting.

ZBB may take different forms, but the prevailing procedure is the following:*

1. The firm is divided into *decision units* (cost or service centers), to which budget decisions naturally relate.
2. Decision units request funds by preparing *decision packages*, which set forth a statement of goals, a program for achieving them, benefits expected, related alternatives, consequences of not being funded, and required expenditures. Decision packages are often grouped as they relate to continuing a minimum level of operations, increasing the level of continuing operations, and initiating new operations.
3. Various levels of management participate in combining and ranking all departments' decision packages.
4. Decision packages ranked higher than management's cutoff point constitute the plans for the firm's master budget.

A major drawback to ZBB is that it is time consuming—and thus costly—for all departments to justify in detail each year all aspects of their operations. Consequently, some firms use traditional budgeting procedures and have what is termed a *zero-based review* of departments every two or three years. ZBB is much more useful in budgeting for support functions—such as research and development or the utility department—than it is for budgeting direct material and labor.

*For a comprehensive treatment of the subject, see P. A. Pyhrr, *Zero-Base Budgeting* (New York: John Wiley & Sons, Inc., 1975).

The major sequential steps in preparing the master budget are as follows (assuming the prior development of long-run goals and plans):

1. Prepare the sales forecast.
2. Determine production volume.
3. Estimate manufacturing costs and operating expenses.
4. Determine cash flows and other financial effects.
5. Formulate projected financial statements.

Estimating sales volume is usually the initial step in constructing a master budget. Once sales are forecast, production volume can be set to reflect desired changes, if any, in finished goods inventories. When production volume is known, reliable estimates can be made for direct material, direct labor, factory overhead, and operating expenses. With estimates of these costs and expenses, cash flows and the related effects on other accounts can be projected. Then, with proper consideration for capital expenditures and related financing, projected financial statements can be prepared. Aspects of the detailed budgets may indicate unacceptable situations such as excessive costs, exceeded capacities, or cash shortages for which revisions must be made. Early identification of these types of potential operating problems is a key advantage of budgeting.

ILLUSTRATIONS OF BUDGETS

The following illustrations outline the development of a relatively simple master budget for Baker Corporation. Budgeted financial statements are not illustrated because they would be virtually identical with the financial statements studied earlier throughout the text.

Sales Budget

The **sales budget** is prepared first. Anticipated unit sales volume is based on a sales forecast that reflects prior periods' sales, expected general economic conditions, related market research, and specific industry trends. This forecast must be prepared very carefully. Overestimating sales volume can lead to large unwanted inventories, which in turn result in extra storage costs and possibly sales price reductions when liquidating the excess inventory. Underestimating sales can lead to loss of sales revenue and customer ill-will stemming from unfilled orders.

The estimated unit sales volume of each product is multiplied by planned unit sales prices to estimate sales revenue. An example of a sales budget is presented in Exhibit 26–1.

Units of Production Budget

The **units of production budget** reflects the quantity of each product to be produced during the budget period. Scheduled production should specifically provide for anticipated sales and desired ending inventories and, of course, consider the beginning inventories of each product. Assume Baker Corporation wants to

EXHIBIT 26–1

Baker Corporation
Sales Budget
For the Quarter Ended June 30, 19XX

	Estimated Unit Sales Volume	Planned Unit Sales Price	Budgeted Total Sales
Product A: East Area	40,000	$10	$ 400,000
West Area	28,000	10	280,000
Total product A	68,000		$ 680,000
Product B: East Area	20,000	$13	$ 260,000
West Area	11,000	13	143,000
Total product B	31,000		$ 403,000
Total sales revenue			$1,083,000

EXHIBIT 26–2

Baker Corporation
Units of Production Budget
For the Quarter Ended June 30, 19XX

	Units of Finished Product	
	A	**B**
Estimated units to be sold	68,000	31,000
Desired ending inventories	12,000	4,000
Amounts to be available	80,000	35,000
Less: Beginning inventories	10,000	5,000
Total production to be scheduled	70,000	30,000

increase its inventory of product A by 20% (from 10,000 to 12,000 units) and decrease its inventory of product B by 20% (from 5,000 to 4,000 units). Baker's production budget appears in Exhibit 26–2. Note that the desired change in inventory of each product is accomplished by scheduling the appropriate production volumes.

Direct Material Budget

The quantities of material to be purchased to meet scheduled production and desired ending inventory requirements are presented in the **direct material budget.** Any beginning material inventory must be considered in estimating purchases for the budget period. The quantities to be acquired are multiplied by the anticipated unit prices to calculate the total dollar amounts of material purchases. In the direct material budget illustrated in Exhibit 26–3, we assume that Baker

EXHIBIT 26–3

Baker Corporation
Direct Material Budget
For the Quarter Ended June 30, 19XX

	X	**Y**
Direct material required:		
Product A: 70,000 × 2.0	140,000	
70,000 × 0.5		35,000
Product B: 30,000 × 2.0	60,000	
30,000 × 2.0		60,000
Desired ending material inventory	40,000	15,000
Total units to be available	240,000	110,000
Less: Beginning material inventory	40,000	30,000
Total units to be purchased	200,000	80,000
Unit purchase prices	× $0.60	× $0.80
Total materials purchases	$120,000	$64,000

Corporation uses only two direct materials, X and Y, in producing products A and B.

Direct Labor Budget

The **direct labor budget** presents the number of direct labor hours necessary for the production volume planned for the budget period. These hours are multiplied by the applicable hourly labor rates to determine the total dollar amounts of direct labor costs to be budgeted. In the direct labor budget for Baker Corporation in Exhibit 26–4, we have assumed that both products A and B require manufacturing work in the Machining and Finishing departments, as follows:

	Machining Department	Finishing Department
Product A	0.5 hours	0.3 hours
Product B	1.0 hours	0.4 hours

Factory Overhead Budget

Recall from earlier chapters that *factory overhead* comprises all factory costs that are not direct material or direct labor. Examples of factory overhead are indirect material, indirect labor, factory supervisory salaries, utilities, depreciation, maintenance, taxes, and insurance. Because of the variety of cost factors, factory overhead includes both variable and fixed cost elements.

The **factory overhead budget** should be determined by using a flexible budget approach. A columnar format flexible factory overhead budget for the Machining Department of Baker Corporation is shown in Exhibit 26–5. Note that the columnar format **flexible budget** separates variable and fixed overhead cost elements and presents budgeted factory overhead costs for three different volumes of direct labor hours. A flexible budget may also be stated as a cost formula. For the Machining Department of Baker Corporation for the quarter ended June 30, the flexible budget formula for factory overhead at the planned operating volume of 65,000 direct labor hours would be:

$$\begin{matrix}\text{Total}\\\text{Factory}\\\text{Overhead}\end{matrix} = \begin{matrix}\text{Total}\\\text{Fixed}\\\text{Overhead}\end{matrix} + \left(\begin{matrix}\text{Variable}\\\text{Overhead}\\\text{per direct}\\\text{labor hour}\end{matrix} \times \begin{matrix}\text{Production}\\\text{Volume}\end{matrix}\right)$$

$$\$169{,}000 = \$104{,}000 + \left(\$1 \times \begin{matrix}\text{65,000 direct}\\\text{labor hours}\end{matrix}\right)$$

Notice that the formula agrees with the related column for 65,000 hours in Exhibit 26–5, the columnar format.

A flexible factory overhead budget should be prepared for each production department. The master budget amount can be calculated using the formula with the appropriate production volume. In our example, the production volume selected is derived from the direct labor budget (65,000 direct labor hours for the Machining Department), as shown in Exhibit 26–4.

Operating Expense Budget

Operating expenses, composed of selling and general administrative expenses, are often budgeted using the flexible budget approach just illustrated for factory overhead. The result is an **operating expense budget.** Certain variable selling and administrative expenses, such as sales commissions, may vary with *sales volume* rather than with production volume. As with factory overhead, for purposes of departmental cost control and performance measurement, various supplemental schedules would be prepared to relate specific portions of total selling and administrative expenses to specific departments or cost centers.

EXHIBIT 26 – 4

Baker Corporation
Direct Labor Budget
For the Quarter Ended June 30, 19XX

	Machining Department	Finishing Department
Direct labor hours required for production:		
Product A: (70,000 units × 0.5 hours)	35,000	
(70,000 units × 0.3 hours)		21,000
Product B: (30,000 units × 1.0 hours)	30,000	
(30,000 units × 0.4 hours)		12,000
Total direct labor hours	65,000	33,000
Hourly rate for direct labor	× $7.00	× $8.00
Total direct labor costs	$455,000	$264,000

EXHIBIT 26 – 5

Baker Corporation
Machining Department
Factory Overhead Budget
For the Quarter Ended June 30, 19XX

		Overhead Costs at		
	Variable Cost per Direct Labor Hour	60,000 Direct Labor Hours	65,000 Direct Labor Hours	70,000 Direct Labor Hours
Variable costs:				
Indirect material	$0.30	$ 18,000	$ 19,500	$ 21,000
Indirect labor	0.40	24,000	26,000	28,000
Factory utilities	0.20	12,000	13,000	14,000
Factory maintenance	0.10	6,000	6,500	7,000
Total variable overhead	$1.00	$ 60,000	$ 65,000	$ 70,000
Fixed costs:				
Supervisory salaries		$ 30,000	$ 30,000	$ 30,000
Depreciation on equipment		15,000	15,000	15,000
Factory utilities		20,000	20,000	20,000
Factory maintenance		12,000	12,000	12,000
Property taxes and insurance		27,000	27,000	27,000
Total fixed overhead		$104,000	$104,000	$104,000
Total factory overhead		$164,000	$169,000	$174,000

EXHIBIT 26–6

Baker Corporation
Capital Expenditures Budget
For the Year Ended December 31, 19XX

	Calendar Quarters Ending			
	March 31	June 30	September 30	December 31
Machinery	$7,000	$10,000		$40,000
Delivery equipment		8,000	$ 8,000	
Conveyor system			40,000	6,000
Computer		32,000		
Totals	$7,000	$50,000	$48,000	$46,000

Budgeted Income Statement

With the information available from the budgets discussed above, a **budgeted income statement** can be prepared. Other income or expense and estimated income taxes would also be incorporated. The budgeted income statement may be supported by a schedule or statement of cost of goods sold.

Capital Expenditures Budget

Expenditures for plant and equipment are among a firm's most important transactions. Chapter 27 considers some approaches to choosing among capital outlay proposals. Because of the large dollar amounts involved and the relatively long lives of capital assets, such expenditures should be well planned. Even companies that are not growing must eventually replace their equipment. For expanding companies—especially those subject to high technological obsolescence—the budgeting of capital expenditures can be most challenging.

In its simplest form, a **capital expenditures budget** is a list of types of equipment and the amounts budgeted for their acquisition in each of a series of future operating periods, as illustrated in Exhibit 26–6. Capital outlay decisions may significantly affect aspects of other budgets, such as production capacities in production budgets, depreciation expense in factory overhead and operating expense budgets, and related cash expenditures in the cash budget. For example, the $50,000 to be spent in the quarter ended June 30 appears as an April cash disbursement in Baker Corporation's cash budget, shown in Exhibit 26–7.

Cash Budget

The **cash budget** portrays the projected flows of cash during the budget period. Cash receipts are shown in terms of their sources, while cash disbursements are shown in terms of their uses. Cash flows are classified into three groups: cash flows from operating activities, cash flows from investing activities, and cash flows from financing activities.

Because of the characteristic time lags between many routine transactions and their related effects on cash, proper cash budgeting often requires the analysis of certain data contained in other budgets to determine their impact on cash flows. Sales precede collections from customers, purchases precede payments on account, depreciation usually does not represent current cash outlays, and, of course, several types of prepayments may call for cash outlays before the

EXHIBIT 26 – 7

Baker Corporation
Cash Budget
For the Quarter Ended June 30, 19XX

	April	May	June
Cash Flows from Operating Activities			
Cash Receipts:			
Cash sales	$ 18,000	$ 15,000	$ 17,500
Collections from customers	341,780	350,000	358,000
Interest income	3,220	6,000	6,500
	$363,000	$371,000	$382,000
Cash Disbursements:			
Manufacturing costs	$280,000	$290,000	$285,000
Operating expenses	60,000	61,000	58,000
Interest expense	4,000	9,000	19,000
Income taxes	—	—	30,000
	$344,000	$360,000	$392,000
Net Cash Flow from Operating Activities	$ 19,000	$ 11,000	$(10,000)
Cash Flows from Investing Activities			
Sale of investments	$ 8,000	—	—
Capital expenditures	(50,000)	—	—
Net Cash Flow from Investing Activities	$(42,000)	—	—
Cash Flows from Financing Activities			
Short-term borrowing	$ 40,000	—	—
Cash dividends	(15,000)	—	—
Net Cash Flow from Financing Activities	$ 25,000	—	—
Net Increase (Decrease) in Cash	$ 2,000	$ 11,000	$(10,000)
Beginning Cash Balance	20,000	22,000	33,000
Ending Cash Balance	$ 22,000	$ 33,000	$ 23,000

related expenses are recognized in the accounts. Generally, the shorter the budget period, the more significant may be the differences between cash flows and related aspects of the firm's operations.

For an example of one important aspect of cash budgeting, assume that Baker Corporation has analyzed the collection of its total credit sales in any month as follows:

1. In the month of sale, 30% is collected and receives a 2% cash discount. (The cash received is thus 30% of the credit sales × 0.98).
2. In the month following sale, 50% is collected and no discounts are involved.
3. In the second month following sale, 18% is collected. The remaining 2% of accounts are written off as uncollectible.

Assuming estimated credit sales of $350,000 in February, $340,000 in March, and $370,000 in April, Baker Corporation's cash receipts from credit customers for April could be budgeted in the following manner:

	Monthly Credit Sales	Collections Received During February	March	April
February:	$350,000 × (30% × 0.98)	$102,900		
	350,000 × 50%		$175,000	
	350,000 × 18%			$ 63,000
March:	340,000 × (30% × 0.98)		99,960	
	340,000 × 50%			170,000
April:	370,000 × (30% × 0.98)			108,780
				$341,780

Baker Corporation's cash budget for the quarter ended June 30, 19XX, in Exhibit 26–7 reflects some of the most common examples of cash receipts and disbursements. Note that virtually every other element of the master budget has affected the cash budget.

Budgeted Balance Sheet

The **budgeted balance sheet** presents anticipated balances for the various balance sheet items at the end of the budget period. Assuming all other budgeting procedures have been properly coordinated, the budgeted balance sheet is extremely useful in reviewing the firm's projected financial position. Management can then identify potential financial problems—for example, by assessing the adequacy of the projected current ratio and equity ratio—and can revise plans or take other necessary corrective actions.

STANDARD COSTS

Budgeted amounts are typically stated in total dollar amounts per accounting period. **Standard costs,** however, are usually stated as cost per unit of finished product. A complex process is used to develop standard costs, involving engineering specifications, time and motion studies, estimates of supply and demand, and analysis of historical trends. Standard costs are useful for a number of purposes, including evaluating management performance, preparing flexible and master budgets, and establishing product selling prices.

DETERMINING AND USING STANDARD COSTS

Standard costs represent the costs per unit that should be incurred during the upcoming year. Reasonably attainable levels of efficiency are typically used to establish standard costs, so the standard costs can serve as a motivating factor and a standard of performance.

Standard costs are usually established prior to the beginning of each year as part of the budgeting process. They should not be updated during the year unless there are major, unexpected changes in vendor costs, wage rates, technology, or product design. One of the important uses of standard costs is to compare them to actual costs to identify significant differences. This comparison process will be most meaningful when the standards used represent the level of efficiency that was planned during the budgeting process.

Standard Cost Accounting

Many companies, especially manufacturing firms, adopt **standard cost accounting** for product costs. When this approach is taken, all inventory accounts—material, work in process, and finished goods—and the Cost of Goods Sold account are stated in terms of standard or predetermined costs rather than actual costs incurred. Specifically, standard costs are used for direct material, direct labor, variable overhead, and fixed overhead.

Standard cost accounting can be used with either job order costing (see Chapter 22) or with process costing (see Chapter 23). When standard cost accounting is used, actual product costs are accumulated separately while standard costs are carried in the inventory accounts and the Cost of Goods Sold account.

The development of standard costs per unit requires the use of eight components: (1) direct material standard price; (2) direct material standard quantity; (3) direct labor standard rate; (4) direct labor standard time; (5) standard variable overhead rate; (6) variable overhead standard capacity; (7) standard fixed overhead rate; and (8) fixed overhead standard capacity. The cost-related components are developed and updated as part of the budgeting process, and quantity and capacity standards are usually developed as part of the product design and engineering process. The eight components are described in the following sections.

Direct Material Standards

The standard cost of direct material used to make a unit of a particular finished product is determined by multiplying the *direct material standard price* by the *direct material standard quantity*:

$$\begin{array}{c}\text{Standard Cost of}\\ \text{Direct Material}\\ \text{per Unit}\end{array} = \begin{array}{c}\text{Direct Material}\\ \text{Standard Price}\end{array} \times \begin{array}{c}\text{Direct Material}\\ \text{Standard Quantity}\end{array}$$

To illustrate this calculation, assume that Gregg Manufacturing Company produces product X, which requires only one type of direct material, M. The standard purchase price of M is $4 per pound, and the standard quantity of M needed to make one unit of product X is three pounds. The standard direct material cost to produce one unit of product X is $12:

$$\begin{array}{c}\text{Standard Cost of}\\ \text{Direct Material}\\ \text{per Unit of X}\end{array} = \begin{array}{c}\text{\$4 per}\\ \text{pound}\\ \text{of M}\end{array} \times \begin{array}{c}\text{3 pounds}\\ \text{of M per}\\ \text{unit of X}\end{array} = \begin{array}{c}\text{\$12 per}\\ \text{unit of}\\ \text{product X}\end{array}$$

There are a number of factors that affect the direct material standard price, including the quality of the material, its availability, and discounts for volume purchases. Factors affecting the direct material standard quantity include material quality, engineering specifications, the skill of the direct labor workers, and the capabilities of the equipment used to process the material.

Direct Labor Standards

The standard cost of direct labor required to produce one unit of a particular product is determined by multiplying the *direct labor standard rate* by the *direct labor standard time*:

$$\begin{array}{c}\text{Standard Cost of}\\ \text{Direct Labor}\\ \text{per Unit}\end{array} = \begin{array}{c}\text{Direct Labor}\\ \text{Standard Rate}\end{array} \times \begin{array}{c}\text{Direct Labor}\\ \text{Standard Time}\end{array}$$

Continuing the Gregg Manufacturing Company illustration, assume that the standard hourly rate for direct labor is $10 and that the standard amount of direct labor needed is two hours per unit of product X. The resulting standard direct labor cost per unit of product X is $20:

$$\text{Standard Cost of Direct Labor per Unit of X} = \text{\$10 per direct labor hour} \times \text{2 direct labor hours per unit of X} = \text{\$20 per unit of product X}$$

The direct labor standard rate represents the expected weighted average of labor rates for all level of workers who undertake direct labor tasks on the product. The rates for the various levels of workers are set by the company or prescribed by labor contract. Direct labor standard times are based primarily on prior employee performance and current time and motion studies.

Variable Overhead Standards

The standard cost of variable overhead needed to manufacture one unit of a particular product is determined by multiplying the *standard* (or predetermined) *variable overhead rate* by the *variable overhead standard capacity*:

$$\text{Standard Cost of Variable Overhead per Unit} = \text{Standard Variable Overhead Rate} \times \text{Variable Overhead Standard Capacity}$$

The basis for determining the standard variable overhead rate (which applies to all products) can be direct labor hours, direct labor dollars, machine hours, or one of the lesser-used bases. The basis selected should be the best common measure of variable overhead capacity utilized during production. The variable overhead capacity standard should also be stated in terms of this basis. If the basis for variable overhead is direct labor hours, then the variable overhead standard capacity will be the same as the direct labor standard time.

In the Gregg Manufacturing Company illustration, assume that the standard variable overhead rate is $3.50 per direct labor hour and that the variable overhead standard capacity is two direct labor hours per unit of product X (same as the direct labor standard time). The resulting standard variable overhead cost per unit of product X is $7:

$$\text{Standard Cost of Variable Overhead per Unit of X} = \text{\$3.50 per direct labor hour} \times \text{2 direct labor hours per unit of X} = \text{\$7 per unit of product X}$$

The standard variable overhead rate is based on the *expected* level of operations. Since a wide variety of cost items is included in variable overhead, there are many different factors that affect the rate. The variable overhead standard capacity is influenced by such factors as prior employee performance, prior machine performance, and current time and motion studies.

Fixed Overhead Standards

The standard cost of fixed overhead to produce one unit of a particular product is determined by multiplying the *standard fixed overhead rate* by the *fixed overhead standard capacity*:

$$\text{Standard Cost of Fixed Overhead per Unit} = \text{Standard Fixed Overhead Rate} \times \text{Fixed Overhead Standard Capacity}$$

The basis for determining the standard fixed overhead rate (which applies to all products) can be the same or different than the basis for variable overhead. The basis selected (direct labor hours, machine hours, and so on) for fixed overhead should be the best common measure of fixed overhead capacity used during production. The fixed overhead standard capacity should be stated in terms of this basis. If the basis for fixed overhead is direct labor hours, then the fixed overhead standard capacity will be the same as the direct labor standard time.

Continuing the Gregg Manufacturing Company example, assume that the standard fixed overhead rate is $4.50 per machine hour and that the fixed overhead standard capacity is 1.5 machine hours per unit of product X. The resulting standard fixed overhead cost per unit of X is $6.75:

Standard Cost of Fixed Overhead per Unit of X	=	$4.50 per machine hour	×	1.5 machine hours per unit of X	=	$6.75 per unit of product X

The standard fixed overhead rate is typically based on the *normal* level of operations, usually a multiple-year average. Factors similar to those affecting the variable overhead standards will affect fixed overhead standards.

Total Standard Costs

The relationships described above are summarized in Exhibit 26–8. Most firms that use standard costs prepare a summary of the standard product costs for each product that they produce. Based on the preceding concepts, Gregg Manufacturing Company's standard cost summary for product X would appear as in Exhibit 26–9. If Gregg were to use standard cost accounting, then all units in their inventories and Cost of Goods Sold would have a product cost of $45.75 per unit, as shown in Exhibit 26–9.

EXHIBIT 26–8

SUMMARY OF COMPONENTS USED TO DETERMINE STANDARD COST PER UNIT OF PRODUCT

Standard Cost of Direct Material per Unit:

Direct Material Standard Price × Direct Material Standard Quantity

Standard Cost of Direct Labor per Unit:

Direct Labor Standard Rate × Direct Labor Standard Time

Standard Cost of Variable Overhead per Unit:

Standard Variable Overhead Rate × Variable Overhead Standard Capacity

Standard Cost of Fixed Overhead per Unit:

Standard Fixed Overhead Rate × Fixed Overhead Standard Capacity

EXHIBIT 26–9

Gregg Manufacturing Company
Standard Cost Summary for Product X

Direct material ($4.00/pound × 3 pounds)	$12.00
Direct labor ($10.00/DLH × 2 DLH)	20.00
Variable overhead ($3.50/DLH × 2 DLH)	7.00
Fixed overhead ($4.50/MH × 1.5 MH)	6.75
Total standard product cost per unit of X	$45.75

DLH = Direct labor hour(s)
MH = Machine hour(s)

Standard costs are also used in determining product cost variances. The remaining sections of this chapter deal with the calculation and use of product cost variances.

Cost Variances

Even in well-managed companies with carefully established and currently maintained cost standards, actual costs often differ from standard costs. The differences should be analyzed for indications of their cause so that appropriate action may be taken.

Suppose that during June, Gregg Manufacturing Company produced 9,800 units of product X for which it incurred the following actual costs (assume no beginning or ending work in process inventories):

Direct material ($4.20 × 28,600 pounds)	$120,120
Direct labor ($9.94 × 20,000 DLH)	198,800
Variable overhead	67,000
Fixed overhead	67,500
Total actual production costs	$453,420

In Exhibit 26–10 the actual costs are compared with standard costs for 9,800 units of product, and the differences, or **variances,** for each cost category are calculated. The standard costs (from our standard cost summary for product X) are multiplied by the actual quantity of 9,800 units produced in June. Note that both favorable and unfavorable variances exist and that the overall net variance of $5,070 is unfavorable. To initiate remedial action, management must analyze the variance for each manufacturing cost element to determine the underlying causal factors related to prices paid, quantities used, and productive capacity used. The following paragraphs present these analyses and the related general journal entries (in summary form) for recording variances.

Material Variances

Variances for direct material stem primarily from paying more or less than the standard price (the **material price variance**) and from using more or less than the standard quantity (the **material quantity variance**). Gregg Manufacturing Company's material variances for June are computed below.

EXHIBIT 26–10

Comparison of Standard and Actual Costs of Product X
For the Month of June, 19XX

	Standard Costs (9,800 units)	Actual Costs (9,800 units)	Total Variances	
Direct material	$117,600	$120,120	$2,520	Unfavorable
Direct labor	196,000	198,800	2,800	Unfavorable
Variable overhead	68,600	67,000	1,600	Favorable
Fixed overhead	66,150	67,500	1,350	Unfavorable
	$448,350	$453,420	$5,070	Unfavorable

The material price variance for Gregg would be:

$$\text{Material Price Variance} = \left(\text{Actual Price} - \text{Standard Price}\right) \times \text{Actual Quantity}$$
$$= (\$4.20 - \$4.00) \times 28{,}600$$
$$= \$5{,}720 \text{ Unfavorable}$$

The material price variance is unfavorable since actual price is greater than standard price. If actual price had been less than standard price, then the material price variance would have been favorable.

The material quantity variance for Gregg would be:

$$\text{Material Quantity Variance} = \left(\text{Actual Quantity} - \text{Standard Quantity}\right) \times \text{Standard Price}$$
$$= (28{,}600 - 29{,}400) \times \$4.00$$
$$= \$3{,}200 \text{ Favorable}$$

The *standard quantity* is the quantity that should have been used to produce 9,800 units (9,800 units × 3 pounds per unit = 29,400 pounds). The material quantity variance is favorable since actual quantity is less than standard quantity. If actual quantity had been greater than standard quantity, then material quantity variance would have been unfavorable.

The total material variance would be:

Material price variance	$5,720	Unfavorable
Material quantity variance	3,200	Favorable
Total material variance	$2,520	Unfavorable

Notice that the total material variance agrees with the amount in Exhibit 26–10.

The unfavorable price variance may have been caused by increases in supplier prices, improper purchasing, or other factors. The favorable quantity variance may have been caused by efficient workers, superior-quality material, or other factors.

The general journal entry to record material costs and variances is:

	Debit	Credit
Work in Process [standard price and quantity]	117,600	
Material Price Variance	5,720	
Material Quantity Variance		3,200
Materials Inventory [actual price and quantity]		120,120
To record direct material costs and related cost variances.		

Note that the journal entry debits Work in Process for standard costs, records the unfavorable variance as a debit, records the favorable variance as a credit, and records the actual costs of material requisitioned during June.[1]

Labor Variances

Variances for direct labor result from paying more or less than the standard wage rates for direct labor (the **labor rate variance**) and from using more or less than the standard amount of direct labor hours (the **labor efficiency variance**). Gregg Manufacturing Company's direct labor variances are computed and recorded as shown below. Note that the basic calculations are the same as for material, but the term *rate* is used instead of *price* and the term *efficiency* is used instead of *quantity*.

$$\text{Labor Rate Variance} = \left(\text{Actual Rate} - \text{Standard Rate}\right) \times \text{Actual Hours}$$

$$= (\$9.94 - \$10.00) \times 20{,}000$$

$$= \$1{,}200 \text{ Favorable}$$

$$\text{Labor Efficiency Variance} = \left(\text{Actual Hours} - \text{Standard Hours}\right) \times \text{Standard Rate}$$

$$= (20{,}000 - 19{,}600) \times \$10.00$$

$$= \$4{,}000 \text{ Unfavorable}$$

Labor rate variance	$1,200 Favorable
Labor efficiency variance	4,000 Unfavorable
Total labor variance	$2,800 Unfavorable

Notice that the total labor variance also agrees with the amount in Exhibit 26–10.

The unfavorable labor efficiency variance might be charged to the production supervisor, who presumably oversees the production teams. The favorable labor rate variance could have resulted from assigning lower-paid employees more than specified, using less overtime, or paying decreased labor rates.

The following journal entry records these costs and variances:

	Debit	Credit
Work in Process [standard rate and hours]	196,000	
Labor Efficiency Variance	4,000	

(entry continues)

[1]In our illustration, we recognize and record the material price variance when the materials start into production. Some firms recognize and record the price variance when materials purchases are recorded.

Labor Rate Variance		1,200
Factory Payroll Payable [actual rates and hours]		198,800
To record direct labor costs and related cost variances.		

The journal entry shown charges Work in Process with standard direct labor costs, records the unfavorable labor efficiency variance as a debit and the favorable labor rate variance as a credit, and records the liability for direct labor at the amount owed, which is determined by actual hours worked and actual rates paid.

Alternative Calculations

Material and labor variances can also be determined using alternative calculations, as outlined in Exhibit 26–11. The total material variance and the total labor variance are determined by comparing total actual cost to total standard cost.

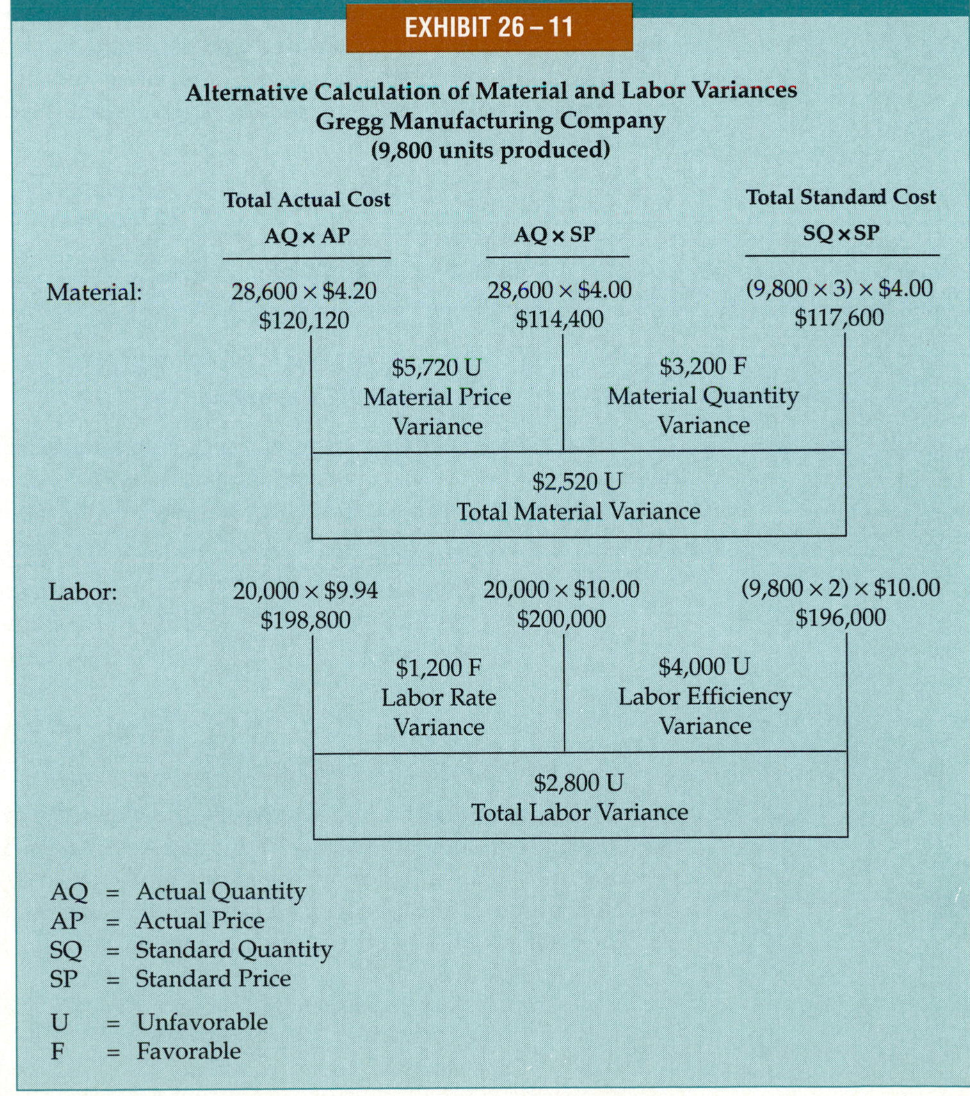
EXHIBIT 26 – 11

Alternative Calculation of Material and Labor Variances
Gregg Manufacturing Company
(9,800 units produced)

	Total Actual Cost AQ × AP	AQ × SP	Total Standard Cost SQ × SP
Material:	28,600 × $4.20 $120,120	28,600 × $4.00 $114,400	(9,800 × 3) × $4.00 $117,600
Labor:	20,000 × $9.94 $198,800	20,000 × $10.00 $200,000	(9,800 × 2) × $10.00 $196,000

Material: $5,720 U Material Price Variance; $3,200 F Material Quantity Variance; $2,520 U Total Material Variance

Labor: $1,200 F Labor Rate Variance; $4,000 U Labor Efficiency Variance; $2,800 U Total Labor Variance

AQ = Actual Quantity
AP = Actual Price
SQ = Standard Quantity
SP = Standard Price

U = Unfavorable
F = Favorable

Material price and labor rate variances are calculated by comparing actual quantity times actual price (total actual cost) to actual quantity times standard price. Material quantity and labor efficiency variances are calculated by comparing actual quantity times standard price to standard quantity times standard price (total standard cost). Note that the resulting variances are the same as those previously calculated.

The standard quantity amounts require further explanation. The standard quantity of material required to produce one unit of product X is three pounds. Therefore, the standard quantity of material allowed to produce 9,800 units of product X is 29,600 pounds (9,800 × 3). Similarly, the standard quantity of labor required to produce one unit of X is two hours, resulting in 19,600 hours (9,800 × 2) allowed to produce 9,800 units of product X.

Variable Overhead Variances

Variances for variable overhead result from paying more or less than planned for items that comprise variable overhead (the **variable overhead spending variance**) and from using more or less than the standard amount of capacity (the **variable overhead efficiency variance**). The variable overhead variances for Gregg Manufacturing Company are computed and recorded as shown below. The calculations are similar to those for material and labor, which, like variable overhead, are variable product cost components. The variable overhead spending variance for Gregg would be:

$$\begin{array}{c}\text{Variable}\\ \text{Overhead}\\ \text{Spending}\\ \text{Variance}\end{array} = \begin{array}{c}\text{Actual}\\ \text{Variable}\\ \text{Overhead}\\ \text{Cost}\end{array} - \left(\begin{array}{c}\text{Variable}\\ \text{Overhead}\\ \text{Actual}\\ \text{Capacity}\\ \text{Used}\end{array} \times \begin{array}{c}\text{Standard}\\ \text{Variable}\\ \text{Overhead}\\ \text{Rate}\end{array}\right)$$

$$= \$67{,}000 - (20{,}000 \times \$3.50)$$
$$= \$3{,}000 \text{ Favorable}$$

The variable overhead spending variance is favorable since actual variable overhead cost ($67,000) is less than actual capacity used times standard price ($70,000).

The variable overhead efficiency variance for Gregg would be:

$$\begin{array}{c}\text{Variable}\\ \text{Overhead}\\ \text{Efficiency}\\ \text{Variance}\end{array} = \left(\begin{array}{c}\text{Variable}\\ \text{Overhead}\\ \text{Actual}\\ \text{Capacity}\\ \text{Used}\end{array} \times \begin{array}{c}\text{Standard}\\ \text{Variable}\\ \text{Overhead}\\ \text{Rate}\end{array}\right) - \left(\begin{array}{c}\text{Variable}\\ \text{Overhead}\\ \text{Standard}\\ \text{Capacity}\\ \text{Allowed}\end{array} \times \begin{array}{c}\text{Standard}\\ \text{Variable}\\ \text{Overhead}\\ \text{Rate}\end{array}\right)$$

$$= (20{,}000 \times \$3.50) - [(9{,}800 \times 2) \times \$3.50]$$
$$= \$1{,}400 \text{ Unfavorable}$$

The variable overhead standard capacity allowed is the capacity that should have been used to produce 9,800 units of product X (9,800 units × 2 direct labor hours per unit of X). The variable overhead efficiency variance is unfavorable because the actual quantity of capacity used is greater than the standard capacity allowed.

The total variable overhead variance would be:

Variable overhead spending variance	$3,000 Favorable
Variable overhead efficiency variance	1,400 Unfavorable
Total variable overhead variance	$1,600 Favorable

Notice that the total variable overhead variance agrees with the amount in Exhibit 26–10.

The general journal entry to record variable overhead costs and variances is:

Work in Process [at standard rate]	68,600	
Variable Overhead Efficiency Variance	1,400	
Variable Overhead Spending Variance		3,000
[Various accounts]		67,000
To record variable overhead costs and related cost variances.		

This journal entry charges work in process with standard variable overhead costs, records the unfavorable variable overhead efficiency variance as a debit and the favorable variable overhead spending variance as a credit.

Fixed Overhead Variances

Variances for fixed overhead stem primarily from paying more or less than planned for the items that comprise fixed overhead (the **fixed overhead spending variance**) and from operating at a level different than the normal level of capacity utilization (**fixed overhead volume variance**). Assuming fixed overhead was budgeted at $67,050, the fixed overhead variances for Gregg Manufacturing Company are calculated and recorded as shown below.

$$\text{Fixed Overhead Spending Variance} = \text{Actual Fixed Overhead Cost} - \text{Budgeted Fixed Overhead Cost}$$

$$= \$67{,}500 - \$67{,}050$$
$$= \$450 \text{ Unfavorable}$$

$$\text{Fixed Overhead Volume Variance} = \text{Budgeted Fixed Overhead Cost} - \left(\text{Fixed Overhead Standard Capacity Allowed} \times \text{Standard Fixed Overhead Rate}\right)$$

$$= \$67{,}050 - [(9{,}800 \times 1.5) \times \$4.50]$$
$$= \$900 \text{ Unfavorable}$$

Fixed overhead spending variance	$ 450 Unfavorable
Fixed overhead volume variance	900 Unfavorable
Total fixed overhead variance	$1,350 Unfavorable

Notice that the total fixed overhead variance agrees with the amount in Exhibit 26–10.

The standard quantity of capacity allowed is the capacity that should have been used to produce 9,800 units of product X (9,800 units × 1.5 machine hours per unit). The fixed overhead volume variance is unfavorable since the amount of fixed overhead applied to product X (standard quantity of capacity allowed × standard fixed overhead rate) is less than the total budgeted fixed overhead cost.

The general journal entry to record fixed overhead costs and variances is:

Work in Process [at standard rate]	66,150	
Fixed Overhead Spending Variance	450	
Fixed Overhead Volume Variance	900	
[Various accounts]		67,500
To record fixed overhead costs and related cost variances.		

Exhibit 26–12 presents a summary of the product cost variances presented in the previous sections of this chapter. These eight variances are important management tools for controlling and analyzing manufacturing operations.

Total Overhead Variances

Some companies choose to analyze variances related only to total overhead rather than analyze separate variances for variable overhead and fixed overhead. It is important to note, however, that separate variances for variable overhead and fixed overhead are generally considered to be superior.

There are two primary approaches to developing total overhead variances: the *three-overhead-variance system* and the *two-overhead-variance system*. Total overhead variances can be determined by combining or relabeling the variances previously determined for variable overhead and fixed overhead. Exhibit 26–13 outlines how the total overhead variances can be determined.

In the Gregg Manufacturing Company illustration, total overhead variances would be calculated as follows:

Three-Overhead-Variance System

Overhead Spending Variance = Variable Overhead Spending Variance + Fixed Overhead Spending Variance

= $3,000 Favorable + $450 Unfavorable

= $2,550 Favorable

Overhead Efficiency Variance = Variable Overhead Efficiency Variance = $1,400 Unfavorable

Overhead Volume Variance = Fixed Overhead Volume Variance = $900 Unfavorable

Two-Overhead-Variance System

Overhead Controllable Variance = Variable Overhead Spending Variance + Fixed Overhead Spending Variance + Variable Overhead Efficiency Variance

= $3,000 F + $450 U + $1,400 U

= $1,150 Favorable

Overhead Volume Variance = Fixed Overhead Volume Variance = $900 Unfavorable

EXHIBIT 26 – 12

SUMMARY OF PRODUCT COST VARIANCES

Direct Material Variances:

$$\text{Material Price Variance} = (\text{Actual Price} - \text{Standard Price}) \times \text{Actual Quantity}$$

$$\text{Material Quantity Variance} = (\text{Actual Quantity} - \text{Standard Quantity}) \times \text{Standard Price}$$

Direct Labor Variances:

$$\text{Labor Rate Variance} = (\text{Actual Rate} - \text{Standard Rate}) \times \text{Actual Hours}$$

$$\text{Labor Efficiency Variance} = (\text{Actual Hours} - \text{Standard Hours}) \times \text{Standard Rate}$$

Variable Overhead Variances:

$$\text{Variable Overhead Spending Variance} = \text{Actual Variable Overhead Cost} - (\text{Variable Overhead Actual Capacity Used} \times \text{Standard Variable Overhead Rate})$$

$$\text{Variable Overhead Efficiency Variance} = (\text{Variable Overhead Actual Capacity Used} \times \text{Standard Variable Overhead Rate}) - (\text{Variable Overhead Standard Capacity Allowed} \times \text{Standard Variable Overhead Rate})$$

Fixed Overhead Variances:

$$\text{Fixed Overhead Spending Variance} = \text{Actual Fixed Overhead Cost} - \text{Budgeted Fixed Overhead Cost}$$

$$\text{Fixed Overhead Volume Variance} = \text{Budgeted Fixed Overhead Cost} - (\text{Fixed Overhead Standard Capacity Allowed} \times \text{Standard Fixed Overhead Rate})$$

In the three-overhead-variance system, the **overhead spending variance** reflects how much more (unfavorable) or less (favorable) was spent on factory overhead than the budget allowed for the actual work completed. The **overhead efficiency variance** shows how much overhead cost was either added or saved as a result of operating above or below the standard level of efficiency. Note that no part of fixed overhead enters into this variance, since fixed overhead should remain constant regardless of the level of efficiency. The **overhead volume variance** reflects the costs associated with using factory capacity at more or less than the

EXHIBIT 26 – 13

TOTAL OVERHEAD VARIANCES

Three-Variance Approach:

Overhead Spending Variance	=	Variable Overhead Spending Variance	+	Fixed Overhead Spending Variance		
Overhead Efficiency Variance	=	Variable Overhead Efficiency Variance				
Overhead Volume Variance	=	Fixed Overhead Volume Variance				

Two-Variance Approach:

Overhead Controllable Variance	=	Variable Overhead Spending Variance	+	Fixed Overhead Spending Variance	+	Variable Overhead Efficiency Variance
Overhead Volume Variance	=	Fixed Overhead Volume Variance				

Note: Overhead Controllable Variance = Overhead Spending Variance + Overhead Efficiency Variance

normal level. Note that variable overhead costs play no role in the volume variance since variable overhead costs respond to the level of production.

In the two-overhead-variance system, the **overhead controllable variance** measures how well the actual factory overhead costs have been kept within the budgetary limits. Both spending and efficiency factors are considered, since these are the factors controllable by management. The overhead volume variance is identical to the overhead volume variance described above.

STANDARD COSTS IN FINANCIAL STATEMENTS

When the standard costs and related variances for direct material, direct labor, variable overhead, and fixed overhead are recorded as previously illustrated, the Work in Process account is debited for each in amounts representing standard quantities and standard prices. All variances—favorable or unfavorable—are carried in separate accounts with appropriate titles. Gregg Manufacturing Company records completed production for June in the following entry (assume no beginning or ending work in process inventories):

Finished Goods Inventory [at standard cost]	448,350	
Work in Process [at standard cost]		448,350
To record completion of June's production of 9,800 units at a standard unit cost of $45.75 ($117,600 material, $196,000 labor, $68,600 variable overhead, and $66,150 fixed overhead).		

As each month's production is sold, the related amounts of standard costs are transferred from Finished Goods Inventory to Cost of Goods Sold.

Standard costs and related variances are usually reported only in financial reports intended for management's use. The following partial income statement illustrates how variances often appear on interim financial statements for internal use (amounts are assumed).

Gregg Manufacturing Company
Partial Income Statement
For the Month Ended June 30, 19XX

Sales	$600,000
Cost of Goods Sold at Standard Cost	400,000
Gross Profit at Standard Cost	$200,000
Less: Net Unfavorable Cost Variance	5,070
Gross Profit	$194,930

The total net variance could be broken down into subvariances or possibly detailed in a schedule of variances accompanying the financial statements.

At year-end, firms commonly close the variance accounts by transferring their balances to Cost of Goods Sold. In effect, this transfer converts the Cost of Goods Sold account from standard costs to actual costs. If large variances exist at year-end and there is evidence that the standards may not apply, a firm may be justified in allocating all or part of the variances to Work in Process Inventory, Finished Goods Inventory, and Cost of Goods Sold.

KEY POINTS FOR CHAPTER OBJECTIVES

1 Describe the budgeting process used by business and other entities (pp. 1001–1002).

- A comprehensive budget provides management with a plan for accomplishing objectives and a basis for controlling operations and measuring performance.
- The budget committee, the budget period, and the master budget are key elements in comprehensive budgeting.

2 Present an illustration of the development of a master budget by a business entity (pp. 1003–10).

- The master budget is usually summarized in the form of budgeted financial statements.
- Key components of the master budget for a manufacturing firm are:

  Sales budget.
  Units of production budget.
  Direct material budget.
  Direct labor budget.
  Factory overhead budget.
  Operating expense budget.
  Capital expenditures budget.
  Cash budget.

- Flexible budgeting allows management to budget amounts that can be compared with costs incurred at actual operating volumes. There are two formats for a flexible budget: columnar and formula.

3 Define *standard costs* and describe their use in standard cost accounting (pp. 1010–11).

- Standard costs represent the costs per unit that should be incurred during the upcoming year. They are established as part of the budgeting process.
- When standard cost accounting is used, all inventory accounts—material, work in process, and finished goods—and the Cost of Goods Sold account are stated in terms of standard costs. Actual costs are accumulated separately.

4 Develop an understanding of the determination of standard costs for direct material, direct labor, variable overhead, and fixed overhead (pp. 1011–13).

- Eight components are required to develop standard product costs:

  Direct material standard price.
  Direct material standard quantity.
  Direct labor standard rate.
  Direct labor standard time.
  Standard variable overhead rate.
  Variable overhead standard capacity.
  Standard fixed overhead rate.
  Fixed overhead standard capacity.

- A standard cost summary is usually prepared for each product that is manufactured.

5 Outline the procedures for determining cost variances for direct material, direct labor, variable overhead, and fixed overhead (pp. 1014–20).

- The following product cost variances are calculated:

  Material price variance.
  Material quantity variance.
  Labor rate variance.
  Labor efficiency variance.
  Variable overhead spending variance.
  Variable overhead efficiency variance.

Fixed overhead spending variance.
Fixed overhead volume variance.

- Each variance can be either favorable or unfavorable.

6 Describe the procedures for calculating total overhead variances (pp. 1020–22).

- There are two schemes for total overhead variances: a three-variance system and a two-variance system.
- Total overhead variances are determined by combining variances calculated individually for variable overhead and fixed overhead.

7 Present and illustrate the use of standard costs in financial statements (pp. 1022–23).

- Standard costs are typically used only in financial statements for internal use by management only.
- Both Gross Profit at Standard Cost and Gross Profit (net of product cost variances) will appear on the income statement.

KEY TERMS USED IN THIS CHAPTER

budgeted balance sheet 1010
budgeted income statement 1008
budgeting 1001
capital expenditures budget 1008
cash budget 1008
continuous budgeting 1002
direct labor budget 1006
direct material budget 1005
factory overhead budget 1006
fixed overhead spending variance 1019
fixed overhead volume variance 1019
flexible budget 1006
labor efficiency variance 1016
labor rate variance 1016
master budget 1002
material price variance 1014
material quantity variance 1014
operating expense budget 1006
overhead controllable variance 1022
overhead efficiency variance 1021
overhead spending variance 1021
overhead volume variance 1021
sales budget 1004
standard cost accounting 1011
standard costs 1010
units of production budget 1004
variable overhead efficiency variance 1018
variable overhead spending variance 1018
variances 1014
zero-base budgeting 1003

SELF-TEST QUESTIONS FOR REVIEW

(Answers are at the end of this chapter.)

1. Which of the following budgets should be prepared before the others?
   (a) Factory overhead.
   (b) Direct material.
   (c) Units of production.
   (d) Direct labor.
2. In what terms are standard overhead rates usually stated?
   (a) Per dollar.
   (b) Per direct labor hour.
   (c) Per unit of product.
   (d) Per month.
3. The formula [(Actual Price − Standard Price) × Actual Quantity] can be used to calculate which cost variance?
   (a) Fixed overhead volume.
   (b) Labor efficiency.
   (c) Material quantity.
   (d) Material price.
4. Which variance considers production capacity not used?
   (a) Fixed overhead volume.
   (b) Labor efficiency.
   (c) Variable overhead spending.
   (d) Material quantity.

5. The gross profit on the interim income statement of a firm using standard costs is computed as:
   (a) Sales less cost of goods sold at standard.
   (b) Sales less cost of goods sold at standard plus net unfavorable variances.
   (c) Sales less cost of goods sold at standard less net unfavorable variances.
   (d) Sales less cost of goods sold at actual.

DEMONSTRATION PROBLEM FOR REVIEW

Crenshaw Manufacturing, Inc., planned to produce 25,000 units of its only product during the year. The standard cost data for this product are:

	Per Unit
Direct material (3 pounds at $2 per pound)	$ 6.00
Direct labor (0.5 hour at $8 per hour)	4.00
Variable overhead (0.5 hours at $4 per hour)	2.00
Fixed overhead (0.5 hours at $6* per hour)	3.00
Total standard cost per unit	$15.00

*Standard fixed overhead rate is computed by dividing total budgeted fixed overhead of $81,000 by normal hours of 13,500 to yield a rate of $6 per hour.

The actual level of production was 24,000 units, with the following actual total costs incurred:

	Total Cost
Direct material (74,000 pounds at $1.80)	$133,200
Direct labor (13,000 hours at $8.10)	105,300
Variable overhead	50,200
Fixed overhead	80,100
Total actual cost	$368,800

The expected level of operations was 12,500 direct labor hours while the normal (multiyear average) level of operations was 13,500 direct labor hours.

REQUIRED

(a) Calculate the variances for material, labor, variable overhead, and fixed overhead.
(b) Show that the difference between total actual cost and total standard cost equals the sum of all the variances.
(c) Determine the total overhead variances if a three variance system is used.

SOLUTION TO DEMONSTRATION PROBLEM

(a)

$$\text{Material Price Variance} = \left(\text{Actual Price} - \text{Standard Price}\right) \times \text{Actual Quantity}$$

$$= (\$1.80 - \$2.00) \times 74{,}000$$

$$= \underline{\underline{\$14{,}800}} \text{ Favorable}$$

$$\text{Material Quantity Variance} = \left(\text{Actual Quantity} - \text{Standard Quantity}\right) \times \text{Standard Price}$$

$$= [74{,}000 - (3 \times 24{,}000)] \times \$2.00$$

$$= \underline{\underline{\$4{,}000}} \text{ Unfavorable}$$

$$\text{Labor Rate Variance} = \left(\text{Actual Rate} - \text{Standard Rate}\right) \times \text{Actual Hours}$$

$$= (\$8.10 - \$8.00) \times 13{,}000$$
$$= \underline{\underline{\$1{,}300}} \text{ Unfavorable}$$

$$\text{Labor Efficiency Variance} = \left(\text{Actual Hours} - \text{Standard Hours}\right) \times \text{Standard Rate}$$

$$= [13{,}000 - (0.5 \times 24{,}000)] \times \$8.00$$
$$= \underline{\underline{\$8{,}000}} \text{ Unfavorable}$$

$$\text{Variable Overhead Spending Variance} = \text{Actual Variable Overhead Cost} - \left(\text{Variable Overhead Actual Capacity Used} \times \text{Standard Variable Overhead Rate}\right)$$

$$= \$50{,}200 - (13{,}000 \times \$4.00)$$
$$= \underline{\underline{\$1{,}800}} \text{ Favorable}$$

$$\text{Variable Overhead Efficiency Variance} = \left(\text{Variable Overhead Actual Capacity Used} \times \text{Standard Variable Overhead Rate}\right) - \left(\text{Variable Overhead Standard Capacity Allowed} \times \text{Standard Variable Overhead Rate}\right)$$

$$= (13{,}000 \times \$4.00) - [(0.5 \times 24{,}000) \times \$4.00]$$
$$= \underline{\underline{\$4{,}000}} \text{ Unfavorable}$$

$$\text{Fixed Overhead Spending Variance} = \text{Actual Fixed Overhead Cost} - \text{Budgeted Fixed Overhead Cost}$$

$$= \$80{,}100 - \$81{,}000$$
$$= \underline{\underline{\$900}} \text{ Favorable}$$

$$\text{Fixed Overhead Volume Variance} = \text{Budgeted Fixed Overhead Cost} - \left(\text{Fixed Overhead Standard Capacity Allowed} \times \text{Standard Fixed Overhead Rate}\right)$$

$$= \$81{,}000 - [(0.5 \times 24{,}000) \times \$6.00]$$
$$= \underline{\underline{\$9{,}000}} \text{ Unfavorable}$$

(b)

Total standard cost ($15 × 24,000)	$360,000
Total actual cost	368,800
Total Variance	$ 8,800 Unfavorable

Material price variance	$ 14,800 Favorable
Material quantity variance	4,000 Unfavorable
Labor rate variance	1,300 Unfavorable
Labor efficiency variance	8,000 Unfavorable
Variable overhead spending variance	1,800 Favorable
Variable overhead efficiency variance	4,000 Unfavorable
Fixed overhead spending variance	900 Favorable
Fixed overhead volume variance	9,000 Unfavorable
Sum of all variances	$ 8,800 Unfavorable

(c)

$$\text{Overhead Spending Variance} = \text{Variable Overhead Spending Variance} + \text{Fixed Overhead Spending Variance}$$

$$= \$1{,}800 \text{ Favorable} + \$900 \text{ Favorable}$$

$$= \underline{\underline{\$2{,}700}} \text{ Favorable}$$

$$\text{Overhead Efficiency Variance} = \text{Variable Overhead Efficiency Variance} = \underline{\underline{\$4{,}000}} \text{ Unfavorable}$$

$$\text{Overhead Volume Variance} = \text{Fixed Overhead Volume Variance} = \underline{\underline{\$9{,}000}} \text{ Unfavorable}$$

QUESTIONS

26–1 What is the difference between budgets and standard costs?

26–2 List and briefly explain three advantages of budgeting.

26–3 What is meant by *continuous budgeting*?

26–4 Define *master budget*.

26–5 List, in the order of preparation, the various budgets that might constitute a master budget for a small manufacturing company.

26–6 Why do most firms prepare the sales budget first?

26–7 Beginning finished goods inventory is 9,000 units, anticipated sales volume is 60,000 units, and the desired ending finished goods inventory is 12,000 units. What number of units should be produced?

26–8 Three pounds of material R (costing $5 per pound) and 4 pounds of material S (costing $6 per pound) are required to make one unit of product T. If management plans to increase the inventory of material R by 500 pounds and reduce the inventory of material S by 800 pounds during a period when 3,000 units of product T are to be produced, what are the budgeted purchases costs of material R and material S?

26–9 What is flexible budgeting? Describe the two formats used for a flexible budget.

26–10 Why is a capital expenditures budget an important budget?

26–11 When should standard costs be established and how often should such standards be changed?

26–12 "Standard costs can be set too high or too low for motivational purposes." Comment.

26–13 Garcia Company used 6,300 pounds of direct material costing $3.90 per pound for a batch of products that should have taken 6,000 pounds costing $4 per pound. What are the material variances?

26–14 Name and briefly describe the two direct labor variances.

26–15 Name and describe the total overhead variances calculated in a three-variance system.

26–16 "Total actual cost exactly equals total standard cost, so everything must be okay." Comment.

26–17 The variable overhead rate is $5 per direct labor hour. 31,000 direct labor hours were used to produce 7,500 units of product. The standard is 4 direct labor hours per unit. Actual variable overhead cost was $152,000. Determine the variable overhead variances.

26–18 Who in the firm might be responsible for each of the following variances?
(a) Material price and quantity variances.
(b) Labor rate and efficiency variances.
(c) Variable overhead spending and efficiency variances.

26–19 Briefly explain how standard cost variances are reported on financial statements.

EXERCISES

Budgeting inventories

26–20 For each independent situation below, determine the amounts indicated by the question marks.

Number of Units	A	B	C	D
Beginning inventory	9,000	?	7,000	?
Produced	15,000	27,000	?	60,000
Available	?	?	26,000	85,000
Sold	18,000	28,000	?	?
Ending inventory	?	13,000	6,000	10,000

Budget preparation

26–21 Taylor Company is preparing its comprehensive budget for July. Use the given estimates to determine the amounts required in each part below. (Estimates may be related to more than one part.)
(a) What should total sales revenue be if territories A and B are estimating sales of 8,000 and 12,000 units, respectively, and the unit selling price is $40?
(b) If the beginning finished goods inventory is an estimated 1,500 units and the desired ending inventory is 3,000 units, how many units should be produced?
(c) What dollar amount of material should be purchased at $4 per pound if each unit of product requires 3 pounds and beginning and ending material inventories should be 5,000 and 4,000 pounds, respectively?
(d) How much direct labor cost should be incurred if each unit produced requires 1.5 hours at an hourly rate of $9?
(e) How much factory overhead should be incurred if fixed factory overhead is $50,000 and variable factory overhead is $1.50 per direct labor hour?
(f) How much operating expense should be incurred if fixed and variable operating expenses are $28,000 and 75 cents per unit sold, respectively?

Budget preparation

26–22 Jacobs Company is preparing its comprehensive budget for May. Use the estimates provided to determine the amounts required in each part below. (Estimates may be related to more than one part.)
(a) What should total sales revenue be if territories A and B are estimating sales of 50,000 and 100,000 units, respectively, and the unit selling price is $18?
(b) If the beginning finished goods inventory is an estimated 12,000 units and the desired ending inventory is 18,000 units, how many units should be produced?

(c) What dollar amount of material should be purchased at $2 per pound if each unit of product requires 2.5 pounds and beginning and ending material inventories should be 35,000 and 25,000 pounds, respectively?
(d) How much direct labor cost should be incurred if each unit produced requires 0.5 hours at an hourly rate of $8?
(e) How much factory overhead should be incurred if fixed factory overhead is $32,000 and variable factory overhead is 85 cents per direct labor hour?
(f) How much operating expense should be incurred if fixed and variable operating expenses are $40,000 and $1.20 per unit sold, respectively?

Using flexible budgets

26–23 The following summary data are from a performance report for Porter Company for June, during which 9,600 units were produced. The budget reflects the company's normal capacity of 10,000 units.

	Budget (10,000 units)	Actual Costs (9,600 units)	Variances over (under) Budget
Direct material	$ 70,000	$ 68,400	($1,600)
Direct labor	140,000	138,600	(1,400)
Variable overhead	48,000	49,200	1,200
Fixed overhead	36,000	36,200	200
Total	$294,000	$292,400	($1,600)

(a) What is the general implication of the performance report? Why might Porter question the significance of the report?
(b) Revise the performance report using flexible budgeting, and comment on the general implication of the revised report.

Budgeting cash collections

26–24 Blaine Company, which sells on terms 2/10, n/30, has had gross credit sales for May and June of $60,000 and $80,000, respectively. Analysis of Blaine's operations indicates that the pattern of customers' payments on account is as follows (percentages are of total monthly credit sales):

	Receiving Discount	Beyond Discount Period	Totals
In month of sale	50%	20%	70%
In month following sale	15%	10%	25%
Uncollectible accounts, returns, and allowances			5%
			$100%

Determine the estimated cash collected on customers' accounts in June.

Budgeting cash flow

26–25 The following various elements relate to Randolph, Inc.'s cash budget for April of the current year. For each item, determine the amount of cash that Randolph should receive or pay in April.
(a) At $24 each, unit sales are 5,000 and 6,000 for March and April, respectively. Total sales are typically 40% for cash and 60% on credit. 30% of credit sales are collected in the month of sale, with the balance collected in the following month. Uncollectible accounts are negligible.
(b) Merchandise purchases were $43,000 and $76,000 for March and April, respectively. Typically, 20% of total purchases are paid for in the month of purchase and a 5% cash discount is received. The balance of purchases are paid for (without discount) in the following month.
(c) Fixed administrative expenses, which total $11,000 per month, are paid in the month incurred. Variable administrative expenses amount to 20% of total monthly sales revenue, one-half of which is paid in the month incurred, with the balance paid in the following month.

(d) Fixed selling expenses, which total $4,200 per month, are paid in the month incurred. Variable selling expenses, which are 5% of total sales revenue, are paid in the month following their incurrence.
(e) A plant asset originally costing $8,000, on which $6,000 depreciation has been taken, is sold for cash at a loss of $400.

Material and labor variances

26–26 The following actual and standard cost data for direct material and direct labor relate to the production of 2,000 units of a product:

	Actual Costs	Standard Costs
Direct material	3,900 pounds @ $5.30	4,000 pounds @ $5
Direct labor	6,200 hours @ $8.40	6,000 hours @ $8.60

Determine the following variances:
(a) Material price.
(b) Material quantity.
(c) Labor rate.
(d) Labor efficiency.

Fixed and variable overhead variances

26–27 Anderson Company considers 6,000 direct labor hours or 3,000 units of product its normal monthly capacity. Its standard variable and fixed factory overhead rates are $4 and $7, respectively, per direct labor hour. During the current month, $24,000 of variable overhead cost and $38,700 of fixed overhead cost were incurred in working 5,600 direct labor hours to produce 2,700 units of product. The fixed overhead budget was $39,200. Determine the following variances, and indicate whether each is favorable or unfavorable:
(a) Variable overhead spending.
(b) Variable overhead efficiency.
(c) Fixed overhead spending.
(d) Fixed overhead volume.

Material, labor, variable overhead, and fixed overhead variances

26–28 The following summarized manufacturing data relate to Barth Corporation's May operations, during which 2,000 finished units of product were produced. Normal monthly capacity is 1,100 direct labor hours and the fixed overhead budget is $4,400.

	Standard Unit Costs	Total Actual Costs
Direct material:		
Standard (2 lb @ $3/lb)	$ 6	
Actual (4,200 lb @ $3.40/lb)		$14,280
Direct labor:		
Standard (0.5 hr @ $8/hr)	4	
Actual (950 hr @ $7.80/hr)		7,410
Variable overhead:		
Standard (0.5 hr @ $2/hr)	1	
Actual		2,150
Fixed overhead:		
Standard (0.5 hr @ $4/hr)	2	
Actual		4,550
Total	$13	$28,390

Determine the material price and quantity variances, labor rate and efficiency variances, variable overhead spending and efficiency variances, and fixed overhead spending and volume variances.

Working with variances

26–29 From the following data, determine the total actual costs incurred for direct material, direct labor, and variable overhead.

	Standard Costs	Variances over (under) Standard
Direct material	$60,000	
Price variance		$1,500
Quantity variance		(2,000)
Direct labor	50,000	
Rate variance		700
Efficiency variance		900
Variable overhead	22,000	
Spending variance		(500)
Efficiency variance		300

Standard costs in financial statements

26–30 For producing and selling 3,500 units of its only product for the month ended April 30, 19XX, Kapp Company's records reflect the following selected data:

	Standard Unit Costs	Total Actual Costs
Direct material	$ 6.00	$22,500
Direct labor	10.00	33,800
Variable overhead	2.00	6,600
Fixed overhead	5.00	18,300

Assuming that the product sells for $48 per unit and that Kapp Company uses standard costs in its general ledger accounts, prepare a partial summary income statement (through gross profit) including total net variances.

PROBLEMS

Budgeting cash

26–31 Manchesters, Inc., sells on terms of 5% discount for "cash and carry" or 2/10, n/30 and estimates its total gross sales for the second calendar quarter of next year as follows: April, $200,000; May, $160,000; and June, $240,000. An analysis of operations indicates the following customer collection patterns:

	Portions of Total Sales
In month of sale:	
Cash at time of sale	25%
On account, during discount period	15%
On account, after discount period	10%
In month following sale:	
On account, during discount period	20%
On account, after discount period	10%
In second month following sale:	
On account, after discount period	15%
Average portion uncollectible	5%
	100%

REQUIRED

Prepare an estimate of the cash to be collected from customers during June.

Monthly cash budget

26–32 During the first calendar quarter of 19X1, Liberty Corporation is planning to manufacture a new product and introduce it in two regions. Market research indicates that sales will be 6,000 units in the urban region at a unit price of $35 and 5,000 units in the rural region at $32 each. Since the sales manager expects the product to catch on, he has asked for production sufficient to generate a 4,000-

unit ending inventory. The production manager has furnished the following estimates related to manufacturing costs and operating expenses.

	Variable (per unit)	Fixed (total)
Manufacturing Costs:		
Direct material:		
A (4 lb @ $2.10/lb)	$8.40	—
B (2 lb @ $3.10/lb)	6.20	—
Direct labor (one-half hour per unit)	5.00	—
Factory overhead:		
Depreciation	—	$ 5,100
Factory supplies	0.60	3,000
Supervisory salaries	—	19,200
Other	0.50	15,300
Operating Expenses:		
Selling:		
Advertising	—	15,000
Sales salaries and commissions*	1.00	10,000
Other*	0.60	2,000
Administrative:		
Office salaries	—	1,800
Supplies	0.10	700
Other	0.05	1,300

*Varies per unit sold, not per unit produced.

REQUIRED

(a) Assuming that the desired ending inventories of materials A and B are 4,000 and 6,000 pounds, respectively, and that work in process inventories are immaterial, prepare budgets for the calendar quarter in which the new product will be introduced for each of the following operating factors:
1. Total sales revenue.
2. Production (in units).
3. Material purchases cost.
4. Direct labor costs.
5. Factory overhead costs.
6. Operating expenses.

(b) Using data generated in requirement (a), prepare a projected income statement for the calendar quarter. Assume an overall effective income tax rate of 30%.

Monthly cash budget

26–33 Gardner, Inc., is a wholesaler for its only product, a deluxe wireless electric drill, which sells for $60 each and costs Gardner $36 each. On December 1, 19X1, Gardner's management requested a cash budget for December. The following selected account balances at November 30 were gathered by the accounting department:

Cash	$ 90,000
Marketable securities (at cost)	140,000
Accounts receivable (all trade)	1,140,000
Inventories (15,000 units)	540,000
Operating expenses payable	93,600
Accounts payable (all merchandise)	388,800
Note payable (due 12/31/X1)	262,000

Actual sales for October and November were 20,000 and 30,000 units, respectively. Projected unit sales for December and January are 50,000 and 40,000, respectively. Experience indicates that 50% of sales should be collected in the month of sale, 30% in the month following sale, and the balance in the second month following sale. Uncollectibles, returns, and allowances are negligible.

Planned purchases should provide ending inventories equal to 30% of next month's unit sales volume. Approximately 70% of the purchases are paid for in the month of purchase and the balance in the following month.

Monthly operating expenses are budgeted at $5.40 per unit sold plus a fixed amount of $126,000 including depreciation of $54,000. Except for depreciation, 60% of operating expenses are paid in the month incurred and the balance in the following month. Interest expense is included in operating expenses.

Special anticipated year-end transactions include the following:

(1) Declaration of a $15,000 cash dividend to be paid two weeks after the December 20 date of record.
(2) Sale of one-half of the marketable securities held on November 30; a gain of $14,000 is anticipated.
(3) Pay off the note payable due December 31, 19X1.
(4) Trade-in of an old computer originally costing $450,000 and now having accumulated depreciation of $360,000 at a gain of $105,000 on a new computer costing $900,000. Sufficient cash will be paid at the time of trade-in so that only 50% of the total price will have to be financed.
(5) Gardner's treasurer has a policy of maintaining a minimum month-end cash balance of $90,000 but wants to raise this to $150,000 at December 31. He has a standing arrangement with the bank to borrow any amount up to a limit of $300,000.

REQUIRED

Prepare a cash budget for Gardner, Inc., for December 19X1. Pattern your solution after Exhibit 26–7.

Flexible budget application

26–34 The Polishing Department of Austin Manufacturing Company operated during April 19X1 with the following factory overhead cost budget based on 5,000 hours of monthly productive capacity:

Austin Manufacturing Company
Polishing Department
Overhead Budget (5,000 hours)
For the Month of April, 19X1

Variable costs:		
Factory supplies	$ 50,000	
Indirect labor	76,000	
Utilities (Usage charge)	34,000	
Patent royalties on secret process	148,000	
Total variable overhead		$308,000
Fixed costs:		
Supervisory salaries	$ 80,000	
Depreciation on factory equipment	72,000	
Factory taxes	24,000	
Factory insurance	16,000	
Utilities (Base charge)	40,000	
Total fixed overhead		232,000
Total factory overhead		$540,000

The Polishing Department was operated for 4,600 hours during April and incurred the following factory overhead costs:

Factory supplies	$ 48,760
Indirect labor	68,080
Utilities (usage factor)	41,400
Utilities (base factor)	48,000
Patent royalties	140,208
Supervisory salaries	84,000
Depreciation on factory equipment	72,000
Factory taxes	28,000
Factory insurance	16,000
Total factory overhead incurred	$546,448

REQUIRED

Using a flexible budgeting approach, prepare a report for the Polishing Department for April 19X1 comparing actual overhead costs with budgeted overhead costs for 4,600 hours. Separate overhead costs into variable and fixed components and show the amounts of any variances between actual and budgeted amounts. Label the report a cost performance report.

Calculate variances

26–35 The following summary data relate to the operations of Mendota Company for April, during which 9,000 finished units were produced. Normal monthly capacity was 20,000 direct labor hours and the fixed overhead budget for April was $40,000.

	Standard Unit Costs	Actual Total Costs
Direct material:		
Standard (4 lb @ $1.80/lb)	$ 7.20	
Actual (38,000 lb @ $1.70/lb)		$ 64,600
Direct labor:		
Standard (2 hr @ $8.20/hr)	16.40	
Actual (18,500 hr @ $8.40/hr)		155,400
Variable overhead:		
Standard (2 hr @ $1.50/hr)	3.00	
Actual		27,200
Fixed overhead:		
Standard (2 hr @ $2.00/hr)	4.00	
Actual		42,000
Total	$30.60	$289,200

REQUIRED

Determine the following variances and indicate whether each is favorable or unfavorable:

(a) Material price and quantity variances.
(b) Labor rate and efficiency variances.
(c) Variable overhead spending and efficiency variances.
(d) Fixed overhead spending and volume variances.

Variances, entries, and income statement

26–36 A summary of Western Company's manufacturing variance report for May follows.

	Total Standard Costs (9,200 units)	Total Actual Costs (9,200 units)	Variances
Direct material	$ 27,600	$ 30,380	$2,780 Unfavorable
Direct labor	138,000	137,740	260 Favorable
Variable overhead	16,560	16,400	160 Favorable
Fixed overhead	6,900	7,600	700 Unfavorable
	$189,060	$192,120	$3,060 Unfavorable

Standard material cost per unit of product is 0.5 pounds at $6 each, and standard direct labor cost is 1.5 hours at $10 per hour. The total actual material cost represents 4,900 pounds purchased at $6.20 per pound; total actual labor cost represents 14,200 hours at $9.70 per hour. Standard variable and fixed overhead rates are $1.20 and 50 cents, respectively, per direct labor hour (based on a normal capacity of 15,000 direct labor hours or 10,000 units of product).

REQUIRED

(a) Calculate variances for material price and quantity, labor rate and efficiency, variable overhead spending and efficiency, and fixed overhead spending and volume.

(b) Prepare compound general journal entries to record standard costs, actual costs, and related variances for material, labor, and overhead.

(c) Prepare journal entries to record the transfer of all completed units to Finished Goods Inventory and the subsequent sale of 8,400 units on account at $38 each (assume no beginning finished goods inventory).

(d) Prepare a partial income statement (through gross profit on sales), showing gross profit based on standard costs, the incorporation of variances, and gross profit based on actual costs.

Variances and journal entries

26–37 Lakeland Company manufactures a single product and uses a standard costing system. The nature of its product dictates that material is used as purchased and no ending material or work in process inventories occur. Per-unit standard product costs are: material, $6 (4 pounds); labor, $5 (one-half hour); variable overhead, $4 (based on direct labor hours); and fixed overhead, $3 (based on a normal monthly capacity of 9,000 direct labor hours—and a fixed overhead budget of $54,000).

Lakeland accounts for work in process and finished goods inventories and cost of goods sold at standard cost and records each variance in a separate account. The following data relate to May, when 17,700 finished units were produced.

REQUIRED

(a) Assuming that 67,000 pounds of material purchased on account at $1.60 per pound were used in May's production, present a compound journal entry to record actual costs, standard costs, and any material variances.

(b) Assuming that 8,900 direct labor hours were worked at an average hourly rate of $9.60, present a compound journal entry to record actual costs, standard costs, and any labor variances.

(c) Assuming that actual variable overhead incurred was $74,200 and that fixed overhead incurred was $54,700, present a compound journal entry to record actual and standard overhead costs and any overhead variances.

(d) Set up T accounts for Work in Process, Finished Goods Inventory, and Cost of Goods Sold, and enter the amounts for requirements (a), (b), and (c). Assume that no beginning inventories exist, that all production was completed, and that all but 500 units produced were sold. Prepare and post journal entries to (1) record production completed and (2) record cost of goods sold at standard costs.

Variances, total overhead variances, and variance reconciliation

26–38 Clancy Company planned to produce 21,000 units of its only product during the year. Clancy established the following standard cost data for this product prior to the beginning of the year:

	Per Unit
Direct material (3 pounds at $2.50 per pound)	$ 7.50
Direct labor (2 hours at $8.75 per hour)	17.50
Variable overhead (2 hours at $3 per hour)	6.00
Fixed overhead (2 hours at $5* per hour)	10.00
Total standard cost per unit	$41.00

*Standard fixed overhead rate is computed by dividing total budgeted fixed overhead of $200,000 by 40,000 normal hours to yield a rate of $5 per hour.

The actual level of production was 22,000 units, with the following actual total costs incurred:

	Total Cost
Direct material (68,000 pounds at $2.40)	$163,200
Direct labor (43,000 hours at $9.00)	387,000
Variable overhead	131,160
Fixed overhead	204,800
Total actual cost	$886,160

The expected level of operations was 42,000 direct labor hours while the normal (multiyear average) level of operations was 40,000 direct labor hours.

REQUIRED

(a) Calculate the variances for material, labor, variable overhead, and fixed overhead.
(b) Show that the difference between total actual cost and total standard cost equals the sum of all the variances.
(c) Determine the total overhead variances if a three-variance system is used.

ALTERNATE PROBLEMS

Budgeting cash

26–31A Milton, Inc., sells on terms of 5% discount for "cash and carry" or 2/10, n/30 and estimates its total gross sales for the third calendar quarter of next year as follows: July, $150,000; August, $100,000; and September, $120,000. An analysis of operations indicates the following customer collection patterns:

	Portions of Total Sales
In month of sale:	
Cash at time of sale	30%
On account, during discount period	20%
On account, after discount period	10%
In month following sale:	
On account, during discount period	20%
On account, after discount period	10%
In second month following sale:	
On account, after discount period	7%
Average portion uncollectible	3%
	100%

REQUIRED

Prepare an estimate of the cash to be collected from customers during September.

Monthly cash budget

26–32A During the first calendar quarter of 19X1, Lincoln Corporation is planning to manufacture a new product and introduce it in two regions. Market research indicates that sales will be 8,000 units in the urban region at a unit price of $53 and 6,000 units in the rural region at $45 each. Since the sales manager expects the product to catch on, he has asked for production sufficient to generate a 4,000-unit ending inventory. The production manager has furnished the following estimates related to manufacturing costs and operating expenses.

	Variable (per unit)	Fixed (total)
Manufacturing Costs:		
Direct material:		
A (2 lb @ $2.00/lb)	$ 4.00	—
B (5 lb @ $1.10/lb)	5.50	—
Direct labor (two hours per unit)	16.00	—
Factory overhead:		
Depreciation	—	$18,000
Factory supplies	0.45	2,000
Supervisory salaries	—	13,000
Other	0.50	7,400
Operating Expenses:		
Selling:		
Advertising	—	10,000
Sales salaries and commissions*	1.00	16,000
Other*	0.40	5,000
Administrative:		
Office salaries	—	12,000
Supplies	0.30	1,000
Other	0.20	4,000

*Varies per unit sold, not per unit produced.

REQUIRED

(a) Assuming that the desired ending inventories of materials A and B are 4,000 and 20,000 pounds, respectively, and that work-in-process inventories are immaterial, prepare budgets for the calendar quarter in which the new product will be introduced for each of the following operating factors:
   1. Total sales revenue.
   2. Production (in units).
   3. Material purchases cost.
   4. Direct labor costs.
   5. Factory overhead costs.
   6. Operating expenses.

(b) Using data generated in requirement (a), prepare a projected income statement for the calendar quarter. Assume an overall effective income tax rate of 35%. (Round income statement amounts to nearest dollar.)

Monthly cash budget

26–33A Glendale, Inc., is a wholesaler for its only product, a deluxe wireless rechargeable electric shaver, which sells for $35 each and costs Glendale $24 each. On June 1, 19X1, Glendale's management requested a cash budget for June. The following selected account balances at May 31 were gathered by the accounting department:

Cash	$ 28,000
Marketable securities (at cost)	80,000
Accounts receivable (all trade)	1,085,000
Inventories (12,000 units)	288,000
Operating expenses payable	98,400

Accounts payable (all merchandise)	451,200
Note payable	300,000

Actual sales for April and May were 30,000 and 50,000 units, respectively. Projected unit sales for June and July are 40,000 and 20,000, respectively. Experience indicates that 50% of sales should be collected in the month of sale, 30% in the month following sale, and the balance in the second month following sale. Uncollectibles, returns, and allowances are negligible.

Planned purchases should provide ending inventories equal to 30% of next month's sales volume. Approximately 60% of the purchases are paid for in the month of purchase and the balance in the following month.

Monthly operating expenses are budgeted at $4.80 per unit sold plus a fixed amount of $144,000 including depreciation of $56,000. Except for depreciation, 70% of operating expenses are paid in the month incurred and the balance in the following month. Interest expense is included in operating expenses.

Special anticipated June transactions include:

1. Declaration of a $30,000 cash dividend to be paid two weeks after the June 20 date of record.
2. Sale of all but $20,000 of the marketable securities held on May 31; a gain of $9,000 is anticipated.
3. Payment of $25,000 installment on the note payable.
4. Trade-in of an old company plane originally costing $150,000 and now having accumulated depreciation of $100,000 at a gain of $80,000 on a new plane costing $1,000,000. Sufficient cash will be paid at the time of trade-in so that only 50% of the total purchase price will have to be financed.
5. Glendale's treasurer has established a policy of maintaining a minimum month-end cash balance of $20,000 and has a standing arrangement with the bank to borrow any amount up to a limit of $200,000.

REQUIRED

Prepare a cash budget for Glendale, Inc., for June 19X1. Pattern your solution after Exhibit 26–7.

Flexible budget application

26–34A The Cutting Department of Anchor Manufacturing Company operated during September 19X1 with the following factory overhead cost budget based on 6,000 hours of monthly productive capacity:

Anchor Manufacturing Company
Cutting Department
Overhead Budget (6,000 hours)
For the Month of September, 19X1

Variable costs:		
Factory supplies	$24,000	
Indirect labor	36,000	
Utilities (Usage charge)	18,000	
Patent royalties on secret process	72,000	
Total variable overhead		$150,000
Fixed costs:		
Supervisory salaries	$48,000	
Depreciation on factory equipment	70,000	
Factory taxes	20,000	
Factory insurance	12,000	
Utilities (Base charge)	16,000	
Total fixed overhead		166,000
Total factory overhead		$316,000

The Cutting Department was operated for 5,500 hours during September and incurred the following factory overhead costs:

Factory supplies	$ 20,200
Indirect labor	33,600
Utilities (usage factor)	19,050
Utilities (base factor)	16,000
Patent royalties	67,000
Supervisory salaries	48,000
Depreciation on factory equipment	70,000
Factory taxes	21,700
Factory insurance	13,500
Total factory overhead incurred	$309,050

REQUIRED

Using a flexible budgeting approach, prepare a report for the Cutting Department for September 19X1 comparing actual overhead costs with budgeted overhead costs for 5,500 hours. Separate overhead costs into variable and fixed components and show the amounts of any variances between actual and budgeted amounts. Label the report a cost performance report.

Calculate variances

26–35A The following summary data relate to the operations of Monona Company for April, during which 4,500 finished units were produced:

	Standard Unit Costs	Total Actual Costs
Direct Material:		
Standard (0.6 lb @ $6/lb)	$ 3.60	
Actual (3,000 lb @ $6.25/lb)		$ 18,750
Direct labor:		
Standard (0.8 hr @ $8.50/hr)	6.80	
Actual (3,800 hr @ $8.30/hr)		31,540
Variable overhead:		
Standard (0.8 hr @ $5/hr)	4.00	
Actual		20,800
Fixed Overhead*:		
Standard (0.8 hr @ $15/hr)	12.00	
Actual		59,200
Total	$26.40	$130,290

*Fixed overhead budget is $60,000 at normal monthly capacity of 4,000 direct labor hours.

REQUIRED

Determine the following variances and indicate whether each is favorable or unfavorable:

(a) Material price variance and quantity variance.
(b) Labor rate variance and efficiency variance.
(c) Variable overhead spending variance and efficiency variance.
(d) Fixed overhead spending variance and volume variance.

Variances, entries, and income statement

26–36A A summary of Wolff Company's manufacturing variance report for June follows.

	Total Standard Costs (7,600 units)	Total Actual Costs (7,600 units)	Variances
Direct material	$ 44,080	$ 43,400	$ 680 Favorable
Direct labor	51,300	54,900	3,600 Unfavorable
Variable overhead	22,800	22,000	800 Favorable
Fixed overhead	68,400	73,000	4,600 Unfavorable
	$186,580	$193,300	$6,720 Unfavorable

Standard material cost per unit of product is 4 pounds at $1.45 each and standard direct labor cost is 0.75 hours at $9.00 per hour. Total actual material cost represents 31,000 pounds purchased at $1.40 per pound; total actual labor cost represents 6,000 hours at $9.15 per hour. Variable and fixed factory overhead rates are $4 and $12, respectively, per direct labor hour (based on a normal capacity of 6,000 direct labor hours or 8,000 units of product).

REQUIRED

(a) Calculate variances for material price and quantity, labor rate and efficiency, variable overhead spending and efficiency, and fixed overhead spending and volume.

(b) Prepare compound general journal entries to record standard costs, actual costs, and related variances for material, labor, and overhead.

(c) Prepare journal entries to record the transfer of all completed units to Finished Goods Inventory and the subsequent sale of 6,400 units on account at $40 each (assume no beginning finished goods inventory).

(d) Prepare a partial income statement (through gross profit on sales) showing gross profit based on standard costs, the incorporation of variances, and gross profit based on actual costs.

Variances and journal entries

26–37A Landover Company manufactures a single product and uses a standard costing system. The nature of its product dictates that material is used as purchased and no ending material or work in process inventories occur. Per-unit standard product costs are: material, $2 (one-half pound); labor, $9 (1.5 hours); variable overhead, $3 (based on direct labor hours); and fixed overhead, $12 (based on a normal monthly capacity of 12,000 direct labor hours and a fixed overhead budget of $96,000).

Landover Company accounts for work in process and finished goods inventories and cost of goods sold at standard cost and records each variance in a separate account. The following data relate to June, when 7,800 finished units were produced.

REQUIRED

(a) Assuming that 4,200 pounds of material purchased on account at $3.70 per pound were used in June's production, present a compound journal entry to record actual costs, standard costs, and any material variances.

(b) Assuming that 12,000 direct labor hours were worked at an average hourly rate of $6.30, present a compound journal entry to record actual costs, standard costs, and any labor variances.

(c) Assuming that actual variable overhead was $23,100 and that actual fixed overhead was $97,100, present a compound journal entry to record actual and standard overhead costs and any overhead variances.

(d) Set up T accounts for Work in Process, Finished Goods Inventory, and Cost of Goods Sold, and enter the amounts for requirements (a), (b), and (c). Assume that no beginning inventories exist, that all production was completed, and that all but 900 units were sold. Prepare and post journal entries to (1) record production completed and (2) record cost of goods sold at standard costs.

Variances, total overhead variances, and variance reconciliation

26–38A Champion Company planned to produce 10,000 units of its only product during the year. Champion established the following standard cost data for this product prior to the beginning of the year:

	Per Unit
Direct material (2 pounds at $5 per pound)	$10.00
Direct labor (1.5 hours at $9 per hour)	13.50
Variable overhead (1.5 hours at $4 per hour)	6.00
Fixed overhead (1.5 hours at $6* per hour)	9.00
Total standard cost per unit	$38.50

*Standard fixed overhead rate is computed by dividing total budgeted fixed overhead of $96,000 by 16,000 normal hours to yield a rate of $6 per hour.

The actual level of production was 9,000 units, with the following actual total costs incurred:

	Total Cost
Direct material (17,000 pounds at $5.20)	$ 88,400
Direct labor (14,000 hours at $8.90)	124,600
Variable overhead	53,500
Fixed overhead	97,100
Total actual cost	$363,600

The expected level of operations was 15,000 direct labor hours while the normal (multiyear average) level of operations was 16,000 direct labor hours.

REQUIRED

(a) Calculate the variances for material, labor, variable overhead, and fixed overhead.

(b) Show that the difference between total actual cost and total standard cost equals the sum of all the variances.

(c) Determine the total overhead variances if a three variance system is used.

BUSINESS DECISION PROBLEM

Highpoint Corporation has just hired Bill Swanson as its new controller. Although Bill has had little formal accounting training, he professes to be highly experienced, having learned accounting "the hard way" in the field. At the end of his first month's work, Bill prepared the following cost variance report:

Highpoint Corporation
Cost Variance Analysis
For the Month of June, 19XX

	Total Actual Costs	Total Budgeted Costs	Variances
Direct material	$108,315	$118,800	$10,485 Favorable
Direct labor	119,340	132,000	12,660 Favorable
Variable overhead	64,000	66,000	2,000 Favorable
Fixed overhead	185,000	187,000	2,000 Favorable
	$476,655	$503,800	$27,145 Favorable

In his presentation at Highpoint's month-end management meeting, Bill indicated that things were going "fantastically." "The figures indicate," he said, "that the firm is beating its budget in all cost categories." Bill's good news made everyone at the meeting happy and furthered his acceptance as a member of the management team.

After the management meeting, Susan Jones, Highpoint's general manager, asked you as an independent consultant to review Bill's report. Susan's concern stemmed from the fact that Highpoint has never operated as favorably as Bill's report seems to imply, and Susan cannot explain the apparent significant improvement.

While reviewing Bill's report, you are provided the following cost and operating data for June: Highpoint has a monthly normal capacity of 11,000 direct labor hours or 8,800 units of product. Standard costs per unit for its only product are: direct material, 3 pounds at $4.50 each; direct labor, 1.25 hours at $12 each; and variable and fixed overhead rates per direct labor hour of $6 and $17, respectively. During June, Highpoint produced 8,000 units of product using 24,900 pounds of material costing $4.35 each, 10,200 direct labor hours at an average rate of $11.70 each, and incurred variable overhead costs of $64,000 and fixed overhead costs of $185,000.

After reviewing Highpoint's June cost data, you tell Bill that his cost report contains a classic budgeting error, and you explain how he can remedy it. In response to your suggestion, Bill revises his report as follows:

	Total Actual Costs	Total Budgeted Costs	Variances
Direct material	$108,315	$108,000	$ 315 Unfavorable
Direct labor	119,340	120,000	660 Favorable
Variable overhead	64,000	60,000	4,000 Unfavorable
Fixed overhead	185,000	187,000	2,000 Favorable
	$476,655	$475,000	$1,655 Unfavorable

Bill's revised report is accompanied by remarks expressing regret at the oversight in the original report.

REQUIRED

In your role as consultant:

(a) Verify that Bill's actual cost figures are correct.

(b) Identify and explain the classic budgeting error that Bill apparently incorporated into his original cost report.

(c) Explain why Bill's revised figures could be considered deficient.

(d) Further analyze Bill's revised variances, isolating underlying potential causal factors. How do your analyses indicate bases for concern to management?

ANSWERS TO SELF-TEST QUESTIONS

1. (c) **2.** (b) **3.** (d) **4.** (a) **5.** (c)

27

CAPITAL BUDGETING

CHAPTER OBJECTIVES

1. Provide a basis for understanding the elements of capital budgeting (pp. 1045–46).
2. Discuss required rates of return and the time value of money (pp. 1046–49).
3. Illustrate the use of present value tables (pp. 1049–52).
4. Discuss and illustrate the determination of after-tax cash flows (pp. 1052–55).
5. Describe the net present value method of capital expenditure analysis (pp. 1055–59).
6. Describe the cash payback and average rate of return methods of capital expenditure analysis (pp. 1059–62).

Prediction is very difficult, especially about the future.

NIELS BOHR

Using accounting data in planning long-term investments in plant assets is known as **capital budgeting.** The term reflects the fact that for most firms the total costs of all attractive investment opportunities exceed the available investment capital. Thus management must ration, or budget, investment capital among competing investment proposals. In deciding which new long-term assets to acquire, management must seek investments that promise to optimize return on the funds employed.

Capital budgeting is most valuable for organizations in which managers are responsible for the long-run profitability of their area of concern and are therefore encouraged to develop new products and more efficient production processes. Firms often make their most capable employees responsible for capital budgeting decisions, because such decisions determine how large sums of money are invested and commit the firm for extended future periods. Furthermore, investment decision errors are often difficult and costly to remedy or abandon.

Managers as well as accountants should be familiar with the special analytical techniques that evaluate the relative attractiveness of alternative uses of available capital. In this chapter, we first discuss the nature and procedures of capital budgeting, how required investment earning rates are determined, the time value of money, and the effect of income taxes on capital expenditure decisions. We conclude by illustrating three approaches to capital expenditure analysis: the *net present value method*, the *cash payback method*, and the *average rate of return method*.

ELEMENTS OF CAPITAL BUDGETING

Many firms have a capital budgeting calendar calling for consideration of capital expenditure proposals at regular intervals—for example, every six months or a year. Proposals are usually examined with respect to (1) compliance with capital budget policies and procedures; (2) aspects of operational urgency, such as the need to replace critical equipment; (3) established criteria for minimum return on capital investments; and (4) consistency with the firm's operating policies and long-run goals. Proposals for relatively small cash outlays may require the approval of low-level management only, whereas comprehensive proposals are subject to approval at high management levels, perhaps including the board of directors. These comprehensive proposals and the decisions based on them profoundly affect a firm's long-run success.

Once approved, capital expenditures should be monitored to ensure that amounts and purposes are consistent with the original proposal. At appropriate intervals, the actual rates of return earned on important expenditures should be compared with projected rates. These periodic reviews encourage those responsible to formulate thorough and realistic proposals, and often provide an incentive for improving overall capital budgeting procedures.

CAPITAL EXPENDITURE ANALYSIS

The scope of capital expenditures varies widely, ranging from the routine replacement of production equipment to the construction of entire factory complexes. Whatever their size, most capital expenditure projects have the following three recognizable stages:

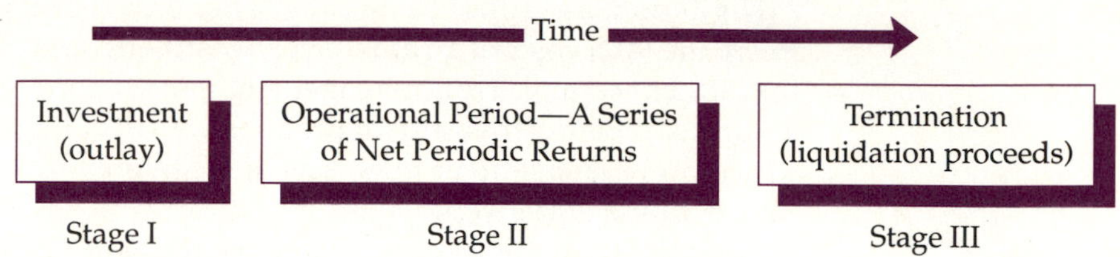

Investment (stage I) consists of the net cash outlay for a project or an asset. Net periodic returns during the life of the project (stage II) may result from either an excess of periodic revenue over related expenses or a periodic saving in some expense. Finally, because most efficient firms replace capital equipment before it becomes worthless, the termination of a project (stage III) often results in some amount of liquidation proceeds.

The attractiveness of a particular investment is determined in large part by the quantitative relationship between the investment in stage I and the receipts expected in stages II and III. This relationship is usually expressed as a ratio known as the *rate of return*:

$$\text{Rate of Return} = \frac{\text{Returns}}{\text{Investment}}$$

All other things being equal, the greater the expected rate of return, the more attractive the investment opportunity. Proposed investments can be ranked according to their expected rates of return, and capital outlays can be allocated among the most attractive investments. In its simplest terms, capital expenditure analysis consists of judging the attractiveness of income-producing or cost-saving opportunities in relation to required investments. The results of this analysis are among the most important input data in capital budgeting decisions.

Three questions of considerable concern in capital budgeting are:

1. How do we determine an acceptable rate of return for a given project?
2. How can we meaningfully compare investments made now with returns to be received in the future?
3. In what terms should investments and returns be measured?

These challenging problems are considered in the following sections of this chapter.

REQUIRED RATES OF RETURN

In determining an acceptable rate of return for a given project, we must consider not only the required capital outlay, but also the costs associated with the acquisition of that capital. The parties providing the funds expect to be reasonably compensated for their use. When the money is borrowed (usually through a bond issue), the interest paid by the firm is a cost of using the funds. When stockholder funds are used, we assume that some combination of dividend payments and increase in the value of the capital stock compensates stockholders for furnishing the investment capital. The cost to the firm of acquiring the funds used in capital investment projects—typically expressed as an annual percentage rate—is called the **cost of capital.**

Determining the actual cost of capital for a firm may require complex calculations, and even well-informed authorities in finance disagree about certain aspects of these calculations. Many firms use an approach that distinguishes among the various sources of financing.

A firm may acquire capital by issuing preferred or common stock, using retained earnings, borrowing, or some combination of these. Consequently, the overall cost of capital for a given project may reflect the cost rates of the several sources of funds in proportion to the amounts obtained from each source. This situation has led to the concept of the **weighted average cost of capital,** illustrated as follows.

Assume that a particular company had acquired capital through all four sources, in the proportions indicated below and with the cost of capital rates as shown.

Source of Capital	Percentage of Total	×	Cost of Capital Rate	=	Weighted Average Cost of Capital Component
Debt	40%		8%		3.2%
Preferred stock	10		9		0.9
Common stock	20		12		2.4
Retained earnings	30		12		3.6
	Weighted average cost of capital				10.1%

Multiplying the percentage of each capital source by its cost of capital rate provides weighted cost factors whose sum is the weighted average cost of capital. This percentage (in this case, 10.1%) can then be used to compare the attractiveness of proposed investments.

Logically, for a capital investment to be considered favorably by a firm, its expected rate of return must be *at least as great* as the cost of capital. Therefore, *the cost of capital represents a minimum required rate of return*. In other words, a firm whose cost of capital is 10% will ordinarily want to invest only in an asset or project whose expected rate of return is greater than 10%. An investment whose return is less than the cost of capital would be economically detrimental, although firms sometimes disregard their cost of capital if qualitative considerations override the quantitative aspects of the decision. Qualitative considerations might include the desire to achieve certain environmental goals, the desire to maintain research leadership in the field, and the need to maintain full employment of the work force during a business slowdown.

Some firms only consider investments whose rates of return are at least a certain number of percentage points higher than the cost of capital. This **buffer margin** acts as a safety factor, because proposals, which rely heavily on estimates of costs and future returns, may involve what will prove to be an erroneous estimated rate of return. Of course, even proposals whose expected rate of return is higher than the **cutoff** or **hurdle rate** (Cost of Capital + Buffer Margin) may be rejected if other investment opportunities offer still higher returns.

THE TIME VALUE OF MONEY

We have seen that in determining the desirability of a proposed capital investment, management compares the amount of investment required at the beginning of a project with its expected returns—typically a series of returns extending several years into the future. This comparison, which is so important in capital outlay decisions, cannot be made properly using the absolute amounts of the future returns because *money has a time value*. As discussed in Appendix B to Chapter 17, the **time value of money** means that the right to receive an amount of money today is worth more than the right to receive the same amount at some future date, because a current receipt can be invested to earn interest over the intervening period. Thus, if 10% annual interest can be obtained on investments, $100 received today is equal in value to $110 received one year from now. Today's $100 has a *future value* of $110 one year from now; conversely, the *present value*[1] of a $110 receipt expected one year from today is $100.

The difference between present and future values is a function of interest rates and time periods. The greater the interest rate or time period involved, the greater the amount by which a future value is reduced, or *discounted*, in deriving its present value. For example, Exhibit 27–1 shows just how significant the time value of money can be at various interest rates and time periods. As the table indicates, $100 five years from now has a present value of $78, $62, or $40 if the applicable interest rates are 5%, 10%, and 20%, respectively. Note also that the greater the time period or the interest rate, the greater the difference between the future value of $100 and its present value. Comparing a current investment with its future returns without discounting the returns to their present value would substantially overstate the economic significance of the returns. We must, therefore, recognize the time value of money in capital budgeting procedures.

We should also recognize that techniques for discounting future cash flows

[1]Students not familiar with present values may wish to review the present value discussion in Appendix B.

EXHIBIT 27–1

PRESENT VALUE OF $100 DISCOUNTED FOR YEARS AND INTEREST RATES SHOWN (ROUNDED TO NEAREST DOLLAR)

Years Discounted	5%	10%	20%
1	$95	$91	$83
2	91	83	69
3	86	75	58
4	82	68	48
5	78	62	40
10	61	39	16
20	38	15	3
30	23	6	—
40	14	2	—
50	9	1	—

KNOWN CUTOFF RATES: YES OR NO?

At least once a year, the senior executives and directors of many corporations address the problem of establishing a capital spending budget and selecting the projects that will be undertaken during the following year. The usual practice is for proposals to be submitted up through the organization; top management selects the most promising proposals, and the directors approve the selection. Some projects are selected for economic reasons; other selections are largely based on nonfinancial considerations such as environmental compliance.

Regardless of the common threads of this process, considerable controversy surrounds the appropriate methodology to be applied to the selection. One of the focal points of this controversy is the determination of capital spending hurdle rates: Should they even be used, and if so, how should they be calculated?

A survey of 136 companies by The Conference Board showed that 62 companies (46%) do not specify minimum cutoff rates for their capital investments. These proportions correspond with my own experience. Many companies do not establish capital spending hurdle rates for three reasons:

1. Management wishes to reserve the prerogative of determining which proposals should be accepted and which should be turned down or referred. They do not wish to discourage the submission of any capital proposals. However, all proposals should be ranked in the order of their desirability.
2. It is difficult to determine what "cutoff" or "hurdle rate" should apply, as risks, capital costs, and strategic considerations vary among projects. Moreover, some projects should be considered on a noneconomic basis.
3. If a hurdle rate is made known to operating management, the figures used in proposals may be "massaged" to pass this rate rather than present the project on an objective basis.

There is merit to the point of view of not using hurdle rates. Good proposals should indeed not be discouraged, particularly those that cannot be supported on a strictly financial basis. It *is* difficult to determine the cost of capital and the impact of risks. Simplistic, arbitrary rates are not a solution either, and operating management *will* tend to play games with capital proposals if hurdle rates are known.

However, not establishing cutoff rates imposes some important disadvantages. Operating managers are not informed about the basic economics of the business. The absence of information encourages the submission of proposals that do not support these economics. It is akin to asking managers to prepare budgets without budget guidelines or objectives, or marketing managers to set selling prices without cost information. Each individual is left to his own devices without any common focus or sense of direction. Unofficial yardsticks as to "what will fly" often emerge from this vacuum. Such yardsticks are communicated through the grapevine and are as apt to provide misinformation as they are to constructively assist with the capital spending proposal and selection process.

From Allen H. Seed, III, "Structuring Capital Spending Hurdle Rates," *Financial Executive*, February 1982, pp. 20–21. Reprinted by permission of Financial Executives Institute.

to their present values apply to both cash receipts and cash outlays. In other words, the current value of the *right to receive*—or the current value of the *obligation to pay*—a sum in the future is its present value computed at an appropriate interest rate. Of course, we maximize our economic position by arranging to receive amounts as early as possible and postponing amounts to be paid as long as possible. The intrinsic role of these generalizations is apparent in the capital budgeting illustrations later in the chapter.

USING PRESENT VALUE TABLES

Widely available present value tables simplify our work considerably in computing present values. Tables I and II give the present values of $1 for a number of rates and time periods. The amounts in these tables are called **present value factors,** or **discount factors,** because we convert any given cash flow to its present value by multiplying the amount of the cash flow by the appropriate factor.

Single Sum Flows

Table I gives present value factors for amounts received in a single sum at the end of a specified number of periods. We use Table I to determine the present value of sporadic cash flows—when the returns expected on an investment, or the expenditures it requires, are unequal amounts or are expected at irregular intervals during or at the end of the life of the investment.

To illustrate the use of Table I, we assume that an investment project promises a return of $2,000 at the end of two years and another $1,000 at the end of five years. The desired rate of return is 10%. The factor in the 10% column of the table for two periods from now is 0.826; the factor for five periods from now is 0.621. The total present value of the combined flows is $2,273, calculated as follows:

Future Receipts			PV Factor		Present Value
2 years from now	$2,000	×	0.826	=	$1,652
5 years from now	1,000	×	0.621		621
					$2,273

TABLE I

PRESENT VALUE OF $1 RECEIVED IN THE FUTURE

Periods Hence	Rate per Compounding Period 5%	6%	8%	10%	12%	15%	20%
1	0.952	0.943	0.926	0.909	0.893	0.870	0.833
2	0.907	0.890	0.857	0.826	0.797	0.756	0.694
3	0.864	0.840	0.794	0.751	0.712	0.658	0.579
4	0.823	0.792	0.735	0.683	0.636	0.572	0.482
5	0.784	0.747	0.681	0.621	0.567	0.497	0.402
6	0.746	0.705	0.630	0.564	0.507	0.432	0.335
7	0.711	0.665	0.583	0.513	0.452	0.376	0.279
8	0.677	0.627	0.540	0.467	0.404	0.327	0.233
9	0.645	0.592	0.500	0.424	0.361	0.284	0.194
10	0.614	0.558	0.463	0.386	0.322	0.247	0.162
11	0.585	0.527	0.429	0.350	0.287	0.215	0.135
12	0.557	0.497	0.397	0.319	0.257	0.187	0.112
13	0.530	0.469	0.368	0.290	0.229	0.163	0.093
14	0.505	0.442	0.340	0.263	0.205	0.141	0.078
15	0.481	0.417	0.315	0.239	0.183	0.123	0.065

Note: A more complete table is presented on page 628.

Annuity Flows

We can compute the present value of a single cash flow sum—or any combinations of single sums—using Table I. Cash flows that are the same each period over two or more periods are an annuity, and using an annuity table is more convenient. Generally, annuity tables are cumulative versions of single sum tables. Table II, for example, is an annuity table based on present value factors from Table I.

To illustrate, we assume a project has expected cash inflows of $1,000 at the end of each of the next three periods, and 8% is the appropriate interest rate. Using Table I, we compute the total present value as the sum of three individual amounts, as shown below:

Periods Hence	Cash Inflows		PV Factor (Table I @ 8%)		Present Value
1	$1,000	×	0.926	=	$ 926
2	1,000	×	0.857	=	857
3	1,000	×	0.794	=	794
					$2,577

Alternatively, using Table II, we need only multiply the periodic cash flow by a single present value factor for three periods at 8%.

TABLE II

PRESENT VALUE OF $1 ANNUITY RECEIVED AT END OF EACH PERIOD

Periods Hence	Rate per Compounding Period						
	5%	6%	8%	10%	12%	15%	20%
1	0.952	0.943	0.926	0.909	0.893	0.870	0.833
2	1.859	1.833	1.783	1.736	1.690	1.626	1.528
3	2.723	2.673	2.577	2.487	2.402	2.283	2.106
4	3.546	3.465	3.312	3.170	3.037	2.855	2.589
5	4.330	4.212	3.993	3.791	3.605	3.352	2.991
6	5.076	4.917	4.623	4.355	4.111	3.784	3.326
7	5.786	5.582	5.206	4.868	4.564	4.160	3.605
8	6.463	6.210	5.747	5.335	4.968	4.487	3.837
9	7.108	6.802	6.247	5.760	5.328	4.772	4.031
10	7.722	7.360	6.710	6.145	5.650	5.019	4.192
11	8.306	7.887	7.139	6.495	5.988	5.234	4.327
12	8.863	8.384	7.536	6.814	6.194	5.421	4.439
13	9.394	8.853	7.904	7.103	6.424	5.583	4.533
14	9.899	9.295	8.244	7.367	6.628	5.724	4.611
15	10.380	9.712	8.560	7.606	6.811	5.847	4.675

Note: A more complete table is presented on page 629.

Periods Hence (in annuity)	Periodic Cash Inflow		PV Factor (Table II @ 8%)		Present Value
3	$1,000	×	2.577	=	$2,577

Note that the present value factor for Table II is applied to the periodic cash flow of $1,000, not to the $3,000 total amount of cash flows in the annuity.

The advantage of Table II is that a single present value factor is provided for two or more equal amounts occurring evenly throughout a series of periods. When analyzing investments involving extended series of equal cash flows, the savings in computational effort can be significant.

Tables I and II both assume that all cash flows occur at the end of the periods shown. This assumption is somewhat simplistic, because cash receipts or cost savings from most industrial investments occur in a steady stream throughout the operating period. Nevertheless, businesses use such tables principally because of their availability and ease of use. These tables will understate present values of flows that are gradual throughout the period, because the present values of cash flows early in the period are greater than similar inflows or outlays at the end of the period. The difference in the factors, however, is normally not material.

MEASUREMENT OF INVESTMENTS AND RETURNS

When present value analysis is used to make investment decisions, investments and returns must be stated in the form of *cash* flows. Present value determinations are basically interest calculations, and therefore only money amounts—cash flows—are properly used in interest calculations. Furthermore, only the *incremental cash flows* that will occur if the project is accepted should be considered in the analysis.

Typically, financial data available in the accounts are not stated in terms of cash flows because accrual basis accounting is used. Amounts compiled on the accrual basis must be restated to the appropriate cash flows for capital budgeting purposes.[2] For example, apportioning the cost of an asset over its life through depreciation accounting is an important feature of accrual accounting. When present value analysis is used, the cost of an asset is treated as a cash outlay when the asset is paid for. In measuring future returns related to the asset, depreciation expense is irrelevant because it does not represent a cash outlay. However, depreciation provisions affect cash flows indirectly by reducing cash outlays for income tax payments.

Likewise, earnings from projects should reflect the cash inflows rather than the revenue amounts computed using accrual accounting. The timing of the cash collections is important, too, because the essence of present value analysis is that cash received can be reinvested.

If specific accruals or deferrals are not material in amount, or if their amounts at the beginning and end of the period are roughly the same, they are often ignored in restating accrual basis amounts to cash flows. Ignoring the impact of accruals and deferrals in these instances will not adversely affect the capital budgeting analysis.

[2]Exhibit 19–3 (page 704) illustrates the process of converting accrual basis amounts to cash flows.

After-tax Cash Flows

Both federal and state income taxes are important to investment decisions; for many large companies, the combined federal and state income tax rate may approach 40%. Generally, income taxes reduce the economic significance of taxable receipts and deductible outlays. For example, assuming a 40% tax rate, a \$40,000 before-tax gain would increase taxable income by \$40,000 and income taxes by \$16,000 (40% × \$40,000), resulting in a \$24,000 after-tax gain. A \$15,000 before-tax expense would reduce taxable income by \$15,000 and income taxes by \$6,000 (40% × \$15,000), resulting in a \$9,000 after-tax expense. Because income tax rates can be substantial, management has a continuing responsibility to minimize the firm's income tax. After-tax cash flows are more relevant than before-tax cash flows because they represent the amounts available to retire debt, finance expansions, or pay dividends. For these reasons, investment decision analyses must be formulated in terms of after-tax cash flows.

Illustration of After-tax Cash Flows

Thinking in terms of after-tax cash flows represents a significant departure from the accrual-based accounting for revenue and expenses that dominates much of our earlier study of accounting. Exhibit 27–2 builds on the traditional income statement to illustrate (1) the conversion of net income to after-tax cash flows, (2) the confirmation of that amount as actual cash flows, and (3) the determination of the individual after-tax cash flow effects of receiving revenue, incurring cash expenses, and recording depreciation. An understanding of Exhibit 27–2 provides a basis for studying the comprehensive illustration of capital budgeting later in the chapter.

The highlighted area in Exhibit 27–2 is the traditional income statement, showing that revenue minus operating expenses and income taxes results in a net income of \$18,000. For simplicity, we assume revenue and cash expenses involve no significant accruals and that depreciation is the same on both the books and the tax return. Ordinarily, net income does not represent after-tax

EXHIBIT 27–2

ILLUSTRATION OF DETERMINING AFTER-TAX CASH FLOWS

		(A) Traditional Income Statement	(B) Income Statement Cash Inflows (Outflows)	(C) Individual After-tax Cash Inflow (Outflow) Effects
Cash revenue (Sales)		\$100,000	\$100,000	\$60,000
Cash operating expenses	\$60,000		(60,000)	(36,000)
Depreciation expense	10,000			4,000
Total operating expenses		70,000		
Pretax income		\$ 30,000		
Income tax expense at 40%		12,000	(12,000)	
Net income		\$ 18,000		
Add back depreciation		10,000		
After-tax cash flow		\$ 28,000	\$ 28,000	\$28,000

cash flows because depreciation expense—a noncash expense—is deducted to derive net income. As indicated in column A of Exhibit 27–2, to convert the $18,000 net income to an after-tax cash flow, we must add back the depreciation of $10,000, resulting in $28,000 of after-tax cash flow.[3] Present value computations are properly applied to this amount.

Column B of Exhibit 27–2 confirms the $28,000 amount of after-tax cash flow determined in column A. This is accomplished by simply listing the amounts in column A that constitute cash inflows (revenue of $100,000) and cash outflows (cash expenses of $60,000 and income tax payments of $12,000). Depreciation is excluded because it does not represent a cash payment.

Column C in Exhibit 27–2 illustrates the determination of the individual amounts of after-tax cash flows for each item on the income statement. We use this approach in the comprehensive illustration of capital budgeting appearing later in the chapter. Amounts in column C are determined as follows (again, a 40% income tax rate is assumed):

Receipt of $100,000 cash revenue: Receipt of $100,000 cash revenue would, by itself, increase taxable income by $100,000, adding $40,000 ($100,000 × 40%) to income taxes. The $60,000 after-tax cash inflow is the difference between the $100,000 cash revenue received and the related $40,000 increase in income taxes (a cash outflow).

Payment of $60,000 in cash operating expenses: Payment of $60,000 in cash operating expenses represents a deductible cash outflow that reduces taxable income by $60,000 and thus reduces income taxes by $24,000 ($60,000 × 40%). The $36,000 net cash outflow is the difference between the $60,000 actually paid out for expenses and the $24,000 of income tax payments avoided by virtue of the tax deductibility of the expenses.

Notice that *avoiding a cash outflow* has the same effect on net cash flows as a cash inflow. In other words, total net cash inflows can be increased by adding to cash inflows or by avoiding cash outflows.

Recording $10,000 of depreciation expense: Although depreciation expense is tax deductible, no related cash expenditure occurs during the period. The $10,000 deduction reduces taxable income $10,000 and income taxes $4,000 ($10,000 × 40%). Because the depreciation deduction results in avoidance of an outflow, its after-tax cash flow effect is that of a cash inflow. Depreciation expense and similar noncash expense deductions are often referred to as *tax shields* because they shield an equal amount of income from whatever income tax rate is applicable.

The depreciation amount that provides a tax shield is the depreciation deduction on the tax return. Tax depreciation deductions are governed by tax regulations and not by generally accepted accounting principles. Often the periodic tax depreciation will differ from depreciation expense on the income statement (in Exhibit 27–2 we assume the amounts are equal). When identifying the depreciation tax shield in capital budgeting analysis, then, it is important to use the depreciation amount on the tax return.

Combining the after-tax cash flow effect of each individual amount in column C again confirms that net cash inflows total $28,000. It is helpful to realize that the after-tax cash flow effect of cash receipts and cash expenses is derived

[3]If present, other amounts of noncash expenses—such as amortization of intangible assets and depletion of natural resources—are also added back.

by multiplying the before-tax amounts by (1 − income tax rate). In contrast, the after-tax cash flow effect of depreciation deductions is derived by multiplying the before-tax amounts by the tax rate. In our example

Cash revenue $100,000 × (1 − 40%)	=	$60,000
Cash expenses $60,000 × (1 − 40%)	=	(36,000)
Depreciation expense $10,000 × 40%	=	4,000
Net cash flow		$28,000

SUMMARY OF CONCERNS UNDERLYING CAPITAL BUDGETING

1. The typical investment pattern involves a present investment of funds resulting in anticipated returns, often extending years into the future.
2. The basic question in capital budgeting is whether present investments are justified by related future returns.
3. Because money has a time value, returns that occur in the future must be discounted to their present values for a proper comparison with present investments.
4. To use discounting (interest) calculations properly, we must state amounts in capital budgeting analyses in terms of cash flows.
5. Because income tax rates are substantial, capital budgeting analyses should be formulated in terms of after-tax cash flows.

In this chapter, we have presented a number of important aspects of capital budgeting as background for the review of several approaches to capital expenditure analysis. These background materials have focused on the analytical concept known as *net present value.* Accountants generally concede that the net present value approach is conceptually and analytically superior to the other two approaches that we illustrate—*cash payback* and *average rate of return.*

NET PRESENT VALUE ANALYSIS

The basic considerations of the **net present value method** are shown schematically in Exhibit 27–3. Referring to the items in the diagram, we can explain the steps in the net present value approach as follows:

❶ Determine in terms of incremental after-tax cash flows the amount of the investment outlay required.

❷ Estimate in terms of incremental after-tax cash flows the amounts and timing of future operating receipts or cost savings.

❸ Estimate any incremental after-tax liquidation proceeds to be received on termination of the project.

❹ Discount all future cash flows to their present value at an appropriate interest rate, usually the minimum desired rate of return on capital.

❺ Subtract the investment outlay from the total present value of future cash flows to determine *net* present value. If net present value is zero or positive (returns equal or exceed investment), then the project's rate of return equals or exceeds the minimum desired rate and should be accepted. Negative net

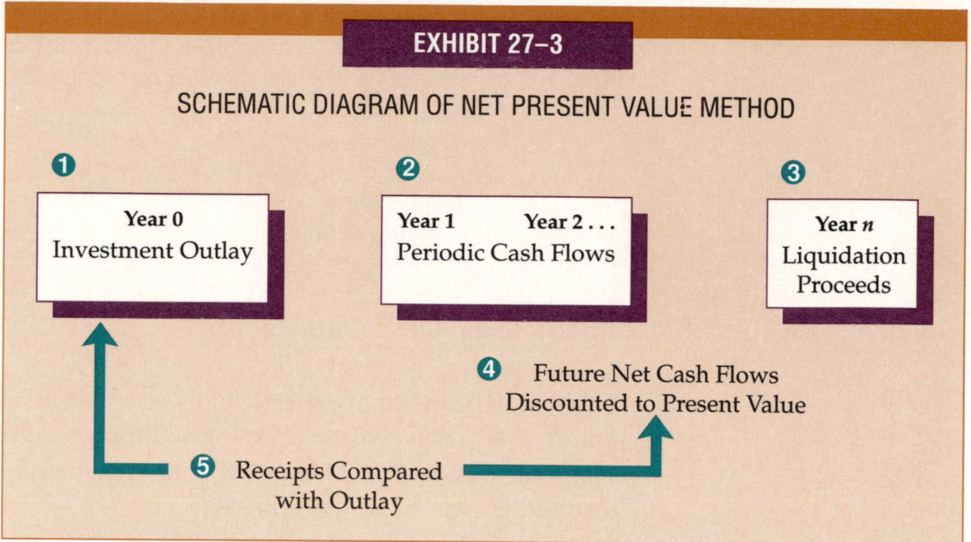

present values indicate that the project's return is less than desired and the project should be rejected.

To illustrate net present value analysis, assume that, with a minimum desired return of 10%, a glass manufacturer is considering the purchase of a $12,000 special shipping rack that will save $5,000 annually in cash operating expenses; have a useful life of three years; be depreciated over three years on the tax return—$2,400 in year 1, $4,800 in year 2, and $4,800 in year 3; and be sold for $2,000 at the end of the third year. Also, assume that all income and gains are taxed at 40%.

Exhibit 27–4 presents a net present value analysis of the shipping rack as an investment project. Note how the format follows the schematic analysis presented in Exhibit 27–3: future returns are stated in terms of after-tax cash flows; then, from Tables I and II, the present values of future cash flows are determined and compared with the investment. The computations shown in Exhibit 27–4 are explained below.

Annual cash expense savings: Cash savings or expense reductions have the same effects as cash revenue, income, or gains. Of course, they also have the same consequence of increasing income taxes. In our example, saving $5,000 in cash expenses each year raises taxable income by $5,000, which leads to a $2,000 ($5,000 × 40%) increase in taxes. Thus, the annual after-tax cash flow is $3,000—the $5,000 savings less the $2,000 tax increase. The $3,000 saved each year for three years can be treated as an annuity. Its present value factor of 2.487 is taken from Table II on the line for three periods and the column for 10% (the minimum return desired). The analysis shows that, with desired return at 10% and income taxes at 40%, saving $5,000 annually for the next three years has a present value of $7,461.

Annual depreciation tax shield: The depreciation deduction on the tax return shields an equal amount of income from taxes. The avoided taxes are equal to the depreciation deduction multiplied by the applicable tax rate. In our illustration, the annual tax savings from the depreciation tax shield are as follows:

EXHIBIT 27–4

ILLUSTRATION OF NET PRESENT VALUE ANALYSIS: AFTER-TAX CASH FLOWS (ROUNDED TO NEAREST DOLLAR)

Analysis of After-tax Cash Flows		Present Value Factors at 10% (Table I or II)	Total Present Value	Projected After-tax Cash Flows Year 0	Year 1	Year 2	Year 3
Annual Cash Expense Savings:							
Annual cash expense saving	$5,000						
Less income tax @ 40%	2,000						
After-tax expense savings	$3,000	(II) 2.487	$ 7,461		$3,000	$3,000	$3,000
Tax Savings from Depreciation Tax Shield:							
Year 1: $2,400 x 40% =	$ 960	(I) 0.909	873		960		
Year 2: $4,800 x 40% =	$1,920	(I) 0.826	1,586			1,920	
Year 3: $4,800 x 40% =	$1,920	(I) 0.751	1,442				1,920
Liquidation Proceeds:							
Sales price of rack	$2,000						
Tax book value (original cost of $12,000 less accumulated depreciation of $12,000)	–0–						
Gain on sale	$2,000						
Income tax on gain @ 40%	800						
After-tax proceeds of sale	$1,200	(I) 0.751	901				1,200
Total present value of future cash flows			$12,263				
Investment required in rack			(12,000)	($12,000)*			
Net positive present value			$ 263				

*Outflow

Year	Depreciation		Tax Rate		Tax Savings
1	$2,400	×	40%	=	$ 960
2	4,800	×	40%	=	1,920
3	4,800	×	40%	=	1,920

The tax savings represent tax payments that are avoided. In analyzing cash flows, tax savings are treated as having an effect similar to that of cash inflows. Present value factors from Table I are used to determine that the present values of these tax savings are $873, $1,586, and $1,442, respectively, for each of the three years.

Liquidation proceeds: The amount realized when an asset is liquidated contributes to the relative attractiveness of an investment in capital equipment. Liquidation proceeds on long-lived assets are sometimes disregarded because their occurrence is so far in the future that the amounts are difficult to predict, and their present values tend to be small. When useful lives are short, however, liquidation proceeds may be a deciding factor in the analysis. In our illustration, the shipping rack costing $12,000 is sold after three years for $2,000. For tax purposes, salvage value may be ignored in computing depreciation, so the machine is fully depreciated over the three years to a zero book value. The rack's sale for $2,000, then, creates a $2,000 gain on the tax return ($2,000 sales price − $0 tax book value). The $2,000 gain increases income taxes by $800, which is deducted from the sales price of $2,000 to produce a net after-tax cash flow of $1,200. Because the $1,200 is a single sum received at the end of year 3, its present value of $901 is derived by multiplying the $1,200 by the 0.751 factor from Table I (three periods hence at 10%).

If an asset is sold before the end of its tax depreciation period, a loss may be generated for tax purposes. The loss operates as a tax shield because it shields an equal amount of income from taxes. To illustrate the calculation of cash flows related to a loss sale, assume that the machine was sold after two years for $3,200. The total after-tax cash flow is computed as follows:

Tax book value of machine ($12,000 original cost − $7,200 accumulated depreciation)	$4,800
Less sales price of machine	3,200
Loss on sale	$1,600
Income tax rate	× .40
Income tax savings from loss	$ 640
Plus sales price of machine	3,200
Total after-tax cash flow from sale	$3,840

Required investment: Proper consideration of the required investment involves neither an income tax nor a present value calculation. The $12,000 investment itself is not tax deductible; the related depreciation deductions are tax deductible, and are, of course, incorporated into our analysis. Since the investment expenditure is immediate, no discounting for present value is required. Thus, $12,000 represents the after-tax present value of the required investment outflow.

DECISION RULE With its annual savings of cash expense, tax savings from the depreciation tax shield, and liquidation proceeds, the $12,000 investment results in future cash flows with a total present value of $12,263 and therefore a net present value of $263. This return on the capital invested, adjusted for the time value of money, exceeds the 10% return rate sought, and the investment is acceptable.

Another interpretation of our analysis is that as much as $12,263 could be paid for the machine and still attain the desired 10% rate of return. Paying more than $12,263 for the machine results in a return of less than 10%.

Excess Present Value Index

Alternative capital expenditure proposals may be compared in terms of their **excess present value index,** defined as

$$\text{Excess Present Value Index} = \frac{\text{Total Present Value of Future Cash Flows}}{\text{Initial Investment}}$$

For the investment presented in Exhibit 27–4, the excess present value index would be

$$\frac{\$12{,}263}{\$12{,}000} = 1.022$$

The higher the ratio of return on investment, the more attractive the proposal. Although the excess present value index may be a convenient measure for ranking various proposals, it does not reflect the amount of the investment. Two proposals, requiring initial cash investments of $5,000 and $5,000,000, respectively, could have identical excess present value indexes but could hardly be considered equal investment opportunities.

CASH PAYBACK ANALYSIS

The **cash payback method** is a form of capital expenditure analysis that evaluates investment proposals in terms of the cash payback period. The **cash payback period** is *the time in years that it takes net future after-tax cash inflows to equal the original investment.*

Assume that a firm is considering purchasing either machine A or machine B, for which the following data are given:

Machine	Investment Required	Estimated Annual Net After-tax Cash Inflows	Useful Life
A	$10,000	$2,500	8 years
B	15,000	5,000	3 years

If annual net cash inflows are *equal,* the cash payback period is computed as

$$\frac{\text{Original Investment}}{\text{Annual Net Cash Inflows}} = \text{Cash Payback in Years}$$

Thus, for the two machines, we obtain

$$\text{A:}\quad \frac{\$10{,}000}{\$2{,}500} = \text{4-year cash payback}$$

$$\text{B:}\quad \frac{\$15{,}000}{\$5{,}000} = \text{3-year cash payback}$$

This analysis shows that machine A will pay back its required investment in four years, and machine B will take only three years. Because the decision rule in cash payback analysis states that *the shorter the payback period the better,* machine B would be considered the better investment.

If annual net cash inflows are *not equal,* the cash payback period is computed by summing the annual cash inflows until the cumulative amount equals the initial investment. For example, assume a $14,000 investment in machine C is also being considered. The investment is expected to generate annual net after-tax cash inflows for six years, as follows:

Year	Estimated Annual Net After-tax Cash Inflows	Cumulative Cash Payback	
1	$3,000	$ 3,000	
2	4,000	7,000	
3	5,500	12,500	
4	6,000	14,000	(requires $\frac{1}{4}$ of $6,000
5	4,000		to reach $14,000)
6	2,500		

As shown in the cumulative cash payback column, the original investment in machine C will be recovered in cash one-fourth of the way through year 4. The cash payback period, then, is $3\frac{1}{4}$ years.

Concern for the payback of investments is quite natural because the shorter a project's payback period, the more quickly the funds invested in that project are recovered and available for other investments. In high-risk investments, the payback period indicates how soon a firm is "bailed out" of an investment should it prove unattractive.

The cash payback method is considered less sophisticated than net present value analysis. A primary limitation to cash payback analysis is that the *relative profitability of various investments is not specifically considered*. Note, for example, that in the foregoing illustration, machine B has the better (shorter) cash payback period. However, its useful life, which is ignored in cash payback analysis, indicates that machine B will stop generating cash inflows just when payback is completed. Consequently, there will be no opportunity to generate profit. In contrast, although machines A and C have longer payback periods they will generate future cash inflows for several years beyond payback and therefore promise to be profitable.

Regardless of its failure to consider profitability, cash payback analysis is widely used in industry, probably because of its relative simplicity. It can be useful in conjunction with other analyses or as a preliminary screening device for investment projects under consideration.

AVERAGE RATE OF RETURN ANALYSIS

Another approach to capital outlay analysis, the **average rate of return method,** relies heavily on accounting determinations of net income. This measure is calculated as

$$\text{Average Rate of Return} = \frac{\text{Average Annual Net Income from Investment}}{\text{Average Investment}}$$

Note that here the focus is not on after-tax cash flows but on traditional accounting net income (with depreciation deducted).

Assume machine D requires an initial investment of $48,000; provides $12,000 annual cash inflows from operations; and has a useful life of 12 years. Assuming no salvage value, annual straight-line depreciation on machine D would be ($48,000/12), or $4,000. With an income tax rate of 40%, the average annual net income from the investment would be $4,800, computed as follows:

Cash inflow from operations	$12,000
Depreciation expense	4,000
Pretax income from investment	$ 8,000
Income tax expense	3,200
Net income from investment	$ 4,800

Of course, if the annual net incomes from investment are unequal, we would compute the average annual net income from investment by (1) summing the annual net incomes and (2) dividing by the number of such incomes.

We may calculate average investment simply by adding the beginning and ending investments and dividing by 2. The ending investment is the expected salvage value. In our illustration, machine D has no salvage value, so the ending investment is zero. Average investment is therefore ($48,000 + $0)/2 = $24,000.

The average rate of return on machine D is

$$\frac{\$4,800}{\$24,000} = 20\%$$

The decision rule for average rate of return analyses states that *the higher the return, the more attractive the investment.*

As an approach to capital expenditure analysis, the average rate of return method is often defended as being most easily understood by management personnel who are accustomed to thinking in accounting terms and concepts. It has two major limitations, however. First, the calculations rely heavily on accounting computations of net income and depreciation, and are thus subject to arbitrary choices, such as the selection of a depreciation method. Second, average rate of return calculations do not consider the time value of money. Future cash flows are treated the same as current cash flows. Our discussion of net present value analysis amply illustrates the often substantial differences between future values and related present values discounted by even moderate interest rates.

As an example of how deceptive the average annual income figures used in average rate of return computations can be, consider three investment proposals that each require a $40,000 initial investment (with a zero salvage value) and promise the annual cash inflows shown in Exhibit 27–5. Note that cash flows

EXHIBIT 27–5

PRESENT VALUE COMPARISON OF EQUAL ANNUAL AVERAGE INCOMES

	Proposals A	B	C
Annual net cash inflows			
Year 1	$46,000	$10,000	$ 1,000
2	1,000	10,000	1,000
3	1,000	10,000	1,000
4	1,000	10,000	1,000
5	1,000	10,000	46,000
Aggregate net cash inflows	$50,000	$50,000	$50,000
Average annual net cash inflows	$10,000	$10,000	$10,000
Less depreciation ($40,000/5)	8,000	8,000	8,000
Average annual net income	$ 2,000	$ 2,000	$ 2,000
Average rate of return on investment $2,000/[($40,000 + $0)/2]	10%	10%	10%
Present value of net cash inflows at 10%:			
(A) One year hence, $45,000 x 0.909	$40,905		
5-year annuity of $1,000 x 3.791	3,791		
	$44,696		
(B) 5-year annuity of $10,000 x 3.791		$37,910	
(C) 5-year annuity of $1,000 x 3.791			$ 3,791
5 years hence, $45,000 x 0.621			27,945
			$31,736

are concentrated in year 1 in proposal A, are uniform in proposal B, and are concentrated in year 5 in proposal C. Because average rate of return calculations fail to consider the timing of cash flows from operations, these three proposals would have identical 10% average rates of return and therefore would be considered equally attractive. Such an implication is hardly defensible in view of the substantial differences in the relative net present values of the operating cash flows. In our illustration, the difference between the present values of A and C is $12,960, an amount equal to 41% of C's present value.

CAPITAL BUDGETING: AN INTRODUCTORY PERSPECTIVE

Because it incorporates aspects of such fields as economics, finance, business management, and accounting, the subject of capital budgeting is too complex to treat comprehensively in an introductory accounting book. In this chapter, we have simply provided some insight into problem-solving techniques in capital budgeting by stating decision rules in their simplest form, showing the relevance of present value concepts and after-tax cash flows, and creating an awareness of the potentials and limitations of several widely used approaches to capital expenditure analysis. The illustrations have highlighted key relationships. The rudiments presented here should serve as a basis for further study and an understanding of related subject areas.

KEY POINTS FOR CHAPTER OBJECTIVES

1 Provide a basis for understanding the elements of capital budgeting (pp. 1045–46).

- Capital budgeting is the planning of long-lived asset investments. Capital expenditure analysis basically examines how well prospective future returns justify related current investments.

2 Discuss required rates of return and the time value of money (pp. 1046–49).

- Cost of capital is a measure of the firm's cost for investment capital; it usually represents the minimum acceptable return for investment opportunities.
- The time value of money concept recognizes that the further into the future cash flows occur, the less current economic worth they have.

3 Illustrate the use of present value tables (pp. 1049–52).

- Present value tables enable us conveniently to convert future cash flows to their present values at appropriate interest rates.
- The present value tables used most frequently in capital budgeting are those for future single sum flows and end-of-period annuity flows.

4 Discuss and illustrate the determination of after-tax cash flows (pp. 1052–55).

- After-tax cash flows probably represent the most relevant measure of the prospective returns of proposed investments.
- We convert cash flows from revenues and expenses into after-tax amounts by multiplying them by (1 − income tax rate). We convert depreciation deductions into their after-tax cash flow effect by multiplying the deduction by the applicable income tax rate.

5 Describe the net present value method of capital expenditure analysis (pp. 1055–59).

- Net present value analysis compares the present value of net future cash flow returns with the investment. Projects having zero or positive net present value are acceptable.
- Alternative investment proposals may be compared in terms of their excess present value index; the higher the index, the more attractive the proposal.

6 Describe the cash payback and average rate of return methods of capital expenditure analysis (pp. 1059–62).

- Cash payback analysis measures the time in years necessary for the net future after-tax cash flows to equal the original investment. In this type of analysis, the shorter the payback period, the more attractive the investment.
- Average rate of return analysis compares the annual average net income with the average investment. The higher this ratio, the more attractive the investment.
- Cash payback analysis fails to consider the relative profitability of alternative projects. Average rate of return analysis fails to consider the time value of money.

KEY TERMS USED IN THIS CHAPTER

SELF-TEST QUESTIONS FOR REVIEW

(Answers are at the end of this chapter.)

1. The cost to a firm of acquiring the funds for capital investment projects is known as the
   (a) Payback period.
   (b) Rate of return.
   (c) Cost of capital.
   (d) Time value of money.
2. All other things remaining the same, when the interest rate used to discount future values increases, the present value amount will
   (a) Decrease.
   (b) Increase in proportion to the interest rate increase.
   (c) Remain the same.
   (d) Increase but not in proportion to the interest rate increase.
3. Although depreciation is a noncash expense, it does have an indirect effect on cash flows because it shelters an equal amount of income from income taxes. This feature is known as a
   (a) Buffer margin.
   (b) Cash payback.
   (c) Depreciation flow.
   (d) Tax shield.
4. Whistler Company is considering four investment proposals, each requiring the same amount of initial cash investment. The excess present value index for each proposal is listed below. Using the index as a selection criterion, identify the index of the most attractive proposal.
   (a) 90 (b) 100 (c) 110 (d) 115
5. The primary limitation of the cash payback method is that it
   (a) Uses before-tax cash flows.
   (b) Identifies the length of time it will take to recover the investment outlay in cash.
   (c) Ignores the profitability of one investment project as compared to another.
   (d) Involves a more sophisticated analysis than the net present value method.

DEMONSTRATION PROBLEM FOR REVIEW

Virlee Company is evaluating a possible $150,000 investment in equipment that would increase cash flows from operations for four years. The equipment will have no salvage value. The income tax rate is 30%. Virlee uses a 15% cutoff rate when using net present value analysis. Other information regarding the proposal is as follows:

	Year 1	Year 2	Year 3	Year 4
Cash inflow from operations (pretax)	$60,000	$87,000	$42,000	$40,000
Depreciation on tax return	50,000	67,000	22,000	11,000
Depreciation in financial statements	37,500	37,500	37,500	37,500
Net income from investment	15,750	34,650	3,150	1,750

REQUIRED

(a) What are the annual net after-tax cash inflows from this proposal?

(b) Compute the net present value and indicate whether it is positive or negative (round amounts to nearest dollar).

(c) Compute the cash payback period.

(d) Compute the average rate of return.

SOLUTION TO DEMONSTRATION PROBLEM

(a) We may compute the individual after-tax cash effects by multiplying (1) the cash inflow from operations by 70% (that is, 1 − income tax rate) and (2) the tax return depreciation by 30% (that is, the income tax rate). Combining the individual after-tax cash effects gives the annual net after-tax cash inflows.

Year 1:	$60,000 × 70% = $42,000		Year 3:	$42,000 × 70% = $29,400
	50,000 × 30% = 15,000			22,000 × 30% = 6,600
	After-tax cash flow $57,000			After-tax cash flow $36,000
Year 2:	$87,000 × 70% = $60,900		Year 4:	$40,000 × 70% = $28,000
	67,000 × 30% = 20,100			11,000 × 30% = 3,300
	After-tax cash flow $81,000			After-tax cash flow $31,300

Alternatively, we may compute the net after-tax cash inflows by subtracting the cash income tax payments from the cash inflows from operations. The annual cash income tax payments are 30% of the cash inflow from operations less the tax return depreciation.

	Year 1	Year 2	Year 3	Year 4
Cash inflow from operations	$60,000	$87,000	$42,000	$40,000
Cash payment for income taxes	3,000	6,000	6,000	8,700
After-tax cash flows	$57,000	$81,000	$36,000	$31,300

(b)

Year	Annual Net After-tax Cash Inflows		Table I Present Value Factors		Present Value
1	$57,000	×	0.870	=	$ 49,590
2	81,000	×	0.756	=	61,236
3	36,000	×	0.658	=	23,688
4	31,300	×	0.572	=	17,904
			Total present value		$152,418
			Investment required in equipment		150,000
			Net positive present value		$ 2,418

(c) The cash payback period is $2\frac{1}{3}$ years, computed as follows:

Year	Annual Net After-tax Cash Inflows	Cumulative Cash Payback	
1	$57,000	$ 57,000	
2	81,000	138,000	
3	36,000	150,000	(requires $\frac{1}{3}$ of $36,000 to reach $150,000)
4	31,300		

(d) Annual net income from investment:

Year 1	$15,750
Year 2	34,650
Year 3	3,150
Year 4	1,750
Total	$55,300

Average annual net income from investment: $55,300/4 = $13,825.
Average investment: ($150,000 + $0)/2 = $75,000.
Average rate of return: $13,825/$75,000 = 18.4%.

QUESTIONS

27–1 What is capital budgeting?

27–2 List three reasons why capital budgeting decisions are often important.

27–3 What are the three stages typical of most investments in plant and equipment?

27–4 Briefly describe the concept of *weighted average cost of capital.*

27–5 In what sense does the cost of capital limit a firm's investment considerations?

27–6 A company plans to accumulate 75% of its needed investment capital by issuing bonds having a capital cost percentage of 10%; the balance will be raised by issuing stock having a capital cost percentage of 14%. What would be the weighted average cost of capital for the total amount of capital?

27–7 Briefly describe the concept of the *time value of money*.

27–8 In which interest rate columns and periods hence lines in a table showing the present values of $1 received in the future would you expect the smallest factors? Why?

27–9 In which interest rate columns and periods hence lines in a table showing the present values of a $1 annuity would you expect the largest factors? Why?

27–10 What is the relationship between a table showing the present values of $1 and a table showing the present values of a $1 annuity, when both tables use the same interest rates and time periods?

27–11 You have the right to receive $20,000 at the end of each of the next four years, and money is worth 8%. Using Table II, compute the present value involved. Illustrate how Table I can be used to confirm your answer.

27–12 A rich uncle allows you to stipulate which of two ways you receive your inheritance: (a) $800,000 one year after his death or (b) $250,000 on his death and $190,000 each year at the end of the first, second, and third years following his death. If money is worth 10%, what is the relative advantage of the more attractive alternative?

27–13 You can settle a debt with either a single payment now of $60,000 or with payments of $16,000 at the end of each of the next five years. If money is worth 10%, what is the relative advantage of the most attractive alternative? If money is worth 12%, would your answer change? Why?

27–14 Explain how to convert before-tax cash operating expenses and depreciation deductions into after-tax amounts.

27–15 What is meant by the term *depreciation tax shield*?

27–16 What amounts are compared in net present value analysis? State the related decision rule.

27–17 What is an excess present value index?

27–18 Define *cash payback period*, state the related decision rule, and specify an important limitation of this analysis.

27–19 Define *average rate of return*, state the related decision rule, and specify an important limitation of this analysis.

EXERCISES

Weighted average cost of capital

27–20 Druland, Inc., plans to finance its expansion by raising the needed investment capital from the following sources in the indicated proportions and respective capital cost rates:

Source	Proportion	Capital Cost Rate
Bonds	45%	12%
Preferred stock	10	8
Common stock	25	10
Retained earnings	20	9
	100%	

Calculate the weighted average cost of capital.

Present value computations

27–21 (a) Assuming money is worth 10%, compute the present value of:
1. $6,000 received 15 years from today.
2. The right to inherit $2,000,000 14 years from now.
3. The right to receive $750 at the end of each of the next six years.
4. The obligation to pay $1,000 at the end of each of the next 10 years.
5. The right to receive $5,000 at the end of the seventh, eighth, ninth, and tenth years from today.

(b) Confirm your answer to part (a)(5) by using Table II and subtracting the present value of a six-year annuity from a ten-year annuity (isolating the four relevant years).

After-tax cash flows

27–22 For each of the following independent situations, compute the net after-tax cash flow amount by subtracting cash outlays for operating expenses and income taxes from cash revenue. The cash outlay for income taxes is determined by applying the income tax rate to the cash revenue received less the cash and noncash (depreciation) expenses.

	A	B	C
Cash revenue received	$75,000	$380,000	$180,000
Cash operating expenses paid	45,000	260,000	120,000
Depreciation on tax return	10,000	25,000	15,000
Income tax rate	30%	40%	20%

After-tax cash flows

27–23 Using the data in Exercise 27–22, (a) calculate—as shown in column C of Exhibit 27–2—the individual after-tax cash flow effect of each relevant item in each independent situation, and (b) sum the individual after-tax cash flows in each situation to determine the overall net after-tax cash flow.

Depreciation tax shields

27–24 Sample Company has purchased equipment for $100,000. After it is fully depreciated, the equipment has no salvage value. Sample may select either of the following depreciation schedules for tax purposes:

Year	Option 1 Depreciation	Option 2 Depreciation
1	$20,000	$10,000
2	32,000	20,000
3	19,200	20,000
4	11,520	20,000
5	11,520	20,000
6	5,760	10,000

Assuming a 40% tax rate and a 12% desired annual return, compute the total present value of the tax savings provided by these alternative depreciation tax shields. Which depreciation schedule would be more attractive to Sample?

Net present value analysis

27–25 Loral Company must evaluate two capital expenditure proposals. Loral's cutoff rate is 15%. Data for the two proposals follow.

	Proposal X	Proposal Y
Required investment	$80,000	$80,000
Annual after-tax cash inflows	16,000	
After-tax cash inflows at the end of years 3, 6, 9, and 12		48,000
Life of project	12 years	12 years

Using net present value analysis, which proposal is the more attractive? If Loral has sufficient funds available, should both proposals be accepted?

Cash payback

27–26 Refer to the data in Exercise 27–25. What is the cash payback period for proposal X? for proposal Y?

Average rate of return

27–27 Breen Company is considering the purchase of equipment for $120,000. The equipment will expand the company's production and increase revenue by $32,000 per year. Annual cash operating expenses will increase by $8,000. The equipment's useful life is ten years with no salvage value. Breen uses straight-line depreciation. The income tax rate is 35%. What is the average rate of return on the investment?

PROBLEMS

After-tax cash flows and present value factors

27–28 Below is a list of aspects of various capital expenditure proposals that the capital budgeting team of Bowman, Inc., has incorporated into its net present value analyses during the past year. Unless otherwise noted, the items listed are unrelated to each other. All situations assume a 40% income tax rate and a 15% minimum desired rate of return.

1. Pretax savings of $4,000 in cash expenses will occur in each of the next three years.
2. A machine is purchased now for $35,000 cash.
3. A long-haul tractor costing $18,000 will be depreciated $6,000, $8,000, $2,700, and $1,300, respectively, on the tax return over four years.
4. Equipment costing $200,000 will be depreciated over five years on the tax return in the following amounts: $25,000; $50,000; $50,000; $50,000; and $25,000.
5. Pretax savings of $8,500 in cash expenses will occur in each of the next six years.
6. Pretax savings of $6,000 in cash expenses will occur in the first, third, and fifth years from now.
7. The tractor described in aspect 3 will be sold after four years for $3,000 cash.
8. The equipment described in aspect 4 will be sold after four years for $20,000 cash.

REQUIRED

Set up an answer form with the four column headings as shown below. Answer each investment aspect separately. Prepare your calculations on a separate paper and key them to each item. The answer to investment aspect 1 is presented as an example.

Investment Aspect	(A) After-tax Cash Flow Effect(s) Inflows (Outflows)	(B) Year(s) of Cash Flow	(C) Applicable Present Value Multiple
1	$2,400	1, 2, 3	(II) 2.283

Calculations:

(1)	Pretax cash savings	$4,000
	Less income tax at 40%	1,600
	After-tax cash inflow	$2,400

(a) Calculate and record in column A the related after-tax cash flow effect(s). Place parentheses around outflows.

(b) Indicate in column B the timing of each cash flow shown in column A. Use 0 to indicate immediately and 1, 2, 3, 4, and so on for each year involved.

(c) When relevant, record in column C the present value multiple from Table I or II that you would apply to the cash flow amount shown in column A.

Net present value analysis

27–29 Tower Company is considering a contract that would require an expansion of its food processing capabilities. The contract covers five years. To provide the required products, Tower would have to purchase additional equipment for $64,000. Tower estimates the contract will provide annual net cash inflows (before taxes) of $24,500. For tax purposes, the equipment will be depreciated as follows:

Year 1	$ 8,000
Year 2	16,000
Year 3	16,000
Year 4	16,000
Year 5	8,000

Although salvage value is ignored in the tax depreciation calculations, Tower estimates the equipment will be sold for $6,000 after five years.

REQUIRED
Assuming a 35% income tax rate and a 15% cutoff rate, compute the net present value of this contract proposal. Using net present value analysis, should Tower accept the contract? (Round amounts to the nearest dollar.)

Net present value, cash payback, and average rate of return methods

27–30 Decker Company is evaluating a possible $84,000 investment in special tools that would increase cash flows from operations for four years. The tools will have no salvage value. The income tax rate is 40%. Decker uses a 12% cutoff rate when using present value analysis. Other information regarding the proposal is as follows:

	Year 1	Year 2	Year 3	Year 4
Cash inflow from operations (pretax)	$30,000	$40,000	$33,000	$24,000
Depreciation on tax return	28,000	37,000	13,000	6,000
Depreciation in financial statements	21,000	21,000	21,000	21,000
Net income from investment	5,400	11,400	7,200	1,800

REQUIRED
(a) What are the annual net after-tax cash inflows from this proposal?
(b) Compute the net present value and indicate whether it is positive or negative (round amounts to nearest dollar).
(c) Compute the excess present value index.
(d) Compute the cash payback period.
(e) Compute the average rate of return.

Excess present value index and average rate of return

27–31 Perrin Company is evaluating five different capital expenditure proposals. The company's cutoff rate for net present value analyses is 12%. A 10% salvage value is expected from each of the investments. Information on the five proposals is as follows:

Proposal	Required Investment	Present Value at 12% of After-tax Cash Flows	Average Annual Net Income from Investment
A	$135,000	$155,015	$18,700
B	100,000	118,390	13,000
C	80,000	86,520	9,600
D	90,000	108,150	13,800
E	64,000	68,495	7,480

REQUIRED
(a) Compute the excess present value index for the five proposals.
(b) Compute the average rate of return for the five proposals.

(c) Assume Perrin will commit no more than $250,000 to new capital expenditure proposals. Using the excess present value index, which proposals would be accepted? Using the average rate of return, which proposals would be accepted?

Cash payback, average rate of return, and net present value methods

27–32 Americana Amusement Park is considering the construction of a new facility to house a curved, multistory movie screen. The facility will cost $400,000 and be useful for ten years, with no salvage value. The facility will be depreciated on a straight-line basis over ten years on both the books and the tax return. The following annual results are expected if the facility is constructed:

Increase in annual cash revenue		$180,000
Increase in expenses:		
Cash operating expenses	$60,000	
Depreciation	40,000	100,000
Pretax income		$ 80,000
Income tax expense (40%)		32,000
Net income		$ 48,000

Americana uses a 15% cutoff rate when analyzing capital expenditure proposals using net present value.

REQUIRED

(a) What are the annual net cash flows (net inflows) from this project?
(b) Compute the cash payback period.
(c) Compute the average rate of return.
(d) Compute the net present value and indicate whether it is positive or negative.
(e) Assume Americana decides to use a 20% cutoff rate when using net present value analysis. Compute the net present value using a 20% cutoff rate and indicate whether it is positive or negative.

Weighted average cost of capital and net present value analysis

27–33 Hartwig Company is considering a proposal to acquire new equipment for its manufacturing division. The equipment will cost $96,000, be useful for four years, and have a $6,000 salvage value. Hartwig expects annual savings in cash operating expenses (before taxes) of $34,000. For tax purposes, the annual depreciation deduction will be $32,000, $43,000, $14,000, and $7,000, respectively, for the four years (the salvage value is ignored on the tax return). The income tax rate is 40%.

Hartwig establishes a cutoff rate for a net present value analysis at the company's weighted average cost of capital plus one percentage point. Hartwig's capital is provided in the following proportions: debt, 50%; common stock, 40%; and retained earnings, 10%. The cost rates for these capital sources are: debt, 10.6%; common stock, 11%; and retained earnings, 13%.

REQUIRED

(a) Compute Hartwig's (1) weighted average cost of capital and (2) cutoff rate.
(b) Using Hartwig's cutoff rate, compute the net present value of this capital expenditure proposal. Under net present value analysis, should Hartwig accept the proposal? (Round amounts to the nearest dollar.)

ALTERNATE PROBLEMS

After-tax cash flows and present value factors

27–28A Below is a list of aspects of various capital expenditure proposals that the capital budgeting team of Space Systems, Inc., has incorporated into its net present value analyses during the past year. Unless otherwise noted, the items listed are unrelated to each other. All situations assume a 30% income tax rate and a 20% minimum desired rate of return.

1. Pretax savings of $5,000 in cash expenses will occur in each of the next three years.
2. A machine is purchased now for $75,000.
3. Special tools costing $90,000 will be depreciated $18,000, $36,000, and $36,000, respectively, on the tax return over a three-year life.
4. A patent purchased for $420,000 will be amortized on a straight-line basis over 15 years on the tax return. No salvage value is expected.
5. Pretax savings of $7,000 in cash expenses will occur in each of the next seven years.
6. Pretax savings of $4,500 in cash expenses will occur in the first, fourth, and seventh years from now.
7. The special tools described in aspect 3 will be sold after three years for $20,000 cash.
8. A truck with a tax book value of $7,200 after two years will be sold at that time for $4,600.

REQUIRED

Set up an answer form with the four column headings as shown below. Answer each investment aspect separately. Prepare your calculations on a separate paper and key them to each item. The answer to investment aspect 1 is presented as an example.

Investment Aspect	(A) After-tax Cash Flow Effect(s) Inflows (Outflows)	(B) Year(s) of Cash Flow	(C) Applicable Present Value Multiple
1	$3,500	1, 2, 3	(II) 2.106

Calculations:

(1)	Pretax cash savings	$5,000
	Less income tax at 30%	1,500
	After-tax cash inflow	$3,500

(a) Calculate and record in column A the related after-tax cash flow effect(s). Place parentheses around outflows.
(b) Indicate in column B the timing of each cash flow shown in column A. Use 0 to indicate immediately and 1, 2, 3, 4, and so on for each year involved.
(c) When relevant, record in column C the present value multiple from Table I or II that you would apply to the cash flow amount shown in column A.

Net present value analysis

27–29A You have an opportunity to invest in a concession at a world exposition. To use the building and exhibits more fully, the venture is expected to cover a six-year period consisting of a preliminary year, the two years of formal exposition, and a three-year period of reduced operation as a regional exposition.

The terms of the concession agreement specify that:

1. At inception, a $50,000 deposit is paid to World Expo, Inc., the promoting organization. This amount is returned in full at the end of the six years if the operator maintains the concession in order and keeps it open during scheduled hours. The deposit is not tax deductible, nor is its return subject to income taxes.
2. The operator must install certain fixtures that will cost $150,000. The fixtures become the property of World Expo, Inc., at the end of the six years.

After careful investigation and consultation with local experts, you conclude that the following schedule reflects the estimated pretax income of the concession (amounts in thousands of dollars):

	Year 1	Year 2	Year 3	Year 4	Year 5	Year 6
Sales (all cash)	$100	$290	$325	$200	$160	$120
Operating expenses:						
Cash	$ 50	$152	$186	$113	$ 93	$ 71
Tax depreciation	30	48	29	17	17	9
Total expenses	$ 80	$200	$215	$130	$110	$ 80
Pretax income	$ 20	$ 90	$110	$ 70	$ 50	$ 40

REQUIRED
Assuming an income tax rate of 40% and a desired annual return of 15%, what is the net present value of this investment opportunity? What is the maximum amount that could be invested and still earn a 15% annual return?

Cash payback, average rate of return, and net present value methods

27–30A At a cash cost of $165,000, Mundt, Inc., can acquire equipment that will save $50,000 in annual cash operating expenses. No salvage value is expected at the end of its five-year useful life. Assume the machine will be depreciated over five years on a straight-line basis on both the books and the tax return. The income tax rate is 30% and Mundt has a 10% cutoff rate when using a net present value analysis.

REQUIRED
(a) What are the annual after-tax cash savings in operating expenses?
(b) What are the annual tax savings from the depreciation tax shield?
(c) Compute the cash payback period.
(d) Compute the average rate of return.
(e) Compute the net present value and indicate whether it is positive or negative (round amounts to nearest dollar).
(f) Compute the excess present value index.

Excess present value index and average rate of return

27–31A Calgary Corporation is evaluating five different capital expenditure proposals. The company's cutoff rate for net present value analyses is 15%. A 15% salvage value is expected from each of the investments. Information on the five proposals is as follows:

Proposal	Required Investment	Net Present Value	Average Annual Net Income from Investment
A	$25,000	$ 4,498	$ 4,550
B	40,000	2,906	6,000
C	55,000	13,517	9,150
D	75,000	3,772	10,750
E	36,000	7,911	6,980

REQUIRED
(a) Compute the excess present value index for the five proposals.
(b) Compute the average rate of return for the five proposals.
(c) Assume Calgary will commit no more than $100,000 to new capital expenditure proposals. Using the excess present value index, which proposals would be accepted? Using the average rate of return, which proposals would be accepted?

Cash payback, average rate of return, and net present value methods

27–32A Lowrey Company is considering whether to enter into a franchise agreement that would give the company exclusive distribution rights in a three-state region to a quality line of leisure spas. The franchise agreement will extend eight years and cost $300,000. There is no salvage value. The franchise cost will be amortized on a straight-line basis over eight years on both the books and the tax return. The following annual results are expected if the franchise is acquired:

Increase in annual cash revenue		$115,000
Increases in expenses:		
Cash operating expenses	$47,500	
Amortization	37,500	85,000
Pretax income		$ 30,000
Income tax expense (35%)		10,500
Net income		$ 19,500

Lowrey uses a 12% cutoff rate when analyzing capital expenditure proposals using net present value.

REQUIRED
(a) What are the annual net cash flows (net inflows) from this proposal?
(b) Compute the cash payback period.
(c) Compute the average rate of return.
(d) Compute the net present value and indicate whether it is positive or negative.
(e) Assume Lowrey decides to use a 10% cutoff rate when using net present value analysis. Compute the net present value using a 10% cutoff rate and indicate whether it is positive or negative.

Weighted average cost of capital and net present value analysis

27–33A Cornell Company is considering a proposal to purchase special equipment at a cost of $320,000. The equipment will be useful for five years and has an expected $30,000 salvage value. Cornell expects annual savings in cash operating expenses (before taxes) of $115,000. For tax purposes, the annual depreciation deduction will be as follows (salvage value is ignored on the tax return):

Year 1	$40,000
Year 2	80,000
Year 3	80,000
Year 4	80,000
Year 5	40,000

The income tax rate is 40%.

Cornell establishes a cutoff rate for a net present value analysis at the company's weighted average cost of capital plus two percentage points. Cornell's capital is provided in the following proportions: debt, 55%; common stock, 25%; and retained earnings, 20%. The cost rates for these capital sources are: debt, 12%; common stock, 13.2%; and retained earnings, 15.5%.

REQUIRED
(a) Compute Cornell's (1) weighted average cost of capital and (2) cutoff rate.
(b) Using Cornell's cutoff rate, compute the net present value of this capital expenditure proposal. Under net present value analysis, should Cornell accept the proposal?

BUSINESS DECISION PROBLEM

Nugent Corporation recently identified an investment opportunity involving the purchase of a patent that will permit the company to modify its line of videocassette recorders. The patent's purchase price is $360,000 and the legal protection it provides will last for five more years. There is no salvage value. However, after preparing the capital expenditure analysis below, Nugent's treasurer has recommended to Nugent's capital budgeting committee that the investment be rejected. Brad Saler, chairperson of the capital budgeting committee, finds it difficult to accept the treasurer's analysis because he "feels intuitively" that the investment is attractive. For this reason, he has retained you to review the treasurer's analysis and recommendation. You are provided with the following data and summary of the treasurer's analysis:

1. Required investment: $360,000 cash for the patent to be amortized on a straight-line basis, five-year useful life, with a zero salvage value.
2. Projected cash revenue and operating expenses:

Year	Cash Revenue	Cash Expenses
1	$ 310,000	$120,000
2	280,000	100,000
3	200,000	85,000
4	125,000	40,000
5	100,000	25,000
	$1,015,000	$370,000

3. Source of capital: Nugent plans to raise 10% of the needed capital by issuing bonds, 30% by issuing stock, and the balance from retained earnings. For these sources, the capital cost rates are 11%, 12%, and 13%, respectively. Nugent has a policy of seeking a return equal to the weighted average cost of capital plus two and one-half percentage points as a "buffer margin" for the uncertainties involved.
4. Income taxes: Nugent assumes an overall income tax rate of 30%.
5. Treasurer's analysis:

Average cost of capital (11% + 12% + 13%) ÷ 3 = 12%		
Total cash revenue		$1,015,000
Total cash expenses	$370,000	
Total amortization	360,000	
Total operating expenses		730,000
Projected net income over five years		$ 285,000
Average annual income ($285,000 ÷ 5)		$ 57,000
Present value factor of five-year annuity at 12%		× 3.605
Present value of future returns		$ 205,485
Required investment		360,000
Negative net present value		$ 154,515

Recommendation: Reject investment because of insufficient net present value.

REQUIRED

(a) Review the treasurer's analysis, identifying any questionable aspects and briefly commenting on the apparent effect of each such item on the treasurer's analysis.

(b) Prepare your own analysis of the investment, including a calculation of the proper cost of capital and cutoff rates, a net present value analysis of the project, and a brief recommendation to Saler regarding the investment (round amounts to nearest dollar).

(c) Because of his concern for the uncertainties of the videocassette recorder business, Saler also has asked you to provide analyses supporting whether or not your recommendation would change:
1. If estimates of projected cash revenue were reduced by 10%.
2. If the "buffer margin" were tripled from 2.5% to 7.5%.

ANSWERS TO SELF-TEST QUESTIONS

1. (c) **2.** (a) **3.** (d) **4.** (d) **5.** (c)

28

INCOME TAXES AND THEIR EFFECT ON BUSINESS DECISIONS

CHAPTER OBJECTIVES

1. Provide an understanding of the purpose and coverage of the tax law (pp. 1077–80).
2. Describe the format for determining tax liability for individuals (pp. 1080–88).
3. Discuss the nature and treatment of capital gains and losses (p. 1084).
4. Illustrate a complete individual tax computation (pp. 1088–90).
5. Describe and illustrate basic elements of corporate taxation (pp. 1091–94).
6. Discuss tax avoidance and related business decisions (pp. 1094–97).

The hardest thing in the world to understand is the Income Tax.

ALBERT EINSTEIN

Except for a brief period during Civil War, the United States had no federal income tax until 1913, when its constitutionality was confirmed by ratification of the Sixteenth Amendment. The numerous revenue acts passed since 1913 were first codified in 1939 and then recodified as the Internal Revenue Code of 1954. With the passage of the Tax Reform Act of 1986, another codification has resulted in the Internal Revenue Code of 1986. The federal income tax system is administered by the Internal Revenue Service, an agency of the Treasury department. Regulations interpreting the code are published from time to time by the IRS, but the ultimate interpretative authority lies with the federal court system, which adjudicates controversies between the IRS and taxpayers.

Of the many revenue acts passed in recent years, some of the most sweeping changes in the incidence of taxation on individuals and corporations were made in the Tax Reform Act of 1986. Some of the major purposes of this act were to shift more of the total tax burden to corporations, to exempt low-income taxpayers from income taxes, to simplify somewhat the computations of tax liability for individuals, to reduce the effectiveness of certain tax avoidance schemes (such as tax shelters), and in general, to produce a more equitable incidence of taxation. Recognize, however, that the tax laws will continue to change in the future, as a result of changes in the political and philosophical view of Congress and the executive branch.

The 1986 Tax Reform Act provided for certain transitional changes during the years following its enactment. For example, the consumer interest deduction is gradually phased out over a five-year period (see page 1083). In addition, the Act scheduled increases in the personal exemption amount (page 1084) through 1989, with the proviso that this amount will be indexed for inflation in 1990 and thereafter. Changes in the standard deduction amount (page 1082) were scheduled only through 1988; this amount is to be indexed for inflation in 1989 and thereafter. For simplicity, in our illustrations, questions, exercises, and problems, we will use the provisions pertaining to the 1989 taxable year whenever possible. For some items, especially where an inflation adjustment is to be made late in 1989 (standard deduction, rate schedule brackets for phasing out certain benefits for high-income taxpayers, and so on), we use 1988 amounts because the adjustments are not known at the time of this writing.

Because of the complexity of tax laws, many of the nation's taxpayers have turned to accountants, attorneys, and others for assistance in preparing their tax returns. These professional consultants may also help to arrange business and personal affairs to minimize tax liability. Few business decisions are made without first considering which possible alternatives judged consistent with the business objective have the most desirable tax effect. Indeed, when large amounts of money are involved, this factor is so important that many accountants and attorneys confine their practices to such special areas as estate planning, pension plans, wage and stock option plans, and reorganizations and mergers. Whether they call on professionals for assistance or not, taxpayers generally benefit from a basic understanding of the tax system structure and the options it provides.

PURPOSES OF THE TAX LAW

The primary purpose of the federal income tax laws is raising revenue to pay for the operations of the government. In addition to the primary revenue-producing purpose, many amendments to the Internal Revenue Code have been enacted for other purposes. Federal taxation has changed since 1913 in both purpose and magnitude. The income tax system has become an instrument of the government for economic and social policy.

Through its taxing powers, the government can attempt to distribute income more equitably, stimulate economic growth, combat inflation and unemployment, and finance projects it considers socially desirable. In addition, a number of changes in the tax laws are the result of political influences on Congress, which formulates tax laws. Thus multidimensional influences have contributed to the complexity of rapidly changing income tax laws. Because of these factors, the business manager must be keenly aware of the changing effect of income taxes on the business decision process.

CLASSIFICATION OF TAXPAYERS

The main entities that are recognized for purposes of federal income taxation are individuals, partnerships, corporations, and estates or trusts. Here we cover individuals, partnerships, and corporations, leaving estates and trusts to an advanced course.

Although they are business entities, sole proprietorships and partnerships are not taxable entities. The owners of such firms must include their shares of business income along with income from other sources in their respective individual tax returns. The allocable shares of their business income are taxed directly to them whether or not they have withdrawn such amounts. In conjunction with this requirement, each partnership must file an **information return** showing the results of the firm's operations and the respective shares of net income accorded to each partner.

As taxable entities, corporations are taxed directly on their earnings. Shareholders receiving distributions of earnings must include these amounts as dividend income on their individual returns. Although this practice has led to the allegation that corporate earnings are subject to "double taxation," it is generally conceded that the bulk of corporate taxes are passed on to the consumer in the long run.

Under Subchapter S of the Internal Revenue Code, certain corporations generally are not taxed but pass income and losses through to their owners like partnerships. Firms meeting the Subchapter S criteria are referred to as **S corporations.**

Because of the many technical differences between the tax computations for individuals and those for corporations, we consider them separately. Thus we first discuss the more salient features of individual income tax and then briefly cover some important features of corporate income tax. Keep in mind that the provisions of the tax laws relating to tax rates, exemption amounts, various prescribed limits, and other details have been changing rapidly and will continue to change.

THOSE TAXING DAYS OF FORM 1040'S INFANCY

If you're about to go crazy doing your federal income tax, just be thankful you weren't around in 1914. That was the first year that Americans had to fill out a Form 1040 after the income tax, or 16th Amendment to the Constitution, was ratified in February 1913. Everything was in a mess.

For one thing, Congress didn't pass the implementing legislation until Oct. 3, 1913, which meant that the handful of officials and clerks authorized by the act had too much to do in too short a time. No tax forms were available until Jan. 8, even though the deadline for submission was March 1. Individuals who planned to be out of the country for the first three months of the year were in a pickle. In fact, a couple of taxpayers simply filled in a sample form printed in their daily newspaper and mailed it before they left. The Internal Revenue people said that was legal, although not preferable. The situation was even worse for Americans living abroad. In Paris, for example, there was almost a storming of consular offices by Americans in search of forms.

The biggest problem was that the Internal Revenue regulations didn't answer all the questions that taxpayers had. "Is the allowance once made a son by his father exempt," wrote one man to his hometown newspaper, "assuming that the father has already paid a tax on this allowance as part of his income? Should presents of money," he went on, "such as Christmas or birthday presents, be included in a statement of income, and, if so, can exemption be claimed on such amounts? . . ." One of the most confusing provisions of Form 1040 was the exemption allowed husband and wife filing a joint return: some taxpayers interpreted the authorizing language to permit a $4,000 exemption for both; others saw it as $7,000 for both; and still others were certain that it meant $3,000 to each.

Hardly a day went by that the Treasury Department did not issue a clarifying interpretation. Yes, indeed, women were required to pay taxes even though they didn't have the vote; by all means, returns could be submitted in person until 6 p.m. Saturday, Feb. 28, but mail returns would be timely if received by Tuesday, March 3. As for married couples who were temporarily separated, the married exemption could be claimed provided their separation "was not due to family differences." When the Manhattan Internal Revenue office was besieged by taxpayers in mid-January over a rumor to the effect that certain exemptions and deductions would be lost if they weren't immediately claimed, its ruling did little to allay anxieties. By Feb. 21, the government threw up its hands, saying that no more clarifying statements would be issued before March 1.

Although only a tiny fraction of the population made enough money to pay the first federal tax, it was still bedlam as the deadline approached—so much so that Col. William H. Osborn, commissioner of Internal Revenue, extended the deadline to Monday, March 2, with local offices on that day staying open until midnight. Of course, his decision may well have been motivated by the fact that his boss, President Wilson, would not be ready to submit the three-page 1040 until that date.

Expectedly, there were numerous errors in the returns. But the Internal Revenue was scarcely precise about the extent of the problem: the range of errors, it announced, was from 30% to 80%. The most common problem involved the tax period covered by the return (March to December 1913), which meant that only five-sixths of income and deductions were to be reported.

A few months later at the National Tax Conference in Denver, experts raked the government's noble experiment with income taxes over the coals. Prof. Charles J. Bullock of Harvard said the tax law was patently discriminatory. "We now have a law," he argued, "that largely exempts holders of corporation securities from the ordinary tax and substantially exempts agricultural industry, while it taxes incomes derived from unincorporated manufacturing or commercial enterprise, and those received in the form of salaries and professional earnings." What was even worse, according to Bullock, were the excessive rates of taxation, rising to 6% on incomes of more than $500,000. "Now the limit of safety, for income taxes," said Bullock, "is probably 10%; and it certainly does not exceed 12. . . ."

A. C. Rearick of New York blamed the confusion of the first year on the taxing verbiage of the congressional act. "To begin with," he said, "the language in which the Act is couched is involved and its rhetoric bewildering. It contains sentences hundreds of words in length, in which clauses are added to clauses and provisos heaped upon provisos." To be sure, Rearick had a better idea. It was called "Simplification of the Federal Income Tax."

Thomas V. DiBacco, "Those Taxing Days of Form 1040's Infancy," *The Wall Street Journal*, March 28, 1985. Reprinted by permission of *The Wall Street Journal*,

TAXATION OF INDIVIDUALS

Generally, individuals who are citizens of the United States are taxed on all income from whatever source, unless it is specifically excluded by law. Thus the gross income reported in an individual's tax return consists of total income and gains *less exclusions*. Various deductions and exemptions are permitted to convert gross income to taxable income. Deductions and exemptions must be enumerated in the individual's return (Form 1040) or in supporting schedules.

Although the manner in which this information is detailed in the return varies, a basic, logical format guides the computation of taxable income and the related tax liability. This format, illustrated in Exhibit 28–1, describes the classifications used in the tax laws and is a useful frame of reference in compiling the information needed to prepare an individual's tax return.

Filing Status

There are basically five possible ways in which individuals may file tax returns: single taxpayer, married taxpayers filing jointly, married taxpayers filing separately, unmarried head of a household, and qualifying surviving spouse with a dependent child. When we refer to *individual* taxpayers in this chapter, we are referring to tax returns filed under these various categories. Tax rates, exemption amounts, and other provisions of the tax laws differ, depending on filing status. In this chapter we will focus mainly on the most prevalent types of returns: joint returns of married individuals, and single taxpayer returns.

EXHIBIT 28–1

FORMAT FOR DETERMINING
TAX LIABILITY OF INDIVIDUALS

Steps		Explanation
Determine:	Total Income	All income from whatever source
Less:	Exclusions	Items of income excluded by law (p. 1081)
Equals:	Gross Income	Income subject to tax (before deductions and exemptions)
Less:	Deductions from Gross Income	Business-related expenses, losses, and specific deductions from gross income (p. 1081)
Equals:	Adjusted Gross Income	Base for computation of limitations on some personal (itemized) deductions
Less:	Itemized Deductions or Standard Deduction	Itemized deductions permitted by law or standard deduction stipulated by law in lieu of itemized deductions (p. 1082)
	Personal Exemptions	An amount stipulated by law for taxpayer, spouse, and each dependent. The amount depends on filing status, and it is phased out at certain income levels (p. 1084)
Equals:	Taxable Income	Amount used to compute the tax from the appropriate tax rate schedule.
Results in:	Income Tax	Taxable income multiplied by appropriate tax rate
Less:	Tax Credits	Specified credits against the tax (p. 1087)
Equals:	Tax Liability	Amount of tax owed by the taxpayer

Gross Income

As shown in Exhibit 28–1, **gross income** is income from all sources, less allowable exclusions. Some of the most common types of income are wages, salaries, unemployment compensation, bonuses, fees, tips, interest, dividends, profits or shares of profits from business, pensions, annuities, rents, royalties, prizes, taxable gains on sales of property or securities, fellowships, and scholarships. The list also includes income from gambling, and even illegal income. (Racketeers and other criminals have often been more easily apprehended through income tax investigations than through regular criminal investigations.) Special rules and procedures apply to certain of these sources of gross income in determining the portion to be included.

Exclusions from Gross Income

Some items excluded by law from gross income include interest on certain state and municipal bonds; Social Security receipts;[1] gifts, bequests, and inheritances; worker's compensation for sickness or injury; certain disability benefits; life insurance proceeds received at the death of the insured; and the portion of scholarships or fellowships for degree candidates that is spent for tuition and course-required materials. (Amounts for room, board, or incidental expenses are not excludable.) The exclusions also exempt amounts of pensions and annuities that are returns of capital invested in them.

Deductions from Gross Income

Individual taxpayers are generally permitted two types of deductions—deductions from gross income to arrive at *adjusted gross income* and deductions from adjusted gross income. The first type is widely characterized as most business expenses and expenses incurred in the production of rents and royalties, whereas the second is generally described as allowable personal deductions.

The calculation of **adjusted gross income** is important in the taxation of individuals becuase it may affect the amount of certain personal deductions. Generally, we determine adjusted gross income to provide a more equitable base for certain other calculations than that provided by a gross income measure. Thus a person who generates a large amount of gross income by incurring large amounts of business expenses or other related costs of producing such income is provided a base for determining personal deductions that is fairly comparable to the income of a wage earner or salaried taxpayer who does not have such business expenses.

Deductions permitted the individual taxpayer in arriving at adjusted gross income are as follows (remember these are subject to change):

1. *Trade and business deductions*—Ordinary and necessary expenses attributable to a trade or business carried on by the taxpayer may be deducted, provided such activity does not consist of performance of services by an employee. (However, if an employee has reimbursed expenses in gross income, they can be deducted.) Only 80% of business meals and entertainment (100% of banquet expense) may be included with trade and business deductions, and certain kinds of entertainment expenses are not deductible.
2. *Losses from sales or exchanges of property*—Losses from the sale or exchange of business or investment property are deductible in arriving at adjusted gross income. However, losses on the sale or exchange of "personal use" property are not deductible.

[1]However, taxpayers with "modified" adjusted gross income in excess of certain specified base amounts may have as much as 50% of their Social Security benefits included in taxable income.

3. *Net operating loss deduction*—Generally, a business's operating loss in a particular year, which is of no tax benefit for that year, may be carried back to the three preceding years and forward to the next 15 years to reduce the tax liability for those years. After certain adjustments, the loss is carried back to the earliest preceding year first, then successively to each succeeding period, if unused. A taxpayer may forego the carryback and only carry the loss forward 15 years. The Tax Reform Act of 1986 imposed a number of technical limitations on certain carryovers; the act should be read to determine if any of these limitations apply.
4. *Other deductions*—Certain other deductions, relating to rents, royalties, pensions, profit sharing, bond purchase plans of self-employed individuals, and individual retirement accounts (IRAs) are allowed. Prior to the Tax Reform Act of 1986, the law allowed an individual to contribute up to $2,000 of compensation to an IRA, plus $250 if there was a nonworking spouse, and deduct the amount contributed. The 1986 Act continues to allow individuals not covered by employer-sponsored qualified pension plans to fully deduct IRA contributions. However, the deduction for IRA contributions is now either limited or completely denied to individuals covered by employer plans. For these individuals, the maximum deduction is phased out between $40,000 and $50,000 of adjusted gross income, if married, and between $25,000 and $35,000, if single.

Itemized Deductions and Standard Deduction

An individual taxpayer may deduct from adjusted gross income certain itemized personal and other expenses specified by the tax law, or may, in lieu of itemizing expenses, take advantage of a **standard deduction.** The amount of the standard deduction for 1988 is given below for single taxpayers and married taxpayers filing jointly.

Single taxpayer	$3,000
Married taxpayers filing jointly	5,000

The above amounts are increased for married individuals if they are elderly or blind by $600 for each condition; for single taxpayers the corresponding amount is $750. In 1989 the standard deduction will be indexed to adjust for inflation. In our illustrations, questions, exercises, and problems, we use the 1988 standard deduction amount because the amount for 1989 is not known at the time of this writing.

Personal expenses that may be itemized and deducted from adjusted gross income are classified as follows:

1. *Medical expenses*—With certain limitations, a taxpayer may deduct his or her medical and dental expenses, and those for dependents, not compensated for by insurance or otherwise. The total medical and dental expenses are deductible to the extent that they exceed 7.5% of adjusted gross income. Prescription drugs and insulin are the only drugs that are considered medical expenses.

   For example, a taxpayer with an adjusted gross income of $30,000 has the following medical expenses: health insurance premiums, $900; prescription drugs, $620; and other medical expenses not compensated for by insurance, $1,400. The deduction is calculated as follows:

Insurance premiums	$ 900
Prescription drugs	620
Other medical expenses	1,400
	$2,920
Less 7.5% of $30,000 adjusted gross income	2,250
Medical deduction	$ 670

2. *Taxes*—State and local income taxes, real estate taxes, and personal property taxes are deductible. State and local sales taxes, which were deductible through 1986, are no longer deductible. Federal taxes do not qualify as itemized deductions, nor do flat fees paid for most types of licenses (auto, driver's, pet, and so on). Variable auto license fees required by some states may be deductible. State and local gasoline taxes are not deductible.
3. *Interest*—Interest on indebtedness incurred to purchase a principal or second home is deductible. However, with certain exceptions, mortgage interest is not deductible on the excess of loans over the purchase price plus improvement costs. The 1986 Tax Reform Act phases out, over five years, the deduction for consumer interest, such as amounts paid for credit card balances and automobile installment loans. The amount of consumer interest to be disallowed is as follows: 1987, 35%; 1988, 60%; 1989, 80%; 1990, 90%; and 1991 and later years, 100%. Interest on a federal tax deficiency is considered consumer interest. (In our illustrations, questions, exercises, and problems, we use the 1989 amount for deductible consumer interest.)
4. *Charitable contributions*—The amount of gifts made to religious, scientific, educational, and other charitable organizations officially recognized by the Internal Revenue Service can be deducted but may not exceed 50% of adjusted gross income. Certain other limitations may also apply, as with noncash contributions and gifts to foundations. Gifts to individuals or labor unions and donations to organizations whose major activity is to influence legislation are not deductible. Prior to January 1, 1987, taxpayers not itemizing personal deductions were permitted to deduct charitable contributions, subject to certain limitations. This deduction for non-itemizers has been eliminated.
5. *Casualty losses*—To the extent that they exceed $100 for each casualty loss plus 10% of adjusted gross income, certain casualty and theft losses are deductible unless compensated by insurance. Casualty losses must be sudden and unexpected: losses from fire, accident, windstorm, and so forth qualify as deductions. Certain "gradual" losses, such as termite damage and Dutch elm disease, usually do not qualify.
6. *Miscellaneous deductions*—Certain itemized miscellaneous deductions are allowed to the extent that they aggregate more than 2% of the taxpayer's adjusted gross income. There are a number of expenses, however, to which the 2% floor does not apply. (For example, gambling losses can still be deducted to the extent of gambling winnings, which must be included in gross income. Also, employee moving expenses are not subject to the 2% floor.) Some of the most common miscellaneous deductions are:

Unreimbursed employee business expenses
Professional dues
Employment agency fees
Employee moving expenses. Not subject to the 2% floor.

Subscriptions to professional publications
Union dues
Cost of job-related work clothing, tools, and safety equipment
Safe-deposit box rental (to store securities)
Fees paid for income tax assistance
Certain educational expenses related to present job, incurred to improve or maintain skills, or to meet employer's requirements
Gambling losses (but only to the extent of gains, which are includible in gross income). Not subject to the 2% floor.

Capital Gains and Losses

Capital gains and losses are those gains and losses that result from the sale or exchange of capital assets. Although they are sometimes difficult to define, capital assets generally include any of the taxpayer's business and investment property except receivables, inventories, real and depreciable business property, certain governmental obligations, and rights to literary and other artistic works. Under certain conditions, however, business real estate and depreciable assets may be treated as capital assets when gains from sales of such assets exceed losses.

Gains or losses on capital assets sold or exchanged are classified as long term if the assets have been held longer than one year (six months for assets acquired after June 22, 1984, and before January 1, 1988). If the assets have been held for one year or less (six months for assets acquired after June 22, 1984, and before January 1, 1988), disposition results in short-term gains or losses.

If a taxpayer has both long-term and short-term transactions during the year, each type is reported separately and gains and losses from each type are netted separately. After this netting process has been achieved, the net long-term capital gain or loss for the year is combined with the net short-term capital gain or loss for the year to arrive at an overall (net) capital gain or loss for the year. If capital gains exceed capital losses, the overall gain is included with the taxpayer's other taxable income and is taxed at the regular tax rates. For many taxpayers, the maximum rate of tax on net capital gains is 28%. For taxpayers subject to the 5% surtax (explained later) the rate may go as high as 33%.

If the net amount from capital transactions is a loss, individuals and other noncorporate taxpayers may offset the loss against ordinary income up to $3,000 in any year. The amount of the losses that are not offset may be carried forward indefinitely to offset capital gains or $3,000 ordinary income in any year.

Personal Exemptions

In arriving at taxable income, the individual taxpayer may deduct an amount for each **personal exemption** he or she may legally claim. Married taxpayers filing jointly are allowed an exemption for each spouse and one for each dependent. Through 1986 additional exemptions were granted taxpayers who are 65 or over or blind, but these were repealed by the Tax Reform Act of 1986. Instead, as mentioned earlier, these individuals receive an additional standard deduction amount.

To qualify for a dependency exemption, a person must (1) be closely related to the taxpayer or live in the taxpayer's household for the entire year as a member of the family; (2) have received more than one-half of his or her support from the taxpayer; (3) if married, not file a joint return with the spouse; (4) have, with certain exceptions, income less than the exemption amount; and (5) be a U.S. citizen or a resident of the U.S., Canada, or Mexico.

The personal exemption amount for 1989 is $2,000. In 1990 the amount will be indexed to adjust for inflation.

The 1986 Tax Reform Act provided for a "phase-out" of the personal exemptions benefit for high-income taxpayers, starting in 1988. As we explain in the next section, first the benefit of the lowest tax rate in the tax schedules is phased out for high-income taxpayers, then the personal exemptions are phased out. For example, in 1988, a single taxpayer begins to lose the personal exemptions benefit when taxable income exceeds $89,560; married taxpayers filing jointly begin to lose their benefit when taxable income exceeds $149,250. The threshold amounts for these and other taxpayers are to be indexed for inflation in 1989.

For 1989, the phase out per exemption is completed at $11,200 of taxable income beyond the threshold amount:

One exemption: $2,000 × 28% = $ 560 tax saved per exemption
$ 560 ÷ 5% = $11,200 taxable income

The method of calculating the phase-out is explained in the following pages.

DETERMINING INDIVIDUAL TAX LIABILITY

Tax Tables and Rate Schedules

Applying the appropriate tax rate to taxable income results in the tax liability, unless there are tax credits (discussed later in this chapter). Individual taxpayers who do not itemize their personal deductions use simplified **tax tables** for various levels of taxable income and the number of claimed exemptions. If deductions are itemized, or if either the taxable income or number of exemptions claimed exceeds those shown in the tables, the taxpayer then uses **tax schedules.** Schedules are provided by the IRS for (1) single taxpayers, (2) married taxpayers filing a joint return (and surviving spouses), (3) married taxpayers filing separately, and (4) unmarried taxpayers who qualify as heads of households.

Head of Household

Unmarried taxpayers who qualify as **heads of households** determine their tax liability from tables or schedules (not shown) that generally determine a tax liability falling between that of single taxpayers and married taxpayers filing jointly. Generally, the qualification can be met by unmarried taxpayers who pay more than one-half the cost of maintaining a home in which a parent resides, if the parent qualifies as a dependent. A taxpayer who pays more than one-half of the cost of maintaining his or her own home where a dependent relative or where unmarried children, adopted stepchildren, or grandchildren reside may also qualify as a head of household.

Phasing out the 15% Bracket

Exhibit 28–2 illustrates the tax rate schedules for the various types of individual taxpayers for 1988. It is expected that the same rates will also be in effect for 1989, except that the threshold and upper amounts for phasing out the 15% tax rate and for phasing out personal exemptions will be indexed for inflation in 1989.

To see how the rate schedules work, let us examine Schedule X for single individuals in Exhibit 28–2. A single individual is subject to a 15% rate on taxable income up to $17,850, and to a 28% rate on the next $25,300 of taxable income ($43,150 − $17,850). However, when the taxpayer's taxable income exceeds $43,150, a 5% surtax (33% − 28%) is imposed, which begins to "phase out" the benefit of the 15% bracket. This surtax rate continues until the taxable income reaches $89,560, at which point the benefit of the 15% bracket is completely phased out. For example, assume that a single taxpayer has exactly $89,560 taxable income. The schedule shows that the tax is $9,761.50 + 33%($89,560 − $43,150) =

EXHIBIT 28–2

1988–89 TAX RATE SCHEDULES

Schedule X: Single Individual

If Taxable Income Is

Over	But Not Over	Tax Is		Of the Amount Over
$ 0	$17,850	———	15%	$ 0
17,850	43,150	$2,677.50 +	28%	17,850
43,150	89,560	9,761.50 +	33%	43,150
89,560	—	Use worksheet below to figure tax.		

Schedule Z: Head of Household

If Taxable Income Is

Over	But Not Over	Tax Is		Of the Amount Over
$ 0	$ 23,900	———	15%	$ 0
23,900	61,650	$ 3,585 +	28%	23,900
61,650	123,790	14,155 +	33%	61,650
123,790	—	Use worksheet below to figure tax.		

Schedule Y-1: Married Filing Jointly or Qualifying Widow(er)

If Taxable Income Is

Over	But Not Over	Tax Is		Of the Amount Over
$ 0	$ 29,750	———	15%	$ 0
29,750	71,900	$ 4,462.50 +	28%	29,750
71,900	149,250	16,264.50 +	33%	71,900
149,250	—	Use worksheet below to figure tax.		

Schedule Y-2: Married Filing Separately

If Taxable Income Is

Over	But Not Over	Tax Is		Of the Amount Over
$ 0	$ 14,875	———	15%	$ 0
14,875	35,950	$2,231.25 +	28%	14,875
35,950	113,300	8,123.25 +	33%	35,950
113,300	—	Use worksheet below to figure tax.		

Worksheet

1. If filing status is: Single, enter $25,076.80; Head of household, enter $34,661.20; Married filing jointly, etc., enter $41,790.00; Married filing separately, enter $33,657.75 . . . . . 1. ________
2. Enter your taxable income . . . . . 2. ________
3. If filing status is: Single, enter $89,560; Head of household, enter $123,790; Married filing jointly, etc., enter $149,250; Married filing separately, enter $113,300 . . . . . 3. ________
4. Subtract line 3 from line 2. Enter the result. (If the result is zero or less, use the schedule above to figure the tax.) . . . . . 4. ________
5. Multiply the amount on line 4 by 28%. Enter the result. . . . . . 5. ________
6. Multiply the amount on line 4 by 5%. Enter the result. . . . . . 6. ________
7. Multiply $560 by the number of exemptions claimed . . . . . 7. ________
8. Enter the smaller of the amounts on lines 6 and 7 . . . . . 8. ________
9. Tax. Add lines 1, 5, and 8 and enter the total here . . . . . 9. ________

Based on instructions to Internal Revenue Service Form 1040 (1988), p. 51.

$25,076.80. The same amount of tax is obtained by multiplying 28% times the entire taxable income of $89,560. Thus, at taxable income of $89,560, the entire benefit of the 15% bracket is relinquished by the taxpayer. The threshold level and the upper level, $43,150 and $89,560 respectively, will be indexed for inflation in late 1989, as well as the corresponding amounts for other taxpayers in the schedules. (Since these amounts are not known at the time of this writing, we will use the 1988 amounts shown in Exhibit 28–2 in all of our questions, exercises, and problems.)

Phasing out the Personal Exemption

Once taxable income exceeds the upper limit for phasing out the benefit of the 15% bracket, the benefit of the taxpayer's personal exemptions is gradually phased out. Therefore, to calculate the tax at these income levels, it is necessary to use the worksheet shown in Exhibit 28–2. This worksheet is designed expressly to phase out the personal exemptions benefit. To illustrate the use of the worksheet, let us assume that a single taxpayer with one exemption has $95,000 taxable income. Following the worksheet, the tax is calculated as follows:

1. Single, enter $25,076.80		$25,076.80
2. Enter taxable income	$95,000.00	
3. Single, enter $89,560	89,560.00	
4. Subtract line 3 from line 2. Enter the result	$ 5,440.00	
5. Multiply amount on line 4 by 28%. Enter the result		1,523.20
6. Multiply amount on line 4 by 5%. Enter the result	272.00	
7. Multiply $560 by the number of exemptions claimed	560.00	
8. Enter the smaller of the amounts on lines 6 and 7		272.00
9. Tax. Add lines 1, 5, and 8 and enter the total here		$26,872.00

The line 1 amount in the calculation is simply the tax on $89,560 from the schedule, $9,761.50 + (33% × $43,150) = $25,076.80. Line 4 shows the taxable income in excess of $89,560, and line 5 is the tax on this excess at 28%, $1,523.20. Next, we must determine how much of the benefit from personal exemptions is lost, and add this amount to compute the total tax amount. This benefit is phased out at a 5% rate. 5% of the $5,440.00 excess taxable income over the $89,560 bracket is $272.00. Because this amount is less than the $560 maximum tax benefit from one personal exemption, the $272 amount is added to the tax. The maximum benefit is 28% of the $2,000 personal exemption for 1989, $560.00. The full $560 benefit from one exemption is lost when the taxable income exceeds the $89,560 bracket by $11,200. ($560/5% = $11,200.)

CREDITS AGAINST THE TAX

Once the income tax has been calculated, certain credits specified in the tax law may reduce the amount owed. Two of the most important of these credits for individual taxpayers are the earned income credit and the dependent care credit.

Earned Income Credit

The earned income credit provides tax relief to low-income working individuals with children. Beginning in 1987 the credit is 14% of the first $5,714 of earned income permitting a maximum credit of $800. However, this amount is gradually phased out at income levels between $9,000 and $17,000. The maximum amount of income against which the credit applies ($5,714) and the beginning phase out level ($9,000) will be indexed for inflation.

Dependent Care Credit

A tax credit is available for taxpayers who maintain a household and incur expenses in caring for a dependent child under 15 years or an incapacitated dependent or spouse, if the expenses incurred permitted the taxpayer to be gainfully employed. The amount of the credit is 20% of the employment-related expenses up to a maximum of $2,400 for one qualifying individual and $4,000 for two or more qualifying individuals.

Two prominent credits that were repealed by the Tax Reform Act of 1986 are the investment tax credit and the political contributions credit. The investment credit was a credit against the tax liability for investments in qualified business property—a stipulated percent of the cost of property meeting certain requirements and used in a trade or business. This credit was repealed, effective for property placed in service after December 31, 1985. The political contributions credit, which permitted a taxpayer to apply 50% of political contributions as a credit against the tax up to a maximum of $50 ($100 in a joint return) was repealed for periods after December 31, 1986.

WITHHOLDING AND ESTIMATED TAX

Ordinarily, tax returns must be filed within $3\frac{1}{2}$ months of the close of the individual's taxable year. Because most taxpayers are on a calendar year basis, they must file their returns by April 15 following the end of the taxable year. During the taxable year, employers of wage earners and salaried employees have withheld tax payments based on the employees' estimated earnings and the number of withholding allowances claimed. Taxpayers who have income not subject to withholding (beyond a certain amount) must estimate income for the current year and file a Declaration of Estimated Tax. The estimated tax, less the amounts expected to be withheld, is paid in four installments. Therefore, when the tax return is filed, the amounts paid through the withholding or declaration process are credits that offset the total tax liability.

INDIVIDUAL TAX COMPUTATION: TWO EXAMPLES

We present two examples of the common elements of individual tax computations. Exhibit 28–3 shows the relevant tax data for the joint return of Brian and Mary Fleming, and Exhibit 28–4 shows data for the single taxpayer return of James Malone. Although some of this information would be shown in separate schedules that reveal more detail, we have condensed the data into single schedules to conserve space. Both returns are for the 1989 calendar year.

Brian and Mary Fleming have one child who qualifies as a dependency exemption. Brian operates a tax service and has paid $600 estimated tax quarterly. Mary works part-time as a nurse and has tax withheld from her salary. During the year, Brian sold at a $1,200 gain securities purchased two years ago. The couple has been contributing $4,000 each year to an individual retirement account

EXHIBIT 28–3

BRIAN AND MARY FLEMING'S
1989 JOINT FEDERAL INCOME TAX RETURN INFORMATION

Net income from Fleming Tax Service:			
Fees collected		$48,000	
Ordinary and necessary expenses		18,000	$30,000
Salary (Mary's)			5,600
Interest on savings accounts (excluding IRA interest)			1,400
Dividend income			650
Net capital gain on sale of securities			1,200
Contribution to Individual Retirement Account			(4,000)
Adjusted Gross Income			$34,850
Deductions from adjusted gross income:			
Taxes:			
Property tax on home	$2,200		
State income tax	1,530	$3,730	
Interest on home mortgage		1,620	
Interest on installment and credit card purchases	$ 500		
Less 80% not deductible	400	100	
Charitable contributions		950	
Professional dues, nurse's uniforms, and other miscellaneous deductions	$ 775		
Less 2% of $34,850 adjusted gross income not deductible	697	78	
Total itemized deductions			6,478
			$28,372
Less exemptions 3 × $2,000			6,000
Taxable income			$22,372
Tax: 15% of $22,372 (rounded)			$ 3,356
Less prepayments:			
Tax withheld from salary		$ 680	
Estimated taxes paid quarterly		2,400	
Total tax withheld or prepaid			3,080
Balance of tax due with return			$ 276

(IRA). Neither Brian nor Mary is covered by an employer-sponsored retirement plan. The Fleming family's medical expenses were not significant during the year. Notice that the Flemings can deduct their $4,000 contribution to an IRA because they are not covered by an employer retirement plan and they fall below the income levels at which these contributions are not deductible. Brian and Mary are each allowed a $2,000 deductible contribution because both are working. Also notice that their miscellaneous deductions are slightly higher than 2% of adjusted gross income, so that they can deduct a small amount of this expense, and that some of their consumer interest (20%) is deductible.

EXHIBIT 28–4

JAMES MALONE'S
1989 FEDERAL INCOME TAX RETURN INFORMATION

Salary				$56,480
Interest (excluding interest on Individual Retirement Account)				2,410
Dividends				2,190
Net capital gain on sale of securities				1,600
Adjusted Gross Income				$62,680
Deductions from adjusted gross income:				
Taxes:				
Property taxes on home and vacation home		$2,250		
State income tax		3,070	$5,320	
Interest:				
On home mortgage		$2,560		
On vacation home mortgage		200	2,760	
Charitable contributions			1,550	
Miscellaneous expenses:				
Employee moving expense		$ 650		
Other (Safe deposit box rental, dues, subscriptions, etc.)	$ 960			
Less 2% of adjusted gross income	1,254	0	650	
Total itemized deductions				10,280
				$52,400
Less one exemption ($2,000)				2,000
Taxable income				$50,400
Tax: $9,761.50 + 33% ($50,400 – $43,150)				$12,154
Less prepayments:				
Tax withheld from salary			$7,100	
Estimated taxes paid quarterly			5,200	12,300
Overpayment of tax				$ 146

James Malone, whose 1989 federal income tax data are given in Exhibit 28–4, is single and is covered by an employer-sponsored retirement program. Malone contributed $2,000 to an IRA as he has done for several years. This amount is not deductible in calculating adjusted gross income (both because he is in a retirement program and because of his income level). However, the interest on his IRA is deferred for tax purposes and is not included in adjusted gross income. Malone was transferred by his employer in 1989 and had unreimbursed moving expenses of $650, which are fully deductible as miscellaneous expenses. Malone's other miscellaneous expenses are not deductible because they fall below 2% of adjusted gross income. Notice that, because of the level of his taxable income, Malone had phased out part of the tax benefit of the 15% tax bracket. During the year Malone paid estimated tax of $1,300 each quarter (total, $5,200) and had $7,100 withheld from his salary.

PARTNERSHIPS

Partnerships are not recognized as separate taxable entities for income tax purposes. Although partnerships are separate business and legal entities, they are treated as conduits for tax purposes, as are S corporations. That is, the ordinary income of the partnership is allocated on a pro-rata basis to the partners, who report this amount on their individual income tax returns (or corporate return, if the partner is a corporation). Items of income other than ordinary income, as well as any deductions that are subject to limitations or special treatment on an individual tax return, are stated separately and flow through to the partners based on their pro-rata shares.

Since each partner must pay the tax on his or her pro-rata share of income, the partners must include the partnership items in adjusted gross income. The partnership pays no federal income tax, but must file an annual information return reflecting the partnership's ordinary income and each partner's individual items. In addition, each partner must include any prospective partnership income in his or her estimate of total personal taxes and pay the related tax quarterly.

TAXATION OF CORPORATIONS

The corporation is a taxable entity, separate from its shareholders, and must file an annual tax return whether or not it owes any tax. Certain corporations—such as banks, insurance companies, and cooperatives—are subject to special tax provisions. Tax regulations even for corporations that are not specially treated can be quite complex. Our discussion is limited to a few of the major distinguishing features of corporate taxation.

Corporate Tax Rates

The Tax Reform Act of 1986 established the following three-tier tax rate structure, effective July 1, 1987:

If Taxable Income Is:		Tax Is:		
Over	**But Not Over**	**Amount Plus**	**% of**	**Excess Over**
$ 0	$50,000	$ 0	15	$ 0
50,000	75,000	7,500	25	50,000
75,000	—	13,750	34	75,000

Corporations with taxable income in excess of $100,000 pay an additional tax equal to the lesser of (a) 5% of the excess over $100,000 or (b) $11,750. This surtax eliminates the benefits of the graduated rates on the first $75,000 of taxable income for corporations with taxable income between $100,000 and $335,000. Corporations with taxable income in excess of $335,000 thus pay tax at a flat 34% rate.

Corporate taxpayers must pay estimated taxes in quarterly installments, similar to certain individuals. Their final returns, however, are due within $2\frac{1}{2}$ months of the close of their calendar or fiscal years.

Corporate Tax Base

The tax base for corporations is taxable income (Gross Income − All Allowable Deductions). There is no adjusted gross income for corporations. Corporation deductions can be classified as ordinary or special. *Ordinary* deductions are the usual expenses (with certain exceptions) of doing business and producing revenue. The most prominent *special* deduction is a credit for 80% of dividends received from other domestic corporations (100% if such other corporations are affiliates).

The deduction for dividends received is intended to reduce the effect of "triple" taxation. Without this deduction, the distributing corporation, the receiving corporation, and individual shareholders of the receiving corporation (if they subsequently received the dividends) would all pay tax on the earnings.

The net operating loss deduction, which also applies to sole proprietorships, offsets business losses of a particular year against the income of other years in calculating the ultimate tax liability for those years. Briefly, an operating loss in a particular year can offset the income of the three preceding years, beginning with the earliest. After this carryback unused losses can be carried forward successively to the next 15 years and used to compute taxable income. In the loss year only, the corporation may forego the carryback and instead only carry the loss forward up to 15 years. The Tax Reform Act of 1986, through some complex rules, curtails the use of certain net operating loss carryovers when there is a substantial change in stock ownership of a loss corporation or failure to meet certain continuity of business enterprise tests. These rules are designed to forestall profitable firms from acquiring a loss corporation solely to offset their own taxable income with the loss corporation's loss carryover.

Prior to the Tax Reform Act of 1986, net capital gains of corporations were subject to a maximum alternative tax rate of 28%. This rate was used when the tax based on that rate was lower than the corporation's regular tax. The new law raises the maximum rate to 34% subject to certain transitional rules.

The excess of a corporation's capital losses over capital gains is not offset against ordinary income. It is carried back three years and forward five years and offset against capital gains in those years in the manner just described for a net operating loss.

Charitable contributions of corporations are limited to 10% of taxable income, computed before considering the contributions and the special deduction for dividends received. Any contribution in excess of the limitation can be carried forward five years.

Corporate Tax Illustration

The effect of the foregoing items on the corporate tax computation is illustrated in Exhibit 28–5. In this example, we use the following data from the firm's income statement for the year ended December 31, 1989:

Gross profit on sales	$500,000
Dividends from unaffiliated domestic corporations	40,000
Gain on sale of capital asset	10,000
	$550,000
Business expenses, including charitable contributions of $20,000	380,000
Reported income before taxes	$170,000

The firm also had an unused net capital loss carryforward of $3,000 from preceding years.

BASIS OF DETERMINING TAXABLE INCOME

Many taxpayers' taxable income is determined on a **cash basis.** Taxable earnings from various sources are includible in gross income when received, and deduc-

EXHIBIT 28–5

CORPORATE TAX COMPUTATION
FOR CALENDAR YEAR 1989

Gross profit		$500,000
Dividends from domestic corporations (unaffiliated)		40,000
Gain on sale of capital asset	$10,000	
Less: Net capital loss carryforward	3,000	7,000
		$547,000
Less: Business expenses, less charitable contributions of $20,000		360,000
		$187,000
Charitable contributions, limited to 10% of $187,000		18,700
		$168,300
Dividends received deduction, 80% of $40,000		32,000
Taxable income		$136,300
Tax:		
Regular tax $13,750 + 34% ($136,300 – $75,000)		$ 34,592
Surtax 5% of ($136,300 – $100,000)		1,815
Total tax liability		$ 36,407

tions are recognized when the allowable related expenditures are paid. Cash-basis taxation has wide appeal because it is fairly simple and requires perhaps the least amount of record keeping.

Even a cash-basis taxpayer should be aware of certain exceptions provided by the law. Although certain income may not be directly paid to the taxpayer, the law may consider the income a *constructive receipt* if the taxpayer effectively controls it. Thus, interest on savings accounts credited to the taxpayer constitutes taxable income whether or not it is withdrawn. Likewise, any checks received that represent taxable income are taxable whether or not they are cashed before the taxable year-end.

Generally, payments made during the taxable year are deductible in determining the year's taxable income if they meet the criteria for deductions. However, expenditures representing prepayments for a period must usually be allocated to the periods involved. For example, the cost of plant assets must be allocated to the periods of use through depreciation accounting. Likewise, prepayments of insurance, rent, and similar items must be allocated to the years involved rather than deducted totally in the year of payment. Under certain circumstances, real estate taxes paid a year in advance may be deducted; also, in certain cases, prepaid interest has been allowed as a deduction when the prepayment period was not extremely long.

Cash-basis taxpayers, particularly those in certain types of service business, sometimes can arrange their pattern of billings and disbursements near year-end to minimize tax liability. For example, an expected tax rate reduction for next year would suggest that billings should be delayed to postpone revenue recognition, but that expenditures qualifying as deductions should be made this year.

For the most part, **accrual basis** accounting must be used by trading or manufacturing firms, because inventories are a factor in determining their income. Revenue must be recognized when sales are made, and inventories must be considered in determining the cost of goods sold.[2] Although some prepayments and accruals may be ignored, the method followed must be consistent and provide a reasonable income determination. Thus, the taxable income of an accrual-basis taxpayer will likely not be substantially affected by altering the pattern of receipts or expenditures.

TAX AVOIDANCE AND BUSINESS DECISIONS

Taxpayers who deliberately misstate their taxable income, whether by omitting income or claiming fraudulently contrived deductions, are practicing **tax evasion.** This, of course, is illegal, and the penalties for such a practice can be severe. However, taxpayers are perfectly within their rights to practice **tax avoidance**—arranging their business affairs to minimize their tax liability. The effectiveness of some methods of tax avoidance, particularly certain tax shelters and deferred methods of income recognition, have been seriously curtailed by the Tax Reform Act of 1986. However, there are still some areas of taxation that permit an informed taxpayer to minimize taxes.

Timing of Transactions

In some instances, taxpayers can minimize taxes by timing certain transactions in a particular way. For example, timing is important when a taxpayer's principal residence is sold at a gain. Under a long-standing Internal Revenue Code provision, the gain is not taxable if an amount at least as great as the selling price[3] is invested in a new residence during the period beginning 24 months before the sale and ending 24 months after the sale. The basis of the new residence is reduced by the gain not recognized; thus the tax is deferred. Another Code provision, however, grants a once-in-a-lifetime exclusion of $125,000[4] of gain on the sale of a residence for a taxpayer who is at least 55 years old and has used the property as his or her principal residence for three of the five preceding years. Because this exclusion can be used only once in a taxpayer's life, he or she must decide when to use it. If a taxpayer sells a residence at a gain of less than $125,000, he or she must speculate on the possibility of a larger gain being realized on a future residence.

For many years, some taxpayers were able to defer taxes by selling property on the installment plan (reporting income for tax purposes as cash is received in installments, rather than when the sale is made). Although the 1986 Tax Reform Act disallowed the benefits of the installment method for many installment transactions, there are exceptions for real property used in a trade or business or held for rental, where the selling price is less than $150,000, and for casual sales of personal property. Also, in some cases the installment method may be beneficial

[2]The Tax Reform Act of 1986 imposed an exception to the accrual method of providing for uncollectible accounts expense. Accrual taxpayers, except for certain financial institutions, must now use the direct write-off method, and take into income the existing balance of the allowance for uncollectible accounts over a four-year period.

[3]Selling price here means *adjusted selling price* as defined by the Code (selling price less expenses of fix-up and sale).

[4]$75,000 for married taxpayers filing separately.

where the portion of installment sales disallowed is low (the amount disallowed is based on the ratio of outstanding debt to the basis of the assets).

Earlier we mentioned the possibility that cash-basis taxpayers may affect their pattern of receipts and expenditures. For example, some taxpayers may be able to concentrate their personal deductions in a particular year. If their itemized deductions are below the standard deduction in the following year (because of the deduction-shifting process), they can take advantage of the standard deduction.

These are just a few examples of how the timing of transactions can alter the impact of income taxes. Because they often deal with the disposition of property, it is wise to investigate thoroughly the tax consequences of a contemplated property disposition and the possible forms it may take.

Tax Shelters

The term **tax shelter** is a somewhat broad term that describes investments which, by their nature, create either tax-exempt income or a probable deductible tax loss, or which defer taxes to the future. We have already mentioned individual retirement accounts, which permit qualified individual taxpayers to defer taxes on their contributions and interest income until the amounts are withdrawn (after age $59\frac{1}{2}$). It is also well known that certain affluent taxpayers often invest in state or municipal securities, the interest on which is exempt from federal income tax. Indeed, this was a very effective method of sheltering income in the past when top individual tax rates were first 70% and then 50%. It can still be a modest method of sheltering investment income. The attractiveness depends on the taxpayer's marginal (top) tax rate. Suppose a taxpayer in the 28% marginal rate bracket had $50,000 to invest in either 9% municipal bonds or 12% industrial bonds (interest taxable) of equal merit. The municipal bonds would provide $4,500 tax-free income, whereas the industrial bonds would provide only $4,320 after-tax income ($6,000 − $1,680). The differential ($180) is not great. However, many taxpayers with high income levels reach a 33% marginal tax rate (because of the phase-out of lower tax bracket rates described earlier in this chapter). A taxpayer in this situation would have after-tax income of $4,020 ($6,000 − $1,980) with the industrial bond investment as compared with a $4,500 return on the municipal bond investment.

Prior to the Tax Reform Act of 1986, a number of tax shelters permitted the taxpayer a tax-free cash inflow on an investment that generated a loss for tax purposes. Sometimes, groups of taxpayers made a joint investment—typically a limited partnership—in such ventures as apartment and condominium properties and oil properties. Revenue from rents and royalties exceeded out-of-pocket (cash) operating costs, so a distributable amount of cash existed; however, because of large accelerated depreciation write-offs, a tax loss was allocable to the investors. Taxpayers could use these losses to offset income from wages, dividends, interest, capital gains, and so on. The new law does not allow the offsetting of such losses against other types of income. The law provides that deductions from "passive" activities (exclusive of dividends, interest, and so on) can be offset only against other "passive" income, or be deductible in full when the taxpayer disposes of his or her entire interest in the activity. Under the law, an activity is passive if it involves the conduct of a trade or business and if the taxpayer does not "materially participate" in the activity. The taxpayer must be involved on a *regular, continuous,* and *substantial* basis. Thus the new law eliminates the effectiveness of many tax shelters. However, working interest in oil and gas properties are exempted from the general rules and therefore allow some individuals a tax shelter.

Forms of Business Organization

Most large businesses operate as corporations to have wider access to capital, limit liability, or enjoy other advantages of incorporation explained in Chapter 15. For small businesses, with perhaps a single owner or a few owners, tax considerations may well influence the form of ownership.

Let us examine some general factors in determining the relative tax effects. First, all income of single proprietorships and partnerships is taxable to the owners as earned, whether or not it is distributed. Second, corporations must pay a tax on earnings, but may deduct reasonable salaries paid to owners. Furthermore, corporations may pay only a portion of the earnings as dividends (as long as accumulations are not deemed unreasonable). Other relevant factors are the amount of the business earnings and the amount of the owners' other separate income.

For example, consider the comparative tax effects of the corporate and sole proprietorship forms of organization for a married individual whose business is expected to generate $50,000 net income annually. Of this amount, $30,000 is withdrawn each year (as a salary, if the corporate form is used). The owner's other income, less all deductions and exemptions, is about $8,000 annually. A comparison of the total tax effect of the two forms of organization is shown in Exhibit 28–6.

The example assumes no distribution of dividends by the corporation. This policy might require justification if questioned by the IRS. Generally, the IRS may impose a penalty on unreasonable retention of earnings without a genuine business purpose. Of course, the owner will be taxed on the $17,000 earnings retained

EXHIBIT 28–6

COMPARATIVE TAX RESULTS IN TWO FORMS OF ORGANIZATION

		Corporation	Sole Proprietorship
Income from business		$50,000	$50,000
Less: Owner's salary		30,000	—
Taxable business income		$20,000	$50,000
Corporate tax on $20,000 at 15%		$ 3,000	
Salary	$30,000		
Other income less deductions and exemptions	8,000		8,000
	$38,000		$58,000
Tax on $38,000: $4,463 + (28% × $8,250)		6,773	
Tax on $58,000: $4,463 + (28% × $28,250)			$12,373
Total tax		$ 9,773	$12,373

($20,000 − $3,000 tax) if distributed in the future. However, it is almost always beneficial to defer taxes to the future.

Obviously, no general rule or formula can determine the most beneficial form of organization for tax purposes. The type of analysis we have illustrated may be modified in response to changes in the levels of business income, other income, reasonableness of salary levels, dividend policy, and other factors. The addition of owners and increases in the size and scope of the business may be influential. Finally, depending on the nature of the ownership, small corporations can sometimes elect to be taxed as partnerships.

KEY POINTS FOR CHAPTER OBJECTIVES

1 Provide an understanding of the purpose and coverage of the tax law (pp. 1077–80).

- The primary purpose of the income tax law is to raise revenue for the operation of the government; however it is also used to distribute income more equitably, stimulate economic growth, combat inflation, and meet other social goals.
- The main entities recognized for tax purposes are individuals, partnerships, corporations, and estates or trusts.

2 Describe the format for determining tax liability for individuals (pp. 1080–88).

- All income less specific exclusions equals gross income.
- Business-related expenses and other specific deductions are subtracted from gross income to obtain adjusted gross income. The latter amount is often used in calculations that limit certain deductions.
- To get taxable income we deduct either itemized deductions or a standard deduction and also an amount of personal exemptions for the taxpayer, spouse, and dependents.

3 Discuss the nature and treatment of capital gains and losses (p. 1084).

- Net gains on sales of capital assets are taxed at regular rates for individuals and corporations, with a maximum rate of 28% for most individuals and 34% for corporations.
- If capital transactions result in a loss, individuals may carry the loss forward to offset capital gains and up to $3,000 of ordinary income in any year. Loss carryforwards of corporations can be offset only against capital gains.

4 Illustrate a complete individual tax computation (pp. 1088–90).

- Once taxable income is determined using the format described in Key Point 2, the tax liability is calculated by using tax tables or tax schedules.
- At certain levels of taxable income, the benefit of the lowest tax bracket is phased out for high income taxpayers; at certain higher levels, the benefit of personal exemptions is phased out.

5 Describe and illustrate basic elements of corporate taxation (pp. 1091–94).

- The tax base for corporations is taxable income (gross income less allowable deductions).
- Ordinary deductions are generally business expenses. Special deductions include an 80% credit for domestic dividends received (100% for affiliates) and the operating loss deduction which can be carried back three years and forward fifteen years.

6 Discuss tax avoidance and related business decisions (pp. 1094–97).

- In many cases taxpayers can reduce taxes by affecting the timing of transactions.
- Some taxpayers shelter income by investing in tax-free securities or investing in shelters not restricted by the 1986 Tax Reform Act.
- Individual retirement plans and other allowed tax-deferred compensation plans are available to some individuals to defer taxes.

KEY TERMS USED IN THIS CHAPTER

accrual basis 1094
adjusted gross income 1081
capital gains and losses 1084
cash basis 1092
gross income 1081
heads of households 1085
information return 1078
personal exemption 1084

S corporations 1078
standard deduction 1082
tax avoidance 1094
tax evasion 1094
tax schedules 1085
tax shelter 1095
tax tables 1085

SELF-TEST QUESTIONS FOR REVIEW

(Answers are at the end of this chapter.)

Note: The following questions are based on tax law effective in 1988.

1. Which of the following is not a deduction from gross income to determine adjusted gross income of a married couple filing a joint return?
   (a) Qualified contribution to Individual Retirement Account.
   (b) Trade and business deductions.
   (c) Deductions for state and local income taxes.
   (d) Net operating loss deduction.
2. A single taxpayer had $30,000 gross income and $24,000 adjusted gross income. Her medical expenses amounted to $2,400. The deduction for medical expenses is:
   (a) $600 (b) $150 (c) $2,400 (d) $-0-
3. Which of the following is not allowed as an itemized deduction?
   (a) Property tax on home.
   (b) State income taxes.
   (c) State sales taxes.
   (d) Mortgage interest on second home.
4. Which of the following is not phased out at certain income levels?
   (a) Benefit of 15% rate bracket for individuals.
   (b) Standard deduction.
   (c) Personal exemptions.
   (d) Deduction for IRA contribution made by person covered by employer sponsored retirement plan.
5. Which of the following statements relating to corporate taxation is not true?
   (a) Corporations are permitted a deduction for 80% of domestic corporation dividends received.
   (b) Corporate contributions are limited to 10% of adjusted gross income.
   (c) Corporate capital losses cannot be offset against ordinary income.
   (d) Corporations must file tax returns within $2\frac{1}{2}$ months after the close of their calendar or fiscal year.

DEMONSTRATION PROBLEM FOR REVIEW

Eric and Victoria Nelson have two teenage children who qualify as dependency exemptions. Eric is a consulting engineer; he collected $160,000 in fees in 1989 and had $18,000 of deductible business expenses. Victoria works for an interior decorating firm; her salary for 1989 was $45,000. For 1989, Eric paid $38,500 in estimated taxes. During 1989, Victoria had $8,400 of income taxes withheld from her salary. The Nelsons had interest income on savings accounts totaling $9,500 in 1989. They also had $840 dividend income and net capital gains on sales of securities of $8,800. In 1989, the couple paid $3,600 for property taxes on their home, and state income taxes of $9,200. Interest on their home mortgage was $12,600 and charitable contributions amounted to $3,800. Miscellaneous deductions for professional dues, subscriptions, income tax advice, and so on totaled $1,600. Unreimbursed medical expenses (surgery for Victoria) amounted to $8,400.

REQUIRED
Prepare the 1989 joint income tax calculation for Eric and Victoria Nelson.

SOLUTION TO DEMONSTRATION PROBLEM

Eric and Victoria Nelson
1989 Joint Federal Income Tax Calculation

Net income from engineering consulting (Eric):			
Fees collected		$160,000.00	
Ordinary and necessary expenses		18,000.00	$142,000.00
Salary (Victoria)			45,000.00
Interest on savings accounts			9,500.00
Dividend income			840.00
Net capital gains			8,800.00
Adjusted Gross Income			$206,140.00
Deductions from adjusted gross income:			
Medical expenses	$ 8,400.00		
Less 7.5% of adjusted gross income (rounded)	15,461.00	$ -0-	
Taxes:			
Property tax on home	$ 3,600.00		
State income tax	9,200.00	12,800.00	
Interest on home mortgage		12,600.00	
Charitable contributions		3,800.00	
Miscellaneous expenses	$ 1,600.00		
Less 2% of adjusted gross income (rounded)	4,123.00	-0-	
Total itemized deductions			29,200.00
			$176,940.00
Less exemptions: 4 × $2,000			8,000.00
Taxable income			$168,940.00
Tax:			
1. Married, filing jointly, enter $41,790.00			$ 41,790.00
2. Enter taxable income		$168,940.00	
3. Married, filing jointly, enter $149,250.00		149,250.00	
4. Subtract line 3 from line 2. Enter the result.		$ 19,690.00	
5. Multiply the amount on line 4 by 28%. Enter the result			5,513.20
6. Multiply the amount on line 4 by 5%. Enter the result		$ 984.50	
7. Multiply $560 by the number of exemptions claimed		2,240.00	
8. Enter the smaller of the amounts on lines 6 and 7			984.50
9. Tax. Add lines 1, 5, and 8 and enter total here			$ 48,287.70
Less prepayments:			
Tax withheld from salary		$ 8,400.00	
Estimated tax payments		38,500.00	46,900.00
Balance of tax due with return			$ 1,387.70

QUESTIONS

Note: In all questions, exercises, and problems use applicable law and rates for 1989.

28–1 In addition to raising revenue, what other purposes are served by the federal income tax?

28–2 Name the major entities recognized for federal income tax purposes.

28–3 How is the net income from sole proprietorships and partnerships taxed? Must either of these business entities file a federal income tax return?

28–4 Describe the general format used to determine an individual's taxable income.

28–5 Which of the following items can be *excluded* from gross income?
1. Interest on savings accounts.
2. Interest on municipal bonds.
3. Social Security payments (benefits).
4. Gambling gains.
5. Bonuses.
6. Life insurance proceeds paid at death of insured.
7. Royalties.
8. Tuition portion of scholarship of a degree candidate, not requiring services.

28–6 Generally describe the deductions allowable in computing an individual's adjusted gross income, and name two examples.

28–7 Why is the concept of adjusted gross income important in the calculation of an individual's taxable income?

28–8 Vera Knight, who operates a real estate agency as a sole proprietorship, had the following expenditures for the current year:
1. Interest on office building mortgage.
2. Interest on home mortgage.
3. Property taxes on home.
4. Expenses of automobile used solely in business.
5. License on business automobile.
6. License on personal automobile (flat amount).
7. State gasoline tax, business automobile.
8. State gasoline tax, personal automobile.
9. Sales taxes on personal items.
10. Church contributions by Knight family.
11. Loss on sale of office building.
12. Net capital loss of $800 on personal investments.
13. Uninsured termite damage to home.

Indicate whether each of these items is (a) deductible in obtaining adjusted gross income, (b) deductible from adjusted gross income, or (c) nondeductible.

28–9 What is meant by a personal exemption? How much is each personal exemption?

28–10 What are the criteria for determining whether a person qualifies as a dependent of a taxpayer?

28–11 Alma Todd, who is single and has no dependents, has adjusted gross income of $42,000 in 1989. Personal expenses qualifying as itemized deductions amount to $2,800. Calculate her tax, using the appropriate schedule in Exhibit 28–2 (page 1086).

28–12 George Mann, a single taxpayer, has taxable income in 1989 of $72,000. Calculate Mann's tax liability using the appropriate schedule in Exhibit 28–2 (page 1086). How much of the benefit of the 15% bracket was phased out?

28–13 An individual has a net capital gain of $6,000 in 1989. What is the maximum rate at which this amount is taxed?

28–14 An individual has a net capital gain of $2,000 in 1989. He also has a capital loss carryforward from preceding years of $8,000. How much of the carryforward can be used in 1989?

28–15 What is meant by a tax credit? Give an example of a tax credit.

28–16 Describe the basic accounting methods taxpayers may use in computing their taxable income.

28–17 What limitations related to adjusted gross income are there for medical expense deductions? For miscellaneous expense deductions?

28–18 Explain the dividends received deduction. Why is it a special deduction for corporations?

28–19 What tax factors might be considered by the owner or owners of a small business in choosing the form of business organization?

28–20 What is the difference between *tax evasion* and *tax avoidance*?

EXERCISES

Adjusted gross income

28–21 Calculate the adjusted gross income for the joint return of Arthur and Mary Bower from the following data in 1989:

Share of partnership net income	$46,200
Interest on municipal bonds	1,000
Dividend income	700
Interest income	220
Lottery prize	500
Gift from relative	1,500
Net capital gain on sale of securities	2,000
Qualified contributions to individual retirement account	2,250

Taxable income

28–22 According to their 1989 joint return, Bart and Irene Lowe have two dependents and their adjusted gross income is $36,000. Using the relevant data from the items shown below, calculate their taxable income.

Real estate taxes	$1,400	State gasoline taxes	$ 140
Interest on home mortgage	2,400	Health insurance premiums	900
Charitable contributions	600	Other medical expenses	2,100
Gift to relative	150	Automobile licenses	36
State income taxes	700	Employee moving expense	400
State sales taxes	280	Union dues	150
Interest on car payments	200	Income tax return preparation	180

Individual tax liability

28–23 Using the appropriate schedule in Exhibit 28–2 (page 1086), calculate the amount of tax due (or overpayment) for Ellen Wade, a single taxpayer (with no dependents) who has given you the following information:

Gross income	$30,000
Deductions to determine adjusted gross income	1,950
Allowable itemized personal expenses	3,500
Tax withheld from salary	3,250
Payments of estimated tax	250

Individual tax; phase-out of 15% rate

28–24 Using the appropriate schedule in Exhibit 28–2 (page 1086), calculate the amount of tax due (or overpayment) for Ben River, a single taxpayer with no dependents. Also calculate how much of the benefit of the 15% rate bracket is phased out for River. The following information is given:

Gross income	$72,000
Deductions to determine adjusted gross income	3,200
Allowable itemized personal expenses	5,400
Tax withheld from salary	12,600
Payments of estimated tax	2,400

Individual tax; phase-out of 15% rate and exemption

28–25 Using the appropriate schedule in Exhibit 28–2 (page 1086), calculate the amount of the 1989 tax liability for John Adams, a single taxpayer with no dependents, who has taxable income of $120,000.

Corporate tax liability

28–26 Verity Corporation has pretax income of $92,000 during the year 1989. In arriving at this amount, the firm included $10,000 in dividends from nonaffiliated domestic corporations and deducted $16,000 of charitable contributions. Calculate the corporation's federal income tax for the year, using the rate schedule given on page 1091.

PROBLEMS

Joint tax return

28–27 Ralph and Jane Burns, who have three school-age children, are filing a joint federal income tax return. Ralph, whose annual salary is $40,000 as an accountant for Byrd Corporation, operates a tax service in his spare time. During the current year, he had $7,200 gross income and $1,600 business expenses in his tax service. He received $120 in dividends from his investments and $600 interest on municipal bonds. Mary had $250 in dividend income on her stocks. In addition, Ralph sold for $45 per share 100 shares of stock purchased five years ago for $30 per share. Income taxes deducted from Ralph's salary for the year amounted to $4,900, and his payments of estimated tax were $560. Personal expenses of the Burns family for the year included the following:

Mortgage payments (of which $1,600 was interest)	$3,600
Real estate taxes	1,800
State income taxes	1,400
State sales taxes	360
Charitable contributions	560
Medical and dental expenses (unreimbursed)	1,920
License fees for auto, pets, etc.	52
Interest on charge accounts	250

REQUIRED
Calculate the amount of tax due (or overpayment) shown on the Burns' joint income tax return for the current year. Use the appropriate schedule in Exhibit 28–2 (page 1086). Round computations to the nearest dollar.

Types of deductions

28–28 The following items relate to the federal income taxes of individuals who itemize their deductions in computing their tax. Consider each item independently.

1. Fee paid employment agency for obtaining employment.
2. Payment of $150 repair bill for damage to pleasure automobile from skid on icy road (not compensated for by insurance).
3. Labor union dues.
4. Contribution to Empty Stocking Fund formed by neighbors for children of a needy family.
5. State income tax paid.
6. Federal cigarette tax.
7. State gasoline tax for pleasure car.
8. State fishing license.
9. Gambling losses in excess of gambling gains.
10. Fee paid by unemployed student to take the CPA examination.
11. Fee paid to Smith & Brown, CPAs, for preparation of personal tax return.
12. Cost of cleaning uniform paid by train conductor.
13. Fair market value of furniture given to the Salvation Army.
14. Entertainment expenses of an outside salesperson, not reimbursed.
15. Life insurance premiums paid.
16. Trade and business expenses of sole proprietorship.
17. Net capital loss of $1,200 on sale of securities.

REQUIRED
Indicate whether each of the above items is (a) nondeductible, (b) deductible in determining adjusted gross income, or (c) deductible from adjusted gross income. If answer (c) is given, indicate if there are limitations on the amount of the deduction.

Joint tax return

28–29 Carl and Lisa Hunt are married and are both under 65 years of age. Their one child, Sally, is 18 years old and a full-time student at a university; they contribute over one-half of her support, and Sally earned $1,500 from part-time work during the year.

Lisa Hunt operates a retail dress shop. Her records are kept on the accrual basis; however, all sales are for cash. The following information is available for the year's operations:

Cash receipts from sales	$86,500
Merchandise inventory, January 1	22,600
Merchandise purchases	48,200
Rent expense	5,400
Utilities and supplies expense	800
Salaries of part-time help	4,600
Insurance expense	700
Merchandise inventory, December 31	24,500

Carl Hunt's annual salary as a purchasing agent for a local firm was $45,000 and income tax withheld was $9,600. Quarterly payments of estimated tax totaled $4,500. The following information for the year was compiled from Hunt's checkbook and other sources:

Dividends received	$1,150
Interest income:	
Savings account	900
Municipal bonds	600
Real estate taxes on home	2,000
State sales taxes	380
Medical expenses (unreimbursed)	1,850
State income taxes paid	1,760
Contribution to United Fund	400
Accountant's services (preparing last year's income tax return)	200
Auto license on personal car	24
Safe deposit box rental (used for jewelry)	32
Subscriptions to professional journals	120
Country club dues	450
Interest expense on home mortgage	1,600
Interest paid on personal loans	500

During the year, Carl sold the following corporate stock:

Security	Holding Period	Cost	Proceeds
Xerox	four years	$5,100	$6,300
Reebok	two years	2,100	1,800
Tenneco	four months	3,850	5,050
Genentech	three months	2,450	1,750

REQUIRED

Compute the amount of tax due (or any overpayment) reported in the Hunt's 1989 joint income tax return. Use the appropriate schedule in Exhibit 28–2 (page 1086). (Round computations to the nearest dollar.)

Corporate tax return

28–30 The following information for the current year is from the records of Eagle Corporation:

Sales	$800,000
Interest earned on corporate bonds	18,000
Dividends received on Nu-tech stock (a domestic corporation)	30,000
Dividends received on Atikokan, Ltd., stock (a Canadian company)	4,000
Cost of goods sold	520,000
Selling and administrative expenses (excluding charitable contributions)	120,000
Charitable contributions	8,000
Net capital gain on sale of property	20,000

In addition, the corporation had a net capital loss carryforward of $8,000 from prior years, and a $16,000 charitable contributions deduction carryforward.

REQUIRED

Prepare a schedule showing the computation of Eagle Corporation's total income tax liability for the year, using the rate schedule given on page 1091.

Tax effects—form of business

28–31 Scott Hilyer, who is married and has one dependent, is opening a business with an estimated annual income of $100,000 before tax and owner's salary. He must decide whether the business should be operated as a corporation (with all shares owned by his wife and himself) or as a sole proprietorship. Hilyer has annual investment income of $16,000, which is fully taxable. He estimates that his annual total itemized deductions are approximately $12,000.

If the business is a corporation, Hilyer expects an annual salary of $40,000 and one-half of the after-tax corporate income in dividends. If the business is a sole proprietorship, he would withdraw $50,000 from the business each year.

REQUIRED
Prepare an analysis showing the expected tax results (to the nearest dollar) of the two types of business organization. Use the corporate tax rate schedule on page 1091 and the appropriate schedule in Exhibit 28–2 (page 1086).

ALTERNATE PROBLEMS

Joint tax return

28–27A Paul and Joan Lang, who have two young children, are filing a joint federal income tax return. Paul's annual salary as a credit manager for the Bond Company is $46,500, from which $5,100 was withheld for federal income tax. Joan works part-time as a free-lance editor; her gross receipts for the year were $5,200 and her business expenses were $1,800. The couple paid $300 estimated tax during the year. The Langs' dividend income during the year amounted to $580. Joan also received a small bequest of $2,500 from a relative who died during the year. During the year, Paul had a long-term capital gain of $2,600 and a short-term loss of $3,800 from the sale of securities.

The family's personal expenses for the year included the following:

Contributions to United Fund and church	$ 850
Flood damage to house (not insured)	3,200
State fishing and hunting licenses	36
Medical and dental expenses (not paid by insurance)	2,100
State sales taxes	480
Real estate taxes	1,900
Interest on home mortgage	3,200
State income taxes paid	2,100

REQUIRED
Calculate the amount of tax due (or overpayment) shown in the Langs' joint income tax return for the current year. Use the appropriate schedule in Exhibit 28–2 (page 1086). Round computations to the nearest dollar.

Types of deductions

28–28A The following items relate to the federal income taxes of individuals who itemize their deductions in computing their tax. Consider each item independently.

1. Purchase of Christmas seals (stamps) from tuberculosis association.
2. Sales taxes incurred in operating a business.
3. Federal excise taxes on telephone calls.
4. Dog license.
5. Tuition for Dale Carnegie course taken by insurance salesperson to improve selling skills.
6. Loss of elm trees due to Dutch elm disease.
7. Cost of spike shoes bought by professional baseball player.
8. Cost of piano and ballet lessons for daughter.
9. Employee moving expenses.
10. Fee paid to employment agency.
11. Net capital loss of $800.
12. Wagering losses of $500 (gains of $900 included in gross income).

13. Advisor's fee for personal investment advice.
14. Cost of professional magazine subscriptions paid by university professor.
15. Transportation expenses driving to and from one's regular place of employment.

REQUIRED
Indicate whether each of the above items is (a) nondeductible, (b) deductible in determining adjusted gross income, or (c) deductible from adjusted gross income. If answer (c) is given, indicate if there are limitations on the amount of the deduction.

Joint tax return

28–29A Rod and Katy Morse are both under 65 years of age and have two dependent children. Rod furnished over one-half the support for his mother-in-law, who lives with them. Her total income consists of $800 interest on a savings account. Katy has no outside employment. Rod owns an office building from which rentals for the year totaled $42,000. During the year, he had the following items related to the building:

Heat	$3,700
Janitor service	2,200
Depreciation	2,500
Interest on mortgage	3,600
Real estate taxes	4,800
Insurance premiums on three-year policy (paid January 1)	1,200

Rod's annual salary as sales manager for an insurance firm was $45,000, from which $6,800 was withheld for federal income taxes during the year. He also paid $4,200 in estimated tax during the year. The following information for the year was compiled from his checkbook and other sources:

Dividends received	$1,620
Interest income:	
Savings account	840
Municipal bonds	1,200
Real estate taxes on home	2,200
State sales taxes	480
Medical expenses (unreimbursed)	4,200
State income taxes paid	3,100
Contributions to United Fund	750
Accountant's services (preparing last year's income tax return)	200
Athletic club dues	450
Auto license on personal cars	48
Safe deposit box rental (used for jewelry)	40
Subscriptions to professional journals	180
Lottery winnings	200
Interest expense on mortgage	4,200

During the year, Rod sold the following corporate stock:

Security	Holding Period	Cost	Proceeds
Heinz	two years	$2,200	$3,400
Olin	three years	1,600	1,300
Chrysler	three months	2,800	2,200
Syntex	five months	3,600	4,100

REQUIRED
Compute the amount of tax due (or any overpayment) reported in the Morses' joint income tax return. Use the appropriate schedule in Exhibit 28–2 (page 1086). (Round computations to the nearest dollar.)

Corporate tax return

28–30A The following information for the current year is from the records of Aztec Company:

Sales	$2,100,000
Cost of goods sold	1,250,000
Interest expense	14,000
Selling and administrative expenses (excluding contributions)	580,000
Dividends received from wholly owned affiliate	12,000
Dividends received from Empire, Inc. (a domestic corporation)	10,000
Net capital gain on sale of assets	24,000
Charitable contributions	34,000

In addition, the corporation had a net capital loss carryforward of $4,000.

REQUIRED
Prepare a schedule showing the computation of Aztec Company's total income tax liability for the year using the rate schedule given on page 1091.

Tax effects—form of business

28–31A Charles Elliot, who is married and has one dependent, is opening a business with an estimated annual income of $160,000 before tax and owner's salary. He must decide whether the business should be operated as a corporation (with all shares owned by his wife and himself) or as a sole proprietorship. Elliot has annual investment income of $20,000, which is fully taxable. He estimates that his annual total itemized deductions are approximately $20,000.

If the business is a corporation, Elliot expects an annual salary of $50,000 and one-half of the after-tax corporate income in dividends. If the business is a sole proprietorship, he would withdraw $50,000 from the business each year.

REQUIRED
Prepare an analysis showing the expected tax results of the two types of business organization. Use the corporate tax rate schedule on page 1091 and the appropriate schedule in Exhibit 28–2 (page 1086).

BUSINESS DECISION PROBLEM

At the beginning of the current year, Wendy Allen received a $100,000 inheritance from a relative. She asks your advice about the income tax treatment of the inheritance and also about several possible investment opportunities. She may invest the $100,000 in a partnership owned by two acquaintances or purchase either 10% high-grade industrial bonds or 7% tax-exempt municipal bonds.

Wendy's annual share of the partnership net income would be 25% of an expected $56,000 for the next several years. If she invests in the partnership, she expects to withdraw only one-half of her share of net income annually.

Wendy is unmarried and under 65 years of age. Her annual salary is $40,000, and she estimates that her total itemized deductions will amount to $10,500 for the year.

REQUIRED

(a) How is the $100,000 inheritance handled for income tax purposes?

(b) Which of the three investment alternatives should Wendy choose if she is basing her decision on receiving the largest after-tax income for the current year? (Ignore the problem of risk in determining the best alternative.) Show calculations of the after-tax income to support your choice.

ANSWERS TO SELF-TEST QUESTIONS

1. (c) **2.** (a) **3.** (c) **4.** (b) **5.** (b)

ANNUAL REPORT PROBLEM FOR PART 6: Whirlpool Corporation

The following problem concludes Part 6 of the text; further, it reflects issues covered throughout the book. The problem uses the actual financial section of the 1988 annual report of Whirlpool Corporation, a major U.S. corporation. This financial section, provided on pages 1110–31, includes management's discussion and analysis of financial condition and results of operations, the consolidated financial statements, notes to the consolidated financial statements, report of the independent auditors, and the report by management on the financial statements.

Although some items in the financial section relate to matters not covered in an introductory accounting course, they are included to illustrate the comprehensive nature of the financial data.

REQUIRED

(a) In presenting its consolidated statements of cash flows, does Whirlpool use the direct method or the indirect method to show the details of cash provided by operating activities?

(b) In computing cash provided by operating activities, the equity in net earnings of foreign affiliates less dividends received, $10.4 million, is deducted from Whirlpool's earnings. Why?

(c) Using data available in the consolidated statements of cash flows and in the consolidated balance sheets, estimate the amount of accumulated depreciation on property, plant, and equipment sold or retired during 1988.

(d) Why do product warranty liabilities appear in both the current liabilities and the other liabilities sections of the consolidated balance sheet?

(e) Whirlpool Corporation has a complex capital structure because it has outstanding stock options (see Note 8). Yet the firm, correctly, does not make a dual presentation of primary earnings per share and fully diluted earnings per share. Why do you suppose this is the case? (Hint: one of the basic principles discussed in Chapter 13 applies here.)

(f) The firm has a 100% interest in Whirlpool Acceptance Corporation, a finance and leasing subsidiary. In previous annual reports, the accounts of this subsidiary were not consolidated with those of the parent company, but they were consolidated in the 1988 annual report. Why? (See Note 1.)

(g) Read Note 1 relating to principles of consolidation, Note 2 relating to acquisitions, and Note 5 relating to affiliated foreign companies. Which of the following companies' accounts are consolidated with those of the parent company, and which are carried on the equity method in the consolidated financial statements: KitchenAid, Inc.; Aspera S.r.l.; Brasmotor S.A.; Inglis Limited; Vitromatic, S.A. de C. V.; N. V. Philips' Gloeilampenfabrieken; Brastemp S. A.; Embraco S. A.; and Consul S. A.?

(h) Using the formulas shown in Chapter 20, compute the following ratios and relationships for Whirlpool's 1988 and 1987 data, and comment on the results: rate of return on assets, rate of return on common stockholders' equity, rate of return on sales (use total revenue), dividend payout ratio, equity ratio, current ratio, quick ratio, inventory turnover, and average collection period for trade receivables (use sales only). At December 31, 1986, Whirlpool's total assets, in millions of dollars, were $2,855.5, and total stockholders' equity, also in millions of dollars, was $1,349.8. In calculating inventory turnover, use ending inventory rather than average inventory (the December 31, 1986, inventory is not given in the 1988 annual report).

Management's Discussion and Analysis of Results of Operations and Financial Condition

Results of Operations

The statements of earnings summarize Whirlpool operating results for the last three years. This section of Management's Discussion highlights the main factors affecting the change in operating results during this three-year period.

On January 1, 1988, the company adopted Financial Accounting Standards Board Statement No. 94, "Consolidation of All Majority-owned Subsidiaries." The 1987 and 1986 consolidated financial statements have been restated to include Whirlpool Acceptance Corporation, a wholly owned subsidiary previously accounted for by the equity method. Whirlpool Acceptance Corporation provides inventory financing services for dealers and distributors marketing products manufactured by the company, its subsidiaries and certain other manufacturers. Whirlpool Acceptance Corporation also provides consumer financing services for retail sales by dealers, lease financing services for the acquisition of general equipment and facilities by business organizations, insurance premium financing, and dealer financing for manufactured homes and recreational vehicles. Its net earnings for 1988, 1987 and 1986 were $15 million, $13 million and $14 million before elimination of intercompany transactions.

Revenues

Revenues were up 5% in 1988 from 1987. Appliance unit volume, up 3% during a period when the industry, overall, was down, accounted for the majority of this increase. The remainder of the improvement consisted of higher non-appliance sales and increased financing services revenue attributable to higher dealer and lease financing volumes. As in 1987, market conditions continued to be very competitive. Price increases were difficult to achieve despite higher costs being incurred by the company for basic raw materials. A price increase averaging 3% was implemented during the fourth quarter of 1988.

As explained earlier, in March, 1988, the company was reorganized into business units along brand lines. Results by business unit were as follows:

- Kenmore Appliance Group sales of $1,440 million were up $63 million from 1987, an increase of 5%.
- KitchenAid Appliance Group sales of $308 million were up $66 million from 1987, an increase of 27%. Stronger sales were experienced across all product categories as the full line roll out continued.
- Whirlpool Appliance Group sales of $1,678 million were down $76 million from 1987, a decrease of 4% over most product categories.
- Inglis Limited sales of $351 million were up $35 million from 1987, an increase of 11%.
- Whirlpool Acceptance Corporation revenues of $107 million were up $13 million from 1987, an increase of 14%.
- Sales of other consolidated companies and business units were $538 million, an increase of $112 million, or 27%, over 1987.

1987 revenues were up 5% from 1986. 1986 sales included $259 million related to the central heating and cooling business which was sold in the fourth quarter of that year. Taking this disposition into account, 1987 revenues were up 12% from 1986. Appliance unit volume was up 6% and accounted for the majority of this increase. The remainder of the 1987 sales improvement was due to a richer sales mix and an increase in financing services revenue from higher dealer and lease financing volumes.

Costs and Expenses

The relationship of cost of products sold to sales was unfavorable in 1988 compared to 1987 and 1986. Price pressures from our supplier base continued in many commodities due to high capacity utilization, strong demand and a relatively weak dollar, while competitive pressures limited the ability to recover these increased costs in our selling prices. The relative mix of sales between brands also had a negative impact on operating results in 1988. Additionally, cost of products sold for 1988 included a warranty charge ($.20 per share) related to the sale of product by a former subsidiary.

Interest expense related to financing services revenue increased in both 1988 and 1987 due to higher levels of borrowings to support improved business levels.

The company's selling and administrative expenses in dollars and as a percent of revenues for 1988 and 1986 were lower than 1987 due primarily to 1987 start-up costs associated with product-line expansion of acquired businesses. Selling and administrative expenses for 1988 were favorably affected by the previously mentioned company reorganizations which reduced salaried head count and an increased emphasis on cost containment.

Costs included research and development expenditures of $73 million, $79 million and $75 million in 1988, 1987 and 1986. Higher levels of investments in equipment and tooling in 1987 and 1986 resulted in depreciation expense of $143 million in 1988, $133 million in 1987 and $120 million in 1986. These costs and investments included expenditures for product improvements and more efficient production methods. The provision for income taxes was 39% of before-tax earnings in 1988, compared to 44% in 1987 and 45% in 1986. The 1988 decrease was due primarily to rate reductions. The 1987 decrease was also affected by rate reductions, which were partially offset by the repeal of the investment tax credit and other items.

Other Income and Expense

Other income increased in 1988 primarily due to more favorable foreign exchange experience. Interest expense was up in 1988 and 1987 due to higher average levels of outstanding borrowings necessary to help fund working capital needs, capital expenditures and investments in affiliated companies.

Earnings from the company's Brazilian affiliates were $16 million, $29 million and $21 million in 1988, 1987 and 1986. The high level of 1987 earnings reflects an unusually strong performance in the latter part of that year. During 1988, those companies continued to operate in an environment which gave rise to variable business conditions, which among other things, created volatility in consumer demand. The decrease in Brazilian earnings for 1988 was partially offset by $3 million in equity earnings from Vitromatic, a Mexican joint venture company established in late 1987 for the manufacture and sale of appliances. The company has a 49% interest in the joint venture.

Operating results for 1986 included a business disposition and consolidation gain of $13 million, consisting of a gain from the sale of the central heating and cooling business, partially offset by a provision for closing a major portion of the St. Joseph, Michigan manufacturing facility.

Net Earnings

As a result of the above factors, earnings from continuing operations before the 1987 accounting change for income taxes were $161 million in 1988, $187 million in 1987 and $202 million in 1986. Corresponding earnings per share figures were $2.33, $2.61 and $2.72.

In late 1988, management took steps to exit the company's kitchen cabinet business, Whirlpool Kitchens, Inc. The decision was made after an assessment of the fit of the business within the company's overall strategic direction. The after-tax loss from discontinuing the business of Whirlpool Kitchens, including operating results, was $67 million ($.97 per share) in 1988, $6 million ($.08 per share) in 1987 and $2 million ($.02 per share) in 1986. The loss for 1988 includes an after-tax loss of $45 million ($.65 per share) consisting primarily of estimated provisions for losses on disposal of assets, lease costs and the write off of goodwill.

In 1987, the company adjusted deferred income taxes to reflect reduced tax rates resulting from the Tax Reform Act of 1986. The cumulative effect of this accounting change increased 1987 earnings by $11 million, or $.15 per share.

After consideration of the 1988 loss from discontinuing the kitchen cabinet business and the 1987 accounting change, net earnings were $94 million in 1988, $192 million in 1987 and $200 million in 1986. Related earnings per share were $1.36, $2.68 and $2.70.

Financial Position

The balance sheets represent the company's financial position at December 31, 1988 and 1987. The statements of cash flows reflect the changes in cash and cash equivalents for the last three years, classifying transactions into three categories—operating, investing and financing activities.

Operating Activities

The company's main source of liquidity is cash from operating activities, which was $366 million, $264 million and $176 million in 1988, 1987 and 1986. Cash from operating activities consists of net earnings from continuing operations before accounting change adjusted by non-cash operating income and expenses and changes in assets and liabilities. The change in cash from operating activities from 1987 to 1988 resulted from a decrease in inventories, partially offset by lower earnings and changes in various other assets and liabilities. Inventories were lower due to an increased emphasis on managing finished goods inventory levels. The change from 1986 to 1987 resulted primarily from a smaller increase in inventories, partially offset by lower earnings.

Investing Activities

The principal recurring uses of cash have been property additions and increased investment in financing receivables and leases. Net property additions consumed $166 million, $223 million and $217 million of cash in 1988, 1987 and 1986. These expenditures were primarily for equipment and tooling related to product improvements and more efficient production methods. Investment in financing receivables and leases (net of payments received) consumed $192 million, $106 million and $268 million in 1988, 1987 and 1986. These expenditures represent an expansion in the business of Whirlpool Acceptance Corporation.

The other main investing activities during the past three years involved new business acquisitions and investments in affiliated businesses to enhance future growth opportunities. In 1988, the company purchased the dishwasher and trash compactor manufacturing facility of Emerson Electric Co. and increased its investment in affiliated foreign companies at a combined cost of $43 million. In 1987, the company acquired an additional interest in Inglis Limited, a Canadian appliance subsidiary, increasing our ownership to approximately 72%. The company also acquired in 1987 a 49% interest in Vitromatic, a Mexican major appliance company, and signed an agreement for a joint venture in India. The cost of the 1987 acquisitions was $72 million in cash and notes payable. In 1986, the company acquired various businesses, including KitchenAid, Inc. and a majority interest in Aspera S.r.l., at a total cost of $209 million, and received proceeds of $156 million from the disposal of its central heating and cooling business.

Financing Activities

Dividends of $76 million ($1.10 per share), $79 million ($1.10 per share) and $76 million ($1.03 per share) were paid in 1988, 1987 and 1986. Also, in 1987 the company repurchased five million shares of its common stock in the open market for $178 million.

Additional funds needed for the above investing and financing activities over those provided by operating activities were obtained through increased borrowings. Short-term debt increased by $68 million, $117 million and $115 million in 1988, 1987 and 1986. Long-term debt increased by $105 million in 1988, $60 million in 1987 and $211 million in 1986. In 1988, the company issued $125 million of 9.1% notes due in 2008 and $21 million of other long-term debt due in 1991 through 1993.

Financial Condition and Other Matters

The financial position of the company remains strong as evidenced by the consolidated balance sheet. As of December 31, 1988, cash and short-term investments totaled $143 million, total assets were $3,410 million, working capital (the excess of current assets over current liabilities) amounted to $429 million, and shareholders' equity equaled $1,321 million.

In addition to its liquidity, the company's broad access to capital markets and internally generated cash flows are believed to be more than adequate to provide for currently anticipated ongoing business needs, as well as support other internal and external business growth opportunities that may arise.

On January 2, 1989, the company acquired for $361 million in cash a 53% interest in a joint venture with N. V. Philips' Gloeilampenfabrieken ("Philips") of The Netherlands. The joint venture consists of the major portion of Philips' worldwide Major Domestic Appliance Division ("MDA") and manufactures, sells and services home appliances under various brand names. It has been accounted for as a purchase transaction and will be consolidated into the company's financial statements beginning in 1989. The acquisition was financed with short-term borrowings until more permanent financing is arranged.

The joint venture will be evaluated during 1991. If it is decided to continue the venture under the existing ownership interests, the company will pay Philips 2.50 million Dfl (approximately $125 million based on the exchange rate at December 31, 1988) plus interest at 7% per annum from January 1, 1989. If no payment is made the relative interests of the venture partners may be adjusted to 50%. If the venture is not continued, either venture partner can cause the company to become sole owner of the joint venture. In this case, the company would pay Philips 1 billion Dfl (approximately $500 million based on the exchange rate at December 31, 1988) plus interest at 7% per annum from January 1, 1989 and a possible additional amount based on the performance of the company's common stock. If a cash payment is required under the above alternatives, it is currently expected that the related funding would take any one or more of several forms of debt issued in the U.S. and/or European markets.

The basic nature of the U.S. and European domestic appliance businesses is similar, although products for the European markets are designed and manufactured differently to meet customers' tastes and lifestyles and governmental requirements existing in various national markets. European gross margins are usually more favorable than in the U.S., although higher selling and administrative costs, generally higher European tax rates and foreign exchange exposure can be offsetting factors.

MDA operating results for 1988 are expected to be improved over those for 1987, primarily as a result of more stringent cost containment programs, a more focused approach to the business and higher market growth. The 1988 pro forma financial implications of the acquisition are more fully explained in Note 2 to the accompanying financial statements in this report. These amounts are based on estimated 1988 MDA financial data and assume the MDA interest was purchased at the beginning of 1988. The pro forma consolidated balance sheet at December 31, 1988 shows an increase in working capital, intangibles and long-term debt required to fund the acquisition. The pro forma ratio of long-term debt to invested capital (long-term debt, minority interests and stockholders' equity) at December 31, 1988 rises to 44% from 26%. The pro forma higher interest costs and amortization of intangibles, generally over 40 years, were more than offset by favorable operating results of the venture. Pro forma earnings from continuing operations for 1988 are estimated to be $166 million ($2.39 per share) on sales of over $6 billion.

Consolidated Balance Sheets

December 31 *(millions of dollars)*	1988	1987
Assets		
Current Assets		
Cash and cash equivalents	$ 97.5	$ 90.4
Short-term investments	45.9	33.1
Trade receivables, less allowances for doubtful accounts (1988—$4.4; 1987—$3.3)	419.5	327.6
Financing receivables and leases, less allowances for doubtful accounts (1988—$3.1; 1987—$3.1)	641.0	545.6
Inventories	536.8	615.6
Prepaid expenses	55.7	49.3
Deferred income taxes	24.9	20.6
Other	6.0	7.8
Total Current Assets	1,827.3	1,690.0
Investments, Long-Term Receivables and Other Assets		
Affiliated foreign companies	247.7	218.8
Financing receivables and leases, less allowances for doubtful accounts (1988—$5.4; 1987—$2.6)	387.1	292.2
Intangibles, less accumulated amortization (1988—$8.1; 1987—$5.1)	110.8	110.2
Other assets	16.9	46.9
	762.5	668.1
Property, Plant and Equipment		
Land	19.9	19.1
Buildings	316.8	312.9
Machinery and equipment	887.9	794.5
	1,224.6	1,126.5
Less allowances for depreciation	404.7	347.9
	819.9	778.6
Total Assets	$3,409.7	$3,136.7

December 31 (*millions of dollars*)	1988	1987
Liabilities and Stockholders' Equity		
Current Liabilities		
Notes payable	$ 695.1	$ 626.9
Accounts payable	351.7	311.2
Payrolls and other compensation	113.0	120.6
Accrued expenses	173.8	142.9
Income taxes	5.1	8.4
Product warranty	24.1	21.4
Current maturities of long-term debt	35.8	38.4
Total Current Liabilities	1,398.6	1,269.8
Other Liabilities		
Deferred income taxes	139.3	118.3
Product warranty	13.3	13.5
Long-term debt	473.8	366.5
	626.4	498.3
Minority Interests	63.8	64.8
Stockholders' Equity		
Capital stock	74.3	74.3
Additional paid-in capital	8.3	7.0
Retained earnings	1,391.9	1,374.0
Foreign currency translation adjustment	24.0	26.1
	1,498.5	1,481.4
Less treasury stock—at cost	177.6	177.6
	1,320.9	1,303.8
Total Liabilities and Stockholders' Equity	$3,409.7	$3,136.7

See notes to consolidated financial statements

Consolidated Statements of Stockholders' Equity

Year Ended December 31 *(millions of dollars)*	1988	1987	1986
Common Stock			
Balance at beginning of year	$ 74.3	$ 74.1	$ 36.7
Two-for-one stock split	—	—	36.7
Stock option transactions	—	.2	.5
Other	—	—	.2
Balance at End of Year	74.3	74.3	74.1
Additional Paid-in Capital			
Balance at beginning of year	7.0	4.7	33.9
Two-for-one stock split	—	—	(36.7)
Stock option transactions	1.3	2.3	5.9
Other	—	—	1.6
Balance at End of Year	8.3	7.0	4.7
Retained Earnings			
Balance at beginning of year	1,374.0	1,260.7	1,136.1
Net earnings	94.1	191.9	199.7
Other	—	—	.5
	1,468.1	1,452.6	1,336.3
Cash dividends paid	(76.2)	(78.6)	(75.6)
Balance at End of Year	1,391.9	1,374.0	1,260.7
Foreign Currency Translation Adjustment			
Balance at beginning of year	26.1	10.3	—
Translation adjustment	(2.1)	15.8	10.3
Balance at End of Year	24.0	26.1	10.3
Treasury Stock—at Cost			
Balance at beginning of year	(177.6)	—	—
Purchase of 5 million shares	—	(177.6)	—
Balance at End of Year	(177.6)	(177.6)	—
Stockholders' Equity at End of Year	$1,320.9	$1,303.8	$1,349.8
Cash dividends per share of common stock	$ 1.10	$ 1.10	$ 1.03

See notes to consolidated financial statements

Consolidated Statements of Earnings

Year Ended December 31 *(millions of dollars except share data)*	1988	1987	1986
Revenues			
Net sales	$4,314.5	$4,114.8	$3,937.6
Financing services	106.9	93.8	76.1
	4,421.4	4,208.6	4,013.7
Expenses			
Cost of products sold	3,505.7	3,264.8	3,107.5
Interest expense related to financing services	47.4	38.8	29.4
Selling and administrative expenses	606.7	608.8	550.8
	4,159.8	3,912.4	3,687.7
Operating Profit	261.6	296.2	326.0
Other Income (Expense)			
Interest and sundry	24.7	14.2	12.2
Interest expense	(53.4)	(30.7)	(22.4)
Business disposition and consolidation	—	—	12.8
Earnings from Continuing Operations Before Income Taxes and Other Items	232.9	279.7	328.6
Income taxes	90.9	122.5	147.1
Earnings from Continuing Operations Before Other Items	142.0	157.2	181.5
Equity in net earnings of affiliated foreign companies	19.5	28.9	20.6
Minority interests in net earnings of subsidiaries	(.2)	.5	(.6)
Earnings from Continuing Operations Before Accounting Change	161.3	186.6	201.5
Loss from discontinued operation	67.2	5.5	1.8
Earnings Before Accounting Change	94.1	181.1	199.7
Cumulative effect on prior years of change in accounting for income taxes	—	10.8	—
Net Earnings	$ 94.1	$ 191.9	$ 199.7
Per share of common stock:			
Earnings from continuing operations before accounting change	$ 2.33	$ 2.61	$ 2.72
Loss from discontinued operation	(.97)	(.08)	(.02)
Cumulative effect of accounting change	—	.15	—
Net Earnings	$ 1.36	$ 2.68	$ 2.70
Average number of common shares outstanding (millions)	69.3	71.7	73.8

See notes to consolidated financial statements

Consolidated Statements of Cash Flows

Year Ended December 31 *(millions of dollars)*	1988	1987	1986
Operating Activities			
Earnings before accounting change	$ 94.1	$ 181.1	$ 199.7
Adjustments to reconcile earnings to cash provided by operating activities:			
Depreciation	142.7	133.3	119.8
Deferred income taxes	16.7	12.0	15.3
Equity in net earnings of affiliated foreign companies, less dividends received	(10.4)	(20.2)	(11.0)
Provision for doubtful accounts	11.5	17.7	6.0
Other	4.7	6.4	(4.3)
Business disposition and consolidation	—	—	(12.8)
Loss from discontinued operation, including in 1988, loss on disposition of $45.0	67.2	5.5	1.8
Changes in assets and liabilities, net of effects of business acquisitions and disposition:			
Increase in receivables	(95.2)	(70.9)	(2.1)
Decrease (increase) in inventories	87.0	(74.8)	(147.3)
Increase in payables	39.3	51.0	3.1
Other—net	8.7	22.8	8.1
	39.8	(71.9)	(138.2)
Cash Provided by Operating Activities	366.3	263.9	176.3
Investing Activities			
Proceeds from business disposition	—	—	156.0
Net additions to properties	(165.9)	(223.4)	(216.8)
Financing receivables originated and leasing assets purchased	(2,133.7)	(1,990.0)	(1,945.9)
Principal payments received on financing receivables and leases	1,941.8	1,884.1	1,677.7
Net (increase) decrease in investment in and loans to affiliated foreign companies	(26.1)	3.3	(38.8)
Acquisitions of businesses	(14.1)	(14.0)	(208.7)
Other	(42.6)	(2.3)	(.5)
Cash Used for Investing Activities	(440.6)	(342.3)	(577.0)
Financing Activities			
Proceeds of short-term borrowings	5,943.3	4,863.8	4,260.7
Repayments of short-term borrowings	(5,875.2)	(4,746.4)	(4,145.7)
Proceeds of long-term debt	145.9	110.0	222.4
Repayment of long-term debt	(41.3)	(50.0)	(11.1)
Acquisition of treasury stock	—	(177.6)	—
Dividends paid	(76.2)	(78.6)	(75.6)
Other	(14.9)	24.6	58.3
Cash Provided by (Used for) Financing Activities	81.6	(54.2)	309.0
Effect of foreign exchange rate changes on cash and cash equivalents	(.2)	.7	1.3
Increase (Decrease) in Cash and Cash Equivalents	7.1	(131.9)	(90.4)
Cash and cash equivalents at Beginning of Year	90.4	222.3	312.7
Cash and Cash Equivalents at End of Year	$ 97.5	$ 90.4	$ 222.3

Year Ended December 31 *(millions of dollars)*	1988	1987	1986
Detail of Cash and Cash Equivalents Provided by Operating Activities from Earnings Before Accounting Change			
Cash received from sales and financing services	$4,337.6	$4,190.1	$3,951.5
Cash paid to suppliers and employees	(3,843.3)	(3,795.6)	(3,633.2)
Dividends received from affiliated foreign companies	9.1	8.7	8.8
Interest received	11.4	13.5	10.4
Interest paid	(100.9)	(59.4)	(49.6)
Income taxes paid	(67.4)	(105.4)	(122.2)
Other—net	19.8	12.0	10.6
	$ 366.3	$ 263.9	$ 176.3

See notes to consolidated financial statements

Notes to Consolidated Financial Statements

(1) Summary of Principal Accounting Policies

Principles of Consolidation: The consolidated financial statements include all majority-owned subsidiaries. Investments in affiliated foreign companies are accounted for by the equity method. On January 1, 1988, the company adopted Financial Accounting Standards Board Statement No. 94, "Consolidation of all Majority-owned Subsidiaries." The 1987 and 1986 consolidated financial statements have been restated to include Whirlpool Acceptance Corporation, a wholly-owned finance and leasing subsidiary previously accounted for by the equity method.

Cash and Cash Equivalents: All highly liquid debt instruments purchased with a maturity of three months or less are considered as cash equivalents.

Inventories: Inventories are stated at last-in, first-out (LIFO) cost, except nonproduction and non-U.S. inventories which are stated at first-in, first-out (FIFO) cost. Costs do not exceed realizable values.

Property, Plant and Equipment: Properties are stated at cost. Depreciation of plant and equipment is computed using the straight-line method based on the estimated useful lives of the assets.

Intangibles: The cost of business acquisitions in excess of net tangible assets acquired is amortized on a straight-line basis over 40 years.

Investment Tax Credits: For financial reporting purposes, investment tax credits relating to Whirlpool Acceptance Corporation leasing transactions prior to the Tax Reform Act of 1986 are deferred and included in lease financing income as earned.

Financing Receivables and Leases: Interest and discount charges are recognized in revenues using the effective yield method. Lease income is recorded in decreasing amounts over the term of the lease contract, resulting in a level rate of return on the net investment in the lease. For transactions entered into after December 31, 1987, origination fees and related direct costs are deferred and amortized as yield adjustments over the lease term, using the effective yield method.

(2) Business Acquisitions and Dispositions

Acquisitions

During 1986, the company purchased for $208.7 million in cash KitchenAid, Inc., a domestic appliance manufacturer, and 65% of Aspera S.r.l., an Italian manufacturer of compressors for refrigeration products. In 1986, the company also purchased 20% of Brasmotor S.A. In 1987, the company increased its majority interest in Inglis Limited, a Canadian appliance manufacturer, to 72% and acquired 49% of Vitromatic, S.A. de C.V., a Mexican appliance manufacturer. The cost of the 1987 acquisitions consisted of $14.0 million in cash and $58.1 million in notes payable. Approximately $43.0 million was paid in 1988 for other acquisitions and investments in affiliated companies. All acquisitions were accounted for as purchase transactions. Pro forma operating results for 1988, 1987 and 1986 would not have been materially different from reported amounts.

On January 2, 1989, the company acquired for cash a 53% interest in a joint venture with N.V. Philips' Gloeilampenfabrieken ("Philips") of The Netherlands. The new joint venture company, which will consist of the major portion of Philips' worldwide Major Domestic Appliance Division ("MDA"), will develop, manufacture, market, sell and service home appliances under various brand names. The cost of the acquisition was 750 million Dfl ($361 million) and has been accounted for as a 1989 purchase transaction. This investment was initially funded with guilder-denominated bank loans and U.S. commercial paper with more permanent financing expected to be arranged during 1989.

Key unaudited pro forma information, based on estimated MDA financial data, assuming the MDA interest was purchased at the beginning of 1988, includes the following:

December 31, 1988 *(millions of dollars)*	
Current assets	$2,600
Intangibles	$ 300
Total assets	$4,700
Current liabilities	$1,800
Long-term debt	$1,200
Stockholders' equity and minority interests	$1,500
Year Ended December 31 *(millions of dollars)*	
Revenues	$6,300
Earnings from continuing operations before accounting change (per share—$2.39)	$ 166

The joint venture agreement provides that the company and Philips will evaluate the venture during the period July through December, 1991. If the parties agree to continue the venture, the company will pay Philips approximately 250 million Dfl (approximately $125 million based on the exchange rate at December 31, 1988) plus interest at 7% per annum commencing January 1, 1989 to retain its current ownership interest; if no such payment is made the relative interests of the venture partners may be adjusted to 50%. If the decision is made to not continue the joint venture, the agreement provides for either party to cause the company to become sole owner of the joint venture. Under this arrangement, the company would pay Philips 1 billion Dfl (approximately $500 million based on the exchange rate at December 31, 1988) plus interest at 7% per annum commencing January 1, 1989 and a possible additional amount based on the performance of the company's common stock.

Disposition and Consolidation

In 1986, the company sold its central heating and cooling business for $156.0 million in cash, resulting in a pre-tax gain of $32.8 million. The central heating and cooling business contributed net sales of $258.8 million and net earnings of $9.5 million to 1986 operating results.

In 1987, the company closed a significant portion of its St. Joseph, Michigan manufacturing facility and relocated production to other manufacturing locations. The 1986 pre-tax provision for the estimated cost of this consolidation was $20.0 million and consisted principally of a provision for loss on the disposal of equipment and facilities and employee severance and related expenses.

Discontinued Operation

During the fourth quarter of 1988, a formal plan was adopted to discontinue operations of Whirlpool Kitchens, Inc., a wholly-owned subsidiary and manufacturer of kitchen cabinets. The operating results of Whirlpool Kitchens have been segregated and are included in the determination of loss from discontinued operation shown in the consolidated statements of earnings. Whirlpool Kitchens' net sales are not material in relation to consolidated amounts.

The loss from discontinued operation consists of the following:

(millions of dollars)	1988	1987	1986
Loss from operations, less applicable income tax benefits (1988—$11.7; 1987—$3.5)	$22.2	$5.5	$1.8
Loss on disposition, less income tax benefit of $15.7	45.0	—	—
	$67.2	$5.5	$1.8

The loss on disposition consists primarily of estimated provisions for losses on disposal of related assets, lease costs and the write-off of goodwill.

The net assets of the discontinued operation are included in other assets in the consolidated balance sheet. These amounts are not significant and represent receivables, inventory, fixed assets and other liabilities. A majority of the operation's assets is expected to be sold in the first quarter of 1989.

(3) Financing Receivables and Leases

December 31 *(millions of dollars)*	1988	1987
Financing receivables	$ 695.7	$ 566.8
Leveraged leases	53.4	47.6
Direct financing leases	297.9	232.9
Other	16.7	12.0
	1,063.7	859.3
Unearned income	(78.7)	(67.3)
Estimated residual value	51.6	51.5
Allowances for doubtful accounts	(8.5)	(5.7)
Total financing receivables and leases	1,028.1	837.8
Less current portion	641.0	545.6
Long-term portion	$ 387.1	$ 292.2

Deferred income tax liabilities relating to leveraged and direct financing leases were $69.1 million and $51.8 million at December 31, 1988 and 1987.

Financing receivables and minimum lease payments receivable at December 31, 1988 mature contractually as follows:

(millions of dollars)	Financing Receivables	Leveraged and Direct Financing Leases	Other
1989	$587.6	$ 83.0	$ 3.9
1990	61.7	71.8	3.5
1991	14.9	65.6	2.9
1992	9.9	43.7	2.5
1993	3.2	29.1	1.8
Thereafter	18.4	58.1	2.1
	$695.7	$351.3	$ 16.7

(4) Inventories

December 31 *(millions of dollars)*	1988	1987
Finished products	$543.0	$603.6
Work in process	56.7	61.3
Raw materials	157.2	155.2
Total FIFO cost	756.9	820.1
Less excess of FIFO cost over LIFO cost	220.1	204.5
	$536.8	$615.6

LIFO inventories represent approximately 79% and 80% of total inventories at December 31, 1988 and 1987.

(5) Affiliated Foreign Companies

The company has direct voting interests, ranging from 20% to 49%, in three Brazilian companies (Brastemp S.A., Embraco S.A. and Consul S.A.) engaged in the manufacture and sale of major home appliances and related component parts and in Vitromatic, S.A. de C.V., a Mexican manufacturer of home appliances. The company also has an interest in Brasmotor S.A., a Brazilian holding company with interests in Brastemp S.A., Embraco S.A. and Consul S. A.

Combined financial information of the affiliated foreign operating companies follows:

(millions of dollars)	1988	1987	1986
Current assets	$421.9	$378.2	$300.0
Other assets	471.3	349.9	218.9
	$893.2	$728.1	$518.9
Current liabilities	$245.9	$236.0	$175.5
Other liabilities	87.0	23.4	23.9
Stockholders' equity	560.3	468.7	319.5
	$893.2	$728.1	$518.9
Net sales	$934.3	$734.8	$604.4
Cost of products sold	$769.5	$620.8	$481.0
Net earnings	$ 47.5	$ 95.3	$ 72.6
Whirlpool share of foreign currency translation losses included in operating results	$ 10.7	$ 14.3	$ 12.8

(6) Financing Arrangements

At December 31, 1988, the company has several unused lines of credit expiring in 1989 permitting borrowings up to $900 million including $185 million of credit lines which are also available to Whirlpool Acceptance Corporation. The company does not have formal compensating balance arrangements with its credit line banks. Generally, the banks are compensated for their credit lines by company operating balances to the extent available in the normal course of business, and/or a fee.

Notes payable consist of the following:

December 31 *(millions of dollars)*	1988	1987
Payable to banks	$ 37.3	$ 82.8
Commercial paper	657.8	544.1
	$695.1	$626.9

The company has entered into forward rate and interest rate swap agreements to fix interest rates on short-term, floating rate notes. At December 31, 1988 and 1987, these agreements had maturities ranging from 2–94 months and 4–35 months on amounts of $101.0 million and $19.0 million. The weighted average interest rate of these agreements was 8.79% in 1988 and 10.01% in 1987.

During 1987, the company entered into an interest rate swap agreement related to a $100 million, 7.125% long-term senior note due in 1991 effectively converting it to a floating rate obligation. The weighted average interest rate on this agreement was 8.09% in 1988 and 7.06% in 1987.

Long-term debt consists of the following:

December 31 *(millions of dollars)*				
Description	Maturity	Interest Rate	1988	1987
Sinking fund debentures	1988 to 2016	9.1 to 11.0%	$285.2	$161.6
Senior notes	1988 to 1993	7.0 to 9.9	201.4	218.9
Other			23.0	24.4
			509.6	404.9
Less current maturities			35.8	38.4
			$473.8	$366.5

At December 31, 1988, the company held debentures in the face amount of $4.7 million which have been deducted from the sinking fund requirements due in 1989 and 1990.

The annual maturities and sinking fund requirements are $35.8 million in 1989, $36.1 million in 1990, $121.5 million in 1991, $12.7 million in 1992 and $18.9 million in 1993.

(7) Stockholders' Equity

The company has 250 million authorized shares of common stock (par value $1 per share) and 10 million authorized shares of preferred stock (par value $1 per share). At December 31, 1988 and 1987, there were 69.3 million and 69.2 million common shares outstanding.

In 1986, the company's Board of Directors declared a two-for-one split of its common stock. All per share and share data have been retroactively adjusted to give effect to the stock split.

Consolidated retained earnings at December 31, 1988 included $95.8 million of equity in undistributed net earnings of the affiliated foreign companies.

During 1988, the company issued a dividend distribution of one Preferred Stock Purchase Right ("Rights") for each outstanding share of common stock. The Rights, which expire May 23, 1998, will become exercisable ten days after a person or group either becomes the beneficial owner of 20% or more of the common stock or commences a tender or exchange offer that would result in such person or group beneficially owning 25% or more of the outstanding common stock. Each Right entitles the holder to purchase from the company one newly-issued unit consisting of one one-hundredth of a share of Series A Participating Cumulative Preferred Stock at an exercise price of $100.00, subject to adjustment.

If (i) any person or group becomes the beneficial owner of 25% or more of Whirlpool common stock, or (ii) the company is the surviving corporation in a merger with a 20% or more stockholder and its common stock is not changed or converted, or (iii) a 20% or more stockholder engages in certain self-dealing transactions with the company, then each Right not owned by such person will entitle the holder to purchase, at the Rights' then current exercise price, shares of the company's common stock having a value of twice the Rights' then current exercise price. In addition, if the company is involved in a merger in which its common stock is converted or sells 50% or more of its assets, each Right will entitle its holder to purchase for the exercise price shares of common stock of the acquiring successor company having a value of twice the Rights' then current exercise price.

The company will be entitled to redeem the Rights in whole, but not in part, at $.05 per Right at any time prior to the expiration of a ten-day period (subject to extension) following public announcement of the existence of a 20% holder or of a 25% or more tender offer. Until such time as the Rights become exercisable, the Rights have no voting or dividend privileges and are attached to, and do not trade separately from, the common stock.

At December 31, 1988, one million shares of preferred stock were reserved for future exercise of Stock Purchase Rights.

(8) Stock Options

The company's stock option plans permit the grant of stock options to key salaried employees of the company and its subsidiaries. The plans authorize the grant of 8.5 million shares as either incentive or non-statutory stock options and, further, authorize the grant of stock appreciation rights and related cash payments independently of or with respect to options granted or outstanding. The stock appreciation rights allow option holders, in lieu of exercising options, to receive payments in cash or shares of common stock or a combination thereof in an amount equal to the excess of the market price of the common stock over the option price.

Options outstanding at December 31, 1988 have expiration dates ranging from June 22, 1989 to December 12, 1998. Stock appreciation rights are outstanding with respect to 577,434 shares under option at December 31, 1988. Rights to receive a supplemental cash payment are outstanding with respect to 50,092 shares under option at December 31, 1988.

A summary of stock option information follows:

	1988		1987	
	Number of Shares	Average Option Price	Number of Shares	Average Option Price
Outstanding at January 1	1,427,544	$24.47	1,447,275	$24.20
Granted	262,000	24.82	190,100	23.34
Exercised	(70,233)	19.50	(164,471)	20.78
Surrendered under stock appreciation rights	(30,580)	19.08	(27,120)	22.48
Cancelled or expired	(37,482)	27.73	(18,240)	27.49
Outstanding at December 31	1,551,249	$24.79	1,427,544	$24.47
Exercisable at December 31	1,145,169	$24.58	1,062,522	$23.48
Available for future grant at December 31	5,408,122		5,632,640	

(9) Income Taxes

The provisions for income taxes for continuing operations follow:

(millions of dollars)	1988	1987	1986
Current:			
Federal	$ 60.4	$ 90.3	$109.9
State and local	13.8	20.2	21.9
	74.2	110.5	131.8
Deferred (credit):			
Federal	15.9	11.9	12.0
Investment tax credits	—	—	4.5
State and local	.8	.1	(1.2)
	16.7	12.0	15.3
	$ 90.9	$122.5	$147.1

In 1987, the company adopted Financial Accounting Standards Board Statement No. 96, "Accounting for Income Taxes." This change in accounting increased 1987 net earnings by $11.1 million ($.15 per share) which consisted primarily of the cumulative effect on prior years.

Reconciliations between the federal statutory income tax rate and the consolidated effective income tax rate for earnings from continuing operations before income taxes, equity earnings, minority interests and cumulative effect of accounting change follow:

	1988	1987	1986
Federal statutory rate	34.0%	40.0%	46.0%
State and local taxes, net of federal tax benefit	4.1	4.2	3.2
Other items	.9	(.4)	(4.4)
Effective income tax rate	39.0%	43.8%	44.8%

Deferred income taxes result from the tax effect of transactions which are recognized in different periods for financial and tax reporting purposes. Significant components of deferred income taxes and their related impact on deferred income tax expense are as follows:

(millions of dollars)	1988	1987	1986
Excess of tax over book depreciation	$ 8.6	$ 5.8	$ 7.1
Direct financing and operating leases:			
Excess of tax over book depreciation	17.3	11.2	10.7
Conversion of lease income from finance method to operating method	(9.0)	(6.6)	(5.8)
Leveraged leases	10.5	13.7	17.3
Provision for facility consolidation	—	—	(9.9)
Other—net	(10.7)	(12.1)	(4.1)
Deferred income tax expense	$ 16.7	$ 12.0	$ 15.3

It is not practicable to determine the amount of income tax liability, if any, that would result if the company's equity in undistributed earnings of foreign affiliates and subsidiaries were remitted. Foreign withholding taxes payable, if these earnings were distributed, would be approximately $26.2 million.

(10) Pension Plans

The company and its subsidiaries have noncontributory defined benefit pension plans covering substantially all U.S. employees. Plans covering salaried employees provide pension benefits that are based on the employee's compensation during a certain period, as defined, before retirement. Plans covering hourly employees provide benefits of stated amounts for each year of service. The company's present funding policy is to generally make the minimum annual contribution required by applicable regulations. Assets held by the plans consist primarily of listed common stocks and guaranteed insurance contracts.

Pension expense for U.S. plans included the following components:

(millions of dollars)	1988	1987	1986
Service cost—benefits earned during the year	$ 19.9	$ 19.8	$ 18.1
Interest cost on projected benefit obligation	49.9	49.5	45.0
Actual return on plan assets	(59.6)	(30.8)	(96.6)
Net amortization	(1.0)	(27.1)	40.5
	$ 9.2	$ 11.4	$ 7.0

Assumptions used in the actuarial determination of pension expense included 8.5% for both the discount rate and the expected long-term rate of return on plan assets, and 5% to 7% for compensation level increases.

The funded status of the company's U.S. pension plans was as follows:

December 31 *(millions of dollars)*	1988	1987
Projected benefit obligation (actuarial present value of projected benefits attributed to employee service to date based on future compensation levels)	$585.9	$588.2
Less plan assets at fair value	751.9	707.0
Plan assets in excess of projected benefit obligation	166.0	118.8
Unrecognized prior service cost	17.6	13.8
Unrecognized net experience gain	(115.4)	(61.0)
Unrecognized net obligation, net of amortization	(55.2)	(59.6)
Net pension asset included in prepaid expenses	$ 13.0	$ 12.0

Included in the projected benefit obligation is the accumulated benefit obligation, which represents the actuarial present value of benefits attributed to employee service and compensation levels to date. At December 31, 1988 and 1987, the accumulated benefit obligation was $499.3 million and $497.2 million. The vested portion was $450.0 million in 1988 and $443.2 million in 1987.

The pension plans provide that in the event of a plan termination within five years following a change in control of the company, any assets held by the plans in excess of the amounts needed to fund accrued benefits would be used to provide additional benefits to plan participants. A change in control generally means one not approved by the incumbent Board of Directors, including an acquisition of 30% or more of the voting power of the company's outstanding stock or a change in a majority of the incumbent Board.

Employees in foreign countries who are not U.S. citizens are covered by various post-employment benefit arrangements. The cost of defined benefit arrangements charged to results of operations in 1988, 1987 and 1986 was $.7 million, $.9 million and $1.4 million. For those arrangements which are funded, assets exceed the actuarially computed vested benefits at December 31, 1988 and 1987.

(11) Contingencies

The company is involved in various legal actions arising in the normal course of business. Management, after taking into consideration legal counsel's evaluation of such actions, is of the opinion that the outcome of these matters will not have a material adverse effect on the financial position of the company.

(12) Business Segment Information

Percentages of consolidated net sales to Sears, Roebuck and Co. were 38% in 1988, 37% in 1987 and 38% in 1986.

Identifiable assets shown below are those assets directly associated with the respective operating activities. Corporate assets consist principally of cash, investments, prepaid expenses, deferred income taxes and property and equipment related to corporate activities.

Consolidated Foreign and Domestic Operations

(millions of dollars)	Domestic	Foreign	Corporate and (Eliminations)	Consolidated
Revenues				
1988	$3,846.2	$601.1	$ (25.9)	$4,421.4
1987	$3,722.2	$516.2	$ (29.8)	$4,208.6
1986	$3,672.9	$368.7	$ (27.9)	$4,013.7
Operating profit (loss)				
1988	$ 256.3	$ (1.9)	$ 7.2	$ 261.6
1987	$ 288.5	$ (2.2)	$ 9.9	$ 296.2
1986	$ 317.0	$ .3	$ 8.7	$ 326.0
Identifiable assets				
1988	$2,598.3	$402.0	$409.4	$3,409.7
1987	$2,363.7	$400.6	$372.4	$3,136.7
1986	$2,051.4	$341.8	$462.3	$2,855.5

Business Segments

(millions of dollars)	Major Home Appliances	Financing Services	Other	Corporate and (Eliminations)	Consolidated
Revenues					
1988	$4,079.3	$ 135.7	$229.4	$ (23.0)	$4,421.4
1987	$3,934.1	$ 117.3	$197.0	$ (39.8)	$4,208.6
1986	$3,833.8	$ 100.4	$112.8	$ (33.3)	$4,013.7
Operating profit (loss)					
1988	$ 235.4	$ 21.6	$ (2.6)	$ 7.2	$ 261.6
1987	$ 280.5	$ 13.1	$ (7.3)	$ 9.9	$ 296.2
1986	$ 298.3	$ 20.7	$ (1.7)	$ 8.7	$ 326.0
Identifiable assets					
1988	$1,659.8	$1,077.0	$263.5	$409.4	$3,409.7
1987	$1,587.0	$ 914.8	$262.5	$372.4	$3,136.7
1986	$1,342.2	$ 827.9	$223.1	$462.3	$2,855.5
Depreciation expense					
1988	$ 119.7	$ 3.9	$ 17.0	$ 2.1	$ 142.7
1987	$ 113.6	$ 2.9	$ 16.4	$ .4	$ 133.3
1986	$ 103.7	$ 1.1	$ 9.7	$ 5.3	$ 119.8
Capital expenditures					
1988	$ 165.6	$ 4.2	$ 8.9	$ 1.0	$ 179.7
1987	$ 216.1	$ 2.6	$ 17.3	$ 2.2	$ 238.2
1986	$ 200.8	$ 2.0	$ 21.8	$ (1.8)	$ 222.8

Whirlpool Acceptance Corporation

Whirlpool Acceptance Corporation provides inventory financing services for dealers and distributors marketing products manufactured by the company and its subsidiaries and certain other manufacturers. Whirlpool Acceptance Corporation also provides consumer financing services for retail sales by dealers, lease financing services for the acquisition of general equipment and facilities by business organizations, insurance premium financing, and dealer financing for manufactured homes and recreational vehicles. Condensed financial statements (before elimination of intercompany transactions) of Whirlpool Acceptance Corporation follow.

Balance Sheets

December 31 *(millions of dollars)*	1988	1987 (Restated)
Assets		
Current assets		
Cash and cash equivalents	$ 13.9	$ 36.1
Financing receivables and leases—net	642.2	546.6
Other current assets	19.5	25.4
	675.6	608.1
Financing receivables and leases—net	392.5	298.7
Other assets	2.6	3.2
Property, plant and equipment	6.3	4.8
Total Assets	$1,077.0	$914.8
Liabilities and Stockholders' Equity		
Current liabilities		
Notes payable	$ 537.9	$406.8
Other current liabilities	90.2	75.5
	628.1	482.3
Long-term debt	211.0	228.3
Other liabilities	70.9	52.5
Stockholders' equity	167.0	151.7
Total Liabilities and Stockholders' Equity	$1,077.0	$914.8

Statements of Earnings

Year Ended December 31 *(millions of dollars)*	1988	1987 (Restated)	1986 (Restated)
Financing services revenue	$135.7	$117.4	$100.4
Interest expense	(60.2)	(48.5)	(38.9)
Operating expenses	(53.9)	(55.8)	(40.9)
Other income	1.3	1.1	1.2
Income taxes	(7.6)	(.7)	(7.8)
Net earnings	$ 15.3	$ 13.5	$ 14.0

(13) Supplementary Expense Information

(millions of dollars)	1988	1987	1986
Maintenance and repairs	$ 95.8	$ 93.5	$ 94.7
Research and development costs	72.9	78.9	74.5
Advertising costs	35.8	41.2	46.4

(14) Quarterly Results of Operations (Unaudited)

	Three Months Ended			
(millions of dollars except share data)	March 31	June 30	September 30	December 31
1988:				
Net sales	$1,041.8	$1,126.9	$1,151.8	$994.0
Cost of products sold	$ 835.4	$ 912.4	$ 947.7	$810.2
Financing services revenue, less related interest expense	$ 14.2	$ 13.7	$ 15.6	$ 16.0
Earnings from continuing operations before accounting change	$ 37.1	$ 46.7	$ 36.6	$ 40.9
Loss from discontinued operation	$ 3.9	$ 5.3	$ 5.1	$ 52.9
Net earnings (loss)	$ 33.2	$ 41.4	$ 31.5	$ (12.0)
Per share of common stock:				
Earnings from continuing operations before accounting change	$ .54	$. 67	$ .53	$ .59
Loss from discontinued operation	$ .06	$ .07	$ .08	$ .76
Net earnings (loss)	$ .48	$ .60	$ .45	$ (.17)
Dividends paid	$ .275	$ .275	$ .275	$ .275
Stock price:				
High	$ 29⅞	$ 29¾	$ 28⅞	$ 28⅛
Low	$ 23½	$ 24½	$ 24⅛	$ 23½
1987:				
Net sales	$ 945.5	$1,118.6	$1,092.7	$958.0
Cost of products sold	$ 738.4	$ 892.9	$ 868.5	$765.0
Financing services revenue, less related interest expense	$ 13.2	$ 13.4	$ 13.8	$ 14.6
Earnings from continuing operations before accounting change	$ 50.1	$ 48.2	$ 46.4	$ 41.9
Loss from discontinued operation	$ 1.4	$ .8	$ 1.8	$ 1.5
Net earnings	$ 59.5	$ 47.4	$ 44.6	$ 40.4
Per share of common stock:				
Earnings from continuing operations before accounting change	$ 0.68	$ 0.66	$ 0.66	$ 0.61

(continued)

Loss from discontinued operation	$ 0.02	$ 0.01	$ 0.03	$ 0.02
Net earnings	$ 0.81	$ 0.65	$ 0.63	$ 0.59
Dividends paid	$ 0.275	$ 0.275	$ 0.275	$ 0.275
Stock price:				
High	$ 40⅞	$ 39¾	$ 40	$ 36⅞
Low	$ 32½	$ 34	$ 33⅝	$ 20¼

Fourth quarter 1988 net earnings were reduced by approximately $10 million ($.14 per share) for a warranty charge relating to the sale of product by a previously owned business.

The loss from discontinued operation for the fourth quarter of 1988 includes a loss on disposition of $45.0 million ($.65 per share). Prior quarters have been restated to reflect the discontinuance of operations. See Note 2.

Report of Ernst & Whinney, Independent Auditors

The Stockholders and Board of Directors
Whirlpool Corporation
Benton Harbor, Michigan

We have audited the accompanying consolidated balance sheets of Whirlpool Corporation and subsidiaries as of December 31, 1988 and 1987, and the related consolidated statements of earnings, stockholders' equity, and cash flows for each of the three years in the period ended December 31, 1988. These financial statements are the responsibility of the company's management. Our responsibility is to express an opinion on these financial statements based on our audits. We did not audit the financial statements of Inglis Limited for 1988, which statements reflect total assets and total revenues constituting 4.0% and 7.9% of the related consolidated totals. We did not audit the financial statements of Whirlpool Acceptance Corporation and Inglis Limited, both consolidated subsidiaries, for 1987 and 1986, which statements combined reflect total assets constituting 33.2% in 1987 and total revenues constituting 9.7% in 1987 and 8.1% in 1986 of the related consolidated totals. Those statements were audited by other auditors whose reports have been furnished to us, and our opinion, insofar as it relates to the amounts included for Inglis Limited and for Whirlpool Acceptance Corporation, is based solely on the reports of the other auditors.

We conducted our audits in accordance with generally accepted auditing standards. Those standards require that we plan and perform the audit to obtain reasonable assurance about whether the financial statements are free of material misstatement. An audit includes examining, on a test basis, evidence supporting the amounts and disclosures in the financial statements. An audit also includes assessing the accounting principles used and significant estimates made by management, as well as evaluating the overall financial statement presentation. We believe that our audits and the reports of other auditors provide a reasonable basis for our opinion.

In our opinion, based on our audits and the reports of other auditors, the financial statements referred to above present fairly, in all material respects, the consolidated financial position of Whirlpool Corporation and subsidiaries at December 31, 1988 and 1987, and the consolidated results of their operations and their cash flows for each of the three years in the period ended December 31, 1988, in conformity with generally accepted accounting principles.

As described in notes 1 and 9 to the financial statements, Whirlpool Corporation changed its method of accounting for income taxes in 1987, and began consolidation of all majority-owned subsidiaries in 1988, retroactively to 1986.

Ernst & Whinney

Chicago, Illinois
January 20, 1989

Report by Management on the Financial Statements

The management of Whirlpool Corporation has prepared the accompanying financial statements. The financial statements have been audited by Ernst & Whinney, independent auditors, whose report, based upon their audits and the reports of other independent auditors, expresses the opinion that these financial statements present fairly the financial position and results of operations of Whirlpool Corporation and its subsidiaries (later referred to as "the company") in accordance with generally accepted accounting principles. Their audits are conducted in accordance with generally accepted auditing standards and include a review of internal controls and tests of transactions.

The financial statements were prepared from the company's accounting records, books and accounts which, in reasonable detail, accurately and fairly reflect all material transactions or dispositions of assets. The company maintains a system of internal controls designed to provide reasonable assurance that the company's accounting records, books and accounts are accurate and that transactions are properly recorded in the company's books and records, and the company's assets are maintained and accounted for, in accordance with management's authorizations. The company's accounting records, policies and internal controls are regularly reviewed by the company's internal audit staff.

The Audit Committee of the Board of Directors of Whirlpool Corporation, which is comprised of three Directors who are not employed by the company, considers and makes recommendations to the Board of Directors as to accounting and auditing matters concerning the company, including recommending for appointment by the Board of Directors the firm of independent auditors who is engaged on an annual basis to audit the financial statements of Whirlpool Corporation and certain of its wholly owned subsidiaries. The Audit Committee meets with the independent auditors at least twice yearly to review the scope of the audit, the results of the audit and such recommendations as may be made by said auditors with respect to the company's accounting methods and system of internal controls.

James R. Samartini

James R. Samartini
Executive Vice President
and Chief Financial Officer
January 20, 1989

Revenue Information

Year Ended December 31 *(millions of dollars)*	Percent	1988	1987	1986
Major home appliances:				
Home laundry appliances	33.6%	$1,485.2	$1,429.3	$1,353.1
Home refrigeration and room air conditioning equipment	33.9	1,500.6	1,429.5	1,278.5
Other home appliances	24.9	1,099.3	1,059.0	1,193.2
	92.4	4,085.1	3,917.8	3,824.8
Other products and services	5.2	229.4	197.0	112.8
Financing services	2.4	106.9	93.8	76.1
	100.0%	$4,421.4	$4,208.6	$4,013.7

GLOSSARY

Chapter numbers at the end of each entry indicate where elaborations on the term may be found.

Absorption costing A product costing method in which all manufacturing costs are treated as product costs. (Ch. 25)

Accelerated cost recovery system (ACRS, MACRS) A system of accelerated depreciation for tax purposes introduced in 1981 and modified starting in 1987; it prescribes depreciation rates by asset classifications for assets acquired after 1980. (Ch. 10)

Accelerated depreciation method Any depreciation method under which the amounts of depreciation expense taken in the early years of an asset's life are larger than those amounts taken later. (Ch. 10)

Account A record of the additions, deductions, and balances of individual assets, liabilities, owners' equity, revenue and expenses. The basic component of a formal accounting system. (Ch. 2)

Accounting The process of recording, classifying, reporting, and interpreting the financial data of an organization. (Ch. 1)

Accounting controls Internal control procedures that help (1) produce accurate and reliable financial data and (2) safeguard assets. (Ch. 7)

Accounting cycle Steps in the processing of accounting transactions during the accounting year: (1) analyzing transactions, (2) recording in journals, (3) posting to general ledger, (4) preparing a trial balance, (5) adjusting accounts, (6) preparing financial statements, (7) journalizing and posting adjusting entries, (8) journalizing and posting closing entries, and (9) preparing a post-closing trial balance. (Chs. 3, 4)

Accounting entity Those people, assets, and activities devoted to a specific economic purpose and for which a separate accounting should be made. (Chs. 1, 13)

Accounting equation An expression of the equivalency in dollar amounts of assets and equities in double-entry bookkeeping; often stated as Assets = Liabilities + Owners' Equity. (Ch. 1)

Accounting period That time period, typically one year, to which accounting reports are related. (Ch. 13)

Accounting principles *See* Generally accepted accounting principles.

Accounting transaction A business activity or event that requires accounting recognition. (Ch. 1)

Accrual basis The accounting basis whereby revenue is recognized in the period earned whether actually received or not and expenses are recognized and matched with the related revenue of the period whether actually paid or not. (Chs. 1, 28)

Accruals Adjustments that reflect previously unrecorded revenues and expenses. (Ch. 3)

Accrued expense An expense incurred but not yet paid for; recognized with an adjusting entry. (Ch. 3)

Accrued revenue Revenue earned but not yet billed or received; recognized with an adjusting entry. (Ch. 3)

Accumulated depreciation A contra account to the related asset account reflecting the cumulative amounts recorded as depreciation for a specific asset or group of assets. (Ch. 3)

Additional income tax assessments An assessment by taxing authorities for an increased income tax payment; if contested, it will be disclosed as a contingent liability by the company that is assessed the additional tax. (Ch. 12)

Adjusted gross income An income tax term denoting the amount obtained by subtracting from gross income certain business expenses and expenses incurred in producing rents and royalties. (Ch. 28)

Adjusted trial balance A trial balance of the general ledger accounts taken after adjustments have been made. (Ch. 4)

Adjusting entries Those entries resulting from an attempt to reflect in the accounts various changes that may be appropriate although no source document is normally available; usually made to align recorded costs or revenue with the accounting period or to reflect previously unrecorded revenue and costs. (Ch. 3)

After-tax cash flow The net amount of any receipt or expenditure after incorporating the effects of income taxes. (Ch. 27)

Aging schedule An analysis that shows how long customers' accounts receivable balances have remained unpaid. (Ch. 8)

AICPA The American Institute of Certified Public Accountants, the national professional organization of CPAs in the United States. (Ch. 1)

Allowance for interest A provision in a partnership profit and loss sharing agreement that allows credit for the relative investments of partners. *See also* Capital ratios. (Ch. 14)

Allowance for uncollectible accounts A contra asset account with a normal credit balance shown on the balance sheet as a deduction from accounts receivable to reflect the expected realizable amount of accounts receivable. (Ch. 8)

Allowance method An accounting procedure whereby in the period in which credit sales occur, the related amount of uncollectible accounts expense is estimated and recorded. (Ch. 8)

Amortization The periodic writing off or charging to expense of some amount of cost (usually associated with intangible assets). (Ch. 11)

Annuity A pattern of cash flows where equal amounts are equally spaced over a number of periods. (App. B)

APB The Accounting Principles Board, a committee of the AICPA responsible for formulating accounting principles until it was replaced in 1973 by the FASB. (Chs. 1, 13)

Applications programs Software that directs the processing of data, including accounting data, through a computer system. (Ch. 6)

Appropriation of retained earnings Segregation or restriction of a portion of retained earnings that reduces the amount that would otherwise be available for dividends. No transfer of funds is necessarily involved, and the aggregate amount of retained earnings remains unchanged. (Ch. 16)

Articles of co-partnership The formal written agreement among partners setting forth important aspects of the partnership such as name, nature, duration, and location of the business, capital contributions, duties, and profit and loss ratios. (Ch. 14)

Articles of incorporation A document prepared by persons organizing a corporation in the United States that sets forth the structure and purposes of the corporation and specifics regarding stock to be issued. (Ch. 15)

Assets Those economic resources of an entity that can usefully be expressed in monetary terms; some examples are cash, accounts receivable, inventories, and plant and equipment. (Ch. 1)

Authorized stock The maximum number of shares in a class of stock that a corporation may issue. (Ch. 15)

Average collection period Trade accounts receivable divided by year's sales multiplied by 365. (Ch. 20)

Average rate of return method A method of capital outlay analysis that focuses on the ratio of expected average annual net income to the related average investment. (Ch. 27)

Balance sheet A financial report showing the financial position of an entity in terms of assets, liabilities, and owners' equity at a specific date. (Ch. 1)

Balance sheet equation Assets = Liabilities + Owners' Equity. (Ch. 1)

Bank reconciliation A procedure or analysis explaining the various items—such as deposits in transit, checks outstanding, bank charges, and errors—that lead to differences between the balance shown on a bank statement and the related Cash account in the general ledger. (Ch. 7)

Bearer One of the terms that may be used to designate the payee on a promissory note; means the note is payable to whomever holds the note. (Ch. 8)

Betterment A capital expenditure that improves the quality of services rendered by a plant asset but does not necessarily extend its useful life. (Ch. 10)

Bond A form of interest-bearing note payable, usually issued by the borrower for relatively long periods to a group of lenders. Bonds may incorporate a wide variety of special provisions relating to security for the debt involved, methods of paying the periodic interest payments, and maturity and retirement provisions. (Chs. 7, 17)

Bond discount Excess of the face value of a bond over its issue price. Bond discount arises when the coupon rate of the bond is below the market rate of interest for that type of bond. (Chs. 7, 17)

Bond interest coverage Income before interest expense and income taxes divided by bond interest. Sometimes called *times interest earned*. (Ch. 20)

Bond premium The excess of the issue price of a bond over its face value. Bond premium arises when the coupon interest rate of the bond is greater than the market rate for that type of bond. (Chs. 7, 17)

Bond sinking fund A fund accumulated through required periodic contributions (and investment income thereon) to be used for the retirement of a specific bond issue. (Ch. 17)

Bonus In the context of partnership admissions, a bonus is the difference between the amount invested by a new partner and the amount credited to the new partner's capital account. (Ch. 14)

Book value The dollar amount carried in the accounts for a particular item. The book value of some items is derived by deducting any related contra account or adding any related premium (or other adjunct) account. (Chs. 3, 17)

Book value per share The dollar amount of net assets represented by one share of stock; computed by dividing the amount of stockholders' equity associated with a class of stock by the outstanding number of shares of that class of stock. (Ch. 15)

Branch accounting The procedures for maintaining the financial records of various outlets of a single firm and coordinating the data with the home office records. (App. C)

Break-even point That level of business volume at which total revenue equals total costs. (Ch. 24)

Budgeted balance sheet A balance sheet projected as of the end of a budget period; a component of a company's master budget. (Ch. 26)

Budgeted income statement An income statement projected over a future budget period; a component of a company's master budget. (Ch. 26)

Budgeting A process of formal financial planning. (Ch. 26)

Buffer margin The number of percentage points added to a firm's cost of capital to derive a cutoff rate for evaluating and selecting capital investment proposals. (Ch. 27)

Byproducts Those products having relatively little sales value compared with other products derived from a process. An example would be the wood shavings generated in a shaping department of a furniture factory. (Ch. 23)

Calendar year A firm whose fiscal year ends in December is on a calendar-year basis. (Ch. 3)

Callable bonds Bonds that allow the borrower to retire (call in) the bonds after a stated date. (Ch. 17)

Capital budgeting Planning long-term investments in plant and equipment. (Ch. 27)

Capital expenditure An expenditure that increases the book value of long-term assets. (Ch. 10)

Capital expenditures budget A list of the types of plant assets and the amounts budgeted for their acquisition in each of a series of future operating periods; a component of a company's master budget. (Ch. 26)

Capital gains and losses Gains and losses from the sale or exchange of certain assets qualifying as "capital assets." Specific tax treatment of capital gains and losses depends on the length of time for which the assets are held (short term for one year or less, long term otherwise) and the net result of combining long- and short-term gains and losses. (Ch. 28)

Capital lease A lease that transfers to the lessee substantially all of the benefits and risks related to ownership of the property. The lessee records the leased property as an asset and establishes a liability for the lease obligation. (Ch. 11)

Capital ratios The quantitative relationship among the balances of partners' capital accounts. This factor is often reflected in the distribution of partnership profits and may be calculated using either beginning or average balances. (Ch. 14)

Capitalization of interest A process adding interest to an asset's initial cost if a period of time is required to prepare the asset for use. (Ch. 10)

Carrying value A term synonymous with book value. *See* Book value. (Ch. 17)

Cash An asset category representing the amount of a firm's paper money, coins, checks, money orders as well as money on demand deposit with a financial institution. (Ch. 7)

Cash basis The accounting basis in which revenue is recognized only when money is received and expenses are recognized when money is paid. (Chs. 1, 19, 28)

Cash budget A document portraying a firm's projected flows of cash during a budget period; a component of a master budget. (Ch. 26)

Cash disbursements journal A special journal used to record all transactions involving cash payments. (Ch. 6)

Cash discount An amount—often 1 or 2% of the purchase price—that a buyer may deduct for paying within the discount period. (Ch. 5)

Cash equivalents Short-term, highly liquid investments that firms acquire with cash in excess of their immediate needs. A statement of cash flows reports the inflows and outflows of a firm's cash and cash equivalents. To qualify as a cash equivalent for the statement of cash flows, an investment must be easily convertible into a known amount of cash and be close enough to maturity so that its market value is not sensitive to interest rate changes; each firm must disclose its policy for deciding which investments are treated as cash equivalents in the statement of cash flows. (Ch. 19)

Cash flow statement *See* Statement of cash flows.

Cash payback method A form of capital expenditure analysis that evaluates investment proposals in terms of the cash payback period. (Ch. 27)

Cash payback period The time in years that it takes net future cash inflows to equal the original investment amount; used in evaluating investment proposals by the cash payback method. (Ch. 27)

Cash receipts journal A special journal used to record all transactions involving cash receipts. (Ch. 6)

Cash short and over An account which contains the amounts by which actual daily cash collections differ from the amounts recorded as being collected. (Ch. 7)

Centralized accounting system In the context of accounting for branches, a system whereby the home office maintains most of the records needed to account for branch operations. (App. C)

Certificate of deposit An investment security available at financial institutions generally offering a fixed rate of return for a specified period. (Ch. 7)

Change in accounting estimate A revision of an estimate used in an accounting analysis, such as revising the useful life of a plant asset. (Ch. 16)

Change in accounting principle A switch from one generally accepted accounting principle to another generally accepted principle, such as changing depreciation methods. (Ch. 16)

Chart of accounts A list of all the general ledger account titles and their numerical code. (Ch. 3)

Check register A special journal used in place of a cash disbursements journal when the voucher system of controlling expenditures is used; a record of all checks written in payment of vouchers. (Ch. 6)

Check truncation Canceled checks are not returned by a bank to its depositors when monthly bank statements are mailed. (Ch. 7)

Classified financial statements Financial statements that separate accounts into various categories to aid in the interpretation of the financial data. (Chs. 5, 16, 19)

Closing procedures A step in the accounting cycle in which the balances in all temporary accounts are transferred to the owner's capital or the Retained Earnings account, leaving the temporary accounts with zero balances. (Chs. 4, 5, 21, App. A, C, F)

Collection bases Those procedures in which revenue recognition is delayed until related amounts of cash are collected. The cost recovery method and the installment method are examples. (Ch. 13)

Commitments A contractual arrangement where both parties to the contract still have acts to perform. (Ch. 13)

Common-size statements A form of financial statement analysis in which only the relative percentages of financial statement items, rather than their dollar amounts, are shown. (Ch. 20)

Common stock Basic ownership class of corporate capital stock, carrying the rights to vote, share in earnings, participate in future stock issues, and share in any liquidation proceeds after prior claims have been settled. (Chs. 7, 15)

Comparative financial statements A form of horizontal financial analysis involving comparison of two or more periods' statements showing dollar and percentage changes. (Ch. 20)

Compensating balance A minimum amount that a financial institution requires a firm to maintain in its account as part of a borrowing arrangement. (Ch. 7)

Completed contract method A point-of-sale (that is, completion of the contract) revenue recognition method for long-term contracts. (Ch. 13)

Complex capital structure A corporate capital structure containing one or more potentially dilutive securities. Complex capital structures normally require a dual earnings per share presentation. (Ch. 16)

Compound journal entry An entry containing more than one debit and/or credit entry. (Ch. 3)

Computer service bureau A company that provides various computing services to clients. (Ch. 6)

Computer software production costs An intangible asset representing the costs incurred (after technological feasibility has been established) to produce computer software product masters. (Ch. 11)

Computer system A system for processing data that utilizes computers. (Ch. 6)

Conceptual framework A cohesive set of interrelated objectives and fundamentals for external financial reporting developed by the FASB. (Ch. 13)

Conservatism An accounting principle dictating that judgmental determinations in accounting should tend toward understatement rather than overstatement of assets and income. (Ch. 13)

Consistency An accounting principle dictating that, unless otherwise disclosed, accounting reports should be prepared on a basis consistent with the preceding period. (Ch. 13)

Consolidated financial statements Financial statements prepared with intercompany (reciprocal) accounts eliminated to portray the financial position and operating results of two or more affiliated companies as a single economic entity. (Ch. 18)

Constant dollar accounting An accounting process that adjusts financial data for changes in the general purchasing power of the dollar. (Ch. 13)

Consumer price index A price-level index of consumer goods and services published monthly by the Bureau of Labor Statistics of the Department of Labor. (Ch. 13)

Contingent liability A potential obligation, the eventual occurrence of which usually depends on some future event beyond the control of the firm. Contingent liabilities may originate with such things as lawsuits, credit guarantees, and contested income tax assessments. (Chs. 8, 12, 13)

Continuous budgeting A budgeting process that breaks the year into quarters (or months) and adds a new quarterly (or monthly) budget as each quarter (or month) expires. (Ch. 26)

Contra account An account related to, and deducted from, another account when financial statements are prepared or when book values are computed. Accumulated depreciation, allowance for uncollectible accounts, discount on notes payable, and sales discounts are examples. (Ch. 2)

Contract (interest) rate The rate of interest stated on a bond certificate. (Ch. 17)

Contribution margin The excess of revenue over variable costs; thus, the amount contributed toward the absorption of fixed cost and eventually the generation of profit. (Ch. 24)

Contribution margin ratio That portion of the sales price that is contribution margin. (Ch. 24)

Control account A general ledger account, the balance of which reflects the aggregate balance of many related subsidiary accounts. Most firms maintain such records for credit customers and for creditors. (Chs. 6, 11)

Controller Usually the highest ranking accounting officer in a firm. (Ch. 1)

Conversion costs The direct labor and factory overhead costs in a manufacturing process. (Ch. 23)

Convertible bond A bond incorporating the holder's right to convert the bond to capital stock under prescribed terms. (Ch. 17)

Copyright An exclusive right that protects an owner against the unauthorized reproduction of a specific written work or artwork. (Ch. 11)

Corporation A legal entity created by the granting of a charter from an appropriate governmental authority and owned by stockholders who have limited liability for corporate debt. (Chs. 1, 15)

Cost behavior analysis Study of the ways in which specific costs respond to changes in the volume of business activity. (Ch. 24)

Cost center Sometimes called an *expense center.* A division of a business with which specific costs can be identified. (Ch. 25)

Cost method A method of accounting by a parent company for investments in subsidiary companies in which the parent company maintains the investment in subsidiary account at its cost, not recognizing periodically its share of subsidiary income or loss. *See also* Equity method. (Ch. 18)

Cost of capital *See* Weighted average cost of capital.

Cost of goods manufactured *See* Manufacturing costs.

Cost of goods sold The cost of merchandise sold to customers during the accounting period. It is calculated by adding the beginning inventory and net cost of purchases and deducting the ending inventory. (Chs. 5, 9)

Cost per equivalent unit report A report for a manufacturing department that identifies the period's production in equivalent units; the current materials and conversion costs; and the current cost per equivalent unit of production. (Ch. 23)

Cost recovery method A revenue recognition method for installment transactions that treats all cash collections as a return of cost until all costs are recovered; the remaining cash collections are considered all gross profit. (Ch. 13)

Coupon bonds Bonds with coupons for interest payable to bearer attached to the bond for each interest period. Whenever interest is due, the bondholder detaches a coupon and deposits it with his or her bank for collection. (Ch. 17)

CPA Certified public accountant, a professional accountant who has passed the Uniform CPA Examination, satisfied other requirements regarding education, professional experience, and character, and been licensed to practice public accounting by a state, district, or territory. (Ch. 1)

Credit card fee A fee charged retailers for credit card services provided by financial institutions. The fee usually ranges from 1/2% to 5% of the credit card sale. (Ch. 8)

Credit (entry) An entry on the right-hand side (or in the credit column) of any account. (Ch. 2)

Credit guarantee A guarantee of another company's debt by cosigning a note; a contingent liability for the guarantor which is usually disclosed in a balance sheet footnote. (Ch. 12)

Credit memorandum A form used by a seller to notify a customer of a reduction in the amount considered owed by the customer. (Ch. 5)

Credit period The period of time a buyer has to pay for goods or services received on account. (Ch. 5)

Cumulative effect of a change in principle An income statement item resulting from a change in accounting principle. It represents the total difference in the cumulative income for all prior years affected by the change had the new principle been used in those years. (Ch. 16)

Cumulative preferred stock A type of preferred stock upon which any dividends in arrears must be paid before dividends can be paid on common stock. (Ch. 15)

Current assets Assets that will either be used up or converted to cash within the normal operating cycle of the business or one year, whichever is longer. (Ch. 5)

Current cost accounting A system of accounting that reflects assets and expenses at their current replacement cost amounts. (Ch. 13)

Current liabilities Obligations that will require within the coming year or the operating cycle, whichever is longer, (1) the use of existing current assets or (2) the creation of other current liabilities. (Chs. 5, 12)

Current ratio Current assets divided by current liabilities. (Ch. 20)

Cutoff rate The minimum acceptable rate of return for an investment proposal; the cutoff rate is equal to the cost of capital + buffer margin. Also known as *hurdle rate.* (Ch. 27)

Debenture bonds Bonds that have no specific property pledged as security for their repayment. (Ch. 17)

Debit (entry) An entry on the left-hand side (or in the debit column) of any account. (Ch. 2)

Decentralized accounting In the context of accounting for branches, a system whereby each branch maintains a comprehensive set of accounting records for its operations and forwards periodic financial statements to the home office. (App. C)

Decision making A process of identifying alternative courses of action and selecting a choice from among the alternatives. (Ch. 25)

Deferrals Adjustments that align previously recorded costs and revenue with the appropriate periods. (Ch. 3)

Deferred revenue A liability representing revenue received in advance. Also called *Unearned revenue.* (Ch. 3)

Deferred tax liability A liability account representing the estimated future income taxes payable resulting from an existing temporary difference between an asset's book value and its tax basis. (Ch. 17)

Deficit A negative (or debit) balance in a corporation's Retained Earnings account. (Ch. 16)

Deflation A decrease in the general level of prices for goods and services. (Ch. 13)

Departmental contribution to indirect expenses The excess of departmental revenue over direct departmental expenses; contributed to the absorption of the firm's pool of indirect expenses. (Ch. 25)

Depletion The allocation of the cost of natural resources to the units extracted from the ground or, in the case of timberland, the board feet of timber cut. (Ch. 11)

Deposits in transit Cash deposits made to a bank account near the end of a month that do not appear on that month's bank statement. (Ch. 7)

Depreciation The decline in economic potential of plant assets originating from wear, deterioration, and obsolescence. (Ch. 10)

Depreciation accounting The process of allocating the cost of plant assets (less salvage value) as expense to the periods benefiting from their use. (Chs. 3, 10)

Differential analysis A concept of limiting consideration in a decision situation to only those factors that differ among alternatives. (Ch. 25)

Direct expenses (costs) Expenses (costs) that can be readily identified with a particular department, product, or activity. (Ch. 25)

Direct labor All labor of workers applying their skills directly to the manufacture of products. The labor of workers indirectly supporting the manufacturing process is accounted for as indirect labor, part of factory overhead. (Ch. 21)

Direct labor budget A document showing the number of direct labor hours necessary for the production volume planned for a budget period; a component of a company's master budget. (Ch. 26)

Direct material All important materials or parts physically making up the product. Incidental amounts of materials are accounted for as indirect materials, part of factory overhead. (Ch. 21)

Direct material budget A document showing the quantities of material to be purchased during a budget period to meet scheduled production and desired ending inventory requirements; a component of a company's master budget. (Ch. 26)

Direct method A presentation of net cash flow from operating activities in a statement of cash flows that shows the major categories of operating cash receipts and payments. (Ch. 19)

Direct write-off method An accounting procedure in which uncollectible accounts are charged to expense in the period they are determined to be uncollectible. (Ch. 8)

Discontinued operations Operating segments of a company that have been sold, abandoned, or disposed of during the operating period. Related operating income (or loss) and related gains or losses on disposal are reported separately on the income statement. (Ch. 16)

Discount factors *See* Present value factors.

Discounting In the context of notes receivable and notes payable, discounting is the exchange of a note for cash at a financial institution where the cash received is less than the note's maturity value. (Ch. 8)

Discount on notes payable A contra account to notes payable. (Ch. 8)

Discount period The number of days beyond the related sales invoice date during which payment entitles the buyer to deduct any cash discount offered (often 1 or 2%). (Ch. 5)

Discounts lost An account reflecting the amount of cash discounts available but not taken. *See* Net price method of recording purchases. (Ch. 5)

Dividend A distribution to a corporation's stockholders usually in cash; sometimes in the corporation's stock (called a *stock dividend*); and much less frequently in property (called a *dividend in kind*). (Chs. 7, 15, 16)

Dividend payout ratio Common stock dividends divided by common stock earnings. (Ch. 20)

Dividend yield Common stock dividends per share divided by the market price per share. (Ch. 20)

Donated capital The amount received by a corporation from the donation of assets or the donation of the corporation's own stock. (Ch. 15)

Double declining-balance depreciation method A depreciation method that allocates depreciation expense to each year in an accelerated pattern by applying a constant percentage to the declining book value of the asset. (Ch. 10)

Double-entry accounting system A method of accounting that recognizes the duality of a transaction (source and disposition) such that any change in one account also causes a change in another account. For example, the receipt of cash would result in an increase in the Cash account but would also require the recognition of an increase in a liability, owners' equity, or revenue account or a decrease in an expense account or in some other asset account. (Ch. 2)

Drawing account A temporary owner's equity account used to accumulate owner withdrawals from the business. (Ch. 2)

Earning process The entire productive effort put forth by an entity to generate and collect revenue. (Ch. 13)

Earnings per share Net income less any preferred dividend requirements divided by the number of common shares outstanding. (Chs. 16, 20)

Effective interest amortization A method of allocating bond premium or discount to various periods that results in a constant effective rate of interest and varying periodic amortization allocations. (Ch. 17, App. B)

Effective (interest) rate The current rate of interest in the market for a bond. When issued, a bond is priced to yield the market rate of interest at date of issuance. (Ch. 17)

Electronic funds transfer (EFT) A system for transferring funds among parties electronically, without the need for paper checks. (Ch. 7)

Employee's Withholding Allowance Certificate (Form W-4) A form used by employees to claim income tax withholding allowances. (Ch. 12)

Entries The information recorded in journals and ledger accounts. (Chs. 2, 3)

Equity method A method of accounting by parent companies for investments in subsidiaries in which the parent's share of subsidiary income or loss is periodically recorded in the parent company's accounts. *See also* Cost method. (Ch. 18)

Equity ratio Stockholders' equity divided by total assets. (Ch. 20)

Equivalent units The smaller number of full measures of work accomplished that is the equivalent of a larger number of partially accomplished work units. For example, 1,000 units 60% processed is equivalent to 600 units fully processed. (Ch. 23)

Evaluation phase A phase of decision making that deals with steps taken to control the outcome of a specific plan of action; performance measures are a part of this phase. (Ch. 25)

Excess present value index Ratio of the total present value of net future cash flows to the related cash investment. (Ch. 27)

Exchange rate The price, in terms of one currency, at which one unit of another currency may be bought or sold. (App. D)

Execution phase A phase of decision making that deals with the steps taken to implement a specific plan of action. (Ch. 25)

Expenses Expired costs incurred by a firm in the process of earning revenue. (Ch. 1)

Extraordinary item A transaction or event that is unusual in nature and occurs infrequently. Gains and losses on such items are shown separately, net of tax effects, in the income statement. (Ch. 16)

Extraordinary repair An expenditure that extends a plant asset's expected useful life beyond the original estimate. (Ch. 10)

Face value (bond) The amount of principal to be repaid at maturity. Also called par value. (Chs. 7, 17)

Factory overhead All manufacturing costs not considered direct material or direct labor, including indirect materials, indirect labor, factory depreciation, taxes, and insurance. (Ch. 21)

Factory overhead budget A written projection of the factory overhead costs that will be incurred during a budget period for the scheduled volume of activity. A factory overhead budget should be prepared on a flexible basis; it is a component of a company's master budget. (Ch. 26)

Fair Labor Standards Act An act establishing minimum wage, overtime pay, and equal pay standards for employees and setting the necessary record-keeping requirements for employers. (Ch. 12)

FASB The Financial Accounting Standards Board, a nongovernmental group organized in 1973 to replace the Accounting Principles Board and to promulgate authoritative rules for the general practice of financial accounting. (Ch. 1)

Federal Unemployment Taxes (FUTA) A federal tax levied against employers to help finance administration of the various unemployment compensation programs operated by the states. (Ch. 12)

FICA tax Federal Insurance Contributions Act tax, under which the income of an individual is taxed to support a national social security program providing retirement income, medical care, and death benefits. Employers pay a matching amount of tax on their eligible employees. (Ch. 12)

FIFO (first-in, first-out) inventory pricing A valuation method that assumes that the oldest (earliest purchased) goods on hand are sold first, resulting in an ending inventory priced at the most recent acquisition prices. (Ch. 9)

Financial accounting Those accounting activities leading primarily to publishable, general-purpose financial statements such as the income statement, balance sheet, and statement of cash flows. (Ch. 1)

Financial reporting objectives A component of the conceptual framework which specifies that financial statements should provide information (1) useful for investment and credit decisions, (2) helpful in assessing the entity's ability to generate future cash flows, and (3) about the entity's resources, claims to those resources, and the effects of events causing changes in these items. (Ch. 13)

Financial statement elements A part of the conceptual framework that identifies the significant components—such as assets, liabilities, owners' equity, revenue, and expenses—used to put financial statements together. (Ch. 13)

Financing activities A section in the statement of cash flows that reports cash flows associated with the obtaining of resources from owners and creditors, returning resources to owners, and repaying amounts borrowed. (Ch. 19)

Finished goods inventory Units of product for which production has been completed. (Ch. 21)

Finished goods ledger card A record of the amounts acquired, sold, and on hand, and the related costs of a specific finished product. In aggregate, finished goods ledger cards are a perpetual inventory record of finished goods and a subsidiary ledger for the Finished Goods Inventory account. (Ch. 22)

Fiscal year The annual accounting period used by a business firm. (Ch. 3)

Fixed assets Sometimes called long-term assets, long-lived assets, or plant and equipment. May include land, buildings, fixtures, and equipment. (Ch. 10)

Fixed costs Costs whose total remains constant within the relevant range even though the volume of activity may vary. (Ch. 24)

Fixed overhead spending variance A fixed overhead variance computed as: Actual Fixed Overhead Cost − Budgeted Fixed Overhead Cost. (Ch. 26)

Fixed overhead volume variance A fixed overhead variance computed as: Budgeted Fixed Overhead Cost − (Fixed Overhead Standard Capacity Allowed × Standard Fixed Overhead Rate). Called *overhead volume variance* in two- and three-overhead-variance systems. (Ch. 26)

Flexible budget A financial plan formulated so that the assumed operating volume can be varied to agree with actual volume of activities attained. (Chs. 24, 26)

F.O.B. (free on board) Term used in conjunction with the terms factory, shipping point, or destination to indicate the point in the delivery of merchandise at which the purchaser bears freight costs. (Ch. 5)

Foreign currency transaction A transaction whose terms are fixed in the amount of foreign currency to be paid or received. (App. D)

Foreign exchange gain or loss A gain or loss arising from a change in exchange rates before a foreign currency transaction is settled. (App. D)

Form W-2 *See* Wage and Tax Statement (Form W-2).

Form W-4 *See* Employee's Withholding Allowance Certificate (Form W-4).

Franchise Generally, an exclusive right to operate or sell a specific brand of products in a given geographical area. (Ch. 11)

Full disclosure An accounting principle stipulating the disclosure of all facts necessary to make financial statements useful to readers. (Ch. 13)

Fully diluted earnings per share An earnings per share presentation for corporations with complex capital structures that assumes all dilutive securities are converted into common stock. (Ch. 16)

Functional currency The currency of the primary economic environment in which a foreign entity operates. (App. D)

Future value The amount a specified investment (or series of investments) will be worth at a future date if invested at a given rate of compound interest. (App. B)

GAAP *See* Generally accepted accounting principles.

General journal A record of original entry in which are recorded all transactions not recorded in the special journals maintained by the business. (Ch. 6)

General ledger A grouping or binding of the accounts in which the activities of an entity are recorded. (Ch. 2)

Generally accepted accounting principles (GAAP) A group of standards or guides to action in preparing financial accounting reports. Their content and usefulness have evolved over many decades. (Chs. 1, 13)

General partnership A partnership in which each partner is individually liable for the firm's obligations regardless of the amount of personal investment. (Ch. 14)

Going concern An accounting principle dictating that, in the absence of evidence to the contrary, a business is assumed to have an indefinite life. (Chs. 1, 13)

Goodwill The value that derives from a firm's ability to earn more than a normal rate of return on its physical assets. Goodwill is recognized in the accounts only when it is acquired through specific purchase and payment (as opposed to gradual development). (Chs. 11, 18)

Governmental accounting A subdivision of accounting practice relating primarily to accounting for federal, state, or local governmental units. (Ch. 1)

Gross income In the context of preparing income tax returns, gross income is income from all sources less allowable exclusions. (Ch. 28)

Gross profit The excess of sales price over the net delivered cost of the product sold (sometimes called gross margin). (Ch. 5)

Gross profit method A procedure for estimating the cost of ending inventories by multiplying the representative cost of goods sold percentage times sales and deducting that amount from goods available for sale. (Ch. 9)

Gross profit percentage Gross profit divided by net sales. (Ch. 5)

Head of household A category of unmarried taxpayers who pay more than one-half the cost of maintaining a home for qualified dependents and whose tax liability generally falls between that of single taxpayers and married taxpayers filing jointly. (Ch. 28)

High–low method A method for dividing costs into variable and fixed components by comparing costs at the highest and lowest levels of activity for which representative cost data are available. The variable cost per activity unit is determined by dividing the difference in costs by the difference in activity. (Ch. 24)

Historical cost The money equivalent of the object given up (and/or obligations assumed) in an exchange transaction. (Chs. 1, 13)

Home office For a firm with several branches, the principal outlet from which the firm's activities are normally directed. (App. B)

Horizontal analysis. *See* Trend analysis.

Hurdle rate *See* Cutoff rate.

Income The increase in the net assets of a firm from its operating activities during a period of time; also known as net income, profits, or earnings. Income is measured by subtracting expenses incurred from revenue earned. (Ch. 1)

Income statement A financial report showing the results of an entity's operations in terms of revenue, expenses, and net income for a period of time. (Chs. 1, 16)

Income Summary account An account used during closing procedures and to which all revenue and expense accounts are closed. At this point, the balance in the Income Summary account summarizes the firm's net income for the period. In turn, the Income Summary account is closed to the owner's capital or the Retained Earnings account. (Ch. 4)

Indirect expenses (costs) Expenses (costs) that are not readily identified with products or activities; usually allocated by some arbitrary formula to various products and activities. (Ch. 25)

Indirect method A presentation of net cash flow from operating activities in a statement of cash flows that begins with net income and applies a series of adjustments to convert the net income to a cash basis amount. Also known as *reconciliation method*. (Ch. 19)

Individual earnings record A detailed record maintained by an employer for each employee showing gross earnings, overtime premiums, all withholding, payroll tax data, and net earnings paid. (Ch. 12)

Inflation An increase in the general level of prices for goods and services. (Ch. 13)

Information return In the context of income tax reporting, a return that is filed to provide certain required information but that is not the basis for computing income taxes owed. For example, a partnership is not a taxable entity, but each partnership must file a return showing the results of the firm's operations and the amount of net income accorded to each partner. (Ch. 28)

Information system The coordinated efforts to record, organize, and present analyses and reports related to specific areas of activity and concern. (Ch. 1)

In-house computer A mainframe or mid-range computer operated on site for a single company. (Ch. 6)

Installment accounts The accounts receivable or payable for which payments or collections are routinely scheduled over extended periods, such as 24 or 36 months. (Ch. 8)

Installment method A method of

revenue recognition for installment transactions that treats each cash collection as part return of cost and part gross profit. (Ch. 13)

Intangible assets A term applied by convention to a group of long-term assets that generally do not have physical existence, including patents, copyrights, franchises, trademarks, and goodwill. (Ch. 11)

Interim financial statements Financial statements prepared at dates other than the firm's accounting year-end. Most monthly and quarterly financial statements are interim statements. (Chs. 4, 13)

Internal auditing A continuing appraisal of a firm's operations accomplished by the firm's own internal audit staff to determine whether management's financial and operating policies are being properly implemented. (Chs. 1, 7)

Internal control structure The policies and procedures established by a firm to provide reasonable assurance that specific entity objectives will be achieved. (Ch. 7)

Internal Revenue Code The codification of numerous revenue acts passed by Congress since 1913. Interpretation and application of the Code is supplemented by extensive Internal Revenue Code Regulations. (Ch. 28)

Inventory A significant current asset for merchandisers and manufacturers. *See also* Finished goods inventory, Materials inventory, Merchandise inventory, and Work in process inventory. (Chs, 5, 9, 21)

Inventory turnover Cost of goods sold divided by average inventory. (Ch. 20)

Investing activities A section in the statement of cash flows that reports cash flows involving (1) the purchase and sale of plant and intangible assets, (2) the purchase and sale of stocks, bonds, and other securities, and (3) the lending and subsequent collection of money. (Ch. 19)

Investments A category on the balance sheet where assets consisting of securities of other companies, sinking funds, and other long-term holdings are reported. Temporary investments in marketable securities are properly shown as current assets. (Chs. 7, 18)

Invoice A document used in business transactions that sets forth the precise terms regarding date, customer, vendor, quantities, prices, and freight and credit terms of a transaction. (Ch. 5)

Invoice register A special journal, sometimes called a purchases journal, in which all acquisitions on account are chronologically recorded. (Ch. 6)

IRS The Internal Revenue Service of the federal government, primarily responsible for applying the current tax codes and regulations and collecting income taxes for the federal government. (Ch. 28)

Issued stock Shares of stock that have been sold and issued to stockholders; issued stock may be either outstanding or in the treasury. (Ch. 15)

Job cost sheets A record of the specific manufacturing costs applied to a given job. When fully recorded, job cost sheets are a subsidiary ledger to the Work in Process Inventory account. (Ch. 22)

Job order cost accounting A method of cost accounting—sometimes called job lot or specific order costing—in which manufacturing costs are assigned to specific jobs or batches of specialized products. (Ch. 22)

Joint costs Costs common to two or more products or activities. (Ch. 23)

Joint products Two or more products having significant value and derived from common inputs such as materials or processing. (Ch. 23)

Journals Tabular records in which business transactions are analyzed in terms of debits and credits and recorded in chronological order before being posted to the general ledger accounts. (Ch. 3)

Labor efficiency variance A labor variance computed as: (Actual Labor Hours − Standard Labor Hours)(Standard Labor Rate). (Ch. 26)

Labor rate variance A labor variance computed as: (Actual Labor Rate − Standard Labor Rate) (Actual Labor Hours). (Ch. 26)

Land improvements Improvements with limited lives made to land sites, such as paved parking lots and driveways. (Ch. 10)

Lawsuit A legal action whereby a plaintiff applies to a court for justice; may lead to a financial statement footnote disclosure by the defendant as a contingent liability. (Ch. 12)

Lease A contract between a lessor (owner) and lessee (tenant) for the rental of property. (Ch. 11)

Leasehold The rights transferred from the lessor to the lessee by a lease. A leasehold account is used to reflect long-term advance lease payments. (Ch. 11)

Leasehold improvements Expenditures made by the lessee to alter or improve leased property. Such improvements typically revert to the lessor on termination of the lease. (Ch. 11)

Lessee The party acquiring the right to the use of property by a lease. (Ch. 11)

Lessor The owner of property that transfers the right to use the property to another party by a lease. (Ch. 11)

Leverage *See* Trading on the equity.

Liabilities Present obligations resulting from past transactions that require the firm to pay money, provide goods, or perform services in the future. (Chs. 1, 12)

LIFO (last-in, first-out) inventory pricing A valuation method that assumes that the most recently purchased goods are sold first, resulting in an ending inventory priced at the earliest related acquisition prices. (Ch. 9)

Limited partnership A partnership in which one class of partners limit their liability for losses to the amount of their investment; there must be at least one general partner in a limited partnership. (Ch. 14)

Liquidation value per share The amount that would be received by a holder of a share of stock if the corporation liquidated. (Ch. 15)

Long-term assets Relatively long-lived assets employed in operating the firm. Some examples are land, buildings, equipment, natural resources, and intangible assets. (Chs. 5, 10, 11)

Long-term liabilities Debt obligations of the firm not due within the firm's current operating cycle or one year, whichever is longer. Examples are mortgage notes payable and bonds payable. (Chs. 5, 17)

Lower of cost or market rule An accounting procedure providing for inventories to be carried at their acquisition price or their replacement price at the balance sheet date, whichever is lower. A similar rule applies to stock investment portfolios. (Chs. 7, 9, 18)

Majority interest The interest owned when a firm owns more than 50% but less than 100% of another firm. (Ch. 18)

Maker The signer of a promissory note. (Ch. 8)

Managerial accounting The accounting procedures carried out by an organization's accounting staff primarily to furnish its management with accounting analyses and reports needed for decision making. (Chs. 1, 25)

Manufacturing costs Those costs—comprising direct material, direct labor, and factory overhead—necessary to bring the product to completion. Selling and nonfactory administrative costs are specifically excluded. (Ch. 21)

Manufacturing margin The excess of revenue over variable manufacturing costs; an amount often presented on variable costing income statements. (Ch. 25)

Manufacturing Summary account An account (used only during closing procedures) to which all temporary manufacturing costs and expenses are closed, resulting in a balance equal to the cost of goods manufactured. In turn, the Manufacturing Summary account is closed to the Income Summary account. (Ch. 21)

Margin of safety The amount by which the actual sales level exceeds the break-even sales level. (Ch. 24)

Marginal cost The cost associated with completing one more unit of production or activity. (Ch. 25)

Marketable securities An asset classification representing temporary investments in highly marketable stocks, notes, and bonds; may also be called short-term investments. (Ch. 7)

Market (interest) rate The current rate of interest in the market for a bond or other debt instrument. (Ch. 17)

Market value per share The current price at which shares of stock may be bought or sold. (Ch. 15)

Mark-up percentage The amount of gross profit expressed as a percentage of sales. (Ch. 5)

Master budget A comprehensive plan comprising all operating budgets related to sales, production, operating expenses, and finance. May include pro forma financial statements for the budgeting period. (Ch. 26)

Matching expenses with revenue An accounting principle requiring that, to the extent feasible, all expenses related to given revenue be deducted from that revenue for the determination of periodic income. (Chs. 3, 13)

Materiality The concept that accounting transactions so small or insignificant that they do not affect one's actions may be recorded as is most expedient. (Ch. 13)

Material price variance A material variance computed as: (Actual Material Price − Standard Material Price)(Actual Material Quantity). (Ch. 26)

Material quantity variance A material variance computed as: (Actual Material Quantity − Standard Material Quantity) (Standard Material Price). (Ch. 26)

Materials inventory All factory materials acquired but not yet placed in production. (Ch. 21)

Materials ledger card A subsidiary record maintained for each type of direct material and indirect material that shows quantities received, issued, and on hand, unit costs, and total amounts. (Ch. 22)

Materials requisition form A form used to authorize the issuance of direct material for various jobs or indirect material. (Ch. 22)

Maturity date The date a note or bond matures. (Ch. 8)

Maturity value (bond) The amount of bond principal to be paid at maturity. (Ch. 7)

Maturity value (note) The amount of principal plus interest on the note to be paid at maturity. (Ch. 8)

Measuring unit The unit of measure in an accounting transaction, typically the base money unit of the most relevant currency. (Chs. 1, 13)

Merchandise inventory An asset account in which is recorded the purchase price of merchandise held for resale. Sometimes simply termed *inventory.* (Ch. 5)

Microcomputer A personal computer. (Ch. 6)

Minority interest That portion of capital stock in a subsidiary corporation not owned by the controlling (parent) company. (Ch. 18)

Monetary assets Cash and other assets that represent the right to receive a fixed number of dollars in the future, regardless of price-level changes. (Ch. 13)

Monetary liabilities Obligations to disburse a fixed number of dollars in the future, regardless of price-level changes. (Ch. 13)

Mortgage note A note combined with a mortgage; the mortgage is a legal agreement pledging certain property of the borrower as security for repayment of the note. (Ch. 17)

Moving average inventory pricing A pricing method under a perpetual inventory system that recomputes an average unit cost of goods on hand each time a purchase occurs and uses that average unit cost to determine the cost of goods sold for each sale. (Ch. 9)

Multinational corporation A corporation that conducts operations in more than one country by locating branches, divisions, or subsidiaries outside its home country. (App. D)

Multiple-step income statement An income statement in which one or more intermediate amounts (such as gross profit on sales) are derived before the ordinary, continuing income is reported. (Ch. 16)

Natural resources Assets such as timber, petroleum, natural gas, coal, and other mineral deposits mined by the extractive industries. (Ch. 11)

Net assets Total assets less total

liabilities. Net assets are equal to owners' equity. (Chs. 1, 11)

Net income The excess of revenue earned over related expenses incurred. (Ch. 1)

Net income to net sales A financial ratio that computes a firm's rate of return on net sales. (Ch. 20)

Net present value method A method of capital outlay analysis that compares a required investment amount with the present value of resulting net future cash flows discounted at the minimum desired rate of return. (Ch. 27)

Net price method of recording purchases An accounting procedure whereby purchases are recorded at amounts that anticipate the taking of any cash discounts available. When discounts are not taken, the amounts paid in excess of the recorded purchase price are charged to a discounts lost account. (Ch. 5)

Net realizable value An asset measure computed by subtracting the expected completion and disposal costs from the asset's estimated selling price. (Ch. 9)

Nominal (interest) rate The rate of interest stated on a bond certificate. (Ch. 17)

Noncash investing and financing activities Investing activities and financing activities that do not affect current cash flows; information about these events must be reported as a supplement to the statement of cash flows. Examples of these activities include the issuance of stocks or bonds in exchange for plant assets and the conversion of long-term debt into common stock. (Ch. 19)

No-par stock Stock that does not have a par value. (Ch. 15)

Normal balance The debit or credit balance of an account corresponding to the side of the account on which increases are recorded (debits for assets and expenses; credits for liabilities, owners' equity, and revenue). (Ch. 2)

Note payable A promissory note owed by the maker of the note. (Ch. 8)

Note receivable A promissory note held by the note's payee. (Ch. 8)

Notes receivable discounted Notes receivable that have been sold to another entity, usually a financial institution. (Ch. 8)

Objectivity An accounting principle requiring that, whenever possible, accounting entries be based on objective (verifiable) evidence. (Chs. 1, 13)

Off-balance-sheet financing The structuring of a financing arrangement so that no liability is reflected on the borrower's balance sheet. (Ch. 11)

Operating activities A section in the statement of cash flows that reports cash flows from all activities of a company that are not classified as investing or financing activities. Generally, the transactions and events reported in the income statement constitute a company's operating activities. (Ch. 19)

Operating expense budget A written projection of the selling and general administrative expenses that will be incurred over a budget period; a component of a company's master budget. (Ch. 26)

Operating lease A lease where the lessor retains the usual risks and rewards of owning the property. Typically, the lessee accounts for an operating lease by charging each lease payment to rent expense. (Ch. 11)

Organization costs Expenditures incurred in launching a business (usually a corporation); may include attorney's fees, various registration fees paid to state governments, and other start-up costs. (Ch. 11)

Outstanding checks Checks issued by a firm that have not yet been presented to its bank for payment. (Ch. 7)

Outstanding stock Shares of stock that are currently owned by stockholders. (Ch. 15)

Overapplied overhead The excess of overhead applied to production over the amount of overhead incurred. Such amounts are shown on interim balance sheets as deferred credits but are closed to cost of goods sold on year-end financial statements. (Ch. 22)

Overhead controllable variance An overhead variance computed as: Variable Overhead Spending Variance + Fixed Overhead Spending Variance + Variable Overhead Efficiency Variance. (Ch. 26)

Overhead efficiency variance An overhead variance that is the same as the variable overhead efficiency variance. *See* Variable overhead efficiency variance. (Ch. 26)

Overhead spending variance An overhead variance computed as: Variable Overhead Spending Variance + Fixed Overhead Spending Variance. (Ch. 26)

Overhead volume variance *See* Fixed overhead volume variance.

Owners' equity The interest or claim of an entity's owners in the entity's assets; equal to the excess of assets over liabilities. (Ch. 1)

Paid-in capital The amount of capital contributed to a corporation by various transactions; the primary source of paid-in capital is from the issuance of shares of stock. (Ch. 15)

Parent company A company holding all or a majority of the stock of another company, which is called a subsidiary. (Ch. 18)

Participating preferred stock Preferred stock that permits holders to share in dividend distributions with common stockholders beyond the preferred stock's regular dividend rate. (Ch. 15)

Partnership A voluntary association of two or more persons for the purpose of conducting a business for a profit. (Chs. 1, 14)

Par value (bond) The face value of a bond (Ch. 7)

Par value (stock) An amount specified in the corporate charter for each share of stock and imprinted on the face of each stock certificate. Usually determines the legal capital of the corporation. (Ch. 15)

Patent An exclusive privilege granted for 17 years to an inventor that gives the patent holder the right to exclude others from making, using, or selling the invention. (Ch. 11)

Payee The company or individual to whom a promissory note is made payable. (Ch. 8)

Payroll register A detailed list, prepared each pay period, showing each employee's earnings and deductions for the period. (Ch. 12)

Pension plan A plan to pay benefits to employees after they retire from the company. The plan may be a defined contribution plan or a defined benefit plan. (Ch. 17)

Percentage depletion A depletion deduction permitted for tax purposes that is a specified percentage of the gross revenue from mining activities, with certain limitations. (Ch. 11)

Percentage of completion A method of revenue recognition that allocates the estimated gross profit on a long-term project among the several accounting periods involved, in proportion to the estimated percentage of the contract completed each period. (Ch. 13)

Performance reports Documents portraying, for a given operating unit, planned amounts of cost, actual costs incurred, and any related variances. (Ch. 25)

Period costs (expenses) Costs (expenses) associated with the period in which they are incurred (rather than with the product being produced). (Ch. 21)

Periodic inventory system A system of accounting for inventories in which no record is made in the Inventory account for the purchase or sale of merchandise at the time of such transactions. (Chs. 5, 9)

Perpetual inventory system A system of accounting for inventories in which both purchases and sales of merchandise are reflected in the Inventory account at the time such transactions occur. (Ch. 9)

Personal exemptions A prescribed amount that a taxpayer may deduct for himself or herself and each qualified dependent in computing taxable income. (Ch. 28)

Petty cash fund A special, relatively small cash fund established for making minor cash disbursements in the operation of a business. (Ch. 7)

Phantom (inventory) profit The increase in net income from the use of FIFO (compared with other inventory pricing methods) during periods of rising prices. (Ch. 9)

Planning phase A phase of decision making that involves goal identification, identifying alternative courses of action, and estimating the qualitative and quantitative effects of the alternative actions on the specified goals. (Ch. 25)

Plant assets A firm's property, plant, and equipment. (Ch. 10)

Pooling method The method used to prepare consolidated financial statements for a business combination treated as a pooling of interests. When the pooling method is used, the book values of the affiliated companies are combined in the consolidated balance sheet; also, parent company and subsidiary earnings for the entire year are combined in the year of acquisition. (Ch. 18)

Pooling of interests Uniting the ownership interests of two or more companies through the exchange of 90% or more of the firms' voting stocks. (Ch. 18)

Post-closing trial balance A list of account titles and their balances after closing entries have been recorded and posted; all temporary accounts should have zero balances. (Ch. 4)

Posting The formal transferring of amounts from the journals to the ledger(s) used in an accounting system. (Ch. 3)

Posting references A series of abbreviations used in the posting step of the accounting cycle that indicate to where or from where some entry is posted; account numbers and one- or two-letter abbreviations of journal titles are typically used. (Ch. 3)

Predetermined overhead rates Estimated overhead rates determined in advance for applying overhead to production during an operating period (usually one year). The rate is calculated by dividing total estimated overhead costs by the estimated amount of the activity (such as direct labor hours) used to assign factory overhead. *See also* Factory overhead. (Ch. 22)

Preemptive right The right of a stockholder to maintain his or her proportionate ownership in a corporation by having the right to purchase an appropriate share of any new stock issue. (Ch. 15)

Preferred dividend coverage Income before interest and taxes divided by the sum of the annual bond interest and preferred dividend requirements. (Ch. 20)

Preferred stock A class of corporate capital stock typically receiving priority over common stock in dividend payments and distribution of assets should the corporation be liquidated. (Ch. 15)

Present value The estimated current worth of amounts to be received (or paid) in the future from which appropriate amounts of discount (or interest) have been deducted. (Ch. 17, App. B, Ch. 27)

Present value factors Sometimes called discount factors. Multipliers found in present value tables formulated to show the present value of $1 (or a $1 annuity) discounted at various interest rates and for various periods. (Ch. 17, App. B, Ch. 27)

Price–earnings ratio The market price of a share of stock divided by the related earnings per share. (Ch. 20)

Price index A series of measurements, stated as percentages, indicating the relationship between the weighted average price of a sample of goods and services at various points in time and the weighted average price of a similar sample of goods and services at a common, or base, date. (Ch. 13)

Primary earnings per share An earnings per share presentation that considers the actual common stock outstanding plus any dilutive common stock equivalents; generally, a required presentation for corporations with complex capital structures. (Ch. 16)

Prior period adjustment A correction of an error made in financial statements of a prior period. (Ch. 16)

Prior service cost The cost of providing retirement benefits earned by employees prior to the adoption or amendment of a pension plan. (Ch. 17)

Process cost accounting A method of assigning costs to relatively homogeneous products in an often continuous, high-volume operation. (Ch. 23)

Product costs All costs necessary to bring a manufactured product to completion. (Ch. 21)

Production cost report A report that allocates a department's total production costs for a period to units transferred out and to units in ending work in process. (Ch. 23)

Production report A report (usually for a department) showing the beginning inventory of units, units started, units finished and transferred out, and any ending inventory of units. (Ch. 23)

Productivity ratio *See* Return on assets.

Product warranties Guarantees against product defects for a designated period of time after sale. (Ch. 12)

Profit center A segment of a business, such as a division or a department, where the manager is responsible for revenue generation as well as cost and expense control. (Ch. 25)

Promissory note A written promise to pay a certain sum of money on demand or at a determinable future time. (Ch. 8)

Proprietorship A form of business organization in which one person owns the business; sometimes termed *sole proprietorship*. (Ch. 1)

Purchase invoice An invoice received by the buyer of merchandise. (Ch. 5)

Purchase method A procedure that treats a business combination from the viewpoint of the acquiring company as a purchase transaction. (Ch. 18)

Purchase order A document completed by the purchasing firm setting forth the quantities, descriptions, prices, and vendors for merchandise to be purchased. (Ch. 5)

Purchase requisition A form used within a firm to initiate the procedures leading to the purchase of needed items. (Ch. 5)

Purchases The title of the account in which is recorded the acquisition price of merchandise purchased by companies using the periodic inventory method. (Ch. 5)

Purchasing power gain or loss on net monetary items The gain or loss in general purchasing power that results from holding monetary assets or owing monetary liabilities during periods of inflation or deflation. (Ch. 13)

Qualitative characteristics of accounting information The characteristics of accounting information that contribute to decision usefulness. *See* Relevance *and* Reliability. (Ch. 13)

Quarterly data Selected quarterly financial information that is reported in annual reports to stockholders. (Ch. 13)

Quick ratio The total of cash, marketable securities, and receivables divided by current liabilities. (Ch. 20)

Rate of return analysis An analysis using financial ratios that deal with a firm's profitability, such as return on assets and return on sales. (Ch. 20)

Realization The conversion of an entity's assets into cash. (Ch. 14)

Realized Revenue is realized when the goods or services are exchanged for cash or claims to cash. (Ch. 13)

Receiving report A document used within a firm to record formally the quantities and descriptions of merchandise received. (Ch. 5)

Recognition criteria The criteria that must be satisfied before a financial statement element may be recorded in the accounts. Essentially, the item must meet the definition for an element, be measurable, and the resultant information about the item must be relevant and reliable. (Ch. 13)

Records of original entry Usually the various journals incorporated in the firm's accounting system. *See also* Journals. (Ch. 3)

Registered bonds Bonds where the issuer (or its trustee) maintains a record of owners and, at the appropriate times, mails out interest payments. (Ch. 17)

Relative sales value method A method of allocating joint product costs among two or more products. The joint cost is allocated to the products in the proportions of their individual sales values to the total sales value of all the joint products at the split-off point. (Ch. 23)

Relevance A qualitative characteristic of accounting information; relevant information contributes to the predictive and evaluative decisions made by financial statement users. (Ch. 13)

Relevant range The range of changes in the volume of activity within which the assumptions made regarding cost behavior patterns are valid. (Ch. 24)

Reliability A qualitative characteristic of accounting information; reliable information contains no bias or error and faithfully portrays what it intends to represent. (Ch. 13)

Remeasurement procedures A process of converting foreign currency financial statements to U.S. dollars which essentially produces the same U.S. dollar financial statements as if the foreign entity's records had been initially maintained in the U.S. dollar. (App. D)

Research and development costs Expenditures made in the search for new knowledge and in the translation of this knowledge into new or significantly improved products or processes. (Ch. 11)

Retail method A procedure for estimating ending inventories by (1) maintaining detailed records of all goods acquired and on hand at both retail and cost prices (and any changes in these), (2) calculating a cost-to-retail percentage, (3) estimating ending inventory at retail prices by subtracting sales from the retail price of merchandise available for sale, and (4) reducing the estimated inventory at retail to cost by applying the cost-to-retail percentage. (Ch. 9)

Retained earnings The amount of stockholders' equity arising from a corporation's retention of assets generated by profit-directed activities. (Chs. 1, 16)

Retained earnings appropriation *See* Appropriation of retained earnings.

Retained earnings statement A statement showing the changes in retained earnings for the accounting period, including net income or loss, dividends declared, appropriations, and corrections of any errors in financial statements of prior periods. (Ch. 16)

Return on assets Income before interest expense and income taxes divided by average total assets. (Ch. 20)

Return on sales Net income divided by net sales. (Chs. 5, 20)

Return on common stockholders' equity Net income less preferred dividends divided by average common stockholders' equity. (Ch. 20)

Revenue The amount of cash received or claims established against customers stemming from the provision of goods or services by the firm. (Chs. 1, 13)

Revenue expenditure An expenditure related to plant assets that is expensed when incurred. (Ch. 10)

Revenue recognition at point of sale An accounting principle requiring that, with few exceptions, revenue be recognized at the point of sale. (Ch. 13)

Reversing entries A bookkeeping technique whereby adjusting entries involving subsequent receipts or payments are literally reversed on the first day of the following accounting period. This procedure permits the routine recording of subsequent related receipts and payments without having to recognize the portions that were accrued at an earlier date. (Ch. 4)

Running balance account An account form having columns for debit entries, credit entries, and for the account balance. Sometimes called the *three-column* account form. (Ch. 2)

Salary allowance A provision in a partnership profit and loss sharing agreement that allows credit for the partners' personal services to the partnership. (Ch. 14)

Sales The title of the account in which revenue from the sale of goods held for resale is recorded for merchandising and manufacturing companies. (Ch. 5)

Sales budget A document showing estimated unit sales volumes and sales revenue for a budget period; a component of a company's master budget. (Ch. 26)

Sales invoice An invoice issued by a seller of merchandise. (Ch. 5)

Sales journal A special journal for recording credit sales transactions. (Ch. 6)

Salvage value The expected net recovery when a plant asset is sold or removed from service. (Ch. 10)

Schedule of accounts payable A list of the account balances in the accounts payable subsidiary ledger. (Ch. 6)

Schedule of accounts receivable A list of the account balances in the accounts receivable subsidiary ledger. (Ch. 6)

S corporations Corporations that qualify for income tax treatment as partnerships. (Ch. 28)

SEC Securities and Exchange Commission, the federal agency that regulates the sale and exchange of most securities. (Ch. 1)

Secured bonds Bonds that pledge specific property as security for meeting the terms of the bond agreement. (Ch. 17)

Segment A subdivision of an enterprise for which supplemental financial information is disclosed. (Ch. 13)

Semivariable costs Those costs, sometimes called *mixed costs*, whose total responds, but less than proportionately, to changes in the volume of activity. (Ch. 24)

Serial bonds Bond issues that stagger the bond maturity dates over a series of years. (Ch. 17)

Service departments Departments or cost centers that provide special support activities to various production departments. Examples are purchasing, personnel, and maintenance departments. (Ch. 23)

Short-term investments *See* Marketable securities.

Simple capital structure A corporate capital structure that does not contain any securities with the potential to dilute earnings per share. (Ch. 16)

Single-step income statement An income statement in which the ordinary, continuing income of the business is derived in one step by subtracting total expenses from total revenue. (Ch. 16)

Sinking fund Cash and other assets accumulated and segregated for some specific purpose such as retiring debt. (Ch. 17)

Sole proprietorship *See* Proprietorship.

Source document Any written document evidencing an accounting transaction, such as a bank check or deposit slip, sales invoice, or cash register tape. (Ch. 3)

Special journals The records of original entry other than the general journal that are designed for recording specific types of transactions such as cash receipts, sales, purchases, and cash disbursements. (Ch. 6)

Specific identification inventory pricing A method involving the physical identification of goods actually sold and goods remaining on hand and pricing the latter at the actual prices paid for them. (Ch. 9)

Standard cost accounting A system of using standard costs in accounting for manufactured products. *See* Standard costs. (Ch. 26)

Standard costs Those costs, usually expressed on a per-unit basis, that should be incurred for direct material, direct labor, and factory overhead. (Ch. 26)

Standard deduction A fixed dollar amount that individual taxpayers are allowed to deduct from adjusted gross income on their income tax returns in lieu of itemizing expenses. (Ch. 28)

State unemployment tax A payroll tax levied on employers by states to finance state unemployment compensation programs. (Ch. 12)

Stated value A nominal amount that may be assigned to each share of no-par stock and accounted for much as if it were par value. (Ch. 15)

Statement of cash flows A financial statement showing a firm's cash inflows and cash outflows for a specific period, classified into operating, investing, and financing categories. (Chs. 1, 19)

Statement of financial position An alternate title for a balance sheet, a financial statement showing an entity's financial position in terms of assets, liabilities, and owners' equity at a specific date. (Ch. 1)

Statement of owners' equity A financial statement reflecting the beginning balance, additions to, deductions from, and the ending balance of owners' equity for a specified period. (Ch. 1)

Statement of owners' equity A financial statement reflecting the beginning balance, additions to, deductions from, and the ending balance of owners' equity for a specified period. (Ch. 1)

Statement of stockholders' equity A financial statement that presents an analysis of all components of stockholders' equity for an accounting period. (Ch. 16)

Stock dividends Additional shares of its own stock issued by a corporation to its current stockholders in proportion to their ownership interests. (Chs. 7, 16)

Stock portfolio A firm's investment in several different stocks. For accounting purposes, stock investments are divided into a current portfolio and a noncurrent portfolio; the portfolios are reported in the balance sheet at the lower of the portfolio's total cost or total market value. (Chs. 7, 18)

Stock split Additional shares of its own stock issued by a corporation to its current stockholders in proportion to their current ownership interests without changing the balances in the related stockholders' equity accounts. A stock split increases the number of shares outstanding and reduces the per-share market value of the stock. (Ch. 15)

Stock subscriptions Contracts for acquiring stock on a deferred payment plan, often used when shares are sold directly rather than through an investment banker. (Ch. 15)

Straight-line depreciation method Allocates uniform amounts of depreciation expense to each full period of an asset's useful life. (Chs. 3, 10)

Subsequent events Events occurring shortly after a fiscal year-end that will be reported as supplemental information to the financial statements of the year just ended. (Ch. 13)

Subsidiary company *See* Parent company.

Subsidiary ledger A group of accounts, not part of the general ledger, that explain or reflect the detail (such as individual customer balances) underlying the balance in a related control account (such as Accounts Receivable) in the general ledger. (Chs. 6, 11)

Sum-of-the-years'-digits depreciation method An accelerated depreciation method that allocates depreciation expense to each year in a fractional proportion, the denominator of which is the sum of the years' digits in the useful life of the asset. (Ch. 10)

Summary of significant accounting policies A financial statement disclosure, usually the initial note to the statements, that identifies the major accounting policies and procedures used by the company. (Ch. 13)

T account An abbreviated form of the formal account; use is usually limited to illustrations of accounting techniques. (Ch. 2)

Tax allocation within a period The apportionment of total income taxes among the various sources of income or loss shown on an income statement. (Ch. 16)

Tax avoidance Arranging business affairs to minimize the impact of income taxes; in contrast to tax evasion, tax avoidance is legal and considered an aspect of sound management. (Ch. 28)

Tax evasion A deliberate misstatement of factors determining taxable income. Tax evasion is illegal and subjects the taxpayer to legal prosecution. *See also* Tax avoidance. (Ch. 28)

Tax schedules Schedules available for individual taxpayers to use to compute their income tax liabilities when they are not eligible to use the simplified tax tables. (Ch. 28)

Tax shelter An investment that by its nature or by qualifying for special tax treatment creates either tax-exempt income or anticipated deductible tax losses (which shelter other income from income taxation). (Ch. 28)

Tax tables Simplified tables available for individual taxpayers to compute their income tax liabilities. (Ch. 28)

Taxable income Gross income less deductions from gross income, itemized deductions or standard deduction, and personal exemptions. (Ch. 28)

Timesharing facilities A remote computer facility that is shared by various users and is accessed through a terminal via telephone lines. (Ch. 6)

Times interest earned *See* Bond interest coverage.

Time ticket A record used in a job order system to accumulate data for each employee on hours worked, jobs worked on, and the labor cost to assign to jobs. (Ch. 22)

Time value of money An expression of the ability of money to earn interest, the total potential for which is a function of the principal amount, the applicable interest rate, and the time period involved. (App. B, Ch. 27)

Trade discounts The differences between suggested retail prices and the prices at which wholesale purchasers are able to buy merchandise. (Ch. 5)

Trademark An exclusive and continuing right to use a certain symbol to identify a brand or family of products. (Ch. 11)

Trade name An exclusive and continuing right to use certain terms or names to identify a brand or family of products. (Ch. 11)

Trade receivables and payables Assets and liabilities arising from the ordinary open account transactions between a business and its regular trade customers or suppliers. (Ch. 8)

Trading on the equity The use of borrowed funds to generate a return in excess of the interest rate that must be paid for the funds. (Ch. 20)

Transaction Any event or activity of the firm leading to entries in two or more accounts. (Ch. 1)

Translation adjustment A component of stockholders' equity (either an increase or a decrease) resulting from the use of translation procedures to convert foreign currency financial statements. The adjustment arises because the same exchange rate is not used to convert all accounts. (App. D)

Translation procedures A process of converting foreign currency financial statements to U.S. dollars which retains, in the converted data, the financial results and relationships among assets and liabilities that were created by the entity's operations in its foreign environment. (App. D)

Transportation In An account for recording the freight charges on merchandise purchased and held for resale. (Ch. 5)

Transportation Out An account for recording the freight charges incurred in the delivery of merchandise sold to customers. (Ch. 5)

Treasury stock Shares of outstanding stock that have been reacquired by the issuing corporation for purposes other than retiring the stock. Treasury stock is recorded at cost and the account is shown on the balance sheet as a deduction from total stockholders' equity. (Ch. 15)

Trend percentages An approach to financial statement analysis involving comparison of the same item over two or more years. Trend percentages are calculated by choosing a base year and stating the amounts of subsequent years as percentages of that base year. (Ch. 20)

Trial balance A list of the account titles in the general ledger, their respective debit or credit balances, and the totals of all accounts having debit balances and all accounts having credit balances. (Chs. 2, 3, 4)

Trustee A party or entity to whom a trust is committed. A bond issuer, for example, may select a bank to act as trustee for bondholders. The trustee may take security title to any pledged property and may initiate appropriate actions if the bond terms are not met. (Ch. 17)

Unadjusted trial balance A trial balance of the general ledger accounts taken before the adjusting step of the accounting cycle. (Ch. 3)

Uncollectible accounts expense The expense stemming from the inability of a business to collect an amount previously recorded as a receivable. Sometimes called bad debts expense. Normally classified as a selling or administrative expense. (Ch. 8)

Underapplied overhead The excess of actual overhead costs incurred over the amounts applied to production. On interim balance sheets such amounts appear as deferred charges but are closed to cost of goods sold on year-end statements. (Ch. 22)

Unearned revenue A liability representing revenue received in advance. Also called *Deferred revenue.* (Ch. 3)

Units of production budget A document showing the quantity of each product to be produced during a budget period; a component of a company's master budget. (Ch. 26)

Units-of-production depreciation method A depreciation method that allocates depreciation expense to each operating period in proportion to the amount of the asset's expected total production capacity used each period. (Ch. 10)

Useful life The period from date of acquisition to date of disposal (or removal from service) for a plant asset or intangible asset. (Ch. 10)

Vacation benefit expense An expense reflecting the cost of employee vacation privileges; this expense is generally accrued over the period employees earn vacations. (Ch. 12)

Variable costing A product costing method in which only variable manufacturing costs are associated with the product; fixed manufacturing costs are treated as period costs in the period incurred. (Ch. 25)

Variable costs Those costs the total of which responds proportionately to changes in volume of activity. (Chs. 24, 25)

Variable overhead efficiency variance A variable overhead variance computed as: (Variable Overhead Actual Capacity Used × Standard Variable Overhead Rate) − (Variable Overhead Standard Capacity Allowed × Standard Variable Overhead Rate). (Ch. 26)

Variable overhead spending variance A variable overhead variance computed as: Actual Variable Overhead Cost − (Variable Overhead Actual Capacity Used × Standard Variable Overhead Rate). (Ch. 26)

Variances Favorable or unfavorable differences between standard costs and actual costs. Variances are usually isolated for price and usage factors for direct material as well as for rate and efficiency factors for direct labor. For factory overhead, variances may be isolated for factors related to spending, efficiency, and volume. (Ch. 26)

Vertical analysis An approach to financial statement analysis highlighting the quantitative relationship between amounts in the same financial statement. (Ch. 20)

Voucher A written authorization form used to support a cash disbursement. (Ch. 6)

Voucher register A special journal or record of original entry (in lieu of a purchases journal) for recording in numerical order all vouchers supporting the disbursement of funds. (Ch. 6)

Voucher system A system for controlling expenditures requiring the preparation and approval of individual vouchers for each contemplated expenditure. (Ch. 6)

Wage and Tax Statement (Form W-2) A form an employer must give each employee annually which shows the employee's total wages paid, federal income tax and FICA tax withheld, and the wages subject to FICA tax. (Ch. 12)

Wasting assets Another name for natural resources. *See* Natural resources. (Ch. 11)

Weighted average cost of capital Expressed as a percentage, the cost to the firm of acquiring investment capital, weighted to reflect the specific cost rates associated with and proportions used from specific sources such as equity securities, debt, and internally generated funds. (Ch. 27)

Weighted average inventory pricing A method that spreads the total dollar cost of all goods available for sale equally among all units. (Ch. 9)

Withdrawals (owners') Amounts that proprietors or partners withdraw, usually in cash and for personal objectives, from the assets of the firm. (Chs. 1, 14)

Working capital The excess of current assets over current liabilities. (Ch. 20)

Working capital turnover The ratio of sales to working capital. (Ch. 20)

Work in process inventory All units of a product that are in the process of being manufactured. (Ch. 21)

Worksheet An informal accounting document used to facilitate the preparation of financial statements. (Chs. 4, 5, 19, 21, App. A, F)

Yield *See* Dividend yield.

Zero-base budgeting A budgeting process that requires each budgetary unit to justify all of its expenditures as if the unit's operations were just starting. (Ch. 26)

HOW TO USE *MICROSTUDY*

Microstudy has been constructed (in cooperation with Delta Software, Inc.) to help you learn faster and learn more about accounting. Study thoroughly the chapter in your textbook first. Then *Microstudy* will be most effective by reinforcing important materials and filling in the gaps. The software is available in forms for both the IBM® PC and compatibles and Apple Macintosh®.

USING *MICROSTUDY* ON THE IBM PC AND COMPATIBLES

The IBM PC and compatibles need a minimum of 192 KB memory. *Microstudy* is not copy-protected, and it is wise to make a backup copy. Because the software is unprotected, you can install it on a hard disk drive or on a 3½-inch diskette if desired. *Do not affix a write-protect label to your Program Disk.* The computer must be allowed to write information on the disk as you use *Microstudy.* Start by booting the PC with any DOS 2.0 or higher disk to obtain an A> prompt. Then replace the DOS disk with the Program Disk. Next enter SIGN or AUTOEXEC (followed by Return). An Operating Environment Screen will appear. Either a color or monochrome monitor (including the IBM standard monochrome) can be used. Specify which one you have. In addition, the speaker can be silenced, or it can be activated to provide useful audio feedback during the learning session.

The Main Menu serves as the hub, and it will appear after one or two introductory graphic screens. You will see eight major options on the screen:

```
                < MICROSTUDY MAIN MENU >

   OPTIONS
   [1]-->  Select Chapter in Textbook for Review.
   [2]-->  Study Chapter Learning Objectives.
   [3]-->  Study a List of Key Terms for the Chapter.
   [4]-->  Vocabulary Building with Matching Exercises.
   [5]-->  Multiple-Choice Question Drill.
   [6]-->  True or False Statement Drill.
   [7]-->  Review Instructions for using Microstudy.
   [8]-->  Stop and Exit from Microstudy.

             PLEASE SELECT YOUR OPTION (1 - 8) _

 1CHPT 2OBJECT 3TERMS 4MATCH 5M-C 6T-F 7HELP 8QUIT 9MENU
```

All of the major options can be triggered by simply pressing a numeric key. This is why the options are labeled <1> through <8>. The Return key need not be pressed after the numeric key is pressed to complete the command.

When you first start to use *Microstudy,* and perhaps once every three or four sessions, it is wise to review the instructions. An abridged set of directions for help can be printed on the screen by pressing the <7> key. A series of three to four screens supply a description of the *Microstudy* program options and, in a sense, represent an abridged version of the guide to this release of *Microstudy.* You can get help in the middle of any learning module by pressing the <7> key in response to the prompt, Press Space Bar to Continue. . .

Any learning module can be accessed directly from another one by pressing a numeric key in response to the prompt, Press Space Bar to Continue. . . This feature allows you to branch from one learning module to the other at will without going through the Main Menu.

The options are arranged in somewhat of a hierarchical order. The first one you select should be <1>—select the chapter from your textbook for review. The computer assumes Chapter 1 if you do not make an initial selection. Suppose, however, you decide to select a new chapter and press <1> to obtain this screen:

```
                    CHAPTERS AVAILABLE FOR REVIEW

  [1]-->  Accounting:  An Information System
  [2]-->  The Double-entry Accounting System
  [3]-->  The Accounting Cycle
  [4]-->  The Accounting Cycle Concluded
  [5]-->  Merchandising Operations
  [6]-->  Data Processing: Manual and Electronic Systems
  [7]-->  Internal Control, Cash, and Short-term Investments
  [8]-->  Trade Accounts and Notes
  [9]-->  Inventories
 [10]-->  Plant Assets: Measurement and Depreciation
 [11]-->  Plant Asset Disposals, Natural Resources, and Intangible Assets
 [12]-->  Current Liabilities and Payroll Accounting
 [13]-->  Accounting Principles and Financial Statement Disclosures
 [14]-->  Partnership Accounting

PLEASE SELECT THE CHAPTER YOU WISH TO REVIEW (1 - 28) _
```

The rest of the chapters can be viewed by pressing the <F1> function key. To respond to the chapter selection prompt, numeric key(s) must be pressed (followed by return or space bar if single digit) to indicate the chapter number you wish to review. From there on, all *Microstudy* learning modules will cover this chapter specifically until you change it again. Be sure that you have inserted the appropriate Question Bank Disk in the computer's second disk drive. The computer will check to be sure that the right disk is available for use.

You must use the Chapter Selection Menu Option if you want to switch chapters and move on to other material from another chapter in the textbook.

Learning Objectives: <2>

Once you have made your chapter selection, the *Microstudy* Main Menu will reappear on the screen and the computer will await further instructions. The logical choice is to look over the learning objectives of the chapter you selected. These are triggered by the <2> key. The learning objectives will appear in a sequence of one or two screens. Study them carefully. They will give you a broad perspective of what you are about to experience and what you are expected to learn about in this chapter. When finished, *Microstudy* advances to the Main Menu and awaits your next selection.

List Key Terms: <3>

If you select Option 3, you can view a list of terms and concepts important to this chapter. The computer will display them in alphabetical order. You may wish to keep your textbook handy, and be sure that you can define every term as it relates to the chapter.

Matching Exercises: <4>

By this time you are building a vocabulary on the subject. One way to test the extent of your vocabulary is to see if you can complete a sentence containing a key term, or pair up descriptions of terms with the terms themselves. The jargon is a crucial dimension of learning any subject, so let's see how many of the key terms in the chapter you can remember.

After selecting Option 4, the computer will build a windowful of terms from the chapter, numbered sequentially. A description of one of the terms will appear. Can you put the two together? If you enter the correct letter, *Microstudy* will let you know. If you choose the wrong term, *Microstudy* will notify you, tally the wrong answer, and wait for another attempt. Your scoring tally will accumulate throughout the session.

You have as many tries as you need. Successive misses do not alter the scoring tally. When you get the correct answer, the next definition will appear as soon as you press the space bar. The window of terms will be reconstructed, and you have one less term from which to choose! The correct answer to the previous definition will have vanished. If you accidentally try to select a term that is no longer in the window, *Microstudy* will recognize your choice is invalid and give you another chance to get it right without adding a wrong answer to your score.

Should you discover that you are unable to correctly match quite a few of the terms, consider reviewing the textbook further. Each time you return to the Matching Exercise, the same window will appear, but *Microstudy* will have scrambled the descriptions completely at random. For a typical chapter, the odds of ever having the same sequence of descriptions appearing twice in a row are less than one in a trillion. Therefore, from an order of appearance standpoint, you will get a different matching quiz whenever you select Option 4.

Multiple-Choice Question Drill: <5>

By far the most popular objective question ever invented is the multiple choice. The odds are only one in four or five of guessing the correct answer, so you are going to have to knuckle down. Enter the letter corresponding to the choice you think is best from those offered. If you miss the question, *Microstudy* will wait until you find the correct answer before advancing. Your instructor will probably use multiple-choice questions for formal testing, so practice now. Remember, if you miss the question, you must try until you select the correct answer.

If you miss a lot of these questions, you need to study the textbook some more. Then take the Multiple-Choice quiz again. The questions will appear in a different order.

True/False Statement Drill: <6>

Option 6 releases a battery of true/false statements. The odds of guessing the correct answer are, of course, 50/50. But can you get all of them right? *Microstudy* will again keep track of your rights and wrongs. Each time you take the True/False quiz the questions will be scrambled in a different order of appearance. Therefore, no two learning sessions will be identical in this respect.

Main Menu: <9>

If you press the <9> key when prompted for the space bar to continue, *Microstudy* will send you back to the Main Menu, thus returning to home base.

USING *MICROSTUDY* ON THE MACINTOSH

The minimum hardware requirements for the Macintosh version of *Microstudy* are 512 KB RAM and a single 800 KB disk drive. Complete operating instructions for the Macintosh version of *Microstudy* are available in the form of a MacWrite file on the Macintosh diskette.

INDEX

A

D

J

L

M

N

O

P

R

S

T

U

A 9
B 0
C 1
D 2
E 3
F 4
G 5
H 6
I 7
J 8

DATE	READING ASSIGNMENT	WRITTEN ASSIGN
1/7	Introduction Present-value concepts	
1/12 1/14 1/19	Ch. 17; Long-term liabilities and Appendix B	17-26A 17-27A 17-28A, 29A
1/21 1/26	Ch. 18; Long-term investments Consolidated financial statements Appendix D	18-18,19,20 18-31A,34A D-2
1/28 2/2	Statement of cash flows Appendix E	19-25,29 19-32A,36A
2/4	Analysis of financial statements	20-25A,26A
2/8	Review for exam	
2/11	***FIRST TERM EXAM*** 7:30-9:00 PM; 179/198ELB	
2/16	Accounting for manufacturing operations	21-25A,28A,30A
2/18 3/2	Job cost accounting	22-17,18 22-30A,32A
3/4 3/9	Process cost accounting	23-18,19 23-24,25,29A
3/11 3/16	Cost-volume-profit relationships	24-17,18,30 24-38A,39A
3/18	***SECOND TERM EXAM*** 7:30-9:00 PM; 179/198ELB	
3/23 3/25	Special analysis for management	25-24,28,30,31 25-39A,40A,33
3/30 4/1 4/6	Budgeting Standard costing Standard costing	26-20,31A,34A 26-26,27 26-36A,37A
4/8 4/13	Capital budgeting	27-20,22,24 27-25,26,30A
4/15 4/20	Current issues in accounting	Class handouts
4/29	♥♦♣♠FINAL EXAMINATION♥♦♣♠ COMPREHENSIVE 7:30-10:30 PM	

16–35A Net income, $420,000
Business Decision Problem (b) 19X7, $29.20; 19X8, $26.80

17–26 (b) Loss on bond retirement, $1,100
17–27 (a)(4) Loss on bond retirement, $5,000
17–28 (a) Book value, end of period 2, $618,252
17–29 (a) Book value, end of period 2, $675,694
17–30 No key figure
17–31 No key figure
17–32 No key figure
17–33 (a) 19X5, $7,800
17–26A (b) Gain on bond retirement, $1,000
17–27A (a)(4) Loss on bond retirement, $2,500
17–28A (a) Book value, end of period 2, $470,832
17–29A (a) Book value, end of period 2, $531,431
17–30A No key figure
17–31A No key figure
17–32A No key figure
17–33A (c) 19X2 year-end, $20,000
Business Decision Problem No key figure

B–1 (a)(1) $37,040;(c) $3,507; (e) $36,390
B–2 Table II: $31,944
B–3 $46,144
B–4 (a) $370,400
B–5 (a) $432,620
B–6 (b) $39,523.22
B–7 (a) $8,576
B–8 (a) $162,960

18–27 Dec. 31, 19X1, adjustment, $3,100
18–28 No key figure
18–29 (a) Goodwill from consolidation, $20,000
18–30 (c) Total consolidated assets, $950,000
18–31 Total consolidated assets, $2,060,000
18–32 Consolidated net income, $92,600
18–33 No key figure
18–34 (c) Total consolidated assets, $3,380,000
18–27A Dec. 31, 19X1, adjustment, $11,500
18–28A No key figure
18–29A (a) Goodwill from consolidation, $24,000
18–30A (c) Total consolidated assets, $1,238,000
18–31A Total consolidated assets, $1,665,000
18–32A Consolidated net income, $111,600
18–33A No key figure
18–34A (c) Total consolidated assets, $1,790,000
Business Decision Problem No key figure

C–1 (b) $100,800
C–2 No key figure
C–3 (d) $176,500
C–4 (b) Corrected balances, $69,100
C–5 (d) $163,500

D–1 (b) July 10, foreign exchange gain, $2,700
D–2 (a) Jan. 18, foreign exchange gain, 1,500
D–3 Nov. 16, foreign exchange loss, $340
D–4 Total assets, $504,600
D–5 Total assets, $534,600

19–32 (b) Net cash provided by operating activities, $10,000
19–33 (b) Net cash provided by operating activities, $96,000
19–34 (b) Net cash provided by operating activities, $115,000
19–35 (b) Net cash used by operating activities, $14,000
19–36 (b) Net cash provided by operating activities, $10,000
19–37 (b) Net cash provided by operating activities, $96,000
19–38 (b) Net cash provided by operating activities, $115,000
19–39 (b) Net cash used by operating activities, $14,000
19–32A (b) Net cash provided by operating activities, $35,000
19–33A (b) Net cash provided by operating activities, $49,000
19–34A (b) Net cash provided by operating activities, $30,000
19–35A (b) Net cash provided by operating activities, $22,000
19–36A (b) Net cash provided by operating activities, $35,000
19–37A (b) Net cash provided by operating activities, $49,000
19–38A (b) Net cash provided by operating activities, $30,000
19–39A (b) Net cash provided by operating activities, $22,000
Business Decision Problem No key figure

E–1 (b) Net cash provided by operating activities, $10,000
E–2 (b) Net cash provided by operating activities, $96,000
E–3 (b) Net cash provided by operating activities, $115,000
E–4 (b) Net cash used by operating activities, $14,000
E–5 (b) Net cash provided by operating activities, $35,000
E–6 (b) Net cash provided by operating activities, $49,000
E–7 (b) Net cash provided by operating activities, $30,000
E–8 (b) Net cash provided by operating activities, $22,000

20–24 (a) Year 5, net sales, 148.8%
20–25 (a) Return on assets, 12.5%
20–26 (b) Net income this year, 6.9%
20–27 (a)(2) 22.20%
20–28 Gross profit, $1,170,000; inventory, $755,000
20–29 (b) Dividends paid per share, $8.57
20–24A (a) Year 5, net income, 194.0%
20–25A (b) Return on sales, 5.56%
20–26A (a) Return on assets this year, 12.31%
20–27A (a)(3) 20.81%
20–28A Gross profit, $1,400,000; inventory, $520,000
20–29A (c) Price–earnings ratio, 7.01
Business Decision Problem This year: (a) 1.87; (g) 11.01%

21–25 Cost of goods manufactured, $453,000
21–26 Cost of goods manufactured, $534,000
21–27 B: Cost of goods manufactured, $1,720
21–28 Work in process inventory, $73,381
21–29 (a) Cost of goods manufactured, $873,200
21–30 (a) Unit production cost, $74.50
21–31 (b) Cost of goods manufactured, $1,166,800
21–32 (b) Cost of goods manufactured, $418,600
21–25A Cost of goods manufactured, $604,000
21–26A Cost of goods manufactured, $831,000
21–27A C: Cost of goods sold, $3,920
21–28A (a) Finished goods inventory, $139,600
21–29A (a) Cost of goods manufactured, $1,010,000
21–30A (a) Unit production cost, $110
21–31A (b) Cost of goods manufactured, $962,800
21–32A (b) Cost of goods manufactured, $1,287,400
Business Decision Problem (b) Cost of goods manufactured, $189,000

F–1 (b) Cost of goods manufactured, $1,166,800
F–2 (b) Cost of goods manufactured, $962,800
F–3 (b) Cost of goods manufactured, $418,600
F–4 (b) Cost of goods manufactured, $1,287,400

22–27 (c) Overhead assigned, $160
22–28 (b) Indirect labor cost incurred, $25,500
22–29 (b) Underapplied overhead, $9,800
22–30 (h) Overapplied overhead, $9,100
22–31 (b) Cost of goods manufactured, $702,000
22–32 (d) Total factory overhead incurred, $10,300
22–33 (c) Ending work in process, $15,400
22–34 (d) Finished goods inventory, $72,280
22–27A (c) Overhead assigned, $360

Paul Sprainitis – 349-4735